REVELATION

REVELATION

ZONDERVAN
Exegetical
Commentary
ON THE
New Testament

BUIST M. FANNING

CLINTON E. ARNOLD
General Editor

ZONDERVAN
ACADEMIC

ZONDERVAN ACADEMIC

Revelation
Copyright © 2020 by Buist Fanning

ISBN 978-0-310-24417-2 (hardcover)

ISBN 978-0-310-10207-6 (ebook)

Requests for information should be addressed to:
Zondervan, 3900 *Sparks Dr. SE*, Grand Rapids, Michigan 49546

Cover design: Tammy Johnson
Interior design: Beth Shagene

Printed in the United States of America

20 21 22 23 24 25 26 27 28 29 30 /LSC/ 25 24 23 22 21 20 19 18 17 16 15 14 13 12 11 10 9 8 7 6 5 4 3 2 1

To Jan
"The best is yet to be . . ."

Contents

Series Introduction

This generation has been blessed with an abundance of excellent commentaries. Some are technical and do a good job of addressing issues that the critics have raised; other commentaries are long and provide extensive information about word usage and catalogue nearly every opinion expressed on the various interpretive issues; still other commentaries focus on providing cultural and historical background information; and then there are those commentaries that endeavor to draw out many applicational insights.

The key question to ask is: What are you looking for in a commentary? This commentary series might be for you if

- you have taken Greek and would like a commentary that helps you apply what you have learned without assuming you are a well-trained scholar.
- you would find it useful to see a concise, one-or two-sentence statement of what the commentator thinks the main point of each passage is.
- you would like help interpreting the words of Scripture without getting bogged down in scholarly issues that seem irrelevant to the life of the church.
- you would like to see a visual representation (a graphical display) of the flow of thought in each passage.
- you would like expert guidance from solid evangelical scholars who set out to explain the meaning of the original text in the clearest way possible and to help you navigate through the main interpretive issues.
- you want to benefit from the results of the latest and best scholarly studies and historical information that help to illuminate the meaning of the text.
- you would find it useful to see a brief summary of the key theological insights that can be gleaned from each passage and some discussion of the relevance of these for Christians today.

These are just some of the features that characterize the new Zondervan Exegetical Commentary on the New Testament series. The idea for this series was refined over time by an editorial board who listened to pastors and teachers express what they wanted to see in a commentary series based on the Greek text. That board consisted of myself, George H. Guthrie, William D. Mounce, Thomas R. Schreiner, and Mark L. Strauss along with Zondervan senior editor at large Verlyn Verbrugge, and former Zondervan senior acquisitions editor Jack Kuhatschek. We also enlisted a board of consulting editors who are active pastors, ministry leaders, and seminary professors to help in the process of designing a commentary series that will be useful to the church. Zondervan senior acquisitions editor Katya Covrett has now been shepherding the process to completion, and Constantine R. Campbell is now serving on the board.

We arrived at a design that includes seven components for the treatment of each biblical passage. What follows is a brief orientation to these primary components of the commentary.

Literary Context

In this section, you will find a concise discussion of how the passage functions in the broader literary context of the book. The commentator highlights connections with the preceding and following material in the book and makes observations on the key literary features of this text.

Main Idea

Many readers will find this to be an enormously helpful feature of this series. For each passage, the commentator carefully crafts a one- or two-sentence statement of the big idea or central thrust of the passage.

Translation and Graphical Layout

Another unique feature of this series is the presentation of each commentator's translation of the Greek text in a graphical layout. The purpose of this diagram is to help the reader visualize, and thus better understand, the flow of thought within the text. The translation itself reflects the interpretive decisions made by each commentator in the "Explanation" section of the commentary. Here are a few insights that will help you to understand the way these are put together:

1. On the far left side next to the verse numbers is a series of interpretive labels that indicate the function of each clause or phrase of the biblical text. The corresponding portion of the text is on the same line to the right of the label. We have not used technical linguistic jargon for these, so they should be easily understood.

2. In general, we place every clause (a group of words containing a subject and a predicate) on a separate line and identify how it is supporting the principal assertion of the text (namely, is it saying when the action occurred, how it took place,

or why it took place?). We sometimes place longer phrases or a series of items on separate lines as well.

3. Subordinate (or dependent) clauses and phrases are indented and placed directly under the words that they modify. This helps the reader to more easily see the nature of the relationship of clauses and phrases in the flow of the text.

4. Every main clause has been placed in bold print and pushed to the left margin for clear identification.

5. Sometimes when the level of subordination moves too far to the right—as often happens with some of Paul's long, involved sentences!—we reposition the flow to the left of the diagram, but use an arrow to indicate that this has happened.

6. The overall process we have followed has been deeply informed by principles of discourse analysis and narrative criticism (for the Gospels and Acts).

Structure

Immediately following the translation, the commentator describes the flow of thought in the passage and explains how certain interpretive decisions regarding the relationship of the clauses were made in the passage.

Exegetical Outline

The overall structure of the passage is described in a detailed exegetical outline. This will be particularly helpful for those who are looking for a way to concisely explain the flow of thought in the passage in a teaching or preaching setting.

Explanation of the Text

As an exegetical commentary, this work makes use of the Greek language to interpret the meaning of the text. If your Greek is rather rusty (or even somewhat limited), don't be too concerned. All the Greek words are cited in parentheses following an English translation. We have made every effort to make this commentary as readable and useful as possible even for the nonspecialist.

Those who will benefit the most from this commentary will have had the equivalent of two years of Greek in college or seminary. This would include a semester or two of working through an intermediate grammar (such as Wallace, Porter, Brooks and Winbery, or Dana and Mantey). The authors use the grammatical language that is found in these kinds of grammars. The details of the grammar of the passage, however, are discussed only when it has a bearing on the interpretation of the text.

The emphasis in this section of the text is to convey the meaning. Commentators examine words and images, grammatical details, relevant OT and Jewish background to a particular concept, historical and cultural context, important text-critical issues, and various interpretational issues that surface.

Theology in Application

This, too, is a unique feature for an exegetical commentary series. We felt it was important for each author not only to describe what the text means in its various details, but also to take a moment and reflect on the theological contribution that it makes. In this section, the theological message of the passage is summarized. The authors discuss the theology of the text in terms of its place within the book and in a broader biblical-theological context. Finally, each commentator provides some suggestions on what the message of the passage is for the church today. At the conclusion of each volume in this series is a summary of the whole range of theological themes touched on by this book of the Bible.

Our sincere hope and prayer is that you find this series helpful not only for your own understanding of the text of the New Testament, but also as you are actively engaged in teaching and preaching God's Word to people who are hungry to be fed on its truth.

CLINTON E. ARNOLD, general editor

Author's Preface

Who can resist sneaking a peek at the last chapter of a book? I often want to know where a book is going before I sign on for the journey. I don't recommend it for mystery novels, but for most books it really helps in understanding the rest of the story if you have an idea where it ends up.

After spending about ten years studying the book of Revelation, I strongly recommend this procedure for the Bible, at least for the typical Bible reader. My grasp and appreciation of the other portions of Scripture have been amazingly enhanced by digging into Revelation. I thought I knew the Gospels and Romans and Hebrews well after teaching them in the church and in the seminary classroom for over forty years, but I understand them so much more after studying Revelation. The same goes for Genesis, Samuel, Kings, the Psalms, and the prophets of the Old Testament— especially the prophets! And I don't mean just an intellectual grasp of the Bible but deep appreciation and commitment to obey it and see others respond in the same way. Revelation is a book that elicits a response of heart and life. In its pages one sees more clearly what's at stake for individuals and society in following God's way or not, and this helps us to read the whole Bible with a fresh intensity.

The influence of two of my teachers from decades ago made me think that I could take on the task of writing a commentary on Revelation. Though they came from very different theological and intellectual backgrounds, S. Lewis Johnson and George B. Caird exemplified for me what a careful and well-informed study of Scripture (and of Revelation in particular) could look like. I took Johnson's seminary course on Revelation in 1972 and listened to several of his sermons on the book. Caird urged me in the early 1980s to read Jewish apocalyptic, and his lively commentary on Revelation has been a help to me, though I don't follow it as much as he might have desired. Both scholars combined academic rigor with a passionate commitment to make the Bible understandable for people in the pews and in the marketplace. I share that passion, in part because of my own story of coming to faith in Christ in my late teenage years after an eye-opening experience of reading what the Bible actually says about the good news of the Christian faith. I was captivated by the grace of God in the cross of Christ, and immediately I was driven to see what else this life-changing book had to say. It gave me a passion to find out what Scripture says and to help others see it too. I was convinced that all people need to understand what the Bible says and respond to it! Even church people need a real, in-depth exposure to its message (my church at that time tended to make the Bible optional).

So I am grateful to have had this chance to dig into Revelation in a deeper way, and my great desire is that it will help pastors and teachers, and all Bible readers, in their important task of leading others to grasp its message and live it out in our day. Revelation contains a special promise for both groups: "Blessed is the one who reads aloud and those who hear the words of this prophecy and obey the things written in it, for the time is near" (1:3). It makes sense that Revelation could bring such blessing even today. If ever the world needed a message about people from "every tribe and language and people and nation" (5:9) formed by Christ's redeeming work into a diverse community that bears witness to God's ways in a broken world, it is today. People need Revelation's message about God bringing real justice to bear against evil and real restoration of his creatures and of his creation, so that human life can flourish as he intended from the beginning. They need to see that God is almighty yet seeks direct communion with his people, that he is faithful to his age-old promises to make things right, and that the godless ideologies of our day have nothing to offer compared to the pathways he has for us as humans. They need to understand God's desire for his people to engage faithfully with the world around them even now instead of yielding to assimilation, isolation, or escapism. When we grasp our real identity and what our future holds, we are better equipped and motivated to live different lives in the present. I urge pastors and teachers to begin their reading of this commentary also at the end. Peruse the summary of Revelation's theology at the back of this volume, and I think you will see what a life-changing book Revelation can be for yourselves and the people you serve.

Anyone who reads this commentary will see what a debt I owe to others who have helped me along the way. A diverse group of writers influenced my ideas on Revelation, but first mention should go to Richard Bauckham and Craig Blaising, as my footnotes will show. Despite the differences between them, I have learned significant things from both. The same can be said for David Aune and Robert Thomas, whose commentaries were a constant companion. The prodigious labor of each of them (again in their quite different ways) helped me greatly. Continuing the theme of diversity in viewpoint, I should also include the indirect influence of R. H. Charles and John Nelson Darby—both graduates of Trinity College, Dublin (in different eras)—who in very different ways had a major impact on the study of Revelation in the last two centuries. This commentary shows that I have learned much from those who learned from them.

A few others deserve specific mention. Thanks to Marc-André Caron, who as my student intern proofread the entire first draft and saved me from many mistakes, as well as contributed fresh ideas to the exposition. Thanks to the invaluable guidance and vision of Clint Arnold and his editorial team and to the editors at Zondervan, especially Christopher Beetham. Zondervan always makes its authors look good. Finally, I express my love and gratitude to my wife Jan who read the entire draft and helped me with it in innumerable ways. Most of all she always knew when to say, "You'll never finish it," and when to say, "Sure, you'll finish it."

BUIST M. FANNING

Abbreviations

BSac	*Bibliotheca Sacra*
BTCB	Brazos Theological Commentary on the Bible
BZNW	Beiheft zur Zeitschrift für die neutestamentliche Wissenschaft und die Kunde der älteren Kirche
CBC	Cambridge Bible Commentary
CBQ	*Catholic Biblical Quarterly*
CC	Continental Commentaries
CEB	Common English Bible
CNT	Commentaire du Nouveau Testament
CSB	Christian Standard Bible
DJG	*Dictionary of Jesus and the Gospels.* 2nd ed. Edited by Joel B. Green, Jeannine K. Brown, and Nicholas Perrin. Downers Grove, IL: InterVarsity, 2013
DLNT	*Dictionary of the Later New Testament and Its Developments.* Edited by Ralph P. Martin and Peter H. Davids. Downers Grove, IL: InterVarsity, 1997
DNTB	*Dictionary of New Testament Background.* Edited by Craig A. Evans and Stanley E. Porter. Downers Grove, IL: InterVarsity, 2000
EDNT	*Exegetical Dictionary of the New Testament.* Edited by Horst Balz and Gerhard Schneider. 3 vols. Grand Rapids: Eerdmans, 1990–1993
EKKNT	Evangelisch-katholischer Kommentar zum Neuen Testament
ESV	English Standard Version
ETL	*Ephemerides Theologicae Lovanienses*
EUS	European University Studies
ExpTim	*Expository Times*
GNS	Good News Studies
GNT	Good News Translation
GNTE	Guides to New Testament Exegesis
GTJ	*Grace Theological Journal*
HALOT	*The Hebrew and Aramaic Lexicon of the Old Testament in English.* Edited by Ludwig Koehler et al. 5 vols. Leiden: E. J. Brill, 1994–2000
HDR	Harvard Dissertations in Religion
HNT	Handbuch zum Neuen Testament
HNTC	Harper's New Testament Commentaries
HNTE	Handbooks for New Testament Exegesis
HTANT	Historisch-theologische Auslegung Neues Testament
HTR	*Harvard Theological Review*
IBC	Interpretation: A Bible Commentary for Teaching and Preaching
ICC	International Critical Commentary
ITSORS	Italian Texts and Studies on Religion and Society

IVPNTC	IVP New Testament Commentary
JBL	*Journal of Biblical Literature*
JETS	*Journal of the Evangelical Theological Society*
JSJ	*Journal for the Study of Judaism*
JSJSup	Supplements to the Journal for the Study of Judaism
JSNT	*Journal for the Study of the New Testament*
JSNTSup	Journal for the Study of the New Testament, Supplement Series
JSPSup	Journal for the Study of the Pseudepigrapha, Supplement Series
JTS	*Journal of Theological Studies*
KEK	Kritisch-exegetischer Kommentar über das Neue Testament
KJV	King James Version
LBS	Linguistic Biblical Studies
LD	Lectio Divina
LSJ	Liddell, Henry George, and Robert Scott. *A Greek-English Lexicon.* 9th ed. Revised and augmented by Henry Stuart Jones and Roderick McKenzie; Oxford: Clarendon, 1940; revised supplement, 1996
LN	Louw, Johannes P., and Eugene A. Nida, eds. *Greek-English Lexicon of the New Testament based on Semantic Domains.* 2nd ed. 2 vols. New York: United Bible Societies, 1989
LNTS	Library of New Testament Studies
LXX	Septuagint
MNTC	Moffatt New Testament Commentary
MSG	*The Message*
MSJ	*The Master's Seminary Journal*
MT	Massoretic Text (Hebrew OT)
NA[28]	*Novum Testamentum Graece.* 28th ed. Edited by B. Aland et al. Stuttgart: Deutsche Bibelgesellschaft, 2012
NABR	New American Bible, Revised Edition
NAC	New American Commentary
NASB	New American Standard Bible
NCB	New Century Bible
NCBC	New Cambridge Bible Commentary
NCCS	New Covenant Commentary Series
NCV	New Century Version
NDBT	*New Dictionary of Biblical Theology.* Edited by T. Desmond Alexander and Brian S. Rosner. Downers Grove, IL: InterVarsity, 2000
NEB	New English Bible
NewDocs	*New Documents Illustrating Early Christianity.* Edited by G. H. R. Horsley and S. Llewelyn. North Ryde, N.S.W.: Ancient History Documentary Research Centre, Macquarie University, 1981–

NET	New English Translation
NIBC	New International Biblical Commentary
NICNT	New International Commentary on the New Testament
NIDNTT	*New International Dictionary of New Testament Theology.* Edited by Colin Brown. 4 vols. Grand Rapids: Zondervan, 1975–1978
NIDNTTE	*New International Dictionary of New Testament Theology and Exegesis.* 2nd ed. Edited by Moisés Silva. Grand Rapids: Zondervan, 2014
NIGTC	New International Greek Testament Commentary
NIV	New International Version
NIVAC	NIV Application Commentary
NJB	New Jerusalem Bible
NKJV	New King James Version
NLT	New Living Translation
NovT	*Novum Testamentum*
NovTSup	Supplements to Novum Testamentum
NRSV	New Revised Standard Version
NT	New Testament
NTC	New Testament Commentary
NTD	Neue Testament Deutsch
NTE	New Testament for Everyone
NTIC	New Testament in Context
NTL	New Testament Library
NTM	New Testament Monographs
NTS	*New Testament Studies*
NTTSD	New Testament Tools, Studies and Documents
OT	Old Testament
OTM	Oxford Theological Monographs
PBM	Paternoster Biblical Monographs
PCS	Pentecostal Commentary Series
PGM	*Greek Magical Papyri*
PTMS	Princeton Theological Monograph Series
REB	Revised English Bible
RSV	Revised Standard Version
SBET	*Scottish Bulletin of Evangelical Theology*
SBG	Studies in Biblical Greek
SBJT	*Southern Baptist Journal of Theology*
SBLGNT	*The Greek New Testament: SBL Edition.* Edited by Michael W. Holmes. Atlanta: Society of Biblical Literature; Bellingham, WA: Logos Bible Software, 2010
SBLMS	Society of Biblical Literature Monograph Series

SCJ	Studies in Christianity and Judaism
SP	Sacra Pagina
TCGNT2	*A Textual Commentary on the Greek New Testament*. 2nd ed. Edited by Bruce M. Metzger. Stuttgart: Deutsche Bibelgesellschaft, 1994
TDNT	*Theological Dictionary of the New Testament*. Edited by Gerhard Kittel and Gerhard Friedrich. Translated by Geoffrey W. Bromiley. 10 vols. Grand Rapids: Eerdmans, 1964–1976
Th.	Theodotion
ThKNT	Theologischer Kommentar zum Neuen Testament
TJ	*Trinity Journal*
TPINTC	TPI New Testament Commentaries
TR	Textus Receptus
TS	Texts and Studies
TTC	Teach the Text Commentary Series
TynBul	*Tyndale Bulletin*
UBS⁵	*The Greek New Testament*. 5th ed. Edited by B. Aland et al. Stuttgart: Deutsche Bibelgesellschaft and United Bible Societies, 2014
VT	*Vetus Testamentum*
WBC	Word Biblical Commentary
WTJ	*Westminster Theological Journal*
WUNT	Wissenschaftliche Untersuchungen zum Neuen Testament
ZECNT	Zondervan Exegetical Commentary on the New Testament
ZNW	*Zeitschrift für die neutestamentliche Wissenschaft*

Introduction

The book of Revelation functions as a kind of literary Rorschach test. An interpretation of it often tells as much about the interpreter as about the message of the book, and this commentary will prove no different. Reactions to Revelation over the centuries have ranged from extremely positive to extremely negative as well as extremely puzzled, usually depending on the religious background and theological stance of the interpreter.[1] This is actually true of all literature, but it is particularly ironic in regard to a book that promises a blessing to those "who hear the words of this prophecy and obey the things written in it" (Rev 1:3; cf. 22:7) and warns against tampering with its message (i.e., adding anything to it or subtracting anything from it; 22:18–19).

Robert Morgan discusses different methods of studying the New Testament and how they contribute to integrating responsible interpretations of its different books, especially Revelation, into a theological whole. He settles on the importance of a chastened historical-critical method for accomplishing the task (i.e., seeking what the author of each text intended in its original setting, without assuming that this is a completely objective task or that one will be initially happy with the message thus discovered). The problem that may arise is that, as he says, "historical exegesis can lead to interpretations which conflict with some Christians' own religious or moral beliefs," and Revelation has proven problematic to many on this score. The options that are open to such Christian interpreters according to Morgan are to "revise their prior beliefs, or . . . engage in theological criticism of the offending text in the light of their own, or the New Testament's, or the biblical author's own better sense of Christianity, or . . . settle for a much looser relationship between their own Christianity and the Bible than the Reformers, for example, envisaged."[2] Such options have all been exercised with John's book.

This commentary, in following an evangelical (i.e., Protestant Reformed) stance on the full authority and truthfulness of Scripture, attempts to follow such a chastened or

---

1. Some extreme examples can be found in Bernard McGinn, "Turning Points in Early Christian Apocalypse Exegesis," in *Apocalyptic Thought in Early Christianity*, ed. Robert J. Daly (Grand Rapids: Baker Academic, 2009), 81–83.

2. Robert Morgan, "The Place of the Book of Revelation in a New Testament Theology," in *Studies in Apocalyptic in Honour of Christopher Rowland*, ed. John Ashton (Leiden: Brill, 2014), 288; the whole essay is valuable (286–304).

receptive historical-critical method and so avoid the later choices Morgan lists (criticism of the text based on my own "better sense of Christianity," opting for a "much looser" relationship with the text). Adjusting "prior beliefs" in line with what the text clearly says and working to be sure that the preferred interpretation is in line with the rest of Scripture is what is attempted here. In addition, this commentary reflects a careful effort to read Revelation in light of its position at the climax of the biblical canon, emphasizing its connections with other Scripture, and in connection with the rich, noncanonical Jewish writings of the first-century world with which Revelation shares many biblical themes (sometimes agreeing, sometimes diverging from their ideas). Working with this material with a receptive, historical-critical method is an attempt to allow John's ancient but inspired book to speak with freshness to us today.

Author

Addressing the question of authorship of a biblical book is important for two reasons: (1) it helps us to gain as clear an idea as possible of the background of the writer and of the audience to which the book was written; and (2) it helps us to establish a basis for the book's authority as Scripture. The first is important for interpretation since its words are the expression of what the author intended to communicate to that audience in that situation. The second is important for the book to carry the privileged authority of inspired Scripture in addressing them as well as others, even if the author is not specifically named in the book. The church looked for certain characteristics to help it assess whether a book carried such privileged authority: Did it have an apostolic connection (authorship by an apostle or one of his associates)? Did it originate in the initial generation of the church's life rather than at a later date? Had it come to be used widely in the life of the church as a whole? Did it cohere with apostolic doctrine as taught by Jesus and his apostles?

For both purposes the evidence of who wrote Revelation places the church on solid ground: for interpretive purposes and for regarding the book as authoritative Scripture.[3] But while the question of the book's authorship does not threaten these two important functions, this does not mean the details are without dispute. The evidence for who the specific author was is quite mixed, and no clear consensus has been reached.

---

3. There were doubts about the canonicity of Rev in some circles, more in the East than in the West and mainly from those who were wary of its apocalyptic character, but it appears in the early list given in the Muratorian Fragment (perhaps as early as AD 170), and Eusebius (*Hist. eccl.* 3.24–25; about AD 325) lists it oddly as first a recognized book and then as possibly a spurious one (i.e., noncanonical) rather than in his middle category of "disputed." Origen also acknowledges it according to Eusebius, *Hist. eccl.* 6.25.3–14. Later it came to full acceptance as canonical, although individual churchmen sometimes struggled with its teachings until even the Reformation. See Adela Yarbro Collins, "Revelation," *ABD* 5:695; Craig R. Koester, *Revelation: A New Translation with Introduction and Commentary*, AYB 38a (New Haven: Yale University Press, 2014), 48–58; Bruce M. Metzger, *The Canon of the New Testament: Its Origin, Development, and Significance* (Oxford: Clarendon, 1987), 203–5, 209–17, 305–15, for details.

The book itself explicitly declares that it came from "John," God's "servant," chosen to be the channel of "the revelation from Jesus Christ" (1:1) that was addressed to the churches of Asia Minor (1:4). This "John" was also a "brother and partner" to those churches (1:9), who wrote out what he heard and saw of God's revelation (22:8). So John produced a work of "prophecy" (1:3; 22:6, 10, 18–19), prophesying (10:11) as God commissioned him to do. So we know the author's name and a few details about his work, but what is not clear is the identity of this "John" who wrote the book.[4]

We must be careful when encountering a name familiar to us from wider biblical usage not to assume unthinkingly that it must represent the person we know. "John" was a widely used name in Jewish and Christian circles of the late first century,[5] so the range of possibilities for the individual named "John" that the readers knew could be great, and some of them could certainly be unknown to us. It seems clear that this person was known to the readers, since he feels no need to give a further description or introduction—he can assume the immediate readers know him by this simple name.

The most likely possibilities for identifying this "John" who wrote Revelation are: (1) John the apostle, who was one of the sons of Zebedee, part of the inner circle of Jesus's early followers (along with his brother James and Peter). John the apostle is often identified as the author of the Fourth Gospel and as the "beloved disciple" mentioned in John (John 13:23; 19:26; 20:2; 21:7; 21:20), although that book has no author named in its text and the two figures could be different. John the apostle lived and served in Ephesus for the latter part of his life according to church tradition.[6] (2) John the "elder" or "presbyter," if different from the apostle, who is named in 2 John 1 and 3 John 1 and in some fragments from the writings of Papias, the bishop of Hierapolis in the early second century.[7] Eusebius (*Hist. eccl.* 3.39) understood this to be a separate person from the apostle, but many others identify the two. Among those who see them as separate, some take "John the elder" to be the author of the Johannine letters but not of the Gospel, and some reverse that identification. (3) A prophet "John," different from the other two, who was active among the churches of Asia Minor in the first century and known to them but unknown to us except for this book.[8]

---

4. It is clear that "John" is not a pseudonym, a false ascription of authorship. This was common among apocalypses in ancient Judaism (e.g., 1 En., 4 Ezra, 2 Bar.) because the name of a respected figure from Israel's past gave an air of authority to a book written much later. This temporal gap is not the case with Rev. In addition, if "John" were a pseudonym, it would likely have been enhanced by further descriptions (the apostle, the beloved disciple, etc.) to give it such authority.

5. Richard Bauckham, *Jesus and the Eyewitnesses: The Gospels as Eyewitness Testimony*, 2nd ed. (Grand Rapids: Eerdmans, 2017), 67–74, 85–91: "John" appears as the fifth most common male name among first-century Palestinian Jews according to studies of names preserved in various ancient sources.

6. Eusebius, *Hist. eccl.* 3.20–23.

7. These fragments have not survived in an intact text of Papias's writings but are quoted by later patristic writers: Eusebius, *Hist. eccl.* 3.39; Jerome, *Vir. ill.* 18; Philip of Side, *Hist. eccl.* 4.6.

8. *Const. ap.* 7.46 (late fourth century) records the earliest bishops of Ephesus as "Timothy, ordained by Paul" and then "John, ordained by John." If this is accurate, it attests to several Ephesian church leaders named John.

Evidence for one or another of these options is debatable, and interpreters have not reached a clear consensus. The primary sticking point is that the external evidence for authorship (drawn from attestation in the early church) seems to be at odds with the internal evidence (drawn from characteristics of the book's style and content). The external evidence points strongly toward authorship by John the apostle (who is assumed to have written also the Gospel and Epistles of John), while the internal evidence makes that identification difficult.

The widespread opinion of early patristic writers was that John the apostle wrote the book of Revelation. Some of these were active in the early second century, and a few have some kind of connection to Asia Minor. The earliest is Justin Martyr (*Dial.* 81.4), whose dialogue with Trypho is set in Ephesus where Justin lived for a time (about AD 132). Another is Irenaeus (*Haer.* 4.20.11; written about AD 180), who was born in Smyrna but spent most of his ministry in Gaul (Lyon). Others who identify John the apostle as the writer of Revelation include Clement of Alexandria (*Quis div.* 42), Hippolytus (*Antichr.* 35–36), Tertullian (*Praescr.* 36.3), and Origen (*Comm. Jo.* 2.4). This external attestation is quite strong.[9]

Only later do we find patristic writers who dispute this identification, most notably Dionysius of Alexandria (mid-third century). In resisting the teaching of an earthly millennium based on Revelation, he denied that it was written by the apostle John (who authored the Gospel and Epistles) but acknowledged that it was an inspired work written by someone else named John. His arguments center on internal differences between Revelation and the other Johannine books: how they present themselves, their ideas, and their literary or grammatical style. He suggests there must have been more than one John serving the church in Ephesus.[10] The differences he observed are picked up by interpreters even today who believe they show that the apostle was not the author of Revelation. What is sometimes said about Dionysius's objections is that they are true in part but exaggerated and that they were due to his theological bias against chiliasm as he understood it.[11]

What is not as often pursued, at least in evangelical circles, is the possible bias that lay behind the judgments of those patristic writers who *espoused* apostolic authorship for Revelation. While we should respect and carefully consider the opinions of church leaders such as Justin, Irenaeus, Tertullian, and others, they were not infallible,[12] and

---

9. Donald Guthrie, *New Testament Introduction*, 4th ed. (Downers Grove, IL: InterVarsity Press, 1990), 931: "There are few books in the New Testament with stronger early attestation."

10. Eusebius, *Hist. eccl.* 7.25.26.

11. Gerhard Maier, *Die Johannesoffenbarung und die Kirche*, WUNT 25 (Tübingen: Mohr Siebeck, 1981), 96–104; Ned Bernard Stonehouse, *The Apocalypse in the Ancient Church: A Study in the History of the New Testament Canon* (ThD diss., Free University of Amsterdam, 1929), 123–28; Robert L. Thomas, *Revelation 1–7* (Chicago: Moody, 1992), 2–11.

12. Eusebius, *Hist. eccl.* 3.31, 39, and Papias as well as Clement of Alexandria (*Strom.* 3.6.52) confuse Philip the apostle (John 1, 12, 14) with Philip the evangelist (Acts 6, 8, 21). Tertullian, *Praescr.* 36.3 reports that John's exile in Patmos came after he was first "plunged in burning oil and suffer[ed] nothing." See John A. T. Robinson, *Redating the New Testament* (Philadelphia: Westminster, 1976), 222–24, for other questions that can be raised about patristic traditions concerning the apostle and Rev.

their accounts do not record the evidence that led them to the conclusions they express. Did Justin have a direct line of information from Ephesus some thirty-five years earlier? What about Irenaeus, who wrote some eighty-five years later in Gaul? Were their judgments about authorship influenced at all by the apologetic value of being able to cite a major apostle instead of a more obscure local prophet? Evaluation of bias should affect how we read all sources, although it does not render their testimony automatically suspect.

The internal evidence of the book's content and style seems to point away from authorship by John the apostle, but this must also be subject to careful assessment since the evidence is mixed. On the one hand, the style and grammar of Revelation are clearly different compared to the Gospel and Epistles of John. The latter books are written in simple Greek, but the style is smooth, consistent, and without grammatical oddities. But Revelation is notable for its grammatical irregularities and is markedly unlike the other Johannine books on a number of counts, while still communicating with power and effectiveness.[13] Scholars must assess how to account for these differences. Are they due to variations in genre, subject matter, or sources that were used? Do they manifest John's skill at varying his style intentionally? Could the use of a secretary or amanuensis have caused the differences? Were the books written at different times and reflect a change in John's abilities to write Greek? Did John write Revelation hurriedly without time to edit his work as with the other books? The last three suggestions are quite unlikely,[14] but the first two explanations merit serious consideration.[15]

Similar things can be said about the book's vocabulary and theological themes. In this area there are noticeable differences as well as clear similarities, including unique expressions characteristic only of Revelation and the Gospel and Epistles of John among the New Testament writings. Interpreters assess these differently as well, some focusing on continuity and seeing the differences as explainable due to the change in setting and purpose,[16] and some focusing on discontinuity although acknowledging some parallels. Where one places the emphasis makes a difference for the decision on authorship of Revelation. See the section at the end of this commentary entitled "Theology of Revelation" for further discussion.

13. See C. F. D. Moule, *An Idiom Book of New Testament Greek*, 2nd ed. (Cambridge: Cambridge University Press, 1959), 3; and G. Mussies, *The Morphology of Koine Greek as Used in the Apocalypse of John: A Study in Bilingualism* (Leiden: Brill, 1971), 351–52, who concludes, "The linguistic and stylistic divergence of the Apc. on the one hand and the Gospel and Letters of St. John on the other, proves beyond any reasonable doubt that all these works as we have them before us were not phrased by one and the same man" (352).

14. See Richard Bauckham, *The Climax of Prophecy: Studies in the Book of Revelation* (Edinburgh: T&T Clark, 1993), x–xiii; idem, *The Theology of the Book of Revelation* (Cambridge: Cambridge University Press, 1993), 3–4; and Nigel Turner, *Style*,

vol. 4 of James Hope Moulton, *A Grammar of New Testament Greek* (Edinburgh: T&T Clark, 1976), 146, on John's thorough attention to detail in composing the book.

15. See G. K. Beale, *The Book of Revelation*, NIGTC (Grand Rapids: Eerdmans, 1999), 34–35; and Vern Sheridan Poythress, "Johannine Authorship and the Use of Intersentence Conjunctions in the Book of Relevation," *WTJ* 47 (1985): 329–36.

16. I. Howard Marshall, *New Testament Theology: Many Witnesses, One Gospel* (Downers Grove, IL: InterVarsity Press, 2004), 570–74; Grant R. Osborne, *Revelation*, BECNT (Grand Rapids: Baker, 2002), 2–6; Stephen S. Smalley, *Thunder and Love: John's Revelation and John's Community* (Milton Keynes: Word, 1994), 57–73.

A further point about internal evidence is the way "John" describes himself in Revelation. If the author is the apostle, why did he not declare his status at some point instead of citing only his simple name and modest descriptions (servant, brother, partner)? Even the claim to write as a "prophet" can be regarded as less authoritative than "apostle." In challenging some of the false teachers in the churches (e.g., 2:6, 14–15, 20–23) and in presenting the Spirit's messages as intended seemingly for other churches beyond the ones he knew (2:7 and parallels), the apostle might be expected to make some reference to his experience of the Lord's earthly ministry and his appointment at its very beginning (cf. 1 John 1:1–5; 2:7). These points would seem to be relevant alongside his commission as a prophet/revealer by the risen Lord (Rev 1:9–11), but we only find the latter. On the other hand, the writer of the Gospel and Epistles is equally modest about any apostolic qualifications to write, being content to ground it in his witness to what he had seen (John 15:27; 20:30–31; 21:24) and his relationship with his audience (2 John 1; 3 John 1).

The authorship question, then, finds careful, faithful interpreters going in different directions. Many affirm authorship by the apostle John with varying degrees of confidence.[17] Some, after setting forth the issues, leave the question essentially unresolved.[18] And some decide that it was written not by the apostle but by another church leader, a prophet known to the churches of Asia Minor, also named John and influenced by the apostle.[19] The final option is the conclusion followed in this commentary. However, all of these would agree with the point argued at the outset of this discussion: none of these conclusions impair our ability to interpret the book within its original setting or to assign inspired authority to its teachings.[20]

Date and Setting

Two sets of dates are generally proposed for the setting of the book: an early date (AD 64–69) near the end of or shortly following Nero's reign as emperor, and a late date (AD 95–98) near the end of or shortly following Domitian's reign. Most interpreters prefer the later date. The external evidence generally favors the later date,

17. D. A. Carson and Douglas J. Moo, *An Introduction to the New Testament*, 2nd ed. (Grand Rapids: Zondervan, 2005), 705–7; Andreas J. Köstenberger, L. Scott Kellum, and Charles L. Quarles, *The Cradle, the Cross, and the Crown: An Introduction to the New Testament*, 2nd ed. (Nashville: B&H Academic, 2016), 931–33; Craig S. Keener, *Revelation*, NIVAC (Grand Rapids: Zondervan, 2000), 54–55; Robert H. Mounce, *The Book of Revelation*, rev. ed. (Grand Rapids: Eerdmans, 1998), 8–15; Osborne, *Revelation*, 2–6; C. Marvin Pate, *The Writings of John: A Survey of the Gospel, Epistles, and Apocalypse* (Grand Rapids: Zondervan, 2011), 372–73; and Stephen S. Smalley, *The Revelation to John: A Commentary on the Greek Text of the Apocalypse* (Downers Grove, IL: InterVarsity Press, 2005), 2–3.

18. Beale, *Revelation*, 34–36; George Eldon Ladd, *A Commentary on the Revelation of John* (Grand Rapids: Eerdmans, 1972), 7–8; and Merrill C. Tenney, *Interpreting Revelation* (Grand Rapids: Eerdmans, 1957), 15–16.

19. George R. Beasley-Murray, "Book of Revelation," in *DLNT* 1031–33; Henry Barclay Swete, *The Apocalypse of St. John*, 3rd ed. (London: Macmillan, 1911), clxxx–clxxxv; Ben Witherington III, *Revelation*, NCBC (Cambridge: Cambridge University Press, 2003), 1–3.

20. Beale, *Revelation*, 35–36.

based primarily on evidence from Irenaeus, *Haer.* 5.30.3, that John wrote toward the end of Domitian's rule, and from Eusebius, *Hist. eccl.* 3.17–20, who quotes Irenaeus and adds his own details about John's exile to Patmos under Domitian and later return to Ephesus.[21] Eusebius also describes Domitian's cruelty and persecution of Christians and the revocation of his honors by the Roman senate after his reign had ended. In his account, Eusebius refers twice to the fact that Roman historians themselves wrote about Domitian's savagery and his subsequent dishonor.[22]

External evidence for a date under Nero relies more on general historical accounts of his persecution of Christians in Rome and the martyrdoms of Peter and Paul there in the mid-to-late 60s AD (e.g., Tacitus, *Ann.* 15.44; Suetonius, *Nero* 16; 1 Clem. 5.3–7; Eusebius, *Hist. eccl.* 2.25) rather than explicit patristic citations that John wrote during his reign. While there is evidence of Christian persecution in Rome in the time of Nero, evidence of such troubles in Asia Minor is lacking. However, scholars of previous centuries often dated Revelation in the late sixties,[23] and it is commonly found today among preterist interpreters of Revelation,[24] as well as a few others.[25]

Internal evidence for dating centers around interpretive issues in Revelation that engender their own debated points apart from how they might provide information for dating the book at the earlier or later time. These include: (1) the condition of the churches in Revelation 2–3 (do they reflect a decline that would not have been true at the earlier date when compared to what we can see of those churches from Acts and the letters of Paul?); (2) the scope and severity of Christian persecution reflected in the book (1:9; 2:13; 6:9; 7:14; 11:7; 12:17; 13:7; 16:6; 17:6; 18:24; 19:2; 20:4); (3) the identity of the Jerusalem temple that is "measured" in 11:1–2; (4) the hints of Nero's return from apparent death (Nero *redivivus*) that may show up in 13:3, 12; 17:8, 16; (5) the list of kings in 17:9–12 (can they show which emperor reigned when John wrote the book?); and (6) the identification of Babylon the prostitute in chapters 17–18 (does she represent Jerusalem, who was judged in AD 70?). These cannot be

---

21. There is also early evidence from the commentary on Rev by Victorinus of Pettau (late third century), who says that Domitian sent John to work in the mines in Patmos during the time that he wrote Rev. According to Victorinus, after Domitian's death John was active in spreading the visions given to him even as an aged man. Cf. William C. Weinrich, ed. and trans., "Victorinus," in *Latin Commentaries on Revelation*, ACT (Downers Grove, IL: IVP Academic, 2011), 13–14.

22. Leonard L. Thompson, *The Book of Revelation: Apocalypse and Empire* (New York: Oxford University Press, 1990), 95–115, argues that the standard Roman historians who wrote in the early second century about Domitian's savagery and demands for worship as divine (Pliny the Younger, Tacitus, Suetonius, Dio Chrysostom) exaggerated his negative traits as a foil for praising Trajan (ruled AD 98–117) in idealized terms. Their portrayal of Domitian influenced later Roman historians.

It is likely that Eusebius referred to some of these (earlier and later Roman writers) in his account of Domitian.

23. This is the observation of Robinson, *Redating*, 224–26; also J. Christian Wilson, "The Problem of the Domitianic Date of Revelation," *NTS* 39 (1993): 587–89.

24. David Chilton, *The Days of Vengeance: An Exposition of the Book of Revelation* (Ft. Worth: Dominion, 1987), 1–6; and Kenneth L. Gentry, *Before Jerusalem Fell: Dating the Book of Revelation*, rev. ed. (Atlanta: American Vision, 1998), 343–53. For evaluation of this specific view, see Mark L. Hitchcock, "A Critique of the Preterist View of Revelation and the Jewish War," *BSac* 164 (2007): 89–100.

25. Albert A. Bell, "Date of John's Apocalypse: The Evidence of Some Roman Historians Reconsidered," *NTS* 25 (1978): 93–102; Robinson, *Redating*, 221–53; Wilson, "Problem," 587–605.

discussed here in detail, but see comments at the passages cited for discussion of their significance for dating. Where these do seem to add something significant for dating the book, they point to the reign of Domitian rather than the reign of Nero.[26]

The scope and severity of Christian persecution should be described here, however, since it is central to understanding the setting and occasion of the book. One of the scenarios often found in older commentaries on Revelation is that under Domitian persecution of Christians was severe, empire wide, and orchestrated from Rome.[27] This is understandable given the general picture of Domitian's rule found in some of the ancient sources. In recent years, however, the broader historical perception has changed, and a different, more nuanced picture has emerged, one that helps us to understand Revelation better.[28] The evidence from the wider historical circumstances as well as from the book itself suggests that Christians in Asia Minor were subject to various kinds of opposition and harassment for their faith, but it was localized and sporadic, not empire wide and organized from the top. It consisted primarily of social opprobrium and economic reprisals for not participating fully in the pervasive idolatry of the religious and commercial life of their communities.[29] It could sometimes lead to imprisonment or even death at the hands of local officials. John's exile in Patmos seems an example of this (1:9), as well as the death of Antipas in Pergamum (2:13). But there is no evidence of more severe and widespread persecution at the time John writes. Yet the broader religious and cultural resistance to their exclusive faith in only one true God and one Lord would leave the churches that John addressed feeling vulnerable and threatened by greater persecution that could break out at any time, and this is what John fears for them as well.[30] The other allusions in the book to martyrdoms, bloodshed, and warfare against God's people (6:9; 7:14; 11:7; 12:17; 13:7; 16:6; 17:6; 18:24; 19:2; 20:4) are primarily descriptions of the intense persecutions to come during the final tribulation leading up to Christ's return. Some of them may include allusions to the broader pattern of righteous suffering in a fallen world throughout the history of God's people over the centuries, but the severe persecution was still to come, perhaps soon, from the perspective of John and his first readers.[31] See discussion at these passages.

26. See also the more focused analysis in Guthrie, *Introduction*, 948–56; Köstenberger, Kellum, and Quarles, *Introduction*, 933–40; Koester, *Revelation*, 71–79.

27. E.g., R. H. Charles, *A Critical and Exegetical Commentary on the Revelation of St. John*, 2 vols., ICC (Edinburgh: T&T Clark, 1920), 1:xci–vii; Swete, *Apocalypse*, lxxxiv–viii, cv; also Thomas, *Revelation 1–7*, 22–23.

28. John Granger Cook, *Roman Attitudes toward the Christians: From Claudius to Hadrian*, WUNT 261 (Tübingen: Mohr Siebeck, 2011), 117–37; Steven J. Friesen, *Imperial Cults and the Apocalypse of John: Reading Revelation in the Ruins* (New York: Oxford University Press, 2001), 143–46; Paul Trebilco,

The Early Christians in Ephesus from Paul to Ignatius, WUNT 166 (Tübingen: Mohr Siebeck, 2004), 342–47.

29. Thomas B. Slater, "On the Social Setting of the Revelation to John," *NTS* 44 (1998): 238, 245–56.

30. Cook, *Roman Attitudes*, 246–51; Köstenberger, Kellum, and Quarles, *Introduction*, 933–35; Koester, *Revelation*, 74–79.

31. Another valuable note is Trebilco's suggestion (*Early Christians in Ephesus*, 346) that John wanted to rouse some of his readers to see dangers—present as well as future—in their situation of which they themselves were unaware because they failed to view them from heaven's perspective.

Genre

The question of genre or type of literature is important because how to understand a written work is inextricably bound up with figuring out what kind of literature it is. An obituary follows a different form than a yearly employee evaluation; a news report should be different from an opinion column. Writers write and readers read with certain expectations of how a certain kind of text should be composed and then understood. If we misunderstand the genre, we will misconstrue the text.

In the very first verses as well as the final verses of Revelation, John provides clear signals of what kind of book he is writing so that readers can operate with the right expectations. He characterizes his work as apocalyptic, prophetic, and epistolary in 1:1–5. He reinforces the latter two genre categories in his epilogue in 22:10–21 and reminds us of its apocalyptic character by using his trademark expression "I saw" (εἶδον) some forty-five times in the book and by structuring its major sections by references to receiving visions "in the Spirit" (1:9–10; 4:1–2; 17:1–3; 21:9–10). Its epistolary character appears again in 1:11 and chapters 2–3.[32]

Of the three major genre types, prophecy is the one John explicitly identifies as most characteristic of his book. He calls the work a "prophecy" five times (1:3; 22:7, 10, 18, 19) and uses the verb "prophesy" of what he is commissioned to do (10:11). In addition, he connects his work with the heritage of the Old Testament prophets by explicit statement (10:7; 11:18; 22:6, 9), by phrasing his "letters" to the churches as prophetic oracles (see comments at 2:1), and by modeling his own commission along the lines of Ezekiel's (10:8–11).[33] While the other two genres are important to the book, prophecy is most central to what John has written. As Bauckham declares, it is "an apocalyptic prophecy in the form of a circular letter."[34]

In reading Revelation as a prophecy then, we must expect to find it declaring God's future for his people and his world both in judgment and in redemption. It is important not to operate, as some do, with a conception of prophecy that focuses only on its claim to speak directly for God to the moral and religious failings of its audience. This is certainly important, but seeing God's future, foretelling what will come because of God's plan, and then calling for a response of repentance and endurance is central to what the Old Testament prophets did[35] and to what John sees

---

32. Bauckham, *Theology*, 1–17.

33. Frederick David Mazzaferri, *The Genre of the Book of Revelation from a Source-Critical Perspective*, BZNW 54 (Berlin: de Gruyter, 1989), 379–83.

34. Bauckham, *Theology*, 2. See also Bert Jan Lietaert Peerbolte, *The Antecedents of Antichrist: A Traditio-Historical Study of the Earliest Christian Views on Eschatological Opponents*, JSJSup 49 (Leiden: Brill, 1996), 115: "It is a prophetic letter describing the present and future of the Christian communities of Asia Minor by means of apocalyptic visions."

35. O. Palmer Robertson, *The Christ of the Prophets* (Phillipsburg, NJ: P&R, 2004), 412–21; Mark F. Rooker, "The Doctrine of the Future in the Prophets," in *Eschatology: Biblical, Historical, and Practical Approaches*, ed. D. Jeffrey Bingham and Glenn R. Kreider (Grand Rapids: Kregel Academic, 2016), 175–93.

his own book doing as a work of prophecy.[36] In the way that it builds on the heritage of the Old Testament prophets, Revelation should be understood as "the climax of prophecy," to co-opt Bauckham's title for his book in which he says, "John was writing what he understood to be a work of prophetic scripture, the climax of prophetic revelation, which gathered up the prophetic meaning of the Old Testament scriptures and disclosed the way in which it was being and was to be fulfilled in the last days."[37]

What is unique about Revelation among the New Testament books is its second genre type, namely, its character as an apocalypse. This was a familiar literary form in ancient Judaism and early Christianity, closely related to prophecy,[38] which included Old Testament examples like Isaiah 24–27, 56–66, parts of Daniel, Ezekiel, Joel, Amos, Zechariah,[39] and New Testament examples like Matthew 24 (and parallels), 2 Thessalonians 2, and possibly others. It flourished from about 200 BC to AD 200 and is represented in several noncanonical works from that period (e.g., 1 En., Sib. Or., 4 Ezra, 2 Bar.). The Greek word ἀποκάλυψις, used in Revelation 1:1 as the title of the book, can be translated as "revelation, unveiling" or as "apocalypse," but not in the technical sense of denoting a genre of literature. However, it fittingly characterizes the book more generally as God's disclosure of the invisible, divine reality that lies behind the visible world of human history as well as his disclosure of the events that will fulfill his sovereign plan for the destiny of this world. In addition, its literary character is parallel to other apocalypses in recording extraordinary visions—often mediated through heavenly beings—that are highly symbolic, dramatic, and often enigmatic. The visions are sometimes puzzling not so much because of their symbolism but because of their impressionistic, nonlinear quality: they pay attention to and even repeat some details, while omitting others or including details in inverted order. They skip to the end of the story without telling what events led to that conclusion.[40] This makes them vivid and true to life (how else could a vision of heavenly or hellish things be written?), but we could wish for greater explanation. Overall, apocalypse as a genre requires special attention to methods of interpretation that are appropriate to such literature (to be discussed below).

The other major genre type of Revelation is its epistolary form, reflected in its prologue, epilogue, and in chapters 2–3. The epistolary opening in 1:4–5 and closing in 22:21 are familiar to us from other New Testament letters. Those features as well

---

36. See comments at 10:6–7; 11:15–18; and the repeated phrase "what must happen soon" or "what must happen after these things" (1:1; 4:1; 22:6; cf. 1:19).

37. Bauckham, *Climax*, xi; also idem, *Theology*, 4–5.

38. The way that John easily juxtaposes "apocalypse" in 1:1 with "prophecy" in 1:3 shows that he sees them as complementary, not at odds with each other.

39. The later sections (apart from Daniel) are sometimes called "proto-apocalyptic" as in Frederick J. Murphy, *Apocalypticism in the Bible and Its World: A Comprehensive Introduction*

(Grand Rapids: Baker Academic, 2012), 27–66. For further introduction to apocalyptic literature, see John J. Collins, *The Apocalyptic Imagination: An Introduction to Jewish Apocalyptic Literature*, 3rd ed. (Grand Rapids: Eerdmans, 2016); and C. Marvin Pate, *Interpreting Revelation and Other Apocalyptic Literature: An Exegetical Handbook*, HNTE (Grand Rapids: Kregel Academic, 2016).

40. These and other features are surveyed in G. Biguzzi, "A Figurative and Narrative Grammar of Revelation," *NovT* 45 (2003): 387–97.

as the specific churches named as recipients in 1:4, 11, and in chapters 2–3 remind us that this composition was written to address a certain occasion or situation in the life of particular first-century readers. It has value also for a wider audience as all Scripture does, but those Christians in that time and place must be figured into our understanding of the book's purpose and meaning. To be sure, other New Testament epistles range across a spectrum from those that are quite "occasional" (written to address a very specific audience and its issues; e.g., Gal, 1 Cor) to others that are more "general" or thematic (written to a wider group of churches or to serve a broader theological purpose; e.g., Rom, Eph, 1 Pet), and Revelation as an epistle fits the latter group.[41] But its address to those original readers must be factored into our interpretation.

A related genre feature concerns the varied ways that John uses to present the accounts of his visions. Sometimes these are recorded in narrative form, telling the story of events that he observed in chronological sequence, but in other cases he uses the mode of a contemporaneous description or report, presenting what he saw as though observing the whole scene at once and moving from one object of attention to another rather than chronologically. Paying attention within individual passages to such issues of microgenre will enhance our understanding as well. See the note at 4:5 for further details.

The mixed character of the genre of Revelation (an apocalyptic prophecy in epistolary form) leads to issues of interpretation. These can be introduced first by focusing on understanding the apocalyptic imagery of Revelation and then by surveying different hermeneutical approaches to the book as a whole.

Imagery and Symbols

The book's apocalyptic symbols alternatively draw us in or repel us depending on how we approach them. They can be frustrating and off-putting or fascinating and uplifting to different readers at the same time or to the same reader at different times. Disputes over how to understand its imagery often result in interpreters talking past each other because they disagree on essential points about what "literal" interpretation means and what "symbolic" or metaphorical interpretation means. The following paragraphs present six axioms to try to bring greater understanding.

1. For interpreting a book like Revelation, *literal* does not automatically equal "real, actual" or "true, accurate," and *symbolic* does not equal "imaginary, existing in

---

41. J. Ramsey Michaels, *Interpreting the Book of Revelation*, GNTE (Grand Rapids: Baker, 1992), 30; also Bauckham, *Theology*, 12–17, who rightly points out that the book addresses some circumstances common to all the churches while targeting other issues peculiar to individual churches. Likewise, not all the Christians he addresses were materially poor or socially oppressed and in need of consolation—some were wealthy and complicit with the idolatrous system and needed rebuke, as chs. 2–3 show.

someone's mind but not existing in the real world" or "untrue, deceptive." *Literal* and *symbolic* concern the way the words and sentences in an utterance or a text refer to entities in the extratextual world, but not to the character of those entities or the truth or falsity of those sentences.[42] Unfortunately, people commonly confuse the two spheres, and so we get an expression like "he literally threw me under the bus" as a way of saying "he actually betrayed me when he should have been loyal." Theologians at both ends of the conservative-liberal continuum have been guilty of misunderstanding or misusing language in this way. To say that the statement, "Jesus is risen," is a metaphor for how he lives on in the hearts of his followers is a way of evading or misrepresenting the New Testament witness to Christ's resurrection. On the other hand, to say, "this must be taken literally, otherwise language has no meaning" is a misunderstanding of how language works, not just in biblical usage but in everyday life.

2. Language that is literal or symbolic can refer to a range of entities of different character and scope. Those entities can be concrete or abstract, and in either case they can be quite specific or very general in scope. Eisenhower's phrase "military-industrial complex" did not mean a manufacturing installation with a specific address but a broad yet concrete set of corporate and governmental interests operating in the US in 1961. If he had said "this tangled web of business and government," the referent would be no different. The context must guide us about what is spoken of and what its character and scope are.

3. A literal description can include emotive or connotative values as well as a denotative or referential sense. *Literal* does not mean "only literal" or "purely referential." Symbols can certainly add greater associated meanings of this sort, but literal description is not devoid of these. When I tell a friend I am going to "New York, New York," it is not greatly different than saying, "the Big Apple." For the related issue of referring to transcendent entities (i.e., realities that cannot be completely captured by human description or explanation), see the discussion of "steno-symbols" versus "tensive symbols" below.

4. A symbol can refer to a real entity without corresponding in a point-by-point way with the reality that it represents.[43] It only needs to correspond in one crucial way to point to that reality, but it may match it in more than one way. This is another thing that is commonly misunderstood. Thus the metaphor, "she's my rock of Gibraltar," may not be the most tactful way to praise a reliable friend who also has a weight problem. We sometimes confuse details about the symbol with its referent, but they are not the same. Being sensitive to the immediate as well as wider contexts of an utterance is required to sort out the degree of correspondence.

---

42. G. B. Caird, *The Language and Imagery of the Bible* (London: Duckworth, 1980), 131–32.

43. This is why Bruce M. Metzger, *Breaking the Code: Understanding the Book of Revelation* (Nashville: Abingdon, 1993), 14, reminds us that in the imagery of Rev, "the descriptions are *descriptions of symbols, not of the reality conveyed by the symbols.*"

5. Norman Perrin introduced the distinction of "steno-symbols" versus "tensive symbols" in discussing Jewish apocalyptic symbols and Jesus's teaching about the kingdom of God.[44] Drawing on the work of others, he defines a *steno-symbol* as having a one-to-one relation with a specific referent and cites symbols in Jewish apocalyptic that refer to specific historical figures or events (e.g., Antiochus IV Epiphanes; Rome's coming). A *tensive symbol* is one that has "a set of meanings that can neither be exhausted nor adequately expressed by any one referent."[45] This basic distinction makes sense, but Perrin pushes the contrast in a way that exaggerates it at both ends: in his view a steno-symbol cannot have evocative or deeper meaning beyond the one-to-one identification, while a tensive symbol carries hardly any definable sense at all. It invites us "to explore the manifold ways in which the experience of God can become an existential reality to man."[46] It refers not "to a single identifiable event which every man experiences at one and the same time [but it] is something which cannot be exhausted in any one event but which every man experiences in his own time."[47] The tensive symbol "tease[s] the mind into ever new evocations of meanings."[48]

Perrin to his credit does not rely solely on these definitions to validate his reading of what Jesus meant by "kingdom of God." He argues the case on source-critical and theological grounds. But these comments about symbols are a distortion of the range of things symbols can do in biblical usage, and others have critiqued his distinction for this distortion.[49] Collins, however, perpetuates the problem by asserting that poetic, mythological, and apocalyptic literature "articulat[es] feelings and attitudes rather than describing reality in an objective way. . . . [it] is expressive rather than referential, symbolic rather than factual."[50] This is a false dichotomy.

It is certainly true that biblical symbols often refer to transcendent entities about God, judgment, and redemption that are hard for humans to grasp or describe fully, especially in literal propositions. Imagery helps to expand our conception of God and his ways without reducing its profound mystery to prosaic terms. But it is important in turn not to reduce God's ways with humans and his plans for his good creation to the purely spiritual and otherworldly. There is an irreducible "earthiness of biblical eschatology" that resists complete spiritualization.[51] God's redemption involves the resurrection of Christ and those who are

---

44. Norman Perrin, "Eschatology and Hermeneutics: Reflections on Method in the Interpretation of the New Testament," *JBL* 93 (1974): 10–13; idem, *Jesus and the Language of the Kingdom* (Philadelphia: Fortress, 1976), 29–32, 43, 59.

45. Perrin, "Eschatology and Hermeneutics," 10–11.

46. Perrin, "Eschatology and Hermeneutics," 13.

47. Perrin, "Eschatology and Hermeneutics," 13.

48. Perrin, "Eschatology and Hermeneutics," 13.

49. Dale C. Allison, *The End of the Ages Has Come: An Early Interpretation of the Passion and Resurrection of Jesus* (Philadelphia: Fortress, 1985), 106–12; Collins, *Apocalyptic Imagination*, 19–24, 128–29.

50. Collins, *Apocalyptic Imagination*, 21.

51. David L. Turner, "The New Jerusalem in Revelation 21:1–22:5: Consummation of a Biblical Continuum," in *Dispensationalism, Israel and the Church: The Search for Definition*, ed. Craig A. Blaising and Darrell L. Bock (Grand Rapids: Zondervan, 1992), 278. See also George Eldon Ladd, *The Presence of the Future: The Eschatology of Biblical Realism* (Grand Rapids: Eerdmans, 1974), 59–64; idem, *A Theology of the New Testament*, rev. ed., ed. Donald A. Hagner (Grand Rapids: Eerdmans, 1993), 680–83.

his to a "spiritual" but *bodily* existence suited for an eternity with him (1 Cor 15; 2 Cor 5). And the coming judgment and redemption of his creation seems also to involve not a casting aside of this world in favor of a purely ethereal existence but a radical renewal that sets it free from the effects of sin (Rom 8). The Old Testament typological parallels that Revelation uses to portray the future events that will consummate such judgment and redemption should lead us to understand that John's symbols likewise do not cast aside this "earthiness" in his portrayal of what is coming (see discussion below of typology and use of the OT).

6. Determining how literal or symbolic a description might be and what the symbol signifies must be assessed in light of its ancient setting. This starts with careful attention to the immediate and wider contexts within Revelation itself, but then moves to the wider New Testament, both its apocalyptic texts (e.g., Mark 13 and parallels; 2 Thess) and others that are nearly apocalyptic or speak to the coming consummation (e.g., Acts 1, 3; Rom 8; 1 Cor 15; 1 Thess). Very important for Revelation is research into its Old Testament allusions. How the Old Testament itself conceives of the prophetic future and represents that by its descriptions and symbols is particularly relevant since John identifies himself with the tradition of the Old Testament prophets as mentioned in the discussion of genre above. The wider search for conceptual parallels should extend from there to ancient Jewish and Christian apocalyptic texts since many of John's symbols occur there also as a further development of Old Testament traditions about God's future for the world. Greco-Roman imagery and conceptual parallels can be important also, but John seems to have mediated these through his Old Testament and apocalyptic heritage (e.g., Balaam, Jezebel, the beast from the sea, Babylon the prostitute) so they do not seem to be as important on their own.[52] It is important, as in all interpretation of ancient texts, not to assume that our modern instincts about what the symbols could or should mean will be reliable.[53] This caveat applies both to some conservative interpreters who jump immediately to a certain feature of modern life that seems parallel (e.g., Cobra attack helicopters, nuclear weapons, embedded microchips as the mark of the beast) as well as to more liberal interpreters with apologetic hesitations about what a modern audience is prepared to believe.[54]

Here are some illustrations of these ideas from Revelation (see specific passages in the commentary for discussion). In 5:6 the "lamb" bears little literal correspondence to Jesus (not wooly, only two eyes and no horns, but slain as a sacrifice and then

---

52. Alan Bandy, "The Hermeneutics of Symbolism: How to Interpret the Symbols of John's Apocalypse," *SBJT* 14 (2010): 49–54, gives similar circles of context.

53. Bauckham, *Theology*, 18–22.

54. See Bandy, "Hermeneutics," 47–48, on the former. See Collins, *Apocalyptic Imagination*, 1–2, on the latter. He mentions Klaus Koch's 1970 book entitled *Ratlos vor der Apokalyptik*

(Gütersloh: Gütersloher Verlagshaus), describing how standard NT critics were "'perplexed' or 'embarrassed' by apocalyptic," and so its texts and ideas were thus "often avoided or ignored by biblical scholarship." Other translations of the word *ratlos* could be "at a loss" or "ashamed." The English title toned it down a notch: *The Rediscovery of Apocalyptic* (1972).

able to stand again after the ordeal), but there is no doubt about the quite specific (earthly as well as transcendent) person and experience that it represents. The four trumpets of Revelation 8 picture hail, fire, and blood pouring from the sky, the seas and inland waters turning to blood and made poisonous, heavenly lights darkened, and all accompanied by lightning, thunder, and an earthquake. It is wrong to fall back on the argument that "these must be spiritual not physical judgments because Revelation uses bizarre apocalyptic symbols." These features are all drawn from Old Testament accounts of God's physical, earthly appearances in judgment and deliverance at Sodom, at the Exodus, at Sinai, and at other divine interventions throughout Israel's history. They are intensified and universalized to be sure, but not changed to a different ontological realm. Revelation 9 has bizarre "locusts" and "scorpions" from the abyss who dress and act, on the one hand, like an earthly cavalry regiment, but on the other hand like no military force ever assembled. Biblical allusions to Exodus 10 and Joel 2–3 as well as details from the passage itself suggest an actual physical attack by demonic beings on ungodly humans at some point in the culminating judgments of the final tribulation rather than a spiritualized glimpse at eternal condemnation. Revelation 13:1–3 presents a "beast coming up from the sea" with various features that evoke the four beasts of Daniel 7. In neither passage is the referent a literal savage animal, although the number four in Daniel 7 is a literal number. Both have fairly specific referents in the world of earthly political history (with some shift from king to kingdom in Dan 7), but they are certainly not devoid of evocative and emotive meanings since they suggest evil empires that have savagely oppressed God's people throughout her history.

Hermeneutical Approaches

Discussion of interpretive approaches to Revelation follows naturally from consideration of its imagery, because its puzzling visions and symbols immediately raise the question of how John's book relates to the actual history and chronology of this world.[55] Does it picture circumstances in the past, from the immediate world of John and his readers? Does it refer to occurrences in the future culmination of the age just prior to the return of Christ to earth and the transformation of all things? Does it give an account of the world or of the church during the whole period from John's day to the final consummation? Or does it portray broad principles of spiritual and earthly life, of God and humans and good and evil, that are true of all times?

These represent essentially the four traditional "approaches" to Revelation that are often surveyed: the preterist, futurist, historicist, and idealist approaches

---

55. As G. B. Caird, *A Commentary on the Revelation of St John the Divine*, HNTC (New York: Harper & Row, 1966), 1, notes in his inimitable way, a person encountering Rev for the first time moves from an initial perplexed question, "What on earth is *this* all about?" to a more reflective question, "What *on earth* is it all about?"

respectively. They provide valuable insight into four possible ways of making sense of John's visions that have been followed by various interpreters through the history of the church.[56] As such, they are important for the modern interpreter to consider as a check on individualistic or idiosyncratic readings. Awareness of how the wider community of Christian interpreters through the centuries has understood the text can help make us more aware of our personal biases and the predispositions of our age and make us more attentive to the text itself. What is missing from the brief descriptions given above is any note of exclusivity in the approaches, the idea that the visions point *only* to the ancient situation or the distant future and so forth. These views have sometimes been held as exclusively valid (e.g., an idealist understanding that the symbols do not refer to any specific persons or events but only to timeless truths),[57] but most interpreters over the centuries have operated with a mixture of these approaches,[58] and an eclectic combination of these elements is more and more characteristic of recent commentaries.[59] The axiom (sometimes true of competing theological views) that each of the approaches is "correct in what it affirms and wrong in what it denies" seems generally true here as well.[60]

So the preterist view is correct in that the visions pointed to challenges that the ancient readers faced in their situation in Roman Asia Minor and gave them hope to remain faithful in the face of opposition from their surrounding culture. But the circumstances and events portrayed were not exhausted by what happened (or failed to happen)[61] in the first century AD (the destruction of Jerusalem) or the fourth or fifth century AD (the Christianization of the Roman Empire or its collapse), as some preterists insist.

Likewise the futurist approach must be given a large place in interpreting Revelation because the book repeatedly orients its visions around events that surround the imminent coming of Jesus to earth and the culmination of God's judgment and

56. For surveys of how such approaches have been used to interpret Rev across the centuries, see Isbon T. Beckwith, *The Apocalypse of John: Studies in Introduction with a Critical and Exegetical Commentary* (New York: Macmillan, 1919), 318–36; Koester, *Revelation*, 29–65; Arthur W. Wainwright, *Mysterious Apocalypse: Interpreting the Book of Revelation* (Nashville: Abingdon, 1993), 21–103. A shorter survey that includes also liturgical and artistic influences is Judith Kovacs and Christopher Rowland, *Revelation, the Apocalypse of Jesus Christ*, BBC (Oxford: Blackwell, 2004), 14–38.

57. E.g., William Milligan, *The Revelation of St. John* (London: Macmillan, 1886), 154–55: "We are not to look in the Apocalypse for special events, but for an exhibition of the principles which govern the history both of the world and the Church. . . . The book thus becomes to us not a history of either early or mediaeval or last events written of before they happened, but a spring of elevating encouragement and

holy joy to Christians in every age."

58. Koester, *Revelation*, xiii.

59. Carson and Moo, *Introduction*, 720–21; Köstenberger, Kellum, and Quarles, *Introduction*, 973. Such an eclectic approach is the recommendation of Tenney, *Interpreting Revelation*, 144–46.

60. Tenney, *Interpreting Revelation*, 143, says this about the idealist approach.

61. *Preterists* are usually understood to include interpreters who take Rev as divine prophecy fulfilled in the ancient situation as well as those who see the book as a purely human and fallible work whose "prophecies" were not fulfilled (sometimes labeled the "historical-critical" approach). See Köstenberger, Kellum, and Quarles, *Introduction*, 966–68; Tenney, *Interpreting Revelation*, 136; also the distinctions cited by Koester, *Revelation*, 57–58.

redemption that will accompany his return (e.g., 1:1, 7; 4:1; 10:6–7; 11:15–18; 21:1–5; 22:6–21), events that are certainly still future. But the book (even chs. 4–22) also spoke to its first readers about events in their day (Rome and its oppression),[62] and in a typological way it speaks of circumstances that recur in preliminary forms throughout the age leading up to their ultimate expression in the final days (nations and individuals exalting themselves against God and his people; difficulties that God's people experience in the present world; God's control over all things and his preliminary judgment of those opposed to him).[63] See discussion of typology below.[64]

It is more difficult to find legitimacy in the historicist approach despite its attractiveness to the Reformers in their polemics against the papacy (utilized also by earlier church leaders who resisted corrupt popes or clerical practices). Revelation simply does not follow the pattern of other ancient apocalypses in tracing the course of the history of God's people or of the world across the centuries up to its own day and into the eschaton (e.g., the animal apocalypse in 1 En. 85–90; the apocalypse of weeks in 1 En. 91 and 93).[65] In comparison with the periodization of history found in Daniel 2 and 7 (four kingdoms) and Daniel 9 (seventy weeks), Revelation chooses to focus only on the culmination of God's kingdom coming to earth (i.e., on the final phase as portrayed in Dan 2:44–45; 7:13–14, 23–27; 9:26–27; 12:1–3), not the centuries-long sequence of events that lead to it. Attempts to correlate its symbols with events in world history have repeatedly met with failure and embarrassment to the groups that espoused these identifications. The invasions of Rome by the Goths or of eastern Europe by the Ottoman Turks, the imprisonment of Pope Pius VI by French forces in 1798, the rise of Mussolini or the European Union or Saddam Hussein—these events are not what the symbols of Revelation are pointing to. Historicist interpretations of Revelation are difficult to find these days,[66] although this is still the standard approach of Jehovah's Witnesses[67] and Seventh-day Adventists,[68] and a form of historicism can be found in some popular attempts to correlate today's

---

62. See Caird, *Language and Imagery*, 258–59, on the ability of the prophets to synthesize a near vision of historical events imminent in their own time with a far vision of the day of the Lord in future events distant from their day. Similar is Bauckham, *Theology*, 152–53.

63. It is simply not true that holding to a pre-tribulation rapture makes most of Rev irrelevant to Christians today as Köstenberger, Kellum, and Quarles, *Introduction*, 972, assert.

64. Carson and Moo, *Introduction*, 720–21, refer to these correspondences of past and future as "prefigurements" of the eschaton.

65. Christopher R. Smith, "The Structure of the Book of Revelation in Light of Apocalyptic Literary Conventions," *NovT* 36 (1994): 380, 390–91, has a valuable analysis of how and why Rev does not follow the "review of history" motif like these earlier apocalypses did.

66. It is omitted, for example, from the Counterpoints volume on Rev edited by C. Marvin Pate, *Four Views on the Book of Revelation* (Grand Rapids: Zondervan, 1998). The views included are: preterist, idealist, progressive dispensationalist, and classical dispensationalist.

67. M. James Penton, *Apocalypse Delayed: The Story of Jehovah's Witnesses*, 3rd ed. (Toronto: University of Toronto Press, 2015), 3–9, 277–81.

68. Ministerial Association of Seventh-day Adventists, *Seventh-Day Adventists Believe: A Biblical Exposition of 27 Fundamental Doctrines* (Washington: Ministerial Association, General Conference of Seventh-day Adventists, 1988), 319–31; George R. Knight, ed., *Seventh-Day Adventists Answer Questions on Doctrine*, annotated ed. (Berrien Springs, MI: Andrews University Press, 2003), 193–97.

headlines with the visions of Revelation (see comments on 13:18; 16:12–16; and "Theology in Application" at the end of ch. 16).[69] The measure of validity that can be found in historicism is best correlated with various typological precursors to the persons and events that Revelation portrays as part of the last days (as mentioned above). Just as the events of 586 BC, 167 BC, and AD 70 foreshadow the attack on Jerusalem by worldwide forces in the final days prior to Christ's return (see comments on 11:15–18; 19:11–21), so other events of world history may prefigure the end-time events that Revelation pictures, but they are not ordered chronologically and do not represent the ultimate fulfillment of those prophetic visions.

The idealist approach is correct in finding timeless principles about God and his dealings with humans in Revelation (as in all of Scripture). The book teaches a great deal about God's character as holy and his sovereign rule over his creation. Its instruction about Christ's divine being and the redemption and victory he accomplished by his sacrifice comes across clearly apart from resolving issues about chronology and specific symbolism. See the section on theology at the end of this commentary for other theological themes. The sinful stubbornness of humans and their need for repentance and submission to God's ways also shows through. The church has always discerned such spiritual and moral truths in the book. But idealism is wrong in refusing to see specific persons and sequences of events portrayed in John's visions.[70] These two (timeless truths and specific referents) are not mutually exclusive. Particular historical circumstances in the first century as well as in the distant future are pictured in Revelation, as the commentary will show.

Use of the Old Testament: Prophecy and Typology

Parallels and allusions to various part of the Old Testament are pervasive in the book of Revelation, occurring in virtually every verse, especially in its visions.[71] Unlike many other New Testament books, however, no explicit citations or formal quotations are found (i.e., OT quotations introduced by formulas such as "it has been written," "as it is written," etc.). John does not quote the Old Testament to demon-

---

69. See Craig A. Blaising and Darrell L. Bock, *Progressive Dispensationalism* (Wheaton: Bridgepoint, 1993), 292–94; Crawford Gribben, *Evangelical Millennialism in the Trans-Atlantic World, 1500–2000* (Basingstoke: Palgrave Macmillan, 2011), xii–xiii; Köstenberger, Kellum, and Quarles, *Introduction*, 968; Osborne, *Revelation*, 18–19.

70. Bauckham, *Theology*, 19, says, "It would be a serious mistake to understand the images of Revelation as timeless symbols. . . . Their resonances in the specific social, political, cultural and religious world of their first readers need to be understood if their meaning is to be appropriated today."

71. G. K. Beale and Sean M. McDonough, "Revelation," in *Commentary on the New Testament Use of the Old Testament*, ed. G. K. Beale and D. A. Carson (Grand Rapids: Baker Academic, 2007), 1081, say Rev is "permeated" by the OT. J. Ramsey Michaels, "Old Testament in Revelation," *DLNT* 850–51, writes, "No other book of the NT is more thoroughly saturated with the thought and language of ancient Scripture than the book of Revelation."

strate its fulfillment in Christ as Matthew does or to support his theological argument as Paul does. But he echoes the prophets and other Old Testament books (especially Gen, Exod, Pss, Isa, Ezek, Dan, Zech) as he pursues his divinely appointed prophetic role of showing the coming fulfillment of all that was announced through the Old Testament prophets (10:7; 11:18; 22:6, 9; see discussion of genre above). In contrast to formal quotations, there are perhaps fifteen informal quotations of the Old Testament in Revelation (as reflected in italicized wording in NA[28]).[72] But scholars have estimated that John alludes to or echoes the Old Testament much more frequently, somewhere between two hundred fifty and a thousand times.[73] Precise counting is tricky because of John's habit of using composite allusions that combine potential parallels from various Old Testament passages in a single sentence or two. Moyise, for example, cites the opening vision (Rev 1:12–18) containing a minimum of eight allusions to Isaiah (2x), Ezekiel (2x), and Daniel (4x),[74] and similar complexes can easily be found in other visions. John seems to utilize the Hebrew text in some allusions and forms of the Greek Old Testament (LXX and others) elsewhere.[75] There are also numerous parallels with ancient noncanonical Jewish and Christian literature rooted in Old Testament prophetic expectation, especially apocalyptic books like Apocalypse of Elijah, Assumption of Moses, 2 Baruch, 1 Enoch, 4 Ezra, Testament of Job, Jubilees, Psalms of Solomon, as well as Didache, 1QM, 11QTemple, and Sibylline Oracles.[76] These are very significant texts for tracing the development of theological ideas from the Old Testament to the New.[77] In comparison, allusions to or shared images from Greco-Roman literature or ancient Near Eastern mythology are relatively rare, and where they do surface they are mediated through Jewish sources that have absorbed them at an earlier point (see commentary at 12:1–4 and 13:11).[78]

72. See Jan Fekkes, *Isaiah and Prophetic Traditions in the Book of Revelation: Visionary Antecedents and Their Development*, JSNTSup 93 (Sheffield: JSOT Press, 1994), 63–64, for this distinction between formal and informal quotations. The UBS[5] Greek text (cf. index, p. 863), following more stringent criteria, does not indicate any OT quotations in Rev (i.e., text set off in bold print).

73. Beale and McDonough, "Revelation," 1082; Steve Moyise, "Revelation and Scripture," in *The Later New Testament Writings and Scripture: The Old Testament in Acts, Hebrews, the Catholic Epistles, and Revelation* (Grand Rapids: Baker Academic, 2012), 111.

74. Moyise, "Revelation and Scripture," 112.

75. Beale and McDonough, "Revelation," 1082–83; Koester, *Revelation*, 123–24; Steve Moyise, *The Old Testament in the Book of Revelation*, JSNTSup 115 (Sheffield: Sheffield Academic Press, 1995), 17.

76. The first eight of these works are indexed in NA[28] (pp. 869–77), and its listing records 129 parallels with these books in Rev. This is not to say that John cites these books specifically but

that they were a part of the world of thought with which he and his readers were acquainted. John and the NT in general were directly dependent alongside these books on the theological heritage of the OT Scripture and shared in developing its traditions through the Second Temple period and beyond. In some of the parallels, John shares a close affinity to these works, but in all such cases their shared ideas are developed from foundational OT texts. For example, see the summary of parallels with 1 Enoch in Loren T. Stuckenbruck and Mark D. Mathews, "The Apocalypse of John, *1 Enoch*, and the Question of Influence," in *Die Johannesapokalypse: Kontexte—Konzepte—Rezeption*, ed. Jörg Frey, James A. Kelhofer, and Franz Töth (Tübingen: Mohr Siebeck, 2012), 231–34.

77. Larry R. Helyer, "The Necessity, Problems, and Promise of Second Temple Judaism for Discussions of New Testament Eschatology," *JETS* 47 (2004): 597–615.

78. Features of the first readers' socioeconomic and cultural-political world in ancient Asia Minor do, of course, appear regularly in the book (e.g., wealth and poverty, power and oppression, production and trade).

Even specific parallels with other Christian sources (e.g., Synoptic traditions, Paul's teaching) are surprisingly minimal, especially at places where they might be expected to appear (see commentary at 19:11–21). Revelation is an explicitly Christian book and exalts God's work in Jesus Christ from start to finish, but it is the Old Testament and its Jewish conceptions of God's salvation and judgment now being fulfilled in Jesus that are central to John's book as a whole.

Since John does not signal that an Old Testament passage or passages lie in the background of his imagery, he appears to know his readers well enough (and they him) to assume that they will understand the significance of the parallels either immediately, through further reflection, or through the repetition of similar ideas throughout the book.[79] Their shared conceptual world grounded in the Old Testament and in the early church's preaching about Jesus and his fulfillment of God's redemptive work gave them a common framework of ideas in which the visions of Revelation would make sense. Our challenge today is to enter into that conceptual world by tracing down the Old Testament allusions and John's use of them in terms that he and his original readers would understand. As Kraft argues, if we do not explore the Old Testament sources to John's prophetic sayings in a given passage, we have not done the job of interpreting Revelation as we ought, since John sees himself not as creating his own prophecies but as continuing and interpreting the work of the Old Testament prophets by the agency of the same Holy Spirit who inspired them.[80]

Reading Revelation in the light of this world of Old Testament and ancient Jewish expectation is, unfortunately, something many interpreters neglect. As Jauhiainen says, "The Jewish character of Revelation is not always fully appreciated in contemporary scholarship. Though John writes as a follower of Jesus, the questions he is answering are Jewish questions and the fulfilments he is offering fulfill Jewish expectations." He adds:

> Revelation shares Zechariah's interest in the restoration of God's people. . . . This reality has perhaps not been given sufficient weight in the contemporary interpretation of Revelation, which often emphasizes the Christian character of the document at the expense of its Jewish features. The hope of the coming restoration was, after all, an essential part of the first-century Jewish worldview, which may have been modified, but not abandoned, by the Jewish followers of Jesus. Though John cannot but see the events of the last days in light of Jesus's life, death and resurrection, he is nevertheless firmly anchored in the Jewish prophetic tradition in the way he offers his vision of the restoration. The process has been set in motion that will culminate in the consummation of Israel's hopes of restoration. What in Zechariah was postponed

79. Bauckham, *Climax*, xi–xii; idem, *Theology*, 18–22.

80. Heinrich Kraft, *Die Offenbarung des Johannes*, HNT 16a (Tübingen: Mohr Siebeck, 1974), 16.

until "that day," finally takes place in John's vision, which he offers as the ultimate fulfillment and closure of ancient prophecies.[81]

Jauhiainen speaks in these lines about "the restoration of God's people" as seen in Zechariah, but a similar thing could be said about broader themes concerning God's fulfillment of his promises to Israel taken also from other Old Testament prophetic voices. Zechariah's theme of restoration itself includes subthemes about Israel's lack of repentance for her sins, her intense suffering during the "final tribulation" preceding restoration that will both cleanse Israel and punish her enemies, and the renewal of Jerusalem itself as the place of the true worship of God and as the center of his rule over the earth in the presence of his people.[82] And as Jauhiainen points out, John is quick to show that this fulfillment has begun already and will be fully consummated through Jesus Christ, who is Yahweh's agent to bring about the consummation and will share his coming rule over the whole earth and his personal presence with those who are his.[83] Similar themes could be traced through various Old Testament prophets and on into John's visions by following the topic of the day of the Lord with its juxtaposition of God's intervention to judge his enemies and to purify Israel in preparation for redeeming her along with the nations who turn to him in faith.[84] Likewise the related theme of the messianic woes, or the time of severe testing prior to the coming of God's deliverer, can be traced through Deuteronomy, Isaiah, Jeremiah, Ezekiel, Daniel, Jesus's eschatological teaching, and then Revelation with similar events in view.[85]

The larger point that Jauhiainen alludes to when he speaks of interpretation that "emphasizes the Christian character of the document at the expense of its Jewish features" surfaces in other debates over the use of the Old Testament in Revelation. One of these is the question of how Old Testament parallels function in the book and whether they are foreign to the original passages from which they are taken. Some propose that John uses Old Testament images and terms with no intention to connect them to the scriptural passages or theological contexts in which they occur. John has his own meanings, and the Old Testament or Jewish features serve his purpose,

---

81. Marko Jauhiainen, *The Use of Zechariah in Revelation*, WUNT 2.199 (Tübingen: Mohr Siebeck, 2005), 160–61, 167. See also Mark Adam Elliott, *The Survivors of Israel: A Reconsideration of the Theology of Pre-Christian Judaism* (Grand Rapids: Eerdmans, 2000), 659–63; Bauckham, *Theology*, 147–48; Joel Willitts, "The Bride of Messiah and the Israel-ness of the New Heaven and New Earth," in *Introduction to Messianic Judaism: Its Ecclesial Context and Biblical Foundations*, ed. David Rudolph and Joel Willitts (Grand Rapids: Zondervan, 2013), 245–54; and idem, "Conclusion," in *Introduction to Messianic Judaism*, 315–19.

82. Jauhiainen, *Zechariah*, 142–53.

83. Jauhiainen, *Zechariah*, 153–62. This is a feature of progressive revelation: God adding further details as he continues over time to reveal his plan and its fulfillment. See Boyd Luter, "Interpreting the Book of Revelation," in *Interpreting the New Testament: Essays on Methods and Issues*, ed. David Alan Black and David S. Dockery (Nashville: Broadman & Holman, 2001), 464.

84. Craig Blaising, "A Case for the Pretribulation Rapture," in *Three Views on the Rapture*, ed. Alan Hultberg (Grand Rapids: Zondervan, 2010), 27–65.

85. Brant James Pitre, *Jesus, the Tribulation, and the End of the Exile: Restoration Eschatology and the Origin of the Atonement*, WUNT 2.204 (Tübingen: Mohr Siebeck; Grand Rapids: Baker Academic, 2005), 127–29, 377–79, 504–18.

not theirs.[86] Other researchers have rightly rejected this approach per se, while acknowledging and offering various explanations of places where John seems to take the meaning in a different direction than his Jewish sources.[87] Even among those who conclude that John's visions are grounded in specific Old Testament passages and ideas, there is debate about how much freedom he exercised in "re-imagining" the Old Testament images and what hermeneutical principles governed that "re-birth."[88] See discussion of typology below.

For those who understand John to be attentive to the Old Testament sense, Beale and McDonough explain the interplay of Old Testament and New Testament usage in Revelation as a choice between two approaches, expressed as follows: "Should Revelation be interpreted in the light of the OT, or should the OT be interpreted in the light of Revelation? Put more pointedly, Which body of material takes interpretive precedence?" In their view these options then boil down to a choice between: (1) John portraying Old Testament promises to ethnic Israel as now fulfilled for "the true eschatological people of God," the multiethnic church; or (2) John presenting the Old Testament promises as understood "in a pedantically 'literal' fashion" that entails the fulfillment of "the promises of physical blessings to Israel in the Holy Land."[89] Their evaluation of these choices is that since John says nothing explicit about the land promises, it is wrong to read it into the text of Revelation. Revelation ought to have priority (i.e., option one) since John was working "from a redemptive-historical stance of greater progressive revelation," and so his understanding of the Old Testament promises should be read back into the Old Testament passages themselves. The New Testament gives the true spiritual and eternal sense of the Old Testament promises that were not understood until the fulfillment that began at Christ's first coming.

This position has a kind of theological plausibility about it, and many interpreters of Revelation follow it. But it can also be seen to impose a later Christian theological construct on a text that is asking and answering a set of ancient Jewish questions (à la Jauhiainen). In the words of Elliott, it raises the question of "whether the Jewish

---

86. For example, Elizabeth Schüssler Fiorenza, *The Book of Revelation: Justice and Judgment* (Philadelphia: Fortress, 1985), 135–40, argues that John as a Christian prophet used the "words, images, phrases, and patterns [of the OT] as a language arsenal in order to make his own theological statement or express his own prophetic vision" independently of OT and Jewish prophetic/apocalyptic traditions (135). Cf. Louis A. Vos, *The Synoptic Traditions in the Apocalypse* (Kampen: J. H. Kok, 1965), 51: "John merely employs the thought and terminology of the Old Testament as the garb in which to clothe his New Testament vision." Moyise tends to side with this approach, although he prefers to picture the NT meaning as in dialogue with the OT rather than supplanting it altogether ("Revelation

and Scripture," 139–42; *Old Testament in Revelation*, 135–46).

87. Bauckham, *Climax*, 297–98; Fekkes, *Prophetic Traditions*, 286–90; Jauhiainen, *Zechariah*, 139–41; David Mathewson, *A New Heaven and a New Earth: The Meaning and Function of the Old Testament in Revelation 21.1–22.5*, JSNTSup 238 (Sheffield: Sheffield Academic Press, 2003), 222–30; Osborne, *Revelation*, 491–94.

88. Michaels, "Old Testament in Revelation," 852, who cites approvingly the book by Austin Farrer, *A Rebirth of Images: The Making of St. John's Apocalypse* (Westminster: Dacre, 1949), and says that in Rev "the language and thought of the OT are not only preserved and reaffirmed but transformed."

89. Beale and McDonough, "Revelation," 1088.

context of Revelation has ever been allowed a serious voice in interpretation. This would require that the Christian Apocalypse be read in light of themes and presuppositions of paramount significance to Jews living in the first century and, it should be added, to Christians who still considered themselves as belonging in some way to that society."[90] The book does not have to be read with pedantic literalism (in the terms Beale and McDonough use) to see its thoroughgoing concern for how God's prophetic words about his people (ethnic Israel) would be fulfilled, including how his rule from Jerusalem over the whole earth would be taken back from the hands of pagan empires who rise up to oppress his people and how his entire creation would be restored from the effects of human sin.[91]

The role of the New Testament in clarifying how the Old Testament prophecies will come to fulfillment can be explained in other ways that are more faithful to what both Old Testament and New Testament passages in their original settings actually say about ethnic Israel and its future in God's redemptive purposes.[92] Old Testament texts about Israel as an ethnic body chosen by God and promised earthly blessing as an outreach to all the nations (e.g., Gen 12; Exod 19) can be expanded to include non-Israelite peoples and spiritual cleansing from sin as the New Testament makes clear, without eliminating or redefining the multitude of promises made to ethnic Israel throughout the Old Testament. To add other recipients of the blessings and clarify how God's Messiah has come to complete God's restoration of all things does not require subtracting the original recipients from the fulfillment or setting aside the promises made to them. The two testaments are complementary on this point, not conflicting. See commentary at Revelation 7:4 and 21:3 for further discussion.

A related issue is the need to give Revelation its due even among New Testament texts on eschatology. A practice sometimes evident among interpreters is to rely on other New Testament passages about Christ's second coming and the consummation of the age, but to shy away from Revelation because it speaks in metaphor and visions or because it is too controversial or hard to interpret. The principle that *clear* texts of Scripture should help shed light on unclear ones is certainly a valid axiom. But what

---

90. Elliott, *Survivors*, 662. A critique of the larger "anti-Jewish" tendency found in much of NT theology, especially in German scholarship of a previous generation, can be found in Jörg Frey, "New Testament Eschatology—an Introduction: Classical Issues, Disputed Themes, and Current Perspectives," in *Eschatology of the New Testament and Some Related Documents*, ed. Jan G. van der Watt, WUNT 2/315 (Tübingen: Mohr Siebeck, 2011), 23–30.

91. See also Willem A. VanGemeren, "Israel as the Hermeneutical Crux in the Interpretation of Prophecy (II)," *WTJ* 46 (1984): 254–97, who argues that the particularity of the OT prophets' messages to Israel must not be obscured by imposing on them a purely spiritual emphasis drawn from a certain reading of the NT.

92. E.g., Craig Blaising, "Biblical Hermeneutics: How Are We to Interpret the Relation between the Tanak and the New Testament on This Question?," in *The New Christian Zionism: Fresh Perspectives on Israel & the Land*, ed. Gerald R. McDermott (Downers Grove, IL: IVP Academic, 2016), 79–105; Darrell L. Bock, "Summary Essay," in *Three Views on the Millennium and Beyond*, ed. Darrell L. Bock (Grand Rapids: Zondervan, 1999), 290–305; Robert L. Saucy, *The Case for Progressive Dispensationalism: The Interface between Dispensational & Non-Dispensational Theology* (Grand Rapids: Zondervan, 1993), 297–323, esp. 311–23.

is too often ignored is that *central* texts should always be allowed to speak and add light to peripheral ones, even if they are debated (e.g., one should study Matt 5 and 19 and 1 Cor 7 on divorce and remarriage, not just Rom 7). So, as Bock argues, "Revelation is the key book for futuristic eschatology because it is devoted to that topic. Thus, it should be given careful attention when this topic is raised. Rather than highlighting its obscurity, it is a central text for this topic that demands our careful attention."[93]

The necessary balance of acknowledging what the Old Testament says about God's future for his people and for the world, as well as the decisively new dimensions of that future that John adds, can be preserved by probing the typological dimensions of the argument of Revelation, how it traces the relationship of Old Testament to New Testament by means of pattern and escalation. Typological interpretation of the Old Testament is more obvious in New Testament books like Matthew, John, Hebrews, 2 Peter, Jude, and some passages in Paul, but it seems equally important in Revelation, and it helps to resolve some of the issues of interpretation surfaced above.

Foulkes's definition of *type* is a good starting point for understanding biblical typology:

> A type is an event, a series of circumstances, or an aspect of the life of an individual or of the nation, which finds a parallel and a deeper realization in the incarnate life of our Lord, in His provision for the needs of men, or in His judgments and future reign. A type thus presents a pattern of the dealings of God with men that is followed in the antitype, when, in the coming of Jesus Christ and the setting up of His kingdom, those dealings of God are repeated, though with a fulness and finality that they did not exhibit before.[94]

Goppelt's description reinforces some of the same points:

> Only historical facts—persons, actions, events, and institutions—are material for typological interpretation: words and narratives can be utilized only insofar as they deal with such matters. These things are to be interpreted typologically only if they are considered to be divinely ordained representations or types of future realities that will be even greater and more complete.[95]

The three basic elements to observe in these definitions are: (1) a shared pattern or correspondence in historical fact; (2) a divinely intended anticipation; and (3) an escalation or intensification in the later part of the correspondence.[96] The second el-

---

93. Bock, "Summary Essay," 298.

94. Francis Foulkes, *The Acts of God: A Study of the Basis of Typology in the Old Testament* (London: Tyndale, 1958), 35.

95. Leonhard Goppelt, *Typos: The Typological Interpretation of the Old Testament in the New*, trans. Donald H. Madvig (Grand Rapids: Eerdmans, 1982 [1939]), 17–18.

96. See the definition of typology in similar terms in Paul M. Hoskins, *That Scripture Might Be Fulfilled: Typology and the Death of Christ* (n.p.: Xulon, 2009), 20–23; also idem, *The Book of Revelation: A Theological and Exegetical Commentary* (n.p.: ChristoDoulos, 2017), 40.

ement is refined a bit further in Beale's definitions to try to clarify how "anticipation" works in actual interpretive practice.[97] The third element also requires clarification, as described below. Because a type is a divinely intended pointer to its more complete counterpart, it operates as a form of indirect prophecy to anticipate God's future for his creation, and so it can be spoken of as "fulfilled" just as prophecy is.[98]

Typological relationships in this sense can be found in the Old Testament itself, in intertestamental Jewish literature, and in rabbinics (an adjustment from Foulkes's definition). The exodus model certainly reappears in various ways as the prophets envision God's future judgment on Israel's oppressors and the restoration of his people. His judgments on Noah's generation, on Sodom and Gomorrah, and on Egypt at the exodus show up as patterns for judgments yet to come either on Israel itself or on pagan nations. Likewise, the reigns of David and Solomon are taken as ideals to be replicated in better times to come.[99] Broad instances of Old Testament typology like these can be found also in Revelation.

Some of the clearest examples of Old Testament types or patterns used in Revelation are the parallels in chapters 8–9 and 15–16 with the Egyptian plagues (Exod 7–12), including (1) specific woes (water turned to blood, frogs, skin boils, hail and fire, locusts, darkness, death); (2) arrangement in a series with increasingly destructive intensity; (3) continued lack of repentance by those targeted by the plagues (from small to great, with Pharaoh as a type of the Roman emperor); and (4) joyous celebration of God's deliverance at the sea. Broader exodus typology shows up also in the ominous signs of God's holy presence (e.g., Rev 4:5; 6:12; 8:5; 11:19) as at Sinai (Exod 19; thunder, lightning, earthquake, darkness), provision of manna (Rev 2:17), Israel's escape into the wilderness on the wings of an eagle in spite of a flood of water (12:14–16), and her restoration as a nation after a new exodus (7:4–8; 14:1–5; 19:7–9; 20:1–10; 21:1–22:5) as in Isaiah 11, 44, 60–66.[100]

Because the use of typology has been invoked in a variety of ways in discussions of the use of the Old Testament in the New, it is important to clarify a few misunderstandings about how it works in Revelation and elsewhere. (1) Typology is not just a matter of Old Testament to New Testament relationships as noted above. It occurs from one part of the Old Testament to another and from the Old Testament to later Jewish literature. This is grounded in observations about God's consistency in working out his purposes across human history.[101] (2) Typology is not limited

97. G. K. Beale, *Handbook on the New Testament Use of the Old Testament: Exegesis and Interpretation* (Grand Rapids: Baker Academic, 2012), 13–14, 19.

98. Beale, *Handbook*, 17–18; Beale and McDonough, "Revelation," 1085–86.

99. E. Earle Ellis, "Biblical Interpretation in the New Testament Church," in *Mikra: Text, Translation, Reading and Interpretation of the Hebrew Bible in Ancient Judaism and Early Christianity*, ed. Martin Jan Mulder (Philadelphia: Fortress, 1988), 715–16; Foulkes, *Acts of God*, 9–22; Goppelt, *Typos*, 23–41.

100. See Fekkes, *Prophetic Traditions*, 80–82, who cites the opinion of Irenaeus (*Haer.* 4.30.2) that the woes of Rev follow the typology of Egypt's plagues.

101. See Beale, *Handbook*, 16–17, 22; Hoskins, *Revelation*, 40–41.

to features of Christology and soteriology, although these are common topics. For example, judgment of the ungodly, opposition to God's ways, and human character traits are some of the patterns that appear (only negatively related to soteriology).[102] (3) Typology does not necessitate a metaphysical shift from physical, geographic, or historic entities in the Old Testament type to spiritual and eternal realities in the New Testament antitype. Sometimes the typological escalation works this way, but it is not necessary for it to do so. For example, the typology of sacrifice in Hebrews and elsewhere (e.g., 1 Cor 5:7) did not mean that Christ offered himself only spiritually or only in the heavenly realms to deal with sin. He experienced real physical suffering, death, and resurrection in time and space, even though his sacrifice was God's full and final provision for sin and provides spiritual, eternal blessings for the redeemed.[103] (4) Typology does not necessitate the abrogation of the type in favor of the antitype. Abrogation is the case in one notable example that is sometimes cited (animal sacrifices as a type of Christ's sacrifice; Heb 9–10). But to take another instance from Hebrews, Adam's role as God's image bearer and ruler over creation (Gen 1; Ps 8) is not revoked for humankind but renewed and restored by Christ (Heb 2; cf. Rev 2:26–27; 20:4, 6; 22:5).[104] (5) The future counterpart or antitype may not be limited to a single, climactic exemplar, although this is often the case. It is also possible for an Old Testament pattern to find more than one future replication on the way to its ultimate fulfillment. Either way it involves "progression toward a final goal" in God's design for history.[105] Beale gives the illustration of Noah (Gen 9:1–2, 7) as an intermediate antitype of Adam (Gen 1:26–28), pointing ultimately to Christ. In the same place he cites day of the Lord prophecies that have a near-term fulfillment as well as an eschatological one.[106] The same can be said of the use in Revelation of Babylon (the ancient empire pointing to Rome and on to an end-time power opposed to God) or of the "beast" that exalts itself against God, desecrates the temple, and oppresses God's people (Antiochus IV Epiphanes, Rome in AD 70, and a future antichrist). See commentary on Revelation 12–13, 17–18.

In addition to the ones already mentioned, other Old Testament typologies of judgment appear in Revelation, including motifs related to the day of the Lord, holy war, and eschatological enemies,[107] as well as Noah's flood, Sodom and Gomorrah, and the broader pattern of "destruction-preservation soteriology."[108] Typologies

---

102. See comments on Balaam (2:14–15), Jezebel (2:20), the Euphrates (9:14; 16:12), Armageddon (16:16–18). Also Elliott, *Survivors*, 387–92, and various OT examples in 2 Pet and Jude.

103. See comments on this issue at Rev 6:16–18; cf. Blaising, "Biblical Hermeneutics," 85–87.

104. See Bock, "Summary Essay," 293–94; see also commentary on 1:6; 5:10; 7:8; 21:3.

105. Hoskins, *Revelation*, 41.

106. Beale, *Handbook*, 16–17; Bock, "Summary Essay," 294–95.

107. See Fekkes, *Prophetic Traditions*, 78–80, 82–85, for these motifs. See commentary at chs. 6, 12–13, and 19 for discussion of these as typological.

108. This is Elliott's description (*Survivors*, 575–637) of a theological construct that sees Israel's deliverance arriving through a process of catastrophic judgment on the world or on the nation because of sin, which leads to the preservation of a remnant that will enjoy God's blessing. This is an abstraction, in part, of the typology of Noah's flood and of the new exodus: restoration of a purified remnant of Israel, not all of

of redemption and blessing also appear in addition to the exodus patterns already mentioned: access to the tree of life (2:7; 22:2, 14), a new name (2:17); God's protective seal or mark (7:2–3); God's Messiah ruling with his saints from Zion (2:27; 11:15; 14:1–5; 20:4); miraculous deliverance from enemies (20:9); Edenic conditions (22:1–5). See commentary on these verses for further discussion.

A typological approach to John's use of the Old Testament in Revelation helps to explain how John's imagery can refer to realities in the first-century world as well as in the final climactic period prior to Christ's second coming (i.e., a preterist-futurist reading as discussed above).[109] The pattern can also be seen as repeated in some measure in various situations involving persecution, temptations, apostasy, or fidelity on the part of God's people as they live in anticipation of his return and then culminating at that time (i.e., an idealist-futurist approach).[110] It also clarifies how Old Testament expectations about ethnic Israel can be, as some interpreters phrase it, "universalized" to include the whole world (i.e., escalated to their ultimate extent) without excluding the expected fulfillment for Israel. The typological pattern is expanded to include all the nations as the Old Testament anticipates in various places, without abrogating Israel's special role in bringing God's redemption to its consummation and then participating in that consummation as an ethnic entity. See commentary on Revelation 7:4; 21:3.

Text

For those accustomed to working with text-critical issues in other parts of the New Testament, Revelation requires important adjustments.[111] Because of its distinctive character and sometimes disputed theology, Revelation was often copied separately

the nation, following a time of purging from sin: "salvation is experienced by means of, as well as in the midst of, danger and judgment" (p. 595). Elliott finds this construct in a number of passages in Second Temple Jewish literature as well as in the OT itself (see his summary of OT themes and passages on p. 596). This is similar to the messianic-woes motif of intense suffering just prior to the renewal of Israel that Pitre, *Tribulation*, 41–65, 127–30, traces through ancient Jewish texts and into the NT Gospels.

109. C. Marvin Pate combines these two foci of Rev (things already true in the first-century world, other things not completed until Christ returns to earth) under the rubric of "already/not yet." See his "A Progressive-Dispensationalist View of Revelation," in *Four Views on the Book of Revelation*, 135–48, 172–75, and idem, *Interpreting Revelation*, 176–84. This is quite appropriate for some points (e.g., defeat of Satan; reign of Christ), but it does not seem to capture very well what John is saying in a great deal of the rest of the book, at least not as well as the typological approach described above.

110. This typological approach leads to similar results as that of Bauckham, *Theology*, 153–56. It is essentially the same as the early part of his argument: God's consistency in his past acts as "models for what he would do in the future" and the excess of prophetic promise over existing fulfillment leading to "hopes for a much greater salvation event" in the future (153–54). But it is harder to see the validity of the latter part of his conclusions: a kind of "eschatological hyperbole" far greater than any possibility of fulfillment in the first century, but not actually predicting events of the distant future beyond an undefined "coming of God's universal kingdom" (155–56). It seems that John claims more for his prophetic role than this (see commentary on 1:1–8; 10:5–6; 11:15–18; 22:6–21).

111. Many commentaries on Rev cover textual issues only superficially or do not reflect the latest developments in the field, but see the excellent surveys in David E. Aune, *Revelation 1–5*, WBC 52A (Nashville: Thomas Nelson, 1997), cxxxiv–clx, and Koester, *Revelation*, 144–50.

from the other groups of New Testament books (e.g., Gospels, Paul, Acts and General Letters), and copied less frequently. Compared to something like seventeen hundred extant Greek copies of portions of the Gospels, eight hundred copies of Paul, and six hundred of Acts and the General Letters, there are a little over three hundred Greek copies of portions of Revelation.[112] This includes seven papyri, twelve majuscules (or uncials), about two hundred ninety minuscules, and no lectionary texts (the Greek church never included Rev in its liturgical readings). Of the non-Greek witnesses, the evidence of ancient versions and patristic quotations can provide support on occasion, but as in the rest of the New Testament, their help is secondary to the Greek evidence.[113] When Revelation was copied along with other books in larger segments, a different exemplar was sometimes used compared to the other portions (e.g., Codex Alexandrinus [A 02] is Byzantine in the Gospels and Alexandrian elsewhere, including Rev). This means that classification of certain manuscripts into familiar text-types (e.g., Alexandrian, Byzantine) based on working with the Gospels or Paul does not automatically carry over to Revelation, and evaluation of the quality and reliability of familiar manuscripts may not be the same in Revelation.

Among the unexpected changes are these: Codex Vaticanus (B 03) will not figure in any textual decisions in Revelation because it does not contain any verses from Revelation (its original final section is missing, omitting the latter part of Heb as well as the Pastorals, Phlm, and Rev). Codex Sinaiticus (ℵ 01) is still an early, valuable Alexandrian manuscript, but its text in Revelation displays more mixture in readings and more careless scribal errors. Even though earlier than A and C (fourth century rather than fifth century), it is regarded as secondary to A and C in its witness to Revelation. Alexandrinus (A 02), however, is regarded as the best witness for Revelation, even though it takes second place to Sinaiticus elsewhere (especially in the Gospels). There are not very many papyri manuscripts, and most of them contain only small fragments of text. The exceptions are $\mathfrak{P}^{47}$ (parts of nine chs.) and $\mathfrak{P}^{115}$ (parts of twelve chs.). Also worth mentioning is $\mathfrak{P}^{98}$, which contains only 1:13–20, but has been dated to the second century, one of the three or four earliest witnesses to any New Testament book. There are no identifiable Western witnesses for Revelation. Finally, the Byzantine or Majority manuscripts are divided into two subgroups rather than being more unified as in the rest of the New Testament (see details in the next paragraph).

---

112. Markus Lembke, "Beobachtungen zu den Handschriften der Apokalypse des Johannes," in *Die Johannesoffenbarung: Ihr Text und Ihre Auslegung*, ed. Martin Karrer and Michael Labahn, ABG 38 (Leipzig: Evangelische Verlagsanstalt, 2012), 20–21 (his count for Rev is 307 manuscripts); D. C. Parker, *An Introduction to the New Testament Manuscripts and Their Texts* (Cambridge: Cambridge University Press, 2008), 232 (306 manuscripts); Ulrich Schmid and Martin Karrer, "Die

neue Edition der Johannesapokalypse: Ein Arbeitsbericht," in *Studien zum Text der Apokalypse*, ed. Marcus Sigismund, Martin Karrer, and Ulrich Schmid, ANTF 47 (Berlin: de Gruyter, 2015), 3–4 (308 manuscripts).

113. For resources on evidence from ancient versions and patristic citations, see Aune, *Revelation 1–5*, cxlviii–clvi, and Parker, *Introduction*, 236–40.

The Greek witnesses to Revelation are widely understood to fall into three groups, based on extensive studies done by J. Schmid.[114] The first two are older forms of the text, both Alexandrian. The most reliable of these ("primary Alexandrian")[115] is represented by the two fifth-century majuscules (uncials), A (02) and C (04), and by three minuscules, 2053, 2062, and 2344 (the first two of these contain the text of Rev that accompanies an early seventh-century commentary on the text by Oecumenius; the third is poorly preserved and sometimes illegible but important when it has clear readings). More recently $\mathfrak{P}^{115}$ has been added to this list of most important witnesses.[116] The second most important group is also Alexandrian and dated early, but it is not as highly regarded as the previous one ("secondary Alexandrian" according to Holmes). The main witnesses in this group are: $\mathfrak{P}^{47}$, $\aleph$ (01), and a few others.[117] The third group is the later body of Byzantine or Majority witnesses, many of which can be classified into at least two subgroups identified by Schmid and others. In the NA^{28} text these are cited as $\mathfrak{M}^A$ and $\mathfrak{M}^K$, the former following the kind of readings found in the sixth-century commentary on Revelation by Andreas (or Andrew) of Caesarea, and the latter following the more typical Koine text of the Eastern Church. $\mathfrak{M}^A$ includes P (025) and about 110 minuscule witnesses, while $\mathfrak{M}^K$ includes 046 and about 85 minuscules.[118] Sometimes these two groups agree on a reading (NA^{28} lists this as "$\mathfrak{M}$" with no superscript), but on many textual questions they are divided. As mentioned above, there are no specifically Western witnesses for Revelation.

More recently, research on the text of Revelation has probed the area of internal evidence, specifically studying scribal habits that can be discerned from careful analysis of textual variation within certain Greek manuscripts themselves. Scholars have studied the text of Revelation as found in $\mathfrak{P}^{47}$, $\mathfrak{P}^{98}$, $\aleph$, A, and C.[119] Several points

---

114. Josef Schmid, *Studien zur Geschichte des griechischen Apokalypse-Textes*, 2 vols. (Munich: Karl Zink, 1955), 2:24–28, 146–51; also Kurt Aland and Barbara Aland, *The Text of the New Testament*, 2nd ed. (Grand Rapids: Eerdmans, 1989), 242–43; Aune, *Revelation 1–5*, clvi–clvii; Parker, *Introduction*, 240–41.

115. Michael W. Holmes, "New Testament Textual Criticism," in *Introducing New Testament Interpretation*, ed. Scot McKnight (Grand Rapids, Baker, 1989), 60.

116. Also included are several other papyri and majuscules that contain only a paragraph or so of text each ($\mathfrak{P}^{18}$, $\mathfrak{P}^{24}$, 0163). Cf. Parker, *Introduction*, 240.

117. Also included are several other majuscules that contain only a few verses each (e.g., 0169, 0207). A further group of minuscules attest a form of the Alexandrian text but cannot be classified consistently with either of the two groups of older witnesses noted above: 1006, 1611, 1841, 1854, 2030, 2050, 2329, 2351, 2377. Cf. Parker, *Introduction*, 240–41.

118. Parker, *Introduction*, 241.

119. Garrick V. Allen, "The Apocalypse in Codex Alexandrinus: Exegetical Reasoning and Singular Readings in New Testament Greek Manuscripts," *JBL* 135 (2016): 859–80; Juan Hernández Jr., "The Apocalypse in Codex Alexandrinus: Its Singular Readings and Scribal Habits," in *Scripture and Traditions: Essays on Early Judaism and Christianity in Honor of Carl R. Holladay*, ed. Patrick Gray and Gail R. O'Day, NovTSup 129 (Leiden: Brill, 2008), 341–58; idem, *Scribal Habits and Theological Influences in the Apocalypse: The Singular Readings of Sinaiticus, Alexandrinus, and Ephraemi*, WUNT 2.218 (Tübingen: Mohr Siebeck, 2006); Dirk Jongkind, *Scribal Habits of Codex Sinaiticus*, TS 3.5 (Piscataway, NJ: Gorgias, 2007); Peter Malik, "Another Look at P.IFAO II 31 (P^{98}): An Updated Transcription and Textual Analysis," *NovT* 58 (2016): 204–17; idem, *P.Beatty III (P47): The Codex, Its Scribe, and Its Text*, NTTSD 52 (Leiden: Brill, 2017); Tobias Nicklas, "The Early Text of Revelation," in *The Early Text of the New Testament*, ed. C. E. Hill and M. J. Kruger (Oxford: Oxford University Press, 2012), 225–38; James Ronald Royse, *Scribal Habits in Early Greek New Testament Papyri*, NTTSD 36 (Leiden: Brill, 2008).

emerge from these studies. First, singular readings (i.e., wording found in only one witness and nowhere else in the textual tradition) are often due to careless errors or spelling variation, and in other cases they are apparently intentional "improvements" by a scribe, but sometimes they preserve the original. Given the smaller number of witnesses for the text of Revelation, we should be prepared to accept readings supported by only a few or even by only one solid witness if it is warranted.[120] Second, the "shorter reading" canon does not always apply; some scribes tend to delete rather than add material.[121] Third, it is important especially in Revelation to look for corrections to a smoother or better form of Greek expression. The unusual grammatical style of Revelation (see next section) was often changed in copying. Fourth, harmonization to match a familiar Old Testament text that is alluded to or to a parallel expression occurring elsewhere in Revelation sometimes occurs, but these are hard to assess. Finally, theological adjustments are sometimes evident, usually to a higher Christology or a more appropriate description of angelic or divine actions. All these items are in some sense conventional wisdom in textual criticism, but recent research has confirmed their importance especially for the text of Revelation.[122]

Another area of current textual research on Revelation that is actively underway is the production of the Editio Critica Maior (ECM) for the book. This is a completely new edition of the Greek New Testament text based on extensive research by a collaborative team of scholars investigating all Greek witnesses, ancient versions, and patristic citations across the first millennium of its existence. Textual readings will be evaluated based on computerized genealogical analysis of variants. The volume on the Catholic Letters has been published, and work on Acts, John, and Revelation is in process. The entire New Testament is expected to be finished by 2030. The results of the work will become the printed text for future editions of NA, as has now happened for NA[28] in the Catholic Letters.[123]

In practice, then, textual decisions should take into account the manuscript support of different readings as weighed in view of Schmid's groupings, with strong preference for readings found in the primary Alexandrian witnesses noted above, especially when they are supported by witnesses from the secondary Alexandrian group. Readings found primarily in the Byzantine or Majority manuscripts should be suspect. But internal considerations must also be examined, particularly the ones

---

120. E.g., Codex Alexandrinus has three singular readings that are almost universally accepted as original: 12:10 (κατήγωρ); 13:10 (ἀποκτανθῆναι); 21:4 (ἀπῆλθαν).

121. See J. K. Elliott, "A Short Textual Commentary on the Book of Revelation and the 'New' Nestle," *NovT* 56 (2014): 70–71, for a more radical statement of this finding. *TCGNT2*, 13*, has a more moderate caveat.

122. See discussion of these points in Allen, "Codex Alexandrinus," 862–66; Hernández, "Codex Alexandrinus," 344–53; and Malik, "Another Look," 213–16.

123. For introduction to this project and its significance for NT textual studies, see Peter J. Gurry, "How Your Greek NT Is Changing: A Simple Introduction to the Coherence-Based Genealogical Method (CBGM)," *JETS* 59 (2016): 675–89; Peter M. Head, "Editio Critica Maior: An Introduction and Assessment," *TynBul* 61 (2010): 131–52; Schmid and Karrer, "Die neue Edition," 3–15.

noted in the preceding paragraph (e.g., issues related to the author's language and style, possible harmonization, omission of wording a scribe might think to be unnecessary or unsuitable). Of course, these are not always easy to evaluate.[124]

Language and Style

It was mentioned in the discussion of authorship that Dionysius of Alexandria (mid-third century) rejected apostolic authorship of Revelation partly on the grounds that its grammar and style were quite different from John's Gospel and Epistles. While acknowledging the writer's inspired and prophetic character, he says about "John" who wrote Revelation, "I perceive that his dialect and language is not very accurate Greek; but that he uses barbarous idioms, and, in some places, solecisms."[125] This observation about the Greek of Revelation can be confirmed by anyone with an intermediate ability in New Testament Greek who reads a chapter or two of the book carefully. It is wrong to say the book displays "bad" or "incorrect" grammar, but it is not standard or normal usage even compared to the simple Greek found in comparable books of the New Testament (e.g., John's Gospel and Epistles; Mark).

Two clarifications are needed in this regard. First, linguistic patterns vary from one person to another even among competent speakers, and spoken language differs from written language under normal circumstances. Usage also varies depending on the social purpose and audience for which it is intended. Part of competence in a language is the ability to adapt grammatical usage and word choice to the intended situation and the expectations associated with that environment. Totally apart from the abbreviated style of today's electronic communications, a quick note to a friend would be written differently than a cover letter to accompany a job application, and they would both differ from how we would express ourselves in person in those situations. But standard or normal usage at the expected level suited to the situation is different from substandard or nonnormal usage.

This is the issue with the unusual grammar of Revelation. In a variety of ways, Revelation displays Greek usage that is not the normal or expected expression. For example, there are problems of agreement in case, number, and gender; proper case usage; nonfinite verbs used as finites; redundant pronouns; severe limitation in choice of conjunctions; a few odd lexical uses.[126] It is clear that John wrote a Semitized form of Greek that reflects various departures from standard Koine or Hellenistic Greek usage (the form of ancient Greek used across the first-century Mediterranean

---

124. See Parker, *Introduction*, 241–42; Elliott, "Short Textual Commentary," 70–72, for brief comments on the practice of textual criticism in Rev.

125. Eusebius, *Hist. eccl.* 7.25.26–27; translation as found in *Eusebius' Ecclesiastical History: Complete and Unabridged,* updated ed., trans. C. F. Cruse (Peabody, MA: Hendrickson, 1998), 264.

126. See the summary given in BDF §§136–37. Details of most of these can be found in Charles, *Revelation* 1:cxlii–cliv; Turner, *Style,* 145–58.

world).[127] He wrote in an idiolect (his individual linguistic patterns and preferences) that sometimes used the expected patterns of Semitized Greek familiar in other New Testament and LXX books but at other times followed patterns that have their own linguistic logic. For example, John frequently uses nominative nouns and participles in apposition to nouns in a nonnominative case, contrary to the normal pattern that puts appositives in the same case (e.g., 1:5; 2:13, 20; 3:12; 20:2).[128] In some of these the appositives could be understood as titles or names, and the idea of using the basic nominative as fundamental to the "naming" function may be John's underlying linguistic logic. It can be argued that this exceptional use calls attention to the Old Testament background or in other ways emphasizes the further identification,[129] but this is not so clear in some cases (cf. 8:9; 9:14), and it nevertheless departs from the normal pattern. Normal Greek usage does not choose this means to show emphasis.

The second clarification is that effective communication is hardly ever obstructed due to such nonnormal usage, and it is certainly not hindered in the book of Revelation. John gets his points across with skill, power, and often eloquence despite grammatical infelicities or unusual expressions. Our perplexity over the sense of various passages is not due to such grammatical oddities but to puzzling imagery or undetected allusions or other problems related to our distance from the original situation of writing.

A few further points of explanation are needed. First, the primary reason for John's unusual linguistic patterns is that he used Greek as a second language, and his idiomatic style often reflects influence from his mother tongue.[130] It is likely that his first language was Aramaic and that he was comfortable also in Hebrew (including biblical Hebrew and some form of later spoken Hebrew similar to Mishnaic Hebrew that is known from later Jewish writings). This should not be taken to mean that Revelation was originally written in Aramaic or Hebrew and then badly translated (by John or others) into Greek, or that we should try to back translate it into a Semitic form if we are truly to understand it.[131] Nor does it mean that John's mastery of Hellenistic Greek was rudimentary or that he struggled to express himself in Greek. He was quite capable, as the book itself shows, and certainly would have

---

127. Aune, *Revelation 1–5*, clxii–iii.

128. See Aune, *Revelation 1–5*, 25, for a dozen examples of this in Rev.

129. G. K. Beale, "Solecisms in the Apocalypse as Signals for the Presence of Old Testament Allusions: A Selective Analysis of Revelation 1–22," in *Early Christian Interpretation of the Scriptures of Israel: Investigations and Proposals*, ed. Craig A. Evans and James A. Sanders, JSNTSup 148 (Sheffield: Sheffield Academic Press, 1997), 423–26; Daniel B. Wallace, *Greek Grammar beyond the Basics: An Exegetical Syntax of the New Testament* (Grand Rapids: Zondervan, 1996), 62.

130. See the brief general survey of this issue in BDF §4

and the detailed analysis of grammatical examples in Aune, *Revelation 1–5*, cxcix–ccvii; Mussies, *Morphology*, 92–101, 165, 171, 177, 311–12, 348–49, 352–53; and idem, "The Greek of Revelation," in *L'Apocalypse johannique et l'Apocalyptique dans le Nouveau Testament*, ed. Jan Lambrecht, BETL 53 (Leuven: Leuven University Press, 1980), 167–77.

131. E.g., Charles Cutler Torrey, *The Apocalypse of John* (New Haven: Yale University Press, 1958), 13–48, argues for an Aramaic original. Supporting a Hebrew original is R. B. Y. Scott, *The Original Language of the Apocalypse* (Toronto: Toronto University Press, 1928), a published dissertation that is not widely available.

operated as an effective communicator in the largely Hellenistic linguistic sphere of first-century Asia Minor. But his Greek linguistic instincts show the influence of the Semitic languages he knew first and used more naturally. Bilingual speakers can communicate quite capably in their second language, and yet their intuitive syntactical choices often are drawn to patterns that correspond to similar features in their first language.[132] For John this can involve the use of some features that are perfectly good Greek but are used more frequently because of parallels to a Semitic language (this is sometimes called "enhancement"). But it can also produce awkward expressions that, while understandable in the second language, would not be used by a native speaker. This can more properly be labeled "interference."[133]

Secondly, by way of explanation, it does not seem to be the case for John that his second language usage was awkward and unnatural to such a degree that his competence as a user of the second language could be called into question. The proposal by some that John had not yet learned Greek very well when he wrote Revelation, or that on Patmos he had no opportunity to give his work the revision and correction it needed, or that he had no secretary available to improve his rough Greek style does not sit well with what can be seen of his effectiveness as a writer despite the book's irregularities.[134] John's impassioned acclamations of praise (e.g., 5:9–14; 11:15–17; 19:1–6) or his accounts of the pathos of judgment (e.g., 6:16–17; 9:5–6; 16:10–11) and the glories of the saints' future reward (e.g., 21:1–4; 22:1–5) can rival the best in world literature.

Thirdly, as an addendum to observations about John's Semitic style, it is sometimes argued that John's Greek is influenced primarily by his immersion in the Greek translations of the Old Testament used by the churches of Asia Minor (the LXX and others). The point is that from his ministry among such churches, as well as from his own intensive study of the Greek Scriptures, he was able to mirror that style of Greek as he wrote. Opinions differ, but often this is thought to have been intentional on his part, out of a sense that elevated religious topics should be treated in elevated, spiritual-sounding language (cf. the practice in older generations of using KJV English for prayers and liturgy). While some of the same Semitic-style Greek would be the result, it is thought to be due not to his own second-language usage or lack of ability in Greek but to this conscious or unconscious mirroring

---

132. See the helpful discussion of bilingualism in G. H. R. Horsley, "The Fiction of 'Jewish Greek,'" in *NewDocs*, 5:6–19; and Jonathan M. Watt, "Some Implications of Bilingualism for New Testament Exegesis," in *The Language of the New Testament: Context, History, and Development*, ed. Stanley E. Porter and Andrew W. Pitts, LBS 6 (Leiden: Brill, 2013), 9–27, and the works on general linguistics they cite.

133. Hugo Baetens Beardsmore, *Bilingualism: Basic Principles*, 2nd ed. (San Diego: College-Hill Press, 1986), 45–47; Watt, "Implications of Bilingualism," 17; also Stanley E. Porter,

"The Language of the Apocalypse in Recent Discussion," *NTS* 35 (1989): 587, 599. Porter resists seeing Semitic "interference" per se in the Greek of Rev, but he discusses primarily examples of tenses and moods of the Greek verb, so his evidence is rather narrow.

134. Guthrie, *Introduction*, 939–40; Porter, "Language of the Apocalypse," 600; and A. T. Robertson, *A Grammar of the Greek New Testament in the Light of Historical Research* (Nashville: Broadman, 1914), 136–37, all mention such ideas.

of "biblical-sounding" diction.[135] This idea covers some of John's idiolectical Greek usage (e.g., use of "and," καί, so frequently; redundant pronouns) but leaves many of the most noticeable irregularities unexplained (issues of agreement and case usage) since these are not characteristic of the LXX.

A variation on this is Beale's view that John uses unusual grammatical phrasing of various kinds to call attention to Old Testament allusions in the book.[136] Sometimes, according to Beale, the unusual phrasing is taken more or less directly from an Old Testament text put into Greek form in order to create a syntactical dissonance for his readers that causes them to take more careful notice and discern the Old Testament connection. But at other times

> the precise grammar from the Old Testament passage is not retained, but stylistic Semitisms or Septuagintalisms are incorporated in order to create the dissonance. This 'dissonance' is one of the ways that John gets the readers' attention, causing them to focus on the phrase and to cause them more readily to recognize the presence of an Old Testament allusion.[137]

The first sort of case makes good sense, and examples of this are not hard to find, including the notable instance in 1:4 (nominatives used after "from," ἀπό, under the influence of Exod 3), 12:5 (use of a neuter form of "male," ἄρσεν, alluding to Isa 66:7), and instances in 11:2 and 14:6.[138] But many of his examples of "stylistic Semitisms and Septuagintalisms" seem to push his claims too far. These display simply idiolectical departures from the normal patterns of usage, and any allusions to the Old Testament are either fairly easy to see on their own or are rather vague even with an extra signal like this (e.g., 1:5; 2:13; 4:1; 9:14; 11:15; 12:7; 14:7). Beale does acknowledge that some solecisms may show emphasis of some other kind (not related to OT allusions), that some are hard to explain on any theory, and that some may simply reflect John's Semitized Greek style in general.[139] These points bring his theory closer to what appears to be the actual pattern of usage, although I would reverse the proportions (i.e., occasionally they help to signal OT allusions but generally not).[140] But when Beale asserts that even these uses—ones that are only peripherally related to his main

---

135. Farrer, *Rebirth of Images*, 24; Robertson, *Grammar*, 136; Daryl D. Schmidt, "Semitisms and Septuagintalisms in the Book of Revelation," *NTS* 37 (1991): 592–603.

136. Beale, "Solecisms in the Apocalypse," 423–26. Bauckham, *Climax*, 286, opts for a closely related view (but not quite the same): "Unusual and difficult phrases in Revelation frequently turn out to be Old Testament allusions." He means by this that such phrases are often "translation Semitisms" (cf. BDF §4) taken from an OT text and roughly translated into a Greek phrase that reflects the Hebrew structure or vocabulary quite closely.

137. Beale, "Solecisms in the Apocalypse," 423; similarly, Jean-Pierre Ruiz, *Ezekiel in the Apocalypse: The Transformation of Prophetic Language in Revelation 16,17–19,10*, EUS 23.376 (Frankfurt am Main: Peter Lang, 1989), 220–23.

138. The latter two are the examples Bauckham, *Climax*, 286–87, mentions (see earlier footnote).

139. Beale, "Solecisms in the Apocalypse," 424–25.

140. Beale does qualify his approach ("Solecisms in the Apocalypse," 426) by claiming that not *all* examples but "*a significant number* of the Apocalypse's grammatical solecisms indicate the presence of Old Testament allusions" (emphasis added).

thesis—are intended by John "to create a 'biblical' effect in the hearer and, hence, to show the solidarity of his writing with that of the Old Testament,"[141] I think this misses the true explanation of John's unusual examples of Greek usage.

Another recent theory about John's unusual style is that he intentionally violates normal grammatical standards as a form of protest against Rome. This is related to an idea that his lexical choices and veiled expressions (e.g., use of polemical titles or images for the empire or emperor contrasted with positive images of Christ) are intended to mock and subvert imperial ideology,[142] but it goes a step further. The further step is that John's grammatical solecisms are meant to "deliberately flout the accepted forms of grammar" to undermine social conventions and establish group identity.[143] But using the language of the empire in a substandard way—and only here and there rather than throughout the work—as a means of undermining its power seems both counterproductive and overly subtle at the same time. Such a thing makes sense in the modern world of identity politics, but evidence for this in the ancient Jewish and Christian world is lacking. John's protest against Rome and world powers like it comes across clearly in the substance of what he says. He does not rely on grammatical irregularities to make his point.

To say that John used a Semitized form of Hellenistic Greek displaying idiolectical patterns peculiar to his own linguistic style is not to say that he followed those patterns without exception. Many have observed that John's solecisms can be put alongside other examples of the same constructions (sometimes in the near context) that follow the normal patterns. The two "from" (ἀπό) phrases in 1:4–5 (using nominative and then genitive objects) are often cited. The same can be said for his use of the participle "saying" (forms of λέγω) to introduce direct speech: sometimes they fail to display the expected agreement (e.g., 4:1, 8) and sometimes they follow it perfectly well (e.g., 6:1, 3, 5–6).[144] But this is to be expected from a second-language user who interacts regularly in different linguistic circles, sometimes in circles where the *unusual* linguistic pattern is followed (or at least is not objectionable) and sometimes where the *normal* pattern is followed.[145]

---

141. "Solecisms in the Apocalypse," 426.

142. John E. Hurtgen, *Anti-Language in the Apocalypse of John* (Lewiston, NY: Mellen, 1993), 90; Harry O. Maier, *Apocalypse Recalled: The Book of Revelation after Christendom* (Minneapolis: Fortress, 2002), 110–12; James L. Resseguie, *The Revelation of John: A Narrative Commentary* (Grand Rapids: Baker Academic, 2009), 48–49. Shane J. Wood, *The Alter-Imperial Paradigm: Empire Studies & the Book of Revelation*, BIS 140 (Leiden: Brill, 2016), 64–69, critiques this idea (not entirely successfully).

143. Koester, *Revelation*, 141. In this he is following Allen Dwight Callahan, "The Language of Apocalypse," *HTR* 88 (1995): 464–70. See also Elisabeth Schüssler Fiorenza, "Babylon the Great: A Rhetorical-Political Reading of Revelation

17–18," in *The Reality of Apocalypse: Rhetoric and Politics in the Book of Revelation*, ed. David L. Barr (Atlanta: SBL Press, 2006), 252–55.

144. Aune, *Revelation 1–5*, ccvi, gives statistics: of fifty-three examples of present participles of λέγω in Rev introducing speech, forty-one display proper agreement and twelve do not. But these do not account for differences due to ad sensum agreement or intervening phrases that affect the agreement pattern (e.g., 5:12, 14; 9:14; 19:1).

145. Baetens Beardsmore, *Bilingualism*, 65–75; Watt, "Implications of Bilingualism," 22–24.

One final point to add to an already complicated discussion: the Greek of Revelation also manifests a variety of inner-Greek linguistic changes that have sometimes been labeled nonnormal or substandard, but should not be. Diachronic developments within ancient Greek itself across the centuries from classical Greek through Hellenistic Greek and into medieval or Byzantine Greek should not figure in this discussion. Regarding some features, Semitized Greek moved further or faster along the continuum of change than non-Semitic forms of Hellenistic Greek, but such changes were characteristic of Hellenistic Greek in general, not of biblical Greek or John's Greek alone. Examples of this are uses of future indicatives instead of subjunctives (with ἵνα or οὐ μή; see note on 3:9; 9:6), use of the aoristic perfect (see note on 5:7), and more generally a tendency to more redundant expression (more prepositions, more pronouns, ἵνα or ὅτι clauses instead of infinitives) and to simpler or more uniform usage (coordinate clauses instead of subordinate ones, direct speech instead of indirect).[146]

Structure and Outline

As with other puzzling features of Revelation, its larger units of text and thematic flow are not immediately transparent, and interpreters have arrived at only a minimal consensus about the book's structure. Some structural features stand out as important, but opinions differ over their significance for an overall outline of contents (e.g., prologue and epilogue at beginning and end; a possible preview of the contents in 1:19, seven letters or messages to the churches; repetition of "in the Spirit" at significant places along the way; three judgment heptads in the middle of the book; contrast of two cities and women toward the end; use of "and I saw," καὶ εἶδον, throughout the book but more prominently in some sections).[147] The larger question of whether there is consistent chronological progression in the book or frequent recapitulation (and where these occur) is a major issue. Thus many different proposed outlines can be found, and they often significantly affect the interpretation of the book.

Osborne surveys "six basic types of outlines" and then adds his own proposal as a seventh.[148] The six are: chiastic arrangements, multi-act dramas, six or seven series of sevens, liturgical arrangements, cycles of recapitulated visions, and structures utilizing discourse analysis. Several of these are based directly on one or more of the structural features just mentioned, but oddly he does not specifically label the

---

146. Maximillian Zerwick, *Biblical Greek Illustrated by Examples*, trans. Joseph Smith (Rome: Pontifical Biblical Institute, 1963), 161–64.

147. Alan S. Bandy, "The Layers of the Apocalypse: An Integrative Approach to Revelation's Macrostructure," *JSNT* 31 (2009): 472–73.

148. Grant R. Osborne, "Recent Trends in the Study of the Apocalypse," in *The Face of New Testament Studies: A Survey of Recent Research*, ed. Scot McKnight and Grant R. Osborne (Grand Rapids: Baker Academic, 2004), 497–504. See his survey for bibliographic details.

approach that has gained more attention in recent years (see following discussion). His own proposal follows this approach through chapter 16 and then departs from it in the final chapters. Bandy also surveys multiple features in Revelation that have been used to discern its larger structure and argument, but he pulls them together in a layered approach that provides better grounds for consensus.[149]

The more common recent approach is to structure the major sections between the prologue and the epilogue according to the literary transitions given by the repetition of "in the Spirit" (ἐν πνεύματι) in four places, accompanied by "I came to be" (ἐγενόμην) in 1:9–10 and 4:1–2 and by "he carried me away" (ἀπήνεγκέν με) in 17:1–3 and 21:9–10. The verb "I will show" (δείξω) occurs in the immediate context of the latter three transitions, while in the first it is a bit further away (the infinitive "to show" in 1:1).[150] These higher-level transitions structure the book into four major visions spread out between the prologue and epilogue, but it leaves two major loose ends to resolve: the large unit of 4:1–16:21 (the second vision) that needs to be sub-divided based on further literary features; and the important section that intervenes between the third and fourth visions (19:11–21:8) that needs to be incorporated in some appropriate way. Both can be handled following one or more of the other structural features listed above.[151] The section between the third and fourth major visions is made up of seven shorter visions that portray the events that will intervene between Babylon's destruction and the coming of the new Jerusalem (signaled by prominent uses of "and I saw," καὶ εἶδον). The second major vision is much more complex, but it is clearly structured according to the three series of seven judgments (seals, trumpets, bowls) with their introduction (the throne-room vision of chs. 4–5) and significant interludes to slow down the impending destruction and fill in important details about God's coming rule on earth. See outline given below and discussion at these points of transition in the commentary.

In addition to the level of major divisions just laid out, it is important to note other ways in which John ties the sections of the book together through interlocking or interweaving literary techniques.[152] Bandy refers to these further levels as "intertextual" (focusing especially on the influence of the OT on John's themes and arrangement of themes) and "intratextual" (focusing on repetition of phrases within the book that trace its larger themes).[153] Some of the intertextual features were mentioned in the section on the use of the Old Testament above (e.g., judgment typologies such as the plagues of Egypt, the day of the Lord, and holy war; also patterns of Israel's

---

149. Bandy, "Layers of the Apocalypse," 469–99.

150. This structure can be found as early as Tenney, *Interpreting Revelation*, 32–34. Bauckham, *Climax*, 2–7, 21–22, gives a convincing presentation of it. See also Bandy, "Layers of the Apocalypse," 475; Wayne Richard Kempson, "Theology in the Revelation of John" (PhD diss., Southern Baptist Theological Seminary, 1982), 95–142; Ladd, *Revelation*, 14–17; Lietaert

Peerbolte, *Antecedents of Antichrist*, 116–18; Mazzaferri, *Genre*, 331–43, 363; Smith, "Structure," 384–87.

151. See discussion of these in Bandy, "Layers of the Apocalypse," 475–81.

152. Koester, *Revelation*, 112–15, discusses some of these features.

153. Bandy, "Layers of the Apocalypse," 481–90.

discipline and restoration). The intratextual features include repeated references to God's prophets and his message through them, features of the theophany from Sinai, the deception as well as redemption of the world's nations, and divine titles.[154]

A further issue about the structure of Revelation is the question of recapitulation versus chronological progression in the book. One larger dimension of this issue was touched on already in the section "Hermeneutical Approaches": whether John's visions refer to events throughout the age or exclusively in the past or distant future (predominantly future seems to be the best approach). But the structural dimension of this question is whether the events described in the major units and subunits of the book progress chronologically or go back and describe the same events again as the chapters move along.[155] The main focus of this debate falls on chapters 6–16 (how do the seal, trumpet, and bowl judgments and their various interludes relate to one another?) and chapters 19–21 (does 20:1–6 recapitulate events described earlier in the book, and do the eschatological battle accounts in 19:11–21 and 20:7–10 refer to the same events?). See discussion in the commentary on chapters 19–21 for the second issue. The following discussion centers on the question in chapters 6–16.

The essence of the recapitulation view of the three series of judgments is that they give three descriptions of the same judgments but with differing viewpoints or levels of detail.[156] The main support for this approach includes the following: (1) general thematic parallels appear frequently among the seals, trumpets, and bowls such as effects on the earth's waters, effects on heavenly bodies, warfare and invasion, scorching heat, widespread human deaths, and lack of repentance by the ungodly.[157] (2) Some inconsistencies arise if we take the three series sequentially: the heavenly bodies that were dramatically affected in the sixth seal (6:12–17) are still in place and are darkened under the fourth trumpet (8:12); the first trumpet (8:7) burns all the green grass, but the locusts of the fifth trumpet are not to harm it (9:4).[158] (3) The seven trumpets and seven bowls seem to end at the same place: the consummation of God's judgment just prior to the start of his rule on the earth (10:5–7; 11:15–18; 16:17; cf. 15:1; the seventh seal is unclear, 8:1).[159] (4) A storm

---

154. See Bauckham, _Climax_, 7–37 and passim.

155. A few commentators see recapitulation in the whole book, not just in chs. 6–16 as described above. For example, William Hendriksen, _More Than Conquerors: An Interpretation of the Book of Revelation_, 2nd ed. (Grand Rapids: Baker, 1940), 16–22, divides the book into seven major sections and argues that "they are parallel and each spans the entire new dispensation, from the first to the second coming of Christ," viewing it from different perspectives and selecting different details to highlight (p. 22). Charles Homer Giblin, "Recapitulation and the Literary Coherence of John's Apocalypse," _CBQ_ 56 (1994): 81–95, structures chs. 4–22 according to three cycles of recapitulation, and Adela Yarbro Collins, _The Combat Myth in the Book of Revelation_, HDR 9 (Missoula, MT: Scholars

Press, 1976), 11–13, 31–44, sees five cycles of recapitulation in chs. 6–22.

156. This was the fundamental point made by Gunther Bornkamm, "Die Komposition der apokalyptischen Visionen in der Offenbarung Johannis," _ZNW_ 36 (1937): 132–49, who influenced several later scholars.

157. George Raymond Beasley-Murray, _The Book of Revelation_, rev. ed., NCB (Grand Rapids: Eerdmans, 1978), 238–41; Frederick J. Murphy, _Fallen Is Babylon: The Revelation to John_, NTC (Harrisburg, PA: Trinity Press International, 1998), 51–52, 201.

158. Koester, _Revelation_, 443–44; Murphy, _Fallen Is Babylon_, 236–38.

159. Beasley-Murray, _Revelation_, 30, 187–88, 233–34.

theophany (lightning, thunder, earthquake, hail) comes at the end of each of the series (8:5; 11:19; 16:18–21). These are taken as evidence that the three series are coextensive and parallel and describe the same events but with different specifics or points of view each time. (5) The sixth seal (6:12–17) describes such changes in the heavenly bodies that it must refer to realities immediately prior to Christ's return.[160]

The final three points make clear that the three series are not purely sequential (i.e., all seven seals followed by all seven trumpets and then all seven bowls). But arguing (as in points 3 and 4) that the series all end at the same time does not speak to whether they begin at the same time. And general parallels (point 1) do not establish identity of events since the three series all draw from Old Testament typologies of judgment (e.g., the day of the Lord, Egyptian plagues, Sodom and Gomorrah) that may recur at separate occasions.[161] The sixth seal does speak of cataclysmic effects, but it is best to see its description as hyperbolic for unmistakable heavenly portents of God's coming judgment, not the end of the cosmic order as a woodenly literal reading would take it (see commentary on 6:12–17).

The evidence for chronological sequence includes the following points, and this approach seems more satisfactory:[162] (1) explicit ordering of the features within each series ("first," "second," etc.) supports a predisposition toward taking the realities they refer to as well as the three series themselves as chronologically sequential. Why portray these features as explicitly sequenced if they represent things that occur at various times in no particular order? (2) The strong typological association with the Egyptian plagues (at least for the trumpets and bowls) suggests that the judgments in all three series are sequential and get progressively worse just as those did and they likewise do not lead to repentance even as they get worse.[163] (3) The intensification within each series and between the series is easier to explain by chronological sequencing than by recapitulation of the same events. For example, the first four seals and first four trumpets are less severe than the later ones in each series, and the scope of destruction increases with each series (one fourth in 6:8, thirds in 8:7–12 and 9:15, 18, including a third of the sea creatures dead; all of the sea creatures die in 16:3, and the other bowls seem to affect the whole world with their woes rather than being partial).[164] (4) The bowl judgments are explicitly called "the last plagues," that "complete" God's judgmental wrath visited on the earth (15:1; 21:9). (5) The contents of the seventh seal and seventh trumpet are left unspecified and are narrated or described so closely with the subsequent series (trumpets and bowls respectively) as

160. Beasley-Murray, *Revelation*, 30–31, regards this as incontrovertible evidence for recapitulation.

161. On the inconsistencies mentioned at point 2, see commentary at the verses listed.

162. See Marko Jauhiainen, "Recapitulation and Chronological Progression in John's Apocalypse: Towards a New Perspective," *NTS* 49 (2003): 543–59; J. Lambrecht, "A Structuration of Revelation 4:1–22:5," in Lambrecht, *Apocalypse johannique*, 80–104; Pate, "Progressive Dispensational View," 161–64; and James L. Resseguie, *Revelation Unsealed: A Narrative Critical Approach to John's Apocalypse*, BIS 32 (Leiden: Brill, 1998), 160–66, for many of these points.

163. Fekkes, *Prophetic Traditions*, 80–82.

164. Bauckham, *Theology*, 40.

to indicate that the trumpets constitute the last seal judgment and the bowls constitute the last trumpet judgment (8:1–6; 10:5–7; 11:15–19; 15:1).[165] This arrangement
is sometimes called *telescoping* or *telescopic* rather than purely sequential.[166] Thus
each series brings the reader up to the end point of the future climactic period of
judgment, just prior to the establishment of God's rule at the return of Christ as King
of kings and Lord of lords (19:11–21).

Within the larger framework of the seals, trumpets, and bowls, chapters 6–16 also
contain various interludes or digressions that can be disorienting but complement
the mainline narration in important ways. They pause the chronological progression
for shorter or longer segments with flashbacks to background events, heavenly previews of the consummation about to come, or glimpses of relevant contemporaneous
circumstances before the judgment sequence is picked up again. These interludes
serve several discernible purposes in the literary design. They relax the tension of
a seemingly breathless but predictable pace and implicitly show that the imminent
end will come on an unexpected timetable controlled by God.[167] They give glimpses
of the heavenly viewpoint on the earthly events portrayed in the images of judgment
in the chronological progression. They also provide needed answers to questions
raised by the judgments (e.g., 6:17, "Who can stand?"; 10:5–7, Why the delay before
the end?). These answers sometimes give encouragement (7:1–8, God will protect
Israel) or hope for redemption in the midst of judgment (7:9–17, a vast multitude
from every nation worshiping God and the Lamb). They provide examples of God's
witnesses for the readers to emulate in their own experiences of hostility and rejection by the surrounding culture (chs. 10–11). They explain the cosmic and historical
background to the present and coming conflict (chs. 12–13). They preview God's
coming triumph as well as the severe judgment about to be consummated (ch. 14).[168]
In summary, a basic chronological progression with embedded flashbacks, previews,
or contemporary glimpses is the most satisfactory way to read the central section of
Revelation (chs. 6–16, most of the second major vision).

With the third major vision (17:1–19:10), John focuses on the destruction of
Babylon, which is roughly contemporaneous with chapters 6–16 in time but also
portrays her past and present evil influence on the world and then the events of
God's judgment on her. This judgment will culminate in divine rule being established
on earth when her power is swept away at the time of Christ's second coming (as
foreshadowed in 11:15–18; 14:1, and stated explicitly in 14:8; 16:10, 19). The fourth
major vision (21:9–22:9) provides a contrasting focus on the new Jerusalem, which

165. Ladd, *Revelation*, 121–23, 145, 160.

166. Larry R. Helyer, *The Witness of Jesus, Paul and John: An Exploration in Biblical Theology* (Downers Grove, IL: Inter-Varsity Press, 2008), 354–55; Murphy, *Fallen Is Babylon*, 236; Thomas, *Revelation 1–7*, 531–43.

167. Resseguie, *Narrative Commentary*, 53.

168. Peter S. Perry, *The Rhetoric of Digressions: Revelation 7:1–17 and 10:1–11:13 and Ancient Communication*, WUNT 2.268 (Tübingen: Mohr Siebeck, 2009), 209–41, discusses some of these purposes and shows that digressions were a part of the communication patterns in the Greco-Roman world with which John's readers would have been familiar.

exists in an eternal future. The vision describes the blessedness of living in direct communion with and service for God. The major section that intervenes between the third and fourth major visions (19:11–21:8) is laid out chronologically and recounts seven shorter visions portraying future events that take place between the collapse of Babylon and the coming of the new Jerusalem with its new heaven and earth.[169] So the larger arrangement of most of the book follows a temporal progression through various events that will culminate this age and lead finally to the new heaven and new earth, events that "must happen soon" (1:1; 22:6).[170]

Outline of Revelation

I. Prologue (1:1–8)
   A. Superscription (1:1–3)
   B. Epistolary Opening and Doxology (1:4–6)
   C. Theme of the Book (1:7–8)
II. First Vision: The Exalted Christ and His Messages to the Churches (1:9–3:22)
   A. Vision of the Exalted Christ (1:9–20)
   B. Messages to the Seven Churches (2:1–3:22)
      1. To the Church in Ephesus (2:1–7)
      2. To the Church in Smyrna (2:8–11)
      3. To the Church in Pergamum (2:12–17)
      4. To the Church in Thyatira (2:18–29)
      5. To the Church in Sardis (3:1–6)
      6. To the Church in Philadelphia (3:7–13)
      7. To the Church in Laodicea (3:14–22)
III. Second Vision: Heavenly Throne Room and Three Judgment Cycles (4:1–16:21)
   A. Vision of God in His Heavenly Throne Room (4:1–11)
   B. The Seven-Sealed Scroll and the Slain Lamb (5:1–14)
   C. The Seven Seals and the Interlude of the Two Multitudes (6:1–8:1)
      1. The First Six Seals (6:1–17)
      2. The Interlude of the Two Multitudes (7:1–17)
      3. The Seventh Seal (8:1)

---

169. See discussion in commentary at 19:11; 20:2, 7, 10.

170. Despite the book's predominant chronological arrangement of its prophetic vision of the future, some interpreters (holding both to recapitulation and to chronological progression) insist on denying that Rev refers to any "specific series of events in time and space" (Koester, *Revelation*, 445) or any specific "sequence of events within this final period of history" (Bauckham, *Theology*, 149; cf. 40–41); see also Giblin, "Recapitulation," 94; and Resseguie, *Narrative Commentary*, 59. This in part is an overreaction to popular writers about the end times who produce overly literal and overly specific accounts of the world's future. It can also come from a false dichotomy between the value of a sequence of prophesied events and their "nature and meaning" (Bauckham, *Theology*, 149–50). Surely these are not mutually exclusive; we should aim to find both if a text presents it (as Rev seems to do).

Select Bibliography

Adams, Edward. *The Stars Will Fall from Heaven: Cosmic Catastrophe in the New Testament and Its World*. LNTS 347. London: T&T Clark, 2007.

Aland, Barbara, et al., eds. *The Greek New Testament*. 5th ed. Stuttgart: Deutsche Bibelgesellschaft, 2014.

Aland, Barbara, et al., eds. *Novum Testamentum Graece*. 28th ed. Stuttgart: Deutsche Bibelgesellschaft, 2012.

Aune, David E. *Revelation*. 3 vols. WBC 52. Nashville: Thomas Nelson, 1997–98.

Balz, Horst, and Gerhard Schneider, eds. *Exegetical Dictionary of the New Testament*. 3 vols. Grand Rapids: Eerdmans, 1990–1993.

Barker, Margaret. *The Revelation of Jesus Christ*. Edinburgh: T&T Clark, 2000.

Barnhouse, Donald Grey. *Revelation: An Expository Commentary*. Grand Rapids: Zondervan, 1971.

Bass, Justin W. *The Battle for the Keys: Revelation 1:18 and Christ's Descent into the Underworld*. PBM. Milton Keynes: Paternoster, 2014.

Bauckham, Richard. *The Climax of Prophecy: Studies in the Book of Revelation*. Edinburgh: T&T Clark, 1993.

———. *The Theology of the Book of Revelation*. Cambridge: Cambridge University Press, 1993.

Bauer, Walter, W. F. Arndt, F. W. Gingrich, and Frederick William Danker. *A Greek-English Lexicon of the New Testament and Other Early Christian Literature*. 3rd ed. Chicago: University of Chicago Press, 2000.

Baynes, Leslie. *The Heavenly Book Motif in Judeo-Christian Apocalypses, 200 B.C.E.–200 C.E.* JSJSup 152. Leiden: Brill, 2012.

Beagley, A. J. *The "Sitz im Leben" of the Apocalypse: With Particular Reference to the Role of the Church's Enemies*. BZNW 50. Berlin: de Gruyter, 1987.

Beale, G. K. *The Book of Revelation*. NIGTC. Grand Rapids: Eerdmans, 1999.

Beale, G. K., and Sean M. McDonough. "Revelation." Pages 1081–161 in *Commentary on the New Testament Use of the Old Testament*. Edited by G. K. Beale and D. A. Carson. Grand Rapids: Baker Academic, 2007.

Beasley-Murray, G. R. *The Book of Revelation*. Rev. ed. NCB. Grand Rapids: Eerdmans, 1978.

Beckwith, Isbon T. *The Apocalypse of John: Studies in Introduction with a Critical and Exegetical Commentary*. New York: Macmillan, 1919.

Blaising, Craig. "Biblical Hermeneutics: How Are We to Interpret the Relation between the Tanak and the New Testament on This Question?" Pages 79–105 in *The New Christian Zionism: Fresh Perspectives on Israel & the Land*. Edited by Gerald R. McDermott. Downers Grove, IL: IVP Academic, 2016.

Blaising, Craig A., and Darrell L. Bock. *Progressive Dispensationalism*. Wheaton: Bridgepoint, 1993.

Blass, Friedrich, Albert Debrunner, and Robert W. Funk. *A Greek Grammar of the New Testament and Other Early Christian Literature*. Chicago: University of Chicago Press, 1961.

Blass, Friedrich, and Albert Debrunner. *Grammatik des neutestamentlichen Griechisch*. Edited by Friedrich Rehkopf. 15th ed. Göttingen: Vandenhoeck & Ruprecht, 1979.

Blount, Brian K. *Revelation: A Commentary*. NTL. Louisville: Westminster John Knox, 2009.

Bock, Darrell L., ed. *Three Views on the Millennium and Beyond*. Grand Rapids: Zondervan, 1999.

Boring, M. Eugene. *Revelation*. IBC. Louisville: Westminster John Knox, 1989.

Boxall, Ian. *The Revelation of Saint John*. BNTC. Peabody, MA: Hendrickson, 2006.

Burton, Ernest DeWitt. *Syntax of the Moods and Tenses in New Testament Greek*. 3rd ed. Edinburgh: T&T Clark, 1898.

Caird, G. B. *A Commentary on the Revelation of St John the Divine*. HNTC. New York: Harper & Row, 1966.

———. *The Language and Imagery of the Bible*. London: Duckworth, 1980.

Cancik, Hubert, and Helmuth Schneider, eds. *Brill's New Pauly: Encyclopaedia of the Ancient World*. Antiquity. 15 vols. Leiden: Brill, 2002–2010.

Cerfaux, Lucien and Jules Cambier. *L'Apocalypse de Saint Jean lue aux Chrétiens*. LD 17. Paris: Cerf, 1955.

Charles, R. H. *A Critical and Exegetical Commentary on the Revelation of St. John*. 2 vols. ICC. Edinburgh: T&T Clark, 1920.

Chilton, David. *The Days of Vengeance: An Exposition of the Book of Revelation*. Ft. Worth: Dominion, 1987.

Culy, Martin M. *The Book of Revelation: The Rest of the Story*. Eugene, OR: Pickwick, 2017.

Dixon, Sarah Underwood. *The Testimony of the Exalted Jesus: The "Testimony of Jesus" in the Book of Revelation*. LNTS 570. London: Bloomsbury T&T Clark, 2017.

Fuller Dow, Lois K. *Images of Zion: Biblical Antecedents for the New Jerusalem*. NTM 26. Sheffield: Sheffield Phoenix, 2010.

Dumbrell, William J. *The End of the Beginning: Revelation 21–22 and the Old Testament*. Homebush West, NSW: Lancer, 1985.

Duvall, J. Scott. *The Heart of Revelation: Understanding the 10 Essential Themes of the Bible's Final Book*. Grand Rapids: Baker, 2016.

———. *Revelation*. TTC. Grand Rapids: Baker, 2014.

Fanning, Buist M. "Discipleship in Revelation." In *Following Jesus Christ: The New Testament Message of Discipleship for Today*. Edited by John K. Goodrich and Mark L. Strauss. Grand Rapids: Kregel, 2019.

———. "Greek Tenses in John's Apocalypse: Issues in Verbal Aspect, Discourse Analysis, and Diachronic Change." Pages 328–53 in *The Language and Literature of the New Testament: Essays in Honour of Stanley E. Porter's 60th Birthday*. Edited by Lois K. Fuller Dow, Craig A. Evans, and Andrew W. Pitts. Leiden: Brill, 2016.

———. *Verbal Aspect in New Testament Greek*. OTM. Oxford: Clarendon, 1990.

Farrer, Austin. *A Rebirth of Images: The Making of St. John's Apocalypse*. Westminster: Dacre, 1949.

Fee, Gordon D. *Revelation: A New Covenant Commentary*. NCCS. Eugene, OR: Cascade, 2011.

Fekkes III, Jan. *Isaiah and Prophetic Traditions in the Book of Revelation: Visionary Antecedents and Their Development*. JSNTSup 93. Sheffield: JSOT Press, 1994.

Ford, J. Massyngberde. *Revelation*. AB 38. Garden City, NY: Doubleday, 1975.

Freedman, David Noel, ed. *Anchor Bible Dictionary*. 6 vols. New York: Doubleday, 1992.

Friesen, Steven J. *Imperial Cults and the Apocalypse of John: Reading Revelation in the Ruins*. New York: Oxford University Press, 2001.

Gentry, Kenneth L. *Before Jerusalem Fell: Dating the Book of Revelation*. Rev. ed. Atlanta: American Vision, 1998.

Giblin, Charles Homer. *The Book of Revelation: The Open Book of Prophecy*. GNS 34. Collegeville, MN: Liturgical Press, 1991.

Glasson, T. F. *The Revelation of John*. CBC. Cambridge: Cambridge University Press, 1965.

Hamilton, James M. *Revelation: The Spirit Speaks to the Churches*. Wheaton, IL: Crossway, 2012.

Harrington, Wilfrid J. *Revelation*. SP 16. Collegeville, MN: Liturgical Press, 1993.

Helyer, Larry R. *The Witness of Jesus, Paul and John: An Exploration in Biblical Theology*. Downers Grove, IL: InterVarsity Press, 2008.

Hemer, Colin J. *The Letters to the Seven Churches of Asia in Their Local Setting*. JSNTSup 11. Sheffield: JSOT Press, 1986.

Hendriksen, William. *More Than Conquerors: An Interpretation of the Book of Revelation*. 2nd ed. Grand Rapids: Baker, 1940.

Hernández Jr., Juan. *Scribal Habits and Theological Influences in the Apocalypse: The Singular Readings of Sinaiticus, Alexandrinus, and Ephraemi*. WUNT 2.218. Tübingen: Mohr Siebeck, 2006.

Hoskins, Paul M. *The Book of Revelation: A Theological and Exegetical Commentary*. n.p.: ChristoDoulos, 2017.

Hughes, Philip Edgcumbe. *The Book of the Revelation: A Commentary*. Grand Rapids: Eerdmans, 1990.

Hultberg, Alan, ed. *Three Views on the Rapture*. Grand Rapids: Zondervan, 2010.

Jauhiainen, Marko. *The Use of Zechariah in Revelation*. WUNT 2.199. Tübingen: Mohr Siebeck, 2005.

Karrer, Martin. *Johannesoffenbarung*. Vol. 1 (1,1–5,14). EKKNT 24.1. Ostfildern: Patmos, 2017.

Keener, Craig S. *Revelation*. NIVAC. Grand Rapids: Zondervan, 2000.

Kiddle, Martin. *The Revelation of St. John*. MNTC. London: Hodder and Stoughton, 1940.

Kistemaker, Simon J. *Exposition of the Book of Revelation*. NTC. Grand Rapids: Baker Academic, 2001.

Kittel, Gerhard, and Gerhard Friedrich, eds. *Theological Dictionary of the New Testament*. Translated by G. W. Bromiley. 10 vols. Grand Rapids: Eerdmans, 1964–1976.

Koehler, Ludwig et al., eds. *The Hebrew and Aramaic Lexicon of the Old Testament*. 5 vols. Leiden: Brill, 1994–2000.

Koester, Craig R. *Revelation: A New Translation with Introduction and Commentary*. AYB 38A. New Haven: Yale University Press, 2014.

Kovacs, Judith, and Christopher Rowland. *Revelation, the Apocalypse of Jesus Christ*. BBC. Oxford: Blackwell, 2004.

Kraft, Heinrich. *Die Offenbarung des Johannes*. HNT 16A. Tübingen: Mohr Siebeck, 1974.

Kraybill, J. Nelson. *Imperial Cult and Commerce in John's Apocalypse*. JSNTSup 132. Sheffield: Sheffield Academic Press, 1996.

Ladd, George Eldon. *A Commentary on the Revelation of John*. Grand Rapids: Eerdmans, 1972.

———. *A Theology of the New Testament*. Rev. ed. Edited by Donald A. Hagner. Grand Rapids: Eerdmans, 1993.

Lang, G. H. *The Revelation of Jesus Christ*. London: Paternoster, 1948.

Levinsohn, Stephen H. *Discourse Features of New Testament Greek: A Coursebook on the Information Structure of New Testament Greek*. 2nd ed. Dallas: SIL, 2000.

Lichtenberger, Hermann. *Die Apokalypse*. ThKNT 23. Stuttgart: Kohlhammer, 2014.

Liddell, Henry George, Robert Scott, Henry Stuart Jones. *A Greek-English Lexicon*. 9th ed. with revised supplement. Oxford: Clarendon, 1996.

Lietaert Peerbolte, Bert Jan. *The Antecedents of Antichrist: A Traditio-Historical Study of the Earliest Christian Views on Eschatological Opponents.* JSJSup 49. Leiden: Brill, 1996.

Lohse, Eduard. *Die Offenbarung des Johannes.* NTD 11. Göttingen: Vandenhoeck & Ruprecht, 1983.

Lorein, Geert Wouter. *The Antichrist Theme in the Intertestamental Period.* JSPSup 44. London: T&T Clark, 2003.

Louw, Johannes P., and Eugene A. Nida, eds. *Greek-English Lexicon of the New Testament Based on Semantic Domains.* 2nd ed. 2 vols. New York: United Bible Societies, 1989.

Lupieri, Edmondo F. *A Commentary on the Apocalypse of John.* ITSORS. Grand Rapids: Eerdmans, 2006.

Luter, Boyd. "Interpreting the Book of Revelation." Pages 457–80 in *Interpreting the New Testament: Essays on Methods and Issues.* Edited by David Alan Black and David S. Dockery. Nashville: Broadman & Holman, 2001.

MacLeod, David J. *The Seven Last Things: An Exposition of Revelation 19–21.* Dubuque, IA: Emmaus College Press, 2003.

Maier, Gerhard. *Die Offenbarung des Johannes.* 2 vols. HTANT. Giessen: Brunnen, 2009–2012.

Mangina, Joseph L. *Revelation.* BTCB. Grand Rapids: Brazos, 2010.

Marshall, John W. *Parables of War: Reading John's Jewish Apocalypse.* SCJ 10. Waterloo, Ontario: Wilfred Laurier University Press, 2001.

Martin, Ralph P., and Peter H. Davids, eds. *Dictionary of the Later New Testament and Its Developments.* Downers Grove, IL: InterVarsity Press, 1997.

Mathewson, David. *A New Heaven and a New Earth: The Meaning and Function of the Old Testament in Revelation 21.1–22.5.* JSNTSup 238. Sheffield: Sheffield Academic Press, 2003.

———. *Revelation: A Handbook on the Greek Text.* BHGNT. Waco: Baylor University Press, 2016.

———. *Verbal Aspect in the Book of Revelation: The Function of Greek Verb Tenses in John's Apocalypse.* LBS 4. Leiden: Brill, 2010.

Mazzaferri, Frederick David. *The Genre of the Book of Revelation from a Source-Critical Perspective.* BZNW 54. Berlin: de Gruyter, 1989.

McNicol, Allan J. *The Conversion of the Nations in Revelation.* LNTS 438. London: T&T Clark, 2011.

Mealy, J. Webb. *After the Thousand Years: Resurrection and Judgment in Revelation 20.* JSNTSup 70. Sheffield: JSOT Press, 1992.

Metzger, Bruce M. *Breaking the Code: Understanding the Book of Revelation.* Nashville: Abingdon, 1993.

———, ed. *A Textual Commentary on the Greek New Testament.* 2nd ed. Stuttgart: Deutsche Bibelgesellschaft, 1994.

Michaels, J. Ramsey. *Interpreting the Book of Revelation.* GNTE. Grand Rapids: Baker, 1992.

———. *Revelation.* IVPNTC 20. Downers Grove, IL: InterVarsity Press, 1997.

Moffatt, James. "The Revelation of St. John the Divine." Pages 279–494 in *The Expositor's Greek Testament.* Edited by W. Robertson Nicoll. Vol 5. London: Hodder & Stoughton, 1910.

Moo, Jonathan A. *Let Creation Rejoice: Biblical Hope and the Ecological Crisis.* Downers Grove, IL: InterVarsity Press, 2014.

Moule, C. F. D. *An Idiom Book of New Testament Greek.* 2nd ed. Cambridge: Cambridge University Press, 1959.

Mounce, Robert H. *The Book of Revelation.* Rev. ed. NICNT. Grand Rapids: Eerdmans, 1998.

Moyise, Steve. *The Old Testament in the Book of Revelation.* JSNTSup 115. Sheffield: Sheffield Academic Press, 1995.

—, ed. *Studies in the Book of Revelation.* Edinburgh: T&T Clark, 2001.

Murphy, Frederick J. *Fallen Is Babylon: The Revelation to John.* NTIC. Harrisburg, PA: Trinity Press International, 1998.

Mussies, G. *The Morphology of Koine Greek as Used in the Apocalypse of John: A Study in Bilingualism.* NovTSup 27. Leiden: Brill, 1971.

Osborne, Grant R. "Recent Trends in the Study of the Apocalypse." Pages 473–504 in *The Face of New Testament Studies: A Survey of Recent Research.* Edited by Scot McKnight and Grant R. Osborne. Grand Rapids: Baker Academic, 2004.

—. *Revelation.* BECNT. Grand Rapids: Baker, 2002.

Pate, C. Marvin. *Four Views on the Book of Revelation.* Grand Rapids: Zondervan, 1998.

—. *Interpreting Revelation and Other Apocalyptic Literature: An Exegetical Handbook.* HNTE. Grand Rapids: Kregel Academic, 2016.

Patterson, Paige. *Revelation.* NAC 39. Nashville: Broadman & Holman, 2012.

Pitre, Brant James. *Jesus, the Tribulation, and the End of the Exile: Restoration Eschatology and the Origin of the Atonement.* WUNT 2.204. Tübingen: Mohr Siebeck, 2005.

Price, S. R. F. *Rituals and Power: The Roman Imperial Cult in Asia Minor.* Cambridge: Cambridge University Press, 1984.

Prigent, Pierre. *L'Apocalypse de Saint Jean.* 3rd ed. CNT. Geneva: Labor et Fides, 2000.

—. *Commentary on the Apocalypse of St John.* Translated by Wendy Pradels. Tübingen: Mohr Siebeck, 2001.

Resseguie, James L. *The Revelation of John: A Narrative Commentary.* Grand Rapids: Baker Academic, 2009.

Richard, Pablo. *Apocalypse: A People's Commentary on the Book of Revelation.* BLS. Maryknoll, NY: Orbis Books, 1995.

Rowland, Christopher. "The Book of Revelation: Introduction, Commentary, and Reflections." Pages 501–743 in *The New Interpreter's Bible.* Edited by Leander E. Keck. Vol. 12. Nashville: Abingdon, 1998.

Ruiz, Jean-Pierre. *Ezekiel in the Apocalypse: The Transformation of Prophetic Language in Revelation 16,17–19,10.* EUS 23.376. Frankfurt am Main: Peter Lang, 1989.

Runge, Steven E. *Discourse Grammar of the Greek New Testament: A Practical Introduction for Teaching and Exegesis.* Peabody, MA: Hendrickson, 2010.

Sandy, D. Brent. *Plowshares and Pruning Hooks: Rethinking the Language of Biblical Prophecy and Apocalyptic.* Downers Grove, IL: InterVarsity Press, 2002.

Satake, Akira. *Die Offenbarung des Johannes.* Edited by Thomas Witulksi. KEK 16. Göttingen: Vandenhoeck & Ruprecht, 2008.

Saucy, Robert L. *The Case for Progressive Dispensationalism: The Interface between Dispensational & Non-Dispensational Theology.* Grand Rapids: Zondervan, 1993.

Schmid, Josef. *Studien zur Geschichte des griechischen Apokalypse-Textes.* Munich: Karl Zink, 1955.

Schüssler Fiorenza, Elizabeth. *The Book of Revelation: Justice and Judgment.* Philadelphia: Fortress, 1985.

Scott, Walter. *Exposition of the Revelation of Jesus Christ.* 4th ed. London: Pickering & Inglis, 1900.

Seiss, J. A. *The Apocalypse: Lectures on the Book of Revelation.* 6th ed. London: Charles C. Cook, 1900.

Siew, Antoninus King Wai. *The War between the Two Beasts and the Two Witnesses: A Chiastic Reading of Revelation 11:1–14:5*. LNTS 283. London: T&T Clark, 2005.

Silva, Moisés, ed. *New International Dictionary of New Testament Theology and Exegesis*. 2nd ed. 5 vols. Grand Rapids: Zondervan, 2014.

Skaggs, Rebecca, and Priscilla Benham. *Revelation: Pentecostal Commentary*. PCS. Blandford Forum, Dorset, UK: Deo, 2009.

Smalley, Stephen S. *The Revelation to John: A Commentary on the Greek Text of the Apocalypse*. Downers Grove, IL: InterVarsity Press, 2005.

———. *Thunder and Love: John's Revelation and John's Community*. Milton Keynes: Word, 1994.

Smith, J. B. *A Revelation of Jesus Christ: A Commentary on the Book of Revelation*. Scottdale, PA: Herald, 1961.

Strecker, Georg. *Theology of the New Testament*. Edited by Friedrich Wilhelm Horn. Translated by M. Eugene Boring. New York: de Gruyter; Louisville: Westminster John Knox, 2000.

Sweet, John. *Revelation*. TPINTC. Philadelphia: Trinity Press International, 1990.

Swete, Henry Barclay. *The Apocalypse of St. John*. 3rd ed. London: Macmillan, 1911.

Tenney, Merrill C. *Interpreting Revelation*. Grand Rapids: Eerdmans, 1957.

Thomas, Robert L. *Revelation*. 2 vols. Chicago: Moody, 1992–1995.

Thompson, Leonard L. *The Book of Revelation: Apocalypse and Empire*. New York: Oxford University Press, 1990.

Wainwright, Arthur W. *Mysterious Apocalypse: Interpreting the Book of Revelation*. Nashville: Abingdon, 1993.

Wall, Robert W. *Revelation*. NIBC 18. Peabody, MA: Hendrickson, 1991.

Wallace, Daniel B. *Greek Grammar beyond the Basics: An Exegetical Syntax of the New Testament*. Grand Rapids: Zondervan, 1996.

Walvoord, John F., Philip E. Rawley, and Mark Hitchcock. *Revelation*. Chicago: Moody, 2011.

Weinrich, William C., trans. "Andrew of Caesarea." Pages 109–208 in *Greek Commentaries on Revelation*. Edited by Thomas C. Oden. ACT. Downers Grove, IL: IVP Academic, 2011.

———, trans. "Oecumenius." Pages 1–107 in *Greek Commentaries on Revelation*. Edited by Thomas C. Oden. ACT. Downers Grove, IL: IVP Academic, 2011.

———. *Revelation*. ACCS. Downers Grove, IL: InterVarsity Press, 2005.

———, ed. and trans. "Victorinus." Pages 1–22 in *Latin Commentaries on Revelation*. ACT. Downers Grove, IL: IVP Academic, 2011.

Wilcock, Michael. *The Message of Revelation: I Saw Heaven Opened*. Downers Grove, IL: InterVarsity Press, 1975.

Witherington III, Ben. *Revelation*. NCBC. Cambridge: Cambridge University Press, 2003.

Wood, Shane J. *The Alter-Imperial Paradigm: Empire Studies & the Book of Revelation*. BIS 140. Leiden: Brill, 2016.

Wright, N. T. *Revelation for Everyone*. NTE. Louisville: Westminster John Knox, 2011.

———. *Surprised by Hope: Rethinking Heaven, the Resurrection, and the Mission of the Church*. New York: HarperOne, 2008.

Zerwick, Maximilian. *Biblical Greek: Illustrated by Examples*. Translated and adapted by Joseph Smith. Rome: Scripta Pontificii Instituti Biblici, 1963.

Zerwick, Maximillian, and Mary Grosvenor. *A Grammatical Analysis of the Greek New Testament*. Rev. ed. Rome: Pontifical Biblical Institute, 1981.

CHAPTER 1

Revelation 1:1–8

Literary Context

The Book of Revelation opens with a prologue that describes the content, origin, genre, and value of the book for all who will read and follow its truths. In addition, it prepares the way directly for John's spectacular vision of the exalted Christ (1:9–20) and the letters Christ commissioned him to write to the seven churches of Asia Minor (chs. 2–3). Many themes of this prologue are repeated in the epilogue that concludes the book (22:10–21).

➡ **I. Prologue (1:1–8)**
   II. First Vision: The Exalted Christ and His Messages to the Churches (1:9–3:22)

Main Idea

This book is a prophetic revelation from God Almighty through John intended to bless the churches by showing how God's redemption will be consummated through the imminent coming of Jesus Christ to rule over the whole earth.

Translation

(See page 72.)

Structure

This prologue to the entire book of Revelation moves through three closely related sections that identify its content and literary form (vv. 1–3), its writer and immediate recipients (vv. 4–6), and its major theme (vv. 7–8). From its very beginning the focus of Revelation is the eternal God and the future completion of his redemption and judgment through Jesus Christ.

Revelation 1:1–8

1a	Title	**The revelation from Jesus Christ,**
b	Description/ Source	which God gave him to show his servants what must happen soon.
c	Action	**And he made it known**
d	Means	by sending his angel to his servant John,
2a	Description	who testifies to the word of God and the testimony of Jesus Christ—
		=
b	Apposition	all the things that he saw.
3a	Beatitude	**Blessed is the one who reads aloud and**
b		**those who hear the words of this prophecy and**
c		**obey the things written in it,**
d	Explanation	**for the time is near.**
4a	Sender	**John,**
b	Recipients	**to the seven churches in the province of Asia:**
c	Greeting	**Grace to you and peace**
d	Source, Series 1	from the one who is and who was and who is to come, and
e	Source, Series 2	from the seven spirits before his throne, and
5a	Source, Series 3	from Jesus Christ,
b	Description 1	the faithful witness,
c	Description 2	the firstborn from the dead, and
d	Description 3	the ruler over the kings of the earth.
e	Doxology	**To him who loves us and**
f		**freed us from our sins by his blood and**
6a		**made us to be a kingdom,**
		priests to serve his God and Father,
b		**to him be glory and might for ever and ever. Amen.**
7a	Prophetic oracle 1	**Indeed, he is coming with the clouds,** (Dan 7:13)
b		**and every eye will see him,**
c		even those who pierced him;
d		**and all the tribes of the earth will mourn over him.** (Zech 12:10)
e	Affirmation	**So it shall be. Amen.**
8a	Prophetic oracle 2	*"I am the Alpha and the Omega,"*
b		**says the Lord God,**
c		*"the One who is and who was and who is to come, the Almighty."*

Exegetical Outline

➡ **I. Prologue (1:1–8)**

    A. Superscription (1:1–3)

        1. Title and Origin (1:1–2)

        2. Blessing on Those Who Read and Obey (1:3)

    B. Epistolary Opening and Doxology (1:4–6)

        1. Sender, Recipients, and Greeting (1:4–5d)

        2. Praise to Jesus (1:5e–6)

    C. Theme of the Book (1:7–8)

        1. Jesus's Coming (1:7)

        2. God's Sovereignty (1:8)

Explanation of the Text

1:1–2 The revelation from Jesus Christ, which God gave him to show his servants what must happen soon. And he made it known by sending his angel to his servant John, 2 who testifies to the word of God and the testimony of Jesus Christ—all the things that he saw (Ἀποκάλυψις Ἰησοῦ Χριστοῦ ἣν ἔδωκεν αὐτῷ ὁ θεὸς δεῖξαι τοῖς δούλοις αὐτοῦ ἃ δεῖ γενέσθαι ἐν τάχει, καὶ ἐσήμανεν ἀποστείλας διὰ τοῦ ἀγγέλου αὐτοῦ τῷ δούλῳ αὐτοῦ Ἰωάννῃ, 2 ὃς ἐμαρτύρησεν τὸν λόγον τοῦ θεοῦ καὶ τὴν μαρτυρίαν Ἰησοῦ Χριστοῦ ὅσα εἶδεν). John's enigmatic book begins clearly enough with a title that succinctly describes its character, source, and intended audience. The opening words in v. 1a are not a full sentence but a phrase or heading, similar to the first verse of several of the prophets of the Old Testament and to some degree Mark ("The beginning of the gospel of Jesus Christ, God's Son").[1] The key word of the title, "revelation" (ἀποκάλυψις),

denotes an unveiling or disclosure of something hidden,[2] referring to either the *action* of revealing (Rom 8:19; 1 Cor 1:7; 1 Pet 1:7) or the *content* that is revealed, as here. This noun and its related verb are used frequently in the New Testament (noun 18x; verb 26x), always of divine disclosure of what is otherwise hidden from humans. They often refer to the "unveiling" that will come in the future consummation of all things,[3] and that is the sense in this verse, as we will see. The English transliteration of the word, "apocalypse," has come to be used as an alternate title for this book, and also as the name of a genre of ancient literature, apocalypse or apocalyptic literature (see introduction). While the word does not carry the technical sense of a genre of literature here, it aptly describes the book in two ways: (1) as God's disclosure of the events that will fulfill his sovereign plan for the destiny of the world (the content of apocalyptic), and

---

1. See Hosea, Joel, Micah, Zephaniah ("The word of the Lord . . ."), Habakkuk ("The oracle of God . . ."), and Malachi ("The oracle of the word of the Lord . . ."). Aune, *Revelation 1–5*, 9–10, mentions other parallels. The larger structure of Rev 1:1–20 is parallel to Jer 1:1–4, Ezek 1:1–3, Hag 1:1, and Zech 1:1 in describing the prophets' works as "the word of the Lord"

and telling the circumstances under which they received their visions. See Wallace, *Grammar*, 49–50, for the nominative used in titles.

2. BDAG 112; T. Holtz, "ἀποκάλυψις," *EDNT* 1:130–32.

3. E.g., Luke 17:30; Rom 2:5; 8:18–19; 2 Thess 2:8; 1 Pet 1:5.

(2) as an unveiling communicated in dramatic, highly symbolic, and often enigmatic ways (the character of apocalyptic).

This "revelation" is described by a genitive phrase ("of Jesus Christ"; Ἰησοῦ Χριστοῦ) to show its source: it is from Jesus Christ (cf. Gal 1:12). The phrase could carry the sense of an objective genitive, "about Jesus Christ," since the initial vision (1:9–20) reveals Jesus Christ in all his glory as the one who holds the keys to human destiny. The rest of the book would then simply fill this out in detail: he who is now unseen will soon appear in glory and power to establish God's rule over all things. Additionally, "the unveiling of Jesus Christ" carries this objective and eschatological sense in other places (1 Cor 1:7; 2 Thess 1:7; 1 Pet 1:7, 13). But the immediate context of 1:1–2 strongly suggests the sense of a subjective or source genitive instead, "revelation given by Jesus Christ" or "revelation from Jesus Christ" (NIV, NLT).[4] The clarifying clauses of vv. 1b–2 set up a full chain of agents of communication from God to Jesus to God's angel to John and then to God's servants. The rest of the book centers on the two final agents in this chain: what Jesus Christ reveals to John about the events that are coming.[5] Ultimately this comes from God the Father, and sometimes we see angels taking a role in mediating what John sees, while the wider recipients are God's people. But Jesus Christ is the primary revealer, as the vision of 1:9–20 shows (especially vv. 17–19).[6] This of course underscores the paramount authority of the message contained in this book and thus its value for all who give attention to its message (cf. 1:3).

The opening title, "the revelation from Jesus Christ," is further clarified by a relative clause (v. 1b) describing the content as well as the beginning and end of the chain of revelation. First, God the Father is the initiator of this disclosure: he gave it to Jesus. The Father's revelation of his will supremely through the Son is a common theme in the Gospel of John (John 1:18; 5:20; 12:49–50; 17:8). And his intent is "to show" (δεῖξαι, infinitive of purpose; cf. parallel use in 22:6)[7] the coming events "to his servants," the ultimate recipients of this revelation. The reference to God's "servants" (δούλοις, those who figuratively are "duty bound only" to their Master and owe him "total allegiance"[8]) may be narrow in scope, that is, his prophets (cf. 10:7 "his own servants the prophets," alluding to Amos 3:7). But a more general scope is more likely, as the subsequent verses show: this revelation is for the churches (Rev 1:4), God's people who belong to him and serve his purpose (2:20; 19:5; 22:3, 6; cf. 1 Cor 7:22; 1 Pet 2:16).

The content of this disclosure is expressed by the very significant phrase "what must happen soon," which provides vital insights into the background and central elements of John's theology in Revelation. The first part of the phrase, "what must happen" (ἃ δεῖ γενέσθαι), is an allusion to Daniel 2 where Daniel is given the interpretation of Nebuchadnezzar's troubling dream. This exact phrase in Revelation 1:1 appears twice in the LXX version of Daniel 2:28–29 (and variations of it occur also in 2:29, 45). Three important theological themes appear in Daniel 2 that are mirrored in John's prologue and throughout Revelation. First, God is the

---

4. Koester, *Revelation*, 211.

5. The conclusion of the book also emphasizes Jesus's active role in revealing: "I, Jesus, have sent my angel to testify about these things for the churches" (22:16).

6. Wallace, *Grammar*, 119–21, argues that in a book title like this we could expect a "plenary" sense for the genitive, i.e., both objective and subjective senses are intended, not one

or the other alone. But the subjective sense alone seems more likely for the reasons cited above.

7. The verb δείκνυμι is used in John and Rev as a synonym of "reveal, unveil" (ἀποκαλύπτω); see G. Schneider, "δείκνυμι," *EDNT* 1:280–81; H. Schlier, "δείκνυμι," *TDNT* 2:25–33.

8. BDAG 260.

only one who can reveal the mysteries of the future (Dan 2:18–19, 28–29, 47). This is the point of Revelation 1:1a as we have seen: God is the origin of this revelation from Jesus Christ. Second, God has predetermined all the events of earthly history, and he is the one who "changes times and seasons and deposes some kings and establishes others" (Dan 2:21). This is the significance of the verb translated "must" in this phrase (δεῖ, "it is necessary"). Certain events "must happen" because they are set out by God in his sovereign plan for this world and its inhabitants.[9] The phrase "must happen" occurs at key places in the literary structure of Revelation to frame the events that are coming in God's purposes (1:1; 4:1; 22:6). It also appears in Jesus's eschatological discourse with a similar allusion to Daniel 2 (Matt 24:6; Mark 13:7; Luke 21:9). Third, the seemingly invincible kingdoms of this world will be swept away by God's kingdom that will be established forever (Dan 2:44, 47). John alludes to these points in the prologue (Rev 1:5–8), and it is a recurring theme throughout (11:15, 17; 12:10; 19:6, 16; 20:4, 6; 22:5).

The final part of the phrase (v. 1b; occurring also in 22:6) tells the time of these momentous events: in God's calendar they will occur "soon" or without delay (ἐν τάχει). The temporal sense of this is debated. Other New Testament uses show that this phrase can denote (1) a brief extent of time once the events begin: "suddenly, swiftly" (Luke 18:8; Acts 12:7; 22:18); or (2) the nearness of the events from the time of writing: "soon, without delay" (Acts 25:4; Rom 16:20; 1 Tim 3:14). The main argument for the former sense is apologetic: to avoid what would appear to be a false prediction if the

second sense is accepted. Almost two thousand years have elapsed, and the events that Revelation describes have, in the view of most interpreters, not yet occurred. On the other hand, taking ἐν τάχει as "soon" is the strongest argument for the preterist view of Revelation (i.e., that its predictions were largely fulfilled in the events of the first century;[10] see introduction), but it is hard to see how the prophecies of Revelation 19–22 (or chs. 6–18 for that matter) have in any real sense been fulfilled already. The second option, "soon, without delay," is supported by the expression in 1:3, "the time is near," as well as by other expressions throughout Revelation (see the use of the adverb "quickly," ταχύ, in 2:16; 3:11; 11:14; 22:7, 12, 20; the use of "be about to," μέλλω, in 1:19; 3:10; as well as the repetition of "the time is near," in 22:10). Other New Testament passages speak in similar terms (Luke 21:28; Rom 13:12; 16:20; Phil 4:5; Jas 5:8–9; 1 Pet 4:7). None of these seems to mean "rapid occurrence once started" (view 1).[11] It is better to understand that these expressions reflect a "soon" occurrence not in the sense of an exact chronology but in a prophetic time frame, describing what is certain to occur and could occur at any time without any delay. The timing, however, is subject to God's calendar, whose timetable is different from human calculation (cf. Ps 90:4; 2 Pet 3:8–9).[12]

The remaining clause of v. 1c–d continues to unpack the chain of communication mentioned in summary in the preceding description. The revelation that God gave to Christ to show to his people was made known through angelic mediation to John, who would serve as Christ's prophet. The ambiguity of the subject reference in "he made . . .

---

9. W. Popkes, "δεῖ," *EDNT* 1:280.

10. Gentry, *Before Jerusalem Fell*, 133, 142–45.

11. See especially Jesus's statement, "I am coming quickly," ἔρχομαι . . . ταχύ, repeated five times in Rev (2:16; 3:11; 22:7, 12, 20). These almost certainly mean "my coming is near in time," not "my coming will be swift once it has started."

12. Hoskins, *Revelation*, 45–46; Koester, *Revelation*, 212, 223; Ladd, *Revelation*, 22–23. See the discussion of temporal expectations in Jewish and NT apocalyptic in A. L. Moore, *The Parousia in the New Testament* (Leiden: Brill, 1966), 7–26, 164–73.

known" (ἐσήμανεν) is clarified by paying attention to the successive links in this chain. While "he made known" could reflect God as the subject (i.e., the same subject as in the preceding clause, "God gave [the revelation] to [Christ] . . . and made it known"; this finds some support in the parallel reference to God in 22:6), it is more likely that the subject is Christ ("God gave the revelation to Christ . . . and Christ in turn made it known by sending his angel"; cf. 22:16). The lexical sense of this verb "made known" (σημαίνω) reflects an important dimension of the literary character of Revelation. This verb is often used in a more pedestrian sense of "to report, announce publicly" (e.g., Acts 11:28; 25:27),[13] but it can take on the nuance of "signify, represent, make known through symbols" (cf. the cognate noun σημεῖον, "sign, symbol"). The latter sense for the verb is seen several times in John's Gospel (12:33; 18:32; 21:19) where the noun σημεῖον also occurs in a distinctive way (a physical event with spiritual significance; John 2:11; 4:54; etc.). This richer meaning of σημαίνω is seen also in Daniel 2:45 ("the great God has signified [LXX ἐσήμανε] to the king what will happen in the last of the days," referring both to the great statue in his dream and its end-time interpretation), a chapter that John seems to have in mind as he writes his prologue. John is thus previewing the abundant symbolism about God's future for the world that characterizes his visions and this book that records them for the churches.[14]

Christ's means for communicating in this way was in sending (ἀποστείλας; participle of means) angels to mediate his message to John (i.e., in visions and especially their interpretation). The text men-tions "his angel" (articular singular, τοῦ ἀγγέλου αὐτοῦ), but this seems to be a generic reference to various angels who serve in this way.[15] Such interpreting angels do not appear explicitly in Revelation until 17:1ff. and 21:9ff. (less clearly in 10:9–11; 12:10–12), but angels appear in John's visions more widely ("angel" is used 67x in Rev), and their unmentioned role in mediating Christ's message to John seems to be implied by this verse and 22:6, 16. It is also true that Christ himself is the revealer in some places (1:12–20; 4:1; perhaps 10:4, 8; 11:1–3), and one of the heavenly elders (perhaps angelic, but this is not made explicit; see discussion at 4:4) helps John several times (5:5; 7:13–17).

It is appropriate that John is mentioned here in the elaboration of the book's title in 1:1, since his role as the human channel of Christ's revelation to the churches is all-important. Here he is described as Christ's servant (δοῦλος) in a similar sense to the earlier reference to all Christians as God's "servants" (v. 1b): he belongs to Christ and is duty bound to him alone. But there is probably the added sense of serving as a prophet of God, drawing from Amos 3:7 (God revealing his secrets to "his servants the prophets"; cf. Rev 10:7). His name appears also at 1:4, 9, and 22:8.[16]

John's important place in God's chain of revela-tion is described in v. 2 as bearing faithful witness in this book to all that God and Christ have shown him. This is the final portion of the title (1:1–2), and it shows the content and character of what is coming in Revelation. John is described in a relative clause as one who "testifies" or "bears wit-ness" (v. 2a).[17] The reference is to John's personal confirmation or attestation of what he has seen

---

13. LN §33.153 ("to indicate clearly").

14. Murphy, *Fallen is Babylon*, 61–62. Aune, *Revelation 1–5*, 15, and BDAG 920 cite the use of this verb in Heraclitus's description of the Delphic oracle: "it does not speak or con-ceal but signifies," since the utterances were mysterious and required interpretation.

15. Bauckham, *Climax*, 253–57, argues that one specific angel is the revealer throughout the book, but this is not made clear anywhere.

16. For discussion of authorship, see introduction.

17. The verb is actually an aorist in Greek (ἐμαρτύρησεν, "testified"), but it is used here in an epistolary sense (a special-

in the heavenly visions given to him, which will now be recounted in this book.[18] What he bears witness to is "the word of God and the testimony of Jesus Christ" (v. 2a–b), which is another way of describing the chain of revelation that started with God and Christ and now passes to John for communication to God's people (1:1), and so the two phrases refer to the same content, not two separate communications.[19] Both of these expressions should be taken as subjective genitives: "the message that God speaks" and "the testimony that Jesus gives" since this is the larger idea of 1:1–2, as we have seen.[20] This shows John's sense of prophetic calling, since the claim to be a mouthpiece for God's word mirrors the opening of a number of Old Testament prophetic books (e.g., Jer 1:2; Hos 1:1; Joel 1:1). And he has been faithful to record the divine message completely, as the final clause of v. 2 shows. Here a relative clause is added to describe the two previous phrases (God's word and Jesus's testimony) as "all that" or "as many things as" (ὅσα) John saw.[21] Here we get a preview of the visionary character of Revelation, a book filled with what

John was enabled to "see" regarding the coming consummation of God's saving work. Variations of "he saw," "I saw," or "you saw" in this sense occur more than fifty times in Revelation.

1:3 Blessed is the one who reads aloud and those who hear the words of this prophecy and obey the things written in it, for the time is near (μακάριος ὁ ἀναγινώσκων καὶ οἱ ἀκούοντες τοὺς λόγους τῆς προφητείας καὶ τηροῦντες τὰ ἐν αὐτῇ γεγραμμένα, ὁ γὰρ καιρὸς ἐγγύς). The second major part of the superscription is a pronouncement of blessing on those who read and respond to what is written in John's book of prophecy (v. 3).[22] This blessedness is rooted in the book's authority because it comes from God and Jesus Christ (vv. 1–2) as well as its urgency because the events it describes are near at hand (v. 3d). The conviction that blessing comes to those who pay attention to what God says is rooted in the Old Testament (Pss 1; 19; 119) and more directly in Jesus's teaching about his own words (Luke 11:28; cf. Matt 7:24–27; Luke 6:46–49; 8:18, 21; John 12:47). To be "blessed" (μακάριος)

---

ized use of the past in letters and other communication, taking the temporal viewpoint not of the author as he writes—this is normal in English—but of the readers as they take up the composition sometime later (Ernest DeWitt Burton, *Syntax of the Moods and Tenses in New Testament Greek*, 3rd ed. [Edinburgh: T&T Clark, 1898], 21; BDR §334; Buist M. Fanning, *Verbal Aspect in New Testament Greek*, OTM [Oxford: Clarendon, 1990], 281–82).

18. The verb μαρτυρέω often carries the sense of "confirm[ing] or attest[ing] something on the basis of personal knowledge" (BDAG 617–18). It is used twice in John's Gospel (3:11, 32) with an "apocalyptic tone" of Jesus's bearing witness on earth to things seen in heaven (J. Beutler, "μαρτυρέω," *EDNT* 2:391). Revelation 22:16, 18, 20 also uses the verb in this sense to refer to Jesus's attestation of what is recorded in Rev.

19. Aune, *Revelation 1–5*, 19; Ian Boxall, *The Revelation of Saint John*, BNTC (Peabody, MA: Hendrickson, 2006), 26.

20. The phrase "word of God" (τὸν λόγον τοῦ θεοῦ) is invariably a subjective rather than objective genitive in the NT (see examples in BDAG 600–601), and in Rev itself the phrase occurs in some form seven times, all in the subjective sense. "The testimony of Jesus Christ" (τὴν μαρτυρίαν Ἰησοῦ Χριστοῦ)

or "of Jesus" occurs six times in Rev, but its meaning varies depending on the context, from the subjective sense as here and in 1:9 to objective in 12:17; 19:10; 20:4; cf. 6:9; 12:11. Only a few versions prefer the objective sense here in v. 2 (cf. CSB, NET). Thus the content of Rev constitutes Jesus's extended attestation of the message God has shown to him, and he has communicated through John to his people. Christ's specific attestation of God's message to John in this way is also the continuation of his testimony about God and his ways that was his mission in earthly life and death (see 1:5).

21. The specialized relative pronoun ὅσος carries a sense of completeness or comprehensive scope: "as much as, everything that, whatever" (BDAG 729).

22. This is the first of seven beatitudes in Rev (cf. 14:13; 16:15; 19:9; 20:6; 22:7, 14), with 22:7 in the epilogue being an abbreviated parallel to this verse. Having seven beatitudes in the book appears to be a conscious choice for John, calculated to signify complete, perfect blessedness for those who follow God's way as laid out in Rev (cf. Bauckham, *Climax*, 29–30).

is to enjoy transcendent good fortune, happiness, or privilege because of God's favor on one's life.[23] The combination of singular ("the one who reads") and plural ("those who hear . . . and obey") comes from the common practice in the ancient world of a lector reading a text out loud in the hearing of others—something required by the lower levels of literacy and publication prevalent in those days. Even private reading was typically done audibly to oneself rather than silently as we are accustomed to do (cf. Acts 8:28–31). In the community setting of the synagogue (Luke 4:16–21; Acts 13:15, 27; 15:21) or church (1 Tim 4:13), reading Scripture in the worship service was the expected practice,[24] and communication addressed to the churches in general would be read aloud to the whole community when they gathered (cf. 1 Thess 5:27; Col 4:16).

The specific content to be read and heard is "the words of this prophecy" (τοὺς λόγους τῆς προφητείας; v. 3b).[25] Here we have John's second description of the character of his book (after "revelation," or apocalypse, 1:1a). What he has written is a "prophecy" (see parallel uses of the noun in 22:7, 10, 18, 19; also the related verb in 10:11), a declaration of God's will and purpose, especially about the fulfillment of his purpose in the last days.[26]

As the verse states, reading and hearing these words is insufficient in itself (cf. Jas 1:22–25). What brings God's blessing is to "obey" (τηρέω; "keep, observe, fulfill")[27] what is read and heard (v. 3c). This verb is used elsewhere in Revelation to describe obedience to Christ's word (3:8, 10), God's commands (12:17; 14:12), and the words of this book (22:7, 9). This makes it evident that the goal of a book like Revelation is not merely to communicate information or arouse curiosity but to transform Christians' behavior and strengthen their resolve to live in God's way despite adversity.

The final clause (v. 3d), introduced by "for,"[28] underscores the urgency of heeding the message of Revelation: the culminating events prophesied in this book are close at hand. John refers to the future period of consummation ("the time" [ὁ . . . καιρός]) as a metonymy for the all-important events that will occur in that period.[29] Just as he did in v. 1 ("what must happen soon"), John asserts that these climactic events are "near" at hand (ἐγγύς; same phrasing in 22:10; cf. also Matt 26:18; Luke 21:31; Rom 13:11; Phil 4:5). This is a statement of imminence: these things can happen at any time, without delay. To know this and live accordingly brings blessing from God.

1:4–5d John, to the seven churches in the province of Asia: Grace to you and peace from the one who is and who was and who is to come, and from the seven spirits before his throne, 5 and from Jesus Christ, the faithful witness, the firstborn from the dead, and the ruler over the kings of the earth (Ἰωάννης ταῖς ἑπτὰ ἐκκλησίαις ταῖς ἐν τῇ Ἀσίᾳ· χάρις ὑμῖν καὶ εἰρήνη ἀπὸ ὁ ὢν καὶ ὁ ἦν καὶ ὁ ἐρχόμενος καὶ ἀπὸ τῶν ἑπτὰ πνευμάτων ἃ ἐνώπιον τοῦ θρόνου αὐτοῦ 5 καὶ ἀπὸ Ἰησοῦ Χριστοῦ,

---

23. BDAG 610. The uses of this word in Matt 5:3–11 and repeated uses in the Psalms (e.g., 1:1; 32:1–2) are the primary illustrations of this blessedness.

24. BDAG 60; H. Balz, "ἀναγινώσκω," *EDNT* 1:77.

25. The noun "prophecy" here is articular (lit. "the prophecy"), but the article is deictic, pointing to this specific book being introduced. See Wallace, *Grammar*, 221.

26. BDAG 889; F. Schnider, "προφητεία," *EDNT* 3:183. John sees his book as continuing the tradition of the OT prophets (Murphy, *Fallen Is Babylon*, 59–60; Bauckham, *Theology*, 1–5).

For discussion of prophecy as a genre and its implications for Rev, see the introduction to this commentary.

27. BDAG 1002.

28. The conjunction "for" (γάρ) adds v. 3d as explanatory support for v. 3a–c.

29. It will be a time period "characterized by some aspect of special crisis, . . . the time of crisis, the last times" (BDAG 498; cf. Mark 13:33; Luke 21:8; 1 Pet 1:5). The article used with this noun ("*the* time") signifies the well-known period of eschatological consummation (Wallace, *Grammar*, 225).

ὁ μάρτυς, ὁ πιστός, ὁ πρωτότοκος τῶν νεκρῶν καὶ ὁ ἄρχων τῶν βασιλέων τῆς γῆς). The next section of John's prologue is a standard first-century epistolary opening (1:4–5d). The customary opening formula consisted of three parts: the writer (Greek nominative case; here "John," Ἰωάννης), the recipients (Greek dative case; here "to the . . . churches," ταῖς . . . ἐκκλησίαις), and a greeting or brief wish for good fortune.[30] This then is the indication of a third genre type that characterizes Revelation: it is in part an epistle as well as an apocalypse and a prophecy. In keeping with its epistolary character, this book can be expected to address the situation of its first-century readers with God-given instruction suited to their particular needs (see introduction for details). Under instruction by Jesus Christ (1:11), John addresses his composition to seven (ἑπτά) specific churches in Asia (listed in detail in 1:11 and in chs. 2–3). The name "Asia" (Ἀσία) is the designation for a Roman province in western Asia Minor formed in the late second century BC, now western Turkey. John refers to "the seven churches" not because these were the only ones in the province but because these were the seven specific churches (the number's literal or denotative value) to whom Jesus commanded him to send his book (v. 11).[31] At the same time the number seven appears to have a symbolic or connotative significance for John, suggesting completeness or totality, so that these seven particular congregations represent all God's churches in general.[32] While the message of the book is intended ultimately for all Christians in

various churches (then and now), it is important to note this address to seven churches first of all. This specific set of recipients will figure in what is said in later verses (cf. 1:11; 2:7, etc.; 22:16).

The third part of this epistolary opening, the greeting, begins in v. 4c. Here, as often in the New Testament, the epistolary greeting is altered and expanded to reflect Christian truth. It is altered from the more standard "greetings" (Greek χαίρειν, as in Acts 15:23; 23:25–26; Jas 1:1) to the wish for "grace and peace" to be theirs.[33] The wish is then expanded with a lengthy description of the origin or cause of this grace and peace ("from," ἀπό, used frequently in NT salutations), adding important Christian elements by rooting such favor in God (v. 4d), his Spirit (v. 4e), and Jesus Christ (v. 5).[34]

The reference to God is not the simple phrase "God our Father" or "God the Father" as found so often in New Testament letter openings (e.g., in all of Paul's letters except 1 Thess). Instead, it is the majestic three-part description of God used only in Revelation (1:4, 8; 4:8; and without the third part in 11:17; 16:5), "the one who is and who was and who is to come." This bears conceptual similarities to Greek philosophical descriptions of the divine as "what was and is and will be" (usually with indicative forms of the verb "to be," εἰμί).[35] But John's phrasing of this is different, and the first part has clearly been molded by the translation of the name of God in the LXX of Exodus 3:14 (ὁ ὤν; "the one who is," a Greek participle of the verb "to be"),[36] which occurs as God's name also in Josephus (1x),

---

30. David E. Aune, *The New Testament in Its Literary Environment* (Philadelphia: Westminster, 1987), 163, 184–86.

31. Aune, *Revelation 1–5*, 24; Caird, *Revelation*, 15.

32. Bauckham, *Climax*, 30; contra Aune, *Revelation 1–5*, 29.

33. See Judith M. Lieu, "'Grace to You and Peace': The Apostolic Greeting," *BJRL* 68 (1985): 161–78.

34. An obvious Trinitarian motif, although it is not developed in any way. See Bauckham, *Theology*, 23–25.

35. F. Büchsel, "εἰμί, ὁ ὤν," *TDNT* 2:398–99; Aune, *Revelation 1–5*, 31–32.

36. John is apparently so intent on using the exact form ὁ ὤν from LXX Exod 3:14 that he preserves the nominative case form even though the syntax of the phrase in 1:4 normally requires a genitive (as object of the preposition "from," ἀπό). See H. Balz, "εἰμί," *EDNT* 1:393; Wallace, *Grammar*, 62–64, 237; BDF §143 for discussion.

Philo (8x), and in four textual variants in the LXX of Jeremiah (1:6; 4:10; 14:13; 39:17).[37] God's proclamation of himself as the self-existent one in Exodus 3:14 naturally implies his ongoing existence as the eternal one, and this is the sense John has captured in his three-part title. In this as in other ways he portrays God as the awesome, almighty Lord who controls history from beginning to end (see discussion of 1:1 above and its allusions to Dan 2).

The second part of the title for God in v. 4d ("the one who was") mirrors the linguistic structure of the first and third parts, but in doing so presses the grammatical form to the breaking point. It uses a Greek article "the" (like the first and third phrases with articular *participles*) but makes it the subject of an *indicative* past-tense verb, even though Greek articles do not normally occur on their own as verbal subjects. Because the Greek verb εἰμί lacks a past-referring participle, John has to adapt the phrasing to what is needed. The phrase is literally "the '[he] was'" (ὁ ἦν). The point is clear—God has always existed in the past as well as the present— but the way it is expressed is quite unusual and would certainly get the listeners' attention.

The third part of the title is also unusual. In the similar descriptions of God mentioned above (e.g., in Greek philosophy, Philo, etc.), the third phrase uses a future form of the verb "to be" (either indicative or participle form). But here John phrases it with a present participle of "to come," ἔρχομαι: "the one who is to come" or "the one who is coming" ("the coming one," ὁ ἐρχόμενος). The present tense of "come" often implies future occurrence in Greek as well as English, so this can very well mean "the

one who will be," synonymous with a future of "to be" (equal to "coming, future, imminent").[38] This is the probable sense of the common English rendering "who is to come" (ESV, NIV, NRSV). But it is more likely that John has added a twist to the three-part temporal scheme by using the future element to refer to God's actual "coming" in the future, his intervention in judgment and redemption that constitutes the culminating earthly event this book describes (cf. CSB, NET: "who is coming").[39]

John has indicated that the grace and peace he wishes for the churches must come from God the Father (v. 4d). He now adds that they come also "from the seven spirits before his throne" (v. 4e). These seven spirits are mentioned also in 4:5 (associated with God's heavenly throne as here and said to be "of God") and in 3:1; 5:6 (also "of God" but closely associated with Jesus as well: he "has/ holds" them). Some argue that this refers to seven important angels or "spirits" associated with God's heavenly rule and sent by him to carry out his will on earth and bless his people with favor.[40] But it is hard to explain juxtaposing a reference to angels between glorious descriptions of God and Christ.[41] The parallel element is much more likely to be a reference to the Spirit, so closely associated with the work of the Father and Son in John's Gospel (1:32–33; 3:34; 7:39; 14:17, 26; 15:26; 16:7; 20:22) and throughout the New Testament. Referring to the Spirit as "the seven spirits" is a metaphor of fullness drawn from Isaiah 11:2, which sees the Lord's Spirit, described by seven attributes, as resting on the ideal king from David's line to guide and empower his future rule. John seems to have

---

37. Something similar appears also in Tg. Ps.-J. (Exod 3:14; Deut 32:29) and in Sib. Or. 3:16. See Bauckham, *Theology*, 28–29.

38. BDAG 394.

39. T. Schramm, "ἔρχομαι," *EDNT* 2:55–56; Bauckham, *Climax*, 435; and idem, *Theology*, 29–30. See comments on 1:8; also 11:17 and 16:5.

40. Aune, *Revelation 1–5*, 34–35; Charles Homer Giblin, *The Book of Revelation: The Open Book of Prophecy*, GNS 34 (Collegeville, MN: Liturgical Press, 1991), 71–72.

41. F. F. Bruce, "The Spirit in the Apocalypse," in *Christ and Spirit in the New Testament*, ed. Barnabas Lindars and Stephen Smalley (Cambridge: Cambridge University Press, 1973), 336.

drawn insight also from Zechariah 4:1–6, where a vision of seven lamps is explained as representing not might nor power but God's Spirit at work in the world (also apparently associated with seven "eyes of the LORD that range through all the earth," Zech 4:10; cf. discussion at Rev 5:6 below).[42] The Spirit positioned "before his [God's] throne" pictures God's heavenly presence as a throne room from which he rules the world (this image will be filled out in detail in the vision of chs. 4–5) as well as the Spirit's readiness to carry out God's royal decrees in all the earth.

Having said that grace and peace come from God and the Spirit, John now adds that they come also "from Jesus Christ" (v. 5a). John again uses the full title for Jesus, just as he does in vv. 1 and 2 (only in these three places in Rev). He continues this elevated, fullness of style by adding three further impressive titles for Jesus.[43] Each of these reflects meditation on the messianic implications of Psalm 89, although the connection to the Psalm is seen most clearly in the third title "the ruler over the kings of the earth." Nevertheless, John seems to have found support for all three titles—and a motive for citing them together here—in the Psalm's celebration of God's faithfulness to David

and his royal line. The first title, "the faithful witness" (ὁ μάρτυς ὁ πιστός)[44] has verbal parallels in Psalm 89:37 (LXX 88:38; καὶ ὁ μάρτυς ἐν οὐρανῷ πιστός).[45] In the context of Revelation, to call Jesus "the faithful witness" is to refer to his mission of publicly testifying about who God is and what he is doing in this world, a mission encompassing his earthly life as well as his death on the cross in fidelity to God's calling (cf. 1:1; 3:14).[46] He was faithful to the very end in revealing God's righteousness and redemptive love to the world, and Christians likewise are called to the same costly witness (see 2:13; 6:9; 12:11; 17:6; 19:10; 20:4).

The second title, "the firstborn from the dead" (ὁ πρωτότοκος τῶν νεκρῶν; v. 5c; see Col 1:18, πρωτότοκος ἐκ τῶν νεκρῶν)[47] is a classic oxymoron referring to Jesus's resurrection and what it means for Christians. His victory over death is prototypical because it guarantees resurrected life for those who are his followers (similar to "the firstfruits of those who have fallen asleep," 1 Cor 15:20; cf. v. 23; see also Rom 8:29). Such a guarantee has deep significance for John's addressees, some of whom faced the possibility of physical death because of following Christ. The title "firstborn" itself is rooted also in Psalm 89. In Psalm 89:27 (LXX 88:28) God

---

42. Bauckham, *Climax*, 162–66.

43. These are added in grammatical apposition to describe Jesus Christ further. But here again John stretches the normal patterns of grammar by putting appositives in the nominative case alongside "Jesus Christ" in the genitive case (appositives usually take the case of the noun they describe). John does this not because of "inattention to agreement" (BDF §136.1) but to emphasize the added titles (cf. Wallace, *Grammar*, 62).

44. These four Greek words could be taken as two separate titles, "the witness, the faithful [person]," but the evidence of Ps 89, the use of this noun and adjective in a single unit in 2:13 and 3:14, and John's habit of grouping elements in triads (see Aune, *Revelation 1–5*, 25, for examples) show that "faithful" is most likely an adjective dependent on "witness," not separate from it.

45. The sense of Ps 89:37b (LXX 88:38b) in its context is debatable. The Hebrew wording can be construed literally as "and a witness in the sky, faithful." English translations usually

follow this sense fairly closely (ESV, NASB, NIV, NJB, NLT, NRSV, REB)—and this is what the LXX has done—although other readings are possible if the words are interpreted differently (cf. NET, RSV). There is still the issue of how the word "witness" is to be connected. It is usually taken as a further description of the "moon" in v. 37a ("like the moon established forever"), which is the second part of the simile of v. 36b, "his [David's] throne will continue before me like the sun." But it could be connected not to the "sun-moon" simile but to the earlier reference to David's royal line (v. 36a "his seed . . . his throne") as an enduring witness to God's provision for Israel.

46. Bauckham, *Theology*, 72–73.

47. The phrase could be rendered "firstborn of the dead," but the genitive τῶν νεκρῶν carries a partitive sense best translated "from." A large number of manuscripts include the preposition "from" ἐκ, but this is likely to be a clarifying addition, influenced by the occurrence of "from" in Col 1:18.

declares that he will make the king in David's line the "firstborn [πρωτότοκος], highest of the kings of the earth," continuing the father-son imagery of 89:26 (found also in 2 Sam 7:14 and Ps 2:7). The human king in Jerusalem is pictured in close relation to God, as one who represents God's rule in the way that a son would represent a father. In these terms the "firstborn" is the one who has the greatest claim to the privilege and authority that derives from the family relationship (similar to Col 1:15; Heb 1:6).[48] Jesus's resurrection and exaltation demonstrates his ascension to kingly rule as well as his victory over death.

Closely related is the third title, "the ruler over the kings of the earth" (ὁ ἄρχων τῶν βασιλέων τῆς γῆς; v. 5d), referring to Jesus's status as the ultimate Davidic king, whose reign over all the world's kingdoms is soon to be accomplished in full (cf. the allusions to Dan 2:44, 47 in Rev 1:1). The phrase "kings of the earth" directly reflects the vision of God's rule expressed through a king in the line of David as seen in Psalm 89:27 as well as Psalm 2:2, 6–7. The world's rulers will resist his reign, but his triumph is sure (Rev 11:15; 17:14; 19:16, 19). This will appear as a central theme in the book from Revelation 11 on (see "Literary Context" for Rev 11:1–19).

1:5e–6 To him who loves us and freed us from our sins by his blood 6 and made us to be a kingdom, priests to serve his God and Father, to him be glory and might forever and ever. Amen (Τῷ ἀγαπῶντι ἡμᾶς καὶ λύσαντι ἡμᾶς ἐκ τῶν ἁμαρτιῶν

ἡμῶν ἐν τῷ αἵματι αὐτοῦ, 6 καὶ ἐποίησεν ἡμᾶς βασιλείαν, ἱερεῖς τῷ θεῷ καὶ πατρὶ αὐτοῦ, αὐτῷ ἡ δόξα καὶ τὸ κράτος εἰς τοὺς αἰῶνας [τῶν αἰώνων]· ἀμήν). Related to the prologue's epistolary opening is a doxology (1:5e–6) that is evoked by the exalted titles for Christ in v. 5a–d (cf. Gal 1:5). Doxologies typically begin as here with the mention of the one to whom glory or praise is to be ascribed (in the Greek dative case, v. 5e–f).[49] In keeping with the just-mentioned earthly life, crucifixion, and resurrection/exaltation of Jesus, John calls attention in this dative phrase to the atoning work of Christ and his unending love that motivated this atonement (similar to Gal 2:20; Eph 5:2, 25). What is unusual here is the combination of a present verb (a substantival participle, "the one who loves us," τῷ ἀγαπῶντι ἡμᾶς)[50] with an aorist (also substantival participle, "and freed us," καὶ λύσαντι ἡμᾶς), highlighting Christ's ongoing, eternal disposition toward people that caused him to act in the specific event of the cross to bring release from sin. Also unusual is the focus on Christ's love that led to the cross—the New Testament more frequently cites the love of God the Father as expressed in the atonement (e.g., John 3:16; Rom 5:8; 8:39; Eph 2:4; 1 John 4:8–10). Of course, these are not at odds with each other.

Redemption from sin is the specific expression of Christ's love cited here. The verb "freed" (from λύω; "loose, release, set free")[51] sometimes denotes a literal release from bonds (e.g., Mark 11:2; Luke 13:15–16; John 11:44; Acts 22:30; Rev 9:14–15;

---

48. H. Langkammer, "πρωτότοκος," *EDNT* 3:189–91; W. Michaelis, "πρωτότοκος," *TDNT* 6:878. There is a typological relationship between OT and NT in which the NT fulfillment in Christ is profoundly escalated.

49. For the characteristic elements of biblical doxologies, see Aune, *Revelation 1–5*, 44–45.

50. This is normally expressed by an aorist verb, focusing on Jesus's specific expression of love in his death on the cross (John 13:1, 34; 15:9, 12–13; Rom 8:37; Gal 2:20; Eph 5:2, 25). A few manuscripts actually read an aorist of "love" here in Rev

1:5, but these are clearly scribal corrections under the influence of the more normal pattern and intended to match the aorist of the parallel verb "released."

51. BDAG 606. A textual variant in some manuscripts reads "washed" (λούσαντι) instead of "freed" (λύσαντι). Both fit the context appropriately, since "cleansing, purifying" from sins by Christ's blood is a fairly frequent concept in the NT (Heb 9:14; 1 John 1:7; Rev 7:14). The two verbs sound alike, and the variant is likely to have arisen accidentally, but "freed" has superior manuscript support (𝔓18, ℵ, A, C, 1611, 2050, 2351).

20:3, 7), but only here in the New Testament is it used of release from sins (also in LXX in Isa 40:2; cf. Sir 28:2). However, words from this same root (e.g., λυτρόω and others) occur also in this important theological sense (Mark 10:45; Luke 1:68; Rom 3:24; Eph 1:7; 1 Tim 2:6; 1 Pet 1:18; cf. Ps 130:8 [129:8]). It pictures humans held captive by the power of sin (especially its guilt and penalty), from which Christ's death has set us free. The phrase "by his blood" (ἐν τῷ αἵματι αὐτοῦ) specifies the means or price of this release:[52] his blood poured out for us (i.e., his death on the cross).[53]

The doxology continues in v. 6. In addition to redemption from sin, John describes the vocation Christ has given to Christians in his great love and mercy.[54] He has appointed them to constitute "a kingdom,[55] priests to serve his God and Father" (v. 6a). These words reflect Exodus 19:5–6 (Israel chosen to be God's nation, a people over whom he reigns as king, who also serve him as "priests" in worshiping him and mediating his blessings to the rest of humanity). In both the Old Testament and the New Testament, this is intended as service

"for God" (the Greek dative phrase, τῷ θεῷ καὶ πατρὶ αὐτοῦ, is smoothed out in the English wording, "to serve . . ."), but also as a witness and influence for him on the rest of humanity, who see the true and living God in his people.[56] Those who are redeemed constitute a community under God, who benefit from and respond to his rule and so represent him to the wider world.[57] The sense in which they are a kingdom for God also implies the sharing of God's rule in the world, but this is not developed here (see comments on 2:26; 5:10; 20:6; 22:5).

The doxology concludes in v. 6b with a renewed reference to Jesus Christ (the dative pronoun "to him," αὐτῷ, resumes the referent of the participles in v. 5e–f, "to him who loves us and freed us"). The attributes that are ascribed to him in this declaration of worship, "glory and might" (ἡ δόξα καὶ τὸ κράτος), are commonly found in New Testament doxologies (cf. Rom 11:36; Phil 4:20; 1 Pet 4:11; Jude 25).[58] The doxology form is a way of acknowledging not only that Christ (in this case) possesses these attributes but that he is truly deserving of them and will exercise them "forever and ever."

---

52. BDAG 328–29.

53. See Acts 20:28; Rom 3:25; 5:9; Eph 2:13; 1 Pet 1:18–19; 1 John 1:7–9; Rev 5:9); also Leon Morris, *The Apostolic Preaching of the Cross*, 3rd ed. (Grand Rapids: Eerdmans, 1965), 121–26.

54. This third verb "made" (ἐποίησεν) is parallel in sense to "loves" and "freed," but it is expressed in a different grammatical form, an indicative rather than a participle like the other two. This is unusual grammar but not unprecedented in Koine and even classical Greek, and the sense is clear (BDF §468.3). The verb "made" followed by two accusatives means "appoint, cause to be" in a certain role (BDAG 840; BDF §157.1; cf. Matt 4:19; John 6:15; Acts 2:36).

55. In v. 6a all the early and most reliable manuscripts have "kingdom" (βασιλείαν), but a number of later Byzantine copies read "kings and" (βασιλεῖς καί) as reflected in KJV, NKJV, and a few later copies read a related word "royal" (βασίλειον). These later readings are clearly attempts to smooth out the rather rough appositional construction with "priests" or to bring it more into line with Exod 19:6.

56. This role is stated in Exod 19:5–6 and renewed in new-exodus fashion in Isa 43:20–21 ("my chosen family, the

people I formed for myself to declare my praise") and 61:6, 11 ("you will be called priests of the Lord. . . . The Lord God will make righteousness and praise spring up before all the nations"). See also 1 Pet 2:9–12 that connects Exod 19:5–6 and Isa 43:20–21 to develop this missiological theme and extend it to the church as God's people.

57. A typological relationship between the OT people of God and the NT people of God can be seen here and in Rev 5:9–10, along with the characteristic escalation that typology often brings. In Exod 19 Israel as a nation was chosen by God to be his special people out of all the nations, but now God redeems some from every nation to constitute his community and represent him in outreach to the whole world. The community is expanded to include others without setting aside faithful ethnic Israel. See W. Edward Glenny, "The Israelite Imagery of 1 Peter 2," in Blaising and Bock, *Dispensationalism, Israel and the Church*, 156–87, for similar typology but different development in 1 Peter. See also comments at Rev 7:4–6; 21:3.

58. The word "might" (κράτος) in a doxology seems to mean not just latent "strength" but the exercise of it in ruling: "dominion, sovereignty" (BDAG 565; cf. Dan 2:37; 4:30; 1 Tim 6:16; 1 Pet 5:11). See comments at Rev 5:13.

1:7 Indeed, he is coming with the clouds, and every eye will see him, even those who pierced him; and all the tribes of the earth will mourn over him. So it shall be. Amen (Ἰδοὺ ἔρχεται μετὰ τῶν νεφελῶν, καὶ ὄψεται αὐτὸν πᾶς ὀφθαλμὸς καὶ οἵτινες αὐτὸν ἐξεκέντησαν, καὶ κόψονται ἐπ᾽ αὐτὸν πᾶσαι αἱ φυλαὶ τῆς γῆς. ναί, ἀμήν). The final section of John's prologue is an evocative theme statement previewing the message of the whole book[59] by means of two prophetic oracles John records (vv. 7–8). It is common to find indications of the larger theme of a work in its prologue since the opening lines set the stage for the whole. These oracles portray Jesus's coming to earth to accomplish final judgment and salvation (v. 7) as well as the eternal, almighty God whose purposes will be fulfilled in those culminating events (v. 8).

The oracle of v. 7 begins with an emphatic word "indeed" (ἰδού; first instance of some twenty-six uses in Rev; here perhaps drawn from Dan 7:13 LXX), giving emphatic validation of what immediately follows.[60] This prophetic declaration pulls together informal quotations (as the NA[28] text shows with italic font; see translation diagram above where a change in font shows the quoted words) from two important Old Testament texts (Dan 7:13; Zech 12:10, 12) and also probably an allusion to Jesus's teaching recorded in Matthew 24:30, which incorporates the same two Old Testament texts (in reverse order). This combination of three important streams of prophetic expectation highlights the importance of v. 7 as a précis of John's message in this book. In each case the force of the quotation or allusion is not limited to the particular phrases repeated here but brings with it the wider import of the context in Daniel 7 (this world's great kingdoms will come under the rule of the Son of Man, who will exert the sovereignty of the eternal God on behalf of God's people), Zechariah 12 (the Lord will defeat all of Jerusalem's enemies and graciously bring her people to repentance and blessing under her Davidic king), and Matthew 24 (after a period of extreme persecution the Son of Man will come at the end of the age to bring judgment, reward, and the renewal of all things).

The first quotation (v. 7a) is from Daniel 7:13, "he is coming with the clouds,"[61] a reference here to Christ's return to earth from heaven—a prominent theme throughout Revelation (seven times Jesus declares, "I am coming," ἔρχομαι; 2:5, 16; 3:11; 16:15; 22:7, 12, 20; cf. also "I will come," 3:3 ἥξω and 3:20 εἰσελεύσομαι). This theme is culminated in chapters 19–22 with his coming to earth in power and glory. Jesus's coming will be the embodiment of God's coming (cf. "the one who is coming," 1:4, 8; 4:8) to accomplish judgment and salvation on the earth. In the vision of Daniel 7:13 the prophet sees "one like a son of man" approaching God ("the Ancient of Days")[62] and receiving eternal rule over all the kingdoms under heaven (Dan 7:13–14, 27–28).

---

59. Jauhiainen, *Zechariah*, 142–44; Osborne, *Revelation*, 68; Thomas, *Revelation 1–7*, 1:76.

60. LN §91.10, 13 cite two functions for ἰδού: (1) to validate what follows as here, "indeed, certainly" (e.g., Rev 1:18; 3:8, 9; 5:5; 21:3, 5; 22:7, 12); and (2) to draw attention to what follows, "look, pay attention" (e.g., Rev 3:20; 4:1, 2; 6:2, 5, 8).

61. This is an informal or adapted quotation, since there are various differences from the OT wording in Dan 7:13. The OT identifies the subject as "one like a son of man," to whom John refers in 1:13 and 14:14, but he does not include the title here. The LXX has "was coming" (ἤρχετο, imperfect of ἔρχομαι), which John appropriately changes to a futuristic present, "is coming." The MT has "with the clouds of heaven," using the preposition "with" (עִם), reflected also in the translation of Theodotion (μετά) as here in 1:7 (also in Mark 14:62). The LXX has "on, upon" (ἐπί) as also in Matt 24:30; 26:64. In this case these prepositions blend together in sense, "surrounded by, in, on" (Mark 13:26 and Luke 21:27 have "in, on" [ἐν]). See the next note for the larger significance of this image.

62. It is surprising in Dan 7 to see the two figures (God as the Ancient of Days and the "one like a son of man") clearly distinguished, and yet the "son of man" is said to be coming "with the clouds." In the OT and wider ANE thought, riding the clouds is a divine prerogative. See Pss 68:4; 104:3–4; Isa 19:1;

No explicit destination of the "coming" is given in Matthew 24:30 or Revelation 1:7,[63] but the clear reference in both contexts includes his coming to earth to exert judicial and regal authority, as Daniel 7 describes.[64] The argument that this "coming" is not to earth but to God's heavenly presence or is Christ's "coming" in judgment against Jerusalem in AD 70,[65] or both,[66] fails to see how John has cited a single phrase in Daniel 7 to bring with it the theological point of the larger passage: universal dominion for the Son of Man and for God's people.

The second quotation (v. 7b–d) is a cluster of key words or concepts from Zechariah 12: "seeing" one who was "pierced" and widespread "mourning" over him. Again, this is not an exact quotation, but it picks up several distinct words or ideas from the Old Testament passage.[67] The oracle of Zechariah 12 concerns the Lord's intent to deliver Jerusalem and the house of David at a future occasion ("on that day," used 6x) when all the nations of the earth are arrayed against it. The Lord will judge those nations while pouring out on his people "a spirit of grace and supplication," bringing them to repentance that will spread throughout the "land" (12:12 LXX ἡ γῆ) and all its "families" (12:14 LXX πᾶσα αἱ φυλαί). In this allusion to Zechariah 12, John has followed Jesus's teaching (Matt 24:30) in expanding the scope of "those who mourn" to include not just the "families" in "the land" of Judah but "all the tribes of the earth" (πᾶσαι αἱ φυλαὶ τῆς γῆς; v. 7d). This expansion is in part due to the influence of Daniel 7 and its vision of worldwide dominion granted to the son of man (Dan 7:14: "all peoples, nations, and languages shall serve him"; 7:27: "all the kingdoms under heaven"). A similar expansion lies behind the statement here that "every eye" (πᾶς ὀφθαλμός) will see him, a universalizing of the event of Zechariah 12 where those who see are limited to the house of David and the people of Jerusalem.[68] His coming will impact every person

---

Jer 4:13; Nah 1:3 and discussion in Tremper Longman III, *Daniel*, NIVAC (Grand Rapids: Zondervan, 1999), 186–88; and idem, "The Divine Warrior: The New Testament Use of an Old Testament Motif," *WTJ* 44 (1982): 295–96.

63. In Dan 7:13 the explicit "coming" is his approach to the Ancient of Days in heaven, but the wider context refers to the earthly effects of this coming to establish God's rule over all the earth's kingdoms (7:14, 27).

64. David L. Turner, "The Structure and Sequence of Matthew 24:1–41: Interaction with Evangelical Treatments," *GTJ* 10 (1989): 18–19; Darrell L. Bock, *Blasphemy and Exaltation in Judaism and the Final Examination of Jesus*, WUNT 2/106 (Tübingen: Mohr Siebeck, 1998), 200–201.

65. The view that "coming with the clouds" in 1:7 refers to God's judgment on Jerusalem in AD 70 is found in Chilton, *Days of Vengeance*, 64–67, and Gentry, *Before Jerusalem Fell*, 123–32. For specific critique of this view, see Mark L. Hitchcock, "A Critique of the Preterist View of Revelation and the Jewish War," *BSac* 164 (2007): 89–93, and Thomas, *Revelation 1–7*, 79.

66. N. T. Wright, *Jesus and the Victory of God* (Minneapolis: Fortress, 1996), 507–28, 625–29; idem, *Surprised by Hope: Rethinking Heaven, the Resurrection, and the Mission of the Church* (New York: HarperOne, 2008), 125–26, 138–39. In his brief commentary, *Revelation for Everyone*, NTE (Louisville: West-

minster John Knox, 2011), 1–5, Wright implies that vv. 7–8 speak about Jesus's "return . . . to set up his rule on earth as in heaven" when "he will indeed come to set everything right at last," a return which "we still await . . . today" (p. 5). But he does not explain how the quotations from Dan 7 and Zech 12 carry that sense in vv. 7–8 if Dan 7 actually refers to his vindication in heaven as shown in the destruction of Jerusalem in AD 70. See Darrell L. Bock, "The Trial and Death of Jesus in N. T. Wright's *Jesus and the Victory of God*," in *Jesus and the Restoration of Israel*, ed. Carey C. Newman (Downers Grove, IL: InterVarsity Press, 1999), 121–24, for response to Wright's understanding of Dan 7:13 in Mark 14:62 and parallels.

67. The MT of Zech 12:10 says people "will look" (LXX ἐπιβλέψονται, a different verb from Matt 24:30 [ὄψονται] and Rev 1:7 [ὄψεται], but synonymous) "at me" (so LXX, but "him" in Matt and Rev), "the one they pierced" (also in NT [John 19:37; Rev 1:7] as well as in the Greek translations of Aquila, Theodotion, and Lucian, but LXX has "mocked, treated spitefully" [κατωρχήσαντο]) and "they will mourn" (so LXX, Matt, and Rev [κόψονται]). The contextual identification of the subjects and object of "see" and "mourn" vary, as discussed above.

68. See the wording of Did. 16:8 (also combining Dan 7 and Zech 12): "Then the world will see [ὄψεται ὁ κόσμος] the Lord coming on the clouds of heaven."

on earth, and all the world will come under his dominion (see Rev 19:11–21).[69] But this expansion beyond Israel to include the whole world does not mean that ethnic Israel itself is set aside in favor of a true or spiritual "Israel."

To the statement "every eye will see him," John adds "even those who pierced him" (v. 7c).[70] This likewise involves a shift in referent compared to Zechariah 12. In Zechariah 12:10 the Lord says, "They will look on me, the one they pierced."[71] In the Old Testament context the most likely interpretation is that this "piercing" of Yahweh is a metaphor for the injury inflicted on the Lord by Israel in its rebellion and resistance to his ways.[72] But in a common typological pattern, what was metaphorical in the Old Testament is replicated in real and profound terms in the New Testament counterpart. The insult against the Lord is inflicted on his Son in violent and deadly fashion: "pierced" denotes injury or death inflicted by stabbing with a sword or spear (Judg 9:54; 1 Chr 10:4).[73] John 19:37 applies this verse from Zechariah 12 specifically to the spear wound inflicted on Jesus during his crucifixion and to those who stood around to watch his execution. Here in Revelation 1:7 it denotes his death more generally and broadens out the sense of "those who pierced him" to include the whole world. All humanity in this sense had a hand in his mortal wounding on the cross, and his death for sinners will be universally understood when he comes in power and glory.

The final part of the oracle—also drawn from Zechariah 12—is the declaration that all the tribes of the earth "will mourn" (κόψονται) over Christ when he comes (v. 7d). The difficult question is the sense of "mourn, wail, lament" in this context, and two opposite answers are possible. In Zechariah 12 Jerusalem's mourning is almost certainly a repentant lamentation, that is, a sorrow over rebellion and a turning back to the Lord as a result of a "spirit of grace and supplication" poured out on them (Zech 12:10). On the other hand, the only other occurrence of the verb "mourn" in Revelation (18:9) describes the grief of the kings of the earth at Babylon's destruction, a despairing sorrow to be sure, but not one involving godly remorse over sin. In fact, a common theme in Revelation is the unrepentant stubbornness of evil humanity even in the face of God's severe judgment (Rev 6:15–17; 9:20–21; 16:9, 11, 21). Revelation 1:7 does not explicitly settle this question, and Matthew 24:30 is also ambiguous: is the "mourning" positive, leading to repentance, or negative, reflecting stubborn despair at the prospect of Christ's coming?[74]

The Greek phrase at the end of Revelation 1:7 may tip the scales toward the positive side. The subject of the verb "mourn" is "all the tribes of the earth" (πᾶσαι αἱ φυλαὶ τῆς γῆς). This has some verbal resonance in Zechariah 12:12, 14 as mentioned above, but the full expression does not appear in Zechariah 12. However, it does show up in Genesis 12:3 (and 28:14), in the promise to Abraham (renewed to Jacob at Bethel) that "all the families of the earth [πᾶσαι αἱ φυλαὶ τῆς γῆς] will be blessed

---

69. "Every eye will see him" is a hyperbole expressing the universal impact of Christ's coming. Speculation about how modern technology now makes this prediction possible is misguided.

70. The Greek conjunction καί here means "including" or "even" instead of its normal "and" (BDAG 495).

71. Some Hebrew manuscripts read "on him," but "on me" is the more difficult reading and is likely to be original.

72. Eugene H. Merrill, *Haggai, Zechariah, Malachi: An Exegetical Commentary* (Chicago: Moody, 1994), 319–22; Ralph

L. Smith, *Micah–Malachi*, WBC 32 (Waco: Word, 1984), 276.

73. BDAG 303.

74. Bauckham, *Climax*, 318–22; Jauhiainen, *Zechariah*, 106–7; Koester, *Revelation*, 219, argue for the positive view, while Beckwith, *Apocalypse*, 432; Ladd, *Revelation*, 28–29; Mounce, *Revelation*, 51; Thomas, *Revelation 1–7*, 78–79, take the negative side. Osborne, *Revelation*, 69, suggests that John leaves the issue open in 1:7 because repentance and judgment "develop side by side" throughout the book.

in you."[75] The phrase also appears in Jesus's words as given in Matthew 24:30. In this oracle that provides a theme statement for John's whole book, it is fitting to find allusions to this Abrahamic promise folded in alongside the concepts already seen in Daniel 7 and Zechariah 12 about God's universal purpose that awaits consummation.[76] People from every nation who look on Jesus with repentant faith will, like the Israelites whom Zechariah prophesies about, find blessing in his renewal of Jerusalem at his coming.

The oracle closes with a formula of solemn affirmation (v. 7e), "So it shall be. Amen." This consists of two words in Greek (ναί, ἀμήν), each of which is commonly used to affirm or pronounce solemn agreement with a declaration or prayer.[77] These words about Jesus's future coming and rule evoke John's—and our—hearty affirmation and longing for it to be so (cf. 22:20: "Even so, come, Lord Jesus").

1:8 "I am the Alpha and the Omega," says the Lord God, "the One who is and who was and who is to come, the Almighty" (Ἐγώ εἰμι τὸ Ἄλφα καὶ τὸ Ὦ, λέγει κύριος ὁ θεός, ὁ ὢν καὶ ὁ ἦν καὶ ὁ ἐρχόμενος, ὁ παντοκράτωρ). The second oracle (v. 8)

completes the theme statement of vv. 7–8—as well as the prologue itself—with a direct address by God (only here and in 21:5–8 in Rev), whose sovereign purposes are consummated in the events the book describes. The spoken words of God are not just the initial phrase ("I am the Alpha and the Omega," as in NET, NJB, NRSV, REB, RSV) but include the threefold predication after "I am," and so extend to the end of the verse as punctuated above (see also CSB, ESV, NABR, NASB, NIV, NLT).[78] The "I am" (ἐγώ εἰμι) structure of this statement is important as a reminder of significant self-revelatory propositions in John's Gospel (John 6:35; 8:12; 11:25; 14:6; 15:5), molded there as well as here on the divine name in Exodus 3:14, "I am who I am" (LXX ἐγώ εἰμι ὁ ὤν; see also the occurrence of ἐγώ εἰμί without a predicate in John 8:58).[79] "I am" declarations appear four times in Revelation, twice spoken by God the Father (here and 21:6) and twice by Jesus (1:17–18; 22:16)—this in itself is reflective of a high Christology.

The first predication here is "the Alpha and the Omega" (τὸ Ἄλφα καὶ τὸ Ὦ),[80] using the first and last letters of the Greek alphabet as a figure for the first and last members of a sequence—and everything in between as well.[81] The origin of this

---

75. The expression appears also in the slightly longer form of Ps 72:17 found in the LXX (71:17). This psalm is a prayer for the Davidic king idealizing his rule of peace and prosperity over all the earth. It concludes the second book of the Psalter.

76. Bauckham, *Climax*, 321–22; Max Wilcox, "Text Form," in *It Is Written: Scripture Citing Scripture: Essays in Honour of Barnabas Lindars, SSF*, ed. D. A. Carson and H. G. M. Williamson (Cambridge: Cambridge University Press, 1988), 201–2.

77. The first word ναί is the basic word for "yes, certainly," but it can carry a more formal tone, "surely, so be it" (BDAG 665; cf. Rev 22:20). The second word is the familiar Hebrew loanword ἀμήν, "amen, let it be so," used often to conclude prayers, doxologies, and other liturgical formulas throughout the NT. It is an expression of agreement and faith in what has been said or prayed (BDAG 53).

78. This is in keeping with John's fondness for triads (see Aune, *Revelation 1–5*, 25), taking the predicates here in the

three units as set off by commas above. The speech citation formula, "says the Lord God," is thus inserted in the middle of the quotation instead of at the beginning or end (see 1:9, 17e–18a; 2:2, 3, 5 for other instances of this).

79. L. Schottroff, "ἐγώ," *EDNT* 1:379–80. See comments on Rev 1:4d.

80. The same expression is used also in Rev 21:6 (spoken also by God) and 22:13 (spoken by Christ). The Greek name of the final letter consists of the symbol by itself (here with an article): τὸ Ὦ. The longer name *omega* that we are more familiar with did not appear in Greek texts until centuries later (BDAG 1101).

81. This is a figure of speech called *merism* where two extremes are mentioned in order to include all that lies between. See examples in Gen 1:1 (heavens and earth = everything); Ps 139:2 (my sitting down and my rising up = all that I do).

is the use of the letter alpha as a cardinal or ordinal numeral meaning "one" or "first,"[82] so this expression would be readily understandable as "first and last, beginning and end" (see 21:6 and 22:13 where these explicit phrases are added alongside "Alpha and Omega").[83] The point is that the Lord God is sovereign over all of time and history.[84] He is the origin and goal of everything that exists or happens[85] (cf. 1 Cor 8:6, "from whom and for whom are all things"). This makes it appropriate that the speaker is identified as "the Lord God" (κύριος ὁ θεός) since this expression, so reminiscent of the Old Testament title of God (cf. Exod 3:15–16; 20:2; Deut 6:4) is frequently used in Revelation in contexts emphasizing his authority to judge and rule (cf. Rev 11:17; 18:8; 19:6; 22:5).

The second set of predications connected to God's "I am" is the threefold description, "the One who is and who was and who is to come" (ὁ ὢν καὶ ὁ ἦν καὶ ὁ ἐρχόμενος). This is identical to the title in v. 4, portraying God as the self-existent, eternal One who will soon intervene to accomplish his will on earth (see discussion above for details). The third predication is "the Almighty" (ὁ παντοκράτωρ). This is a distinctive and characteristic title for God in Revelation, since it occurs nine times in the book and only once elsewhere in the New Testament (in an OT quotation in 2 Cor 6:18).[86] But it is rooted in the Old Testament, being used frequently in the LXX to translate the phrase "Lord of hosts/Lord Sabaoth,"[87] a title often invested with nuances of complete dominion and victory over all enemies (cf. 2 Sam 7:8; Amos 4:13; 9:5; Hag 2:6–9; very frequent in Zech, Mal). This squares with the sense it carries in Revelation also, as seen in its use five times in hymnic thanksgiving for God's majesty, sovereignty, and imminent assumption of rule over all the earth (Rev 4:8; 11:17; 15:3; 16:7; 19:6).[88]

Theology in Application

The Blessing of God's Revelation

God has spoken to us in this book and in the Scripture as a whole. He has not left us in the dark. He wants to show us who he is and what he is about in this world (Rev 1:1–3). Who are we as humans? How can there be such amazing human nobility and appalling human evil in the world? How did we get ourselves in this situation, and where will it go from here? The book of Revelation fills us in on that story, both how it will end and what has come before. It shows us especially how Jesus

---

82. Ancient Greek used letters also as numerals (like Latin's use of I, V, X, etc.). So "1, 2, 3" or "first, second, third" could be written as "α, β, γ" (sometimes using a keraia or acute accent to note the numeral use, e.g., α´). See BDAG 1, 48, and the Greek titles of NT epistles like 1 Cor, 1 Thess, etc.

83. The phrase "beginning and end" appears here also in some manuscripts (א, 1854, 2050, 2329), but this is more likely to have been added due to familiarity with the later verses (Rev 21:6; 22:13).

84. These ideas about God are expressed similarly in Isa 44:6; 48:12 and their larger contexts, where the Lord's statements, "I am the first and the last," are connected to his status as Creator and his ability to accomplish his redemptive purposes in the affairs of this world. See Bauckham, *Theology*, 27–28, and David Mathewson, "Isaiah in Revelation," in *Isaiah in the New Testament*, ed. Steve Moyise (London: T&T Clark, 2005), 193–94.

85. Boxall, *Revelation*, 35.

86. The occurrences of "Almighty" (παντοκράτωρ) in Rev include seven times with "Lord God" (1:8; 4:8; 11:17; 15:3; 16:7; 19:6; 21:22) and two times with "God" alone (16:14; 19:15). See Bauckham, *Climax*, 33, for discussion.

87. BDAG 755; W. Michaelis, "παντοκράτωρ," *TDNT* 3:914–15; H. Langkammer, "παντοκράτωρ," *EDNT* 3:11–12; Aune, *Revelation 1–5*, 57–58.

88. Bauckham, *Climax*, 304.

Christ is the fulcrum point of the story of God's creation and his desire for us as his creatures. Holding on to faith in him and living to serve his purpose in the world is how he wants us to fit into that story, whether our current circumstances are hard and painful or rich and wonderful. Because this book comes from God, there is abundant blessing for those who pay attention to what he reveals and then consistently live by it (1:3). God wants us to know about what is coming, not to satisfy our curiosity or puzzle us about specific timing but so that we would obey him and be transformed by that knowledge.

The Centrality of Christ

By his death and resurrection, Jesus Christ takes the central role in God's redeeming work. Through his faithfulness to God and his unending love for us, he shed his blood on the cross to set us free from enslavement to sin and its penalty, and so God exalted him as ruler over all (Rev 1:5–6). He will also be the focal point of God's judgment and redemption in the future. Soon Christ will come to bring his rule to earth completely, just as it already exists in heaven (1:7). Until that time, we should remember what he saved us *from* and what he saved us *for*.[89] We live for him, not for ourselves, in order to represent the true and living God to the wider world.

God Who Is and Who Was and Who Is to Come

God, as "the Alpha and the Omega . . . the Almighty" (1:8), is the source of existence of all things and is sovereign over all things.[90] All of life begins and ends with God, the all powerful and incomparable One, and he should be honored above all. He has been and is now actively engaged with his world, though it is possible for us to lose sight of him. But he will intervene climactically through the imminent return of Christ to bring judgment and renewal to his creation. These events "must happen soon" (1:1), and everything in heaven and earth will be brought under his rule. This calls Christians to worshipful and eager readiness, as they live in light of Christ's coming and assess the value of all things accordingly. Time as we know it will not go on forever. Who and what are we really living for? We must hold our attachments to this present world loosely, living in the world but not of it, "using the world but not making full use of it, because this world in its present form is passing away" (1 Cor 7:31).

---

89. J. Scott Duvall, *Revelation*, TTC (Grand Rapids: Baker, 2014), 28.

90. Bauckham, *Theology*, 27: "God precedes all things, as their Creator, and he will bring all things to eschatological fulfillment. He is the origin and goal of all history. He has the first word, in creation, and the last word, in new creation."

Revelation 1:9–20

Literary Context

Following its prologue, the main body of Revelation starts with John's spectacular vision of the exalted Christ (1:9–20). This is the direct introduction to the letters that Christ commissioned John to write to the seven churches of Asia Minor (chs. 2–3) and is foundational to the visions that constitute the rest of the book (chs. 4–22).

> I. Prologue (1:1–8)
> ➡ **II. First Vision: The Exalted Christ and His Messages to the Churches (1:9–3:22)**
> **A. Vision of the Exalted Christ (1:9–20)**
> B. Messages to the Seven Churches (2:1–3:22)

Main Idea

Through a vision of Jesus Christ in all his resurrected glory, John is commissioned to write down for Christ's churches what the Spirit shows him about God's future for the world.

Translation

(See pages 91–2.)

Structure

As John moves from the prologue to the body of his book, he describes the overarching vision that set in motion the chain of God's revelation through him as mentioned in vv. 1–2. This astounding vision of Jesus Christ in his glory is the central content of 1:9–20. The first few verses (vv. 9–11) tell of John's situation on Patmos when he received the vision and was commissioned to send it to the churches.

Revelation 1:9–20

9a   Character Entrance/   **I, John,…**
    Setting

b   your   brother and
                         partner in the   tribulation and
                                   kingdom and
                                   perseverance that are in Jesus,

c   **… came to be on   the island called Patmos**

d   Cause   because of   the word of God and
                                  the testimony of Jesus.

10a   Action/Setting   **I came to be in the Spirit on the Lord's day,**

b   Theophany/   **and I heard behind me a loud voice like a trumpet …**
      Character Entrance

11a   … saying,

b   Prophetic   *"Write in a scroll what you see, and*
      commission

c   *send it to the seven churches,*

d   Recipients   *to Ephesus and to Smyrna and to Pergamum and to Thyatira and to Sardis ✍*
                                      and to Philadelphia and to Laodicea."

12a   Action/Vision   **Then I turned to see who was speaking to me, and**

b   when I turned

c   Character Entrance   **I saw   seven golden lampstands, and**

13a   in the middle of the lampstands

b   Character Entrance   **one like a son of man,**
                         clothed   with an ankle-length robe and

c

d   with a golden belt wrapped around his chest.

14a   Descriptions (of 13b)   **Now the hair of his head was white**   **like white wool, like snow,**

b   **and his eyes were**   **like a flame of fire,**

15a   **and his feet were**   **like gleaming bronze, refined in a furnace,**

b   **and his voice was**   **like the sound of many waters;**

16a   **and in his right hand he held seven stars,**

b   **and from his mouth came a sharp double-edged sword,**

c   **and his face was**   **like the sun shining in its full force.**

17a   Response (to 12–16)   And
                       when I saw him,

b   **I fell at his feet as though dead.**

Continued on next page.

Continued from previous page.

c	Reassurance	**But he laid his right hand on me, saying,**
d		*"Don't be afraid.*
e		*I am the first and*
		the last and
18a		*the living one.*
b		*"And I died,*
c		*but indeed I am alive forever and ever, and*
d		*I have the keys of Death and of Hades.*
19a	Recommissioning	*"So then write what you have seen, and*
b		*what they mean, and*
c		*what events are destined to take place after these things.*
20a	Identification	*"As for the mystery of the seven stars you saw in my right hand and*
	(of 12c, 16a)	*the seven golden lampstands,*
b		*the seven stars are the angels of the seven churches, and*
c		*the seven lampstands are the seven churches."*

The dazzling appearance of Jesus himself as the glorious Son of Man among his churches dominates the middle part of the passage (vv. 12–16). The final verses repeat John's commission to write down what he had seen, along with brief explanations of some of the details of the vision (vv. 17–20). The commands for John to "write" what he sees (vv. 11, 19) bracket the vision at its beginning and end.

Exegetical Outline

→ **II. First Vision: The Exalted Christ and His Messages to the Churches (1:9–3:22)**

    A. Vision of the Exalted Christ (1:9–20)

        1. John's Situation and Commission to Write (1:9–11)

            a. John on Patmos (1:9)

            b. His prophetic commission to write to the seven churches (1:10–11)

        2. A Vision of the Glorious Son of Man (1:12–16)

            a. John's vision of Jesus and seven lampstands (1:12–13)

            b. Detailed description of the Son of Man in glory (1:14–16)

        3. Reassurance and Renewed Commission (1:17–20)

            a. Reassurance from the resurrected Jesus (1:17–18)

            b. Renewed commission to write down the future events God has revealed (1:19)

            c. Explanation of the stars and the lampstands (1:20)

Explanation of the Text

1:9 I, John, your brother and partner in the tribulation and kingdom and perseverance that are in Jesus, came to be on the island called Patmos because of the word of God and the testimony of Jesus (Ἐγὼ Ἰωάννης, ὁ ἀδελφὸς ὑμῶν καὶ συγκοινωνὸς ἐν τῇ θλίψει καὶ βασιλείᾳ καὶ ὑπομονῇ ἐν Ἰησοῦ, ἐγενόμην ἐν τῇ νήσῳ τῇ καλουμένῃ Πάτμῳ διὰ τὸν λόγον τοῦ θεοῦ καὶ τὴν μαρτυρίαν Ἰησοῦ). After the prologue of 1:1–8, the rest of Revelation 1 relates John's vision of the glorious Christ, beginning first with a description of John's situation when Christ appeared to him and commissioned him to write this book (1:9–11). John speaks of his own personal bond in Christ with his readers (v. 9a–b) before explaining his circumstances when the vision came to him (vv. 9c–10). He refers to himself directly, "I, John" (ἐγὼ Ἰωάννης) in a way reminiscent of other apocalyptic works and their narration of visionary experiences (e.g., "I, Daniel," 9x in Dan 7–12).[1] John adds two nouns in apposition to portray his spiritual connection with the readers (v. 9b): first, "your brother" picks up the family imagery used so commonly in the New Testament of the living union between all who have come to spiritual life under God the Father through Jesus Christ ("fellow Christian").[2] The second appositive describes a more specific connection: "and partner in the tribulation and kingdom and perseverance that are in Jesus." The basic noun in this phrase, "partner" (συγκοινωνός),[3] emphasizes a

shared relationship, a mutual participation joining people together in some reality or experience.[4]

The condition that they share as Christians is the paradoxical experience of persecution in this world, sometimes severe, while patiently and faithfully waiting for the full glory of Christ's future reign—all lived out in the power Christ provides. This is expressed by a prepositional phrase (introduced by "in," ἐν) with three closely connected objects ("the tribulation and kingdom and perseverance") modified at the end by another prepositional phrase ("in Jesus," ἐν Ἰησοῦ). The three objects are joined closely—more closely than by the simple conjunction "and"—by the presence of a single definite article "the" that governs all three (τῇ θλίψει καὶ βασιλείᾳ καὶ ὑπομονῇ). A single article like this denotes a greater unity or cohesiveness among the items it governs.[5] The first feature of their shared reality as Christians is "tribulation, affliction, distress" (θλίψις).[6] This is not merely the annoying problems of life in an imperfect world; it is the trouble that Christians encounter because of their allegiance to Christ in a world set against him, as seen in a number of New Testament uses (e.g., John 16:33; Acts 14:22; 1 Thess 3:3–4). John has experienced such tribulation (as his presence in Patmos seems to show, Rev 1:9c), and he knows that the churches of Asia Minor have done so too—and may soon see greater persecution for their fidelity to Christ (cf. 2:9–10; 2:13). Such affliction,

---

1. Aune, *Revelation 1–5*, 75, cites similar expressions from visions in 1 En., 2 Bar., and 4 Ezra.

2. J. Beutler, "ἀδελφός," *EDNT* 1:28–30.

3. This word is a compound, "fellow-partaker," related to the common word for "fellowship," κοινωνία, so important in describing the shared life of Christians.

4. BDAG 952; *NIDNTTE* 2:706–13; the related verb συγκοινωνέω is used with "tribulation" in Phil 4:14.

5. The article signals a greater *unity* but not *identity* in a case like this, since the nouns refer to things and not persons.

Taking the construction with impersonals as showing identity is a common misunderstanding (e.g., Aune, *Revelation 1–5*, 75–76, who misstates the point and then somewhat confusedly corrects himself). The clearest and best-researched treatment of this, the so-called Granville Sharp "rule" and related construction, is Wallace, *Grammar*, 270–90, especially 287; see also his larger work, Daniel B. Wallace, *Granville Sharp's Canon and Its Kin: Semantics and Significance*, SBG 14 (New York: Peter Lang, 2009), 90, 93, 170, 187–210.

6. BDAG 457.

which is seen in the New Testament as the normal lot of Christians throughout the present age, will culminate with extreme intensity at the end of the age. This is sometimes called "(the) great tribulation" (Matt 24:21; Rev 7:14). Mark 13:19 describes it as "such tribulation as has not been from the beginning of the creation" (based on Dan 12:1–2, which promises that God's deliverance and the resurrection of the dead will follow that time of intense trouble; see comments on Rev 3:10).

This reminder in normal times of those extraordinary days of culmination that will come "soon" is perhaps why John felt no compunction about including "kingdom" (βασιλεία) as the second closely related reality shared by all Christians. We may find "tribulation and kingdom" to be a terribly mixed-up picture, and it is certainly paradoxical. But John has already said (v. 6a) that Christ has made his people to be a "kingdom," the people he already rules as king. The present experience of being his royal people and serving him with ultimate allegiance, however, is only the firstfruits of Christ's future reign in a visible, earthly kingdom yet to come—one in which his people will share (see Rev 5:10; 11:15; 12:10; 19:16; 20:4, 6; 22:5). John and his readers are partners in both realities in Christ, and their experience of tribulation is a reminder that the kingdom has not yet arrived in its fullness (see Paul's reflections in Rom 8:18–25 on Christian "groaning" in this interim time between firstfruits and full harvest).

This naturally leads to the third reality that they share together: "perseverance," the trait of patient endurance in the midst of adversity.[7] In the following letters to the churches, John commends believers for such perseverance four times (2:2, 3, 19; 3:10), and twice later in the book he calls for it in the face of horrific opposition against God's people (13:10; 14:12). It is "both to wait upon God and to stand up against the temptations and evil of the world."[8] When suffering in tribulation, while eagerly anticipating the arrival of Christ's kingdom in full form, Christians must exercise such active, faithful endurance. And the only way to do it is reflected in the phrase that is added, "in Jesus."[9] Christian identity is rooted in a vital connection with Christ, but it is also true that such a union inevitably means participation in his suffering (Rom 8:17; 2 Cor 1:5; 4:10–11; 12:9–10; Phil 3:10; Col 1:24; 1 Pet 4:13), and the ability to persevere comes from this life-giving connection.[10] John shares in these realities with the Christians he is addressing in this book.

Having highlighted these connections, John presents the circumstances he found himself in when he received his glorious vision of Christ (v. 9c): "I came to be on the island called Patmos."[11] This is a small rocky island off the coast of Asia

---

7. The word "perseverance" (ὑπομονή) denotes "fortitude, steadfastness," "the capacity to hold out or bear up in the face of difficulty" (BDAG 1039).

8. Osborne, *Revelation*, 80.

9. The phrase "in Jesus" relates to all three of the nouns (tribulation, kingdom, perseverance), since the one article joins them all together, and as noted above all three are inextricably linked in the reality of Christian living in a fallen world. It is a misunderstanding of what the verse says to surmise, as Aune does, that tribulation "cannot be understood" as "in Jesus" (*Revelation 1–5*, 63), or that "in Jesus" is "joined more closely to ὑπομονή [perseverance] than to the other two nouns," as Mounce says (*Revelation*, 54).

10. The preposition ἐν here "designate[s] a close personal relation in which the referent . . . is viewed as the controlling influence: under the control of, under the influence of, in close association with" (BDAG 327–28).

11. The three aorist verbs used in vv. 9–12a narrate the circumstances of John's vision. Their past time value looks back from John's time of writing to an earlier occasion when he found himself on Patmos. But this in itself does not tell us whether he was still on Patmos when he wrote or how much time had passed since his visionary experience occurred. Those verbs merge naturally with v. 12c where we find the aorist verb "I saw" (εἶδον), John's standard way of introducing the visions he recounts throughout the book.

Minor near ancient Miletus, unremarkable in every way except for this reference in Revelation 1:9, which made it a center of pilgrimage and Christian devotion in subsequent centuries. John does not dwell on what his living situation was or specify clearly how he came to be on Patmos.[12] We can make certain guesses based on the remaining part of the verse, on reports from later patristic writers, and on general historical information from the ancient world. The rest of the verse (v. 9d) adds that he came to be on Patmos "because of the word of God and the testimony of Jesus" (διὰ τὸν λόγον τοῦ θεοῦ καὶ τὴν μαρτυρίαν Ἰησοῦ).[13] The preposition "because of" (διά) tells the cause of an action, but it may have a prospective sense ("in the interest of, for the purpose of") or a retrospective sense ("caused by, resulting from").[14] So he may have been on Patmos proclaiming God's message (prospective) or serving a penalty imposed on him by certain authorities as a result of such a preaching ministry (retrospective). We cannot be sure from the wording of the text itself. Church tradition uniformly attests to the latter scenario: various patristic writers (Clement of Alexandria, Origen, and Eusebius among others) report that John was exiled to Patmos by a Roman emperor (Eusebius says by Domitian), presumably as a penalty for

Christian ministry.[15] While it is possible that they had no independent information about this and simply surmised it based on Revelation 1:9, this explanation makes better sense of the verse than any alternative. It seems less likely that John would have left the wide opportunities in Asia Minor to go and preach in a relatively obscure and sparsely populated island off the coast. We also know from Roman sources that such banishment (at various levels of severity) was practiced in the first-century world as a form of punishment.[16] So while certainty is impossible, it is more likely that John was on Patmos in involuntary exile at the time of his vision because of his efforts to proclaim God's message that was at the same time an expression of the testimony Jesus bore in his life and teaching (see 1:1).

1:10–11 I came to be in the Spirit on the Lord's day, and I heard behind me a loud voice like a trumpet 11 saying, "Write in a scroll what you see, and send it to the seven churches, to Ephesus and to Smyrna and to Pergamum and to Thyatira and to Sardis and to Philadelphia and to Laodicea" (ἐγενόμην ἐν πνεύματι ἐν τῇ κυριακῇ ἡμέρᾳ καὶ ἤκουσα ὀπίσω μου φωνὴν μεγάλην ὡς σάλπιγγος 11 λεγούσης, Ὃ βλέπεις γράψον εἰς βιβλίον καὶ πέμψον ταῖς ἑπτὰ ἐκκλησίαις, εἰς Ἔφεσον καὶ εἰς Σμύρναν καὶ εἰς Πέργαμον καὶ εἰς Θυάτειρα καὶ εἰς Σάρδεις

---

12. The verb John uses to say "I came to be" (or "I was," ESV, NASB, NET, NIV, NRSV) is the aorist ἐγενόμην (from γίνομαι, "become, come to be"), focusing on the circumstances of his arrival there rather than on his ongoing sojourn there in the past (for which the imperfect of "to be," ἦν, would serve better). All of the examples of the aorist of γίνομαι used with ἐν that BDAG 199 lists under the sense "be in a certain place" (Matt 26:6; Mark 9:33; Acts 7:38; 13:5; 2 Tim 1:17; Rev 1:9) are better taken as "arrive, come to be," denoting a change of location (Thomas, *Revelation 1–7*, 87, 89).

13. See 1:2 for discussion of the phrases "the word of God" and "the testimony of Jesus." Here also it seems best to take both expressions as subjective genitives (see Bauckham, *Climax*, 161), although "the testimony of Jesus" is often construed as objective here ("testimony about Jesus"; see CSB, NABR, NET,

NJB, REB). Having introduced the phrase and reinforced its subjective sense in 1:1 ("the witness Jesus bore"), John most likely intends the same sense here.

14. BDAG 225; BDF §222; Boxall, *Revelation*, 39. See Rom 4:25 for illustration of each sense.

15. Clement of Alexandria, *Quis div.* 42; Eusebius, *Hist. eccl.* 3.20.8–9; 3.23.1, 6; Jerome, *Vir. ill.* 9; Origen, *Comm. Matt.* 16.6. See Aune, *Revelation 1–5*, 77–78, for details.

16. Aune, *Revelation 1–5*, 78–79. It also seems that Patmos was primarily a military post or fortress island intended to protect the approaches to Miletus from hostile forces (ibid., 76–77). This makes it more likely to be a place of involuntary exile than a preaching post.

καὶ εἰς Φιλαδέλφειαν καὶ εἰς Λαοδίκειαν). In dramatic but modest fashion[17] John now describes how and when he received the vision of the exalted Christ. He "came to be in the Spirit" (ἐγενόμην ἐν πνεύματι),[18] an understated but powerful depiction of the state of Spirit-possession he entered into at that time.[19] The reference to the Spirit is without the article in Greek (ἐν πνεύματι), but this should not be taken to mean solely "in spirit" (i.e., a reference to John's human spirit or consciousness only).[20] It is "in the Spirit's control," referring to John's "condition of visionary rapture attributed to the action of the divine Spirit"[21] and not to any exertion or qualification on his part. Under the Spirit's influence his normal consciousness was altered, and he saw and heard a scenario other than his normal surroundings in Patmos. Another argument for seeing the Spirit's influence is the similarity of John's description to Ezekiel's prophetic commission in Ezekiel 2:2 and 3:12, where God's Spirit "came on him" or "lifted him up" and then he "heard" from heaven. In John's vision here, there is no indication that he was "carried away," as in the similar experiences in Revelation 17:3 and 21:10 (these are like Ezek 3:14; 8:3; 11:1, 24; 37:1; 43:5, but even these may be visionary rather than bodily transfers). But the explicit parallels between 1:10 and 4:1–2 show that John by the Spirit was given a vision representing God's presence in heaven (4:1–2) and of the glorious Christ exalted there as the Lord of the churches (1:10b–20).[22]

John adds a further detail about the circumstances when this vision of Christ came to him by the Spirit: it was "on the Lord's day" (ἐν τῇ κυριακῇ ἡμέρᾳ). This almost certainly refers to Sunday, the first day of the week, when Christians gathered for worship, instruction, and fellowship (Acts 20:7; 1 Cor 16:2).[23] Sundays had become the Lord's day

---

17. No conjunction is present to connect this new sentence (v. 10) to the preceding one. Sentence opening conjunctions are so common in Greek that grammarians have a technical term, *asyndeton*, for the lack of one as here. Asyndeton is a device that can deftly tie the new sentence closely to the preceding and also lend it a dramatic or solemn force. See BDF §§462–63; Stephen H. Levinsohn, *Discourse Features of New Testament Greek: A Coursebook on the Information Structure of New Testament Greek*, 2nd ed. (Dallas: SIL, 2000), 118–21. For the understated reserve of his description, see the further comments on the present verse concerning John being "in the Spirit."

18. The repetition of ἐγενόμην ἐν πνεύματι at 4:2 and of ἐν πνεύματι at 17:3 and 21:10 serves as a literary device marking major sections in the structure of the book. Each of these passages also includes the invitation to John to "come/come up and I will show you . . ." See introduction and Bauckham, *Climax*, 3.

19. Similar to ἐγενόμην in v. 9 (denoting a change of location) the same aorist verb here denotes a change of mental condition on a particular occasion, not an ongoing, characteristic state of mind. The translation "was" in the Spirit/spirit as in CSB, ESV, NASB, NET, NIV, NRSV, RSV tends to obscure this difference. The REB rendering, "the Spirit came upon me," is closer to the point.

20. The phrase with or without the article (ἐν τῷ πνεύματι or ἐν πνεύματι) and with no further description (i.e., no "Holy" or "of God" added) occurs some twenty times in the NT, usually referring nonetheless to the Holy Spirit (e.g., Matt 22:43; Luke 2:27; 4:1; Acts 19:21; Rom 8:9; Eph 3:5). Sometimes, to be sure, there is an intermingling of human spirit and divine Spirit to produce a sense of "human spirit/consciousness under the influence of the divine Spirit" (John 4:23–24; Gal 6:1; Rev 22:6; cf. 2 Tim 1:7).

21. Bauckham, *Climax*, 133, 150–59. See also Bruce, "Spirit in the Apocalypse," 339–40. Aune, *Revelation 1–5*, 82–83, prefers to take πνεῦμα as human spirit, meaning John's vision "took place not 'in the body' but 'in the spirit,' i.e., in a vision trance" (p. 83). He cites Paul's "contrast" of spirit and mind in 1 Cor 14:15, but Paul's point there is that both are desirable in worship, not spirit alone without the mind.

22. Bauckham, *Climax*, 153–54.

23. A less likely suggestion is that the "Lord's day" refers to the "day of the Lord" in the sense that the vision of Jesus had thrown John into the experience of the first phase of that final day of eschatological judgment and blessing (Isa 13:6, 9; Joel 1:15; Amos 5:18, 20; Acts 2:20; 1 Thess 5:1; 2 Thess 2:2; 2 Pet 3:10). But there seems to be no explanation for why John would not use the normal terminology for the "day of the Lord," consistently ἡμέρα κυρίου, if that is what he meant.

(the "dominical" day, the day belonging to the Lord),[24] because it was the day of the Lord's resurrection (Matt 28:1; John 20:1, 19; cf. Did. 14:1).[25] The relevance of this detail for introducing the vision is that it reinforces the sense of Christ's glory as the one raised from the dead (cf. Rev 1:18). It may also suggest that the vision arose from John's experience of worship and reflection, either alone or with a group of Christians gathered there on Patmos with him on that Sunday.[26]

Having laid out his circumstances and connection to his readers (vv. 9–10a), John begins to describe the visionary experience itself (v. 10b). But the first part of his vision was something he heard rather than saw: "And I heard behind me a loud voice like a trumpet."[27] The vision unfolds in stages as the authoritative voice arrests John's attention and gives him a command about what he will see (v. 11)—after which he finally begins to see but in measured phases (vv. 12–16). Hearing a voice "behind him" is natural to why he does not see Christ at first, but it also suggests John's likeness to Ezekiel who also heard a great sound behind him under the Spirit's influence (Ezek 3:12; see also Ezek 2:2), had a vision of God's glory, and received his commission to prophesy to God's people (Ezek 1–3). The voice John heard could not be missed: it was "like a trumpet" in its volume and authority.[28]

In v. 11 John records his heavenly commission to write out the revelation God gave him and send it to the seven churches of Asia Minor (see previous mention in 1:4), starting with the content of the vision just underway.[29] This command is closely tied to the description of the "loud voice like a trumpet" in v. 10b, by a participle (v. 11a; "saying," λεγούσης) that refers back to that experience.[30] This authoritative voice lays out two specific commands for John to follow (v. 11b–c): "write" (γράψον) and "send" (πέμψον).[31] The former command in this same aorist form is repeated throughout Revelation as John's commission to "write" is renewed and made more specific at various places (1:19; 14:13; 19:9; 21:5; plus 7x in Rev 2–3; in one place John is told not to write, μὴ . . . γράψῃς, 10:4). Here his literary commission is supplemented by the added phrase "in a scroll" (εἰς βιβλίον),[32] and this noun is repeated in the epilogue seven times as an *inclusio* looking back to the basic commission here (22:7, 9, 10, 18 [2x], 19 [2x]). The command to "send" is expanded at greater length, picking up the reference

---

24. For the only other NT use of this adjective derived from "Lord," κύριος, see 1 Cor 11:20, "the Lord's supper"; BDAG 576; J. A. Fitzmyer, "κύριος," *EDNT* 2:331.

25. Richard Bauckham, "The Lord's Day," in *From Sabbath to Lord's Day*, ed. D. A. Carson (Grand Rapids: Zondervan, 1982), 221–50, and Aune, *Revelation 1–5*, 82–84.

26. Boxall, *Revelation*, 40.

27. The phrasing is "as of a trumpet," ὡς σάλπιγγος, using a subjective or source genitive in the comparative phrase.

28. The likeness of heavenly voices or sounds to a "trumpet" (σάλπιγξ) is rooted in Israel's experience at Sinai (Exod 19:16, 19; 20:18) and evokes reverential awe for God's majesty and holiness (Heb 12:19).

29. The command to write "what you see," treats the vision of vv. 12–20 that he was about to receive (βλέπεις, futuristic present) as a single entity (singular pronoun, "what, that which," ὅ). Later he broadens this out with a plural "the things which" (ἅ, v. 19).

30. The Greek participle "saying," λεγούσης, actually agrees with "trumpet" (σάλπιγγος) instead of the expected "voice" (φωνήν), but this is a matter of attraction to the nearest noun in the construction.

31. Both of these are aorist imperatives carrying their typical sense of instruction to be done once (as a whole, not instantaneously) in a specific situation either now or in the future. Such commands are very common in NT narrative accounts, which is what this apocalyptic narration represents. See BDF §335 and Fanning, *Verbal Aspect*, 327–35.

32. As BDAG 176 indicates, the Greek word used here (βιβλίον) may denote a brief document (Matt 19:7; Mark 10:4), but here it is clearly a longer composition written in either a book form (i.e., a codex with pages stitched together to form the ancient counterpart of today's book) or more likely a scroll (sheets of papyrus or leather fastened together to form a roll; cf. Luke 4:17, 20; 2 Tim 4:13). See André Lemaire, "Writing and Writing Materials," *ABD* 6:1003–4, for information on ancient writing materials.

to the "seven churches" (ταῖς ἑπτὰ ἐκκλησίαις) from 1:4 but then specifying the location of each church in turn. These seven place-names are probably arranged according to a normal travel pattern beginning with the main city, Ephesus, on the coast and moving in a circuit counterclockwise to the north (Smyrna, Pergamum) and then south and east (Thyatira, Sardis, Philadelphia, Laodicea) and then westward back to Ephesus along the Lycus Valley.[33] See chapters 2–3 for comments on each location.

1:12 Then I turned to see who was speaking to me, and when I turned I saw seven golden lampstands (Καὶ ἐπέστρεψα βλέπειν τὴν φωνὴν ἥτις ἐλάλει μετʼ ἐμοῦ, καὶ ἐπιστρέψας εἶδον ἑπτὰ λυχνίας χρυσᾶς). This marks the transition from the first section of this vision narrative (John's situation, vv. 9–11) to the second (the vision itself, vv. 12–16). Having heard such a commanding voice in his visionary trance, John naturally turns to see the speaker, but the sight that first catches his eye is a set of multiple lampstands made of gold. With great skill John narrates these events in a measured style intended to slow the reader down in order to

pay attention to this significant juncture in the vision[34] and prepare the way for the appearance of its central figure (see vv. 13–16). The phrasing of "I turned to see who was speaking" (v. 12a) is sometimes viewed as an awkward mixture of terms and attributed to John's unpolished style, because the literal wording is "I turned to see the voice that was speaking." But as Aune has shown, this idiom is attested elsewhere (Exod 20:18; Ezek 3:13; Dan 7:11) and it should be seen as a vivid—if perhaps also rough—synecdoche in which "voice" represents the "source of the voice or sound."[35] John could not see the *voice*, but he was understandably keen to see the one "who was speaking to him."[36] But when he turned (adverbial participle ἐπιστρέψας), he saw first "seven golden lampstands" (ἑπτὰ λυχνίας χρυσᾶς). The word λυχνία refers not directly to lamps themselves (for which the word is λύχνος, a vessel of metal or clay with a wick for burning oil) but properly to holders or racks on which such lamps were placed.[37] However, here as in many places "lampstands" refer naturally to the stands as well as the burning lamps they support, so the appearance of seven golden stands would

---

33. There is no evidence, however, that this constituted some kind of ecclesiastical postal system with a regular circuit and each of the seven churches serving as a central node of communication to other churches in their surrounding area as argued in W. M. Ramsay, *The Letters to the Seven Churches of Asia* (London: Hodder and Stoughton, 1904), 29–31, 188–92. This idea is sometimes found in commentaries on Rev but is not substantiated historically as Steven J. Friesen, "Revelation, Realia, and Religion: Archaeology in the Interpretation of the Apocalypse," *HTR* 88 (1995): 300, has pointed out.

34. Repetition of the same verb "turn" in two contiguous clauses (i.e., "tail-head linkage") slows the narrative down in order to highlight the events that follow. Levinsohn, *Discourse Features*, 197–98; Steven E. Runge, *Discourse Grammar of the Greek New Testament: A Practical Introduction for Teaching and Exegesis* (Peabody, MA: Hendrickson, 2010), 163–77. Osborne's speculation (*Revelation*, 86) about the repetition suggesting a metaphorical sense ("a 'turning point' for the church" when God's purposes begin to find fulfillment) is a misunderstanding of this feature of discourse structuring.

35. Aune, *Revelation 1–5*, 87–88. Aune does note, however, that Philo remarks in several places about the voice said to be visible in Exod 20:18, but this seems due to Philo's desire to see deeper meaning in the text, not to a failure to catch the figure of speech.

36. Here the imperfect ἐλάλει ("was speaking") appears in a string of aorists to portray an action simultaneous to the main verbal action: he turned while the voice was still speaking. See Fanning, *Verbal Aspect*, 241–44, and Aune, *Revelation 1–5*, 64. The phrase "to me" more normally means "with me" (μετʼ ἐμοῦ), but John regularly uses λαλέω μετά to mean "speak to" in a context where a heavenly being addresses a human (1:12; 4:1; 10:8; 17:1; 21:9, 15). This seems to be under the influence of the same idiom used several times in the LXX in such situations (Gen 35:13–15; Judg 6:17; Ezek 3:10; 44:5; Dan 8:18; 9:22; 10:11, 15, 19).

37. BDAG 606; W. Michaelis, "λυχνία," *TDNT* 4:324–27.

be an impressive image of fiery illumination. The specific symbolism explained to John later in the vision (v. 20, they represent the seven churches) would not have occurred to him yet—nor would he assume the reader to think in these terms at this point. But the "seven golden lampstands" would evoke associations with several Old Testament passages: Exodus 25:31; 1 Kings 7:49; 2 Chronicles 13:11 (the seven-branched golden lampstand in the tabernacle and temple); and Zechariah 4:2 (a golden lampstand with seven lamps in Zechariah's vision).

1:13 And in the middle of the lampstands one like a son of man, clothed with an ankle-length robe and with a golden belt wrapped around his chest (καὶ ἐν μέσῳ τῶν λυχνιῶν ὅμοιον υἱὸν ἀνθρώπου ἐνδεδυμένον ποδήρη καὶ περιεζωσμένον πρὸς τοῖς μαστοῖς ζώνην χρυσᾶν). This continues the same verbal construction from v. 12c, giving a second object that came into John's sight: "I saw . . . lampstands and . . . one like a son of man." Here the central figure of the vision finally comes into sight after some delay (vv. 10b–13a). Slowing the narration down in this way heightens the dramatic effect and draws the reader's attention to this "one like a son of man." It is unimportant at this stage that the lampstands symbolize the churches (1:20)

and this figure walks among them (2:1) and they could be removed from their place (2:5). This will come later. Even the phrase "one like a son of man" (ὅμοιον υἱὸν ἀνθρώπου)[38] is understated (no article "the," no added descriptions like "glorious," "powerful"), despite its significant allusions to Daniel 7:13–14 and Jesus's own words about himself ("son of man" is Jesus's most frequent self-designation in the Gospels). And the specific identification of this figure as Jesus Christ is not certain until v. 18 (reference to death and resurrection). Nevertheless, the allusion to Daniel's vision of a human-like figure approaching God and receiving eternal authority to exercise on behalf of God's people (Dan 7:13–14, 27; see discussion at Rev 1:7; 14:14) is powerful and important on its own.

Also impressive are the additional descriptions of the central figure's appearance in John's vision (beginning in v. 13c and running through v. 16). The descriptions begin with two perfect participles, "clothed . . . and . . . wrapped." He is "clothed with an ankle-length robe" (ἐνδεδυμένον ποδήρη),[39] reminiscent of the high priest's garb in Old Testament worship (Exod 28:4, 31; 29:5; Zech 3:4; cf. Sir 45:8)[40] and otherwise notable in itself (of Moses's robe, Wis 18:24; of the heavenly figure with the writing case in Ezekiel's vision, Ezek 9:2, 3, 11 LXX).[41] He is also girded or "wrapped"[42] with

---

38. This phrase consists of a comparative adjective "a similar one, one like," ὅμοιον, used substantivally as a compound object of "I saw" (v. 12b), with a related noun filling in the one with whom comparison is made "(similar) to," υἱόν. The related word is usually given in the dative case (see BDAG 706; BDF §182.4), but here it is drawn over to the same case as the object, another of Revelation's solecisms.

39. The noun ποδήρης means a garment "reaching to the feet, ankle-length," derived from the word πούς, "foot" (BDAG 838). The accusative used here is the normal Greek idiom with verbs of "clothing" for the garment that is put on, usually phrased in English as "clothed with" (cf. double accusative of thing, BDF §155.5; Wallace, *Grammar*, 181–82).

40. Beale, *Revelation*, 208–9; Boxall, *Revelation*, 42–43. Aune, *Revelation 1–5*, 93–94, however, resists such priestly

allusions since various Greek words are used in the LXX to portray the high priest's robe, and so ποδήρης is not a technical term guaranteed to evoke this association. The vision seems to draw from various OT images of glorious heavenly beings, not just from Zech 3–4 (a high priestly connection). Jauhiainen, *Zechariah*, 79–81, leaves open the question of a high priestly image in Rev 1.

41. These three verses in Ezek use the same verb "to clothe," ἐνδύω, in the perfect tense as in Rev 1:13, along with the noun ποδήρης.

42. The verb περιζώννυμι means "to put a belt or sash around, gird about" (BDAG 801), here in a perfect participle focusing on the condition that results from the action. Like the verb in the previous clause this also is used with an accusative of the object one puts on (BDF §155.5; Wallace, *Grammar*, 181–82).

"a golden belt . . . around his chest." The "golden belt" (ζώνην χρυσᾶν) adds to the dazzling, majestic appearance (probably an allusion to the angel of Dan 10:5;[43] cf. Rev 15:6). Belts or sashes were commonly worn to secure such robes in the ancient world—usually around the waist—but here the location is said to be "at/against the breasts" (πρὸς τοῖς μαστοῖς), that is, around the lower rib cage.[44]

1:14 Now the hair of his head was white like white wool, like snow, and his eyes were like a flame of fire (ἡ δὲ κεφαλὴ αὐτοῦ καὶ αἱ τρίχες λευκαὶ ὡς ἔριον λευκόν ὡς χιών καὶ οἱ ὀφθαλμοὶ αὐτοῦ ὡς φλὸξ πυρός). John's portrayal of the heavenly son of man continues with an evocative collection of images alluding to various Old Testament visionary experiences, each of which adds to the sense of awe and wonder at this majestic figure.[45] The description of "the hair of his head"[46] alludes surprisingly to Daniel 7:9—not that Daniel 7 is surprising, since 7:13 was quoted in the previous verse ("one like a son of man"). But in this case the wording, "was white like white wool, like snow," comes from Daniel's earlier depiction of "the Ancient of Days," that is, of God Most High, to whom the son of man comes in Daniel 7:14 to receive eternal dominion. Here as in many places John affords Jesus a level of honor

given elsewhere only to God.[47] The influence of Daniel 7:9 (LXX) is what seems to have produced the repetition of the adjective "white," since John picks up the key parts of the comparative phrase "like white wool" (ὡς ἔριον λευκόν) from the "like white pure wool" (ὡσεὶ ἔριον λευκὸν καθαρόν) in the LXX of Daniel 7:9. This simply makes the stated predicate adjective more intense: "white [λευκαί] like white wool." The comparison to white wool is reinforced further by "like snow" (ὡς χιών)—his hair was gleaming, pure white. This also strengthens the allusion to Daniel 7:9 where "like snow" is used of the white raiment of the Ancient of Days. The point of the description of "white hair" in both passages is great wisdom like that of the aged and the corresponding honor owed to such a person.

The second clause of v. 14 reflects the influence of Daniel 7:9 as well as 10:6 in its depiction of his eyes as "like a flame of fire" (ὡς φλὸξ πυρός; cf. Rev 2:18; 19:12). This mirrors the wording of Daniel 7:9 (LXX ὡσεὶ φλὸξ πυρός), but there it describes the *throne* of the Ancient of Days, not his eyes. In Daniel 10:6 the angelic figure's eyes are said to be "like torches of fire" (ὡσεὶ λαμπάδες πυρός). It is hard to unpack the specific attribute this is intended to convey in John's vision,[48] but it certainly adds to the arresting appearance of the exalted son of man.

---

43. The LXX of Dan 10:5 says the angel's loins were "girded" (same verb as here) but "with linen," while the MT and Theodotion's Greek translation have "his loins were girded with gold."

44. BDAG 621. Aune, *Revelation 1–5*, 94, refers to frescos or bas-reliefs in various places depicting Mithras in a shorter garment but wearing a belt cinched just below the chest.

45. The conjunction that opens v. 14 is different (δέ instead of καί as used 4x in vv. 12–13). Δέ is quite rare in Rev (only 7x) so John's pattern of usage is unclear, but in other books it is used to signal a development or change in the flow of argument. See Aune, *Revelation 1–5*, cxcv; Runge, *Discourse Grammar*, 28–36. In this case the description of Christ that follows takes a different form. The four clauses of vv. 14–15 occur without explicit main verbs, but imply the verb "to be" in their adjectival

or comparative constructions. This produces a rapid-fire series of descriptions piled one on another for cumulative effect.

46. This phrase is somewhat literally "his head and [his] hairs," but the "and" (καί) here is epexegetical (BDAG 495; Aune, *Revelation 1–5*, cxcv, 65), "that is, namely," so a smoother English rendering is "the hair of his head."

47. Bauckham, *Climax*, 174–75; cf. 137–40.

48. Aune, *Revelation 1–5*, 95, cites a range of examples of this metaphor (eyes like fire) in Jewish as well as Greco-Roman literature of the ancient world, but no definitive sense seems to attach to it across the board. The repetition of this phrase in 2:18 and especially in 19:12 may associate "fiery eyes" with the indignation of judgment against all who oppose his rule (see comments on those verses).

1:15 And his feet were like gleaming bronze, refined in a furnace, and his voice was like the sound of many waters (καὶ οἱ πόδες αὐτοῦ ὅμοιοι χαλκολιβάνῳ ὡς ἐν καμίνῳ πεπυρωμένης καὶ ἡ φωνὴ αὐτοῦ ὡς φωνὴ ὑδάτων πολλῶν). The third clause in this sequence of vv. 14–15 moves from the head and eyes down to the feet: they were "like gleaming bronze, refined in a furnace" (v. 15a), again focusing on the resplendent glory of this exalted figure.[49] The key term in the comparison "like gleaming bronze" is a rare word (χαλκολίβανος) occurring only here (and in 2:18 referring back to this) in extant Greek literature. However, it is formed from the root that means "copper, brass, bronze," and it seems to mean some kind of "fine brass" or "burnished, polished bronze."[50] This metal is further described as "refined in a furnace" (ὡς ἐν καμίνῳ πεπυρωμένης),[51] using the common imagery of removing impurities from metal through heating.[52] In this set of phrases there are clear allusions to the visions of Daniel 10:6 (the angel has arms and feet "like bronze that flashes like lightning"; LXX: ὡσεὶ χαλκὸς ἐξαστράπτων) and of Ezekiel 1:7 (the four celestial creatures' feet "gleamed [lit. were sparks] like bronze that flashes like lightning"; LXX: σπινθῆρες ὡς ἐξαστράπτων χαλκός). The overall effect is to add to the sense of the dazzling, heavenly glory of the son of man.

The fourth clause in the sequence adds a further awe-inspiring depiction: "His voice was like the sound of many waters" (v. 15b). Earlier the volume and authority of the voice was likened to a trumpet (v. 10), but here the overwhelming power and impressiveness seems to be the point, with the voice perhaps being a metonymy for the person himself: one whose power and authority cannot be resisted. The "sound of many waters" is a fairly frequent biblical metaphor, used of the Lord's voice (Ps 29:3), of a powerful sound in general (Ps 93:4), of the sound of Babylon in its greatness (Jer 51:55), of the wings of the four heavenly beings (Ezek 1:24), and of the glory of God returning to his temple (Ezek 43:2).[53] This metaphor is in several places paired with the metaphor of the sound of thunder (Pss 29:3; 93:4; Ezek 1:24; Rev 14:2; 19:6), reinforcing the sense of overwhelming power.

1:16 And in his right hand he held seven stars, and from his mouth came a sharp double-edged sword, and his face was like the sun shining in its full force (καὶ ἔχων ἐν τῇ δεξιᾷ χειρὶ αὐτοῦ ἀστέρας ἑπτὰ καὶ ἐκ τοῦ στόματος αὐτοῦ ῥομφαία δίστομος ὀξεῖα ἐκπορευομένη καὶ ἡ ὄψις αὐτοῦ ὡς ὁ ἥλιος φαίνει ἐν τῇ δυνάμει αὐτοῦ). Three additional short clauses in v. 16—quite vivid and detailed—complete this description of the exalted son of man

---

49. See the similar description of a mighty angel in Rev 10:1, "his legs were like pillars of fire."

50. BDAG 1076; LN §2.57; Colin J. Hemer, *The Letters to the Seven Churches of Asia in Their Local Setting*, JSNTSup 11 (Sheffield: JSOT, 1986), 111–17. Bronze is technically an alloy of copper and tin, while brass is an alloy of copper and zinc, but something like one of those two—gleaming or polished bright—is what is in view here.

51. The grammatical connection and use of the Greek participle "refined," πεπυρωμένης, is problematic, and this is reflected in several textual variants attempting to smooth out the text. The genitive singular form is most likely since it is the harder reading grammatically and best explains the rise of the others. In this form the participle is best seen as a genitive absolute in which the related pronoun αὐτῆς ("it," referring

to the bronze) has been left out (this occurs occasionally; cf. BDF §423.6). It probably refers to the bronze (neuter) but has been drawn over to the gender of furnace (feminine) due to proximity. Here the genitive absolute construction is adverbial of manner, introduced by "as," ὡς (cf. similar uses of ὡς in 5:6; 9:8; 13:2; 14:2; 16:3) to give the comparative sense (the action that is the basis for comparison). See BDAG 899; BDR §423.10; and Aune, *Revelation 1–5*, 65–66.

52. The verb πυρόω usually means "burn," but when used of metals, "melt, make to glow red hot" and so "refine" (BDAG 899) as in Job 22:25; Pss 12:6 (LXX 11:7); 66:10 (65:10); Prov 10:20; Zech 13:9. Here it occurs in a perfect passive form, emphasizing the purified quality that results from such burning.

53. Several of these occur in visions of God or heaven (Ezek 1:24; 43:2).

(1:12–16), suggesting further his great authority and glory.[54] The first clause speaks of "seven stars" that he holds "in his right hand," symbolizing initially his control over these heavenly bodies ("stars, constellations, planets").[55] Very soon these will be identified as "seven angels" (v. 20; cf. 8:12; 9:1), who are associated with the seven churches (2:1, 8, etc.), but at this point they provide an impressive general glimpse of the son of man's glorious authority. A second clause, quite detailed and boldly metaphorical, portrays "a sharp, double-edged sword" (ῥομφαία δίστομος ὀξεῖα) "coming out from his mouth." Of the range of Greek words for "sword" used in the Bible, this one refers to "a large and broad sword"[56] like the flaming one guarding the way to the tree of life (Gen 3:24 LXX; cf. Num 22:23; Josh 5:13). The fact that it is "sharp" and "double-edged" adds to the picture of violent effectiveness (cf. Ps 149:6; Sir 21:3; and using a different word for sword, Judg 3:16; Prov 5:4). But here the sword proceeds from his mouth (v. 16b) like the tongue or speech. The metaphor of one's speech or words as a sword is a readily understandable one (e.g., Pss 52:2; 57:4; Prov 12:18; Isa 49:2; of God's word: Eph 6:17; Heb 4:12 [both using μάχαιρα, a short, thrusting sword]). Here the additional point is that God's word effects powerful judgment when he pronounces vindication for his people or swift retribution on his enemies (see Rev 19:15, 21; Isa 11:4;

49:2; cf. Wis 18:15–16; Pss. Sol. 17:23–25; 4 Ezra 13:8–11). Particularly important as background for this image are Isaiah 11:4 (the future Davidic ruler will judge with fairness and "he will strike the earth with the rod of his mouth and slay the wicked with the breath of his lips") and 49:2 (God will show his glory through his servant whose mouth is "like a sharp sword [μάχαιραν ὀξεῖαν]").

The final description compares "his face" (ἡ ὄψις αὐτοῦ)[57] to the rays of the sun at their brightest: "Like the sun shining in its full force."[58] A face radiant as the sunshine seems to speak of heavenly "glory," as reflected by Moses when he came down from talking to God on Sinai (Exod 34:29)[59] or by Jesus at the transfiguration (Matt 17:2) or the mighty angel coming down from heaven (Rev 10:1).[60]

1:17–18a And when I saw him, I fell at his feet as though dead. But he laid his right hand on me, saying, "Don't be afraid. I am the first and the last 18 and the living one (Καὶ ὅτε εἶδον αὐτόν, ἔπεσα πρὸς τοὺς πόδας αὐτοῦ ὡς νεκρός, καὶ ἔθηκεν τὴν δεξιὰν αὐτοῦ ἐπ᾽ ἐμὲ λέγων, Μὴ φοβοῦ· ἐγώ εἰμι ὁ πρῶτος καὶ ὁ ἔσχατος 18 καὶ ὁ ζῶν). This marks the transition from the second part of this vision narrative (vision of the glorious Son of Man, 1:12–16) to its finale (reassurance and John's renewed commission, 1:17–20). Here John reacts

---

54. The last two clauses (v. 16b–c) have the same grammatical structure as those of vv. 14–15 (equative clauses with the verb "to be" understood). But the first clause (v. 16a) is a little different since it contains a participle "holding" (ἔχων). However, this is best understood here as part of a periphrastic verb phrase with the main verb "to be" omitted, so the resulting sense is "he was holding/he held." See Rev 6:2, 5; 10:2; 21:14 for the same construction.

55. BDAG 145; W. Foerster, "ἀστήρ," TDNT 1:503–5.

56. BDAG 907.

57. The Greek word ὄψις could be general, his "appearance," as in John 7:24, or specific, his "face," as in John 11:44 (of Lazarus's coming forth with his face wrapped in a cloth

[BDAG 746]). In this sequence of specific descriptions, the latter is more likely.

58. This clause expresses a full simile, literally, "as the sun shines in its strength/power," using a present indicative verb φαίνει, rendered as a participle, "shining," to smooth out the English.

59. The LXX of Exod 34:29 reads, "The appearance of the skin of his face shone [lit. was glorified]," δεδόξασται ἡ ὄψις τοῦ χρώματος τοῦ προσώπου αὐτοῦ. See H. Hegermann, "δόξα," EDNT 1:346 for "light, glory" as a visible manifestation of divine perfection.

60. These two NT texts speak of the face (different Greek word, πρόσωπον) shining or being "like the sun."

to the vision in the only appropriate way: stunned astonishment and reverent submission. The narrative skillfully renews the previous section's reference to what John had seen—more specifically *whom* he had seen, "and when I saw him . . ." (cf. vv. 12c–13). Overwhelmed by the sight, John fell "at the feet" of the glorious Son of Man as one who was dead (v. 17b).[61] Vision accounts in the Bible often record such reactions of falling prostrate, at times in sheer terror and at times in reverent awe, before a heavenly being (Gen 17:3; Josh 5:14; Ezek 1:28; Dan 8:17; Luke 24:5; Acts 9:4; see also 1 En. 14:14, 24; 4 Ezra 4:11). Sometimes the accounts mention a sudden loss of strength, even to the point of being "like a dead person" as here (Matt 28:4; Dan 10:8–9; cf. 4 Ezra 10:30; T. Ab. 9:1). But in response to John's incapacity the glorious one reaches out with a gentle touch, "but he laid his right hand on me," and reassuring words (v. 17c–d).

The glorious one calms the fears that have, with good reason, gripped John: "Don't be afraid" (μὴ φοβοῦ),[62] a reassurance common in such experiences (cf. Dan 10:12, 19; Matt 17:7; Luke 1:13, 30). This is followed by a series of self-descriptions that abundantly provide the basis for this reassurance, phrased initially in the form of an "I am" (ἐγώ εἰμι) statement (on the background and significance of this, see 1:8 above) with three predicates. The first two of these predicates are "the first and the last" (ὁ πρῶτος καὶ ὁ ἔσχατος; cf. 2:8), very similar in meaning to God the Father's statement in 1:8, "I am the Alpha and the Omega,"[63] and likewise rooted in Isaiah 44:6; 48:12 (Yahweh's self-descriptions). The fact that John records within the scope of a few

verses an oracle from God the Father (v. 8) and a vision from Jesus Christ (v. 17) declaring parallel attributes shows John's high Christology as well as the basis in divine revelation for seeing Christ in such exalted terms. "The first and the last" (as seen in Isa) signifies Christ's status (with God) as the origin and goal of everything, especially his role at the beginning and end of history, that is, in forming and then moving God's creation toward its divinely intended purpose.

The third predicate (v. 18a) follows a very unhelpful verse division in most Bible versions, but it should be linked closely to the other predications in this "I am" statement: "and the living one" (καὶ ὁ ζῶν). This Greek verb ζάω is used several times in the aorist tense in Revelation to denote resurrection, "coming to life" (an ingressive aorist; cf. 2:8; 13:14; 20:4, 5). The present tense, as here, could build on that and emphasize the ongoing life that results from resurrection; this is the likely sense a few words later in v. 18c, "I am alive [ζῶν] forever and ever," in contrast to his death on the cross in the preceding clause. On the other hand, in a present substantival participle as here the sense is more likely generic and unrestricted as to time—true of all time—as the constant character and essence of Christ, "the living one," throughout all of history from first to last. This generic sense comes out in the common biblical (especially NT) expression, "the living God," which occurs five times elsewhere in Revelation (4:9, 10; 7:2; 10:6; 15:7; all present participles of ζάω, either adjectival or substantival). "I am . . . the living one" seems to be a transfer of that meaningful description from God the Father

---

61. John's response in 1:17 (falling in reverent worship before Christ, as the heavenly beings do in 5:8, 14) assumes greater significance in light of the end the book, where his falling prostrate before an angel is rebuked because God is the only one worthy of worship (19:10; 22:8–9; cf. Acts 10:26).

62. A negated present imperative as here, μὴ φοβοῦ, when used in a specific situation rather than as a general prohibition,

means, "stop doing/feeling what you are now doing/feeling" (e.g., 5:5). See Fanning, *Verbal Aspect*, 335–38; Wallace, *Grammar*, 724.

63. See 22:13 where "Alpha and Omega" and "the first and the last" are combined—also on the lips of Jesus (Bauckham, *Climax*, 33–34, has a helpful presentation of the four statements of 1:8, 17; 21:6; 22:13 together).

to Jesus Christ.[64] At the same time this serves as a foundation for the further self-description in v. 18b–d (i.e., one whose essence is life cannot be conquered by death).

1:18b–d And I died, but indeed I am alive forever and ever, and I have the keys of Death and of Hades

(καὶ ἐγενόμην νεκρὸς καὶ ἰδοὺ ζῶν εἰμι εἰς τοὺς αἰῶνας τῶν αἰώνων καὶ ἔχω τὰς κλεῖς τοῦ θανάτου καὶ τοῦ ᾅδου). The threefold "I am" statement (vv. 17e–18a) is followed by this succinct threefold description of Jesus's death, resurrection, and resulting authority over death and the grave—in fact, these lines give the first definitive identification in the whole vision that this "one like a son of man" is the exalted Jesus. He "died" (phrased as "became dead," ἐγενόμην νεκρός)[65] in his sacrifice of himself for the redemption of the world (cf. 5:9, 11). But death could not hold "the living one." Instead,[66] Jesus says, "indeed I am alive forever and ever" (ἰδοὺ ζῶν εἰμι εἰς τοὺς αἰῶνας τῶν αἰώνων).[67] As outlined above, here the verb "live" (ζάω) refers to the life Jesus took up again after death and now continues to live.[68] In fact, its extent

is "forever and ever," (literally "to the ages of the ages," a common way of expressing "for eternity, for evermore").[69]

His resurrection is then related to his authority over death and the grave, expressed by the image of holding "the keys" to those realms (v. 18d).[70] Actually "Death" and "Hades" can both be viewed in the New Testament as (1) places containing the dead (Matt 16:18; Rev 20:13) or as (2) personifications of mortality or supernatural beings who rule over mortal or dead humans (Rom 5:12, 14; Rev 6:8; 20:14). Correspondingly the phrases "of death" and "of Hades" can be either (1) objective genitives (keys that open or lock these places, i.e., "keys to" them) or (2) possessive genitives (keys belonging to these supernatural beings, which they use to control humans). The former sense seems better here. John mentions Death and Hades together like this in the two other places just cited, but he never clarifies the relationship between them explicitly.[71] Their referents were undergoing change in Jewish conceptions of the afterlife at the time of the New Testament, and the New Testament itself seems to use the terms differently in different places.[72]

---

64. Aune, *Revelation 1–5*, 101–2, argues that this is "a double entendre referring both to a traditional Jewish designation for God and to the triumph of Jesus over death through his resurrection."

65. Again, ἐγενόμην as an aorist of γίνομαι (cf. vv. 9–10), "become, come to be," denotes the transition into this condition, an ingressive aorist (cf. ESV, NLT, RSV "died"), not a past stative "was dead" (CSB, NASB, NET, NIV, NJB, NRSV, REB), for which the imperfect of εἰμί would be better suited.

66. Here the conjunction καί, so frequently translated as "and" in Rev, takes an adversative sense in contrast to the preceding clause (a "surprising or unexpected" turn; BDAG 495).

67. The exclamation "indeed, look, behold," ἰδού, is used here as in 1:7 to confirm the truth of what follows (Aune, *Revelation 1–5*, 103).

68. The construction ζῶν εἰμι is a periphrastic participle phrase expressing the same basic idea as the simple verb ζῶ, "I live, am alive," but with a greater focus on the ongoing, characteristic nature of that restored life (a customary present). See Fanning, *Verbal Aspect*, 312–13.

69. BDAG 32. The full expression "forever and ever" (εἰς τοὺς αἰῶνας τῶν αἰώνων) is used 4x in Rev of God, "who lives forever and ever" (4:9, 10; 10:6; 15:7).

70. See Matt 16:19 ("the keys of the kingdom of heaven"); Luke 11:52 ("the key of knowledge"); Rev 9:1; 20:1 ("the key of the abyss") and slightly different, 3:7 ("the key of David," see the imagery in Isa 22:22). To see Christ as the one who holds these keys directly contradicts the position of Hecate as the "keyholder" to Hades, a belief that David E. Aune, "The Apocalypse of John and Graeco-Roman Revelatory Magic," *NTS* 33 (1987): 484–89, argues was widespread in western Asia Minor of the first century.

71. It is unclear whether either realm is a place of punishment. The term "hell, Gehenna" (γέεννα) and, in Rev, "the lake of fire," are certainly used for that, and they are spoken of as eternal. Death and Hades seem to be temporary abodes that hold the dead until the resurrection.

72. See J. Jeremias, "ᾅδης," *TDNT* 1:146–49, for details.

John for his part seems to treat them as coextensive, as two different ways to refer to the same evil realm or power, to which the unredeemed dead are subject. This comes out most clearly in 20:11–15 (see comments there). The unredeemed dead will be released only to a resurrection that leads to "the second death, the lake of fire" (Rev 20:11–15; cf. John 5:25–29). The point in this verse is that by his redeeming death and resurrection Jesus gained authority over humanity's "last enemy," death (1 Cor 15:20–28; Heb 2:14–15; cf. Rev 21:4).[73]

1:19 So then write what you have seen, and what they mean, and what events are destined to take place after these things (γράψον οὖν ἃ εἶδες καὶ ἃ εἰσὶν καὶ ἃ μέλλει γενέσθαι μετὰ ταῦτα). The words of the exalted Christ continue, not in self-description but in resumption and expansion of the commission to write given at the outset of the vision (v. 11).[74] This commission gives the revelatory paradigm for the whole book of Revelation: John must record what he has seen in his vision and what those things signify, and thus what they reveal about God's future for the world (cf. 1:1).[75] The same specific command "write" (γράψον; v. 11) is repeated here followed by further details about what is to be written down. The content is structured in three relative

clauses introduced by "what" or "the things that" (ἅ, plural). These three are often regarded as a preview of the outline of the book. What is debated within this view is whether the clauses should be seen as three parallel segments[76] or as one overarching element ("what you have seen") followed by two subsidiary points that unpack it ("that is, what is [now] and what is destined to take place after these things").[77] The conjunction "and" (καί) can mean "that is" (epexegetical use),[78] but the shift in tenses seems to favor the normal sense "and," which yields three parallel units. Also, the reference to what will "happen after these things" is a clear allusion to 4:1, where according to this view the third section would begin. The main objection to a threefold division is that the different sections (especially chs. 4–22) contain a mixture of past, present, and future events. But the predominant temporal character of the three sections is still clear despite some overlap: chapter 1 is what John has just seen,[79] chapters 2–3 address the current condition of the churches in Asia Minor, and chapters 4–22 portray what is yet to occur, as 4:1 indicates.

A different approach to v. 19 that makes more sense than either of these views is to understand the middle clause as "what they are [i.e., represent,

---

73. This reference to Jesus's possession of the "keys" can be taken as an allusion to his "descent into hell" according to the Apostles' Creed and ancient church tradition. It seems more likely that this is not the case, but see Justin W. Bass, *The Battle for the Keys: Revelation 1:18 and Christ's Descent into the Underworld*, PBM (Milton Keynes: Paternoster, 2014) for a careful defense of this position.

74. The conjunction "so then," οὖν, introducing this verse could be inferential, "therefore" (based on what Christ has just declared himself to be, vv. 17b–18), but it is better to see it as resumptive (BDAG 736; cf. Levinsohn, *Discourse Features*, 85–90, on this use in John's Gospel), picking up the command of v. 11, "write . . . what you see," after the details of what he has seen and heard (vv. 12–18).

75. The word translated "are destined" (μέλλει) can denote simply future occurrence ("what will take place"), but here it parallels the idea of 1:1; 4:1; 22:6 (what "must" happen) in

alluding to God's plan for the future (BDAG 628; cf. 3:10; 12:5; Matt 17:12, 22; Acts 26:22).

76. Charles, *Revelation*, 1:33; Ladd, *Revelation*, 34; Paige Patterson, *Revelation*, NAC 39 (Nashville: Broadman & Holman, 2012), 70–71; Thomas, *Revelation 1–7*, 113–16. So the three units of the book would be: (1) what you have seen (1:9–20); (2) what is (2:1–3:22); and (3) what will happen after these things (4:1–22:9).

77. This is the view of many recent commentators and is reflected in some translations. See Aune, *Revelation 1–5*, 105–6; Beale, *Revelation*, 168–70; Koester, *Revelation*, 248; Osborne, *Revelation*, 97; also ESV, CEB, GNB, MSG, NJB, NLT.

78. See Aune, *Revelation 1–5*, cxcv, 67.

79. The verb "you have seen" (aorist εἶδες, v. 19a), spoken by Christ in the midst of John's vision, refers to what John just saw rather than to the visions of the whole book as Koester, *Revelation*, 248, 255, takes it.

mean, or refer to]." John is to record the details from his present vision and what those details signify particularly in regard to future events in God's program of redemption.[80] This is the sense that the verb "are" (εἰσίν) carries in 1:20 (cf. also "you saw," εἶδες, in both verses). The stars and the lampstands *represent* the churches, and chapters 2–3 exhort these churches about their present conduct especially in light of God's judgment and reward that will come in the future. So v. 19 is not intended to provide an outline of the book's contents but a literary pattern for John to follow in recounting his visions. This pattern (what John has seen, what it means, and what it shows about the future) is the template not only for his most recent vision but for all the visions that will be included in the book. It can be seen (especially the verb "be" as "mean, represent") in later passages in the book (e.g., Rev 4:5; 5:6, 8; 7:14–17).[81]

1:20 As for the mystery of the seven stars you saw in my right hand and the seven golden lamp- **stands, the seven stars are the angels of the seven churches and the seven lampstands are the seven churches** (τὸ μυστήριον τῶν ἑπτὰ ἀστέρων οὓς εἶδες ἐπὶ τῆς δεξιᾶς μου καὶ τὰς ἑπτὰ λυχνίας τὰς χρυσᾶς· οἱ ἑπτὰ ἀστέρες ἄγγελοι τῶν ἑπτὰ ἐκκλησιῶν εἰσιν καὶ αἱ λυχνίαι αἱ ἑπτὰ ἑπτὰ ἐκκλησίαι εἰσίν). Christ adds to John's renewed commission to "write" by interpreting two of the visionary symbols that are particularly relevant to the letters John will write in the next two chapters. The topics of this interpretation are highlighted at the beginning of the verse: "As for the mystery of the seven stars . . . and the seven golden lampstands."[82] The particular sense of "mystery" (μυστήριον) in this verse is seen in its usage eight times in Daniel 2:18–47, where the symbolic meaning or interpretation of what the king has seen in his dream is revealed to Daniel.[83] So the topic is the symbolic meaning of "the seven stars"[84] depicted earlier in v. 16a, as well as "the seven golden lampstands."[85]

The main part of the sentence then very quickly

---

80. J. Ramsey Michaels, *Revelation*, IVPNTC 20 (Downers Grove, IL: InterVarsity Press, 1997), 62, writes, "Jesus is telling John to write not only the visions he will see but whatever explanations may accompany them so as to shed light on the future."

81. This view was common in the nineteenth century (e.g., Seiss) but it can be found also in Georg Strecker, *Theology of the New Testament*, ed. Friedrich Wilhelm Horn, trans. M. Eugene Boring (New York: de Gruyter; Louisville: Westminster John Knox, 2000), 530. The best recent defense of this view is J. Ramsey Michaels, "Revelation 1.19 and the Narrative Voices of the Apocalypse," *NTS* 37 (1991): 604–20. Michaels, 608–17, surveys other verses in Rev where this literary pattern occurs.

82. The two nouns "mystery" and "lampstands" (μυστήριον, λυχνίας) should be taken as accusatives of reference, giving the topic of discussion to follow: "in reference to," "as for" (Wallace, *Grammar*, 203–4; Maximillian Zerwick and Mary Grosvenor, *A Grammatical Analysis of the Greek New Testament*, rev. ed. (Rome: Pontifical Biblical Institute, 1981), 744; cf. ESV, NASB, NRSV, RSV). Other suggestions are: (1) accusatives in apposition to the relative clauses of v. 19 ("what you have seen . . . , that is, the mystery . . ."; v. 20b would then be a separate sentence; see ASV); (2) accusatives absolute (Charles, *Revelation*, 1:33–34); (3) the noun "mystery" is a pendant nominative (like

Rev 2:26; 3:12, 21; cf. John 7:38; Acts 7:40; but here without the repetition of a pronoun in the main clause that refers to the same item), and the noun "lampstands" functions in parallel to the genitive "of the stars" but has been drawn into the accusative by the case of the relative pronoun in the phrase just before it ("stars that you saw," ἀστέρων οὓς εἶδες). Aune, *Revelation 1–5*, 67–68, argues for the third option. None of these is without problems, but accusatives of reference seem to have fewer complications than options (1) and (3) and are more common in NT usage than option (2).

83. See also Rev 17:7, "I will tell you the mystery of the woman and of the beast . . ."

84. The article "the" is anaphoric, referring back to v. 16a, where "seven stars" is without the article (the typical sequence in Greek is anarthrous first mention followed by articular renewed mention; Wallace, *Grammar*, 217–20; Levinsohn, *Discourse Features*, 150–51). The same is true of "seven golden lampstands" (v. 12b) and "the seven . . . lampstands" (vv. 13a, 20a).

85. Here John reverts back to the accusative of reference "and (as for) the seven golden lampstands," but the larger sense of the previous phrase ("the *mystery* of the . . . stars") is implied: the symbolic meaning of both images is in view.

gives the sense of the symbols: "The seven stars are the angels of the seven churches and the seven lampstands are the seven churches."[86] These identifications add immeasurably to our appreciation of what the vision is intended to communicate, although while the vision was unfolding these meanings were beyond the reader's grasp. They also prepare the reader in important ways for the seven letters to follow. Christ standing "in the middle of" the lampstands, that is, the churches (vv. 13, 20) is a significant image of his close concern and relationship with these congregations and of their role as witnesses to God's truth (cf. Matt 5:14–16; John 5:33–35). He is not distant even in his glorified present condition; he knows their triumphs and their failures as they try to represent God in the world, because he is vitally connected to them, right in their midst (see also 2:1 "he walks among them"). The fact that he holds the seven stars, that is, "the angels of the churches," in his right hand (vv. 16, 20) denotes his authority and control over them. But who these "angels" are and how they relate to the churches is more enigmatic.

The most likely sense is that these "angels . . . of the seven churches" are holy angels, that is, supernatural messengers or instruments of God, who serve as guardians or representatives of the congregations.[87] This role of angels regarding the churches is not clearly attested elsewhere in the New Testament, but several clues make this the most plausible understanding. Symbolizing an angel as a "star" occurs in 9:1 (also Judg 5:20; Job 38:7 LXX), and in general angels appear frequently in apocalyptic literature and in Revelation itself (readers would more likely expect the term to mean "angel" rather than "messenger"). Angels are viewed as guardians or representatives for individual humans (Matt 18:10; Acts 12:15; cf. Tob 12:15; 2 Macc 11:6) or for earthly nations (Dan 10:13, 20, 21; 12:1; Deut 32:8 LXX; Sir 17:17), and they seem to be attentive to the life of the church (1 Cor 11:10; Eph 3:10). Most interpreters follow this view.[88] Its weakness is that it is hard to explain why the messages that follow in chapters 2–3 are addressed to such an angelic representative and not to the churches directly (see further at 2:1). Another possible interpretation is that "angel" (ἄγγελος) here has its more basic sense of "messenger, envoy" (e.g., Luke 7:24; 9:52; also Mark 1:2; Mal 3:1) and refers to a human figure, either an emissary who will take John's message from Patmos back to the church or one of its leaders who represents the church before God.[89] A third suggestion is that "angel" evokes the kind of heavenly guardian envisioned by the first view, but only as a personification or symbol of the prevailing character or ethos of the church itself.[90] But such a sequence of images seems too convoluted to follow (star in his hand equals

---

86. As in Dan 2, the interpretation involves identifying the *referent* of the symbols: "This is what they represent" ("are," εἰσίν = "mean, signify"; BDAG 284). Sometimes the referents are quite specific ("the seven churches"), and sometimes they are more general but still concrete entities ("a third kingdom").

87. The word "angel," ἄγγελος, denotes a supernatural being everywhere else in Rev (some 58x), referring usually to a holy angel but at times to a demonic being (e.g., 9:11; 12:7, 9).

88. See Beale, *Revelation*, 217–19; G. Kittel, "ἄγγελος," *TDNT* 1:86–87; Koester, *Revelation*, 248–49; Osborne, *Revelation*, 98–99. This view goes back to one of the earliest commentators; see William C. Weinrich, trans., "Andrew of Caesarea,"

in *Greek Commentaries on Revelation*, ed. Thomas C. Oden, ACT (Downers Grove, IL: IVP Academic, 2011), 119.

89. Patterson, *Revelation*, 71–72; Thomas, *Revelation 1–7*, 117–18. A variant reading in 2:20 could give support to this view: Jezebel as "your wife" (instead of "the woman"), meaning the wife of the church angel/leader, but this is not a likely reading based on the textual evidence.

90. Beasley-Murray, *Revelation*, 69–70; Beckwith, *Apocalypse*, 445–46 ("identif[ying] the angel and the sphere of his activity" as "an *ideal conception* of its immanent spirit"); Mounce, *Revelation*, 63; Resseguie, *Narrative Commentary*, 81.

an angel over the church equals the ethos of the church addressed as a person). Moreover, it is hard to see how "angel" could represent such a mean-

ing. The problem for both latter approaches is that throughout Revelation "angel" consistently means "supernatural being."

Theology in Application

An Authoritative Message from a Credible Witness

In commissioning him as a witness (1:2) to the things that must be written to the churches, God enhanced John's credibility as a channel of revelation with two important qualifications that show up in this passage. First, God enriched his ability to urge them toward fidelity in suffering by ensuring that John himself had experienced what that meant. As their "brother and partner in the tribulation and kingdom and perseverance that are in Jesus" (1:9), John could pen a believable message about costly faithfulness from his enforced exile on Patmos. I taught fervent lessons on "what the Bible says about parenting" before I ever had children, but not very convincingly. My lessons on parenting were much better (and more humble) in later years, after our four children grew to be devoted followers of Christ by the grace of God. People will always learn more from us as pastors and teachers when we give them a glimpse of our struggles than they ever will from stories of our victories. But more important for John's authoritative testimony is the astounding vision of the resurrected Christ that is recorded in these verses. What he saw by the Spirit about Christ's divine glory, his victory over death, and his vigilant care for the churches qualified John to write a book that demands our utmost attention and obedience. As chapters 2–3 will show, Christ knew them in their joys and difficulties, their successes and failures, just as he knows us through and through. What the Spirit showed John about God's future for the world is an authoritative, believable, and practical message for us too.

The Keys of Death and of Hades

John's glorious vision of the resurrected Jesus establishes another authoritative baseline that John returns to again and again in the later chapters of Revelation: Christ's victory over death for himself and for his people. He could call Christians to the utmost level of human devotion (e.g., 2:10 "be faithful unto death, and I will give you the crown of life"), because he himself "died" in fidelity to God and now is "the living one" who is "alive forever and ever" (1:18). He overcame the power of death and now possesses authority over death and the grave: he holds "the keys" to unlock them for those who are his. Some of the most comforting promises in the Bible relate to the victory over death that is ours in Christ (John 11:25–26; 1 Cor 15:20–22; Phil 3:20–21; 1 Thess 4:13–14). For Christians the sting of death is gone (1 Cor 15:54–57), the fear of death is gone (Heb 2:14–15), we need not mourn as those who have no hope (1 Thess 4:13), and we long for that day when death itself is abolished (1 Cor 15:26) and there will be no more death, mourning, weeping, or pain (Rev 21:4). We grieve over loved ones facing death and struggle with thoughts of our own mortality, but John's vision here along with the rest of the Bible can give us comfort and hope in Jesus. And because of Christ's victory and his own example, we can ask if necessary for grace not to love our own physical lives more than him (Rev 12:11)—and certainly not to love the trappings of our lives in this world more than him either.

Revelation 2:1–7

Literary Context

This paragraph begins John's messages[1] to the seven churches of Asia Minor (chs. 2–3), and it shows that the seven messages are closely connected to the first chapter as well as the final chapters of the book of Revelation as a whole. The seven churches have been mentioned already in chapter 1, where John was commissioned to send his entire "revelation" to them (1:4, 11). According to some interpreters, chapters 2–3 also constitute the second portion of what the glorious Christ specifically commanded John to write (1:19 NASB: "the things which are"; see comments on 1:19). Descriptions of Christ from John's vision are invoked in specific detail at the beginning of each of the messages (2:1, 8, 12, 18, etc.). The vision had pictured Christ as vitally connected to his churches and vigilant for their care (1:13, 20). And the concluding portion of each message gives promises that point to the consummation of God's redeeming work described in the final chapters of Revelation (e.g., the tree of life, deliverance from the second death).

John is commanded to address each of the churches individually, and he begins with the church at Ephesus (2:1–7). There is no indication that the messages were sent separately to each church prior to their being gathered together in these chapters.[2] In fact, they are explicitly intended to be read as a unit and to speak in a wider way to all of the churches together (see the repeated call to hear what the Spirit says "to the churches" in 2:7, etc.) as well as reflecting, as we will see, the particular character

---

1. These are generally called "letters" to the churches, and this is appropriate since some of the features of epistolary form appear in 1:4; 22:21; and in chs. 2–3. But they are more precisely Christ's prophetic messages to be sent in written form to the churches. Each message contains the phrase "says this" (τάδε λέγει), which appears in a prophetic address in Acts 21:11 and repeatedly in the OT prophets (used over 250 times in the LXX to translate "thus says the LORD"; cf. the prophetic messages in written form used in 2 Chr 21:12–15 and Jer 29:1–32). See

David E. Aune, "The Form and Function of the Proclamations to the Seven Churches (Revelation 2–3)," *NTS* 36 (1990): 197–204; and Beale, *Revelation*, 224–25, for detailed discussion.

2. Charles, *Revelation*, 1:43–47, holds that the letters were previously sent to the individual churches and were subsequently edited for inclusion here, but the evidence for this is not convincing and they fit appropriately into the flow of the book as they stand (cf. 1:4, 11).

of the individual churches and Christ's concern for each one.[3] While the messages apply to churches across the ages, they are not written to portray the course of church history during the interadvent period.[4]

Main Idea

Jesus commends the church in Ephesus for their faithful endurance in the true faith but calls them to repent for their failure to love God and people as they once did.

Translation

(See page 112.)

3. Pierre Prigent, *Commentary on the Apocalypse of St John*, trans. Wendy Pradels (Tübingen: Mohr Siebeck, 2001), 149, 161; and Jürgen Roloff, *The Revelation of John*, trans. John E. Alsup, CC (Minneapolis: Fortress, 1993), 41–42. As Bruce W. Longenecker, "Rome, Provincial Cities and the Seven Churches of Revelation 2–3," in *The New Testament in Its First Century Setting*, ed. P. J. Williams et al. (Grand Rapids: Eerdmans, 2004), 291, writes: Instead of the cities' tendency to compete with each other in showing honors to Rome, Jesus's address to all of them together should "[draw] the churches together in a common relationship of accountability before their exalted Lord.... They should be seeking to outdo each other not in gaining esteem in relation to the empire.... Instead they should outdo each other in finding honour before the sovereign Lord of the universe."

4. Some interpreters (mostly dispensational) understand these messages as prophecies that lay out in chronological order the predominant spiritual characteristics of the worldwide church through seven ages of its existence from Christ's first coming to his second coming. This is usually combined with understanding them to be addressed to specific churches in the first century as well as representing patterns that apply to individual churches across the centuries. See the varying presentations of these ideas in Walter Scott, *Exposition of the Revelation of Jesus Christ*, 4th ed. (London: Pickering & Inglis, 1900), 54–56; J. B. Smith, *A Revelation of Jesus Christ: A Commentary on the Book of Revelation* (Scottdale, PA: Herald, 1961), 61–62; John F. Walvoord, Philip E. Rawley, and Mark Hitchcock, *Revelation* (Chicago: Moody, 2011), 51–53. For the best discussion of this view (for and against, respectively), see James L. Boyer, "Are the Seven Churches of Revelation 2–3 Prophetic?," *GTJ* 6 (1985): 267–73; and Thomas, *Revelation 1–7*, 505–15. But this approach should be rejected for two reasons. First, there is no convincing evidence in the text itself that these messages should be read in this "prophetic" way, and second the correspondences with different ages of church history are invariably impressionistic and colored by an overly pessimistic (and anti-Catholic) view of most of church history as well as an all-too-positive view of other eras (e.g., the eighteenth and nineteenth centuries as an age of evangelism and missionary advance rather than also of orthodoxy's submission to the Enlightenment). Such prophetic readings yield unpersuasive results.

Revelation 2:1–7

1a	Command	**To the angel of the church in Ephesus write:**
b	Speaker	*"The one ...*
	Description 1	*who firmly grasps the seven stars in his right hand,*
	Description 2	*who walks in the midst of the seven golden lampstands,*
	Action	*... says this:*

2a	Commendation	*'I know your works,*
	Explanation	*that is, your labor and endurance, and*
b		*that you cannot tolerate evil people, and*
c		*you tested those who claim they are apostles and are not, and*
d		*you found them to be false.*
3a		*You possess endurance, and*
b		*you tolerated much for the sake of my name, and*
c		*you have not grown weary.*

| 4a | Rebuke | *But I have against you* |
| b | | *that you abandoned the love you had at first.* |

5a	Exhortation	*So remember how far you have fallen and*
b		*repent and*
c		*do the works you did at first.*

d		*But if not,*
e	Warning	*I am coming against you and*
f		*I will remove your lampstand from its place,*
g		*unless you repent.*

| 6a | Reassurance | *But this you do have,* |
| b | | *that you hate the works of the Nicolaitans, which I also hate.* |

7a	Command	*Anyone who has an ear must listen to what the Spirit says to the churches.*
b	Promise	*To the one who overcomes I will give to eat from the tree of life*
c		*that is in God's paradise.'"*

Structure

The seven messages in Revelation 2–3 all display a similar pattern, with very close parallels between them at the beginning and end of each message and greater flexibility in the middle. The parallel elements are easily observable on an initial reading, but subtle differences show up on further examination. Eight distinct parts are usually discussed, but related elements can be grouped together, resulting in fewer major sections.

The eight parts are:[5] (1) address: "to the angel of the church in . . ."; (2) command to John: "write"; (3) prophetic speech introduction: "says this" or "the words of" (τάδε λέγει); (4) description of Christ (drawn primarily from 1:12–20): e.g., "the one who holds the seven stars"; (5) condition of the church: "I know . . ." (οἶδα); (6) exhortation or warning (usually with imperatives and references to future dangers or judgments, often introduced by "therefore" [οὖν]): e.g., "remember . . . and repent"; (7) command to listen (repeated verbatim in each message): "The one who has ears, let him hear what the Spirit says to the churches";[6] (8) promise to the overcomer: "To the one who overcomes I will give . . ." Since several of these are closely related, commentators have often condensed these eight elements into three to five major sections that are more manageable. A three-part option (with subsections under each) is to see introduction (elements 1–4), body (elements 5–6), and conclusion (elements 7–8).[7] A four-part structure is adopted in this commentary: introduction (elements 1–4), condition of the church (element 5), exhortation or warning (element 6), and conclusion (elements 7–8). This more carefully reflects the consistent pattern of the "body" of the messages, while allowing for adjustments as appropriate for individual differences (e.g., the exhortation or warning section can be reassuring or threatening).[8]

The message to the Ephesian church follows this structure quite closely. The assessment of the church's condition is both positive (vv. 2–3) and negative (v. 4). The consequent warning is strongly worded (v. 5) but is followed by reassurance (v. 6).

---

5. Aune, "Form and Function," 183–94; idem, *Revelation 1–5*, 119–24. This list follows the order in the Greek text. In English versions the third and fourth elements are sometimes reversed.

6. This is the order of the final two elements in the first three messages, but their order is reversed in the remaining four messages.

7. Osborne, *Revelation*, 105–6.

8. Hermann Lichtenberger, *Die Apokalypse*, ThKNT 23 (Stuttgart: Kohlhammer, 2014), 82–83, and Akira Satake, *Die Offenbarung des Johannes*, KEK 16 (Göttingen: Vandenhoeck & Ruprecht, 2008), 149–52, adopt a five-part structure (putting elements 3–4 and elements 5–6 together in single units).

Exegetical Outline

II. First Vision: The Exalted Christ and His Messages to the Churches (1:9–3:22)

   A. Vision of the Exalted Christ (1:9–20)

   B. Messages to the Seven Churches (2:1–3:22)

➡   **1. To the Church in Ephesus (2:1–7)**

         a. Introduction (2:1)

            (1) Address and command to write (2:1a)

            (2) Description of Christ who is speaking (2:1b)

         b. Knowledge of the church's condition (2:2–4)

            (1) Commendation for their faithful endurance (2:2–3)

            (2) Rebuke for abandoning their first love (2:4)

         c. Exhortation in view of Christ's coming (2:5–6)

            (1) Call for repentance and renewal (2:5)

            (2) Reassurance for resisting Christ's opponents (2:6)

         d. Conclusion (2:7)

            (1) Command to hear the Spirit's message (2:7a)

            (2) Promise to the overcomer (2:7b)

Explanation of the Text

2:1 To the angel of the church in Ephesus write: "The one who firmly grasps the seven stars in his right hand, who walks in the midst of the seven golden lampstands, says this (Τῷ ἀγγέλῳ τῆς ἐν Ἐφέσῳ ἐκκλησίας γράψον· Τάδε λέγει ὁ κρατῶν τοὺς ἑπτὰ ἀστέρας ἐν τῇ δεξιᾷ αὐτοῦ, ὁ περιπατῶν ἐν μέσῳ τῶν ἑπτὰ λυχνιῶν τῶν χρυσῶν). This command clearly opens a new section of the book (the messages to the seven churches), but it follows along without interruption[9] from the words addressed to John by Jesus Christ, the glorious Son of Man, beginning in 1:17. The seven messages in chapters 2–3 constitute a more specific expression of God's word to these churches in the book of Revelation

as a whole (1:1, 4, 11). The specific addressee here is "the angel of the church," but the heavenly being is understood to be the representative of this community of God's people on earth (see discussion at 1:20). The two become interchangeable as the later messages proceed (singular "you" is used predominantly, but the plural "you" is mixed in freely as well; e.g., ten times in 2:10, 13, 23, 24, 25). It becomes clear also, especially in the conclusion to each letter where Jesus addresses "anyone who has an ear" and makes a promise to "the one who overcomes" that the messages largely apply also to the individuals who make up the congregations as well as to the churches as corporate groups.[10]

---

9. In a way that is unusual for Greek style, there is no explicit conjunction to mark the transition to a new section (see note on 1:10 above and BDF §§462–63 on asyndeton). But the dative form of address ("to the angel," τῷ ἀγγέλῳ), mention of the specific location of the church, and imperative verb

(γράψον; see 1:11 for use of aorist tense here) clearly mark a new line of thought.

10. Weinrich, "Andrew of Caesarea," 119, uses an apt illustration to explain how Jesus addresses the church through its angel: "He converses with the church through the angel, just as

Asia Minor came under Roman rule during the second century BC, but from the time of Augustus the province of Asia was stable, peaceful, and prosperous. There was a Roman governor or proconsul, but his direct administrative role was minimal. Political life was organized primarily around the major cities and towns of the province, but that did not mean that Rome had little influence. Instead municipalities competed to demonstrate their allegiance to Rome and gain greater favor from it.

The cities themselves were an ethnic mixture of Greeks, Romans, native Anatolians, and migrants (such as Jews) from other eastern parts of the empire. The coastline of western Asia Minor had been settled long ago by colonists from Greece who also moved up the main river valleys to settle in key trade centers and in areas with promising agricultural potential and natural resources (e.g., quarries, mines). This pattern of ethnic mixture increased under the Romans.[11]

IN DEPTH: Ephesus

Ephesus itself in the first century AD was the most important city of Asia Minor (with Pergamum and Smyrna as its rivals) and one of the three most important cities in the eastern Mediterranean (alongside Alexandria and Syrian Antioch). It was the Roman provincial capital and was a major port for trade and the entry point for sea travel from Italy and Greece to the west.[12] A system of quite serviceable roads connected it to coastal areas to the north and south and to inland regions to the east. It was a populous city (estimates range from 175,000 to 250,000 inhabitants, probably closer to the lower range) and bustling with trade as well as cottage industries and craft workshops of various kinds. Impressive public and private buildings and numerous religious structures (temples, shrines, monuments, statues) dominated the urban scene of Ephesus, especially the gigantic temple of Artemis or Diana. Other religious sites honored Roma, Julius Caesar, Augustus, and the Flavian emperors as well as more traditional western and eastern deities such as Cybele, Hestia, Serapis, and Zeus. There was a Jewish community in Ephesus from the third century BC (according to Josephus, *Ag. Ap.* 2.39). An important church had existed there since the time of Paul or earlier (Acts 18–20; Eph; 1 Tim 1), and Paul's two-year ministry there in the early AD 50s was a catalyst for the spread of Christianity in the whole province (Acts 19:10). We know of other early Christians who ministered in Ephesus both before and after Paul's two-year stay there (Priscilla and Aquila, Apollos, Timothy). Revelation 1–3 as well as the letters of Ignatius, the Martyrdom of

someone might speak to the student through a pedagogue. The teacher naturally assumes as his own that which pertains to his student, whether that is failures or accomplishments, that is, he is zealous that the student become like himself."

11. J. Albert Harrill, "Asia Minor," *DNTB* 130–31; S. R. F. Price, *Rituals and Power: The Roman Imperial Cult in Asia Minor* (Cambridge: Cambridge University Press, 1984), 1–2; Thompson, *Revelation*, 146–67.

12. It was also the closest of the seven cities to Patmos (some 56 miles [90 km] across the sea to the southwest of Ephesus).

Polycarp, and later patristic references attest to the ongoing life of the church in Ephesus.[13]

It is appropriate for many reasons that the first message to the churches in Asia Minor would be addressed to Ephesus (see "In Depth: Ephesus"). In this message the connection to the vision of chapter 1 is unmistakable, since the description of Christ in 2:1b almost exactly parallels 1:13 and 1:16. Where the wording does differ slightly, the changes communicate more strongly Christ's resilient and intimate connection with the angel and church he addresses in this message. Instead of "holds/held" (ἔχων) the stars as in 1:16, this verse says he "grasps/holds firmly" (κρατῶν, connoting an unshakable grip and firm direction of his service; cf. 2:13, 25; 3:11). John previously saw Christ in the midst of the lampstands (1:13), but here Christ declares that he "walks" (περιπατῶν) in their midst, a picture of active engagement with his churches in their everyday experience of life. He knows intimately their hard circumstances (cf. vv. 2–3, 6) and their successes, as well as their failings, and is vigilant to guard their fidelity.

This is the Christ then who authoritatively speaks to his own in what follows. As mentioned earlier,[14] the introductory phrase "says this" (τάδε λέγει)[15] is a formula used to communicate an inspired message. It was used hundreds of times in the Old Testament to introduce God's words to his people spoken through his prophets (e.g., Isa 29:22; Jer 2:2; Ezek 11:5; Amos 1:6; Mic 2:3; Zech 1:3). Using such a resonant phrase for these messages from Christ reflects the divine status that Revelation regularly assigns to Jesus himself.[16]

2:2–3 'I know your works, that is, your labor and endurance, and that you cannot tolerate evil people, and you tested those who claim they are apostles and are not, and you found them to be false. 3 You possess endurance, and you tolerated much for the sake of my name, and you have not grown weary (Οἶδα τὰ ἔργα σου καὶ τὸν κόπον καὶ τὴν ὑπομονήν σου καὶ ὅτι οὐ δύνῃ βαστάσαι κακούς, καὶ ἐπείρασας τοὺς λέγοντας ἑαυτοὺς ἀποστόλους καὶ οὐκ εἰσίν καὶ εὗρες αὐτοὺς ψευδεῖς, 3 καὶ ὑπομονὴν ἔχεις καὶ ἐβάστασας διὰ τὸ ὄνομά μου καὶ οὐ κεκοπίακες). The heavenly Christ's penetrating knowledge[17] of the church's condition reflects both matters to commend (vv. 2–3) and a major failing he must rebuke (v. 4). He commends them generally for their conduct ("works"; ἔργα),[18]

---

13. Koester, *Revelation*, 256–61; Richard E. Oster, "Ephesus," *ABD* 2:542–49; Trebilco, *Early Christians in Ephesus*, 11–52. See the introduction for traditions about the apostle John's activities in Ephesus.

14. See note in the "Literary Context" section above.

15. The phrase τάδε λέγει is a somewhat archaic form of Greek. It would sound biblical (used more than 250x in the LXX) or traditional and underline the solemnity and authority of the message, like our "thus saith the Lord" (Aune, *Revelation 1–5*, 121).

16. Bauckham, *Theology*, 23–30; idem, *Climax*, 118–20, 133–40; Larry W. Hurtado, *Lord Jesus Christ: Devotion to Jesus in Earliest Christianity* (Grand Rapids: Eerdmans, 2003), 591; Satake, *Offenbarung*, 149.

17. The verb "I know" (οἶδα) appears at this point in five of the seven messages to begin the second major section in the message. In this context "I know" assumes the risen Lord's profound insight into the condition of his churches and of all human affairs.

18. The triad of "work, labor, endurance" appears also in 1 Thess 1:3 with genitives to fill in the details further: "work of faith, labor of love, endurance of hope." But no allusion, even unconsciously, to such a text is likely here, since John uses "work" in the plural with the more general sense of "deeds, conduct," either good or bad (see Rev 2:2, 5, 6, and nine other times in Rev 2–3).

which is then specified further[19] as their "labor and endurance." The Ephesian Christians have worked hard and long for the sake of their faith. The word "labor" (κόπος and the related verb κοπιάω) is often used in the New Testament for Christian service that requires the utmost a person can give—heartfelt and rewarding effort, but expended often in difficult circumstances (John 4:38; Rom 16:6, 12; 1 Cor 3:8; 15:58; 1 Thess 2:9; Col 1:29; 1 Tim 4:10; Rev 14:13).[20] The Ephesian Christians have not given up in the face of their adversities (see "endurance" also in v. 3). This is a central theme in Revelation: the call to remain faithful to Christ even when assailed by seductive and opposing influences (1:9; 13:10; 14:12).

Remaining faithful requires the difficult task of gauging the fidelity of others ("testing" them, assessing their true character),[21] especially those who make claims to leadership among God's people, and then acting with resolve and courage if they fail to measure up. The Ephesian church had resisted certain "evil" or destructive people,[22] seeing through their pretense (cf. 2:9, 20; 3:9) and refusing to allow them[23] to harm the church. Claiming to be an "apostle" probably meant passing themselves off as itinerant but authoritative Christian teachers or missionaries, similar to the sense of "apostle" in 2 Corinthians 8:23 and Philippians 2:25, not claiming the preeminent status of the Twelve or Paul (e.g., Rev 21:14). It was all too common even in the earliest eras of Christian history for teachers and prophets to travel from community to community under a claim of legitimacy while misleading believers with false doctrine (cf. 2 Cor 11:13–15; 1 Thess 5:20–21; 1 John 4:1–3; as well as Did. 11.1–12; 13.1–2).[24] At earlier stages in their history Paul too warned the leaders of the Ephesian church against the threat of false teachers from outside and inside the church and the need to guard against it (Acts 20:28–32; 1 Tim 1:3–7). All churches must heed this call for vigilance (Rev 2:7a).

Christ's commendation continues[25] with a reinforcement of what has just been said but also building ominously toward the contrast that will come with his rebuke in v. 4. Three words (or related words) from v. 2 are repeated here to reiterate their laudable "endurance" and "toleration" (this time in a positive sense, "bearing up under trials") and "labor" that could have caused them to give up in exhaustion. But they instead "have not grown weary"[26] and abandoned their loyalty to Christ. Such loyalty was demonstrated by their bearing up "for the sake of [his] name," where "name" is representative of the character and essence of the person (cf. 2:13; 3:8; Matt 6:9; Acts 3:16; 4:12; 5:41). In this phrase John reflects a theme found elsewhere in the New Testament: the call to identify with Christ even if it brings rejection and persecution (Matt 10:22; Mark 13:13; John 15:21).[27]

2:4 But I have against you that you abandoned the love you had at first (ἀλλὰ ἔχω κατὰ σοῦ ὅτι τὴν ἀγάπην σου τὴν πρώτην ἀφῆκες). Notwithstanding these previous commendations (and they

---

19. The conjunction καί rendered here as "that is" can carry an explanatory, specifying sense (cf. BDAG 494; Aune, *Revelation 1–5*, 134; Prigent, *Apocalypse*, 157).

20. F. Hauck, "κόπος," *TDNT* 3:827–30.

21. BDAG 792–93.

22. "Evil" here means "harmful, pernicious." Moral evil per se is not in view but conduct that brings ruin and destruction. See 16:2 for the only other use of this adjective in Rev, and similar uses in Acts 9:13; Rom 12:17, 21; 1 Pet 3:9.

23. They were "unable to tolerate" such people in that they did not permit them to exert their destructive influence. The verb "tolerate, bear, put up with" (βαστάζω) is used in a positive way in v. 3.

24. Aune, *Revelation 1–5*, 145; Prigent, *Apocalypse*, 158.

25. The Greek conjunction καί at the start of v. 3 signals a connection that English often idiomatically leaves implicit (omitting "and").

26. BDAG 558.

27. L. Hartman, "ὄνομα," *EDNT* 2:519–20. See 2:17; 3:4, 12; 11:13; 19:12 for distinctive uses of "name" in Revelation.

are real),[28] Christ's intimate knowledge of them includes the profoundly troubling charge—actually a sharp rebuke—that they no longer exercise the cardinal Christian virtue of love for God and for people. This is worded as a personal offense they have committed against him ("I have against you"; see same phrasing used in Matt 5:23; Mark 11:25).[29] The offense is that their persevering toil and vigilance against false teaching for the sake of Christ has become all "hands and head" with no heart.[30] It is a veneer of busy outward activity without the inward motivation of sincere love in response to God's great love for them in Christ and without the grace and love toward others that is needed. They have "abandoned" (CSB, ESV, RSV) or "forsaken" (NIV)[31] the heartfelt love that once characterized their Christian conduct.[32]

Throughout the Bible God calls his people to sincere love for himself and for others as displayed in obedient and faithful actions (Lev 19:18; Deut 6:4–6; Mark 12:28–31; John 13:34–35; Rom 13:9–10; Gal 5:22–23; 1 Pet 4:7–11). The actions themselves, admirable and important as they may be, count for little apart from genuine love (1 Cor 13:1–13; 1 Tim 1:5; 1 John 4:11, 19–21). In addition, our grasp of what fidelity and obedience require is often severely limited by lack of heartfelt love (cf. v. 5, "do the works you did at first"). Even otherwise mature and strong believers must be called back to the freshness and vitality of their earliest response to God, since as in any relationship this tends to cool over time (cf. Jer 2:2; Ezek 16:8).

2:5–6 So remember how far you have fallen and repent and do the works you did at first. But if not, I am coming against you and I will remove your lampstand from its place, unless you repent. 6 But this you do have, that you hate the works of the Nicolaitans, which I also hate (μνημόνευε οὖν πόθεν πέπτωκας καὶ μετανόησον καὶ τὰ πρῶτα ἔργα ποίησον· εἰ δὲ μή, ἔρχομαί σοι καὶ κινήσω τὴν λυχνίαν σου ἐκ τοῦ τόπου αὐτῆς, ἐὰν μὴ μετανοήσῃς. 6 ἀλλὰ τοῦτο ἔχεις, ὅτι μισεῖς τὰ ἔργα τῶν Νικολαϊτῶν ἃ κἀγὼ μισῶ). Christ's message to the church moves from commendation and rebuke (vv. 2–4) to exhortation and reassurance (vv. 5–6). As frequently in these messages (cf. 2:16; 3:3, 19), the exhortation is a direct inference from what he intimately knows about them (introduced by "so"; οὖν). The church must "remember and repent" or face severe consequences. Here what they must remember is both negative (they have fallen; they

---

28. The use of the Greek conjunction ἀλλά ("but") after a negated phrase or clause sets up a counterpoint-to-main-point structure. Christ's commendations in vv. 2–3, while retaining their validity, prepare the way for the more significant point of v. 4, how the church has fallen short. It does not set aside the genuine commendation Jesus gives in vv. 2–3 but corrects the inward motivation (love and devotion toward God) and outward tone and spirit (love and grace toward people) for all of their service. See Levinsohn, *Discourse Features*, 114–16; Runge, *Discourse Grammar*, 92–100.

29. This phrase (ἔχω κατὰ σοῦ) is used also in Rev 2:14, 20. A very similar expression using πρός instead of κατά for "against" is used of a more formal, legal accusation in Acts 19:38; 24:19; 25:19; 1 Cor 6:1.

30. Some commentators (Beckwith, *Apocalypse*, 450; Koester, *Revelation*, 269; James Moffatt, "The Revelation of St. John the Divine," in vol. 5 of *The Expositor's Greek Testament*, ed. W. Robertson Nicoll [London: Hodder & Stoughton, 1910],

350) surmise that the Ephesian Christians had maintained a strong love for God and Christ (as evidenced by their doctrinal loyalty described in vv. 2–3) but lacked love for one another (e.g., due to divisions that have arisen from false teaching). But it is more likely that love for God and love for people are seen together and both have cooled (Boxall, *Revelation*, 49–50; Hoskins, *Revelation*, 74–75; cf. 1 John 3:16–18).

31. The verb "abandon" (ἀφίημι) can mean "set aside, neglect," especially to leave out what should be kept central (e.g., Matt 23:23; Mark 7:8).

32. The phrase "the love you had at first" is expressed as their "first" love (πρῶτος). The adjective "first" could mean "primary, most important" (Matt 20:27; 22:38; 1 Cor 15:3), but the point here is not that less important things have captured their affection. It is that the vibrant love they had in their early days as Christians has faded over years of opposition and difficulty. See v. 19 for a similar expression that makes this clear.

must return to their former conduct) and positive (they once had a deep love for God and people and lived it out in their actions). Their failure to love as God desires is not insignificant ("how far" underlines what a regrettable shortcoming this is),[33] but Christ's call to make it right by rebuilding and restoring a previous pattern of conduct ("do the works you did at first") makes the task attainable.

Their serious failure, however, requires two urgent responses to set things right.[34] They must change their course[35] and return to the deeds of devotion and service they once practiced in genuine love for God and others ("the works you did at first"; cf. v. 4). The Ephesian Christians' status quo is unacceptable to the Lord who walks among his churches (2:1) and cares for those he loves (3:19). If they do not change,[36] Christ will personally visit them in judgment: "I am coming against you."[37] Christ's declaration "I am coming" (ἔρχομαι) occurs frequently in Revelation (2:5, 16; 3:11; 16:15; 22:7, 12, 20; also "I will come," 3:3 [ἥξω] and 3:20 [εἰσελεύσομαι]; see 1:7 for discussion of related phrases). Many of these clearly refer to his return in glory to consummate God's salvation and judgment (3:11; 16:15; 22:7, 12, 20), but in this verse (along with 2:16; 3:3; and 3:20)

Christ's oversight and discipline of his people within history is in view.[38] He will come and deal with their refusal to repent by removing their "lampstand from its place." The sense of this symbolism is clear enough at its core: he will visit the consequences of their resistance on them by regarding them as no longer part of the circle of his churches (1:20; 2:1). The metaphor of "lamps" as shining witnesses to Christ's salvation for all to see is a central theme here as well as later in Revelation (cf. the two witnesses as "lamps" in 11:3–4), and it expresses the larger principle that Christians are lights in a dark world, testifying to God's love in Christ only in so far as they live in love themselves (John 13:34–35; Phil 2:14–16). Consistent failure to exhibit this cardinal Christian virtue forfeits their right to bear the name of Christ. Just as some individuals claimed to be apostles but were not (Rev 2:2), so churches that fail to bear the identifying mark of Christian love will be exposed as counterfeits.

In a further reassurance that Christ regards their failings as recoverable (v. 6), the hortatory section of his message closes with a commendation reminiscent of vv. 2–3. Just as they saw through the pretense of false apostles (v. 2), so they

---

33. *The Message* implies an allusion here to Satan's rebellion ("Do you have any idea how far you have fallen? A Lucifer fall!"; cf. Isa 14:12; Rev 12:9; see also Lichtenberger, *Apokalypse*, 86; John Sweet, *Revelation*, TPINTC [London: SCM, 1979], 79–81), and this makes some sense when we remember that this message is addressed to the *angel* of the church. But the word "fall" (πίπτω) is commonly used of human moral or religious failings (e.g., 1 Cor 10:12; Heb 4:11; Jas 5:12) and the message is for the angel and the church seen together (see discussion at 1:20; 2:1). But this is not an irretrievable fall like Satan's was.

34. The commands "repent" and "do" are both aorist tense in Greek, unusual in a context like this (the first imperative "remember" is the more standard present tense, calling for a regular course of conduct, a characteristic attitude of mind). In such contexts, the aorist is rhetorically stronger, demanding urgent action, but still implying a regular practice to be followed thereafter. See Fanning, *Verbal Aspect*, 369–70, and examples like 2 Tim 1:8; 4:2.

35. Repentance (μετανοέω) is not merely sorrow for sin or

"change of mind" as it is sometimes glossed, but involves also a turning (or returning in Rev 2–3) to godly conduct (e.g., Rev 9:20–21; 16:9, 11; *NIDNTTE* 3:292; J. Behm, "μετανοέω," *TDNT* 4:1003–4).

36. The supposition "but if not" is first expressed without the verb in an idiomatic expression (εἰ δὲ μή) that means "otherwise, or else" (BDAG 278; Burton, *Moods and Tenses*, 111) and then with the verb denoting change included, "unless you repent."

37. The "you" (σοί) is a dative of disadvantage (Wallace, *Grammar*, 142–44; Aune, *Revelation 1–5*, 135), not merely "to you" (as in CSB, ESV, NASB, NIV, RSV).

38. Aune, *Revelation 1–5*, 147, 155; Satake, *Offenbarung*, 157; Smalley, *Revelation*, 62. The Lord's "coming" to discipline his people within the normal course of human history cannot be completely separated from his final coming to consummate his judgment and renewal of all things (Rev 19). These purifying visitations establish a pattern that anticipates his coming in ultimate judgment of all people. See Prov 11:31; Jer 25:29; Ezek 9:6; 1 Cor 11:32; 1 Pet 4:12–19.

characteristically resist (μισεῖς; a customary or general present) what "the Nicolaitans" were trying to accomplish in Ephesus. Resistance to their deeds is described as hatred, which Christ himself shares (v. 6b). In the common biblical sense of the term, to "hate" is not to show emotional hostility or intense ill will against something but to act in strong opposition to it, to renounce or reject it.[39]

"Nicolaitans" is a term that means "followers of Nicolaus,"[40] presumably a sectarian leader and group known among the Christians in Asia Minor (here and in 2:15 the article is used: "*the* Nicolaitans"), but Revelation does not tell us anything specific about this person Nicolaus.[41] About a century later, Irenaeus (*Haer.* 1.26.3) identifies him as the Nicolaus mentioned in Acts 6:5, but his account shows that he has no information about the situation in Pergamum except what can be surmised from these New Testament texts. The description of the group in Revelation 2:14–15, however, sheds some light on the movement's teachings and impact. It seems to have advocated accommodation to the surrounding pagan culture and its idolatrous practices (see comments on 2:14–15 and 2:20 for details). In his reassurance (v. 6), Jesus underlines the importance of their fidelity to the truth that he commended in vv. 2–3: the motivation and tone of their resistance to such false teaching need to be changed (v. 4), but that resistance itself must continue.

2:7 Anyone who has an ear must listen to what the Spirit says to the churches. To the one who overcomes I will give to eat from the tree of life that is in God's paradise'" (ὁ ἔχων οὖς ἀκουσάτω τί τὸ πνεῦμα λέγει ταῖς ἐκκλησίαις. τῷ νικῶντι δώσω αὐτῷ φαγεῖν ἐκ τοῦ ξύλου τῆς ζωῆς, ὅ ἐστιν ἐν τῷ παραδείσῳ τοῦ θεοῦ). The conclusion of the message is a command to hear (v. 7a) and a promise to the overcomer (v. 7b). The command to hear is very similar to Jesus's words describing the purpose of his parables (Matt 13:9; Mark 4:9; Luke 8:8), where he acknowledges that some are unreceptive and will not comprehend the spiritual truths veiled within the parable, but he calls all those to whom God has granted understanding to obey what they hear. This fulfills what is seen in Isaiah 6:9–10 about stubborn people continuing to resist even a word from God. While these circumstances are different (the messages to the churches are not cryptic),[42] the command of v. 7a acknowledges that some will be receptive and some not, and it calls on individuals within the community to respond ("anyone who has an ear"). There will be some in the churches who are not prepared to heed the message, who will go their own stubborn way.[43] However, the clear intent is to provoke an active response by those who are receptive: they must pay attention and obey.[44] It is a wake-up call for the faithful in the Ephesian church, but in this way it is a positive

39. BDAG 652–53.

40. BDAG 673.

41. It is possible that there was no specific person named "Nicolaus," and the name is a wordplay or symbolic name expressing a critique of the movement. By popular etymology the names "Nicolaus" and "Balaam" could be construed to mean "conqueror of the people" or "destroyer of the people" (see Duane F. Watson, "Nicolaitans," *ABD* 4:1106–7, for linguistic details and wider discussion). But when Rev uses symbolic names, they bring with them OT resonances (e.g., Jezebel, 2:20; Sodom and Egypt, 11:8; Babylon 17:5). "Nicolaus" is better taken as an actual proper name known in Ephesus and Pergamum.

42. Roloff, *Revelation*, 45–46. Likewise, this is not an invitation to seek a deeper, esoteric meaning in Christ's message, as Anne-Marit Enroth, "The Hearing Formula in the Book of Revelation," *NTS* 36 (1990): 602–8, shows.

43. Beale, *Revelation*, 234. See also Jer 5:21; Ezek 3:27; 12:2; and Rev 13:9–10 (the other command to hear in Rev outside of chs. 2–3); and 22:11 (persistent stubbornness).

44. The significance of using an aorist imperative, "must listen" (ἀκουσάτω), here in v. 7 seems to be the same as in v. 5: to express an urgent command (see note). It is not a "specific message" as Aune, *Revelation 1–5*, 135, suggests.

encouragement for them to heed the exhortations of vv. 5–6 and so receive the promised blessing of v. 7b (cf. also 1:3).

Yet the audience for this message is broader than the Ephesian Christians alone. As in all the messages in Revelation 2–3 (2:11, 17, 29; 3:6, 13, 22), Christ speaks here by the Spirit[45] to all "the churches," the other six named here as well as other and later congregations who meet in his name.[46] In this way the messages to the churches in Revelation 2–3, just as the other letters to churches in the New Testament (e.g., Rom, 1 Pet, 1 John), speak beyond their ancient situation to other Christian congregations across the centuries. To the degree that other churches fit the patterns seen here, they should take encouragement or rebuke from what the Spirit says to these churches (cf. Col 4:16).

The message closes (v. 7b) with a promise that points beyond current difficulties to God's future consummation (Rev 21–22). Again, the individual Christian is addressed ("the one who overcomes"), but the action referred to has a corporate, even cosmic, dimension. "Overcoming"[47] alludes to the universal and age-long struggle of all that is evil, including the devil and the world system that he controls (1 John 2:13–17; 4:2–4), against God Almighty and the saving purpose he is bringing to fulfillment in his entire creation. Christians are caught in the middle of this conflict and are called to faithful endurance even if it means suffering and martyrdom (John 16:32–33a; Rev 1:9; 13:10; 14:12). However, Christ has already won the decisive victory (John 16:33b; Rev 3:21; see comments on 5:5), and his followers will be victorious not by their own efforts but by their faith in him (1 John 4:4; 5:4–5; Rev 12:11; 15:2; 17:14; 21:5–7).[48]

Because of these parallels in the rest of Revelation and in the wider Johannine literature, it is clear that "the one who overcomes" is the one who genuinely believes in Christ and who by virtue of God's new birth finds the ability to endure in that faith against idolatry and persecution (1 John 4:4; 5:4–5; Rev 13:10; 14:12; 21:5–7). This victory is not limited to those who suffer martyrdom for their faith[49] or to a group of more committed or obedient Christians over against other believers who are less spiritual.[50] Another argument against these views is the benefits promised in Revelation 2–3 to the overcomer, since according to the rest of Revelation these benefits accrue to all believers in Christ, not only to a limited group of them (e.g., 22:2–3, 14, 19).

Whatever difficulties may come to faithful Christians in this life, they pale in comparison to

---

45. Bruce, "Spirit in the Apocalypse," 340; and Boxall, *Revelation*, 51. In Rev the Spirit is associated with God and with Christ (1:4–5; 4:5; 5:6), but is especially seen as mediating prophetic visions and messages (1:10; 4:2; 14:13; 17:2; 19:10; 21:10; 22:6).

46. Smalley, *Revelation*, 63–64.

47. The word νικάω captures a characteristic Johannine theme. It can be rendered "overcome" (ASV, KJV, NASB), "conquer" (ESV, NET, NRSV, RSV), "be/prove victorious/be the victor" (CSB, NABR, NIV, NJB, NLT), or "prevail" (cf. BDAG 673). The articular present participle (τῷ νικῶντι) carries a generic sense: the present-tense usage is not progressive, repetitive, or customary ("keeps on overcoming," etc.). See Burton, *Moods and Tenses*, 56–57; Fanning, *Verbal Aspect*, 411–12.

48. Two further subthemes in Rev are God's reversal of what appears to be the irresistible victory of evil in the world and the Lamb's subversion of how victory is obtained (see 5:5; 6:2; 11:7; 12:11; 13:7; 21:7).

49. Caird, *Revelation*, 32–33; Charles, *Revelation*, 1:54; Martin Kiddle, *The Revelation of St. John*, MNTC (London: Hodder and Stoughton, 1940), 62–63. See arguments against this view in I. Howard Marshall, *Kept by the Power of God: A Study of Perseverance and Falling Away*, 3rd ed. (Carlisle: Paternoster, 1995), 253–54.

50. Donald Grey Barnhouse, *Revelation: An Expository Commentary* (Grand Rapids: Zondervan, 1971), 43–44; Joseph C. Dillow, *The Reign of the Servant Kings: A Study of Eternal Security and the Final Significance of Man* (Hayesville, NC: Schoettle, 1992), 478–87. See arguments against this view in James E. Rosscup, "The Overcomer in the Apocalypse," *GTJ* 3 (1982): 261–86.

the glorious blessing promised to them at the consummation. "To eat from the tree of life that is in God's paradise" picks up two images of ultimate deliverance, life-giving restoration, and communion with God that echo the entire biblical story of divine redemption from beginning to end. These powerful images (tree of life, God's paradise) are pervasive in biblical and nonbiblical texts and point to a divine renewal of all God's creation, not just to the spiritual salvation of individual humans.[51] The "tree of life" is a symbol of God's provision for all of humanity's needs in a life lived in obedience to and intimate fellowship with him.[52] "Paradise" represents the original, Edenic context for such a life—a life that humans lost in the fall but that God intends to restore in his renewal of all things in the future.[53]

Theology in Application

Good News and Bad News

As in many of the messages in chapters 2–3, Jesus's words to the Ephesian church do not give a completely positive or negative picture. In such cases we can learn to imitate their successes but avoid their failings. The Ephesians displayed a mix of admirable Christian conduct with tragic shortcomings and neglect. We too are called to live in discerning and lasting fidelity to God's truth and God's ways, but to do it all from a heart of love for God and for people. We must be wary of excusing our failings in one area by assuring ourselves that they are okay since we are doing so well in another area: "My running roughshod over people doesn't matter because I'm such a strong leader for God." It is also important to see that sound doctrine and heartfelt love are not mutually exclusive. It is a common misunderstanding to think that we can uphold truth and godly conduct but that it will make us unloving, or we can really care about people and fudge on the truth, but we cannot have both. No, they go naturally together and complement each other as John 1:14 (Jesus was full of grace and truth) and Eph 4:15 (real maturity in Christ is to live out the truth in love) demonstrate.

Moralistic Therapeutic Deism

Like the Ephesians, our churches need to know the truth of God and be discerning enough to uphold it against theological errors, but to do so in a winsome, Christlike way. Our passion to stand for the gospel should flow from a life transformed by God's grace and devotion to him, a life that also reflects his grace and love to others by

---

51. For development of this theme see commentary on Rev 21–22.

52. See "tree of life" in Gen 2:9; 3:3, 22–24; Rev 22:2, 14, 19; cf. Ezek 47:7–12. For parallel noncanonical texts, see commentary on Rev 22:2.

53. See "paradise" in Ezek 28:13; 31:8–9; Luke 23:43; 2 Cor 12:3–4; cf. Rev 22:1–5 and noncanonical texts cited there.

the power of the Spirit. Resisting false teaching sometimes focuses on specific core doctrines (e.g., deity of Christ, salvation by faith alone in Christ alone). But often our challenges come from more pervasive intermingling of secular attitudes and lifestyles that are advocated as acceptable Christianity (very similar to what the ancient churches of Asia Minor faced). One contemporary example is what researchers have called *moralistic therapeutic deism*. This label describes what sociologists found in an extensive survey of religious beliefs of American teenagers (the National Study of Youth and Religion, 2001–2015). This version of Christian faith seems to reflect the beliefs not only of many young people but also of their parents and churches as well. It is a religion of relational niceness, feeling good about oneself, and a distant paternalistic God. Its tenets are: (1) the central importance of being nice; God is benevolent and nonjudgmental, and his only demand on me is that I should be nice as well; (2) the importance of feeling good about myself and living out my dreams; the main purpose of religion is to help me find happiness, peace, and personal fulfillment; and (3) a laid-back deity who makes no demands of me but is available for emergencies if I ever need him. But for most of life, I am on my own and don't need to pay much attention to him. It is clear that this "Christian-ish"[54] religion fails on both points that Jesus speaks to the Ephesians about (vv. 2–5): fidelity to God's truth and heartfelt love for God and people.

The Indispensible Christian Virtue

Jesus makes clear that service without love is deficient service. Even great accomplishments without love amount to nothing (see 1 Cor 13). Active obedience and vigilance for God's truth, if done apart from love, fall short on both inward and outward grounds. They lack the devotion toward God that should undergird all that we do, and they lack the gracious spirit and tone we should have toward others with whom we interact. Our conception of what is needed to be faithful to God and to serve others is often severely limited by our lack of heartfelt love. Love for the true and living God with our whole being is the great commandment that Jesus gave, and love for our neighbor is likewise central to Christian character (Mark 12:28–31). No matter how mature and battle tested we may become in Christian living, Jesus calls us never to leave behind the vitality and freshness of our love for God and others. We should always remember that he showed us his love and grace when we were undeserving (1 John 4:10, 19) and that his great love for us calls us to love others in that same way (John 13:34–35).

---

54. Kenda Creasy Dean, *Almost Christian: What the Faith of Our Teenagers Is Telling the American Church* (Oxford: Oxford University Press, 2010), 3. This description of moralistic therapeutic deism is drawn from her survey of what the researchers found (pp. 3–24).

CHAPTER 4

Revelation 2:8–11

Literary Context

See the connections discussed under "Literary Context" for 2:1–7 in chapter 3, page 110.

Main Idea

Jesus exhorts the church in Smyrna to remain faithful in their present and future afflictions in view of his promise to bring life out of death.

Translation

(See the next page.)

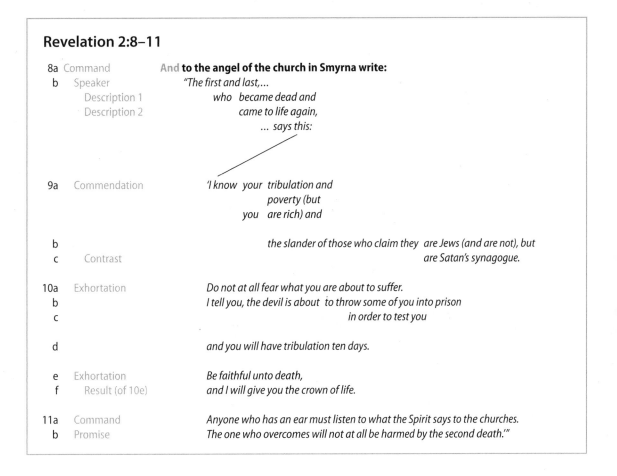

Revelation 2:8–11

8a	Command	**And** **to the angel of the church in Smyrna write:**
b	Speaker	*"The first and last,...*
	Description 1	*who became dead and*
	Description 2	*came to life again,*
		... says this:
9a	Commendation	*'I know your tribulation and*
		poverty (but
		you are rich) and
b		*the slander of those who claim they are Jews (and are not), but*
c	Contrast	*are Satan's synagogue.*
10a	Exhortation	*Do not at all fear what you are about to suffer.*
b		*I tell you, the devil is about to throw some of you into prison*
c		*in order to test you*
d		*and you will have tribulation ten days.*
e	Exhortation	*Be faithful unto death,*
f	Result (of 10e)	*and I will give you the crown of life.*
11a	Command	*Anyone who has an ear must listen to what the Spirit says to the churches.*
b	Promise	*The one who overcomes will not at all be harmed by the second death.'"*

Structure

See 2:1–7 for discussion of the four-part structure common to all the messages.

The message to the church in Smyrna follows the general structure closely, except that Christ's knowledge of them brings unmixed praise for the church's conduct amid difficult circumstances (v. 9). The exhortations then are meant to support them as they face even greater adversity in the future (v. 10).

Exegetical Outline

II. First Vision: The Exalted Christ and His Messages to the Churches (1:9–3:22)

A. Vision of the Exalted Christ (1:9–20)

B. Messages to the Seven Churches (2:1–3:22)

  1. To the Church in Ephesus (2:1–7)

  ➡ 2. To the Church in Smyrna (2:8–11)

    a. Introduction (2:8)

      (1) Address and command to write (2:8a)

      (2) Description of Christ who is speaking (2:8b)

    b. Knowledge of the church's spiritual wealth despite opposition (2:9)

    c. Exhortation in view of suffering to come (2:10)

      (1) Courage amid trials (2:10a–d)

      (2) Fidelity even to death (2:10e–f)

    d. Conclusion (2:11)

      (1) Command to hear the Spirit's message (2:11a)

      (2) Promise to the overcomer (2:11b)

Explanation of the Text

2:8 And to the angel of the church in Smyrna write: "The first and last, who became dead and came to life again, says this (Καὶ τῷ ἀγγέλῳ τῆς ἐν Σμύρνῃ ἐκκλησίας γράψον· Τάδε λέγει ὁ πρῶτος καὶ ὁ ἔσχατος, ὃς ἐγένετο νεκρὸς καὶ ἔζησεν). The address formula (v. 8a) for this letter is identical to v. 1a except for the changed place name and the conjunction "and" to link the two messages together. See commentary on v. 1 for shared expressions. Christ the speaker is presented in words drawn from the vision in chapter 1, "the first and the last" (see commentary on 1:17; cf. 22:13). These titles, rooted in Isaiah 44:6 and 48:12, remind the church that God and Christ are the origin and goal of all things. As the Christians in Smyrna face hardships and likely martyrdom (vv. 9–10), Christ's sovereign control over their life and destiny must be their strong anchor. And the further description of his death and resurrection (cf. 1:18)[1] is exactly what these Christians need as the backdrop for the following promise of resurrection life for those who are faithful until death (vv. 10b–11). Christ's resurrection is the guarantee that all who are his will also be raised (1 Cor 15:20–26; Phil 3:20–21).

The city of Smyrna occupied an extremely favorable site on a large harbor at the end of a long gulf about forty miles north of Ephesus. It survives today as Izmir, the third largest city in Turkey. In the first century it had the additional advantage of being the northwestern terminus of a major

---

1. The verb in the phrase "came to life again" (ἔζησεν) is changed slightly from 1:18. It is an ingressive aorist here instead of the emphatic present phrase "am living/am alive" used there. An ingressive sense ("to become alive, to live again") for the aorist of this verb occurs also in Luke 15:32; Rom 14:9; Rev 13:14; 20:4–5. See Fanning, *Verbal Aspect*, 138, 261–62. For the verb phrase "became dead," see comments on 1:18.

land route leading inland to Sardis, Philadelphia, Laodicea, and on to distant Syria. It chose loyalty to Rome in some of the earliest political changes leading to Roman rather than Hellenistic control of Asia Minor. Smyrna built a temple to Roma in 195 BC and much later was made the "temple warden" for a temple to the emperor in AD 26. It was, like Ephesus, a thriving commercial center and was regarded as one of the four chief cities of Asia (with Ephesus, Pergamum, and Sardis). In addition to the temples just mentioned, it had temples or shrines to honor Aphrodite, Apollo, Artemis, Cybele, Dionysus, Tyche, and Zeus.[2] There was a Jewish population at Smyrna as expected in an eastern Mediterranean city of this era. Ignatius wrote to the church at Smyrna (about AD 110) and later (AD 155) Polycarp, the bishop of Smyrna, was martyred there as recorded in *Martyrdom of Polycarp*.[3]

2:9 'I know your tribulation and poverty (but you are rich) and the slander of those who claim they are Jews (and are not), but are Satan's synagogue (Οἶδά σου τὴν θλῖψιν καὶ τὴν πτωχείαν, ἀλλὰ πλούσιος εἶ, καὶ τὴν βλασφημίαν ἐκ τῶν λεγόντων Ἰουδαίους εἶναι ἑαυτοὺς καὶ οὐκ εἰσὶν ἀλλὰ συναγωγὴ τοῦ Σατανᾶ). In this second major section, Christ's intimate knowledge of the church's condition is expressed (as frequently in the other messages) with the verb "I know" (οἶδα), but without the equally frequent "your works."[4] The focus instead is on their spiritual well-being despite hardships and opposition. The Lord knows the "tribulation" (θλῖψιν; trouble, oppression)[5] they are suffering at the hands of their opponents (v. 9b) and the material hardships they are experiencing, probably also due to economic and social opprobrium in Smyrna against their Christian allegiance.[6] Christ reminds them, however, of the paradoxical status of God's people in a sinful world: they are often poor in this world's wealth (outward, material, ephemeral) but "rich" inwardly, spiritually, and eternally (Luke 6:20; 1 Cor 3:21–23; 2 Cor 6:10; 8:2, 9; Jas 2:5; cf. Rev 3:17–18 for an opposite example).

Connected to their troubled circumstances is the experience described in v. 9b: "the slander" directed against them by certain people who falsely claim to be "Jews." "Slander" (βλασφημία; CSB, ESV, NIV, NRSV, RSV) could be translated "blasphemy" (KJV, NASB, NLT). The latter sense is appropriate if we understand their opposition to the Christians in Smyrna ultimately to be a sacrilege against God and true worship of him (cf. 13:1, 5–6; 17:3). But this verse more likely refers to malign accusations made against Christians to pagan officials in the city. Their reports apparently included not just disputes about Christian teaching but defamatory and unjust charges that left the church vulnerable to harassment (e.g., accusations of atheism or disloyalty to Rome).[7]

---

2. Koester, *Revelation*, 271–74; D. S. Potter, "Smyrna," *ABD* 6:73–75.

3. See comments on v. 9.

4. Five of the seven messages have a reference to "works" at this point, and this appears as a textual variant here in 2:9 (supported by ℵ, one of the best three ancient copies for Rev, and the bulk of later Byzantine minuscules) and is reflected in the KJV. But the reference is omitted in the other two most valuable manuscripts (A, C, as well as P and later copies), and it is much more likely that "works" was added here due to parallels with the other messages. See similar issue at 2:13.

5. BDAG 457. See this sense for "tribulation" in 1:9; 2:10; also Mark 4:17; John 16:33; Acts 11:19; 14:22; 1 Thess 3:3. For the relation of this to the "great tribulation," see discussion at 3:10 and 7:14.

6. To be a Christian could mean exclusion from opportunities to earn a living (and thus "poverty," πτωχεία) as well as seizure or loss of property due to religious hatred (Heb 10:34).

7. Longenecker, "Seven Churches," 282, describes how resistance to local manifestations of Roman imperial cults could bring charges of "atheism," i.e., not revering the gods, including the divinized emperor. This could lead to severe consequences. See examples from ancient sources in Claudia Setzer, *Jewish Responses to Early Christians: History and Polemics, 30–150 C.E.* (Minneapolis: Fortress, 1994), 100–101, 208–9.

But who are these opponents who "claim they are Jews (and are not)"? One suggestion is that they are a rival Christian group advocating observance of the Old Testament law (like the opponents of Paul in Galatia, Philippi, or Colossae).[8] A few decades later Ignatius warned the churches in nearby Magnesia and Philadelphia (but not Smyrna) against certain Judaizers (Ign. *Magn.* 8–10; *Phld.* 6.1). But this seems unlikely to lead to the kind of official proceedings against Christians implied by v. 10. It would also be odd to describe them as a "synagogue" (v. 9c). A more plausible view is that the Jewish community in Smyrna allied itself with local pagan authorities in opposing Christian witness in the city. Such opposition arose decades earlier across the eastern Mediterranean (Acts 13:43–45; 14:1–7; 17:13; 18:5–17; Gal 1:13–14, 23; 1 Thess 2:14–16), and there is evidence of it in Smyrna itself a half-century later (Mart. Pol. 12.2; 13.1; 17.2). The Jewish community's own status in the local power structure might have been quite precarious, as was true for most of diaspora Judaism after the Jewish revolt against Rome (AD 66–73). Opposing and exposing a marginal group that outsiders could misconstrue as closely related to their own may have seemed a necessary strategy.[9]

The response to their claim to be "Jews" is strongly rejected by Christ: they "are not" Jews but, even worse, "are Satan's synagogue" (v. 9b–c; cf. 3:9).

Raising the issue of who is truly Jewish is sometimes taken to reflect a widespread conviction among early Christians that the church is the new Israel, the true Jewish people, and that ethnic Israel has been set aside in God's purposes.[10] But as in other New Testament texts that speak in these terms,[11] the point here is not that gentile Christians are now the real Jews but that ethnic Jews who turn away from and oppose God's saving work through Christ are showing themselves to be Jewish only by physical descent, not by inward devotion and faith like that of Abraham (Rom 2:28–29; Gal 6:15; Phil 3:3; cf. Deut 10:16; 30:6; Jer 4:4; 9:25). And just as the Jewish leaders resisted Jesus and handed him over to Pilate (John 8:31–44; 16:1–3; 19:14–16) and as Paul persecuted the church (Acts 9:4; 26:9–11), so the Jews in Smyrna who worked with pagan authorities to oppose the church were in reality doing Satan's bidding, not God's (cf. v. 10).[12]

2:10 Do not at all fear what you are about to suffer. I tell you, the devil is about to throw some of you into prison in order to test you and you will have tribulation ten days. Be faithful unto death, and I will give you the crown of life (μηδὲν φοβοῦ ἃ μέλλεις πάσχειν. ἰδοὺ μέλλει βάλλειν ὁ διάβολος ἐξ ὑμῶν εἰς φυλακὴν ἵνα πειρασθῆτε καὶ ἕξετε θλῖψιν ἡμερῶν δέκα. γίνου πιστὸς ἄχρι θανάτου, καὶ δώσω σοι τὸν στέφανον τῆς ζωῆς). In this third section of the message, Christ calls his people at Smyrna to

8. Christopher Rowland, "The Book of Revelation: Introduction, Commentary, and Reflections," in *The New Interpreter's Bible*, ed. Leander E. Keck, vol. 12 (Nashville: Abingdon, 1998), 577. A further possibility along this line is that they were a syncretistic Jewish-gnostic-Christian community in Smyrna that had accommodated itself to the local imperial authorities and values. They claimed to be the true followers of Moses and Christ, but in reality were allied with Satan (cf. 2:9c, 13, 24; 3:9).

9. J. Nelson Kraybill, *Imperial Cult and Commerce in John's Apocalypse*, JSNTSup 132 (Sheffield: Sheffield Academic Press, 1996), 168–72; Keener, *Revelation*, 115.

10. Aune, *Revelation 1–5*, 175–76; Prigent, *Apocalypse*, 168; Hemer, *Letters*, 67.

11. See Markus N. A. Bockmuehl, *The Epistle to the Philippians*, BNTC (London: Black, 1998), 191; James D. G. Dunn, *The Epistle to the Galatians*, BNTC (London: Black, 1993), 344–46. This is the conclusion about this passage drawn by Jan Lambrecht, "Jewish Slander: A Note on Revelation 2,9–10," *ETL* 75 (1999): 421–29.

12. Sweet, *Revelation*, 85; Smalley, *Revelation*, 65–66. The phrase "Satan's synagogue" uses a possessive genitive (τοῦ Σατανᾶ): their assembly belonged to and served Satan, the adversary of God and accuser of God's people (BDAG 916–17; cf. Rev 12:9–10).

courage and faithfulness amid suffering that will come upon them soon. The prohibition "do not at all fear" commands a characteristic attitude of courage in all that they do,[13] even in the face of severe tests to the genuineness of their Christian commitment. The Lord, who knows them intimately, wants to fortify them for the spiritual and emotional battle that is coming.[14] Their suffering, modeled in important ways after the suffering of Job (Job 1:6–12; 2:1–6) and the temptation of Jesus (Matt 4:1; Luke 4:2), will be instigated by the devil[15] to test their character. The Lord informs them of this serious challenge by using a rhetorical device to slow down the statement and call special attention to it ("I tell you"; ἰδού, often translated "behold").[16]

This testing will take the form of official persecution that some of the Christians[17] in Smyrna will undergo (v. 10b). To be thrown "into prison" would be not just sporadic mob action or pervasive social or economic exclusion but hostile proceedings by authorities in Smyrna, probably responding (as v. 9 implies) to complaints by the local Jewish community. In the Greco-Roman world, imprisonment brought lasting shame regardless of the party's actual guilt or innocence. Such action would also be serious, since imprisonment in the ancient world was not imposed as a term of punishment for minor offenses. It was temporary custody to force compliance with an official demand, to hold the accused for trial, or to hold someone for execution.[18] Any of these could be in prospect for these believers, including execution as v. 10e implies.

Some of them would face imprisonment as a specific test of faith, but all would experience more general "tribulation."[19] This tribulation will be more intense than they are already experiencing (cf. same word θλῖψις in v. 9; see note there), but Christ's assurance is that it will be limited in time. The reference to "ten days" is probably not literal but is perhaps an allusion to Daniel 1:12, 14–15, where the Hebrew young men were tested (LXX πειράζω) for a limited period and in that case achieved a favorable outcome.[20] But more generally it reminds the church that however fierce the affliction, it is only temporary compared to God's

---

13. The Greek present tense here (φοβοῦ) communicates a customary, habitual attitude, and it is negated by a stronger form of the word "not" (μηδέν; "not at all, in no way"; BDAG 647; cf. Mark 5:26). The traditional idea that a negated present imperative must mean "stop doing [what is already going on]" (e.g., Thomas, *Revelation 1–7*, 166) is not valid. See BDF §335 and Fanning, *Verbal Aspect*, 335–40.

14. The verb translated "about to" (μέλλω, used twice in v. 10) here means "to be at the point of or on the verge of" occurring (Rev 10:4, 7; cf. Mark 13:4; see BDAG 627).

15. The "devil" (διάβολος; "slanderer, adversary"; BDAG 226–27) and "Satan" (Σατανᾶς; "enemy"; BDAG 916–17) are two titles that refer to the same spiritual being, the archenemy of God and his people. Both titles (and a range of others) occur in Rev 12:9–10 and 20:2. See G. H. Twelftree, "Spiritual Powers," *NDBT* 797–802.

16. The word ἰδού often means "behold" (ESV, KJV, NASB, RSV) or "look" (CSB), but in this context the rhetorical or emphatic force is more important. Something like "beware" (NRSV), "indeed" (NABR), "listen" (GNT), or "I tell you" (NCV, NIV) is better.

17. The plural "you" appears here for the first time in ch. 2

(see comment on 2:1). The phrase "throw some of you" is literally "throw from/of you [plural]" (βάλλειν . . . ἐξ ὑμῶν), and the Greek prepositional phrase implies the partitive idea "[ones] from among you" (BDF §164; BDAG 297; Aune, *Revelation 1–5*, 158; cf. 5:9; 11:9; Luke 21:16; John 16:17; 2 John 4).

18. Brian M. Rapske, "Prison, Prisoner," *DNTB* 827–30; Graham Shipley et al., eds., *Cambridge Dictionary of Classical Civilization* (Cambridge: Cambridge University Press, 2006), 723.

19. The verb "you will have" (ἕξετε) is also second-person plural (see note on v. 10b) and is best seen not as a further purpose of imprisonment (parallel to "test you") but as a separate statement about what is soon coming for all of them (parallel to "the devil is about to throw"). See translation.

20. Hemer, *Letters*, 69–70, mentions a bare possibility that "ten days" could allude to a literal period during which gladiatorial contests were held in Smyrna (an inscription from Smyrna honors the sponsor of "five days" of such contests). Christians could be threatened by such contests either by being forced into the competitions or by the danger of unruly crowds who would attend. But he prefers the conclusion stated above (indefinite, limited period).

reward for those who endure (vv. 10e–11; cf. Rom 8:18; 2 Cor 4:17–18; 1 Pet 1:6–7).

So they must "be faithful,"[21] even if the worst prospect turns out to be real—"unto death" (v. 10e). We find again this central theme in Revelation: God's people must endure in faith (13:10; 14:11–12), to the point of physical death if necessary. Jesus was the ultimate model of this (1:5; 3:14), and Antipas exemplified it nearby (2:13). This allegiance to Christ above all, even to the point of giving up one's own life, is rooted in what Jesus called his disciples to years earlier (Mark 8:35–37 and parallels; John 12:25; cf. Rev 14:11), and in the adverse circumstances that Revelation addresses we find it reiterated here.

The sterling promise that closes this verse, "and I will give you the crown of life" (v. 10f), also mirrors Jesus's earlier teaching about how to find real life.[22] The "crown" (στέφανος) here symbolizes not royalty (as "diadem" does in 12:3; 13:1; 19:12) but joyful victory or celebration of accomplishment, especially to recognize difficult, self-sacrificing service (e.g., 1 Cor 9:24–26; Jas 1:12; 1 Pet 5:4; Rev 3:11). Such a crown (a garland or wreath of greenery) honors commendable service or conduct.[23] Here the crown consists of life,[24] that true

and lasting life with God that is the reward of all of God's people (Rev 21:3–7).

2:11 Anyone who has an ear must listen to what the Spirit says to the churches. The one who overcomes will not at all be harmed by the second death'" (ὁ ἔχων οὖς ἀκουσάτω τί τὸ πνεῦμα λέγει ταῖς ἐκκλησίαις. ὁ νικῶν οὐ μὴ ἀδικηθῇ ἐκ τοῦ θανάτου τοῦ δευτέρου). The conclusion of the message as in v. 7 consists of a command to hear (v. 11a) and a promise to the overcomer (v. 11b). For the command to hear, see comments on v. 7a (identical in wording to v. 11a). This promise to the overcomer reflects the theme of death and life laid out in the foregoing message. The person who genuinely believes in Christ and endures in faith[25] will certainly not suffer harm[26] from the second death. This reinforces from the negative side Christ's pledge at the end of v. 10 to award "the crown of life" to the one who is faithful. "The second death" (20:6, 14; 21:8)[27] is the destiny of unbelieving humans,[28] identified also in Revelation as the lake of fire, the fate of those who will not experience the first resurrection or the blessings of the new Jerusalem and whose names are not written in the Lamb's book of life (19:20; 20:4–6, 14–15; 21:7–8).

---

21. The command "be faithful" (γίνου πιστός) uses the verb "become" (γίνομαι) but in the specialized sense of "prove to be, be found, show yourself to be" (BDAG 199). The present tense expresses a general precept, a customary sense for the action, not a focus on the process or a command to "keep doing" (BDF §335; Fanning, *Verbal Aspect*, 327–35).

22. When "and" (καί) links an imperative and a future indicative as here, it often denotes "and so" (e.g., Eph 5:14; Jas 4:7).

23. BDAG 943–44; W. Grundmann, "στέφανος," *TDNT* 7:630–31; cf. 615–29 on the background of "crowns" in the ancient world.

24. This is a genitive of apposition or epexegetical genitive (cf. Wallace, *Grammar*, 95–100; David Mathewson, *Revelation: A Handbook on the Greek Text*, BHGNT [Waco: Baylor University Press, 2016], 26).

25. See commentary on 2:7b for discussion of what it means

to "overcome" in Rev 2–3. In this message the overcomer is especially the person who maintains fidelity to Christ in the midst of suffering and persecution even to the point of death (v. 10). The promise of resurrected life and God's commendation awaits such a person, as Jesus himself has shown by his victory over the grave (v. 8).

26. The Greek verb for "harm" (ἀδικέω) sometimes has the more general moral sense (in the active) of "commit injustice, do wrong," but in Rev the consistent meaning is "to do harm, injure" (BDAG 20; e.g., 9:10, 19; 11:5). Here it occurs as a subjunctive with οὐ μή as an emphatic denial of a future possibility (BDF §365; Wallace, *Grammar*, 468–69).

27. The phrase is always articular in Rev, pointing to a fate assumed to be well-known (Wallace, *Grammar*, 225).

28. The wording "second death" occurs also in Jewish Targums distinguishing the physical death of the righteous in this world (first) from spiritual death of the wicked in the world

Theology in Application

Forewarned and Undaunted

This message of commendation from Christ to faithful Christians who faced affliction, poverty, and slander should catch today's believers up short in our unconscious expectations that if we really love God we will always be prosperous, happy, and well received by our culture. Scripture is clear about the inevitability of opposition, rejection, and suffering for faithful Christians (Matt 5:10–12; Acts 14:22; 2 Tim 3:12), but Jesus's call not to fear when facing persecution rings true nonetheless (Rev 2:10). Economic oppression (denial or loss of employment or of business opportunities), slander (misrepresentation or rejection of our stance on controversial issues), and ostracism (family conflict or social exclusion for countercultural views) seem hardly possible to many Christians in the secular Western world. But we should be aware that in many parts of the globe persecution rages unchecked even now, and our fellow Christians pay a terrible price for their loyalty to Christ. We can mourn over their suffering and be encouraged and inspired by their example, while doing all we can to alleviate their plight (prayer, advocacy, financial help). We must also prepare ourselves to live faithful and obedient lives amid changes that will certainly come as our societies become increasingly post-Christian and anti-Christian.

Comfort and Resolve from the Living Lord

The encouragement that the risen Christ gives in this message to suffering believers has a resonance beyond its immediate reference to present and future persecution for the faith. It provides a rich reminder of Jesus's own experience of suffering and death for our deliverance that led then to his powerful resurrection to an undying life: he is "the first and last, who became dead and came to life again" (v. 8; cf. 1:17–18). Because of his own death and resurrection, he can urge Christians to "be faithful unto death" and promise that he personally will give them "the crown of life" and that they "will not at all be harmed by the second death" (vv. 10–11). The enslaving threat of affliction and death in this world has been transformed for the Christian by the liberating hope of our own bodily resurrection (Rom 8:18–25) in likeness to "his glorious body" (Phil 3:21). Whether we face physical suffering and death through persecution or through disease, accident, or old age, death is still an enemy, but its

---

to come (second). The targum on Deut 33:6 paraphrases it as "may Reuben live in this world [or live an everlasting life] and not die the second death of the wicked in the world to come" (Tg. Onq. Deut. 33:6; Tg. Neof. Deut. 33:6; cf. Tg. Jer. 51:39, 57; Tg. Isa. 22:14; 65:5–6, 15). McNamara discusses the relation of these texts to Rev in Martin McNamara, *Targum and Testament Revisited: Aramaic Paraphrases of the Hebrew Bible: A Light on the New Testament*, 2nd ed. (Grand Rapids: Eerdmans, 2010), 223–27.

power and sting has been taken away (1 Cor 15:55–57). The divine comfort Jesus offers to all who face death comes not from one aloof and distant from our experience but one who knows it firsthand (Heb 2:17–18; 4:15–16). Our ultimate deliverance is not focused on a physical healing or cure that will last only for a time but on bodily resurrection to enjoy God's presence forever.

Revelation 2:12–17

Literary Context

See the connections discussed under "Literary Context" for 2:1–7 in chapter 3, page 110.

I. Prologue (1:1–8)

II. First Vision: The Exalted Christ and His Messages to the Churches (1:9–3:22)

  A. Vision of the Exalted Christ (1:9–20)

  B. Messages to the Seven Churches (2:1–3:22)

    1. To the Church in Ephesus (2:1–7)

    2. To the Church in Smyrna (2:8–11)

    3. To the Church in Pergamum (2:12–17)

    4. To the Church in Thyatira (2:18–29)

Main Idea

Jesus commends the church in Pergamum for their faithfulness despite deadly persecution, but they will face his judgment unless they turn away from idolatrous influences in their midst.

Translation

(See page 134.)

Revelation 2:12–17

| 12a | Command | **And** **to the angel of the church in Pergamum write:** |
| b | Speaker | *"The one who has the sharp, double-edged sword says this:* |

13a Commendation   *'I know where you live—where Satan's throne is.*
 b   *Yet you hold firmly to my name*
 c   *and you did not renounce your faith in me,*
 d   *even in the days of Antipas,*
     my faithful witness,
 e   *who was killed among you—*
       where Satan lives.

14a Rebuke   *But I have*   *a few things against you:*
 b   Explanation   *that you have some there who hold to the teaching of Balaam,*
 c   Identification

     who taught Balak to entice the children of Israel to sin
 d   *so that they ate meat offered to idols and*
 e   *committed sexual immorality.*

15   *So likewise you also have some who hold to the teaching of the Nicolaitans.*

16a Warning   *So repent.*
 b   *But*
     if not,
 c   *I am coming against you soon, and*
 d   *I will wage war against them with the sword of my mouth.*

17a Command   *Anyone who has an ear must listen to what the Spirit says to the churches.*
 b   Promise   *To the one who overcomes I will give some of the hidden manna, and*
 c   *I will give a white stone and*

 d   *inscribed on the stone*
      a new name that no one knows
 e   *except the one who receives it.'"*

Structure

See 2:1–7 for discussion of the four-part structure common to all the messages. The message to the church in Pergamum follows the general structure closely and includes both commendation and rebuke in describing the church's condition (vv. 13–15). The exhortation to repentance is stern (v. 16) but reflects within it the larger faithfulness for which they are commended.

Exegetical Outline

II. First Vision: The Exalted Christ and His Messages to the Churches (1:9–3:22)

  A. Vision of the Exalted Christ (1:9–20)

  B. Messages to the Seven Churches (2:1–3:22)

    1. To the Church in Ephesus (2:1–7)

    2. To the Church in Smyrna (2:8–11)

  ➡ **3. To the Church in Pergamum (2:12–17)**

      a. Introduction (2:12)

        (1) Address and command to write (2:12a)

        (2) Description of Christ who is speaking (2:12b)

      b. Knowledge of the church's condition (2:13–15)

        (1) Commendation for their faithfulness in a dark and deadly place (2:13)

        (2) Rebuke for tolerating influences towards idolatry (2:14–15)

      c. Exhortation to repent or face judgment (2:16)

      d. Conclusion (2:17)

        (1) Command to hear the Spirit's message (2:17a)

        (2) Promise to the overcomer (2:17b)

Explanation of the Text

2:12 And to the angel of the church in Pergamum write: "The one who has the sharp, double-edged sword says this (Καὶ τῷ ἀγγέλῳ τῆς ἐν Περγάμῳ ἐκκλησίας γράψον· Τάδε λέγει ὁ ἔχων τὴν ῥομφαίαν τὴν δίστομον τὴν ὀξεῖαν). The address formula for this letter (v. 12a) is identical to v. 8a except for the changed place name. See commentary on vv. 1, 8a for shared expressions. Again, Christ as speaker (v. 12b) is described with words taken from the vision in chapter 1: he has "the sharp, double-edged sword" (the article "the" refers back to the sword mentioned there). See comments on 1:16 for discussion of the symbolism and Old Testament background of Christ's authoritative word spoken in judgment (cf. also 19:15, 21). The phrase is picked up again at the end of this message as a stern motivation to avoid judgment on those who fail to act on what Christ says here (2:16). In Pergamum this reference may resonate in contrast

to the power of Roman officials to wield the *ius gladii*, the power of the sword, to execute those who threatened its authority (v. 13).

Pergamum was not on the coast like Ephesus and Smyrna, but inland about 16 miles (25 km) and 65–70 miles (110 km) north of Smyrna (the northernmost of all the seven cities). Its location featured an acropolis rising about a thousand feet (300 m) above a plain through which the Caicus River ran, a perfect site for a strategic military outpost. The Hellenistic kingdom of the Attalids ruled there between Alexander's successor Lysimachus and a peaceful transfer to Roman power around 130 BC. The Attalids in the interim had turned a fortress town into an impressive and beautiful Greco-Roman city and growing cultural center. The city's loyalty to Rome was rewarded when the province's first temple dedicated to the emperor cult was built in Pergamum soon after Augustus consolidated his power in 31 BC (see notes on v. 13). Arrayed near it on the acropolis was a temple to Athena, an altar to Zeus, and temples to Dionysus and to Demeter. On the edge of town was a large complex for the worship of Asclepius where the sick could go to seek healing. As in other cities of Asia Minor at this time, wealthy citizens vied for the distinction (and expense) of serving as priests and priestesses and of hosting banquets in honor of these deities. Various trade associations and community groups would participate in such festivities, and Christians would face questions about what level of involvement was acceptable.[1]

2:13 'I know where you live—where Satan's throne is. Yet you hold firmly to my name and you did not renounce your faith in me, even in the days of Antipas, my faithful witness, who was killed among you—where Satan lives (Οἶδα ποῦ κατοικεῖς, ὅπου ὁ θρόνος τοῦ Σατανᾶ, καὶ κρατεῖς τὸ ὄνομά μου καὶ οὐκ ἠρνήσω τὴν πίστιν μου καὶ ἐν ταῖς ἡμέραις Ἀντιπᾶς ὁ μάρτυς μου ὁ πιστός μου, ὃς ἀπεκτάνθη παρ᾽ ὑμῖν, ὅπου ὁ Σατανᾶς κατοικεῖ). Christ immediately acknowledges their perilous situation in Pergamum. They "live" where Satan[2] lives (same verb at start and end of this verse, κατοικέω, to reside or dwell) and where Satan even has his "throne," his locus of evil ruling authority.[3] This seems to say that satanic power is especially entrenched in Pergamum,[4] but the way in which this is true is not immediately clear. Did "Satan's throne" refer to a specific location in late first-century Pergamum? We know of several good candidates,[5] but it is hard after twenty centuries to be certain about whether one or any of these are specifically in view. What is certain, however, is that Satan's evil was particularly virulent in Pergamum and constituted a continuing menace to the Christians there, in the form of both deadly persecution from outside the church and doctrinal deception within the church.[6]

Despite the peril they faced,[7] at the time of this message the church was characterized[8] by strong loyalty to Christ: they "hold firmly to [his] name" (v. 13b).[9] The backdrop and unmistakable proof of their current commitment was courageous fidelity during a notable ordeal they had previ-

---

1. Koester, *Revelation*, 282–86; D. S. Potter, "Pergamum," *ABD* 5:229–30.

2. See note on 2:10 for the name "Satan."

3. "Throne" is an important symbol of ruling authority in Rev: of God and Christ (1:4; 3:21; 4:2; 5:1; 22:1, 3), of other heavenly beings associated with God's presence (4:4; 11:16), as well as of evil powers opposed to God (13:2; 16:10).

4. Boxall, *Revelation*, 58–59, rightly points to the broader truth in Rev that a throne rivaling God's true rule "has been set up on the earth, not only in Pergamum but wherever opposition to God's kingdom manifests itself," but this verse seems to imply some more intensive facet of Satan's rule in Pergamum.

5. Three viable options for "Satan's throne" are: (1) the huge altar to Zeus (now on display at the Pergamon Museum in Berlin) and its related temples to Zeus and Athena situated on the high acropolis that towered over the city; such an image of a throne set on a high mountain has biblical echoes (Ps 48:2; Isa 14:13–14; also 1 En. 25:3); (2) the temple to Augustus and Roma built in 29 BC where the emperor was acknowledged as divine (Dio Cassius, *Rom. Hist.* 51.20.7; Tacitus, *Ann.* 4.37); or (3) the sanctuary of Asclepius the healer- and savior-god on the outskirts of town, whose symbol was the serpent (cf. Rev 12:9). See *BNPauly* 10:754–71; Hemer, *Letters*, 84–85. Adela Yarbro Collins, "Pergamon in Early Christian Literature," in *Pergamon: Citadel of the Gods*, ed. Helmut Köster (Harrisburg, PA: Trinity Press International, 1998), 163–84, makes a strong case for option (1), and until further evidence turns up that should probably be seen as the preferred identification.

6. Steven J. Friesen, "Satan's Throne, Imperial Cults and the Social Settings of Revelation," *JSNT* (2005): 351–67, rejects all of the identifications of "Satan's throne" in Pergamum mentioned above since similar features could be found in the other seven cities. His view is that Pergamum stood out from the others because of the death of Antipas mentioned in v. 13—an unmistakable mark of satanic opposition against the church there.

7. The conjunction "yet" (καί) in v. 13b is normally translated "and," but here it has a contrastive sense.

8. The verb translated "hold firmly" (κρατεῖς) is used here as a customary present.

9. See comments on 2:3. One's "name" was seen as inseparable from the person himself (BDAG 712).

ously endured. "You did not renounce your faith in me,"[10] Christ says as he reflects on those past events.[11] What follows is a terse recounting of a set of circumstances in Pergamum so hostile to the Christians that tragically one of their number was killed: "Antipas[12] . . . who was killed among you." No further details of this episode or this person "Antipas" are preserved for us,[13] and the wording "was killed" does not indicate whether his death was due to mob action (e.g., Stephen's stoning in Acts 8) or official execution (e.g., James's death in Acts 12; cf. death sentences under Pliny in Bithynia two decades later [*Ep.* 10.96–97] or Polycarp's martyrdom in Smyrna in the mid-second century [Mart. Pol. 10–18]). Antipas's costly allegiance to Christ is commended ("my faithful witness")[14] in terms that mirror Christ's own faithfulness to God even until death (1:5; 3:14) as well as the ultimate witness that many Christians would give in the terrible times to come (1:2, 9; 6:9; 12:11, 17; 17:6; 19:10; 20:4). Mention of one specific death likely means that others had not occurred,[15] but Christians in Pergamum would nevertheless have lived under the fearful prospect that deadly hostility could flare up again at any time.

2:14–15 But I have a few things against you: that you have some there who hold to the teaching of Balaam, who taught Balak to entice the children of Israel to sin so that they ate meat offered to idols and committed sexual immorality. 15 So likewise you also have some who hold to the teaching of the Nicolaitans (ἀλλ᾽ ἔχω κατὰ σοῦ ὀλίγα ὅτι ἔχεις ἐκεῖ κρατοῦντας τὴν διδαχὴν Βαλαάμ, ὃς ἐδίδασκεν τῷ Βαλὰκ βαλεῖν σκάνδαλον ἐνώπιον τῶν υἱῶν Ἰσραήλ φαγεῖν εἰδωλόθυτα καὶ πορνεῦσαι. 15 οὕτως ἔχεις καὶ σὺ κρατοῦντας τὴν διδαχὴν [τῶν] Νικολαϊτῶν ὁμοίως). The Lord's knowledge of conditions in the Pergamene church included both commendation (v. 13) and a contrasting rebuke (vv. 14–15). The first portion of this rebuke sets up a typological parallel of false teaching from the Old Testament (v. 14) that is replicated in the congregation at Pergamum (v. 15). The introduction to the rebuke, "I have a few things against you" (v. 14a) moderates its force a little ("a few things," ὀλίγα; cf. similar wording without ὀλίγα in 2:4, 20), and this softening appears again in the pronoun shift in v. 16c–d ("I am coming against *you* soon, and I will wage war against *them*"). The rebuke was deserved, and a change was necessary (v. 16a), but in

---

10. The genitive phrase rendered "faith in me" (τὴν πίστιν μου) carries a clearly objective sense (similarly 14:12, "faith in Jesus"; cf. the subjective genitive in 13:10: "the endurance and faith of the saints").

11. The tense of the verb "did not renounce" (aorist οὐκ ἠρνήσω; also 3:8) summarizes their response during the events of those prior days. Such a repudiation or denial of Christ could occur in the context of judicial proceedings or in everyday social interactions (Matt 26:70, 72; Luke 12:9; Acts 3:13–14; 2 Tim 2:12; 1 John 2:22–23; Jude 4). Renouncing all allegiance to Christ was what Pliny the Younger says he required of the Christians he examined as a Roman official a few decades later in Bithynia (*Ep.* 10.96). He insisted that a verbal denial of Christ must be followed by calling out to the Roman gods, offering wine and incense to images of the emperor and the gods, and cursing Christ.

12. The name "Antipas" is indeclinable in Greek but is used here as a genitive. The phrase that follows ("my faithful wit-

ness") is nominative in apposition to Antipas. This is not the normal case for apposition in Greek, but it occurs commonly in Rev (BDF §136.1; e.g., 1:5; 2:20; 3:12; 14:12).

13. Bruce W. Longenecker, *The Lost Letters of Pergamum*, 2nd ed. (Grand Rapids: Baker Academic, 2016), provides an insightful account of how this may have happened, presented in the form of a fictionalized correspondence vividly reflecting the social and religious situation of Christians in the first-century Mediterranean world.

14. The phrase "my faithful witness" implies his loyal testimony "to Christ" (i.e., "my" [μου] is an objective genitive). The word μάρτυς later came to mean "martyr, one who dies as a witness to his faith," but it does not carry this technical sense in the NT. See Allison A. Trites, "Μάρτυς and Martyrdom in the Apocalypse: A Semantic Study," *NovT* 15 (1973): 72–80; J. Beutler, "μαρτυρία, μάρτυς," *EDNT* 2:392–95; contra BDAG 620.

15. Roloff, *Revelation*, 51; Friesen, "Satan's Throne," 365–66.

the wider perspective the congregation as a whole had been firm in their commitment (v. 13) despite tolerating grave error from "some" in their midst.[16] This group advanced syncretistic teachings that promoted idolatrous practices, powerfully evoked by the mention of Balaam and Balak from the Old Testament.[17] In intertestamental Judaism and early Christianity, Balaam had become the exemplar of a false prophet who, instead of speaking for God, for his own purposes led people away from worship of the true God. This is what Balaam did according to Numbers 25:1–3; 31:8, 15–16.[18] The "teaching of Balaam" is not a specific set of doctrines but a pattern of deceptive, self-serving ministry that promotes false religion.[19]

This picture of Balaam comes out in the description, "who taught Balak to entice the children of Israel to sin" (v. 14c; cf. "Balaam's word," Num 31:16, understood in connection with Num 24:12–14 to be counsel given to Balak).[20] "Entice . . . to sin" (NIV) is literally "put/place a stumbling block before" (CSB, ESV, NABR, NASB, RSV), a metaphor for influencing others toward sin or apostasy (cf. Josh 23:13; Judg 2:3; 8:27; Ps 106:36; Hos 4:17 LXX; Matt 16:23; 18:7; Rom 14:23; 16:17).[21] The two

Greek infinitives that follow give the result of this enticement (in this case an actual historical result in Israel's experience): "So that they ate meat offered to idols and committed sexual immorality" (v. 14d–e). These two could be understood to refer to spiritual idolatry alone,[22] since "sexual infidelity" often appears in the Bible as a metaphor for apostasy from the Lord by worshiping a false god (e.g., 2 Kgs 9:22; 1 Chr 5:25; Ps 73:27; Isa 1:21; Jer 3:6; Ezek 23:19; Rev 2:20; 17:2; 18:3, 9). Numbers 25:1–3 does refer to Israel's spiritual as well as physical "harlotry" under Balaam's influence, and that is the focus of this verse. Spiritual infidelity was clearly a temptation to the Christians in Pergamum (see v. 13), but it is not so obvious that sexual immorality was a major failing. See discussion in the next verse and in comments on 2:20 (where εἰδωλόθυτα are mentioned again).

Verse 15 completes the typological pattern set up by the description of Balaam in v. 14. The parallelism is signaled by the two adverbs "so likewise" (οὕτως, ὁμοίως) that bracket v. 15 at both ends in the Greek, as well as by the shift in tenses from v. 14c–e (past) to v. 15 (present): "They [did] . . . so likewise some among you [do] . . ."[23] The problem,

---

16. "Some . . . who hold" is the translation of a Greek substantival participle without an article (κρατοῦντας), used as an indefinite noun (likewise in v. 15; cf. 4:2).

17. "Balaam" is not the name this group would choose for itself, but it is the description Christ uses (speaking through John) to show their true character. See comments on the next verse for a possible wordplay on the name.

18. The story of Balaam in Num 22–24 has its positive elements, including the messianic prophecy of 24:15–19, but it also contains suggestions of pride and greed that Jewish tradition came to interpret in light of Num 25:1–3; 31:15–16. According to 31:16, it was "Balaam's word" that caused Israel to worship Baal and so provoked the Lord's judgment against them (25:1–3). This line of thought about Balaam can be found in Philo, *Moses* 1.294–99; *Migr.* 113–14; Josephus, *Ant.* 4.6.6, §§126–30; b. Sanh. 105; and also in 2 Pet 2:15–16; Jude 11. See Geza Vermes, "The Story of Balaam," in *Scripture and Tradition in Judaism* (Leiden: Brill, 1961), 127–77; K. G. Kuhn, "Βαλαάμ," *TDNT* 1:524–25.

19. On Balaam as an OT type or pattern in these verses, see Hoskins, *Revelation*, 86–87, and discussion of typology in the introduction to this commentary.

20. The verb "taught" is a Greek imperfect (ἐδίδασκεν) describing his customary, repeated instruction during extended encounters with Balak (Num 22–24).

21. BDAG 926.

22. Keener, *Revelation*, 124; Koester, *Revelation*, 288–89.

23. See the use of οὕτως to connect typological parallels in Matt 12:40; 17:12; 24:37; 24:37, 39; John 3:14; Rom 5:18–19, 21; 2 Tim 3:8; Heb 5:5, and of ὁμοίως to reinforce such a parallel in Luke 17:28. See Heikki Räisänen, "The Nicolaitans: Apoc 2; Acta 6," in *Challenges to Biblical Interpretation: Collected Essays 1991–2000* (Leiden: Brill, 2001), 145n20, for a similar view. Some (Aune, *Revelation 1–5*, 188; Smalley, *Revelation*, 69) take the "likewise" (ὁμοίως) to connect this reference back to 2:6 where Nicolaitans in Ephesus are mentioned, but this seems too far back in the text to be likely.

shown in the repeated words from v. 14 ("you have some there who hold to the teaching"), is that the church as a whole tolerated a group among them ("some") who advocated misleading doctrines. As in 2:6 these are labeled "the Nicolaitans,"[24] and as in that verse, no specific description of their teaching is given in v. 15 itself.[25] But the surrounding context gives more evidence to guide us. Christians in Pergamum were under threat from some notable feature(s) of satanic influence, perhaps focused on centers of pagan worship located there (v. 13). These Nicolaitans mirror the pattern of Balaam's influence toward compromise with idolatrous practices long ago (v. 14). This is the main point to be drawn from Christ's rebuke in vv. 14–15. In the cities of Asia Minor at this time, Christians would have felt constant pressure to participate in and assimilate to the pagan idolatry all around them. Political and economic life was inextricably intertwined with religious observances of various kinds, and this posed great difficulties for faithful Christians.[26] This had produced a particularly tragic outcome among the Christians in Pergamum in the death of Antipas (v. 13).

Reference to eating "meat offered to idols" (2:14, 20; cf. Num 25:2)[27] suggests some possible examples of accommodation the Nicolaitans advocated that Christ rebukes here. The frequent sacrifices of animals at the many altars and temples in a first-century city like Pergamum set off repercussions for the social, economic, and religious life of the city far beyond the sacred precincts themselves, although the impact would start there. Often the sacrificed animal would be eaten in the temple precincts as a sacred meal in honor of the deity. Family and associates of a worshiper could be invited to share in such a banquet at the temple or in a private home. Such a meal could also form a part of public (i.e., community-wide) or semipublic (i.e., clubs or trade guilds) celebrations that reflected social connections and community loyalty. Portions of the meat could even be simply sold in the public markets for private use.[28] The widespread Jewish and Christian stance on these activities was to forbid any participation with such meals due to their associations with idolatrous worship (Acts 15:20, 29; 21:25; cf. 4 Macc. 5:1–3; Did. 6.3; Justin, *Dial.* 34; Irenaeus, *Haer.* 1.6.3). Paul granted some range of freedom to Christians who clearly understood that the idols were nothing, but he also forbade meals in the idol temple—and participation in other ways if it misled a weaker Christian (1 Cor 8:1–13; 10:14–33). The Nicolaitans apparently endorsed much greater participation, and Jesus (speaking through John here) calls for Christians in Pergamum to resist their influence.

Beyond this influence toward idolatry, it is less clear whether the Nicolaitans also encouraged

---

24. There is textual variation here as to whether the article "the" should be included, but its presence is certain in 2:6. The likelihood is that it should be included here as well, since manuscript evidence (while very evenly divided) marginally favors inclusion, and the article may have been omitted to match the parallel anarthrous name in v. 14, "the teaching of Balaam" (τὴν διδαχὴν Βαλαάμ). Christ speaking through John could assume that the church knew this group and its activities among them.

25. The "also" in v. 15 does not mean an additional, separate group from those who teach like Balaam did (v. 14). The typological parallelism (i.e., "you like Israel at the time of Balaam") means that the same group is described in vv. 14–15. See Charles, *Revelation*, 1:63–64; Caird, *Revelation*, 38–39.

26. Koester, *Revelation*, 289; Longenecker, "Seven Churches," 281–84.

27. The phrase "meat offered to idols" in Rev 2:14, 20 is a paraphrase of the Greek compound adjective εἰδωλόθυτος meaning "something slain for an idol," a Jewish-Christian word for an animal sacrificed in worship of a pagan image (BDAG 280). The LXX of Num 25:2 does not use this specific word, but makes the same point.

28. Aune, *Revelation 1–5*, 191–94; Friesen, *Imperial Cults*, 193; *NewDocs*, 1:5–9; Keener, *Revelation*, 124–25; Ramsay MacMullen, *Paganism in the Roman Empire* (New Haven: Yale University Press, 1981), 36–42, 57.

licentious sexual practices in the pattern of Numbers 25:1 (also 1 Cor 10:8; 2 Pet 2:13–14; Jude 7, 11). It seems best to conclude that this was not the case.[29] While sexual immorality and religious idolatry were often found together in the ancient world, John's focus in Revelation is almost exclusively on the pervasive spiritual infidelity that threatened his readers (Rev 2:22; 14:8; 17:1–5; 18:3, 9; 19:2).[30] It is true that a number of decades later the church in Asia Minor was threatened by gnostic groups that may have combined sexual licentiousness with doctrinal heresy.[31] Patristic accounts regularly connect late second-century gnostic groups to the Nicolaitans of Revelation 2:6, 15, and they sometimes identify the Nicolas of Acts 6:5 as their early leader.[32] But such accounts appear to be interpretations of these New Testament texts and not independent information about the first-century group. Some have seen an early form of Gnosticism behind the Nicolaitans as well as "Jezebel" in 2:20 ("knowing the deep things of Satan" in 2:24 could refer to gnostic secrets),[33] but Revelation says nothing at all about some central features of later Gnosticism (e.g., dualism or docetism) and does not say much, if anything, of its libertinism as mentioned above. It is preferable to concentrate on what Revelation makes central about the Nicolaitans, that is, their influence on Christians to compromise their allegiance to the true God.

2:16 So repent. But if not, I am coming against you soon, and I will wage war against them with the sword of my mouth (μετανόησον οὖν· εἰ δὲ μή, ἔρχομαί σοι ταχὺ καὶ πολεμήσω μετ᾽ αὐτῶν ἐν τῇ ῥομφαίᾳ τοῦ στόματός μου). In wording very similar to 2:5, Christ commands repentance (μετανόησον), a change of conduct[34] away from their toleration of destructive teachings (vv. 14–15).[35] If they fail to heed his command, he will "soon" visit Pergamum in disciplinary judgment (same wording as in 2:5 [see comments there] except that "soon," ταχύ, is used to sharpen the consequence of such failure).[36] He will take decisive action especially against those who seek to mislead his people (note the pronoun shift: "you" to "them"). The insistent tone is reinforced by the battle imagery that returns to the description of Christ's "sharp sword" in v. 12: "And I will wage war against them with the sword of my mouth." War imagery often refers to cosmic conflict in Revelation (e.g., 12:7; 13:4; 17:14), but here Christ pledges decisive opposition against the Nicolaitans similar to that which Balaam ultimately suffered (see the same word "sword," ῥομφαία, used of the false prophet's fate in Num 31:8; also the parallel Hebrew word in Josh 13:22). He will

---

29. Koester, *Revelation*, 288–89; Räisänen, "Nicolaitans," 152–60.

30. Revelation mentions sexual sins only three times, in lists of various moral violations by unrepentant humans (9:21; 21:8; 22:15).

31. Patristic accounts describe these opponents as sexual libertines, but there is some question about whether this is a distortion of their actual practice (Kurt Rudolph, "Gnosticism," *ABD* 2:1034).

32. Irenaeus, *Haer.* 1.26.3; 3.11.1; Hippolytus, *Haer.* 7.24; Clement of Alexandria, *Strom.* 2.20; 3.4; and Eusebius, *Hist. eccl.* 3.29.

33. Adolf Schlatter, *The Church in the New Testament Period* (London: SPCK, 1955), 133–36; C. K. Barrett, "Gnosis and the Apocalypse of John," in *The New Testament and Gnosis* (Edinburgh: T&T Clark, 1983), 127–35; and Smalley, *Revelation*, 63.

34. See lexical note on repentance (μετανοέω) at 2:5.

35. The inferential conjunction "so" or "therefore" (οὖν) is a frequent part of the exhortation section of these seven messages (e.g., 2:5; 3:3, 19), but it is omitted by some important manuscripts here in v. 16 (א, P, 025, 2053, 2329), and a scribe may have added it because of its occurrence in these other places. But it is included in equally valuable copies (A, C, 046, 1006, 1611), and it may have been dropped accidentally due to similar-looking letters at the end of μετανόησον (haplography).

36. The word "soon" in v. 16c could show that Christ's final coming is in view (in light of the use of "soon" elsewhere in Rev; see 3:11; 22:7), but as noted in 2:5 these comings are typologically related and thus are hard to separate completely.

defend his people, both near term and in his ultimate victory, by his authoritative pronouncement of judgment against all the enemies of their faith (see the imagery of "sword" and "mouth" in Rev 1:16; 19:15, 21; cf. Job 4:9; Ps 33:6; Isa 11:4; 2 Thess 2:8; also Ps 7:11–12, God's "sword" as his righteous judgment against the unrepentant).

2:17 Anyone who has an ear must listen to what the Spirit says to the churches. To the one who overcomes I will give some of the hidden manna, and I will give a white stone and inscribed on the stone a new name that no one knows except the one who receives it" (ὁ ἔχων οὖς ἀκουσάτω τί τὸ πνεῦμα λέγει ταῖς ἐκκλησίαις. τῷ νικῶντι δώσω αὐτῷ τοῦ μάννα τοῦ κεκρυμμένου καὶ δώσω αὐτῷ ψῆφον λευκήν, καὶ ἐπὶ τὴν ψῆφον ὄνομα καινὸν γεγραμμένον ὃ οὐδεὶς οἶδεν εἰ μὴ ὁ λαμβάνων). The conclusion of the message to Pergamum as in the previous two consists of a command to hear (v. 17a) and a promise to the overcomer (v. 17b–e). For the command to hear, see comments on v. 7a (identical in wording to v. 17a). In this conclusion the promise to the overcomer[37] has multiple parts ("I will give . . ." occurs twice, and the second clause has two objects that Christ pledges to give to the overcomer).

The first gift that is promised is "some of the hidden manna" (τοῦ μάννα τοῦ κεκρυμμένου),[38] in clear contrast to the food of idol-meat offered by the Nicolaitans (vv. 14–15). Alluding to God's life-sustaining provision for Israel in the wilderness (Exod 16:4, 14–36; Num 11:6–7),[39] this image speaks of how Christ's deliverance will provide all that his people truly need for human life as God designed it to be lived in his renewed creation (John 6:25–40; Rev 7:16–17; 21:1–7; 22:1–3).[40] The initiation of this deliverance has already been accomplished because Jesus came from heaven and gave himself on the cross so that all who believe may have eternal life (John 6:41–59).[41] But the full-orbed consummation awaits the time when Christ "will raise them up" (John 6:54) and God renews all things as described in Revelation 21–22. This appears to be the point of the description of this manna as "hidden." It is concealed in the sense that it is out of human sight but preserved in heaven until it is made evident on earth in the final days (cf. Col 3:1–4). God's provision of nourishment from heaven at the exodus (Exod 16:4) anticipates the coming of his ultimate and complete provision for his people in the last days (a feature of eschatological expectation among some Jews as seen in 2 Bar. 29:8; Sib. Or. 7:141–49; Mek. on Exod 16:25).[42]

---

37. See commentary on 2:7b for discussion of what it means to "overcome" in Rev 2–3. In this message the overcomer is especially the person who does not renounce his faith in Christ (v. 13) by following influences that lead to compromise with satanic idolatry in Pergamum (vv. 13–15).

38. The genitive τοῦ μάννα after the verb "give" (which usually takes an accusative object, as here in v. 17c–d) carries a partitive sense, "some of" (BDAG 743; cf. similar phrase with preposition ἐκ in 1 John 4:13).

39. The patterns of God's dealings with Israel in the Exodus from Egypt are evoked again and again in subsequent parts of the Bible to describe how God delivers his people in recurring situations of peril and enslavement to evil (cf. the new-exodus imagery involving provision of food in Isa 49:9–10). And these all point by typological escalation to God's ultimate provision in the eschaton (see Rev 7:16–17; 19:9; 21:1–7; 22:1–3).

40. As in the previous promises to the overcomer (2:7, 11), this verse speaks of features of God's ultimate redemption described in the final chapters of the book.

41. His sacrifice for believers is remembered in the celebration of the Lord's Supper (John 6:52–58), which also anticipates the consummation to come (Matt 26:29; 1 Cor 11:26).

42. A more esoteric story in Jewish tradition, found in 2 Macc 2:4–8 and 2 Bar. 6:7–10, is not likely to be related to the "hidden" manna here. In that story the ark and other sanctuary furnishings were sealed in a cave by Jeremiah or buried in the earth by angels at the time of Nebuchadnezzar's destruction of the temple (586 BC) to be disclosed only in the latter days. This could include the manna Moses put in a jar inside the ark of the covenant (Exod 16:32–34; Heb 9:4), but neither 2 Macc nor 2 Bar. mention manna, and 1 Kgs 8:9 says the ark contained only the tablets of the law when the temple was dedicated under Solomon.

The second gift Christ will give is "a white stone" and with it "a new name" that is "inscribed on the stone" (v. 17c–d). These items are simply and clearly worded, but the range of possibilities for what they signify is daunting to a modern-day interpreter. Presumably they were more transparent to John and his early readers, but we do not share their intuitive cultural associations and struggle to grasp the connotations. In context they almost certainly pertain to privileges the faithful will receive at their final deliverance, since that is the character of the overcomer promises in all seven messages. But specific nuances are more elusive, and no firm conclusion can be drawn from the available evidence.

The word "stone" (ψῆφον) can refer to a pebble or small rock (Lam 3:16), a precious stone or gem (e.g., a ring stone; perhaps given to recognize someone's status), an amulet (e.g., a stone thought to have magical powers or used in divination), a token (signifying initiation or membership; e.g., an entrance pass), or by specific association a tally-stone or vote (since pebbles were cast and counted to decide a court case or public election; Acts 26:10; 4 Macc. 15:26).[43] Several of these could fit nicely in the context of Revelation 2:14, but none stands out as the most appropriate above all others. The further issue to consider is which of these could more fittingly carry an inscription of "a new name"? An ancient amulet or magic charm would often carry the name(s) of a deity whose power the stone was thought to carry.[44] Evidence is lacking for "stone" in one of the other senses having a name inscribed, but it is not hard to conceive of ways this might be fitting (e.g., an entry pass belonging to a person or a favorable verdict for someone). It is possible that

this image derives from Zechariah 3:9 where an inscribed stone (λίθος) is perhaps related to removal of sin. But the interpretation of that verse is unclear, and evidence of an allusion or echo of that verse here in Revelation 2:17 is also murky.[45]

The further question then is whose name should be understood to stand written on the stone? In 3:12 the names of God and of the new Jerusalem as well as Christ's "new name" are written on the overcomer himself (cf. 22:4). So here in 2:17 a stone with a divine name could represent Christ's recognition or authorization of the overcomer as one of his own, no longer part of Satan's realm. But the gift of "a new name" also seems to connect to the larger vision of God's renewal of his people and of all creation in Isaiah (Isa 43:18–19; 65:17; 66:22; cf. Rev 21:1–2, 4), since according to Isaiah God's people will be given a "new name" (Isa 62:2–4; 65:15). In biblical usage, giving a new name speaks of spiritual or moral transformation (e.g., Abraham, Jacob).[46]

The further description in v. 17e, "that no one knows except the one who receives it," also individualizes the reference since if it were Christ's name (19:12; 22:4) others would know it. So it seems to represent individual identity and transformation in that future day.[47] While God's redemptive consummation has a number of important corporate dimensions (Rev 5:9–14; 7:9–10; 21:1–7), at the level of this transformation each Christian relates to Christ intimately and personally in a way that no one else can fathom. It is likely also, along the lines of Christ's name that only he knows (19:12; see comments there), to understand that the "new name" for each Christian is not a previously unknown name or identity but the full flowering of

---

43. BDAG 1098; see LSJ 2022–23 for a number of ancient illustrations. *New Docs* 1:84; 4:209 cite ancient inscriptions in which "white stones" signify favorable or acquittal votes.

44. E.g., Artemidorus, *Onir.* 5.26; cf. *PGM* 1.146; 12.6–20.

45. Jauhiainen, *Zechariah*, 82–83.

46. The "new name" or "other name" in Isa 62:2–4; 65:15 is corporate (for Jerusalem or Israel), but to extend the sense to an individual's name as here is not unreasonable in light of wider biblical imagery.

47. Fekkes, *Prophetic Traditions*, 128–30.

the individual character that God has in mind for each of his children in Christ. Our ultimate conformity to the image of Christ (Rom 8:29; 1 John 3:2) will bear the family likeness but will reflect God's design for each of its members, whom he calls by name (John 10:3).

Theology in Application

Very Personal Communication

In this message as well as in the other messages of the risen Christ to the churches, it is clear that he knows them completely and is fully aware of their circumstances and their response to it (cf. "I know where you live," v. 13). The old spiritual that laments, "Nobody knows the trouble I've seen, nobody knows my sorrow," is not true for the believer. Actually, in the version that Louis Armstrong recorded the next stanza says, "Nobody knows but Jesus." His intimate knowledge of his people extends to all churches then and now, as well as the individual Christians who make up those congregations. He knows us profoundly, even if no one else does or cares to. He walks among us (2:1), sees our struggles and our successes, and will act authoritatively in judgment or reward (vv. 12, 16–17). Whether his all-seeing knowledge of us is a source of comfort or distress depends on our response to him.

Future Hope and Present Identity

Those who live in anticipation of the fulfillment of God's prophecies of future redemption are often caricatured as "too other-worldly to be of any earthly good." They are viewed as pessimistic escapists, happy to see the culture decay with no investment in what is just or good in today's society. But this passage, and all of Revelation, shows that not to be the case, either corporately or individually. Because of its vision of the future, Revelation calls Christians to stand firm in the present against the dominant ideology of religious and moral apostasy and to bear consistent witness in life and word to the true God. We are called to resistance and gracious outreach, not assimilation or withdrawal or isolation, even in the face of insidious and deadly opposition (1:5; 2:13; 6:9; 12:11; 19:20).[48] We do this in part because the church as a whole is "an inaugurated form of the future kingdom of God"[49] on earth. It displays ahead of time what God's redeemed and reconciled human society can look like in pursuing righteousness, joy, and peace among people of diverse backgrounds.

Yet also as individual Christians we are called to live toward the future God has for us. I will receive a new name from Jesus, an identity and character hardly

---

48. Bauckham, *Theology*, 160–61; Richard B. Hays, *The Moral Vision of the New Testament—Community, Cross and New Creation: A Contemporary Introduction to New Testament Ethics* (New York: HarperOne, 1996), 176–81.

49. Blaising and Bock, *Progressive Dispensationalism*, 286; cf. 285–91.

imagined now but which represents the full transformation of my person and gifts according to God's good design for me in Christ. Who am I in Christ and what community or extended family do I belong to because of him? How I see myself now and in the future largely controls how I live in the present, and God's revelation in Scripture should inform that image. I must discover and inhabit Christ's intent for my life, not my own self-chosen identity or one molded by the overpowering culture around me (autonomous, self-absorbed, without God).[50] Our identity and conduct in the present is formed from our history as well as from our destiny and hope for the future.

---

50. See this point explored especially regarding sexual identity and ethics (both hetero- and same-sex conduct) in Stanton L. Jones and Mark A. Yarhouse, "Anthropology, Sexuality, and Sexual Ethics: The Challenge of Psychology," in *Personal Identity in Theological Perspective*, ed. Richard Lints, Michael S. Horton, and Mark R. Talbot (Grand Rapids: Eerdmans, 2006), 118–36.

Revelation 2:18–29

Literary Context

See the connections discussed under "Literary Context" for 2:1–7 in chapter 3, page 110.

I. Prologue (1:1–8)

II. First Vision: The Exalted Christ and His Messages to the Churches (1:9–3:22)

    A. Vision of the Exalted Christ (1:9–20)

    B. Messages to the Seven Churches (2:1–3:22)

        1. To the Church in Ephesus (2:1–7)

        2. To the Church in Smyrna (2:8–11)

        3. To the Church in Pergamum (2:12–17)

        4. To the Church in Thyatira (2:18–29)

        5. To the Church in Sardis (3:1–6)

Main Idea

Jesus commends the church in Thyatira for their growth in Christian character and exhorts them to hold fast, but he rebukes their toleration of idolatrous teaching and warns them of judgment for any who follow it.

Translation

(See page 146.)

Revelation 2:18–29

18a	Command	**And to the angel of the church in Thyatira write:**
b	Speaker	*"The Son of God,...*
	Description 1	*the one who has eyes like a flame of fire and*
	Description 2	*whose feet are like gleaming bronze,*
		... says this:

19a	Commendation	*'I know your works, that is,*
b	Explanation	*your love and faith and service and endurance,*
c		*and your last works are greater than the first.*

20a	Rebuke	*But I have against you*
		that you tolerate the woman Jezebel,
b	Description 1	*who claims she is a prophetess but*
c	Description 2	*teaches and misleads my servants*
d		*to commit sexual immorality and*
		eat meat offered to idols.

21a	Warning	*And I gave her time to repent,*
b		*but she is not willing to repent of her sexual immorality.*
22a		*I tell you, I am going to throw her onto a sickbed and*
b		*those who commit adultery with her into great ☜*
		tribulation,
c	Qualification (of 22b)	*unless they repent of her works.*

23a	Warning Cont.	*And I will kill her children with a deadly disease.*
b	Result	*Then all the churches will know that I am the one who searches minds and hearts, and*
c		*I will give to each of you according to your works.'*
24a	Exhortation	*But I say to the rest of you in Thyatira*
b	Description 1	*who do not hold this teaching,*
c	Description 2	*who did not learn Satan's so-called deep secrets,*
d	Declaration	*'I do not put any further burden on you.*
25	Command	*Only hold fast to what you have until I come.*

26a	Promise	*To the one who overcomes and*
		keeps my works until the end
b	Promise	*I will give authority over the nations—*
27		*and he will shepherd them with a rod of iron,*
		as earthen pots are broken to pieces— (Ps 2:9)

28a	Comparison (to 26b)	*just as I received authority from my Father.*
b	Promise	*And I will give him the morning star.*
29	Command	*Anyone who has an ear must listen to what the Spirit says to the churches.'"*

Structure

See 2:1–7 for discussion of the four-part structure common to all the messages. The message to the church in Thyatira follows the general structure in most respects. After the introduction (v. 18), it describes the church's condition with a succinct commendation and longer rebuke and warning (vv. 19–23). The exhortation is an encouragement for the faithful to maintain their godly conduct (vv. 24–25). In the conclusion (vv. 26–29) the order of the promise to the overcomer and the command to hear is reversed compared to the earlier addresses, and this new order is followed in the remaining three addresses.

Exegetical Outline

II. First Vision: The Exalted Christ and His Messages to the Churches (1:9–3:22)

    A. Vision of the Exalted Christ (1:9–20)

    B. Messages to the Seven Churches (2:1–3:22)

        1. To the Church in Ephesus (2:1–7)

        2. To the Church in Smyrna (2:8–11)

        3. To the Church in Pergamum (2:12–17)

        4. To the Church in Thyatira (2:18–29)

           a. Introduction (2:18)

               (1) Address and command to write (2:18a)

               (2) Description of Christ who is speaking (2:18b)

           b. Knowledge of the church's condition (2:19–23)

               (1) Commendation for their fruitful and growing Christian conduct (2:19)

               (2) Rebuke for tolerating idolatrous teaching and warning to its adherents (2:20–23)

           c. Exhortation for the faithful to hold fast (2:24–25)

           d. Conclusion (2:26–29)

               (1) Promise to the overcomer (2:26–28)

               (2) Command to hear the Spirit's message (2:29)

Explanation of the Text

2:18 And to the angel of the church in Thyatira write: "The Son of God, the one who has eyes like a flame of fire and whose feet are like gleaming bronze, says this (Καὶ τῷ ἀγγέλῳ τῆς ἐν Θυατείροις ἐκκλησίας γράψον· Τάδε λέγει ὁ υἱὸς τοῦ θεοῦ, ὁ ἔχων τοὺς ὀφθαλμοὺς αὐτοῦ ὡς φλόγα πυρὸς καὶ οἱ πόδες αὐτοῦ ὅμοιοι χαλκολιβάνῳ). The formula of address for this letter (v. 18a) is identical to v. 8a except for the changed place name. See commentary on 2:1, 8a for shared expressions. Here Christ is described (v. 18b) in a way that is especially suitable for how the message concludes (vv. 26–28), as well as with appropriate words taken from the vision in chapter 1. The title "Son of God," so common in the rest of the New Testament and especially in the Gospel and Epistles of John, is used only here in Revelation, but references to God as "my Father" (2:28; 3:5, 21) and "his Father" (1:6; 14:1) frequently portray Jesus's divine sonship. This would be in direct conflict with the worship of the Roman emperor as *divi filius*, "son of a god," a title conferred on many emperors since the time of Augustus.[1] Seeing Jesus as "the son of God" comes into even greater conflict with Roman ideology in light of the Christian understanding of an Old Testament text like Psalm 2 (quoted at the end of this address) that associates Jesus's divine sonship with authority to rule the whole world (see discussion of vv. 26–28 below; also comments at Rev 11:15–19).

This picture of Christ in glorious authority is reinforced by the two descriptions drawn from the vision of him in 1:14–15. First, he "has eyes like a flame of fire," a description drawn from Daniel 10:6 (cf. 1:14), but also repeated in Revelation 19:12, where it evokes the sense of divine indignation expressed ultimately in judgment against all who oppose his ruling authority (cf. "in a flame of fire" in Isa 66:15–16; 2 Thess 1:7–8). Second, his "feet are like gleaming bronze," reinforcing his resplendent, heavenly glory (see Rev 1:15), but also perhaps indirectly making a connection to the well-known metalworking trade of Thyatira.[2] The word rendered "gleaming bronze" (χαλκολίβανον; found only here and in Rev 1:15 in all of extant Greek literature) seems to refer to a type of fine brass or bronze, and it could be a specialized term familiar in the local area.[3] In any case it also serves to connect the glorious vision of Christ (1:15) with his appearance in judgment, perhaps alluding in this case to his future coming in irresistible power as Lord of all (19:11–16).

Thyatira was a medium-sized city located further inland in a wide valley on the main road going southeast from Pergamum to Sardis. Its location made it an important commercial center with a thriving textile industry (wool trade, weaving, dyeing). Lydia as mentioned in Acts 16:14 was a merchant from Thyatira who sold purple cloth. Inscriptions give evidence of various other trades that flourished in the city (coppersmiths, tanners and leather workers, potters, slave traders). See comments about these trade guilds at v. 20. Not much archeological work has been done there since, as with Smyrna/Izmir, it is the site of a sizable modern town Akhisar. From coins and inscriptions we know that there were shrines to local deities who

---

1. Friesen, Imperial Cults, 31–32, 75–76; Koester, *Revelation*, 297–98; Mark Reasoner, "The Emperor Cult," in *DLNT* 324–25.

2. Hemer, *Letters*, 111–17.

3. BDAG 1076; Dan 10:6, as the source of this imagery (see notes on Rev 1:15), does not use this rare word but refers to "bronze that flashes like lightning," a polished, high-quality metal.

had been assimilated to the Greco-Roman Apollo and Artemis, and to Helios, Meter, and Tyche. There is no extant evidence of a Jewish population from this time, but it is likely to have had one.[4]

2:19 'I know your works, that is, your love and faith and service and endurance, and your last works are greater than the first (οἶδά σου τὰ ἔργα καὶ τὴν ἀγάπην καὶ τὴν πίστιν καὶ τὴν διακονίαν καὶ τὴν ὑπομονήν σου, καὶ τὰ ἔργα σου τὰ ἔσχατα πλείονα τῶν πρώτων). As in 2:2 Christ's knowledge of the church's condition begins with a commendation for their conduct in general (their "works") and then specifies further dimensions of their characteristic actions.[5] They are commended first for their exercise of "love," the cardinal Christian virtue (see comments on 2:4). They also consistently display "faith" (often called for in Rev; cf. 2:13; 13:10; 14:12), which is at times coupled in the New Testament with love as one of several most important Christian traits (Col 1:4; 1 Thess 3:6; 5:8; 1 Tim 1:14; 2 Tim 1:13; Phlm 5). Commentators sometimes assert that "faith" (πίστις) here does not mean "belief, trust" but "faithfulness,"[6] but these should not be separated. As a character trait πίστις means "trust, confidence, firm commitment" toward God or Christ that endures in spite of difficult times.[7] The third characteristic is "service" (only here in Rev), which speaks broadly of action taken to help others, providing aid or support in a variety of ways both material and spiritual.[8] By his example and teaching Jesus established this as a central characteristic for his followers, especially in its concern

for others rather than for oneself (Mark 10:43–45; Luke 22:27), and it is also associated with the other traits cited here (e.g., work, love; cf. Heb 6:10; 1 Pet 4:8–10; cf. Gal 5:13; Phil 2:1–5). Finally, along with their persevering faith mentioned above, Christ commends them for their "endurance" (ὑπομονή), a quality mentioned at key points throughout Revelation in light of the opposition the readers were facing (Rev 1:9; 2:2–3; 13:10; 14:12).

In deliberate contrast to what was said to the Ephesian church, where some of these same commendations occur (2:2–3), Christ does not need to rebuke them for spiritual regression (2:4–5: "You abandoned the love you had at first. . . . Do the works you did at first"). Instead they are moving forward in Christian conduct (v. 19c): "Your last works are greater than the first,"[9] undeterred by adverse circumstances (cf. 2 Cor 10:15; Eph 4:15–16; Phil 1:25; Col 1:6, 10; 1 Tim 4:15; 2 Pet 3:18).

2:20 But I have against you that you tolerate the woman Jezebel, who claims she is a prophetess but teaches and misleads my servants to commit sexual immorality and eat meat offered to idols (ἀλλὰ ἔχω κατὰ σοῦ ὅτι ἀφεῖς τὴν γυναῖκα Ἰεζάβελ, ἡ λέγουσα ἑαυτὴν προφῆτιν καὶ διδάσκει καὶ πλανᾷ τοὺς ἐμοὺς δούλους πορνεῦσαι καὶ φαγεῖν εἰδωλόθυτα). Paradoxically, in light of v. 19 the church in Thyatira must be rebuked and warned (vv. 20–23) for failure to do what the Ephesian church had done (2:6, preventing false teaching in their midst). Despite their exemplary conduct in other ways (v. 19), Christ takes them to task[10] for

---

4. Koester, *Revelation*, 295–97; John E. Stambaugh, "Thyatira," *ABD* 6:546.

5. The Greek conjunction translated as "that is" (καί) here carries an explanatory, specifying sense (cf. BDAG 494; Aune, *Revelation 1–5*, 202).

6. Aune, *Revelation 1–5*, 202; Roloff, *Revelation*, 54; Sweet, *Revelation*, 94.

7. See BDAG 818–20, and passages listed above (also Heb 11:1, 13, 39).

8. See διακονία and cognate words in BDAG 229–31; A. Weiser, "διακονέω," *EDNT* 1:302–4.

9. The clause in v. 19c is a new sentence, but it continues Jesus's commendation given in v. 19a–b.

10. The words "but I have against you that" (ἀλλὰ ἔχω κατὰ σοῦ ὅτι) are exactly parallel to the opening words of 2:4 (see for comments; cf. also 2:14).

allowing ("you tolerate," ἀφεῖς; similar to vv. 14–15 but the opposite of vv. 2, 6) a certain false teacher to operate freely within their congregation (v. 20a). This person is a woman, well-known in the congregation,[11] to whom Christ assigns the symbolic name "Jezebel" (cf. other such names in 11:8; 17:5). This could hardly have been her personal name or one she would have welcomed. The title she did claim was that of "prophetess," a woman who speaks for God, but Christ implicitly rejects that label (see the similarity of v. 20b "who claims she is"[12] to vv. 2, 9; 3:9, 17).[13] "Jezebel," as with the name "Balaam" in v. 14, evokes the Old Testament typology of false prophecy again, not because the Old Testament Jezebel herself claimed a prophetic gift but because, along with her husband Ahab, she was a notorious influence on Israel toward idolatry, and she supported the prophets of Baal and Asherah while opposing God's true prophets including Elijah (1 Kgs 16:31–32; 18:4; 19:1–3; 21:17–26; 2 Kgs 9:7, 22).[14]

The evidence that this woman in Thyatira is not a true prophetess and instead is like Jezebel of old is that in her teaching[15] she "misleads my servants to commit sexual immorality and eat meat offered to idols" (v. 20c–d). Leading God's people astray

(πλανάω) is the work of the devil, the beast, and the false prophet in Revelation (cf. 12:9; 13:14; 18:23; 19:20; 20:3, 8, 10), especially in influencing them to offer worship to false gods. This is likewise the cardinal indicator of false prophecy in the Old Testament (Deut 13:5–8; Jer 23:13, 32; cf. Mark 13:22). Here we should understand that her impact on the church, Christ's "servants," was not extensive (note Christ's generous praise in v. 19 and see v. 24), but some smaller number had been affected. Her influence on Christians in Thyatira is probably not toward physical fornication[16] but spiritual infidelity: both phrases, "to commit sexual immorality and eat meat offered to idols" (v. 20d), seem to describe entanglement with idolatrous worship that constitutes disloyalty to the true God (see v. 21, which seems to summarize both as "her sexual immorality," τῆς πορνείας αὐτῆς). The same two items appear in vv. 14–15, but as argued there the Nicolaitans of Pergamum likewise advocated not sexual sin but spiritual disloyalty disguised as participation in certain rituals of their pagan culture.

A number of commentaries note the presence of trade guilds in Thyatira and suggest that their meetings and ceremonies or banquets would unavoidably have implicated Christian participants

---

11. She is referred to as *the woman* (τὴν γυναῖκα), i.e., one known to them. A textual variant (attested in A, 046, 1006, 1841, 1854) adds a genitive "your" (σου, a genitive of relationship, "your wife"). The phrase without σου has slightly better manuscript support (א, C, P, 2053, 2329, 2344), and the addition seems to have arisen from a sense on the part of later copyists that a "Jezebel" must have an "Ahab" to give her a base of authority and that the "angel" of the church was the local monarchical bishop (see 1:20; 2:1 for discussion).

12. The Greek participle behind this English phrase (ἡ λέγουσα) is a nominative in apposition to an accusative phrase "the woman Jezebel" (τὴν γυναῖκα Ἰεζάβελ). This does not follow normal Greek agreement, but it sometimes occurs and the sense is clear enough (cf. Phil 3:19; Zeph 1:12 LXX). This is corrected in some manuscripts to two versions of more standard wording, but the nominative is the harder reading and has superior textual support (א, A, C, 2053, 2329).

13. She is rejected as a true prophetess because of her

teaching and evil influence, not because of her gender. Women who exercised the true prophetic gift clearly served in OT Israel (Exod 15:20; Judg 4:4; 2 Kgs 22:14; Isa 8:3) and in the NT (Luke 2:36; Acts 2:17–18; 21:9; 1 Cor 11:5).

14. Hoskins, *Revelation*, 95, who also notes that Jezebel contributes to the portrait of Babylon as the great prostitute in Rev 17–18, both in killing God's prophets (1 Kgs 18:4; Rev 17:6; 18:24; 19:2) and in leading Israel into idolatry (1 Kgs 16:31–33; 21:25–26; Rev 17:1–5; 18:3; 19:2).

15. See the brief further glimpse into her "teaching" in v. 24.

16. Some argue that ancient pagan celebrations would inevitably bring temptations to sexual sin as well as idolatry (Smalley, *Revelation*, 73–74), but Rev does not otherwise take this up as a topic of needed exhortation. The main issue seems to be the more subtle entanglements with pagan society that Christ (through John) regarded as idolatrous but that this "Jezebel" advocated as a supposed prophetess of God. See Koester, *Revelation*, 288–89.

in worship dedicated to various local gods.[17] This is certainly true, but it should be expanded in two ways: such guilds existed not only in Thyatira but in all the cities addressed in Revelation 2–3, and similar issues faced Christians when they participated in various other civic and even family gatherings, not just in regard to trade guilds.[18] Questions of what constituted idolatry and thus should be avoided were more pervasive for Christians in the ancient Roman world, and it is likely that "Jezebel" and others were advocating not abandonment of Christianity altogether but compromise or syncretism, that is, idolatrous emperor worship along with the worship of Jesus. We cannot reconstruct enough of the details to judge where they should have drawn the lines, but Jesus (speaking through John) challenges the church in Thyatira to avoid the approach "Jezebel" was taking.

2:21 And I gave her time to repent, but she is not willing to repent of her sexual immorality (καὶ ἔδωκα αὐτῇ χρόνον ἵνα μετανοήσῃ, καὶ οὐ θέλει μετανοῆσαι ἐκ τῆς πορνείας αὐτῆς). Christ's message continues to fill out why he is against the church's toleration of this "Jezebel" (v. 20a) by describing her further response to his intervention in the past. He "gave her time to repent" (ἔδωκα αὐτῇ χρόνον ἵνα μετανοήσῃ),[19] acting most likely either through John or through the local leadership of the Thyatiran church to call her to change her sinful actions (see comments on "repent" at 2:5). The way Christ's intervention is described in vv. 21–23

(giving "time to repent" and pledging disciplinary judgment on her and others when there is no repentance) echoes the process of church discipline touched on in other parts of the New Testament. Action is taken in a step-by-step way, hopeful of and allowing time for a repentant response, but involving the wider congregation and escalating the consequences if sinful action persists (Matt 18:15–17). The goal of such action is the purity of the church as well as the restoration of the sinful church member (1 Cor 5:1–5, 11–13; Gal 6:1–2). The sinful person is treated as no longer part of the community, while still being appealed to as a brother or sister (2 Thess 3:6, 11–15). God's judgment on grave sin can extend to physical sickness or even death (Acts 5:1–11; 1 Cor 5:5; 11:31–34; see vv. 22–23 below).

Sadly, in this case "Jezebel" has shown, even up to the present, no willingness to change her ways (v. 21b).[20] She continues to be "not willing to repent" (the present tense of θέλει reflects her ongoing resistance to Christ's appeal to cease her evil influence).[21] As noted above, what she refuses to turn from is "her sexual immorality," a metaphorical summary of what the two verbs of v. 20d describe.[22] In leading others to spiritual infidelity, she is guilty of idolatrous "prostitution" herself. This wording is mirrored in the extended description of Babylon, "the great harlot" (14:8; 17:1–5; 18:3, 9), who causes the nations and their leaders to join in her idolatry.[23]

---

17. This is a theme that Ramsay, *Letters*, 324–30, and Hemer, *Letters*, 107–9, 120, 127–28, develop.

18. Koester, *Revelation*, 295–96; Thompson, *Revelation*, 152–54. Ramsay, *Letters*, 346–53, also cites this more pervasive influence, but not all commentators who refer to him include this point.

19. In the Greek expression, χρόνον ἵνα μετανοήσῃ, the ἵνα-clause does not show purpose but instead explains the temporal word, "time for repenting." See similar uses in John 12:23; 13:1; 16:2, 32; Rev 9:15.

20. The καί at the beginning of v. 21b adds a clause that is in contrast to v. 21a, so it is translated as "but" (BDAG 495; see 1:18; 2:13).

21. One important manuscript (A) uses an aorist here, "was [not] willing" (ἠθέλησεν), in parallel to the aorist of v. 21a ("I gave"), but this is likely to be a scribe's misreading of the past-present-future sequence of the actions of vv. 21–23.

22. See comments at v. 14 on the frequent OT imagery of idolatry as "sexual infidelity."

23. Bauckham, *Climax*, 377–78. See note on v. 20a above.

2:22 I tell you, I am going to throw her onto a sick-bed and those who commit adultery with her into great tribulation, unless they repent of her works (ἰδοὺ βάλλω αὐτὴν εἰς κλίνην καὶ τοὺς μοιχεύοντας μετ᾿ αὐτῆς εἰς θλῖψιν μεγάλην, ἐὰν μὴ μετανοήσωσιν ἐκ τῶν ἔργων αὐτῆς). The false prophetess in Thyatira has resisted Christ's call for repentance (v. 21), and so he declares his coming judgment on her and those she has influenced (vv. 22–23a). He begins with a rhetorical device to slow down the declaration and call special attention to it ("I tell you"; ἰδού, often translated "behold").[24] The judgment on her is physical sickness, intended to prompt repentance as mentioned above (cf. 1 Cor 5:5; 11:31–34). Being "thrown into a sickbed" (v. 22a) is an idiom for falling sick (a passive or intransitive),[25] but it is phrased here as an action Christ will do to her (to "strike her" with an illness).[26] Likewise those who share in her violations ("who commit adultery with her")[27] Christ will "throw . . . into great tribulation" (the main verb "I will throw" carries over to both objects: "her" and "those . . . with her"). In parallel with v. 22a ("a sickbed"), "great tribulation" (θλῖψιν μεγάλην) in v. 22b seems to carry the sense of "severe distress" (cf. θλῖψις μεγάλη in Acts 7:11 referring to famine and starvation in Joseph's time), that is, difficult physical suffering or need (cf. 2 Cor 6:4; 8:2; Phil 4:14; Jas 1:27). See additional comment in next paragraph. But just as "Jezebel" was offered a chance to repent (v. 21a; and there is still hope that

she will), so this judgment on her co-idolaters can be averted. Verse 22c expresses this possibility and reinforces her own culpability for their misdeeds: "Unless they repent of her works."

Unlike the reference in v. 22b ("great tribulation"), the phrases "great tribulation" (Matt 24:21) or "the great tribulation" (Rev 7:14) have a technical, eschatological sense drawn from Daniel 12:2 (a "time of trouble such as has never been" that will occur in the final days; cf. Rev 3:10: "Time of testing that will come upon the whole world"). "Great tribulation" in Acts 7:11 and here in Revelation 2:22 (as well as "tribulation" in Rev 1:9; 2:9–10) are related but not identical. They prefigure a pattern or typology of serious but lesser difficulties that will be replicated in the ultimate expression of the pattern in the final days.[28]

2:23 And I will kill her children with a deadly disease. Then all the churches will know that I am the one who searches minds and hearts, and I will give to each of you according to your works' (καὶ τὰ τέκνα αὐτῆς ἀποκτενῶ ἐν θανάτῳ. καὶ γνώσονται πᾶσαι αἱ ἐκκλησίαι ὅτι ἐγώ εἰμι ὁ ἐραυνῶν νεφροὺς καὶ καρδίας, καὶ δώσω ὑμῖν ἑκάστῳ κατὰ τὰ ἔργα ὑμῶν). This verse completes the declaration of future consequences for the sins of Thyatira's "Jezebel" (v. 23a) and adds a wider lesson for all the churches to learn from this (v. 23b–c). If there is no repentance on the part of "Jezebel" and her followers, Christ declares, "I will kill her children

---

24. See comment on 2:10.

25. The phrase occurs several times with a perfect passive of the verb denoting someone's current condition: "laid/lying on a (sick)bed" (Matt 9:2; Mark 7:30; cf. Matt 8:6, 14); but also with the verb *fall* on a (sick)bed (Jdt 8:3; 1 Macc 1:5) or an implied verb *be* on a (sick)bed (Ps 41:3 [40:4 LXX]).

26. BDAG 549. The word translated "sickbed" (κλίνη) is more commonly rendered "bed," and it could refer to a "reclining couch" used in the ancient world around a low dinner table for a formal meal (Esth 7:8; Ezek 23:41; Mark 7:4 [variant reading]) or it could be a metaphor for sexual relations (Prov 7:16; Song 1:16; Sir 23:18; similar to Heb 13:4 "let the [mar-

riage-]bed be kept pure," but a different word for bed, κοίτη occurs there). Neither of these fits as the primary reference in v. 22a, but because of the sexual imagery in vv. 20–22 there could be a play on "bed" in the latter sense: she will take to her sickbed because she defiled her spiritual bed (the principle of associative punishment: the penalty is exacted in close relation to how the violation was committed; cf. 16:2, 6; also Roloff, *Revelation*, 188).

27. See the next verse for how this group differs from "her children" in v. 23.

28. See Smalley, *Revelation*, 196, for a similar view, and see comments on 3:10.

with a deadly disease." This harsh consequence is clearly of a piece with the two judgments declared in v. 22: sickness and physical distress as the first stage of divine discipline intended to lead supposed Christians to repentance and renewed fidelity (see comments above). But it overtly states the fatal punishment that could eventuate for those who refuse to repent (cf. 1 Cor 11:31–34). To "kill . . . with a deadly disease" can be construed in two different senses, but both point to physical death inflicted as Christ's discipline for sin.[29]

Mention in vv. 22–23 of judgment on two groups of people in addition to the prophetess herself ("her co-adulterers" and "her children") leads to some uncertainty about who the actual referents are in Thyatira. Some suggest that the co-adulterers could be pagans in Thyatira with whom she associates in idolatrous ceremonies, while the children are fellow Christians who follow her in these sinful entanglements.[30] But if it is correct to connect these verses to the theme of church discipline as suggested above, pagan fellow-idolaters should not be in view (cf. 1 Cor 5:9–13). A better suggestion is that the mention of children who are put to death is added as an allusion from the Old Testament to the fate of Ahab's (and Jezebel's) sons who were slain as part of God's judgment on their parents (2 Kgs 9:7; 10:7), while still symbolizing this woman's spiritual followers (cf. 2 John 1, 4). The two metaphors (co-adulterers and children) then would simply be two

ways to picture the same group of Christians who were influenced by this "Jezebel" to engage in her idolatrous practices and, if unrepentant, will be caught up in her punishment as well.

In v. 23b–c, the address moves to the resulting lesson[31] that all the churches will learn about Christ and his judgment from this warning to "Jezebel" in Thyatira. The significance of the individual messages for "all the churches" (i.e., for the seven churches in Asia Minor as well as other congregations) is a theme repeated in the concluding section of each message (2:7, 11, 17, 29; 3:6, 13, 22; cf. 1:4; 22:16). But Christ's coming judgment on those who advocate or engage in idolatry calls for most careful attention. What the churches will understand as they reflect on this is that Christ will judge every person based on his searching knowledge of that person's inward motives and outward actions. The true righteousness of someone's conduct and intentions may not always be obvious, and "Jezebel's" authoritative persona had evidently overwhelmed the discernment of some in the church. But not Christ's. God's penetrating awareness of all human desires and affections is a common biblical affirmation (Ps 7:9; Prov 24:12; Jer 11:20; 17:10; 20:12–13; Acts 1:24; Rom 8:27; Heb 4:12–13; cf. 1 Cor 2:10 of the Spirit). Here the Son of God (v. 18b) claims that divine knowledge for himself (cf. John 2:24).[32] And so Christ will not be fooled or show favorites in his judgment (Rev 2:23c): "I will give to each of you according to your works,"[33] whether that

---

29. The phrase is literally "I will kill . . . by death" (ἀποκτενῶ ἐν θανάτῳ), but "by death" can be taken as a Semitic-style reinforcing phrase, "certainly kill, strike dead" (ESV, NIV, NRSV, RSV; cf. Exod 22:18 LXX) or as carrying a specialized sense for the word "death" (i.e., "pestilence, fatal illness"; BDAG 443; CSB, NASB; cf. Rev 6:4; 18:8; Num 14:36–38; Job 27:15; Jer 15:2; Ezek 33:27). The latter sense is much more likely here.

30. Boxall, *Revelation*, 65; Rowland, "Revelation," 581.

31. The "then" (καί) of v. 23b carries the sense of result: "and so" (see 5:4; 8:8; BDAG 495; Aune, *Revelation 1–5*, 198).

32. What Christ is said to search is human "minds and hearts" (νεφροὺς καὶ καρδίας; cf. CSB, NASB, NRSV), two terms

that appear together in several of the OT texts cited above. The translation "minds" is an attempt to put into English idiom the word νεφρός ("kidney"; cf. KJV "reins"), an internal organ used as a metaphor for one of the unseen parts of the human make-up that leads to outward actions (LN §26.11; H. Preisker, "νεφρός," *TDNT* 4:911.

33. The "you" that appears twice in these words (v. 23c) is second-person plural in each case, shifting from the singular "you" in vv. 19–20 (referring to the angel and the church seen together). The "you" plural continues in vv. 24–25 (twice in each verse), referring to individual church members as here.

judgment be the final assize (20:12; 22:12; cf. Matt 16:27; Rom 2:16) or his preliminary visitations that foreshadow it (Rev 2:5, 16; 3:3, 20). The prospect of facing his discerning and fully righteous judgment should prompt all humans to cry out for mercy and commit themselves to true obedience.

2:24–25 But I say to the rest of you in Thyatira who do not hold this teaching, who did not learn Satan's so-called deep secrets, 'I do not put any further burden on you. 25 Only hold fast to what you have until I come (ὑμῖν δὲ λέγω τοῖς λοιποῖς τοῖς ἐν Θυατείροις, ὅσοι οὐκ ἔχουσιν τὴν διδαχὴν ταύτην, οἵτινες οὐκ ἔγνωσαν τὰ βαθέα τοῦ Σατανᾶ ὡς λέγουσιν· οὐ βάλλω ἐφ' ὑμᾶς ἄλλο βάρος, 25 πλὴν ὃ ἔχετε κρατήσατε ἄχρι[ς] οὗ ἂν ἥξω). Moving from his rebuke for permitting "Jezebel" to gain a following in the church (vv. 20–23),[34] Christ now (v. 25) exhorts the Christians at Thyatira to hold firm to their spiritual progress mentioned in v. 19. But he prepares for this command by describing how the larger body of faithful Christians there had refused to be taken in by her influence (v. 24). He

addresses his words to "the rest of you in Thyatira,"[35] but the content of what he says to them is delayed until vv. 24d–25 (no "further burden.... Only hold fast"). The two intervening clauses that commend their resistance to "Jezebel" give us in a roundabout way a further glimpse into what she was espousing—which "the rest" had resisted. First there is the general point about their ongoing conviction, they "do not hold[36] this teaching" (cf. v. 20), and then more specifically they "did not learn[37] Satan's so-called deep secrets." The prophetess had purported[38] to offer insights into "secret" teachings, hidden from humans except through her divinely given utterances.[39] "Deep secrets" was her claim; Christ speaking through John adds the word "Satan's" to show the diabolical character of her teachings (cf. similar "editorial additions" in 2:9; 3:9).[40] That the larger group of Christians in Thyatira had seen this as well was certainly to be commended.

In vv. 24d–25 Christ declares to the faithful Christians in Thyatira what he had begun to say

---

34. The conjunction translated "but" (δέ) is not primarily a contrastive word in Greek, although that is often the best way to render it into English. It serves instead to signal an advance (either major or minor) in the flow of argument to a new line of thought. See Runge, *Discourse Grammar*, 28–36.

35. The phrase "the rest of you" does not imply a minority of the church members, but simply the ones not discussed in the preceding vv. 20–23 (BDAG 602; Swete, *Apocalypse*, 44; cf. 9:20; 19:21; 1 Thess 4:13). The "you" is a plural here and in vv. 24d, 25.

36. A customary present, denoting their characteristic conviction at the time of writing. To "hold" (ἔχουσιν) here means to possess a certain belief or religious stance (BDAG 420–21; cf. 6:9; 12:17; 19:10; 2 Tim 1:13). The stronger word that is sometimes used for this is κρατέω (Rev 2:14–15; cf. Mark 7:8; 2 Thess 2:15; Heb 4:14; see a related sense in Rev 2:25; cf. 2:13; 3:11).

37. This is an aorist of the verb "to know" (γινώσκω) with an ingressive sense: did not learn, realize, come to know.

38. The description of the "so-called" or "purported" (ὡς λέγουσιν) "deep secrets" refers to the false claims of "Jezebel" and her followers (see the use of λέγω in this sense in 2:2, 9, 20; 3:9, 17).

39. The phrase "deep secrets" renders the adjective βαθέα, "deep things." A related noun refers in 1 Cor 2:10 to profound truths about God revealed by the Spirit. See LN §28.76; A. Strobel, "βάθος," *EDNT* 1:190; and Job 12:22; Dan 2:22; Rom 11:33; also similar concepts in 1 En. 63:3; 65:6; 3 En. 11:1; T. Job 37:6. The gnostic teachers of the late second-century AD also claimed to teach "hidden" things (H. Schlier, "βάθος," *TDNT* 1:517), but as the preceding texts show, these concepts are not found only in Gnosticism. Fringe Jewish or Christian groups could claim exclusive access to divine revelation to lure followers.

40. It is not clear that there were ever gnostic groups who professed knowledge of satanic secrets without in any way sullying their spirituality, since according to Gnosticism every created thing and all worldly evil are illusory anyway. Such ideas like its supposed libertine sexual ethic could be simply accusations by patristic writers who distorted gnostic teachings in their refutations of them (Kurt Rudolph, "Gnosticism," *ABD* 2:1034). But it is unlikely that a group operating in some measure in a Christian church in late first-century AD would overtly claim such a satanic connection.

at the beginning of v. 24: he assigns to them no further responsibility in this regrettable "Jezebel" matter but wants them to focus on maintaining their godly conduct described already in v. 19. Putting no "further burden"[41] on them does not deny that they must take responsibility to ensure that she is not allowed to teach freely within their congregation—this is the point of v. 20, and Christ does not rescind that expectation. But the intervening verses were addressed largely to the prophetess and her followers, not to the Thyatiran faithful (vv. 21–23), and ultimately they cannot force the others to come to their senses. For their part what the faithful must be sure to do (v. 25)[42] is "hold fast[43] to what you have," a reference to their exemplary and flourishing conduct described in v. 19. The addition of "until I come" indicates both the challenging extent of Christian living (godly, fruitful conduct is our calling as long as life shall last) and the note of hope that is needed to carry on (one day, perhaps soon, our journey with Christ will be lifted to a glorious new level).

2:26–28 To the one who overcomes and keeps my works until the end I will give authority over the nations—27 and he will shepherd them with a rod of iron, as earthen pots are broken to pieces—28 just as I received authority from my Father. And I will give him the morning star (καὶ ὁ νικῶν καὶ ὁ τηρῶν ἄχρι τέλους τὰ ἔργα μου, δώσω αὐτῷ ἐξουσίαν ἐπὶ τῶν ἐθνῶν 27 καὶ ποιμανεῖ αὐτοὺς ἐν ῥάβδῳ σιδηρᾷ ὡς τὰ σκεύη τὰ κεραμικὰ συντρίβεται, 28 ὡς κἀγὼ εἴληφα παρὰ τοῦ πατρός μου, καὶ δώσω αὐτῷ τὸν ἀστέρα τὸν πρωϊνόν). The ending of the message to Thyatira (as in the remaining three messages in ch. 3) reverses the order of the two concluding elements compared to the three previous messages: the promise to the overcomer comes first (vv. 26–28) and then the command to hear (v. 29).[44] In addition, a further description of the overcomer is added here alone: "and keeps[45] my works until the end," a reinforcement of v. 25 (hold fast, until Christ comes, to the "works" praised in v. 19) and a clear contrast to "her works" (v. 22). What Christ promises to the faithful Christian[46] is a share in his rule over the whole world at the

---

41. It is possible that "burden" (βάρος) indicates an allusion to the wording of the apostolic decree of Acts 15:19–35; 21:25, since this word as well as the connective "only" (πλήν) occur together in Acts 15:28 and two of the requirements there pertain to "meat offered to idols" and "sexual immorality" as here in Rev 2:14, 20. Such an allusion would add to the credibility of what is said here, since it evokes the wider church policy on these matters. On the other hand, this choice of words might simply flow from what needs to be said on this occasion (the two repeated words are common enough in occurrence) and from OT language for confronting idolatry. In addition, the prohibition in Acts concerning "sexual immorality" may have a narrower sense ("incest"); see Eckhard J. Schnabel, *Acts*, ZECNT (Grand Rapids: Zondervan, 2012), 645–46.

42. The connective "only," πλήν, is used for "breaking off a discussion and emphasizing what is important" (BDAG 826; cf. BDF §449.2).

43. The imperative "hold fast" (κρατήσατε) is aorist, not to refer to a "single decisive effort" (Swete, *Apocalypse*, 45) but to communicate an urgent command that views the action in summary and so envisions carrying it through to its accomplishment (not just to work at this but to carry it out). See BDF

§337; Fanning, *Verbal Aspect*, 369–70; Smalley, *Revelation*, 77; see comments on 2:5.

44. This shift structures the seven messages in a "3 + 4" sequence as compared to the "4 + 3" arrangement of the seals, trumpets, and bowls that will follow in chs. 6–16. Perhaps this subtle change adds to an intended distinction between the seven messages and the threefold series of seven judgments (Bauckham, *Climax*, 9–10).

45. The verb "keep" (τηρέω) means "persist in obedience [to], observe, fulfill" (BDAG 1002), and it usually takes an object like "words" (3:8, 10; 22:7), "what is written" (1:3), "what you received and heard" (3:3), or "commands" (12:17; 14:12; frequently in Gospel of John). This use is a slight extension of the sense: "keep the works [that I have commanded]."

46. See comments on "the overcomer" at 2:7. In this verse (and in 3:12, 21; cf. John 7:38) reference to the overcomer occurs in a nominative phrase initially (ὁ νικῶν καὶ ὁ τηρῶν), but this construction is not carried through to the end of the sentence (a pendent nominative, a type of anacoluthon; BDF §466.4; Zerwick, *Biblical Greek*, 9). Instead here and in 3:21 the overcomer is included again in the main clause as a dative pronoun αὐτῷ (not translated above).

dawning of God's coming renewal of all creation (v. 26b).[47] This is expressed initially as "authority over the nations" (ἐξουσίαν ἐπὶ τῶν ἐθνῶν). The prospect that God's people will reign (βασιλεύω) with Christ over the nations of the world appears also in Revelation 5:10; 20:4, 6; 22:5—in fact, they already represent his rule in a preliminary form in the present (1:6; 5:10), and this will be brought to its consummation in the future. This expectation of sharing divine rule over the whole world is rooted in the vision of Daniel 7:9–14,[48] in which "one like a son of man" appears before the Ancient of Days and receives rule (βασιλεία) and everlasting authority (ἐξουσία) over all the nations of the earth. The further explanation in Daniel 7:18, 22 is that "the saints of the Most High" are given dominion (βασιλεία, βασίλειον) that replaces the evil world empires previously described. This came to be understood in early Christianity as a reference to God's future rule through his Messiah and his redeemed people (Matt 19:28; 1 Cor 6:2–3; 2 Tim 2:12; Heb 2:5–9; see also Wis 3:7–8).

The allusion to Daniel 7 is expanded in Revelation 2:27 with a parenthetical[49] quotation of Psalm 2:9 (cf. allusions also in Rev 12:5; 19:15). Psalm 2 speaks of the rule of God's "anointed" (v. 2), who is also his "king on Zion" and "son" (vv. 6–7),[50] to whom God will grant dominion over "the nations" and "the ends of the earth" (v. 8). God's pledge to the son in Psalm 2:9 is transferred here to the over-comer: "He will shepherd them with a rod of iron, as earthen pots are broken to pieces." These harsh statements reflect the atmosphere of Psalm 2 that portrays the kings of the earth in arrogant rebellion against God, a context that is not foreign to the situation in Revelation. Such haughty defiance of God's sovereignty is futile (in Psalm 2:4 God derides their feeble resistance), and the wording of Psalm 2:9 vividly pictures how decisively his rule will be established over them: they will be summarily crushed (cf. Rev 19:19–21; see too 2 Thess 2:8).[51] In the Hebrew text of Psalm 2:9, both verbs, translated here as "shepherd" (רעע) and "broken to pieces" (נפץ), carry the sense of "break, shatter," and the "rod of iron" denotes a ruler's scepter. But the LXX translates the first verb as "shepherd" (ποιμαίνω; this is preserved in the three citations in Rev: 2:27; 12:5; 19:15), since the Hebrew lettering can be construed either as "shatter" (רעע) or as "shepherd" (רעה). To care for his flock, the shepherd must at times act harshly toward threats to its safety, and this sense fits quite well in the contexts of Psalm 2 as well as Revelation.[52] Suggestion of God's renewing work that follows his judgment of evil will come in Revelation 2:28b.

Following the quotation, v. 28a resumes the basic declaration started in v. 26b. The derived authority Christ will grant to the overcomer is associated with the supreme authority granted to Christ already: "Just as I received[53] authority from my Father."

---

47. The two parallel promises to the overcomer are "I will give authority" (v. 26b) and "I will give him the morning star" (v. 28b).

48. See further discussion at Rev 1:6–7; 5:9–10.

49. The words from the psalm enrich but also interrupt the larger sentence of vv. 26b–28: "I will give him authority . . . as I received authority."

50. The title "son" in the immediate context of Ps 2:6–7 referred to the human Davidic king installed as the representative of God's rule on earth, and so metaphorically he could be called God's son. The NT picks up the title "son" from Ps 2:6–7 as a pattern or type that finds its escalated fulfillment in Christ's res-urrection and exaltation as the one who comes to share God's rule because he shares God's essence (Acts 13:33; Heb 1:5; 5:5). See Buist M. Fanning, "Hebrews," in *Biblical Theology of the New Testament*, ed. Roy B. Zuck and Darrell L. Bock (Chicago: Moody, 1994), 384–88.

51. Imagery from Ps 2 appears also in wider Jewish messianic expectation: 1 En. 90:18; Pss. Sol. 17:21–25; 18:5–7; Sib. Or. 8:248.

52. Beale and McDonough, "Revelation," 1095.

53. The verb "I received" (εἴληφα) is a Greek perfect tense, but it probably carries an aoristic sense rather than a true perfect idea. It refers in summary to Christ's reception of authority at his exaltation. See discussion of aoristic perfects at Rev 5:7.

In his resurrection and exaltation, Christ has already been installed in the position of greatest authority in God's presence in heaven,[54] now awaiting the full establishment of that authority on earth at his second coming (Rev 19:11–21). The governing role that the saints will exercise in that future realm will take place only because of their relationship to Christ who will wield his scepter as "King of kings and Lord of lords" (19:15–19).

The second promise to the overcomer (parallel to v. 26b, "I will give authority") is "I will give him the morning star" (δώσω αὐτῷ τὸν ἀστέρα τὸν πρωϊνόν; v. 28b). Revelation 22:16 tells us that Christ himself is "the bright morning star" (ὁ ἀστὴρ ὁ λαμπρὸς ὁ πρωϊνός),[55] but this image ties into the larger cluster of messianic expectations surfaced in the previous allusions to Daniel 7:9–22, Zechariah 12:10, and Psalm 2:9 (in Rev 1:7; 2:26b–27).

These texts lead also to Genesis 49:10, Numbers 24:17, and Isaiah 11:4, which share the reference to the Messiah's "scepter" (Heb שֵׁבֶט) of judgment but also assert his rising like a morning "star" (ἀστήρ) to draw the nations to the dawn of God's full salvation (Gen 49:10; Num 24:17; Ps 2:8; Isa 11:9–10; cf. Isa 60:1–3; 2 Pet 1:19).[56] Given this background of thought, to "give him [the overcomer] the morning star" is a promise that the faithful Christian will share in God's complete redemption represented even now in Christ who is "the bright morning star" (22:16), whose appearance presages the full light of day.[57]

2:29 Anyone who has an ear must listen to what the Spirit says to the churches'" (ὁ ἔχων οὖς ἀκουσάτω τί τὸ πνεῦμα λέγει ταῖς ἐκκλησίαις). For this command to hear, see comments on v. 7a (identical in wording to v. 29).

Theology in Application

Shepherds and Wolves

Toleration of false teaching in a church reveals the church leaders' dereliction of duty toward those entrusted to their spiritual care. Those who shepherd a flock of God's people must protect them from the wolves of doctrinal and behavioral error (Acts 20:28–32; 1 Tim 1:3–7; Titus 1:9).[58] Why is this so rare in many churches? We have all too often imbibed the relativism and pluralism of the wider culture. We grasp at straws to justify doing nothing: "Well at least it's meeting a need for some people." "He has a lot of influence in the community and he's a big giver, so how can we ask him not to teach?" "Give them time and they'll come around." "Our church has a big tent." "Who are we to judge?" Yet our desire to avoid controversy or unpleasantness ends up causing real harm to vulnerable people. It is not "showing Christian love" to

---

54. See Acts 2; Eph 1; Heb 1–2; as well as Rev 5 for the acclamation of Christ's authority due to his death, resurrection, and exaltation.

55. The "morning star" is a reference to Venus, the bright planet that signals the coming of day even when nighttime persists a while longer (BDAG 145, 892).

56. Bauckham, *Climax*, 322–26; Beale and McDonough, "Revelation," 1096.

57. There may also be a note, as with the promise of authority (vv. 26b–28a), that just as Christ is the bright morning star, so his people will shine now and forever as testimonies to God's glorious mercy (Dan 12:3; Phil 2:15; see also Sir 50:6–7; 1 En. 14:2; 4 Ezra 7:97).

58. For wise and biblical advice about why and how to practice church discipline, see Mark Dever, *Nine Marks of a Healthy Church*, 3rd ed. (Wheaton: Crossway, 2013), 181–205, 263–67.

permit such damage. Church members for their part should appreciate leaders who take this responsibility seriously and carry it out in a gentle but firm way (2 Tim 2:23–26). Jesus the Good Shepherd makes clear that any attempt to lead his sheep astray will provoke a strong, protective response from him (Rev 2:21–23; see also Luke 17:1–4).

The Glory of Everyday Faithfulness

In our world of short attention spans and fascination with celebrities, it seems so pedestrian to ask for solid continuity and steady progress. How unglamorous! Yet this is what Jesus acclaims in this church: they have held fast to God's ways and continued to grow and advance in Christian character (love, faith, service, endurance, maturity). They were not taken in by Jezebel's esoteric teachings ("deep things") that really came from Satan himself. Our world's penchant for what is fresh and new, "the latest thing," can be a trap for the unsuspecting. Amid unprecedented change and turmoil all around us, we need to see the value of spiritual continuity and fidelity, the old pathways of following Jesus in enduring faith and sacrificial service. We will be surprised by how fresh and new such a walk with him will turn out to be even in this world! And as vv. 26–27 show, such faithful followers are the ones who will someday share his rule in the future kingdom: "If we endure, we will also reign with him" (2 Tim 2:12). Nothing pedestrian about that.

Revelation 3:1–6

Literary Context

See the connections discussed under "Literary Context" for 2:1–7 in chapter 3, page 110.

Main Idea

Jesus rebukes most of the church in Sardis for their spiritual lethargy and commands them to wake up or face his judgment, but the faithful few among them will experience holiness with him forever.

Translation

(See page 160.)

Revelation 3:1–6

1a	Command	**And to the angel of the church in Sardis write:**
b	Speaker	*"The one …*
		who has the seven spirits of God and
		the seven stars
		… says this:
c	Rebuke	*'I know your works,*
d		*that you have a reputation of being alive, but*
e		*you are dead.*
2a	Exhortation	*Wake up and*
b	Exhortation	*strengthen the things that remain, that were about to die,*
c	Basis	*for I have not found your works adequate before my God.*
3a	Exhortation	*So remember what you received and heard and*
b		*keep it and repent.*
c	Condition	*So*
		if you do not wake up,
d	Warning	*I will come as a thief, and*
e		*you will not at all know the hour when I will come against you.*
4a	Reassurance	*But you have a few individuals in Sardis who have not defiled their garments, and*
b		*they will walk with me in white,*
c		*for they are worthy.*
5a	Promise	*The one who overcomes will be clothed like them in white garments, and*
b		*I will never erase his name from the book of life, and*
c		*I will confess his name before my Father and*
		before his angels.
6	Command	*Anyone who has an ear must listen to what the Spirit says to the churches.'"*

Structure

See 2:1–7 for discussion of the four-part structure common to all the messages. The message to the church in Sardis is almost entirely negative, and this seems to cause departure from the general structure. The church's deplorable spiritual condition is presented in vv. 1c–2 with fierce irony, prompting several imperatives prior to the actual exhortation section. The exhortation itself begins with "so" (οὖν) as is common and includes several further demands for action, yet also includes a reassuring promise about future blessing (vv. 3–4) that is normally included later in other messages. In the conclusion (vv. 5–6) the promise to the overcomer continues with the theme of blessing as well as further assurance for the minority in Sardis who prove faithful.

Exegetical Outline

II. **First Vision: The Exalted Christ and His Messages to the Churches (1:9–3:22)**

A. Vision of the Exalted Christ (1:9–20)

B. Messages to the Seven Churches (2:1–3:22)

   1. To the Church in Ephesus (2:1–7)

   2. To the Church in Smyrna (2:8–11)

   3. To the Church in Pergamum (2:12–17)

   4. To the Church in Thyatira (2:18–29)

➡   **5. To the Church in Sardis (3:1–6)**

     a. Introduction (3:1a–b)

      (1) Address and command to write (3:1a)

      (2) Description of Christ who is speaking (3:1b)

     b. Knowledge of the church's condition (3:1c–2)

      (1) Reputation versus reality (3:1c–e)

      (2) Stir up and build up what remains (3:2)

     c. Exhortation and reassurance (3:3–4)

      (1) Remember and repent or be judged (3:3)

      (2) Assurance for a faithful few (3:4)

     d. Conclusion (3:5–6)

      (1) Promise to the overcomer (3:5)

      (2) Command to hear the Spirit's message (3:6)

Explanation of the Text

3:1a–b And to the angel of the church in Sardis write: "The one who has the seven spirits of God and the seven stars says this (Καὶ τῷ ἀγγέλῳ τῆς ἐν Σάρδεσιν ἐκκλησίας γράψον· Τάδε λέγει ὁ ἔχων τὰ ἑπτὰ πνεύματα τοῦ θεοῦ καὶ τοὺς ἑπτὰ ἀστέρας). The formula of address for this letter (v. 1a) is identical to 2:8a except for the changed place name. See commentary on 2:1, 8a for shared expressions. The description of Christ who speaks (v. 1b) comes from the vision of 1:16, 20 ("who has . . . the seven stars"; cf. also 2:1) but also from 1:4 ("the seven

spirits of God"). The Trinitarian motif in 1:4–5 shows that "seven spirits" is a figurative way to describe the Holy Spirit in his fullness (in an allusion to Isa 11:2 and Zech 4:6, 10).[1] To say that Christ "has" or possesses the Spirit is the common idiom for the Spirit's empowering presence and activity in someone's life (Rom 8:9; 1 Cor 6:19; 7:40; 2 Cor 4:13; Jude 19). To add "and the seven stars" shows that his authority over the angels of the churches (see 1:20; 2:1) is infused with the Spirit's full power as he oversees and exhorts the churches through

---

1. See discussion at 1:4; 4:5; and 5:6; also Steve Moyise, *The Later New Testament Writings and Scripture: The Old Testament in Acts, Hebrews, the Catholic Epistles and Revelation*

(Grand Rapids: Baker Academic, 2012), 113–14; Prigent, *Apocalypse*, 192.

these angelic mediators.[2] This is quite relevant in the call for revival of true spiritual vitality and holiness in the message that follows (vv. 1b–2, 4).

Sardis was a historically significant city located to the southeast of Thyatira and about 50 miles east of Smyrna. It was on the Persian "royal road" that ran between Smyrna and eastern parts of Anatolia all the way to Susa in Persia (Herodotus, *Hist.* 5.52–54). It was the ancient capital of the kingdom of Lydia (from the seventh to the sixth century BC) and then was conquered by the Persians and subsequently fought over in its battles with Greek forces around 500 BC. It was later controlled by the Seleucids (as their provincial capital) and then by the Attalids (from Pergamum) until the Romans established direct rule over all of Asia Minor around 130 BC. Because of its strategic location it continued to flourish as an important inland trade center, and after a devastating earthquake in AD 17, Tiberias provided help with its reconstruction (Tacitus, *Ann.* 2.47). This led to many new structures as well as rebuilding of existing ones, and the city in turn expressed its gratitude by dedicating a local cult to Tiberias.[3] It previously had a temple to Augustus and a cult to Roma as well as a huge temple to Artemis and Zeus. A variety of other Greco-Roman and eastern deities were honored in the city as well. Like the other cities of Revelation 2–3, Sardis had numerous trade and cultic associations whose members participated in various ways in the civic and religious life of the city. At a later date (third century AD) one of the more prominent buildings in the center of town was a large Jewish synagogue, and this most likely reflects a sizable and influential Jewish community even in the late first century.[4]

3:1c–2 'I know your works, that you have a reputation of being alive, but you are dead. 2 Wake up and strengthen the things that remain, that were about to die, for I have not found your works adequate before my God (Οἶδά σου τὰ ἔργα ὅτι ὄνομα ἔχεις ὅτι ζῇς, καὶ νεκρὸς εἶ. 2 γίνου γρηγορῶν καὶ στήρισον τὰ λοιπὰ ἃ ἔμελλον ἀποθανεῖν, οὐ γὰρ εὕρηκά σου [τὰ] ἔργα πεπληρωμένα ἐνώπιον τοῦ θεοῦ μου). The description of the church's condition begins, as frequently in these messages, with a reference to their conduct ("your works," in the general sense of "behavior, characteristic actions," usually commendable; cf. 2:2, 19; 3:8), but it takes an ironic twist in the clause that follows.[5] Instead of praise we find biting censure: "You have a reputation of being alive, but you are dead" (v. 1d–e). The lofty opinion they had of themselves—and assumed that others shared[6]—is summarily contradicted by Christ.[7] They were purportedly spiritually healthy and vigorous ("alive"), but[8] in reality they had no life from God, as genuine Christians have (John 3:36; 5:24; 6:53; 20:21); they were "dead"

---

2. Because the "spirits" and the "stars" (i.e., angels) are mentioned together in v. 1b, several commentators understand the "seven spirits of God" as the seven angels or archangels standing before God in 8:2, 6 (possibly also sent out by him in 5:6), who are either identical to the angels of the churches ("and," καί, is taken as explanatory; Aune, *Revelation 1–5*, 219) or rule over them in their work (Roloff, *Revelation*, 58). But this misses the influence of Isa 11 and Zech 4 in John's thought, as mentioned above.

3. Smyrna instead of Sardis was chosen by Rome as the location for a provincial temple to show Asia's gratitude to Tiberias (built in AD 26). See Tacitus, *Ann.* 4.55–56; *Brill's New Pauly* 12:991.

4. J. A. Harrill, "Asia Minor," *DNTB* 132; Koester, *Revelation*, 309–12; John Griffiths Pedley, "Sardis," *ABD* 5:983–84.

5. The "that" (ὅτι) clause is explanatory of the "works," as in 3:15, which also expresses criticism of the church's conduct.

6. "Reputation" (ὄνομα, commonly "name") here denotes what they were known for or how they regarded themselves (BDAG 714; LN §3.265; cf. Gen 11:4; Deut 22:14; Mark 6:14).

7. See his response to a similar self-delusion by the Laodiceans in 3:17.

8. The conjunction "but" is not the normal translation for καί, but here it is contrastive; cf. Aune, *Revelation 1–5*, 215.

(cf. Eph 2:1–2). As Christ assessed their conduct, he saw mainly[9] empty claims to Christian commitment without the fruit of transformed lives to confirm its inward reality (Rev 3:2b; cf. John 14:21, 23; Eph 2:10; Jas 2:14, 20; 1 John 2:3–6, 29; 3:9–10). They were Christian in name only. This is the start of a wordplay using "name" as a theme in this letter (ὄνομα is used 4x in Rev 3:1–6). The occurrence in v. 1b ("reputation") departs from the almost uniform biblical usage that "name" reflects the reality of the person, but later uses return to that pattern.

This bleak assessment triggers an immediate call to remedy the situation before a further note about their condition to round out this section of the message (v. 2). The first remedy is to "wake up" from their lethargy and self-deception (v. 2a).[10] This summons to moral and spiritual alertness mirrors Jesus's teaching (Matt 24:42–44; Mark 13:34–36; Luke 12:37–40) as well warnings in the rest of the New Testament (1 Cor 16:13; 1 Thess 5:6; 1 Pet 5:8), especially about his imminent coming.[11] Secondly, in a note of hope Christ calls them to "strengthen the things that remain" (v. 2b). What is weak or dying out among their congregation in Sardis needs to be reinforced and sustained.[12] Many commentators understand these "things that remain" to refer to people in the church despite its neuter gender in Greek (τὰ λοιπά).[13] This is possible grammatically and fits better with the next clause ("about to die"), but none of the references to the "remaining people" in Revelation are neuter, and in this context Christ's attention is on their conduct (neuter "works" in vv. 1c, 2c) and what they received and heard and must keep (v. 3a–b). The "things that remain" are the vestiges of godly conduct, weak as they have been,[14] that still exist in a congregation that is largely dead (v. 1e). The path forward for this church is to cultivate such signs of genuine life (vv. 3a, 4) and challenge the deadly status quo (v. 3b).

The reason ("for," γάρ) they must wake up and strengthen any remaining traces of life is that according to Christ's assessment[15] their present spiritual condition falls far short in God's view, however satisfactory it may be in their self-estimation (v. 1d). God's evaluation is that their "works" (i.e., conduct

---

9. There were in fact traces of real life among some in the congregation at Sardis (cf. vv. 3a, 4).

10. The translation "wake up" (most modern English versions) comes from a Greek expanded verb phrase, γίνου γρηγορῶν, an unusual periphrastic expression using a form of the verb "become" (γίνομαι) instead of the normal "be" (εἰμί), plus a present participle (cf. BDF §98.1; 354.1; Fanning, *Verbal Aspect*, 310, 312). This strengthens the expression compared to the nonperiphrastic verb. In addition, γίνομαι carries its normal sense of "become, come to be" (cf. 2:10), emphasizing the necessary transformation from their current condition. See Matthew Black, *An Aramaic Approach to the Gospels and Acts*, 3rd ed. (Oxford: Clarendon, 1967), 130; contra Turner, *Style*, 155.

11. This "wakefulness" (γρηγορέω) implies not watching for eschatological signs but staying alert morally and spiritually, a readiness to welcome the master's coming because of a life of purity and obedience (cf. vv. 2b–3a; 16:15).

12. The word translated "strengthened" (στηρίζω) is used in the NT for spiritual fortitude ("establish firmly") as in Luke 22:32; Rom 1:11 (especially in view of persecution or judgment to come: 1 Thess 3:2, 13; Jas 5:8; 1 Pet 5:10; see G. Schneider, "στηρίζω," *EDNT* 3:276).

13. Smalley, *Revelation*, 81; Swete, *Apocalypse*, 48; Thomas, *Revelation 1–7*, 249, take it to refer to personal or impersonal features of church life—whatever needs reviving in the church's service for God.

14. The main verb in "were about to die" (ἔμελλον ἀποθανεῖν) is imperfect tense, denoting past occurrence (as in ASV, NASB, NET) but in this case one that continued in the past and up to the present moment (Burton, *Moods and Tenses*, 13–14; cf. Luke 2:49; Rom 15:22; 1 John 2:7). Most English translations render this as a simple present (CSB, ESV, KJV, NIV, NRSV, RSV), perhaps as an epistolary imperfect (cf. Charles, *Revelation*, 1:79; Smalley, *Revelation*, 81), but this is attested nowhere else in NT Greek.

15. "I have not found" (εὕρηκα), using a perfect tense, denotes the present (negative) verdict resulting from his evaluation of their conduct (see BDAG 412; cf. John 18:38; 19:4, 6; Acts 13:28; 23:9; 24:20; 2 Pet 3:10 for εὑρίσκω as a metaphor for judicial decisions).

in general; cf. 2:2; 3:1c) are not adequate, that is, "fulfilled" (πεπληρωμένα) or accomplished to a degree reflective of genuine Christian life.[16] The rest of the New Testament warns of the absence of conduct that confirms a claim of genuine life from God (e.g., Matt 7:21–23; Jas 2:14; 1 John 3:17–19; 4:20). Faith is what overcomes, but genuine faith is seen in behavior that shows forth the new life that is within.

3:3–4 So remember what you received and heard and keep it and repent. So if you do not wake up, I will come as a thief, and you will not at all know the hour when I will come against you. 4 But you have a few individuals in Sardis who have not defiled their garments, and they will walk with me in white, for they are worthy (μνημόνευε οὖν πῶς εἴληφας καὶ ἤκουσας καὶ τήρει καὶ μετανόησον. ἐὰν οὖν μὴ γρηγορήσῃς, ἥξω ὡς κλέπτης, καὶ οὐ μὴ γνῷς ποίαν ὥραν ἥξω ἐπὶ σέ. 4 ἀλλὰ ἔχεις ὀλίγα ὀνόματα ἐν Σάρδεσιν ἃ οὐκ ἐμόλυναν τὰ ἱμάτια αὐτῶν, καὶ περιπατήσουσιν μετ᾽ ἐμοῦ ἐν λευκοῖς, ὅτι ἄξιοί εἰσιν). After laying out their grim condition (vv. 1c–2), Christ draws the positive inference from it ("so," οὖν) in the three commands that follow in the exhortation section (vv. 3–4).[17] The pathway to renewal begins with recalling how they became

a Christian community in the first place: "Remember what[18] you received and heard" (v. 3a). What they should recall is the gospel proclaimed to them (they "heard"[19] it), which at least some of them "received" in faith.[20] In this verse "receive" (λαμβάνω) does not refer directly to accepting Christian tradition passed down from others (cf. παραλαμβάνω in 1 Cor 11:23; 15:1; 1 Thess 4:1).[21] Instead it means acknowledging in faith the proclamation about God's salvation in Christ (e.g., Matt 13:20; Mark 4:16; John 12:48; 17:8), which is closely related to accepting Christ and his authority by faith (John 1:12; 5:43; 13:20). The second command (v. 3b) is to "keep" (τήρει, i.e., obey, fulfill) that message they received and heard.[22] This is where they are currently failing to follow through with the Christian beginning they previously seemed to have made. To "hear and keep" is a sequence found earlier in 1:3, and it brings with it the expectation of consistent obedience to the implications of what is heard (e.g., conduct commanded by Christ as in 2:26).[23] This puts the focus again on their conduct—active deeds of real Christian obedience that Christ has said was lacking among them (v. 1c, 2c). The third command (also v. 3b) summarizes the previous two: "repent" (i.e., change their ways, return to godly conduct;

---

16. The sense of this perfect participle of πληρόω is similar to the frequent use in John's Gospel and Epistles of Christian joy brought to its full measure (e.g., John 15:11; 17:13; 1 John 1:4), but it shades over also into the idea of completion or accomplishment (i.e., something actually done or carried out faithfully) as in Acts 12:25; 2 Cor 10:6; cf. related adjective in 2 John 8.

17. The exhortation of 2:5 is very similar (also "so remember"), but in that case the backward look was negative ("how far you have fallen"), while here it is positive.

18. This is literally "how" (πῶς) introducing an indirect question (cf. 2:5 "how far," πόθεν), but in NT Greek πῶς often shades over into "that" or "what," i.e., not manner but fact or content. See BDAG 901; Beckwith, *Apocalypse*, 474; Smalley, *Revelation*, 82.

19. The two actions are cited in v. 3 in reverse order, but this is common in Rev (cf. 3:17; 4:11; 6:4; 10:9; 20:4; 22:14).

The second event (here "receiving") in actual sequence is put first in textual order to show its importance (Beckwith, *Apocalypse*, 243–44; Aune, *Revelation 1–5*, 221; Resseguie, *Narrative Commentary*, 51); "heard" refers to listening to a proclamation of the gospel message (Mark 4:15–20; John 5:24; Acts 4:4; 15:7; Rom 10:14; Eph 1:13; Col 1:23).

20. The verb "received" (εἴληφας) is an aoristic perfect (see Zerwick, *Biblical Greek*, 97–98, and note on 5:7).

21. This is the view of Koester, *Revelation*, 313; Osborne, *Revelation*, 176.

22. The Greek verb "keep" has no explicit object, but clearly implies keeping the thing just referred to (what was received and heard). Greek readily omits nonemphatic pronoun objects that are easily supplied from the context, but English idiom requires them (e.g., Mark 12:15–16; John 2:8).

23. See comments on 1:3 and 2:26.

cf. 2:5, 16, 21–22; 3:19). This comes last, apparently to capture in a sharp summary[24] what is called for in the other two commands. Reversal of their current moral and spiritual trajectory is urgently required.

Verse 3c–e reinforces this urgent necessity of correcting their lifeless ways by resuming the reference to spiritual alertness ("wake up") from v. 2a.[25] If they fail to prepare themselves[26] in character and obedience (see comments on v. 2a), he will come against them with no prior notice.[27] Several of the other New Testament texts that call for such alertness (cited at v. 2a) also use the image of "coming as a thief" (16:15; Matt 24:43–44; Luke 12:39–40; 1 Thess 5:2, 4; 2 Pet 3:10–12). The point of the simile is certainly that the coming is unexpected—this is reinforced in v. 3e: they cannot know when he will come. But the second point is that a thief's coming is a hostile, unwelcome thing (v. 3e: "against you"), one that a person should prepare for and prevent if possible. The Christians in Sardis must take heed and prepare themselves spiritually so that Christ's coming will not have that hostile character for them.[28]

After a sharp challenge (v. 3) this exhortation section moves to reassurance (as in 2:5–6). The situation in the church at Sardis is largely dark (v. 1c–e), but it contains "a few individuals" (ὀλίγα ὀνόματα) whose lifestyle has not betrayed their Christian profession (v. 4a). The contrast between the collective whole[29] and a small number of godly Christians viewed according to their particular character is carried by the word "name(s)" used to denote individual people.[30] Their conduct has not sullied[31] the purity and godliness given to them by Christ's redemptive work (symbolized by "their garments" that he provided for them and washed or made white paradoxically in his sacrificial blood).[32] As encouragement to this faithful group and an indirect appeal to the larger congregation, Christ describes the exalted prospect in store for them: "And they will walk with me in white" (v. 4b). The image of "walking with"[33] Christ while clothed "in white" is a picture of the direct divine communion that his people will enjoy in the new creation and new Jerusalem, when God will dwell among them as their God (21:3) and the redeemed from all nations "will walk" in the light of God and of the Lamb (21:24). This unparalleled blessing is grounded[34] in their worthiness to receive it (v. 4c). As John's conclusion reveals, all the evil and impure will be excluded (21:8; 22:15). However, this is not a merit of their own but is one granted to them freely

---

24. The imperative "repent" (μετανόησον) is an urgent command in the aorist tense. The previous two imperatives of v. 3 were customary presents.

25. In v. 3c the "so" (οὖν) does not draw a conclusion (as in v. 3a) but resumes the earlier line of thought from v. 2a (for this sense, see 1:19; also BDAG 736; Runge, *Discourse Grammar*, 44–45; Smalley, *Revelation*, 82–83; Swete, *Apocalypse*, 50).

26. The aorist subjunctive in "you do not wake up" (γρηγορήσῃς) is ingressive (i.e., become alert).

27. The verb phrase "you will not at all know" uses the double negation, οὐ μή (16x in Rev), strongly denying this future possibility (Zerwick, *Biblical Greek*, 149–50).

28. See discussion of Jesus's coming in judgment in Rev 2:5 (cf. also 2:16).

29. The contrast reflects a conscious play on the word "name," ὄνομα, which means "(false) reputation" in v. 1c and "individual person" (i.e., one's personal name as truly capturing

his or her particular character and identity as a person) in v. 4a.

30. BDAG 714; and LN §9.19. This is clearly attested but not frequent: Num 1:2, 18, 20; Acts 1:15; Rev 11:13. For uses in Greek papyri, see *NewDocs* 2:113; 4:58.

31. The word "defile" (μολύνω) means to make dirty, pollute, or stain; it is used of ritual (Rev 14:4) or moral impurity (1 Cor 8:7).

32. Roloff, *Revelation*, 58, 90. Clothing imagery in Rev is expressed by a variety of words including "garment" (ἱμάτιον), "clothed" (περιβάλλω), and "white" (λευκός) as in vv. 4–5. See 3:18; 6:11; 7:9, 13–14; 19:7–8, 13; 22:14.

33. "Walking" is of course a common biblical metaphor for living one's life in general, but in some places it implies a closer intimacy or deeper sharing of life together (e.g., 2:1; see too Gen 5:22, 24; 6:9; 17:1; Mic 6:8).

34. The word "for" (ὅτι) in v. 4c introduces a causal clause.

through the sacrifice of Christ (1:5; 5:9; 7:14; 21:6; 22:16), a status that they, to be sure, have reflected in their conduct by their consistent life of godliness and devotion (cf. Matt 3:8; 10:37–38).[35]

3:5 The one who overcomes will be clothed like them in white garments, and I will never erase his name from the book of life, and I will confess his name before my Father and before his angels

(ὁ νικῶν οὕτως περιβαλεῖται ἐν ἱματίοις λευκοῖς καὶ οὐ μὴ ἐξαλείψω τὸ ὄνομα αὐτοῦ ἐκ τῆς βίβλου τῆς ζωῆς καὶ ὁμολογήσω τὸ ὄνομα αὐτοῦ ἐνώπιον τοῦ πατρός μου καὶ ἐνώπιον τῶν ἀγγέλων αὐτοῦ). The first promise to the overcomer (v. 5a)[36] is closely related to the previous verse by the continued theme of "white garments" and reinforced by the phrase "like them"[37] that modifies the verb "will be clothed."[38] This verb appears elsewhere in Revelation (3:18; 4:4; 7:9, 13; 19:13) along with other expressions that use the imagery of "white" garments or appearance (1:14; 6:11) to denote the holiness of God, of his heavenly company, or most frequently of humans when they are cleansed from sin and God's own holiness and purity has come to be theirs.[39]

The second promise to the overcomer is:

"I will never[40] erase his name from the book of life" (v. 5b). This expresses the idea negatively as a way of asserting the positive sense more powerfully:[41] the overcomer will always be included among those who will live forever with God. The verb translated "I will never erase" carries the sense of "wipe away" (of tears from the eye; 7:17; 21:4), "wipe out, blot out, erase" (of words in ink from a papyrus sheet; Exod 32:32; Ps 68:29 LXX [69:28]), or more generally "obliterate, remove so that no trace remains" (of sins or charges against someone; Ps 50:11 LXX [51:9]; Acts 3:19; Col 2:14).[42]

The image of a heavenly ledger of names, a "book" or "book of life," is widely attested in the Old Testament, ancient Judaism, and early Christianity.[43] John utilizes this symbolism frequently in Revelation, but adapts it in significant ways to express his Christian theology. One distinctive of his usage is that while he briefly mentions in one place "books" from which people are judged at the end time (20:12), he gives repeated attention to a single "book of life" (as here; also 13:8; 17:8; 20:12, 15; 21:27). References in Daniel (7:10, "books"; 12:1, "book") preserve this distinction as well and seem to be the primary influence on Revelation.[44] Another clearly Christian difference

---

35. This focus on being "worthy" in a context that also employs the image of suitable clothing is perhaps rooted in Jesus's parable of the marriage feast (Matt 22:1–14), where those who refused the open invitation to the feast were judged not "worthy" (ἄξιοι; v. 8), but among those who later came freely one was found to have no wedding garment (ἔνδυμα γάμου) and was excluded (vv. 11–12).

36. See general comments on "the overcomer" at 2:7.

37. "Like them" (NET, NIV, NRSV, REB) is the translation of οὕτως (often rendered "in this way, thus"). Some manuscripts read "this [overcomer]" (οὗτος; cf. KJV), but the evidence for οὕτως is much stronger (א, A, C, 1006, 2329, 2344).

38. The verb translated "will be clothed" (περιβαλεῖται) is not passive but middle intransitive. In itself it does not express a causative agent who "will clothe" them in this way, but related verses (3:18; 6:11; 7:14; Ps 51:7; Is 1:18) show that, when the imagery is unpacked, God is the one who cleanses from sin and causes humans to possess the holiness to which "clothed

in white" refers.

39. See also Ps 51:7; Isa 1:18; Dan 11:35; 12:10; also 4 Ezra 2:40.

40. The double negation (οὐ μή) plus a future indicative emphatically denies this future possibility (see note on 9:6).

41. See the use of this rhetorical device in Heb 2:11; 4:15; 6:10; 7:20; 13:17.

42. BDAG 344–45.

43. Ezek 13:9; Dan 7:10; 12:1–2; Mal 3:16; Luke 10:20; Phil 4:3; cf. also Wis 4:20; Odes Sol. 9:11; 1 En. 47:3; 90:20; 108:3; Jub. 30:19–23; 36:10; Jos. Asen. 15:3; 1QM 12:2; Birkat Haminim (12th of the Eighteen Benedictions or Amidah). For a valuable survey of these texts, see Leslie Baynes, *The Heavenly Book Motif in Judeo-Christian Apocalypses, 200 B.C.E.–200 C.E.*, JSJSup 152 (Leiden: Brill, 2012).

44. Passages like Exod 32:32; Ps 69:28 are not as important to this theme in Rev. See Beale, *Revelation*, 281.

is that "the book of life" belongs to the Lamb (it is "the Lamb's book of life," 13:8; 21:27), by virtue of his sacrificial death (13:8 "who was slain"; cf. 5:9), and it is this sacrifice that opens the way to life with God for those whose names appear in it. The third unique feature of "the book of life" in Revelation is that names are enrolled in it "from the foundation of the world" (17:8; cf. 13:8), symbolizing God's initiative to select individuals for eternal life based on his mercy and love apart from their own merit or demerit.[45] This focus on God's gracious election coheres with other texts in the New Testament (e.g., John 6:35–44, 65; 10:26; 17:2, 6–9, 12, 24; Acts 13:48; Rom 8:28–30; 9:11–12; 11:5–6; 1 Cor 1:26–31; Eph 1:4–5, 11). It also suggests that the enrollment symbolizes "life" beyond the bounds of earthly time and place.

These three distinctives show that it is wrong to understand the promise of v. 5b as "conditional predestination"[46] or as a veiled threat (i.e., that genuine Christians will be taken off God's list if they fail to live up to these commands). None of the three promises in v. 5 has a condition attached, and it is risky to read one in even when the promise is phrased negatively as in this clause. Jesus's teaching as recorded in the Gospel of John is em-phatically clear about the absolute security of those who are genuinely part of his flock (John 6:35–40; 10:26–30).[47]

Picking up the "name" rubric one final time in this message, the third promise (v. 5c) pledges Christ's heavenly advocacy for the overcomer: "I will confess his name before my Father and before his angels." As in v. 3, this wording reflects Jesus's teaching to his disciples (Matt 10:32; Luke 12:8), and the situation addressed there is parallel to this one. His disciples must live and speak for Christ on earth in open acknowledgment of their Christian commitment even when this brings rejection and persecution (e.g., Matt 10:17–23). In correspond-ing loyalty to the one who confesses him "before humans," he will confess that person before his Fa-ther (Matt 10:32) and before the angels (Luke 12:8). The word "confess" in this context means to profess allegiance, to acknowledge loyalty or personal as-sociation with someone,[48] and it speaks of Christ vouching for the overcomer in the future judgment.

3:6 Anyone who has an ear must listen to what the Spirit says to the churches'" (ὁ ἔχων οὖς ἀκουσάτω τί τὸ πνεῦμα λέγει ταῖς ἐκκλησίαις). For this command to hear, see comments on 2:7a (identical in wording to 3:6).

Theology in Application

The Curse of Nominalism

It happens in all spheres of life. The educational institution or school district that still awards diplomas but no longer provides a real education. Businesses that keep the doors open and file their annual reports but have forgotten who they serve or why they exist. The army that brings in recruits and pays out pensions but can't mount an effective defense of its country. The church with its beautiful buildings, prominent location, and godly heritage that holds regular "services" but has become empty of

---

45. See Beale, *Revelation*, 279–82; Caird, *Revelation*, 49.

46. Caird, *Revelation*, 49: "A man cannot earn the right to have his name on the citizen roll, but he can forfeit it."

47. 1 John 2:19 clarifies that some who abandon the Chris-tian community show by their leaving that they were not truly a part of it.

48. BDAG 708–9.

real spiritual life. It no longer really serves its surrounding community, its own congregation, or its God. All of these "have a reputation of being alive, but . . . are dead" (3:1). They exist in name only. The curse of nominalism is that such an *appearance* of vitality often prevents real life from ever springing up again—it inoculates its participants against the real disease. In the religious sphere we get "Churchianity" instead of real Christianity, a form of godliness that denies and resists its true power (2 Tim 3:5). Our desperate need in that situation whether as corporate churches or individual believers is spiritual revival, to "wake up" to our real condition and stir up the dying embers of our Christian heritage, to "strengthen" what remains of our true vitality and restore the habits that nourish real health (Rev 3:2–3). For many this will mean anchoring our lives in Scripture once again and in the vibrant creeds of our church tradition that somehow were lost in misguided efforts to "relate to the modern world." We must find our life in Christ once again before we can offer it to our contemporaries. Or it will mean saying no to the myriad of distractions that fill our lives to the brim, to the good things that squeeze out the best things. We think we can "have it all," but peripheral matters have a habit of choking the life out of what is really central in church life as well as in the believer's individual walk with the Savior.

The Value and Power of the Few

Amid this largely negative message to the church in Sardis that calls for the majority of its members to take desperate and decisive action or face certain judgment, Jesus does not forget the "few individuals in Sardis who have not defiled their garments" (v. 4). Even when he must paint with broad brushstrokes, he doesn't lose the fine touch of personal knowledge and attention. He knows and values his faithful ones, his godly remnant, even if they are small in number, and their future reward with him is assured. They can also serve as catalysts to trigger a return to life and health for the majority that has lost its way. But to do so they must be persevering and winsome. A fickle and belligerent minority is likely to provoke resistance rather than real change. But in God's hands a few well-placed embers, a small spark of real fire, can revitalize even the coldest congregations or at least stir the flames for a few others.

Revelation 3:7–13

Literary Context

See the connections discussed under "Literary Context" for 2:1–7 in chapter 3, page 110.

Main Idea

Jesus commends the church in Philadelphia for fidelity despite weakness, and he pledges to vindicate them against their enemies and protect them from the unprecedented testing that will fall on the whole world.

Translation

(See page 170.)

Revelation 3:7–13

7a	Command	**And to the angel of the church in Philadelphia write:**
b	Speaker	*"The holy one,...*
		the true one,
		the one who has the key of David,
		who opens and no one will close and closes and no one opens,
		... says this:
8a	Commendation	*'I know your works.*
b		*I tell you, I have set before you an open door that no one is able to close.*
c		*I know that you have only a little power,*
d		*yet you have kept my word and*
e		*have not renounced my name.*
9a	Promise 1	*I tell you, I will cause certain ones*
		who belong to the synagogue of Satan,
b		*who claim they are Jews and are not—*
c		*I tell you, I will make them come and*
d		*bow down before your feet and*
e		*acknowledge that I have loved you.*
10a		*Since you have kept my word about endurance,*
b	Promise 2	*I also will keep you from the hour of testing*
c		*that is destined to come on the whole world*
d		*to test those who live on the earth.*
11a	Exhortation	*I am coming soon.*
b		*Hold fast what you have,*
c		*so that no one will take your crown.*
12a	Promise	*The one who overcomes I will make a pillar in the temple of my God, and*
b		*he will never depart from it.*
c		*And I will write on him the name of my God and*
		the name of the city of my God, the new Jerusalem
d		*that comes down out of heaven*
		from my God, and
e		*my new name.*
13	Command	*Anyone who has an ear must listen to what the Spirit says to the churches.'"*

Structure

See 2:1–7 for discussion of the four-part structure common to all the messages.

This message gives unqualified commendation of the church in Philadelphia (similar to the message to Smyrna, 2:8–11). Praise for the church's condition (vv. 8–10) is thus a bit longer compared to the other messages and includes promises of vindication and protection that come from their fidelity to Christ, while the exhortation section is quite brief (v. 11). The conclusion likewise gives a lengthy promise to faithful overcomers in Philadelphia, one that all the churches should hear carefully as well (vv. 12–13).

Exegetical Outline

II. First Vision: The Exalted Christ and His Messages to the Churches (1:9–3:22)

  A. Vision of the Exalted Christ (1:9–20)

  B. Messages to the Seven Churches (2:1–3:22)

    1. To the Church in Ephesus (2:1–7)

    2. To the Church in Smyrna (2:8–11)

    3. To the Church in Pergamum (2:12–17)

    4. To the Church in Thyatira (2:18–29)

    5. To the Church in Sardis (3:1–6)

➡   **6. To the Church in Philadelphia (3:7–13)**

      a. Introduction (3:7)

        (1) Address and command to write (3:7a)

        (2) Description of Christ who is speaking (3:7b)

      b. Commendation and pledge of support (3:8–10)

        (1) Loyalty despite weakness (3:8)

        (2) Promise of vindication against opponents (3:9)

        (3) Promise of protection from the coming time of testing (3:10)

      c. Exhortation to hold firm (3:11)

      d. Conclusion (3:12–13)

        (1) Promise to the overcomer (3:12)

        (2) Command to hear the Spirit's message (3:13)

Explanation of the Text

3:7 And to the angel of the church in Philadelphia write: "The holy one, the true one, the one who has the key of David, who opens and no one will close and closes and no one opens, says this (Καὶ τῷ ἀγγέλῳ τῆς ἐν Φιλαδελφείᾳ ἐκκλησίας γράψον· Τάδε λέγει ὁ ἅγιος, ὁ ἀληθινός, ὁ ἔχων τὴν κλεῖν Δαυίδ, ὁ ἀνοίγων καὶ οὐδεὶς κλείσει καὶ κλείων καὶ οὐδεὶς ἀνοίγει). The formula of address for this message (v. 7a) is identical to 2:8a except for the changed place name. See commentary on 2:1, 8a for shared expressions.

The town of Philadelphia was located about 30 miles east of Sardis, on the road that led to Hierapolis and Laodicea. Situated on the edge of a fertile plateau with a tributary of the Hermus River to its north and a high ridge of Mount Tmolus looming over it to the south, it benefitted from trade along that route to the interior and from productive vineyards and grazing land for sheep. Viticulture, woolen textiles, and leather working were some of its main industries. It was the youngest of the seven cities, since it was founded in the mid-second century BC by the Attalid rulers of Pergamum after they had annexed this region to their territory. On whether it was established with a "missionary" purpose to spread Hellenism further inland, see brief comments on v. 8 below. In AD 17 it suffered destruction by the same earthquake that leveled parts of Sardis and received help from Tiberius likewise (Tacitus, *Ann.* 2.47). Philadelphia expressed its gratitude on inscriptions and coins and took the name "Neocaesarea" for a time in his honor. Later it took the name "Flavia Philadelphia" in honor of Vespasian and Domitian. Its primary deity was the goddess Anaitis, a Persian-Anatolian mix that represented the mother goddess. Various other Greco-Roman and eastern deities were honored in the city. Not much is known of the Jewish population of Philadelphia prior to Revelation. A few decades later Ignatius briefly warned the Philadelphian church against Judaizers (Ign. *Phld.* 6.1). For conflict between the Jewish and Christian communities at the time of Revelation, see comments on v. 9.[1]

The description of Christ in v. 7b has an important connection to the vision at the end of chapter 1 (the "key," 1:18; see below), but it begins with a broader set of christological titles not cited previously in Revelation.[2] "The holy one" (ὁ ἅγιος) is an Old Testament title for God (Isa 40:25; 43:15; Hab 3:3; with "of Israel," 2 Kgs 19:22 and numerous times in Pss and Isa), used here of Christ (see also "the holy one of God" in Mark 1:24; Luke 4:34; John 6:69). The longer title, "holy one of Israel,"

is often used in contexts denoting the one "set apart" or unique, the true and living God as opposed to humans or false gods, the one who alone can and will redeem and renew the whole world (e.g., Isa 40:25; 43:3–4; 45:11–14; 49:6–7; 60:9–14).[3] This nuance comes across also with the second title "the true one" (ὁ ἀληθινός), used elsewhere to refer to the one true God and Jesus Christ his Son (John 1:9; 7:28; 17:3; 1 John 5:20). Here it underscores his uniqueness and divinity as compared to idols: he alone can save and redeem.[4]

The next description, "the one who has the key of David" harks back to 1:18 ("I have the keys of Death and of Hades") and seems to carry a sense complementary to it.[5] In 3:7b this "key" relates to opening and closing in a context that speaks of "an open door" (v. 8b) and access to the new Jerusalem (v. 12), and so it refers to Christ's control over the eternal destiny of humans (cf. Matt 16:19: "keys of the kingdom of heaven"). The connection with David is drawn directly from Isaiah 22:22 (with allusions to Isa 9:7; 16:5; 55:3). Isaiah 22 does not directly refer to God's messianic deliverer in the line of David (cf. Rev 5:5; 22:16) but to an official in the royal household who would exercise the king's authority[6] and do so with firm control: "Who opens and no one will close and closes and no one opens."[7] But in the typology of Isaiah 22, the firm rule of a human official in David's house intensifies to represent Christ's inviolable divine sovereignty

---

1. Koester, *Revelation*, 321–23; W. Ward Gasque, "Philadelphia," *ABD* 5:304–5.

2. Both terms, "holy and true," describe the Lord God in 6:10.

3. O. Procksch, "ἅγιος," *TDNT* 1:93–94. Several of these passages include elements that appear in the next few lines of Rev 3:7–9. For example, open gates (Isa 60:11), bowing (Isa 45:14; 49:7; 60:14), God's beloved (Isa 43:4).

4. Prigent, *Apocalypse*, 201; *NIDNTTE* 1:239–40.

5. Roloff, *Revelation*, 61.

6. The targum to Isaiah paraphrases 22:22a as "I will place the key of the sanctuary and the authority of the house of David

in his hand," representing perhaps the idea of access to God's temple reflected here in v. 12 (Bruce D. Chilton, *The Isaiah Targum*, vol. 11 of *The Aramaic Bible: The Targums*, ed. Martin McNamara (Edinburgh: T&T Clark, 1987), 44.

7. This wording is dependent on the MT of Isa 22:22, not the LXX. The second verb in each pair varies from future ("will close"; κλείσει) to present ("opens"; ἀνοίγει), but the sense is almost identical (gnomic in both places). A textual variation that reads a future form ("will open") for the latter verb has inferior manuscript support and represents a scribal effort to smooth out the difference in tense.

over human afterlife. His authority to "open" the way to God is mentioned immediately in v. 8.

3:8 'I know your works. I tell you, I have set before you an open door that no one is able to close. I know that you have only a little power, yet you have kept my word and have not renounced my name (Οἶδά σου τὰ ἔργα, ἰδοὺ δέδωκα ἐνώπιόν σου θύραν ἠνεῳγμένην, ἣν οὐδεὶς δύναται κλεῖσαι αὐτήν, ὅτι μικρὰν ἔχεις δύναμιν καὶ ἐτήρησάς μου τὸν λόγον καὶ οὐκ ἠρνήσω τὸ ὄνομά μου). The section on the church's condition begins as usual (cf. 2:2, 19; 3:1) with the general statement about their conduct, "I know your works" (v. 8a). But instead of the normal elaborations seen in the other messages, this one moves immediately[8] (v. 8b) to express a benefit from Christ suggested by what was just said in v. 7b, before describing the details of their commendable conduct (v. 8c–e). The benefit is that he has "set before"[9] them "an open door." But how should this image be understood? Bible students might readily think of Paul's "open door" as a metaphor for wider ministry opportunities, especially in evangelism (1 Cor 16:9; 2 Cor 2:12; Col 4:3; cf. Acts 14:27) and understand that same sense here.[10] But related images in this context (Christ's authority over the

eternal destiny of people in v. 7b and indications in vv. 9 and 11 that these Christians truly belong to him) make it more likely that this "open door" assures their own access to God rather than success at leading others to him.[11] Christ's own divine authority guarantees that their access will never be taken away ("no one is able to close" it; v. 8b).[12]

The following sentence[13] fills in what Christ has seen in their conduct: consistent Christian obedience and loyalty despite human weakness. The words "you have only a little power" (v. 8c) highlight at the outset their difficult situation in Philadelphia (similar to 2:9, 13). In this clause Christ sympathetically acknowledges a fact of which these Christians themselves were all too well aware: their own weakness in worldly status and influence in the pagan environment in which they lived.[14] Their faithfulness commended in the rest of the verse testifies to their grasp of the wider Christian truth that God's strength must supply what they lack in their own spiritual resources (cf. 1 Cor 1:26–29; 2 Cor 12:9–10; Phil 4:13). The following clauses (v. 8d–e) describe their spiritual strength despite this weakness[15] in terms seen elsewhere in these chapters. They "have kept[16] [his] word" (i.e., have

---

8. "I tell you" reflects the use of ἰδού (often "behold, look") for emphasis as in 2:10 to interject the statement about "an open door" (v. 8b).

9. The verb "I have set" is from the word usually rendered "give" (δίδωμι), but here it carries a nuance associated with the Hebrew word "give." Cf. Aune, *Revelation 1–5*, 229; Matthew Black, "Some Greek Words with 'Hebrew' Meanings in the Epistles and Apocalypse," in *Biblical Studies: Essays in Honour of William Barclay*, ed. Johnston R. McKay and James F. Miller (London: Collins, 1976), 145.

10. Ramsay, *Letters*, 391–95; 404–6; Hemer, *Letters*, 154–55, 172, 174 (related to Philadelphia's role in "evangelizing" its area with Hellenistic culture); Charles, *Revelation*, 1:87; Swete, *Apocalypse*, 53; Walvoord, Rawley, and Hitchcock, *Revelation*, 83.

11. Aune, *Revelation 1–5*, 236; Kraft, *Offenbarung*, 81; Prigent, *Apocalypse*, 203. This sense for "open door" appears also in Odes Sol. 42:17–18. Boxall, *Revelation*, 72, takes a different view, related to the "open door in heaven" that John would soon see (4:1): these Christians and all who heed John's insights are

given a chance to view their circumstances from a heavenly perspective. But this is not as persuasive as the conceptual clues from this immediate context.

12. Cf. v. 7b and Job 12:13–14.

13. The main verb from v. 8a ("I know") is inserted here in the English translation to pick up the train of thought after v. 8b that was somewhat parenthetical (an open door set before them). The conjunction (ὅτι) in the phrase "[I know] that" can be taken in a causal sense (CSB, KJV, NASB), but the parallels in 2:2; 3:1, 15 make the sense "that" (i.e., content, indirect discourse) much more likely (ESV, NET, NIV, NRSV, RSV).

14. Boxall, *Revelation*, 72.

15. The word "yet" represents the simple conjunction καί ("and"), used here to add an unexpected element (BDAG 495; Zerwick, *Biblical Greek*, 153).

16. The verb "you have kept" is an aorist in Greek (ἐτήρησας), here referring to various unspecified past acts viewed in summary with perhaps a consummative sense (the action was done despite difficulties). In English the present

been obedient to his teaching; see comments at 1:3; 2:26; also John 8:51; 17:6), and they "have not renounced [his] name" (i.e., have not repudiated or turned back on their allegiance to Christ; see the positive expression of this in 2:13, "hold firmly to my name" and its parallel phrase about "renouncing faith" in Christ).[17]

3:9 I tell you, I will cause certain ones who belong to the synagogue of Satan, who claim they are Jews and are not—I tell you, I will make them come and bow down before your feet and acknowledge that I have loved you (ἰδοὺ διδῶ ἐκ τῆς συναγωγῆς τοῦ Σατανᾶ τῶν λεγόντων ἑαυτοὺς Ἰουδαίους εἶναι, καὶ οὐκ εἰσὶν ἀλλὰ ψεύδονται. ἰδοὺ ποιήσω αὐτοὺς ἵνα ἥξουσιν καὶ προσκυνήσουσιν ἐνώπιον τῶν ποδῶν σου καὶ γνῶσιν ὅτι ἐγὼ ἠγάπησά σε). Christ continues to commend their spiritual condition in an animated style and draws again on the imagery from Isaiah evoked in v. 7b. The emphatic expression "I tell you" (or "look" [ἰδού]; see v. 8a and 2:10 for explanation) occurs twice in this verse, and it causes an adjustment in the sentence structure, breaking off the original phrasing and starting again with a new main verb ("I tell you, I will cause certain ones . . . I tell you, I will make them . . .")—all evidence of lively speech in written form.[18] This verse continues to assure these outwardly powerless but faithful Christians of their eternal status with God (an "open door" to him, v. 8b), but it does so by speaking of how they will

benefit from a reversal of fortune in the end times at the expense of certain antagonists of theirs in Philadelphia. In phrasing very similar to 2:9 (the message to Smyrna), Christ mentions members of "the synagogue,"[19] who take the label of "Jews," but as in 2:9 he denies the legitimacy of that label ("they . . . are not") and describes their gathering instead as a "synagogue of Satan" (v. 9a–b). These are Jews outwardly and ethnically, but in their rejection of Christ they are not truly Jews inwardly, and in their opposition to the gospel[20] they are actually allied with God's enemy, Satan.[21] It is likely that these two minority religious groups in Philadelphia competed for influence in the wider pagan culture. Based on what Christ says here, it is easy to envision some in the Jewish community mocking and castigating an outwardly powerless church as rejected by their God and certain to be judged in the future.

Christ's assurance to them, however, is the opposite. He says, "I will cause[22] [them]," "I will make them," to see things differently (v. 9a, c). This reversal of status (and of human opinion about it) is expressed using imagery drawn from the later chapters of Isaiah, already evoked by references to Christ as the holy and true God and the bearer of Davidic authority in v. 7b. In some of the same passages cited above, God promises Israel that the gentile world powers who had oppressed them would at the time of his future renewal of all things

---

perfect verb ("have done") is the best way to express this indefinite past sense (cf. CSB, ESV, NASB, NET, NIV, NRSV). The same is true of the final verb in this verse, "you have not renounced" (aorist, ἠρνήσω). See Fanning, *Verbal Aspect*, 260, 263–65.

17. See comments on 2:13 for further explanation.

18. Such a break due to an intervening clause is an example of anacoluthon that often occurs in animated, popular Greek style of the first century (BDF §467; Robertson, *Grammar*, 437–39).

19. The Greek phrase translated "certain ones who belong to the synagogue" (ἐκ τῆς συναγωγῆς) is a partitive expression

referring to "*some* from the synagogue" (see BDF §164; BDAG 297, and other comments at 2:10; 5:9).

20. Jewish hostility to the church in Smyrna is explicit in 2:9, but nothing clear is said here about actual opposition in Philadelphia. It is likely that there was a tense relationship between the groups, as mentioned above.

21. See further discussion at 2:9.

22. The verb "I will cause" is διδῶ, the word that normally means "give," used here as a futuristic present. The sense "cause, make" is another Hebraic nuance similar to the usage noted in v. 8b above.

come and bow down before their feet,[23] and they would be compelled to acknowledge the love[24] that the true God of redemption has for his people Israel (Isa 43:4; 45:14; 49:23; 60:14; see also 1QM 19:5–7; Jub. 1:25). In an ironic twist this reversal is now seen to apply also (v. 9c–e) to unbelieving Jews who in the future will be forced to recognize God's favor on gentile Christian believers they currently regard as unworthy.[25]

3:10 Since you have kept my word about endurance, I also will keep you from the hour of testing that is destined to come on the whole world to test those who live on the earth (ὅτι ἐτήρησας τὸν λόγον τῆς ὑπομονῆς μου, κἀγώ σε τηρήσω ἐκ τῆς ὥρας τοῦ πειρασμοῦ τῆς μελλούσης ἔρχεσθαι ἐπὶ τῆς οἰκουμένης ὅλης πειράσαι τοὺς κατοικοῦντας ἐπὶ τῆς γῆς). After the interjected statements about their future vindication (v. 9), Christ resumes the line of thought that ended v. 8 (they have loyally kept his word) as a basis[26] for a further promise

about their future. The initial clause ("since you have kept my word about endurance") repeats the same verb, object, and possessive pronoun from v. 8d, "you have kept my word" (ἐτήρησάς μου τὸν λόγον), but adds the description "of/about endurance" and puts the possessive "my" in a different place (ἐτήρησας τὸν λόγον τῆς ὑπομονῆς μου). This connection with the sense of v. 8 tips the scale toward understanding this phrase in v. 10a as "my word about [your] endurance," that is, Christ's call for his followers to maintain faith in him despite difficulties (cf. CSB, NIV, NJB, REB).[27] The Christians in Philadelphia had maintained such faith in obedience to his word.

Christ's promise in response is to deliver them from the uniquely terrible period of fearful judgments that will test all God's enemies across the entire world (v. 10b–d). The wording, "I also will keep you," uses the same verb "keep" (τηρέω) to maintain the parallelism with v. 10a, but the sense shifts from

---

23. The Greek construction of Rev 3:9, "I will make them come and bow down," uses a clause introduced by ἵνα with future indicative verbs (lit., "that they will come and will bow down"). This use of a ἵνα-clause where other writers would normally use an infinitive in Greek is characteristic of the Gospel of John as well as Rev (BDF §§369.2; 392.1; 408; 476.1; Aune, *Revelation 1–5*, 230). Verbs in ἵνα-clauses are usually subjunctives, but in vernacular Hellenistic Greek the future indicative is sometimes used instead with no change in sense (Zerwick, *Biblical Greek*, 117; cf. Rev 6:4, 11; 8:3; 9:4, 5, 20; 13:12; 14:13; 22:14).

24. The verb "I have loved" in Rev 3:9 is an aorist (ἠγάπησα), denoting indefinite past acts viewed in summary; see comment on the aorist verbs in v. 8d–e. This refers to God's redemption and ongoing care for them even during times when they had no power or status of their own (vv. 7–8).

25. God's promises through Isaiah are seen as a typological anticipation of the greater, humanly unexpected fulfillment that will come about through Christ. The pattern here is similar to Paul's citation of Hos 2:25; 2:1 LXX in Rom 9:24–26: just as the northern tribes of Israel were taken into judgment as though in some sense they were "not God's beloved people" and then later restored to him, so also (but in an unexpectedly greater way) gentiles who truly had not been God's people will be made his own alongside believing Israel.

26. The initial clause of v. 10 is causal, giving the ground or reason (BDAG 732) for his promise in the rest of the verse. The Greek conjunction ὅτι, translated here as "since" (NIV) or "because" (CSB, ESV, NABR, NASB, NRSV), usually follows its main verb, but here it precedes (cf. John 1:50; 20:27; 1 Cor 12:15) in order to establish the connection back to v. 8 more easily.

27. This rendering takes the genitive "of endurance" as objective to "word" (message/command about endurance) and the genitive "my/of me" as subjective also to "word" (the message I speak). See this interpretation in Zerwick and Grosvenor, *Grammatical Analysis*, 748; Aune, *Revelation 1–5*, 231. In a string of genitives the final possessive pronoun can sometimes skip the immediately preceding noun and connect to an earlier head noun (Wallace, *Grammar*, 87–88; Zerwick, *Biblical Greek*, 15; they observe this with attributive-genitive phrases, but it can occur more broadly). The alternative interpretation also takes "of endurance" as objective to "word," but takes "my/of me" as subjective to "endurance": "the message about my perseverance" (cf. NASB; Swete, *Apocalypse*, 55; Prigent, *Apocalypse*, 205), but Christ's own endurance, while true and important, is not mentioned elsewhere in this context and is thus less likely.

"keep, obey" to "keep safe, preserve, protect."[28] What they will be protected "from" (ἐκ) is "the hour of testing that is destined to come on the whole world,"[29] a period of unprecedented judgment and suffering that ancient Judaism and early Christianity expected to occur in the last days just prior to God's renewal and restoration of all things.[30] This culminating period has general connections to Old Testament prophetic warnings about the day of the Lord with its judgment on sinful Israel as well as its pagan enemies.[31] Such judgments were seen to fall on God's people and their world at various times in their history in repeated patterns of heaven-sent calamities visited on sinful humans.[32] But a few texts begin to speak in typological escalation of a period similar to these judgments but unprecedented in its severity and significance, a "great" tribulation, having worldwide impact, such as has never occurred before (Dan 12:1; Matt 24:21; Mark 13:19; Rev 7:14; cf. T. Mos. 8:1).[33] The "hour of testing" in Revelation 3:10 certainly appears to fit this unprecedented level of intensification since it comes "on the whole world" and tests "those who live on the earth" without exemption.[34]

The question that interpreters have debated regarding Revelation 3:10 is how Christ's promised protection of the Philadelphian Christians from this period of testing should be seen to operate in light of the key terms used here and the broader evidence of the rest of the book and the Bible as a whole. One important distinction to note in this discussion is the difference between troubles that God's people suffer throughout this age (from the time of Christ's ascension until his future return in glory) and the unprecedented sufferings that will come at the end of the age just prior to his return. These are related to each other in a patterned way, but the escalation at the end must not be simply collapsed into the general experience of difficulties that anticipate it. The terms for "testing" and related words like "tribulation" are used elsewhere to describe sometimes the general experience of the godly in a fallen world (John 16:33; Acts 11:19; 14:22; 20:19; Rom 5:3; 1 Cor 10:13; 2 Cor 1:4–8; 4:8, 17; 8:2; Col 1:24; 1 Thess 3:3–7; Heb 10:33; Jas 1:27; 1 Pet 1:6; 4:12; Rev 1:9; 2:9–10; 2:22) and sometimes the intense sufferings of the final period (Matt 24:21, 29; Mark 13:19, 24; Rev 7:14; cf. Dan 12:1).[35] As just noted, some texts in Revelation seem to denote the former and some the latter. It is

---

28. BDAG 1002.

29. For the sense "is destined" (for the verb μέλλω), see BDAG 628; cf. 1:19; 12:5; 17:8; Matt 17:12, 22; Acts 26:22.

30. For a detailed survey of this theme in early Judaism, see Pitre, *Tribulation*, 41–130, especially his summary on 127–30; also Stanley E. Porter, "Tribulation, Messianic Woes," in *DLNT* 1179–82.

31. Characteristic terms used to describe this suffering include "trouble, tribulation" (θλῖψις; Isa 33:2; Jer 15:11; Dan 12:1; these include texts that have the parallel Hebrew term צָרָה but render it differently in Greek translation); "birth pains or woes," referred to in later literature as "messianic woes" or "birth pangs" of the messiah (ὠδίν, ὠδίνω); "trial, test" (πειρασμός, πειράζω); "punish, chastise" (παιδεία, παιδεύω).

32. For the "tribulation" as a pattern of woes or judgments prefigured in the OT prophets and in the Olivet Discourse and finding its fulfillment in the final days of woe described in Rev, see Blaising, "Case," 32–52, 58–65.

33. The term "great" (μεγάλη) when describing "tribulation"

is not a technical term that ensures the phrase always refers to this final period of intense trouble. In Acts 7:11 and Rev 2:22 it describes severe difficulties (e.g., famine, sickness); see comments at 2:22.

34. This is the first use of the phrase "those who live on the earth" in Rev, but it occurs repeatedly hereafter, always with a negative sense: the earth-dwellers who under Satan's deception resist God to the very end (3:10; 6:10; 8:13; 11:10; 13:8, 14; 17:8; cf. 13:12; 17:2). See A. Boyd Luter and Emily K. Hunter, "The 'Earth Dwellers' and the 'Heaven Dwellers': An Overlooked Interpretive Key to the Apocalypse," *Faith and Mission* 20 (2003): 3–5 for a helpful survey. Phrases like this are common in noncanonical apocalyptic literature since they speak of events with cosmic or worldwide scope (e.g., 1 En. 40:6–7; 54:6; 60:5; 4 Ezra 3:34–35; 5:1; 7:74; 12:24; 2 Bar. 25:1; 48:32, 40; see others listed in Aune, *Revelation 1–5*, 240), but they do not always carry this negative connotation.

35. The references in the Lord's Prayer are debated: Matt 6:13; Luke 11:4.

the latter texts that deserve our attention in asking how the promise of protection in Revelation 3:10 should be understood.

On the one hand, clearly some followers of Christ will suffer terribly in the judgments of this final intense period. For example, the great multitude before God's throne in 7:14 are the blessed dead who have come "from the great tribulation" (ἐκ τῆς θλίψεως τῆς μεγάλης), and they seem to be identified with, if not coextensive with, the martyrs slain because of their witness for Christ who cry out for vindication in 6:9–11.[36] These seem to have suffered death during the outpouring of divine wrath signified by the six seals (cf. 6:16–17). So it is difficult to argue as many do that 3:10 promises preservation "in the midst of" or "through" the cataclysmic judgments rather than exemption from them.[37] At best this would mean "protecting" them so that they die faithfully in these trials rather than denying their Lord. It is tempting to cite partial parallels to the wording of 3:10 like John 17:15 ("I do not ask that you take them from the world, but that you keep them from [ἐκ] the evil one") or Jas 1:27 ("to keep oneself unspotted from [ἀπό] the world"). These clearly denote a level of protection of people who directly experience what threatens, but the wording is not completely parallel to 3:10. Here the keeping is not from the "trial" alone but "from the hour of trial" (ἐκ τῆς ὥρας τοῦ πειρασμοῦ). Refer-

ring to the time period of the threat marks a clearer contrast between "keeping from" and "protecting in" or "through" its experiences. The other partial parallels that are sometimes cited involve references to "saving/delivering from" trial, especially several references to Jesus being "saved from death" (Heb 5:7; Jas 5:20) or "the hour" of death (John 12:27). Again it must be said that "saving from" is different than "keeping from" an experience or its time period.[38] The language of "deliverance from" an experience of judgment does, however, suggest another typology of judgment and deliverance from the Old Testament, one drawn from the story of Sodom and Gomorrah whom God destroyed by fire as an "example" (ὑπόδειγμα) of his judgment on the ungodly (2 Pet 2:6). In that episode God "rescued righteous Lot" (δίκαιον Λὼτ . . . ἐρρύσατο; 2:7) showing that "the Lord knows how to rescue the godly from trial" (οἶδεν κύριος εὐσεβεῖς ἐκ πειρασμοῦ ῥύεσθαι; 2:9), that is, by giving them "absolute immunity (cf. 2 Peter 2:9), . . . escape from [the trial] entirely,"[39] as Lot experienced.

This suggests that in Revelation 3:10 Christ promises to "keep" the Christians in Philadelphia "from" the future period of severe worldwide "trial" by taking them away from the earthly scene entirely.[40] This coheres exactly with Paul's description of a "rapture" of Christians that catches them up from the earth to be with Christ forever as one facet

---

36. Likewise the group described in 12:10–12. See commentary on these passages for discussion.

37. Cf. Prigent, *Apocalypse*, 206: they "cannot hope to escape the tribulation, but . . . they are preserved in it." Also Aune, *Revelation 1–5*, 240: "Not that they will be physically absent but rather that they will not be touched by that which touches others." This would be parallel to the experience of Noah who was delivered "through water" (1 Pet 3:20), a play on the word "through" (διά; "in the midst of" as well as "by means of").

38. One important difference is that when the verb is "keep" and not "save," the preposition "from" (ἐκ) does not necessitate "prior existence in" or "emergence from" a circumstance. It means "independence from" or "outside of." See Aune, *Revelation 1–5*, 231; LN §89.121.

39. Moffatt, "Revelation," 368. He poses this as an option for Rev 3:10 but draws no conclusion of his own.

40. One of the earliest commentators on Rev (Andrew of Caesarea, sixth century), suggests that this could refer to protection of Christians during Roman persecution (e.g., under Domitian), but he prefers to see it as deliverance in the end-times: "He speaks of the universal coming of the antichrist against the faithful at the end of time. From this coming he pledges to free those who are zealous, for they will beforehand be seized upward by a departure from there, lest they be tempted beyond what they are able to endure" (Weinrich, "Andrew of Caesarea," 125–26).

of the Lord's coming at the end of the age (1 Thess 4:16–17). This will be done in connection with delivering Christians from God's wrath that will be visited on the ungodly in the judgments of the day of the Lord (1 Thess 1:10; 5:2, 9). In Revelation these judgments are portrayed in chapters 6–19.[41] It is important in reading Revelation to distinguish between those followers of Christ addressed in the seven messages, who represent Christians throughout the present age from Christ's first coming up to this phase of his second coming, as over against followers of Christ who will live during the future period of final "tribulation."[42]

3:11 I am coming soon. Hold fast what you have, so that no one will take your crown (ἔρχομαι ταχύ· κράτει ὃ ἔχεις, ἵνα μηδεὶς λάβῃ τὸν στέφανόν σου). In the section normally given over to exhortations and warnings (e.g., 2:5–6, 10–11, 16; 3:3–4) this exhortation to the church in Philadelphia is comparatively brief. Christ again asserts his soon coming (v. 11a; cf. 2:5, 16), in this case as both an encouragement since he comes to rescue his people and a reminder to be morally prepared (cf. 3:2–3; 16:15; 22:12). The only command he lays on them is to maintain[43] their commendable spiritual and moral condition (v. 11b). In v. 8 he mentioned that they "have" only a little strength, but that by itself is not in view here; what they "have" in this case is the same kind of general character or spiritual health cited in several other messages as the "possession" of those Christians (cf. 2:3, 6, 25). The goal Christ

sets before them for staying spiritually alert in this way[44] is the "crown" or commendation already in store for them (cf. 2 Tim 4:8) in acknowledgment of their faithful service to Christ (v. 11c). The "crown" (στέφανος) represents the joyful celebration of accomplishment awaiting them when Christ comes.[45] The phrasing "that no one will take" does not imply a zero-sum competition for Christ's commendation ("if others serve more devotedly, you may fall short") but is again a rhetorical expression of the negative in order to assert the positive counterpart more powerfully ("so that you will without question receive what is waiting for you"; see 3:5).

3:12 The one who overcomes I will make a pillar in the temple of my God, and he will never depart from it. And I will write on him the name of my God and the name of the city of my God, the new Jerusalem that comes down out of heaven from my God, and my new name (ὁ νικῶν ποιήσω αὐτὸν στῦλον ἐν τῷ ναῷ τοῦ θεοῦ μου καὶ ἔξω οὐ μὴ ἐξέλθῃ ἔτι καὶ γράψω ἐπ᾽ αὐτὸν τὸ ὄνομα τοῦ θεοῦ μου καὶ τὸ ὄνομα τῆς πόλεως τοῦ θεοῦ μου, τῆς καινῆς Ἰερουσαλήμ ἡ καταβαίνουσα ἐκ τοῦ οὐρανοῦ ἀπὸ τοῦ θεοῦ μου, καὶ τὸ ὄνομά μου τὸ καινόν). Christ's promise to the overcomer[46] returns metaphorically to the theme that began this message, the motif of open access to God granted by Christ (vv. 7b–8b) and full vindication of these Christians as God's own when his redemption is made complete (v. 9). This is expressed initially by the image of God's people as a building or more specifically a

---

41. See comments especially at 6:8 and 6:17.

42. This promise should not be limited to the Christians in Philadelphia alone (contra Aune, *Revelation 1–5*, 240). In the same way that all the messages are ultimately addressed "to the churches" (3:13; see comment on 2:7), so all Christians, in obeying Christ's call to faithful endurance, can expect his preservation from the future period of cataclysmic wrath at the time when he comes for them (1 Thess 4–5).

43. "Hold fast" (κράτει) is a present imperative commanding this as a characteristic course of life (customary present).

The same verb is used to give an urgent command, using the aorist in 2:25 (κρατήσατε; see note).

44. The clause introduced by "so that" (ἵνα) shows the purpose of "holding fast."

45. See comments at 2:10.

46. In this verse as in 2:26 and 3:21 "the overcomer" is expressed as a pendant nominative that is resumed in the main clause by a pronoun in another case. See 2:26 for brief discussion.

"temple" to God (cf. 1 Cor 3:16–17; Eph 2:19–22), in which (i.e., among whom) God dwells in intimate communion and receives their joyful worship (v. 12a–b).[47] Using that image these Christians are pictured as ones who are notable members of the community or have central importance for it (see the sense of "pillar," στῦλος, in Gal 2:9; also Philo, *Migr.* 124; 1 Clem. 5.2). Despite their current weakness (v. 8) and in contrast to what their antagonists may say (v. 9), in God's future redemption they will have a privileged position among God's people that will never be taken away.[48] The overcomer "will never depart from" that role in God's community.[49]

This assertion of the overcomer's full acceptance and security is augmented by a further picture added to the image of the "pillar," in this case a threefold inscription on it or him (v. 12c–e).[50] The main verb "I will write" has three objects: three "names" that Christ will inscribe to denote the overcomer's eternal identity and citizenship. The "name of my God" shows his full acceptance with God provided by Christ's redeeming work (i.e., this person belongs to God). The "name of the city of my God" certifies the overcomer's right to dwell in the "new Jerusalem" (the heavenly origin of which is recited; see further discussion of "coming down out of heaven from God" at 21:2). Finally, Christ declares he will write "my new name" on the overcomer. After the mention of God's name just above, the genitive "my" would seem most naturally to mean Christ's own name (i.e., this person belongs to Christ as well). But it is more difficult to understand what is "new" about this. It could mean "new" to that person; a change of ownership has come for him. But "my" can easily mean "from me" (a genitive of source), denoting a new identity for the individual Christian made possible by Christ's transforming work (cf. 2:17), and this seems more likely.

3:13 Anyone who has an ear must listen to what the Spirit says to the churches (ὁ ἔχων οὖς ἀκουσάτω τί τὸ πνεῦμα λέγει ταῖς ἐκκλησίαις). For this command to hear, see comments on 2:7a (identical in wording to 3:13). Here it is significant to note that what is promised to the Christians in Philadelphia (3:10) is addressed more broadly to the other churches in Asia Minor as well as those in other places and times down to the present day.

Theology in Application

His Power and Honor in Our Weakness and Shame

After speaking of his own absolute authority, especially over eschatological blessing or judgment (3:7), Jesus alludes to something of which the Christians in ancient Philadelphia were themselves all too aware: their own lowly status in worldly

---

47. Because this "temple" is a metaphor of God's people—even in its future expression—it is not in conflict with the vision of chs. 21–22 of the new Jerusalem as a city in which there is "no [literal] temple" (21:22) because God and the Lamb are its temple, and God's people worship them there. Both images speak of God in perfect communion with his people forever (21:3–7; 22:3–4).

48. In later descriptions of God's new community it is made clear that not all humans have access to God in this way; clear demarcations have been made (cf. 21:27; 22:15).

49. The wording in v. 12b ("he will never depart from it") is quite emphatic about not ever being excluded from God's temple. It says literally "he will not at all go outside any longer" (ἔξω οὐ μὴ ἐξέλθῃ ἔτι), using a subjunctive with οὐ μή to deny in strongest terms even the possibility of this occurring in the future (see note on 2:11) plus the adverb "still, any longer."

50. The phrase "on him" (ἐπ᾽ αὐτόν; masculine singular) can refer to the pillar or the person (both masculine singular grammatically).

power and influence in the pagan environment in which they lived: "I know that you have only a little power" (3:8). Yet by drawing on God's strength they had stayed faithful to the gospel and had not denied Christ even in the face of shame and oppression. Their lives displayed the paradox of following a suffering but victorious Savior. Like the other churches in ancient Asia Minor—and many Christians in our world today—they were denigrated by the elites, mocked by the rich and powerful, and disadvantaged even by their social peers. They were taking it on the chin with seemingly no one to defend them, yet they remained steadfast. In profound irony Jesus promises them (and all Christians), who are excluded from prosperity and power at present, that they will also be excluded from the time of severe judgment that will come against the world's ungodly inhabitants in the future time of severe tribulation (3:10). Even more, Jesus pledges that they will receive future glory in the place of present suffering, a destiny of being honored by God himself and claimed as his own forever. Those whose lives were subject to such vulnerability and insecurity in this age will in the future become unshakable pillars of God's new community, the heavenly Jerusalem to be established on earth in the end times (3:12).

The Heritage of Israel

This is the second of Jesus's messages that mention the Asian churches' conflict with Judaism in their day (3:9; cf. 2:9). No Christian should read Jesus's assurance to the church in Philadelphia about its ethnic Jewish opponents as a justification for anti-Jewish animus today. As the whole New Testament makes clear, gentile Christians have no grounds for arrogance or hostility against Jewish people (e.g., Rom 11:17–24). We should instead honor and value the Jewish background of our Christian faith and be grateful to be included in the circle of blessing that God has brought to the world through Abraham and his ethnic descendants. We should love Jewish people as God loves them. We should grieve over the harm that Christians have inflicted on Jews over the centuries in the name of Christ and be energetic and gracious in extending the gospel to Jewish people so that they can share in the blessings intended for them first through their Messiah.

Revelation 3:14–22

Literary Context

See the connections discussed under "Literary Context" for 2:1–7 in chapter 3, page 110.

Main Idea

Jesus rebukes the church in Laodicea for their uselessness and their pitiable self-sufficiency; only he can provide what they need, and he appeals to them to repent and renew their fellowship with him.

Translation

(See page 182.)

Revelation 3:14–22

14a	Command	**And to the angel of the church in Laodicea write:**
b	Speaker	"The Amen,…
		the faithful and true witness,
		the ruler of God's creation,
		… says this:
15a	Rebuke	'I know your works,
b		that you are neither cold nor hot.
c		I wish that you were cold or hot.
16a	Warning	So…
		because you are lukewarm and neither hot nor cold,
b		… I am about to spit you out of my mouth.
17a	Cause (for 18)	Because you say, "I am rich and
		I have become wealthy and
		I do not need a thing," but
b		you do not know that you are wretched and
		pitiable and
		poor and
		blind and
		naked,
18a	Invitation	I counsel you to buy from me (1) gold refined by fire
		so that you may be wealthy, and
b		(2) white garments
		so that you may be clothed and
		the shame …
		of your nakedness
		… may not be exposed, and
c		(3) salve to anoint your eyes
		so that you may see.
19a	Exhortation	Those whom I love I rebuke and discipline.
b		So be zealous and repent.
20a		Here I am! I stand at the door and knock.
b		If anyone hears my voice and opens the door,
c		I will come in to him and
d		share a meal with him and
e		he with me.
21a	Promise	To the one who overcomes
		I will give the right to sit with me on my throne,
b		as I myself overcame and
c		sat down with my Father on his throne.
22	Command	Anyone who has an ear must listen to what the Spirit says to the churches.'"

Structure

See 2:1–7 for discussion of the four-part structure common to all the messages.

The message to the church in Laodicea is even more negative than the one to Sardis (3:1–6), but ends with a warm appeal for renewed fellowship. Christ who is full of truth and ruler of all (v. 14) strongly rebukes their conduct (vv. 15–18), but he reminds them of his love even in chastening and invites them to repentance and restoration of intimacy (vv. 19–20). The promise to the overcomer looks to the continuation of that intimacy in sharing Christ's rule in the new age (v. 21). The message is structured in inverted parallelism moving through three main themes: rule (vv. 14, 21), dining fellowship (vv. 15–16, 19–20), and true prosperity (vv. 17–18).[1]

Exegetical Outline

II. **First Vision: The Exalted Christ and His Messages to the Churches (1:9–3:22)**

    A. Vision of the Exalted Christ (1:9–20)

    B. Messages to the Seven Churches (2:1–3:22)

       1. To the Church in Ephesus (2:1–7)

       2. To the Church in Smyrna (2:8–11)

       3. To the Church in Pergamum (2:12–17)

       4. To the Church in Thyatira (2:18–29)

       5. To the Church in Sardis (3:1–6)

       6. To the Church in Philadelphia (3:7–13)

       ➡ **7. To the Church in Laodicea (3:14–22)**

          a. Introduction (3:14)

            (1) Address and command to write (3:14a)

            (2) Description of Christ who is speaking (3:14b)

          b. Knowledge of the church's condition (3:15–18)

            (1) Their repulsive conduct (3:15–16)

            (2) Self-sufficiency versus true prosperity (3:17–18)

          c. Exhortation and appeal (3:19–20)

            (1) Loving call for repentance (3:19)

            (2) Appeal for intimate relationship (3:20)

          d. Conclusion (3:21–22)

            (1) Promise to the overcomer (3:21)

            (2) Command to hear the Spirit's message (3:22)

---

1. Craig R. Koester, "The Message to Laodicea and the Problem of Its Local Context: A Study of the Imagery in Rev 3.14–22," *NTS* (2003): 411–13.

Explanation of the Text

3:14 And to the angel of the church in Laodicea write: "The Amen, the faithful and true witness, the ruler of God's creation, says this (Καὶ τῷ ἀγγέλῳ τῆς ἐν Λαοδικείᾳ ἐκκλησίας γράψον· τάδε λέγει ὁ Ἀμήν, ὁ μάρτυς ὁ πιστὸς καὶ ἀληθινός, ἡ ἀρχὴ τῆς κτίσεως τοῦ θεοῦ). As elsewhere in these messages this formula of address (v. 14a) is identical to 2:8a except for the changed place name. See commentary on 2:1, 8a for shared expressions.

Laodicea was the city located farthest south and east among the seven cities, about 50 miles southeast of Philadelphia in the Lycus River valley, with Hierapolis a few miles to its north and Colossae a few miles to its south. The Seleucids founded it in the mid-third century BC on the site of earlier settlements. The location was advantageous for agriculture and herding as well as strategic for trade, and the city prospered immediately. It was at a major intersection of highways, one running west-to-east from Ephesus to Iconium and on to Syria, and one running northwest-to-southeast from Smyrna and Sardis to Colossae and Attalia. Strabo, writing about AD 25, extolled its rapid growth, its wealth, and the soft black wool it produced (*Geogr.* 12.8.16). Tacitus records its severe damage from an earthquake around AD 60 from which it recovered from its own resources without any help from Rome (*Ann.* 14.27). Its extant ruins reflect a large city with impressive public buildings including two theaters, monumental gates, a colonnaded main street, and a stadium built in AD 79 in honor of the emperor Titus. For issues related to its water supply, see discussion at vv. 15–16 below. The god Zeus had been traditionally worshiped in Laodicea along with other gods, but at later times a local cult to Domitian was established. A Jewish community existed for a long time in Laodicea according to several anecdotes recorded by Josephus (*Ant.* 12.147–53; 14.241–43) and another by Cicero (*Flac.* 67–68). Paul's letter to the Colossians mentions a Christian community in Laodicea as a part of his circle of churches in the early 60s (Col 2:1; 4:13–16).[2]

The description of Christ in this final message (v. 14b) is related explicitly to what is said about him in 1:5, and this sets the stage for what is said to the Laodiceans. The middle phrase here, "the faithful and true witness," is identical to 1:5 ("the faithful witness"), but is expanded by the further adjective "true" (ἀληθινός).[3] Jesus in his earthly life and supremely in his death embodied completely reliable testimony about God and his redemption, and his trustworthy witness continues in the revelation he now communicates through John (cf. 22:20; also 2:13: Antipas, "my faithful witness"). The addition of the adjective "true" suggests how the preceding description came to be used here. The title "the Amen" (ὁ Ἀμήν) is transliterated from the Hebrew אָמֵן (meaning "surely," from the verbal root "be firm, trustworthy").[4] As a title it is likely drawn from Isaiah 65:16 that refers twice to God's people counting on "the God of truth," translated in the LXX as "the true [reliable] God" (τὸν θεὸν τὸν ἀληθινόν). This theme of Christ as fully reliable in bearing witness to the truth should encourage this church to accept his forthcoming counsel about their true condition and its remedy (vv. 17–18).

---

2. F. F. Bruce, "Laodicea," *ABD* 4:229–31; Koester, *Revelation*, 333–35; Edwin Yamauchi, *The Archaeology of New Testament Cities in Western Asia Minor* (Grand Rapids: Baker, 1980), 135–46.

3. This adjective can mean "genuine, authentic" (LN §73.2),

but when it appears with "faithful" (πιστός) as here, it shades over into "reliable, trustworthy" (cf. Rev 19:11; 21:5; 22:6; BDAG 43), especially when describing "witness" as in this phrase (cf. John 19:35).

4. HALOT 64.

The third title for Christ in v. 14b ("the ruler [ἡ ἀρχή] of God's creation") is also drawn thematically from 1:5, but the wording is similar rather than identical ("the ruler [ἄρχων] over the kings of the earth"). The key word in 3:14 (ἀρχή) is translated in a variety of ways: "beginning" (ESV, KJV, NASB, NLT, RSV),[5] "source, prime source, origin, originator" (CSB, NABR, NET, NRSV, REB), and "ruler" (NIV). The sense of "source, originator" is thought to be a way of expressing Christ's role as agent in God's creation of all things (John 1:1–3, 10; 1 Cor 8:6; Col 1:15–18; Heb 1:2–3, 10),[6] and its explicit use in Colossians 1:18 is seen to support this. But Colossians 1:18 speaks of Christ not as God's agent in the physical creation of all things (this comes in Col 1:15–17)[7] but of his role in resurrection ("the firstborn from the dead") or more broadly of his sovereignty because of his resurrection and exaltation (vv. 18–20). Moreover, while God is regularly seen in Revelation as the creator of all things (Rev 4:11; 10:6; 14:7; also of the new creation: 21:2, 5), Christ is never presented in this book as creator or agent of creation.[8] The connection with 1:5 (see above) suggests that "ruler, authority" (paralleling 1:5, "ruler [ἄρχων] over the kings of the earth") is a better sense for ἀρχή here.[9] Revelation speaks often about God's sovereign rule over all things (1:8; 11:17; 15:3; 19:6) or Christ's (1:5; 2:26–27;

3:21; 12:5; 17:14; 19:15–16; 20:4–6) or God's and Christ's together (5:12–13; 11:15; 12:10). Within this immediate context the ideas seem to flow in an inverted thematic structure by which this verse is parallel to v. 21 in speaking about Christ's authority or rule with his Father, and this is done in preparation for the vision (chs. 4–5) of the heavenly throne room where every creature offers worship to God and the Lamb (5:13).[10]

The connection of Jesus as "the Amen, the faithful and true witness" to his role as "ruler" or "beginning" of God's creation has led some to understand "creation" here as primarily the new creation (Rev 21–22), since these concepts all appear in Isaiah 65:16–18 (God is faithful to create new heavens and a new earth for his chastened people). This is then understood to indicate that the new creation is already in existence, inaugurated in Christ's resurrection.[11] These themes are certainly found in Isaiah, and the new creation appears in Revelation 21–22, but there is scant evidence in this message to the church (vv. 14–22) that new creation alone is in view and that Christ is its "inaugurator." Instead the letter closes with a focus on the overcomer sharing Christ's "rule" with the Father over all things (v. 21), a rule that is picked up again in Revelation 20:4–6 as well as 22:1–5, not in the new creation alone.[12]

---

5. BDAG 137–38. This is the rendering of ἀρχή used of God and of Christ in the phrase "the beginning and the end" (Rev 21:6; 22:13; also in a textual variant in 1:8). The fact that Rev can speak of God and Christ in this way as existing prior to time and into eternity shows that ἡ ἀρχή "of God's creation" does not mean "the first part or beginning of God's creation," i.e., "first created" as BDAG 138 allows.

6. These verses are seen as an echo of how God used "wisdom" in creating all things according to Prov 8:22–30; cf. Wis 6:22; Sir 24:3, 9.

7. And Col 1:15–17 as well as the other NT verses cited here never speak of Christ as the direct source or originator of creation but always of his agency under God the creator.

8. Koester, "Message to Laodicea," 412; Michael J. Svigel, "Christ as Ἀρχή in Revelation 3:14," *BSac* 161 (2004): 229.

9. The noun ἀρχή in 3:14 denotes "rule, authority" in a more abstract way as opposed to the personal noun ἄρχων (ruler) in 1:5 (cf. Luke 20:20; 1 Cor 15:24; Eph 1:21; Col 2:10; Jude 6). But ἀρχή itself can refer to the person who rules, usually in the plural "rulers, authorities" (Luke 12:11; Rom 8:38; Eph 3:10; 6:12; Col 1:16; 2:15; Titus 3:1), but occasionally in the singular "ruler, one who exercises authority" (Hos 1:11; Neh 9:17; also P.Hal. 1.226). Col 1:18 in speaking of Christ's preeminent rule over all enemies including death may have influenced the choice of terms here.

10. Koester, "Message to Laodicea," 411–12.

11. Beale, *Revelation*, 297–301; Beale and McDonough, "Revelation," 1097–98. They also connect Isa 43:10–12, 19 (God's people as his witnesses that he will do a new thing).

12. Svigel, "Christ as Ἀρχή," 226–27.

3:15–16 'I know your works, that you are neither cold nor hot. I wish that you were cold or hot. 16 So because you are lukewarm and neither hot nor cold, I am about to spit you out of my mouth (οἶδά σου τὰ ἔργα ὅτι οὔτε ψυχρὸς εἶ οὔτε ζεστός. ὄφελον ψυχρὸς ἦς ἢ ζεστός. 16 οὕτως ὅτι χλιαρὸς εἶ καὶ οὔτε ζεστὸς οὔτε ψυχρός, μέλλω σε ἐμέσαι ἐκ τοῦ στόματός μου). Christ begins a lengthy section on the church's spiritual condition (vv. 15–18) by referring to their general conduct, using an expression familiar in these messages: "I know your works" (2:2, 19; 3:1, 8). He then captures their behavior specifically[13] with a powerful metaphor, sharply rebuking how useless and displeasing their conduct is to him. It is the metaphor of cold, hot, or lukewarm water—in this case specifically drinking water, since v. 16b refers to expelling it "out of my mouth." Construing the appropriate sense for this can be challenging because we must be careful to understand the ancient cultural and linguistic setting and not just impose what seems natural to our modern situation. Most modern readers are likely to take "lukewarm" and "neither hot nor cold" to mean half-hearted, indifferent, vacillating, and in religious matters perhaps also nominal or syncretistic.[14] This would be in contrast to "hot" as fervent, ardent, enthusiastic (cf. the related verb in Acts 18:25; Rom 12:11) and "cold" as lifeless, aloof, hard-hearted (cf. related verb in Matt 24:12). There may be evidence for this in the command of v. 19 to be earnest or zealous (ζήλευε). But is this really

the point of Christ's rebuke? The context suggests that "lukewarm" is the only negative here, and "hot" or "cold" are equally desirable alternatives. Does Christ actually prefer even outright spiritual hostility or rejection rather than half-heartedness (v. 15c: "I wish that you were cold or hot")?[15]

One approach leading toward a better understanding has been advanced by a number of recent commentaries and aims to incorporate cultural insights drawn from studies of the ancient site of Laodicea and its surrounding area. These studies focused on the water supply of Laodicea and the nearby cities of Colossae and Hierapolis. Literary and archeological evidence from the ancient world suggests that Colossae had an abundant supply of fresh, cool water for drinking and Hierapolis was known for hot mineral waters (evident even today to visitors to the site). Both could be seen as desirable and useful for human use and consumption. In contrast, it was thought that the site of Laodicea itself lacked a ready water supply, and pipes that carried hot waters from another site (five miles away) provided only a tepid and mineral-laden supply. Given these notable local conditions, being "lukewarm," it is argued, means not half-hearted or indifferent but useless or ineffective, "providing neither refreshment for the spiritually weary, nor healing for the spiritually sick."[16]

This interpretation itself seems essentially correct, but the archeological evidence to support it has been seriously questioned in recent years,[17] and

---

13. The "that" (ὅτι) clause explains and specifies "works" (cf. 3:1b).

14. See Caird, *Revelation*, 56–57; Prigent, *Apocalypse*, 215; Roloff, *Revelation*, 64.

15. The logic is sometimes stated as "stubborn outsiders have a better chance to realize their great need and be converted while the self-satisfied pious will always be blind to their true condition." This is the stance that Thomas, *Revelation 1–7*, 306–7, adopts. Or the reference in v. 15c could be ironic. But as M. J. S. Rudwick and E. M. B. Green, "The Laodicean Lukewarmness," *ExpTim* 69 (1958): 177, point out, whether the

wish is sincere or ironic, if "cold" means "antagonistic to true faith," we would expect v. 15c to say, "I wish you were hot or even cold" (ὄφελον ζεστὸς ἦς ἢ καὶ ψυχρός) to highlight the unexpected element.

16. Rudwick and Green, "Lukewarmness," 178. See also Hemer, *Letters*, 186–91. It is followed in large measure by Beale, *Revelation*, 303; Osborne, *Revelation*, 205–6; Smalley, *Revelation*, 98.

17. Koester, *Revelation*, 336–37; Prigent, *Apocalypse*, 210–11; Thompson, *Revelation*, 202–4 (a broader critique of Hemer's methods).

it fails to explain certain details from the text. This reading sees the value of hot water to lie in its healing and soothing properties for bathing, while the text seems to imply water for *drinking* at all three temperature levels. The reason for "spitting" out the displeasing water is not due to its high mineral content, as implied by some explanations just noted, but is due to its tepid temperature,[18] which for some reason was not preferred compared to hot or cold. A better suggestion is to ground the sense in ancient practices more broadly rather than in local conditions understandable only in Laodicea. Koester has found evidence of common dining practices across the Greco-Roman world that explain the imagery of Revelation 3:15–16 more satisfactorily than the localized explanations. For example, drinks taken with a meal (water as well as wine) were not always served at room temperature. If a host could manage it, there was a preference for cold drinks on some occasions and for hot on others, depending on the climate. Diners desired cold drinks when it was hot and hot drinks when it was cold according to Plato (*Rep.* 437 d–e), and other writers reflect this too.[19] At a minimum this background for the imagery of 3:15–16 suggests that Christ faults the Laodicean church not so much for half-hearted commitment or passivity as for conduct repulsive to him, conduct that he vehemently rejects (he is about to "spit" it from his mouth, v. 16b). Their conduct

is further described in vv. 17–18 as self-sufficient and satisfied with material wealth (see below), which certainly displeases the Lord. Koester takes the analogy a bit further and suggests that Christ desires followers whose character and conduct set them off from the surrounding society, who refuse to adopt the lifestyle of outsiders whose wealth lulls them into self-sufficiency.[20]

3:17 Because you say, "I am rich and I have become wealthy and I do not need a thing," but you do not know that you are wretched and pitiable and poor and blind and naked (ὅτι λέγεις ὅτι Πλούσιός εἰμι καὶ πεπλούτηκα καὶ οὐδὲν χρείαν ἔχω, καὶ οὐκ οἶδας ὅτι σὺ εἶ ὁ ταλαίπωρος καὶ ἐλεεινὸς καὶ πτωχὸς καὶ τυφλὸς καὶ γυμνός). Verses 17–18 form a unit that develops further the deplorable conduct of the Laodicean Christians that vv. 15b–16 portrayed metaphorically. Within this unit v. 17 gives the reason or basis for the counsel that Christ gives in v. 18 (CSB, KJV, NASB, NET).[21] The reason is their utter misapprehension of their own wretched spiritual condition. They cheerily tell themselves[22] that they are doing quite well (v. 17a), but[23] Christ's sad diagnosis is the complete opposite (v. 17b). Their self-perception as "wealthy"[24] and needing nothing is an intermingling of the metaphorical and the real sense: they possess material, earthly riches, and they suppose that this represents true and lasting prosperity.[25] In this regard they are

18. Stanley E. Porter, "Why the Laodiceans Received Lukewarm Water (Revelation 3:15–18)," *TynBul* 38 (1987): 146–49, makes this point clear.

19. Koester, "Message to Laodicea," 412–15; he cites also Plautus, *Curc.* 292–93; Athenaeus, *Deipn.* 3.123; Martial, *Epigrams* 5.64.1–2; 14.103–5; Seneca, *Ep.* 78.23; Xenophon, *Mem.* 2.1.30.

20. Koester, "Message to Laodicea," 415. He cites examples from ancient literature of diners spitting out food that was distasteful and the use of lukewarm water to cause vomiting.

21. The causal clause (v. 17; introduced by ὅτι) comes before the main clause (v. 18). Some versions reflect this with two separate sentences joined by "therefore" or "so" at the start of v. 18 (NEB, NRSV, RSV).

22. This is another use of "say" for a false—even if in this case sincere—claim (cf. 2:2, 9, 20, 24; 3:9).

23. The word normally translated "and" (καί) is used here with a contrastive sense.

24. The phrase "I have become wealthy" is a Greek perfect tense verb (πεπλούτηκα) denoting the act of acquisition that leads to wealth. This verb is a cognate of the adjective "rich" (πλούσιος) in the previous clause, and the two clauses are in reverse order (see note on 3:3).

25. This is a common human condition throughout history and frequently lamented in the Bible (Ezek 28:4–10; Hos 12:7–8; Zech 11:5; Luke 12:19–21; 1 Cor 4:8; 1 Tim 6:9–10, 17–19; Jas 1:10–11; 2:5).

the opposite of the church in Smyrna (2:9), but they foreshadow Babylon (18:7–8, 16–19). Their true situation is that they are "not rich toward God" (Luke 12:21). Spiritually and ethically they are in great need, and Christ lays bare their true condition in a crescendo[26] of woeful descriptions: "wretched and pitiable"[27] as well as "poor and blind and naked." The last three are figurative for their true spiritual bankruptcy, ignorance, and shameful exposure as evil and helpless. See the further unpacking of these figures in v. 18, in which Christ prescribes the remedy for each of these.

3:18 I counsel you to buy from me gold refined by fire so that you may be wealthy, and white garments so that you may be clothed and the shame of your nakedness may not be exposed, and salve to anoint your eyes so that you may see (συμβουλεύω σοι ἀγοράσαι παρ᾽ ἐμοῦ χρυσίον πεπυρωμένον ἐκ πυρὸς ἵνα πλουτήσῃς, καὶ ἱμάτια λευκὰ ἵνα περιβάλῃ καὶ μὴ φανερωθῇ ἡ αἰσχύνη τῆς γυμνότητός σου, καὶ κολλούριον ἐγχρῖσαι τοὺς ὀφθαλμούς σου ἵνα βλέπῃς). This verse is the main clause of the extended sentence that began in v. 17 and gives Christ's resultant counsel[28] for the spiritual and moral ills of the Laodicean church identified in that verse. The three failings expressed figuratively at the end of v. 17 (poor, blind, naked) are taken up here in close parallels, and Christ stipulates the cure for them. But the most important point of the verse is that the remedy in each case is something beyond their own vaunted resources

(see their clueless self-sufficiency portrayed in v. 17a) and must be obtained from Christ. The image of "buying from me" (ἀγοράσαι παρ᾽ ἐμοῦ) does not imply that they have any means of payment for such benefits, but it emphasizes the true source of what is required. It alludes to the Lord's words in Isaiah 55:1 inviting the needy to "buy" (repeated twice in MT; LXX has ἀγοράσατε) without money or payment (alluded to also in Rev 21:6; 22:17).[29]

What they must obtain from Christ is detailed in three parallel objects of "buy," each followed by a clause telling the benefit this will bring (v. 18).[30] The first one picks up the initial image from the final three metaphors at the end of v. 17 (poor): "gold refined by fire," that is, the purest gold, wealth that is truly valuable, not sham treasure as their outward riches are (v. 17). This will produce true spiritual wealth, the heritage of life forever with God (cf. Matt 6:19–21; 1 Tim 6:19). The second object they need mirrors the final image of v. 17 (naked): "white garments," which bring two complementary benefits, "that you may be clothed and the shame of your nakedness may not be exposed." These represent the cleansing and purity that comes with the forgiveness Christ provides by his sacrificial death (see comments on "white garments" at 3:4–5) and the removal of the humiliation and judgment that sin brings (cf. 16:15; 17:16; also Gen 2:25; 3:10–11; Isa 20:3–4). The third object he can offer corresponds to the middle of the three images at the end of v. 17 (blind): from Christ they can get relief from

---

26. This repeated use of "and" (καί) in a series adds power or pathos (BDF §460.3; see also 5:12).

27. On "wretched" (ταλαίπωρος) see Rom 7:24 (and Wis 3:11), except that Paul knew and deeply felt his desperate condition, while here they fail to realize it. "Pitiable" (ἐλεεινός) means "miserable," "deserving of sympathy" (BDAG 315). Some translations say "pitiful" (CSB, Message, NEB, NET, NIV, REB), but in American English this increasingly carries a nuance of contempt that seems inappropriate here.

28. The main verb "I counsel" (συμβουλεύω) carries the nuance of providing wise advice to someone facing a critical decision (e.g., Exod 18:19; 1 Kgs 1:12; John 18:14; cf. 1 Clem. 58.2).

29. It is possibly also an ironic counter to their self-sufficient idea that their wealth would enable them to purchase on their own whatever they needed.

30. The three ἵνα-clauses of v. 18 tell the purpose of obtaining the object in each case. See the parallels displayed in the structured translation at the start of this chapter.

their spiritual darkness "so that [they] may see." Use of a healing "salve" for eye problems was widely known and recommended in the ancient world,[31] but Christ stretches the image here to cover healing even of blindness. The image of blindness and sight speaks of the spiritual enlightenment that comes with Christian conversion and instruction (cf. John 1:4–5; 8:12; 9:39–41; 12:46; 2 Cor 4:4). Already in this passage Christ has begun to open their minds to truth about themselves they had been oblivious to (Rev 3:17). In a larger way the "revelation" given through John in this whole book (1:1, 11) enables the churches to see the realities of life both present and future that are otherwise hidden from our eyes.

3:19–20 Those whom I love I rebuke and discipline. So be zealous and repent. 20 Here I am! I stand at the door and knock. If anyone hears my voice and opens the door, I will come in to him and share a meal with him and he with me (ἐγὼ ὅσους ἐὰν φιλῶ ἐλέγχω καὶ παιδεύω· ζήλευε οὖν καὶ μετανόησον. 20 Ἰδοὺ ἔστηκα ἐπὶ τὴν θύραν καὶ κρούω· ἐάν τις ἀκούσῃ τῆς φωνῆς μου καὶ ἀνοίξῃ τὴν θύραν, εἰσελεύσομαι πρὸς αὐτὸν καὶ δειπνήσω μετ' αὐτοῦ καὶ αὐτὸς μετ' ἐμοῦ). After his stinging rebuke (vv. 15–18), Christ reassures the Laodicean church of his loving concern for their welfare and appeals to them to renew their intimacy with him both now and in the age to come (vv. 19–20). This reassurance of his love despite his harsh reproof[32] is based on Proverbs 3:11–12, grounding his chastening[33] in loving concern for their growth in godliness (Rev 3:19a). The word used to express his "love" (φιλέω) is not the more common New Testament verb (ἀγαπάω; this is used in Prov 3:12 LXX; cf. Rev 1:5; 3:9). While the two are often used with almost no difference in sense, this verb (φιλέω) sometimes carries the nuance of "love or affection based upon interpersonal association" (cf. Matt 10:37; John 11:3, 36; 16:27; 20:2),[34] and that fits nicely into Christ's reassurance here. His loving concern for their spiritual guidance and welfare has motivated all that he said above as well as the commands he now gives[35] to "be zealous and repent" (v. 19b). Their situation demands their earnest attention[36] and a decisive change of direction (see comments on "repent" at 2:5; cf. 2:16, 21; 3:3).

Christ's solicitous and affectionate tone continues in v. 20 with an explicit resumption (from vv. 15–16) of the theme of sharing food and drink

---

31. Koester, "Message to Laodicea," 418–19, 422–23. The verb for "anoint" (ἐγχρίω) used here means to "smear on" or "apply" a substance to the eye (BDAG 275; cf. Tob 6:9). Many interpreters understand the three issues in this verse to have a special local significance in ancient Laodicea because of its particular status as a banking, textile, and medical center. Some support for each of these can be teased out of ancient literary and archeological evidence, but similar evidence can be found for several of the other cities mentioned in Rev 2–3. It is more likely that these three images were chosen because they had a widespread cultural relevance (and would speak cogently to all the churches; see the conclusion of each message). See Koester, "Message to Laodicea," 216–24, for discussion.

32. The verb "rebuke" (ἐλέγχω) is used in one of the main manuscripts (B) of Prov 3:12 and carries the sense of "expose" wrongdoing (John 3:20; 16:8; Eph 5:11) and thus sharply calls for its correction, to "reprove, rebuke" (Matt 18:15; Luke 3:19; 1 Tim 5:20; BDAG 315).

33. The verb "discipline" (παιδεύω) is used rather than ἐλέγχω (see previous note) in another main manuscript (א) of Prov 3:12, but its related noun (παιδεία) occurs in 3:11 of both manuscripts (א and B). This word denotes training (especially children) toward maturity by positive instruction as well as correction when needed (1 Cor 11:32; 2 Tim 2:25; Titus 2:12; Heb 12:6–7, 10; BDAG 749).

34. LN §§25.33, 43.

35. The inferential conjunction "so" (οὖν) builds on v. 19a but reaches back through it to the diagnosis of their spiritual condition in vv. 15–18 (just as οὖν connects the "exhortation" section to the "condition" section in 2:5, 16; 3:3).

36. The verb ζήλευε translated "be zealous" (ESV, KJV, NASB, RSV) or "be earnest" (NET, NIV, NRSV) occurs only here in the NT, but it is related to the frequent words ζῆλος/ ζηλόω denoting zeal or jealousy. It could be taken as a further rebuke to indifference, vacillation, or syncretism (cf. CSB "be committed"; Prigent, *Apocalypse*, 218), but see discussion of "lukewarm" at vv. 15b–16. Here it is intended to stir them to serious attention to their spiritual condition.

together. With great emphasis[37] he uses the bold figure of patiently seeking readmittance to mutual fellowship with "anyone" (τις) of the Laodicean Christians who will welcome it. The picture of Christ standing outside and knocking on the door has important connections to Jesus's parable of the servants who are alert to their master's knock when he comes from the wedding feast, to whom the master himself then serves a banquet (Luke 12:35–38).[38] This parable has an eschatological reference, anticipating the coming messianic banquet or marriage supper of the Lamb (Isa 25:6–8; Matt 8:11; 26:29; Luke 14:15; 22:30; Rev 19:9) that the redeemed will enjoy when Christ returns.[39] The warmth of relationship spoken of here ("I will come in to him[40] and share a meal[41] with him and he with me") likewise pictures the deep communion they will experience with their God in the new age (7:15–17; 21:3, 7). But the escalated sense of those ultimate future blessings does not obviate the present and repeated opportunities for humans (both believing and unbelieving) to respond to Christ's

appeal to enjoy ever-deepening relationship with him (cf. John 14:23; Eph 3:17).[42] This pattern of blessed visitation by the Savior anticipates the far greater fulfillment to come.[43]

3:21 To the one who overcomes I will give the right to sit with me on my throne, as I myself overcame and sat down with my Father on his throne (ὁ νικῶν δώσω αὐτῷ καθίσαι μετ᾽ ἐμοῦ ἐν τῷ θρόνῳ μου, ὡς κἀγὼ ἐνίκησα καὶ ἐκάθισα μετὰ τοῦ πατρός μου ἐν τῷ θρόνῳ αὐτοῦ). This promise that the overcomer[44] will share Christ's authority[45] returns to the theme of Christ's rule over all creation that the message started with (v. 14b). As in the other messages the overcomer can look forward to experiencing the blessed consummation of God's salvation portrayed in the final chapters of Revelation. Here the promise returns to the theme of God's people ruling alongside the Messiah as seen in Revelation 2:26–28 (cf. Matt 19:28; Luke 22:30) and grounded in the vision of Daniel 7:9–14, 22, 27.[46] But the statement "I sat down with my Father

---

37. The phrase "here I am!" (NIV) in v. 20a attempts to bring out the emphatic use of ἰδού (see discussion at 2:10; 3:8–9).

38. Roloff, *Revelation*, 65. This resonates with the picture of the good shepherd whose sheep recognize his "voice" (John 10:4) and perhaps also the beloved "knocking" and saying, "Open to me, my sister" (Song 5:2). The theme of eschatological expectancy because the Lord is "at the door" (Matt 24:33; Mark 13:29; Jas 5:9) seems also to be in the background here.

39. Pictured also in 1 En. 62:13–14.

40. It is important to note this wording carefully and in its contextual sense to avoid a common popular misunderstanding of the verse. It does not speak of Christ entering and indwelling a person (i.e., "I will come into him"), but of entering someone's home ("come into"; εἰσέρχομαι) and proceeding to where the person is ("to/toward/up to him"; πρὸς αὐτόν) in order to share a meal together in warm fellowship.

41. The relational significance of sharing a meal together—with friends or with strangers—was far deeper and richer in the ancient world compared to some cultures in our own time. See M. A. Powell, "Table Fellowship," *DJG* 925–31; Timothy Wiarda, "Revelation 3:20: Imagery and Literary Context," *JETS* 38 (1995): 207–10.

42. Oecumenius, one of the earliest commentators on Rev (sixth century), points out how this appeal shows the Lord's "humble and peaceful nature" in contrast to the devil who "'with hatchet and hammer' smashes the doors of those who do not receive him" (William C. Weinrich, trans., "Oecumenius," in *Greek Commentaries on Revelation*, ed. Thomas C. Oden, ACT [Downers Grove, IL: IVP Academic, 2011], 20).

43. See comments on 2:5, 16; 3:3 for a similar pattern of Christ's present and future comings in corrective judgment. This same pattern can be seen in the church's regular observance of the Lord's Supper as an anticipation of the ultimate banquet of salvation that Jesus-followers will enjoy in the future (Matt 26:29; Luke 22:14–18; 1 Cor 11:26).

44. See comments on what it means to be an "overcomer" at 2:7. On the grammatical construction used here (pendant nominative resumed by a dative pronoun in the main clause) see 2:26.

45. The phrase "I will give the right to sit" uses the verb "give" (δίδωμι) with an infinitive to mean "grant the right or privilege" to act in a certain way (BDAG 243).

46. See comments at 2:26–28. See this shared rule also in Matt 19:28; Luke 22:30; 1 Cor 6:2–3; Eph 2:6; 2 Tim 2:12.

on his throne" also clearly alludes to Psalm 110:1 ("sit at my right hand"), understood as in many places in the New Testament[47] to point to Christ's rule alongside God—a rule inaugurated already in heaven at his exaltation and still to be consummated in the future on earth when he returns to reign as King of kings and Lord of lords (19:16).

Christ entered this co-regency with God as a result of his fidelity to the Father demonstrated fully in his incarnation, death, and resurrection by which, as he says here, "I myself overcame" (κἀγὼ ἐνίκησα; cf. John 16:33; Rev 5:5, 9) and so God exalted him to greatest authority at his right hand in heaven (Acts 2:33; Rom 8:34; Phil 2:5–11; Heb 12:2; seen also in Rev 5:5–6; 7:9–10). But as Revelation will go on to show, this rule will be established on earth as well, first in Christ's intermediate messianic reign (the millennium; 20:4, 6) and then transitioning into his rule with God forever in the new heaven and new earth (21:1–7; 22:1–5; cf. 1 Cor 15:24–28).

3:22 Anyone who has an ear must listen to what the Spirit says to the churches'" (ὁ ἔχων οὖς ἀκουσάτω τί τὸ πνεῦμα λέγει ταῖς ἐκκλησίαις). For this command to hear, see comments on 2:7a (identical in wording to 3:22).

Theology in Application

Wealth or Poverty?

"You made us for yourself, O Lord, and our heart is restless until it finds its rest in you" (Augustine, *Confessions* 1.1.1). Love for our material possessions makes us useless for Christ and his kingdom. Instead we live for ourselves in self-absorption and self-sufficiency rather than for God or for others. Yet material things can never satisfy the human soul, and they leave us greedy for more. And as Jesus tells the Laodiceans, he finds such conduct disgusting in the extreme. We have faith not in him but in our bank accounts or our sizeable income. We are preoccupied with our large houses (and garages and rented storage facilities) filled with all the things we thought at some point that we couldn't live without. Just as the Laodiceans did, we frequently think of spiritual and material riches as coextensive: when we experience financial well-being, we myopically think all's right in our world, but if our bank accounts are thin we wonder what God has against us. Those who base their well-being on material possessions couldn't be more wrong about their true condition, as Jesus powerfully communicates (3:17). Our constant need instead is to draw real and lasting life from Christ rather than from property we amass (3:18). When we get these things backward, we are of no use to God, to others, or even to ourselves.

---

47. Ps 110 is quoted or alluded to in the NT more frequently than any other OT passage (e.g., 110:1 in Matt 22:44; 26:64; Mark 12:35–37; 14:62; Luke 20:42; 22:69; Acts 2:33–36; 5:31; Rom 8:34; 1 Cor 15:25; Eph 1:20; Col 3:1; Heb 1:3, 13; 8:1; 10:12–13; 12:2; 1 Pet 3:22). See David M. Hay, *Glory at the Right Hand: Psalm 110 in Early Christianity*, SBLMS 18 (Nashville: Abingdon, 1973), 163–65.

The Wounds of a Friend

The most loving thing anyone can do for us is to help us, in all gentleness and sensitivity, to see the truth about ourselves and about God. When we are self-deceived and sinning, we don't need sentimental reinforcement that we're doing fine and that everything will be okay. Proverbs's down-to-earth wisdom tells us that real friends will not coddle our foolishness (Prov 27:5–6), and God himself will take the role of a loving parent to discipline an erring child and set him back on the right path (3:11–12). When we utterly misapprehend our own wretched spiritual condition (Rev 3:17–18), we likewise need Jesus's challenging love (v. 19) to call us back to repentance and renewed fellowship (v. 20). A good church or good Christian friend can be Jesus's instrument to do this for us if we will allow it, but our society resists such "interference" and "violation of privacy." The sentiment that such correction is hateful and out of line is another sign that our Christian walk may be more like the compromising Laodiceans than we'd like to admit. This message from Jesus, like several of the others, shows that John's book is written not just to comfort the afflicted but to afflict the comfortable, to stir them out of complacency and sinfulness toward true repentance and change.

Revelation 4:1–11

Literary Context

The phrases that introduce this passage, "after these things I looked" (4:1) and "I came to be in the Spirit" (4:2; also in 1:10), indicate that 4:1–2 is a major transition in the structure of the book of Revelation (cf. the similar phrase "he carried me away in the Spirit" in 17:3 and 21:10). These expressions signal a new phase in the complex of visions that began in 1:9–10 and are now extended in 4:1–2 and will be extended further in 17:3 and 21:10 (see introduction).

After its prologue, Revelation opens with a spectacular vision of the exalted Christ (1:9–20) and the messages Christ commissioned John to write to the seven churches of Asia Minor (chs. 2–3). Now John experiences a second magnificent vision of the Lord God on his heavenly throne and of Jesus Christ the slain lamb, both receiving the worship of all creation for their majesty, sovereignty, and redemptive purpose (chs. 4–5). This serves as the grounding vision to orient the reader to the descriptions of wrath and redemption that will follow in the subsequent chapters: to chapters 6–16 most specifically (the seals, trumpets, and bowls) as well as to chapters 17–22 (the further descriptions of judgment and salvation that finish out the body of the book).[1] John's vision of the scene in heaven gives "the appropriate perspective from which to view and make sense of what is happening on earth"[2] in his own day and in days to come.

---

1. As Beale, *Revelation*, 314–19 shows, John's vision in chs. 4–5 when taken together mirror the structure of Dan 7:9–28 and reflect the theological motifs present there. Seeing God on his heavenly throne is the foundation for tracing the establishment of God's kingdom on earth through his Messiah, replacing the rule of world empires that oppress his people.

2. Boxall, *Revelation*, 79. See also M. Eugene Boring, *Revelation*, IBC (Louisville: John Knox, 1989), 102: "This scene is the theological fountainhead and anchor point for the whole document."

Main Idea

All the creatures in the heavenly throne room continually worship the Lord God Almighty as the eternal creator and sovereign of all things.

Translation

Revelation 4:1–11

1a	Action/Vision Introduction	**After these things I looked**
b		**and beholda door standing open in heaven,**
c		**and the earlier voice ... said,**
d		which I had heard speaking with me like a trumpet,
e	Invitation	*"Come up here,*
f	Promise	*and I will show you what must happen after these things."*
2a	Circumstance	**At once I came to be in the Spirit,**
b		**and behold, a throne was standing in heaven,**
c	Character Entrance 1	**and there was someone sitting on the throne.**
3a	Description	**And the one who was sitting was like** **a jasper stone and**
		a carnelian in appearance,
b		**and a rainbow was around the throne like** **an emerald in appearance.**
4a		**And around the throne I saw** **twenty-four thrones,**
b	Character Entrance 2	**and on the thrones there were** **twenty-four elders sitting,**
c	Description	clothed in white garments with golden crowns on their heads.
5a	Setting	**And from the throne come** **flashes of lightning and**
		rumblings and
		peals of thunder,
b		**and there were seven fiery torches burning before the throne,**
c		which are the seven spirits of God,
6a		**and before the throne was something like a glass sea—like crystal.**

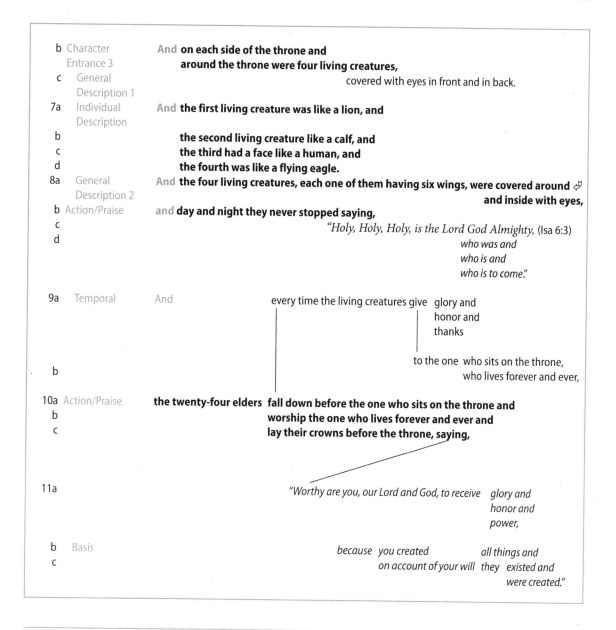

Structure

John's second major vision (4:1–5:14) falls into two parts, focusing first on God on his heavenly throne (4:1–11) and then the Lamb who was slain to accomplish God's redemption (5:1–14). This initial portion in chapter 4 begins as did John's first major vision (1:9–20), with a brief description of the circumstances in which he received the vision (4:1–2a) followed by the introduction of three main actors in the vision with accompanying descriptions: God on his heavenly throne (4:2b–3), twenty-four elders (4:4), and four living creatures (4:6b–7)—interrupted briefly by a broader description of the heavenly setting (4:5–6a). The only actions in this part of the vision center on acclamations of praise offered to the Lord God Almighty by the living creatures (4:8) and then, in response, by the twenty-four elders (4:9–11).

Exegetical Outline

III. Second Vision: Heavenly Throne Room and Three Judgment Cycles (4:1–16:21)

➡ **A. Vision of God in His Heavenly Throne Room (4:1–11)**

   1. The Circumstances of John's Renewed Vision (4:1–2a)

   2. The Lord God on His Heavenly Throne (4:2b–3)

   3. The Heavenly Council and Its Setting (4:4–7)

      a. Twenty-four elders on their thrones (4:4)

      b. Lightning, thunder, fire, and a glass sea (4:5–6a)

      c. Four living creatures around the throne (4:6b–7)

   4. Worship of God by the Elders and the Living Creatures (4:8–11)

      a. Praise for God's holiness (4:8)

      b. Praise for God's creation of all things (4:9–11)

Explanation of the Text

4:1 After these things I looked and behold, a door standing open in heaven, and the earlier voice, which I had heard speaking with me like a trumpet, said, "Come up here, and I will show you what must happen after these things" (Μετὰ ταῦτα εἶδον, καὶ ἰδοὺ θύρα ἠνεῳγμένη ἐν τῷ οὐρανῷ, καὶ ἡ φωνὴ ἡ πρώτη ἣν ἤκουσα ὡς σάλπιγγος λαλούσης μετ᾽ ἐμοῦ λέγων, Ἀνάβα ὧδε, καὶ δείξω σοι ἃ δεῖ γενέσθαι μετὰ ταῦτα). This verse starts a major new unit of the book, with clear thematic links back to the beginning of Revelation itself as well as the opening of the previous main section.

The phrase "after these things I looked [or saw]" (μετὰ ταῦτα εἶδον) occurs frequently to signal John's shift to a new vision (7:9; 15:5; 18:1; cf. 7:1; 19:1 for similar uses).[3] What John "saw" in this vision encompasses all of chapter 4 and leads to new dimensions of the same vision in chapter 5, but he leads us into it step by step. In this verse John first calls special attention[4] to a striking phenomenon that launches his vision, "a door standing open in heaven" (v. 1b), symbolizing unlocked access between earth and heaven.[5] While God's heaven seems distant and alien to everyday reality on

---

3. The phrase "these things" in v. 1a refers to the vision of the exalted Son of Man and his messages to the churches of Asia Minor in 1:9–3:22, and "after these things" denotes the sequence of John's reception of the visions (chs. 1–3, then ch. 4 and following).

4. The expression "I looked and behold" (εἶδον καὶ ἰδού) followed by a nominative word in Greek frequently introduces visionary experiences in Rev (4:1; 6:2, 5, 8; 7:9; 14:1, 14;

cf. 19:11). "Behold" (ἰδού) functions here as a "presentative particle" (BDAG 468), introducing something into the story or account. This can be translated "here is/was," "there is/was" (CSB, NET, NIV), or simply "behold" followed by the thing(s) emphatically introduced into the story (ESV, NASB).

5. See 19:11 where "heaven standing open" (τὸν οὐρανὸν ἠνεῳγμένον) signals Christ's triumphant return to earth with the armies of heaven. Elsewhere it describes God's provision

earth, it is close at hand and pervades all that takes place on earth, as John will be shown.[6] While this is not the case for all of John's visions, the heavenly "time" of this vision, as well as the related one in chapter 5, is portrayed as contemporaneous with John's earthly time, since songs of worship in both chapters celebrate creation and the cross as already past (4:11; 5:6, 9) yet anticipate the seal judgments and the saints' reign on earth as yet future (5:9–10).[7]

This leads immediately to a second notable experience, "the earlier voice"[8] that John had heard (1:10–12), "speaking . . . like a trumpet." The voice came from Christ, the one "speaking with [him]"[9] earlier (1:12), "like a trumpet" (1:10) and like "many waters" (1:15). This explicit reference back to the vision of chapter 1 is an important part of this transition to a new section (see also v. 2 and comments on "Literary Context" above).

What Christ now invites John to do is "come up here" (v. 1e)[10] so that he can receive a vision of future events on earth and in heaven. The phrase "what must happen"[11] ($\mathring{\alpha}$ δεῖ γενέσθαι) with a temporal phrase ("soon" or "after these things") as well as the verb "I will show" (δείξω) are significant thematic markers because they occur in the prologue and epilogue of the whole book to summarize its contents (1:1; 22:6). The verb "I will show" (v. 1f)[12] also carries thematic import since it is used in other verses that mark major transitions in the book (4:1; 17:1; 21:9; see "Literary Context" above). What Christ unveils in this chapter and in the accompanying visions of chapters 5–16 constitute the heart of "the revelation from Jesus Christ" that God gave to John (1:1). Some understand the final phrase in v. 1f ("after these things"; μετὰ ταῦτα) also to connect with the vision of chapter 1, indicating that what John will now see moves us into the third part of the preview given in 1:19, "what events are destined to take place after these things" ($\mathring{\alpha}$ μέλλει γενέσθαι μετὰ ταῦτα). But see 1:19 for a different view of that verse. Nevertheless "after these things" in 4:1f denotes not just the sequence in which John

---

from heaven (Ps 78:23), relates to the Spirit's coming upon Jesus at his baptism (Matt 3:16), or represents access to heavenly revelation (Ezek 1:1; Acts 7:56; 10:11; cf. 1 En. 14:15; T. Levi 5:1).

6. Wright, *Revelation for Everyone*, 42–43.

7. See comment on 5:13 about the timing of its events in the future.

8. The phrase "the earlier voice" could be rendered "the first voice" (ἡ φωνὴ ἡ πρώτη) as in most English versions, but in Greek "first" is sometimes used for "former, earlier" (πρότερος; see BDAG 892–93, and 2 Kgs 1:14; Isa 43:18; Dan 7:24; 1 Tim 5:12; Rev 2:4; 21:4), and "earlier" helps to show the connection to Rev 1:10–12.

9. The participle "speaking" in v. 1c (λαλούσης) is genitive to agree with "trumpet" (as in 1:11a), but some scribes supposed that it should be accusative to agree with the object "which [I heard]" (א) or nominative to agree with "voice" (1854, 2329). It could conceivably agree with any of these, but the genitive makes acceptable sense, and it is the harder reading internally. The later verb in v. 1c "said/saying" (λέγων) does display a lack of grammatical agreement in gender (a masculine referring to the feminine noun "voice") that some manuscripts also correct (e.g., P). This is a case of "agreement according to sense" where the masculine is used to refer to the *person* speaking in this "voice."

10. The same command (in the plural) is used in 11:12 to summon the two witnesses to heaven. In that instance they are caught up bodily and visibly into heaven, but 4:2 seems to indicate that John's "going up" was done in a visionary trance rather than in bodily form (see comments on v. 2). A common view among some dispensationalists is that "come up here" in 4:1 speaks at least symbolically of the rapture of the church prior to the judgments of chs. 6–16 (*New Scofield Reference Bible* [New York: Oxford University Press, 1967], 1356; J. A. Seiss, *The Apocalypse: Lectures on the Book of Revelation*, 6th ed. [London: Charles C. Cook, 1900], 95–99; Walvoord, Rawley, and Hitchcock, *Revelation*, 98–99). But this does not square with the clear sense of the verse (referring only to John; not a bodily removal; not a permanent transfer to heaven, etc.). See critique in Koester, *Revelation*, 351; and Michael J. Svigel, "The Apocalypse of John and the Rapture of the Church: A Reevaluation," *TJ* 22 (2001): 28–30.

11. See 1:1 for discussion of the influence of Dan 2:28–29, 45 and the theological meaning of the verb "must" (δεῖ) in this context.

12. The verb "show" (δείκνυμι) is a synonym for "reveal, unveil," (ἀποκαλύπτω) in John and Rev (H. Schlier, "δείκνυμι," *TDNT* 2:27–30; G. Schneider, "δείκνυμι," *EDNT* 1:280–81). See comments on 1:1.

received the visions (as in 4:1a). It designates the time frame subsequent to his and his addressees' present circumstances, moving on ultimately to the final days when God's full judgment and renewal of all things will occur. This future sense is not entirely clear in chapter 4 itself, but it becomes evident as the complementary visions of chapters 5–16 and 17–22 unfold.[13]

4:2 At once I came to be in the Spirit, and behold, a throne was standing in heaven, and there was someone sitting on the throne (εὐθέως ἐγενόμην ἐν πνεύματι, καὶ ἰδοὺ θρόνος ἔκειτο ἐν τῷ οὐρανῷ, καὶ ἐπὶ τὸν θρόνον καθήμενος). As John presents the circumstances in which he received the vision, he describes the state of Spirit possession ("in the Spirit") he entered immediately after Christ's call (v. 1e) to "come up here." The expression "I came to be in the Spirit" (v. 2a; also in 1:10) and the related phrase "he carried me away in the Spirit" in 17:3 and 21:10 mark crucial transitions between units in the whole book of Revelation (see introduction and "Literary Context" above). In his visionary trance[14] John begins to see through the "door standing open in heaven" and to glimpse details of the heavenly scene.[15] Two central features appear right away: a locus of ruling authority in heaven and someone who wields that authority. As in several of his later vision accounts, John's style is somewhat impres-

sionistic, somewhat minimalist at first and then adding descriptive details as he moves along (see comments at 20:4). In a masterful way John gently unfolds for the reader—most likely mirroring the way Christ did so for him—this overwhelming, luminous vision (as we discover in the verses that follow) of God Almighty in his glorious throne room surrounded by his heavenly retinue. But here John presents with restrained simplicity first a throne "standing in heaven" (v. 2b) representing the place from which the whole universe is ruled (cf. 1 Kgs 22:19; Ps 47:8; Isa 6:1; 66:1; Ezek 1:1, 26; 10:1; Dan 7:9; cf. 1 En. 14:8–25; T. Levi 5:1), but introduced here as though unfamiliar to the readers (without the article in Greek, θρόνος, "a throne"). Likewise unidentified is the second central item in the vision: "Someone sitting on the throne" (ἐπὶ τὸν θρόνον καθήμενος; v. 2c).[16] John will soon identify this one explicitly as "the Lord God Almighty" (vv. 8–9), who "lives forever and ever" (v. 10), and "our Lord and God" (v. 11), but he holds this in suspense for now, allowing the reader to experience the vision—and have its impact settle in—in stages.[17]

4:3 And the one who was sitting was like a jasper stone and a carnelian in appearance, and a rainbow was around the throne like an emerald in appearance (καὶ ὁ καθήμενος ὅμοιος ὁράσει λίθῳ ἰάσπιδι καὶ σαρδίῳ, καὶ ἶρις κυκλόθεν τοῦ θρόνου

---

13. This is the sense that the similar expressions carry in Dan 2:28–29, 45 ("what must happen in the last of the days"). See comments on 1:1; cf. 2 Bar. 10:3.

14. See comments on 1:10 for the meaning of "in the Spirit" and its background in Ezekiel. See also Bauckham, *Climax*, 133–34, 150–59.

15. Whether this implies his transfer to heaven in bodily form or instead in a state of altered consciousness is hard to decide (see Paul's own uncertainty about this question in 2 Cor 12:1–7). The latter seems more likely, but the more important point is that this experience came to him by the influence of God's revealing Spirit (cf. Bauckham, *Climax*, 158: "Indicat[ing] that the whole revelation came to him ἐν πνεύματι . . . was a theological claim as much as a psychological statement").

16. Here the substantival participle καθήμενος is without the Greek article, giving an indefinite sense (see note on 2:14). The same participle is used of the Lord God ten further times in Rev, always with the article and the word "throne," "the one sitting [on the throne]"; cf. also 20:11: "A great white throne and the one sitting on it."

17. This "unfamiliar" feel for v. 2 is clearly due to John's literary strategy rather than a lack of awareness of such things on the part of his readers. He assumed without hesitation just a bit earlier in the book that they knew about God the Father's throne (3:21) and his ruling authority over the world (2:26–28). On John's narrative style, see Resseguie, *Narrative Commentary*, 47–48.

ὅμοιος ὁράσει σμαραγδίνῳ). The one sitting on heaven's throne (v. 2c) is immediately portrayed in v. 3, but reverently and discretely, through images of precious and beautiful gems rather than with specific details. John's wording has clearly been influenced by Ezekiel's vision of the Lord's throne and his glory described in similar terms (Ezek 1:26–28).[18] How could humans picture the glorious God of heaven except by depicting what he is "like" (ὅμοιος; cf. 1:13, 15; 14:14) or how he appears ("in appearance," ὁράσει, used twice) in his glory? The gemstones mentioned here are difficult to identify in any technical way since ancient terms were used of a range of stones that had some outward similarities in color or consistency. "Jasper" is usually understood to be a greenish, opaque stone, but a range of other colors may be possible,[19] and Revelation 21:11 uses "jasper" of something that is crystal clear (possibly a diamond). "Carnelian" or sardius is taken to mean a reddish-brown or orange stone, and "emerald" is the bright green gem more familiar to modern readers.[20] These three appear along with other stones in Exodus 28:17–18; 39:10–13; Ezekiel 28:13; and Revelation 21:11, 18–20. In those texts as well as here these precious stones seen together portray the impressive value and beauty of what they describe. They are unlikely to have individual symbolic significance. The other image used here is the "rainbow" (ἶρις) around the throne (v. 3b). Some have preferred to render this as "halo" since it is not multicolored like a rainbow, but the likely connection to Ezekiel 1:28 ("like the appearance of a bow when it is in the cloud on a rainy day") makes "rainbow" preferable even if it has a single color.[21] An emerald rainbow opens up the vista of the throne scene and adds to the impressive effect. An early commentator who makes much of the symbolic meaning of the precious jewels of v. 3 explained that unlike a natural rainbow whose multiple colors come from sunlight filtered through clouds, this rainbow around the heavenly throne has a single hue but consists of hovering angels whose color symbolizes their deeds of service (green for their life-giving quality).[22]

4:4 And around the throne I saw twenty-four thrones, and on the thrones there were twenty-four elders sitting, clothed in white garments with golden crowns on their heads (καὶ κυκλόθεν τοῦ θρόνου θρόνους εἴκοσι τέσσαρες, καὶ ἐπὶ τοὺς θρόνους εἴκοσι τέσσαρας πρεσβυτέρους καθημένους περιβεβλημένους ἐν ἱματίοις λευκοῖς καὶ ἐπὶ τὰς κεφαλὰς αὐτῶν στεφάνους χρυσοῦς). With God's throne (and his implicit presence on it)[23] as the central focus, John proceeds to describe other beings and phenomena associated with his heavenly presence. An important part of this glorious scene is the group of twenty-four elders[24] described in v. 4 as the very first thing after God and his throne and

---

18. The common LXX Greek terms are "throne," "appearance," precious "stone" (but not the ones listed here), and "rainbow" (using a different word). See also the unmistakable parallels with Ezek 1 in Rev 4:6–8 (see comments there).

19. BDAG 465.

20. BDAG 913, 933.

21. Ezek 1:28 LXX uses a different Greek word for "rainbow" or "bow" (τόξον), but the concept is more determinative than the specific word. Some suggest that "rainbow" (using either term) alludes to God's pledge not to destroy the world again (Gen 9:13–16), but this seems foreign to the heavenly scene portrayed in this chapter. A focus on God's glorious presence is the point here (as well as in Ezek 1:28).

22. Weinrich, "Oecumenius," 21.

23. A broad characteristic of references to heaven in Rev is a reverential hesitation to refer to God himself directly. Worship is offered before the throne, and declarations come from the throne (5:13; 7:9, 11; 8:3; 14:3; 16:17; 19:5; 21:3, 5), but rarely is God himself cited as in heaven (11:16; 12:5; 19:4).

24. The word "elders" (as well as "crowns" later in the verse) are accusative nouns in the Greek text because they are understood as direct objects of a verb that John leaves unexpressed. The most plausible transitive verb to supply in this report of his vision is "I saw" as in 4:1 and many other vision texts in the book.

then repeatedly cited in later chapters as a way of referring back to this heavenly scene or to heaven's involvement in earthly events (e.g., 5:5, 6; 7:11, 13). While these "elders" are prominent in John's vision of heaven (especially in chs. 4–5), their identity is not made clear, and interpreters differ over how to understand their role.

The prominence of these "elders" comes across unmistakably in the way John portrays them here and in later visions. First, like a royal council they sit on thrones arranged in a circle around God's throne (v. 4a–b). The fact that other thrones exist in God's presence does not detract from his unique supremacy already recognized (vv. 2–3) and acknowledged repeatedly (e.g., v. 10; 5:8, 14).[25] Second, they are "clothed in white garments," symbolizing the holiness expected of those who approach God. Third, they have "golden crowns on their heads," representing their exalted status and perhaps victory in the face of struggle. In later verses they offer worship to God (4:10–11; 5:8–14; 19:4) and interact with John in his visionary experiences (5:5; 7:13–14).

John gives attention to describing these "elders" and their activities, but he tells us nothing explicit about their being or identity. Are they angelic or human?[26] If human, do they represent Old Testament worthies, New Testament saints, or God's people from all ages? John saw no need to specify

such matters. We are left to ponder possible clues based on what John does tell us about them. Of the descriptions mentioned already, offering worship to God in heaven does not seem to be distinctive since 5:11–14 shows both angels and humans doing so. Wearing of white is likewise shared by Christ, angels, and humans (1:14; 3:4–5; 6:11; 7:9, 13). Enthronement and possession of a "crown" or victory wreath is sometimes thought to tip the scales toward seeing them as glorified humans, since these are promised to faithful Christians (2:10; 3:11, 21). But crowns may denote a broader sort of victory or exalted status in Revelation (6:2; 9:7; 12:1; 14:14) and elsewhere.[27] Finally, the significance of their number, "twenty-four," is likewise debatable. This possibly symbolizes the whole people of God, representing the sum of both Israel (the twelve tribes as in 7:4–8; 21:12) and the church (the twelve apostles as in 21:14). Or it may picture them as a heavenly order of priestly ministers in heaven like the twenty-four Levitical orders of 1 Chronicles 24:4; 25:9–31.

The fact that these are called "elders" seems to be rooted in the term's use for leaders among the people in the Old Testament and later Judaism, a group of officials who shared various social and tribal responsibilities as a ruling council (e.g., Exod 17:5; 18:12; Num 11:30; 2 Sam 5:3). This favors the view that these elders are a council of heavenly be-

---

25. Other thrones or ruling authorities representing shared or delegated authority under God's supreme rule have already been mentioned in 2:26–28; 3:22 and will be noted again in 5:10; 20:4, 6; 22:5.

26. Among the commentaries taking these as heavenly beings or angels—a more common view in recent years—are Charles, Ladd, Mounce, Thomas, Osborne; also Ned B. Stonehouse, "The Elders and the Living Beings in the Apocalypse," in *Paul before the Areopagus* (Grand Rapids: Eerdmans, 1957), 88–108. For the view that these are glorified human beings see Patterson, Swete, Walvoord, Rawley, and Hitchcock; also David J. MacLeod, "The Adoration of God the Creator: An Exposition of Revelation 4," *BSac* 164 (2007): 198–218. Koester, *Revelation*,

360–63, argues that they are neither angels nor humans but "heavenly representatives of God's people" (360). Beale, Boxall, Murphy, and Smalley take a similar view (angels or figures in angelic form who represent the faithful of both testaments before God).

27. This word for "crown" is στέφανος, a wreath of foliage or other material (here of gold formed into a wreath). This is often associated with joyous celebration or recognition of victory (see BDAG 943, and comments at 2:10) and is different from the diadem or headband symbolizing royal authority (e.g., 19:12). Yet it can also speak of high position or ruling status (e.g., Zech 6:11–14; also the mocking crown given to Jesus as "king of the Jews"; Matt 27:29; Mark 15:17; John 19:2).

ings who surround God's throne (as seen, e.g., in 1 Kgs 22:19; Job 1:6; Ps 89:7; Dan 7:9–10; possibly Isa 24:23).[28] Also favoring this view is the fact that John seems to distinguish the "elders" from martyred earthly saints who have come to be present in heaven after their physical deaths (Rev 7:13–14) and from redeemed saints whether on earth or in heaven (14:1–3).[29]

4:5–6a And from the throne come flashes of lightning and rumblings and peals of thunder, and there were seven fiery torches burning before the throne, which are the seven spirits of God, 6 and before the throne was something like a glass sea—like crystal (καὶ ἐκ τοῦ θρόνου ἐκπορεύονται ἀστραπαὶ καὶ φωναὶ καὶ βρονταί, καὶ ἑπτὰ λαμπάδες πυρὸς καιόμεναι ἐνώπιον τοῦ θρόνου, ἅ εἰσιν τὰ ἑπτὰ πνεύματα τοῦ θεοῦ, 6 καὶ ἐνώπιον τοῦ θρόνου ὡς θάλασσα ὑαλίνη ὁμοία κρυστάλλῳ). Continuing to orient everything to God's throne as the center of what he saw, John notes three further impressive features of this heavenly scene. The first set of items ("flashes of lightning and rumblings and peals of thunder"; v. 5a) represent God's awesome presence taken from Israel's Sinai experience (Exod 19:16–19) and repeated often thereafter

as symbols of theophany and portents of coming judgment (Judg 5:4–5; Pss 18:7–15; 68:7–8; 77:18; Isa 13:13; 64:2–4; Jer 10:10; Ezek 1:13; Hag 2:6–7, 21). In Revelation the same three phenomena (with additions) appear also at the end of the three series of judgments (8:5; 11:19; 16:18), linking them to this vision of God in his heavenly rule as the source of the seals, trumpets, and bowls that will prepare the way for his rule on earth.[30] John reports these phenomena using a present-tense verb, "[they] come, are coming" (ἐκπορεύονται; NASB, NRSV) to draw the reader into his visionary experience more directly.[31]

The second striking feature is "seven fiery torches"[32] burning in front of the throne (v. 5b–c). These contribute to the scene's dazzling and fearful visual impression, but they also represent, as John reports, "the seven spirits of God." John has already mentioned these "seven spirits who are before God's throne" in 1:4, and in that context they clearly refer to the fullness of the Holy Spirit.[33] In understanding the torches here as "the seven spirits of God," John has been influenced by Zechariah 4:1–14 in two important ways. One is to see this throne room in heaven as also exhibiting parallels with the earthly sanctuary or temple where God is

---

28. G. Bornkamm, "πρεσβύτερος," *TDNT* 6:655–61, 668.

29. Another argument for seeing the elders as part of redeemed humanity is the textual variation in 5:9–10 where according to some manuscripts the elders say, "you redeemed *us* for God . . . you made *us* to be a kingdom and priests" (see KJV). But the more likely text leads to a third-person sense ("them") rather than first person in both places, distinguishing the elders from the redeemed. See the comments and textual notes at 5:9, 10. For arguments supporting "us" as the superior readings in both places, see MacLeod, "Exposition of Revelation 4," 209–12.

30. Bauckham, *Climax*, 202–4; Beale, *Revelation*, 326.

31. See Mussies, *Morphology*, 333–36, 340, who posits three types of presentation in the visionary material of Rev. One subtype recounts the contents of a vision in a nonnarrative genre. This takes the form of a description or report of the contents as events currently taking place. This draws the reader into the

vision more directly to see the events along with John as he relives his prior experience of seeing and hearing the details of the vision. For further discussion of John's modes of presentation, see Buist M. Fanning, "Greek Tenses in John's Apocalypse: Issues in Verbal Aspect, Discourse Analysis, and Diachronic Change," in *The Language and Literature of the New Testament: Essays in Honour of Stanley E. Porter's 60th Birthday*, ed. Lois K. Fuller Dow, Craig A. Evans, and Andrew W. Pitts (Leiden: Brill, 2016), 341–49.

32. The Greek word for "torches" (λαμπάδες) can denote the more domesticated "(oil) lamps" (Matt 25:1–8), but here a flaming "torch" is in view (cf. Gen 15:17; Nah 2:5; Dan 10:6; John 18:3). This feature is also influenced by Ezek 1:13.

33. See comments at 1:4–5 where they, alongside God and Jesus Christ, are a source of grace and peace for the churches. These "spirits" are closely associated with Jesus also in 3:1 and 5:6 (see comments).

approached in worship (cf. also Isa 6:1–7).[34] Here the seven torches parallel the lampstand with its seven lamps in the outer chamber of the tabernacle (Exod 25:31–40; 40:4, 24–25). The other insight from Zechariah 4 is to see the lamps or torches as symbolic of God's ability to see and act powerfully by his Spirit to accomplish his will across the whole earth (Zech 4:2–6, 10; see discussion at Rev 5:6).[35]

The third feature, also "before the throne," is "something like a glass sea—like crystal" (v. 6a).[36] This is also drawn from Ezekiel's vision (Ezek 1:22) as well as Israel's experience at Sinai (Exod 24:10) and may likewise reflect a heavenly parallel to the furnishings of the earthly sanctuary, the bronze laver or "sea" (Exod 30:18–21; 40:7, 30; 1 Kgs 7:23–25). As it appears to John in his vision, it is like a gleaming, translucent floor stretching out in front of God's throne, reinforcing the astounding impression of the glory and purity of heaven.[37]

4:6b–7 And on each side of the throne and around the throne were four living creatures, covered with eyes in front and in back. 7 And the first living creature was like a lion, and the second living creature like a calf, and the third had a face like a human, and the fourth was

like a flying eagle (Καὶ ἐν μέσῳ τοῦ θρόνου καὶ κύκλῳ τοῦ θρόνου τέσσαρα ζῷα γέμοντα ὀφθαλμῶν ἔμπροσθεν καὶ ὄπισθεν. 7 καὶ τὸ ζῷον τὸ πρῶτον ὅμοιον λέοντι καὶ τὸ δεύτερον ζῷον ὅμοιον μόσχῳ καὶ τὸ τρίτον ζῷον ἔχων τὸ πρόσωπον ὡς ἀνθρώπου καὶ τὸ τέταρτον ζῷον ὅμοιον ἀετῷ πετομένῳ). After describing the heavenly throne, the one sitting on it, and other accompanying features of the heavenly scene rather quickly (vv. 2b–6a), John connects one other group of beings to the throne and pays greater attention to their appearance and activities in heaven (vv. 6b–9). These are the "four living creatures" (τέσσαρα ζῷα), directly drawn from the vision of Ezekiel 1 but with important changes and omissions compared to Ezekiel's account. These must be understood as an order of angels, although John never gives them a specific label beyond "living creatures."[38] They are similar in appearance and activity, however, to both Ezekiel's "living creatures" (which Ezekiel later identifies as "cherubim"; Ezek 1:5–22; 9:3; 10:15, 20)[39] and Isaiah's "seraphim" (Isa 6:1–7). Their location is what John mentions first, again orienting them to God's throne: they form the innermost circle around God himself.[40] They are "on each side of the throne and around the throne" (v. 6b),[41] offering worship and service to

---

34. See in the later verses prayers and incense (Rev 5:8; 8:3–4), an altar (6:9; 9:13), incense altar (8:3), ark of the covenant (11:19), bronze laver (15:2), and heavenly tabernacle (15:5, 8), as well as songs of praise and worship (4:8–11; 5:9–14; 7:10–12).

35. Bauckham, *Climax*, 162–66.

36. As in v. 2, the best John can do is work with comparisons (cf. 5:6; 6:6; 8:8). The translation "something like a glass sea" comes from the Greek ὡς θάλασσα ὑαλίνη, "as a glass sea," followed by ὁμοία κρυστάλλῳ, "similar to crystal." See 4 Ezra 11:37 and 14:39 for similar wording for things seen in apocalyptic visions.

37. See the parallel reference to "glass sea" (θάλασσα ὑαλίνη) in 15:2 and discussion there.

38. "Living creature" (ζῷα) means an "animal," wild or domesticated (BDAG 431; cf. Gen 1:21; Heb 13:11; 2 Pet 2:12; Jude 10), but without the connotations of "dangerous, ferocious" often carried by "beast" (θηρίον) as in Gen 1:24; 3:1; Dan

7:3–23; Acts 28:4; Rev 6:8; 13:1, 11 (BDAG 455–56; LN §4.2–4). KJV uses "beast" for ζῷα (here in 4:6) as well as θηρίον (13:1, 11), but this is not followed by modern versions.

39. The presence of cherubim in the heavenly throne room may add to its character as also a sanctuary-temple (see comments on v. 5 above), since the cherubim overshadowing the ark of the covenant were a well-known feature of the tabernacle and the later temple (Exod 25:18–20; 1 Kgs 6:27–28; 8:6–7). The Lord who was present there among his people could be referred to as "the one enthroned above the cherubim" (1 Sam 4:4; 2 Sam 6:2; 2 Kgs 19:15; Pss 80:1; 99:1; Isa 37:16).

40. Although the "elders" were noted first as "around the throne" (v. 4), later verses seem to locate them in a second ring, with the "living creatures" closest to God (5:6, 11).

41. The phrase "on each side of the throne" (v. 6b) is expressed as "in (the) midst of the throne" (ἐν μέσῳ τοῦ θρόνου). This seems to be an adaptation of Ezek 1:4–5, which initially places the living creatures "in the midst of the fire" that accom-

God and guarding his purity and holiness (cf. Gen 3:24; Ps 18:10; Isa 6:2–7; Ezek 1:11–21; 28:14, 16).

In later verses John will devote attention to such activities of the living creatures (4:8b–9; 5:8–14; 6:1–8), but first he portrays their enigmatic appearance (vv. 6c–8a). They are "covered with eyes in front and in back" (v. 6c).[42] Such "eyes" should probably be understood to refer to complete vigilance in protecting God and doing his bidding (cf. Rev 2:18; 5:6; see Zech 4:10 where they seem to represent knowledge or understanding).

Continuing to replicate but adapt features from Ezekiel 1, John describes the appearance of each of the creatures in turn by noting its resemblance[43] to a living being known on earth (v. 7). In Ezekiel 1:10 each being has four "faces" (human, lion, calf, eagle), simplified here in that each creature has a likeness in general to just one of these earthly animals (same Greek words as in Ezek 1:10 LXX). The first is like a lion, and the second is like a calf or ox.[44] The "face" of the third is specified as "like a human" (ὡς ἀνθρώπου), and the fourth "like a flying eagle." Each of these is illustrative of God's good, varied, and noble creation (e.g., the added description of the fourth as a "flying" eagle). It is hard to determine whether these likenesses for the four angelic creatures have symbolic significance, but in light of v. 11 (continual praise to God as the creator of all things), they may represent his

good and useful creation, fully devoted to him as it ought to be.

4:8 And the four living creatures, each one of them having six wings, were covered around and inside with eyes, and day and night they never stopped saying, "Holy, Holy, Holy, is the Lord God Almighty, who was and who is and who is to come" (καὶ τὰ τέσσαρα ζῷα, ἓν καθ᾽ ἓν αὐτῶν ἔχων ἀνὰ πτέρυγας ἕξ, κυκλόθεν καὶ ἔσωθεν γέμουσιν ὀφθαλμῶν, καὶ ἀνάπαυσιν οὐκ ἔχουσιν ἡμέρας καὶ νυκτὸς λέγοντες, Ἅγιος ἅγιος ἅγιος κύριος ὁ θεὸς ὁ παντοκράτωρ, ὁ ἦν καὶ ὁ ὢν καὶ ὁ ἐρχόμενος). John provides one final feature of the creatures' appearance that, based on Scripture, is evocative also of their continual activity that he begins now to relate. Two features of Ezekiel's vision contribute to this description, their "wings" (8x in Ezek 1:6–24 LXX) and "eyes" (Ezek 1:18; 10:12).[45] But the image of "winged" angelic creatures clearly evokes also Isaiah 6:1–7, the other significant passage that has influenced John's description here. Isaiah's overwhelming vision of God in his heavenly throne room/temple includes glorious six-winged creatures (seraphim; Isa 6:2–3) who worship God in a similar way.[46]

Here in v. 8b–d and carrying over into v. 9 (and then expanding to include the twenty-four elders in vv. 10–11), John presents the primary events that he sees in his vision. In doing so he portrays

---

panies God's presence (v. 4) and then simply "in the midst" (ἐν τῷ μέσῳ; v. 5). John uses "in the midst" to mean "in the middle of each side" of the throne, i.e., closely encircling it (BDAG 635; Moffatt, "Revelation," 380).

42. This detail is taken from Ezek where initially the creatures' wheels (1:18) and later their whole bodies (10:12) are said to be "full of eyes all around" (LXX πλήρεις ὀφθαλμῶν κυκλόθεν). John's vision is simpler since he says nothing about the wheels and rapid movements that dominate Ezekiel's vision (cf. Rowland, "Revelation," 592).

43. The adjective "like" (ὅμοιος) is used three times and the conjunction "as" (ὡς) once.

44. The word "calf" (μόσχος) usually denotes a young bovine (BDAG 660; LN §4.17; Exod 32:4; Luke 15:23; Heb 9:12; cf. KJV, NASB), but this is often translated here as "ox" (CSB, ESV, NET, NIV, NLT NRSV, RSV).

45. Ezekiel's creatures had four wings, while John saw six-winged creatures like Isaiah did. But the picture of heavenly beings "covered around and inside" (i.e., on the inner surfaces of their wings) is drawn from Ezek 1:18; 10:12 (see notes on v. 6 above).

46. John emphasizes the possession of six wings by "each one of them," using two distributive expressions: "one by one of them" (ἓν καθ᾽ ἓν αὐτῶν) and "six wings apiece" (ἀνὰ πτέρυγας ἕξ). See BDAG 58, 293, 512; and Mathewson, *Handbook*, 65.

the constant activity of the four living creatures before God's throne in heaven in such a way that his readers can experience the vision's power for themselves.[47] The creatures sing praise to God continually,[48] uttering in part the same words Isaiah heard in his vision (Isa 6:3),[49] "Holy, Holy, Holy, is the Lord God Almighty" (Rev 4:8c). They, like Isaiah's seraphim, marvel unceasingly at the character of the God who is "set apart," unmatched, the true and living God (see comments at 3:7 on the sense of "holy"; ἅγιος). The threefold repetition drives home his uniqueness as Lord and God above all others. The title "Almighty" (παντοκράτωρ) appears in LXX Isaiah 6:3 in a form transliterated from the Hebrew (צְבָאוֹת; σαβαώθ), "Sabaoth." This acknowledges God's absolute dominion and sovereignty over all.[50] It is appropriately addressed to God in worship utterances elsewhere in Revelation (11:17; 15:3; 16:7; 19:6), and John has already recorded its use as a self-designation by God in the prologue at the start of the whole book (1:8). Also appearing in 1:8 as well as in John's opening salutation in 1:4 is the phrase that concludes the living creatures' refrain of praise here in 4:8d: "Who was and who is and who is to come" (ὁ ἦν καὶ ὁ ὢν καὶ ὁ ἐρχόμενος).[51] The expression draws on God's own self-disclosure in Exodus 3:14 and acknowledges

him as the eternal, self-existent One[52] who controls history from beginning to end (a significant foundation for the complementary vision that will follow in 5:1–14).[53] Its third part also highlights his engagement with his creation: "who is to come" refers not only to his future existence but to his "final coming to bring all things to fulfilment in his eternal future."[54]

4:9 And every time the living creatures give glory and honor and thanks to the one who sits on the throne, who lives forever and ever (καὶ ὅταν δώσουσιν τὰ ζῷα δόξαν καὶ τιμὴν καὶ εὐχαριστίαν τῷ καθημένῳ ἐπὶ τῷ θρόνῳ τῷ ζῶντι εἰς τοὺς αἰῶνας τῶν αἰώνων). This temporal clause (v. 9) launches the compound sentence that finishes John's description of the living creatures' actions in his vision (vv. 9–11). The implication of the clause[55] is that, as seen in v. 8b, the living creatures offer their unceasing praise to God (v. 9), and the twenty-four elders join in (vv. 10–11). To "give glory and honor" to someone is to acknowledge that person's rightful possession of those high attributes. It does not bestow those traits but recognizes and celebrates the glory and honor the person has and displays.[56] Likewise to give "thanks" in parallel with the other traits is more than to "say thanks"; it is a declaration about someone's character, an acknowledgment

---

47. Both main verbs of v. 8 are present indicative as in a direct report or description. See note on v. 5.

48. "They never stop saying" is phrased as "they do not have rest" (ἀνάπαυσιν οὐκ ἔχουσιν; cf. 14:11), used with genitives of time, "day and night." Similar visions (based on the same OT texts) of unceasing worship by hosts of angels before God's throne in heaven are found in 1 En. 39:12–14; 61:9–12; 2 En. 21:1; 22:2–3; and T. Levi 3:4–9.

49. All but the final word of this line is a verbatim citation of Isa 6:3 LXX.

50. See discussion at 1:8.

51. The first and second predications are reversed in 1:4, 8 ("the one who is and who was and who is to come") compared to the order here.

52. This is reinforced by John's description of God twice in vv. 9b, 10b as the one "who lives forever and ever."

53. See 1:4 for further discussion of the grammar and meaning of this phrase.

54. Bauckham, *Theology*, 28–30 (quotation from p. 30).

55. The clause is introduced by a temporal conjunction (ὅταν; "whenever") translated here as "every time." Such clauses usually contain subjunctive verbs to denote indefinite occurrences that can happen at various times rather than a definite or specific action at a particular time (as with ὅτε plus indicative verbs). In NT and vernacular Hellenistic Greek the future indicative can replace the subjunctive with a similar range of meanings.

56. See 1 Chr 16:28–29; Pss 66:2; 68:34; Isa 42:12; Luke 17:18; Rev 14:7; 19:7; also see comments on 5:12.

that the person deserves gratitude for blessings bestowed.

After repeated references to "the throne" in the intervening verses, v. 9a returns to an explicit focus on "the one who sits on the throne" (not seen since vv. 2–3). But a further description is added (v. 9b), "who lives forever and ever."[57] This phrase (drawn primarily from Dan 4:34; 6:26; 12:7) is repeated also in v. 10b and complements what v. 8d already asserted about God's eternal existence, reinforcing the point about his sovereignty over all of this world's history. The universal scope of God's dominion is a central proposition in the passages in Daniel that influenced John's description of this heavenly worship (see especially Dan 4:34–35 and 6:26–27).[58]

4:10–11 the twenty-four elders fall down before the one who sits on the throne and worship the one who lives forever and ever and lay their crowns before the throne, saying, 11 "Worthy are you, our Lord and God, to receive glory and honor and power, because you created all things and on account of your will they existed and were created" (πεσοῦνται οἱ εἴκοσι τέσσαρες πρεσβύτεροι ἐνώπιον τοῦ καθημένου ἐπὶ τοῦ θρόνου καὶ προσκυνήσουσιν τῷ ζῶντι εἰς τοὺς αἰῶνας τῶν αἰώνων καὶ βαλοῦσιν τοὺς στεφάνους αὐτῶν ἐνώπιον τοῦ θρόνου λέγοντες, 11 Ἄξιος εἶ, ὁ κύριος καὶ ὁ θεὸς ἡμῶν, λαβεῖν τὴν δόξαν καὶ τὴν τιμὴν καὶ

τὴν δύναμιν, ὅτι σὺ ἔκτισας τὰ πάντα καὶ διὰ τὸ θέλημά σου ἦσαν καὶ ἐκτίσθησαν). In the heavenly scene that John describes, the twenty-four elders also join the living creatures in worshiping God with their own overt physical expressions of adoration (v. 10) as well as declarations of praise for him (v. 11). They "fall down"[59] or prostrate themselves before God as a sign of humble adoration (e.g., Gen 17:3; Matt 2:11; often in Rev: 1:17; 5:8, 14; 7:11; 11:16; 19:4; see discussion at 5:8). In bowing down before him, they symbolize their "worship"[60] to the eternal God (cf. v. 9). Their graphic demonstration of homage toward God is culminated when they "lay their crowns"[61] in front of his throne (v. 10c). The crowns that represented their own honored status in heaven in proximity to God's throne itself (v. 4) are now rightly offered back to God in acknowledgment that all creaturely honor is dependent on God's gifts and must redound to the creator's praise.[62]

Just as the living creatures declare their praise to the Almighty God in a hymn of worship in v. 8, so the elders sing of God's perfections here in v. 11 to conclude John's vision. Addressing their song to God directly, they exalt God as the one deserving[63] of all acclaim (v. 11a) and cite his creation of all things as the ground of his worthiness (v. 11b).[64] To say that he is "worthy . . . to receive" is to extol the perfections he possesses and displays. The things

---

57. This phrase is used of Christ in 1:18 and of God again in 4:10; 10:6; 15:7.

58. Beale, *Revelation*, 333–34.

59. The three Greek future-tense verbs in v. 10 ("fall," "worship," "lay") continue the indefinite or "whenever" sense that began in v. 9 (see note on v. 9a). These have a gnomic sense (Wallace, *Grammar*, 571) rendered here as English general presents.

60. The verb "worship" (προσκυνέω) is a fitting complement to "fall down before," since it "indicates not only a body position but also an attitude and activity of reverence or honor" (LN §17.21). The two verbs often occur together (Matt 2:11; 4:9; 18:26; Acts 10:25; 1 Cor 14:25; Rev 4:10; 5:14; 7:11; 11:16; 19:4,

10; 22:8), but at times προσκυνέω means "fall prostrate, show honor" without the religious sense of "worship" (e.g., Rev 3:9).

61. The verb used here (βάλλω) is often translated "cast" or "throw" (CSB, ESV, KJV, NASB, NRSV, RSV), but it can mean "put, place, or lay" (BDAG 163; LN §85.34; cf. NIV, NLT), which seems better in this context.

62. This sort of obeisance (laying a wreath or crown at the feet of a superior) can be found, for example, in two ancient histories (Arrian, *Anab.* 7.23.2; Tacitus, *Ann.* 15.29).

63. For the word "worthy" (ἄξιος) see 3:4; 5:2, 4, 9, 12; 16:6.

64. See the focus on God as creator also in Rev 3:14; 10:6–7; 14:7; 21:5.

he "receives" are his creatures' declarations ascribing exalted attributes and privileges to him (note the complementary verb "give" in 4:9).[65] Here the elders sing of his "glory and honor," just as the living creatures did in v. 9, and the addition of "power" (δύναμις) especially befits their worship of him as creator in v. 11b–c.

To acclaim God as creator (as here and in 10:6–7; 14:7) is also to acknowledge his control over the history of the world he created.[66] To the creator belongs the right to direct the course of the world and its creatures according to his intent and timing. This point is reinforced in v. 11c by the citation of God's "will" by which they "existed and were created."[67] This final acclamation of chapter 4 sets the stage for the vision of chapter 5, which launches God's plan for the coming judgment and redemption that will unfold in subsequent chapters. The songs of praise recorded here are only the beginning of repeated acclamations of worship that will follow in anticipation of God's great victory to come (7:10, 12; 11:15, 17; 12:10; 15:3–4; 19:1–7).

Theology in Application

The Majesty of God

All healthy Christian living and service is rooted in a right view of God, the biblical view of him rather than our cultural or personal distortions. As Tozer wrote, "What comes into our minds when we think about God is the most important thing about us."[68] Do we see him in his majesty, sovereignty, and goodness, or do we create him in our image as something far less? According to Packer, modern people, "though they cherish great thoughts of man, have as a rule small thoughts of God. When the man in the Church, let alone the man in the street, uses the word 'God,' the thought in his mind is rarely of divine *majesty*." He adds:

> Today, vast stress is laid on the thought that God is *personal*, but this truth is so stated as to leave the impression that God is a person of the same sort as we are— weak, inadequate, ineffective, a little pathetic. . . . He is personal, but unlike us He is *great*. In all its constant stress on the reality of God's personal concern for His people, and on the gentleness, tenderness, sympathy, patience, and yearning compassion that He shows towards them, the Bible never lets us lose sight of His majesty, and His unlimited dominion over all His creatures."[69]

---

65. See further discussion at 5:12.

66. See a similar line of thought in Sir 18:1–2; 4 Ezra 6:6–7; 3 Macc. 2:1–3.

67. These two verbs reverse the normal order of events, a common pattern in Rev. See note on 3:3 for other examples and its possible significance. Two textual variants are worthy of note in this verse. A few manuscripts (P, 1854, 2050, plus part of the Byzantine minuscules) read "are/exist" (present tense εἰσίν), which appears in the KJV: "They are and were created." One manuscript (046) has a negative with the past tense (οὐκ ἦσαν) producing the sense "they were not/did not exist and [then] were created." This reading is defended by J. M. Ross, "Some Unnoticed Points in the Text of the New Testament," *NovT* 25 (1983): 72. Both readings seem more likely to be scribal attempts at resolving what appeared to them as an improper sense.

68. A. W. Tozer, *The Knowledge of the Holy* (New York: Harper & Row, 1961), 1.

69. J. I. Packer, *Knowing God* (Downers Grove, IL: InterVarsity Press, 1973), 73–74.

This is the dominant point of John's vision in chapter 4: God's eternal majesty and sovereignty above all that exists. The descriptions of his heavenly throne room and the angelic retinue offering him constant worship are relevant only insofar as they show us the majestic God in all his heavenly glory and worth. Everything that follows in the remaining chapters of Revelation is set in its proper framework by seeing God on his throne receiving worship for his perfect holiness and his eternal power to create and sustain all things. The preoccupation, even obsession, of such heavenly worship of God himself in all his glory and honor and power should be our model—or at least our aspiration—for the corporate and individual worship that we engage in today in our earthly setting that is so different. The degree to which we imitate such worship will speak worlds about how healthy our Christian life and service actually are.

The Tension of God's Sovereignty

John's great vision of God on his heavenly throne and of Jesus the Lamb who will consummate God's worldwide judgment and redemption (chs. 4–5) is perfectly placed. On one side of this picture of the majestic God ruling and directing the world's destiny, we see seven accounts of churches in John's day suffering and struggling to live for Christ amid first-century idolatry and hostility to the true God (chs. 2–3). On the other side, we see unprecedented divine judgment poured out on a future world in which that idolatry and hostility have grown exponentially (chs. 6–19). The tension between John's vision of God being worshiped and in control in heaven, and human empires and individuals vehemently resisting his rule on earth, could not be more blatant. Our own earthly experience displays the same paradox. Intermingled with periods of peace and stability in our personal lives and in the wider world, we also confront episodes of unspeakable agony and tragedy, of seemingly uncontrollable chaos and turmoil that make us wonder if anyone is at the helm. Yet this is one of the purposes of revelatory or apocalyptic visions such as the one John provides in this book: to see all of life from a heavenly perspective that rises above the earthly hysteria and disorientation that can easily overwhelm us. To see God as sovereign, as creator, as redeemer and judge is the all-important theological foundation for understanding the rest of the book as well as the rest of our lives. The judgments that follow should not be seen in isolation but in light of God's sovereign right as creator. His promises of victory and renewal ring true in light of his control of all things, according to his plan in Christ to establish his kingdom in its fullness on earth as it is in heaven. Heartfelt worship and faithful service for such a God, even in our less-than-heavenly circumstances, is the only appropriate response to this vision.

CHAPTER 11

Revelation 5:1–14

Literary Context

As mentioned at 4:1, John's visions in chapters 4–5 pick up from the vision of chapter 1 and lead into the descriptions of judgment and salvation that will follow in chapters 6–22. The majestic scene in chapter 4, for all its glory, sets the stage for the stunning events—with far-reaching implications—that John witnesses in chapter 5. Jesus Christ, who was not seen in chapter 4, now appears in surprising, dramatic fashion to assume his God-given role as the one who fulfills the royal and redemptive promises of the Old Testament and puts into operation God's sovereign plan to judge sin, redeem his worldwide people, and accomplish his purpose for all creation.

I. Prologue (1:1–8)

II. First Vision: The Exalted Christ and His Messages to the Churches (1:9–3:22)

III. Second Vision: Heavenly Throne Room and Three Judgment Cycles (4:1–16:21)

    A. Vision of God in His Heavenly Throne Room (4:1–11)

→   **B. The Seven-Sealed Scroll and the Slain Lamb (5:1–14)**

    C. The Seven Seals and the Interlude of the Two Multitudes (6:1–8:1)

Main Idea

All of creation continually worships the Lord God and Jesus Christ for their sovereign plan to accomplish both judgment against sin and redemption for God's people through the sacrifice of Christ.

Translation

(See pages 209–10.)

Revelation 5:1–14

1a	Action/Vision Introduction	**And I saw** **in the right hand of the one sitting on the throne**
		a scroll
b	Descriptions	written inside and on the back,
c		sealed with seven seals.

2a	Vision/Character Entrance	**And I saw** **a mighty angel proclaiming with a loud voice,**
b	Question/ Challenge	*"Who is worthy to open the scroll and break its seals?"*
3	Plot Tension/Crisis	**And no one …**
		in heaven or
		on earth or
		under the earth
		… was able to open the scroll or
		look into it.

4a	Response to 3	**So I began to weep bitterly**
b	Reason	that no one was found worthy
c	Explanation	to open the scroll or
		look into it.

5a	Response to 4	**Then one of the elders said to me,**
b	Prohibition	*"Stop weeping!*
c	Explanation	*See, the Lion of the tribe of Judah,…*
		the Shoot of David,
		… has won the victory
d	Purpose of 5c	*so that he can open the scroll and*
		its seven seals."

6a	Vision/Character Entrance	**And I saw**
		amid the throne area and
		the four living creatures and
		amid the elders
		a Lamb standing,
b	Descriptions	looking like it had been slain,
c		with seven horns and seven eyes,
d	Identification	which are the seven spirits of God
e	Description	sent out into all the earth.

7	Action	**Then he went and took the scroll from the right hand of the one sitting on the throne.**

8a	Time/Tail-Head Linkage	And when he had taken the scroll,
b	Action/ Response to 7	**the four living creatures and**
		the twenty-four elders **fell down before the Lamb,**
c	Description	each holding a kithara and golden bowls full of incense,
d	Identification	which are the prayers of the saints.

Continued on next page.

Continued from previous page.

9a Action/
    Response to 7
 b   Praise
 c   Reasons
 d

And **they sang a new song, saying,**

        "Worthy are you to take the scroll and open its seals,
            for   *you were slain*
            and by your blood *you ransomed for God members of every* *tribe and*
                                            language and
                                            people and
                                            nation,

10a

            and   *you made* *them to be* *a kingdom and*
                                      priests to serve our God,

 b

            and   *they will reign on the earth."*

11a Action/Vision
    Introduction
 b Action/Character
    Entrance

And **I saw,**

and **I heard the sound of many angels around the throne and**
                  of the living creatures and
                  the elders,

 c   Description
12a
 b   Praise

and **the number of them was myriads of myriads and thousands of thousands,**
                saying with a loud voice,
                    "Worthy is the Lamb who was slain, to receive *power and*
                                              wealth and
                                              wisdom and
                                              might and
                                              honor and
                                              glory and
                                              blessing!"

13a Action/Character
    Entrance

And **every creature** **in heaven and**
                        on earth and
                        under the earth and
                        in the sea, and

        all that is in them, I heard saying,
 b   Praise   *"To the one sitting on the throne and*
                        to the Lamb be *blessing and*
                                      honor and
                                      glory and
                                    might

                          forever and ever!"

14a Coda/
    Responses to 13
 b

And **the four living creatures were saying,** *"Amen!"*

and **the elders fell down and**
                  worshiped.

Structure

The literary structure of the chapter is clearly reflected in the fourfold repetition of the Greek phrase καὶ εἶδον ("and I saw") at the beginning of vv. 1, 2, 6, and 11. The phrase is more difficult to trace in most English versions since it is not translated uniformly. This repetition marks four additional phases of John's vision that began in chapter 4 and continues here in dramatic fashion.[1]

The first phase (5:1) connects the further parts of the vision to the central figure of chapter 4 (the Lord God sitting on his heavenly throne), but sets the stage for new developments by introducing the seven-sealed scroll in God's right hand. The second phase (5:2–5) poses the challenge of the scroll: Is anyone in heaven or on earth worthy to open it? The third phase (5:6–10) constitutes the dramatic high point of the chapter, the revelation of Jesus Christ as the slain Lamb who alone is qualified to open the scroll (vv. 6–7) and the heavenly worship that acknowledges his redemptive sacrifice and its cosmic significance (vv. 8–10). An ever-widening crescendo of praise, to the Lord God and to the Lamb, continues this response as the final phase of the vision (5:11–14).

Exegetical Outline

III. Second Vision: Heavenly Throne Room and Three Judgment Cycles (4:1–16:21)

    A. Vision of God in His Heavenly Throne Room (4:1–11)

➡   **B. The Seven-Sealed Scroll and the Slain Lamb (5:1–14)**

        1. The Seven-Sealed Scroll (5:1)

        2. The One Worthy to Open the Scroll (5:2–5)

           a. Problem: Is anyone worthy? (5:2–4)

           b. Solution: Judah's victorious Lion! (5:5)

        3. Worship of the Sacrificed Lamb (5:6–10)

           a. The sacrificed Lamb steps forward (5:6–7)

           b. Praise for the Lamb's redeeming sacrifice (5:8–10)

        4. Worship of God and of the Lamb (5:11–14)

           a. All of heaven's company praises the Lamb (5:11–12)

           b. All of creation praises God and the Lamb (5:13–14)

---

1. Aune, *Revelation 1–5*, 329, 338; Osborne, *Revelation*, 247.

Explanation of the Text

5:1 And I saw in the right hand of the one sitting on the throne a scroll written inside and on the back, sealed with seven seals (Καὶ εἶδον ἐπὶ τὴν δεξιὰν τοῦ καθημένου ἐπὶ τοῦ θρόνου βιβλίον γεγραμμένον ἔσωθεν καὶ ὄπισθεν κατεσφραγισμένον σφραγῖσιν ἑπτά). John continues describing the vision of the heavenly throne room begun in the preceding chapter, adding four new stages. These are signaled by the repetition of the phrase "and I saw" as here (καὶ εἶδον; see "Structure" above). The reference to "the one sitting on the throne" (cf. 4:2, 3, 9, 10) shows that the new phases of the vision are built directly on the image of the sovereignty and majesty of God just seen in chapter 4. This connection is important not only for the arrangement of chapter 5 but also its theology, since it maintains the focus on God's heavenly rule over all things (e.g., God's "throne" mentioned 17x in chs. 4–5) and anticipates the establishment of his rule on the earth in full measure. Verse 1 sets the stage for dramatic new developments in the vision by referring to the seven-sealed scroll John sees "in the right hand" of God (v. 1a). The scroll itself represents God's sovereign plan for his creation (as discussed below), and the fact that God holds it in his hand suggests that he initiates and controls the events recorded in it[2] (the detail of the "right" hand may reinforce the point, since the right side often rep-

resents the position of ruling, delegated authority; cf. Rev 1:16, 17, 20; 2:1; Ps 110:1).

The descriptions of this "scroll"[3] tell us two important facts (v. 1b): first, that it is "written inside and on the back." This indicates that it contains a full, comprehensive account of its subject matter. Scrolls were normally written only on the inside, but because writing materials were expensive, the reverse side was sometimes used if the contents extended beyond the limits that the front side could hold.[4] This wording also clearly alludes to a significant Old Testament passage with similar imagery, Ezekiel 2:9–10. Ezekiel was also shown a scroll (βιβλίον) with things written "on the back and on the front" (γεγραμμένα . . . τὰ ὄπισθεν καὶ τὰ ἔμπροσθεν). In his case the scroll contained "words of lamentation, mourning, and woe" (Ezek 2:10), that is, messages of judgment that Ezekiel was commissioned to proclaim to Israel (3:1–4).

Ezekiel's scroll was immediately unrolled before him, but the scroll that John saw was "sealed with seven seals" (v. 1c), that is, entirely secured to keep its contents secret ("seven" seals denoting completeness).[5] This also suggests important Old Testament parallels, especially Isaiah 29:11 and Daniel 12:4, 9. In both passages the sealing of a scroll prevents premature disclosure of its contents, and the sealed scroll represents an account

---

2. Ladd, *Revelation*, 82–83.

3. As BDAG 176 indicates, the Greek word used here (βιβλίον) may denote a brief document (Matt 19:7; Mark 10:4), but here it is clearly a longer composition written in either a book form (i.e., a codex with pages stitched together to form the ancient counterpart of today's book) or more likely a scroll (sheets of papyrus or leather fastened together to form a roll; cf. Luke 4:17, 20; 2 Tim 4:13). See André Lemaire, "Writing and Writing Materials," *ABD* 6:1003–4, for information on ancient scrolls and codices.

4. Instead of taking "written inside and on the back" this way, some scholars understand this to refer to a doubly written document, something like the deed described in Jer 32:10–12

(cf. Eduard Lohse, *Die Offenbarung des Johannes*, NTD 11 [Göttingen: Vandenhoeck & Ruprecht, 1983], 37–38; Roloff, *Revelation*, 74). The content is written twice, once on the inside, which is then sealed to ensure it cannot be changed, and then again (same content) on the outside so all can read its terms. But if the content is given on both sides, John could hardly be heartbroken that no one was able to "look inside" (vv. 3–4). This also does not fit the parallel with Ezek 2:9–10 noted above.

5. Aune, *Revelation 1–5*, 346; Ladd, *Revelation*, 82. John reinforces this by using a compound form of the verb for sealing, κατασφραγίζω, meaning "seal up (completely)" (used only here in the NT).

of future events known only to God until revealed at the time of his choosing. In Isaiah 29 (similar to Ezek 2) the events specifically concern judgment and subsequent blessing on Israel as well as on the nations that fight against her.[6] At the time of such future events the words of the scroll would be plain for all to understand.

These basic points lead to the larger question of the scroll's significance in Revelation 5, especially regarding its form, content, and literary function in this and subsequent chapters. The most likely answer closely follows the prophetic account of future events just mentioned from the Old Testament. But other possibilities have been explored. One view that might present itself is to identify it with the "Lamb's book of life" cited in Revelation (13:8; 21:27; similarly, 3:5; 17:8; 20:12, 15), since we have here a scroll or "book" (KJV) that the Lamb alone is worthy to open because of his redemptive sacrifice (5:6–10). But the book of life does not seem to be opened until 20:12, while the events that unfold when the seals of this book or scroll are broken (6:1–16; 8:1–5) have little or nothing to do with disclosing the names of the redeemed.

Another suggestion about the scroll's form is to see it as some kind of legal document (e.g., a title deed, a last will or testament), secured with the personal seals of witnesses who could guarantee its authenticity.[7] The Lamb's ability to take the scroll from God's hand thus signifies his reception of authority over creation or his right to give or to receive an inheritance. While this view receives some support from first-century legal customs[8] and from the possible parallel in Jeremiah 32:10–12, nothing in this passage refers clearly to ownership or inher-

itance. As noted above, the parallels with Ezekiel 2, Isaiah 29, and Daniel 12 make the prophetic form—a scroll revealing future events that will unfold according to God's plan—more persuasive.[9]

Understanding the form of the scroll in this way is confirmed when we trace the contextual clues in Revelation itself for interpreting the content and literary function of this scroll. We have seen in Revelation 4:1 that John's vision concerns "what must take place after this." The vision of God's majesty and sovereignty (4:2–11) continues with a focus on the sealed scroll he holds in his hand (5:1). The only one worthy to open this scroll is the Lamb whose sacrificial death effected worldwide redemption and rule (5:9–10). When the seals are opened, the result is not just disclosure of the scroll's contents but also putting into operation on earth the events it describes (6:1–17).[10] In fact, 6:16–17 describe the seal judgments as the wrath of the Lamb and of the one sitting on the throne, clearly connecting them to the scroll scene in chapter 5. And the sequence does not end there, since the seven trumpets follow and then seven bowls and further visions that continue the same course of events. These trace not only a series of unprecedented judgments to come but also proclamations about God's salvation and kingdom finally coming on earth (11:15, 17; 12:10; 19:1; 19:16; 20:4, 6; 22:5).

The scroll then represents the divine plan for redemption and restoration through Christ. It "symbolizes God's salvific plan, to assert his sovereignty over a rebellious world, and to achieve his loving purposes in creation through the victory of the Lamb."[11] As long as it remains sealed, these purposes cannot be made known and cannot be

---

6. Similarly in Jer 36:1–3, 27–29, the prophet is instructed to write in a scroll an account of the judgments God intends to bring upon Israel, Judah, and the nations.

7. Beale, *Revelation*, 340–41, 344–46.

8. See Keener, *Revelation*, 184–85, for citation and discussion of ancient parallels.

9. Bauckham, *Climax*, 248–49.

10. Beale, *Revelation*, 344–45; Caird, *Revelation*, 71; Smalley, *Revelation*, 130; also Jan Lambrecht, "The Opening of the Seals (Rev 6:1–8:6)," *Bib* 79 (1998): 218.

11. Smalley, *Revelation*, 126; cf. Aune, *Revelation 1–5*, 34.

fulfilled. But through Christ's victory on the cross (5:9–10) and his revelation through John (cf. 1:1–2), God's purposes are to be unveiled and accomplished. No wonder John wept when it seemed this was impossible (5:4); no wonder all creation erupted in worship and adoration when Christ's victory was made clear (5:8–14).

As mentioned in "Literary Context" above, this vision of a sealed scroll thus provides the literary framework for the chapters that follow, at least through 16:21 (the seals, trumpets, and bowls), but more likely all the way through 22:5 (all the visions of judgment and restoration that form the remaining body of the book). However, the scroll figures into this series of visions in two stages, since it reappears in 10:1 as an open document, not a sealed one.[12] The seal-breaking initiates the first phase of fulfillment (the somewhat less severe judgments of the seven seals and six trumpets, 6:1–9:21), while John's prophetic commissioning (10:9–11) prepares him to reveal the consummation of "the mystery of God" (10:7) in the following chapters, including the most severe judgments of the seven bowls (15:1–16:21). Because of this it is possibly better to envision the seven seals placed at different spots on the top of the rolled cylinder instead of all together along the flat outer edge of the scroll. As each seal is broken, another portion of the scroll's contents is revealed and enacted (see ch. 6 below).[13]

5:2 And I saw a mighty angel proclaiming with a loud voice, "Who is worthy to open the scroll and break its seals?" (καὶ εἶδον ἄγγελον ἰσχυρὸν κηρύσσοντα ἐν φωνῇ μεγάλῃ, Τίς ἄξιος ἀνοῖξαι τὸ βιβλίον καὶ λῦσαι τὰς σφραγῖδας αὐτοῦ). The expression "and I saw" (v. 2a) marks the second phase of John's vision (see "Structure" above). These verses (5:2–5) raise the dramatic tension of the scene by posing the challenge of "who is worthy to open" the seven-sealed scroll (v. 2b). As John watches, this issue is raised in the heavenly throne room by a "mighty angel." Such a description is rare in Revelation (angels are directly described as "mighty" only 3x out of some 67x in the book; the 3x do not likely refer to the same figure, since the next occurrence says "another angel, a mighty one"; 10:1;[14] cf. 18:21). "Mighty" may reflect a high position in the angelic ranks,[15] but it could instead be just one of several expressions John employs to portray angels in general as powerful and authoritative servants of God (e.g., 18:1). This is reinforced when his proclamation[16] is said to be "with a loud voice." This expression is often used in Revelation, especially when the announcement is intended for a widespread audience (cf. 7:2; 8:13; 11:15; 14:7, 9; 18:2; 19:17)—here the whole creation (cf. v. 3a).

The question that the angel poses seems a natural one, given the paradoxical significance of the scroll as seen in v. 1. It contains God's cosmic plan for accomplishing justice and redemption in the whole creation, yet it is sealed completely, its truths undisclosed and its execution stymied. But his question also must be seen against the biblical background of such heavenly scenes: a combination of (1) posing questions in the heavenly council as a way to move things along to a conclusion (1 Kgs 22:20–21; Isa 6:8), and (2) questions raised in a visionary experience to clarify the significance

---

12. See 10:2 for discussion of the identity of the two scrolls.

13. Thomas, *Revelation 1–7*, 381. Beale, *Revelation*, 344, notes that while this is not the normal way of sealing a scroll, an apocalyptic image need not conform to literal convention in order to communicate its points.

14. This is one of several parallels between ch. 5 (the seven-sealed scroll) and ch. 10 (the little scroll).

15. Aune, *Revelation 1–5*, 347.

16. The Greek verb κηρύσσω is often used in the NT of Christian/gospel preaching, but in its broader background it refers to official, public proclamations, as here (BDAG 343–44).

of what is seen (Dan 8:13–14; 10:20; 12:5–13; Zech 4–5).[17] Both nuances enrich the sense of the question here.

The adjective "worthy" (ἄξιος) carries the basic meaning of "fit, deserving,"[18] but it is filled in significantly by its contextual usage, especially in Revelation 4:11 and 5:9, 12. This is not so much a moral or spiritual worthiness in the normal sense but a status, rank, or eminence gained by a combination of inherent being or nature and the accomplishment of actions that accord with and flow from that nature. So in 4:11 (see above), the Lord God Almighty is proclaimed "worthy" of worship because he alone is the creator and sustainer of all things: this comes from his inherent being as God Almighty, but both his nature and his concordant actions are celebrated. In 5:9, 12 a similar status or rank is accorded to the Lamb because of his inherent nature and his redemptive accomplishment on the cross (see discussion below).

The order of the infinitives "to open . . . and break" (v. 2b) seems backward, but the "and" (καί) here is explanatory, denoting not order of occurrence but complementary parts of the same action ("to open . . . by breaking" or "to open . . . , that is, to break").[19]

5:3–4 And no one in heaven or on earth or under the earth was able to open the scroll or look into it. 4 So I began to weep bitterly that no one was found worthy to open the scroll or look into it (καὶ οὐδεὶς ἐδύνατο ἐν τῷ οὐρανῷ οὐδὲ ἐπὶ τῆς γῆς οὐδὲ ὑποκάτω τῆς γῆς ἀνοῖξαι τὸ βιβλίον οὔτε βλέπειν αὐτό. 4 καὶ ἔκλαιον πολύ, ὅτι οὐδεὶς ἄξιος εὑρέθη ἀνοῖξαι τὸ βιβλίον οὔτε βλέπειν αὐτό). The answer to the heavenly question of v. 2 is immediately obvious: no one is "able" (ἐδύνατο; ability is a partial synonym for "worthiness" in v. 2) to open the scroll (v. 3). "No one . . . was able to open the scroll" is reinforced by "or look into it" (i.e., "or see it," οὔτε βλέπειν αὐτό, but the sense is clearly "to view its contents when it is opened").[20] The exclusive sense of "no one" (οὐδεὶς) is strongly reinforced by the threefold description "in heaven or on earth or under the earth." This characteristic division of the entire universe into three parts goes back to the Decalogue (Exod 20:11; Deut 5:8) and is expressed in slightly different form in Philippians 2:10. See also Revelation 5:13, which adds a fourth part, the sea, as in Job 11:8–9 (a different tripartite division of "heaven, earth, and sea" appears in Rev 10:6; 12:12; 14:7; and 21:1; cf. Ps 146:6; Acts 4:24; 14:15). The absolute failure to find anyone worthy to open the scroll (repeated in v. 4) anticipates the unique status of the Lamb recognized in vv. 5–10.[21] Theologically this shows how futile and meaningless all of history ultimately is apart from Christ. Human destiny, and that of the universe, hinges on the person and work of Jesus Christ.[22]

The latter half of v. 4 summarizes and reinforces the disappointment of vv. 2–3 ("no one was found worthy . . .").[23] John's reaction to this is described vividly in v. 4a: overwhelming grief. The conjunction "and" (καί) is used here to mark the result of what has come before, "(and) so."[24] In such a

---

17. Bauckham, *Climax*, 136; Keener, *Revelation*, 185.

18. BDAG 93–94; in Rev this can be positive (3:4; 4:11; 5:2, 4, 9, 10, 12) or negative (16:6).

19. Aune, *Revelation 1–5*, 322; Osborne, *Revelation*, 251; BDAG 495; BDF §442. Beale, *Revelation*, 338, notes that v. 9 shows the main action to be the opening of the scroll; breaking the seals is a part or means of that larger act. It can also be seen that "to open" is repeated in vv. 3, 4, 5, while "to break" is omitted.

20. BDAG 179; Osborne, *Revelation*, 252. As Osborne says, the present tense βλέπειν suggests a more detailed examination after the summary act of opening the book (aorist ἀνοῖξαι).

21. Aune, *Revelation 1–5*, 348; Bauckham, *Climax*, 136.

22. Ladd, *Revelation*, 82.

23. Osborne, *Revelation*, 252, observes that the third occurrence of "open the scroll" in only three verses heightens our focus on the scroll's contents.

24. BDAG 495.

context the imperfect verb "I wept" (ἔκλαιον) probably has an inceptive sense, marking the beginning of an action that is then seen to continue (ESV, NASB, NET, NLT).[25] John adds the adverb "bitterly" (πολύ, which means more generally "much, greatly, strongly").[26] Contextually this could carry slightly different nuances: "wept and wept" (CSB, NIV; cf. MSG), "shed many tears" (NABR), "wept loudly,"[27] or "wept bitterly" (NET; NLT). John's reason for crying is not just foiled curiosity, the pang of disappointment at not being privy to the scroll's contents. In view of the cosmic significance of this scroll, his bitter grief is over the apparent frustration of God's redemptive purpose. It is the deep lament shared by God's people through the ages, including his readers in the first-century, when everything they have hoped and prayed for under God seems to have come to nothing. Fortunately for John, such weeping lasts only for a season, and what reassures John should give all God's people renewed courage and faith as well.

5:5 Then one of the elders said to me, "Stop weeping! See, the Lion of the tribe of Judah, the Shoot of David, has won the victory, so that he can open the scroll and its seven seals" (καὶ εἷς ἐκ τῶν πρεσβυτέρων λέγει μοι, Μὴ κλαῖε, ἰδοὺ ἐνίκησεν ὁ λέων ὁ ἐκ τῆς φυλῆς Ἰούδα, ἡ ῥίζα Δαυίδ, ἀνοῖξαι τὸ βιβλίον καὶ τὰς ἑπτὰ σφραγῖδας αὐτοῦ). A member of the heavenly company responds to John's grief with sharp but most welcome words, communicating the first part of the resolution of his despair. Instances of interaction between a human visionary and figures seen in the vision are common features of prophetic and apocalyptic literature, as a way of advancing the revelatory process (cf. Dan 7:15–16; 8:14–19; 10:15–21; 12:8–13; Zech 1–6; Rev 7:13–14 [elder]; 17:1, 7, 15; 19:9–10; 21:9; 22:6). One of the elders[28] around the throne of God (see discussion at 4:4, 10) speaks[29] to John personally, to rebuke his tears and proclaim why they have no place. In view of v. 4 ("I began to weep"), the prohibition in v. 5b clearly calls on John to cease an action that is already in progress, "stop weeping."[30]

With great forcefulness[31] the heavenly informant gives John the initial answer to his despair by pointing to the decisive victory of the one who fulfills the royal promises of the Old Testament (v. 5c–d). Such a person, of course, possesses the status or "worthiness" to put into operation God's sovereign plan as revealed in the scroll. This vic-

---

25. Wallace, *Grammar*, 544–45. This is often seen when the imperfect follows a rapid series of events in a narrative, and the imperfect verb then pays vivid attention to the ongoing action triggered by those events. Cf. Fanning, *Verbal Aspect*, 252–53.

26. BDAG 849.

27. BDAG 849.

28. Osborne, *Revelation*, 252 and Thomas, *Revelation 1–7*, 386 point out that this use of a form of εἷς followed by ἐκ in a partitive sense (cf. BDAG 297; BDF §164) is fairly common in John's Gospel (12x) and Rev (8x) and comparatively uncommon in the rest of the NT (10x), a fact that supports the view that these books have a common authorship.

29. The verb λέγει is used here as a historical present, normally translated into English as a simple narrative past, "said" (other uses of λέγει/λέγουσιν occur as historical presents in Rev 10:9, 11; 17:15; 19:9, 10; 21:5; 22:9, 10). The historical present in Greek is a highlighting feature that is generally anticipatory or "kataphoric"; it attracts attention not usually to the event

or statement it relates but to the one that follows, in this case, v. 6. For further discussion, see Levinsohn, *Discourse Features* §§12.2; 14.3; 15.1; and Fanning, "Greek Tenses," 345–46.

30. This is not because present prohibitions in Greek "usually" have this sense, as Aune, *Revelation 1–5*, 349 and Thomas, *Revelation 1–7*, 386 state. In fact, they usually express a general precept, "make it your practice not to do . . ." (cf. BDF §§335–36; Fanning, *Verbal Aspect*, 327–40). But if the prohibition refers to a particular attitude or action already underway in the specific context (as here), it clearly carries the sense "stop doing . . ." (Fanning, *Verbal Aspect*, 335–38).

31. The elder's statement is doubly emphatic at its outset: the interjection "see" (ἰδού) denotes "strong emphasis" on what follows (BDAG 468), and the verb "has won the victory" (ἐνίκησεν) comes before its subject phrase. This highlights the subject phrase as well, since it stands between the verb and its modifying infinitive at the end of the sentence.

tory (ἐνίκησεν)[32] was cited already in Revelation 3:21, when the exalted Christ encouraged the Christians of Asia Minor (who are urged 7x in chs. 2–3 to "overcome, be victorious" in their spiritual struggles): "The one who overcomes" (ὁ νικῶν) will receive "the right to sit with me on my throne, just as I myself overcame [ἐνίκησα] and sat down with my Father on his throne" (cf. Ps 110:1). In Revelation 3:21 and here in 5:5, the "victory" in view is the decisive triumph Christ won in his death, resurrection, and exaltation (note allusions to his death in 5:9, 12; and his resurrection and exaltation in 3:21 and 5:6 ["standing amid the throne area"]; cf. also John 16:33; 1 Cor 15:54). But as in the rest of the New Testament, Revelation views this victory in an "already/not yet" tension: it has been decisively won in the past but remains to be consummated fully in the future. The complete accomplishment portrayed in chs. 6–22 is yet to be fulfilled, but this will be nothing more than the extension—visibly and on earth—of the triumph and rule Christ already enjoys at the right hand of God in heaven.[33]

The note of mighty victory is clear in the two messianic titles used in the subject phrase (v. 5c): "the Lion of the tribe of Judah" and "the Shoot of David." "The Lion of the tribe of Judah" is Jacob's portrayal of one of Judah's descendants with the strength and ferocity of a lion, who will wield the scepter of rule over his enemies and to whom the nations will render obedience (Gen 49:8–10).[34] "The Shoot of David" (ἡ ῥίζα Δαυίδ) is a title drawn from Isaiah 11:1–10, where the phrase is actually "the root of Jesse" (ἡ ῥίζα [τοῦ] Ἰεσσαί; vv. 1, 10; cf. Rom 15:12).[35] But the passage speaks of a coming "shoot" or "branch" (ῥάβδος) as well as a "flower" (ἄνθος) springing from Jesse's stock (v. 1; i.e., new growth coming up from what appears to be his dead stump—clearly a restoration of David's line), anointed and equipped by the Lord's Spirit (v. 2), exerting righteous judgment and peaceful rule over the whole earth (vv. 3–9), including the gentile nations as well as the exiles of Israel regathered from the corners of the earth (vv. 10–12).[36] Jesus's connection with Judah and especially David is widely noted in the New Testament (Matt 1:1, 17; Mark 11:10; 12:35–37; Luke 1:32; 2:11; Acts

---

32. This verb denotes "winning in the face of obstacles" (BDAG 673). It is translated "has overcome" (NASB), "has triumphed" (NIV), "has conquered" (CSB, ESV, NET, MSG, RSV), "has won the victory" (NLT), "hath prevailed" (KJV). Syntactically this is a consummative aorist (Wallace, *Grammar*, 559–61) emphasizing the summary accomplishment of the action despite opposition. The consistent translation as an English present perfect seen above is not because the aorist takes on the sense of the Greek perfect (focus on results of the action). In English idiom expression of a past indefinite action (referring to an act done at an unspecified time in the past) requires the present perfect (Fanning, *Verbal Aspect*, 260–61).

33. Ladd, *Revelation*, 84–85; Erich Sauer, *The Triumph of the Crucified*, trans. G. H. Lang (London: Paternoster, 1951), 25, 29, 51–52, 143.

34. This image is used as a reference to the messiah in various ancient Jewish texts: 4 Ezra 11:37; 12:31–34; T. Jud. 24:5; Tg. Neof. and Tg. P-J. Gen 49:8–10.

35. "Shoot of David/Jesse" denotes a descendant of David or Jesse, one coming from their stock. The Greek word ῥίζα can mean "root," and this is the common English translation of Isa

11 as well as Rev 5 (CSB, ESV, KJV, NASB, NET, NIV, RSV), but it can also denote "shoot, scion" ("that which grows from a root"; BDAG 903–4; cf. C. Maurer, "ῥίζα," *TDNT* 6:986–89) and so figuratively "descendant." A few have taken ῥίζα to mean "root, source, originator" and the genitive "of David" as "producing David/from which David comes," in the sense that Jesus as divine is the ultimate spiritual source of the messianic line (Beasley-Murray, *Revelation*, 342; G. H. Lang, *The Revelation of Jesus Christ* [London: Paternoster, 1948], 390; Swete, *Apocalypse*, 309). But as Beale, *Revelation*, 1146–47 argues, the use of ῥίζα in Isa 5:24; 53:2 (and even 11:10; see also Sir 47:22) shows that "shoot, scion; descendant" is the more likely sense. So the genitive means "produced by David/coming from David" (cf. *TDNT* 6:989).

36. The expectation of future rule by a descendant of David is based on God's promise to him in 2 Sam 7 (reflected also in Pss 89; 110; 132). The themes of Isa 11 are picked up also in Jer 23:15; 33:15; Zech 3:8; 6:12. As Ladd, *Revelation*, 83–84 notes, Isa 11 speaks of societal, political restoration as well as individual, spiritual salvation. See 5:10 below for further discussion.

2:22–36; 13:32–41; Rom 1:3; 2 Tim 2:8; Heb 7:14) and referred to elsewhere in Revelation as well (3:7; 22:16; cf. also 19:11–16 with further allusions to Isa 11:4).

The final part of the verse comes back to the burning focus of vv. 2–4: Christ's victory has qualified him "to open the scroll and its seven seals."[37] As in v. 2, the order of "scroll and seals" appears to be backward, but opening the seals is the subsidiary means for accomplishing the main action of opening the scroll (see comment at v. 2 above).

The larger point about the significant christological titles of v. 5c is that they are completely appropriate and expected in a context like this. The mighty angel (v. 2) asked for a figure who is worthy, one with obvious credentials, status, and acclaim, whom all would acknowledge as qualified and capable. And the figure described in Genesis 49 and Isaiah 11 certainly fits the bill: glorious, regal, forcefully and effortlessly exerting rule over all the world in fulfillment of the Old Testament promises. All of this is true about Jesus Christ, but it is not the complete picture, as v. 6 reveals.

5:6 And I saw amid the throne area and the four living creatures and amid the elders a Lamb standing, looking like it had been slain, with seven horns and seven eyes, which are the seven spirits of God sent out into all the earth (Καὶ εἶδον ἐν μέσῳ τοῦ θρόνου καὶ τῶν τεσσάρων ζῴων καὶ ἐν μέσῳ τῶν πρεσβυτέρων ἀρνίον ἑστηκὸς ὡς ἐσφαγμένον ἔχων κέρατα ἑπτὰ καὶ ὀφθαλμοὺς ἑπτὰ οἵ εἰσιν τὰ [ἑπτὰ] πνεύματα τοῦ θεοῦ ἀπεσταλμένοι εἰς πᾶσαν τὴν γῆν). The expression "and I saw"

marks the third phase of John's vision (see "Structure" above). Here John sees Jesus Christ as the slain Lamb, the only one worthy to open the scroll (vv. 6–7), as well as the heavenly worship that celebrates his redemptive sacrifice (vv. 8–10). It is important to note the actual sequence of John's experience in vv. 5–6. The contrast between what he just *heard* (v. 5) and what he now *sees* (v. 6) is significant.[38] This constitutes the most dramatic surprise of the vision: John hears about the victorious regal Lion, but when he turns to look, he sees a sacrificed Lamb. As noted above, this is completely contrary to expectations. It compels deeper consideration and raises the issue of how exactly Christ accomplished God's purpose and showed himself worthy above all others. (See the "Theology in Application" for reflections.)

When John turns to look at this "worthy" one, he sees him in the location of highest honor, in the center of the heavenly throne room (v. 6a; cf. 4:6; 7:17 for the construction "amid the throne area"; cf. also 5:7 for the Lamb's approach to the throne itself) and among the heavenly beings that surround God's throne in worshipful adoration (cf. 4:4–11 for explanation of these "creatures" and "elders"). The figure that he sees, as noted above, is a lamb (ἀρνίον; first of 29x in Rev), bearing the marks of having been slaughtered,[39] but standing alive and strong among the heavenly company (v. 6a–b). The text says that the lamb was "looking like it had been slain" (i.e., "as slain"; ὡς ἐσφαγμένον), but this does not mean the killing was in appearance only and was not reality. Verses 9 and 12 unequivocally say

---

37. The infinitive ἀνοῖξαι is either purpose ("in order to") or result ("so as to"), but given the larger significance of "opening the scroll" (i.e., revealing and accomplishing God's redemptive purposes), purpose is a better option. His triumph was aimed at fulfilling God's plan, and he is seen to be the only one able to carry that out.

38. Bauckham, *Theology*, 74; Caird, *Revelation*, 73–74.

39. The verb σφάζω means to kill violently, "slaughter, murder, butcher" (BDAG 979). It is used of Cain's murder of Abel in 1 John 3:12. See also Rev 5:9, 12; 6:4, 9; 13:3, 8; 18:24. Here it appears in perfect tense, highlighting the continued effect of his having been slaughtered (Wallace, *Grammar*, 574–76; Fanning, *Verbal Aspect*, 291–95). The present effect is not that he remains dead but that his appearance shows he was slain as a sacrifice, though now he is standing alive amid the heavenly company.

he was slain. But now the Lamb, though once dead, stands triumphant in the heavenly throne room (cf. 1:18: "I am . . . the living one. And I died, but indeed I am alive forever and ever"; also 2:8).

The figure of a lamb along with the reference to "slaughter" evokes the picture of sacrificial death—note how v. 9 connects the Lamb's slaying to redemption by means of blood. But it probably does so by drawing not on a single Old Testament precedent but several. The most important Old Testament models evoked here are the Passover Lamb of Exodus 12:1–24 (slain so that its blood could be applied to the door to avert judgment) and the Suffering Servant of Isaiah 53:7 (led like a lamb to the slaughter, within the larger picture of his vicarious suffering in 52:13–53:12).[40] John's word for "Lamb" in Revelation is ἀρνίον (29x, all referring to Christ except 13:11; the word occurs outside Rev only at John 21:15), originally a diminutive ("little lamb"; cf. Ps 114:4, 6 [113:4, 6 LXX]; Jer 11:19; 50:45 [27:45 LXX]) from an older word for lamb, ἄρης or ἀρήν (root ἀρν-; cf. Luke 10:3), but the diminutive sense seems to have dropped away in the New Testament. The image of a lamb, sheep, or paschal lamb pictures Christ's redemptive sacrifice elsewhere in the New Testament, but the specific words used are different (ἀμνός in John 1:29, 36; 1 Pet 1:19; πρόβατον and ἀμνός in Acts 8:32, quoting Isa 53:7; and πάσχα in 1 Cor 5:7).

The initial glimpse of a slain Lamb certainly contrasts with that of the Lion of Judah, descendant of the great King David (Rev 5:5). The Lamb's sacrifice, suffering, vulnerability, and weakness even to death in the service of God are all shockingly different from what v. 5 led us to expect. But as John describes this Lamb further, we discover he is no longer a meek and helpless victim. He is a figure with overwhelming power and divine wisdom (v. 6c). The "seven horns," while bizarre in visual terms, represent fullness of strength and authority (cf. "horns" in Deut 33:17; Pss 18:2; 112:9; Dan 7:7, 20; Rev 12:3; 13:1, 11; 17:3, 7, 12, 16). The "seven eyes" represent complete wisdom and understanding (e.g., "eye" = insight: Mark 12:11; Luke 19:42; Eph 1:18; esp. of divine knowledge, 2 Chr 16:9; Ps 34:15; Prov 15:3; 1 Pet 3:12; Heb 4:13), but this image is immediately augmented by John's explanation (v. 6d–e), "which are the seven spirits of God sent out into all the earth" (see similar parenthetical elaboration at the end of v. 8). We have already encountered this reference to "seven spirits" in Revelation, said to be "before [God's] throne" (1:4) and "of God" (3:1; 4:5), and held by Jesus Christ (3:1). There is a clear allusion to Isaiah 11:2 (cf. v. 5, "shoot of David," from Isa 11:1, 10), noting that the Lord's Spirit, described by seven attributes, will rest on the ideal king from David's line to guide and empower his future rule. The phrase "sent into all the earth" alludes to Zechariah 4:2, 6, 10, where seven torches represent the seven "eyes of the Lord that range through the whole earth," and the Lord acts "not by might or power but by [his] Spirit." These seven eyes/spirits represent the fullness of the divine Spirit that rests on Christ as he carries out God's redemptive mission to all the world (cf. the Spirit in John 1:32–33; 3:34; 14:26; 20:22).

The Lamb will appear repeatedly in the rest of Revelation, and the value of his sacrificial death is continually evoked, but he is no longer seen as a slain victim but instead as consistently dominant and mighty (e.g., Rev 6:16; 14:10; 17:14; 22:3).[41] The word "Lamb" rather than "Lion" continues to

---

40. Both these passages in the LXX use the words slay or slaughter (σφάζω, σφαγή) and several words for lamb or sheep (e.g., πρόβατον, ἀμνός). Exod 12:5 uses the word ἀρήν for lamb, sheep; this is the base form for the word John uses in Rev 5:6.

41. Cf. Aune, *Revelation 1–5*, 367–73; Bauckham, *Theology*, 66–76; Boxall, *Revelation*, 98; Osborne, *Revelation*, 256.

be used to refer to him, but even as the Lamb he clearly acts as powerful ruler and judge. It is wrong to think that his Davidic role is reinterpreted in 5:5–6 to strip away any military or national elements and defines him only as a symbol of self-sacrificial suffering and nonviolent martyrdom, as some interpreters argue.[42] In his acts of judgment and redemption Christ continues to be both Lion and Lamb, without collapsing one into the other (cf. 19:11–16).[43]

One final comment is in order regarding this and subsequent references in Revelation to Christ as the "Lamb." These give us valuable insights into how the somewhat bizarre imagery of Revelation often works. Christ as the "Lamb" certainly symbolizes important truths about a specific and real person, but clearly there is no literal correspondence between the visual symbol and the actual referent.[44] Christ does not actually look like a lamb, especially one with seven horns and seven eyes. Nor does John see Christ in some future actual manifestation and describe him as best he can as lamb-like (literally but imperfectly). This will be important as we tackle some of the imagery later in Revelation (e.g., the locusts of 9:3–10; the beasts of 13:1, 11). What John sees in a vision often does not correspond literally to what exists or occurs but rather powerfully symbolizes a real referent in the present or future (see "Imagery and Symbols" in the introduction).

5:7 Then he went and took the scroll from the right hand of the one sitting on the throne (καὶ ἦλθεν καὶ εἴληφεν ἐκ τῆς δεξιᾶς τοῦ καθημένου ἐπὶ τοῦ θρόνου). After the lengthy description of the Lamb he saw (v. 6), John narrates the series of events occurring next.[45] The Lamb "stepped forward" (NLT)[46] before the throne and without further ado took possession[47] of the scroll held by the Lord God. The latter half of the verse repeats the wording of v. 1a, "[from] the right hand of the one sitting on the throne," showing that the Lamb has met the challenge that occupied the narrative in vv. 2–5. In keeping with the imagery of v. 1 (in the Lord's "hand" denotes control, sovereignty), for the Lamb to "take the scroll" (vv. 7, 8a) means his assumption of authority, as the Lord's agent, to initiate and control the events recorded in the scroll.

Some have described this scene as the "enthronement" of the Lamb,[48] but the terminology of

---

42. Bauckham, *Climax*, 213–15; Caird, *Revelation*, 74–75; Sweet, *Revelation*, 124–26.

43. Koester, *Revelation*, 387–88 and Joseph L. Mangina, *Revelation*, BTCB (Grand Rapids: Brazos, 2010), 87–90, give a better balance between the two. See also Steve Moyise, "Does the Lion Lie Down with the Lamb?" in *Studies in the Book of Revelation*, ed. Steve Moyise (Edinburgh: T&T Clark, 2001), 181–94.

44. For example, we know "the bulls are running on Wall Street" does not mean actual cattle in New York. The king of Greece (Dan 8:21) is not literally a "goat with a great horn between his eyes" (v. 5), nor does he look somewhat like that to someone dazzled by the sight of him.

45. Greek καί (usually rendered "and") is used here to portray events in a close sequence, reflected best in English by "then" or "next" (cf. Rev 10:7 and NET footnote on 5:7).

46. Forms of ἔρχομαι (here ἦλθεν) without further qualification can be used with another verb "to denote that a person, in order to do someth[ing], must first come to a certain place" (BDAG 394). This frequently occurs in John and Rev (BDAG notes John 1:39, 46; 6:15; 11:34, 48; 12:22; 19:38; 20:19, 26; 21:13; Rev 17:1; 21:9), another pointer toward common authorship.

47. The verb translated "took" is a Greek perfect tense (εἴληφεν), most commonly "has taken." It occurs here in a series of aorists, likely with an aorist sense (BDF §343; Fanning, *Verbal Aspect*, 299–303; Mussies, *Morphology*, 264–65) to express a simple past event. This is part of a late development in Hellenistic and Byzantine Greek in which the perfect assumes the sense of the aorist. Rev has several examples of this (7:14; 8:5; 11:17; 19:3). See discussion in Fanning, "Greek Tenses," 347–49. Alternatively, this occurrence may be used to give a more lively or dramatic narration. See elaboration of this idea in K. L. McKay, *A New Syntax of the Verb in New Testament Greek* (SBG 5; New York: Peter Lang, 1994), 50; Robertson, *Grammar*, 896–97; Wallace, *Grammar*, 578–79; also Aune, *Revelation 1–5*, 324; and Smalley, *Revelation*, 133.

48. Roloff, *Revelation*, 72–73; Sweet, *Revelation*, 121–27.

"seating/crowning" does not occur here. Revelation consistently presents Jesus Christ as already positioned with God in the place of ruling authority, both before and after this text (3:21; 7:17; 22:1). While flashbacks to earlier events are possible in Revelation (cf. 12:1–5), even in this passage the Lamb is seen standing in the center of things from the very first time John notices him (v. 6 "amid the throne-area" and the heavenly council). He does not proceed from the outer fringes to approach the throne, but simply steps around to face the Lord and take the scroll. A better label than enthronement would be "ratification" or public confirmation of someone in a role he already possesses. Heavenly recognition of the Lamb as worthy to "take the scroll" means consummating God's predetermined plan, so that what is decreed can be made actual, the inaugurated brought to fulfillment, the hidden made visible. The scene is patterned on Daniel's vision of "one like a son of man," given authority by the Ancient of Days to establish an everlasting kingdom (Dan 7:9–14).[49] The connection with Daniel's vision will provide insight into many of the details to come in Revelation 5.

5:8 And when he had taken the scroll, the four living creatures and the twenty-four elders fell down before the Lamb, each holding a kithara and golden bowls full of incense, which are the prayers of the saints (καὶ ὅτε ἔλαβεν τὸ βιβλίον, τὰ τέσσαρα ζῷα καὶ οἱ εἴκοσι τέσσαρες πρεσβύτεροι ἔπεσαν ἐνώπιον τοῦ ἀρνίου ἔχοντες ἕκαστος κιθάραν καὶ φιάλας χρυσᾶς γεμούσας θυμιαμάτων, αἵ εἰσιν αἱ προσευχαὶ τῶν ἁγίων). The next several verses (5:8–10) show the heavenly response to the Lamb's dramatic reception of the scroll from the hand of the Lord God. The key words from v. 7 are repeated here at the outset ("when he had taken the scroll," v. 8a, using the aorist ἔλαβεν in this case for the decisive act of "taking").[50] What ensues is heavenly adoration, worship, and acclamation declaring the worthiness of the Lamb. Remarkably, it follows the pattern of worship offered to the Lord God by these same "living creatures" and "elders" in 4:4–11 (see comments there for identification of these beings). They "fell down before" the Lamb (v. 8b), just as they previously showed obeisance[51] to God on his throne (4:10).[52] This is significant in Revelation since heavenly beings repeatedly give such worship to God (4:10; 7:11; 11:16; 19:4). When John tries on two occasions to honor an angelic messenger in this way (19:10; 22:8–9), the angel rebukes him and insists, "Worship God [alone]!" But Jesus Christ receives such honor here, as well as in 1:17 (John falling before the exalted Christ) and 5:14 (worship to God and the Lamb).[53]

"Falling before" someone in obeisance or worship in the ancient world usually meant bowing with one's face to the ground or assuming a completely prostrate position (e.g., on the ground, Mark 14:35; on one's face before someone, Gen 17:3, 17;

---

49. Aune, *Revelation 1–5*, 336–38; Beale, *Revelation*, 356–57.

50. This discourse feature is known as "tail-head linkage," a form of repetition that slows down the presentation to highlight what is said next. See Levinsohn, *Discourse Features*, 197–99; Runge, *Discourse Grammar*, 163–67.

51. The verb in both verses (4:10; 5:8) is πίπτω, to "throw oneself to the ground as a sign of devotion or humility" (BDAG 815); cf. 1:17; 5:14; 7:11; 11:16; 19:4.

52. Other features of this pattern of worship are (1) acclamation of worthiness for their person and work (4:11; 5:9, 12); (2) chanting or singing of praise hymns to them (4:8, 11; 5:9, 12–13); and (3) ascription of glory, honor, power, and other

virtues to them (4:9, 11; 5:12–13). These will be developed further in subsequent verses.

53. For this point and further discussion of the Christology of Rev, see Bauckham, *Theology*, 58–63, and Richard Bauckham, "The Worship of Jesus," *ABD* 3:812–19. Aune, *Revelation 1–5*, 355 notes a reservation from this verse in how the worship of Jesus is portrayed: the verb "worship" itself (προσκυνέω) does not appear in 5:8. It was used in 4:10 (worship of God alone), but not here (toward Christ). But this does not seem significant since the other features of the pattern of worship are parallel throughout vv. 8–14 (see previous note), and the verb is used in 5:13–14 regarding worship of God and the Lamb together.

Matt 26:39; Luke 5:12; or at someone's feet, Luke 8:41; John 11:32; Acts 10:25). Here the picture presumably is of falling to their knees (cf. Gen 41:43; 1 Kgs 19:18; 2 Kgs 1:13; Ezra 9:5; Isa 45:23), since the heavenly beings continue to hold instruments of worship, as noted below.

The fullness of their worship is represented by the instruments of praise and devotion these heavenly beings have in their hands (v. 8c).[54] Each holds a "kithara" or box lyre (κιθάρα),[55] a musical instrument long associated with playing and singing praises to God (e.g., 2 Chr 9:11; Pss 33:2; 43:4; 98:5; 147:7). The heavenly beings are clearly ready to offer the hymns of praise described in Rev 5:9–10 and 12–13 (cf. 14:2–3; 15:2–3). Each one also holds a golden bowl full of incense,[56] another traditional implement and substance associated with worship (cf. 8:3–5; Exod 30:1, 7–9, 37; Lev 16:12–13; Mal 1:11; Luke 1:10–11). Here John further explains that the "incense" (θυμιαμάτων, a plural in Greek, but normally translated as a singular mass noun in English; cf. 8:3, 4; 18:13) is "the prayers of the saints" (v. 8d). Prayer metaphorically rising up

to God as a pleasing aroma also has roots in the devotional life of ancient Israel (Ps 141:2; perhaps also Luke 1:10–11; see similar spiritualizing of sacrifices in general in Pss 40:6; 51:16–17). The symbolism of heavenly beings bringing the prayers of God's people, "the saints,"[57] before the heavenly throne also has parallels in ancient Judaism (Tob 12:15; 3 Bar. 11:4–5). In this passage the prayers probably include expressions of praise, adoration, and thanksgiving (in keeping with the near context, vv. 9–14) as well as pleas for vindication and God's justice to be established on earth (in keeping with the wider context, 6:9–11; 8:4–6).[58] Their symbolic appearance in the heavenly scene reminds us of how significant and welcome our prayers are before God and in the advancing of his purposes.

5:9–10 And they sang a new song, saying, "Worthy are you to take the scroll and open its seals, for you were slain and by your blood you ransomed for God members of every tribe and language and people and nation, 10 and you made them to be a kingdom and priests to serve our God, and they

---

54. There is ambiguity in the expression "each holding" (ἔχοντες ἕκαστος), since this may refer only to the elders (the Greek participle is masculine plural, agreeing with "elders," πρεσβύτεροι, but not with "creatures," ζῷα, a neuter plural). Also, the "twenty-four elders" may mirror the twenty-four orders of Levites in 1 Chr 25:1–31, who provided musical accompaniment for OT worship in the temple (the kithara, κιθάρα, however, is not one of the instruments specifically mentioned in 1 Chr). But Greek participles often take masculine form—representing common personal reference—when the antecedents are personal beings (cf. 4:8 where a masculine participle refers to ζῷα; 5:6, 13; 19:4, 14), and the impression in vv. 8–9, as well as 4:8–11; 7:11; and 19:4 is that of joint participation in all the activities of worship (despite separate mention in 4:9–10; 5:14).

55. BDAG 544 gives "harp, lyre" as glosses for the word κιθάρα. It is traditionally translated "harp" (most English versions). But a kithara was somewhat different, and the distinction would have been well known in the ancient world. A kithara was an instrument with strings of equal length like a lyre, not strings of graduated length like a harp. Its soundbox was rectangular with two arms extending up to a cross-piece

to which the strings were attached. See note on 14:2 for more information.

56. John switches from the distributive singular ("each holding a kithara") to the collective plural ("and bowls of incense"), but it is clear that each being holds one of each object. It is still awkward to conceive of these worshipers using both objects at the same time, but we should take this as a summary portrayal, not delving into details of actual usage. See further in Aune, *Revelation 1–5*, 355.

57. The plural of the Greek adjective ἅγιος, "holy," is commonly used in the NT, especially in Paul, to refer to Christians, God's consecrated people, "the saints" (e.g., Acts 9:13, 32; Rom 8:27; 1 Cor 6:1; Heb 6:10), but it has roots also in the OT (e.g., Pss 16:3; 34:9), not least Dan 7:18–27. The latter passage, with its reference to the oppression and defeat of God's people followed by God's judgment in their favor and their reception of a universal kingdom, is particularly significant here. The preceding paragraph of Dan 7 (vv. 9–14, the vision of one like a son of man approaching the Ancient of Days to receive an everlasting kingdom) was alluded to in Rev 5:6–7.

58. Osborne, *Revelation*, 258–59.

will reign on the earth" (καὶ ᾄδουσιν ᾠδὴν καινὴν λέγοντες, Ἄξιος εἶ λαβεῖν τὸ βιβλίον καὶ ἀνοῖξαι τὰς σφραγῖδας αὐτοῦ, ὅτι ἐσφάγης καὶ ἠγόρασας τῷ θεῷ ἐν τῷ αἵματί σου ἐκ πάσης φυλῆς καὶ γλώσσης καὶ λαοῦ καὶ ἔθνους 10 καὶ ἐποίησας αὐτοὺς τῷ θεῷ ἡμῶν βασιλείαν καὶ ἱερεῖς, καὶ βασιλεύσουσιν ἐπὶ τῆς γῆς). The second and third elements of the pattern of worship that the heavenly beings offer to the Lord God in 4:4–11 (see v. 8 for the first) are directed to the Lamb here at the outset of v. 9: singing of praise hymns to him (4:8, 11; 5:9; see also 5:12–13) and acclamation of worthiness for his person and work (4:11; 5:9; see also 5:12). The four living creatures and twenty-four elders "sang a new song,"[59] a phrase that occurs also in 14:3 (and in 15:3 but without "new")[60] and has significant Old Testament echoes. Singing a "new song" (ᾠδὴν καινήν) to the Lord appears in this exact Greek form only in Ps 144:9 (LXX 143:9), but the underlying Hebrew expression appears also in Pss 33:3; 40:3 [40:4 MT]; 96:1; 98:1; 149:1; and Isa 42:10, with "song" translated by a synonym in Greek. In all these the sense of a "new song" is praise "freshly inspired"[61] by the Lord's gracious deliverance. But the use in Isaiah 42:10 almost certainly adds an eschatological nuance (cf. 42:9: "the former things are past; I now declare new things," i.e., things concerning the Lord's Servant establishing justice and freedom over all the earth and "as a light to the gentiles"; 42:1–8). This is made more likely by the use of "new," καινός, elsewhere in Revelation (2:17; 3:12; 21:1, 2, 5), pointing to the coming deliverance and restoration of all creation (cf. 21:5, "See, I make all things new"). To sing a "new song" in 5:9 is to celebrate the Lamb's victory that sets in motion this coming renewal.[62]

Their praise-song acclaims the Lamb's "worthiness" (v. 9b; cf. v. 2). He alone possesses the status or rank commensurate with the task of taking the scroll and opening its seals (vv. 2, 3, 4, 5, 7, 8), as the preceding part of the vision has dramatized. The basis for his worthiness is set forth in the next clause.

The Lamb's unparalleled accomplishments establish his worthiness, as expressed by the statements in vv. 9c–10a (three parallel, aorist indicative verbs in Greek, "you were slain and . . . ransomed . . . and made . . . ," introduced by the conjunction "for," ὅτι, showing the basis or cause[63]). By his sacrificial death the Lamb has redeemed and constituted a community of people—from and for the whole world—to serve God and fulfill his cosmic purposes. The decisive impact and universal scope of these achievements are stunning. It is clear that for John in the first century this is a vision of God's intent in the death of Christ and the trajectory of what is yet to come based on Christ's decisive work. While the actualization of this redemption is not yet fulfilled even in our day, it has been initiated, and we can see clearly the scope God intends the gospel to have.

"You were slain" (v. 9c) repeats and begins to unpack the meaning of John's initial vision of the Lamb in v. 6: "Standing, looking like it had been slain" (see also v. 12). As noted earlier, this verb σφάζω denotes a violent, merciless killing.[64] John uses it

---

59. The verb "sang" is a historical present ᾄδουσιν, like "said," λέγει, in v. 5 (see note there for the general significance of the historical present). In this case the usage points forward to the crescendo of worship (vv. 11–14) that follows this immediate utterance of praise (vv. 9–10).

60. The further connection in 15:3 is that the martyrs in heaven hold "kitharas," κιθάρας, and sing "the song of Moses . . . and the song of the Lamb."

61. Keener, *Revelation*, 188.

62. Beale, *Revelation*, 358; Ladd, *Revelation*, 90; Osborne, *Revelation*, 259.

63. BDAG 732.

64. The sense is to "slaughter, murder, butcher" (BDAG 979).

here probably under the influence of Isaiah 53:7, which, in context, describes one led "to slaughter" (σφαγή) like an innocent lamb bearing the sins of others. The verb "you ransomed" (ἠγόρασας) fills out the theological significance of this death with the picture of redemption, paying a costly price to buy someone out of slavery or captivity (v. 9d).[65] The beneficiary and the price paid are specified: "for God"[66] indicates that the redeemed become his "property" to serve his purposes, as v. 10 begins to elaborate; "by your blood" is the expression of the cost or price paid for the purchase.[67] The Lamb's "blood" represents his violent death and reinforces the sacrificial imagery seen already in "slain" (v. 6). Mention of his blood in this way suggests another significant parallel, Revelation 1:5–6. There John speaks of Christ "who loves us and freed us from our sins by his blood [ἐν τῷ αἵματι αὐτοῦ]" and refers to our appointment to be "a kingdom, priests to serve his God," a preview of what 5:10 adds here.

There is a textual issue in this part of v. 9, affecting the sense of the verse, as the translations show. The KJV and NKJV say "ransomed us," while most modern versions give something like "ransomed/ purchased people" or "men" (e.g., CSB, ESV, NASB, NIV, NLT, RSV). The latter reading (omitting "us" and thus giving no explicit object) is preferred on strong internal grounds.[68] The construction without an explicit object fits into a fairly common Greek idiom in Revelation (2:7, 10; 3:9; 11:9), a partitive ἐκ phrase used as a substantive (noun),[69] here as a direct object. The resulting English translation fills in the understood generic sense of the partitive expression: "Ransomed [some/people/men] from every tribe . . ." (see translations noted above).

The final part of v. 9 presents a glorious vision of what God intends to accomplish in human history through the sacrifice of the Lamb. This is theologically significant for both soteriology and Christology. The verse speaks of redeeming for God "members of every tribe and language and people and nation." This is the first of seven occurrences in Rev of a remarkably consistent four-fold phrase referring to the multicultural impact of the gospel (5:9; 7:9; 10:11; 11:9; 13:7; 14:6; 17:15).[70] Each of the four nouns carries its distinctive sense, but the

---

65. The verb ἀγοράζω means to "buy, purchase, acquire as property" (BDAG 14). It carries a theological sense in 1 Cor 6:20; 7:23; 2 Pet 2:1; Rev 14:3, 4. See the related verb ἐξαγοράζω in Gal 3:13; 4:5.

66. In Greek τῷ θεῷ, a dative of advantage (Wallace, *Grammar*, 142–44).

67. The Greek phrase is ἐν τῷ αἵματί σου; ἐν plus the dative here expresses instrument or means, a paraphrase for the genitive of price (BDAG 328–29). The dative alone can carry a similar sense, as seen in Rom 3:25; 5:9; 1 Pet 1:18–19. The latter passage is significant in citing Christ's blood, pictured as that of a sacrificed lamb (ἀμνός), as the high price of redemption (λυτρόω, "redeem, set free by paying a ransom," a near synonym of ἀγοράζω).

68. The reading "us" (ἡμᾶς) is found in many manuscripts (including ℵ, 2050, 2344, most of the Byzantine minuscules, and several ancient versions), sometimes before "for God," sometimes after "for God," and in a few copies omitting "for God" altogether in favor of "us" alone. On the other hand, "us" is omitted and no object is explicitly expressed in manuscript A (a fifth-century uncial regarded as the best witness for Rev). While this is a very narrow base in terms of external evidence,

on internal grounds this reading (no explicit object) is very likely to be original, since it best explains the origin of the other readings. Adding "us" smooths out and clarifies the phrasing "you redeemed for God by your blood," which seems awkward on first glance. It is harder to see why "us" would occur in various places and be omitted in A if it was the original reading. See the note on 4:4 for further discussion.

69. BDAG 297; BDF §164; Aune, *Revelation 1–5*, 325; e.g., as object, Matt 23:34; Luke 11:49; 21:16; 2 John 4; Rev 2:7, 10; as subject, Rev 11:9; as indirect object, Rev 3:9. In such cases English idiom must supply a proxy word to smooth out the phrase; e.g., Rev 2:10: "The devil will throw [some] of you into prison" (lit., "throw from/of you into prison").

70. See Bauckham, *Climax*, 326–37, who surveys the wording, OT roots, and significance of these occurrences. The same four nouns (as here) occur in every place except 10:11 and 17:15 where a different word is substituted for "tribe" φυλή; however, the order of the nouns is never the same. As Bauckham argues, Rev's story of the nations' turning to God also includes their oppression for a time by God's enemies who must be overcome, a point very relevant for John's first-century audience living as subjects of the Roman empire.

main point is the serial mention of closely related words, along with the use of "every" at the outset, to reinforce the same idea. No grouping of humans is excluded; every society, culture, populace, and tradition conceivable will be part of God's redeemed community. This is the soteriological and missiological significance of the heavenly beings' song of praise.

The conviction that Christ's redemption is for the whole world and all its peoples was taught to John and other early Christians by Jesus himself (Matt 28:19–20; Luke 24:47; John 10:16; Acts 1:8). But it also has deep roots in the Old Testament, and this verse shows signs of John's reflection on that background, especially Daniel 7 (as we have seen above). Seven times in Daniel the threefold Aramaic expression for "peoples, nations, and languages" occurs (Dan 3:4, 7, 29; 4:1 [MT 3:31]; 5:19; 6:25; 7:14; except for 3:4 they contain "all" at the beginning as well). The Greek versions of Daniel translate them with some combination of the words used for these phrases in Revelation (noted above).[71] A quick survey of the passages in Daniel reveals the sad truth that gripped John in the first century (and should grip us today): all the early references portray "all the peoples, nations, and languages" under the dominion of God's enemies! Only in Daniel 6:25–26 do we find the nations urged to fear "the living God [whose] kingdom will never be destroyed." In addition, in Daniel 7:1–28 there is the vision of a series of rapacious human kingdoms oppressing God's people, only to be finally overcome by God's rule. This rule is expressed through the authority of "one like a son of man" to whom "all peoples, nations, and languages" will give worship, whose "kingdom will never be

destroyed" (7:13–14). John has seen, and the vision of Revelation 5 has vividly reinforced, that this son of man is Jesus Christ the Lamb, whose sacrifice and victory has worldwide significance.

The vision's christological meaning is rooted in its message about the global scope of the Lamb's sacrifice. What kind of status must he have, what kind of person must he be, to have this sort of stunning impact on the destiny of the world and its peoples?[72] He alone is worthy to open the scroll, to reveal and set in motion God's redemptive plan that reaches "every tribe and language and people and nation" because of the surpassing merits of his sacrificial death. The parallel declarations of worthiness in 4:11 and 5:9 are instructive at this point. As noted earlier, in 4:11 the Lord God is proclaimed "worthy" of worship because he is the creator and sustainer of all things. His action of creating and sustaining the universe, however, is not seen in isolation. It is a reflection of his inherent being as God Almighty (4:8), and so both his nature and his concordant actions are seen together. Here in 5:9 (and 5:12) the status of "worthy" is acknowledged for the Lamb as well. In this case his worthiness is seen in his unparalleled accomplishment of worldwide redemption. Yet it is also seen in his inherent nature as a divine person, and the redemption is grounded in this reality. No self-sacrifice at the purely human level can redeem a world in sin; no merely human agent can accomplish such a feat.

The third part of the causal clause of vv. 9c–10 (the basis for the Lamb's worthiness) expresses not the origin of the redeemed but their destiny and assigned duty under God. As an inherent part of their redemption "for God" (v. 9d), the Lamb has appointed[73] them,[74] all of them, to a significant

---

71. See Bauckham, *Climax*, 328–31, for details.

72. See this line of thought developed in G. B. Caird, *New Testament Theology*, ed. L. D. Hurst (Oxford: Clarendon, 1994), 279–81.

73. The verb here is simply "you made," ἐποίησας, but "make"

can denote "appoint, cause to be" in a certain role (BDAG 840; cf. Matt 4:19; Mark 3:14; Acts 2:36).

74. Almost all ancient manuscripts read "them" here (see most English translations), but a few Greek copies and several ancient versions have "us" (see KJV, NKJV), perhaps under the

service for God (τῷ θεῷ ἡμῶν, dative of advantage, "for our God," here expanded as "to serve our God"). They serve him by being "a kingdom" (βασιλείαν), the people he rules as king,[75] and "priests" (ἱερεῖς), who live in holiness and worship of God all their days (v. 10a; cf. 20:6). John has already asserted such roles for Christians in 1:6 in almost the same words ("he made us a kingdom, priests to serve his God"), and in this he is echoing the role God intended for his people Israel (Exod 19:6). Their service for God includes providing a witness to the wider world about the character of their redeeming God. This is true for all of Christ's redeemed regardless of ethnic background. See comments on 1:6 for further discussion.

The final clause of v. 10 picks up another central theme of Daniel 7: not only are God's people "his holy ones/saints" in this world (Dan 7:27), but God will eventually judge their pagan oppressors and give the world's sovereignty to "his saints" (7:18, "they will receive the kingdom"; 7:22, "they possess the kingdom"; 7:27, "the rule, authority, and greatness of the kingdoms under all of heaven will

be handed over to the people who are the saints of the Most High"). The heavenly beings rejoice that God's redeemed "will reign[76] on the earth" (Rev 5:10b). John speaks of this also in Revelation 2:26–27; 3:21; 20:4, 6; 22:5, referring to Christians exerting authority over the nations, sharing in Christ's throne or reign, and ruling with him a thousand years upon his return as King and then forever.[77] Here and in 20:4, 6 it seems clear that this anticipates a physical, geographical reign on this earth,[78] not one that is spiritual and otherworldly only (see Dan 7:27, "under all of heaven"; Jer 3:17, rule from Jerusalem).[79] This coregency with Christ is a recapitulation of God's intent for humans to exert delegated dominion over creation (Gen 1:26–27; Ps 8:3–8; Heb 2:5–9; see comments at Rev 22:5).[80] John sees that the full victory of the "son of man," the "Lamb," will be both spiritual and earthly (Dan 7:13–14; Rev 5:5, 9–10; 11:15), and he longs for that consummation to come.[81]

5:11–12 And I saw, and I heard the sound of many angels around the throne and of the living

---

influence of that reading in v. 9 and a few copies that say "we will reign" in v. 10b. Despite such meager support, both of these readings oddly made it into the printed Textus Receptus, the Greek text that lies behind the KJV, but "them" is certainly a better reading.

75. The word "kingdom," βασιλεία, is used of (1) the exercise of ruling, "royal rule, royal power"; or (2) the realm or "territory ruled by a king" (BDAG 168–69). As an outgrowth of the latter sense, here and in 1:6 it means not the place but the people he rules.

76. A twofold textual issue appears here, but the best reading is "they will reign," βασιλεύσουσιν, future tense, third-person plural. A few late copies read "we will reign," but this apparently arose from the (less likely) reading "us" in vv. 9c–10a (see above; this is the reading of the printed TR and so the KJV; see also NKJV). Of the many manuscripts that attest the "they" form, an almost equal number read the present "they reign" (A, 1006, 1611, 1841, 2329, and part of the Byzantine minuscules) as those that read the future "they will reign" (ℵ, 1854, 2050, 2053, 2344, 2351, and part of the Byzantine minuscules). It is debatable which is the harder reading in v. 10 (perhaps "you made them to be a kingdom" would cause a change from future

to present; or the present would be changed to fit the future orientation of 2:26; 3:21; 20:6). The very reliable manuscript A has the present here as well as in 20:6, but in the latter verse it is a distinctly inferior reading. The future seems marginally better here in 5:10 (cf. *TCGNT2*, 666–67).

77. These ideas appear in different forms in a range of texts like Matt 5:5; 19:28; 1 Cor 4:8; 6:2; 2 Tim 2:12; and perhaps Rom 5:17. See also Ps 47:1–9; Jer 3:17.

78. The preposition ἐπί ("on" the earth) means exerting "power, authority, control . . . *over*" (BDAG 365), but at the same time denotes the sphere or location of that rule (cf. 5:3, 13; Matt 6:10; 9:6): "on/over the earth" (see ESV, KJV, NASB, NIV, NKJV, NLT, RSV).

79. Ladd, *Revelation*, 93; Osborne, *Revelation*, 261. There are larger biblical-theological issues involved here, of course; see 20:1–6 for further discussion.

80. Keener, *Revelation*, 72; Erich Sauer, *The King of the Earth: The Nobility of Man according to the Bible and Science* (Grand Rapids: Eerdmans, 1971), 72–100.

81. Cf. Paul's longing for both spiritual and earthly/cosmic restoration in Rom 8:17–25.

creatures and the elders, and the number of them was myriads of myriads and thousands of thousands, 12 **saying with a loud voice, "Worthy is the Lamb who was slain, to receive power and wealth and wisdom and might and honor and glory and blessing!"** (Καὶ εἶδον, καὶ ἤκουσα φωνὴν ἀγγέλων πολλῶν κύκλῳ τοῦ θρόνου καὶ τῶν ζῴων καὶ τῶν πρεσβυτέρων, καὶ ἦν ὁ ἀριθμὸς αὐτῶν μυριάδες μυριάδων καὶ χιλιάδες χιλιάδων 12 λέγοντες φωνῇ μεγάλῃ, Ἄξιόν ἐστιν τὸ ἀρνίον τὸ ἐσφαγμένον λαβεῖν τὴν δύναμιν καὶ πλοῦτον καὶ σοφίαν καὶ ἰσχὺν καὶ τιμὴν καὶ δόξαν καὶ εὐλογίαν). The words "and I saw" make the transition to the fourth phase of John's vision, where praise to the Lamb and to the Lord God rings out in ever-widening circles (vv. 11–14). Here the vision (what John "saw") focuses immediately on the sounds he experienced ("and I heard"; cf. 6:1; 8:13) as he witnessed this overwhelming heavenly scene. He heard "the sound of many angels" adding their praises to the Lamb (vv. 11b–12). Here a vast host of angels (not seen before in the vision of chs. 4–5) joins itself to the company of the living creatures and elders (cf. 4:8–11; 5:8–10) in giving worship to the Lamb.[82] Because of the position the elders and living creatures were previously seen to have (4:4, elders simply "around the throne"; 4:6, living

creatures closer in, "amid and around the throne"), we should probably view this vast angelic company as occupying a further concentric circle (v. 11b; see also 7:11).[83] Most impressive is the incalculable number of these worshiping angels: "myriads of myriads and thousands of thousands."[84] This is a further powerful allusion to the vision of Daniel 7, in which the sovereign "Ancient of Days" is seen on his heavenly throne, attended by "a thousand thousands" and "ten thousand ten thousands" (Dan 7:10). This in turn is rooted in Deuteronomy 33:2 and Psalm 68:17, where the Lord is said to be served by "ten thousands of holy ones" and "twice ten thousand, thousands upon thousands."[85] The order of Revelation 5:11 (myriads then thousands) is unexpected and reverses the order in Daniel 7:10, but the sense is no different, and it is perhaps influenced by the sequence in Psalm 68:17.

Verse 12 continues directly from v. 11, giving the content of what the angels, elders, and living creatures were acclaiming forcefully in John's hearing.[86] In a further song of praise[87] they repeat the central points from v. 9 (this time more formally, in third person instead of second person): the Lamb who has been slain[88] is worthy (v. 12b). In this way the verse has already given us two elements of the fourfold pattern of worship seen earlier between

---

82. Thomas, *Revelation 1–7*, 403.

83. Osborne, *Revelation*, 262.

84. A "myriad," μυριάς and related words, can be a group of "ten thousand" items (e.g., Acts 19:19), but usually it represents "a very large number, not precisely defined" (BDAG 661; cf. Ps 3:6; Matt 18:24; Luke 12:1; Acts 21:20; 1 Cor 4:15; Rev 9:16).

85. These OT texts influenced a number of later Jewish and Christian writings in their portrayal of God's innumerable angelic attendants (e.g., 1 En. 1:9; 14:22; 40:1; 60:1; 71:8; Apoc. Zeph. 4:1–2; 8:1–2; 1 Clem. 34.6; cf. Jude 14; Heb 12:22).

86. The participle "saying" (λέγοντες) ties this utterance into v. 11, but it is an instance of anacoluthon in Greek (not continuing the original grammatical construction; cf. BDF §§458, 466–70). Such participles usually agree grammatically with those who are speaking (often masculine nominative plural; e.g., v. 9 "they sang . . . saying"), but in v. 11c those

words are genitive plural (either "angels," "living creatures," or "elders," or most likely all three). It is not uncommon in such situations for the participle to revert as here to the idiomatic, more frequently occurring, masculine nominative plural (e.g., 2 Cor 1:7; 7:5; 8:4; 11:6; Eph 4:2–3; Rev 7:9; 11:15).

87. Instead of "sing" (v. 9) the more general verb "say" (λέγω) is used here (as in 4:8, 10; 5:13), but it is clear from the parallels in content (between 5:9, 12–13 and 4:8, 10–11) that "singing" a song of praise (cf. NLT) is the more specific sense (see also 7:10–12; 15:3; 19:1–8).

88. Here John uses the perfect tense of σφάζω, "slay," again, as in v. 6 (the aorist or summary past was used in v. 9). The perfect draws attention to some ongoing effect of the past act of slaughter; here perhaps his redemptive accomplishment through the cross—and the worship he is due as a result.

chapter 4 and chapter 5 (see note at 5:8 above): (1) singing of praise to God or to the Lamb (4:8, 11; 5:9, 12–13) and (2) acclamation of worthiness for their person and work (4:11; 5:9, 12).

Now v. 12b adds a third element in the pattern: ascription of glory, honor, power, and other virtues to them (4:9, 11; 5:13). Even though there is an outward parallel between this verse together with 4:11 on the one hand, and 5:9 on the other ("worthy to receive/take," ἄξιον / ἄξιος ... λαβεῖν; cf. "take" in v. 7), the different objects make the sense of "receive/take" quite different.[89] Instead λαβεῖν in this verse and 4:11 means to "receive" declarations ascribing exalted attributes and privileges (note the complementary verb "give," δώσουσιν, in 4:9). This ascription of virtues (4:9, 11; 5:12–13) is a form of doxology,[90] glorifying or honoring someone for their status by reciting various perfections they possess (the speaker does not bestow these qualities but acknowledges them). David's acclamation of the Lord in 1 Chronicles 29:10–11 is a likely influence on the doxology in v. 12, since two of the key terms are repeated from the LXX wording (δύναμις and ἰσχύς), and two others are cognates or near synonyms ("blessed/blessing" and "pride/ glory").[91] It is christologically significant that ascriptions of praise in Revelation are offered to God alone (4:9, 11; 7:12; 19:1), to God and to the Lamb (5:13), or to Christ alone (1:6; 5:12).[92]

Here the list of attributes and privileges (v. 12b) is sevenfold (as in 7:12, symbolizing completeness of virtue).[93] While the composite impression of such a list is important,[94] the individual qualities are worth noticing briefly as well. A paradoxical one to ascribe to the Lamb is power, capability (δύναμις). It is frequently attributed to God and seems especially connected with sovereign rule and victory (cf. 5:5) over all enemies (1 Chr 29:11; Mark 13:26; 1 Cor 1:24; Rev 4:11; 7:12; 19:1; also 11:17; 12:10; 15:8). Wealth, riches (πλοῦτος) is a way of celebrating the vast resources of God and the benefits Christ can bestow on his followers (1 Chr 29:11; cf. Eph 3:8; Phil 4:19). Wisdom, understanding (σοφία) is a divine perfection bestowed on Christ by the Spirit's anointing (Rev 7:12; cf. Isa 11:2; Rom 11:33; 1 Cor 1:24; Col 2:3). Might, strength (ἰσχύς) is closely related to "power" (listed first) and is also bestowed by the Spirit (Rev 7:12; cf. Isa 11:2). Honor or deserved respect (τιμή) is of course naturally due to God, but in Christ's case it is often seen as the result of obedient suffering (Rev 4:9, 11; 5:13; 7:12; cf. Pss 29:1 [28:1 LXX]; 96:7 [95:7 LXX]; 1 Tim 1:17; 6:16; Heb 2:9; 2 Pet 1:17). Likewise glory or splendor/radiance as a symbol for perfection (δόξα) is frequently cited as a divine attribute or something to be ascribed to God by right, but it is used also of what Christ received after his humiliation (Pss 29:1 [28:1 LXX]; 96:7

---

89. Contra Aune, *Revelation 1–5*, 364; Osborne, *Revelation*, 262.

90. See also 5:13b below. For detailed discussion of the "doxology" form, see Aune, *Revelation 1–5*, 43–45.

91. Beale, *Revelation*, 364. Another influence is Dan 2:37, but there the "glory" of Nebuchadnezzar as "king of kings" is attenuated by Daniel's declaration that "the God of heaven has given you [LXX the rule and] the kingdom and the might and the honor and the glory" (three of the nouns in Rev 5:12). In context Daniel's "doxology" takes as much as it gives: Nebuchadnezzar is the vision's "head of gold" (2:38), but only because the God of Israel has granted him such a status.

92. Bauckham, *Climax*, 139, notes that John displays an important "sensitiv[ity to] monotheism in worship," while

regarding Christ as divine. This is an important issue in early Christology because Christian understanding of Jesus's person developed within the Jewish heritage of strict monotheism. The worship of Christ as divine in v. 12 "leads to the joint worship of God and Christ" in v. 13, because "Christ cannot be seen as an alternative object of worship alongside God, but shares in the glory due to God." See also Bauckham, *Theology*, 60; and L. W. Hurtado, "Christology," in *DLNT* 176–77.

93. Bauckham, *Climax*, 30–31.

94. The single Greek article before the first item serves to link all the items together in some way—not as identical but as closely associated (e.g., Matt 24:3; Acts 20:21; 2 Cor 13:11; Phil 1:19; 2 Thess 2:1). See Wallace, *Grammar*, 286–90.

[95:7 LXX]; Mark 13:26; John 1:14; 17:5; 1 Cor 2:8; 1 Tim 1:17; Heb 1:3; 2:9; 2 Pet 1:17; Jude 25; Rev 4:9, 11; 5:13; 7:12; 19:1). The rubric of suffering and then honor/glory fits the scene of Revelation 5 most auspiciously since Christ's adoration here is due to his redemptive sacrifice (vv. 6, 9, 12; cf. Phil 2:5–11 where this theme appears as emptying and then exaltation). Finally blessing, praise (εὐλογία) in the sense of "praiseworthiness"[95] is most appropriate as a conclusion (also as the initial item, cf. 5:13; 7:12) since it denotes the general character of deserving to be spoken well of, to be admired, extolled, and adulated (Rev 5:13; 7:12; cf. cognate words in 1 Chr 29:10; Pss 41:13; 89:52; Rom 1:25; 2 Cor 11:31; Eph 1:3; 1 Pet 1:3; and "thanksgiving," εὐχαριστία, in Rev 4:9; 7:12).

5:13 And every creature in heaven and on earth and under the earth and in the sea, and all that is in them, I heard saying, "To the one sitting on the throne and to the Lamb be blessing and honor and glory and might forever and ever!" (καὶ πᾶν κτίσμα ὃ ἐν τῷ οὐρανῷ καὶ ἐπὶ τῆς γῆς καὶ ὑποκάτω τῆς γῆς καὶ ἐπὶ τῆς θαλάσσης καὶ τὰ ἐν αὐτοῖς πάντα ἤκουσα λέγοντας, Τῷ καθημένῳ ἐπὶ τῷ θρόνῳ καὶ τῷ ἀρνίῳ ἡ εὐλογία καὶ ἡ τιμὴ καὶ ἡ δόξα καὶ τὸ κράτος εἰς τοὺς αἰῶνας τῶν αἰώνων). In a growing and ever-widening crescendo every

created being is now heard to join the chorus of praise.[96] It is only right that every creature (κτίσμα) should honor God since he is the creator and sustainer of all (4:11, κτίζω used twice) and should honor the Lamb since his redemption extends to every part of humanity (5:9).[97] This universality of worship is emphasized by the fourfold subdivision into heaven, earth, underworld,[98] and sea (see the threefold division in 5:3 and details cited there) and also by the reinforcing "and all that is in them" (v. 13a). As John recorded this vision, he and his readers were well aware that the enemies of God were still active in God's world and resistant to the worship of the Lamb. Yet John was convinced that the victory of the cross had made a decisive difference for all of creation, and the future fulfillment of this vision was sure (cf. Phil 2:9–11; Col 1:20).[99] What he saw "in the Spirit" (4:2) unveils what is true in heaven as a preview of what will come to be true on earth as well (cf. Matt 6:10).

The expression of praise from all creatures comes in the form of a more standard doxology (v. 13b),[100] offered to God and the Lamb together. This joint worship of "the one sitting on the throne" (cf. 4:2, 3, 9, 10; 5:1, 7; identified as God in 7:10; 19:4) and of the Lamb (cf. 5:6, 8, 12)[101] provides an important culmination for the heavenly vision

---

95. Osborne, *Revelation*, 264.

96. This extension is an echo of Ps 103:19–22. Because the Lord rules over all from his heavenly throne (v. 19), he should be praised by his angels and heavenly hosts (vv. 20–21) as well as by "all his works in every part of his dominion" (v. 22).

97. This is the point at which John's vision of heavenly events shifts from being descriptive (what did or could happen in heaven at the time John was alive and then wrote) to being prescriptive or determinative (a preview of what will yet come to pass in God's will). See Beale, *Revelation*, 319; Caird, *Revelation*, 60–61.

98. This refers metaphorically to the realm of the unredeemed dead and the demons that are held captive until the coming judgment (cf. Job 11:8–9; 2 Pet 2:4; Jude 6). Willingly or unwillingly all will one day recognize the lordship of God and the Lamb (cf. Phil 2:9–11). This portrayal, however, does not

indicate universal salvation (i.e., all of God's enemies and even the unconverted dead brought ultimately to salvation). John makes it clear throughout Rev that some will resist the gospel to the end and suffer eternal judgment (e.g., Rev 9:20–21; 13:8; 20:11–15).

99. Caird, *Revelation*, 77; Ladd, *Revelation*, 93.

100. The more standard form includes (1) dative phrase denoting recipient(s); (2) nominative phrase, usually including "glory," δόξα, normally articular (cf. Aune, *Revelation 1–5*, 326 and examples he cites), denoting the qualities ascribed to the recipients; (3) expression of temporal extent, usually "forever" in some form; and (4) a concluding "amen." See Aune, *Revelation 1–5*, 43–45, for details. These elements appear also in Rev 1:5b–6; 7:12.

101. See the significance of this for Christology and monotheism in the comments on 5:12.

in chapters 4–5.[102] The most significant point of the entire vision is the divine status and cosmic sovereignty that God and the Lamb share. This prepares the way for the following chapters that trace the outworking of their divine plan of justice and redemption as symbolized by the seven-sealed scroll.[103] Here the qualities ascribed to them in worship are fourfold,[104] repeating three elements from v. 12 ("blessing and honor and glory"; see above for discussion) and adding one not seen there. The addition is "might," κράτος, referring to strength but more specifically in a doxology to the "exercise of ruling ability . . . sovereignty"[105] (as in 1 Tim 6:16; 1 Pet 4:11; 5:11; Jude 25; Rev 1:6; cf. Dan 2:37 [Th.]; 4:30 [LXX]). Finally, the doxology, as normally, tells how long God and the Lamb will possess these perfections: "forever and ever" (εἰς τοὺς αἰῶνας τῶν αἰώνων), literally, "unto the ages of the ages."[106]

5:14 And the four living creatures were saying, "Amen!" and the elders fell down and worshiped (καὶ τὰ τέσσαρα ζῷα ἔλεγον, Ἀμήν· καὶ οἱ πρεσβύτεροι ἔπεσαν καὶ προσεκύνησαν). The coda to the stirring scene of worship in chapters 4–5 is this response by the heavenly beings to the doxology of praise sung by all creation in v. 13. How fitting that the elders who appeared early in chapter 4 seated on twenty-four thrones surrounding the throne of God (4:4), and the living creatures who filled the throne room with cries of worship day and night (4:6b–9), should honor God and the Lamb together with these final acts of worship to conclude the vision. The living creatures repeatedly[107] affirm the song of praise by interjecting cries of "amen."[108] And the elders bow down in humble adoration and worship (cf. 4:10; 5:8),[109] an especially suitable conclusion to the chapter.

Theology in Application

The Triumph of the Crucified[110]

The most important theme in Revelation 4–5 as a unit is God's sovereignty over all of the world and its history. This begins with John's vision in 4:1–11 of the majestic,

---

102. Thomas, *Revelation 1–7*, 407.

103. This verse is the first of seven places in Rev (5:13; 6:16; 7:10; 14:4; 21:22; 22:1, 3) where God and the Lamb are referred to together, as Bauckham, *Climax*, 34 notes.

104. Bauckham, *Climax*, 31 brilliantly observes that the fourfold doxology in v. 13b is likely to be influenced by the fourfold description of creation in v. 13a. Other doxologies in Rev contain two (1:5b–6), three (4:9, 11; 19:2) or seven qualities (5:12; 7:12).

105. BDAG 565.

106. BDAG 32; cf. further details at 1:6.

107. The imperfect verb ἔλεγον in a context describing specific action often highlights repetition within a narrow time frame (Fanning, *Verbal Aspect*, 242–43, 286–88).

108. See treatment at 1:6, 7. As BDAG 53 says, this is a transliteration of the Hebrew word for "truly," used as a response in congregational worship, "let it be so, truly, amen" (e.g., 1 Chr 16:36; 1 Cor 14:16) or to affirm and conclude a doxology (e.g.,

Rev 1:6; 7:12; see also Rom 11:36; Gal 1:5; Eph 3:21; Phil 4:20; 1 Tim 1:17; 2 Tim 4:18; Heb 13:21; 1 Pet 4:11; 5:11; Jude 25).

109. The elders' response is expressed by two aorists, ἔπεσαν and προσεκύνησαν, summarizing these acts of worship and reinforcing each other. Both verbs occur also in 4:10; 7:11; 11:16; 19:4, 10; and 22:8. In the preferred Greek text the verb "worshiped" has no stated object, although a few late copies insert "the one who lives forever and ever" under the influence of 4:9–10 (clearly an inferior reading externally and internally, which unfortunately made it into the TR and thus the KJV; see also NKJV). The implied objects of "worshiped" are easily seen as the two beings addressed in the doxology of v. 13: God and the Lamb. See also comments on vv. 8, 12 above.

110. The titles used with these points are taken, respectively, from the title of Erich Sauer's 1951 book, from the title of a 1971 sermon by S. Lewis Johnson, and from the 1963 "I Have a Dream" speech by Martin Luther King, Jr.

almighty God sitting on his heavenly throne, being worshiped as the creator and sustainer of all the universe. He reigns over all, and everything exists from and for his sovereign will (4:11). All that "must happen after these things" (4:1) issues from his throne room. In 5:1–14 this sovereign will, while remaining cosmic in scope, is focused on the victory of Jesus Christ, the Crucified. All of God's purposes will be accomplished through Jesus Christ and his sacrifice. He alone, because "he was slain," will reveal and set in motion the divine plan of justice and redemption symbolized by the seven-sealed scroll. The dramatic imagery of these chapters powerfully communicates the centrality of God and the centrality of the cross.

Revelation 5:1–14 also shows how the cross is the connecting point for the story of the whole Bible. All that came before in the creation and fall of humankind and in the saga of God's people Israel can now be seen to point toward the Crucified One. He is the focus and fulcrum of God's intent for all of humanity. This includes his choice of Abraham and his deliverance of Israel from Egypt to be his people among all the nations of the world, his royal promises to David, and the visions of Daniel about "a son of man" establishing God's everlasting dominion over the rebellious kingdoms of the world. All that "will take place after this" decisively turns on the triumph of the Crucified. John sees these things as presently inaugurated in heaven and in microcosm in the church and anticipates their ultimate universal consummation in the future on earth.

This vision serves as a vital reality check for John's audience, who risked persecution by the greatest empire the world had known for their confession of Jesus as Lord. The Romans regarded their empire as the focal point of world history, their glorious emperor as the gift of the gods to humankind and the one who should receive universal submission. An unknown peasant executed for treason in some far corner of the empire was worthy of nothing but contempt and oblivion. Even today, of course, Christianity has its "cultured despisers." They may give lip service to Jesus as a wonderful example and teacher or as a tragic case of martyrdom for his revolutionary ideas. But to assert the centrality and exclusivity of his sacrifice as the way to world redemption is beyond disdain.

Nevertheless, John has given us here a glimpse into the divine perspective on the course and meaning of the world's history. The Gospel of John began its narrative of Jesus's life by recording the Baptist's words, "Look, the Lamb of God, who takes away the sin of the world" (John 1:29, 36), and now Revelation portrays Jesus's continued significance by pointing to heaven's celebration of the victory of the Lamb, the Lion of Judah and Shoot of David.

The words of the hymn writer, John Bowring (1792–1872), celebrate this theme in a wonderful way: "In the cross of Christ I glory, towering o'er the wrecks of time; all the light of sacred story gathers round its head sublime."[111]

---

111. "In the Cross of Christ I Glory" (1825). Public domain.

The Christology of Heaven

The rock opera *Jesus Christ Superstar* features the lines, "Jesus Christ. Jesus Christ. Who are you? What have you sacrificed?"[112] Earthly opinions about Jesus over the centuries have, of course, run the gamut. Even within Christendom the range of answers to those questions seems unlimited. Who is he really? A myth? An iconoclastic peasant philosopher? A Marxist revolutionary before his time? A new-age spirit-being bringing enlightenment? A divine spirit who only appeared human? A cipher on whom we can imprint our own dreams and desires?

After all is said and done on earth, John's vision in Revelation 5:1–14 portrays the heavenly viewpoint on these questions. What Christology prevails in the throne room of heaven? How is Jesus viewed there? The answer to this question is in fact a paradox. John's vision gives us a remarkable mixture of majesty and meekness, celebration and suffering, worship and woe, divine glory and abject humiliation. Just when we think heaven's Christology is all as we expected, John upsets our categories.

The heavenly scene virtually glows with greatness and prestige. God Almighty on his throne, his heavenly attendants with their thrones and crowns, the great seven-sealed scroll expressing God's will for the universe—it is an overwhelming picture of eminence, status, and privilege of the highest order. Amid this scene a mighty angel issues the ultimate challenge: Who is worthy to take the scroll and open its seals? We all nod in agreement when the Lion of Judah, the Shoot of David, is announced as worthy. Of course, such a one would qualify.

The biggest surprise, and a most significant point for Christology, is revealed when John turns and sees a Lamb standing as slain. The ultimate person is known "by the prints of the nails in his hand."[113] What does it take to be a VIP in heaven's eyes? It takes surrender, sacrifice, suffering, obedience, and endurance. C. S. Lewis's mighty Lion Aslan restores and rules Narnia only because he submits to the White Witch's knife. Jesus himself is the ultimate demonstration of his teaching that we must follow him in servanthood (Mark 8:31–35; 9:33–35; 10:41–45), even though our service will not bring the cosmic effects that his produced.

This brings us back to the point about Christology. The heavenly chorus sees the Lamb's death not as the contradiction of his divinity but as the confirmation of it. What kind of person must he be for his sacrifice to produce such world-redeeming, world-changing effects? No merely human martyrdom or execution, even for the most noble of causes and from the loftiest motives, could produce these results. His meek and lowly human service must also reflect his divine character and holiness in offering himself for the sins of all humanity and the restoration of God's creation.

---

112. Murray Head, vocalist, "Superstar," by Andrew Lloyd Webber and Tim Rice, recorded October 10, 1969, track 3 of side 4 of *Jesus Christ Superstar*, Decca/MCA, 1969.

113. Fanny Crosby, "My Savior First of All" (1894). Public domain.

For John it was the cross, truly understood, that revealed the glory of Jesus in the ultimate way (John 7:39; 12:16, 23; 13:31–32; 17:1, 4–5; 21:19). Here in Revelation 5, it is his God-given role as the slain Lamb that causes the heavenly beings and all creation to worship Christ in the same ways and with the same breath they use to worship the Lord God.

The Christian doctrines of the Trinity and of the divine and human natures of God the Son were not worked out in detail until the church councils of the fourth and fifth centuries. However, from the earliest days Christians began to see that Jesus of Nazareth shared fully in the deity of God the Father. In doing this they were in fact reflecting the Christology of heaven.

The Table of Brotherhood

John's vision captures in a beautiful way another profound paradox of Christianity. Because there is only one true and living God and only one atoning sacrifice—the cross of Christ—to bring us to God, the many diverse peoples of the world are all the objects of his grace and destined to find true union in him. We make a grave mistake in today's world when we think that diversity can only mean division and that unity of truth and of human destiny cannot survive the multiplication of cultures on earth. Sometimes we hear statements that go like this: "In earlier times it made more sense for Christians to think that Jesus was the only way to God and that the God of the Bible was the only true God, because people lived in greater cultural isolation in those days. Now that the world is getting smaller due to ease of travel and widespread immigration and commerce, we can no longer believe such provincial ideas."

No one who has actually studied the world of the first-century would ever fall for such a line as that. Jesus, John, Paul, and the early Christians lived in an incredibly diverse mix of nations, philosophies, cultures, religious ideas, and claims for allegiance often enforced at the point of a sword. If we ever decide that the price we must pay for allegiance to Christ and the gospel is too great, let us never deceive ourselves that after all our intellectual and religious situation is more difficult than theirs.

But Revelation 5 gives us a more positive vision to draw us forward, the vision of every tribe and language and people and nation united in Christ. God's intent from the beginning as creator and redeemer has been to bring all humanity together in communion and worship of himself as the one true and living God. John's vision makes it clear that this is only right and proper: God's sovereign plan to accomplish judgment against sin and redemption for his people through the sacrifice of Jesus Christ should evoke heartfelt worship from every part of creation.

When we truly worship God, it does not efface our differences but focuses them on something more important. It brings them together to contribute to something larger than our group alone. True worship centers us on God, and in so doing it unites us with others we may otherwise have excluded in our provincialism and self-centeredness. It humbles our sense of ethnocentric superiority as we gather on the level ground at the foot of the cross to acknowledge that our redemption is purely by the free grace of God in Christ. It exalts Christ to realize that he will receive universal acclaim. He deserves to be worshiped by all the nations of the world.

Anyone who has ever thrilled at the climax of Handel's *Messiah*—Revelation 5:12–13 sung in a mighty crescendo of voices and instruments—can begin to imagine, in small measure at least, the glory of that day when the redeemed from every tribe and language and people and nation will unite in worship of the Lord God and of the Lamb.

Revelation 6:1–17

Literary Context

John's vision in chapters 4–5 that concluded with all of creation worshiping God and the Lamb (5:11–14) now moves along to the next, quite different phase of the heavenly scene (6:1–17). Again John "looked" (εἶδον, v. 1a; cf. 4:1; 5:1, 2, 6, 11) and a rapid-fire series of heavenly events presents itself, but this time with unmistakable earthly consequences. As seen in chapter 5, the contents of the sealed scroll consist of future events that will unfold according to God's plan (see discussion of OT background at 5:1). The Lamb is found worthy to take the scroll and open its seals (5:1–7), and in doing so he unveils the scroll's contents and more importantly puts into operation on earth the events it describes. This further phase of John's vision now unfolds in opening the first six seals (6:1–17) and discloses what those future events will be.

The calamities that come in connection with Christ's opening of the six seals are the initial expression of God's judgment on sin in anticipation of completing worldwide redemption. John was permitted to glimpse and then reveal to others the severe woes, including the later series of trumpet and bowl judgments, that will be visited on earth in the final days (cf. 1:1–2). On the question of how the seals, trumpets, and bowls relate to one another, see "Structure and Outline" in the commentary's introduction.

These woes are portrayed figuratively, but their vivid symbols refer to quite real, this-worldly suffering that the earth and its inhabitants will experience as judgments from God during the future climactic events of this age (see "Imagery and Symbols" in the introduction). They are manifestations of God's wrath (vv. 16–17), and they reflect real-world judgments such as the flood at the time of Noah, the destruction of Sodom and Gomorrah, and the plagues visited on Egypt at the exodus. These patterns reappear in the Old Testament prophets as parts of the "day of the Lord" judgments. Jesus associates the same features with the time of severe testing that Daniel foresaw in connection with a future "abomination of desolation" and unprecedented "tribulation" (Dan 9:27; 11:31; 12:1, 11; Matt 24:15, 21). The judgments connected with these seven seals begin the time of worldwide distress or tribulation mentioned in Revelation 3:10.[1]

I. Prologue (1:1–8)

II. First Vision: The Exalted Christ and His Messages to the Churches (1:9–3:22)

III. Second Vision: Heavenly Throne Room and Three Judgment Cycles (4:1–16:21)

    A. Vision of God in His Heavenly Throne Room (4:1–11)

    B. The Seven-Sealed Scroll and the Slain Lamb (5:1–14)

➡   **C. The Seven Seals and the Interlude of the Two Multitudes (6:1–8:1)**

        1. The First Six Seals (6:1–17)

        2. The Interlude of the Two Multitudes (7:1–17)

        3. The Seventh Seal (8:1)

Main Idea

As the first six seals on the Lamb's scroll are opened, waves of calamities such as military invasion, civil war, famine, disease and death, and fearful cosmic disturbances assault the earth's inhabitants as expressions of divine wrath, causing them to cower in desperate terror while faithful martyrs in heaven appeal for justice from God.

Translation

(See pages 237–8.)

Structure

The events associated with the opening of the first six seals are recorded in 6:1–17, while the seventh comes in 8:1 after an interlude of two visions (7:1–17). The first four seals (vv. 1–8) repeat a shared pattern that gives them a unity distinct from the subsequent three seal openings.[2] This consists of: (1) a temporal clause with an explicit enumeration of the seal ("when he opened the ___ seal"), (2) the voice of one of the four living creatures, also enumerated ("I heard the ___ living creature say, 'Come!'"), (3) the appearance of a horse and rider whose destructive actions are briefly described. The woes associated with these four seals, while calamitous,

---

1. Blaising, "Case," 25–52. See also the comments at 3:10 and at the end of 6:8.

2. A similar grouping can be found for the trumpets and less clearly for the bowls. See Bauckham, *Climax*, 9–15.

Revelation 6:1–17

1a	Action/1st Seal Opening	**And I looked when the Lamb opened one of the seven seals,**
b	Summons	**and I heard one of the living creatures saying with a voice like thunder,** *"Come!"*
2a	Character Entrance	**And I looked, and behold, a white horse,**
b	Description/Effects	**and the one sitting on it had a bow**
c		**and a crown was given to him,**
d		**and like a conqueror he rode out in order to conquer,**
3a	Action/2nd Seal Opening	And when he opened the second seal,
b	Summons	**I heard the second living creature saying,** *"Come!"*
4a	Character Entrance	**And another horse, a red one, rode out,**
b	Description/Effects	**and the one sitting on it was given authority to take peace from the earth**
c		so that people would in fact slaughter each other,
d		**and a large sword was given to him.**
5a	Action/3rd Seal Opening	And when he opened the third seal,
b	Summons	**I heard the third living creature saying,** *"Come!"*
c	Character Entrance	**And I looked, and behold, a black horse, and**
d	Description/Effects	**the one sitting on it held a balance scale in his hand.**
6a		**And I heard something like a voice in the midst of the four living creatures saying,**
b	Offers	*"A quart of wheat for a denarius*
c		*and three quarts of barley for a denarius,*
d	Prohibition	*and do not spoil the olive oil and the wine."*
7a	Action/4th Seal Opening	And when he opened the fourth seal,
b	Summons	**I heard the voice of the fourth living creature saying,** *"Come!"*
8a	Character Entrance	**And I looked, and behold, a sickly green horse, and**
b		**the one sitting on it had the name Death,**
c	Character Entrance	**and Hades was following with him.**
d	Description/Effects	**And authority was given to them over a fourth of the earth**
e	Explanation	to kill with sword and with famine and with pestilence and by the wild beasts of the earth.
9a	Action/5th Seal Opening	And when he opened the fifth seal,
b	Character Entrance	**I saw**
	Location	**under the altar**
	Object	**the souls of those who had been slaughtered**
	Reason	**because of the word of God and**
	Reason	**because of the testimony they maintained.**

Continued on next page.

Continued from previous page.

10a	Action	And **they cried out with a loud voice saying,**
b	Entreaty	*"How long, O Sovereign Lord, holy and true,*
		will you not judge and
c		*avenge our blood on those who live* ↵
		on the earth?"

11a	Response	And **a white robe was given to each of them,**
b		and **they were told to rest for a little while longer**
c		until both their fellow servants and
		their brothers and sisters …
		who were going to be killed as they also had been
		… would come to their full number.

12a	Action/6th Seal Opening	And **I looked when he opened the sixth seal,**
b	Cosmic Effects	and **a great earthquake took place,**
c		and **the sun became black like sackcloth made of hair,**
d		and **the whole moon became like blood,**
13a		and **the stars of the sky fell to the earth**
b	Comparison	like a fig tree sheds its new figs
c		when shaken by a great wind,

14a		and **the sky was split apart like a torn scroll rolling up,**
b		and **every mountain and island were moved from their place.**
15	Human Response	And **the kings of the earth and**
		the nobles and
		the commanders and
		the wealthy and the powerful and
		everyone, slave and free,…
		… **hid themselves in the caves and rocks of the mountains.**

16a	OT Quotation	And **they said to the mountains and the rocks,**
b	Entreaty	*"Fall on us*
		and
c		*hide us from the presence of the one who sits on the throne and*
		from the wrath of the Lamb, (Hos 10:8)

17a	Reason	*because the great day of their wrath has come, and*
b		*who is able to stand?"*

are not as intense as the ones that follow in the subsequent seals, trumpets, and bowls. The first four seal judgments are not more severe as they go along but are interrelated calamities with some sense of sequence implied (invasion, civil strife, famine, death), since the earlier two seem to lead to the latter two. The fifth and sixth seals (6:9–17) present events of a different character from the first four, focusing on terrifying cosmic disturbances as well as the reactions accompanying these woes, first by martyred saints in heaven and then by the earth's inhabitants desperate to escape these manifestations of divine wrath.[3]

Exegetical Outline

III. Second Vision: Heavenly Throne Room and Three Judgment Cycles (4:1–16:21)

    A. Vision of God in His Heavenly Throne Room (4:1–11)

    B. The Seven-Sealed Scroll and the Slain Lamb (5:1–14)

    C. The Seven Seals and the Interlude of the Two Multitudes (6:1–8:1)

➡   **1. The First Six Seals (6:1–17)**

        a. Four seals, four horsemen (6:1–8)

          (1) First seal and horseman: international conquest (6:1–2)

          (2) Second seal and horseman: civil war (6:3–4)

          (3) Third seal and horseman: severe famine (6:5–6)

          (4) Fourth seal and horseman: widespread disease and death (6:7–8)

        b. Fifth seal: cry of the martyrs (6:9–11)

        c. Sixth seal: wrath of the Lamb (6:12–17)

          (1) Cosmic disturbances (6:12–14)

          (2) Response of earth-dwellers (6:15–17)

Explanation of the Text

6:1–2 And I looked when the Lamb opened one of the seven seals, and I heard one of the living creatures saying with a voice like thunder, "Come!" 2 And I looked, and behold, a white horse, and the one sitting on it had a bow and a crown was given to him, and like a conqueror he rode out in order to conquer (Καὶ εἶδον ὅτε ἤνοιξεν τὸ ἀρνίον μίαν ἐκ τῶν ἑπτὰ σφραγίδων, καὶ ἤκουσα ἑνὸς ἐκ τῶν τεσσάρων ζῴων λέγοντος ὡς φωνὴ βροντῆς, Ἔρχου. 2 καὶ εἶδον, καὶ ἰδοὺ ἵππος λευκός, καὶ ὁ καθήμενος ἐπ’ αὐτὸν ἔχων τόξον καὶ ἐδόθη αὐτῷ στέφανος καὶ ἐξῆλθεν νικῶν καὶ ἵνα νικήσῃ). The close connections of this passage to chapters 4–5 are evident as John describes the first seal opening using the same words that appeared in 5:1, 5 ("seven seals"), in 5:2–5, 9 ("open"), and in 5:6, 12–13 ("the Lamb"), and the voice that he heard using the same phrase as in 4:6, 8 ("four

---

3. See the introduction to the commentary ("Structure and Outline") for how the seals, trumpets, and bowls relate to one another.

living creatures").[4] Since both the Lamb and the living creatures were seen as central in God's throne room (4:6; 5:6), their actions here must be understood as direct expressions of God's sovereign plan for the world he created and redeems (4:11; 5:9–12; cf. 7:11; 14:3; 15:7). At the breaking of this first seal, John heard one of the living creatures uttering "with a voice like thunder"[5] the command, "Come" (ἔρχου; v. 1b). This could be taken as an invitation to John, "come (and see),"[6] but in context it commands the horseman who appears in v. 2 to launch his divinely intended mission of judgment.

The appearance of this emissary is emphatically signaled in v. 2 by the phrase "and I looked, and behold" (also in vv. 5, 8; see note on 4:1). What John saw was a fearful military image, "a white horse" and its rider, "the one sitting on it." The three horses to follow (vv. 4, 5, 8) all vary in color, and the four individual colors establish an allusion to Zechariah's visions (Zech 1:8, 10; 6:1–3) of four sets of powerful horses of similar colors (white, red, black, and sorrel or dappled, but not in a set order). In Zechariah these are sent by the Lord to patrol the whole earth, symbolizing his worldwide dominion. The details are different in John's vision, but the larger point is the same: God's sovereign plan of judgment and salvation will be accomplished in all the earth, beginning with a series of terrible woes.

The four horsemen, as in Zechariah, represent effects that impact the entire world as represented in its four proverbial corners. They most likely refer not to specific personal beings (human or angelic) sent by God to bring his judgment but disastrous calamities that will be loosed on the world and its peoples. For further discussion of how these calamities should be understood, see comments at v. 8.

The elements unique to this first horse and rider have led to widely differing interpretations of his identification and significance. One distinctive feature is the white color of this horse (v. 2a). In Revelation "white" seems to be a symbol of goodness and purity (e.g., 3:4–5; 4:4; 6:11), and a white horse appears again in 19:11 ridden by Jesus Christ who is crowned with "diadems" as Lord of all and identified as the "Word of God" (vv. 11–16). Here in 6:2 the rider has a "crown" (στέφανος) and rides out "like a conqueror . . . in order to conquer,"[7] perhaps related directly to Christ's victory just mentioned (5:5; see also 3:21). To see this rider as Christ leading his heavenly army out to conquer all foes (e.g., the last enemy, death [cf. 6:8]) or as the gospel about Christ going forth first to win converts to salvation ahead of the worldwide judgment (cf. Matt 24:14) were the dominant interpretations in the early centuries of the church and still attract some support.[8] But these connections to the figure in 19:11 are too

---

4. John uses a series of aorist verbs in vv. 1–2 to narrate both his reception of the visionary experience ("looked" [2x]; "heard") and its contents. In the latter case the events of the vision are recounted as prior actions viewed in summary ("opened"; "was given"; "rode out"). See Mussies, *Morphology*, 333–36, 340; Fanning, "Greek Tenses," 341–46.

5. "With a voice like thunder" translates a comparative particle (ὡς; "like, as") followed by an attributive genitive phrase (φωνὴ βροντῆς), meaning a thunder-like voice. This phrase does not appear in the parallel verses below (vv. 3, 5, 7). It could have been phrased as a dative φωνῇ, "with a voice" (and some manuscripts correct the text to a dative), but comparative clauses are often elliptical, and the nominative φωνή fits quite well on its own (i.e., "as a voice of thunder [speaks or sounds]").

6. Some manuscripts contain the additional words, "and

see," in two forms (καὶ ἴδε or καὶ βλέπε; cf. KJV; also in vv. 3, 5, 7). But better manuscripts (A, C, P, 1006, 1611, 1854, 2053) support the shorter reading, and the occurrence of two different verbs for "see" makes the longer readings suspect. They are a later addition. When Rev expresses the idea "come and see," it uses "come, I will show you" (δεῦρο, δείξω σοι; 17:1; 21:9).

7. This phrase is more exactly "conquering . . . in order that he may conquer" (νικῶν . . . ἵνα νικήσῃ). The participle of manner "conquering" and the purpose clause reinforce this rider's dominant function of military victory and domination over other nations.

8. E.g., Sweet, *Revelation*, 137–39 (a reference to Christian witness that destroys the world's illusions about itself); Prigent, *Apocalypse*, 266–68; Rowland, "Revelation," 611–12.

tenuous to overrule the strong contextual parallels that show the first horseman to be a destructive evil force like the other three (and the remaining seals as well). The color white may be taken from Zechariah 1:8 and 6:3 without special significance, or it can represent a satanic parody of the true king or his more general attempt to deceive Christians,[9] just as the beast later "conquers" both the two witnesses (11:7) and the saints (13:7).[10] A more likely possibility than these is the association of white horses with victory celebrations or military dominance: the warrior rides on a white horse in recognition of his overpowering conquest (cf. Herodotus, *Hist.* 9.63; Dio Cassius, *Rom. Hist.* 43.14.3).

Three other unique elements, mentioned already in passing, are the "bow" carried by this rider, the "crown" he is given, and his purpose of conquest (v. 2b–d). These seem to suggest a specific first-century allusion as well as a more general symbolic sense that matches it: the sense of military invasion or conquest. To take these in reverse order, "conquering" in a list of terrible earthly calamities naturally suggests military struggle and subjugation of peoples, especially foreign peoples, with all its accompanying human woes. A "crown," here awarded in anticipation of the rider's victory, is what is given to a military conqueror in celebration of his triumph (στέφανος; cf. locusts with such crowns in 9:7).[11] And a mounted archer with his "bow" represents an especially threatening kind of warrior (see images of God exacting his judgment through sword, arrows, and chariots in Deut 32:41–42; Ps 7:13; Isa 5:23; Jer 4:29; 6:23;

Lam 2:4; Hab 3:8–9). In the first-century Roman world of John and his readers, the Parthians were likely to come to mind when horse and bow were mentioned, since the archetypal Parthian warrior was a mounted archer.[12] Parthia was the imperial power to the east and south of Mesopotamia (Armenia and Persia) that Rome was never able to conquer fully and against whom it had suffered several stinging defeats in the late first-century. They benefited from a larger-than-life reputation as fierce fighters, and Romans were regularly set on edge by rumors of a Parthian invasion sweeping in from the east (cf. notes on 16:12). To John's first readers an allusion to a Parthian-like figure would present a powerful image of destructive conquest by outsiders.[13] By analogy, the coming of such a catastrophe would strike fear in subsequent generations of readers as well.

6:3–4 And when he opened the second seal, I heard the second living creature saying, "Come!" 4 And another horse, a red one, rode out, and the one sitting on it was given authority to take peace from the earth so that people would in fact slaughter each other, and a large sword was given to him (Καὶ ὅτε ἤνοιξεν τὴν σφραγῖδα τὴν δευτέραν, ἤκουσα τοῦ δευτέρου ζῴου λέγοντος, Ἔρχου. 4 καὶ ἐξῆλθεν ἄλλος ἵππος πυρρός, καὶ τῷ καθημένῳ ἐπ᾽ αὐτὸν ἐδόθη αὐτῷ λαβεῖν τὴν εἰρήνην ἐκ τῆς γῆς καὶ ἵνα ἀλλήλους σφάξουσιν καὶ ἐδόθη αὐτῷ μάχαιρα μεγάλη). In a virtual duplication of v. 1, John repeats the first two parts of his parallel formula (see "Structure" above) to describe the opening of the second seal and the second living

---

9. Beale, *Revelation*, 377.

10. A few interpreters take the first horseman to be the antichrist, and some support can be marshaled for this (e.g., Matt 24:23–25, the end-time rise of false Christs). See Matthias Rissi, "The Rider on the White Horse: A Study of Revelation 6:1–8," *Interpretation* 18 (1964): 407–18; Barnhouse, *Revelation*, 122–23; Patterson, *Revelation*, 179; Daniel K. K. Wong, "The First Horseman of Revelation 6," *BSac* 153 (1996): 222–25.

But the other three horsemen represent impersonal evil forces, so direct reference to a personal figure seems out of place in this sequence.

11. H. Kraft, "στέφανος," *EDNT* 3:274.

12. See Tacitus, *Ann.* 15.10–15; Vergil, *Aen.* 12.857–58; *Georg.* 4.313–14.

13. Boring, *Revelation*, 122; Smalley, *Revelation*, 150–51.

creature's summons (v. 3).[14] This time a "red" horse appeared in view (drawn from Zech 1:8; 6:2),[15] and this color is fitting given the references to slaughter and bloodshed in v. 4b–c. Its rider had been "given authority to take peace from the earth,"[16] a theme similar to v. 2 (invasion or conquest). Ancient Romans who prided themselves on the Pax Romana provided by the emperor would be particularly sensitive to any threat to that stability, and John's Christian readers need to see clearly that the emperor's power has been delegated by God and can be removed at any time (Dan 2:21; 4:25; Rom 13:1). How this loss of peace relates to the closely related image of conquest in v. 2 is suggested by the next clause (v. 4c), "so that people would in fact slaughter each other" (καὶ ἵνα ἀλλήλους σφάξουσιν).[17] The two significant points to note are the horrific word "slaughter" (σφάζω; acts of butchery; used for killing sacrificial animals) and the reciprocal objects of this bloody killing: "each other" or "one another." This seems to speak of civil war or internecine struggle within a nation rather than foreign invasion as in v. 2. The final description of this rider adds to the gruesome prospect: by God's permission he wields "a large sword,"[18] symbolizing widespread carnage on the earth as the effect of this act of judgment from heaven (v. 4d).

6:5–6 And when he opened the third seal, I heard the third living creature saying, "Come!" And I looked, and behold, a black horse, and the one sitting on it held a balance scale in his hand. 6 And I heard something like a voice in the midst of the four living creatures saying, "A quart of wheat for a denarius and three quarts of barley for a denarius, and do not spoil the olive oil and the wine" (Καὶ ὅτε ἤνοιξεν τὴν σφραγῖδα τὴν τρίτην, ἤκουσα τοῦ τρίτου ζῴου λέγοντος, Ἔρχου. καὶ εἶδον, καὶ ἰδοὺ ἵππος μέλας, καὶ ὁ καθήμενος ἐπ᾽ αὐτὸν ἔχων ζυγὸν ἐν τῇ χειρὶ αὐτοῦ. 6 καὶ ἤκουσα ὡς φωνὴν ἐν μέσῳ τῶν τεσσάρων ζῴων λέγουσαν, Χοῖνιξ σίτου δηναρίου καὶ τρεῖς χοίνικες κριθῶν δηναρίου, καὶ τὸ ἔλαιον καὶ τὸν οἶνον μὴ ἀδικήσῃς). Here again the first two parts of John's parallel structure are repeated (see comments on v. 1) to describe the opening of the third seal and the third living creature's summons to a horse and rider (v. 5a–b). The phrase "and I looked, and behold" (as in v. 2; not found in v. 4) calls attention to the third horse, a "black" one.[19] This rider has "a balance scale" in his hand (v. 5d), a device for measuring grains or

---

14. Between "come!" (v. 3b) and the introduction of the horse and rider (v. 4a), one manuscript (א) includes the words "and I looked, and behold." These are not found in the other manuscripts (e.g., A, C, 2053, 2329), and they probably were added under the influence of vv. 2, 5, 8.

15. The same Greek word for "red" (πυρρός) occurs in LXX Zech 1:8; 6:2. This word is related to the word for "fire" (πῦρ), so it is sometimes translated "fiery red" (CSB, NET, NIV) or "bright red" (ESV, RSV). This is not a natural color for horses, but it could certainly be used in a striking apocalyptic image (cf. Rev 12:3 "a red dragon"). But πυρρός is used for the color of foxes and wolves and of the "red heifer" (Num 19:2), and the related verb can describe a sunrise or sunset (Matt 16:2; BDAG 899–900) so a reddish-brown or chestnut hue is possible.

16. The word "authority" is not explicit but is implied (see expressions with "given" plus an infinitive where "authority" is included in 6:8; 7:2; 13:5b, 7a). The passive "was given" (ἐδόθη) is used here in vv. 2, 4 (twice), 8, 11 with God as the implied agent: this was granted to him by God for the outworking of the divine purpose (cf. BDF §130.1; Joachim Jeremias, *New Testament Theology: The Proclamation of Jesus*, trans. John Bowden [New York: Scribner's, 1971], 13–14). Authority on earth to maintain peace or to shatter its peace comes ultimately from the Lord Almighty (Dan 2:21, 37–38; 4:17, 25).

17. The Greek καί (normally rendered "and") is used here to intensify the following clause ("even, in fact"). The third-person plural verb σφάξουσιν carries an indefinite or impersonal sense: "that they [i.e., unspecified people] would slaughter . . ." (cf. BDF §130.2).

18. This word for "sword," μάχαιρα, refers to a shorter sword used for thrusting, slashing blows (as in Mark 14:43, 47) as compared to a large broad sword, ῥομφαία, as here in v. 8 and in 1:16 (see comments on 1:16; also LN §6.32–33).

19. Black (μέλας) is the color of horses in Zech 6:2, and generally represents threatening or evil times (fitting here, but the same sense would fit any of these four woes).

other bulk goods for sale (cf. v. 6).[20] However, his balance scale is not the harbinger of prosperity and plenty but of scarcity and hard times to come, as the next verse shows.

Just as the summons from the living creatures to the horsemen (vv. 1–8) represents a command from the very throne room of God (see comment on v. 1), so now "something like a voice" (v. 6a) from among the living creatures explains the significance of the balance scale by describing the circumstances that will exist when the effects of this wave of God's judgment are felt on earth. The price quote, "a quart of wheat for a denarius . . ." (v. 6b–c) gives the picture of weighing out basic food staples for sale at exorbitant prices.[21] It symbolizes critical food shortages caused by war or crop failure and the economic distress and human suffering that come when basic supplies break down. Conditions of near starvation like this are a common motif in descriptions of God's judgment to come (e.g., Lev 26:26; Deut 28:51; Ezek 4:10–16; Joel 1:10–12; Mic 6:15).[22] The call not to "spoil the olive oil and the wine" (v. 6d) is debated. It is sometimes taken to represent economic oppression of the poor whose basic foods are rationed, while luxury foodstuffs for the wealthy are not restricted.[23] But in the Old Testament oil and wine were not regarded as luxuries but as basic supplies along with grains to provide

for life (cf. Deut 7:13; 11:14; Neh 5:11; Joel 2:19), and this makes more sense here as well. The sense of "do not spoil" (μὴ ἀδικήσῃς)[24] is "see to it that the oil and wine are kept safe to be used wisely." These as well as the grains must be treated as precious and all-too-scarce commodities. The earthly situation portrayed in these words from heaven is one of scarcity and desperation to find the basic necessities for life—for all groups of humanity.

6:7–8 And when he opened the fourth seal, I heard the voice of the fourth living creature saying, "Come!" 8 And I looked, and behold, a sickly green horse, and the one sitting on it had the name Death, and Hades was following with him. And authority was given to them over a fourth of the earth to kill with sword and with famine and with pestilence and by the wild beasts of the earth

(Καὶ ὅτε ἤνοιξεν τὴν σφραγῖδα τὴν τετάρτην, ἤκουσα φωνὴν τοῦ τετάρτου ζῴου λέγοντος, Ἔρχου. 8 καὶ εἶδον, καὶ ἰδοὺ ἵππος χλωρός, καὶ ὁ καθήμενος ἐπάνω αὐτοῦ ὄνομα αὐτῷ [ὁ] Θάνατος, καὶ ὁ ᾅδης ἠκολούθει μετ' αὐτοῦ καὶ ἐδόθη αὐτοῖς ἐξουσία ἐπὶ τὸ τέταρτον τῆς γῆς ἀποκτεῖναι ἐν ῥομφαίᾳ καὶ ἐν λιμῷ καὶ ἐν θανάτῳ καὶ ὑπὸ τῶν θηρίων τῆς γῆς). For one final time the first two parts of John's parallel structure are repeated (see comments on v. 1) in presenting the opening of the fourth seal and the fourth living creature's summons[25] to a horse and

---

20. Rowland, "Revelation," 612, argues that this is better understood as "yoke" (a common sense for the word ζυγός in the NT: Matt 11:29–30; Acts 15:10; Gal 5:1; 1 Tim 6:1), as a metaphor for slavery or economic oppression (alluding to the evils of Babylon in ch. 18). Economic woes are certainly indicated in v. 6, but it is hard to see this in the word ζυγός in v. 5 (unless it is a wordplay exploiting the double sense of the term).

21. A "quart" (χοῖνιξ) of wheat is said by Herodotus (*Hist.* 7.187) to be a soldier's basic ration per day, while a "denarius" is given as the going daily wage for a farm worker (Matt 20:2). While the standard price for grain in ancient times is hard to calculate based on evidence from different centuries and geographical areas, the grain prices here could be as high as sixteen times the normal rate (see Cicero, *Verr.* 3.81.188 and other texts cited in David E. Aune, *Revelation 6–16*, WBC 52B

[Nashville: Thomas Nelson, 1998], 397).

22. Most of these texts mention shortages of wheat, oil, and wine. Joel 1 mentions barley as well as the other three included here.

23. Boring, *Revelation*, 122; Thomas, *Revelation 1–7*, 433.

24. This verb (ἀδικέω) can carry a more general sense of "do wrong, commit injustice" (Acts 25:10; 1 Cor 6:8; Col 3:25; Rev 22:11), but often in Rev it means "harm, damage, spoil" (2:11; 7:2–3; 9:4, 10, 19; 11:5; cf. Luke 10:19). With a negative as here, it means "leave unaffected, guard, protect" (e.g., Rev 7:2–3; 9:4).

25. In this verse alone the normal phrase "I heard the . . . living creature saying" adds the word "voice" (omitted in some copies but solidly attested in the best manuscripts: 𝔓24, ℵ, A, 1006, 1841, 2344).

rider (v. 7). The phrase "and I looked, and behold" (as in vv. 2, 5) is used to bring the fourth horse on the scene (v. 8a). Here again the color is appropriate to the character of the distress that it represents: a "sickly green"[26] horse, pointing to the pallor of disease and death described below. Its rider even bore the name "Death," and "Hades" was accompanying him.[27] Death and Hades are realms in which dead humans are held captive (Pss 6:5; 49:14; Matt 16:18; Rev 1:18; 20:13–14), but they can also be personified as here (cf. Hos 13:14; Rom 5:12, 14; 1 Cor 15:26, 54–55) to represent hostile forces that attack and enslave mortals to bring them into their domain.

After setting the key actors in place, John summarizes the gruesome role God has permitted them[28] to play in inflicting extensive suffering and death over a large portion of humanity (v. 8d–e). As seen earlier (vv. 2, 4), the phrase "authority was given to them" (ἐδόθη αὐτοῖς ἐξουσία) implies that God is the one who authorized their part in these visitations of judgment. And their actions carry an extremely wide impact, "a fourth of the earth," something not attributed to the earlier three.[29] It is unclear whether this should be taken as their potential range in which to operate or as

the actual effectiveness of their mission of death. In any case, though it is widespread, it just begins to approach the scope of later cataclysmic judgments (cf. 6:14; 8:7–12; 9:15, 18; 16:3, 20). But their grisly mission was clear and multifaceted: "To kill with sword[30] and with famine and with pestilence[31] and by the wild beasts of the earth." Death and Hades could be expected to "kill," of course, but the verse specifies the variety of horrific ways in which they will carry this out. These four (sword, famine, pestilence, wild beasts) should be understood as the culminating effects of human anarchy and societal decay associated with the woes of the other three seal judgments (invasion, civil strife, and famine), but launched into motion from heaven as the expression of God's judgment on sinful humanity.[32] This ultimate divine source can be seen in the Old Testament passages John has certainly drawn on for these ideas that speak of punishment from the Lord on his people as well as their enemies, but specify these very four items as the means by which God's judgment will be carried out. One passage refers to two of these (Jer 43:11), some to three of these (Jer 14:12; 21:7; 24:10; 42:17; Ezek 5:12; 33:27), and some to all four (Jer 15:2–3; Ezek 5:17; 14:21).

---

26. This color does not appear in Zechariah's visions (Zech 1:8–10; 6:1–3). Depending on the context, it means the fresh "green" of healthy grass and plant life (Gen 1:30; Mark 6:39; Rev 8:7; 9:4) or the pallor of the dead or dying, as here (used for this in ancient medical texts; see LSJ 1995; BDAG 1085–86).

27. John does not specify but Hades is probably understood to follow along on foot (Beasley-Murray, *Revelation*, 134) or as riding together with Death (O. Böcher, "ᾅδης," *EDNT* 1:31) rather than on a separate horse.

28. The pronoun "them" (αὐτοῖς) could refer to the four horsemen together, and this final sentence of v. 8 would summarize the dolorous impact of all four. But this interrupts the tight parallelism of vv. 1–8 in which other uses of "was given to ___" applied to individual horsemen ("him," αὐτῷ; vv. 2, 4). The "sickly green" horse represents an intensification of the deadly effects the other three have brought about, but it is better to take "them" as referring to Death and Hades alone.

29. John has perhaps been influenced in his thinking by Ezek 5:1–12 in the LXX, which pledges various judgments

on Jerusalem, each affecting a fourth of its inhabitants. This pattern of judgment has been escalated here to take in a fourth of the world's inhabitants.

30. The word for "sword" used here is ῥομφαία. Some OT passages (LXX) cited later in the paragraph above use the Greek word μάχαιρα (see note on v. 4), but all of them have the same Hebrew word חֶרֶב in the MT.

31. The word rendered "pestilence" (θάνατος) more commonly means simply "death," but is used here in a specialized sense. See note at 2:23.

32. In light of repeated references to the Lamb opening the seals and the living creatures from God's throne room summoning each of these "horsemen" in vv. 1–8, it is misguided to think as some do (e.g., Duvall, *Revelation*, 100; Osborne, *Revelation*, 272) that these woes are due simply to human evil, allowed by God to occur but not specifically sent by him. These features signal specific divine direction behind these earthly phenomena, not merely that they are, as all things, ultimately under God's control.

Because of these allusions to the day-of-the-Lord judgments of the Old Testament (as mentioned also in "Literary Context" above) and because of the severity and widespread impact of these four woes (vv. 1–8), the first four seals should be understood as features of God's climactic judgments in the end times, not just as human forces that operate throughout history in various places beginning with Christ's ascension.[33] To be sure, patterns of God's judgment may appear in preliminary forms throughout the interadvent age as pointers to the intensified calamities of the final days. And the first four seal judgments are comparatively less severe compared to the intensity of the calamities that come with the sixth seal and beyond. But the Old Testament parallels show that even these somewhat lesser judgments are manifestations of God's wrath as part of his day-of-the-Lord judgments on earth.[34]

Jesus associates such woes in his eschatological discourse (Matt 24; Mark 13; Luke 21) with the concentrated era of intense testing that Daniel spoke about as an "abomination of desolation" and unprecedented "tribulation" (Dan 9:27; 11:31; 12:1, 11). In his address Jesus refers to some troubles that constitute "the beginning of birth pangs" (Matt 24:8; Mark 13:8) as over against more severe woes that follow (Matt 24:21; Mark 13:19), but both contain patterns of judgment characteristic of the Old Testament motif of the day of the Lord. Both should be understood as the end-times "tribulation," the concentrated period of seven years (according to Daniel) that immediately precedes Jesus's return, although the latter half can be labeled "great tribulation" (Matt 24:8; Luke 21:23) as over against messianic woes in general.[35] John has followed Jesus in understanding this complex of less severe and then more severe woes as judgments that come with the "day of the Lord" or the time of final severe tribulation that leads to redemption and restoration.[36]

6:9–10 And when he opened the fifth seal, I saw under the altar the souls of those who had been slaughtered because of the word of God and because of the testimony they maintained. 10 And they cried out with a loud voice saying, "How long, O Sovereign Lord, holy and true, will you not judge and avenge our blood on those who live on the earth?" (Καὶ ὅτε ἤνοιξεν τὴν πέμπτην σφραγῖδα, εἶδον ὑποκάτω τοῦ θυσιαστηρίου τὰς ψυχὰς τῶν ἐσφαγμένων διὰ τὸν λόγον τοῦ θεοῦ καὶ διὰ τὴν μαρτυρίαν ἣν εἶχον. 10 καὶ ἔκραξαν φωνῇ μεγάλῃ λέγοντες, Ἕως πότε, ὁ δεσπότης ὁ ἅγιος καὶ ἀληθινός, οὐ κρίνεις καὶ ἐκδικεῖς τὸ αἷμα ἡμῶν ἐκ τῶν κατοικούντων ἐπὶ τῆς γῆς). With the opening of the fifth seal (v. 9a), events in John's vision change dramatically. Instead of the series of four horsemen whose actions begin in heaven and shift to calamities that take place on earth (vv. 1–8), the fifth seal focuses on interaction in the heavenly throne room that alludes to earthly events in the near past (martyrdom of God's servants) and in the future (God's vindication on their killers). But the specific

---

33. As argued by Beale, *Revelation*, 370–71; Caird, *Revelation*, 72; Hoskins, *Revelation*, 141–42.

34. Occurrences of the key themes of vv. 1–8 (e.g., war, ruin, pestilence, sword, famine) along with references to God's wrath (ὀργή) and the day of the Lord appear, for example, in Isa 34:5–8; Jer 46:10; Ezek 7:10–15, 23–27; 30:1–4; Joel 3:9–16; Zeph 1:14–18.

35. Blaising, "Case," 37–47. Pitre, *Tribulation*, 318–25, distinguishes two stages of messianic woes, only the second of which he labels "great tribulation," but "great tribulation" is not a technical term in any case (see notes on 3:10).

36. While there is a general correlation between the woes in Rev 6 and in the Synoptic eschatological discourses (Matt 24; Mark 13; Luke 21), it is clear that John has drawn from the wider OT and Jewish background as well as from Jesus's teaching. Attempts to draw precise parallels between Rev and the Synoptics are misguided. See Fekkes, *Prophetic Traditions*, 80–82; Koester, *Revelation*, 357–58.

element seen here—severe persecution against God's people—clearly fits the pattern of eschatological woes anticipated in the Old Testament, in early Judaism, and in the New Testament. These were seen already in the first four seals and will continue into the sixth seal and beyond.[37]

John mentions for the first time "the altar" (v. 9b; using the Greek article: τοῦ θυσιαστηρίου), which he assumes his readers can identify because of the heavenly scene he has already portrayed from 4:1 onward.[38] Isaiah's vision of God on his heavenly throne pictures the throne room as also a temple (Isa 6:1) with an altar (6:6; θυσιαστήριον), and John has incorporated this into his own vision of God's presence (see comments on 4:5–6). This altar is mentioned seven additional times in Revelation, all within the section on judgments that flow from the heavenly scene in chapters 4–5, and it figures prominently in heaven's orchestration of the judgments that fall on the earth (e.g., 8:5; 9:13; 14:18).[39] To locate the souls of these martyrs "under the altar" in heaven is a bold association with important implications. At the least it symbolizes their nearness

to God after death: they are brought into the very presence of God (cf. 2 Cor 5:8; Phil 1:23), there to await the resurrection of the body (1 Cor 15:20–23; Phil 3:20–21; Rev 20:4).[40] It is likely also that it connects their "slaughter" (v. 9) and shedding of blood (v. 10) in loyalty to God to the faithful sacrifice that Jesus Christ, the Lamb, exemplified (cf. 5:6, 9). The Old Testament incense altar was not the scene of actual sacrifices, but blood from those sacrifices was applied to its "horns" as part of the ritual (e.g., Lev 4:6–7, 16–18).[41] The location of their souls "under the altar" represents their martyrdom as an act of worship, a costly offering of themselves to God who is worthy of all devotion.

The glimpse that John provides on the heavenly scene is both sobering and strengthening for God's people. It leaves no room for illusions that a world opposed to their Lord will welcome those who are loyal to him, as these souls certainly were. Their violent killing, pictured as the "slaughter" of an animal,[42] was due to their Christian witness (v. 9b) as exemplified and commended throughout Revelation (1:2, 9; 2:10; 3:8, 10; 12:11, 17; 19:10;

---

37. E.g., Dan 7:21; 11:31–35; 12:1; 1 En. 100:7; 104:3; Jub. 23:23–24; 2 Bar. 70:1–10; Matt 24:9–13; Mark 13:9–13; Luke 21:12–19.

38. An item can be identifiable or definite because it is associated with a known entity with which it is connected in the culture. See Levinsohn, *Discourse Features*, 148–49.

39. The word "altar" by itself does not clarify whether it is seen as corresponding to the larger bronze altar of burnt offering outside the OT sanctuary (Exod 38:1 [38:22 LXX]; 1 Kgs 8:64; 2 Kgs 16:14–15; 2 Chr 1:5–6) or the smaller golden altar of incense inside it (Exod 30:1, 27), since the Greek OT uses the same term for both (θυσιαστήριον). Both earthly altars were places of sacrifice or offering (of blood sacrifices or of incense) and had four "horns" or raised corners. In Rev 6:9, John does not make clear which heavenly counterpart is in view, but the next set of uses (8:3 [twice], 5; 9:13) distinctly identify it as the incense altar ("golden"; connected with "incense" offering), and that seems to set the pattern for the remaining occurrences in the book (11:1; 14:18; 16:7). On typological grounds (cf. Heb 9:11–12, 24), the altar located in the very presence of God in heaven would seem to correspond to the

earthly altar inside the sanctuary rather than the one in the outside courtyard. It seems unnecessary to posit one heavenly altar that represents the functions of both earthly altars (as suggested by Boxall, *Revelation*, 113; Koester, *Revelation*, 398; Mounce, *Revelation*, 146).

40. Their "souls" (τὰς ψυχὰς) or immaterial selves were under the altar, anticipating the resurrection and full redemption yet to come (BDAG 1098; Luke 12:20; Acts 20:10; Rev 20:4; cf. also 4 Ezra 4:35).

41. Some interpreters see the area "under the altar" in 6:9 as quite graphically the place where sacrificial blood was poured out (i.e., at the altar of burnt offerings, Lev 4:7b, 18b) and so connect these "souls" directly to such sacrificial imagery (e.g., Boxall, *Revelation*, 113; Osborne, *Revelation*, 284–85; Sweet, *Revelation*, 142). But this misconstrues which altar is in view and takes the imagery too far.

42. Their death is described in v. 9b as "slaughter" or "slaying" (σφάζω; same verb in 18:24; cf. 5:6 of the Lamb's death). The parallel in 20:4 is even more graphic: "The souls of those beheaded."

20:4). They stood up for the gospel, the "word" that comes from God about his saving work in Christ,[43] and they "maintained"[44] their own witness by life and word to its truths.

Such faithful witness on earth even to the point of death is the background to the heavenly scene John narrates (v. 10). Because of the context in which this vision comes (associated with the fifth seal), these martyrs should be understood to be Christ's followers killed for their faith during the time of the preceding judgments (see 7:13–17 for a similar group explicitly said to have died in "the great tribulation"). The entire period of intense tribulation leading up to Christ's return will be characterized by severe opposition on the part of God's enemies (both angelic and human) against God's people (11:7–10, 18; 12:10–12, 17; 13:7, 15). The martyrs' loud and plaintive appeal is for the Lord to exact his perfect justice, unhurried but sure, against the evils of those who opposed God and them.[45] The impatience of righteous sufferers who wonder that God has not yet visited his judgment against sinners ("how long, O Lord?") has a long tradition in Israel, and prayers that ask such a question are easy to find (e.g., Ps 79:5–7; Zech 1:12; 4 Ezra 4:33–37; cf. Luke 18:7). Part of the dilemma is that they know God is the "Sovereign Lord"[46]

and that he is "holy and true" (see comments on 3:7), and yet he has not accomplished judgment and justice[47] against their persecutors or against human evil more widely.[48] This cry for vengeance is more understandable since it is directed against those guilty of murdering people for their service to God (cf. v. 10, "our blood"; v. 9, "slaughtered").[49] See "Theology in Application" below for further discussion.

6:11 And a white robe was given to each of them, and they were told to rest for a little while longer until both their fellow servants and their brothers and sisters who were going to be killed as they also had been would come to their full number (καὶ ἐδόθη αὐτοῖς ἑκάστῳ στολὴ λευκή καὶ ἐρρέθη αὐτοῖς ἵνα ἀναπαύσονται ἔτι χρόνον μικρόν, ἕως πληρωθῶσιν καὶ οἱ σύνδουλοι αὐτῶν καὶ οἱ ἀδελφοὶ αὐτῶν οἱ μέλλοντες ἀποκτέννεσθαι ὡς καὶ αὐτοί). Heaven's response to the martyrs' cry was not a specific eschatological timetable but a reminder of the larger purpose that God would soon accomplish on earth despite human evil. They were each given "a white robe," symbolizing heavenly purity and perhaps reassurance that they bore no guilt for what had been perpetrated against them (v. 11a).[50] Their question about divine timing (v. 10b) is not answered directly, but the unspoken

---

43. "The word of God" (τὸν λόγον τοῦ θεοῦ) is a subjective genitive phrase (see comments at 1:2).

44. "They maintained" (εἶχον) is an imperfect tense denoting their habitual conduct in earthly life (cf. 12:17; 19:10 for "having testimony").

45. Their question "how long . . . ?" (v. 10) does not imply that God's judgment against the "earth dwellers" has not yet begun at the time of the fifth seal, as Luter and Hunter, "The 'Earth Dwellers,'" 8–10, and Luter, "Interpreting the Book of Revelation," 472–73, conclude. It has certainly begun in the form of the first four seals (see comments on v. 17 below). The appeal here is for God's judgment against their persecutors to be brought to completion and for the martyrs' own redemption to be accomplished in full.

46. The title used here is ὁ δεσπότης, emphasizing his complete dominion (cf. Luke 2:29; Acts 4:24; 2 Pet 2:1; Jude 4).

47. Both these verbs (κρίνω and ἐκδικέω) are used of God's actions against Babylon in Rev 19:2. The verb "avenge" (ἐκδικέω) means to exact a suitable penalty for injustice that has been committed (BDAG 300; G. Schrenk, "ἐκδικέω," *TDNT* 2:442–46; cf. Deut 32:43 LXX; Rom 12:19; and related terms in 1 Thess 4:6; 2 Thess 1:8; 1 Pet 2:14).

48. "Those who live on the earth" is Rev's frequent description of humanity obdurately opposed to God, who will suffer his judgment in the final days. See 3:10 for discussion.

49. See similar references to God's justice against those who shed righteous blood: Gen 4:10; Deut 32:43; 2 Kgs 9:7; Ps 79:10; Matt 23:35.

50. "White robes" are mentioned also in 7:9, 13–14 (on a group of martyrs like these). On white garments see comments on 3:4–5.

reply is similar to God's answer to similar questions previously, that is, "this is not for you to know" (cf. Mark 13:32; Acts 1:7; 1 Thess 5:1–2; cf. 2 Bar. 21:8). Instead in v. 11b they are encouraged to enjoy their present "rest" (ἀναπαύω), that stage of blessed relief from struggle and sin now granted to them in God's presence (cf. 14:11–13; 19:2).[51]

The full answer to their cry for God's justice will come after only "a little while longer" (ἔτι χρόνον μικρόν).[52] This time indication is filled in further, however, by a temporal clause (introduced by "until," ἕως) that explains, in part, the events in God's plan that must occur before his full answer will be seen (v. 11c). The temporal clause specifies two groups of people (not denoting the same individuals) that have not yet reached their "full number."[53] The two groups are shown by a "both . . . and" (καί . . . καί) parallelism joining two noun phrases that are subjects of "be completed" (v. 11c). The first is "their fellow servants," a reference to others who, in the purpose of God, will come to faith in Christ and serve him faithfully as these martyrs have done. This reflects a common eschatological theme that God's delay in bringing his judgment is due in part to his mercy in allowing more time for the gospel to be proclaimed across the world (cf. Matt 24:14) and for more individuals to "come to repentance" (2 Pet 3:9). The second group is "their brothers and sisters,"[54] but this group is specified further: those who will "be killed" for their faith, just as the heavenly martyrs were. This sad indication, that even heaven ac-

knowledges martyrdoms yet to come, is a reminder of the heartbreaking reality of the events associated with these seal openings: these are the messianic woes, the time of intense suffering that the world and its people—even God's people—must endure before the full blessedness of his redemption will be experienced. But God's full justice will come soon, as the next seal opening shows.

6:12–14 And I looked when he opened the sixth seal, and a great earthquake took place, and the sun became black like sackcloth made of hair, and the whole moon became like blood, 13 and the stars of the sky fell to the earth like a fig tree sheds its new figs when shaken by a great wind, 14 and the sky was split apart like a torn scroll rolling up, and every mountain and island were moved from their place (Καὶ εἶδον ὅτε ἤνοιξεν τὴν σφραγῖδα τὴν ἕκτην, καὶ σεισμὸς μέγας ἐγένετο καὶ ὁ ἥλιος ἐγένετο μέλας ὡς σάκκος τρίχινος καὶ ἡ σελήνη ὅλη ἐγένετο ὡς αἷμα 13 καὶ οἱ ἀστέρες τοῦ οὐρανοῦ ἔπεσαν εἰς τὴν γῆν, ὡς συκῆ βάλλει τοὺς ὀλύνθους αὐτῆς ὑπὸ ἀνέμου μεγάλου σειομένη, 14 καὶ ὁ οὐρανὸς ἀπεχωρίσθη ὡς βιβλίον ἐλισσόμενον καὶ πᾶν ὄρος καὶ νῆσος ἐκ τῶν τόπων αὐτῶν ἐκινήθησαν). With the opening of the sixth seal (vv. 12–14) and the response of those on earth who suffer its associated judgments (vv. 15–17), John portrays the intensity and severity of earthly woes characteristic of the final phases of the great tribulation period. We come right to the brink of seeing God's consummation, but the full picture is

---

51. Their rest will be consummated in their future bodily resurrection amid God's future renewal of all things as Rev 20–22 describes. See God's promise of this "rest" through its OT anticipations leading toward its future fulfillment in Heb 4:1–11.

52. This answer in v. 11b gives an indefinite time, of course, but it encourages them to wait in patience as well as reassuring them that the wait will not be long. See discussion at 1:1 for statements about God's eschatological timing in Rev.

53. "Come to their full number" is an idiomatic translation to bring out the sense of the verb πληρωθῶσιν ("be filled full/ be completed"; see LN §59.33). This implies a foreordained number in each group known only to God. See 4 Ezra 4:36–37 for very similar wording.

54. The phrase "their brothers and sisters" (οἱ ἀδελφοὶ αὐτῶν) denotes both male and female fellow Christians (ἀδελφοί can mean "brothers," but more commonly in the NT denotes "siblings, brothers and sisters").

delayed while John sketches out other significant details in chapters 7–16.[55] We also encounter phenomena far beyond the normal range of even horrific earthly occurrences like war, famine, death, and martyrdom as seen in vv. 1–11. The sixth seal brings violent shakings of the created world and ominous heavenly portents that seem hardly understandable in our normal frame of earthly experience. However, they are more distinctly characteristic of the day of the Lord predicted in many of the Old Testament prophets and in Jesus's eschatological discourse (Mark 13 and parallels),[56] phenomena that the prophets and Jesus attribute directly to God's punishment of sinful humanity. Within the Greco-Roman world of John's day, they would be read as omens of real-life disaster against the powerful elites of Asia Minor (cf. vv. 15–17).[57]

The first event that John narrates[58] from his vision is "a great earthquake" (v. 12b; σεισμὸς μέγας), a feature of God's theophany at Sinai (Exod 19:16–19) that became an important part of a judgment typology related to the complex of events associated with Israel's deliverance from Egypt (the ten plagues and God's appearance to Israel in the giving of the law). God's awesome shaking of creation is cited repeatedly in the later Old Testament as a warning of similar judgment to come (Judg 5:4–5; Pss 18:7–15; 68:7–8; 77:18; Isa 13:13; 64:2–3; Jer 10:10; Ezek 38:19; Hag 2:6–7, 21). Such quaking is likewise a feature of God's wrath poured

out on the earth in the day of the Lord (Isa 13:13; 24:14–23; Joel 3:14–16; Nah 1:5–6; Zech 14:4–5, 8–10) and is included in Jesus's predictions of the messianic woes that precede his coming (Matt 24:7; Mark 13:8; Luke 21:11).[59]

The second and third events are paired: ominous changes in the sun and moon (v. 12c–d). The sun appearing to be "black like sackcloth made of hair" and the moon "like blood"[60] comes quite close to how they look during solar or lunar eclipses, and these in themselves can be alarming to the unsophisticated eye. But such portents are also a standard part of Old Testament day-of-the-Lord imagery (this is very close to Joel 2:30–31; see also Isa 13:9–11; Joel 3:14–15; Amos 5:18–20; 8:9–10; Zeph 1:14–15; also Matt 24:29; Mark 13:24–25; Luke 21:25), and coupled with the celestial effects described in vv. 13–14 they too must be regarded as severe disruptions of the created order. The cumulative effect of these things would be terrifying.

The subsequent phenomena (vv. 13–14) are even more cataclysmic and raise sober questions about how they and the related features of v. 12 should be interpreted. On the one hand "the stars of the sky fell to the earth"[61] (v. 13a) could be taken to describe comets or meteor showers, and our normal understanding of how our universe works would not be disturbed. We could even read this as a veiled narrative of the fall of Satan and his angels (cf. 12:4, 9) or as purely figurative for upheaval

---

55. Resseguie, *Narrative Commentary*, 131–32; Roloff, *Revelation*, 92.

56. See notes on vv. 7–8 and v. 9 above; the earlier seal judgments also fit the day-of-the-Lord pattern, but the parallels are not as overt.

57. Andrew Chester, "Chaos and New Creation," in Ashton, *Studies in Apocalyptic*, 338–39.

58. A series of aorist verbs in vv. 12–14 narrate the phenomena John saw.

59. These texts, as well as the reaction of those who experience such "shaking" (vv. 15–17), show that it is misguided to separate God's glorious manifestation (theophany) from his

wrath in judgment (punishment) in these images as Boring, *Revelation*, 115–16, suggests. His treatment of these verses a bit later (126–27) makes more sense.

60. Other descriptions of darkness could have been chosen, but "sackcloth" and "blood" suggest a creation subjected to mourning and violence. The note about the "whole" moon being affected adds to the unnerving impact.

61. The comparison with fig trees dropping their figs is wonderfully illustrative, and it also points directly to Isa 34:4 as an influence on John's description here (and in v. 14: the sky rolling up).

in the social and political order,[62] a shaking of all that seems secure and reliable in life but not going beyond the natural order of creation. Something similar could be said about the descriptions of v. 14. The sky[63] "split[ting] apart like a scroll when it is rolled up" (NASB)[64] does not easily fit our understanding of the real world, but could it refer to horrible weather systems approaching? Mountains and islands are physically fixed in place; how can "every" one of them be "moved from its place"?[65] But purely naturalistic readings (i.e., seeing these as essentially normal occurrences) or purely figurative readings (i.e., social or political upheaval) fail to do justice to the typological character of the descriptions or to how the Old Testament prophets and Jesus himself seemed to use such images.[66] It is better to take these as severe disruptions in the visible sky, as dramatic portents of the coming cosmic re-creation but not the actual dissolution of the creation yet. The text itself indicates that the world does not immediately come to an end (6:15–17, people have time to hide and lament what is still to come; 7:3, there is delay so that God's servants can be sealed from judgments still to come). But these severe disruptions point forward to the ultimate escalation soon-to-come, the dissolution of the present sky and earth in connection with the arrival of the new creation of Revelation 21–22 (cf. 20:11, sky and earth "fled"; 21:1, first sky and first earth "passed away"; 21:23; 22:5, no need of sun or moon).[67]

6:15–17 And the kings of the earth and the nobles and the commanders and the wealthy and the powerful and everyone, slave and free, hid themselves in the caves and rocks of the mountains. 16 And they said to the mountains and the rocks, "Fall on us and hide us from the presence of the one who sits on the throne and from the wrath of the Lamb, 17 because the great day of their wrath has come, and who is able to stand?" (καὶ οἱ βασιλεῖς τῆς γῆς καὶ οἱ μεγιστᾶνες καὶ οἱ χιλίαρχοι καὶ οἱ πλούσιοι καὶ οἱ ἰσχυροὶ καὶ πᾶς δοῦλος καὶ ἐλεύθερος ἔκρυψαν ἑαυτοὺς εἰς τὰ σπήλαια καὶ εἰς τὰς πέτρας τῶν ὀρέων 16 καὶ λέγουσιν τοῖς ὄρεσιν καὶ ταῖς πέτραις, Πέσετε ἐφ᾽ ἡμᾶς καὶ κρύψατε ἡμᾶς ἀπὸ προσώπου τοῦ καθημένου ἐπὶ τοῦ θρόνου καὶ ἀπὸ τῆς ὀργῆς τοῦ ἀρνίου, 17 ὅτι ἦλθεν ἡ ἡμέρα ἡ μεγάλη τῆς ὀργῆς αὐτῶν, καὶ τίς δύναται σταθῆναι). In vv. 15–17 John narrates the final portion of this vision, the response of those who experience the cataclysmic events of the sixth seal (vv. 12–14). His portrayal captures the universal impact these woes will have, the desperation people will feel when faced with such catastrophes, and their recognition that such judgments represent God's anger against human sin. He also masterfully connects this entire section (6:1–17) with what precedes (chs. 4–5)

---

62. This is the suggestion even of Scott, *Exposition*, 157–58, who usually opts for the most literal sense possible.

63. Here the "sky" or "heaven" (οὐρανός) refers to the visible "heaven" as opposed to God's invisible heavenly realm (BDAG 737–38; LN §1.5).

64. It is difficult to fit these two phrases together coherently (rolling up an intact scroll is hard to fit with the sky being split). Some posit a stronger sense of "was split" (ἀπεχωρίσθη), i.e., "vanish, depart, go out of view" (LN §15.14; cf. ASV, ESV, KJV, NIV, NRSV, RSV). But the image seems to liken the visible sky to a scroll that is torn and then rolls up on either side (e.g., NABR: "The sky was divided like a torn scroll curling up"). The visual effect would be that the sky is withdrawing toward the horizons.

65. See 16:20 (seventh bowl): every island fled, every mountain not found.

66. These are signs of God's judgment within ongoing history, not the immediate end of history, but they are patterns of greater earthly judgment to come (e.g., Ps 97:5; Isa 42:15; 54:10; Jer 4:23–28; Ezek 38:20; Mark 13:24–27). See Boring, *Revelation*, 126–27.

67. Edward Adams, *The Stars Will Fall from Heaven: Cosmic Catastrophe in the New Testament and Its World*, LNTS 347 (London: T&T Clark, 2007), 243–48; Ladd, *Revelation*, 106–9; Mounce, *Revelation*, 150–51.

and follows (7:1–17). To communicate that such judgments affect the whole world of humanity (cf. 3:10), John uses a list of groups drawn from Old Testament prophecies about the day of the Lord (Isa 24:1–4, 21; 34:12), emphasizing especially that not even the privileged and powerful of the earth will be exempt (v. 15).[68] He refers first to a series of elites in the plural: "The kings of the earth and the nobles and the commanders and the wealthy and the powerful."[69] Shifting to the generic singular and including a contrasting disadvantaged class shows that all are included: "Everyone, slave and free."[70] What they all do is try to escape God's judgment by "hiding themselves,"[71] desperately seeking protection "in the caves and rocks of the mountains," another set of images from texts about the day of the Lord (Isa 2:10–21; cf. Jer 4:29; Matt 24:16; Mark 13:14; Luke 21:21, escape to the mountains).

These images from Isaiah 2 and Jeremiah 4 suggest also the hyperbolic words (almost verbatim in LXX) of Hosea 10:8: "They said[72] to the mountains and the rocks, 'Fall on us and hide us'" (v. 16a–b).[73] Hosea 10 portrays Samaria's desperation in the face of Assyrian invasion, and Jesus quotes Hosea 10:8 to portray the destruction of Jerusalem in AD 70 in advance (Luke 23:30).[74] These historical episodes illustrate the typological pattern of judgments that fall time and again as foreshadowings of the inten-

sified wrath to come in the last days. As previously, so in the future tribulation period, humans will be so fearful that natural perils, even rockslides, will seem preferable to facing God's punishment.

John portrays their cry for protection using key phrases from chapters 4–5 to anchor the connection of these judgments to his vision of the holy God enthroned in heaven and of the victorious Lamb (4:2–3; 5:5–7): "Hide us from the presence of the one who sits on the throne" and also "from the wrath of the Lamb" (v. 16c). Referring to "the wrath of the Lamb" epitomizes the mystery of God's kindness and severity (Rom 11:22). The Lamb is the one who willingly gave himself as the redeeming sacrifice for sin (Rev 5:9) and who forever will bear the marks of that "slaughter" (5:6), but in his victory over sin and death he is now the ultimate king of David's line who will rule the nations with a rod of iron (5:5; 19:15). The "wrath" (ὀργή) against human sin that these desperate people cannot escape comes both from the Lamb and from God Almighty enthroned in heaven (v. 16c; see v. 17, "their wrath").

John adds one further clause to their plea for deliverance (v. 17), giving the reason ("because," ὅτι) that they urgently desire to be hidden. Here again he masterfully phrases their rationale to capture the larger significance of this vision of the six seal

68. Similar listings appear later in Rev to describe those who are forced to give allegiance to the beast (13:16) and those defeated when Christ returns (19:18).

69. For "kings of the earth" in opposition to God, see Ps 2:1–2. "Nobles" (CSB, REB) is the term μεγιστᾶνες (see 18:23; also Isa 34:12; Mark 6:21), translated as "great ones/great men" (ESV, NASB, RSV) or "magnates" (NRSV). "Commanders" is a military term, χιλίαρχοι (a tribune, who commands six hundred Roman soldiers; BDAG 1084).

70. Rev 13:16 and 19:18 mention "all, the small and the great, and the rich and the poor, and the free and the slaves" and "all, both free and slaves and small and great."

71. "Hiding" is perhaps an intentional allusion to sinful humanity's primeval reaction to God in Eden (Gen 3:8).

72. The LXX of Hos 10:8 has a future tense "they will say" (also the sense of the MT), but Rev 6:16 has a present, "they say" (λέγουσιν), used as a historical present. This highlights the significance not of the utterance it introduces (vv. 16–17) but of what follows. It points forward to the judgments of the seventh seal, the trumpets, and the bowls (chs. 7–16). The horrors portrayed in the seal judgments clearly embody the wrath of God and of the Lamb, but wrath's end has not yet arrived. See the note on the historical present at 5:5.

73. The link words that clearly connect these texts are "rocks," "caves," and "hide."

74. It is natural in the face of an overwhelming military defeat for the losing side to look for escape and protection wherever it can be found. Cf. Judg 6:2; 1 Sam 13:6; and Fekkes, *Prophetic Traditions*, 79n40.

openings and to build a bridge into the next chapter. The eschatological woes just portrayed (6:1–16) must be understood as judgments of the day of the Lord predicted by Old Testament prophets and by Jesus Christ himself. This is the realization that the suffering people described in vv. 15–16 express: "The great day of their wrath has come" (ἦλθεν; v. 17a).[75] As noted in several comments about the preceding verses, the day-of-the-Lord predictions regularly characterize its judgments as manifestations of divine wrath (ὀργή), and the wording here makes that explicit ("the great day . . ."). The start of the outpouring of wrath just portrayed in 6:1–17 will find its consummation in the later two series of judgments, and 15:1 announces its end, tying the seals, trumpets, and bowls together (the bowls as "seven plagues—the final ones, because in them God's anger will be completed"). John shows at numerous points in Revelation his awareness that

the Lamb shares the divine status of the Almighty God, and he reinforces that by labeling judgments said in the Old Testament to be "the Lord's" first as "the wrath of the Lamb" (v. 16c) and then as "their wrath" (v. 17a).[76]

The hopeless question that closes the chapter ("who is able to stand?") is another feature of day-of-the-Lord prophecies that John incorporates into his portrayal (cf. Joel 2:11; Nah 1:6; Mal 3:2). The implied answer is, of course, "no one." None can resist or withstand his judgment when it arrives at last. All attempts at protection or escape are futile. The question is left unanswered in chapter 6. However, John skillfully uses this question to lead the reader into the interlude (7:1–17) that he has inserted between the sixth seal (6:12–17) and the seventh (8:1). Some humans in fact will be able to stand in that day because God himself will protect and enable them to do so.

---

75. This is an aorist that refers in summary to an action or series of actions that have recently occurred (i.e., in the six seals just recorded). For this "recent past" idea English requires the present perfect (Burton, *Moods and Tenses*, 23–27; Fanning, *Verbal Aspect*, 260–61). Thomas, *Revelation 1–7*, 457–60, calls this a constative aorist summarizing the events of the six seals, but he translates it "has come"; to be sure, the "recent past" sense is simply a constative aorist that requires a special translation pattern in English. To call ἦλθεν an ingressive ("began to come") or proleptic/futuristic sense ("is about to come") is motivated by the correct observation that what the seals of ch. 6 describe is simply the beginning phase of a series of catastrophic end-time judgments that will climax in the personal intervention of Christ, who decisively conquerors all foes and establishes his kingdom on earth (19:11–20:6). What it gets wrong, however, is its resistance to seeing the day-of-the-Lord elements as present until the very end of the tribulation period (i.e., with the trumpets and bowls only). For this view see Fekkes, *Prophetic Traditions*, 78–80, 86, 158–66. Likewise, Alan Hultberg ("A Case for the Prewrath Rapture," in Hultberg, *Three Views on the Rapture*, 87, 147, 260) wants to take

this aorist as "has arrived," by which he means a futuristic or impending sense (i.e., "is about to appear," beginning with the trumpets), and the same critique applies. See the same verb (ἦλθεν) used with "wrath" (ὀργή) as its subject in a recent past sense in 11:18.

76. There is a textual variant for the phrase "their wrath" (v. 17a). Several good manuscripts, including the most reliable one (A; along with P, 046, 1006, 1841, 2351, most Byzantine minuscules) have the reading "his wrath," referring to the Lamb, as v. 16c just stated. The external evidence for "their" is also substantial (א, C, 1611, 1854, 2053, 2329, 2344), and the internal evidence is debatable. *TCGNT2*, 668 thinks that scribes would have corrected "their" because it seemed ambiguous, while Aune, *Revelation 6–16*, 386, argues that "his" is John's clear point from the immediately preceding phrase of v. 16c, but scribes would have broadened this to reflect the larger reference to "the one who sits on the throne and . . . the Lamb." All in all the "their" reading seems more likely, since scribes would, I think, have the closest referent in mind as they copied and would change "their" to "his" accordingly.

Theology in Application

The Four Horsemen of the Apocalypse

For thousands of years church altars, biblical manuscripts, and even tapestries in fine homes have been embellished with illustrations of the four harbingers of God's judgment presented in Revelation 6:1–8, including a famous woodcut by Albrecht Durer (1498). As fascinating and beautiful as such artistic pieces are, they portray horrendous events: devastating international and civil war, terrible famine, and disease and death on a massive scale. When we ponder the destruction and human suffering that comes with such events in real life (e.g., when we catch glimpses of such things in news reports from across the world or in archival photos of events from the past), it should make us cringe in horror. They also raise challenging theological and moral questions for all who read these verses. How can a loving God allow, or in fact cause, such things to happen in this world? But the questions we pose to challenge the biblical text, though fruitful and necessary for our growth in knowledge and faith, also turn around and put us as its readers to the test as well. What perspective do we bring to the text and what standing do we have to call God's actions into question?

When we read these verses not in isolation but in light of the larger story of the Bible, it brings a broader perspective and a deeper understanding of God and his work of both judgment and redemption.[77] The paradoxical phrase used to describe these events, "the wrath of the Lamb" (6:16), helps to open our eyes to such a background. The whole Bible shows us that God is holy and good, just and merciful, all-powerful and forgiving. We can count on the fact that "the judge of all the earth will do what is just" (Gen 18:25), even in regard to human evil that came into the world through rebellion against him (Gen 3). In his plan to set things right he sent his own Son to provide atonement for human sin, an atonement offered freely to all who trust him. His patient appeal is for humans to turn to him as their creator and Savior. But for those who refuse, his patience eventually will come to an end, and "God's wrath [will be] revealed from heaven against all godlessness and wickedness of humans who suppress the truth in wickedness" (Rom 1:18). As Mangina has written, Revelation

> helps to purge us of [our] fantasies concerning God. God is not whatever we would like him to be. God is God. He is the Creator and *Pantokrator* glimpsed in the heavenly worship—power indeed, but not power at human disposal and control—and he is also the Lamb, the slaughtered victim-as-victor. If the image of the all-powerful Creator frees us of our sentimentalism concerning God, the image of the Lamb of God should free us of our fear.[78]

---

77. Osborne, *Revelation*, 38–40, has a valuable discussion of "theodicy" in Rev, a defense of God's character in judging the world's evil.

78. Mangina, *Revelation*, 97.

Crying Out for Justice

Is a prayer for vengeance (6:9–11) truly Christian, when Jesus himself called for loving our enemies and praying for those who persecute us (Matt 5:44) and then asked for God's forgiveness for his killers (Luke 23:34)? Yet Jesus himself declared, "Will not God bring about justice for his chosen ones who cry to him day and night? . . . I tell you that he will bring about justice for them quickly" (Luke 18:7–8). The difference is one of tone and focus. These martyrs are not asking for personal retribution against their persecutors but for God's justice to prevail among humans, who reject his ways and so bring his name into disrepute (Rev 6:10; cf. Ps 79:10–12). They are examples of leaving vengeance to the Lord rather than taking it in their own hands to pay back evil for evil (Rom 12:17–21). In addition, their appeal for justice is directed against an extreme act of injustice, the crime of murdering people for serving the true God. We sometimes want to lash out at others because they inconvenience us momentarily or cause a detour in our personal pathway to success and status. But their martyrdom was an act of self-abnegating worship, a costly offering of themselves to God who is worthy of all devotion. They valued faithfulness over personal comfort and safety, over life itself. This truly reflects their likeness to Christ, who came not to do his own will but the Father's (Luke 22:42; John 5:30). Even for those whose experience of unfair treatment does not measure up to theirs, these verses reassure us that we can and should leave vengeance, if it is deserved, to the all-wise, all-powerful Lord of heaven to take care of as he sees fit, rather than take it into our own hands.

Revelation 7:1–17

Literary Context

After the breathtaking pace of judgments associated with the first six seals, John pauses before continuing with the seventh seal, which will unfold in further judgments heralded by seven trumpets (8:1ff). This respite is similar to the interlude that will come between the sixth and seventh trumpets (10:1–11:14). Such interludes give time to add background and related details, but they also increase the dramatic tension of the narrative, since it is clear that further judgments are impending and cannot be put off for long.[1] The pause here in chapter 7 consists of two separate visions,[2] each of which responds in some way to the plaintive question of 6:17: "Who is able to stand?" (cf. "standing" in vv. 1, 9).

III. **Second Vision: Heavenly Throne Room and Three Judgment Cycles (4:1–16:21)**
    A. Vision of God in His Heavenly Throne Room (4:1–11)
    B. The Seven-Sealed Scroll and the Slain Lamb (5:1–14)
    C. The Seven Seals and the Interlude of the Two Multitudes (6:1–8:1)
        1. The First Six Seals (6:1–17)
→   **2. The Interlude of the Two Multitudes (7:1–17)**
        3. The Seventh Seal (8:1)
    D. The Seven Trumpets and Further Interludes (8:2–14:20)

Main Idea

Further calamities are delayed until a large company of God's servants from all of Israel is marked for protection from the coming judgments on earth while an innumerable multitude from every nation joins in the heavenly worship of God.

---

1. Boxall, *Revelation*, 121; Resseguie, *Narrative Commentary*, 135.

2. Cf. v. 1, "after this I saw"; v. 9, "after these things I looked."

Translation

Revelation 7:1–17

1a	Vision Intro/ Character Entrance	**After this I saw four angels**
b	Descriptions	standing at the four corners of the earth, holding back the four winds of the earth
c	Purpose	so that no wind could blow on the earth or on the sea or against any tree.
2a	Character Entrance	And **I saw another angel**
b	Descriptions	coming up from the rising of the sun
c		having the seal of the living God,
d	Action	and **he cried out with a loud voice** **to the four angels to whom it was given to harm the earth and the sea,**
3a	Command	saying, *"Do not harm the earth or* *the sea or* *the trees,*
b	Intention	*until we seal the servants of our God on their foreheads."*
4a	Action/Effect	And **I heard the number of those who were sealed,**
b	Apposition	a hundred and forty-four thousand sealed from every tribe of the sons of Israel.
5	Specification	From the tribe of Judah twelve thousand sealed, from the tribe of Reuben twelve thousand, from the tribe of Gad twelve thousand,
6	Specification	from the tribe of Asher twelve thousand, from the tribe of Naphtali twelve thousand, from the tribe of Manasseh twelve thousand,
7	Specification	from the tribe of Simeon twelve thousand, from the tribe of Levi twelve thousand, from the tribe of Issachar twelve thousand,
8	Specification	from the tribe of Zebulun twelve thousand, from the tribe of Joseph twelve thousand, from the tribe of Benjamin twelve thousand sealed.
9a	Vision Intro/ Character Entrance	**After these things I looked and behold, a great multitude**
b	Description	that no one could number,
c	Origin	from every nation and tribe and people and tongue,

d   Action   standing   before the throne and
                                                                       before the Lamb,

e   Description   clothed   in white robes and
                                                      with palm branches in their hands,

10a   Action   **and they cried out with a loud voice saying,**

b   Praise   *"Salvation to our God who sits on the throne and*
                                            to the Lamb."

11a   Character Entrance   **And all the angels and**
                                  the elders and
                                  the four living creatures

                                        stood   **around the throne,**

b   Action   **and**   **they**   **fell on their faces**   **before the throne**

c   Action   **and**   **worshiped God,**

12   Doxology   saying, *"Amen.*
                                           Blessing and
                                           glory and
                                           wisdom and
                                           thanks and
                                           honor and
                                           power and
                                           strength   *to our God forever and ever.*
                                           Amen."

13a   Action   **And one of the elders replied, saying to me,**

b   Questions   *"Who are these clothed in the white robes and*

c   *where have they come from?"*

14a   Intermediate   **And I said to him,** *"My lord, you know."*
        Response

b   Answer   **And he said to me,**

c   Description   *"These are the ones who come out of the great tribulation and*

d   *they have washed their robes and*

e   *made them white in the blood of the Lamb.*

15a   Result of 14d–e   *For this reason*
                               they are before God's throne

b   *and serve him day and night in his temple,*

c   Results of 14d–15b   *and*
                            the one who sits on the throne will shelter them.

16a   *They will not hunger any more*

b   *nor will they be thirsty any more*

c   *and*
                                the sun will never beat down on them
                                nor any scorching heat, (Isa 49:10)

17a   Reasons for 15c–16   *because the Lamb in the center of the throne will shepherd them*

b   *and he*   *will guide them to springs* ↻
                                                    of the waters of life.

c   *And God will wipe away every tear from their eyes."* (Isa 25:8)

Structure

Chapter 7 contains two visions that intervene between the first six seals (6:1–17) and the seventh seal (8:1). These are signaled by the parallel phrases "after this/these things I saw/looked" in 7:1 (μετὰ τοῦτο εἶδον) and 7:9 (μετὰ ταῦτα εἶδον). The first gives John's vision of a brief delay in further judgments while 144,000 of God's Israelite servants are sealed (7:1–8), and the second a vision of an innumerable multitude from every nation joining in the heavenly worship of God (7:9–17).

Exegetical Outline

III. **Second Vision: Heavenly Throne Room and Three Judgment Cycles (4:1–16:21)**

   A. Vision of God in His Heavenly Throne Room (4:1–11)

   B. The Seven-Sealed Scroll and the Slain Lamb (5:1–14)

   C. **The Seven Seals and the Interlude of the Two Multitudes (6:1–8:1)**

      1. The First Six Seals (6:1–17)

➡   2. **The Interlude of the Two Multitudes (7:1–17)**

         a. Sealing on earth of 144,000 from the twelve tribes of Israel (7:1–8)

           (1) Preparation for sealing (7:1–3)

           (2) Enumeration of those sealed from all the tribes of Israel (7:4–8)

         b. Worship in heaven from an innumerable multitude of tribulation martyrs (7:9–17)

           (1) A multinational assembly joins the heavenly worship of God (7:9–12)

           (2) Heavenly identification and protection of these martyrs (7:13–17)

Explanation of the Text

7:1 After this I saw four angels standing at the four corners of the earth, holding back the four winds of the earth so that no wind could blow on the earth or on the sea or against any tree (Μετὰ τοῦτο εἶδον τέσσαρας ἀγγέλους ἑστῶτας ἐπὶ τὰς τέσσαρας γωνίας τῆς γῆς, κρατοῦντας τοὺς τέσσαρας ἀνέμους τῆς γῆς ἵνα μὴ πνέῃ ἄνεμος ἐπὶ τῆς γῆς μήτε ἐπὶ τῆς θαλάσσης μήτε ἐπὶ πᾶν δένδρον). After what John saw in connection with the six seals, he now recounts two separate visions[3] with quite

a different tone and pace. Instead of the panic and desperation of those who suffer God's outpouring of wrath (6:12–17), we see God's protection of one group of his people on earth (7:1–8) and the relief enjoyed by another group who have passed through that wrath into his heavenly presence (7:9–17). The first vision begins with some preparatory details as a way of further slowing down the relentless pace of 6:1–17. Before focusing on God's "sealing" of his servants (vv. 4–8), John narrates the interaction

---

3. The phrase "and . . . I saw" occurred in 6:1, 2, 5, 8, 9, 12. Now in 7:1 "after this I saw" (μετὰ τοῦτο εἶδον) signals the temporal sequence of John's next vision, since "this" refers either to what he saw of the six seals as a whole or more likely

to the vision of the sixth seal (v. 12). It probably reflects also the general sequence of the events of the last days that these visions portray since the sealing provides protection against the more severe woes of the trumpets and bowls.

of several angels who implement God's actions throughout the whole earth (vv. 1–3).

A common way of conceiving of the world in its entirety is by reference to "the four corners of the earth" in relation to "the four winds of the earth" (v. 1a–b) oriented along the cardinal points of the compass (cf. 1 Chr 9:24; Isa 11:12; Ezek 7:2; Dan 8:8; 11:4; Zech 2:6; 6:5; Mark 13:27; Rev 20:8). These winds are understood to be ultimately under the control of angels who, as God's servants, direct their force toward the accomplishment of his purposes on earth (e.g., the angel of the waters, Rev 16:5; cf. 1 En. 60:11–22; 66:2; 69:22; Jub. 2:2). The winds are often seen as destructive, as part of God's judgment against evil (Jer 49:36; Dan 7:2–3; Hos 13:15; cf. Sir 39:28–29; 1 En. 76:1–14). In John's vision, however, the four angels are "standing" (ἑστῶτας; same word as in 6:17, "Who is able to stand?") at the four corners and "holding back" the four winds, which by implication are ready to be unleashed in further widespread punishment from God. But the purpose of their current restraint (v. 1c)[4] is to prevent the winds of judgment (as representative of wider calamities about to come; e.g., hail, fire; 8:7ff.) from bringing their destructive effects against the earth and its inhabitants until the time is right.[5]

7:2–3 And I saw another angel coming up from the rising of the sun having the seal of the living God, and he cried out with a loud voice to the four angels to whom it was given to harm the earth and the sea, 3 saying, "Do not harm the earth or the sea or the trees, until we seal the servants of our God on their foreheads" (καὶ εἶδον ἄλλον ἄγγελον ἀναβαίνοντα ἀπὸ ἀνατολῆς ἡλίου ἔχοντα σφραγῖδα θεοῦ ζῶντος, καὶ ἔκραξεν φωνῇ μεγάλῃ τοῖς τέσσαρσιν ἀγγέλοις οἷς ἐδόθη αὐτοῖς ἀδικῆσαι τὴν γῆν καὶ τὴν θάλασσαν 3 λέγων, Μὴ ἀδικήσητε τὴν γῆν μήτε τὴν θάλασσαν μήτε τὰ δένδρα, ἄχρι σφραγίσωμεν τοὺς δούλους τοῦ θεοῦ ἡμῶν ἐπὶ τῶν μετώπων αὐτῶν). The further development of the same vision[6] is the appearance of "another angel" who commands the angels of the winds to delay releasing their destructive force long enough for God's servants to be protected. Delaying impending judgment to permit important things to occur first is a feature in other apocalyptic works, often expressed in terms similar to John's vision here.[7] This angel is said to "com[e] up from the rising of the sun" (v. 2b), that is, "from the east" (CSB, KJV, NET, NIV),[8] which in a context like this is associated with God's deliverance (Ezek 43:1–5; Luke 1:78; Rev 2:28; 22:16; cf. Sib. Or. 3:652). A second description is that he "ha[s] the seal of the living God" (v. 2c), a detail directly relevant to the purpose of the delay. This word "seal" (σφραγίς) occurred ten times already in chapters 5–6 to refer to a waxy drop bearing an official imprint that keeps a scroll closed up. The same noun is used by association for the "signet" used to imprint such an official "seal." Likewise the related verb "to seal" (σφραγίζω; vv. 3, 4, 5, 8) denotes the action of imprinting or "marking" something to identify

---

4. Verse 1c is a purpose clause introduced by "so that" (ἵνα).

5. The translation "on the earth or on the sea or against any tree" (cf. ESV, NRSV, RSV) reflects a change in Greek case from genitives (earth, sea) to accusative (tree), the accusative indicating more direct effect "against" the object (cf. BDAG 366 [12.b]). The objects move from general to more specific targets of the wind's destructive force (earth in general, then sea and trees; see 8:7–9 where these three suffer devastation). In the phrase "no wind . . . against any tree" the combination of a negative (μή) with "all, every" (πᾶς) is a Semitism in Greek

where "not . . . every" denotes in English "not any" (BDAG 782; BDF §302; Zerwick, *Biblical Greek* §446).

6. In v. 2a "and I saw" is used to continue the same vision rather than introduce a different one (cf. 5:1, 2, 6, 11; 21:2).

7. For example, in 1 En. 66:1–2 angels ready to flood the earth are delayed by the Lord's command so that the ark can be built first. In 2 Bar. 6:4–5 four angels are poised to burn Jerusalem in 586 BC, but an angel delays them while the temple furnishings are secured.

8. BDAG 74.

it or certify it as genuine.[9] In this case the "signet" belongs to the true and eternal God (cf. "living God" in Deut 32:39–40; Jer 10:10; Rev 15:7) and certifies that whatever bears the mark of his "seal" belongs to him.

The angel's command not to "harm the earth or the sea or the trees" (v. 3a) is a call not to release the judgments that are presently held back. This is expressly intended to provide time to "seal the servants of our God on their foreheads" (v. 3b).[10] The nature of the mark or seal is not specified, but 14:1 indicates that it represents the name of the Lamb and of his Father.[11] The objects of the sealing are "the servants of our God" (τοὺς δούλους τοῦ θεοῦ ἡμῶν), a phrase that often in Revelation denotes all God's people in general (1:1; 19:5; 22:3, 6), but sometimes refers to a narrower group of his servants specified in the context (2:20; 10:7; 19:2; cf. 15:3 [sg.]). The referents in this passage are debated, but see the discussion of vv. 4–8 below.

The implication is that this identifying seal will protect them from the onslaught of judgment that will soon be released against the wider world. Such protection is clearly implied here in 7:1–8, although it must be defined further, and it is confirmed when we consider the Old Testament background of the passage in Ezekiel 9:1–11 and the later mention of these who are sealed in

Revelation 9:4; 14:1–5; 22:4.[12] In Ezekiel 9 the prophet has a vision of God's slaughter of everyone in Jerusalem as judgment for apostasy. The only ones to be spared are those who "mourn over its abominations" (v. 4), whom an angel identifies by placing a "mark on their foreheads" (vv. 4, 6).[13] When judgment then seems to engulf everyone, Ezekiel asks whether "the entire remnant of Israel" will be destroyed in the "outpouring of wrath on Jerusalem" (v. 8). God's answer gives no hope for Ezekiel's day (vv. 9–11; 11:13), but it promises the restoration of a remnant in the future when God will renew them spiritually and regather Israel in its own land from all the places where he had scattered them in judgment (11:14–21).[14] Just as in the cataclysmic judgments of Ezekiel's day (and in the typological parallels in Gen 4 and Exod 12; see note below), so when faced with the outpouring of God's wrath in the future, unprecedented tribulation that John is describing (Rev 6–16), one is led to wonder what will become of God's people in the midst of judgment. Will God's promised re-gathering and restoration be abandoned in his future torrent of wrath? The further part of John's vision (vv. 4–8) answers that question.

7:4 And I heard the number of those who were sealed, a hundred and forty-four thousand seal-

---

9. BDAG 980.

10. The action of sealing is anticipated ("until we seal," ἄχρι σφραγίσωμεν) but not described here in v. 3 or in subsequent verses (even in vv. 4–8 it is portrayed as already accomplished). The pronoun reference in "until we seal" implies that other angels will assist in this task.

11. In a number of ways this "seal" or mark (σφραγίς) on God's servants' foreheads is the opposite of the "mark" (χάραγμα) that the beast will require his followers to receive on their hand or forehead, representing his name and thus their allegiance to him (13:16–17; 14:9, 11; 16:2; 19:20; 20:4).

12. E.g., in 9:4 destructive "locusts" are given permission to "harm" (ἀδικέω) the people "who do not have God's seal on their foreheads."

13. Ezekiel's vision mirrors the stories of how God spared

Jewish homes marked with blood from his final plague on Egypt (Exod 12:1–32) and how God marked Cain so that no one would kill him during his wanderings imposed on him for his sin (Gen 4:11–16).

14. Daniel I. Block, *The Book of Ezekiel 1–24*, NICOT (Grand Rapids: Eerdmans, 1997), 300–10; 338–56; Lamar Eugene Cooper, *Ezekiel*, NAC 17 (Nashville: Broadman & Holman, 1994), 125–29; 141–44. Relevant parallels can be found also in ancient Jewish apocalyptic works (CD-B 19:12; Pss. Sol. 15:4–9; 2 Bar. 27–30; Apoc. Ab. 29:14–21). The last three works describe eschatological tribulation or distress similar to the calamities of Rev 6 that the Lord will pour out on the whole world prior to the Messiah's coming. But they pledge God's protection in the midst of these for those marked out as the faithful remnant of Israel.

ed from every tribe of the sons of Israel (καὶ ἤκουσα τὸν ἀριθμὸν τῶν ἐσφραγισμένων, ἑκατὸν τεσσεράκοντα τέσσαρες χιλιάδες, ἐσφραγισμένοι ἐκ πάσης φυλῆς υἱῶν Ἰσραήλ). John continues to recount the vision he "saw" (vv. 1a, 2a) by identifying further "the servants of our God" who were sealed (v. 3b) as a large number of Israelites.[15] This identification consists of several specific facts that John "heard" about these servants. First, the number of those sealed totals "a hundred and forty-four thousand" (v. 4a–b). There is debate over whether this number should be understood literally. Contrary to what is often said, not all numbers in Revelation are figurative. For example, the referents of "the seven churches in the province of Asia" (1:4) are literally the seven churches that are listed specifically in 1:11 and chapters 2–3. However, the significance in that case is not *merely* or *only* literal, since the number seven can connote completeness or totality and so the seven churches represent in some sense "God's church" more broadly.[16] The number here in 7:4 is contrasted with "a great multitude that no one could count" (v. 9), so it is hard to conclude that 144,000 is symbolic for "a very large number" and hard also to take the two groups as identical when John explicitly portrays one as numbering a certain amount (even a large round number) and the other as innumerable (whether the two groups are the same is discussed further

below). On the other hand, multiples of the number twelve clearly resonate with significance for redemptive history and prophecy (e.g., features of the New Jerusalem symbolizing the twelve tribes of Israel and the twelve apostles in Rev 21:12, 14; cf. Jesus's selection of the twelve as representative of Israel in Matt 19:28; Mark 3:16–19; Luke 22:30).[17] It is likely that 144,000 represents ideas of fullness and completeness whether or not it intends to give an actual or approximate count of these "servants" (see further below).[18]

The second specific identification of those sealed is that they are "from every tribe of the sons of Israel" (v. 4b). John's choice of words strongly emphasizes an Israelite origin for these servants: not just "from Israel" or "from the sons of Israel" or "from the tribes of the sons of Israel," but "from every tribe of the sons of Israel."[19] This phrasing is then reinforced with almost tortured repetition in vv. 5–8 as each of the tribes is specified and its contribution to the total is tallied. On the face of it, the meaning of this description is quite straightforward: they are ethnic Israelites, physical descendants of the sons of Jacob. The parallel in 14:1–5 narrows the scope by showing that they are followers of the Lamb,[20] thus Jewish Christians, not Israelites from the days prior to Christ's coming or Jews who refuse Christ. Some of the earliest patristic commentators understood vv. 4–8 in this way, either of

---

15. In narrating his vision John does not describe the action of sealing itself. It is anticipated in v. 3b and spoken of as already done in v. 4 (the Greek participles translated "sealed," ἐσφραγισμένων and ἐσφραγισμένοι, are perfect tense, denoting the existing result of a past action). Apocalyptic visions can be elliptical and uneven, so the vision itself very likely jumped from the prospect to the result without including the extended action of sealing such a large group.

16. So the address to them also addresses other churches in the first-century and today (see comments on 1:4; 2:7).

17. See Scot McKnight, "Jesus and the Twelve," in *Key Events in the Life of the Historical Jesus*, ed. Darrell L. Bock and Robert L. Webb (Tübingen: Mohr Siebeck, 2009), 196–97.

18. See Bauckham, *Climax*, 218–19, who takes the 144,000 as symbolic, but not "purely symbolic"; it represents an army to which it is "possible" that "each tribe supplies twelve battalions of a thousand men each."

19. In order to be gender inclusive, some versions omit "sons" and read "people of Israel" (NRSV) or "all the tribes of Israel" (NIV, NLT) but here it is important to preserve the reference to Jacob's male sons who became tribal chiefs in Israel, even though of course they represent in many ways all of their descendants, male and female, as God's people.

20. For the other descriptions of them given in 14:1–5, see comments on those verses.

Jewish believers in Christ who were preserved from destruction in AD 70 (Oecumenius)[21] or of a final turning of Jews to Christ at the end times (Andrew of Caesarea, Irenaeus, Jerome, Victorinus).[22] Given the explicit contextual contrasts between this group (vv. 4–8) and the multitude described in vv. 9–17,[23] taking these servants as ethnic Israelites appears to be the most straightforward reading of the text, and this interpretation is taken by a number of recent commentators.[24]

It is possible, however, to construe the references to "the twelve tribes of Israel" as figurative for the whole church, that is, Christians regardless of ethnic background, especially if one is inclined to view the wider biblical theology of God's people in this way. If the church is the "new Israel" that replaces ethnic Israel and takes over its promises of redemption, then vv. 4–8 can be seen as some kind of ultimate spiritual protection for God's redeemed people as a whole. Many recent commentaries adopt this view of vv. 4–8.[25] This approach is usually then coupled with taking vv. 9–17 as referring to the same group viewed from a different perspective (see discussion of this at v. 9). Yet arguments for this view that are

taken from vv. 4–8 are not entirely convincing. Here are some of the arguments and brief responses:

1. It is said that the phrase "servants of God" (v. 3) often describes all redeemed people in Revelation, so it cannot mean just Jewish-Christians here.[26] But as noted at v. 3, it occurs a few times with a narrower group specified in the context (2:20, Christians misled by Jezebel; 10:7, prophets; cf. 15:3, Moses; 19:2, martyrs of the great prostitute).

2. Since the ten northern tribes had been so absorbed into the surrounding peoples, they no longer actually existed in the first century, and so no one could conceive of a literal regathering of them.[27] But contrary to our modern estimates, first-century people actually did think in these terms and anticipated God's restoration of all Israel (e.g., Luke 2:36; Josephus, *Ant.* 11.133).[28]

3. Irregularities and Christian influences in the listing of the tribes (vv. 5–8) show that it cannot mean literal Israel but must be symbolic of the church.[29] But there is no actual "regular" list in the Old Testament. It is true that moving Judah to the initial spot probably reflects Christian concern to put Jesus's tribe first, but even purely

21. Weinrich, "Oecumenius," 34–35.

22. Irenaeus, *Haer.* 5.30.2; Jerome, *Hom. Mark* 82; cf. Koester, *Revelation*, 355; Kovacs and Rowland, *Revelation*, 102; Weinrich, "Andrew of Caesarea," 137–40; William C. Weinrich, *Revelation*, ACCS (Downers Grove, IL: InterVarsity Press, 2005), 102–10.

23. The contrasts include: numbered vs. innumerable; from Israel vs. from every nation, tribe, people, and language; on earth vs. in heaven; protected in the midst of trouble vs. sheltered from all woe by exiting the great tribulation (see comments on v. 14 for how they "come out of" it).

24. T. F. Glasson, *The Revelation of John*, CBC (Cambridge: Cambridge University Press, 1965), 51–53; Kraft, *Offenbarung*, 126–27; Patterson, *Revelation*, 193–99; Rowland, "Revelation," 620; Thomas, *Revelation 1–7*, 475–78; Walvoord, Rawley, and Hitchcock, *Revelation*, 139–41. See J. A. Draper, "The Heavenly Feast of Tabernacles: Revelation 7:1–17," *JSNT* 19 (1983): 136–37. This is also the interpretation presented by Joel R. White, "The 144,000 in Revelation 7 and 14: Old Testament and Intratextual Clues to Their Identity," in *From Creation to New*

Creation: Biblical Theology and Exegesis, ed. Daniel M. Gurtner and Benjamin L Gladd (Peabody, MA: Hendrickson, 2013), 179–97. White, however, understands their sealing differently (it ensures spiritual but not physical protection) and identifies these 144,000 Jewish believers as part of, not separate from, the innumerable, multiethnic crowd of 7:9–10 (Jewish believers are included with gentile believers).

25. Beale, *Revelation*, 416–23; Osborne, *Revelation*, 311–15; Prigent, *Apocalypse*, 282–86; Smalley, *Revelation*, 184–88; Gerhard Maier, *Die Offenbarung des Johannes: Kapitel 1–11*, HTANT (Giessen: Brunnen, 2009), 355–62; Satake, *Offenbarung*, 227–29. Also C. Maurer, "φυλή," *TDNT* 9:248–49.

26. Prigent, *Apocalypse*, 282; Smalley, *Revelation*, 188.

27. Caird, *Revelation*, 95; Mounce, *Revelation*, 158; Smalley, *Revelation*, 185.

28. Maier, *Offenbarung 1–11*, 355–56.

29. Ladd, *Revelation*, 114–15; Christopher R. Smith, "The Portrayal of the Church as the New Israel in the Names and Order of the Tribes in Revelation 7:5–8," *JSNT* 39 (1990): 114–16; Swete, *Apocalypse*, 98.

Jewish texts sometimes list Judah first. The arrangement of the names in itself is not a hermeneutical key.[30] See more detailed comments on vv. 5–8 below.

4. Whatever protection from coming woes such "sealing" provides for this group cannot be the exclusive privilege of only one part of the church (i.e., true for only Jewish-Christians and not all Christians). Thus the group must include all Christians.[31] But this depends very much on properly understanding God's purpose for the protection. It is broadly agreed that Christians in the tribulation are not all protected from suffering or from physical death. A clear grasp of what the sealing signifies mitigates the force of this argument.

5. The emphasis in Revelation (as in the NT in general) on the inclusion of gentiles among the people of God (e.g., 5:9, redeemed by the Lamb "from every tribe and tongue and people and nation"; 15:4, "all the nations" worshiping God and included in the New Jerusalem [21:24, 26; 22:2]) is often cited as evidence that ethnic Israel has been set aside and the church has assumed her spiritual privileges.[32] But the inclusion of gentiles does not necessitate the exclusion of Israel or the revocation of God's repeated promises to her (many of them strongly reinforced even in the face of her sinful ways; cf. Isa 66:18–22; Jer 31:33–37). The extension of God's blessing to include non-Israelites accompanies his restored favor to Israel; it does not mean he sets her aside. Verses in Revelation and elsewhere in the New Testament (e.g., 2:29, 3:9; 21:12, 14; Rom 2:29; Gal 6:16; Jas 1:1; 1 Pet 2:9–10) that purportedly show the church as the "new Israel" are subject to the same misunderstanding; at least they are subject to the same debate and do not without further discussion prove the disputed point here.[33]

Instead of taking Israel as the church in these verses, a strong case can be made that John affirms the widespread ancient Jewish expectation of the regathering in the end-times of all the tribes of ethnic Israel from their exile among the nations.[34] This is God's pledge throughout the Old Testament (Deut 30:1–5; Isa 11:10–16; 27:12–13; 49:5–6; Jer 3:18; 23:5–8; 31:7–10; Ezek 11:13–21; 37:15–28; 47:13–14; 48:30–35; Mic 2:12; Zech 10:8–10), and it reverberates through early Jewish literature as well (Tob 13:3–5; Sir 36:11–17; 48:10; 4 Ezra 13:39–50; 2 Bar. 62:5–6; 77:19–78:7; T. Jos. 19:1–4; T. Benj. 9:2; 10:5–9; 1QM 2:1–3; 3:13–14; 5:1–2; 11QTemple 57:5–6; m. Sanh. 10.3; Shemoneh Esreh 10).[35] Jesus's choosing of twelve disciples to be with him

30. See the negative response by Richard Bauckham, "The List of the Tribes in Revelation 7 Again," *JSNT* 42 (1991): 100–102, to two of the three features of arrangement that Smith, "Portrayal," 114–16 finds persuasive.

31. Charles, *Revelation*, 1:200; Maier, *Offenbarung 1–11*, 361; Smalley, *Revelation*, 186.

32. Prigent, *Apocalypse*, 284–85; Smalley, *Revelation*, 185–87; cf. Roloff, *Revelation*, 97: "The church [is] the end-time people of salvation who have taken up Israel's inheritance.... Christians have assumed the rights of Israel in every respect."

33. For arguments from wider biblical-theological evidence that dispute the idea that the church is the new or true Israel and ethnic Israel is set aside, see Craig A. Blaising, "The Future of Israel as a Theological Question," *JETS* 44 (2001): 435–50; Ronald E. Diprose, *Israel and the Church: The Origin and Effects of Replacement Theology* (Rome: Istituto Biblico Evangelico Italiano, 2000); R. Kendall Soulen, *The God of Israel and Christian Theology* (Minneapolis: Fortress, 1996); Michael J. Vlach, *The Church as a Replacement of Israel: An Analysis of Supersessionism* (New York: Peter Lang, 2009); and essays in Gerald R. McDermott, ed., *The New Christian Zionism: Fresh Perspectives on Israel & the Land* (Downers Grove, IL: IVP Academic, 2016).

34. See E. P. Sanders, *Jesus and Judaism* (Philadelphia: Fortress, 1985), 95–98, who cites a number of canonical and noncanonical texts (96–98) and calls this expectation "widespread" in the first century (98).

35. McKnight, "Jesus and the Twelve," 196–97; Pitre, *Tribulation*, 33–40; James M. Scott, "And Then All Israel Will Be Saved (Rom 11:26)," in *Restoration: Old Testament, Jewish, and Christian Perspectives*, JSJSup 72 (Leiden: Brill, 2001), 489–526 (see the ancient texts listed on p. 519).

represents this intent also (Mark 3:13–19), and his declaration that in the coming renewal, when he sits on "his glorious throne," they will likewise "sit on twelve thrones judging the twelve tribes of Israel" (Matt 19:28; Luke 22:30) speaks to this promise of national restoration in the end times.[36] John's emphasis here in 7:4–8 on all twelve tribes captures the same anticipation that God has not abandoned Israel,[37] but in his judgment and renewal of all things he will restore them through his Messiah, the promised king of David's line (Rev 5:5; 22:16).[38]

That John would record a vision of the preservation of Israel as a whole at this juncture in Revelation relates to a particular purpose that the future time of tribulation will serve in regard to ethnic Israel. In addition to its function to embody God's climactic judgment against his (and Israel's) enemies in the wider gentile world, the tribulation was intended to discipline his people Israel in preparation for their restoration in the land he promised to Abraham, Isaac, and Jacob under a renewed Davidic rule (Deut 4:29–30; 28:58–59; Isa 10:20; 26:16–21; 27:5–13; Jer 30:4–11; Zeph 3:11–20; Zech 13:7–9; Dan 12:1–3, 10).[39] As John reaches this transition between the series of judgments connected to the earlier seals (6:1–17) and confronts the more severe outpourings of God's wrath to come (8:1ff), it is appropriate to confirm here that among those who "are able to stand" (6:17) is the full complement of regathered, faithful Israel. They have turned or

will turn to Christ in faith at some point during this time of severe trouble and are protected by God so that they will be able to stand with their Messiah (among other Christians) in Jerusalem when he begins his earthly reign there (14:1–5; 20:1–10).[40] Israel will not be destroyed but refined by these judgments. These woes are God's restorative discipline of his erring people, not a sign of their rejection. To be sure, the focus on "Israel as a whole" (e.g., the symbolism of the number 144,000 and the emphasis on every tribe) means that the sealing should not be understood as a guarantee that every individual Jewish person who turns to Christ during the tribulation will be physically protected from its judgments. Instead it ensures that a substantial number will be preserved in order to constitute a full regathering of Israel when Christ establishes his millennial reign.[41]

7:5–8 From the tribe of Judah twelve thousand sealed, from the tribe of Reuben twelve thousand, from the tribe of Gad twelve thousand, 6 from the tribe of Asher twelve thousand, from the tribe of Naphtali twelve thousand, from the tribe of Manasseh twelve thousand, 7 from the tribe of Simeon twelve thousand, from the tribe of Levi twelve thousand, from the tribe of Issachar twelve thousand, 8 from the tribe of Zebulun twelve thousand, from the tribe of Joseph twelve thousand, from the tribe of Benjamin twelve thousand sealed (ἐκ φυλῆς Ἰούδα δώδεκα χιλιάδες

---

36. McKnight, "Jesus and the Twelve," 202–9; John P. Meier, *A Marginal Jew: Rethinking the Historical Jesus*, vol. 3: *Companions and Competitors*, ABRL (New York: Doubleday, 2001), 148–54.

37. See also Paul's concern to defend God against any supposition that he has abandoned his people Israel (Rom 11:11–32).

38. Albert Geyser, "The Twelve Tribes in Revelation: Judean and Judeo-Christian Apocalypticism," *NTS* 28 (1982): 388–99.

39. Elliott, *Survivors*, 575–637 ("destruction-preservation soteriology"); Pitre, *Tribulation*, 59–65.

40. Several ancient texts connect the regathering and pro-

tection of Israel in the final cataclysmic judgments explicitly to their presence in the land (Apoc. Ab. 29:14–17; 2 Bar. 29:1–3; 32:1–2; 40:2; 71:1; 1 En. 99:6–10; 100:4–5; 4 Ezra 9:7–8; 13:40, 48–49; Pss. Sol. 15:4–7). See Allison, *End of the Ages*, 20–22; and Aune, *Revelation 6–16*, 443–45.

41. See essentially the same view as presented here in Rebecca Skaggs and Priscilla Benham, *Revelation: Pentecostal Commentary*, PCS (Blandford Forum, Dorset, UK: Deo, 2009), 86–87. Aune, *Revelation 6–16*, 443, presents a similar conclusion about the preservation of this group through the horrors of the coming judgments, but he does not limit it to ethnic Israel.

ἐσφραγισμένοι, ἐκ φυλῆς Ῥουβὴν δώδεκα χιλιάδες, ἐκ φυλῆς Γὰδ δώδεκα χιλιάδες, 6 ἐκ φυλῆς Ἀσὴρ δώδεκα χιλιάδες, ἐκ φυλῆς Νεφθαλὶμ δώδεκα χιλιάδες, ἐκ φυλῆς Μανασσῆ δώδεκα χιλιάδες, 7 ἐκ φυλῆς Συμεὼν δώδεκα χιλιάδες, ἐκ φυλῆς Λευὶ δώδεκα χιλιάδες, ἐκ φυλῆς Ἰσσαχὰρ δώδεκα χιλιάδες, 8 ἐκ φυλῆς Ζαβουλὼν δώδεκα χιλιάδες, ἐκ φυλῆς Ἰωσὴφ δώδεκα χιλιάδες, ἐκ φυλῆς Βενιαμεὶν δώδεκα χιλιάδες ἐσφραγισμένοι). In repetitive but powerful detail, John specifies in vv. 5–8 the contribution of each of the twelve tribes to the "hundred and forty-four thousand sealed from every tribe of the sons of Israel" (v. 4b). The verses display an obvious parallelism broken only by the bracketing effect of including the word "sealed" with the first and last tribes. The number "twelve thousand" for each tribe seems clearly to be a round number extrapolated from the total that represents completeness (see comment at v. 4). It does not seem to denote an absolutely literal census, but the larger sense of equivalent representation and large-scale protection of God's servants across all of ethnic Israel is certainly intended.

Two further issues that require brief examination are the overall arrangement of the tribes and the inclusion or omission of certain tribes in the list. As mentioned above, there is no standard way of arranging the tribes in biblical passages where they are listed. One author finds thirty Old Testament lists of the tribes and classifies them into four basic systems based on the interplay of genealogical and geographical factors.[42] The idea that John's list is so "irregular" that it cannot refer to literal Israel[43] is discredited simply by looking at the biblical evidence. Placing Judah first (v. 5a) is almost certainly due to Christian conviction about Jesus as descended from David and Judah (Rev 5:5; 22:16; Matt 1:1, 6; Luke 1:32; Rom 1:3; 2 Tim 2:8; Heb 7:14), but the Davidic connection was important in the Old Testament as well.[44] Since the two sons of Joseph are often included as separate tribes in the Old Testament (cf. Josh 14:4), and Levi is often omitted since his tribe had no separate geographical inheritance, the "twelve" tribes were actually thirteen depending on how they were enumerated. Here Levi is included (v. 7), and Joseph is listed separately (v. 8) along with Manasseh (v. 6), but Ephraim and Dan are not listed. It is possible that Joseph is cited instead of Ephraim because Ephraim was associated too closely with the idolatry of the northern tribes—something restored Israel would leave behind forever. Dan's omission may similarly be due to associations with Rehoboam's idolatrous altars (1 Kgs 12:25–33; 2 Kgs 10:29; cf. also Judg 18:30; T. Dan 5:6).[45] Despite these questions about arrangement and omission, the larger focus of vv. 5–8 on all Israel as a complete people is clear.

7:9–10 After these things I looked and behold, a great multitude that no one could number, from every nation and tribe and people and tongue, standing before the throne and before the Lamb, clothed in white robes and with palm branches in their hands, 10 and they cried out with a loud voice saying, "Salvation to our God who sits on the throne and to the Lamb" (Μετὰ ταῦτα εἶδον, καὶ ἰδοὺ ὄχλος πολύς, ὃν ἀριθμῆσαι αὐτὸν οὐδεὶς ἐδύνατο, ἐκ παντὸς ἔθνους καὶ φυλῶν καὶ λαῶν καὶ γλωσσῶν ἑστῶτες ἐνώπιον τοῦ θρόνου καὶ ἐνώπιον

---

42. Zecharia Kallai, "The Twelve-Tribe Systems of Israel," *VT* 47 (1997): 57, 90.

43. Ladd, *Revelation*, 114–16. The contention of Smith, "Portrayal," 115–17, that certain features of the arrangement constitute an overwhelming argument against taking this as ethnic Israel is likewise overstated.

44. Judah could be listed first in the OT for various reasons as well; e.g., Num 2:3; 7:12; 10:14.

45. The tradition that the antichrist would arise from Dan (possibly a misreading of Gen 49:17) does not appear earlier than the late second century (Irenaeus, *Haer.* 5.30.2; Hippolytus, *Antichr.* 14). See also Weinrich, "Andrew of Caesarea," 139. Testament of Dan 5:9–10 (second century BC) portrays Dan as restored from its idolatry in the end-times. See Bauckham, *Climax*, 222–23.

τοῦ ἀρνίου περιβεβλημένους στολὰς λευκὰς καὶ φοίνικες ἐν ταῖς χερσὶν αὐτῶν, 10 καὶ κράζουσιν φωνῇ μεγάλῃ λέγοντες, Ἡ σωτηρία τῷ θεῷ ἡμῶν τῷ καθημένῳ ἐπὶ τῷ θρόνῳ καὶ τῷ ἀρνίῳ). Following the first vision (vv. 1–8) recorded in this interlude between the sixth and seventh seals, John signals the beginning of a separate vision (vv. 9–17) with the phrase "after these things I looked, and behold" (v. 9a).[46] He describes a "great multitude," somewhat parallel to the 144,000 (i.e., a large number of people) portrayed in vv. 4–8, but otherwise contrasting sharply with them. They cannot be counted, even symbolically; they are from all the peoples of the world rather than from Israel; they stand joyfully before the heavenly throne rather than needing to be protected from earthly destruction (v. 9b–d).[47] As argued above, this is almost certainly a different group of people, gentile Christians set apart in heaven (vv. 11–13), no longer threatened by the great tribulation (v. 14), sheltered and blessed by God forever (vv. 15–17).[48]

Despite these contrasts, many interpreters understand the two visions to describe the same group (the Christian church of all ages or of the final days) but viewed in radically different settings. First they are seen as needing God's protection amid severe troubles (vv. 1–8) and then seen as victorious over these woes and enjoying heavenly sanctuary (vv. 9–17). It is easy to find in these verses the contrasting settings suggested by this approach, but

why does John describe the people themselves so differently? The answer commonly given is that this is a feature of John's literary style as well as theological presentation. The complete number of "Israel" is what John *hears* (v. 4), but what he *sees* (v. 9) is the vast international multitude of Christians. The nationalistic Old Testament expectation that is heard is reinterpreted in light of Christ, and in lively, unexpected fashion the Christian fulfillment of the same thing is juxtaposed by what John sees. The parallel that interpreters cite is how Christ is presented in 5:5–6. John is first told that "the Lion of Judah, the root of David" is worthy to open the sealed book (v. 5), but what he sees is a slain Lamb (v. 6), a transformation of Jewish militaristic expectations into Christian sacrifice and victory through martyrdom (see comments on 5:6).[49]

This explanation, while plausible, is not convincing. On literary grounds the parallel with 5:5–6 is minimal. In 1:10–13 where John uses a hearing-then-seeing sequence, the two parts are parallel and additive, not contrasting or reinterpreting (so also 9:16–17; cf. 22:8). The verb "hear" does not actually occur in 5:5–6 to set up the supposed contrasting structure. Also, what John is told in 5:5 is very brief and is then filled in quickly by what he sees (5:6), but what John hears here in vv. 4–8 is quite extensive and elaborate, followed by a sharper transition to a new vision ("after these things I saw).[50] In theological terms, the degree of

---

46. Compare 7:1: "After this I looked." This use of "behold" (ἰδού) is seen also in 6:2, 5, 8 (see note on 4:1).

47. See Rebecca Skaggs and Thomas Doyle, "Revelation 7: Three Critical Questions," in *Imagery in the Book of Revelation*, ed. Michael Labahn and Outi Lehtipun (Leuven: Peeters, 2001), 165–73, for recitation of various contrasts between the two groups. As Hultberg says ("Prewrath Rapture," 145), it is as though John "goes out of his way to describe them in opposing terms." See also Aune, *Revelation 6–16*, 466: "This represents an intentional contrast with 7:4."

48. Walvoord, Rawley, and Hitchcock, *Revelation*, 147, suggest that juxtaposing the two groups in close proximity as John

has done implies that the 144,000 are specifically appointed Jewish evangelists whose witness leads this innumerable multitude to faith. Thomas, *Revelation 1–7*, 474–75, 478, has a similar view: the 144,000 are protected for period of witness or evangelism after which they are martyred (cf. Rev 11:3–8). There is very little support for these ideas in the text itself.

49. Bauckham, *Climax*, 215–16; Beale, *Revelation*, 425; Boxall, *Revelation*, 124–25; Caird, *Revelation*, 96; Koester, *Revelation*, 424; Resseguie, *Narrative Commentary*, 136–38; Smalley, *Revelation*, 184.

50. Hultberg, "Prewrath Rapture," 145–46.

reinterpretation from Old Testament expectation to Christian fulfillment is not as great as these interpreters make it out to be. Such an interpretation of 5:5 does an injustice to how Christ will fulfill the Old Testament Davidic hope, and this reading of the vision of Israel's regathering in 7:4–8 is a Christian theological imposition on the exegetical sense of Jeremiah 30 and Isaiah 66, for example, in their own biblical contexts. See comments on 2:27–28; 5:5; 19:15 for further discussion.

If as suggested above vv. 9–17 portray a different group than vv. 4–8, they are still complementary since the Old Testament expectation of Israel's endtime restoration invariably includes gentiles also coming to worship the God of Israel (e.g., Isa 2:2–5; 11:10; 49:5–6; 56:6–8; Mic 4:1–4; Zech 2:10–12; 14:16). A form of the phrase "every nation and tribe and people and tongue"[51] (v. 9c) occurs seven times in Revelation to speak of the multicultural impact of God's redemption that begins with Israel (cf. Gen 12:1–3; Exod 19:5–6) but expands to the whole world.[52] This anticipation that in the endtime people from every nation will worship God and the Lamb is not just a dream for the future. It constitutes a mission that Jesus gave his followers at the beginning and continues throughout the age (Matt 28:19–20; Luke 24:47; John 10:16; Acts 1:8).

John describes this scene (v. 9d–e) in terms that connect it back to the grounding vision for all of chapters 6–16, the vision of God and the Lamb in the heavenly throne room (chs. 4–5). The innumerable multitude is "standing before the throne and before the Lamb" (v. 9d; cf. 4:2; 5:6; 6:17),[53] no longer facing tribulation but now in the very presence of the Lord God (4:10–11) and of the Lamb who redeemed them (5:9), joined by God's angelic court in worshiping him (4:4, 6; 5:8, 11; 7:11). Christ's sacrifice has made them pure from sin, as symbolized by their "white robes" (v. 9e; cf. v. 14).[54] The "palm branches in their hands" represent their festive celebration[55] before God as they cry out in praise to him.

Shouts of praise from the redeemed multitude (v. 10) anticipate the larger body of heavenly beings joining them in worship (see vv. 11–12 below).[56] But before that the uncountable crowd for its part offers worship by acknowledging that "salvation," their full-orbed deliverance from all evil including victory over powerful enemies, is due to God and to the Lamb (v. 10b).[57] The Greek datives reflected

---

51. The Greek wording for this phrase shifts from an initial singular ("every nation") to a series of plurals ("and tribes and peoples and tongues") but the universal sense of the "every" carries over to all of the nouns by agreement according to sense (cf. BDF § 282.3). See ESV, NASB, NRSV, RSV for an attempt to render this more literally.

52. See Bauckham, *Climax*, 326–37, for details of their occurrences in Rev and the connection of these ideas to Dan 7.

53. The description "standing" is a plural participle in Greek (ἑστῶτες), agreeing in sense but not grammatically with the singular "multitude" (ὄχλος).

54. The phrase "clothed [in white robes]" (περιβεβλημένους) contains a Greek participle that is accusative. The accusative occurs due to the influence of the transitive "I saw" in v. 9a, although that construction was broken by the intervening "behold" with its nominative "multitude" and "standing" (see previous note). The Greek of this verse is very colloquial but powerfully expressive.

55. "Palm branches" (φοίνικες) could suggest a heavenly reenactment of the Festival of Booths (Lev 23:39–43; Neh 8:13–18; Zech 14:16–19), with which both "palm branches" (φοίνικες) and "booths" or "shelters" (σκηναί) were associated (see Rev 7:15, "shelter," σκηνόω). But palm branches were a symbol of joyful celebration more broadly, and that may explain the symbolism sufficiently (cf. 1 Macc 13:51, communal celebration of victory over enemies).

56. The phrase "they cried out" is a historical present in Greek (κράζουσιν), used to draw attention to the events that follow, the worship from the heavenly company in vv. 11–12 (see 5:5 for further discussion of this usage).

57. The word "salvation" (σωτηρία) in its use in Rev (7:10; 12:10; 19:1) resonates with an eschatological sense drawn from texts like Isa 49:6; 52:10 (God's salvation reaching "the ends of the earth" through his victory over evil). See BDAG 986, and W. Foerster, "σωτηρία," *TDNT* 7:997–98.

in the phrase "to our God . . . and to the Lamb" (τῷ θεῷ ἡμῶν . . . καὶ τῷ ἀρνίῳ) along with the understood wish, "may it be," are a standard way of ascribing a quality or an admirable action to God in praise or doxology (e.g., 1:5–6; 5:13; 7:12; a variant of this appears in 4:9).[58] The same meaning can be expressed by a genitive (i.e., "belongs to God") as in 19:1,[59] a clear parallel to this verse. All credit for their deliverance goes to God and Christ, and they joyfully acknowledge it.[60]

7:11–12 And all the angels and the elders and the four living creatures stood around the throne, and they fell on their faces before the throne and worshiped God, 12 saying, "Amen. Blessing and glory and wisdom and thanks and honor and power and strength to our God forever and ever. Amen" (καὶ πάντες οἱ ἄγγελοι εἱστήκεισαν κύκλῳ τοῦ θρόνου καὶ τῶν πρεσβυτέρων καὶ τῶν τεσσάρων ζῴων καὶ ἔπεσαν ἐνώπιον τοῦ θρόνου ἐπὶ τὰ πρόσωπα αὐτῶν καὶ προσεκύνησαν τῷ θεῷ, 12 λέγοντες, Ἀμήν, ἡ εὐλογία καὶ ἡ δόξα καὶ ἡ σοφία καὶ ἡ εὐχαριστία καὶ ἡ τιμὴ καὶ ἡ δύναμις καὶ ἡ ἰσχὺς τῷ θεῷ ἡμῶν εἰς τοὺς αἰῶνας τῶν αἰώνων· ἀμήν). As in 4:8–11 and 5:8–14, one offering of praise to God triggers an ever-widening crescendo of adoration and worship in his throne room. The praise of redeemed humans in v. 10 is extended as all the angels

present add their voices and physical expressions of adoration and acclaim. "All the angels" and "the elders" and "the four living creatures"[61] surrounded the throne[62] and prostrated themselves in humility and devotion[63] before him (v. 11a–b). Their bodily posture of adoration is then followed by vocal expression of praise to God. The final clause of v. 11 states the general point, "they worshiped God," but v. 12 fills in how this was carried out: by spoken declarations of worship.

What they express is a sevenfold ascription of sterling attributes (symbolizing perfection in virtue; as also in 5:12) for which God deserves praise (v. 12). These are bracketed at the beginning and end by the strong affirmation "amen, let it be so,"[64] but the first affirms what was said by others in v. 10 (as in 5:14; 19:4; 22:20), while the last "amen" reinforces what the angelic host themselves declare in v. 12 (as in 1:6, 7). As discussed in 4:9 and 5:12, such an ascription of attributes is an honorific recitation of perfections that the person possesses. The speakers do not bestow these qualities but declare and celebrate his possession and display of such worthy traits. Even the mention of items like "blessing" (εὐλογία) and "thanks" (εὐχαριστία) used in conjunction with the other traits do not denote simply the creature's offering of blessing or

---

58. See Aune, *Revelation 6–16*, 43–45 on doxological forms; also comments on 5:13.

59. See also Ps 3:8 (MT and LXX 3:9) where the Hebrew has "salvation to the Lord" (לַיהוָה הַיְשׁוּעָה), and the Greek uses a genitive (τοῦ κυρίου ἡ σωτηρία).

60. In a bizarre inversion of much of what 7:1–17 says, Jehovah's Witnesses understand the "great multitude" of vv. 9–17 to be a group of the redeemed with a second-class status, who will enjoy a paradise on earth, ruled by the select group of 144,000 who will rule over them with Christ from the heavenly Zion (7:4–8; 14:1–5). Only the 144,000 (a literal number) will experience the privilege of being in heaven. See Penton, *Apocalypse Delayed*, 273–76; and Watch Tower Bible and Tract Society of Pennsylvania, *What Does the Bible Really Teach?* (Wallkill, NY: Watchtower Bible and Tract Society of New York, 2014), 74–85, 213–15.

61. See these three groups cited in 5:11. The three phrases in 7:11 are articular, referring back to the beings described in chs. 4–5, so it is presumably not "all the angels" that exist but all of the "many angels" mentioned in 5:11 as being "around the throne."

62. The verb "stood" is a Greek pluperfect (εἱστήκεισαν) that consistently carries a past stative meaning in the NT (not a true past perfect, "had stood," as Aune, *Revelation 6–16*, 430, claims; cf. BDAG 482). It is followed by the aorists "fell" and "worshiped" to narrate in sequence what John witnessed.

63. NET translates the phrase "fell on their faces" (ἔπεσαν . . . ἐπὶ τὰ πρόσωπα αὐτῶν) as "threw themselves down with their faces to the ground."

64. BDAG 53.

thanks to God. Instead it acknowledges that God is "praiseworthy" and "deserving of gratitude" for benefits he has bestowed. As in 5:12, the composite impression of the sevenfold list is valuable to note, but the individual qualities nevertheless carry their own importance. For the sense of specific items, see the brief notes on them at 4:9, 11, or 5:12–13, where each of these is mentioned in an ascription of praise. The one to whom they are ascribed here is "our God" (Greek dative τῷ θεῷ ἡμῶν), and as is common in doxologies, he is said to possess these perfections not only in this situation but "forever and ever" (see comments at 1:6; 5:13).

7:13–14 And one of the elders replied, saying to me, "Who are these clothed in the white robes and where have they come from?" 14 And I said to him, "My lord, you know." And he said to me, "These are the ones who come out of the great tribulation and they have washed their robes and made them white in the blood of the Lamb" (Καὶ ἀπεκρίθη εἷς ἐκ τῶν πρεσβυτέρων λέγων μοι, Οὗτοι οἱ περιβεβλημένοι τὰς στολὰς τὰς λευκὰς τίνες εἰσὶν καὶ πόθεν ἦλθον; 14 καὶ εἴρηκα αὐτῷ, Κύριέ μου, σὺ οἶδας. καὶ εἶπέν μοι, Οὗτοί εἰσιν οἱ ἐρχόμενοι ἐκ τῆς θλίψεως τῆς μεγάλης καὶ ἔπλυναν

τὰς στολὰς αὐτῶν καὶ ἐλεύκαναν αὐτὰς ἐν τῷ αἵματι τοῦ ἀρνίου). Having described the participants in his heavenly vision and their interaction with one another (vv. 9–12), John now recounts his own engagement with one of the heavenly figures and the explanation that he received about the identity, origin, and destiny of this multitude (vv. 13–17).[65] As in 5:4–5, "one of the elders" responds[66] to the scene John has witnessed—as well as probably to John's unspoken bewilderment at it—by gently addressing him with questions that John himself was pondering (v. 13). The questions focus first on the "multitude" of people and their heavenly condition: "Who are these clothed in the white robes?"[67] The second question is added without delay: "Where have they come from?" (πόθεν ἦλθον).[68] Their varied national origins had been made clear (v. 9), but how did they come to be in the heavenly situation John has seen them in?

John perceives correctly that these questions were not due to the elder's uncertainty but his own, and so he politely defers to him to provide heavenly insight into what has been witnessed (v. 14a).[69] John's simple response[70] mirrors what Ezekiel said to God in a similar situation (Ezek 37:3, "Lord God, you know"). The elder's explanation continues to

---

65. As in 1:17; 5:4–5; 10:8–11; and elsewhere, John describes a vision that he did not merely witness from afar but one that he participated in directly. This is not uncommon in ancient apocalyptic literature, especially in conversations about the significance of what the seer witnesses in the vision (see note on v. 14a).

66. In 5:4–5 an elder responds to John's explicit dismay and grief at what he was witnessing ("I began to weep"). Here his perplexity is implicit.

67. In the Greek wording of this, the phrase "these clothed in the white robes" is put first for emphasis, followed by the interrogative words "who are they?" The wording is identical to v. 9e except that articles are added here to refer back to *the ones clothed* and to *the white robes* (both anarthrous in v. 9e).

68. On this use of the aorist for indefinite past action(s) viewed in summary, see the note on 3:8. The same action is described with a present tense of the same verb in v. 14, "the ones coming."

69. This is not quite identical but still very similar to the interaction between humans and a heavenly interpreter often seen in ancient apocalyptic literature. Having received a perplexing vision, the human turns to an angel or to the Lord for explanation of what he has just seen (e.g., 1 En. 18:13–16; 21:3–10; 25:1–5; 4 Ezra 10:29–57; cf. Dan 7:15–27; Zech 4:2, 4–6; Rev 17:6–8).

70. The phrase "I said" is expressed in Greek as a perfect tense verb (εἴρηκα), but the normal sense of the perfect (existing result of a prior act) simply does not fit this context. Since it is surrounded in the narrative by aorists (vv. 11b, 11c, 13a, 14b), this is clearly an example of a perfect coalescing in sense with the aorist, a phenomenon that increasingly occurred in late Hellenistic Greek. See Fanning, "Greek Tenses," 347–49, and the note on Rev 5:7 above.

the end of the chapter (Rev 7:14c–17). Where they have come from (cf. 13c) is "out of the great tribulation" (ἐκ τῆς θλίψεως τῆς μεγάλης; v. 14c), referring to the unprecedented period of end-time judgment whose beginning phase had just been portrayed in relation to the six seal openings (6:1–17). Jesus himself described the latter portion of it as an unparalleled "great tribulation" in Matthew 24:21 (θλῖψις μεγάλη), and John called it "the great day of their wrath," that is, of God and the Lamb (6:17), and "the hour of testing that is destined to come on the whole world" (3:10).[71] Some interpreters minimize these clear references to unprecedented end-time woes and understand even "the great tribulation" here to mean the difficulties that Christians are destined to encounter through the entire interadvent age. This "coming out of the great tribulation" in that view denotes simply the time of death when the faithful achieve spiritual victory over earthly woes and enter heaven's bliss.[72]

The most likely interpretation is that this "great tribulation" (v. 14) refers to the ultimate escalation of such troubles in the end-time, represented by John's three series of seven woes (chs. 6–16).[73] But even on this view the phrase "the ones who come from the great tribulation" does not specify exactly how they left such dire earthly circumstances behind and are now safe in heaven. Some understand this to denote a single act of deliverance in which Christians are taken to heaven before the worst outpourings of judgment.[74] This approach takes "the great tribulation" (coextensive also with "wrath" and "the day of the Lord") to designate only the cataclysmic judgments that come later in the (seven-year) tribulation or at the very end just prior to Christ's second coming to earth in severe judgment (Rev 19:10–21). It is better to take the phrase to mean various "exits" from the earthly scene due to repeated individual deaths (whether by martyrdom or natural death) during the entire

---

71. The parallel in Luke 21:23 calls it "great distress" (ἀνάγκη μεγάλη) and Mark 13:19 calls it "tribulation" (θλῖψις), using the same language about unprecedented trouble ("such as has not occurred from the beginning until now") as in Matt 24:21. Daniel 12:1 is the background for all of these references: a day of unprecedented "tribulation" (LXX θλῖψις). The phrase is used also in Herm. Vis. 2.2.7. These end-time woes were foreshadowed by a pattern of severe persecutions against Judah under Antiochus Epiphanes (cf. 1 Macc 9:27) that Daniel predicted (Dan 9:27; 11:31; 12:1, 11). The typological pattern of judgment was experienced also in the destruction of Jerusalem in AD 70.

72. Boxall, *Revelation*, 127; Caird, *Revelation*, 72, 102; Koester, *Revelation*, 421–22. Smalley, *Revelation*, 196, takes a middle position. See discussion of this issue in relation to typology of judgment at 2:22 (where the phrase "great tribulation" occurs also) and at 6:8.

73. Ladd, *Revelation*, 117–18; Mounce, *Revelation*, 164; Thomas, *Revelation 1–7*, 496–97 (who takes "the great tribulation" to be the final half of the intense end-time woes).

74. Hultberg, "Prewrath Rapture," 136–37; Luter and Hunter, "The 'Earth Dwellers,'" 9–13. In the latter essay (p. 13) much is made of the sequence indicated by the statement in Joel 2:31, "The sun will be turned into darkness and the moon to blood before the great and terrible day of the Lord comes."

Thus, according to Luter and Hunter (and others), the day of the Lord proper does not begin until sometime after the cosmic signs of 6:12–14; it cannot begin with the first seal judgment. But this fails to reckon with (1) the specific point that Joel is making in 2:31 in the sequence of his larger argument, and (2) the typological significance throughout the Bible of such theophanic signs taken from God's fearful presence at Sinai in Exod 19–20 (see Bauckham, *Climax*, 199–209). Joel traces two phases of the day of the Lord: a time of judgment for Israel, carried out by foreign nations acting as God's instrument, intended to lead her to repentance (Joel 1:15; 2:1, 11–17), followed by God's direct judgment on gentile nations who attack Israel and his merciful restoration of his people to enjoy peace and security in their land (Joel 2:28–3:17). While these phases are generally seen as a unity in the Bible, Joel 2:31 refers specifically to the second phase. See Craig Blaising, "A Pretribulation Response," in Hultberg, *Three Views on the Rapture*, 246–48; and Hans Walter Wolff, *Joel and Amos: A Commentary on the Books of the Prophets Joel and Amos*, Hermeneia (Philadelphia: Fortress, 1977), 54–70. It is a misunderstanding of Joel 2 to think that it describes the start of the entire day of the Lord complex.

seven-year period of great suffering and persecution of God's people.[75] In contrast to the 144,000 Jewish believers who are sealed and protected by God during this time (vv. 1–8), these Christians from various ethnic backgrounds fall victim to natural deaths or to martyrdom for their faith.[76] The Greek present tense participle (οἱ ἐρχόμενοι) used in the phrase "the ones who come out of the great tribulation" more naturally carries a distributive sense (repetition consisting of various individual acts viewed together; e.g., Rev 14:13, "the dead who die in the Lord").[77]

The final portion of v. 14 explains their "white robes" (cf. vv. 9, 13) in a bold metaphor that specifies the multitude's Christian identity. Their robes were "washed" and "made . . . white in the blood of the Lamb." John's image of washing garments as a symbol of religious consecration or sinful acts being "made white" perhaps was influenced by Old Testament examples (Exod 19:10, 14; Ps 51:7; Isa 1:18), but the paradox of cleansing "in blood"[78] comes from John's view that Christ's blood (i.e., sacrificial death) atoned for human sins (1:5; 5:9; cf. 22:14; Acts 15:9; Rom 3:25; Heb 9:14; 1 John 1:7).[79]

7:15 For this reason they are before God's throne and serve him day and night in his temple, and the one who sits on the throne will shelter them (διὰ τοῦτό εἰσιν ἐνώπιον τοῦ θρόνου τοῦ θεοῦ καὶ λατρεύουσιν αὐτῷ ἡμέρας καὶ νυκτὸς ἐν τῷ ναῷ αὐτοῦ, καὶ ὁ καθήμενος ἐπὶ τοῦ θρόνου σκηνώσει ἐπ᾽ αὐτούς). In addition to explaining the multitude's identity and origin (v. 14b–c), the elder describes further the privileges that they enjoy in God's very presence in heaven. With the introductory phrase "for this reason," he emphasizes that their presence "before God's throne" (cf. v. 9) and their worshipful service there (cf. vv. 10–11) is due to Christ's atoning work on their behalf.[80]

The picture of Christians finally victorious over earthly trials and joining with the whole angelic host in worship[81] that continues "day and night in [God's heavenly] temple" (here and in 5:8–14; 15:2–4) is a powerful and widespread popular conception of the blessed destiny of all Christians for all time. Coupled with the benefits the elder describes in vv. 15c–17, this forms an encouraging and wonderful prospect to place before Christians who are struggling with earthly trials (cf. Rom 8:18; 2 Cor 4:17–18).

But as valuable as this may be in some respects, we should ask further as we move through the next two-and-a-half verses: Who exactly is pictured

---

75. The fact that "no one could number" them (v. 9) does not necessitate that they include the saints of all the ages rather than only from the time of cataclysmic judgment just before Christ's return. "Innumerable" is not to be intended as a precise description in either case.

76. Aune, *Revelation 6–16*, 475, 480; Thomas, *Revelation 1–7*, 482. Because the martyrs of the fifth seal were given "white robes" (6:11), it is possible to take these "white-robed" people (7:9, 13–14) likewise to be exclusively Christians killed for their faith. But white garments are promised to all Christians (3:5, 18; cf. 19:8) and are more broadly the garments of heaven (19:14). They cannot be taken as the sign of a martyr's death.

77. Fanning, *Verbal Aspect*, 410–12. The aorist indicative used in v. 13 does not in itself indicate a single act of departure; it is most likely a summary of various indefinite past acts (see comment there). Both Aune, *Revelation 6–16*, 430, and Smalley, *Revelation*, 196, make a simple error of observation when they assert that the participle "coming" takes on a past temporal sense from the aorist verbs "washed" and "made . . . white" (ἔπλυναν, ἐλεύκαναν) in v. 14d–e. The verb "are" (εἰσιν) in v. 14c is the main verb that sets the temporal frame for the participle, and the aorists then add a recent past sense (see note on 6:17). The "coming" overlaps with their condition at the time the angel describes them to John: a multitude is present before God's throne already, and others will join them as time goes on.

78. This is an instrumental use of ἐν as in 1:5; 5:9.

79. It is possible that the idea of washing a robe "in blood" is an allusion to Gen 49:11, but the imagery is quite different there. See Fekkes, *Prophetic Traditions*, 167–69.

80. "For this reason" (διὰ τοῦτο) refers to the cleansing they received through Christ's blood (v. 14d–e).

81. The verb translated "serve" (λατρεύω) means to perform religious duties or rites, to worship (BDAG 587; LN §53.14; cf. Rev 22:3).

here, and when in their experience does this scene occur? Is it their final destiny or an intermediate stage? Is this an entirely accurate picture of the eternal destiny of all God's people? Will "heaven" be their eternal home, or will it be the new heaven and new earth, the New Jerusalem that comes down from heaven to earth (Rev 21:1–22:5)? One problematic element that appears here (and must be taken into account for vv. 15b–17) is the reference to this multitude worshiping "in his temple" (ἐν τῷ ναῷ αὐτοῦ). The heavenly "temple" of God is often referred to in Revelation (11:19; 14:15, 17; 15:5, 8; 16:1, 17), but 21:22 specifically records the absence of a temple in the eternal conditions of the New Jerusalem. It seems then that John sees them in an intermediate stage, enjoying the blessings of God in heaven but not yet in their resurrected state. The heavenly Jerusalem has not yet come down to earth as Revelation 21–22 portrays it. See further discussion of the verses that follow.

The last clause of v. 15 begins a series of heavenly blessings (vv. 15c–17) enjoyed by this multicultural body of Christians. The elder's words as reported by John portray these blessings as future (cf. six future indicative verbs in vv. 15c–17 plus a future-referring aorist subjunctive), but it seems best to take these as beginning already at the time of their appearance before God's throne (i.e., the present time of v. 15a–b), and running on from there to be finally consummated in the eternal New Jerusalem. First, they experience "shelter" (i.e., protection) from the sovereign Lord (v. 15c).[82] This protection

or "shelter" is phrased literally as "he will shelter over them" (σκηνώσει), using the verb "dwell, live" (σκηνόω), followed not by "with them" as in 21:3 (μετ᾽ αὐτῶν) or "among them" as in Ezek 37:27 (ἐν αὐτοῖς) or Zechariah 2:10 (LXX 2:14; ἐν μέσῳ σου)[83] but the prepositional phrase "over them" (ἐπ᾽ αὐτούς).[84] The verb σκηνόω (related to the noun "tent, shelter" [σκηνή]) often means "dwell, live" as in 21:3 (also 12:12; 13:6), but it can also reflect the sense of "spread a tent over to protect."[85] However, in this context, protection is closely related to the promise that he will live with or among his people (Ezek 37:27; Rev 21:3), so the expanded translation "will shelter them with his presence" (ESV, NIV, RSV) is certainly appropriate.[86]

7:16–17 They will not hunger any more nor will they be thirsty any more and the sun will never beat down on them nor any scorching heat, 17 because the Lamb in the center of the throne will shepherd them and he will guide them to springs of the waters of life. And God will wipe away every tear from their eyes (οὐ πεινάσουσιν ἔτι οὐδὲ διψήσουσιν ἔτι οὐδὲ μὴ πέσῃ ἐπ᾽ αὐτοὺς ὁ ἥλιος οὐδὲ πᾶν καῦμα, 17 ὅτι τὸ ἀρνίον τὸ ἀνὰ μέσον τοῦ θρόνου ποιμανεῖ αὐτοὺς καὶ ὁδηγήσει αὐτοὺς ἐπὶ ζωῆς πηγὰς ὑδάτων, καὶ ἐξαλείψει ὁ θεὸς πᾶν δάκρυον ἐκ τῶν ὀφθαλμῶν αὐτῶν). In words quoted almost verbatim from Isaiah 49:10[87] and from Isaiah 25:8 (supplemented by elements from Ps 23:1–3; Jer 2:13; and Ezek 34:24), the elder describes a series of further provisions God will make for this heavenly multitude of Christians

---

82. "The one who sits on the throne" as the ruler of all will protect them. This phrase is used six times in chs. 4–5; also in 6:16; 21:5. He is identified as "God" in 7:10; 19:4.

83. The KJV renders σκηνώσει ἐπ᾽ αὐτούς in Rev 7:15 as "shall dwell among them," but this is not quite the sense.

84. Cf. BDAG 363.

85. Cf. BDAG 363, 929.

86. Ezek 37:27 lies behind this verse as well as Rev 21:3 where God dwelling "with them" accompanies the assurance

as in Ezek that "they will be his people and he will be their God" (see also Zech 8:3, 8). Here, as commonly in the NT, God's promise to ethnic Israel is expanded to include gentiles as part of his future redeemed people but without retracting his promise to Israel.

87. This is one of the few clear instances of an OT *quotation* in Rev (OT allusions on the other hand are quite frequent). See Fekkes, *Prophetic Traditions*, 68–69, 170.

(vv. 16–17). Isaiah 49 declares how God's Servant will regather Jacob and make them a light for the nations (Isa 49:6). He will release those imprisoned in darkness (v. 9) and provide all that they need, just as a shepherd ensures that his sheep are well fed and protected from the elements (v. 10). The sense of never suffering from "hunger," "thirst," or the sun's "scorching heat"[88] in Revelation 7:16 refers, as in Isaiah 49, to God's abundant sustenance and protection of his redeemed. In their earthly troubles they suffered physical hunger, thirst, and lack of shelter, but such deficiencies will never threaten them again (note the repetition in v. 16 of the word "any more," ἔτι, added to the basic wording from Isa 49:10).

The reason (note "because"; causal ὅτι) they will never lack provision for such needs again is that Jesus Christ, the "Lamb" who shares with God in his sovereign rule over all creation,[89] will care for them as a shepherd does for his sheep (v. 17a–b). The shepherd imagery comes also from Isaiah 49:10, but instead of "the one who shows them compassion" as in Isaiah, the shepherd is here identified (from the grounding vision of chs. 4–5) as the Lamb, whose atoning death exemplified God's compassion (1:5; 5:9). His pastoral role is expressed using verbs perhaps drawn from Psalm 23:1–3 and Ezekiel 34:23: "He will shepherd" (ποιμανεῖ, to "tend, lead to pasture") and "he will guide" (ὁδηγήσει) as a good shepherd directs his sheep. But in this case, he leads them to "springs of the waters of life." "Springs of waters" comes from Isaiah 49:10, and "of life" (perhaps drawn from Jer 2:13) adds the spiritual, eternal nuance on top

of the physical, earthly image (cf. John 4:14; 10:28; 1 John 1:2; Rev 21:6; 22:1, 17).

The glorious picture from Isaiah 49 of how the Lamb will shepherd God's people and provide all that is needed even for eternal life suggests a further blessing pictured in Isaiah that Christ will fulfill for this multitude from all peoples (v. 17c). Isaiah 25:7–8 speaks of God abolishing death forever, the threat that casts a pall over all nations, and wiping away tears from every face. John sees that God has initiated through the Lamb the fulfillment of this promised blessing as well. For this multitude from the great tribulation, suffering of all kind is now over,[90] and God's eternal consolation is theirs.

The blessings that are said to be in store for these Christians (vv. 15c–17) raise the question of how to fit this scene into the sequence of events John presents in the course of his visions in Revelation. These benefits are unmistakably repeated in the vision of the New Jerusalem of chapters 21–22. God's sheltering "over them" (7:15c) or "with them" in the way that Ezekiel 37:27 portrays figures prominently in Revelation 21:3. God's provision of their every need, especially through "springs of the waters of life" as in Isaiah 49:10, appears along with other images of full provision "for the nations" in Revelation 21:6 and 22:1–2 (also the nations "serving" in the presence of God and the Lamb; 7:15b and 22:3–4). And God's abolition of death's curse and of all pain and grief in "wiping away every tear" as in Isaiah 25:8 comes up again in Revelation 21:4 and 22:3. Since these are all features of the New Jerusalem (21:1–22:5), it is easy to conclude that the vision of 7:9–17 places the multitude from every nation in the New Jerusalem already. The problem,

---

88. See the negative parallel in 16:8–9.

89. The phrase "in the center of the throne" (v. 17a; cf. BDAG 57) pictures his central position in God's throne room, symbolizing his share in God's rule. See comments on similar expressions in 4:6; 5:6.

90. To "wipe away every tear" is a metonymy for removing the causes of sorrow or grief of every kind, including death, and extending to all sorts of woes that plague fallen humanity. Note Paul's "groaning" in the midst of present sufferings in anticipation of God's final redemption for humans and for the whole creation (Rom 8:18–25).

however, as mentioned in comments on v. 15, is that the New Jerusalem will have no temple since the direct presence of God and the Lamb obviates the need for holy precincts in which to approach God (21:22). The presence of this multitude before God's heavenly throne, serving in his heavenly temple (7:15), shows that they are not yet in God's New Jerusalem (similar to the situation of those portrayed in 6:9–11), but are enjoying his presence nonetheless.[91] In their penultimate state they have begun to experience the rich provision that is to come when the final state of blessedness arrives.

Theology in Application

God Has Not Rejected His People

John's vision of protection from judgment for twelve thousand believers in Jesus from every tribe of ethnic Israel displays in a graphic way the truth of Paul's words, "God has not rejected his people" (Rom 11:1). Just as Paul declares that in the end times not just a remnant as now but Israel as a whole "will be saved" because "the gifts and the calling of God are irrevocable" (Rom 11:25, 29), so John gives a picture of God's faithfulness to his ancient people Israel in the final days before Christ's return. In terms that Jeremiah uses to affirm God's faithfulness to Israel, just as the fixed and reliable order of the times and seasons he established can be counted on to continue without fail (Jer 31:35–40), so his promises to Abraham and his descendants will certainly be fulfilled—Israel will never "cease to be a nation before [him] forever" (Jer 31:36). This example of God's constancy and mercy to uphold his promises to Israel (cf. Isa 54:4–10) should be a great reassurance to non-Jewish followers of Christ as well. We can all rely on God's promises of future salvation and blessing and be confident that their fulfillment is secured ultimately not by our fidelity to him but by his own purpose and grace displayed in Christ Jesus toward all those who believe in him (2 Tim 1:8–10).

Our Future, Our Present

The significant theological point that immediately complements God's faithfulness to Israel (Rev 7:1–8) is John's repeated emphasis on the multiethnic impact of God's redemption that begins with Israel but expands to include the whole world, his gracious salvation of people from "every nation and tribe and people and tongue" (7:9–17). But God's intent that people from every nation will know and worship him is not just a dream for the future. John's vision of an innumerable multitude from every nation is a reminder of the crosscultural mission that Jesus gave his followers at the very beginning, which continues until today (Matt 28:19–20; Luke 24:47; John

---

91. Wright, *Revelation for Everyone*, 75–76.

10:16; Acts 1:8). The gospel is not just for "people like us," but for all peoples across the earth. We are intended to share the blessings of forgiveness and communion with God and the Lamb before their throne forever (7:14–17; cf. 22:1–5). Our churches and their witness and outreach should model this multiethnic vision even now.

Revelation 8:1–13

Literary Context

After the significant pause in 7:1–17 from the first six seal openings (6:1–17), John now resumes the series of judgments described in chapters 6–16 with the seventh seal (8:1), which is shown to consist of seven trumpet judgments that run from 8:2 to 11:19. Compared to the seal judgments, the seven trumpets display more explicit parallels with the plagues on Egypt (Exod 7–12). Like those plagues, the trumpets will visit judgment against the oppressive world powers opposed to God and his people. Just as with the seals, the trumpets are grouped in units of four and then three, with the final three announced with additional solemnity as three "woes" directed against the world's inhabitants (8:13; 9:12; 11:14). This motif helps to hold the narrative of the trumpets together despite the lengthy accounts of the fifth (9:1–12) and sixth (9:13–21) trumpets and then further interludes (10:1–11:14) prior to the seventh trumpet (11:15–19).

Main Idea

After a period of heaven's silent attention to the prayers of God's people, seven angels prepare themselves and pour out fiery and destructive judgment onto the earth in connection with the sounding of the first four trumpets.

Translation

Revelation 8:1–13

1a	Action/7ᵗʰ Seal Opening	And	when he opened the seventh seal,
b	Event		**there came to be silence in heaven for something like half an hour.**
2a	Character Entrance	**And**	**I saw the seven angels who stand before God,**
b	Action	**and**	**seven trumpets were given to them.**
3a	Character Entrance	**And**	**another angel came and stood at the altar,**
b	Description		having a golden censer,
c	Action	**and**	**a great quantity of incense was given to him**
d	Purpose		to offer with the prayers of all the saints on the golden altar
e	Description		that was before the throne.
4	Action/Effect	**And**	**the smoke of the incense, with the prayers of the saints, went up before God from the hand of the angel.**
5a	Actions	**And**	**the angel took the censer**
b		**and**	**filled it from the fire of the altar**
c		**and**	**threw it onto the earth,**
d	Effects	**and**	**there came peals of thunder and rumblings and flashes of lightning and an earthquake.**
6	Action/Preview	**And**	**the seven angels who had the seven trumpets prepared themselves to sound them.**
7a	Action/1ˢᵗ Trumpet	**And**	**the first angel sounded his trumpet,**
b	Action	**and**	**there came hail and fire mixed with blood,**
c	Action	**and**	**it was thrown onto the earth,**
d	Effects	**and**	**a third of the earth was burned up,**
e		**and**	**a third of the trees were burned up,**
f		**and**	**all the green grass was burned up.**

Continued on next page.

Continued from previous page.

8a	Action/2nd Trumpet	**And the second angel sounded his trumpet,**
b	Action	**and something like a great mountain burning with fire was thrown into the sea,**
c	Effects	**and a third of the sea became blood,**
9a		**and a third of the living creatures in the sea died,**
b		**and a third of the ships were destroyed.**

10a	Action/3rd Trumpet	**And the third angel sounded his trumpet,**
b	Actions	**and a great star burning like a torch fell from heaven,**
c		**and it fell on a third of the rivers and on the springs of water,**
11a	Description	**and the name of the star was called "Wormwood,"**
b	Effects	**and a third of the waters became wormwood**
c		**and many people died from the water**
d	Reason	because it became poisonous.

12a	Action/4th Trumpet	**And the fourth angel sounded his trumpet,**
b	Action	**and a third of the sun and a third of the moon and a third of the stars were struck,**
c	Effects	so that a third of them was darkened and
d		the day did not shine for a third of it, and
e		the night likewise.

13a	Action/Preview	**And I looked, and I heard an eagle** flying high in the sky,
b		saying in a loud voice,
c	Announcement	*"Woe, woe, woe to those who live on the earth*
d	Reason	*because of the remaining trumpet blasts*

that the three angels are about to sound."

Structure

The account of the seventh seal (8:1ff.) begins in much the same way as the previous six (cf. 6:1–7) but is quickly diverted to a different course. Prior to the actual events that the seventh seal represents (i.e., the trumpets), several angels attend to the incense altar in heaven, and there is silence in heaven to give attention to the prayers of God's faithful people on earth (vv. 2–5). Then the first four trumpets are narrated rather briefly in numbered order (vv. 6–12). The last verse previews the final three trumpets, describing them as three woes that are about to fall on the earth's inhabitants (v. 13).

Exegetical Outline

III. Second Vision: Heavenly Throne Room and Three Judgment Cycles (4:1–16:21)

    A. Vision of God in His Heavenly Throne Room (4:1–11)

    B. The Seven-Sealed Scroll and the Slain Lamb (5:1–14)

    C. The Seven Seals and the Interlude of the Two Multitudes (6:1–8:1)

        1. The First Six Seals (6:1–17)

        2. The Interlude of the Two Multitudes (7:1–17)

➡   **3. The Seventh Seal (8:1)**

    D. The Seven Trumpets and Further Interludes (8:2–14:20)

        1. The First Four Trumpets (8:2–13)

            a. The seventh seal: seven trumpets and the saints' prayers in heaven (8:1–5)

                (1) The seventh seal and silence in heaven (8:1)

                (2) Seven angels receive seven trumpets (8:2)

                (3) The saints' prayers in heaven and omens of judgment on earth (8:3–5)

            b. Four trumpets (8:6–12)

                (1) The first trumpet: fiery hail burns the earth, trees, and grasslands (8:6–7)

                (2) The second trumpet: fiery destruction on the sea and its creatures (8:8–9)

                (3) The third trumpet: fiery poisoning of rivers and springs of water (8:10–11)

                (4) The fourth trumpet: partial darkening of sun, moon, and stars (8:12)

            c. Announcement of the three woes of the remaining three trumpets (8:13)

Explanation of the Text

8:1–2 And when he opened the seventh seal, there came to be silence in heaven for something like half an hour. 2 And I saw the seven angels who stand before God, and seven trumpets were given to them (Καὶ ὅταν ἤνοιξεν τὴν σφραγῖδα τὴν ἑβδόμην, ἐγένετο σιγὴ ἐν τῷ οὐρανῷ ὡς ἡμίωρον. 2 καὶ εἶδον τοὺς ἑπτὰ ἀγγέλους οἳ ἐνώπιον τοῦ θεοῦ ἑστήκασιν, καὶ ἐδόθησαν αὐτοῖς ἑπτὰ σάλπιγγες). The series of seal openings resumes here after the intervening two visions of chapter 7, but without the immediate action or further vision that follows each of the first six seals in the previous chapter (see comments at the end of v. 2 about the significance of this inaction). The introductory form is initially quite similar (see "when he opened the ___ seal [with an ordinal number]"),[1] but the period of "silence in heaven" that follows is unique (v. 1b). The absence of noise was not characteristic of any of the seals of chapter 6 or of John's visions in chapters 4, 5, or 7. Coming here in the seventh seal, it certainly carries an unexpected and dramatic effect, and like the interlude of chapter 7 it increases the narrative tension by postponing yet further the cataclysm of judgment that seems imminent in the story.

---

1. A minor variation is the use of a slightly different word for "when" (ὅταν instead of ὅτε), but the two seem synonymous in this context, signaling a definite time as in 6:1, 3, 5, 7, 9, 12 (BDAG 731; BDF §382.4). Several solid manuscripts have ὅτε as a variant (ℵ, P), but ὅταν is the reading of other good manuscripts (A, C), and scribes would more likely have changed to ὅτε for consistency with ch. 6.

Yet is there a further significance for this "silence" beyond the literary effect, and does it help us to understand these verses more clearly? Interpreters have offered three suggestions that seem most viable. First, silence may be associated with God's judgment, and so this portends the intensified judgments that are about to come.[2] This certainly fits the context of Revelation 8:1, but it does not seem to be the actual point of the Old Testament and other Jewish texts that are cited to support this idea. People are silent in Sheol after God's judgment (Pss 6:5; 115:17; Isa 38:18), and humans can offer no defense and so are silent before the divine judge (Exod 14:14; Isa 23:2; 41:1; 47:5; Lam 2:10; Amos 8:2–3; Zeph 1:7; Zech 2:13), but this is not the same as "silence in heaven." Second, some apocalyptic texts connect the primeval silence and inactivity prior to God's first creation with a repetition of such silence prior to his re-creation of the universe in the end-times (4 Ezra 6:39; 7:30–31; 2 Bar 3:7). This makes some sense, but it seems to come too late in the sequence of visions (why not prior to the seals if the idea is "destructive chaos and then re-creation"?[3]) or too early (why here seemingly in the middle of the destruction and not closer to the visions of renewal in chs. 20–22?). Third, this silence may be associated with Jewish traditions about incense offering in the heavenly temple as the time when the angels of heaven fall silent and God gives special attention to the prayers of his people on earth.[4] These traditions are found in various rabbinic works as well as in *Testament of Adam* 1:12 and can be traced back to before AD 70.[5] The silence is not due to God's inability to hear human prayers while angelic worship is going on[6] but represents instead his attentiveness to his people who cry out to him in prayer. This view fits more naturally into the context of this prelude to the trumpet judgments, since Revelation 8:3–5 connect the judgments to the heavenly incense offering as well as the prayers of the saints (see comments on vv. 3–5).[7]

The period of silence is brief (v. 1b) but adequate to allow for the events in vv. 2–5 to occur before the outpouring of judgment begins under the seven trumpets (vv. 6ff.). The significance of "something like half an hour" is likely to be more nearly literal (a brief but adequate time) and not completely figurative, as is sometimes suggested.[8] John uses "hour" like many writers to mean a period of time that may be either quite lengthy or more literal (e.g., 3:10, "the hour of testing"; 9:15, "prepared for the hour, day, month, and year"; 11:13, "and in that hour").[9] To divide this in half simply denotes a brief period, but enough time for the events specified to occur.[10]

---

2. Beale, *Revelation*, 446–53.

3. This is what Sweet, *Revelation*, 159, implies.

4. Charles, *Revelation*, 1:223–24 (a version of this view), followed by Beasley-Murray, *Revelation*, 150–51, and Caird, *Revelation*, 106–7. See Bauckham, *Climax*, 70–83, for a more detailed and revised presentation of this view.

5. See Bauckham, *Climax*, 71–81. See also Luke 1:10.

6. An objection raised by Aune, *Revelation 6–16*, 507; Smalley, *Revelation*, 211.

7. It also incorporates some of the dimensions of the view that liturgical practice demands silence before God in preparation for prayer and worship (Aune, *Revelation 6–16*, 507–8; Smalley, *Revelation*, 212). This view on its own does not explain why the previous worship scenes in Rev were so noisy or why human prayers require silence in heaven.

8. Resseguie, *Narrative Commentary*, 142 (cf. also 30–31), cites Lupieri to the effect that "half" a number in Rev denotes a "fractured period," an interruption or breaking of a complete event. Thus, whatever the related number symbolizes, a half represents an imperfect or disrupted form of that. Since "hour" refers in Rev to the time of "momentous events" (e.g., 11:13; 14:7, 15), half an hour must signal "the interruption of a complete, finalized event"; thus, according to Resseguie it signals here a delay in the sequence of action leading to the end. This seems to be an unduly complicated pathway to reach essentially the same result as a literal reading.

9. See BDAG 1102–3; LN §§67.1, 42, 148, 199.

10. The sense of "something like" (ὡς) is not quite the normal use of ὡς with a numeral (i.e., "about, approximately"; BDAG 1105), but reflects John's common resort to analogy in

Verse 2 begins to set the stage for the events that will occur when this brief pause is complete, especially the trumpet judgments that begin in v. 6. In his vision John "saw" (εἶδον; used 14x in chs. 4–7) "seven angels" standing ready to serve God,[11] whom John assumes were familiar to his readers since he uses the article: "*The* seven angels."[12] Jewish tradition at the time of the New Testament knew of seven archangels (cf. Tob 12:15; 4 Ezra 4:36; they are all named in 1 En. 20:1–8), two of whom are named in the Old Testament or New Testament (Gabriel; Michael).[13] Perhaps it is these seven who are in view here. The mission of divine judgment that will follow is important enough to be entrusted to God's chief angels.[14]

An important structural issue is raised by the lack of specific judgment associated with the seventh seal. There appears to be a close relationship between the seventh seal of v. 1 and the seven trumpets introduced in v. 2, suggesting that the seven trumpets constitute the actual content of the seventh seal. A similar telescoping or nesting together of the series of judgments is likely also in 11:15 where the seventh trumpet has no separate content but consists of the seven bowls that come in chapters 15–16. The effect of this telescoping

at the end of the series of sevens is that each of the series actually brings us to the verge of the consummation of judgment, but the ultimate cataclysm is then delayed by a further unpacking of the final details.[15]

To set the stage more specifically for vv. 6–12, John records in summary the seven angels' reception[16] of "seven trumpets" (v. 2b). Trumpets in the biblical tradition are used to herald various momentous events,[17] but in this context they signal end-time destruction and judgment often associated with the day of the Lord (e.g., Isa 58:1; Joel 2:1–2; Zeph 1:14–16; Zech 9:14–15).[18] Their connection with devastating judgment is a possible allusion to God's victory at Jericho so long ago (Josh 6:13). When the angels blow their trumpets, starting in v. 7, devastating judgments will follow. Before this occurs, however, and during the short period of silence in heaven, another angel intervenes in ways that foreshadow what the trumpets will signal (vv. 3–5).

8:3–4 And another angel came and stood at the altar, having a golden censer, and a great quantity of incense was given to him to offer with the prayers of all the saints on the golden altar that

---

describing a bewildering vision in human language (e.g., "as" or "like" in 1:10–16; 4:1–6). This is not an exact time, but how it seemed to John as he witnessed the vision.

11. They "stand before God" in his throne room (ἑστήκασιν, a perfect that carries a present stative sense, here used of their customary, characteristic position), ready to serve at his beck and call.

12. The article could refer back to the angels of the seven churches (1:20ff.) or the seven spirits who likewise are "before the throne" (1:4; cf. 4:5; 5:6), but both of these groups are too far back in the text to make this reference clear, and the seven spirits should be understood not as angels but as a description of the fullness of the Holy Spirit (see notes on 1:4; 4:5; 5:6). This article is not anaphoric but "well-known" (cf. Wallace, *Grammar*, 225), i.e., a feature of general cultural knowledge rather than something cited earlier in the text itself.

13. See Smalley, *Revelation*, 213–14, and Swete, *Apocalypse*, 105, for more detail about the Jewish background.

14. The "seven angels" introduced without an article in 15:1 (who will pour out the bowls of judgment) have a similar function, but are apparently not identical to these archangels. The angels of the seven bowls or "last plagues" are referred to with anaphoric articles and identified specifically with the bowls in six subsequent verses (15:6, 7, 8; 16:1; 17:1; 21:9).

15. For further discussion of how the seals, trumpets, and bowls relate to one another, see "Structure and Outline" in the commentary's introduction.

16. The verb phrase "were given" is a Greek aorist passive (ἐδόθη), quickly recounting the action as a whole, with the passive implying God as the agent who equips them in this way.

17. See G. Friedrich, "σάλπιγξ," *TDNT* 7:76–88; *NIDNTTE* 4:235–36.

18. None of these seven, however, corresponds specifically with the trumpets mentioned in Matt 24:31; 1 Cor 15:52; or 1 Thess 4:16.

**was before the throne. 4 And the smoke of the
incense, with the prayers of the saints, went up
before God from the hand of the angel** (Καὶ ἄλλος
ἄγγελος ἦλθεν καὶ ἐστάθη ἐπὶ τοῦ θυσιαστηρίου
ἔχων λιβανωτὸν χρυσοῦν, καὶ ἐδόθη αὐτῷ θυμιάματα
πολλά, ἵνα δώσει ταῖς προσευχαῖς τῶν ἁγίων πάντων
ἐπὶ τὸ θυσιαστήριον τὸ χρυσοῦν τὸ ἐνώπιον τοῦ
θρόνου. 4 καὶ ἀνέβη ὁ καπνὸς τῶν θυμιαμάτων
ταῖς προσευχαῖς τῶν ἁγίων ἐκ χειρὸς τοῦ ἀγγέλου
ἐνώπιον τοῦ θεοῦ). These verses provide some
confirmation that heaven was silent so that God
could focus on the prayers of his people (see comments on v. 1). Here John narrates certain events
occurring in heaven during the period of silence
that postpone the sounds of the seven trumpets just
mentioned. The events occur in rapid sequence:
"another angel" different from the seven of v. 2
approaches and stands at the "altar" (v. 3a).[19] As
in Isaiah's vision (Isa 6:1, 6), John's visions reveal a
throne room in heaven that serves also as a temple
with an altar. The altar mentioned here corresponds
to the altar of incense inside the earthly tabernacle
or temple (see note at 6:9 for discussion). So the
"altar" at the beginning of v. 3 is the same as the
"golden altar" at the end of the verse (cf. Exod
37:25–26; 1 Kgs 7:48), whose location "before the
throne" corresponds to the earthly altar of incense
"before the ark" (Exod 40:5) or "before the Lord"
(Lev 4:7). The angel is poised to carry out the ritual

of incense offering (cf. Exod 30:7–8; Lev 16:12–13;
Luke 1:9–10; m. Tamid 5–6) because he has with
him "a golden censer" (λιβανωτὸν χρυσοῦν)[20] or
fire pan (Exod 27:3; 1 Kgs 7:50) in which to carry
coals to the altar of incense to make the offering
(Rev 8:3b).

John adds the detail (v. 3c) "a great quantity of
incense was given to him" (by God or by an assist-
ing angel). This was for offering it[21] by sprinkling it
on the fiery coals the angel would place on the altar
of incense (v. 3d). An additional striking image is
that the incense would be offered "with the prayers
of all the saints" (cf. 5:8),[22] symbolizing the prayers
of God's people[23] presented as an act of worship
"before his throne." The fact that these prayers are
from "all" of God's people nicely reinforces the
detail in the preceding clause that the angel was
given "a great quantity of incense." It also indicates
that the prayers come from a wider group than
the martyrs described in 6:9–11, a natural but not
exact parallel to this passage. Judging from how the
events of vv. 3–6 flow together, however, it seems
correct to understand these as prayers for relief and
vindication similar to those of 6:10.[24] In various
places Revelation alludes to the suffering of the
righteous at the hands of God's enemies (13:7; 16:6;
17:6; 18:24; 20:9), so this is not foreign to the content of the book. God's people throughout history
have cried out to him for deliverance and justice

---

19. Because of his duties connected with the heavenly altar's coals of fire (vv. 3–5), this is possibly the "angel who had
authority over the fire" mentioned in 14:18.

20. This Greek word, not used in this sense in the LXX or
other ancient Greek texts known to us, usually means "(frank)
incense" (see a related word in 18:13; Matt 2:11), but with
the adjective "golden" is clearly used here by association for
"censer," a vessel used to carry coals on which incense could
be burned. See BDAG 594; W. Michaelis, "λιβανωτός," *TDNT*
4:264; *NewDocs* 4:129.

21. The English infinitive "to offer" translates a Greek ἵνα-
clause (ἵνα δώσει), indicating purpose. See the note at 3:9 for
this use of ἵνα with the future indicative and of the occurrence

of a ἵνα-clause where another writer would have used a Greek
infinitive.

22. A dative of association in Greek. This symbolism is
expressed as a direct metaphor in 5:8, "incense(s) which are
the prayers of the saints" (see comments there).

23. On "the saints," i.e., "the holy ones" (οἱ ἅγιοι), as God's
people, see the note at 5:8.

24. See this theme also in 1 En. 47:1–2; 99:3. The cries of
the Israelite slaves in Egypt (Exod 2:23–25; 3:7–9; Neh 9:9–11;
Ps 106:44–45), which God answers by means of the ten plagues
and the exodus, had perhaps the greatest influence on John's
imagery here.

amid opposition from a fallen world (e.g., Gen 4:10; Deut 32:43; 2 Kgs 9:7; Ps 79:10; Matt 23:35), and here in John's vision of the trumpet judgments God's sure answer is about to be disclosed.

The angel fulfills the first part of his service in the heavenly temple (i.e., offering incense on the altar, v. 3d), as indicated by "the smoke of the incense" rising as a sweet aroma "before God" (v. 4).[25] The picture of the smoke floating up from the altar suggests how human prayers could be associated symbolically with the incense, as Psalm 141:2 also reflects: "May my prayer be counted as incense before you" (cf. also the image of "lifting up" prayer to God; e.g., 2 Kgs 19:4; Isa 37:4; Jer 7:16; 11:14). This association of the saints' prayers with incense is repeated here for emphasis as a preparation for what will happen next (v. 5).

8:5 And the angel took the censer and filled it from the fire of the altar and threw it onto the earth, and there came peals of thunder and rumblings and flashes of lightning and an earthquake (καὶ εἴληφεν ὁ ἄγγελος τὸν λιβανωτὸν καὶ ἐγέμισεν αὐτὸν ἐκ τοῦ πυρὸς τοῦ θυσιαστηρίου καὶ ἔβαλεν εἰς τὴν γῆν, καὶ ἐγένοντο βρονταὶ καὶ φωναὶ καὶ ἀστραπαὶ καὶ σεισμός). In dramatic and unexpected fashion, the angel follows his act of worship with a gesture of judgment that foreshadows the outpouring of punishment on the earth accompanying the seven trumpets that follow. In particular, the angel's action of "throwing fire" from the heavenly altar anticipates the character of the first four trumpet judgments especially: they visit destruction on earth but originate directly from heaven.[26] His three

rapid actions in the heavenly throne room ("took," "filled," "threw"; v. 5a–c)[27] are followed by omens of God's appearance to judge the whole cosmos (v. 5d). When the angel took up his censer again, filled it with fire from the heavenly altar, and threw the coals of fire onto the earth, he was following a pattern of judgment seen earlier in Ezekiel 10 (a passage that significantly influenced John's vision of heaven at Rev 4:6–8). In Ezekiel 10:2–7 an angel is commanded to pour out on Jerusalem coals of fire from the heavenly throne room as a judgment for her sins (a portent that had its earthly fulfillment when Nebuchadnezzar destroyed the city soon after). Notable expressions of the same pattern of judgment occurred when God "rained sulfur and fire from heaven" on Sodom and Gomorrah (Gen 19:24) and when he visited "hail and fire" from heaven on Egypt in the seventh plague (Exod 9:23–24; cf. Ps 18:10–14; 2 Kgs 1:10–14). This pattern will be intensified in the judgments of the first three trumpets (Rev 8:7–10).

The ominous portents of v. 5d look backward and forward in Revelation, from the grounding throne vision of chapters 4–5 (cf. 4:5) to the culmination of the trumpet judgments (11:19) as well as the bowl judgments (16:18–21). As discussed at 4:5 the phenomena of "peals of thunder and rumblings and flashes of lightning" represent God's awesome presence as experienced by Israel at Sinai (Exod 19:16–19), but when they are replicated here at 8:5 (and in ever-expanding form in 11:19 and 16:18–21) with the addition of "an earthquake," they portend God's judgment on the whole universe.[28]

---

25. Mention of the smoke going up "from the hand of the angel" is a subtle touch that shows he has carried out his assigned duty in the ritual. This, together with the note that he had "a great quantity of incense" (v. 3c), may also be a reminder that it was customary to offer "handfuls" of incense (Lev 16:12), not just a pinch or two.

26. Roloff, *Revelation*, 109–10; Smalley, *Revelation*, 216–17.

27. In Greek these verbs are one perfect followed by two

aorists. The aorists fit the typical tense sequence that John uses when he narrates his visions (see note on 6:1). In this context the perfect verb "he took" (εἴληφεν) almost certainly carries simply an aoristic sense rather than the normal perfect meaning (see examples of this at 5:7 and 7:14).

28. See Bauckham, *Climax*, 202–4, and comments above at 4:5.

The theophany at Sinai included the "trembling" of the mountain (Exod 19:18 MT) as well as the other features of a colossal thunderstorm, but the later Old Testament saw these phenomena as a pattern of judgment that would be repeated in the future in more intense and widespread visitations of judgment—on all the nations and on the wider heavens and earth (Judg 5:4–5; Pss 18:7–15; 68:7–8; 77:18; Isa 13:13; 29:6; 64:2–4; Jer 10:10; Hag 2:6–7, 21).

8:6–7 And the seven angels who had the seven trumpets prepared themselves to sound them. 7 And the first angel sounded his trumpet, and there came hail and fire mixed with blood, and it was thrown onto the earth, and a third of the earth was burned up, and a third of the trees were burned up, and all the green grass was burned up (Καὶ οἱ ἑπτὰ ἄγγελοι οἱ ἔχοντες τὰς ἑπτὰ σάλπιγγας ἡτοίμασαν αὐτοὺς ἵνα σαλπίσωσιν. 7 Καὶ ὁ πρῶτος ἐσάλπισεν· καὶ ἐγένετο χάλαζα καὶ πῦρ μεμιγμένα ἐν αἵματι καὶ ἐβλήθη εἰς τὴν γῆν, καὶ τὸ τρίτον τῆς γῆς κατεκάη καὶ τὸ τρίτον τῶν δένδρων κατεκάη καὶ πᾶς χόρτος χλωρὸς κατεκάη). Resuming the scene from v. 2 after the intervening events of vv. 3–5, v. 6 sets the stage again for the series of seven trumpet judgments.[29] Once again we see "the seven angels," and here "the seven trumpets" carries an anaphoric article (referring back to v. 2 where the phrase was anarthrous to introduce them to the scene). But the activity of this verse is purely anticipatory: they "prepare themselves"[30] for what will come next, the

actual sounding of the first four trumpets one by one in vv. 7–12.

The seven trumpets that follow are clustered in two groups, just as the seals were: the first four (vv. 7–12) and then the final three (v. 13ff.). The first four trumpets affect primarily the natural world (earth, sea, fresh water, sky), albeit with substantial collateral effects on humans (cf. vv. 7, 9, 11), while the final three target humans specifically. The final three are enumerated also as three "woes" that are formally announced in sequence (8:13; 9:12; 11:14). Just as with the seals, the seventh trumpet heralds an effect different from the other six (11:15–19).

Verse 7 begins the ordered sequence of the first four trumpets by recounting simply, "the first angel sounded his trumpet."[31] The trumpet blast signals the onslaught of a preternatural barrage of "hail and fire mixed with blood" that was "thrown onto the earth." This judgment follows the pattern of the punishment of Sodom and Gomorrah (Gen 19:24, fire and sulfur), the seventh plague on Egypt (Exod 9:23–24, hail and fire), and Ezekiel's visions of Jerusalem's destruction (Ezek 10:2, fire) and of God's defeat of Gog and Magog (Ezek 38:22, pestilence, blood, hail, fire, sulfur).[32] The earlier Old Testament judgments from God were destructive but localized. The pattern will be intensified in this end-time replication by being more widespread, as the final clauses of v. 7 indicate (one-third of the earth, trees, all the grass).[33] This proportion

---

29. John recounts this as simply the next step in the unfolding narrative (cf. the aorist verb of v. 6, "prepared" [ἡτοίμασαν], like the predominant aorists of vv. 1–5), but it clearly resumes the line of thematic development from v. 2.

30. The pronoun "themselves" (αὐτούς [SBLGNT] or αὑτούς [above and NA²⁸]) could possibly be read as "them" (i.e., the trumpets), but the gender should be feminine (αὐτάς) for that sense. But forms of the personal pronoun αὐτός often serve in the NT for the reflexive sense (like forms of ἑαυτοῦ). Another way of analyzing this is to say that αὐτούς is a contraction of ἑαυτούς, and editors may choose to spell out the contraction or not (cf. BDAG 268–69; BDF §64.1).

31. The first seal opening was phrased as "one [μίαν] of the seven seals" (6:1), but with the trumpets John uses ordinal numerals from the start.

32. On this typology of judgment, especially related to the Egyptian plagues, see the comments on v. 5 and the wider discussion in the commentary introduction ("Use of the Old Testament: Prophecy and Typology"). See also Irenaeus, *Haer.* 4.30.2, who observes that the woes of Rev against all the nations follow the typology of the plagues against Egypt at the exodus.

33. Note here the pattern of threes that John incorporates into the effects of the trumpet judgments (also in 8:12, 13; 9:4, 17–18). Cf. Resseguie, *Narrative Commentary*, 144.

perhaps mirrors Old Testament prophetic models as well,[34] and while it represents an escalation over the "one-fourth" of the earth affected by the fourth seal (6:8), it is nonetheless an indication that the final, greatest cataclysm is still to come (e.g., 16:3). The verb phrase "burned up" (κατεκάη) used three times in the final clause of v. 7 carries the strong sense of "consume by fire, destroy by burning,"[35] and the Old Testament parallels cited earlier (Sodom and Gomorrah, Jerusalem) make it difficult to minimize the catastrophic damage described in this verse. The burning of "all the green grass" adds to the severity of this blow to the earth and its inhabitants.[36]

8:8–9 And the second angel sounded his trumpet, and something like a great mountain burning with fire was thrown into the sea, and a third of the sea became blood, 9 and a third of the living creatures in the sea died, and a third of the ships were destroyed (Καὶ ὁ δεύτερος ἄγγελος ἐσάλπισεν· καὶ ὡς ὄρος μέγα πυρὶ καιόμενον ἐβλήθη εἰς τὴν θάλασσαν, καὶ ἐγένετο τὸ τρίτον τῆς θαλάσσης αἷμα 9 καὶ ἀπέθανεν τὸ τρίτον τῶν κτισμάτων τῶν ἐν τῇ θαλάσσῃ τὰ ἔχοντα ψυχάς καὶ τὸ τρίτον τῶν πλοίων διεφθάρησαν). Moving quickly through these first four trumpet judgments, John takes up the second (vv. 8–9), whose destructive effects focus on the sea rather than the earth (cf. vv. 6–7). The image of "a great mountain burning with fire" that is cast "into the sea" (v. 8b)[37] is likely drawn from a variety of sources, including apocalyptic metaphors (e.g., 1 En. 18:13–14, angels in heaven that appear like

"great burning mountains"; cf. 1 En. 21:3; 108:4) as well as perhaps the eruption of Thera (Santorini) in AD 46/47 or of Vesuvius in AD 79. In biblical material Babylon is seen as a fiery "destroying mountain" that will in turn be destroyed (Jer 51:24–26, 63–64; God uses it to judge Judah, but pledges to judge it as well), and "mountain" in itself can symbolize a kingdom or empire (Dan 2:35, 45). It does seem that this judgment, which so drastically affects the sea and its commerce (fishing, ship-born trade, etc.), foreshadows the destruction of "Babylon" and its commercial empire as described in chapters 17–18 (especially 18:21). It would be a mistake, however, to take this resonance with chapters 17–18 as the sole symbolic significance of this judgment (i.e., evil commercial empires suffering collapse at various times in history). The pattern of judgments like those that fell on Egypt—but in the end-times escalated to extreme and cosmic proportions—strongly suggests that the trumpet judgments will be supernatural plagues from God that have horrific natural effects.

The parallel with the plagues on Egypt is picked up in vv. 8c–9b as John begins to cite the effects[38] of the preternatural phenomenon just described. The water of the sea becoming "blood" mirrors the first plague where the waters of the Nile (as well as in pools, ponds, and storage vessels across Egypt) became blood (Exod 7:14–25; Ps 78:43–44). As in v. 7d–e the proportion of the sea affected is "a third," an immense but limited amount. This then leads to further effects related to sea creatures ("a third . . .

---

34. Cf. Ezek 5:1–2, 12 and Zech 13:8–9, although in the former text the "one-thirds" add up to encompass the whole city of Jerusalem that suffers judgment in some way. Cf. also Sib. Or. 3.544 (only a third survives).

35. BDAG 517; LN §14.66; e.g., Acts 19:19; Heb 13:11 (cf. Exod 29:14, 34).

36. Reference to burning of trees and grass perhaps comes from the parallel in Gen 19:25 that "what grew from the ground" was burned up. In Rev 9:4 some recovery prior to

the fifth trumpet is indicated, but the grim results of this first trumpet are clear.

37. John resorts to his use of "something like" (ὡς) to present what is virtually indescribable in normal human terms (see note on v. 1).

38. The "and" (καί) that begins the last clause of v. 8 carries the sense of result: "and so" (see 2:23; 5:4; BDAG 495).

died")[39] and sea trade ("a third of the ships were destroyed").[40] Later we see that the second bowl judgment (16:3) increases the severity by turning "the sea," presumably all of it, to blood and causing the death of "every living creature" in the sea.

8:10–11 And the third angel sounded his trumpet, and a great star burning like a torch fell from heaven, and it fell on a third of the rivers and on the springs of water, 11 and the name of the star was called "Wormwood," and a third of the waters became wormwood and many people died from the water because it became poisonous (Καὶ ὁ τρίτος ἄγγελος ἐσάλπισεν· καὶ ἔπεσεν ἐκ τοῦ οὐρανοῦ ἀστὴρ μέγας καιόμενος ὡς λαμπάς καὶ ἔπεσεν ἐπὶ τὸ τρίτον τῶν ποταμῶν καὶ ἐπὶ τὰς πηγὰς τῶν ὑδάτων, 11 καὶ τὸ ὄνομα τοῦ ἀστέρος λέγεται ὁ Ἄψινθος, καὶ ἐγένετο τὸ τρίτον τῶν ὑδάτων εἰς ἄψινθον καὶ πολλοὶ τῶν ἀνθρώπων ἀπέθανον ἐκ τῶν ὑδάτων ὅτι ἐπικράνθησαν). The third trumpet judgment mirrors the second quite closely (a large heavenly object hurled into earthly waters) and fills out the pattern of the first plague on Egypt (not the sea but fresh water sources affected). In this case the object is not a great fiery mountain but a similar "great star burning like a torch" (v. 10b). Here the verb "fall" is used instead of "throw" as in vv. 5, 7, 8, but the accompanying phrases in this context ("were thrown onto" the earth or sea versus "fell from heaven") imply almost no difference in meaning for the larger expressions. With both verbs the point is that destruction on earth originates in heaven (see note on v. 5).

In Revelation a "star" can represent an angelic figure (e.g., 1:20; 9:1) and "a great star" falling to earth could be related to Satan's rebellion (Luke 10:18; Rev 12:9). But these seem quite foreign to this context. The parallel with vv. 8–9 (and with v. 7) makes this "great star" more like an escalation of the destructive objects that rained down in judgment from heaven on Sodom and Gomorrah and Egypt. Just as the imagery of v. 8 may have been enriched by contemporary accounts of volcanic eruptions, so the portrayal of a star "burning like a torch" may be influenced by sightings of comets shooting through the sky but go beyond them.

This destruction from heaven fell (v. 10c) "on a third of the rivers" and "on the springs of water." Because the preposition "on" (ἐπί) occurs twice, this could refer separately to one third of the rivers and *all* of the springs. But when the ill effects are summarized in v. 11b, the two are put together as "a third of the waters," implying this proportion for both.[41] These refer then to freshwater sources in contrast to seawater as in vv. 8–9. In this way, John continues to evoke the first plague on Egypt (Exod 7:14–24), but emphasizes different dimensions (here the ill effects the contaminated water has on humans).

The further difference from v. 8 is that instead of turning into blood, the waters are poisoned (v. 11d). This contamination is signaled by the name of the burning star, "Wormwood" (ὁ Ἄψινθος), because a third of the waters "became wormwood" (ἐγένετο ... εἰς ἄψινθον; v. 11b). The (middle) English term "wormwood" is the name for a shrub or herb whose leaves are used in making a bitter-tasting medicine to treat intestinal parasites

---

39. John describes the sea creatures in a somewhat awkward way, "a third of the creatures, the ones in the sea, that is, the ones having life." The participle at the end (neuter nominative plural, "the ones having life," τὰ ἔχοντα ψυχάς) is in apposition either to "a third" (neuter nominative singular, but with a collective plural sense) or to "the creatures, the ones in the sea" (neuter genitive plural). Either way the participle fails to agree

exactly with its head term, but these types of inexact agreement are common features of popular Greek style of the first century. See Zerwick, *Biblical Greek* §13 for the second option.

40. This effect on "ships" also anticipates the devastation of "Babylon's" commerce by sea (cf. 18:17–18).

41. See comments on the significance of "a third" at vv. 7, 9.

and other ailments.[42] It contains a compound that is safe yet quite bitter in low concentrations, but can cause fatal seizures in higher amounts. That so much of the fresh water supply is contaminated in this way inevitably produces disastrous results for humans. John records that "many people died" because of the water.[43] The added clause "because it [i.e., the water] became poisonous" (v. 11d) literally reads "because it was made bitter" (ἐπικράνθησαν), but the bitterness here is toxic. The Old Testament associates punishment for sin with bitter drink or bitterness that often leads to death (Num 5:24, 27; Deut 29:18; Prov 5:4; Jer 9:15; 23:15; Lam 3:19), and in this case the death-dealing effect is made clear in Revelation 8:11c.

8:12 And the fourth angel sounded his trumpet, and a third of the sun and a third of the moon and a third of the stars were struck, so that a third of them was darkened and the day did not shine for a third of it, and the night likewise (Καὶ ὁ τέταρτος ἄγγελος ἐσάλπισεν· καὶ ἐπλήγη τὸ τρίτον τοῦ ἡλίου καὶ τὸ τρίτον τῆς σελήνης καὶ τὸ τρίτον τῶν ἀστέρων, ἵνα σκοτισθῇ τὸ τρίτον αὐτῶν καὶ ἡ ἡμέρα μὴ φάνῃ τὸ τρίτον αὐτῆς καὶ ἡ νὺξ ὁμοίως). With the final trumpet in this first group of four, again we see plagues directed against a feature of the natural world, in this case the sun, moon,

and stars. A further parallel is the proportion of judgment measured in thirds as in each of the first three trumpets, indicating substantial but not final disruption. This blow was struck[44] against "a third" each of the main heavenly bodies, sun, moon, and stars (v. 12b), and the result[45] was that those thirds in each case were "darkened," prevented from shining their light (v. 12c).

This punishment is broadly reminiscent of the ninth plague on Egypt (Exod 10:21–23, a palpable darkness over all of Egypt for three days), but it also incorporates details from certain day-of-the-Lord passages that speak of the day's darkness and gloom by citing its effects on the sun, moon, and stars (e.g., Joel 2:10, 31; 3:14–15; Amos 5:18–20; 8:9; cf. Ezek 32:7–8).[46] The further effect described here (v. 12d–e) is similar to Amos 8:9 (darkness for a portion of the day) and different from Exodus 10:22 (darkness for three entire days). The blows result in complete darkness for a third of the daytime and of the nighttime: "The day did not shine for a third of it, and the night likewise."[47]

8:13 And I looked, and I heard an eagle flying high in the sky, saying in a loud voice, "Woe, woe, woe to those who live on the earth because of the remaining trumpet blasts that the three angels are about to sound" (Καὶ εἶδον, καὶ ἤκουσα ἑνὸς ἀετοῦ πετομένου ἐν μεσουρανήματι λέγοντος

---

42. See BDAG 161; Mitchell G. Reddish, "Wormwood," *ABD* 6:973. The herb wormwood is sometimes known as "absinth(e)" (from the Greek ἄψινθος), and this name is used for an alcoholic drink flavored with small amounts of wormwood.

43. The preposition "from" (ἐκ) carries a causal sense here (BDAG 296–97).

44. The verb translated "were struck" (ἐπλήγη) means "to strike with force," and in this form it shares a root with the noun "plague, blow" (πληγή) used of God's judgment, e.g., in Exod 11:1; Num 11:33; Jer 30:14; Rev 9:18, 20.

45. Here the Greek conjunction ἵνα indicates the result of this plague (cf. 9:20; 13:13; BDAG 477; BDF §391.5).

46. Beale, *Revelation*, 481–83, cites texts from Wis 17 that interpret the physical darkness the Egyptians experienced as symbolic also of their religious idolatry and spiritual pun-

ishment, and then suggests that "darkness" in Rev 8:12 is "probably not literal but refers to all those divinely ordained events intended to remind the idolatrous persecutors that their idolatry is folly and that they are separated from the living God" (482). But this dichotomy of the "literal, physical" versus the "metaphorical, spiritual" is unnecessary, and it departs even from the ideas of Wis 17. It is more likely to be a literal darkness that has connotative value (see "Imagery and Symbols" in the commentary introduction).

47. With the verb "shine" (φαίνω; "produce light," give light; BDAG 1046), the word "day" (ἡμέρα) refers by metonymy to the light of day (cf. Luke 24:29; Acts 27:29, 39; 2 Pet 1:19), and John extends this to imply "the light(s) of the night" (i.e., moon and stars) in the final clause.

φωνῇ μεγάλῃ, Οὐαὶ οὐαὶ οὐαὶ τοὺς κατοικοῦντας ἐπὶ τῆς γῆς ἐκ τῶν λοιπῶν φωνῶν τῆς σάλπιγγος τῶν τριῶν ἀγγέλων τῶν μελλόντων σαλπίζειν). In a new part of the same vision (see v. 2, "and I saw"; καὶ εἶδον), John presents a transition from the first four trumpets (vv. 2–12) to the final three that are further identified as three "woes" (cf. 9:12; 11:14). Most prominent in this part of the vision is what John "heard" (as in 5:11), "an eagle"[48] heralding the impending distress that will accompany the final three trumpets. The eagle is a common image for swift, overwhelming destruction (e.g., Deut 28:49; Jer 4:13; Lam 4:19; Hos 8:1; Hab 1:8), and an eagle "flying high in the sky"[49] implies its ability to swoop down at will on unsuspecting and vulnerable targets. The eagle here, however, gives loud warning[50] of the intense distress that will come soon with the threefold exclamation, "woe, woe, woe."[51] Such "woes" are pronounced also in the Old Testament (e.g., 1 Sam 4:7–8; Isa 1:4, 24; Jer 4:13; Zeph 2:5; see the double "woe, woe" in Ezek 16:23; Amos 5:16) and frequently by Jesus as well (e.g., Luke 6:24–26). Here the triple lament is pronounced regarding "those who live on the earth,"[52] a frequent description in Revelation referring to the world of humanity opposed to God (see note on 3:10), whom God will judge by these woes. The threefold exclamation intensifies the emotional expression, but it also provides the structure for grouping the final three trumpet judgments together. The threefold structure is introduced here and reiterated in 9:12 and 11:14. The "trumpet blasts"[53] by the three remaining angels are the reason for these cries of lament.[54]

Theology in Application

God's Attention to Prayers from the Crucible

Every year in late April or early May, Israelis observe a day of commemoration for the victims of the Nazi Holocaust, Yom HaShoah. In addition to public ceremonies and services of remembrance, the whole country comes to a complete halt and stands in silent reflection for two minutes beginning at 10:00 am. It is a solemn ritual of pausing the hurried pace of life to honor millions of innocent victims who suffered unprecedented acts of horror. The silence in heaven in Revelation 8:1 has a similar

---

48. The reading "eagle" has strong manuscript support (א, A, 1006, 1611, 1854, 2053, 2329, 2344), but some copies (P, part of the Byzantine tradition) read "angel" (ἀγγέλου), and this found its way into the KJV and the printed TR. The variant is most likely a scribal correction: an angel was thought to be more fitting for this announcement (as in 14:6).

49. The phrase "high in the sky" is "in midheaven" (ἐν μεσουρανήματι), using an astronomical term for "high overhead," "at the zenith" of the sky (BDAG 635). Among the English versions "directly overhead" (ESV) and "high overhead" (CSB) are much better than "through the midst of heaven" (KJV), "in midair" (NIV), or "in midheaven" (NASB).

50. A "loud voice" (φωνὴ μεγάλη) is a recurrent description in Rev of significant announcements of what has or will come (e.g., 11:15; 12:10; 14:7, 9; 16:17; 21:3; cf. "strong voice," 18:2).

51. As an exclamation, "woe" is an expression of pain or lament over what is or is to come (12:12; 18:10, 16, 19), but "woe" can also refer to the state of hardship that someone might lament over (9:12; 11:14; 1 Cor 9:16; see BDAG 734; LN § 22.9).

52. The phrase "to those who live . . ." (τοὺς κατοικοῦντας) is a Greek accusative of reference or respect as in 12:12; cf. BDF §160; 190.2, although there are textual variants in both places— probably scribal corrections, not original—that have datives of respect (or disadvantage) instead of accusatives.

53. "Trumpet blasts" or "the . . . sounds of the trumpet" (τῶν . . . φωνῶν τῆς σάλπιγγος) is an attributive or identifying genitive phrase, i.e., "trumpet sounds" (BDAG 1071; Wallace, *Grammar*, 86–88).

54. See BDAG 296–97, 734, for this causal sense for the Greek preposition ἐκ.

significance, but is directed toward the future instead of the past and is focused on God's alertness to the prayers of his people, as vv. 3–5 show. The prayers of God's people are presented as an act of worship "before his throne," like the sweet aroma of incense offered to him, a somber ritual that symbolizes God's attentiveness to his people who cry out to him for justice and relief (similar to the martyrs' appeal in 6:10). He is not too busy to pause and take note of their plight. And though his answer may seem a long time in coming, according to his own wise timetable he will not neglect their cries. As Jesus said, "Will not God bring about justice for his chosen ones, who cry out to him day and night? Will he keep putting them off? I tell you, he will see that they get justice, and quickly. However, when the Son of Man comes, will he find faith on the earth?" (Luke 18:7–9 NIV). God's sure answer is about to be disclosed, but our concern should be to endure in faith and engage with others so that they too can embrace the Son of Man in faith.

The Tragedy of Sin and Judgment

When we see the outworking of human evil and its disastrous effects in this world, we should be filled not with a sense of satisfaction or resignation but of horrible melancholy and longing for a better way. This is true whether we witness deep personal tragedies (e.g., drug abuse, family breakdown, murderous violence) or worldwide conflict and suffering (e.g., terrorism, warfare, preventable famine and disease). We cry out within ourselves, "Why does it have to be like this? What's wrong with us? Why can't people change from these destructive patterns that happen over and over?" If this holds true of the human misery we witness in our world now, how much more when we read about the intense afflictions that the people of the world will suffer in the end times. What John reveals of divine punishment against sin in the vision of these early trumpet judgments should fill us with anguish and a desire for something better. The story that Revelation tells of the final outpouring of God's wrath just prior to Christ's return is a deeply wrenching one. In this section of the book we read about terrible but just judgments (6:1–8; 8:7–12) interspersed with divine warnings (e.g. 8:13) and, sadly, lack of a repentant response to those warnings and judgments (6:15–17; 9:20–21). Those who have any awareness of biblical history should realize that God's inescapable judgment will come at last, just as it came against Noah's defiant generation, wicked Sodom and Gomorrah, and unrepentant Egypt. If sin and evil bring such inevitable disaster, why not change our ways? Why not help others to see the danger that is coming around the corner if they stay on that pathway? Why not help them see the good news about a Savior who came to deliver them from their own inability to change and from the horror that looms ahead if they refuse him?

15

Revelation 9:1–21

Literary Context

After the ominous foreshadowing of 8:13, the first and second of the three "woes," which are also the fifth and sixth trumpet judgments, follow immediately in 9:1–21. These are narrated in greater detail compared to the first four trumpets and present painful calamities targeting humans more directly and carried out by fearsome demonic attackers. The appearance of overtly demonic forces in both plagues foreshadows the appearance of Satan's chief end-time protagonist, the beast of chapter 13, and the war against God and his people that he will wage in the days immediately prior to Christ's return.

III. Second Vision: Heavenly Throne Room and Three Judgment Cycles (4:1–16:21)

   A. Vision of God in His Heavenly Throne Room (4:1–11)

   B. The Seven-Sealed Scroll and the Slain Lamb (5:1–14)

   C. The Seven Seals and the Interlude of the Two Multitudes (6:1–8:1)

   D. The Seven Trumpets and Further Interludes (8:2–14:20)

     1. The First Four Trumpets (8:2–13)

➡   **2. The Fifth Trumpet—First Woe (9:1–12)**

     3. The Sixth Trumpet—Second Woe (9:13–21)

     4. Two Revelatory Interludes: God's Prophets (10:1–11:14)

Main Idea

The fourth and fifth trumpet judgments bring severe torment from demonic assaults and widespread human death from a huge demonic force, but the survivors stubbornly refuse to repent.

Translation

Revelation 9:1–21

1a	Action/5th Trumpet	And **the fifth angel sounded his trumpet,**
b	Action/Character Entrance	and **I saw a star that had fallen from heaven onto the earth,**
c		and **the key to the shaft of the bottomless pit was given to him,**
2a		and **he opened the shaft of the bottomless pit,**
b		and **smoke went up from the shaft like smoke from a great furnace,**
c		and **the sun and the air were made dark by the smoke from the shaft.**
3a	Effects	And **from the smoke locusts came out onto the earth,**
b		and **they were given power**

like the power that the earth's scorpions have,

c	Comparison	
4a	Commission	and **they were told not to harm the grass of the earth or any green growth or any tree,**

but only   the humans
who do not have God's seal on their foreheads.

b	Specification	
5a	Qualification	And **they were not permitted**
b	Commission	**to kill them but to torment them for five months,**

c	Comparison	and **their torment was like the torment inflicted by a scorpion**
d		**when it stings a person.**
6a	Effects	And **in those days people will seek death,**
b		and **they will not find it,**
c		and **they will long to die,**
d		and **death flees from them.**
7a	Description/ Comparison	And **the appearance of the locusts was like horses prepared for battle,**
b		and **on their heads were something like crowns similar to gold,**
c		and **their faces were like the faces of humans,**
8a		and **they had hair like the hair of women,**
b		and **their teeth were like those of lions,**
9a		and **they had chests like iron breastplates,**
b		and **the sound of their wings was like the sound of chariots with many horses charging into battle.**
10a		And **they have tails and stingers like scorpions,**
b		and **their power to harm people for five months is in their tails.**

Continued on next page.

Continued from previous page.

11a		**They have a king over them,**
		the angel of the bottomless pit,
b	Description	whose name in Hebrew is Abaddon and
c		in Greek he has the name Apollyon.
12a	Review	**The first woe has passed.**
b	Preview	**Behold, two woes are still to come after these things.**
13a	Action/6th Trumpet	And **the sixth angel sounded his trumpet,**
b	Action	and **I heard a voice from the horns of the golden altar that is before God,**
14a		saying to the sixth angel who had the trumpet,
b	Command	*"Release the four angels that are bound at the great river Euphrates."*
15a	Response	And **the four angels were released,**
b	Description	who had stood ready for the hour and
		day and
		month and
		year,
c	Commission	in order to kill a third of humanity.

16a	Preview	And **the** number of the armies of cavalry was twice ten thousand times ⤴
		ten thousand.
b	Affirmation	**I heard their number.**
17a	Explanation	And **this is how I saw** the horses in my vision as well as those who sit on them:
b	Description	the horsemen have breastplates
c		that are fiery red and
		dark blue and
		sulfurous yellow in color, and
d		the heads of the horses are like lions' heads; and
e		fire and smoke and sulfur come from their mouths.

18a	Effect	**From these three plagues a third of humanity was killed,**
		from the fire and
		the smoke and
		the sulfur
b		that came from their mouths.
19a	Explanation	For **the power of the horses is in their mouths and**
		in their tails,
b		for **their tails which are like serpents have heads,**
c		and **they inflict harm with them.**

20a	Effect	**And the rest of humanity …**		
		who were not killed in these plagues		
		… did not repent of the works of their hands		
b	Result	so as not to worship	demons and	
			idols of	gold and
				silver and
				bronze and
				stone and
				wood,
			which cannot	see or
				hear or
				walk,
21	Effect	**and they did not repent of**	**their murders or**	
			their sorceries or	
			their sexual immorality or	
			their thefts.	

Structure

The heavenly announcement of 8:13 leads directly into the first of the three "woes," which is also the fifth trumpet judgment (9:1–12). Within this unit, the opening of the bottomless pit (vv. 1–2) sets the stage for the human suffering caused by demonic "locusts" from the pit (vv. 3–12). The second woe, announced in v. 12, finishes out the chapter with the events of the sixth trumpet in vv. 13–21. A huge demonic "cavalry" that assaults the earth kills a third of humanity (vv. 13–19), but this brings no repentance on the part of the humans who survive these attacks (vv. 20–21).

Exegetical Outline

Explanation of the Text

9:1–2 And the fifth angel sounded his trumpet, and I saw a star that had fallen from heaven onto the earth, and the key to the shaft of the bottomless pit was given to him, 2 and he opened the shaft of the bottomless pit, and smoke went up from the shaft like smoke from a great furnace, and the sun and the air were made dark by the smoke from the shaft (Καὶ ὁ πέμπτος ἄγγελος ἐσάλπισεν· καὶ εἶδον ἀστέρα ἐκ τοῦ οὐρανοῦ πεπτωκότα εἰς τὴν γῆν, καὶ ἐδόθη αὐτῷ ἡ κλεὶς τοῦ φρέατος τῆς ἀβύσσου 2 καὶ ἤνοιξεν τὸ φρέαρ τῆς ἀβύσσου, καὶ ἀνέβη καπνὸς ἐκ τοῦ φρέατος ὡς καπνὸς καμίνου μεγάλης, καὶ ἐσκοτώθη ὁ ἥλιος καὶ ὁ ἀὴρ ἐκ τοῦ καπνοῦ τοῦ φρέατος). At the sounding of the fifth trumpet (v. 1a), John witnesses a further portion of the trumpet visions (see "I saw/looked" in 8:2, 13) that begins with "a star" (ἀστέρα) fallen[1] from heaven to earth (v. 1b). Because of the actions this "star" is permitted to take (vv. 1c–2), it should be understood as representing an angelic being (a common image; cf. 1:16, 20; Judg 5:20; Job 38:7),[2] who as God's holy emissary sets in motion acts of

---

1. The verb translated "that had fallen" is a Greek perfect participle (πεπτωκότα) that portrays not the *process* or action of falling (as implied by KJV, "I saw a star fall from heaven") but the *result* of such an action (located now on earth, ready to carry out heaven's mission here).

2. "Stars" refer to (evil) angels in 1 En. 88:1; 90:24–27, where reference is also made to their judgment by confinement in a fiery abyss. The angel of Rev 9:1, however, was not locked in the pit but came from heaven. One text of 1 En. 20:3 portrays a holy angel who has charge over Tartarus (the abyss).

divine judgment against sinful humans (in this case, carried out by demonic agents). To portray him here as "a star . . . fallen from heaven onto the earth" (v. 1b) underscores the cosmic significance of his earthly mission. A parallel that supports taking this "star" as an angel is 20:1–3, where a being John explicitly calls "an angel" comes down from heaven with the key to the bottomless pit so that he can lock Satan away in it for a thousand years. This parallel provides evidence also that the angel in 9:1 is not "fallen" in a spiritual sense despite possible parallels with the "fall" of Satan or his demons from heaven (e.g., Luke 10:18, "fall"; Rev 12:8–9, "was thrown"; possibly Isa 14:12; cf. also Jude 13, "erring stars").[3] In this verse, "fall" ($\pi\acute{\iota}\pi\tau\omega$) denotes movement to a lower level (as in 6:13, 16; 8:10), not spiritual ruin or lapse into sin or rebellion (e.g., 2:5).[4] Likewise the "star" (angel) in v. 1 should not be identified with the angel named in v. 11 as king over the creatures of the bottomless pit (see further discussion there).[5]

Having come to earth, the angel was granted God-given authority over access[6] to "the shaft of the bottomless pit" ($\tau o\hat{\upsilon}$ $\varphi\rho\acute{\epsilon}\alpha\tau o\varsigma$ $\tau\hat{\eta}\varsigma$ $\mathring{\alpha}\beta\acute{\upsilon}\sigma\sigma o\upsilon$). This phrase pictures a narrow vertical opening or "shaft"[7] that leads to a well-known domain, "the bottomless pit,"[8] pictured as being deep underground (v. 1c). The Greek word for this, $\mathring{\alpha}\beta\upsilon\sigma\sigma o\varsigma$

(often brought directly over into English versions as "abyss"; cf. ASV, CSB, NIV, NET) denotes a depth ($\beta\upsilon\theta\acute{o}\varsigma$) with no limit (negative prefix α-). In the LXX it often translates תְּהוֹם (e.g., Gen 1:2; Ps 78:15), meaning the depths of the sea or the powers thought to control the primeval "sea," but in later Judaism and the New Testament it came to denote an unfathomable depth conceived of as below the earth because it was the opposite of "heaven" conceived as above the earth and skies. In this way "the bottomless pit" or "Abyss" referred to the general "underworld" that subsumed both Sheol or Hades (the realm of the righteous and unrighteous dead; cf. Ps 71:20; Rom 10:7) and Gehenna or Hell (the place of torment or of imprisoned spirits awaiting condemnation; Luke 8:31; cf. 2 Pet 2:4; also 1 En. 18:14–16; 21:1–6; 4 Ezra 7:36; Jub. 5:6–10).[9] Revelation uses this term seven times, always to refer to the place of torment or imprisonment (9:1, 2, 11; 11:7; 17:8; 20:1, 3). This verse draws from the common expectation that in the end-times God would allow demons or demonically inspired forces some measure of greater freedom to oppress and deceive humans as part of his culminating judgments (e.g., 2 Thess 2:9; Rev 12:12; 13:2).

God's purpose in giving this angel "the key" is not to seal up access to the pit (as in 20:1–3) but to

---

3. Ancient noncanonical Jewish-Christian literature describes the expulsion from heaven of both Satan (1 En. 86:1; Apoc. El. 4:11) and his demons (1 En. 86:3; 88:1; 90:24; T. Sol. 20:14–17).

4. See BDAG 815–16.

5. Some interpreters understand the "star" of v. 1 (whether or not it is the same as the angel in v. 11) as an evil angel or even Satan (e.g., Beale, *Revelation*, 491–92; Caird, *Revelation*, 117–18; Charles, *Revelation*, 1:238–39), but for reasons cited above it is better to see it as a holy angel serving God's purpose of judgment (see Koester, *Revelation*, 455–56; Osborne, *Revelation*, 362; Smalley, *Revelation*, 225–26; Robert L. Thomas, *Revelation 8–22* [Chicago: Moody, 1995], 27).

6. This authority to control access is symbolized by "the key" (ἡ κλείς; see discussion at 1:18) that "was given" (ἐδόθη) to

him by God (v. 1c). See BDAG 243, and the note on the divine passive at 6:4 ("was given" is a very common divine passive in Rev).

7. The word "shaft" (φρέαρ) is used of a deep well (Gen 24:20; John 4:11–12) or pit (Ps 55:23 [54:24 LXX]; Luke 14:5) from which water or objects can be drawn (BDAG 1065). Sometimes such deep wells were covered by a large stone to hide or secure them when not in use (e.g., Gen 29:2–3).

8. The phrase is articular in Greek even at its first mention here in v. 1, showing that John could assume that his readers were familiar with it through general cultural knowledge (Wallace, *Grammar*, 225).

9. J. Jeremias, "ἄβυσσος," *TDNT* 1:9–10; O. Böcher, "ἄβυσσος," *EDNT* 1:4; BDAG 2.

open it wide, and v. 2a narrates that fateful action. This sets in motion the fearful attacks on humanity that follow (vv. 5–11). But in his narration of these events John first lays out several preparatory details that build tension before the full terror and scope of the judgment is made clear. The immediate effect of opening the shaft is an ominous cloud of "smoke" that rises "from the shaft" (v. 2b). Its appearance is "like smoke from a great furnace," wording similar to the accounts of judgment on Sodom and Gomorrah (Gen 19:28) and of God's threatening presence at Sinai (Exod 19:18), but also reminiscent of the fires of judgment associated with Gehenna (Matt 5:22; 13:42; 18:9; Mark 9:43; Jas 3:6; cf. 4 Ezra 7:36). The foreboding is only increased when "the smoke from the shaft" is said to darken "the sun and the air" (v. 2c). This indicates the extensive effect of the cloud of smoke, yet it also evokes a prominent feature of the Lord's day of judgment (cf. Joel 2:10; 3:15; Amos 5:18–20; 8:9; Zeph 1:15).

9:3–4 And from the smoke locusts came out onto the earth, and they were given power like the power that the earth's scorpions have, 4 and they were told not to harm the grass of the earth or any green growth or any tree, but only the humans who do not have God's seal on their foreheads (καὶ ἐκ τοῦ καπνοῦ ἐξῆλθον ἀκρίδες εἰς τὴν γῆν, καὶ ἐδόθη αὐταῖς ἐξουσία ὡς ἔχουσιν ἐξουσίαν οἱ σκορπίοι τῆς γῆς. 4 καὶ ἐρρέθη αὐταῖς ἵνα μὴ ἀδικήσουσιν τὸν χόρτον τῆς γῆς οὐδὲ πᾶν χλωρὸν οὐδὲ πᾶν δένδρον, εἰ μὴ τοὺς ἀνθρώπους οἵτινες οὐκ ἔχουσι τὴν σφραγῖδα τοῦ θεοῦ ἐπὶ τῶν μετώπων). The evocative forebodings of the previous two

verses are horrifically fulfilled when preternatural creatures bringing fearful judgment appear from the cloud of smoke that rises from the pit (v. 3a). As with the earlier trumpets (8:7, 8, 10, 12), this imagery is drawn largely from the pattern of the Egyptian plagues (here the eighth one, the locust plague; Exod 10:12–20; Pss 78:46; 105:34–35), but Joel's picture of the day of the Lord as cloudy darkness and as an innumerable invading army desolating the land (Joel 2:1–11) has an unmistakable influence as well (see comments on vv. 7–9 below). But these "locusts," like Joel's, are even worse than the scourge from a natural plague of locusts who strip the land of everything green but are unable to harm the human population directly. They are more fearful, first of all, because they are equipped (by God)[10] with scorpion-like "power"[11] to inflict excruciating pain (v. 3b–c). Humans seem to have a natural phobia regarding scorpions (as with snakes) wherever they are found because of their punishing stings and ability to hide and then strike from unexpected places (cf. Deut 8:15; 1 Kgs 12:11, 14; Luke 10:19; cf. Sir 39:28–31)—how much worse to have such creatures swarming everywhere.

They are worse, secondly, because unlike natural locusts these are assigned to target not the earth's plant life but that large portion of its human population left unprotected by God (v. 4). The passive (i.e., "they were told")[12] is used again to indicate what is ultimately God's mandate for these invaders from the pit. They are "not to harm"[13] the green growth that locusts normally consume voraciously: things like the earth's grass or "any green growth or

---

10. Again, the divine passive "were given" (ἐδόθη; v. 3b) implies permission from God to torment humans in the ways vv. 3–6 describe.

11. The word translated "power" (ἐξουσία) sometimes means "authority, official warrant," but here it denotes the related "capability, might" as in v. 19 (BDAG 353; LN §76.12).

12. The phrase "they were told" (v. 4a) is a smoother English rendering of the literal "it was told to them" (ἐρρέθη αὐταῖς).

13. This phrase appears in v. 4a as an indirect command expressed by ἵνα with the future indicative (Robertson, *Grammar*, 1046; Zerwick, *Biblical Greek*, 117; Aune, *Revelation 6–16*, 486). The verb "harm" (ἀδικέω) is used also in 7:2–3 to describe damage to the world of nature that was postponed until the 144,000 could be sealed.

any tree."[14] Instead[15] they must mete out painful "harm" on the greater part of earth's humanity that were not protected by God's seal (7:3–4). So the only ones not targeted will be those who have God's seal "on their foreheads" (ἐπὶ τῶν μετώπων), wording repeated from 7:3 to describe the thousands from all Israel whom God will protect through these judgments and restore to the land of Israel when their Messiah comes to reign on earth (see discussion at 7:3–4).[16]

9:5–6 And they were not permitted to kill them but to torment them for five months, and their torment was like the torment inflicted by a scorpion when it stings a person. 6 And in those days people will seek death, and they will not find it, and they will long to die, and death flees from them (καὶ ἐδόθη αὐτοῖς ἵνα μὴ ἀποκτείνωσιν αὐτούς, ἀλλ᾽ ἵνα βασανισθήσονται μῆνας πέντε, καὶ ὁ βασανισμὸς αὐτῶν ὡς βασανισμὸς σκορπίου ὅταν παίσῃ ἄνθρωπον. 6 καὶ ἐν ταῖς ἡμέραις ἐκείναις ζητήσουσιν οἱ ἄνθρωποι τὸν θάνατον καὶ οὐ μὴ εὑρήσουσιν αὐτόν, καὶ ἐπιθυμήσουσιν ἀποθανεῖν καὶ φεύγει ὁ θάνατος ἀπ᾽ αὐτῶν). These creatures from the pit who bring torture on the large body of earth's humanity are limited (v. 5a–b) in the harm

that God has allowed them to inflict—if in fact it can be regarded as a limitation. John's reflections in v. 6 are perhaps intended to bring the reader to an opposite opinion—the suffering they inflict is more severe than death itself. The divine passive appears one more time in the expression "they were not permitted" (v. 5a),[17] implying the scope of damage God allows them to cause. Their warrant "not . . . to kill . . . but to torment" (v. 5b)[18] is reminiscent of Job's suffering (Job 2:6), although here the victims of evil agents are not limited to the righteous. The torment they are allowed to inflict is severe,[19] but it is limited also in time, "for five months." But whatever sense one gives to the number "five" here, whether strictly literal or as indicating "several" months,[20] this indicates a period of longer agony (i.e., some months, not seconds or minutes) than anyone would care to endure even if it is not unending. John brings up again the terrifying comparison with earthly scorpions from v. 3, by likening ("as"; ὡς) the torments these infernal locusts inflict with the severe pain a scorpion delivers[21] to a human through its sting (v. 5c–d).

Shifting his discourse mode from narrative to argument or report (v. 6),[22] John describes conditions that will prevail in the future when what

---

14. Note the threefold enumeration cited at 8:7, where the "earth," "trees," and "green grass" were seen to suffer under the first trumpet judgment.

15. The words "but only" (v. 4a) are a translation of the Greek εἰ μή denoting a contrastive exception to the instruction not to bring harm (BDAG 278; LN §89.131).

16. The comments at 7:3–4 describe also the OT background of this protection in Ezek 9:1–11 (also Gen 4:11–16; Exod 12:1–32).

17. See the passives in vv. 3–4. As in v. 4 the Greek expression in v. 5a, "it was given to them that they might not . . ." (ἐδόθη αὐτοῖς ἵνα μὴ . . .), is rendered in English as "they were not permitted" (see BDAG 243, for "give" in the sense of God's allowance or permission).

18. The Greek expressions translated as "to kill . . . to torment" are clauses introduced by the conjunction ἵνα ("that they may not kill . . . but that they may be tormented"). They show the content that was "permitted" (cf. Wallace, *Grammar*, 474–75).

19. The Greek verb and related nouns translated "torment" (v. 5c) are used of severe suffering or agony as from serious illness (Matt 8:6), birth pains (Rev 12:2), or the torments of the lake of fire (Rev 14:10–11; 20:10). See BDAG 168.

20. Aune, *Revelation 6–16*, 530; C. J. Hemer, "πέντε," *NID-NTT* 2:689–90; Prigent, *Apocalypse*, 314. But several of the examples they cite for an indefinite sense actually argue for a literal meaning (e.g., Matt 14:17, 19; 15:34; 16:9–10, where the count "five loaves" or "seven loaves" is repeated twice and then recalled later in exactly the same count; see also 15:34 for the use of "a few fish" for an indefinite count).

21. Both phrases in v. 5c, "their [i.e., the locusts'] torment" (ὁ βασανισμὸς αὐτῶν) and "the torment inflicted by a scorpion" (literally "a scorpion's torment"; βασανισμὸς σκορπίου), are subjective genitives: the genitive shows who inflicts the pain.

22. See note on 4:5.

he has seen in his vision comes to pass on earth. From the events just recounted he now anticipates the end-time cosmic judgment they portray (see similar examples of this shift in 5:10; 7:15–16; 20:6c–8). In contrast to the aorists of vv. 1–5, John now uses three future indicative verbs (plus a general or customary present referring to the same circumstances). These are introduced by the temporal phrase "in those days" to point not backward (to the time of his vision) but forward from John's day to its end-time occurrence.[23] Tragically the humans experiencing those torments will long for death's release from suffering but will be completely unable to escape their anguish.[24] In poignant language John repeats these points a second time and personifies death as repeatedly eluding those who pursue it in their pain. The human plight he describes is heartbreaking, but common enough throughout human history (cf. Job 3:21; Jer 8:3).

9:7–9 And the appearance of the locusts was like horses prepared for battle, and on their heads were something like crowns similar to gold, and their faces were like the faces of humans, 8 and they had hair like the hair of women, and their teeth were like those of lions, 9 and they had chests like iron breastplates, and the sound of their wings was like the sound of chariots with many horses charging into battle (Καὶ τὰ ὁμοιώματα τῶν ἀκρίδων ὅμοια ἵπποις ἡτοιμασμένοις εἰς πόλεμον, καὶ ἐπὶ τὰς κεφαλὰς αὐτῶν ὡς στέφανοι ὅμοιοι χρυσῷ, καὶ τὰ πρόσωπα αὐτῶν ὡς πρόσωπα ἀνθρώπων, 8 καὶ εἶχον τρίχας ὡς τρίχας γυναικῶν, καὶ οἱ ὀδόντες αὐτῶν ὡς λεόντων ἦσαν, 9 καὶ εἶχον θώρακας ὡς θώρακας σιδηροῦς, καὶ ἡ φωνὴ τῶν πτερύγων αὐτῶν ὡς φωνὴ ἁρμάτων ἵππων πολλῶν τρεχόντων εἰς πόλεμον). After narrating the origin and infernal power entrusted to these locusts (vv. 1–6), John explains further how fearsome and diabolical they are by describing their appearance in a variety of ways (vv. 7–11).[25] As in 1:13–16 and 4:4–7 John repeatedly uses comparative words,[26] in this case to portray creatures almost unimaginably horrible. After noting a broad likeness in appearance to "horses prepared for battle" (v. 7a), he specifies in rapid sequence their "heads" (crowned with gold in a sinister honor; v. 7b) and "faces" (human-like, perhaps representing evil intelligence along with their brute power; v. 7c),[27] and then their "hair" ("like the hair of women," perhaps approximating the appearance of their insect-like antennae; v. 8a)[28] and "teeth" (powerful and rapacious like "lions"; v. 8b). Finally, he notes their "chests" ("like iron breastplates"; v. 9a)[29] and "wings" (sounding like multi-horse chariots rushing to battle; v. 9b). Some of these similes may be suggested by features

---

23. "Those days" refers to end-time events in Matt 24:19, 22, 29 (likewise "that day" in Luke 10:12; 17:31; 2 Thess 1:10). Cf. BDAG 302.

24. "They will not find it" appears in v. 6b as a future indicative with the double negation οὐ μή (also in 18:14). This is equivalent in sense to a subjunctive with οὐ μή (e.g., 2:11; 3:5, 12) in expressing an emphatic denial of a future possibility (BDF §365; Wallace, *Grammar*, 468–69, 571).

25. John uses a series of aorists for standard narration of the vision's events in vv. 1–5, then switches to the future for the portrayal of v. 6. The imperfects of vv. 7–9 resume the narrative mode but provide background to the earlier events. Then vv. 10–11 shift to nonnarrative description using customary present tenses in vv. 10–11. See comments at 4:5 on modes of presentation in John's visions.

26. Words meaning "like, similar to," (ὁμοίωμα, ὅμοιος, ὡς) appear 9x in vv. 7–10.

27. "Faces of humans" (πρόσωπα ἀνθρώπων; cf. similar use in 4:7) could mean "the faces of men" (i.e., adult males) in contrast to "women" in v. 8a, since ἄνθρωπος occasionally means "male, husband" when the context specifically contrasts it with "woman" (γυνή). But ἄνθρωπος in Rev almost always means "human, person" and not "husband, male" (cf. ἀνήρ in 21:2). See BDAG 81.

28. Or this could be an allusion to Roman fears of invasion by long-haired Parthian warriors (cf. Plutarch, *Crass.* 24.2; Suetonius, *Vesp.* 23.4).

29. The same Greek word θώραξ can refer to the piece of armor that covers the chest or trunk ("breastplate") or the body part underneath it ("chest, thorax"). See BDAG 463; LSJ 814.

of actual locusts (e.g., antenna, thorax), but associating a locust plague with an overwhelming host of armed, ruthless invaders is a frequent image in the Old Testament as noted in v. 3 above, and some of those texts have certainly influenced John toward the martial comparisons seen here in vv. 7–9. Joel's predictions of the day of the Lord speak of locusts having teeth like lions (Joel 1:6) and an appearance like battle horses and rumbling chariots (2:4–5). Joel uses a natural attack of locusts as the vehicle for warning about a vicious Assyrian or Babylonian army that will overwhelm Israel or Judah in the Lord's day of judgment (1:15; 2:1–11). Other texts picture large armies of invading cavalry and chariots as deafening clouds of locusts covering and devastating the land (Judg 6:5; 7:12; Job 39:19–25; Jer 46:23; 47:3; 51:14, 27).

But what actual realities in the world of that future day (or of any time) do these images represent? Do they symbolize the spiritual pain and devastation of life and health that humans are subject to in any era if they submit to demonic influences?[30] The connections to patterns of earthly judgment drawn from Old Testament passages about the day of the Lord as well as parallels to the plagues on Egypt in the first four trumpets (8:7–12) seem to show that these demonic attackers represent more than spiritual and personal torments. But does the parallel with Joel mean that they symbolize a military attack by some human army with sophisticated and destructive weaponry?[31] It seems to fit more of the textual evidence to understand these as demons functioning in some way like an invading army, but bringing an escalation of physical horror and suffering beyond that of human warfare.[32]

9:10–11 And they have tails and stingers like scorpions, and their power to harm people for five months is in their tails. 11 They have a king over them, the angel of the bottomless pit, whose name in Hebrew is Abaddon and in Greek he has the name Apollyon (καὶ ἔχουσιν οὐρὰς ὁμοίας σκορπίοις καὶ κέντρα, καὶ ἐν ταῖς οὐραῖς αὐτῶν ἡ ἐξουσία αὐτῶν ἀδικῆσαι τοὺς ἀνθρώπους μῆνας πέντε, 11 ἔχουσιν ἐπ' αὐτῶν βασιλέα τὸν ἄγγελον τῆς ἀβύσσου, ὄνομα αὐτῷ Ἑβραϊστὶ Ἀβαδδών, καὶ ἐν τῇ Ἑλληνικῇ ὄνομα ἔχει Ἀπολλύων). John's presentation of his vision shifts in vv. 10–11 from standard narration (using aorists and imperfects as in vv. 1–5, 7–9) to report or description mode (using customary present verbs to portray what he saw as though it were occurring directly in front of his readers).[33] These descriptions continue to show how fearsome and diabolical these future invaders from the pit will be. John briefly repeats and fills out several particulars from vv. 3–5 about their likeness to earthly scorpions (v. 10a): they possess scorpion-like "tails and stingers,"[34] an extremely menacing detail to add to the alarming features already given. The latter part of the verse supplements what vv. 4–5 said about their "power to harm

30. Hendriksen, *More Than Conquerors*, 145–46; Philip Edgcumbe Hughes, *The Book of the Revelation: A Commentary* (Grand Rapids: Eerdmans, 1990), 109–11. Patterson, *Revelation*, 221, sees this as "spiritual agony and destruction," "an unimaginable spiritual devastation," rather than any kind of physical attack, but one that comes during the final tribulation period, not in any or every era of the church age.

31. The often-cited example of this is from Hal Lindsey, *There's a New World Coming: A Prophetic Odyssey* (Santa Ana, CA: Vision House, 1973), 138–39 (helicopter gunships spraying Agent Orange from their tails). As Metzger, *Breaking the Code*, 14, observes, John's visions give "descriptions of symbols, not of the reality conveyed by the symbols." See the section "Imagery and Symbols" in the commentary introduction.

32. D. Brent Sandy, *Plowshares and Pruning Hooks: Rethinking the Language of Biblical Prophecy and Apocalyptic* (Downers Grove, IL: InterVarsity Press, 2002), 179; most of the commentaries speak in these terms without going into detail.

33. See comments on 4:5; 9:7–9.

34. The word "stinger" (κέντρον) can denote, as here, the sharp instrument used to inflict a piercing wound (Acts 26:14) or the wound or damage itself (i.e., "sting"; 1 Cor 15:55–56). See BDAG 539–40; LN §8.45.

people for five months" (see above) by locating that power in their scorpion-like tails (v. 10b).

John's final description[35] of the locusts (v. 11) also reinforces an earlier theme: their origin in the world of the dead and the damned (cf. vv. 1–2). Unlike the reputation that natural locusts sometimes had (i.e., they need no king, Prov 30:27), these have "a king over them" who is identified initially as "the angel of the bottomless pit." Although control over the pit's access (vv. 1–2) and rule over its occupants as "king" (v. 11a) are parallel in some ways, this angel is not identical to the "fallen star" entrusted with the key to the pit (v. 1).[36] Nor should he be identified as Satan who with other evil angels opposes God's work on the earth (12:3–17) until he is imprisoned in the bottomless pit during the millennium (20:1–3, 7–10). This "angel of the bottomless pit" seems to be an evil angel with intermediate authority, not their high prince like Satan, but exercising rule over these subordinate demons who appear as "locusts" to attack the earth's inhabitants.[37] More important for John's descriptive purpose is the angel's character as revealed in his horrible names (v. 11b–c). His name in Hebrew is

"Abaddon" (Ἀβαδδών), a direct transliteration of the Hebrew word אֲבַדּוֹן into Greek. The name in Hebrew means "destruction," from the verb "perish, destroy" (אבד), and its significance is seen by its occurrences in synonymous parallelism with "Sheol" (Job 26:6; Prov 15:11; 27:20), death (Job 28:22), or the grave (Ps 88:11 [88:12 MT]). In all of these Old Testament texts the LXX translates "Abaddon" as "destruction, ruin" (ἀπώλεια), the abstract noun related to the word "Apollyon" (Ἀπολλύων)[38] that John cites as the angel's name "in Greek." An evil angel with such a name—and the swarm of demons he rules over—can only bode ill for the world's inhabitants in the end-times.

9:12 The first woe has passed. Behold, two woes are still to come after these things (Ἡ οὐαὶ ἡ μία ἀπῆλθεν· ἰδοὺ ἔρχεται ἔτι δύο οὐαὶ μετὰ ταῦτα). This verse picks up the thematic links laid down at 8:13 (three woes to come signaled by the final three trumpet blasts) to mark the transition between the fifth and sixth trumpets. "The first woe"[39] points to the torments just described (9:1–11),[40] and these are in view also in the temporal expression "after these things" in v. 12b.[41] The woe, although actually

---

35. The beginning of v. 11 is an example of asyndeton (lack of a sentence opening conjunction), a relatively rare thing in Rev (but see vv. 12, 18). Asyndeton heightens the solemnity and prominence of this verse as a conclusion to the paragraph. See BDF § 462.2; and Levinsohn, *Discourse Features*, 118–21.

36. The star in v. 1 descends from heaven to carry out a divine commission and opens the pit, while the angel of v. 11 shares the diabolical nature of its "locusts" and appears to be confined with them in the underworld until the release of vv. 2–3.

37. The fact that he is called "*the* angel of the bottomless pit" using a Greek article does not mean he would be well known to the readers or others. He is definite or known because of his association with "the bottomless pit," similar to "the angel of the waters" in 16:5 or "the one who had authority over the fire" in 14:18 (except that he is an evil angel, not a holy one).

38. The name "Apollyon" is a present participle, "one who destroys, destroyer," from the verb ἀπόλλυμι, to destroy. This sense, but no exact verbal links, may suggest a connection also to the action of angelic "destroyers" in Exod 12:23 (using a dif-

ferent Hebrew word and the Greek verb ὀλοθρεύω, "destroy," in the LXX as well as in Heb 11:28) and in Num 21:6 (no explicit mention of destruction in OT or LXX, but see Paul's account of this in 1 Cor 10:10, "they were destroyed by the destroyer"; ἀπώλοντο ὑπὸ τοῦ ὀλοθρευτοῦ).

39. The expression "the first woe" (ἡ οὐαὶ ἡ μία) is phrased as "the one woe," illustrating how the cardinal number "one" can serve in Greek as an ordinal (followed in 11:14 by the Greek ordinals "second," δεύτερος, and "third," τρίτος). See BDAG 293; also Titus 3:10.

40. "Woe" in this verse denotes not directly a cry of lament but the trouble or distress that someone would lament over (see BDAG 734; LN §22.9; and note at 8:13).

41. Some manuscripts either drop the "and" (καί) at the start of v. 13 or move it prior to "after these things" (μετὰ ταῦτα) in v. 12 or add another conjunction in order to read the temporal phrase as beginning v. 13. But "after these things" at the end of v. 12 (cf. 1:19; 4:1) before the "and" of v. 13 has good manuscript support (A, P, 1611) and best explains the rise of the other readings.

yet to occur in the end-times, "has passed" just now in the sense that John has portrayed its events in his visionary narration and will now move on to the next vision account.[42] In his visionary sequence two additional woes are about to come (11:14 signals the transition between these two).[43] The first of these appears immediately in 9:13.

9:13–14 And the sixth angel sounded his trumpet, and I heard a voice from the horns of the golden altar that is before God, 14 saying to the sixth angel who had the trumpet, "Release the four angels that are bound at the great river Euphrates" (Καὶ ὁ ἕκτος ἄγγελος ἐσάλπισεν· καὶ ἤκουσα φωνὴν μίαν ἐκ τῶν [τεσσάρων] κεράτων τοῦ θυσιαστηρίου τοῦ χρυσοῦ τοῦ ἐνώπιον τοῦ θεοῦ, 14 λέγοντα τῷ ἕκτῳ ἀγγέλῳ, ὁ ἔχων τὴν σάλπιγγα, Λῦσον τοὺς τέσσαρας ἀγγέλους τοὺς δεδεμένους ἐπὶ τῷ ποταμῷ τῷ μεγάλῳ Εὐφράτῃ). Picking up the sequence of trumpet blasts again from 9:1, John begins the events of the sixth trumpet by recording first of all the heavenly interaction between the sixth angel and a certain "voice"[44] from the heart of God's throne room.[45] The fact that the voice comes "from the horns of the golden altar that is before God"[46] (v. 13b) shows that it speaks with divine authority—it is either God himself speaking or more likely an overseeing angel directing his deputy angels in carrying out God's purpose (cf. Ps 103:19–21).[47] The punishments that follow, horrible as they are and executed by evil agents, are directed by God in fulfilling his purposes in judgment and redemption (cf. Rev 6:16–17).

The voice from heaven directly addresses[48] the angel who sounded the sixth trumpet (v. 14a). This angel alone among the seven has a further role to play after his trumpet blast. He must give the signal for four additional angels to play their part in the judgments about to be poured out (v. 14b).[49] The voice commands him to "release" those four angels

---

42. The verb translated "has passed" (ἀπῆλθεν) is an aorist that refers in summary to an action or actions that have just now happened (also in 11:14). Such a reference requires a present perfect verb in English idiom (see Fanning, *Verbal Aspect*, 260–61; see also the note at 6:17).

43. Both 9:12 and 11:14 use the verb "are . . . to come" in a present tense form ("comes, is coming, ἔρχεται). Here in v. 12 the verb is singular because it views the two woes as a single unit. As often with verbs of coming and going, this present tense carries a futuristic sense of what is already on its way and will arrive in the near future. See Fanning, *Verbal Aspect*, 221–22.

44. "A voice" is the translation of φωνὴν μίαν, in which the numeral "one" (μίαν) is used with an indefinite sense (BDAG 292; cf. 8:13).

45. Because this "voice" is the initiating event after the trumpet blast, John does not use his standard "I saw" (εἶδον) to introduce the vision in v. 13b but "I heard" (ἤκουσα) instead ("I saw" comes later, v. 17).

46. Its horns and its gold overlay identify this clearly as the incense altar in the heavenly temple (see 8:3 and Exod 30:1–3; also the note at Rev 6:9). There is a textual variant in v. 13b that does not affect the larger sense but changes the specific wording: several good manuscripts including most of the Byzantine minuscules (P, 046, 1006, 1841, 1854, 2329, 2351) have the word "four" with "horns" (cf. ESV, KJV, NASB, NIV, NRSV).

But several better manuscripts (𝔓[47], A, 1611, 2053, 2344) omit the word (cf. ASV, NEB, NET). Metzger, *TCGNT2*, 670, judges the omission to be accidental: a scribe could have skipped the word "four" (τεσσάρων) since three words in the phrase have the same ending (τῶν τεσσάρων κεράτων). On the other hand, it could have been added to match the "four angels" of v. 14b or to contrast with "a voice" in v. 13b (literally "one voice," φωνὴν μίαν; note on that phrase). It seems best to follow the better manuscripts and omit the word "four."

47. John hears a heavenly voice also in 10:4, 8; 11:12; 12:10; 14:2, 13; 18:4; 19:1. In 18:4 it could be God who speaks in first person (but the wording shifts to third person in 18:5); in 12:10 and 19:1 the voice speaks about God in third person.

48. The participle in v. 14a, "saying" (λέγοντα; a masculine), does not reflect normal grammatical agreement with "voice" (φωνήν; a feminine). This is a case of "agreement according to sense," referring to the person whom the voice represents (cf. 4:1; 11:15).

49. In v. 14b the phrase "the four angels that are bound" (τοὺς τέσσαρας ἀγγέλους τοὺς δεδεμένους) contains the article in Greek neither to refer back to the angels of 7:1–3 nor because John assumes his readers are familiar with these angels already. The reader (actually, the hearer) in view in the phrase is the sixth angel who is addressed by the heavenly voice; this angel is assumed to know already about these four agents in the angelic chain of command, whom he should release when the time is

because they are currently "bound,"[50] held back from their task of destruction until God's time for it arrives (cf. v. 15), in the same way that the four angels in 7:1–3 restrained the earth's destructive winds until the time was right. These are "bound" not because they are fallen, evil angels (i.e., not as Satan will be "bound," 20:2; cf. Mark 3:27); they are holy angels who visit God's punishments on the objects of his judgment (cf. Ps 78:49 ["angels who bring calamity," not "evil angels" as KJV has it]; Ezek 9:1–7; Matt 13:41).[51]

A very significant addition is that they are bound "at the great river Euphrates" (v. 14b). The importance of this will be seen more clearly in the transition between vv. 15 and 16 (see discussion there). The Euphrates, of course, was the "great" river that, with the Tigris River to its east, defined the boundaries of Mesopotamia, the prominent center of ancient Near Eastern civilization. In addition, it proverbially defined the eastern boundary of the land God promised to Abraham and to Israel (Gen 15:18; Exod 23:31; Deut 1:7; 11:24; Josh 1:4). As a result, the Euphrates River was associated with invading armies from Mesopotamia such as Assyria (Isa 8:5–8) and Babylon (2 Kgs 24:7; Jer 46:10), whom God used as instruments of judgment against Israel. At a later time, first-century Roman civilization developed a phobia about hordes of Parthians attacking from the east (across the Euphrates, a natural obstacle against invasion; cf. Tacitus, *Hist.* 5.9; *Ann.* 15.17), and this may have influenced John's wording here. This association of the Euphrates with the threat of an outside attack (see also Rev 16:12) represents a further feature of the typology of judgment mentioned earlier (cf. 6:8, 12, 14, 16), which John expects to be repeated and intensified in the end-times.[52] The future fulfillment of the pattern does not necessitate an invading army only from the east, as some interpreters insist. Destructive invasions converging on Israel from any direction would replicate the pattern sufficiently. But it is essential to see this association of "the great river Euphrates" with attacks by vast forces from the outside in order to follow the narrative through the next several verses.[53]

9:15–16 And the four angels were released, who had stood ready for the hour and day and month and year, in order to kill a third of humanity. 16 And the number of the armies of cavalry was twice ten thousand times ten thousand. I heard their number (καὶ ἐλύθησαν οἱ τέσσαρες ἄγγελοι οἱ ἡτοιμασμένοι εἰς τὴν ὥραν καὶ ἡμέραν καὶ μῆνα καὶ ἐνιαυτόν, ἵνα ἀποκτείνωσιν τὸ τρίτον τῶν ἀνθρώπων. 16 καὶ ὁ ἀριθμὸς τῶν στρατευμάτων τοῦ ἱππικοῦ δισμυριάδες μυριάδων, ἤκουσα τὸν ἀριθμὸν αὐτῶν). The command of v. 14b to release the four angels is carried out right away (v. 15a), and the

---

right. Commentaries consistently misconstrue this detail and assume that the four angels must be known to John's readers as well. Often the internal and external addressees overlap, but not here.

50. "Bound" is a perfect passive participle (δεδεμένους), showing their condition at the outset of the vision (see also the perfect participle of v. 15b).

51. Interpreters disagree over this question. Most argue that these must be evil angels due to the parallel with Satan as "bound" (e.g., Beale, *Revelation*, 506–8; Osborne, *Revelation*, 379; Smalley, *Revelation*, 236–37). Aune, *Revelation 6–16*, 536–37, suggests that these are good angels due to parallels with 7:1 and other texts suggesting holy angels as agents of judgment (cf. Charles, *Revelation*, 1:248–51; Swete, *Apocalypse*, 118–19).

52. The typological pattern shows that the association of the Euphrates River with invading armies in both 9:13–16 and 16:12–16 cannot be taken as persuasive evidence that the sixth trumpet and the sixth bowl "depict the same event from different viewpoints" (Beale, *Revelation*, 507; also Smalley, *Revelation*, 237; quotation from Smalley). The accounts of the two are quite different except for this detail.

53. See Osborne, *Revelation*, 379, for forces crossing the Euphrates as "a symbol of foreign invasion" throughout Israel's history. Thomas, *Revelation 8–22*, 43–44, argues that "Euphrates" must be literal because it is used that way in the OT, but this is not persuasive.

significance of their being held back is made clear: they "had stood ready"[54] to act, but did not proceed until God's predetermined time came. With his extended description, "for the hour and day and month and year" (v. 15b),[55] John emphasizes God's sovereign coordination of his agents of judgment. A fundamental premise of Revelation, as with apocalyptic literature in general, is that God is in control of the events of this world and they occur according to his timetable. This is seen especially in John's use of "time, season" (καιρός; 1:3; 11:18; 12:12; 22:10) and of what "must" happen in the future (δεῖ; 1:1; 4:1; 17:10; 20:3; 22:6). In this case the horrific but God-ordained task that the four angels were released to accomplish is "to kill a third of humanity" (v. 15c).[56] Just as in the first four trumpets (8:7–12) where the proportion "a third" is noted repeatedly as the measure of destruction (see note on 8:7 for the OT background), this portrays a staggering level of anguish and devastation, and it targets the earth's human population directly like the fifth trumpet does (9:1–11).

To the modern reader v. 16 begins rather abruptly in introducing a vast army that will occupy John's attention in vv. 16–19, since the connection with the angels of vv. 13–15 is not made explicit. What the angels are assigned to do in v. 15c (to kill a third of humanity) is directly attributed to the actions of this army in v. 18a (a third of human-

ity was killed; see also v. 20a), but how these are related seems rather puzzling. It is also enigmatic how John can introduce "the armies of cavalry"[57] into the narrative, using an articular Greek phrase (τῶν στρατευμάτων τοῦ ἱππικοῦ) as though the reader is familiar with them already (v. 16a). The answer to this puzzle seems to be the mention of "the great river Euphrates" in v. 14b as the location of the four angels. This should not be read as geographical trivia. John's assumption is that his readers would associate the Euphrates River with past invasions by vast armies across Israel's borders as a manifestation of God's judgment. With that allusion in mind, a reader could understand what "*the* armies" are: they are the armies of God's judgment conventionally associated with invasion across the great river.[58] The role of the overseeing angels is to set these attacking hordes in motion, and so their destructive effects can be attributed to the armies (v. 18a) or to the angels themselves (v. 15c).

The census of the troops (v. 16a) is a staggering number, "twice ten thousand times ten thousand." This, like the multiple large numbers in 5:11,[59] seems to be a way of expressing an unimaginably large body of military forces. A literal count (whether exact or rounded) is not intended but rather the sense that such an army would wreak unspeakable levels of destruction.[60] The fact that such a number is astounding explains John's narrative

---

54. The phrase "who had stood ready" translates a perfect passive participle (ἡτοιμασμένοι) denoting their state of preparedness (cf. the perfect participle in v. 14). See also 12:6, "a place prepared by God" and the NT use of "prepare" to denote God's plans for future events (Matt 25:34, 41; Mark 10:40; Luke 2:31; 1 Cor 2:9).

55. See the final three (day, month, year) cited in sequence in Num 1:1; Hag 1:15; Zech 1:7. Mark 13:32 has only the first two in reverse order (day, hour).

56. The infinitive phrase "to kill" is a smoother English translation of the Greek purpose clause ἵνα ἀποκτείνωσιν, "that they might kill" (cf. v. 5), which shows more clearly the angels' role in this ravaging judgment.

57. In this phrase the plural "armies" suggests wave after wave of military forces (cf. 19:14, 19), and they consist of swift and formidable mounted troops, "cavalry."

58. This is like John's reference to "the altar" in 6:9 (see note there). Once the scene of a heavenly temple has been established in the narrative, related items can be spoken of as definite by association. So here mention of the river evokes the image of invading armies.

59. See the note at 5:11 for the likely OT background of these numbers (Dan 7:10; see too Deut 33:2; Ps 68:17).

60. This is why the translation "two hundred million" (CSB, NASB, NET, NLT, NRSV) may seem too precise, though it too is an astonishing size for an army.

aside, "I heard their number," as an affirmation that this was not merely his own estimate but part of the heavenly vision (v. 17b; cf. 7:4).

9:17 And this is how I saw the horses in my vision as well as those who sit on them: the horsemen have breastplates that are fiery red and dark blue and sulfurous yellow in color, and the heads of the horses are like lions' heads; and fire and smoke and sulfur come from their mouths (καὶ οὕτως εἶδον τοὺς ἵππους ἐν τῇ ὁράσει καὶ τοὺς καθημένους ἐπ᾽ αὐτῶν, ἔχοντας θώρακας πυρίνους καὶ ὑακινθίνους καὶ θειώδεις, καὶ αἱ κεφαλαὶ τῶν ἵππων ὡς κεφαλαὶ λεόντων, καὶ ἐκ τῶν στομάτων αὐτῶν ἐκπορεύεται πῦρ καὶ καπνὸς καὶ θεῖον). Mention of the mounted troops in v. 16 leads to a detailed description of their appearance as well as their dreadful power to kill humans (vv. 17–19). Beginning with his standard "and . . . I saw" (καὶ . . . εἶδον), John recounts how things appear in the vision that he started narrating at v. 13 (the sixth trumpet),[61] but his description takes the form of a concurrent report using present-tense verbs (see comment on vv. 10–11). He mentions first "the horses" and then adds their riders, "those who sit on them" (v. 17a), and his descriptions follow in reverse order (v. 17b–e). The riders are protected by "breastplates" of various ominous colors: "fiery red," "dark blue," and "sulfurous yellow,"[62] colors that foreshadow the three fiery "plagues" these forces will inflict on humans (vv. 17e–18). The horses for their part have heads "like lions' heads," suggestive of the ferocity with which they will attack and kill their human prey (v. 17d). The bizarre

images continue as these horses appear finally like fire-breathing dragons, whose mouths[63] breathe out "fire and smoke and sulfur" (v. 17e). These three destructive elements appear again in v. 18 as well as in 14:10–11, and they are almost certainly drawn from the pattern of judgment seen first at Sodom and Gomorrah (see sulfur, fire, and smoke in Gen 19:24–28) and repeated elsewhere in the Old Testament (see comment at 8:7).

Here again (as in vv. 7–9) we are faced with the question of how to understand the strange imagery of v. 17. Does it refer to spiritual warfare in the human soul, to fierce human armies, or to demonic forces unleashed against sinful humanity in the final days of tribulation? As in vv. 7–9 the last option seems best in this passage also (see discussion at v. 9).

9:18–19 From these three plagues a third of humanity was killed, from the fire and the smoke and the sulfur that came from their mouths. 19 For the power of the horses is in their mouths and in their tails, for their tails which are like serpents have heads, and they inflict harm with them (ἀπὸ τῶν τριῶν πληγῶν τούτων ἀπεκτάνθησαν τὸ τρίτον τῶν ἀνθρώπων, ἐκ τοῦ πυρὸς καὶ τοῦ καπνοῦ καὶ τοῦ θείου τοῦ ἐκπορευομένου ἐκ τῶν στομάτων αὐτῶν. 19 ἡ γὰρ ἐξουσία τῶν ἵππων ἐν τῷ στόματι αὐτῶν ἐστιν καὶ ἐν ταῖς οὐραῖς αὐτῶν, αἱ γὰρ οὐραὶ αὐτῶν ὅμοιαι ὄφεσιν, ἔχουσαι κεφαλὰς καὶ ἐν αὐταῖς ἀδικοῦσιν). Verse 18 begins without an introductory conjunction (i.e., asyndeton; cf. v. 11) as befits its very close connection with what was said in v. 17. The referents of "these three plagues"[64] (v. 18a)

---

61. To clarify his focus on appearance, John inserts two elements: the words "this is how" (οὕτως, "thus, in this way") and "in my vision" (ἐν τῇ ὁράσει).

62. Each of these colors has a "fiery" connection: "fiery red" (πύρινος) or "red like fire" is related to the color term used in 6:4; 12:3. "Dark blue" (ὑακίνθινος, "hyacinth") is the color of a flower, but vv. 17e–18 make it parallel to "smoke," so it may

denote a hot, blue flame. "Sulfurous yellow" (θειώδης) is related to the word "sulfur, brimstone" (θεῖον). See comments on v. 17d for the OT background of these words.

63. Verse 19a confirms that "from *their* mouths" refers to the horses, not the riders.

64. This is the first of sixteen occurrences in Rev of the word "plague" (πληγή). In a few places it carries its more gen-

are clearly the three destructive elements that proceed from the horses' mouths as v. 17e records, and the wording of that clause is repeated virtually verbatim in v. 18a (the three elements that were anarthrous now have anaphoric articles to refer back to v. 17e). The deadly consequence of these "plagues," that "a third of humanity was killed" (v. 18a), was also anticipated earlier (v. 15c), but here it is presented not as something about to occur but as a starkly tragic fact.[65]

John adds one more peculiar element to his description of these horses by clarifying ("for")[66] where their phenomenal power lies (v. 19a).[67] Their destructive "power" (ἐξουσία)[68] is "in their mouths" from which they breathe out deadly fire, smoke, and sulfur as vv. 17–18 indicated. But to this he adds "and in their tails," with a further explanation (another "for" [γάρ] clause) quite unexpected from the image of horses and horsemen given previously. These "horses" are like mythical dragons not only because they breathe out fire (v. 17e) but also because they have serpent-like, multiheaded tails.[69] With these "heads" they are able to "inflict harm" (ἀδικοῦσιν), so presumably the heads are snake-like and deadly to humans just like the fire-breathing mouths of the horses are. This verse reveals the similarities of this cavalry troop to the locusts of vv. 1–11, since they also have "power" (vv. 3, 10)

to inflict "harm" (vv. 4, 10) with tails that have a punishing sting (v. 10).[70]

9:20–21 And the rest of humanity who were not killed in these plagues did not repent of the works of their hands so as not to worship demons and idols of gold and silver and bronze and stone and wood, which cannot see or hear or walk, 21 and they did not repent of their murders or their sorceries or their sexual immorality or their thefts (Καὶ οἱ λοιποὶ τῶν ἀνθρώπων, οἳ οὐκ ἀπεκτάνθησαν ἐν ταῖς πληγαῖς ταύταις, οὐδὲ μετενόησαν ἐκ τῶν ἔργων τῶν χειρῶν αὐτῶν, ἵνα μὴ προσκυνήσουσιν τὰ δαιμόνια καὶ τὰ εἴδωλα τὰ χρυσᾶ καὶ τὰ ἀργυρᾶ καὶ τὰ χαλκᾶ καὶ τὰ λίθινα καὶ τὰ ξύλινα, ἃ οὔτε βλέπειν δύνανται οὔτε ἀκούειν οὔτε περιπατεῖν, 21 καὶ οὐ μετενόησαν ἐκ τῶν φόνων αὐτῶν οὔτε ἐκ τῶν φαρμάκων αὐτῶν οὔτε ἐκ τῆς πορνείας αὐτῶν οὔτε ἐκ τῶν κλεμμάτων αὐτῶν). In this final tableau John summarizes the spiritual and religious aftermath of the punishing attacks that the sixth trumpet will unleash in the end-times. After such deadly and widespread attacks by the horrific armies just seen in John's vision (vv. 16–19), one might have expected a wholesale turning to the God of heaven for protection and solace, but as elsewhere in Revelation (e.g., 2:21; 6:15–17; 16:9, 11, 21) no repentance by rebellious humanity is forthcoming (vv. 20–21).[71] John sees in his vision that the two-thirds

---

eral sense of "wound, blow" (e.g., 13:3, 12, 14; cf. Luke 10:30; Acts 16:23), but it frequently evokes typological connections with the divine "plagues" against Egypt (Exod 7–12) as noted by G. Schwarz, "πληγή," *EDNT* 3:103.

65. For this level of ruin, see 8:7–12; cf. 6:7 (one fourth); in Ezek 5:12 and Zech 13:8 only one third survives (also Sib. Or. 3:538–44).

66. The "for" (γάρ) of v. 19a is explanatory, telling how these attackers could inflict such extreme casualties (BDAG 190; Runge, *Discourse Grammar*, 51–54).

67. Two present customary verbs in v. 19 show that John has switched again to his report mode of presentation (see vv. 10–11, 17).

68. See note about "power" at v. 3.

69. The verb in v. 19b translated "have heads" (ἔχουσαι) is a participle showing by its agreement that the "tails" have heads.

70. These parallels should not lead us to conflate the two or see the sixth trumpet as a repetition of the fifth since the other details are distinctive.

71. This stubborn refusal to repent is part of the exodus-plagues motif that John reflects in all three series of judgments. Just as Pharaoh hardened his heart despite increasingly severe punishment (e.g., Exod 7:22; 8:15, 19, 32), so the enemies of God and his people in the future will continue to resist him. Cf. Fekkes, *Prophetic Traditions*, 80–82.

of humanity who survived those attacks (cf. one-third killed, vv. 15, 18) "did not repent" (i.e., change their course of life; see note on this verb at 2:5). This verb phrase occurs twice to underline their failure to turn from their idolatry (violations against worship of the true God; v. 20) and their failure to cease from their moral offences (violations against other people; v. 21).

The description of their idolatry (v. 20b) is phrased in terms common to ancient Jewish critique of such practices: idols are merely "the works of [human] hands" (Deut 31:29; Ps 115:4–7; Isa 2:8; Jer 1:16), fashioned from various materials the true God created (Dan 5:4, 23 cites six such materials: the five listed here plus "iron"; cf. 2 Kgs 19:18; Isa 37:19; Jer 10:1–16). They have no ability to deliver from trouble since they cannot even "see or hear or walk" (Deut 4:28; Ps 115:4–7; Jer 10:4–5; cf. Wis 13:1–19). Instead, to worship such man-made images is to worship false gods, "demons" who oppose God and deceive humanity (Exod 20:3–6; Deut 32:17; Ps 95:5; 1 Cor 10:19–22; cf. 1 En. 19:1). In the end-times this pattern of human deception and false worship will reach its ultimate escalation in worldwide worship of the dragon Satan and his "beast," through the image of the beast made by the "false prophet" who compels humans to offer such worship and oppose God (Rev 13:4–8, 11–15; 14:9, 11; 16:13–14; 19:20; 20:10). The bitter irony of Revelation 9 is that those who worship demons are not somehow exempt from demonic violence but rather will suffer severe attacks from these satanic hordes and remain unrepentant.

Their failure to repent from moral offences (v. 21) is likewise expressed in wording central to Old Testament ethical teaching, that is, actions prohibited in the Decalogue (Exod 20:13–15), such as "murders," "sexual immorality," and "thefts" (cf. Mark 10:19; Luke 18:20; Rom 13:9). The additional item, "sorceries" (φαρμάκων),[72] was associated with false worship and its actions against other humans to deceive them into its idolatry (Exod 7:11; 8:14; 9:11; 2 Kgs 9:22; Nah 3:4). The widespread Jewish-Christian conviction was that departure from worship of the true God inevitably leads to false worship and moral debauchery (2 Kgs 17:15–17; Jer 13:22–27; Acts 7:42; Rom 1:21–32; cf. 2 Bar. 54:17–18; 1 En. 99:6–16; Wis 14:22–31). Clinging to sinful acts in the face of such judgment reveals the irresistible power of evil that holds humankind in its grip. But the sure judgment of God will come on all such human evil when the third woe (the seventh trumpet) comes to pass (portrayed after two interludes in 11:14).

Theology in Application

The Nightmare of Sin and Its Consequences

You wake up in a cold sweat from a terrifying nightmare about some bizarre creature or terrible accident from which you couldn't escape. What a relief to find that it was just a bad dream! But at some point in the future of this fallen world, the nightmarish scenario will be devastatingly real as Revelation 9 reveals: a bottomless, smoke-filled pit teeming with demonic locusts/scorpions, who pour out onto the

---

72. The word translated "sorceries" (φάρμακον; cf. CSB, ESV, KJV, NASB, NRSV, RSV) refers to "magic arts" (NIV), the use of potions, spells, or related practices to gain power over spirits or humans (BDAG 1049–50). Related words appear in Exod 7:11; Deut 18:10; Dan 2:2; Gal 5:20; Rev 18:23; 21:8; 22:15.

earth and target the earth's ill-fated inhabitants with horrifying pains. Their suffering is worse than death, but relief eludes them. Or an infernal horde of horses/serpents spewing fire, smoke, and sulfur gallop across the earth, bringing death to billions of people. Although the depth of agony is hardly comparable, this scene reminds us of the desperate straits people find themselves in even today because of sinful choices they make. As vv. 20–21 show, most of these who suffer from the terrible wounds or painful deaths inflicted by demonic forces will be ones who are actually on the same side of the end-time cosmic conflict Revelation portrays. Satan's demons are all too happy to visit mayhem even on their own human "followers" if given the chance. The New Testament teaches that those who turn away from God become darkened in their understanding of what is really at stake in their lives. At some point in this sinful derangement, they come to believe that allegiance to Satan and his evil—in whatever deceptive form it presents itself to them—would be to their advantage. What a shock when they belatedly see what he and his minions are like! What a shock to find that the "choices" for sin they felt free to make have turned around and made them who they are (i.e., people trapped in false worship and its attendant moral enslavements, vv. 20–21). The visions of Revelation are given to dispel such deception and show the truth of how the world of good and evil really works and what is at stake in their choices.

Refusing the Gift of Repentance

Revelation 9:20–21 reminds us that, even in the late hour of redemptive history described here, God's intent is to bring people to repentance, not destruction (cf. 2:21; 6:15–17; 16:9, 11, 21). The chapter notes that amid widespread devastation there are still limits to God's punishment (e.g., 9:5, 15, 18), and in his patience he offers time for billions to turn away from evil before the final judgments fall. Despite this, people will stubbornly refuse to repent. These verses illustrate the indivisible link between worship and ethics.[73] What we worship and how we conduct ourselves always go together. The ideology we adopt (even if we refuse to acknowledge the "religious" commitment that is at its core) affects our lifestyle and vice versa. And our vaunted autonomy to choose our own way proves to be a mirage, since as mentioned above, the choices we make always make us who we are. In biblical teaching, sin is not something we opt for but is a hostile and enslaving force whose bonds we cannot break on our own (Rom 5:12, 21). It is "a self-perpetuating cycle of idolatry and falsehood from which, humanly speaking, there is no escape."[74] But God, through his emancipating grace in Christ, freely offers deliverance from its power (Rom 3:24; 6:23; Rev 21:6; 22:17). This is a gift no one should refuse.

---

73. Thanks to Marc-André Caron for this insight.   74. Mangina, *Revelation*, 127.

Revelation 10:1–11

Literary Context

Just as chapter 7 gives two complementary visions as an interlude between the sixth and seventh seals, so 10:1–11:14 relates a twofold vision between the sixth and seventh trumpets. While these sections are labeled "interludes," they reflect the central themes of the book in remarkable ways. In this phase of the vision (10:1–11), the pause in the action makes clear that the surrounding events of judgment (seals, trumpets, and later the bowls) are anchored in prophetic revelation—given through John among others—about God's eternal plans for the peoples of his world (cf. 10:7, 11). By revisiting John's prophetic call (after his initial commission in 1:9–11, 17–19), divine messengers remind John in 10:8–11 that he, like Ezekiel of old, is charged with the bittersweet task of prophesying about God's worldwide work of judgment and redemption. He is also assured that in this task he is joining a train of God's prophets across the centuries and that God is about to accomplish his hidden plan for creation revealed through these messengers (10:6–7). The two witnesses whose contested ministry is traced in the next section (11:1–14) will be a faithful manifestation of the same prophetic tradition in the final days.

III. **Second Vision: Heavenly Throne Room and Three Judgment Cycles (4:1–16:21)**

    A. Vision of God in His Heavenly Throne Room (4:1–11)

    B. The Seven-Sealed Scroll and the Slain Lamb (5:1–14)

    C. The Seven Seals and the Interlude of the Two Multitudes (6:1–8:1)

    D. **The Seven Trumpets and Further Interludes (8:2–14:20)**

        1. The First Four Trumpets (8:2–13)

        2. The Fifth Trumpet—First Woe (9:1–12)

        3. The Sixth Trumpet—Second Woe (9:13–21)

➡   4. **Two Revelatory Interludes: God's Prophets (10:1–11:14)**

            a. **John and the little scroll (10:1–11)**

            b. Temple measurements and the two witnesses (11:1–14)

Main Idea

The series of judgments seen in John's visions signal the imminent fulfillment of what God has revealed about the world's future through prophets like John whom he has commissioned.

Translation

Revelation 10:1–11

1a	Vision Intro/ Character Entrance	And **I saw another angel,**
b	Description	a mighty one,
c		coming down from heaven,
d		clothed with a cloud, and
e		a rainbow was above his head, and
f	Comparison	his face was like the sun, and
g		his legs were like pillars of fire,
2a	Description/Plot Tension	**and he had in his hand a little scroll lying open.**
b	Setting	And **he put his right foot on the sea and his left foot on the land,**
3a	Action/Comparison	and **he cried out in a loud voice like a lion roars.**
b	Time	And when he cried out,
c	Action	**the seven thunders spoke with their own voices.**
4a	Time	And when the seven thunders spoke,
b	Response to 3c	**I was about to write,**
c	Counterresponse to 4b	and **I heard a voice from heaven saying,**
d	Command	*"Seal up the things that the seven thunders said and do not write them down."*

Continued on next page.

Continued from previous page.

5 Action   And **the angel I saw standing**
                      on the sea and
                      on the land
           raised his right hand toward heaven

6a   and   **swore by the one**
                          who lives forever and ever,

b   Description   who created
                          the heaven and the things in it and
                          the earth and the things in it and
                          the sea and the things in it,

c   Declaration 1   *"There will be no more delay,*

7a   Circumstance/   *but*   *in the days of the sound of the seventh angel,*
      Temporal
b   Clarification   *when he will sound his trumpet,*
c   Declaration 2   *then*
               the mystery of God will be completed

d   Confirmation   *as he announced*
                             to his own servants
                             the prophets."

8a   Action/Resumption   And **the voice that I heard from heaven I heard again,**
      (from 4c)

b   speaking with me and
                   saying,
c   Command   *"Go take the scroll*
d   Description   *that is lying open in the hand of the angel*
e   Description   *who is standing on the sea and*
                               on the land."

9a   Response to 8c–e   So **I went to the angel,**
b   requesting him to give me the little scroll.

c   Response to 9b   And **he said to me,**
d   Command   *"Take*
                  and eat it,
e   Result   *and it will make your stomach bitter,*
f   Contrast   *but in your mouth it will be sweet like honey."*
10a   Response to 9d   And **I took the little scroll from the hand of the angel**
                   and **I ate it,**
b   Result   and **in my mouth it was sweet like honey,**
c   Contrast   but **when I ate it my stomach was made bitter.**
11a   And **I was told,**
b   Commission   *"You must prophesy again about peoples and*
                               nations and
                               languages and
                               many kings."

Structure

The initial vision (10:1–11) of this interlude before the seventh trumpet comes in two related sections. First, in vv. 1–7 John sees and hears a powerful angel holding a little scroll, whose roar in heaven finds a response from "seven peals of thunder." As in 5:4 John reacts to the events of the vision, in this case by starting to record what he has heard, but he is distinctly forbidden to do so (vv. 1–4). Then the mighty angel solemnly affirms that the events of the seventh trumpet will bring without delay the completion of what God has revealed through his prophets (vv. 5–7). In the second section, John is pulled into the vision even more directly by being told to take the little scroll from the mighty angel's hand and eat it (vv. 8–9). He finds it a mixed experience and is told that it represents his divine commission to prophesy further about the peoples of the world (vv. 10–11).

Exegetical Outline

III. **Second Vision: Heavenly Throne Room and Three Judgment Cycles (4:1–16:21)**
    A. Vision of God in His Heavenly Throne Room (4:1–11)
    B. The Seven-Sealed Scroll and the Slain Lamb (5:1–14)
    C. The Seven Seals and the Interlude of the Two Multitudes (6:1–8:1)
    D. The Seven Trumpets and Further Interludes (8:2–14:20)
        1. The First Four Trumpets (8:2–13)
        2. The Fifth Trumpet—First Woe (9:1–12)
        3. The Sixth Trumpet—Second Woe (9:13–21)
        4. Two Revelatory Interludes: God's Prophets (10:1–11:14)
            a. John and the little scroll (10:1–11)
                (1) A mighty angel with a little scroll: God's mystery completed (10:1–7)
                    (a) An angel, the little scroll, and seven thunders: command not to write (10:1–4)
                    (b) The angel's oath: no further delay in completing God's plan (10:5–7)
                (2) John and the little scroll: prophecy about the future of the world (10:8–11)
                    (a) Command to eat the little scroll (10:8–9)
                    (b) Bittersweet task of prophesying about the world's peoples (10:10–11)

Explanation of the Text

10:1–2a And I saw another angel, a mighty one, coming down from heaven, clothed with a cloud, and a rainbow was above his head, and his face was like the sun, and his legs were like pillars of fire, 2 and he had in his hand a little scroll lying open (Καὶ εἶδον ἄλλον ἄγγελον ἰσχυρὸν καταβαίνοντα ἐκ τοῦ οὐρανοῦ περιβεβλημένον νεφέλην, καὶ ἡ ἶρις ἐπὶ τῆς κεφαλῆς αὐτοῦ καὶ τὸ πρόσωπον αὐτοῦ ὡς ὁ ἥλιος καὶ οἱ πόδες αὐτοῦ ὡς στῦλοι πυρός, 2 καὶ ἔχων ἐν τῇ χειρὶ αὐτοῦ βιβλαρίδιον ἠνεῳγμένον). John's next vision ("and I saw"; cf. 9:1, 17) represents a pause before he narrates the seventh trumpet blast (i.e., the third "woe," cf. 11:14–15). This vision concerns the interaction between "another angel" who was mighty (v. 1), impressive voices from heaven (vv. 3, 4, 8), and John, who receives a prophetic commission in the process (vv. 10–11). During the vision the mighty angel solemnly announces that the completion of God's revealed purpose will be delayed no further (vv. 6–7). The same vision carries over also to further events in 11:1–19.

The initial protagonist in the story is "another angel, a mighty one" (ἄλλον ἄγγελον ἰσχυρόν; v. 1a–b), who is thus distinguished from the angel with the sixth trumpet as well as the four angels who released the hordes of judgment in the previous vision (9:13–15). The added trait, "mighty,"[1] begins a series of impressive descriptions that show his heavenly credentials for the role he will play in the vision. He descends "from heaven" as God's emissary (cf. 18:1; 20:1). The other features in v. 1 reinforce the heavenly splendor of this one who comes to carry out the divine will on earth. Some have argued that the "cloud" and "rainbow" must identify this angel as Jesus Christ or the Lord God himself (appearing as "the angel of the Lord" known from the OT).[2] Likewise a face "like the sun" and legs (or feet)[3] "like pillars of fire"[4] are features of the glorified Christ in 1:15–16 and 2:18. But the term "angel" is not used to refer to Christ or God anywhere else in Revelation (out of 67 total occurrences). If the Old Testament "angel of the Lord" was John's intent in this passage, we might have expected the longer phrase to be used for clarity. Like other "angels" who have regularly appeared in John's visions (e.g., 5:2; 7:1–2; 8:2–5; 9:14–15), this one is best understood as an agent of God but not divine, and these glorious descriptions are cited to underscore his nearness to God (cf. Exod 34:29–30;

---

1. The whole phrase could be translated "another mighty angel" (cf. CSB, ESV, KJV, NIV, NRSV, RSV), and this could imply a specific contrast with the "mighty angel" of 5:2 or some connection with "a certain mighty angel" in 18:21 (as though these three "mighty" ones are thought of together). Neither of these can be justified from the phrases themselves or the contexts in which they occur.

2. Beale, *Revelation*, 523–24. Some support for this can be seen in the "rainbow" around the heavenly throne in 4:3 (cf. Ezek 1:28) and the frequent OT association of a "cloud" with God's coming or presence (e.g., Exod 16:10; 19:9; 1 Kgs 8:10–11; Isa 19:1). But the rainbow can also be seen as a feature of gleaming light associated with God as well as his glorious angels (both are in view in Rev 4:2–8 and Ezek 1:4–28), and the cloud likewise can be a broader figure for heaven or transport to or from heaven (cf. Dan 7:13; Acts 1:9; 1 Thess 4:17;

Rev 11:12). See 14:14–16 for similar issues about the significance of a "cloud" there.

3. The word translated "legs" here in 10:1 is more commonly rendered "feet" (πόδες), but it can occasionally include the leg as well (cf. BDAG 858; MM 531–32), and "pillar" is more naturally a figure for the whole leg.

4. A further debatable point is whether the mention of "cloud" and "pillars of fire" alludes to the frequent OT accounts of God's presence and guidance of Israel in the wilderness (e.g., Exod 13:21; 14:19, 24; Num 14:14; Neh 9:12, 19), used here as a new exodus motif (God is present with his people to bring them through to peace and safety). Since these two elements are mentioned here in separate descriptions and have a sense that seems to come from different OT texts (Ezek 1; Dan 10), not exodus passages, it seems unlikely that such an allusion is intended.

Matt 13:43) and his heavenly origin and mission (like the glorious beings in Ezek 1:7, 13–14; Dan 10:5–6; cf. 4 Ezra 7:97; 2 En. 1:5; 19:1).

While the appearance of "another angel" who is mighty (v. 1; cf. 5:2) does not in itself relate this episode to 5:1–7 (a scroll, in God's hand sealed with seven seals), the angel's possession of "a little scroll lying open" (v. 2a) makes the two accounts parallel in at least some respects. Is this the same scroll as in 5:1, now reappearing after its unsealing in 6:1–8:1, or is it a different one perhaps symbolizing a similar point (unveiling and unfolding of God's plan for judgment and redemption)? When seen as representing a similar point, the issue of whether the two are identical or different becomes less important.[5] The word for "little scroll" (βιβλαρίδιον)[6] used in 10:2, 9, 10 is different from "scroll" (βιβλίον) used six times in 5:1–8, but βιβλίον also appears as a synonym for βιβλαρίδιον here in 10:8, and the meaning of the two is close enough to allow for both to point to the same referent. It makes more sense overall to see this "little scroll" as a reappearance of the same "scroll" from chapter 5, now "lying open" after its seals have been broken.[7] It comes back on the scene as part of the transition between the beginning judgments of 6:1–9:21 and the culminating judgments that follow (11:15ff.) when "the mystery of God will be completed" (10:7). In any case the "little scroll" is mentioned only briefly here to set the stage; the significant events surrounding it are narrated in vv. 8–11.

10:2b–4 And he put his right foot on the sea and his left foot on the land, 3 and he cried out in a loud voice like a lion roars. And when he cried out, the seven thunders spoke with their own voices. 4 And when the seven thunders spoke, I was about to write, and I heard a voice from heaven saying, "Seal up the things that the seven thunders said and do not write them down" (καὶ ἔθηκεν τὸν πόδα αὐτοῦ τὸν δεξιὸν ἐπὶ τῆς θαλάσσης, τὸν δὲ εὐώνυμον ἐπὶ τῆς γῆς, 3 καὶ ἔκραξεν φωνῇ μεγάλῃ ὥσπερ λέων μυκᾶται. καὶ ὅτε ἔκραξεν, ἐλάλησαν αἱ ἑπτὰ βρονταὶ τὰς ἑαυτῶν φωνάς. 4 καὶ ὅτε ἐλάλησαν αἱ ἑπτὰ βρονταί, ἤμελλον γράφειν· καὶ ἤκουσα φωνὴν ἐκ τοῦ οὐρανοῦ λέγουσαν, Σφράγισον ἃ ἐλάλησαν αἱ ἑπτὰ βρονταί, καὶ μὴ αὐτὰ γράψῃς). With the mighty angel on the scene, the events of John's new vision move rapidly along, although an important diversion from the main narrative develops when other figures including John enter the story. Taking an imposing stance that represents the cosmic reach of what he has come to reveal (vv. 6–7), the angel straddles both sea[8] and land (v. 2b). In vv. 1–2 as well as in v. 5 this picture encompasses all three of the commonly cited realms of God's created universe: heaven, earth or land, and sea (v. 6; cf. 5:13; 14:7; see other biblical texts cited at v. 6 below); this angel's actions will have cosmic significance. In this dramatic pose the angel then utters a loud cry "like a lion roars,"[9] apparently to garner attention for what he will declare in vv. 6c–7. But the angel's cry prompts a response from "the

---

5. There are certainly contrasts between the two (sealed vs. open; in God's hand vs. in the angel's hand; in heaven vs. on earth; the Lamb's role in its unveiling vs. John's role, etc.), but these are complementary, not mutually exclusive. John's dependence on Ezek 2:8–3:3 in both helps to meld the chapters together too. See Resseguie, *Narrative Commentary*, 153, for this narrowing of the distinctions.

6. The ending -ιον is a diminutive suffix in Greek, and it probably retains its sense of "a smaller one" (see BDAG 176; BDF §111.3; Aune, *Revelation 6–16*, 558). The textual evidence for βιβλαρίδιον and βιβλίον in 10:2, 8–10 is quite mixed, but

the readings accepted by the printed editions of NA[28]/UBS[5] (reflected in the commentary above) are likely to be correct.

7. See comments at 5:1. Bauckham, *Climax*, 243–57, provides the most extensive defense of this view.

8. Apocalyptic imagery, like other figurative language, is not constrained by normal physical realities. Just as mountains can skip like rams (Ps 114:4), so an angel can stand on the sea.

9. God's voice is pictured as the roar of a lion in Hos 11:10; Joel 3:16; Amos 1:2; 3:8 (especially God speaking through his prophets). Here the angel is God's spokesperson.

seven thunders," creating a short diversion in the storyline (vv. 3b–4). It is not clear who these "seven thunders" are who reply "with their own voices" to the loud voice of the mighty angel. John presents them as familiar to his readers (*the* seven thunders), but no ancient sources give evidence of well-known phenomena like this. This may represent seven angels who interact from heaven with the mighty angel (cf. 7:2–3; 14:17–18, where angelic interaction is portrayed in John's visions; see also John 12:29). It could be a reference to the fullness of God's voice (like "the seven spirits of God" denoting the Holy Spirit in Rev 1:4; 5:6). Psalm 29:3–9 (where "the voice of the LORD" is mentioned seven times and portrayed as a rainstorm "thundering" over the earth) could be a source for such an idea.[10]

Whoever the actual speaker or speakers were, John was impressed enough with the voices of the seven thunders that he "was about to write"[11] down what he heard (an activity he was commanded to do on other occasions, 1:11, 19; 14:13; 19:9; 21:5). But in this instance a heavenly voice gives him the opposite instruction: "Do not write" (μὴ . . . γράψῃς; v. 4d).[12] Instead, he must "seal up" the things[13] the thunders had spoken. The image of "sealing" what had been revealed is drawn from Daniel 8:26 and 12:4, 9 (Rev 10:5–6 is strongly influenced by Dan 12). In Daniel the implication is that revelation about the distant future should be secured and its authenticity ensured (the image of a seal as marking ownership or authenticating something as valid) until the end draws near. At that time it will be available to show the significance of the events

that occur. Here the import seems to be more like that of the "seals" of 5:1–4 before the Lamb is found to open them (i.e., they are closed off from wider knowledge). The things the thunders have said should remain inaccessible. Though he has not even written them yet, they are to be sealed off in John's mind only and not written down for others to read. So the things John heard are divine secrets, never to be made known more widely (cf. 2 Cor 12:4). We can still wonder what purpose is served for John (under inspiration) to record this part of the vision that tantalizes the reader with heavenly secrets only to withhold them in the end. Why not just omit this portion of the vision? One suggestion is that it is an overt reminder that God's counsel has depths that humans will never see or understand. Prior to its fulfillment—and even after—the details of God's purposes that he has chosen to reveal through his prophets will always be a partial glimpse of his plan and seen only "through a glass darkly" (1 Cor 13:12). It is always a salutary thing for proud humans to be reminded of their limitations and to leave some matters to a trustworthy God.

10:5–7 And the angel I saw standing on the sea and on the land raised his right hand toward heaven 6 and swore by the one who lives forever and ever, who created the heaven and the things in it and the earth and the things in it and the sea and the things in it, "There will be no more delay, 7 but in the days of the sound of the seventh angel, when he will sound his trumpet, then the mystery of God will be completed as he an-

---

10. Thunder is one of the features of God's appearance at Sinai (Exod 19:16), and this is repeated with other frightful phenomena in Rev 4:5; 8:5; 11:19; 16:18–21, but this is never specified as "the seven thunders."

11. In the context of v. 4 the sense of "was about to" (μέλλω) is almost equal to "began to," as BDAG 627 points out (similar sense in v. 7; also 3:2; 8:13; 12:4).

12. The verbs "seal up" and "do not write" reflect the typical use of the aorist tense in commands or prohibitions: they give instructions for a specific situation, not for broad or customary action (BDF §§335–37; Fanning, *Verbal Aspect*, 327–40).

13. Even though John had apparently not yet written anything on a scroll that could be closed up, "sealing" here carries the broader sense of "keeping secret, not disclosing."

nounced to his own servants the prophets" (Καὶ ὁ ἄγγελος, ὃν εἶδον ἑστῶτα ἐπὶ τῆς θαλάσσης καὶ ἐπὶ τῆς γῆς, ἦρεν τὴν χεῖρα αὐτοῦ τὴν δεξιὰν εἰς τὸν οὐρανὸν 6 καὶ ὤμοσεν ἐν τῷ ζῶντι εἰς τοὺς αἰῶνας τῶν αἰώνων, ὃς ἔκτισεν τὸν οὐρανὸν καὶ τὰ ἐν αὐτῷ καὶ τὴν γῆν καὶ τὰ ἐν αὐτῇ καὶ τὴν θάλασσαν καὶ τὰ ἐν αὐτῇ, ὅτι χρόνος οὐκέτι ἔσται, 7 ἀλλ᾽ ἐν ταῖς ἡμέραις τῆς φωνῆς τοῦ ἑβδόμου ἀγγέλου, ὅταν μέλλῃ σαλπίζειν, καὶ ἐτελέσθη τὸ μυστήριον τοῦ θεοῦ, ὡς εὐηγγέλισεν τοὺς ἑαυτοῦ δούλους τοὺς προφήτας). After something of a digression in vv. 3b–4 (the seven thunders), John picks up the main events of his vision from v. 2b where he first presented the angel who was "standing on the sea and on the land" (v. 5a). The main content of the vision, in terms of its relevance for the sequence of the seven trumpets, is presented in the angel's solemn declaration about the completion of God's purposes without further delay (vv. 6–7). His declaration is recorded in terms drawn closely from Daniel 12:5–13.[14] The angel's dramatic oath by the God "who lives forever" and affirmed with hand raised "toward heaven" mirrors Daniel 12:7 almost exactly (see also Gen 14:22; Deut 32:40). Here the gravity of "swearing" by the living God is increased from Daniel's oath formula by adding the threefold description of God's creative work in heaven, earth, and sea (Rev 10:6b) commonly found in the Old Testament (e.g., Gen 1:26; Exod 20:11; Neh 9:6; Ps 146:6; Jonah 1:9; cf. Acts 4:24; 14:15). The angel's

announcement must certainly be taken as an iron-clad declaration of God's truth and its significance for John's portrayal of coming events duly noted. The seventh trumpet (and the seven bowls associated with it; cf. comments at 11:15) will bring cataclysmic changes for the world.

The content of his declaration (vv. 6c–7) concerns God's timing and purpose in the events that John described as "what must happen soon" (1:1; cf. 4:1; 22:6–7). Amid the seals and trumpets of these chapters, God through his emissary now affirms (v. 6c), "There will be no more delay" (χρόνος οὐκέτι ἔσται).[15] This time indication is oriented, of course, not to John's time of writing but to the time referred to in this preview of future judgments, the time of the seventh trumpet (v. 7a–b). "No further delay" is oriented in part toward the failure of humans to repent despite severe suffering under the sixth trumpet, just as under the sixth seal (6:15–17; 9:20–21); they should have taken the opportunity to turn to the true God previously because full judgment is near (cf. 2:21; 2 Pet 3:4, 9). But it speaks also to the nearness of full salvation for God's people; they do not have long to wait when this point is reached (cf. Rev 6:10–11).

"No more delay" is thus defined more precisely by the temporal indications of v. 7a–b, pointing to the imminent blast of the seventh trumpet (11:15ff.) as the time of culmination.[16] That time is reinforced by the clause "when he will sound his

---

14. In Dan 12 the glorious angel of Dan 10 is asked when the events portrayed in Dan 11 will reach "completion" (Dan 12:6; LXX, συντέλεια). His response is a time period ("a time, times, and half a time," v. 7) that appears in adapted form in Rev 11:2, 3.

15. Here the word translated "delay" (χρόνος; cf. NIV, ESV, NASB, NRSV) does not denote time as an abstract or philosophical entity (as the KJV's rendering, "that there should be time no longer," or the Geneva Bible, "that time should be no more"), and is sometimes wrongly understood. Instead it means a duration or period of time, especially a time of respite

or delay prior to some occurrence. See 2:21; 6:11; 20:3; cf. Wis 12:20; Josephus, *J.W.* 4.188; *Life* 370 (cf. also the related verb in Matt 24:48; 25:5; Luke 1:21; Heb 10:37).

16. The wording of v. 7a–b is a bit rough and repetitive. The translation given above sticks fairly closely to the structure of the Greek original: "But in the days of the sound of the seventh angel, when he sounds his trumpet" (cf. KJV, NASB). Some modern versions smooth this out (see CSB, ESV, NIV, RSV), but the sense is the same.

trumpet."[17] When that occurs,[18] what God revealed across the ages through his prophets, that is, "the mystery of God" (τὸ μυστήριον τοῦ θεοῦ), will be brought to completion,[19] just as he "announced" to them in various ways over the centuries (v. 7c–d). Here John uses the term "mystery" in its revelatory sense, of something held secret in the divine counsel but unveiled and then brought to fulfillment in God's time.[20] The nuance of something secret or hidden from humans but revealed by God can be seen in Daniel 2:18–19, 28–30, 47. In the New Testament the word is used of God's redemptive purpose, conceived in eternity past but now revealed in the gospel of Christ and proclaimed to all (Rom 16:25–26; 1 Cor 2:1; 4:1; Eph 1:9; 3:9; 6:19; Col 1:26–27; 4:3). Here John emphasizes how God made the divine counsel known[21] "to his own servants the prophets" (Jer 7:25; Dan 9:6; Amos 3:7; Zech 1:6) as a prelude to vv. 8–11 where his own commissioning as a prophet of "the mystery of God" is symbolized. The following vision (11:1–14)

also represents the ministry of God's prophets across the ages right up till the time of the consummation to come, a ministry with which John identifies himself and his present work (1:3; 22:6, 10, 18–19).

This passage reveals the larger sense in which Revelation can aptly be called "the climax of prophecy."[22] John's own contribution to the Old Testament prophetic tradition is not to counter or redirect what the prophets have said but to show how it will soon be fulfilled in God's work of judgment and redemption directed toward Israel and all the nations of the world. His message particularly builds on what is said in central Old Testament texts such as Daniel 7, Zechariah 12, Psalm 2, and numerous passages from Isaiah, Jeremiah, and Ezekiel that tell of the establishment of God's coming reign on earth, even in the face of powerful worldly empires and their kings that oppose his rule and oppress God's people.[23]

This announcement that God's saving plan is

---

17. The phrase "when he will sound" (ὅταν μέλλῃ σαλπίζειν) is also a smoother rendering to suit English idiom. The Greek conjunction translated "when" (ὅταν) denotes an indefinite time in the future: "at whatever time," and the phrase "he will sound" contains a verb (μέλλω) that can mean "to be about to, to verge on" (cf. NASB, NET, NIV) or even "to begin to," but it can also simply express future occurrence ("will blow"; CSB; cf. ESV, NRSV, RSV), and that fits this context best.

18. After the temporal clauses of v. 7a–b, the word "then" signals a close temporal sequence (a special use of the Greek conjunction καί, usually rendered "and"; cf. 5:7; Luke 2:21).

19. The verb "will be completed" (ἐτελέσθη) in v. 7c is a proleptic or futuristic aorist in Greek (Zerwick, *Biblical Greek*, 84–85; Fanning, *Verbal Aspect*, 269–70). When the aorist follows a phrase pointing to the future, it denotes the whole action as done at that time. Since Greek is an aspect-prominent language, its tense-aspect forms tend to focus on the aspect value even if it goes against the normal temporal sense. In English, however, as a tense-prominent language, the most idiomatic expression goes the other way.

20. See NEB, REB, "the hidden purpose of God"; CSB, "the mystery of God's will."

21. The verb "announced" in v. 7d is one of only two occurrences in Rev of the verb that often means "preach the gospel, evangelize" (εὐαγγελίζω). Here it has the more general sense

of "announce, proclaim a welcome message" (cf. Luke 1:19; 1 Thess 3:6), but in the other occurrence (Rev 14:6) it has its more specialized meaning (BDAG 402).

22. This is the title for Bauckham's book of essays on Rev, in which he argues that John's use of the OT is "an essential key to . . . understanding" the book, since it arises from his "pattern of disciplined and deliberate allusion to specific Old Testament texts." He adds, "John was writing what he understood to be a work of prophetic scripture, the climax of prophetic revelation, which gathered up the prophetic meaning of the Old Testament scriptures and disclosed the way in which it was being and was to be fulfilled in the last days. His work therefore presupposes and conveys an extensive interpretation of large parts of Old Testament prophecy" (Bauckham, *Climax*, x–xi).

23. See Allan J. McNicol, *The Conversion of the Nations in Revelation*, LNTS 438 (London: T&T Clark, 2011), 14–16, whose thesis is that John's central theme is "grounded in prophetic models of what will take place in the last days. These models, found in the Psalms and major prophets, moulded and nourished John to seek fervently their fulfillment. On the basis of the Christ-event, this expectation was deepened. The language has been reformulated. Yet the basic patterns of earlier eschatological thinking remain in place." John's expectation was for "an actual Day of the Lord which, long delayed, he believes will take place."

about to be completed without any more delay (vv. 6c–7) is the first of a series of anticipatory declarations in the coming chapters of the defeat of all enemies and the arrival of God's kingdom (e.g., 11:15–18; 12:10–12; 14:7–8; 15:1; 18:2; 19:2). God's heavenly rule over all things means that this can be proclaimed as already done even while its earthly consummation is still in process. The temporal indicators in these verses (10:6c–7) and elsewhere in the book show that John does in fact present a fairly clear sequence of events revealed in the Old Testament prophets and confirmed here in Revelation.[24]

10:8–10 And the voice that I heard from heaven I heard again, speaking with me and saying, "Go take the scroll that is lying open in the hand of the angel who is standing on the sea and on the land." 9 So I went to the angel, requesting him to give me the little scroll. And he said to me, "Take and eat it, and it will make your stomach bitter, but in your mouth it will be sweet like honey." 10 And I took the little scroll from the hand of the angel and I ate it, and in my mouth it was sweet like honey, but when I ate it my stomach was made bitter (Καὶ ἡ φωνὴ ἣν ἤκουσα ἐκ τοῦ οὐρανοῦ πάλιν λαλοῦσαν μετ᾽ ἐμοῦ καὶ λέγουσαν, Ὕπαγε λάβε τὸ βιβλίον τὸ ἠνεῳγμένον ἐν τῇ χειρὶ τοῦ ἀγγέλου τοῦ ἑστῶτος ἐπὶ τῆς θαλάσσης καὶ ἐπὶ τῆς γῆς. 9 καὶ ἀπῆλθα πρὸς τὸν ἄγγελον λέγων αὐτῷ δοῦναί μοι τὸ βιβλαρίδιον. καὶ λέγει μοι, Λάβε καὶ κατάφαγε αὐτό,

καὶ πικρανεῖ σου τὴν κοιλίαν, ἀλλ᾽ ἐν τῷ στόματί σου ἔσται γλυκὺ ὡς μέλι. 10 καὶ ἔλαβον τὸ βιβλαρίδιον ἐκ τῆς χειρὸς τοῦ ἀγγέλου καὶ κατέφαγον αὐτό, καὶ ἦν ἐν τῷ στόματί μου ὡς μέλι γλυκύ· καὶ ὅτε ἔφαγον αὐτό, ἐπικράνθη ἡ κοιλία μου). The final four verses of the chapter tie together the central theme of this vision by demonstrating John's prophetic role in revealing the consummation of God's saving plan for the peoples of the world (vv. 8–11). Verses 8–9 show how the protagonists and props introduced earlier will figure in commissioning John as God's prophet. "The voice that he heard from heaven" (as described in v. 4, the one that told him not to write what the thunders said) again addresses[25] John with specific personal instructions (v. 8). He must approach the mighty angel who straddles the sea and the land (as seen in vv. 1–2, 5) and "take the scroll that is lying open in [his] hand" (as v. 2 related). In v. 8c a slightly different word is used for "scroll" (βιβλίον), but it refers to the same one elsewhere called a "little scroll" (βιβλαρίδιον; vv. 2, 9–10).[26] John responds immediately, approaching the angel and asking for the little scroll (v. 9a–b), a daunting venture given how majestic this angel must have seemed, but a command from heaven would certainly encourage bold action.

The angel is happy to comply, but replies[27] with peculiar instructions and a warning for John: "Take and eat it, and it will make your stomach bitter, but in your mouth it will be sweet like honey" (v. 9d–f). As John received and wrote down this part of the

---

24. These indicators are an important counterbalance to the disclaimers found in many commentaries to the effect that Rev does not predict a sequence of future events. See the discussion of this point at the end of the section "Structure and Outline" in the introduction to this commentary.

25. In v. 8a–b there is a problem of agreement between the word for "voice" (φωνή; nominative) and the two participles "speaking" (λαλοῦσαν; accusative) and "saying" (λέγουσαν; accusative). The sense connections are clear, but the grammatical agreement goes awry because "voice" has no verb expressed, and the participles agree instead with the accusative relative

pronoun (ἥν) that refers to "voice." For its part "voice" (φωνή) is a pendant nominative (BDF §466; Aune, *Revelation 6–16*, 551; see note at 2:26), left hanging when the construction moves on, and its main verb ("I heard") becomes redundant. A verb has been supplied to smooth out the English wording.

26. See v. 2 for comments on these synonyms and on textual variants in these verses.

27. The verb "he said" (λέγει) in v. 9c is a historical present that points forward to John's response (v. 10) to what the angel says. See explanation at 5:5.

vision and as his first-century audience heard or read it, they would have quickly associated these actions with Ezekiel's account of his prophetic appointment in Ezekiel 2:1–3:15 and understood the vision's significance accordingly. God called Ezekiel to go and speak as a prophet to the stubborn and rebellious people of Israel (Ezek 2:1–7). In his vision a hand offered a scroll to him filled with words of "lamentation, mourning, and woe" (2:8–10), and he was told to eat the scroll, to fill his belly with it, and then go and speak for God.[28] When he ate it, Ezekiel found it "sweet as honey in his mouth" (3:1–3). But as he went out to preach he found the people unwilling to listen (3:7–9), and he went about his task discouraged and "in bitterness" (3:14–15).

John's experience in his vision was the same as Ezekiel's. In almost point-by-point repetition of the angel's instructions from Revelation 10:9, John recounts his response, "I took the little scroll . . . and I ate it" (v. 10a), as well as its mixed result. It was "sweet like honey" in his mouth (v. 10b), echoing a description commonly used of the value and attractiveness of God's word for those who receive it willingly (Pss 19:10; 119:103; Prov 24:13–14; cf. Jer 15:16). But in truly absorbing the message, God's prophet cannot help but be affected deep within ("my stomach was made bitter"; v. 10c) when the message meets with stubborn unbelief and resistance, and he knows that God's judgment will be the result (cf. Ezek 2:5–10). A commission to proclaim judgment is an unwelcome task, and this vision forewarns John about what is ahead for him. Amid bitter angst about their messages of judgment, however, prophets are sometimes

given a glimpse of hope about God's restoration and renewal that are in store after the cataclysm of punishment has passed (cf. Isa 6:8–13; Ezek 14:22–23; 36:22–36). John has seen this already (Rev 10:7; also 5:9; 7:9–10), and v. 11 is a further reminder of this hope.

10:11 And I was told, "You must prophesy again about peoples and nations and languages and many kings" (καὶ λέγουσίν μοι, Δεῖ σε πάλιν προφητεῦσαι ἐπὶ λαοῖς καὶ ἔθνεσιν καὶ γλώσσαις καὶ βασιλεῦσιν πολλοῖς). A solemn heavenly proclamation[29] serves as the coda to John's symbolic commissioning as a prophet. His divine assignment (what he "must" do) is to "prophesy again," an indication that this is not a vision of his *initial* prophetic appointment inserted here without regard for the sequence of events portrayed in the visions surrounding it (see the explicit signal of that sequence in v. 7). His initial commission to write this "prophecy" is portrayed in 1:9–20. Instead, this is a renewal of his prophetic call along the way, at a critical juncture in its accomplishment. John's awareness of his role as a prophet appears at the start and end of Revelation (1:3; 22:7, 10, 18–19), but God solidifies his resolve just here as his portrayal of the completion of God's "mystery" reaches a phase of cataclysmic judgment and then victory (v. 7).

John's references to peoples and nations and languages across the book of Revelation share this paradoxical thematic feature (i.e., conflict, then redemption). These references appear seven times (5:9; 7:9; 10:11; 11:9; 13:7; 14:6; 17:15), often with "tribes" added (but not here), and often with related words as well (like "kings" here). These are drawn

---

28. Fourth Ezra 14:38 pictures prophetic inspiration as a fiery drink to be consumed before the prophet could speak with wisdom from God.

29. The translation "I was told" (v. 11a) renders an impersonal third-person verb phrase (λέγουσίν μοι, "they said to me") that is a paraphrase of the passive (Aune, *Revelation 6–16*, 553). The verb is also a historical present, pointing forward to John's prophetically symbolic act of measuring in 11:1–2 and its significance regarding the peoples of the world in relation to Jerusalem.

primarily from Daniel's picture of the nations of the world, first suffering under the dominion of hostile powers and then turning to the true God when he defeats those powers and establishes his everlasting kingdom on earth (Dan 3:4, 7, 29; 5:19; 6:25; 7:14).[30] This Old Testament background as well as the use of these phrases in Revelation show that John's prophetic words "about[31] the peoples and nations and languages and kings" in the chapters that follow will not be just a message of doom and judgment but of hope and worldwide redemption as well.[32] The historical present "I was told" in v. 11a (see note on that phrase) highlights the events of 11:1–2 and their importance for John's prophetic message about God and the nations at the end-times.

Theology in Application

The Blessing and Unity of God's Revelation in Scripture

This passage reminds us of the unsurpassed gift of God's revelation to us in Scripture. John's recommissioning here (after his initial prophetic call in 1:9–20 and mirroring the call of Ezekiel in Ezek 2:1–3:15) anchors his words not in his own human insight but in the authority of the Lord. And here as elsewhere, John identifies himself and his work with the prophets of old (Rev 1:3; 22:6, 10, 18–19). Through all these messengers God has graciously unveiled his "mystery" (10:7), the previously hidden truth about his plan to redeem Israel and then, through her, people from all the nations of the world. John's visions reflect the unity of what he has seen with what God revealed through the Old Testament prophets, through Jesus's own teaching, and through the apostles and prophets of the New Testament. We are not left to mere human speculation or opinion about the future of the world. Though we sometimes long for greater clarity in our grasp of his truth, God has not left us uninformed about what he will do to bring his full redemption to earth in both judgment and restoration.

Bittersweet Words

Many of us know what it is like to live in a family or organization or workplace where only good news is welcomed, where the operating principle is "if you don't have anything nice to say, don't say anything at all." Sometimes this social constraint is appropriate, but it is not a healthy way to run our lives in general. Hard truths—spoken with gentleness and humility—are sometimes the most important things we can say in the situation at hand. If I am lying to myself, the most loving thing someone can do for me (whether it's "nice" or not) is to tell me the truth (e.g., Rev 3:17–19).

---

30. See comments at 5:9.

31. The preposition translated "about" (ἐπί) denotes the topic ("about, concerning"; CSB, ESV, NASB, NIV, NRSV, RSV), not "before" (KJV) or "against" (as in Luke 12:52–53; Acts 11:19). See BDAG 366; and John 12:16; Heb 11:4; Rev 22:16.

32. Bauckham, *Climax*, 326–37.

Paul knew this about church life (e.g., Gal 6:1; Eph 4:15) and especially about Christian preaching and teaching (Gal 1:9–10; 1 Tim 5:1–2; 2 Tim 4:2). At one level it seems that ministry of God's word would always be an unmixed blessing. How sweet to think of speaking for the true and living God, or for those who listen, of hearing from God himself. Who would not want a part in that! But John's experience (Rev 10:9–11) reveals a bitter side. A message of rebuke and judgment (cf. Ezek 2:1–10) is hardly pleasant for the hearers, and it is gut-wrenching even for the speaker. Only the fact that it is God's word, a message from the all-wise, all-loving Creator and Savior, makes it possible to speak and welcome such a word. Preachers as well as their listeners must be wary of the tendency brought on by our modern sensitivities of only ever speaking what is "nice" to say and hear.

Revelation 11:1–19

Literary Context

This chapter includes material from two larger sections. Its early verses (11:1–14) give the second part of the narrative interlude between the sixth and seventh seals (10:1–11:14), part of the same vision with 10:1–11 (John's prophetic commissioning). John continues to be directly engaged with the events of the vision, but the focus changes to God's temple and the holy city Jerusalem, the focal point of God's conflict with the nations in the final days before Christ's return. The later verses (11:15–19) describe the seventh trumpet that foreshadows God's coming rule on earth. This section, however, leads to further interludes that preview the destruction of Babylon, the end-time rival for worldwide dominion (12:1–14:20). Both sections assume a larger significance when seen in light of the major themes of the book. The work of God's prophets is shown in the context of severe trouble for Israel and the world, exacerbated by Satan's minion, a "beast" of a figure (v. 7), who will lead the earth's people against God's spokesmen. This foreshadows further intense conflict described in later chapters. This is in fact the major theme of the last part of the book: warfare waged by the powers of this world under Satan's instigation against God and his Messiah, who will summarily defeat them, leading to "regime change" for the whole world.[1] The sounding of the seventh trumpet in 11:15–19 announces this arrival of God's kingdom on earth displacing the nations who rage against him; it also signals the coming appearance of God himself to judge and redeem.

---

1. This phrase is taken from Poul F. Guttesen, *Leaning into the Future: The Kingdom of God in the Theology of Jürgen Moltmann and in the Book of Revelation* (Eugene, OR: Pickwick, 2009), 123–41, who writes, "Revelation 11:15–19 is the most succinct statement of the book's eschatological hope," and he proceeds to show how the book foresees "the time when the powers that now have usurped the position of authority in the world will be defeated" (123). See also McNicol, *Conversion*, 56–57 ("a central theological focus of the Apocalypse" is "a vision of the transition of power" as seen, for example, in the use of Ps 2 in Rev 11:15–19).

III. **Second Vision: Heavenly Throne Room and Three Judgment Cycles (4:1–16:21)**
   A. Vision of God in His Heavenly Throne Room (4:1–11)
   B. The Seven-Sealed Scroll and the Slain Lamb (5:1–14)
   C. The Seven Seals and the Interlude of the Two Multitudes (6:1–8:1)
   D. **The Seven Trumpets and Further Interludes (8:2–14:20)**
      1. The First Four Trumpets (8:2–13)
      2. The Fifth Trumpet—First Woe (9:1–12)
      3. The Sixth Trumpet—Second Woe (9:13–21)
      4. **Two Revelatory Interludes: God's Prophets (10:1–11:14)**
         a. John and the little scroll (10:1–11)
   ➡   b. **Temple measurements and the two witnesses (11:1–14)**
      5. **The Seventh Trumpet—Third Woe: Anticipating God's Rule (11:15–19)**
      6. Two Further Interludes: Anticipating Babylon's Fall (12:1–14:20)

Main Idea

John glimpses God's future for Jerusalem and its people when two prophets speak for God in its streets during days of severe persecution before Christ's return (11:1–14), and there is heavenly rejoicing following the seventh trumpet as a preview of God's wrath in the seven bowl judgments that lead to his coming rule over the world (11:15–19).

Translation

(See pages 323–5.)

Structure

Chapter 11 provides the bridge between two larger units, as noted above. John is summoned to perform a symbolic prophetic action (measurement of the temple), representing God's future for Jerusalem and for its people Israel. This leads immediately to the story of the two witnesses or prophets who will speak for God in Jerusalem during its days of terrible trouble just prior to Christ's return (11:1–14). In the second part of the chapter the seventh trumpet sounds, launching a further interlude prior to the series of bowl judgments (15:1–16:21) that will consummate God's victory over evil and the establishment of his kingdom on earth. John records the jubilant heavenly worship that anticipates God's coming rule (11:15–19).

Revelation 11:1–19

1a	Action	And **a measuring rod like a staff was given to me,**
b		and **I was told,**
c	Commands	"Get up and measure the temple of God and
		the altar and
		those who worship in it,
2a		but leave out the courtyard that is outside the temple
b		and do not measure it,
c	Reason	because it has been given over to the gentiles,
d		and they will trample the holy city for forty-two months.
3a	Assertion	And I will give authority to my two witnesses,
b		and they will prophesy for twelve hundred and sixty days clothed in sackcloth."
4a	Identification	**These are the two olive trees and**
		the two lampstands
b	Description	who stand before the Lord of the earth.
5a	Circumstance	And if anyone intends to harm them,
b	Consequence	**fire comes out of their mouths**
		and **consumes their enemies.**
c	Circumstance	If anyone intends to harm them,
d	Consequence	**he must be killed in this way.**
6a	Description of 4a	**These have the authority to close the sky**
b	Purpose	so that no rain falls during the days of their prophesying,
c	Description of 4a	and **they have authority over the waters**
d	Explanation	to turn them into blood and
e		to strike the earth
		with any kind of plague
f	Time	as often as they want.
7a	Time	And when they have completed their testimony,
b	Action	**the beast that comes up from the bottomless pit will wage war against them and**
		overcome them and
		murder them.
8a	Effect of 7b	And **their dead bodies will lie in the public square of the great city,**
b	Identification 1	which in spiritual terms is called Sodom and
		Egypt,
c	Identification 2	where their Lord also was crucified.

Continued on next page.

Continued from previous page.

9a	Effects of 8a	And **individuals from the peoples and**
		tribes and
		languages and
		nations …
		… **look at their dead bodies for three-and-a-half days,**
b		and **they do not allow their dead bodies to be placed in a tomb.**
10a		And **those who live on the earth gloat over them and celebrate.**
b		And **they will send gifts to one another,**
c		because these two prophets tormented those who live on the earth.

11a	Time	And after the three-and-a-half days
b	Actions	**a spirit of life from God entered them,**
c		and **they stood on their feet,** (Ezek 37:5, 10)
d	Effect of 11c	and **great fear fell on those who watched them.**
12a	Action	And **they heard a loud voice from heaven saying to them,**
b	Command	*"Come up here."*
c	Effects of 12b	And **they went up into heaven in a cloud,**
d		and **their enemies watched them.**
13a	Actions	And **in that hour a great earthquake took place,**
b		and **a tenth of the city fell,**
c		and **seven thousand people were killed in the earthquake,**
d	Effects of 13a–c	and **the rest became terrified and**
		gave glory to the God of heaven.

14a	Review	**The second woe has passed.**
b	Preview	**Behold, the third woe is coming soon.**

15a	Action/7th Trumpet	And **the seventh angel sounded his trumpet,**
b	Action	and **there came loud voices in heaven saying,**
c	Announcement	*"The kingdom of the world has become the kingdom of our Lord and of his Messiah,*
d		*and he will reign forever and ever."*
16	Response to 15c–d	And **the twenty-four elders who were sitting on their thrones fell on their faces and worshiped God,**
17a		saying,
b	Thanksgiving	*"We thank you, Lord God Almighty,*
		the One who is and was,
c		*because you have taken your great power and begun to reign.*

18a	Declaration	And the nations have raged
b		but your wrath has come,
c		and the time has come
d	Explanation of 18c	for the dead to be judged and
e		to reward your servants the prophets and the saints and those who fear your name, the small and the great, and
f		to ruin those who ruin the earth."
19a	Actions	**And the temple of God in heaven was opened,**
b		**and the ark of his covenant appeared in his temple,**
c		**and there came flashes of lightning and rumblings and peals of thunder and an earthquake and large hail.**

Exegetical Outline

III. Second Vision: Heavenly Throne Room and Three Judgment Cycles (4:1–16:21)

    A. Vision of God in His Heavenly Throne Room (4:1–11)

    B. The Seven-Sealed Scroll and the Slain Lamb (5:1–14)

    C. The Seven Seals and the Interlude of the Two Multitudes (6:1–8:1)

    D. The Seven Trumpets and Further Interludes (8:2–14:20)

        1. The First Four Trumpets (8:2–13)

        2. The Fifth Trumpet—First Woe (9:1–12)

        3. The Sixth Trumpet—Second Woe (9:13–21)

        4. Two Revelatory Interludes: God's Prophets (10:1–11:14)

           a. John and the little scroll (10:1–11)

➡   **b. Temple measurements and the two witnesses (11:1–14)**

              (1) Measuring the temple (11:1–2)

              (2) The witnesses' earthly ministry (11:3–6)

              (3) Their defeat by the beast (11:7–10)

              (4) Resurrection of the witnesses and judgment on Jerusalem (11:11–14)

        5. The Seventh Trumpet—Third Woe: Anticipating God's Rule (11:15–19)

           a. Heavenly announcement of God's reign (11:15)

           b. The elders' praise for God's wrath against evil (11:16–18)

           c. Cosmic signs of God's impending presence (11:19)

Explanation of the Text

11:1-2 And a measuring rod like a staff was given to me, and I was told, "Get up and measure the temple of God and the altar and those who worship in it, 2 but leave out the courtyard that is outside the temple and do not measure it, because it has been given over to the gentiles, and they will trample the holy city for forty-two months (Καὶ ἐδόθη μοι κάλαμος ὅμοιος ῥάβδῳ, λέγων, Ἔγειρε καὶ μέτρησον τὸν ναὸν τοῦ θεοῦ καὶ τὸ θυσιαστήριον καὶ τοὺς προσκυνοῦντας ἐν αὐτῷ. 2 καὶ τὴν αὐλὴν τὴν ἔξωθεν τοῦ ναοῦ ἔκβαλε ἔξωθεν καὶ μὴ αὐτὴν μετρήσῃς, ὅτι ἐδόθη τοῖς ἔθνεσιν, καὶ τὴν πόλιν τὴν ἁγίαν πατήσουσιν μῆνας τεσσεράκοντα [καὶ] δύο). After John's reappointment as a prophet portrayed in 10:8–11, he is pulled further into the events of the same vision (11:1–2) to perform a symbolic prophetic act (cf. Isa 20:1–6; Ezek 12:1–7). But John's small role is quickly left behind as the focus shifts to God's temple, the holy city Jerusalem, and the witness of God's prophets in Jerusalem during the fateful days of its judgment that will come prior to its restoration (Rev 11:3–13). John was given "a measuring rod like a staff"[2] and instructed[3] to

"measure" God's temple and some of its accompanying features (v. 1c).[4]

Interpreters have puzzled over the connotations of this "measuring" and why some features are or are not to be measured (vv. 1c–2b). Further questions arise over which "temple of God" and which "holy city" is in view (see below). The significance of "measuring" as a prophetic act is clarified significantly by examining the Old Testament passages that seem to have most influenced John's account.[5] The most important of these are Ezekiel 40 and Zechariah 1–2. In each of those passages the prophet has a vision of an angel measuring Jerusalem and its temple at a time when it had been destroyed by gentile nations, and measurement symbolized God's claim of ownership and indicated that he would again show Israel his mercy and prosper his people in their land. "Measuring" in that case was God's pledge to rebuild the city and its temple and restore his people to the land he had promised them to worship him there (see similar point in Jer 31:38–39 without as many details). He would not allow its desecration and destruction (es-

---

2. The word for "measuring rod" in v. 1a (κάλαμος) denotes a straight stalk or cane used for determining the length of an area or a building (BDAG 502; cf. 21:15–16), in this case quite a long one, since it is compared to a "staff" (ῥάβδος), i.e., a walking stick (Mark 6:8) or a ruler's scepter (Rev 19:15).

3. The phrase "and I was told" (v. 1b) is a smoother English rendering of the Greek λέγων ("saying"), which implies a personal speaker. Verse 3 shows that God or Christ is speaking to John since the directly quoted instructions continue there and refer to "my two witnesses," i.e., those who bear divine witness (cf. 2:13, "Antipas, my [Christ's] faithful witness").

4. One of the topics of discussion among technical commentaries is a proposal by some that 11:1–2 and possibly 11:3–13 originated among non-Christian Jews in the days leading up to the destruction of Jerusalem in AD 70. According to this view John incorporated an earlier Jewish oracle into his material here with varying degrees of editorial adjustment. See Aune, *Reve-*

lation 6–16, 594–96; Beckwith, *Apocalypse*, 584–88; Charles, *Revelation*, 1:270–73; and Osborne, *Revelation*, 415–16. While ideas like these could have circulated among Jews and Christians in the late first century, there is little evidence that John would have slavishly or sloppily used such material. The OT itself (Ezek 40; Zech 1–2) exerted a far greater influence than any contemporary source (see commentary).

5. As Marko Jauhiainen, "The Measuring of the Sanctuary Reconsidered (Rev 11,1–2)," *Bib* 83 (2002): 509, 514–19, 525, points out, we are not seeking what the word "measure" (μετρέω) *denotes* (this would be its lexical definition, i.e., "to take the dimensions of" something; BDAG 643) but what it *connotes* or implies in various contexts. Sometimes the result of measuring is destruction (2 Sam 8:2; 2 Kgs 21:13; Lam 2:8), and sometimes it is associated with preservation or protection (2 Sam 8:2; Jer 31:38–39; Zech 2:1–5).

pecially as the symbol and center of Israel's national life and its relation to the Lord) to be the final word. This would entail God's preservation or protection of his people,[6] but it is much richer, more detailed, and more complex than commonly noted. One of the complexities is that the act of measuring that Ezekiel and Zechariah observed was a pledge not of safety in the present circumstances but of ultimate future restoration and protection, something that John's vision seems to reflect as well (cf. Rev 11:2c, 7–10 and comments below).[7]

To identify the referent of "the temple of God"[8] in v. 1c, the first step is observing that its outside courtyard "has been given over to the gentiles" (v. 2c), and they "will trample the holy city" (v. 2d) for a period of time (cf. Luke 21:24). This must represent some form of earthly temple.[9] Only by quite a stretch can this be taken as the heavenly temple, somehow defiled by God's enemies.[10] In addition, the widely held view that "temple" here is figurative in some sense for God's people (either at the time of the end or throughout the church's history) seems likewise to be an imposition from other passages[11] rather than a careful engagement with these verses and their Old Testament background. Various symbolic views related to God's people have been advanced, but they struggle to define the significance of measuring (i.e., protecting) God's people and who or what is included and excluded from such protection.[12]

---

6. Beale, *Revelation*, 557–65; Koester, *Revelation*, 484–86, 495; Osborne, *Revelation*, 410–12.

7. Koester, *Revelation*, 483–84 observes that these earlier prophecies concerned restoration but asserts that John has modified this to speak of protection only, but it is hard to see how this can be justified in Rev (see the notes of earthly restoration along the lines that the prophets predicted in 11:15–18; 14:1–5; 19:1–10; 21:1–5, 10, 24–26).

8. Because of how the outer courtyard is distinguished in v. 2, "the temple of God" (τὸν ναὸν τοῦ θεοῦ) in v. 1c could denote the two-chambered sanctuary that was at the heart of the temple precincts as well as the inner courtyard(s) directly associated with its worship functions (i.e., the areas containing the sacrificial altar, the laver, etc.; in Herodian times these inner areas included courts for priests only, for other Jewish males, and for Jewish women). A related word, ἱερόν, is generally used for the much larger temple complex, including a court for gentiles that was used as a market (cf. Mark 11:15–16 and parallels). But these two words are not technical terms, and "temple" (ναός) could refer to the two-chambered sanctuary only, excluding the inner courts. See comments at v. 2 and Aune, *Revelation 6–16*, 605–6.

9. See Aune, *Revelation 6–16*, 605; and Antoninus King Wai Siew, *The War between the Two Beasts and the Two Witnesses: A Chiastic Reading of Revelation 11:1–14:5*, LNTS 283 (London: T&T Clark, 2005), 91–103.

10. This is the view of Michaels, *Revelation*, 137, and Osborne, *Revelation*, 410 (the heavenly temple but figurative for God's people). See also Charles Homer Giblin, "Revelation 11:1–13: Its Form, Function and Contextual Integration," *NTS* 30 (1984): 438, 440, and Michael Bachmann, "Himmlisch: der 'Tempel Gottes' von Apk 11:1," *NTS* 40 (1994): 474–80.

Their argument that "temple" and "altar" are consistently heavenly in Rev and therefore they must be so here is simply to ignore the specific evidence of this context. See v. 19 where John specifically describes "the temple of God in heaven" in contrast to this one (for text critical issue there see note on v. 19). Koester, *Revelation*, 484–85, notes that when John has in mind the heavenly temple he consistently makes this explicit, a feature that is absent here.

11. It is true that "temple" is used metaphorically of Christians in 1 Cor 3:16–17; 2 Cor 6:16; Eph 2:21–22; 1 Pet 2:4–10; and Rev 3:12, but those texts specifically speak of people: "you," "we," or "the overcomer." This figurative sense cannot be carried over to all other uses of "God's temple," "the Lord's temple," or "holy temple" regardless of context (cf. Matt 26:61; Luke 1:9; 2 Thess 2:4; Rev 11:19). It is likewise not a sound argument to say that everything is figurative in Rev and so this must be also (cf. Caird, *Revelation*, 131) or that Rev shows no interest in ethnic Israel or earthly Jerusalem and its temple, so this must be purely symbolic (Bauckham, *Climax*, 272). It certainly has metaphorical extensions (i.e., it is not *merely* literal; the temple and the city imply also Israel as well as the nations who will benefit from her future prosperity; cf. Zech 2:10–12), but those are built on the literal reference as a base.

12. Read Smalley, *Revelation*, 272–74, for examples of the interpretive agility required to read both the temple (v. 1) and the holy city (v. 2) as symbolizing God's people in some way, who are alternatively measured (protected) or not measured (subject to persecution). Likewise Murphy, *Fallen is Babylon*, 260–61. Aune, *Revelation 6–16*, 597–98, criticizes the "over-allegorization" that comes when "the clear apocalyptic orientation that the passage exhibits" is minimized. Thus the verses themselves can exercise "little restraint" on interpretive

A possible literal reading of "the temple" in this passage is to take the referent as the Second Temple (vv. 1–2) and Jerusalem in general (vv. 8, 13) either prior to or after their destruction by the Romans in AD 70 (depending on the date that John wrote). This view is supported by preterist interpreters who understand most or all of the prophecies of Revelation to have been fulfilled in the events of AD 70.[13] The main problem for this view is to define what "measuring" means if the temple is in fact destroyed. The explanations given are subject to the charge of "over-allegorization" and imposition of meanings that do not seem to be subject to the text, according to Aune.[14] A further question concerns the time period of gentile trampling: in what sense does "forty-two months" fit the preterist view that this predicts the total destruction of Jerusalem in the first century?[15]

A better option is that the vision anticipates an earthly temple that will exist in Jerusalem at the cataclysmic time of future judgment just prior to the return of Christ to earth (i.e., at the time when the seal, trumpet, and bowl judgments occur as presented in chs. 6–16; cf. 2 Thess 2:4 that also assumes this scenario).[16] This vision, given to John at a time when Herod's temple in Jerusalem lay in ruins (AD 90s), symbolizes God's ownership of the sanctuary and its surroundings and his pledge of its future restoration at the center of national life among a renewed people who will worship him with true hearts. Just as in the Old Testament passages cited above (Ezek 40; Zech 1–2), the reference to "measuring" the temple indicates God's intent to restore it in the future after the time of chastening that Israel will experience. The time indications in Revelation 11:2c–3 ("forty-two months"; "1,260 days") lend support to this view, since they correlate with other texts from Daniel (e.g., Dan 7:25; 8:13–14; 9:24–27; 12:1, 11) that point to the period of final "tribulation" immediately preceding Christ's second coming (see discussion below). These Old Testament texts also contain details often overlooked by spiritualizing or idealist interpretations of Revelation 11:1–2, details reflecting the prophets' national and geographical focus on Jerusalem and its temple, which are made explicit here in vv. 8 and 13 as well. This is another indicator of the wholesale neglect on the part of many interpreters of what Revelation explicitly says about Israel and its future.[17]

Other details about this temple in the tribulation period and its construction and usage are not given to us. Perhaps it will initially be built by Jews with no faith in Jesus as a step toward restoring Israel's worship in Jerusalem. Ezekiel 40–48 seems to envision a restored temple during the millennial

---

variations (598). See also Beckwith, *Apocalypse*, 584–88, who mentions what he calls an "allegorical" reading of the passage (i.e., "Jerusalem is the Church, the temple and outer courts are respectively the faithful and faithless Christians, the two Witnesses are the testimony borne by the whole body of Christian teachers, saints, and martyrs"). Then he adds, "There is in the passage itself no intimation that such was the author's meaning. . . . [This is] a form of exegesis which reads into the Apocalypse anything to which a figurative parallel can be found there" (585–86).

13. A. J. Beagley, *The "Sitz im Leben" of the Apocalypse: With Particular Role to the Role of the Church's Enemies*, BZNW 50 (Berlin: de Gruyter, 1987), 59–64 (looking back to AD 70); Gentry, *Before Jerusalem Fell*, 165–67; Roloff, *Revelation*, 129.

14. Aune, *Revelation 6–16*, 597–98.

15. For discussion of this issue and others, see Mark L. Hitchcock, "A Critique of the Preterist View of the Temple in Revelation 11:1–2," *BSac* 164 (2007): 222–26.

16. Patterson, *Revelation*, 240; Thomas, *Revelation 8–22*, 80–86. Cf. Siew, *War*, 92–96, as well as Hitchcock, "Critique of the Preterist View," 226–36, for further defense of this approach. This view was articulated clearly in the early patristic period (Irenaeus, *Haer.* 5.30.4; Hippolytus, *Antichr.* 6).

17. See comments on 2:9; 3:9; 7:4–8; 12:1–2; 14:1–5 and the section "Use of the Old Testament: Prophecy and Typology" in the introduction to this commentary. See the critique of this neglect in Elliott, *Survivors*, 662; John W. Marshall, *Parables of War: Reading John's Jewish Apocalypse*, SCJ 10 (Waterloo, Ontario: Wilfrid Laurier University Press, 2001), 1–24; and Willitts, "Bride of the Messiah," 245–47.

reign (Rev 20), but the relation of the two temples is unclear. See comments on 21:22 for further discussion of Ezekiel 40–48.

Two additional features associated with the temple are to be "measured" as well (v. 1c): the "altar"[18] and "those who worship in it [i.e., in the temple]."[19] It seems unnatural to refer to "measuring" people, but we could plausibly understand the verb to shift its sense to accommodate the new object (i.e., "measure" becomes "count, number"; cf. CSB, NABR, NLT).[20] But 2 Samuel 8:2 uses a compound of this verb (διαμετρέω) for "marking out or distinguishing" groups of people for different treatment. In the imagery of v. 1c God seems to be pledging to restore both the incense altar as representative of his presence with his people in the temple[21] as well as his scattered people as faithful worshipers (along with others from every nation; cf. Jer 3:17; Mic 4:2; Zech 2:10–13; 8:22; 9:9–10; 14:16).

In contrast,[22] what John must "leave out" and "not measure" (v. 2a–b) is "the courtyard that is outside the temple." In Solomon's temple as well as Herod's, the larger temple district included an inner area for functions pertaining more directly to worship as well as an outer area serving more civic purposes (king's palace, market areas, etc.; 1 Kgs 6:36; 7:9, 12; Mark 11:15–16; also, in Ezekiel's vision, 40:17–20, 23). In New Testament times this outer area was as close as non-Jews could come to the temple itself, and a low wall blocked the way between the outer and inner courts (Josephus, *J. W.* 5.193–200; 5.226–27).[23] This outer, less-sacred precinct of the temple could be the area that John is instructed not to measure. But there are good indications that in referring to this "courtyard" that is not to be measured, John has in mind the area immediately outside the sanctuary itself, the one containing the altar of burnt offering. The command "leave out" (ἔκβαλε) is quite strong (v. 2a), with the sense of "pay no attention to, reject."[24] This wording seems to be based on the MT of Daniel 8:11 (RSV: "the place of the sanctuary was overthrown"), and it describes the anticipated desecration of the temple in connection with the "abomination of desolation" that disrupts the temple offerings (Dan 8:10–14; 9:27; 11:31; 12:11; cf. Matt 24:15).[25] The symbolic meaning of the command not to measure this courtyard is clarified in the clauses that follow.

The reason ("because"; ὅτι) for not including

---

18. "The altar" (τὸ θυσιαστήριον) is most likely the incense altar inside the sanctuary itself rather than the altar of burnt offering in the inner court leading to the sanctuary (see note on 6:9).

19. In attempting to solve other interpretive issues in these verses (e.g, what is to be measured and what is not, what "leave out" means in v. 2, what is symbolized overall), a few interpreters argue that the final two occurrences of the conjunction "and" (καί) in v. 1 carry a contrastive sense ("but" instead of "and") and an explicative sense ("that is") respectively (Jauhiainen, "Measuring of the Sanctuary," 519–21) or the explicative sense and the normal sense respectively (Rob Dalrymple, "The Use of Καί in Revelation 11:1 and the Implications for the Identification of the Temple, the Altar, and the Worshippers," *Bib* 87 [2006]: 387–94). But the normal sense is more likely for both of these.

20. On the other hand, this could be a case of zeugma (omission of a verb such as "number, count," resulting in an odd collocation of objects; cf. BDF §479; e.g., 1 Tim 4:3).

21. See the association of the smoke of the incense in the sanctuary with God's presence among his people (Lev 16:13; cf. Exod 25:21–22).

22. The conjunction at the start of v. 2 is καί (normally "and"), but here it adds an idea that is contrastive, "but" (Aune, *Revelation 6–16*, 578). To be clear, the conjunction itself is simply additive or continuative, but here it joins two clauses that are themselves adversative in thought (Levinsohn, *Discourse Features*, 124–25; Runge, *Discourse Grammar*, 23–26; cf. Mathewson, *Handbook*, 146, comment on 11:7).

23. See John D. Currid and David P. Barrett, *Crossway ESV Bible Atlas* (Wheaton, IL: Crossway, 2010), 134–36, 176–77, 214–20; and Emil Schürer, *The History of the Jewish People in the Age of Jesus Christ*, rev. ed., ed. Geza Vermes, Fergus Millar, and Matthew Black (Edinburgh: T&T Clark, 1979), 2:296–99.

24. See BDAG 299; cf. Ps 50:16; Luke 6:22; 1 Clem. 35.8 (fig. for rejecting instruction).

25. Bauckham, *Climax*, 266–73.

the outer court is that God in his redemptive plan has permitted gentiles to control and to defile it along with the rest of Jerusalem (v. 2c–d),[26] especially at the period in the future that the heavenly voice identifies (future-tense verb "will trample"; πατήσουσιν, with the temporal extent specified, "for forty-two months"). To speak of "trampling" Jerusalem alludes to a pattern of judgment that God has allowed Israel and its temple-city to endure at various times in the past, and this verse suggests that the pattern will occur again in escalated form in the period of time leading up to Christ's return to earth. Jerusalem's fall to Babylon in 586 BC was the cardinal instance of gentile conquest and destruction that Old Testament prophets portrayed as a "trampling" by Israel's enemies, and it became the paradigm that foreshadows an ultimate attack by the nations in the future.[27] The same pattern is seen to recur in 167 BC when Antiochus Epiphanes desecrated the Jerusalem temple and halted its sacrifices for a period of time (1 Macc 3:45, 51),[28] and Jesus uses the language of Daniel 8:13 (desolation and trampling, καταπάτημα, of the holy place) to point at least typologically to the time of his future return (Mark 13:14).[29]

The command then to exclude this "courtyard that is outside the temple" (v. 2a) from John's symbolic measurement represents God's intent not to restore or rebuild the temple precinct (or the wider city as portrayed here) in such a conquered and desecrated condition. Its "trampled" state during the tribulation will not be its final condition. This also explains why the rebuilt temple itself and its altar and worshipers will need the restoration that is symbolized by the measuring commanded for it (v. 1).

The influence of Daniel is clear also in the extent of time that is given for this trampling (v. 2d). "Forty-two months" or its general equivalence is cited in several places in Daniel as the future time period when God's people will suffer intense oppression just prior to God's kingdom being established on earth (Dan 7:25; 8:14; 9:27; 12:7, 11, 12).[30] Reference to "forty-two months" (Rev 11:2; 13:5) or "twelve hundred and sixty days" (11:3; 12:6), since they are so specific, can only with difficulty be taken as "an indefinite period of time" or "a standard symbol for that limited period of time during which evil would be allowed free rein" or a reference to the whole era from Christ's resurrection till his return.[31] In light of Daniel's central influence on John's visions of the end times (e.g., Rev 1:7, 13;

---

26. "The holy city" clearly refers in this context to earthly Jerusalem, although it is an ironic or paradoxical description of the desecration of the place that God intended to be holy and that in the future he will restore to holiness (Rev 21:2, 10; 22:19; cf. Matt 4:5). For how this identification relates to "the great city" in v. 8, see the discussion there.

27. Isa 63:18; Dan 8:13; Zech 12:3. These verses in the LXX use the verb καταπατέω or the noun καταπάτημα. These prophets seem to have the destruction of 586 BC in mind as they envision an additional (and ultimate) future attack that God will decisively repel.

28. Many understand Dan 8:13 to have the events of 167 BC in view as well, reflecting on 586 BC as well as looking forward to a more severe end-time fulfillment. Cf. Wood, *Daniel*, 212–19; 261–62.

29. Luke 21:24 seems to point to Jerusalem's destruction in AD 70 as a further replication of the typological pattern that will be climaxed at Christ's future return. See also the discussion

in Mark L. Strauss, *Mark*, ZECNT (Grand Rapids: Zondervan, 2014), 577–80, who takes AD 70 as the "primary reference" of Mark 13:13 but in a way that foreshadows Christ's future coming.

30. John J. Collins, *Daniel: A Commentary on the Book of Daniel*, Hermeneia (Minneapolis: Fortress, 1993), 322–24; 357–60; Pitre, *Tribulation*, 51–62; D. S. Russell, *The Method and Message of Jewish Apocalyptic, 200 BC—AD 100* (Philadelphia: Westminster, 1964), 194–95; Leon James Wood, *A Commentary on Daniel* (Grand Rapids: Zondervan, 1973), 199–202; 247–63; 315–29. Among commentaries on Rev, see Glasson, *Revelation*, 67–70, 74; Osborne, *Revelation*, 414–15, 420, 464; Patterson, *Revelation*, 241–42; and Thomas, *Revelation 8–22*, 84–85. See comments at 3:10 on this future period of tribulation.

31. See Smalley, *Revelation*, 274; Mounce, *Revelation*, 215; and Beale, *Revelation*, 566–67, respectively. For the argument that 12:5–6 convincingly establishes the third option as the correct one (cf. Beale, *Revelation*, 567; Hoskins, *Revelation*, 190–93), see comments at that passage.

7:14; 11:15; 20:4; 22:5), a more precise, literal sense for this time frame is much more likely.[32]

11:3–4 And I will give authority to my two witnesses, and they will prophesy for twelve hundred and sixty days clothed in sackcloth." 4 These are the two olive trees and the two lampstands who stand before the Lord of the earth (καὶ δώσω τοῖς δυσὶν μάρτυσίν μου καὶ προφητεύσουσιν ἡμέρας χιλίας διακοσίας ἑξήκοντα περιβεβλημένοι σάκκους. 4 οὗτοί εἰσιν αἱ δύο ἐλαῖαι καὶ αἱ δύο λυχνίαι αἱ ἐνώπιον τοῦ κυρίου τῆς γῆς ἑστῶτες). The continued quotation (vv. 1c–3) shows that vv. 1–2 (temple measurement) and vv. 3–13 (two witnesses) present connected episodes in John's vision. They are linked also by reference to Jerusalem (vv. 2, 8, 13), by the time frame cited (vv. 2, 3, 9), and by strong allusions throughout to passages from Zechariah (e.g., Zech 4:2–6; 12:3; 14:2). The story of the "two witnesses" recounts their earthly activity (vv. 3–6), their celebrated murder by the beast (vv. 7–10), and their stunning resurrection followed by God's judgment on Jerusalem (vv. 11–13).[33]

The heavenly voice presents the two witnesses as definite or known ("the two witnesses of mine") because they are identified by the accompanying possessive "my" (v. 3a).[34] What must be understood about them beyond their relationship to God or Christ follows in these verses, beginning with the divine appointment they will receive in days to come (the verbs of v. 3 continue the future orientation set in v. 2d).[35] The result or focus of this heavenly commission is that "they will prophesy" (v. 3b), an assignment similar to John's (cf. 10:11),[36] and the time frame of their prophecy ("twelve hundred and sixty days") also matches the period specified for the holy city's desecration in v. 2d ("forty-two months"). God appointed them to proclaim his message during the final three-and-a-half years leading up to Christ's return to earth,[37] and the somber tone of their ministry, as could be expected, is symbolically reflected in their attire, "clothed in sackcloth" (v. 3b). They will speak for God authoritatively[38] and accompanied by miraculous deeds of power (see discussion at vv. 5–6), yet all the while with an attitude of mourning over God's coming judgment and the desperate need for their listeners to repent (cf. "sackcloth" in Gen 37:34; Jer 4:8; Jonah 3:5–6, 8; Matt 11:21).[39]

The further description of them in v. 4 is adapted from Zechariah 4 and identifies them as Spirit-inspired spokesmen for God at a time of great crisis for Israel and the wider world.[40] After Zechariah's visions of Jerusalem and Israel rebuilt after judgment (Zech 1–2), he speaks in

---

32. A future period of three and a half years when the antichrist devastates Jerusalem just prior to Christ's return is the interpretation reflected in Irenaeus, *Haer.* 5.30.4.

33. For the question of whether the two witnesses can be specifically identified, see comments on vv. 5–6.

34. Commentaries puzzle over how John or his readers would be familiar already with these two, but this is a misunderstanding of how the article is used in phrases like this in Rev. John never uses "my" (μου) with an anarthrous noun (except the vocative in 7:14, for which there is no corresponding article). The possessive identifies the item as specific, and thus an article is used. See similar usage with "her" in 12:14 ("her place").

35. In v. 3a John abbreviates his common expression "to give authority" (2:26; 6:8; 9:3; 13:2, 4, 5, 7) by leaving "authority" to be implied by the verb itself and its indirect object ("I will

give to them") and jumps immediately to how they will act in keeping with this commission ("and they will prophesy").

36. They will serve God as both prophets (vv. 3, 6, 10) and witnesses (vv. 3, 7) in the ways that the following verses describe. John was charged with the same combined task in writing this book (cf. 1:2–3).

37. This is the interpretation given by Hippolytus, *Antichr.* 64.

38. BDAG 890; F. Schnider, "προφητεύω," *EDNT* 3:184.

39. Siew, *War*, 216–19, emphasizes the witnesses' mourning over Jerusalem's desecration prior to the arrival of God's kingdom.

40. Shifting from the future-tense verbs of vv. 2d–3, John describes the two witnesses in his vision using customary present verbs in vv. 4–6. This is his report mode (see discussion at 4:5; 9:6, 10–11).

complementary visions about the nation's spiritual renewal through God's messianic "Branch"
in a future day (3:8–10) and God's power at work
through his representatives to restore Jerusalem as
a light for all the world (4:6, 14). Zechariah initially
speaks of "two olive trees" and one "lampstand"
(4:2–3, 11–12) and later of "two anointed ones"
who represent "the Lord of all the earth" (4:14),[41]
referring in that context to Joshua and Zerubbabel,
through whom God was at work in rebuilding the
temple at that time. John adapts these and takes
them as patterns of two representatives of God in
the future judgment and restoration of Jerusalem
in the final days. They are "the two olive trees" and
also "the two lampstands" (Rev 11:4; identified as
well known by the article).[42] John can assume his
readers' familiarity with Zechariah's vision after
the allusion to Zechariah 1–2 in the measuring
motif of vv. 1–2 and also from his near quotation
of Zechariah 2:14, "who stand before the Lord of
the earth" (Rev 11:4b). This description is another
reminder that the Lord is sovereign over the whole
world and his judgment and subsequent blessing
on Jerusalem will impact all the world's peoples.

**11:5–6 And if anyone intends to harm them, fire
comes out of their mouths and consumes their
enemies. If anyone intends to harm them, he must
be killed in this way. 6 These have the authority to
close the sky so that no rain falls during the days
of their prophesying, and they have authority
over the waters to turn them into blood and to
strike the earth with any kind of plague as often
as they want** (καὶ εἴ τις αὐτοὺς θέλει ἀδικῆσαι πῦρ
ἐκπορεύεται ἐκ τοῦ στόματος αὐτῶν καὶ κατεσθίει
τοὺς ἐχθροὺς αὐτῶν· καὶ εἴ τις θελήσει αὐτοὺς

ἀδικῆσαι, οὕτως δεῖ αὐτὸν ἀποκτανθῆναι. 6 οὗτοι
ἔχουσιν τὴν ἐξουσίαν κλεῖσαι τὸν οὐρανόν, ἵνα μὴ
ὑετὸς βρέχῃ τὰς ἡμέρας τῆς προφητείας αὐτῶν,
καὶ ἐξουσίαν ἔχουσιν ἐπὶ τῶν ὑδάτων στρέφειν
αὐτὰ εἰς αἷμα καὶ πατάξαι τὴν γῆν ἐν πάσῃ πληγῇ
ὁσάκις ἐὰν θελήσωσιν). John's description of these
end-time spokesmen for God highlights the divine authority that will energize their ministry,
which will include highly charged conflict as well
as displays of divine power similar to what Elijah
and Moses experienced. Continuing in his report
mode, John recounts what he sees in his vision by
using present-tense verbs (see note on v. 4), even
though he has already indicated that these events
will occur on earth in the future, at the time of the
culminating judgments just prior to Christ's return.
Far from being cloistered holy men, these witnesses
will speak for God in an atmosphere of sharp opposition and resistance, as indicated by references
to "their enemies" (v. 5b) and some who want to
"harm" them (twice in v. 5), as well as by what happens to them when they finish their God-given period of ministry (vv. 7–10). Their defenses against
such hostility are phrased in terms that evoke the
God-given power that Elijah displayed against his
foes: destructive fire from heaven (v. 5b; see 2 Kgs
1:9–16 [possibly also Moses; Num 16:17–35]) and
no rainfall for three-and-a-half years (v. 6a–b; see
1 Kgs 17:1; cf. Luke 4:25; Jas 5:17), or like Moses's
power in Egypt: water turned to blood (v. 6c–d; see
Exod 7:14–21) and various plagues as necessary
(v. 6e–f; see Exod 7–12).

The fact that John pictures the work of the two
witnesses in these terms does not mean that Elijah and Moses will personally reappear on earth
in the end times.[43] Rather, John sees Elijah and

---

41. The number of witnesses cited in Rev 11:3 seems to
come primarily from these parallels in Zech 4, but the Jewish expectation that two or more witnesses were required to
establish the truth of a matter (Deut 17:6–7; 19:15) may lie in
the background.

42. Wallace, *Grammar*, 225.
43. Contra Smith, *Revelation*, 168–70; Thomas, *Revelation
8–22*, 88–89.

Moses as representative of a pattern of prophetic ministry that will be exercised in that future time of crisis (similar to the typology of heresy seen in Rev 2:14–15, 20–23; see comments there).[44] Since John does not use the names Elijah or Moses (or any others that could be suggested),[45] it would be overstepping the evidence to think that their personal appearance is what Malachi 4:5–6 intends.[46] It seems most likely, however, that we should understand the witnesses as unnamed individual spokesmen for God in that future day rather than as representatives of a wide body of Christian prophets bearing witness at that time or of the church in its prophetic role throughout the age. The imagery of vv. 7–12 becomes very unwieldy or even incoherent when read corporately (killed by the beast, bodies lie unburied, etc.).[47]

One further puzzle in the symbolism of these verses is how to read things like "fire com[ing] out of their mouths and consum[ing] their enemies" and their enemies thus being "killed" (v. 5b, d).[48] Some suggest this is a strong portrayal of the force of their prophetic ministry: the "fire" is not a destructive weapon but the power of their words to overcome the opposition (cf. 2 Sam 22:9; Jer 5:14), similar to the symbolic "sword" coming out of Jesus's mouth (Rev 1:16; 19:15).[49] It is true that "fire" and "sword" are symbolic for speech in these cases, but they seem to be words pronouncing immediate punishment, in this case against those who threaten

the divine proclamation in those critical future days. It is hard to give an appropriate sense to v. 5d (the foe "must be killed in this way") if this "fire" represents simply forceful persuasion. Given the hostility against God's work in that future day (cf. vv. 7–10), it is only right to understand these witnesses as able to call down from heaven the kinds of tangible punishment against their opponents that Elijah and Moses exercised in earlier days.

11:7–8 And when they have completed their testimony, the beast that comes up from the bottomless pit will wage war against them and overcome them and murder them. 8 And their dead bodies will lie in the public square of the great city, which in spiritual terms is called Sodom and Egypt, where their Lord also was crucified (καὶ ὅταν τελέσωσιν τὴν μαρτυρίαν αὐτῶν, τὸ θηρίον τὸ ἀναβαῖνον ἐκ τῆς ἀβύσσου ποιήσει μετ' αὐτῶν πόλεμον καὶ νικήσει αὐτοὺς καὶ ἀποκτενεῖ αὐτούς. 8 καὶ τὸ πτῶμα αὐτῶν ἐπὶ τῆς πλατείας τῆς πόλεως τῆς μεγάλης, ἥτις καλεῖται πνευματικῶς Σόδομα καὶ Αἴγυπτος, ὅπου καὶ ὁ κύριος αὐτῶν ἐσταυρώθη). After the previous account of the witnesses' powerful ministry (vv. 3–6), it is a shock to read next of their peremptory defeat and murder by the beast (vv. 7–10). The whole account turns on the theological backdrop of the initial clause of v. 7, "when they have completed their testimony," because it captures the reminder of God's sovereign plan for their work, seen previously in the indication that

---

44. See also Resseguie, *Narrative Commentary*, 161–62; and Roloff, *Revelation*, 131.

45. See Matthew Black, "The 'Two Witnesses' of Rev. 11:3f. in Jewish and Christian Apocalyptic Tradition," in *Donum Gentilicium: New Testament Studies in Honour of David Daube*, ed. E. Bammel and C. K. Barrett (Oxford: Clarendon, 1978), 227–37; and Daniel K. K. Wong, "The Two Witnesses in Revelation 11," *BSac* 154 (1997): 344–54.

46. Malachi's prophecy is understood in a typological way in Matt 17:10–12; Mark 9:11–13; Luke 1:17. John the Baptist's reply in John 1:21 was a denial that he was Elijah in person.

47. Patterson, *Revelation*, 242–45; Walvoord, Rawley, and Hitchcock, *Revelation*, 181–82. Osborne, *Revelation*, 418, suggests that these will be two individual prophets in the final days who also represent "the witnessing church in its suffering and triumph." Ladd, *Revelation*, 154, expresses a view similar to Osborne's.

48. Water turning "into blood" and being able to "strike the earth with any kind of plague" (v. 6c–e) seems more likely to be literally true in that future day, following the intensification of the Egyptian plagues as seen already in the trumpet judgments (see, e.g., comments on 8:7–12).

49. Resseguie, *Narrative Commentary*, 162–63.

"they will prophesy for twelve hundred and sixty days" (v. 3b). When God's assigned work for them is completed, then the overpowering evil of those final days will have its way—at least for a short time (cf. vv. 11–13). The entire verse looks ahead to the culminating events of the seven-year period of tribulation (cf. three future verbs in the main clause), and so it gives a brief preview of "the beast that comes up from the bottomless pit" (v. 7b),[50] the central figure of evil whose opposition to God will dominate that period. The main account of this "beast" begins in 13:1, and he figures prominently in Revelation from there until his final demise in 20:10. This evil world leader (a person who is represented as a wild animal to picture his savage brutality; cf. Dan 7:3–27, and see discussion at Rev 13:1) will step in by God's permission and summarily wipe out the witnesses' annoying opposition to his regime. This human figure is said to "come up from the bottomless pit" because his rise to prominence and exercise of power is under Satan's control, not because he is himself a demonic spirit (see notes at 9:1; 13:1–2).

The beast's attack against the witnesses appears to be part of a larger campaign against God's people, and that larger story is presented in 13:7 ("it was given to him to wage war against the saints and to overcome them"; cf. Dan 7:21). The assault against these two individuals (11:7) seemingly will come at the end of that full-scale persecution. Their God-given ability to defend themselves from harm (vv. 5–6) prevents any prior efforts to eliminate them. But when God's three-and-a-half-year mission for them is done, the beast will quickly "overcome them and murder them" (v. 7b).

Their slaying will apparently be intended as a brutal public example for all to see, because v. 8a records that "their dead bodies[51] will lie in the public square of the great city" (see also vv. 9–10). The reference to "the public square"[52] underscores the open nature of this gruesome display, obvious to all and continuing for three-and-a-half days (v. 9).

There are mixed signals concerning the identity of "the great city" mentioned in v. 8, but it quite clearly refers to Jerusalem. In later chapters of Revelation "the great city" is consistently Babylon-Rome (16:19; 17:18; 18:10, 16, 18, 19, 21), and some argue that the mention of "peoples and tribes and languages and nations" viewing the corpses (11:9) as well as its association with the beast indicates a world wider than Jerusalem itself, that is, the "city" or world opposed to God as represented by Babylon. Further, when John actually names the city in this passage, he cites "mystical" or "spiritual" names rather than a literal one ("Sodom and Egypt"; v. 8b), and so a figurative rather than literal space is intended.[53] But do these names undercut the straightforward declaration of v. 8c that seems

---

50. John uses an articular expression to bring this figure into the narrative for the first time (contrary to the normal Greek pattern that would use an anarthrous phrase). But this is part of his individual narrative style, to give a brief preview of a major figure or item prior to its full discussion in the story. He seems to use the "well known" article because of the item's importance to end-time events, even though it may be new to the story here. This adds tension to the narrative by heightening the readers' awareness of central figures. See Beckwith, *Apocalypse*, 247–48, and Resseguie, *Narrative Commentary*, 51–52, for other examples.

51. The phrase "their dead bodies" (τὸ πτῶμα αὐτῶν) is a singular collective here and in v. 9a ("their dead body," i.e., corpse) since these clauses picture the dead as a single entity.

The plural "their dead bodies" occurs in v. 9b, perhaps because burial suggests more individual attention.

52. The word translated "public square" (πλατεία) when used as a noun denotes a wide space or road. In the plural it tends to mean streets (e.g., Matt 6:5; Luke 10:10; 14:21) and in the singular a market plaza or city square (e.g., Gen 19:2; Judg 19:15–20; Ezra 10:9; cf. Rev 21:21; 22:2). The article is used here because it is definite by association with the city (see note on 6:9). This would mean some specifically public space in the city, usually the center of civic life. In Jerusalem it may mean the public courtyard outside the temple (cf. v. 2).

53. Koester, *Revelation*, 500; Osborne, *Revelation*, 426–27; Resseguie, *Narrative Commentary*, 164; Roloff, *Revelation*, 133.

to identify the city unequivocally as Jerusalem: "Where their Lord also was crucified"? It is true that in theological terms "Babylon" is opposed to what the cross represents and that the evil of the whole world sent Jesus to the cross, but this statement is a very opaque way of making such a point.[54] John does not explicitly name the city "Jerusalem," and he postpones the crucial identifying clause till the very last, but v. 8c despite its indirectness clearly identifies "the great city" as earthly, literal Jerusalem.[55]

Verse 8 simply continues the focus on Jerusalem that started in vv. 1–2. The larger vision (vv. 1–13) pertains to Jerusalem at the end of the tribulation period, and so we should understand John's attitude toward Jerusalem as both negative (it will be subjected to severe judgment because of its sinful rejection of Christ) and positive (this is God's disciplinary punishment leading to its forgiveness and restoration). This explains the mixed description found in vv. 2, 8: "the holy city" and "the great city,"[56] but also "in spiritual terms is called Sodom and Egypt." The names "Sodom and Egypt" reflect a pattern of evil, labeling Jerusalem as guilty of widespread wickedness like Sodom and of idolatry like Egypt (Deut 29:23; Isa 1:9–10; 3:9; 19:1; Jer 23:14; 49:18; Ezek 20:7; 23:27), both of which God judged severely. For Jerusalem to be the place where Israel's messiah was crucified (Rev 11:8c) adds to the paradox, but it is understandable

that God's witnesses would complete their ministry there and that Jerusalem would be the locus for judgment and repentance when the witnesses are spectacularly vindicated after three-and-a-half days (vv. 11–13).[57]

11:9–10 And individuals from the peoples and tribes and languages and nations look at their dead bodies for three-and-a-half days, and they do not allow their dead bodies to be placed in a tomb. 10 And those who live on the earth gloat over them and celebrate. And they will send gifts to one another, because these two prophets tormented those who live on the earth (καὶ βλέπουσιν ἐκ τῶν λαῶν καὶ φυλῶν καὶ γλωσσῶν καὶ ἐθνῶν τὸ πτῶμα αὐτῶν ἡμέρας τρεῖς καὶ ἥμισυ καὶ τὰ πτώματα αὐτῶν οὐκ ἀφίουσιν τεθῆναι εἰς μνῆμα. 10 καὶ οἱ κατοικοῦντες ἐπὶ τῆς γῆς χαίρουσιν ἐπ᾽ αὐτοῖς καὶ εὐφραίνονται καὶ δῶρα πέμψουσιν ἀλλήλοις, ὅτι οὗτοι οἱ δύο προφῆται ἐβασάνισαν τοὺς κατοικοῦντας ἐπὶ τῆς γῆς). The ruthless treatment of God's witnesses by the beast is matched by the watching world's indifferent and even gleeful reaction to the murders of these two whom they regard as dangerous enemies. In vv. 9–10a John switches from predominantly future verbs (vv. 3, 7) to his descriptive present mode (as in vv. 4–6) and then back again to the future in v. 10b (with a background aorist in v. 10c), as he tells what he has seen and then anticipates its actual occurrence in the end times.[58] The relevant authorities, certainly

---

54. Perhaps "by whom" he was crucified or "who" oppose their Lord would denote this broader point, but "where" and a definite historical event, "was crucified," seems an odd way to express a nonliteral identification.

55. Aune, *Revelation 6–16*, 619–21; Charles, *Revelation*, 1:287–88; Thomas, *Revelation 8–22*, 93–94.

56. The OT celebrates Jerusalem as "the city of the great King" (Ps 48:2), set "in the center of the nations" (Ezek 5:5), to which the nations will come to seek the Lord (Jer 3:17; Mic 4:2; Zech 2:10–12; 8:22; 9:9–10; 14:16). But in departing from their God, Jerusalem will be mourned as a "great city" under judgment (Jer 22:1–9).

57. In addition to ironically identifying the city, this reference to Jesus's crucifixion suggests the pattern of discipleship that the two witnesses have faithfully followed until death. They died serving God in the same city where their Lord also gave his life in fulfilling God's will, and all Christians are called to such fidelity as witnesses for Christ (Luke 24:48; Acts 1:8; Rev 1:5; 2:13).

58. See note on 11:4.

under the beast's direction, "do not allow"[59] the slain bodies to be buried (v. 9b). In the ancient world (as today) this represents a final act of insult and desecration against the dead (cf. Jer 9:22; 16:4–7; cf. Tob 1:17–20; 2:3–8; 2 Macc 5:10; also Sophocles, *Ant.* 21–30). This public disgrace continues for "three-and-a-half days," a period that in a reduced form mirrors their predetermined time of ministry (v. 3) and approximates their Lord's time in a tomb outside Jerusalem (see note on discipleship at v. 8c). During this time people from the whole world[60] will view their dead bodies, apparently without concern or revulsion at the horror of this public spectacle. Reference to "peoples and tribes and languages and nations" (v. 9a) does not require a symbolic interpretation of the city as Babylon-Rome or as the world in general as some suggest,[61] but it does indicate what a center of world attention Jerusalem will be in those trouble-filled days and how the whole world will follow the beast's actions after his rise to prominence (cf. 13:3, 12–13; 17:8). At the same time, it continues to be a sign of hope for the possibility that at the end of that final period of domination by evil forces some from all the nations of the world could respond to God's redemption through Christ (cf. v. 13).[62]

This worldwide but wicked audience for these events is reinforced in v. 10 by the phrase "those who live on the earth," used at both ends of the verse to highlight the contrasting actions recounted in between (celebration vs. torment). "Those who live on the earth" is John's frequent designation of the general population of the world who oppose God and will suffer his judgment in the final days.[63] John describes them as "gloat[ing]" and "celebrat[ing]" the murder and desecration of the two witnesses (v. 10a).[64] They will even take this as an opportunity for exchanging gifts of special celebration, a kind of diabolical Christmas or Boxing Day (see Neh 8:10–12; Esth 9:19 for examples of such community-wide rejoicing in the ancient world).[65] Their rationale for this is to some degree understandable, as v. 10c indicates. When John says, "these two prophets tormented" the earth dwellers,[66] it refers not to their annoyance at such preaching[67] but to the witnesses' exercise of divine powers in executing judgment on any who opposed them over their three-and-a-half-year ministry (v. 6, drought, bloody water, every plague; cf. "torment" in 9:5; 14:10). Their exuberance and relief in seeing these two lying dead in the public square, however, will set them up for a great reversal, as v. 11 shows.

---

59. The verb translated "they do not allow" (ἀφίουσιν) is an impersonal third-person plural usually denoting "people" in general as the subject. Sometimes this is equivalent to a passive since the actual agents are not relevant (e.g., Luke 12:20). But the context here suggests that "they" are the governing authorities, especially the primary actor of v. 7 (the beast), rather than the multicultural crowd of v. 9a.

60. The phrase "individuals from the peoples" represents a partitive phrase with the preposition "from" (ἐκ). See note on 2:10 for further comment on the grammatical construction. This means that some from all these groups will view this scene at one time or another during the three-and-a-half days.

61. E.g., Caird, *Revelation*, 138.

62. See comments on 5:9 and 7:9 about John's use of the words "peoples and tribes and languages and nations" and their OT background.

63. See note on 3:10 for further discussion. In 6:9–10 these

earth-dwellers are charged with the martyrdom of those "slaughtered because of the word of God and because of the testimony they maintained." The woes of the final three trumpets are directed against them in 8:13.

64. The verbs for "gloat" (χαίρω) and "celebrate" (εὐφραίνω) normally denote rejoicing over something genuinely delightful (e.g., χαίρω in Matt 2:10; 18:13; 1 Thess 3:9; εὐφραίνω in Pss 16:9 [15:9 LXX]; 19:8 [18:9 LXX]; Luke 15:23; both verbs in Luke 15:32) instead of the Schadenfreude (taking delight in someone's pain) indicated in this context.

65. Here John projects into the future again with the verb "they will send" (πέμψουσιν).

66. This description of the two witnesses (cf. vv. 3, 7) as "prophets" returns to the role John indicated for them back in vv. 3 and 6.

67. This is suggested by BDAG 168; Giblin, "Revelation 11.1–13," 444.

11:11–12 And after the three-and-a-half days a spirit of life from God entered them, and they stood on their feet, and great fear fell on those who watched them. 12 And they heard a loud voice from heaven saying to them, "Come up here." And they went up into heaven in a cloud, and their enemies watched them (καὶ μετὰ τὰς τρεῖς ἡμέρας καὶ ἥμισυ πνεῦμα ζωῆς ἐκ τοῦ θεοῦ εἰσῆλθεν ἐν αὐτοῖς, καὶ ἔστησαν ἐπὶ τοὺς πόδας αὐτῶν, καὶ φόβος μέγας ἐπέπεσεν ἐπὶ τοὺς θεωροῦντας αὐτούς. 12 καὶ ἤκουσαν φωνῆς μεγάλης ἐκ τοῦ οὐρανοῦ λεγούσης αὐτοῖς, Ἀνάβατε ὧδε. καὶ ἀνέβησαν εἰς τὸν οὐρανὸν ἐν τῇ νεφέλῃ, καὶ ἐθεώρησαν αὐτοὺς οἱ ἐχθροὶ αὐτῶν). In an astounding—and very public—reversal of fortune, God's prophets go from slaughter and desecration on earth to resurrection and welcome into heaven, while their previously rejoicing enemies gape in terror. After shameful exposure and mocking for three-and-a-half days, the witnesses are completely vindicated as God's servants by being raised from the dead for all to see (v. 11b–c). The language of resurrection used here is drawn almost word for word from the LXX of Ezekiel 37:5 ("a spirit of life"; πνεῦμα ζωῆς)[68] and 37:10 (the spirit "entered" them, εἰσῆλθεν; "they stood" on their feet, ἔστησαν), replicating God's promise of new life from dead bones. John notes explicitly that the spirit of life came[69] "from God" to underscore heaven's affirmation of their ministry and sacrifice. Their obvious return to vitality— "they stood on their feet"—demonstrated the work of God as well, as indicated by the onlookers' "great fear." This is the normal human response when faced with an undeniable display of supernatural power (e.g., Exod 15:14–16; Jonah 1:10; Luke 1:12,

65; Acts 5:5; 19:17), and given the earlier actions of these two (vv. 5–6), such a reaction is justified.

An even greater mark of their vindication by God came about (v. 12a–b) when a commanding "voice from heaven" (cf. 10:4, 8; 14:2, 13) instructed the two to "come up here" (ἀνάβατε ὧδε).[70] John records that they did so immediately, ascending "up into heaven in a cloud." Here the influence of two typologies that are intermingled in this passage come together in one image: just as a cloud received Christ as he ascended to heaven (Acts 1:9) and as Elijah was taken up in a whirlwind into heaven (2 Kgs 2:11; cf. 1 En. 39:3), so these two prophets are transported visibly to their welcome by God on high in public recognition of their faithful service. This evidence of divine approval is witnessed in this case, however, not by beloved followers but by terrified foes: "Their enemies watched them" (v. 12d; same verb as in v. 11d).

11:13 And in that hour a great earthquake took place, and a tenth of the city fell, and seven thousand people were killed in the earthquake, and the rest became terrified and gave glory to the God of heaven (Καὶ ἐν ἐκείνῃ τῇ ὥρᾳ ἐγένετο σεισμὸς μέγας καὶ τὸ δέκατον τῆς πόλεως ἔπεσεν καὶ ἀπεκτάνθησαν ἐν τῷ σεισμῷ ὀνόματα ἀνθρώπων χιλιάδες ἑπτά καὶ οἱ λοιποὶ ἔμφοβοι ἐγένοντο καὶ ἔδωκαν δόξαν τῷ θεῷ τοῦ οὐρανοῦ). In the final verse of this section we find the conclusion not only to the story of the two witnesses (vv. 3–12) but also to the account of God's temple being measured as a sign of its restoration (vv. 1–2). References here to the city and its people under judgment and their initial responses of repentant reverence toward God remind us that spiritual

---

68. Gen 6:17 and 7:15 contain this phrase as a description of existing physical life on earth. Genesis 2:7 reflects a similar image of God giving "life" to Adam at creation, but different words for "breath/spirit" are used in both Hebrew and Greek.

69. In vv. 11–13 John returns to standard narration of the

events he saw: every main verb is aorist (11x), recounting the events of the vision in sequence. These picture what will happen in the climactic future days just prior to Christ's return.

70. John received the same summons in 4:1 (ἀνάβα ὧδε) but his was a visionary ascent, while theirs is an actual bodily one.

and national renewal will come only through disciplinary judgment. The specific time indication, "in that hour" (v. 13a), reestablishes the consistent temporal frame (cf. vv. 2, 3, 7, 9, 11) focused on the final three-and-a-half years of the tribulation period leading up to Christ's return and earthly reign (19:11–20:10). When the witnesses ascend in ultimate victory, their opponents in Jerusalem are left to face God's culminating wrath in the form of a "great earthquake" (a pattern of judgment stretching back to Exod 19; see comments on 4:5; 6:12) that destroys "a tenth" of the city's structures (v. 13a–b). The human toll[71] is also large, "seven thousand people," a number that resonates with significance as the reversal of the remnant that God counted as faithful Israelites in the time of Elijah (1 Kgs 19:14–18; Rom 11:4).[72] The remaining number,[73] the survivors of the catastrophe, "became terrified and gave glory to the God of heaven" (v. 13d). Their terror (ἔμφοβοι) matches the initial response of "great fear" (φόβος μέγας) in v. 11d but goes beyond it. There is some debate over whether rendering glory to God in v. 13d represents genuine spiritual repentance or merely external, cowering submission to judgment. The phrase "the God of heaven" naturally identifies Israel's God as supreme in contexts where many acknowledged other gods (used 13x in Ezra-Nehemiah; cf. 2 Chr 36:23; Dan 2:18–19; Jonah 1:9). It is likely that Daniel 2:37 and 2:44 have influenced John's choice of words in a greater way, since those verses speak of earthly rule coming only from Israel's God and of a future

day when [through Israel] his lasting kingdom will replace all the earth's human kingdoms. In later verses John associates fearing and glorifying God with true worship (14:7) and blaspheming God with lack of repentance (16:9, 11). The combination of "fear" and "glory" here in 11:13 seems to reflect a positive, repentant response to what has happened.

11:14 The second woe has passed. Behold, the third woe is coming soon (Ἡ οὐαὶ ἡ δευτέρα ἀπῆλθεν· ἰδοὺ ἡ οὐαὶ ἡ τρίτη ἔρχεται ταχύ). The structure of the final three woes announced in 8:13 surfaces here again as it did in 9:12, following the fifth trumpet. The announcement does not follow immediately after 9:21 where the events of the sixth trumpet end. Its location here signals that the intervening sections about the little scroll (10:1–11) and the temple measurement and two witnesses (11:1–13) should be associated with the sixth trumpet, that is, the second woe.[74] The time indications cited in these intervening accounts (e.g., 10:6–7; 11:2–3, 11, 13) confirm that the events they describe will occur in the final half of the tribulation and run right up to its culmination at Christ's return. The "third woe" refers to the cataclysmic judgments that immediately precede and accompany that return. This warning that it "is coming soon" (v. 14b) mirrors the wording used at several places in the book to describe Christ's own imminent coming (2:16; 3:11; 22:7, 12, 20). The end of the "third woe" is not explicitly signaled later in the book, because John

---

71. The word "people" in the phrase "seven thousand people" translates a Greek phrase meaning "names of humans" (ὀνόματα ἀνθρώπων), used here to denote "individual humans," seven thousand of whom were killed (cf. 3:4; BDAG 714).

72. Just as God's announcement to Elijah was likely to be a literal, if rounded, number, so John's number here seems intended to be literal, but not merely or only literal—it has a connotative or allusive sense as well.

73. Since the portion cited earlier (v. 13b, "a tenth of the city") referred to buildings, etc., not to people, the "seven

thousand" gives no basis for estimating the city's population, contrary to the suggestions of some.

74. Lambrecht, "Structuration," 92–93; Siew, *War*, 114–15. Several interpreters attribute the location of this announcement here to confusion or incompetence on the part of later editors or John himself in a final redaction of his earlier composition (Aune, *Revelation 6–16*, 630; Roloff, *Revelation*, 134–35). It seems always better to accept the presentation that a text gives if possible rather than rewriting it according to what we think is best.

indicates its content in other ways (see comments on the seventh trumpet in v. 15a).

11:15 And the seventh angel sounded his trumpet, and there came loud voices in heaven saying, "The kingdom of the world has become the kingdom of our Lord and of his Messiah, and he will reign forever and ever" (Καὶ ὁ ἕβδομος ἄγγελος ἐσάλπισεν· καὶ ἐγένοντο φωναὶ μεγάλαι ἐν τῷ οὐρανῷ λέγοντες, Ἐγένετο ἡ βασιλεία τοῦ κόσμου τοῦ κυρίου ἡμῶν καὶ τοῦ Χριστοῦ αὐτοῦ, καὶ βασιλεύσει εἰς τοὺς αἰῶνας τῶν αἰώνων). With the trumpet blast from the seventh angel (v. 15a) the series of trumpets that began in 8:2–7 is completed. But just as the opening of the seventh seal in 8:1 signaled no immediate judgments (unlike the first six seals; 6:1–17), so no explicit judgments follow the seventh trumpet blast. Instead, the seven bowls that eventually follow in chapters 15–16 will fill out the judgments of the seventh trumpet (as the seven trumpets fill out the seventh seal; cf. comments on 8:1–2). The cumulative effect of this telescoping of each of the seven judgments in this way is that each of the series brings the reader right up to the climax of God's coming judgment and redemption. The heavenly preview of the seventh trumpet in 10:6–7 sets the stage for this consummation (i.e., no further delay; God's mystery will be completed when the seventh angel sounds), and the description of the seven bowls as "the seven last plagues" (15:1) reinforces it at the other end.

Instead of an onslaught of judgment, the immediate effect of the seventh trumpet is "loud voices in heaven"[75] proclaiming God's everlasting victory over the whole world (v. 15b–d). This is another in the series of heavenly announcements in these chapters of the imminent arrival of God's full judgment and redemption (10:6–7; 12:10–12; 14:7–8; 15:1; 18:2; 19:2; see comments at 10:7). Giving heaven's perspective on earthly events, the voices proclaim the establishment of God's rule on earth, overcoming the existing evil empires: "The kingdom of the world has become the kingdom of our Lord and of his Messiah" (v. 15c). The full accomplishment has not yet come—the seven last plagues are still to be poured out (15:1–16:21) and Babylon must be defeated (17:1–18:24)—but God's rule on earth is already decided, and so it is certain and near at hand. The imminent victory is phrased using an aorist ("has become"; ἐγένετο[76]) as well as a future verb ("will reign"; βασιλεύσει) to signal that what is anticipated has already been decreed and is about to come to pass on earth.[77]

The wording of this acclamation is strongly influenced by Daniel 2:44 and 7:13–27 as well as Psalm 2:1–12. The point is not simply God's eternal rule as the great King of heaven (as in 2 Kgs 19:14–19; Pss 22:28; 93:1–2; 95:3; Dan 4:3, 34) but

---

75. The phrase "loud voice" (singular) appears often in Rev (in the near context, see 11:12; 12:10), but this is the only occurrence of the plural. But see the singular phrase in 14:2 and 19:1 where the voice or sound comes from multiple sources in heaven.

76. This aorist pictures the accomplishment as a recent past event viewed in summary, and so the translation "has become" (almost all recent English versions; cf. NLT "has now become"), because English prefers a present perfect for recent past actions (cf. 6:17; 9:12; Fanning, *Verbal Aspect*, 260–61). This is not a futuristic or proleptic aorist (cf. Aune, *Revelation 6–16*, 638; Smalley, *Revelation*, 289), but what the futuristic reading gets right is the sense that God's rule is certain and imminent. It could be labeled a "consummative" aorist because of the sense

that it has actually been accomplished despite opposition (Fanning, *Verbal Aspect*, 263–65), but it is the recent past idea that requires "has become" in English. Rowland, "Revelation," 643, is simply wrong in asserting that γίνομαι in Rev usually means "is" or "was" and that ἐγένετο in 11:15 should be translated "was" in the sense of "belonged to" (i.e., the kingdom of the world has always been God's). His comments show that he does not understand the aorist "recent past" tense usage (he confuses it with the Greek perfect), and he misses the theological point of 11:15.

77. Thompson, *Revelation*, 60–64, describes such liturgical passages in Rev (e.g., 10:6–7; 11:15–18; 12:10–12; 14:7–8; 15:1; 18:2; 19:2) as the celebration of heavenly realities that will soon come down to earth.

that he is about to establish that rule in actuality on earth (cf. Matt 6:10). John sees here the fulfillment of Daniel's visions of the savage gentile kingdoms of the world that are ultimately defeated by "one like a son of man" (Dan 7:13–14, 22, 27), who rules on behalf of "the saints of the Most High" (7:18, 22, 25, 27).[78] Likewise the nations' furious opposition "against the LORD and against his anointed" (Ps 2:1; cf. Rev 11:18) will finally be subdued by the earthly reign of God's Davidic king who will rule from Zion over all the nations (Ps 2:6–9; cf. Rev 2:26–28; 12:5; 19:5).[79] John's use of the specific word "world" (κόσμος) in v. 15c is not taken from Daniel or Psalm 2 (although the concept is there). The term refers to "human society, temporarily controlled by the powers of evil, organized in opposition to God,"[80] a usage characteristic of the Gospel and Epistles of John (John 7:7; 15:18–19; 16:33; 1 John 2:15–17; 5:19; see also Matt 4:8). Satan is the present ruler of this world (John 12:31; 14:30; 16:11; see also Matt 4:8 and Luke 4:5–6), but Christ has already decisively overcome him in the cross (John 16:11, 33). However, that victory remains to be brought to its full earthly accomplishment in the events that Revelation 4–19 represent. The final clause of 11:15 declares the future extension of that rule, once established, into all eternity, "and he will reign forever and ever."[81] This clause in effect previews the account that John gives in Revelation 20–22

(Christ's rule in the millennium that transitions into the eternal rule of God in a new heaven and new earth; cf. 1 Cor 15:23–28).

11:16–17 And the twenty-four elders who were sitting on their thrones fell on their faces and worshiped God, 17 saying, "We thank you, Lord God Almighty, the One who is and was, because you have taken your great power and begun to reign (καὶ οἱ εἴκοσι τέσσαρες πρεσβύτεροι [οἱ] ἐνώπιον τοῦ θεοῦ καθήμενοι ἐπὶ τοὺς θρόνους αὐτῶν ἔπεσαν ἐπὶ τὰ πρόσωπα αὐτῶν καὶ προσεκύνησαν τῷ θεῷ 17 λέγοντες, Εὐχαριστοῦμέν σοι, κύριε ὁ θεὸς ὁ παντοκράτωρ, ὁ ὢν καὶ ὁ ἦν, ὅτι εἴληφας τὴν δύναμίν σου τὴν μεγάλην καὶ ἐβασίλευσας). Just as in the vision of chapters 4–5, the twenty-four elders who surround God's heavenly throne, sitting on their own thrones (4:4), now join the acclamation of the heavenly voices (11:15b) with their own worshipful posture (v. 16; cf. 4:10; 5:8, 11, 14) and song of thanksgiving (v. 17).[82] Their heavenly declaration of gratitude is reminiscent of 4:9 and 7:12, and is addressed to the Lord here using titles appropriate to the theme of their thanksgiving. The Lord God is "Almighty" (παντοκράτωρ), a characteristic title for God in Revelation,[83] rooted in the Old Testament (see comments at 1:8) and denoting his all-powerful sovereignty over the affairs of his created universe.[84] As in 1:8 and 4:8, the name "Lord God Almighty" is accompanied by

---

78. See also the time period ("time, times, and half a time") during which one of the savage gentile rulers tramples God's people under his feet (Dan 7:23–25), alluded to in Rev 11:2–3, 7 above.

79. See 12:10 for another acclamation of the rule of God and of "his Messiah."

80. Smalley, *Revelation*, 289; see also H. Sasse, "κόσμος," *TDNT* 3:894–95.

81. These words closely reflect several OT texts (Exod 15:18; Pss 10:16; 146:10; Isa 24:21–23; Obad 1:21; Mic 4:5–8; Zech 14:9; see also Wis 3:8). On the phrase "forever and ever," see note on Rev 1:6.

82. The elders' declaration of thanks continues as a direct

quotation to the end of v. 18 (see second-person pronouns in vv. 17b–18), but v. 19 is John's further description of events in his vision (see third-person reference to God).

83. This term occurs nine times in Rev (7x with "Lord God": 1:8; 4:8; 11:17; 15:3; 16:7; 19:6; 21:22; and 2x with "God" alone: 16:14; 19:15) and only one additional time in the NT (an OT quotation in 2 Cor 6:18).

84. As Bauckham, *Theology*, 30, notes, the term "indicates not so much God's abstract omnipotence as his actual control over all things." See also Bauckham, *Climax*, 33; H. Langkammer, "παντοκράτωρ," *EDNT* 11–12. The term "Almighty" is associated with God's "reign" as king over the earth also in 15:3 and 19:6.

the title "the One who is and who was" (11:17b), signifying his eternal, self-existent deity. The latter is rooted in Exodus 3:14 (see comment on 1:4 for discussion of the grammar and theology of this phrase). In 1:8 and 4:8 a third epithet is included, "and who is to come," but here and in 16:5 this phrase is omitted because its sense of God's future coming has now been made real (see 1:4). The reason ("because"; ὅτι) for giving thanks (v. 17c) is that God has "taken" in hand (cf. NLT, REB: "assumed") his "great power" in order to exert it in ruling authority on earth: "You have begun to reign" (ἐβασίλευσας).[85]

11:18 And the nations have raged but your wrath has come, and the time has come for the dead to be judged and to reward your servants the prophets and the saints and those who fear your name, the small and the great, and to ruin those who ruin the earth" (καὶ τὰ ἔθνη ὠργίσθησαν, καὶ ἦλθεν ἡ ὀργή σου καὶ ὁ καιρὸς τῶν νεκρῶν κριθῆναι καὶ δοῦναι τὸν μισθὸν τοῖς δούλοις σου τοῖς προφήταις καὶ τοῖς ἁγίοις καὶ τοῖς φοβουμένοις τὸ ὄνομά σου, τοὺς μικροὺς καὶ τοὺς μεγάλους, καὶ διαφθεῖραι τοὺς διαφθείροντας τὴν γῆν). The elders' declaration of gratitude to the Lord God continues to trace the imminent consummation of God's judgment and redemption, moving from wrath against those who resist (v. 18a–b) to judging both righteous and unrighteous dead (v. 18c–d) to reward for the righ-

teous (v. 18e) and back to judgment again (v. 18f). Here the background of hostility by pagan nations against God and his people, implied by allusions to Daniel 7 and Psalm 2 in vv. 15 and 18, is made explicit by referring to the futile "rage" of the nations in resisting God's coming rule (Ps 2:1; cf. Exod 15:14; 2 Kgs 19:28; Ps 99:1). But God's response is the arrival[86] of his "wrath" (ὀργή; cf. Jer 30:23) in judgment and justice against these enemies.[87] Also arriving[88] is the "time" or season (καιρός) for three culminating acts of God that define or explain what occurs during this time (expressed by the three epexegetical or explanatory infinitives that follow). The first of these is for "the dead to be judged" (v. 18d), a general reference to both the righteous as well as unrighteous "dead" who will face God's assessment for good or for ill (cf. 14:7; 22:12). This judgment is then defined both positively and negatively by the two infinitives that follow ("to reward" and "to ruin").

The positive side then is "to reward" (δοῦναι τὸν μισθὸν) those who have been faithful to God (v. 18e).[89] These are specified in two groups with further descriptions of the final group. First mentioned are God's "servants the prophets," two designations that seem to belong as a unit under the influence of 10:7 and the common Old Testament phrase that lies behind it.[90] Although John can sometimes use "servant" to refer to all of God's people (e.g., 1:1; 2:20; 19:2, 5; 22:3, 6), here he narrows

---

85. The verb "you have begun to reign" (ἐβασίλευσας) is an ingressive aorist (cf. 19:6, ἐβασίλευσεν) but translated into English here as a perfect present because of the contextual focus on the recent past event of starting his earthly rule (see note on v. 15). The verb "you have taken" (εἴληφας) is a Greek perfect but is used in an aoristic sense as a parallel to the aorists of vv. 15, 17 (see notes on 5:7; 7:14).

86. The verb "has come" is another aorist denoting a recent past action (see note on 11:15): from heaven's point of view God's wrath and the time for judgment and reward have already come. The verb ἦλθεν carries this sense also in 6:17; 14:7, 15; 18:10; 19:7.

87. The words describing God's "wrath" (ὀργή) and "anger" (θυμός) appeared sparingly in the early chapters of Rev (e.g., only ὀργή twice in 6:16–17), but they will occur 11x from here to the end of the book.

88. The verb translated "has come" (ἦλθεν) is omitted in the clause about "the time . . . for the dead to be judged," etc., but it is clearly implied by the preceding clause. See also 14:7 that speaks of the "hour" of God's judgment as having come (ἦλθεν).

89. See 2:23 and 22:12 where the concept of reward is also expressed (both with and without using the term μισθός).

90. See 2 Kgs 9:7; 17:13, 23; 21:10; 24:2; Ezra 9:11; Jer 7:25; 25:4; Ezek 38:17; Dan 9:6, 10; Amos 3:7; Zech 1:6.

it to a more specific group. These servant-prophets would include both Old and New Testament prophets (e.g., the prophets Isaiah, Ezekiel, Daniel, Zechariah to whom John often alludes, as well as John himself and the two prophets of vv. 3–13), vehicles of God's progressive unveiling of his mystery of redemption (10:7). Mentioned second is a general group, "the saints," that is, God's people in general (οἱ ἅγιοι; for the sense of this term, see note on 5:8), perhaps singled out here under this term due to the influence of Daniel 7:18, 22, 25, 27 (alluded to in Rev 11:15). "The saints" are frequently portrayed in coming chapters as suffering and under attack by the forces of evil (e.g., 13:7, 10; 17:6; 18:20; in 16:6 and 18:24 "saints" are mentioned with "prophets" as two persecuted groups).

References to fearing God, as in the next phrase in v. 18e, also occur in the coming chapters (14:7; 15:4; 19:5; but not at all earlier in Rev; ἔμφοβοι in v. 13d has a different sense), and they seem to describe the same group as "the saints," that is, God's people in general (see 19:5 where "those who fear him" is parallel to "all his servants" in its general sense).[91] So the "and" (καί) after "saints" adds an explanatory phrase rather than a different group who will be rewarded. John adds, then, one more phrase to describe further "the ones who fear your name" (just as he does in 19:5; cf. also Ps 115:13).

All social and economic classes, "the small and the great,"[92] will be rewarded among God's people, just as all ethnic groups will be represented (cf. 5:9; 7:9).

The negative side of God's time of judgment that has now arrived is "to ruin those who ruin the earth" (v. 18f). This is a clear reference to the coming judgment of the great harlot Babylon who "corrupted the earth with her sexual immorality" (19:2),[93] using a play on words. The verb "ruin" (διαφθείρω and its cognate words) can refer either to physical decay or outright destruction (8:9; cf. Luke 12:33; 2 Cor 4:16) or to moral or spiritual corruption (Rev 19:2; cf. Gen 6:11; 1 Cor 15:22; 2 Cor 7:2; 11:3; 1 Tim 6:5). John uses the verb with its double sense to describe God's destructive judgment against those who lead others astray morally and spiritually (see Paul's play on the simple verb in 1 Cor 3:17; also 2 Pet 2:12; Jude 10). In our day of environmental concern, to "ruin the earth" may seem to denote ecological destruction,[94] but in this context "earth" refers by metonymy to the world's inhabitants whom Babylon leads away from God (cf. Rev 17:2; 18:3, 9, 23). The related verb καταφθείρω is used twice in LXX Genesis 6:12 to describe the corruption of the earth as well as "all flesh" and is then used in 6:13 to declare God's imminent "corruption" or destruction of the earth and humanity in the flood of Noah's day.

---

91. John does not show any signs of using "those who fear God" to specify gentiles who are drawn to the God of Israel, as Acts does in a few places (Acts 10:2, 22, 35; 13:16, 26; also six other times using the verb σέβω, "reverence, worship"). Nor does he seem to extend Luke's sense to mean gentile believers in Christ in contrast to "the saints" as Jewish Christians, as Aune, *Revelation 6–16*, 645, suggests.

92. The phrase "the small and the great" in v. 18e appears as an accusative in Greek (τοὺς μικροὺς καὶ τοὺς μεγάλους), although in normal syntax it should be dative to agree with "those who fear your name." A few manuscripts read the dative for "the small and the great," but this is an inferior reading on external and internal grounds (cf. *TCGNT2*, 672). Mussies, *Morphology*, 100, suggests that this could be due to an overly

literal rendering of a possible Hebrew wording of the phrase. Mathewson, *Handbook*, 154, gives a more likely suggestion: the accusative may come from an allusion to Ps 115:13 [113:21 LXX] where "those who fear the Lord both small and great" are accusatives.

93. The verb "corrupted" in 19:2 is the simple form φθείρω, related to the verb "ruin" (διαφθείρω) used here, although a few manuscripts in 19:2 have the compound form διαφθείρω. The verb διαφθείρω is also used in Jer 51:1, 25 [28:1, 25 LXX] to describe what ancient Babylon did to the whole earth and what God will do to her.

94. For some it is hard to resist imposing contemporary concerns on the ancient text instead of allowing the text to speak (see Prigent, *Apocalypse*, 364).

11:19 And the temple of God in heaven was opened, and the ark of his covenant appeared in his temple, and there came flashes of lightning and rumblings and peals of thunder and an earthquake and large hail (καὶ ἠνοίγη ὁ ναὸς τοῦ θεοῦ ὁ ἐν τῷ οὐρανῷ καὶ ὤφθη ἡ κιβωτὸς τῆς διαθήκης αὐτοῦ ἐν τῷ ναῷ αὐτοῦ, καὶ ἐγένοντο ἀστραπαὶ καὶ φωναὶ καὶ βρονταὶ καὶ σεισμὸς καὶ χάλαζα μεγάλη). In the culminating event that John witnesses in the heavenly scene following the seventh trumpet in v. 15,[95] he now experiences ominous portents of the very presence of God, who is ready to invade the earthly scene to accomplish the consummation announced in vv. 15–18. God's appearance is represented first by the opening of his temple in heaven, even to its innermost sanctum (v. 19a–b). John records that God's heavenly temple "was opened," a unique access that will be repeated when John picks up the sequence of final judgments again in 15:5–8.

Access into God's heavenly throne room was opened to John previously in chapters 4–5, and he even observed God on his throne at the center of his heavenly retinue, ready to set in motion his plan for worldwide judgment and redemption (see 5:1, 5, 7–9). Here and there in the ensuing visions, features of that heavenly temple have come into view (6:9; 7:9–11; 8:3, 5; 9:13; 11:16). But the vision of chapters 4–5 and subsequent glimpses of it have simply foreshadowed what John witnesses now in its culmination: God's own imminent appearance as judge and ruler of all the earth. The reference to "the ark of [God's] covenant" coming into view[96] in heaven further represents the appearance of God himself ready to assert his sovereignty over the earth. This is the only mention in the Bible of a heavenly ark of the covenant, but from the beginning of the earthly tabernacle's construction, it was understood that an archetype of that place of worship and its furnishings existed in heaven and that Moses was shown its features (Exod 25:40; Heb 8:1–5). The Old Testament envisioned God as a ruling presence even in the earthly sanctuary: he was "enthroned above the cherubim" (1 Sam 4:4; 2 Sam 6:2; 1 Chr 13:6), and this was associated with God's rule over all the earth's kingdoms (2 Kgs 19:15; Isa 37:16).

The ominous signs of God's coming judgment reappear in v. 19c (as in 4:5; 8:5; 16:18). These represent God's awesome presence taken from Israel's Sinai experience (Exod 19:16–19) and repeated often thereafter as symbols of theophany and portents of coming judgment.[97]

Theology in Application

Witness in a Time of Warfare

This passage—with its focus on God's temple, the holy city Jerusalem, and the testimony of God's prophets there while the world watches—gives us a précis of what will happen in the land of Israel during the fateful days of judgment prior to

---

95. It is debatable whether v. 19 goes better with 11:15–18 or with 12:1ff. But the portents of God's imminent presence in judgment and victory (v. 19) seem to fit the preceding a bit more naturally. The "signs" in heaven (a woman, a dragon) beginning in 12:1 move into a separate visionary phase. The connection of v. 19 with 11:15–18 (heavenly voices celebrating God's imminent coming to reign on earth) is thematically stronger.

96. The verb "appeared" in v. 19b is an aorist passive (ὤφθη) with an intransitive sense, "appeared" (CSB, NASB) or "was visible" (NET). It is not a true passive "was seen" (ESV, KJV, NIV, NRSV). See BDAG 719; BDF §313. This verb occurs also in 12:1, 3.

97. See comments on 4:5 and 8:5; see also Bauckham, *Climax*, 199–204.

its restoration. It also represents, in an intensified form, the larger conflict that has raged throughout world history since humans fell into sin. Since that time the powers of this world under Satan's instigation have waged war against God and his Messiah and have co-opted the world's fallen inhabitants into that cosmic struggle. Those who are called to stand and bear witness to God's truth in such a world will find miraculous success as well as powerful opposition. When we experience these in our life and witness for Christ, it should not surprise us since we too fit into that larger story of age-long, but perhaps less intensified, conflict. But like God's two end-time witnesses, we must accept God's call to reach out to an unwelcoming world with our gospel witness, even if it proves difficult and sometimes costly. We must testify to the truth about God's gracious salvation in Jesus Christ, offered even to those who are antagonistic to him. By speaking and living out the truth of God in Christ, we truly exemplify his instructions to love our enemies and to pray for and do good to those who hate us (Luke 6:27–28). Instead of withdrawing from the hostile world and leaving it to its deserved judgment, Christians are to bear winsome witness by their conduct and their verbal testimony to the Lamb who "by [his] blood ransomed for God members of every tribe and language and people and nation" (5:9). The stakes are high because divine judgment awaits those who continue to refuse God's grace in Christ, and Satan's deceptive and destructive power will come to bear more and more against such testimony. But his defeat is assured, and God is even now building his kingdom among all the nations of the world despite desperate opposition.

Victory Guaranteed

Joe Namath guaranteed that his New York Jets would win Super Bowl III at the end of the 1968 American professional football season. Crowds scoffed at him because his team was an 18-point underdog going into the game. But the Jets shocked everyone (except perhaps themselves) by winning 16 to 7. Many other brash athletes and people in other walks of life have given confident predictions about one kind of victory or another that failed miserably. But this passage records heaven's declaration ahead of time that God's victory over evil is certain and that his rule will soon be established on earth despite the world's powers raging against the Lord and his Messiah (v. 15; cf. Ps 2:2). In his death, resurrection, and exaltation to heaven, Jesus has already accomplished a decisive defeat of the forces of evil and now reigns in heaven at God's right hand. It only remains for God's great power and divine justice to assert that victory in full over the earth as well. This is a victory we can count on even before we see the final score. We can rejoice like exuberant sports fans and join with heaven's choruses in singing the praises of the Lord God Almighty (Rev 11:17). And when we seem to face long odds in life, we can be encouraged that the game is not over yet, and our victory in Christ is guaranteed.

CHAPTER 18

Revelation 12:1–18

Literary Context

The topic of the world's warfare instigated by Satan against God and his Messiah continues in chapter 12. Here the cosmic background to this conflict is revealed by the appearance of two great signs in heaven, a glorious woman and a great dragon, and the dramatic interaction that ensues between them when she gives birth to a son. This continues the essentially negative side to the narrative of God's kingdom coming to earth as announced in 11:15–19, although that kingdom is celebrated again along the way (12:10). The interludes in chapters 12–14 will move the story along to the culminating events of judgment that have been announced and will begin to fall upon the earth in God's crescendo of last plagues to be described in chapters 15–16.

Main Idea

In the past God preserved Israel and her Messiah from attack by Satan, and he will continue to do so during the intense satanic warfare against God's people in the end times.

Translation

Revelation 12:1–18

1a	Vision Intro/ Character Entrance	And **a great sign appeared in heaven,**
b	Descriptions	a woman clothed with the sun and
c		the moon was under her feet and
d		on her head was a crown of twelve stars,
2a		and she was pregnant.
b	Description/Plot Tension	And **she cried out, suffering labor pains and in torment to give birth.**
3a	Vision Intro/ Character Entrance	And **another sign appeared in heaven,**
b	Descriptions	and behold, a great red dragon
c		having seven heads and
		ten horns and
		on his heads
		seven diadems,
4a	Action	and **his tail swept away a third of the stars of heaven,**
b		and **he threw them to the earth.**
c		And **the dragon stood before the woman who was about to give birth**
d	Purpose of 4c	so that whenever she gave birth he might devour her child.
5a	Action	And **she bore a son, a male,**
b	Identification	who is destined to shepherd all the nations with an iron rod,
c	Action	and **her child was caught up to God and** **to his throne.**
6a	Action	And **the woman fled into the wilderness,**
b	Description	where she has a place prepared by God,
c	Purpose/ Temporal Extent	so that she would be nourished ⟲ for twelve hundred and sixty days.
7a	Action	And **war broke out in heaven,**
b	Specification	Michael and his angels waging war against the dragon.
c	Action	And **the dragon and his angels waged war,**

8a	Effects of 7c	and **he did not prevail,**
b		and **there was no longer any place for them in heaven.**
9a	Action	And **the great dragon was thrown down,**
		the ancient serpent,
b	Identification	who is called the devil and Satan,
c		who leads the whole world astray;
d	Repetition of Action in 9a	**he was thrown to the earth,**
e	Additional Action	and **his angels were thrown down with him.**
10a	Action/Response to 9d–e	And **I heard a loud voice in heaven saying,**

b Announcement

> "Now the salvation and
> > power and
> > kingdom of our God and
> > the authority of his Messiah ...
> > > ... have come,

c Reason

> because the accuser of our brothers and sisters was ↩
> > thrown down,

d Description

> who accused them
> > before our God
> > day and night.

11a Assertions

> And they overcame him
> > because of the blood of the Lamb and
> > because of the word of their testimony,

b

> and they did not love their lives to the death.

12a	Command	So then rejoice, you heavens and you who live in them.
b	Warning	Woe to the earth and the sea,
c	Reason	because the devil has come down to you, having great anger
d	Reason	since he knows that he has only a little time."

13a	Time	And when the dragon saw that he was thrown to the earth,
b	Action	**he persecuted the woman who gave birth to the male child.**
14a	Response to 13b	And **the two wings of a great eagle were given to the woman**

b Purpose

> that she might fly
> > into the wilderness
> > to her place,

c Location/Time

> where she is nourished for a time,
> > times and
> > half a time
> away from the presence
> > of the serpent.

Continued on next page.

Continued from previous page.

15a	Action	And **the serpent spewed**
		from his mouth water like a river after the woman
b	Purpose	**to sweep her away in a torrent.**

16	Action	And **the earth helped the woman and**
		opened its mouth and
		swallowed up the river that the dragon spewed from his mouth.

17a	Action	And **the dragon became enraged at the woman and**
		went away
b	Purpose	**to wage war against the rest of her offspring,**
c	Description	**who keep God's commands and hold to Jesus's** ☙
		testimony.

| 18 | Preview/Setting | And **he stood on the sand of the seashore.** |

Structure

The passage falls into three sections that symbolically and elliptically tell the story of Satan's efforts to thwart God's salvation through Israel and her Messiah. First the chief actors are introduced, and both the Messiah (in the past) and Israel (in the future) escape Satan's attacks (12:1–6). Next the backstory of Satan's future expulsion from heaven and enraged attacks on the earth in the final tribulation are portrayed (12:7–12). Then the story of his attacks on Israel and her national preservation in the end times is resumed, but it includes a preview of Satan's continued warfare on parts of faithful Israel during that intense period (12:13–18). This warfare on Israel and the wider world is portrayed in subsequent chapters.

Exegetical Outline

   III. Second Vision: Heavenly Throne Room and Three Judgment Cycles (4:1–16:21)

      A. Vision of God in His Heavenly Throne Room (4:1–11)

      B. The Seven-Sealed Scroll and the Slain Lamb (5:1–14)

      C. The Seven Seals and the Interlude of the Two Multitudes (6:1–8:1)

      D. The Seven Trumpets and Further Interludes (8:2–14:20)

         1. The First Four Trumpets (8:2–13)

         2. The Fifth Trumpet—First Woe (9:1–12)

         3. The Sixth Trumpet—Second Woe (9:13–21)

         4. Two Revelatory Interludes: God's Prophets (10:1–11:14)

         5. The Seventh Trumpet—Third Woe: Anticipating God's Rule (11:15–19)

→ **6. Two Further Interludes: Anticipating Babylon's Fall (12:1–14:20)**

　　a. The dragon's war against the woman (12:1–13:18)

　　　(1) The woman, her son, and the dragon (12:1–18)

　　　　(a) Two dramatic signs in heaven: a woman with her son and a great dragon (12:1–6)

　　　　　(i) Introducing the three actors in the drama (12:1–4b)

　　　　　(ii) Intense interaction between them (12:4c–6)

　　　　(b) War in heaven: the dragon thrown down to bring woe on the earth (12:7–12)

　　　　　(i) The dragon expelled from heaven (12:7–9)

　　　　　(ii) Rejoicing in heaven but woe to the earth (12:10–12)

　　　　(c) War on earth: the woman flees but her other children are threatened (12:13–18)

　　　　　(i) The dragon's persecution of the woman (12:13)

　　　　　(ii) The woman's escape to a place of refuge (12:14–16)

　　　　　(iii) The dragon prepares to attack her remaining children (12:17–18)

Explanation of the Text

12:1–2 And a great sign appeared in heaven, a woman clothed with the sun and the moon was under her feet and on her head was a crown of twelve stars, 2 and she was pregnant. And she cried out, suffering labor pains and in torment to give birth (Καὶ σημεῖον μέγα ὤφθη ἐν τῷ οὐρανῷ, γυνὴ περιβεβλημένη τὸν ἥλιον, καὶ ἡ σελήνη ὑποκάτω τῶν ποδῶν αὐτῆς καὶ ἐπὶ τῆς κεφαλῆς αὐτῆς στέφανος ἀστέρων δώδεκα, 2 καὶ ἐν γαστρὶ ἔχουσα, καὶ κράζει ὠδίνουσα καὶ βασανιζομένη τεκεῖν). John begins here a series of vignettes revealing the cosmic struggle that forms the background of the woes described in these chapters as well as the means by which God's victory announced in 11:15–19 will be accomplished.[1] He describes three chief actors in the drama (vv. 1–4b) and then the first of several intense interactions between them (vv. 4c–6). The first two characters are introduced as signs appear-

ing in heaven (vv. 1a, 3a). The word "sign" (σημεῖον) in apocalyptic literature sometimes means a prophetic "portent" to signal a crucial event that is about to occur (Isa 7:11, 14; 8:18; Dan 6:28 [Th.]; Matt 24:3; Mark 13:4; Luke 21:7, 11, 25), but here "sign" means a visual or physical symbol pointing to something beyond itself, especially something with a spiritual significance (Rev 12:1, 3; 15:1; cf. Josh 4:6; Dan 5:9 LXX; similar to "signs" in John's Gospel).[2] The first sign is "a woman clothed with the sun" (v. 1b), an impressive image in itself (similar to what is said about the Lord in Ps 104:1–2). When John adds references to "the moon . . . under her feet" and "twelve stars" crowning her head (v. 1c–d), it suggests that this "woman" represents ethnic Israel by allusion to Jacob and Rachel along with Joseph and his brothers (Gen 37:9–10; cf. T. Naph. 5:1–5; T. Ab. [B] 7:4–16).[3] Later verses

---

1. Fekkes, *Prophetic Traditions*, 86; Willitts, "Bride of the Messiah," 249–51.

2. Aune, *Revelation 6–16*, 679; Smalley, *Revelation*, 313–14.

3. A very common interpretation of the woman is to see her as the ideal or true Israel, the people of God, the faithful community, or "the church," which essentially leaves ethnic Israel out of the picture (Beale, *Revelation*, 625–27; Boxall,

Revelation, 178–79; Smalley, *Revelation*, 315). But in this case, it is important to note that ethnic Israel must be included as the core group that births the "male child who will shepherd all the nations" (v. 5). The Messiah does not emerge from the gentile or multinational church but vice versa (cf. Rom 9:4–5). With this in mind, it seems more natural to understand the "woman" as ethnic Israel, God's OT people, who figure so prominently

lend greater support to this identification (see Rev 12:2, 5–6, 13–17). What is quite surprising after her glorious portrayal in v. 1 is John's terse description of her in v. 2 as "pregnant" and in the last agonizing stages of labor "to give birth."[4] This too evokes Old Testament pictures of Israel as an expectant mother who suffers in birth pangs during God's judgment but anticipates God's redemption and renewal as the joyful result of such suffering (Isa 26:16–21; 66:6–13; Mic 4:9–10; Jer 4:31; cf. also 4 Ezra 10:40–49; 1QH 3:5–18 [alluding to the child of Isa 9:5–6]).[5]

12:3–4 And another sign appeared in heaven, and behold, a great red dragon having seven heads and ten horns and on his heads seven diadems, 4 and his tail swept away a third of the stars of heaven, and he threw them to the earth. And the dragon stood before the woman who was about to give birth so that whenever she gave birth he might devour her child (καὶ ὤφθη ἄλλο σημεῖον ἐν τῷ οὐρανῷ, καὶ ἰδοὺ δράκων μέγας πυρρὸς ἔχων κεφαλὰς ἑπτὰ καὶ κέρατα δέκα καὶ ἐπὶ τὰς κεφαλὰς αὐτοῦ ἑπτὰ διαδήματα, 4 καὶ ἡ οὐρὰ αὐτοῦ σύρει τὸ τρίτον τῶν ἀστέρων τοῦ οὐρανοῦ καὶ ἔβαλεν αὐτοὺς εἰς τὴν γῆν. καὶ ὁ δράκων ἔστηκεν ἐνώπιον τῆς γυναικὸς τῆς μελλούσης τεκεῖν, ἵνα ὅταν τέκῃ τὸ τέκνον αὐτῆς καταφάγῃ). A second character comes into view as "another sign" appearing in

heaven (v. 3a; cf. v. 1a), to which John calls special attention ("behold"; ἰδού).[6] This is "a great red dragon," fearful in size (cf. NIV, "enormous"; NET, "huge") and bizarre in appearance, in that it has "seven heads and ten horns" with "seven diadems"[7] on its heads. These heads, horns, and diadems do not figure in the events of this chapter,[8] but they generally symbolize ruling power (cf. comments at 5:6; also Dan 7:7–8) and make a clear connection to the "beasts" in 13:1 and 17:3 (see comments there). The figure of a "dragon" (δράκων) is also familiar in the Old Testament as a representation of cosmic opposition to God as well as more mundane enemies of God's people like Egypt and Babylon (Ps 74:13–14; Isa 27:1; 51:9–10; Ezek 29:3; 32:2). In v. 9 John will identify the dragon specifically as the ultimate adversary of God ("the ancient serpent, who is called the devil and Satan, who leads the whole world astray"), but as chapters 13–18 show, the devil uses earthly kingdoms in his efforts to oppose God's people.

The dragon's struggle against God and his people Israel is represented here first generally (v. 4a–b) and then specifically (v. 4c–d). Picturing the writhing, violent action of such a huge dragon in the heavens, John describes his powerful "tail" (cf. 9:10, 19) as having "swept away" and casting to the earth "a third of the stars of heaven" (v. 4a). It is unclear how this image should be understood.

---

in God's plan to redeem and renew the world (cf. John 4:22). At various places Rev clearly refers to the extension of Israel's salvific blessings to include gentiles (e.g., 5:9–10; 14:6), but interpreters are too quick to see all of Rev this way and read Israel out of the picture entirely. Cf. Willitts, "Bride of the Messiah," 250n17.

4. The verb in v. 2b, "she cried out" (κράζει), is a Greek historical present, pointing forward to the introduction of the second character in the drama in v. 3 and the plot intensification in v. 4c; see discussion at 5:5.

5. J. Massyngberde Ford, *Revelation*, AB 38 (Garden City, NY: Doubleday, 1975), 195–96. Some have identified the woman as the Virgin Mary, but it is hard to square this with the details of her flight and persecution in vv. 6, 13–17. Cf.

Kovacs and Rowland, *Revelation*, 137; and Murphy, *Fallen Is Babylon*, 382–83.

6. This phrase (consisting of a verb of "appearing" or "seeing" and "behold" as a "presentative particle" with a nominative following; cf. BDAG 468) is similar to the construction in 4:1 and elsewhere (see note at 4:1).

7. A "diadem" (διάδημα) was a royal crown or headband, usually of precious metal (cf. 13:1; 19:12), different from the victor's wreath (στέφανος; see comments at 2:10 and 4:4).

8. Since John does not exploit the heads and horns at all, it is misguided to speculate about possible historical referents. See Kovacs and Rowland, *Revelation*, 140–44, for a range of speculative identifications that have been proposed.

The "stars" may represent angels who fall into sin in Satan's primeval rebellion against God and thus populate the earth as his evil angels (i.e., demons) opposing God's work. This may be the point of vv. 7–9 where the dragon, Satan, and "his angels" are said to be "thrown to the earth" from heaven. But the imagery of v. 4a–b seems to come from Daniel 8:10 that pictures an end-time adversary of God and Israel (prefigured in the 160s BC by the Syrian tyrant Antiochus IV Epiphanes) who "threw some of the stars to the earth." In the context of Daniel 8 this seems to mean an attack against God's good angels or against his people Israel or possibly a combination of the two.[9]

More important for the plotline of these verses is the dragon's specific attack against God's work that is pictured in v. 4c–d. With two of the central characters in place, the dramatic action of the story begins in earnest and brings the third major figure into the scene (the male child, v. 5). In the events of John's vision, the dragon "stood before the woman"[10] who was straining in labor, and he was ready to "devour her child" at the moment of birth. Many of John's readers would understand this imagery against the background of ancient pagan myths about evil creatures poised to kill at birth a child who was destined to defeat them (e.g., the birth of Apollo).[11] But this story fits also the Jewish understanding that evil powers are arrayed against Israel (e.g., Jer 51:34 [LXX 28:34] says that Babylon

"devoured," κατέφαγεν, Jerusalem) or more broadly against the offspring of Eve who will finally defeat the serpent (Gen 3:15). As v. 5 will clearly state, her child is the one who will rule the whole world if the dragon does not slaughter him first.

12:5–6 And she bore a son, a male, who is destined to shepherd all the nations with an iron rod, and her child was caught up to God and to his throne. 6 And the woman fled into the wilderness, where she has a place prepared by God, so that she would be nourished for twelve hundred and sixty days (καὶ ἔτεκεν υἱόν ἄρσεν, ὃς μέλλει ποιμαίνειν πάντα τὰ ἔθνη ἐν ῥάβδῳ σιδηρᾷ. καὶ ἡρπάσθη τὸ τέκνον αὐτῆς πρὸς τὸν θεὸν καὶ πρὸς τὸν θρόνον αὐτοῦ. 6 καὶ ἡ γυνὴ ἔφυγεν εἰς τὴν ἔρημον, ὅπου ἔχει ἐκεῖ τόπον ἡτοιμασμένον ἀπὸ τοῦ θεοῦ, ἵνα ἐκεῖ τρέφωσιν αὐτὴν ἡμέρας χιλίας διακοσίας ἑξήκοντα). In apocalyptic visions events do not always flow smoothly or in expected directions, and this is certainly true of vv. 4c–6. With a huge dragon menacingly awaiting her delivery (v. 4c–d), the woman "bore a son" destined for world rule who is immediately snatched away to heaven (v. 5), while she herself escapes to safety in the wilderness (v. 6). This fragmented sequence is obviously not intended to fill in details or explain contingencies, and it should not be taken to describe events that occur in close temporal sequence (see below). Instead it represents major events that lie in the background of God's judgment

---

9. In Dan 8:10 the "hosts of heaven" and "stars" may refer to righteous angels or to God's people (e.g., Dan 8:24; 12:1–3; cf. Collins, *Daniel*, 331–32; Stephen R. Miller, *Daniel*, NAC 18 [Nashville: Broadman & Holman, 1994], 225–26; Wood, *Daniel*, 213–17).

10. The verb "stood" in v. 4c is the common translation of a Greek verb that can be parsed two different ways. (1) In the standard printed Greek texts (NA[28], UBS[5], SBLGNT) it is written as ἕστηκεν, a perfect indicative of ἵστημι, which carries a present stative sense, "he stands/is standing" (cf. 3:20; 8:2). Rev uses the perfect of ἵστημι frequently (and does not use the alternate στήκω except for this possible occurrence), but its normal

present-stative sense does not fit easily into the tense sequence of these verses. (2) The same spelling with a different breathing mark could form the verb ἔστηκεν, an imperfect of στήκω, with the past sense, "he stood/was standing" (same issue in John 8:44 where most printed editions read ἕστηκεν). This form fits the tense sequence far better as a descriptive imperfect within the narrative sequence of aorists and historical presents found in vv. 1–6. See BDAG 944; BDF §73; Mussies, *Morphology*, 265; Aune, *Revelation 6–16*, 652; and discussion of John's narrative style at 4:5 and 9:6, 10–11.

11. Aune, *Revelation 6–16*, 667–74; Boxall, *Revelation*, 176–77.

and redemption soon to be consummated (10:6–7; 11:15–18; 12:10). In God's plan the woman (Israel) is his human channel to bring into the world's history a "son" (v. 5a), an anointed ruler in the line of David (Ps 2:2, 9; cf. Pss. Sol. 17:21–25), through whom "the kingdom of the world" will become God's kingdom forever, as Revelation 11:15 has said (v. 5b). So v. 5b represents the "not yet" of the son's future earthly rule (he is "destined to shepherd"[12] the nations), juxtaposed with the "already" of his heavenly ascension and exaltation that v. 5c describes in symbolic terms: "Her child was caught up to God and to his throne."[13]

It is transparent that the "son" in this vision represents Jesus Christ, but the reference is greatly enriched by the Old Testament images evoked in this description of him. The wording of "a son, a male" (v. 5a) is a little odd, because it is influenced by the phrasing of Isaiah 66:7, where in a context about restoring his people in Jerusalem (66:5–14), the Lord declares that Zion "brought forth a male" (ἔτεκεν ἄρσεν), that is, "a nation born in a moment" (66:8).[14] In John's vision, however, the corporate image of Isaiah 66 is narrowed to focus on the individual Israelite through whom the nation will be restored, using the wording from Psalm 2:9

about "shepherd[ing] all the nations with a rod of iron."[15] Psalm 2:2 referred to this one as the Lord's "anointed" or messiah (cf. Rev 11:15; 12:10) and also as the Lord's "son" (2:7, 12) to whom he will give "the nations as an inheritance" and "the ends of the earth as a possession" (2:8).[16] Isaiah 9:6–7 likewise speaks of an individual in David's line, "a child" or "son" born to Israel, who will establish widespread peace and God's righteous rule.

From the New Testament perspective this transfer of royal rule to Jesus as Messiah and son of David has already been accomplished in his cross, resurrection, ascension, and exaltation to God's right hand in heaven. He already has been vindicated as God's son and has taken his seat in the position of greatest authority in heaven, as Psalm 110:1 anticipated. Jesus cites Psalm 110:1 as messianic (Mark 12:35–37), and numerous writers all across the New Testament affirm its fulfillment in his present position in heaven (Acts 2:33–36; Rom 8:34; Heb 1:13; 1 Pet 3:22).[17] In contemporary Christian theology the cross and resurrection have a central place, and this is appropriate, but Christ's ascension and heavenly exaltation are too often treated with relative neglect compared to their important place in biblical theology. This explains some of the un-

---

12. The word translated "is destined" (μέλλει) denotes what is sure to happen because it is decreed by God (BDAG 628; W. Radl, "μέλλω," *EDNT* 2:404). Cf. 1:19; 3:10; 17:8; Matt 17:12, 22; Acts 26:22.

13. See 3:21 for Christ's promise that Christians will "sit with me on my throne, as I myself overcame and sat down with my Father on his throne" (cf. 22:1, 3: "The throne of God and of the Lamb"). "His throne" at the end of v. 5c refers to God's throne (nearer antecedent), not the child's.

14. The phrase in Rev "a son, a male" (υἱόν, ἄρσεν) is strange because it places together a masculine noun ("a son") and a neuter adjective used in apposition ("a male"). The more natural phrase in Greek would be for the adjective to agree in gender with the noun (i.e., ἄρσην). In Isa 66:7 of the LXX the neuter adjective by itself is fine because it implies the neuter noun "child" (τέκνον).

15. Ps 2:9 is cited also in Rev 2:27; 19:15. See comments on 2:27 for discussion of the meaning of "shepherd" here.

16. Svigel, "Apocalypse," 23–74, presents a well-argued but unconvincing case for seeing the "son" here as corporate and not individual. Siew, *War*, 160–62, follows Svigel in this interpretation. Svigel's essay was published in a slightly revised form most recently as "What Child Is This? A Forgotten Argument for the Pretribulation Rapture," in *Evidence for the Rapture: A Biblical Case for Pretribulationism*, ed. John F. Hart (Chicago: Moody, 2015), 225–53. An early version of this view can be found in Andrew of Caesarea (sixth century), who cites Methodius for the view that the "male child" represents Christians and takes this "catching up" as a reference to the rapture of the church, as in 1 Thess 4:17 (Weinrich, "Andrew of Caesarea," 154–57).

17. In addition to his present, invisible, heavenly rule (the "already"; e.g., Rev 12:5c), these texts also expect the further consummation of that rule in a future, visible, earthly form (the "not yet"; e.g., v. 5b). See Acts 3:19–21; 1 Cor 15:24–26; Phil 3:20–21; Heb 2:5–9.

ease interpreters have felt at the seemingly deficient summary of Jesus's course of life that Revelation 12:5 provides: How can a Christian portrayal of Christ, even a fragmented visionary one, skip from his birth to his ascension without mentioning the cross and resurrection?[18] The explanation is that for John, especially in a context building toward the actualization of Christ's reign on earth, to cite his ascension and exaltation includes within itself a reference to the victory already won by his cross and resurrection. The climactic step in the journey entails the intermediate steps along the way (as shown by Rev 12:11; see too 1:5–6; 5:9–10; 7:14; 19:13). In terms of the visionary portrayal, this ascension to heaven represents not merely a frantic escape from the clutches of the dragon but the decisive victory of this "child" over him (see further in 12:13). But the vision skips ahead: the ascension does not follow immediately after the birth.

The woman's escape "into the wilderness" (v. 6a) likewise does not begin immediately after the snatching away of the son.[19] But her protection in this way completes the intense interaction (vv. 4c–6) between the three figures that John introduced in vv. 1–4b. The quick summary in v. 6 of her escape and protection will be expanded in vv. 13–17 after the intervening section on war in heaven (vv. 7–12), which precedes her flight (see v. 13). Her escape "into the wilderness" to find there "a place prepared by God" where she could be "nourished"[20] in safety (v. 6) represents God's preservation of ethnic Israel especially through the severe time of judgment to come in the years just prior to Christ's return. The duration of God's special care for her in the wilderness, "twelve hundred and sixty days" (v. 6c), repeats the time period of three-and-a-half years previously given as the time of intense suffering during the final half of the tribulation period (11:2, 3; cf. 12:14; 13:5).[21] Commentators have noted that "wilderness" in the Old Testament sometimes connoted a place of safety and God's special provision, as for Hagar (Gen 16:6–16; 21:14–21), Elijah (1 Kgs 17:2–6; 19:3–18), and supremely for Israel in their exodus from Egypt (Exod 13:18; 16:10, 32; Deut 2:7; 8:2, 15–16; 29:4–6; 32:10; Pss 78:15–16, 23–25, 52–55; 136:13), and this is a valuable point. What should be added, however, is that the pattern of Israel's experience in the wilderness was multivalent. It could just as easily evoke notions of sinful rebellion, exile, and judgment by God (Exod 14:11–12; Num 14:2, 32–35; 26:64–65; 32:10–15; Pss 78:17–22, 40–41; 95:8–11; 106:13–18). Israel's deliverance from Egypt and protection in the wilderness was a reminder of God's faithful deliverance, yet it was also a call to trust the Lord in adversity and not rebel against him. This will certainly be true for ethnic Israel during its days of intense discipline in that future time.[22]

---

18. Some explain this as John's poor editing of an earlier Jewish source (cf. Charles, *Revelation*, 1:307–9; Aune, *Revelation 6–16*, 664–66, 688–89). Others (e.g., Caird, *Revelation*, 149) argue that the son's "birth" in v. 5 represents not Christmas but Easter (cf. John 16:20–22; Acts 13:33–34). See also Svigel, "Apocalypse," 62–67, who takes the nonmention of the cross and resurrection as prime evidence that the "son" is not Jesus individually but the church that is identified with him and will share in his future rule over the nations (cf. 2:27). The description of its being "caught up to God" (v. 5c) is then a reference to the rapture of the church (same Greek verb ἁρπάζω as in 1 Thess 4:17).

19. The view that the time period of twelve hundred and sixty days (v. 6c) begins at Christ's exaltation and runs all the way to his second coming (Beale, *Revelation*, 567; Hoskins, *Revelation*, 216 [cites many others]; Koester, *Revelation*, 547, 562) misreads the elliptical character of the vision and fails to account for its anchoring in Dan 8:13–14; 9:27; 12:7, 11–12.

20. The verb translated "nourished" is an active in Greek (τρέφωσιν), an impersonal third-person verb that carries a passive sense as in 10:11; 13:16.

21. See discussion at 11:2, 3.

22. There is little evidence for reading this as a reference to the escape of Jewish Christians to Pella in the Decapolis just prior to the destruction of Jerusalem in AD 70 as Eusebius, *Hist. eccl.* 3.5.3 records. In any case, Pella in the first century was a prosperous city and would not be regarded as "wilderness."

12:7–9 And war broke out in heaven, Michael and his angels waging war against the dragon. And the dragon and his angels waged war, 8 and he did not prevail, and there was no longer any place for them in heaven. 9 And the great dragon was thrown down, the ancient serpent, who is called the devil and Satan, who leads the whole world astray; he was thrown to the earth, and his angels were thrown down with him (Καὶ ἐγένετο πόλεμος ἐν τῷ οὐρανῷ, ὁ Μιχαὴλ καὶ οἱ ἄγγελοι αὐτοῦ τοῦ πολεμῆσαι μετὰ τοῦ δράκοντος. καὶ ὁ δράκων ἐπολέμησεν καὶ οἱ ἄγγελοι αὐτοῦ, 8 καὶ οὐκ ἴσχυσεν οὐδὲ τόπος εὑρέθη αὐτῶν ἔτι ἐν τῷ οὐρανῷ. 9 καὶ ἐβλήθη ὁ δράκων ὁ μέγας, ὁ ὄφις ὁ ἀρχαῖος, ὁ καλούμενος Διάβολος καὶ ὁ Σατανᾶς, ὁ πλανῶν τὴν οἰκουμένην ὅλην, ἐβλήθη εἰς τὴν γῆν, καὶ οἱ ἄγγελοι αὐτοῦ μετ᾽ αὐτοῦ ἐβλήθησαν). The further story of the woman's flight into the wilderness under persecution by the dragon (v. 6) will be resumed in vv. 13–17, but a series of related events must be presented first (vv. 7–12). The trigger for that persecution is the dragon's expulsion from heaven (v. 13a), so John includes that story here (vv. 7–9), followed by a heavenly celebration of the signifi-cance of his expulsion (vv. 10–12). The events of vv. 7–9 begin dramatically with the outbreak of "war . . . in heaven."[23] The combatants in this conflict are "Michael and his angels" (v. 7b) against the dragon already introduced in v. 3 along with "his angels" (v. 7c). The angel Michael is mentioned in Daniel 10:13 as "one of the chief princes," who is also said to be "the great prince who has charge of your people [i.e., Israel]" (Dan 12:1; cf. Dan 10:21, "your prince").[24] Daniel 10 likewise provides clear glimpses of angelic conflict that lies behind earthly events (Dan 10:13–14, 20–21). Jesus himself alludes to angelic armies both holy (Matt 26:53; cf. also 2 Kgs 6:17) and evil (Matt 25:41).[25] Daniel 12:1–2 names Michael as Israel's chief defender at the unprecedented time of great distress to come. Without narrating any details about this heavenly conflict, John simply emphasizes the two sides and their battle with one another (words denoting "war" occur three times in this one verse).[26]

John quickly moves to the all-important outcome of this angelic combat for the dragon: he is defeated[27] and expelled from heaven along with his angels (vv. 8–9). The phrase "no longer any

---

23. The phrase "broke out" (cf. CSB, NET, NIV, NRSV, REB) or "arose" (ESV, RSV) is a better translation for the aorist Greek verb ἐγένετο than "was" (KJV, NASB). See note at 11:15 and BDAG 197. On the question of when this conflict occurs, see discussion at the end of the comments on vv. 7–9.

24. In early Judaism, Michael is identified as one of the four or seven archangels (1 En. 9:1; 20:1–7; 40:1–10; 54:6; 71:3, 8–9; 2 En. 22:6; 1QM 9:15–16; cf. Jude 9). Of these only Michael and Gabriel are named in the canonical OT or NT books. In other ancient Jewish texts Michael is the angel charged with carrying out God's judgment against the evil angels to prepare for God's renewal of the earth in righteousness (1 En. 10:11–11:2; cf. T. Dan 6:1–5; T. Mos. 10:1–4; 1QM 17:6–8). See Duane F. Watson, "Michael," in *ABD* 4:811.

25. This background and John's repetitive use of the word "war" cast doubt on the suggestion of Caird, *Revelation*, 154–56; Beale, *Revelation*, 661–63, that what is in view here is not a military struggle but a forensic one, with competing advocates arguing their cases until God rules the dragon out of order.

26. The phrase "waging war" in v. 7b translates a Greek infinitive with the genitive article (τοῦ πολεμῆσαι). This is a common translation equivalent in LXX Greek for the Hebrew infinitive construct introduced by the preposition lamed (ל). This construction is used in a thematically related passage, Dan 10:20, where Theodotion's Greek has τοῦ πολεμῆσαι to translate "to make war." This wording may have influenced John's usage here, since the infinitive with τοῦ occurs nowhere else in Rev (see inferior textual variants at 9:10; 14:15). The infinitive in v. 7b is epexegetical, explaining the noun "war" (πόλεμος) in v. 7a (BDF §400.8). The subject of a Greek infinitive would usually be accusative, but John uses the nominative (ὁ Μιχαὴλ καὶ οἱ ἄγγελοι αὐτοῦ). If this goes directly with the infinitive, it could be an instance of John's "barbarous Greek" (Moule, *Idiom Book*, 129). More likely it assumes a further occurrence of an indicative form of γίνομαι from v. 7a, carrying the sense "(they) came on the scene, came to be present" (BDAG 199; cf. 16:18; John 1:6; 1 John 2:18). See Beale, *Revelation*, 653–54.

27. The verb in the phrase "did not prevail" (ἰσχύω; v. 8a) denotes "to be in control, have power," but in the aorist as here it means to "win out, prevail" (BDAG 481; cf. Dan 7:21 Th.; Acts 19:16) and with the negative, "to lose power, be overcome."

place . . . in heaven"[28] (v. 8b) is the lead-in to their expulsion (v. 9). At the start of v. 9 John initially mentions this expulsion ("was thrown down"; ἐβλήθη), but adds an extensive identification of the dragon before repeating the same verb in v. 9d ("was thrown to the earth"; ἐβλήθη εἰς τὴν γῆν). Previously in this chapter the only term used to refer to this evil opponent was "dragon" (vv. 3, 4, 7 [2x]), but now John adds four additional titles or descriptions in v. 9 and one more in v. 10. These titles serve not only to identify but to characterize this evil being and to anchor his current and future opposition in reminders of his prior history and perennial strategies.

The title "the ancient serpent" (v. 9a) specifies the dragon as the creature who deceived Eve in the garden (Gen 3:1–15; cf. 2 Cor 11:3). Genesis does not identify the serpent as Satan or the devil, but this became the traditional Jewish understanding (cf. Wis 2:23–24; 1 En. 13:1; 3 Bar. 9:7; Apoc. Ab. 23:1–14), and Paul reflects this as well (2 Cor 11:3 with Rom 16:20). The next two titles are much more common in the New Testament and in Revelation (see below). "Devil" (Διάβολος) derivationally carries the sense of "slanderer,"[29] and this may still resonate with reminders of the serpent's defamation of God in Genesis 3:1–5. But this was the LXX Greek word most often used to translate "Satan" from the Hebrew of the Old Testament, so it probably came into early Christianity as a more conventional title for the spiritual adversary of God. John and the New Testament seem to use "devil" and "Satan" almost interchangeably (see Rev 2:9–10). The title "Satan" is transliterated from the Hebrew שָׂטָן, meaning "adversary, accuser" (e.g., Job 1–2; Zech 3:1–2).[30] In Revelation the two terms occur at almost the same frequency ("devil," 5x;

"Satan," 8x), and the same is true for the New Testament as a whole ("devil," 37x; "Satan," 36x). The final description of the dragon in v. 9 is "who leads the whole world astray," using a participle of the verb "deceive, lead astray" (πλανάω). Misleading humans is, of course, Satan's archetypal function throughout the Bible, and Revelation reflects this in its portrayal of his role in the end times. The participle form of this verb is used in 20:10 (of the devil who deceives the nations at the end of the millennium). But the verb is used elsewhere of his deceptive work directly (20:3, 8) or through his agents: Jezebel (2:20), the beast from the earth or false prophet (13:14; 19:20), Babylon the prostitute (18:23).

The readers knew these titles already, and John had previously used "Satan" (2:9, 13 [2x], 24; 3:9) and "devil" (2:10) to warn them about this one's insidious influence in the world of their day. But gathering these descriptions together in one place as here (also four of them again in 20:2) provides an unmistakable reinforcement to strengthen the readers' resistance for the future. Knowing their enemy and his ruthless schemes will serve them well.

The "no longer" of v. 8b reminds us that Satan and his angels previously had some right of entry to God's presence in heaven, as Daniel 10:13–21 and Job 1:6–12 illustrate. This is why v. 10c–d speaks of the dragon as "the one who accused [Christians] before our God day and night" (cf. Zech 3:1). But as a result of this defeat in battle, the dragon and his minions are cut off completely from such access and restricted to the earthly sphere alone. This is pictured as being "thrown" from heaven or "thrown to the earth," and it is the fate of both the dragon and his evil angels (v. 9d–e). When v. 12 reflects

---

28. Greek can use the passive of "find" to mean "is, exists, remains" (cf. 20:11; Dan 2:35 Th.; Rev 14:5, reflecting Isa 53:9; Zeph 3:13).

29. BDAG 226; O. Böcher, "διάβολος," *EDNT* 1:297–98.

30. BDAG 917; O. Böcher, "σατανᾶς," *EDNT* 3:234.

on this expulsion, it is taken as a sign of intensified woe and anger against the earth because the devil knows "that he has only a little time" (v. 12d).

What is not immediately clear from these verses is the time when this heavenly conflict and expulsion takes place. The language of being "thrown to the earth" (v. 9) could suggest Satan's primordial fall from heaven, as many Jewish and Christian interpreters understand to be portrayed at least typologically in Isaiah 14 and Ezekiel 28 (cf. LAE 12:1–16:3). However, the limits to Satan's actions described in Revelation 12 (e.g., no access to heaven, intense anger because his time is short) have hardly characterized his career since that primeval event itself.[31] Possibly this later expulsion repeats and intensifies key features of the pattern of that original fall. A second quite plausible option is the decisive defeat of Satan at the death, resurrection, and exaltation of Christ.[32] Verse 5c in this vision focuses on the exaltation of the woman's male child, and several references in John's Gospel point to Jesus's coming death as the decisive judgment of Satan (John 12:31; 16:11; Luke 10:17–18 is sometimes read this way[33]). But it seems unlikely that Satan is understood to have no more access to accuse Christians before God (v. 10) for the entire period after the cross of Christ. It makes more sense to understand a decisive victory to have come at the cross, resurrection, and exaltation (Col 2:15), but that this victory awaits its full accomplishment in the end times (see comments on v. 5c; cf. 1 Cor 15:20–28; Heb 2:8–9, 14–15). A third interpretation takes this expulsion as a yet-future event[34] just prior to the arrival of "the kingdom of our Lord and of his Messiah" on the earth (Rev 11:15; cf.

12:10a), at the time of the seventh trumpet when God's revealed plan for redemption is brought to completion without further delay (10:6–7). This coheres with the point that the devil's brief remaining time to inflict his anger will bring great woes for the earth and sea (v. 12b), and that the woman will need protection from him for a period of three-and-a-half years in the future (vv. 6, 14; cf. 11:2–3; 13:5).

12:10–11 And I heard a loud voice in heaven saying, "Now the salvation and power and kingdom of our God and the authority of his Messiah have come, because the accuser of our brothers and sisters was thrown down, who accused them before our God day and night. 11 And they overcame him because of the blood of the Lamb and because of the word of their testimony, and they did not love their lives to the death (καὶ ἤκουσα φωνὴν μεγάλην ἐν τῷ οὐρανῷ λέγουσαν, Ἄρτι ἐγένετο ἡ σωτηρία καὶ ἡ δύναμις καὶ ἡ βασιλεία τοῦ θεοῦ ἡμῶν καὶ ἡ ἐξουσία τοῦ Χριστοῦ αὐτοῦ, ὅτι ἐβλήθη ὁ κατήγωρ τῶν ἀδελφῶν ἡμῶν, ὁ κατηγορῶν αὐτοὺς ἐνώπιον τοῦ θεοῦ ἡμῶν ἡμέρας καὶ νυκτός. 11 καὶ αὐτοὶ ἐνίκησαν αὐτὸν διὰ τὸ αἷμα τοῦ ἀρνίου καὶ διὰ τὸν λόγον τῆς μαρτυρίας αὐτῶν καὶ οὐκ ἠγάπησαν τὴν ψυχὴν αὐτῶν ἄχρι θανάτου). Amid these visions of cosmic conflict, John hears "a loud voice in heaven" (cf. 11:15) that provides heavenly commentary on the significance of what he has seen, in the form of both praise to God (vv. 10–12a) and a warning to the earth (v. 12b–d). This voice apparently comes from a group of Christians in heaven (possibly the group in 6:9–11) rather than the angelic company because v. 10c speaks of earthly Christians as "our brothers and sisters."[35]

31. Osborne, *Revelation*, 467–73.

32. Bauckham, *Climax*, 185–86; Beale, *Revelation*, 636–37, 650–61; Rowland, "Revelation," 516–17.

33. See discussion in Simon Gathercole, "Jesus's Eschatological Vision of the Fall of Satan: Luke 10.18 Reconsidered,"

ZNW 94 (2003): 143–63, who takes it however as a fall yet to come in the end times.

34. Glasson, *Revelation*, 76–77; Mounce, *Revelation*, 235–39; Thomas, *Revelation 8–22*, 128–29.

John records their words as a direct quotation in vv. 10b–12. This is the next in a series of announcements of God's impending victory over all enemies that occur in these chapters of Revelation (see comments at 10:6–7; 11:15). These consist of declarations that in heaven's eyes God's kingdom has already arrived on earth (10:6–7; 15:1; 18:2) or such declarations combined with calls to worship God as a response to his saving work (11:15–18; 14:7–8; 19:1–3). Here the aorist in v. 10b, "have come" (ἐγένετο; see comments and note on 11:15; cf. 18:2), is reinforced by the adverb "now" (ἄρτι): "Just now this has been accomplished and its complete actualization on earth in the immediate future is certain." What has now come about is "the salvation and power and kingdom of our God,"[36] as well as "the authority of his Messiah" (cf. 2:26–28), referring not directly to their rule and authority in an eternal, heavenly sense but to the coming of this rule to earth (as seen in 19:11–20:6; 21:1–22:5). This mention of God's "power" (δύναμις) is significant in this context because it reminds us that the victory of Michael and his company over Satan (vv. 7–9) will be due ultimately to God's ruling power and Christ's victorious authority. God's holy angels are the instruments of his sovereign purpose in the universe.

The evidence of God's imminent accomplishment of victory ("because," v. 10c) is his ever-tightening rein on Satan as v. 9 revealed.[37] Verse 10c repeats the key verb "was thrown down" (ἐβλήθη) from v. 9 but shines a new light on Satan's expulsion from heaven by using a further title for him to add to the titles in v. 9: "the accuser" (ὁ κατήγωρ). For ages his characteristic practice[38] had been to appear before God to "accuse" God's people of sin and insincere worship and to use persecution and deception if necessary to lead them into such evils (Job 1:6–12; 2:1–6; Zech 3:1).[39] His accusations in God's presence have now come to an end, but as vv. 12b–17 will show, his angry persecution of God's people will intensify for the limited time that will remain for him on earth in that future day.

Just as God's angels have a role in defeating Satan's purposes but will carry it out only by divine power, so too must Christians play a role in vanquishing him based on Christ's victory on the cross and their imitation of him in their faith and practice (v. 11). Verse 11 continues the quoted declaration by the heavenly voice that began in v. 10b, and the pronoun in *they* overcame refers to "our brothers and sisters" in v. 10c, that is, followers of Christ. The aorist (ἐνίκησαν) translated "overcame" (v. 11a) declares their victory to be already accomplished in heaven's eyes,[40] even though the larger context describes intense persecution and judgment as yet to come (vv. 12–17; chs. 13–16). Here we glimpse the ultimate victory in a struggle

---

35. Angels seem to identify as "fellow servants" with faithful Christians on earth but reserve the term "brothers and sisters" for the human fellowship of Christ's followers (e.g., 19:10; 22:9). See Charles, *Revelation*, 1:326–27; Prigent, *Apocalypse*, 390; Thomas, *Revelation 8–22*, 132.

36. These echo the declarations of 7:10 and 19:1 (salvation); 4:11, 7:12, 11:17, and 19:1 (power); and 11:15, 17, and 19:6 (kingdom or rule).

37. See Jesus's parable of the strong man in Luke 11:20–22. Overcoming demonic power signals the arrival of God's kingdom (v. 20).

38. The customary or characteristic sense comes from the title "the accuser" (ὁ κατήγωρ), from the present tense of the participle that follows (a customary present, "the one accusing";

ὁ κατηγορῶν), and from the temporal phrase "day and night" added to the participle. This participle draws its past time frame ("who accused") from the time of its leading verb ("was thrown down"), as is normal for present participles.

39. Prigent, *Apocalypse*, 391.

40. This aorist probably summarizes various past events as a single whole with a focus on actual accomplishment despite opposition (a consummative aorist; cf. Fanning, *Verbal Aspect*, 263–65): "overcame" (e.g., CSB, KJV, NASB, NET, NIV). Alternatively, it denotes recent past events viewed in summary ("have overcome"; e.g., ESV, NLT, NRSV) along the same lines as in v. 10a: the heavenly voice declared a series of actions as having just been accomplished (see "now" in v. 10a and comments there).

that still lies ahead (cf. 15:2), but indicating how it will be gained. Use of the word "overcome" alludes to the promises Jesus expressed to "overcomers" in his messages to the churches (cf. 2:7, etc.) as well as to the description of his victory at the cross (3:21; 5:5–6) that alone provides the grounds and pattern for his followers to overcome Satan.

This theological point is reflected also in the two phrases with "because . . ." that follow the verb in v. 11a.[41] The future victory of Christ's followers will be due to "the blood of the Lamb," that is, his sacrificial death for them (1:5; 5:9; 7:14) as the decisive blow against sin and rebellion from God that Satan fostered. Ultimately it is not Christians' action but Christ's that defeats the dragon. However, a Christian's vital connection with Christ's victory is displayed in practice through imitation of his fundamental sacrifice and witness to God's redemption. This is expressed here in the second "because" phrase as well as the clause that follows in v. 11b. "The word of their testimony" (τὸν λόγον τῆς μαρτυρίας αὐτῶν) combines two subjective-genitive phrases[42] and speaks of the message about God that they bear witness to by their words and actions. The need for Christians to testify faithfully to God's saving work through Christ despite persecution and even martyrdom is a major theme throughout Revelation, and terms like "word, message" and "testimony, witness" repeatedly occur, especially in contexts that speak of their being killed

for such faithfulness (1:9; 6:9; 11:7; 17:6; 20:4). Jesus as God's "faithful witness" is their model in this (1:5; 3:14; cf. Antipas, 2:13). Such discipleship is powerfully reinforced in the summary statement of v. 11b, "they did not love their lives to the death."[43] This word for "life" (ψυχή) mirrors Jesus's statements about losing one's life for his sake and the gospel's (Mark 8:34–35; John 12:24–26). In real-world terms, "overcoming" Satan means remaining faithful to Jesus and the gospel despite deceptive and potentially deadly opposition from satanic evil in the world (see "overcoming" in the messages to the churches, chs. 2–3).

12:12 So then rejoice, you heavens and you who live in them. Woe to the earth and the sea, because the devil has come down to you, having great anger since he knows that he has only a little time" (διὰ τοῦτο εὐφραίνεσθε, οὐρανοὶ καὶ οἱ ἐν αὐτοῖς σκηνοῦντες. οὐαὶ τὴν γῆν καὶ τὴν θάλασσαν, ὅτι κατέβη ὁ διάβολος πρὸς ὑμᾶς ἔχων θυμὸν μέγαν, εἰδὼς ὅτι ὀλίγον καιρὸν ἔχει). The quoted words from the heavenly voice conclude with this summons to joy in heaven (v. 12a) and warning of woe on earth (v. 12b–d). The inferential phrase "so then" (διὰ τοῦτο) draws its conclusion most directly from v. 10c–d (the dragon's exclusion from heaven). Heaven can exult in this closer step toward God's judgment of evil and restoration of righteousness in the universe.[44] A similar call for heaven to rejoice occurs in 18:20 (over God's judg-

---

41. The preposition translated "because" (διά) normally denotes basis or reason (ultimate or effective cause) when it has accusative objects as here (cf. 1:9; 6:9; 20:4). With Christ's "blood" as its object in the *genitive* case, it is used several times in the NT to denote means or instrument (intermediate or efficient cause; e.g., Eph 1:7; Col 1:20; Heb 9:12; 13:12), and translations often adopt this rendering in this verse as well (CSB, ESV, KJV, NIV, NRSV, RSV). But with the accusative case as here, and with the contextual features noted in the comments above, it is better to understand these as causal in sense (cf. CEB, NASB; BDAG 226). See Swete, *Apocalypse*, 153 (the blood of the Lamb is "the primary cause"; their testimony

is "secondary cause"); Zerwick and Grosvenor, *Grammatical Analysis*, 761.

42. The genitive "of the testimony" (τῆς μαρτυρίας) is subjective ("the message that their testimony communicates"), and the genitive "their" (αὐτῶν) is also subjective ("the witness that they give").

43. This elliptical statement is clear enough, but somewhat indirect. Its idea is: "They did not value their physical lives [more than fidelity to Christ], even to the point of dying [in loyalty to him]."

44. The "heavens" (οὐρανοί) here does not mean the visible sky around the earth but the invisible realm where God exists,

ment of Babylon), and both reflect Old Testament celebrations of God as king, judge, and redeemer (Ps 96:10–11; Isa 44:23; 49:13). The warning is added to this without an explicit conjunction in Greek (asyndeton) but clearly in contrast to the gladness of v. 12a: "Woe to the earth and the sea" (v. 12b).[45] This "woe" is a general reference to the third woe that was announced in 11:14 (also 8:13; 9:12), but the more specific manifestation of the third woe (i.e., the seventh trumpet, 11:15) will come in the seven bowl judgments (15:1–16:21). The sea as well as the earth and its peoples will certainly experience great distress in those judgments (cf. 16:2–3).

Another distinction between this woe and the third woe is its source, since these troubles are said to come from the devil's frenzy of "anger" (θυμός; v. 12c) at being thrown to earth, while the bowl judgments constitute the final outpouring of "the anger of God" (ὁ θυμὸς τοῦ θεοῦ; 15:1). The devil's frustrated persecution of Israel and the followers of Jesus (12:13, 17) are intensified by his awareness that "he has only a little time" (v. 12d). This temporal note adds to other indicators that focus these events on the final years leading up to Christ's return to earth (6:11; 10:6; 11:18 as well as 11:2–3; 12:6, 14; cf. Dan 12:7).

12:13–14 And when the dragon saw that he was thrown to the earth, he persecuted the woman who gave birth to the male child. 14 And the two wings of a great eagle were given to the woman that she might fly into the wilderness to her place, where she is nourished for a time, times and half a time away from the presence of the serpent

(Καὶ ὅτε εἶδεν ὁ δράκων ὅτι ἐβλήθη εἰς τὴν γῆν, ἐδίωξεν τὴν γυναῖκα ἥτις ἔτεκεν τὸν ἄρσενα. 14 καὶ ἐδόθησαν τῇ γυναικὶ αἱ δύο πτέρυγες τοῦ ἀετοῦ τοῦ μεγάλου, ἵνα πέτηται εἰς τὴν ἔρημον εἰς τὸν τόπον αὐτῆς, ὅπου τρέφεται ἐκεῖ καιρὸν καὶ καιροὺς καὶ ἥμισυ καιροῦ ἀπὸ προσώπου τοῦ ὄφεως). Having now recounted the conflict in heaven leading to the dragon's banishment to earth and the heavenly commentary on those events (vv. 7–12), John now returns to the story of the woman and the dragon from vv. 1–6. To resume that story the first step is to cite the key point from the intervening section (vv. 7–12), that is, the dragon "thrown to the earth" (v. 13a, which also picks up the thread of "woe to the earth" in v. 12b–d). Then John is ready to move the narrative along further.

The dragon's angry response (v. 13b) is to "persecute" the woman Israel, whose child Jesus Christ ultimately caused his expulsion from heaven (see comments on vv. 5, 10). Verse 14 continues to resume points of the story from v. 6 (her escape into the "wilderness" to a "place" prepared by God to "nourish" her for twelve hundred and sixty days). What is added here are details that restate and fill in that narrative. How did she escape from such a fierce foe? It was by miraculous, God-given means portrayed in symbolic language drawn from the exodus story: by "flying" into the wilderness on "the two wings of a great eagle"[46] (v. 14a–b; cf. Exod 19:4; Deut 32:11; more generally, Isa 40:29–31) to escape the dragon (cf. Pharaoh as the dragon, Ezek 29:3; 32:2). Provision is made for her there (v. 14c, "she is nourished") for the same period of time as in v. 6, "a time, times, and half a time" (a veiled way

---

and those "who live in them" (cf. 13:6) are the spiritual beings and the souls of the righteous dead who serve and worship him there (e.g., 4:4–6; 5:11; 6:9–11; 7:9–12).

45. John often thinks of heaven, earth, and sea together (e.g., 5:13; 10:6; 21:1), so with heaven addressed in v. 12a, the other two are treated in v. 12b–c.

46. The Greek articles in the phrase describing the eagle in v. 14a (τοῦ ἀετοῦ τοῦ μεγάλου) carry a generic sense rather than referring to a specific eagle and so have been translated "a great eagle" instead of "the great eagle"; see Thomas, *Revelation 8–22*, 146–47; cf. CSB, KJV, NET, NIV, NLT).

of referring to three-and-a-half years; cf. Dan 7:25; 12:7; see discussion of the time frame at Rev 11:2) so that she finds refuge in this case from "the serpent," another name for the dragon given in 12:9 (see both titles used in vv. 15–16). This imagery gives us almost no insight into how such an escape might be accomplished in actual earthly terms, but it powerfully portrays the unfailing supernatural help that will preserve a corporate group of ethnic Israel from complete destruction in the final days of that future cataclysmic period (i.e., the final half of the tribulation).[47]

Beyond the question of how to interpret the imagery, v. 14 (as well as v. 6) presents another conundrum. If the "woman" is a corporate symbol representing ethnic Israel as a whole (as argued above), how does that sense fit into this account of "her" escape and protection in her own refuge "prepared by God" (v. 6) during those days of earthly suffering to come? Does this mean every ethnic Jew or every ethnically Jewish believer living at that time? Or does it refer to a representative group of all ethnic Israel or of believing Jewish people? This question arises again in v. 17 with the distinction between the woman (who has escaped Satan's attacks) and "the rest of her offspring" whom he goes to wage war against (i.e., who have not found refuge as the woman is said to have done). It seems best to understand those who are protected in their refuge (v. 14) as a representative group, but see v. 17 for further discussion.

12:15–16 And the serpent spewed from his mouth water like a river after the woman to sweep her away in a torrent. 16 And the earth helped the woman and opened its mouth and swallowed up the river that the dragon spewed from his mouth (καὶ ἔβαλεν ὁ ὄφις ἐκ τοῦ στόματος αὐτοῦ ὀπίσω τῆς γυναικὸς ὕδωρ ὡς ποταμόν, ἵνα αὐτὴν ποταμοφόρητον ποιήσῃ. 16 καὶ ἐβοήθησεν ἡ γῆ τῇ γυναικί καὶ ἤνοιξεν ἡ γῆ τὸ στόμα αὐτῆς καὶ κατέπιεν τὸν ποταμὸν ὃν ἔβαλεν ὁ δράκων ἐκ τοῦ στόματος αὐτοῦ). The saga does not end with her initial escape into the wilderness, as vv. 15–16 show (see also the note at v. 6 about the "wilderness" as both positive and negative for Israel). The serpent (or dragon, v. 16, who controls the rivers and seas; cf. Ezek 29:3; 32:2) intends to destroy the woman even in the wilderness with a flood of "water like a river" disgorged like a weapon "from his mouth" (v. 15a). But the earth itself comes to the woman's aid by "swallow[ing] up" the dragon's river of water (v. 16). This imagery seems to be based on the exodus pattern of deliverance also, but with a strategic twist. Instead of Israel going on dry land through a sea of water that sweeps away the Egyptians, the earth delivers Israel from the flood that the dragon unleashes against her (see Exod 14:13–29; 15:4–13; also Ps 74:12–15 that seems to adapt exodus imagery in a similar way).[48] Similar symbolism about the Lord delivering his people through "floods" of adversity occurs more generally in the Old Testament (Pss 18:4; 32:6; 124:4; Isa 43:2) and sometimes refers to armies that attack like an overwhelming flood (e.g., Isa 8:7–8; Jer 46:7–8; 47:2–3). Again, it is unnecessary to speculate about how such a satanic attack and divine deliverance will take place in future earthly terms. The exodus typology communicates the broader truth without dictating the specific ways it will be replicated in the end times.

---

47. Walvoord, Rawley, and Hitchcock, *Revelation*, 200–1, are content to see this language as symbolic rather than as a literal flood. Thomas, *Revelation 8–22*, 140, is ambivalent. For one attempt to specify how this could happen in literal terms, see Smith, *Revelation*, 190–91.

48. Exod 15:12 LXX says that the earth "swallowed" the Egyptians to defeat them (same verb, κατέπιεν, as in Rev 12:16c).

12:17–18 And the dragon became enraged at the woman and went away to wage war against the rest of her offspring, who keep God's commands and hold to Jesus's testimony. 18 And he stood on the sand of the seashore (καὶ ὠργίσθη ὁ δράκων ἐπὶ τῇ γυναικί καὶ ἀπῆλθεν ποιῆσαι πόλεμον μετὰ τῶν λοιπῶν τοῦ σπέρματος αὐτῆς τῶν τηρούντων τὰς ἐντολὰς τοῦ θεοῦ καὶ ἐχόντων τὴν μαρτυρίαν Ἰησοῦ. 18 καὶ ἐστάθη ἐπὶ τὴν ἄμμον τῆς θαλάσσης). The escape and protection of the woman despite the dragon's herculean efforts (vv. 13–16) does not cause him to stand down but simply stirs his ire further against her (cf. "anger," v. 12). So in rage against the woman (v. 17a), he goes to press his attack against "the rest of her offspring" (v. 17b). This distinction between the "woman" who will escape and "the rest of her offspring" who will still suffer attack is a conundrum that interpreters have solved in various ways. The explanation that makes the most sense is to understand the "woman" protected in her refuge (vv. 6, 14) as a representative body of ethnically Jewish followers of Jesus (who are described also as the sealed 144,000 from every tribe of Israel in 7:4–8; 14:1–5)[49] and "the rest of her offspring" as other ethnically Jewish believers who will not escape satanic persecution in those terrible days to come. They along with believers in Christ from other ethnic origins will face great persecution, and many of them will be killed for their loyalty to Christ (6:9–11; 7:14–15; 12:10–12; 20:4).

A different reading of this puzzling distinction is to orient "the rest of her offspring" not in contrast to the woman herself but to her specific descendant that was mentioned earlier in the chapter: the

"male child" born to her (vv. 5, 13). So "the rest of her offspring" would be her other (spiritual) children, and they consist of whatever group the interpreter has taken the woman to represent, usually the church, the true Israel, God's faithful people on earth who are subject to satanic attack.[50] This fits the larger scheme of the dragon's attempts to kill first her specific child (vv. 4–5) and then her remaining children. But it skips over his persecution of the woman (vv. 13–16) and the specific contrasts in the near context that focus the contrast between the woman and "the rest," rather than between the two mentions of her children.

Another suggestion that stays within the "woman versus offspring" contrast is the view that the woman represents the heavenly, ideal church, and the "rest" are the earthly church subject to the dragon's warfare.[51] It is true that the woman was seen at first in heavenly glory (v. 1), but the story thereafter spoke of her herself (not her remaining offspring) as subject to the dragon's persecution in quite earthly terms (vv. 6, 13–16). A different reading sees the distinction as a somewhat historical one, between the early, mostly Jewish church (the woman) versus the mostly gentile church that came later. Satan tried but failed to stamp out the church in its early, formative days, and then in the latter first century—and continuing to the last days—he directs his attacks against Christians.[52]

Among those who understand the woman to be ethnic Israel, a variety of suggestions remain about what "the rest of her offspring" represents. Smith explains the woman who escapes the dragon's clutches as those believing Jews who live in Judea at the time of the end and flee his attacks

---

49. See comments especially at 7:4–8.

50. Michaels, *Revelation*, 153–54; Mounce, *Revelation*, 242; Smalley, *Revelation*, 333–34.

51. Beale, *Revelation*, 676–78; Ladd, *Revelation*, 167, 174; Osborne, *Revelation*, 484–85.

52. Hughes, *Revelation*, 137–43; Glasson, *Revelation*, 73–78 (who sees the woman as ethnic Israel). Similar to Glasson is Hoskins, *Revelation*, 212–13, 224.

(vv. 13–16), while "the rest" are Jews who live elsewhere and become his victims.[53] Thomas takes a similar view but specifies further: the woman represents believing Israelites who escape to the wilderness, and "the rest" are the 144,000 sealed Jewish believers who are "active witnesses throughout the world" and thus incur the beast's opposition (ch. 13) and then are seen as "victorious victims of his persecution after the conflict is over" (14:1–5).[54] It is true, as Thomas argues, that 14:1–5 (the vision of the 144,000 on Mount Zion) is closely tied to chapters 12–13 (satanic opposition against God's people), but understanding the 144,000 as martyrs does not fit either 7:4–8 or 14:1–5 very well (see commentary at those places).

The descriptions of this group of Israelites (v. 17c) clearly mark them out as followers of Christ: "who keep God's commands and hold to Jesus's testimony." "Keep[ing] God's commands" is a phrase used also in 14:12 as a description of God's faithful saints who believe in Jesus (a wider group than here since it would include non-Jewish believers as well). It is also similar to other uses of "keep" (τηρέω) in Revelation that call on the readers to obey or faithfully observe what is written in the book (1:3; 22:7, 9) or Christ's message (3:8, 10) or the works he commands (2:26) or generally what they have received and heard (3:3). The second description in v. 17c, holding to "Jesus's testimony" (τὴν μαρτυρίαν Ἰησοῦ), is sometimes taken as subjective in sense (the faithful witness that Jesus gave and gives, in his earthly life and possibly in this

book itself). He is called a "faithful witness" (1:5; 3:14), he declares that this book is his testimony (22:20), and the phrase "testimony of Jesus" should almost certainly be taken with a subjective sense in 1:2, 9 due to the context of the book's prologue and opening vision (see comments there).[55] But here (as well as in 19:10; 20:4) an objective sense seems better (cf. CSB, NET, NIV, NLT, RSV; to, for, or about Jesus).[56] Two of these are texts about suffering persecution or martyrdom (here and 20:4; cf. 17:6), and 6:9 has a similar phrase, "holding to one's testimony" (without "of Jesus" added). In these contexts, the focus seems to be on bearing loyal testimony by actions and speech to the truths about Jesus when challenged to renounce him (see this above in 12:11). Even though the related expression "word of God" is subjective, nothing demands that both genitives have the same sense. The phrases are complementary: standing up for God's message about Christ and maintaining their conviction regarding what it says about him.

It is easy to see that v. 18 ("And he [the dragon] stood on the sand of the seashore") is a hinge verse, connecting closely to what has just been presented as well as to the visions of chapter 13. As can be seen in modern printed Bibles (both English and Greek), translators and editors have debated whether the verse goes more closely with chapter 12 as the final verse of that section or with chapter 13 as the beginning of a new one (whether or not they print a verse number beside it). A textual variant for the verb "he stood" (ἐστάθη) reflects the

---

53. Smith, *Revelation*, 191–92. He explains (correctly) that "the rest" (λοιποί) in v. 17b does not carry the technical sense of "remnant" (i.e., that relatively small number of Jews who believe in Jesus; cf. Rom 9:27 [ὑπόλειμμα or variant κατάλειμμα]; 11:5 [λεῖμμα]).

54. Thomas, *Revelation 8–22*, 141–42. Smith, *Revelation*, 192, also includes the 144,000 as well as others among those who suffer martyrdom under the beast.

55. The phrase "the testimony of Jesus" (ἡ μαρτυρία Ἰησοῦ) occurs six times in this book. J. Beutler, "μαρτυρία," *EDNT*

2:392–93, holds that all of them are subjective. Bauckham, *Climax*, 161, espouses the same opinion.

56. Some are happy to see both subjective and objective senses in this phrase (a general or plenary genitive; Wallace, *Grammar*, 119–21): witness that Jesus expressed that Christians in turn express about him (e.g., Beale, *Revelation*, 679; Osborne, *Revelation*, 485). But in most contexts, it is better to choose one sense or the other. Language does not usually allow such a broad range of flexibility.

latter opinion: it reads "I stood" (ἐστάθην), as in KJV, NJKV, to align more closely with "and I saw" of 13:1.[57]

The specific paragraph divisions are actually not so important as long as the verse is clearly understood to tie the two narratives together. The dragon that pursues the woman and her offspring (ch. 12) continues his warfare against them by empowering the two beasts of chapter 13. The dragon is explicitly linked to them in 13:2, 4, and the same time period is mentioned in 13:5 (cf. 12:6, 14). Moreover, the same words for "war" appear in 13:4, 7 (cf. 11:7; 12:7, 17). John sees the dragon standing on the shore of the sea, eagerly awaiting the first of his two end-time agents to appear from its depths to begin his nefarious work.

Theology in Application

A Struggle Bigger Than Ourselves

John's vision of the great signs in heaven in Revelation 12 fills us in on Satan's cosmic and age-long warfare directed against God, his Messiah, and his people. Satan's implacable struggle against God began long ago and continues through the present age despite the decisive defeat he suffered in Christ's death and resurrection (2:10–13; 3:21; 5:5; 12:3–9). And he will wage war against God and his people with heightened intensity in the days immediately preceding Christ's second coming (12:10–13, 17; 13:7). This wider pattern of aggressive, satanic evil should actually reassure us and strengthen our resolve to resist him (Jas 4:7; 1 Pet 5:8–9; 1 John 4:4). Such struggles do not come upon us due to our sins alone, and victory is not gained due to our virtues alone. The conflict is bigger than our situation by itself, but we are called to take our place in the line of battle that stretches back a long way. And Revelation confirms that Christ's decisive victory already accomplished in the cross will soon be fulfilled completely when he returns to the earth to overthrow Satan and his evil rule completely (chs. 19–20).

What Our Victory Will Look Like

When we read about followers of Jesus who "overcome" or become victorious over Satan (v. 11) in the future days of final tribulation, it is important to grasp what it means to overcome and what the battle itself will look like as we face Satan's opposition in our times. In other texts in Revelation, we discover (as expected) that sometimes such attacks come in the form of overt persecution, including social ostracism, personal slander, economic discrimination, physical assault or imprisonment, and even death (1:9; 2:9–10, 13; 12:13, 17; 13:15–17). These are times of great difficulty and danger for Christians. But, perhaps unexpectedly, Satan's opposition also

---

57. The external evidence favors "he stood" (𝔓[47], ℵ, A, C, 1854, 2344, 2351) over "I stood" (P, 046, 1006, 1611, 1841, 2053, 2329, most Byzantine minuscules). On internal grounds "I stood" seems to be an attempt to clarify the sense and tie the sentence more closely to 13:1.

manifests itself in times of peace and prosperity, in the form of false teachings (2:2, 20, 24) or temptations that lull us into complacency (3:17–19) and easy conformity to the sinful practices of the world (2:20; 18:3–4). These are possibly even more challenging and threatening. But this should be no surprise since Satan is the great deceiver and accuser (12:9–10; 13:14), whose wiles include masquerade and duplicity (2 Cor 2:11; 11:13–15) as much as overt violence. But no matter what form this conflict takes in our situations, we are called to faithful endurance even if it means costly suffering and martyrdom (1:9; 13:10; 14:12). For us to be victorious or prevail in this struggle means resisting evil and falsehood in our lives and in our churches, staying faithful to God by not conforming to the world's values or worshiping false gods (see the exhortations in chs. 2–3; also 18:4). This is the sense in which Christ's followers are said to "overcome" Satan (12:11) and the beast (15:2). But such a victory will be gained by virtue of what Christ has already accomplished and by enduring faith in him, not by human attainment (1 John 4:4; 5:4–5; Rev 21:5–7).

Revelation 13:1–18

Literary Context

This passage presents a new stage of the vision in chapter 12, showing how the dragon will wage war against the woman's offspring (12:17) through his surrogates, the beast-like figures who emerge from the sea (13:1–10) and from the earth (13:11–18). This picture of satanic warfare against Israel and the world at large in chapters 12–13 then leads to visions of victory for the Lamb and corresponding defeat of the enemies of God in chapter 14. These interludes anticipate the outpouring of God's intense judgments in the seven last plagues of chapters 15–16.

Main Idea

During the future period of final tribulation a ruthless world leader with a deceptive propagandist at his side will, under Satan's authority, persecute God's people and dominate the whole world.

Translation

Revelation 13:1–18

1a	Vision Intro/ Character Entrance	And **I saw a beast**
		coming up from the sea,
b	Descriptions	having ten horns and seven heads, and
c		on his horns were ten diadems, and
d		on his heads were blasphemous names.
2a	Comparisons	And **the beast that I saw was like a leopard**
b		and **his feet were like a bear's**
c		and **his mouth was like the mouth of a lion.**
d	Action	And **the dragon gave him his power and**
		his throne and
		great authority.
3a	Description	And **one of his heads looked like it had been mortally wounded,**
b	Contrast	but **his mortal wound had been healed.**
c	Results	And **the whole earth was amazed and**
		followed the beast,
4a		and **they worshiped the dragon**
b	Reason for 4a	because he had given authority to the beast,
c		and **they worshiped the beast, saying,**
d	Exclamation	*"Who is like the beast*
e		*and who can war against him?"*
5a	Actions	And **he was given a mouth speaking great boasts and blasphemies,**
b		and **he was given authority to act for forty-two months.**
6a		And **he opened his mouth in blasphemies against God,**
b	Purpose	to blaspheme his name and
		his dwelling,
		even those who dwell in heaven.

7a	Actions	And **it was given to him to wage war against the saints and**
		to overcome them,
b		and **authority was given to him over every tribe and**
		people and
		language and
		nation.
8a	Effect of 7b	And **all those who live on the earth will worship him,**
b	Specification	whose names are not written
		in the book
		of life
		of the Lamb
c	Description	who was slain before the foundation ⤷
		of the world.
9a	Premise	If anyone has an ear,
b	Exhortation	**let him hear.**
10a	Premise	If anyone is destined for captivity,
b	Consequence	**to captivity he goes.**
c	Premise	If anyone is to be killed with the sword,
d	Consequence	**he is to be killed with the sword.**
e	Conclusion	**Here is the endurance and faith of the saints.**
11a	Vision Intro/	And **I saw another beast coming up from the earth,**
	Character Entrance	
b	Description	and **he had two horns like a lamb,**
c	Comparison	and **he was speaking like a dragon.**
12a	Actions	And **he exerts all the authority of the first beast before him,**
b		and **he causes the earth and**
		those who live in it to worship the first beast
c	Description	whose mortal wound was healed.
13a	Action	And **he performs great signs,**
b	Explanation	even to cause fire to come down from heaven to earth for anyone to see,
14a	Action	and **he deceives those who live on the earth**
b	Basis	because of the signs that he was permitted to perform in the beast's presence,
c	Means	telling those who live on the earth
d	Command	to make an image for the beast
e	Description	who has the wound of the sword but came to life.
15a	Action	And **he was permitted to give breath to the beast's image,**
b	Purposes	so that the beast's image might even speak, and
c		he might cause all who would not worship the beast's image to be killed.

Continued on next page.

Continued from previous page.

16a	Action	And **he causes all,**
		the small and the great, and
		the rich and the poor, and
		the free and the slaves,
b	Content of 16a	to be given a mark on their right hands or
		on their foreheads
17a	Purpose of 16b	so that no one is able to buy or sell
b	Exception	except the one who has the mark,
c	Apposition	that is, the name of the beast or
		the number of his name.
18a	Basis for 18b	**Here is wisdom.**
b	Exhortation	**Let the one who has understanding calculate the number of the beast,**
c	Explanation	**for it is the number of a person**
d	Specification	**and his number is six hundred and sixty-six.**

Structure

The two main sections of this chapter are clearly set out by the occurrence of the words "and I saw" (καὶ εἶδον) in 13:1 and 13:11, coupled with the parallels "a beast coming up from the sea" (v. 1) versus "another beast coming up from the earth" (v. 11). In recounting the character and career of the beast from the sea (13:1–10) and the beast from the earth (13:11–18), John shows how they work together under Satan's authority (vv. 2, 4) to persecute God's people and to deceive and dominate the whole world during the period of final tribulation.

Exegetical Outline

III. Second Vision: Heavenly Throne Room and Three Judgment Cycles (4:1–16:21)

    A. Vision of God in His Heavenly Throne Room (4:1–11)

    B. The Seven-Sealed Scroll and the Slain Lamb (5:1–14)

    C. The Seven Seals and the Interlude of the Two Multitudes (6:1–8:1)

    D. The Seven Trumpets and Further Interludes (8:2–14:20)

        1. The First Four Trumpets (8:2–13)

        2. The Fifth Trumpet—First Woe (9:1–12)

        3. The Sixth Trumpet—Second Woe (9:13–21)

        4. Two Revelatory Interludes: God's Prophets (10:1–11:14)

        5. The Seventh Trumpet—Third Woe: Anticipating God's Rule (11:15–19)

6. Two Further Interludes: Anticipating Babylon's Fall (12:1–14:20)

a. The dragon's war against the woman (12:1–13:18)

  (1) The woman, her son, and the dragon (12:1–18)

  (2) The dragon and his beasts from the sea and from the earth (13:1–18)

    (a) The beast from the sea (13:1–10)

      (i) His character and relationship to the dragon and the earth's response (13:1–4)

      (ii) The domination of the world God allows him to exert (13:5–8)

      (iii) Exhortation to be warned and endure what is coming (13:9–10)

    (b) The beast from the earth (13:11–18)

      (i) His character and relationship to the first beast (13:11–12)

      (ii) His deceptive miracles and their effect on earth dwellers (13:13–17)

      (iii) Exhortation to be discerning and identify the beast when he comes (13:18)

Explanation of the Text

13:1–2 And I saw a beast coming up from the sea, having ten horns and seven heads, and on his horns were ten diadems, and on his heads were blasphemous names. 2 And the beast that I saw was like a leopard and his feet were like a bear's and his mouth was like the mouth of a lion. And the dragon gave him his power and his throne and great authority (Καὶ εἶδον ἐκ τῆς θαλάσσης θηρίον ἀναβαῖνον, ἔχον κέρατα δέκα καὶ κεφαλὰς ἑπτὰ καὶ ἐπὶ τῶν κεράτων αὐτοῦ δέκα διαδήματα καὶ ἐπὶ τὰς κεφαλὰς αὐτοῦ ὄνομα βλασφημίας. 2 καὶ τὸ θηρίον ὃ εἶδον ἦν ὅμοιον παρδάλει καὶ οἱ πόδες αὐτοῦ ὡς ἄρκου καὶ τὸ στόμα αὐτοῦ ὡς στόμα λέοντος. καὶ ἔδωκεν αὐτῷ ὁ δράκων τὴν δύναμιν αὐτοῦ καὶ τὸν θρόνον αὐτοῦ καὶ ἐξουσίαν μεγάλην). Chapter 13 begins a new phase of John's vision of the signs in heaven (12:1–18), in which he observes ("and I saw," καὶ εἶδον; 13:1, 11) two wild animals or "beasts" through whom the dragon will "wage war" against the offspring of the woman (12:17). The "beast . . . from the sea" is the more important figure in this warfare (13:1–10), and the "beast . . . from the earth" plays a supporting role in coercing allegiance to the first beast (13:11–18). See below for discussion of what these symbolize. John's initial description in v. 1a, "a beast coming up from the sea," suggests a dependence on Daniel 7:3 ("four great beasts coming up out of the sea") that is confirmed more and more as other details are added. This first beast was mentioned briefly already at 11:7 as the "beast who comes up from the bottomless pit" (cf. also 17:8) and "wages war" on the two witnesses and kills them.[1] But from here till the middle of chapter 20, he will play a central role in Revelation. The bizarre description John adds next, "having ten horns and seven heads" (v. 1b; cf. also 17:3), has been seen already when another figure, the dragon, was first pictured in 12:3, but both are drawn largely from Daniel 7 where one of the beasts is said to have four heads and another has ten horns (Dan 7:6–7). John will develop the significance of the horns and heads in

---

1. This correlation between the "bottomless pit" (ἄβυσσος) and the "sea" (θάλασσα) comes from a broad background in the ancient world that regarded the depths of the sea as a realm of chaos and evil, one that God tamed at the creation and will finally conquer at his restoration of the whole universe (cf. 9:1–2; 21:1).

Revelation 17:9–13 (they represent two types of ruling authority),[2] but Daniel 7:6 prepares the way for this (the beast with the four heads was given dominion). This significance is related also to the angelic interpretation given in Daniel 7:24 (the ten *horns* are ten kings arising in the kingdom that the fourth beast represents).

The intermingling of the imagery of heads and horns is suggested further by the description of the beast as having "ten diadems" on his ten horns (v. 1c), representing royal status (see the dragon of 12:3 with diadems on his seven *heads*).[3] The final phrase (v. 1d) moves in a slightly different direction: the beast has "blasphemous names" on his heads (cf. 17:3), a suggestion of the traits that vv. 5–6 will develop further. This is drawn from Daniel 7:8 (also Dan 7:20; 8:11, 23–25; 11:36–39) that speaks of an arrogant, godless ruler (with "a mouth speaking great boasts") arising from the fourth beast or kingdom in Daniel's vision.

The savage and frightful character of Daniel's four beasts (Dan 7:2–27) comes out more clearly in what Revelation 13:2 says about this beast from the sea. He combines the ferocious traits of Daniel's first three beasts in being like a leopard, bear, and lion (v. 2a–c; Dan 7:4–6) with the destructive and overwhelming strength of the fourth beast (Dan 7:7–8, "different from all the beasts that were before it"). John perceives (v. 2d) that the ruling power represented in the beast's heads and horns comes from Satan himself, the dragon whose war against the woman's offspring (12:17) and against God (13:5–6) is set out in these chapters. The dragon is the one who provided this beast with "his power and his throne and great authority" (v. 2d; see comments on v. 3 for the parody of God and Christ that begins here). As v. 7b will show,

the beast is "given authority over every tribe and people and language and nation," but his exercise of this authority will be limited to "forty-two months" (v. 5b). Later the fifth bowl of judgment will specifically target "the throne of the beast" and will plunge his kingdom into darkness (16:10), another sign that the devil has only a little time left (12:12).

The connection with Daniel 7 gives some important evidence to consider in weighing the identity or historical referent of this "beast from the sea." The visions in Daniel use images of a great statue (Dan 2) or of savage animals (Dan 7–8) or they provide more direct narration (Dan 9–11) to refer to world kingdoms or empires as well as individual kings or rulers of those empires. The personal referents (kings) are merged with the institutional (empires), but the symbols have specific historical referents (e.g., Persia, Greece, the messiah). Daniel focused on the final days of suffering for Israel that lead to her redemption and restoration. John's vision of the first beast presents a composite of four empires that suggests a pattern of arrogant, godless rule over the world's inhabitants that rears its head at various times but most intensely in the last days. While the imagery used here in Revelation 13 is powerfully connotative (signaling savagery and satanic evil) and allusive (connecting this being to the oppressive empires of Dan 7), it refers ultimately not to an impersonal evil force or demonic personal being or generic human rulers who arise at various times in world history but to a specific human ruler and the empire he rules in the last days (the referent can shift from one to the other depending on the context). In the typology of evil used here and elsewhere in Revelation (i.e., the connection of this beast to Babylon the great prostitute), the pattern may have various

---

2. According to 17:9–13 the heads are seven kings preceding the beast in his line of succession, and the horns are ten kings allied to the beast; see comments there.

3. See diadems in Esth 1:11; 2:17; Isa 62:3; cf. 1 Macc 11:13, 54; Sir 47:6.

historical manifestations that foreshadow the ultimate intensification of the type (e.g., Antiochus IV Epiphanes; Rome in AD 70; see comments at 14:8), but the primary referent is the one who appears in the final days just prior to Christ's second coming. More about this savage "beast" of a man and his kingdom in what follows.[4]

13:3–4 And one of his heads looked like it had been mortally wounded, but his mortal wound had been healed. And the whole earth was amazed and followed the beast, 4 and they worshiped the dragon because he had given authority to the beast, and they worshiped the beast, saying, "Who is like the beast and who can war against him?" (καὶ μίαν ἐκ τῶν κεφαλῶν αὐτοῦ ὡς ἐσφαγμένην εἰς θάνατον, καὶ ἡ πληγὴ τοῦ θανάτου αὐτοῦ ἐθεραπεύθη. καὶ ἐθαυμάσθη ὅλη ἡ γῆ ὀπίσω τοῦ θηρίου 4 καὶ προσεκύνησαν τῷ δράκοντι, ὅτι ἔδωκεν τὴν ἐξουσίαν τῷ θηρίῳ, καὶ προσεκύνησαν τῷ θηρίῳ λέγοντες, Τίς ὅμοιος τῷ θηρίῳ καὶ τίς δύναται πολεμῆσαι μετ' αὐτοῦ). In vv. 3–4 the details of John's vision move from the basic imagery of Daniel 7 to develop the portrait of this "beast" in a distinctive direction. One[5] of the "heads" (i.e., a ruler in the reigning line of the kingdom that the beast represents) clearly appears to have received a fatal wound (v. 3a; lit., "as though slain unto death"; ὡς ἐσφαγμένην εἰς θάνατον), but amazingly he was healed from this fatal blow (v. 3b). This portrayal is reinforced in v. 12 (wording like v. 3b: his mortal

wound was healed) and v. 14 (worded differently: he received the blow of the sword and came back to life; ἔχει τὴν πληγὴν τῆς μαχαίρης καὶ ἔζησεν).[6] In all three places (vv. 3, 12, 14) his resuscitation is central to an effort to use miraculous signs to deceive the earth's inhabitants into offering divine worship to the dragon and to the beast. In addition, John has worded this marvel in v. 3a (lit., "as though slain unto death," ὡς ἐσφαγμένην εἰς θάνατον) so that it unmistakably mirrors what was said in Revelation 5:6 about Christ as a Lamb "standing as though slain" (ἑστηκὸς ὡς ἐσφαγμένον; cf. also "the Lamb who was slain" in 5:12).[7] As noted in the comments on v. 2d, John discerns in the career of the beast from the sea a diabolical parody of the Father, Son, and Holy Spirit: the dragon as the ultimate authority who uses the beast as his agent, bolstered by the deceptive influences of the beast from the earth (vv. 11–18). Verse 3c records that the beast's remarkable recovery has a widespread effect: "the whole earth" becomes his wide-eyed followers,[8] and this theme will be repeated below (vv. 7b–8a, 12, 14, 16; except for a few who refuse to follow, vv. 7a, 8b, 10, 15). Humanity's susceptibility to satanic deception in the end times is reflected also in 2 Thess 2:9–12 (cf. also Rev 20:3).

The response portrayed in v. 3c (amazed followers) develops into full worship of the dragon and the beast in v. 4, reinforcing the Trinitarian parody seen in vv. 2b–3. The whole world "worshiped the dragon"[9] (v. 4a) according to John, since the beast

---

4. Further evidence that this "beast" is an individual person rather than an impersonal force or empire in general is found in Rev 13:18. The beast's number is "the number of a person." See comments there.

5. The Greek of v. 3 is unusual in beginning with an accusative "one" (μίαν). This appears to be due to the transitive verb "I saw" in v. 1 that is implied here too.

6. It is hard to be sure whether this should be understood as a miracle allowed by God or as a deception to fool the gullible. See also the "signs" or miracles of vv. 13–15 (cf. v. 14b: "That he was permitted to perform").

7. Cf. v. 14e that reflects what 1:18 says about Christ: "I died but indeed I am alive forever and ever."

8. The phrase "was amazed and followed the beast" is an attempt to smooth over an ellipsis in Greek (lit., "were amazed after the beast"). See BDAG 445 on "amaze" (θαυμάζω); cf. the uses of "after" (ὀπίσω) in Mark 8:34; John 12:19; Acts 5:37; 20:30; 1 Tim 5:15.

9. The subject of v. 3c, "the whole world," is continued in the "they" pronoun reference of the verb "they worshiped" (v. 4a), a collective singular being unpacked as a plural in sense.

exercises ruling authority that originated with the dragon (v. 4b; cf. v. 2d). It is not made clear whether the beast's followers consciously intend to offer worship to Satan, but this is John's theological evaluation of their actions. But the emphasis of v. 4c–e (as well as vv. 8, 12, 15) is that the beast is the immediate focus of their worship and allegiance, and this will include some kind of adoration or obeisance to "an image" of the beast (vv. 14–15). They offer reverence to the beast with exclamations of his incomparability and invincibility (v. 4d–e): "Who is like the beast and who can war against him?" John and his Christian readers would surely bristle at this misuse of worship formulas offered in Scripture to the true God (e.g., Exod 15:11; Job 9:19; 41:10–11; Ps 89:6; Isa 40:25; 46:5; Nah 1:6) recited in honor of a satanic substitute. The exclamation about "war" (Rev 13:4e) is a reminder that the dragon and his protégé, the beast, are intent on battling God and his people in the short period that remains for them prior to Christ's return (cf. 11:7; 12:17; 13:7), at which time the one truly powerful enough to "war against" the beast will conquer him decisively (17:14; 19:19–21; cf. 2 Thess 2:8).

This parody of the second person of the Trinity, particularly the parallels regarding one who was fatally "slain" but miraculously healed and worshiped (vv. 3–4) and his authority over the whole world (v. 7 below), suggests that John views this beast as the antichrist, the eschatological enemy of God and his Messiah.[10] Revelation does not use this specific term, and it appears only in a rather general sense in a few places in the wider New Testament (1 John 2:18, 22; 4:18; 2 John 7).[11] But this person is described in 2 Thessalonians 2:1–12 as "the man of lawlessness" who exalts himself as divine and deceives many, a description that is also dependent on Daniel 7 (vv. 8, 20, 25; also 11:36) and reflected in Revelation 13:5–6, 8, 14. The antichrist figure is developed more extensively in patristic writers, who consistently associate the beast of Revelation 13 with the person described in Daniel 7; 2 Thessalonians 2; and 1 John 2.[12] For the beast's likely typological foreshadowing in the Roman world of John's day and further discussion of his end-time identification, see comments on Revelation 13:18.

13:5–6 And he was given a mouth speaking great boasts and blasphemies, and he was given authority to act for forty-two months. 6 And he opened his mouth in blasphemies against God, to blaspheme his name and his dwelling, even those who dwell in heaven (Καὶ ἐδόθη αὐτῷ στόμα λαλοῦν μεγάλα καὶ βλασφημίας καὶ ἐδόθη αὐτῷ ἐξουσία ποιῆσαι μῆνας τεσσεράκοντα [καὶ] δύο. 6 καὶ ἤνοιξεν τὸ στόμα αὐτοῦ εἰς βλασφημίας πρὸς τὸν θεὸν βλασφημῆσαι τὸ ὄνομα αὐτοῦ καὶ τὴν σκηνὴν αὐτοῦ, τοὺς ἐν τῷ οὐρανῷ σκηνοῦντας). The beast's profane arrogance that was hinted at in v. 1 ("blasphemous names" on his heads) is described in full measure in vv. 5–6, along with a time limit for his oppressive rule. Twice in v. 5 (and twice more in v. 7) actions or authority are said to be "given" or permitted (ἐδόθη) to the beast. The agent who granted these things could be the dragon, because vv. 2b and 4b have just indicated that the dragon "gave" him his authority or power. But more broadly in Revelation, God is understood to be the sovereign one who grants permission for events, even evil or catastrophic events, to occur in these

---

10. See Lietaert Peerbolte, *Antecedents of Antichrist*, for summaries of the themes of the eschatological enemy or antichrist in the NT and patristic literature (pp. 206–20) and in early Jewish literature (pp. 340–45). Geert Wouter Lorein, *The Antichrist Theme in the Intertestamental Period*, JSPSup 44 (London: T&T Clark, 2003), gives a more recent treatment of the topic in intertestamental Judaism (a summary of his findings can be found on pp. 219–43).

11. J. Ernst, "ἀντίχριστος," *EDNT* 1:111.

12. E.g., Barn. 4:1–5; Did. 16:3–4; Irenaeus, *Haer.* 5.28.2; Justin, *Dial.* 32; 110; Hippolytus, *Antichr.* 49; Weinrich, "Andrew of Caesarea," 159–63.

final days (6:2, 4, 8, 11; 7:2; 9:3, 5; 16:8), and that is the more likely reading here as well.[13] The phrase "a mouth speaking great boasts" (v. 5a; στόμα λαλοῦν μεγάλα) follows the wording of Daniel 7:8, 20 LXX, and such self-exaltation is mentioned elsewhere in Daniel as well (8:11, 23–25; 11:36–39). Speaking "blasphemies" also comes from Daniel, both 7:25 ("he will speak words against the Most High") and 11:36 ("he will speak horrendous things against the God of gods"). Daniel 7:25 (the little horn permitted to operate for "a time and times and half a time") is also the source of the time frame specified in v. 5b: "forty-two months" (see 11:2–3; 12:6, 14). In addition, the use of the verb "to act, be active" (ποιέω) in this sense has parallels in Daniel 8:24; 11:28.[14]

The targets of the beast's blasphemous speech (v. 5a) are specified in v. 6. His disrespectful and denigrating words are directed "against God" and against "his name" or character and reputation.[15] One irreverence to which faithful Jews and Christians in the ancient world particularly objected was any claim to rivalry or equality with God. For a human to claim divine status was blasphemy of the highest order.[16] This is what Daniel's visions showed the ancient pagan empires and emperors to be guilty of, and the beast represents an escalation of the same violation against the true God of heaven. His disrespect is shown also against God's "dwelling" (σκηνή), meaning the center of God's activity in heaven, his divine throne room and heavenly "tabernacle" or temple (see comments at 8:3 about God's throne and the use of σκηνή for the locus of worship in the OT where God lived among his people; cf. Exod 29:42–43; 40:34–35).

Slandering this seems to represent a defamation of God's rule over his world. The final phrase of v. 6 adds a further explanation of this "dwelling,"[17] by focusing on an additional dimension of God's "place" in heaven, the beings (angels and deceased humans) "who dwell in heaven" with him (cf. Rev 7:15; 12:12; 21:3).

In the first-century world of John's readers, Roman emperors represented one expression of the pattern that Daniel had set out: they were arrogant rulers of powerful empires who accepted adulation, and in some locales (e.g., Asia Minor) they were honored with temples and shrines that accorded them divine status. At an earlier period (AD 38–41) under Caligula, the Roman governor had permitted mobs to set up images of the emperor in Jewish synagogues in Alexandria (Philo, *Flaccus* 41–43; *Embassy*, 134–38), and Caligula ordered a statue of himself to be erected in the temple in Jerusalem (Philo, *Embassy* 200–3, 265, 337). While delaying tactics by the local governor obstructed this order and the emperor's assassination at Rome ended the threat, Jews and Christians across the Roman world would have been put on notice about what could happen.

13:7–8 And it was given to him to wage war against the saints and to overcome them, and authority was given to him over every tribe and people and language and nation. 8 And all those who live on the earth will worship him, whose names are not written in the book of life of the Lamb who was slain before the foundation of the world (καὶ ἐδόθη αὐτῷ ποιῆσαι πόλεμον μετὰ τῶν ἁγίων καὶ νικῆσαι αὐτούς, καὶ ἐδόθη αὐτῷ ἐξουσία ἐπὶ πᾶσαν φυλὴν καὶ λαὸν καὶ γλῶσσαν καὶ ἔθνος.

---

13. See especially the divine role in things that are said to have a similar time limit as the "forty-two months" of v. 5b (11:2–3; 12:6, 14).

14. BDAG 841.

15. See comment on "name" at 2:3.

16. Cf. βλασφημία in BDAG 178; and LN §33.400.

17. The phrase "those who dwell in heaven" is in grammatical apposition to "God's dwelling." Appositives are not always referential equivalents to their head terms; they may clarify the head noun by referring to a part of what it consists of.

8 καὶ προσκυνήσουσιν αὐτὸν πάντες οἱ κατοικοῦντες ἐπὶ τῆς γῆς, οὗ οὐ γέγραπται τὸ ὄνομα αὐτοῦ ἐν τῷ βιβλίῳ τῆς ζωῆς τοῦ ἀρνίου τοῦ ἐσφαγμένου ἀπὸ καταβολῆς κόσμου). The influence of Daniel 7 continues to show up in John's description of what God will allow the beast from the sea to accomplish in those future days (vv. 7–8). He will be permitted to make "war against the saints" (cf. Rev 12:7) and defeat them (v. 7a; cf. Dan 7:21, 25). He will be allowed to exercise military and political power (i.e., his "authority"; cf. vv. 2, 5) over "every tribe and people and language and nation" (v. 7b),[18] just as Daniel's fourth kingdom is said to devour, trample, and crush all the earth (Dan 7:23). And he will elicit widespread religious devotion alongside this military and political authority, according to v. 8. This "worship" of the beast is explained in more detail in vv. 11–18 when the work of the second beast is presented. Here John simply declares,[19] "All those who live on the earth will worship him" (v. 8a).[20] Whether this will be sincere devotion or a calculating submission to one whose rule cannot be resisted can be seen more clearly in vv. 12–17 (probably a mixture of both). Verse 8b reinforces the negative cast John ascribes to the ones he calls "all those who live on the earth," but it also suggests a notable exception to the "all" he used in that previous phrase.[21] Those earth-dwellers who will worship the beast are the ones whose names are *not* written in the Lamb's book of life (cf. 17:8), implying another group who will not show such

devotion to the beast because of God's sovereign and eternal claim on them.[22] The phrase "foundation of the world" (v. 8c) refers to the start of the created universe (cf. Luke 11:50; Heb 4:3; 9:26) and is used several times in the New Testament to describe the prior extent of God's electing love for a person. Here it reveals the divine commitment to Christ's atoning sacrifice that began in eternity past (cf. Matt 25:34; John 17:24; Eph 1:4; 1 Pet 1:20). The destiny of the people whose names *are* written in the Lamb's book will be recounted in 21:27 (the new Jerusalem). A stark division of humanity will surface in the cataclysmic final days of the tribulation, and this prompts the words of warning that follow in vv. 9–10.

13:9–10 If anyone has an ear, let him hear. 10 If anyone is destined for captivity, to captivity he goes. If anyone is to be killed with the sword, he is to be killed with the sword. Here is the endurance and faith of the saints (Εἴ τις ἔχει οὖς ἀκουσάτω. 10 εἴ τις εἰς αἰχμαλωσίαν, εἰς αἰχμαλωσίαν ὑπάγει· εἴ τις ἐν μαχαίρῃ ἀποκτανθῆναι, αὐτὸν ἐν μαχαίρῃ ἀποκτανθῆναι. Ὧδέ ἐστιν ἡ ὑπομονὴ καὶ ἡ πίστις τῶν ἁγίων). The sobering predictions (vv. 7–8) of the beast's attacks on God's people and the division in humanity that he will bring should provoke an active response by those who are receptive to them. Enduring loyalty to God and to the Lamb must be the pathway for Christians despite the cost (vv. 9–10). These verses give John's hortatory aside between the vision accounts about the two beasts

---

18. See comments on 5:9 on this series of words and its occurrence in Rev.

19. John shifts from past (aorist) tense verbs in vv. 1–7 (narrating his vision) to the future "will worship" (declaring what will occur in the end times). See Mussies, *Morphology*, 334–36, 340; also notes on 4:5; 9:6, 10–11.

20. See comments at 3:10; 8:13; and 11:10 for the negative connotation of the commonly occurring phrase "those who live on the earth" (the earth's general population who resist God and will suffer his judgment).

21. Descriptions of "all" or "every" must be understood in their context of usage and do not invariably mean "without exception." Here "all" means the large group of earth dwellers viewed as a corporate whole, but not "every single person" among that group. See J. William Johnston, *The Use of Πᾶς in the New Testament*, SBG 11 (New York: Peter Lang, 2004), 75–79, 93.

22. See comments on the theology of such a "book of life" at 3:5. See also 17:8; 20:12, 15; 21:27; cf. Dan 12:1.

(vv. 1–8 and vv. 11–18) and are reminiscent of Christ's exhortations through John to the churches (chs. 2–3). The warning "if anyone has an ear, let him hear" (v. 9) is virtually identical to the command repeated at the end of each of those messages (e.g., 2:7). So in the face of the evil that will inexorably come just prior to God's ultimate victory, one cannot blithely expect to be exempted from suffering. In his sovereign plan God will permit the beast to exert savage control over the ungodly in the world (vv. 7b–8), and so "if anyone is destined for [such] captivity"[23] to the beast's overwhelming and autocratic power, there will be no escape (v. 10b). Likewise, as John has shown earlier (v. 7a), God will permit the beast to persecute even God's people severely for a time, and so if a Christian is faced with execution[24] for his allegiance to Christ (v. 10c–d), so be it—it is only an earthly and temporary setback prior to God's ultimate victory (v. 10d). What this should call forth[25] on the part of God's people, however, is persevering conviction, "the endurance and faith of the saints" (v. 10e).[26] Christ's messages to the churches were filled with commendations and exhortations for steadfast faith (2:2–3, 13, 19; 3:10; also 1:9),[27] and such will be called for in the following chapters as well (14:12; 17:14). The circumstances John is about to portray will certainly require faithfulness to Christ

even to death, and such allegiance will be worth it when his victory is finally won (20:4).

13:11–12 And I saw another beast coming up from the earth, and he had two horns like a lamb, and he was speaking like a dragon. 12 And he exerts all the authority of the first beast before him, and he causes the earth and those who live in it to worship the first beast whose mortal wound was healed (Καὶ εἶδον ἄλλο θηρίον ἀναβαῖνον ἐκ τῆς γῆς, καὶ εἶχεν κέρατα δύο ὅμοια ἀρνίῳ καὶ ἐλάλει ὡς δράκων. 12 καὶ τὴν ἐξουσίαν τοῦ πρώτου θηρίου πᾶσαν ποιεῖ ἐνώπιον αὐτοῦ, καὶ ποιεῖ τὴν γῆν καὶ τοὺς ἐν αὐτῇ κατοικοῦντας ἵνα προσκυνήσουσιν τὸ θηρίον τὸ πρῶτον, οὗ ἐθεραπεύθη ἡ πληγὴ τοῦ θανάτου αὐτοῦ). As a complement to John's vision of the beast coming up out of the sea (13:1–10), he now records what he "saw" (εἶδον; cf. v. 1) of "another beast," this one "coming up from the earth" (v. 11a). This portrayal seems to be John's adaptation of Daniel 7 also, where Daniel 7:17 interprets all four of Daniel's beasts that came up from the sea (v. 3) as four kings arising "from the earth." Although John makes this distinction between the two (one from the sea, one from the earth), it serves no further purpose for him, since he never again refers to this figure as coming from the "earth" or even as a "beast" (θηρίον; this term is reserved

---

23. The noun "captivity" (αἰχμαλωσία) has biblical associations with being a prisoner of war or taken into exile after a foreign invasion (Deut 28:41; 2 Kgs 24:14; Ezra 2:1; Jer 15:2; Dan 11:33; Zech 14:2). The note of foreordination in v. 10a comes from the use of the preposition "for" (εἰς) to show the intended end or goal with an implied verb "to be," as in Jer 15:2; 43:11; cf. also Rev 22:2.

24. A number of manuscripts formulate v. 10a–d to speak in various ways of one who perpetrates evil rather than suffers evil (captivity or the sword) and say that the perpetrator himself will be punished in kind (cf. KJV, NKJV). But the text given above (followed by most recent English versions) best explains the rise of the other readings and is found in the most reliable manuscript (A).

25. The expression "here is . . ." is used in varying forms in

13:18; 14:12; 17:9 to imply as here, "this calls for . . ." or "what is needed in this situation is . . ." (see BDAG 1101). This final phrase uses asyndeton (i.e., it has no introductory conjunction like "and" or "so"; see note at 9:11) because the deictic sense of "here" in pointing to what has just been said obviates the need for a connective. Mathewson, *Handbook*, 176, understands the adverb "here" (ὧδε) to be used "substantivally as the subject of ἐστιν . . . like a demonstrative pronoun"). This is to mistake a possible English gloss (e.g., BDAG 1101, "this calls for endurance") as a guide to Greek syntax. The word is still an adverb in Greek, and "endurance" is the subject of the verb.

26. This is a subjective-genitive phrase: the saints must believe and endure.

27. See also the examples of faithfulness even to death in 6:9; 11:7; 12:11; 20:4.

henceforth for the first beast alone). In the rest of this chapter John uses pronoun reference only (separate pronouns or third-singular verbal suffixes) to cite this second beast, and all the references to him in later chapters call him "the false prophet" (Rev 16:13; 19:20; 20:10). The description of this beast in v. 11b has some connection to the animal imagery of Daniel 7, but again John alters it significantly. The paradoxical mix of weakness ("like a lamb," v. 11b) and savagery ("like a dragon," v. 11c) masterfully captures the deceptive but demanding—and ultimately deadly—influence he assumes in his mission of compelling the whole world to worship the first beast. Taken together, the description of this beast "from the earth" and his association with the dragon and the first beast throughout as the third member of this infernal trinity shows that he takes the role of a personal aide to the first beast, who acts to deceive humans into worshiping and serving him.[28]

It is appropriate that he is said to "speak like a dragon" (v. 11c), since as v. 12a reveals, the authority of the dragon that was delegated to the first beast (v. 2; cf. vv. 5, 7) is entrusted in turn to the second beast who "exerts"[29] all of the authority of the first beast" under his watchful eye ("before him"). A great measure of his diabolical "authority" will consist of ability to perform miracles (cf. vv. 13, 15) in support of his primary role in this partnership, which is to cause[30] worldwide adulation and submission to the first beast (v. 12b–c; cf. vv. 4, 8, 15). John reminds us that a great influence toward such worship is the beast's apparent recovery from the deadly wound that he had received (v. 12c; cf. vv. 3, 14).

13:13–14 And he performs great signs, even to cause fire to come down from heaven to earth for anyone to see, 14 and he deceives those who live on the earth because of the signs that he was permitted to perform in the beast's presence, telling those who live on the earth to make an image for the beast who has the wound of the sword but came to life (καὶ ποιεῖ σημεῖα μεγάλα, ἵνα καὶ πῦρ ποιῇ ἐκ τοῦ οὐρανοῦ καταβαίνειν εἰς τὴν γῆν ἐνώπιον τῶν ἀνθρώπων, 14 καὶ πλανᾷ τοὺς κατοικοῦντας ἐπὶ τῆς γῆς διὰ τὰ σημεῖα ἃ ἐδόθη αὐτῷ ποιῆσαι ἐνώπιον τοῦ θηρίου, λέγων τοῖς κατοικοῦσιν ἐπὶ τῆς γῆς ποιῆσαι εἰκόνα τῷ θηρίῳ, ὃς ἔχει τὴν πληγὴν τῆς μαχαίρης καὶ ἔζησεν). Continuing his description of how the second beast promotes worldwide worship of the first beast (v. 12), John records the supernatural power God permits him to exercise and his deceptive and even idolatrous intent in this effort (vv. 13–14).[31] God allows him to perform miraculous deeds[32] as "signs" of the otherworldly power and invincibility of the beast (cf. v. 4). Biblical writers warn against deceptive "signs and wonders" (Deut 13:1–3), especially in the last days when they are expected to intensify (Matt 24:24; Mark 13:22; 2 Thess 2:9). Even calling down "fire . . . from heaven" (v. 13b),[33] a notable

28. Irenaeus, *Haer.* 5.28.2 calls him the first beast's "armor-bearer." F. F. Bruce, "Revelation," in *The International Bible Commentary*, ed. F. F. Bruce, H. L. Ellison, and G. C. D. Howley (London: Pickering, 1986), 1616, calls him the first beast's "Minister of Propaganda."

29. A shift occurs here from description of what John saw as a past narrative (imperfects in v. 11b–c) to description in a report mode using a series of presents in vv. 12–14, 16. See notes at 4:5; 9:6, 10–11 on John's use of tenses in different modes of presentation.

30. See vv. 16–17 as well as 3:9; John 11:37; Col 4:16 for this specialized use of ποιέω plus a ἵνα-clause. See BDAG 840.

31. This report of what John saw in his vision does not follow his more typical narrative style (past-tense verbs recounting a series of events in temporal sequence) but uses present-tense verbs in a spatial progression from one facet of the scene to another (see note on v. 12a).

32. The phrase "he was permitted" (v. 14b) is a translation of ἐδόθη αὐτῷ ("it was given to him"), implying God as the agent. See comments at v. 5 and the verses cited there.

33. The phrase in v. 13b "for anyone to see" is phrased in Greek as "before human beings" (ἐνώπιον τῶν ἀνθρώπων), using a Greek generic article (cf. 14:4; 21:3). So the sense is "in public, as an open display."

sign of the true God and his prophet in Elijah's day (1 Kgs 18:38–39; 2 Kgs 1:10–14; cf. Luke 9:54; Rev 20:9), can be, as here, a misleading sign. This uncertainty about such miracles follows the pattern seen in the exodus, where Moses and Aaron were given "signs" to perform to authenticate their divine calling (Exod 4:9, 17, 30–31), but Pharaoh's magicians were able to counter with their own wondrous deeds (Exod 7:9–12). The early Christians often encountered false prophets and popular teachers who used magic arts to attract a following (Acts 8:9–11; 13:6–10; 16:16–18; 19:13–19). The second beast will exploit to the full this potential of the miraculous to mislead gullible humanity (v. 14a): "he deceives" (cf. 12:9; 19:20) the mass of humanity, who are hostile to God anyway.[34] God will allow him to perform miracles "in the beast's presence" (v. 14b), apparently referring to demonstrations of power with the beast himself on hand, as a way of convincing people of his power and authority.

In addition, this is an opportunity for demanding that the crowds "make an image for the beast" to stimulate greater allegiance (v. 14c–d). The beast's presence apparently would provoke more severe consequences for noncompliance too, as vv. 15–17 will show. Such an idolatrous statue of the beast suggests parallels with Daniel 3:1–7, the story of Nebuchadnezzar's towering golden image to which all were required to bow down (cf. v. 15 below). John inserts again (v. 14e) the extraordinary feature of the beast (mentioned in vv. 3, 12) that would certainly make the crowd more likely to comply: he "has the wound of a sword but came to life."[35] This seems to indicate that even after his recovery from

a fatal wound, the beast continues to bear obvious marks of that horrible blow.

13:15 And he was permitted to give breath to the beast's image, so that the beast's image might even speak, and he might cause all who would not worship the beast's image to be killed (καὶ ἐδόθη αὐτῷ δοῦναι πνεῦμα τῇ εἰκόνι τοῦ θηρίου, ἵνα καὶ λαλήσῃ ἡ εἰκὼν τοῦ θηρίου καὶ ποιήσῃ [ἵνα] ὅσοι ἐὰν μὴ προσκυνήσωσιν τῇ εἰκόνι τοῦ θηρίου ἀποκτανθῶσιν). Another deceptive—and destructive—miracle that God permits the second beast to perform is to animate the first beast's image so that it can pronounce a demand for worship on penalty of death. This is an intensification of the pattern of Nebuchadnezzar's statue of gold in Daniel 3; there the statue remains lifeless and mute, while the king's herald shouts the royal command to bow down or face death (Dan 3:4–6). Here the statue itself is given "breath"[36] to pronounce the demand for all to worship the beast (v. 15b). In the Greco-Roman world, people commonly understood images of the gods to be inhabited by the deities themselves rather than as simply inanimate statues, and sometimes it was claimed that they pronounced oracles.[37] So here the beast's ability to "speak" is focused on the proclamation that "all who would not worship" would suffer execution (v. 15c).

13:16–17 And he causes all, the small and the great, and the rich and the poor, and the free and the slaves, to be given a mark on their right hands or on their foreheads 17 so that no one is able to buy or sell except the one who has the mark, that is, the name of the beast or the number of

---

34. See note at v. 8a on "those who live on the earth."

35. The verb "has" (v. 14e) continues the use of present tense in Greek as in the other series of descriptions in vv. 12–14, 16. The shift to an ingressive aorist for "came to life" is the typical use of a past tense to provide background within report mode. See Fanning, "Greek Tenses," 340–41, 343.

36. The image is given "breath" (ESV, NASB, NIV; πνεῦμα, i.e., "spirit") in order to be able to speak, not "life" (KJV, NET, NLT) in the sense that it moves about and so on.

37. Cf. Lucian, *Syr. d.* 10; *Philops.* 33; Plutarch, *Cor.* 37.3; also Aune, *Revelation 6–16*, 762–64; Koester, *Revelation*, 593–94.

his name (καὶ ποιεῖ πάντας, τοὺς μικροὺς καὶ τοὺς μεγάλους, καὶ τοὺς πλουσίους καὶ τοὺς πτωχούς, καὶ τοὺς ἐλευθέρους καὶ τοὺς δούλους, ἵνα δῶσιν αὐτοῖς χάραγμα ἐπὶ τῆς χειρὸς αὐτῶν τῆς δεξιᾶς ἢ ἐπὶ τὸ μέτωπον αὐτῶν 17 καὶ ἵνα μή τις δύνηται ἀγοράσαι ἢ πωλῆσαι εἰ μὴ ὁ ἔχων τὸ χάραγμα, τὸ ὄνομα τοῦ θηρίου ἢ τὸν ἀριθμὸν τοῦ ὀνόματος αὐτοῦ). A more insidious exercise of the authority of the first beast and of Satan himself (vv. 2, 4, 12) is the "mark" that the second beast is able to compel people to accept before they can engage in the commercial life of their communities. No one is exempt from this requirement, as John emphasizes with the word "all" in v. 16a (also "no one" in v. 17a) and his recitation of all parts of society that must comply, privileged or unprivileged, without exception.[38] They are all forced to accept[39] a "mark" or identifying sign (perhaps on the pattern of the first-century branding of slaves or animals)[40] that certifies their loyalty to the beast. This mark of the beast is mentioned five additional times in Revelation and is always cited together with "worship" of him on the part of those who receive the mark (14:9, 11; 16:2; 19:20; 20:4). This sinister "mark" contrasts with the divine "seal" that the one hundred and forty-four thousand receive on their "foreheads" as a sign of God's protection (7:2–3; 9:4; 14:1; cf. Ezek 9:1–11). Its location on the hand or forehead may simply reflect the most obvious places for an identifying mark, but it could parody the reminders of God's faithfulness or of his law worn by Israelites "on the hand" or "between the eyes" (Exod 13:9, 16; Deut 6:8; 11:18).

The universal enforcement of this requirement is through a ban on commerce ("not able to buy or sell") for any person who does not have such a mark (v. 17). The later portrayal (cf. Rev 18:3, 11–19) of the economic dominance of "Babylon" in worldwide trade and commerce shows how the beast and his system could impose and enforce such a ban. The messages to the seven churches also allude to the pattern of ancient trade guilds infused with Roman imperial loyalties that could easily shut out religious nonconformists from their area of commercial life.[41] John describes such a system in the coming days, but one intensified so much that it cuts off all the necessities of life from anyone who resists. In the world of John's first-century readers, just as the emperor fleshed out in some measure the pattern of the first beast (cf. comments on v. 6), so the economic, civic, and religious influences of emperor worship in Asia Minor would have foreshadowed the pattern of this "beast from the earth."[42]

The "mark" that everyone must have is described further by the phrase, "the name of the beast or the number of his name" (v. 17c; see later verses that mention one or the other: 14:11; 15:2). This suggests that the mark would be the beast's name in either of two forms: (1) written in normal form or abbreviated; or (2) expressed in a numerical representation based on the quantitative value of its constituent letters. In Hebrew and Greek, the standard letters of the alphabet could be used also as numerals (e.g., A = 1, B = 2, etc.). The "number" of a word or name would be the sum of the values of its individual letters (cf. v. 18).[43]

---

38. See comments at 6:15 on the background of phrases like "the small and the great and the rich and the poor and the free and the slaves" (cf. also 11:18; 19:5, 18; 20:12).

39. The verb phrase "to be given" is an impersonal "they" used as a passive ("that they may give to them"; δῶσιν αὐτοῖς); see note at 10:11; 12:6.

40. See 3 Macc 2:29 describing Jews in third-century-BC Alexandria forcibly branded with a symbol of Dionysus (using χαράσσω, the verb related to the noun "mark," χάραγμα, that occurs here).

41. For various ancient parallels of such marking that may have come to mind for the first readers of Rev, see Edwin A. Judge, "The Mark of the Beast, Revelation 13:16," *TynBul* 42 (1991): 158–60.

42. Koester, *Revelation*, 589–90, 599–604.

43. Examples of this from the ancient world are given in

13:18 Here is wisdom. Let the one who has understanding calculate the number of the beast, for it is the number of a person and his number is six hundred and sixty-six (Ὧδε ἡ σοφία ἐστίν. ὁ ἔχων νοῦν ψηφισάτω τὸν ἀριθμὸν τοῦ θηρίου, ἀριθμὸς γὰρ ἀνθρώπου ἐστίν, καὶ ὁ ἀριθμὸς αὐτοῦ ἑξακόσιοι ἑξήκοντα ἕξ). Mention of the "number of his name" (v. 17c) prompts another hortatory aside from John, similar to v. 10: "here is wisdom," meaning that such a numerical representation of the name requires careful thought and skill.[44] The need for "wisdom" (σοφία) and "understanding" (νοῦς; translated as "mind" in 17:9) in sorting out the meaning of apocalyptic visions goes back to Daniel 11:33; 12:10 (see also Matt 24:15; Mark 13:14; cf. 2 Bar 28:1; 4 Ezra 12:37–38; 14:13–18).[45] Wisdom is needed to "calculate,"[46] or count up the beast's "number" (v. 18b), that is, the number associated with his name (v. 17c). It is a number puzzle that must be decoded carefully before its meaning will be grasped. In this context, what is called for is the practice of numerology or

gematria, unpacking the number of the beast's name by identifying and adding up the values of its constituent letters. This sense for the "calculation" that is needed comes out also in the explanatory clause, "for it is the number of a person" (NRSV; v. 18c). The word translated "a person" denotes here a human individual, referred to indefinitely,[47] to whom the "number" belongs (cf. NEB, "it represents a man's name"). The final clause gives the key to the puzzle, the sum that represents the beast's name: "His number is six hundred and sixty-six" (v. 18d). This number is spelled out in Greek words (ἑξακόσιοι ἑξήκοντα ἕξ) in a few manuscripts (A; also ℵ, 025, 1854 with minor spelling variation), but others express the number using Greek letters followed by a keraia or acute accent (χξϛ´) or written with a line above them to show their numerical use (𝔓⁴⁷, 046, 051, 1611, 2329, and most Byzantine minuscules).[48]

Calculating or discerning a person's name numerically can involve decoding something that is otherwise hidden (or at least partly veiled; e.g., the

---

Adolf Deissmann, *Light from the Ancient East*, trans. Lionel R. M. Strachan (London: Hodder & Stoughton, 1910), 276–78. He cites two graffiti from Pompeii: "The number of her honorable name is 45 (or 1035)," and "I love her whose number is 545" (p. 277). See *Sib. Or.* 5.12–51; 12.39–271 for an extensive set of other examples (Roman emperors designated by their initials in numeral form).

44. See note on "here is . . ." at v. 10.

45. Some argue that this "wise understanding" does not pertain to "solving a math problem" or decoding the referent of a symbol but is ethical only: godly people will reflect on these things and choose to live in faithfulness and obedience. See Beale and McDonough, "Revelation," 1130; Rowland, "Revelation," 659. Their motive for this argument is a worthy one, to delegitimize confused attempts to identify contemporary referents of apocalyptic symbols—a practice that over the centuries has proven to be consistently wrong and embarrassing to biblical interpretation. But it is a false dichotomy to argue that such understanding is either ethical or referential. Both are true: those who live in the final days spoken of here must see the real character of the figures who influence their world, in order to resist their deceptions and endure faithfully as Christians (v. 9–10; Matt 24:14–19).

46. The word "calculate" (ψηφίζω) denotes a numerical reckoning (cf. Luke 14:28; also the compound συμψηφίζω in Acts 19:19) to understand the meaning of the name (BDAG 1098; LSJ 2022; G. Braumann, "ψηφίζω," *TDNT* 9:607). The more general sense of "interpret, figure out" (cf. BDAG 1098) is unattested elsewhere.

47. See this indefinite sense of ἄνθρωπος (singular anarthrous) meaning "a person, someone, an individual (human)" in several passages (e.g., John 3:4, 27; 5:7; 7:46; 11:50; 16:21; others in BDAG 81). Some emphasize here a qualitative sense of "human" as sinful, fallen, finite (Rowland, "Revelation," 659; cf. RSV, "it is a human number"). This is unsatisfactory on two counts: (1) attributive or qualitative genitives usually refer to an abstract entity (e.g., glory, sin, flesh); this genitive is best taken as possessive; (2) an article is needed for ἄνθρωπος to mean "humankind"; see Matt 4:4; John 2:25.

48. A few manuscripts give the number as "six hundred sixteen" or "616" (𝔓¹¹⁵, C), and Irenaeus is aware of this reading but regards it as an intentional change (*Haer.* 5.30.1). This variant has weak manuscript support and was likely motivated by interpretive considerations. But the number 616 can yield the same identification with Nero mentioned in the paragraphs above, since the Latin word "Nero" (without the final consonant

emperors' initials cited in *Sib. Or.* 5.12–51; 12.39–271), or it can involve reflection on the deeper significance of a name by numerical wordplay or riddle (e.g., the name "Rome" converted to numbers to show the years that will elapse before its downfall comes in *Sib. Or.* 8.145–50).[49] An example of the latter usage comes from Suetonius, *Nero*, 39, where a popular insult against the emperor is recorded: "Count the numerical values of the letters in Nero's name, and in 'murdered his own mother': you will find their sum is the same."[50] This is likely to be the significance of John's invitation to "calculate the number of the beast, for it is the number of a person" (v. 18b–c). If the letters for the Greek words "beast" (θηρίον) and "Nero Caesar" (Νέρων Καῖσαρ) are transliterated into *Hebrew* letters and then calculated numerically, they add up to 666, thus showing his true character.[51] Taking the number 666 as a reference to Nero in some way is widely accepted among recent commentaries,[52] but others prefer an alternative such as sixes as symbolic for more general human incompleteness or evil in contrast with sevens representing completeness

or 888 as the numerical value of the name "Jesus" in Greek.[53]

If John intends the number 666 as a reference to Nero (and this is the most likely interpretation of ch. 13), it would be a further example of his use of typological patterns (e.g., Balaam, 2:14–15; Jezebel, 2:20; prophets like Elijah and Moses, 11:6), in this case to foreshadow the escalated fulfillment in the future antichrist. John does not foresee Nero himself returning but one like Nero, characterized by even greater savagery and madness.[54] This use of the later perception and reputation of Nero (see introduction for dating of the book at AD 95–98, some three decades after Nero's death) exploits the Nero redivivus myth (the popular legend that Nero had not actually died in AD 68 but had escaped to Parthia and would someday return to take back his empire) without affirming it.[55] John takes up the popular dread or even desire to see Nero restored to illustrate the true character of the final "Nero," the antichrist, and to show how insecure the empire's vaunted power and stability could be. See comments on 17:11 and "In Depth: The Number of the Beast through the Centuries."

---

as in Greek), if transliterated into Hebrew, has the value of 616. Also, the Greek word "beast" in the genitive form as in v. 18b (θηρίου) equals 616 in Hebrew letters. See Bauckham, *Climax*, 387, 390. P. J. Williams, "P[115] and the Number of the Beast," *TynBul* 58 (2007): 151–53, reviews the same information and adds the point that the reading 616 found in 𝔓[115] may be used to imitate the divine name "Jesus," because the line over the letters to indicate their use as numerals is used also to abbreviate the divine name "Christ Jesus" (*nomina sacra*). The scribe may preserve or produce this mimicry of the divine name by the way he writes the numeral 616.

49. Bauckham, *Climax*, 385–86; Koester, *Revelation*, 597–98.

50. Suetonius, *The Twelve Caesars*, trans. Robert Graves, rev. Michael Grant (Harmondsworth: Penguin, 1979), 236.

51. Some object that transliterating into Hebrew letters would make no sense to John's readers in Hellenistic Asia Minor (e.g., Beale, *Revelation*, 718–21; Thomas, *Revelation 8–22*, 184–85), but some of them would certainly know Hebrew, and other examples of this practice from ancient inscriptions

and literature can be cited (Bauckham, *Climax*, 389; Koester, *Revelation*, 597).

52. E.g., Aune, *Revelation 6–16*, 770–73; Bauckham, *Climax*, 384–90; Beckwith, *Apocalypse*, 403–6; Charles, *Revelation*, 1:367–68; Koester, *Revelation*, 596–99; Osborne, *Revelation*, 520–21 (hesitantly). See also Francis X. Gumerlock, "Nero Antichrist: Patristic Evidence for the Use of Nero's Naming in Calculating the Number of the Beast (Rev 13:18)," *WTJ* 68 (2006): 347–60, for answers to the charge that no patristic writers understood Nero to be in view in 13:18.

53. Beale, *Revelation*, 721–28; Ladd, *Revelation*, 186–87; Smalley, *Revelation*, 352–53.

54. J. Daniel Hays, J. Scott Duvall, and C. Marvin Pate, "Nero Redivivus," in *Dictionary of Biblical Prophecy and End Times* (Grand Rapids: Zondervan, 2007), 303; Koester, *Revelation*, 570–71; Osborne, *Revelation*, 521.

55. For details about this Nero legend, see Bauckham, *Climax*, 407–23; Edward Champlin, *Nero* (Cambridge, MA: Belknap/Harvard, 2003), 1–35; and Friesen, *Imperial Cults*, 136–37.

IN DEPTH: The Number of the Beast through the Centuries

In the course of his discussion of the coming antichrist and varied interpretations of the "number of his name" in Revelation 13:17–18, Irenaeus warns his readers against futile speculation about who this antichrist might be. Many had been deceived even in his day by confident identifications of specific figures that had proved erroneous. His counsel is that Christians should simply wait for the actual fulfillment, at which time the antichrist's identity would be abundantly clear from the surrounding circumstances and his characteristic actions. This, Irenaeus says, is "more certain and less hazardous" to Christian credibility.[56] We could wish that numerous interpreters over the centuries had heeded this advice instead of confidently but erroneously naming one prominent figure in current history after another as the antichrist. The list is a long and embarrassing one: from Saladin in the twelfth century to the Ottoman Turks in the sixteenth and then the current pope through much of the Reformation and post-Reformation eras. In modern times the names include Napoleon, Stalin, Franco, Mussolini, Hitler, Sadat, Kissinger, Gorbachev, Saddam Hussein, or the latest US president (whoever he may be).[57] Preachers, blog posters, and popular writers about prophecy would better serve the cause of Christ by refusing to join this ignominious train of error, even if it means attracting a smaller crowd, less traffic to their sites, and lower book sales. The same counsel applies to speculation about how the latest technology could be precisely how the beast's "mark" and its ban on commerce will be accomplished.

Theology in Application

Two of the most important applications from this chapter come from the places where John pauses to reflect on his vision and highlight the need for mature Christian virtues to shine forth in response to what has been seen (vv. 10, 18).

---

56. Irenaeus, *Haer.* 5.30.1–3.

57. See the extensive list in the index of Paul Boyer, *When Time Shall Be No More: Prophecy Belief in Modern American Culture* (Cambridge, MA: Belknap/Harvard, 1992), 451–52; also Koester, *Revelation*, 534–38; and Bernard McGinn, *Antichrist: Two Thousand Years of the Human Fascination with Evil* (New York: HarperSanFrancisco, 1994), whose entire book surveys different identifications of the antichrist over the centuries. See pp. 250–80 for developments during the last century.

The Need for Endurance and Faith

John's vision of the fierce and blasphemous "beast from the sea" (vv. 1–10) provides plenty of reason for Christian endurance and faith to shine forth. These verses portray severe satanic opposition against God's people in the days of final tribulation in the future, but they mirror the struggle of the faithful with the evil powers of Satan's fallen world through the ages. Even at a lower level of intensity, Christians must struggle mightily against the authority exerted in this world through the devil's lackeys in our day. They on the one hand seem to experience impressive success to the amazement of all (vv. 3–4), while God's people for their part suffer defeat (v. 7)—What could be worse for American Christians than to *lose*! And that loss could be of an unimaginable kind: to be subject to imprisonment or even death at the hands of those who oppose the gospel and our God (v. 10). When faced with such opposition or things that even approach it, we will certainly need a strong and courageous faith and an enduring resolve to remain faithful to Christ no matter what. Such faith and endurance can only come through practice and consistent progress to maturity. Like David who first experienced God's faithfulness when he faced the lion and the bear and then was ready to stand firm against Goliath (1 Sam 17:37), so we are called to grow in persevering faith.

The Need for Discerning Wisdom

The other godly virtues John calls for in this chapter are wisdom and understanding (v. 18). Such discernment is needed not only to decipher the number of the beast from the sea but to grasp his true character amid all that John's vision has revealed about his role in the world. He is Satan's savage point man, assisted by the beast from the earth in attacking humans both by frontal assault and by deceptive enticement to false worship. Satan and his agents have always used duplicity and coercion to subvert God's work and hoodwink God's people. Some of his tricks on display here are wiles that Christians at all times need to be on guard against. We must not assume that outward power and success are signs of what is good and right or that the majority must be right. We cannot blithely follow the dominant cultural influences and ideologies of our day no matter who vouches for them. We need to examine even seemingly miraculous events with godly wisdom and spiritual discernment. Even in the religious sphere large crowds and adoring followers are not always signs of a godly, doctrinally sound ministry. We should be prepared if necessary to resist the power of the crowd, the tyranny of the majority. When faced with direct coercion, we must discern the most winsome strategy possible, being "as wise as serpents and innocent as doves" (Matt 10:16). Perhaps a gentle appeal will work better than belligerence. Even if gentleness and patience fail, faithful witness for Christ should be the goal rather than cowardly evasion or angry retaliation.

Revelation 14:1–20

Literary Context

This final part of the interlude of chapters 12–14 contrasts sharply with the previous two chapters. The picture of satanic warfare against Israel and the world at large in chapters 12–13 now opens into visions of victory for the Lamb and corresponding judgment of God's enemies in chapter 14. Vivid images of judgment in the latter part of the chapter anticipate the outpouring of God's wrath in the seven last plagues of chapters 15–16 and even look ahead briefly to the fall of Babylon (14:8) that is the topic of chapters 17–18.

Main Idea

Visions of victory for the Lamb and contrasting judgment against the ungodly world call for fear of God on the part of unbelievers and faithful endurance on the part of believers.

Translation

Revelation 14:1–20

1a	Action/Vision Introduction	**And I looked,**
b	Character Entrance	**and behold, the Lamb standing on Mount Zion and with him a hundred and forty-four thousand**
c	Description	having his name and his father's name written on their foreheads.
2a	Action	**And I heard a voice** **from heaven** **like the sound of many waters and** **like the sound of loud thunder,**
b	Expansion of 2a	and **the voice that I heard was like kithara players playing on their kitharas.**
3a	Expansion of 2b	And **it was as though they sang a new song before the throne and** before **the four living creatures and the elders,**
b	Expansion of 3a	and **no one was able to learn the song**
c	Exception	except the one hundred and forty-four thousand who were redeemed from the earth.
4a	Identification 1	**These are the ones who were not defiled with women,**
b	Explanation	for **they are virgins.**
c	Identification 2	**These follow the Lamb wherever he goes.**
d	Identification 3	**These were redeemed from among humans as firstfruits to God and to the Lamb,**
5a		and **in their mouths no lie was found;** (Isa 53:9; Zeph 3:13)
b		**they are blameless.**
6a	Vision Intro/ Character Entrance 1	**And I saw another angel** flying high in the sky,
b	Description	having an eternal gospel
c	Purpose/ Recipients	to proclaim to the inhabitants of the earth, that is, to every nation and tribe and language and people,

7a	Description	saying with a loud voice,
b	Commands	"Fear God and give him glory,
c	Reason	because the hour of his judgment has come,
d		and worship the one who made the heaven and
		the earth and
		the sea and
		the springs of waters."

8a Character Entrance 2 **And another angel, a second one, followed saying,**

b Announcement *"Fallen, fallen is Babylon the great,*
c *who has made all the nations drink from the wine*
of the passion
of her sexual ☙
immorality."

9a Character Entrance 3 **And another angel, a third one, followed them saying with a loud voice,**

b Premise *"If anyone   worships the beast and his image and*
receives a mark   on his forehead or
on his hand,

10a Consequences *he also will drink from the wine of God's anger,*
b Description *which is mixed full strength in the cup of his wrath,*
c *and he will be tormented in fire and sulfur   before the holy angels and*
before the Lamb."

11a Result **And the smoke of their torment rises up forever and ever,**
b **and those who worship the beast and his image—**
as well as anyone who receives the mark of his name—
have no respite day and night.

12a Conclusion **Here is the endurance of the saints,**
b Description who keep God's commands and their faith in Jesus.

13a Action **And I heard a voice from heaven saying,**
b Command *"Write: 'Blessed are the dead who die in the Lord from now on.'"*

c Affirmation *"Yes,"* **says the Spirit,** *"that they may rest from their labors.*
d Affirmation *For their works follow them."*

14a Action/Vision **And I looked,**
Introduction
b Character Entrance 1 **and behold, a white cloud, and**
sitting on the cloud one like a son of man,
c Description having on his head a golden crown and
in his hand a sharp sickle.

Continued on next page.

Continued from previous page.

15a	Character Entrance 2	**And another angel came out from the temple,**
b	Description	crying with a loud voice to the one sitting on the cloud,
c	Command	*"Put in your sickle and reap,*
d	Reasons for 15c	*because the hour for reaping has come,*
e		*because the harvest of the earth is ripe."*
16a	Response to 15c	**And the one sitting on the cloud swung his sickle over the earth,**
b	Effect	**and the earth was reaped.**
17a	Character Entrance 3	**And another angel came out from the temple in heaven,**
b	Description	he also having a sharp sickle.
18a	Character Entrance 4	**And another angel came out from the altar,**
b	Description	the one who had authority over the fire,
c	Action	**and he called with a loud voice to the one who had the sharp sickle saying,**
d	Commands	*"Put in your sharp sickle*
e		*and gather the clusters of the earth's vineyard,*
f	Reason	*because its bunches have reached their prime."*
19a	Action/Response to 18d	**And the angel swung his sickle onto the earth,**
b	Action/Response to 18e	**and he gathered the earth's grapes,**
c	Effects	**and he put them into the great winepress of God's anger.**
20a		**And the winepress was trodden outside the city,**
b		**and blood went out from the winepress up to the horses' bridles for sixteen hundred stadia.**

Structure

The chapter clearly falls into three sections (vv. 1–5; 6–13; 14–20), with each section introduced as a separate visionary phase by the common expression "and I looked/saw" (καὶ εἶδον). The first section is a joyful scene of victory, while the second and third portray primarily judgment with brief messages of encouragement to the faithful and even to those who still need to turn in faith to the true God (14:6–7, 12–13).

Exegetical Outline

III. Second Vision: Heavenly Throne Room and Three Judgment Cycles (4:1–16:21)

A. Vision of God in His Heavenly Throne Room (4:1–11)

B. The Seven-Sealed Scroll and the Slain Lamb (5:1–14)

C. The Seven Seals and the Interlude of the Two Multitudes (6:1–8:1)

D. The Seven Trumpets and Further Interludes (8:2–14:20)

1. The First Four Trumpets (8:2–13)

2. The Fifth Trumpet—First Woe (9:1–12)

3. The Sixth Trumpet—Second Woe (9:13–21)

4. Two Revelatory Interludes: God's Prophets (10:1–11:14)

5. The Seventh Trumpet—Third Woe: Anticipating God's Rule (11:15–19)

6. Two Further Interludes: Anticipating Babylon's Fall (12:1–14:20)

a. The dragon's war against the woman (12:1–13:18)

➡ **b. Preview of judgment and victory for the Lamb (14:1–20)**

(1) Victory for the Lamb and his protected remnant from Israel (14:1–5)

(a) The Lamb and the protected remnant on Mount Zion (14:1)

(b) A new song before the heavenly throne (14:2–3)

(c) The purity of the protected remnant (14:4–5)

(2) Three angelic announcements and a beatitude (14:6–13)

(a) Good news for all the earth (14:6–7)

(b) The fall of Babylon the great (14:8)

(c) Punishment for the beast's followers (14:9–12)

(d) Blessings for the righteous dead (14:13)

(3) Two harvests of judgment (14:14–20)

(a) The Son of Man reaping the grain harvest of all the earth (14:14–16)

(b) Gathering grape clusters for the winepress of God's wrath (14:17–20)

Explanation of the Text

14:1 And I looked, and behold, the Lamb standing on Mount Zion and with him a hundred and forty-four thousand having his name and his father's name written on their foreheads (Καὶ εἶδον, καὶ ἰδοὺ τὸ ἀρνίον ἑστὸς ἐπὶ τὸ ὄρος Σιὼν καὶ μετ᾽ αὐτοῦ ἑκατὸν τεσσεράκοντα τέσσαρες χιλιάδες ἔχουσαι τὸ ὄνομα αὐτοῦ καὶ τὸ ὄνομα τοῦ πατρὸς αὐτοῦ γεγραμμένον ἐπὶ τῶν μετώπων αὐτῶν). In a chapter contrasting sharply with chapter 13, John begins with the greatest contrasts in vv. 1–5. Instead of the savage beast and those forced to bear his mark, we see the Lamb and those identified with him standing in triumph on Mount Zion and celebrated by the heavenly company in a preview of God's imminent victory. As in each of the three sections of the chapter (vv. 1–5, 6–13, 14–20), this one is introduced with John's frequent visionary formula "and I looked/saw" (καὶ εἶδον), but here he adds "and behold" (καὶ ἰδού) to emphasize the contrast with what came before (v. 1b).[1] Reference to "the Lamb standing on Mount Zion" alludes on the one hand to John's vision of the heavenly throne room in chapters 4–5, in which the Lamb "stood" (5:6) not only as the slain and resurrected Lamb but also as "the Lion of the tribe of Judah, the Shoot of David" who had "won the victory" (5:5). He had become the only one worthy to bring God's plan for judgment and redemption to its full accomplishment. On the other hand, it pictures the consummation of that victory on earth. In this case the victorious Lamb is seen standing not in heaven but on earth.[2] So the vision of 14:1–5 anticipates the scene, soon to be presented in full (19:11–20:6), when Christ will return to earth as "King of kings and Lord of lords" (19:16) to conquer the beast and his armies and establish his rule from the earthly Mount Zion in fulfillment of what God had spoken repeatedly through his prophets (10:7). The reference to Mount Zion is an allusion to Psalm 2 that describes the nations in rebellion against the Lord and his Messiah (as seen in 11:18, right before these interludes were launched). God's victory over them will come through his king established on Zion, who is granted the nations and the ends of the earth as his dominion (Ps 2:6, 8). This expectation that God will rule the earth from Jerusalem is communicated in the Old Testament sometimes in general terms (e.g., Ps 48:1–2; Isa 24:23; 31:4; cf. Jub. 1:28–29; Sib. Or. 5:414–33). But in other places more specific descriptions are given, both of God's victory over the pagan nations through his Davidic king and of the regathering of dispersed Israel to experience blessing again in the land he promised to them (Isa 11:9–12; Joel 2:30–3:3; Mic 4:1–8; Zech 12:8–12; 14:3–5; cf. 4 Ezra 13:29–50; 2 Bar. 40:1–4).[3]

John's anticipation of the regathering of Israel as a whole (not just a small remnant) is expressed in this vision, as in 7:1–8, through the appearance of the "one hundred and forty-four thousand" who stand with the Lamb on Mount Zion (v. 1b).[4] In 7:3–4 twelve thousand from "every tribe of the sons of Israel" are sealed "on their foreheads" as a mark of God's ownership and protection. Their number (12 x 12,000) is symbolic of their complete regathering as a people. Even though additional descriptions of these Israelites are given in 14:3c–5 that did not appear in 7:3–8, their total number and

---

1. See note on 4:1 for "and I looked and behold" (cf. 6:2, 5, 8; 7:9; 14:14).

2. Aune, *Revelation 6–16*, 803–4. In contrast, Smith, *Revelation*, 208–9, understands them to be standing in the heavenly Jerusalem (also Mounce, *Revelation*, 264–65), partly because they hear the "new song" sung in the heavenly throne room (v. 4). But John hears this song as a sound "from heaven" (v. 2), and presumably the 144,000 can too at that future time of victory. Boxall, *Revelation*, 200, takes the location as completely spiritual: "Not the Temple Mount or even the heavenly Mount Zion . . . but that spiritual Zion which is nowhere and everywhere. . . . [a] state of openness toward God and protection by him."

3. This is the only place in Rev where the name "Zion" (Σιών) appears. In Heb 12:22 "Mount Zion" is identified with the "heavenly Jerusalem" to which Christians have already come. But that represents only the first step of what Christ has accomplished. Rev clearly expects a fulfillment of God's redemption in stages: first, Christ's reign at God's right hand in heaven (2:28; 3:21; 5:5; 12:5); then his righteous rule from earthly Zion for a thousand years (2:26–27; 5:10; 20:4–6); and finally the eternal rule of God and the Lamb from the heavenly Jerusalem that comes down to earth as the center of a new heaven and earth (21:1–2; 22:1–5). There is no reason to postpone the fulfillment of this scene to the time of the heavenly Jerusalem's descent to earth in 21:2 (as do Koester, *Revelation*, 616–17; Ladd, *Revelation*, 189–90). It pictures Christ's victory in Rev 19–20 (so Thomas, *Revelation 8–22*, 189–93; Walvoord, Rawley, and Hitchcock, *Revelation*, 220–21), which foreshadows the new heaven and new earth that follow (see comments on 20:4).

4. See the discussion in 7:3–8 of this identification of the 144,000 as ethnic Israelites. The passage in 4 Ezra 13:29–50 cited above expresses in a distinct form a similar late first-century Jewish expectation that all the dispersed tribes of Israel will be restored to the land in the end times, gathered around the Messiah who will stand as ruler on Mount Zion.

their marking with the names of God and the Lamb "written on their foreheads" (v. 1c) make clear that this is the same group, now standing in triumph with Christ.[5]

Both passages (7:1–8 and 14:1–5) suffer in the commentaries from an unfortunate neglect of ethnic Israel in the interpretation of Revelation and a tendency to collapse Old Testament prophetic expectations about the future into a type of Christian eschatology that is either supersessionist or that effaces all ethnic differences among the redeemed. As a result, important clues for interpretation of what the text actually says in the context of its ancient background are missed or misconstrued.[6] See comments on this at 7:4; 11:1–2; 12:1–2.

14:2–3 And I heard a voice from heaven like the sound of many waters and like the sound of loud thunder, and the voice that I heard was like kithara players playing on their kitharas. 3 And it was as though they sang a new song before the throne and before the four living creatures and the elders, and no one was able to learn the song except the one hundred and forty-four thousand who were redeemed from the earth (καὶ ἤκουσα φωνὴν ἐκ τοῦ οὐρανοῦ ὡς φωνὴν ὑδάτων πολλῶν καὶ ὡς φωνὴν βροντῆς μεγάλης, καὶ ἡ φωνὴ ἣν ἤκουσα ὡς κιθαρῳδῶν κιθαριζόντων ἐν ταῖς κιθάραις αὐτῶν. 3 καὶ ᾄδουσιν [ὡς] ᾠδὴν καινὴν ἐνώπιον τοῦ θρόνου καὶ ἐνώπιον τῶν τεσσάρων ζῴων καὶ τῶν πρεσβυτέρων, καὶ οὐδεὶς ἐδύνατο μαθεῖν τὴν ᾠδὴν εἰ μὴ αἱ ἑκατὸν τεσσεράκοντα τέσσαρες χιλιάδες, οἱ ἠγορασμένοι ἀπὸ τῆς γῆς). After John witnesses the initial earthly scene of v. 1, "a voice from heaven" grabs his attention (v. 2a),[7] although the majestic sound that he hears will relate to the people who stand with the Lamb, as vv. 3b–5 indicate. The heavenly sound is impressive, loud, and beautiful at the same time, as John's comparisons attempt to express: like torrents of water, peals of thunder, and musicians[8] playing and singing a song of great celebration (v. 2a–b; cf. 1:15 and comments there on the OT background of these images; also 19:6). John's attempt to describe what he hears continues in v. 3a: "It was as though they sang a new song" (or "they sang something like a new song").[9] It is not clear whether "they" (included in the verb "they sang") refers to the 144,000 (v. 1), the kithara players (singing as well as playing), or to some

---

5. Their identification with the Lamb and with God is in clear contrast to the beast's followers who are marked on the hand or forehead with his "name or the number of his name" (13:16–17).

6. For example, Mounce, *Revelation*, 264, gives prominence to 2 Esd 2:42–47 as an ancient parallel that shows the same scene as Rev 14:1–5 and confirms that it takes place in heaven. He refers to 2 Esd 13 along with passages from Micah, Joel, and Isaiah as Jewish texts pointing to earthly Zion but discounts those. Closer attention to "2 Esdras" as a source would show that 2 Esdras 1–2 is in fact a supersessionist Christian text (dependent on Rev and other NT books) sometimes labeled 5 Ezra. It was written significantly later than 2 Esdras 3–14 (usually labeled 4 Ezra), a Jewish text from around AD 100. See Aune, *Revelation 6–16*, 803–4; and Charles, *Revelation*, 2:4–5.

7. See the similar shifts from a scene on earth to a voice or sound from heaven in 10:4, 8; 18:4.

8. The words referring to a "kithara" (actually three words that denote one who plays a kithara, the act of playing it, and the instrument itself; κιθαρῳδός, κιθαρίζω, κιθάρα) refer technically not to a "harp" as in most English translations (CSB, ESV, KJV, NASB, NIV, NLT, NRSV, REB, RSV) but to a box lyre or kithara. In contrast to a harp, a Greco-Roman kithara had strings of equal length (usually seven) and a rectangular soundbox with two arms extending up to a cross-piece or yoke to which the strings were attached. See *BNPauly* 9:354–58; Eckhard J. Schnabel, "Singing and Instrumental Music in the Early Church," in *Sprache Lieben—Gottes Wort Verstehen: Festschrift für Heinrich Von Siebenthal*, ed. Walter Hilbrands (Giessen: Brunnen, 2011), 331–34; and M. L. West, *Ancient Greek Music* (Oxford: Clarendon, 1992), 48–56. Cf. 5:8; 15:2; 18:22; 1 Cor 14:7.

9. The textual evidence differs over whether the "something like" or "as" (ὡς) should be included or omitted from the text at this point. It is omitted from a larger number of good manuscripts ($\mathfrak{P}^{47}$, ℵ, 1611, 1854, 2053, 2329, 2344), but several solid copies, including what is generally the most reliable one (A), include it (see also C, 051, 1006, 1841). Moreover, the inclusion is a bit awkward here, so the greater likelihood is that scribes dropped it rather than added it in the process of transmission.

heavenly singers in general (an impersonal "they"; see note at 10:11). The first option does not seem likely since v. 2 seems to change the scene (a sound "from heaven" as opposed to the location on Mount Zion). The difference between the latter two choices is less important since some of those who are present for this singing (the living creatures and the elders) were seen in 5:8–9 also to possess "kitharas" and to sing "a new song" in the heavenly throne room as here. In any case, to "sing a new song" reflects a number of Old Testament passages that indicate praise to the Lord inspired afresh by his gracious deliverance, especially culminating in his coming renewal of all things (cf. Isa 42:9–10 and discussion at Rev 5:9). Such a new song is an appropriate backdrop for the scene of victory on Mount Zion that v. 1 presents.

John's difficulty in describing what he heard (v. 3a, "as though they sang a new song") may be due to its ineffable character that he identifies in v. 3b–c: "No one was able to learn the song" except the redeemed who stood with the Lamb. Here "learn" (μανθάνω) does not mean "learn to sing and thus join in" but "learn and thus understand the song's significance" (cf. 1 Cor 4:6).[10] Only those who will stand with the Lamb (v. 1) at his victorious return as King of kings (19:16) can grasp the import of the heavenly song of triumph that John hears. The song must therefore pertain especially to God's gracious restoration of his people Israel in fulfillment of what v. 1 represents for them (see comments above). The 144,000 Israelites who "were redeemed from the earth" (v. 3c) and regathered from their dispersion are able to enter fully into the great song of victory from heaven. John's parallel comment later (v. 4d), "redeemed from among humans as firstfruits,"

indicates that these Israelites are just the initial ingathering of the redeemed from all the nations, who in their turn will enter into the celebration.

14:4–5 These are the ones who were not defiled with women, for they are virgins. These follow the Lamb wherever he goes. These were redeemed from among humans as firstfruits to God and to the Lamb, 5 and in their mouths no lie was found; they are blameless (οὗτοί εἰσιν οἳ μετὰ γυναικῶν οὐκ ἐμολύνθησαν, παρθένοι γάρ εἰσιν, οὗτοι οἱ ἀκολουθοῦντες τῷ ἀρνίῳ ὅπου ἂν ὑπάγῃ. οὗτοι ἠγοράσθησαν ἀπὸ τῶν ἀνθρώπων ἀπαρχὴ τῷ θεῷ καὶ τῷ ἀρνίῳ, 5 καὶ ἐν τῷ στόματι αὐτῶν οὐχ εὑρέθη ψεῦδος, ἄμωμοί εἰσιν). The special purity and consecration of these Israelites who were sealed for God (7:3–8) is now emphasized (vv. 4–5). What comes out clearly in these verses is their exceptional role as the vanguard of all of God's redeemed who will suffer but find victory during those terrible final days. Others will go through this journey with them, from ethnic Israelites as well as from all the nations of the world, but they above and beyond the others receive God's unique protection and exemplify a commensurate special purity. Commentators struggle to interpret the unexpected descriptions of sexual purity in v. 4a–b ("not defiled with women," "virgins"). Revelation does use the imagery of illicit sexual relations to represent religious infidelity or idolatry (2:14, 20–22; 14:8; 17:1–5; 18:3, 9; 19:2), and this sense for v. 4 is often suggested.[11] But this language seems to go beyond that. It would be easy enough for John to speak of "harlotry" or "fornication" as he does to symbolize idolatry in the verses cited above. But v. 4 describes those who have refrained from all sex-

---

10. LN §32.14; K. H. Rengstorf, "μανθάνω," *TDNT* 4:407–8.

11. This is almost obligatory for those who understand the 144,000 "Israelites" of 7:3–8 to represent all of God's people. "Virgins" in this case cannot have a literal sexual sense. See

Hughes, *Revelation*, 157–59; Ladd, *Revelation*, 189–91; Mounce, *Revelation*, 266–68; and Smalley, *Revelation*, 357–58.

ual relations.[12] This is rooted not so much in Old Testament images of spiritual adultery (e.g., 1 Chr 5:25; Jer 3:6; Ezek 23:19) but instead in the language of ritual purity expected of those who enter God's presence or serve him in holy war (Exod 19:14–15; Lev 15:16–18; Deut 23:9–14; 1 Sam 21:5; 2 Sam 11:9–13; cf. 1QM 7:3–7).[13] These who stand with the Lamb on Mount Zion as part of his conquering army must possess such consecration above and beyond the others who share in the Lamb's redemption (cf. 5:9).[14]

John adds four additional descriptions of the extraordinary character of this group of faithful Israelites (vv. 4c–5). They are dedicated disciples of Christ (v. 4c, "they follow the Lamb wherever he goes"), a reference to their costly self-sacrifice and consecration to God and his gospel (cf. Mark 8:34–38 and parallels).[15] Second, they are the vanguard of God's redemptive harvest in the final cataclysmic events of the end times (v. 4d, "redeemed from among humans as firstfruits to God and to the Lamb"). Just as the offering of the first portion of the harvest symbolized Israel's grateful acknowl-

edgment that all of it was from God (cf. "firstfruits" in Deut 26:1–11), so Christ's purchase of ethnic Israelites by his blood (5:9), who thus experience spiritual and national renewal in fulfillment of God's promises, will constitute the forefront of God's salvation and renewal of all humanity and all of his creation in the end times.[16] Thirdly, in sharp contrast to the false prophet's deceit just portrayed repeatedly in 13:12–15, these Christ-followers cannot be charged with any falsehood (v. 5a, "in their mouths no lie was found"). This description comes directly from the Old Testament,[17] most notably from a prophetic passage that anticipates the future great day when God judges all the nations and restores his people Israel in Jerusalem as a godly remnant in whose mouth no deceit will be found (Zeph 3:13 LXX: οὐ μὴ εὑρεθῇ ἐν τῷ στόματι αὐτῶν γλῶσσα δολία).[18] Finally in summary, they fully exemplify God's redeemed people (v. 5b, "they are blameless," a frequent NT description of the moral condition that Christians will attain at the consummation of God's sanctifying work in them; e.g., Eph 1:4; 5:27; Col 1:22; Jude 24).

---

12. Charles, *Revelation*, 2:4–10; Glasson, *Revelation*, 85; Thomas, *Revelation 8–22*, 194–97. The view of Thomas is that these celibate 144,000 are: (a) the sealed of 7:3–8, (b) a special group of Jewish-Christians, who (c) were killed during the tribulation but return to earth in Christ's heavenly army and thus (d) stand on Mount Zion with him at the start of the millennium. Points (a), (b), and (d) make sense, but (c) seems not to fit the contextual sense of "sealing" in 7:3–8. Charles argues for (a), (c), and (d), but not (b).

13. Bauckham, *Climax*, 229–32, focuses on the ritual purity of a holy army as a metaphor for the "moral purity" that is "characteristic of a Christian life" (p. 231). As noted above, it seems more likely that this sexual purity is literal but is limited to a narrow group within the redeemed: the group of ethnic Jewish followers of Jesus (7:3–8) who are protected through the final tribulation (12:12–16) and enter Christ's millennial earthly rule (chs. 19–20) as representatives of regathered Israel as a whole.

14. This does not imply that sexual relations within marriage are sinful or impure but represents the kind of extraordinary consecration to God that is called for in some situations. See Paul's balance in these issues in 1 Cor 7:1–7, 25–35.

15. It is not, however, a veiled way of saying that they will suffer certain martyrdom (i.e., following the Lamb in being slaughtered as he was). Their dedication is firm, but God will protect them from physical harm so that they can serve a different purpose, as noted above.

16. Cf. "firstfruits" (ἀπαρχή) in Rom 16:5; 1 Cor 15:23; 16:15; 2 Thess 2:13. That Jewish Christians will form a prominent "frontline" among all the redeemed in the end times is similar to Paul's thought in Rom 1:16, "to the Jew first and to the Greek" (cf. also Eph 1:12). See White, "The 144,000 in Revelation 7 and 14," 188–97, for the OT background to this imagery and its significance for understanding the relationship of Jewish believers to the rest of the church (their ethnicity is not effaced; Israel is not "replaced" by the church).

17. The marginal note in NA[28] cites Zeph 3:13 and Isa 53:9 as OT parallels. Fekkes, *Prophetic Traditions*, 191–92, argues that Zeph 3:13 (a group with no guile) exerts the primary influence on John's use of this description in v. 5a, but that Isa 53:9 (an individual with no guile) cannot be ruled out. In these traits these pure Israelites follow the Lamb as v. 4c says.

18. Falsehood or lying (ψεῦδος) is among the sinful practices explicitly excluded from God's new Jerusalem (21:27; 22:15).

14:6–7 And I saw another angel flying high in the sky, having an eternal gospel to proclaim to the inhabitants of the earth, that is, to every nation and tribe and language and people, 7 saying with a loud voice, "Fear God and give him glory, because the hour of his judgment has come, and worship the one who made the heaven and the earth and the sea and the springs of waters" (Καὶ εἶδον ἄλλον ἄγγελον πετόμενον ἐν μεσουρανήματι, ἔχοντα εὐαγγέλιον αἰώνιον εὐαγγελίσαι ἐπὶ τοὺς καθημένους ἐπὶ τῆς γῆς καὶ ἐπὶ πᾶν ἔθνος καὶ φυλὴν καὶ γλῶσσαν καὶ λαόν, 7 λέγων ἐν φωνῇ μεγάλῃ, Φοβήθητε τὸν θεὸν καὶ δότε αὐτῷ δόξαν, ὅτι ἦλθεν ἡ ὥρα τῆς κρίσεως αὐτοῦ, καὶ προσκυνήσατε τῷ ποιήσαντι τὸν οὐρανὸν καὶ τὴν γῆν καὶ θάλασσαν καὶ πηγὰς ὑδάτων). Verse 6 begins a new unit within chapter 14 (vv. 6–13) in which John records his vision of three angels who announce God's imminent judgment on the earth and call for a response. The new unit is signaled by the expression "and I looked/saw" (καὶ εἶδον) as in vv. 1 and 14. Here John sees "another angel" (as in 10:1; 18:1 there is no intention to contrast this one closely with a previous angel), one who is "flying high in the sky" (v. 6a)[19] so that he can announce God's good news, a message with eternal significance (v. 6b), to all the world's inhabitants. His elevated vantage point is symbolic of the wide intended audience for the gospel message (there is no need to think of this as a proclamation that literally reaches the whole world in a single instance). In v. 6c John uses a slightly different phrase to describe "the inhabitants of the earth" (τοὺς καθημένους ἐπὶ τῆς γῆς, "those who sit/ live on the earth") compared to his normal "those who inhabit/live on the earth" (τοὺς κατοικοῦντας ἐπὶ τῆς γῆς; see 3:10 for comments and references).

This slight variation may suggest a more hopeful attitude about humans' responses to the gospel compared to the quite negative implication of the more common phrase in 13:8, 14 (humans led astray to worship the beast).[20] The phrases that describe the world's "inhabitants" further, "every nation and tribe and language and people" (v. 6c) tend to support this more positive attitude. John uses this expression six other times in Revelation with slight variations, sometimes to lament how the world's peoples are dominated by evil (11:9; 13:7; 17:15), but also to celebrate the deliverance of some from every nation by God's saving work through Christ (5:9; 7:9; 10:11). This more hopeful prospect is rooted in how these phrases are used in Daniel (especially Dan 6:25–26; 7:13–14) to anticipate God's coming dominion over the whole earth. See comments at 5:9 and 10:11.

In fact, the words that John hears the angel declare "with a loud voice" (v. 7a) may allude to the royal decree that Daniel 6:25 records ("give fear and reverence to the God of Daniel"). Here the angel commands the earth's peoples to "fear God and give him glory" (Rev 14:7b; cf. 15:4), especially because they are faced with imminent divine judgment: "The hour of his judgment has come" (v. 7c).[21] They must also "worship" God (v. 7d), in clear contrast to worship of the dragon and the beast repeatedly described in the previous chapter (13:4, 8, 12, 15). Here as in 10:6 (and commonly in the OT; see Jer 27:4–7 and texts cited in comments on Rev 10:6), worship of the true God is demanded because he is the creator of all things. False gods are capable of nothing and warrant no one's allegiance, but the true and living God, the maker of all, deserves to be worshiped by all people. John's addition of "springs

---

19. See the note on this phrase in 8:13.
20. This more positive tone is the suggestion of Bauckham, *Climax*, 240–41.

21. The verbal phrase "has come" represents a Greek aorist, ἦλθεν, denoting what is from heaven's point of view a recently completed event (as in 6:17; 11:18; 18:10; cf. 14:15). See notes on 6:17 and 11:15, 18.

of waters" to the more common triad of heaven, earth, and sea perhaps reflects his sense that God is the sustainer as well as creator of life (cf. 7:17; 8:10; 16:4; 21:6: God withholds or provides life-giving water in his judgment or blessing of humans).

14:8 And another angel, a second one, followed saying, "Fallen, fallen is Babylon the great, who has made all the nations drink from the wine of the passion of her sexual immorality" (Καὶ ἄλλος ἄγγελος δεύτερος ἠκολούθησεν λέγων, Ἔπεσεν, ἔπεσεν Βαβυλὼν ἡ μεγάλη ἣ ἐκ τοῦ οἴνου τοῦ θυμοῦ τῆς πορνείας αὐτῆς πεπότικεν πάντα τὰ ἔθνη). The second in the series of three angels in vv. 6–13 appears in John's vision with a dramatic announcement that foreshadows much of the content of chapters 16–18. For the first time in Revelation the name "Babylon" explicitly appears,[22] but Babylon's presence in the lives of John's first-century readers—and its ultimate intensification in the last days still to come—has formed the backdrop of much of the book to this point.[23] In an abrupt preview of the story that follows, the angel declares the final destruction of the great imperial city that has spread its idolatry and opposed God and his people for so long.[24] The wording of this declaration is drawn from the Old Testament prophecies in Isaiah 21:9 and Jeremiah 51:8 of the ultimate fall of Judah's great oppressor and destroyer (586 BC), the great Babylonian Empire.[25] The dramatic heavenly announcement (v. 8b), "fallen, fallen is Babylon,"

is phrased with the double occurrence of a Greek aorist verb (ἔπεσεν, ἔπεσεν) to portray Babylon's destruction as having just been accomplished in its totality (also in 18:2).[26]

John uses "Babylon" here and later in Revelation not to refer literally to the city in Mesopotamia but as a typology of evil drawn from the ancient and prominent imperial enemy of God's people in the Old Testament that destroyed Jerusalem and its temple and exiled its population.[27] Ancient Babylonia was a cardinal example of a pagan empire that opposed God and his people, and such examples would be repeated throughout history (e.g., the Seleucids in the 160s BC). Rome was the replication of the type in the first-century world, most notably in its destruction again of Jerusalem and its temple in AD 70 and its pressure on Christians to engage in idolatrous practices. It also united a variety of nations in its godless rule as Babylon had done. This evil pattern will appear in its greatest form in the end-time opposition to God portrayed in Revelation 12–19.

The brief description of Babylon's activity that accompanies this announcement (v. 8c) establishes clear thematic links with the discussion of the beast's career in chapter 13 (the world is compelled to worship him) and the later descriptions of Babylon as a "harlot" who entices the nations to follow her idolatrous ways (cf. 17:1–6, 15; 18:3, 15, 19, 23).[28] The metaphor of Babylon offering fine wine to intoxicate her victims (repeated almost exactly

---

22. The name "Babylon" appears again in 16:19; 17:5; 18:2, 10, 21; she is called "great" apart from that name also in 17:1; 19:2 (great prostitute) and in 17:18; 18:10, 16, 18, 19 (great city).

23. See, e.g., the warnings about idolatry and oppression in chs. 2–3, the career of the two witnesses in ch. 11, the heavenly and earthly conflict in ch. 12, and the rule of the dragon and his beasts in ch. 13.

24. This is the celebration of heavenly realities that will soon come down to earth as in 11:15; 12:10. See Thompson, *Revelation*, 63–64; Fekkes, *Prophetic Traditions*, 88.

25. In the Hebrew of Isa 21:9 the verb "fell, has fallen" (נָפְלָה)

occurs twice, but in the LXX only one verb appears, a Greek perfect (πέπτωκεν). In Jer 51:8 (also in Amos 5:2) the same Hebrew verb occurs once, while the LXX (Jer 28:8) has the aorist (ἔπεσεν) as here, but only once.

26. See the notes on 14:7 and 15:4 for examples and discussion. In English idiom, recent past events are expressed in the present perfect: "has/is fallen."

27. See notes on 17:5 for further discussion of the identity of "Babylon" in Rev.

28. The imagery of "sexual immorality" as spiritual idolatry reveals broader thematic connections with 2:14, 20–21.

in 18:3 and with more variation in 17:2) will be turned against her in later passages in portraying her as drunk with impurity and the oppression of the saints (17:4, 6) and as forced by God's just retribution to drink the cup of his wrath (16:19; 18:6; cf. also 14:10, wrath on the beast's followers).[29]

14:9–10 And another angel, a third one, followed them saying with a loud voice, "If anyone worships the beast and his image and receives a mark on his forehead or on his hand, 10 he also will drink from the wine of God's anger which is mixed full strength in the cup of his wrath, and he will be tormented in fire and sulfur before the holy angels and before the Lamb" (Καὶ ἄλλος ἄγγελος τρίτος ἠκολούθησεν αὐτοῖς λέγων ἐν φωνῇ μεγάλῃ, Εἴ τις προσκυνεῖ τὸ θηρίον καὶ τὴν εἰκόνα αὐτοῦ καὶ λαμβάνει χάραγμα ἐπὶ τοῦ μετώπου αὐτοῦ ἢ ἐπὶ τὴν χεῖρα αὐτοῦ, 10 καὶ αὐτὸς πίεται ἐκ τοῦ οἴνου τοῦ θυμοῦ τοῦ θεοῦ τοῦ κεκερασμένου ἀκράτου ἐν τῷ ποτηρίῳ τῆς ὀργῆς αὐτοῦ καὶ βασανισθήσεται ἐν πυρὶ καὶ θείῳ ἐνώπιον ἀγγέλων ἁγίων καὶ ἐνώπιον τοῦ ἀρνίου). The reversal of imagery just described is immediately employed in the next angel's pronouncement of judgment for anyone who worships the beast (vv. 9–10). The declaration of the third angel in this series (cf. vv. 6, 8) and responses to it will carry through to v. 13 before John relates a new vision in vv. 14–20. Again, as in v. 7, this warning of judgment is delivered "with a loud voice" to underscore its importance, and compared to v. 7

the contrast with chapter 13 is made abundantly clear. In an extended conditional sentence (the if-clause is v. 9b; the conclusion is v. 10),[30] the angel announces divine wrath and fiery torment upon anyone who "worships the beast and his image" (cf. 13:4, 8, 12, 14–15) and "who receives a mark on his forehead or on his hand (cf. 13:16–17). This warning is a direct challenge to the dictates of the false prophet that anyone not worshiping the beast would be killed (13:15) and that all of humanity must bear the beast's mark because without it one could neither buy nor sell (13:16–17).

In declaring the consequences (v. 10) for anyone who accepts the beast's dictates, the angel reverses the imagery of Babylon's intoxicating enticements from v. 8 (implicitly revealing the alliance of the beast and the harlot of Babylon that ch. 17 will portray). The beast's follower will suffer God's wrath in full measure (v. 10a–b), expressed here as drinking from "a cup of his wrath" (cf. 16:19; 18:6; Isa 51:17–22) that contains "the wine of God's anger" (cf. Rev 14:19; 19:15) which is "full strength" or undiluted (cf. LXX of Ps 75:8 and Jer 25:15). Changing the imagery of what God's judicial anger will entail, the angel speaks of it as being "tormented in fire and sulfur" (v. 10c),[31] a preview of the punishment of the beast and the false prophet in the lake of fire (19:20) as well as of the dragon (20:10) and unredeemed humanity (20:13–15; 21:8). This is said to be "before the holy angels and before the Lamb" as

---

29. The phrase in v. 8c translated "of the passion" (τοῦ θυμοῦ) fits this scenario in one of two ways: (1) θυμός has its normal sense of "rage, anger, wrath" as a genitive of purpose, "the wine that brings [God's] anger against her sexual immorality"; or (2) it means "uncontrolled feeling, passion, strong desire" as a genitive of apposition or epexegetical genitive (Wallace, *Grammar*, 95–100), "the wine that is the passion of her sexual immorality" [τῆς πορνείας is a genitive of source or producer; i.e., her passion that immorality produces]. θυμός in Rev often means God's anger or wrath (e.g., 14:10, 19; 15:1, 7; 16:1), but see 16:19; 19:15 where with ὀργή it seems to denote God's passionate or furious wrath (τοῦ θυμοῦ τῆς ὀργῆς αὐτοῦ;

cf. BDAG 461). The first option above seems to stretch too far what a genitive phrase can do; the second sense seems more likely. See LN §25.19; Aune, *Revelation 6–16*, 786.

30. The "if . . . [then]" conditional sentence of vv. 9–10 shows that the Greek καί at the start of v. 10 does not have its normal sense of "and" but means "also, too, indeed" (CSB, ESV, NASB, NIV, NRSV).

31. "Fire" and "sulfur" reflect the typology of judgment that goes back to Sodom and Gomorrah (Gen 19:24; cf. Ps 11:6; Isa 34:9–10; Ezek 38:22) that will reach its ultimate escalation in the future eternal judgment of the ungodly.

an allusion to its initial stages that will take place at the return of Christ to earth with his heavenly armies (19:11–14).

14:11 And the smoke of their torment rises up forever and ever, and those who worship the beast and his image—as well as anyone who receives the mark of his name—have no respite day and night (καὶ ὁ καπνὸς τοῦ βασανισμοῦ αὐτῶν εἰς αἰῶνας αἰώνων ἀναβαίνει, καὶ οὐκ ἔχουσιν ἀνάπαυσιν ἡμέρας καὶ νυκτὸς οἱ προσκυνοῦντες τὸ θηρίον καὶ τὴν εἰκόνα αὐτοῦ καὶ εἴ τις λαμβάνει τὸ χάραγμα τοῦ ὀνόματος αὐτοῦ). The theme of judgment continues from v. 10, but there seems to be a shift here from the angel's declaration quoted in vv. 9b–10 to John's further description of what he has seen (v. 11) and the response that this demands of his readers (v. 12).[32] John describes the punishment of these who suffer God's wrath (again expressed as those loyal to the beast in phrases repeated from v. 9) as unending and continuous. Using the imagery of fiery torment from v. 10c, he states that its "smoke . . . rises up forever and ever" (ὁ καπνὸς . . . εἰς αἰῶνας αἰώνων ἀναβαίνει). This language, drawn from Isaiah 34:10, is repeated in 19:3 concerning God's judgment of Babylon (cf. also Jesus's comment about humans condemned to "eternal fire reserved for the devil and his angels," Matt 25:41). This is similar also to the language of 20:10 (the devil, the beast, and the false prophet "will be tormented day and night forever and ever") that John uses here to describe their punishment as continuous: "They have no respite day and night." Such constant suffering directly contrasts with the "rest" that the blessed dead are said to experience in v. 13 (cf. also 6:11).

The idea of unending torment for those who reject Christ seems so horrendous that even several evangelical theologians have argued that such a harsh judgment cannot be squared with the biblical view of God, even of God's justice.[33] How just is it for temporal, earthly sin to be punished by eternal and conscious torment? Their alternative is annihilationism, the view that the wicked are destroyed (i.e., obliterated, removed from existence) in hell rather than eternally punished.[34] But such a view is unsupportable even in the biblical texts that use the terms "destroy, destruction" (ἀπόλλυμι, ἀπώλεια), since in speaking of God's punishment for sin the words do not mean "annihilate" but "ruin, take away all that is valuable; suffer ultimate loss."[35] The same texts that speak of "eternal" life refer also to "eternal" punishment (e.g., Matt 25:41, 46). Reference to the unending experience of suffering for humans who reject the infinitely glorious God are found throughout the New Testament (e.g., Mark 9:43–48; Phil 3:18–19; 2 Thess 1:9; Heb 6:2; Jude 7). A fitting appreciation of the infinite majesty of God puts into perspective in some measure the justice of such a judgment for those who spurn him.

14:12 Here is the endurance of the saints, who keep God's commands and their faith in Jesus (Ὧδε ἡ ὑπομονὴ τῶν ἁγίων ἐστίν, οἱ τηροῦντες τὰς

---

32. Such a shift is indicated by the change from indefinite singular in v. 10c ("he will be tormented") to indefinite plural in v. 11a ("their torment") as well as the change from future verbs in v. 10 to general presents in v. 11.

33. For surveys of both sides of this issue, see P. S. Johnston, "Hell," in *NDBT* 542–44. For arguments against annihilationism in Rev and in the Bible in general, see Gregory K. Beale, "The Revelation on Hell," in *Hell Under Fire*, ed. Christopher W. Morgan and Robert A. Peterson (Grand Rapids: Zondervan, 2004), 111–34; Robert A. Peterson, "Does the Bible Teach Annihilationism?," *BSac* 156 (1999): 13–27; and Andy Saville, "Arguing with Annihilationism: An Assessment of the Doctrinal Arguments for Annihilationism," *SBET* 24 (2006): 65–90.

34. Another alternative (usually found among nonevangelicals) is universalism, the teaching that God will ultimately reconcile all humanity through Christ.

35. A. Oepke, "ἀπόλλυμι, ἀπώλεια," *TDNT* 1:394–97: "Not a simple extinction of existence . . . but an everlasting state of torment and death" (397).

ἐντολὰς τοῦ θεοῦ καὶ τὴν πίστιν Ἰησοῦ). Without using an introductory conjunction John interjects, as in 13:10, a call for endurance on the part of God's people.[36] The dreadful fate just seen for those who turn away from God shows how important it is for Christians to persevere[37] doggedly in obedience and in their faith in Jesus[38] despite suffering, persecution, and even martyrdom. Such persistence is a frequent theme in Revelation (1:9; 3:10; 13:10) as is the need for obedience (2:26; 3:8; 12:17; 22:7) and faith (2:13, 19; 13:10).[39]

14:13 And I heard a voice from heaven saying, "Write: 'Blessed are the dead who die in the Lord from now on.'" "Yes," says the Spirit, "that they may rest from their labors. For their works follow them" (Καὶ ἤκουσα φωνῆς ἐκ τοῦ οὐρανοῦ λεγούσης, Γράφον· Μακάριοι οἱ νεκροὶ οἱ ἐν κυρίῳ ἀποθνῄσκοντες ἀπ᾽ ἄρτι. ναί, λέγει τὸ πνεῦμα, ἵνα ἀναπαήσονται ἐκ τῶν κόπων αὐτῶν· τὰ γὰρ ἔργα αὐτῶν ἀκολουθεῖ μετ᾽ αὐτῶν). Just as in 13:9–10, the heavenly vision links a call for costly endurance with reassurance to Christians facing physical death. For those who die "in the Lord"[40]—that is, the Lord who himself died and is now alive again (1:18; 2:8; cf. Rom 14:9)—the sting of death is eclipsed by the promise of resurrected life (Rev 20:4–6; cf. 1 Cor 15:54–58). So John hears again (cf. v. 2) an unidentified voice from heaven (see note at 9:13) instructing him to record[41] the blessedness that

will come for Christians in general who pass away (the blessed "rest" of v. 13c applies to all Christians). But there is a particular focus on Christians who suffer martyrdom because of their loyalty to Christ in the horrible events that John is about to record. This special relevance is what is intended by the temporal phrase, "from now on." This beatitude is only the second of seven expressions of "blessedness" in Revelation (see note at 1:3, the first of the seven). A further confirmation of the special focus on Christians who suffer in the final days before the end is seen in the fact that six of the beatitudes occur from here to the end of the book (see the remaining ones in 16:15; 19:9; 20:6; 22:7, 14).

In addition to what the unnamed voice from heaven said about the Christian dead, John records the Holy Spirit's affirmation (see "yes," ναί, in 16:7; 22:20) and further explanation (v. 13c–d). They are blessed because death in the Lord means deliverance from earthly opposition, struggles, and weariness (e.g., 2 Cor 6:5; 11:23)[42] into the relief and rest that will be theirs in the presence of God (Rev 6:11; cf. Dan 12:13; Heb 4:9). The added explanation ("for," γάρ) that "their works follow them" makes clear that God in heaven will not forget the faithful deeds of service and obedience they have lived out on earth (cf. 1 Tim 5:24–25). Their costly sacrifice in allegiance to him will be rewarded when they enter his presence.

---

36. See note at 13:10 about the use of "here" and asyndeton in Rev to imply "this calls for . . ." or "what is needed in this situation is . . ." (cf. BDAG 1101).

37. The phrase "the endurance of the saints" (ἡ ὑπομονὴ τῶν ἁγίων) is a subjective genitive, i.e., "the saints [must] endure."

38. In this context "faith in Jesus" (objective genitive) is the best rendering of the Greek phrase τὴν πίστιν Ἰησοῦ (cf. 2:13).

39. The participle translated "who keep" (οἱ τηροῦντες) is a Greek nominative used in apposition to "the saints" (τῶν ἁγίων), a genitive. This is not the normal pattern for apposition, but it is one of the characteristics of John's idiolect (individual grammatical style) in Rev. See the note on 2:13 for other examples. Mathewson, *Handbook*, 195, suggests that "who keep"

is in apposition to "here" (a substantival adverb used as the subject of "is"), but this is a misunderstanding of the Greek construction (see note on 13:10).

40. Being and acting "in the Lord" is a common expression in Paul to describe all of existence lived in union with Christ. A similar concept is found in John's Gospel and Epistles under the rubric of "remaining" or "abiding" in Christ. This is the only use of the phrase in Rev, but it expresses a similar idea.

41. Commands in Rev for John to "write" pertain at times to the whole book (1:11, 19) and at other times to specific messages (2:1, etc. in chs. 2–3; also 19:9; 21:5).

42. Cf. BDAG 611.

14:14 And I looked, and behold, a white cloud, and sitting on the cloud one like a son of man, having on his head a golden crown and in his hand a sharp sickle (Καὶ εἶδον, καὶ ἰδοὺ νεφέλη λευκή, καὶ ἐπὶ τὴν νεφέλην καθήμενον ὅμοιον υἱὸν ἀνθρώπου, ἔχων ἐπὶ τῆς κεφαλῆς αὐτοῦ στέφανον χρυσοῦν καὶ ἐν τῇ χειρὶ αὐτοῦ δρέπανον ὀξύ). The final unit of chapter 14 (vv. 14–20) begins with the phrase "and I looked/saw" (καὶ εἶδον), as the previous two did in vv. 1 and 6 respectively. This section points to God's culmination of judgment that is about to fall on the earth, using the imagery of two harvests—a grain harvest (vv. 14–16) and a grape harvest (vv. 17–20). Here what John sees initially and calls special attention to ("and behold") is "a white cloud" with "one like a son of man" sitting on it (v. 1b). This heavenly figure representing Jesus Christ will, in interaction with the angel of v. 15, initiate "the harvest of the earth" (vv. 15b–16). However, the identity of this one "like a son of man" (ὅμοιον υἱὸν ἀνθρώπου) in v. 14b is debated. The same wording appears in 1:13 to refer to Jesus Christ in terms drawn from Daniel 7:13, from which the common New Testament messianic title "Son of Man" is taken. Several translations reflect this identification of the figure by using the article and capital letters (e.g., KJV, "the Son of man"; CSB, NRSV, "the Son of Man"). But the wording could refer instead to an angelic being as "like a son of man." A similar phrase ("one like the sons of man") is used in Daniel 10:16 to describe an angel. Also in these verses it seems odd for the exalted Christ to take orders from an angel (cf. v. 15), the figure is said to be "sitting" instead of "coming" on the cloud

as in Daniel 7, and the wording of v. 15 "another angel came out" may imply that the figure of v. 14 is also an angel.[43] The fact that he wears "a golden crown" is not determinative; this clearly denotes an honored figure, but it is not reserved only for the one most honored (cf. 4:4, 10; 9:7). Overall, however, because of the clear parallel with 1:13 and Daniel 7:13, it seems better to understand this figure as Jesus Christ who takes a leading role in the judgment that is coming, and his "golden crown" alludes at least to his victory if not his royal status.[44] His part in the judgment is represented by the final detail of v. 14: he has a "sharp sickle" (δρέπανον ὀξύ) in his hand. This "sickle" was a cutting tool, usually with a long, curved blade mounted on a long handle for cutting stalks of grain (Deut 16:9; Mark 4:29), but the same word can describe a shorter instrument used in harvesting grapes (Rev 14:17–20; cf. Isa 18:5). See the comments on v. 15 concerning "harvest" as a symbol for judgment.

14:15–16 And another angel came out from the temple, crying with a loud voice to the one sitting on the cloud, "Put in your sickle and reap, because the hour for reaping has come, because the harvest of the earth is ripe." 16 And the one sitting on the cloud swung his sickle over the earth, and the earth was reaped (καὶ ἄλλος ἄγγελος ἐξῆλθεν ἐκ τοῦ ναοῦ κράζων ἐν φωνῇ μεγάλῃ τῷ καθημένῳ ἐπὶ τῆς νεφέλης, Πέμψον τὸ δρέπανόν σου καὶ θέρισον, ὅτι ἦλθεν ἡ ὥρα θερίσαι, ὅτι ἐξηράνθη ὁ θερισμὸς τῆς γῆς. 16 καὶ ἔβαλεν ὁ καθήμενος ἐπὶ τῆς νεφέλης τὸ δρέπανον αὐτοῦ ἐπὶ τὴν γῆν καὶ ἐθερίσθη ἡ γῆ). "Another angel" appears in John's vision,[45] carrying

---

43. Aune, *Revelation 6–16*, 841–42; Kiddle, *Revelation*, 275–77.

44. Beale, *Revelation*, 770–71; Osborne, *Revelation*, 550–53; Smalley, *Revelation*, 371–72; Thomas, *Revelation 8–22*, 218; Fekkes, *Prophetic Traditions*, 194–95. The later description of Christ as the conquering "King of kings" who "treads the winepress of God's anger" (19:11–16) says that he wears

"many diadems" (using the word διάδημα, not στέφανος as here). See comments on 2:10 for discussion of these two words for "crown."

45. John uses the phrase "another angel" to commonly introduce additional angelic beings into his narrative, sometimes without any implication of a close contrast with another being (e.g., 10:1; 14:6; 18:1). At other times there is close interaction

authoritative instructions from God's throne room or "temple" in heaven (see comments on 9:13) for Christ, the one seen "sitting on the cloud" in v. 14. Even the Lamb acts in concert with God's instructions, especially in judgment (5:7; 22:1, 3; cf. John 5:19–22). The instruction that he proclaims is that "the hour for reaping has come" and "the harvest of the earth is ripe" (v. 15d–e).[46] The terms for "reaping" or "harvesting" (θερίζω, θερισμός) used in this verse usually denote a grain harvest (i.e., mowing, cutting stalks of grain; cf. Matt 13:30; Jas 5:4 and see the LXX Ruth 1:22; 2:23; 1 Sam 6:13). This is a common symbol for judgment (e.g., Jer 51:33; Hos 6:11; Mic 4:12–13; Matt 13:30, 39; Gal 6:7–9; cf. also 4 Ezra 4:28–32; 2 Bar. 70:2). The angel's command (v. 15c), "Put in your sickle and reap" (πέμψον τὸ δρέπανόν σου καὶ θέρισον), is similar to the wording of Joel 3:13,[47] a context describing God's judgment against the nations at the day of the Lord. Some interpreters take the "grain harvest" imagery in vv. 15–16 as a picture of judgment including both the righteous and unrighteous[48] or even of the ingathering of the righteous only.[49] This would distinguish it from the imagery of the "grape harvest" in vv. 17–20, which in light of v. 19 (God's anger) and in comparison with 19:15 clearly refers to judgment against the unrighteous. But given the background in Joel 3 mentioned above and the fact that nothing clearly signals the presence of the righteous in this grain harvest, it seems best to understand both passages as symbols of God's judg-

ment on the unrighteous.[50] The first (vv. 14–16) is a more general and the second (vv. 17–20) a more detailed picture of the same action.[51] The imagery of rebellious humanity being summarily cut down like stalks of grain at the edge of a sickle is a graphic and terrible warning of judgment to come. But just as anyone who is observant can tell that it is the season for harvest in a positive sense (John 4:35–37), so the world's inhabitants should be aware that the time is drawing near for the harvest of God's judgment to break in upon them. The warnings are clear; the time for repentance has come.

Following the call for judgment to begin (v. 15), v. 16 summarizes in broad terms God's judgment that will come when the Son of Man returns to earth as its king. This is expressed in the vision's renewed reference to the figure "sitting on the cloud" (v. 14), who in the imagery of a grain harvest "swung his sickle" over the earth (v. 16a), and so the earth was "reaped" (v. 16b). John uses past tenses (aorists) to narrate what he saw in his vision, which in this case sums up in advance the end-time acts of judgment to be portrayed in more detail in the immediately succeeding chapters (chs. 15–20).

14:17–18 And another angel came out from the temple in heaven, he also having a sharp sickle. 18 And another angel came out from the altar, the one who had authority over the fire, and he called with a loud voice to the one who had the sharp sickle saying, "Put in your sharp sickle and gather the clusters of the earth's vineyard,

---

with another being, as here (the "son of man" in v. 14; cf. 7:2; 8:3; 14:8, 9, 17, 18), but it is unnecessary to read it as "another being like the one just described."

46. The term for a "ripe" harvest (ξηραίνω, to dry) also comes from grain harvesting practices since it denotes grain heads that have reached maturity and are "dry" and ready to be reaped and threshed (cf. BDAG 684).

47. The expression "put in" in v. 15 (the Greek verb is "send," πέμπω) mirrors the verbs in Joel 3:13 (LXX 4:13: ἐξαποστέλλω; MT 4:13: שׁלח ["send, put"]). The imagery of Joel 3 is that of a grape harvest, which John's vision moves to in vv. 17–20.

48. Beckwith, *Apocalypse*, 661–64; Mounce, *Revelation*, 278.

49. Bauckham, *Climax*, 289–96; idem, *Theology*, 94–98; Koester, *Revelation*, 626–29; Osborne, *Revelation*, 549–53; Smalley, *Revelation*, 372–74. Gathering a "harvest" can be an image of evangelism, i.e., of bringing people into relationship with God (Luke 10:2; John 4:35–37), and the reference to "firstfruits" (v. 4) may prepare the way for picturing a larger harvest of the righteous in vv. 14–16.

50. Aune, *Revelation 6–16*, 801–3; Beale, *Revelation*, 772–79; Thomas, *Revelation 8–22*, 219–20.

51. A suggestion made by Fekkes, *Prophetic Traditions*, 193.

because its bunches have reached their prime" (Καὶ ἄλλος ἄγγελος ἐξῆλθεν ἐκ τοῦ ναοῦ τοῦ ἐν τῷ οὐρανῷ ἔχων καὶ αὐτὸς δρέπανον ὀξύ. 18 Καὶ ἄλλος ἄγγελος [ἐξῆλθεν] ἐκ τοῦ θυσιαστηρίου [ὁ] ἔχων ἐξουσίαν ἐπὶ τοῦ πυρός, καὶ ἐφώνησεν φωνῇ μεγάλῃ τῷ ἔχοντι τὸ δρέπανον τὸ ὀξὺ λέγων, Πέμψον σου τὸ δρέπανον τὸ ὀξὺ καὶ τρύγησον τοὺς βότρυας τῆς ἀμπέλου τῆς γῆς, ὅτι ἤκμασαν αἱ σταφυλαὶ αὐτῆς). The final part of John's vision presents two additional angels who reenact the imagery of a vast harvest of the earth, this time picturing it as a vineyard to be cut back and its fruit trodden in the winepress (vv. 17–20). The first of these two angels appears in v. 17 carrying "a sharp sickle," just as the Son of Man did in v. 14. Both angels are seen to spring into action based on divine authorization, the first coming out "from the temple in heaven" (v. 17a) and the second "from the altar" of incense in the midst of the temple (v. 18a; cf. 8:3, 5; and comments at 6:9; 9:13). The latter angel apparently had regular "authority" or responsibility to tend the fire of the incense altar (v. 18b), but here he adds the duty of commanding the earth's judgment to begin (v. 18c). We see the command of v. 15 again, with the added description, "Put in your sharp sickle" (v. 18d). The different words that follow portray the coming judgment of the whole earth as a grape harvest: "Gather the clusters of the earth's vineyard" (v. 18e). The word translated "vineyard" (ἄμπελος) usually means the plant or grapevine itself (e.g., Mark 14:25; John 15:4; Jas 3:12), but it sometimes is used more broadly for the place where vines are planted, a "vineyard" (ἀμπελών is the more common word for this; e.g., Matt 21:33; Luke 13:6). But "vineyard" makes better sense for

the word ἄμπελος here (CSB).[52] God's judgment portrayed as the cutting (and then trampling, vv. 19–20) of grapes at harvest time is an image also drawn from the Old Testament (Isa 18:5; 63:1–6; Lam 1:15; Joel 3:13). The message of v. 15d–e about the imminence of judgment is repeated here at the end of v. 18: "Its bunches have reached their prime,"[53] and in the symbolism they are ripe for God's judgment to fall.

14:19–20 And the angel swung his sickle onto the earth, and he gathered the earth's grapes, and he put them into the great winepress of God's anger. 20 And the winepress was trodden outside the city, and blood went out from the winepress up to the horses' bridles for sixteen hundred stadia (καὶ ἔβαλεν ὁ ἄγγελος τὸ δρέπανον αὐτοῦ εἰς τὴν γῆν καὶ ἐτρύγησεν τὴν ἄμπελον τῆς γῆς καὶ ἔβαλεν εἰς τὴν ληνὸν τοῦ θυμοῦ τοῦ θεοῦ τὸν μέγαν. 20 καὶ ἐπατήθη ἡ ληνὸς ἔξωθεν τῆς πόλεως καὶ ἐξῆλθεν αἷμα ἐκ τῆς ληνοῦ ἄχρι τῶν χαλινῶν τῶν ἵππων ἀπὸ σταδίων χιλίων ἑξακοσίων). In response to the heavenly command, the second angel carries out his harvesting duties over the whole earth as a representation of the massive scale of God's judgment that is to come. In a rapid sequence of five past-tense (aorist) verbs John portrays what he saw of this judgment in broad summary, using the imagery of a grape harvest. The angel "swung his sickle onto the earth" (v. 19a; cf. v. 16), cutting off the ripe clusters of grapes. Then he "gathered the earth's grapes" (v. 19b).[54] These were put "into the great winepress," but at this point the reality behind the figure breaks more clearly into the wording (v. 19c):[55] it is the great winepress "of God's anger"

---

52. BDAG 54.

53. The verb translated "have reached their prime" (ἀκμάζω) means to be at a high point, "to be in full bloom, at the prime" (LSJ 51; cf. a related word in 1 Cor 7:36), in this case "to be ripe" (ESV, KJV, NASB, NIV) or ready for harvest.

54. The word translated "grapes" is ἄμπελος, which is more commonly rendered "vine" or "vineyard" as in v. 18d; here the collective word is used for the individual portions that were cut.

55. See Caird, *Language and Imagery*, 152, 163–67, for illustrations of biblical metaphors that intermingle the "vehicle" and the "tenor" of the figure.

(τοῦ θυμοῦ τοῦ θεοῦ; cf. 14:10). To be sure, the immense scale of worldwide judgment has been made quite transparent already by the repeated uses in these verses of "earth" (vv. 15e, 16b, 18e, 19b) in connection with this "harvest," as well as the use of "great" to describe the winepress (v. 19c). But to identify this image with God's anger makes the picture more fearful still.

The Old Testament picture of treading out grapes in the winepress as a figure for judgment (Isa 18:5; 63:2; Lam 1:15; Joel 3:13) now is added to the harvest imagery: "The winepress was trodden outside the city" (v. 20a). This is a preview of one of the descriptions of Christ's judgment of his enemies at his glorious return (Rev 19:15). Adding the detail that this is done "outside the city" locates this overpowering retribution near Jerusalem. Jerusalem or Zion (cf. 14:1), the locus of God's restoration of his people Israel (14:1) and the center of Christ's millennial reign (20:4–6), is the setting spoken of in many of the Old Testament prophecies that

John has alluded to in this chapter, especially those that anticipate a final battle of the dragon and his minions against the Lord God and the Lamb (Isa 62:6–63:6; 66:10–17; Joel 3:1–17; Zech 12:8–12; 14:3–5; cf. Rev 19:19–21).

The final ghastly feature of the winepress imagery is the utterly exaggerated picture of "blood" running out from the winepress for "sixteen hundred stadia" (about 200 miles) at the depth of "horses' bridles" (v. 20b).[56] Again the vehicle and tenor of the metaphor are intermingled (see comment on v. 19c) since "blood" is not generally a part of treading out grapes but of the defeat or killing of enemies in battle.[57] Making the real sense more transparent does not, however, mean that this should in any way be taken literally. Blood will not be five or six feet deep for two hundred miles at Christ's second coming. But the cataclysmic defeat, submission, and destruction of all enemies arrayed against him in that day will be unimaginably vast.

Theology in Application

Visions of Victory, Visions of Judgment

In John's literary arrangement of the surrounding chapters, he mingles visions of heavenly and earthly worship (11:15–19; 14:1–5; 15:2–4) with glimpses of horrible evil, conflict, and judgment (chs. 12–13, the rest of chs. 14–16). This intermixture is explicitly intended to produce an appropriate response on the part of those who read or hear these chapters (cf. 1:3; 22:7). On the one hand, believers should have their eyes lifted above the immediate struggle and their faith strengthened by these pictures of the Lamb's victory. Seeing the heavenly celebrations of God's almighty power and anticipations of his kingdom coming to earth are a powerful encouragement to endure in faith and obedience in the here and now of our lives (14:12). Our own private and corporate experiences of worship should mirror such celebrations in refocusing our hearts and minds on the one whose grace and faithfulness we can

---

56. The precise length of a stade (Greek: στάδιον; Latin: *stadium*) is debated, but BDAG 940 gives a figure of 192 meters (about 630 feet).

57. Passages that speak of stains from treading out grapes as "blood" (e.g., Isa 63:1–3) illustrate the point about mixing the vehicle and the tenor; they do not disprove it.

count on at all times. On the other hand, those who are not followers of Christ should soberly assess their situation before it is too late. Everyone in a farming community can see the signs of a ripening harvest well ahead of the time when the reaping and gathering will begin. It should be no surprise. The moral and religious world that God made is like that too. If we pay attention, we can see what is coming and turn to him in good time. The angel's eternal gospel proclaimed to everyone on earth (14:6–7) calls for all to fear God in true reverence and give glory to him above all else. Nothing is more important or urgent than this. The time for turning to God through Christ is now, before the terrible harvest of judgment comes. The good news of God's salvation precedes the bad news of his judgment, but timing is everything.

A Division of Humanity

For the unreflective, most of life is a mixed-up jumble. Daily events come to us willy-nilly, and we react to them but have little time to see the larger pattern. Instead of making deliberate choices, our choices seem to make themselves—and make us who we are whether we think about them or not. But this chapter makes one of life's choices crystal clear and unavoidable. It makes it obvious, just as the rest of the Bible does, that God's offer of grace in Christ confronts us with a stark choice. Jesus Christ himself represents an unavoidable fork in the road amid human life. Some New Testament texts, drawing from Isaiah 8 and 28, picture Christ as a "stone" that looms in our pathway. We can either stumble over him and fall to destruction or build our lives on him as our unshakable foundation (Rom 9:32–33; 1 Pet 2:6–8), but neutrality is not an option. Likewise, Revelation 14 shows that we cannot avoid choosing sides in the cosmic conflict between God and evil: we can follow the Lamb or worship the beast (vv. 4, 9), but being too busy to pay attention is a choice in itself. Everything depends on our response to the angel's "eternal gospel" (vv. 6–7), including consequences for this life as well for all eternity in the life to come (vv. 11, 13). Will we stumble over Christ or base our lives on him?

CHAPTER 21

Revelation 15:1–8

Literary Context

Chapter 15 introduces the series of seven bowl judgments (16:1–21) by relating three brief scenes from heaven (each beginning with "and I saw/looked"; vv. 1, 2, 5) to set the stage for the culminating earthly judgments. John used the same technique to prepare for the previous two judgment series: heavenly visions in chapters 4–5 prior to the seal judgments (6:1–17) and in 8:2–5 prior to the trumpet judgments (8:6–11:19). John also bridges across the series of intervening visions between the trumpets and the bowls (chs. 12–14) by calling what he sees here "another sign in heaven" (v. 1a; cf. 12:1, 3). The structure of three series of sevenfold judgments—with interludes that slow down the action but build dramatic tension—will finally come to its conclusion in these two chapters (chs. 15–16).

III. Second Vision: Heavenly Throne Room and Three Judgment Cycles (4:1–16:21)

    A. Vision of God in His Heavenly Throne Room (4:1–11)

    B. The Seven-Sealed Scroll and the Slain Lamb (5:1–14)

    C. The Seven Seals and the Interlude of the Two Multitudes (6:1–8:1)

    D. The Seven Trumpets and Further Interludes (8:2–14:20)

→   **E. The Seven Bowl Judgments (15:1–16:21)**

        1. Heavenly Preparation for the Bowl Judgments (15:1–8)

        2. The Seven Bowls of God's Wrath Poured Out (16:1–21)

Main Idea

Seven angels are commissioned to pour out bowls of God's wrath on the earth, while others in heaven celebrate God's justice and holiness expressed in his judgment against evil.

Translation

Revelation 15:1–8

1a	Action/Vision Introduction	**And I saw another sign in heaven, great and astonishing,**
b	Character Entrance	seven angels having seven plagues—
		the final ones,
c	Reason	because in them God's anger ✍
		will be completed.

2a	Action/Character Entrance	**And I saw something like a glass sea mixed with fire and**
		those who conquered the beast and
		his image and
		the number of his name,
b	Descriptions	standing beside the glass sea,
c		holding kitharas of God.

3a	Action	**And they sang the song of Moses, God's servant, and**
		the song of the Lamb saying,

b	Exclamations of Praise	*"Great and astonishing are your works, Lord God Almighty.* (Pss 111:2; 139:14; ✍
		Amos 3:13)
c		*Just and true are your ways, King of the nations.* (Deut 32:4; Ps 145:17; Jer 10:7)
4a	Rhetorical Question	*Who will not fear, Lord, and*
		glorify your name, (Jer 10:7; Ps 86:9)
b	Reasons for 4a	*because you alone are holy,*
c		*because all the nations will come and*
		worship before you, (Ps 86:9; Isa 2:2; ✍
		66:23)
d		*because your righteous acts have been made evident."*

5	Action/Vision Introduction	**And after these things I looked,**
		and the temple of the tabernacle of testimony in heaven was opened,
6a	Character Entrance 1	**and the seven angels who had the seven plagues came out from the temple**
b	Descriptions	clothed in pure bright linen and
c		girded around their chests with gold sashes.

7a	Character Entrance 2	**And one of the four living creatures gave the seven angels seven golden bowls**
b	Description	filled with the anger of the God
c	Identification	who lives forever and
		ever.

Continued on next page.

Continued from previous page.

8a	Action	**And the temple was filled with smoke**
		                    from the glory of God and
		                    from his power,

b	Effect	**and no one could enter the temple**
c	Time Extent	until the seven plagues of the seven angels were completed.

Structure

As though postponing something terrible that nevertheless must happen, John takes this chapter to set the stage for the final series of judgments that have been anticipated as far back as 10:6–7 and 11:15–19 (the seventh trumpet). Recounting the bowl judgments themselves will come in chapter 16, but this chapter introduces them in three sections (v. 1, vv. 2–4, 5–8). As in chapter 14, each section is a separate but related vision introduced with "and I looked/saw" (καὶ εἶδον).

Exegetical Outline

III. Second Vision: Heavenly Throne Room and Three Judgment Cycles (4:1–16:21)

    A. Vision of God in His Heavenly Throne Room (4:1–11)

    B. The Seven-Sealed Scroll and the Slain Lamb (5:1–14)

    C. The Seven Seals and the Interlude of the Two Multitudes (6:1–8:1)

    D. The Seven Trumpets and Further Interludes (8:2–14:20)

    E. The Seven Bowl Judgments (15:1–16:21)

➡   **1. Heavenly Preparation for the Bowl Judgments (15:1–8)**

        a. Another heavenly sign: seven angels with seven bowls of wrath (15:1)

        b. Victors praising God beside the crystal sea (15:2–4)

           (1) Beast-conquerors beside a glass sea (15:2)

           (2) Praise to the Almighty from Moses's songbook (15:3–4)

        c. The seven angels commissioned for God's work of judgment (15:5–8)

           (1) The seven plague-angels emerge from the heavenly temple (15:5–6)

           (2) The seven receive bowls of God's wrath, and heaven awaits their work (15:7–8)

Explanation of the Text

15:1 And I saw another sign in heaven, great and astonishing, seven angels having seven plagues—the final ones, because in them God's anger will be completed (Καὶ εἶδον ἄλλο σημεῖον ἐν τῷ οὐρανῷ μέγα καὶ θαυμαστόν, ἀγγέλους ἑπτὰ ἔχοντας πληγὰς ἑπτὰ τὰς ἐσχάτας, ὅτι ἐν αὐταῖς ἐτελέσθη ὁ θυμὸς τοῦ θεοῦ). This first heavenly scene (v. 1) provides a preview of the coming series of seven judgments (or "plagues," v. 1b; cf. vv. 6, 8; 16:9) that pour out God's anger in its dreadful finality in chapter 16. The phrase "another sign in heaven" (v. 1a) alludes to the start of chapter 12 (cf. 12:1, 3) and bridges across the series of intervening visions (chs. 12–14) back to the seventh trumpet (11:15–19).[1] John describes the sign[2] as "great and astonishing," the latter adjective denoting here not just wonder or amazement but a note of dread foreboding as well (cf. Deut 28:59 LXX; Pss 93:4; 106:22; Mic 7:15). What he sees are "seven angels" with "seven plagues" (πληγὰς ἑπτά, "blows" or calamities as at the time of the exodus; cf. Rev 9:18, 20; 11:6; see Exod 11:1; 12:13), ready to be unleashed on the earth at heaven's command (Rev 16:1).[3]

The "seven plagues," like the "seven angels," are introduced as items not previously known to the readers (both without articles in Greek), but John immediately adds "the final ones" (τὰς ἐσχάτας) to describe the plagues further.[4] The clause that follows in v. 1c ("because," ὅτι) gives the theolog-

ical significance of calling them "the final ones": because they will finish out "God's anger"[5] poured out on the earth in the three series of judgments that will come in the last days (cf. 6:16–17). The verb translated "will be completed" is an aorist indicative in Greek (ἐτελέσθη), used here as a summary of the events about to be described in 16:1–21—and yet to occur on the earth in events future to John's time as well as our own.[6]

15:2 And I saw something like a glass sea mixed with fire and those who conquered the beast and his image and the number of his name, standing beside the glass sea, holding kitharas of God (Καὶ εἶδον ὡς θάλασσαν ὑαλίνην μεμιγμένην πυρὶ καὶ τοὺς νικῶντας ἐκ τοῦ θηρίου καὶ ἐκ τῆς εἰκόνος αὐτοῦ καὶ ἐκ τοῦ ἀριθμοῦ τοῦ ὀνόματος αὐτοῦ ἑστῶτας ἐπὶ τὴν θάλασσαν τὴν ὑαλίνην ἔχοντας κιθάρας τοῦ θεοῦ). The second heavenly scene that John records (vv. 2–4) in preparation for the bowl judgments begins here with his second "and I saw" (καὶ εἶδον) in the chapter. In this vision of heaven, he observed "a glass sea" as well as a group of victorious Christians standing by the sea, ready to worship God for his righteous acts of deliverance. In 4:6 John had witnessed such a "glass sea" in the heavenly throne room and likewise struggled to describe what he had seen. The best he can do in both places is to phrase a comparison (v. 2a),

---

1. These are the only occurrences in Rev of "sign," σημεῖον, in the singular.

2. Here the word "sign" means a portent or omen of something momentous or calamitous to come (e.g., Luke 21:11, 25; BDAG 921).

3. BDAG 825. There may also be an allusion to Lev 26:21 (cf. 26:18, 24, 28), threatening God's sevenfold retribution against Israel for her sins of rebellion. In the tribulation period God's disciplinary judgment will fall on Israel to prepare her for restoration.

4. Once introduced, both these phrases are hereafter always

articular: "the seven angels" and "the (seven last) plagues" (cf. vv. 6, 7, 8; 16:1, 9; 17:1; 21:9).

5. A subjective-genitive phrase that occurs also in 15:7; 16:1. See the lexical note at 16:19 on the nuances of "anger, fury" (θυμός) and "wrath" (ὀργή) in Rev.

6. This is a proleptic or futuristic aorist (see explanation in note on 10:7). Reference to the seven "last" plagues that are about to be portrayed in ch. 16 (and yet to occur in reality) is the contextual feature that triggers a temporal shift in how the verb is expressed in English as compared to Greek: future rather than past.

"something like a glass sea" (ὡς θάλασσαν ὑαλίνην; see note at 4:6 for possible OT influences).[7] More important for this vision is the group he sees standing "beside the glass sea,"[8] "the ones who had conquered" (τοὺς νικῶντας), that is, had faithfully resisted all the compulsion and deception of Satan to tear them away from allegiance to Christ. Such victory or "overcoming" is what John has summoned Christians to do throughout the messages to the churches (cf. 2:7, 11, etc.; also 12:11; 21:7), but here it is couched in the language he used to portray the deadly opposition (13:7) of the dragon, his beast, and false prophet: they instead overcame "the beast" (13:1), "his image" (13:14), and "the number of his name" (13:18).[9] This group of "conquerors" would certainly include Christian martyrs now present in heaven who had resisted the beast on earth and been killed as a result (13:10, 15). But the essence of their victory was enduring faith in Christ in the face of idolatry and persecution (1 John 4:4; 5:4–5; Rev 13:10; 14:12; 21:5–7), so the group could include many who had passed on in death from other causes and were now rejoicing in heaven as well. The final phrase in v. 2, "holding kitharas of God,"[10] reinforces the heavenly character of the scene (cf. 5:8; 14:2), but it also leads into the worship song presented in vv. 3–4.

15:3–4 And they sang the song of Moses, God's servant, and the song of the Lamb saying, "Great and astonishing are your works, Lord God Al-mighty. Just and true are your ways, King of the nations. 4 Who will not fear, Lord, and glorify your name, because you alone are holy, because all the nations will come and worship before you, because your righteous acts have been made evident (καὶ ᾄδουσιν τὴν ᾠδὴν Μωϋσέως τοῦ δούλου τοῦ θεοῦ καὶ τὴν ᾠδὴν τοῦ ἀρνίου λέγοντες, Μεγάλα καὶ θαυμαστὰ τὰ ἔργα σου, κύριε ὁ θεὸς ὁ παντοκράτωρ· δίκαιαι καὶ ἀληθιναὶ αἱ ὁδοί σου, ὁ βασιλεὺς τῶν ἐθνῶν· 4 τίς οὐ μὴ φοβηθῇ, κύριε, καὶ δοξάσει τὸ ὄνομά σου; ὅτι μόνος ὅσιος, ὅτι πάντα τὰ ἔθνη ἥξουσιν καὶ προσκυνήσουσιν ἐνώπιόν σου, ὅτι τὰ δικαιώματά σου ἐφανερώθησαν). The victors in heaven at the end times sing[11] a song of praise to God for his mighty acts of justice and faithfulness to his people in judging the godless empires who oppress them. Their song—and God's faithfulness and justice thus celebrated—will follow the same pattern as the song that Israel sang under Moses after their deliverance from Egypt (Exod 15:1–18), because God's faithful deliverance will follow the same glorious and invincible pattern. This is why the song is called "the song of Moses, God's servant, and the song of the Lamb" (v. 3a).[12] It is not two songs but one, and the lyrics are not intended to mirror the exact wording of Exodus 15, but its typological likeness. God used his faithful servant Moses (cf. Exod 14:13–31; Num 12:7; Deut 34:5; Josh 1:2, 7; 14:7) to accomplish an astonishing deliverance from Israel's bondage to Pharaoh and

---

7. "Mixed with fire," used here but not at 4:6, reflects the heavenly throne scene of Dan 7:9–10, symbolic of divine glory and holiness, and perhaps of judgment (cf. Rev 8:7).

8. The phrase "beside the . . . sea" (ἐπὶ τὴν θάλασσαν) could mean "on the sea" (CSB, KJV, NASB), but in preparation for the imagery of Israel's Red Sea deliverance (v. 2; Exod 15), "beside" makes better sense here (ESV, NRSV, NIV, REB, RSV; cf. BDAG 363).

9. The expression "conquered the beast" is worded in v. 2a using the verb νικάω plus a preposition ἐκ that usually means "from, out of." This phrasing carries the richer sense of "victorious over" plus "deliverance from" (BDAG 296; BDF §212;

Moffatt, "Revelation," 443; Swete, *Apocalypse*, 191).

10. In the phrase "kitharas of God" (see 5:8; 14:2 for identification of this instrument), the genitive can indicate source ("from God, God-given") or more likely purpose ("for God," as a shorthand way to say "for [worship of] God").

11. The verb "sing/sang" (ᾄδουσιν) is a Greek historical present anticipating the significant events of vv. 5–8; see discussion of the historical present at 5:5.

12. Here the genitives "of Moses" (subjective genitive: sung by Moses and the people) and "of the Lamb" (objective genitive: about the Lamb; e.g., 5:9–14) are syntactically opposite, but the songs express the same pattern of God's great deliverance.

Egypt. But even greater will be God's judgment and victory through the Lamb over the beast and all the nations under his sway.[13]

The actual content of the song (vv. 3b–4) reflects themes of praise that can be found frequently in the Old Testament, and some of its phrases can be traced more directly to certain passages.[14] God's "great and astonishing" deeds (v. 3b) are celebrated in Exodus 34:10; Psalms 111:2; 139:14, and his "just and true" pathways (v. 3c) in Deuteronomy 32:4 and Psalm 145:17 (cf. Rev 16:5, 7; 19:2). The common Old Testament title "Lord God" is similar to the worship address in 4:11, and "Almighty" (v. 3b) is used frequently in the Old Testament as well as in Revelation (see discussion at 1:8). These forms of address, as well as "King of the nations"[15] (cf. Jer 10:7), are especially fitting for their celebration of God's defeat of all enemies and of his sovereign rule over the whole world. As in the exodus so in his future act of judgment and redemption, God deserves heartfelt praise for his amazing deliverance and his righteous and faithful actions.

The quotation of Jeremiah 10:7 continues in v. 4a with the rhetorical question, "Who will not fear," implying the assertion, "everyone will/must fear you."[16] The force of the question carries over to a line from Psalm 86:9 (quoted also later in v. 4),

"and glorify your name" (cf. LXX Isa 42:10; 66:5; Mal 1:11). These obligations to give the Lord reverence and glory are grounded in three causal clauses that follow (v. 4b–d). Having three such clauses in a row is somewhat repetitive but understandable in such a context. The first ground is that the Lord "alone [is] holy" (v. 4b; cf. Deut 32:4; Ps 144:17 LXX), highlighting his uniqueness and perfection above all other creatures or supposed gods.[17] He alone deserves the ultimate devotion and reverence of all humanity. The second reason is the prophetic anticipation that one day "all the nations will come and worship" the Lord (v. 4c; Ps 86:9; Isa 2:2; 60:3–5; 66:23; Jer 16:19; cf. Rev 21:24). This turning of the nations to the true God will be the positive outcome of the Lord's defeat of evil and its domination over the world of humanity. Finally, as a third reason, the song proclaims that the Lord's "righteous acts have been made evident" (v. 4d; Ps 98:2).[18] What heaven knows of God's just and faithful character will soon be displayed on earth for all to see.

15:5–6 And after these things I looked, and the temple of the tabernacle of testimony in heaven was opened, 6 and the seven angels who had the seven plagues came out from the temple clothed in pure bright linen and girded around their

13. Bauckham, *Climax*, 296–97; Hoskins, *Revelation*, 286–87; Roloff, *Revelation*, 183–84.

14. Bauckham, *Climax*, 296–307.

15. A textual variant "king of the ages" (ὁ βασιλεὺς τῶν αἰώνων) occurs here with solid external evidence (𝔓⁴⁷, א*, C, 1006, 1611, 1841). But evidence for "nations" (τῶν ἐθνῶν) is also quite good (A, P, 046, 1854, 2053, 2062, 2329, 2344, most Byzantine minuscules), and the wording may have been changed to "ages" due to liturgical influences along the lines of 1 Tim 1:17; Tob 13:7 ("king of the ages"). The wording "king of [the] saints" (ὁ βασιλεὺς τῶν ἁγίων; TR; KJV; NKJV) is almost completely unattested in Greek manuscripts (see *TCGNT*2, 679–80 for comments).

16. The question in v. 4a is a Greek subjunctive with double negation (οὐ μὴ φοβηθῇ) to express an emphatic denial of a future possibility. As a rhetorical question it implies a strong

assertion of the positive sense: "will certainly fear" (Wallace, *Grammar*, 467–69; John Beekman and John Callow, *Translating the Word of God* [Grand Rapids: Zondervan, 1974], 238–45, 353–57). See other examples in Luke 18:7–8; John 18:11.

17. H. Balz, "ὅσιος," *EDNT* 2:536.

18. The aorist verb translated "have been made evident" (ἐφανερώθησαν) expresses a "recent past" action (see note on 9:12 and Fanning, *Verbal Aspect*, 260–61). This is one of several aorists in the later chapters of Rev (see 11:15, 12:10) that communicate an action (1) just accomplished from a heavenly point of view and so celebrated in heaven; but (2) on the verge of being presented as an earthly set of events in John's portrayal of the end that is coming; and (3) providing assurance of God's justice and deliverance that Christians look for in the future consummation of God's redemption on earth.

chests with gold sashes (Καὶ μετὰ ταῦτα εἶδον, καὶ ἠνοίγη ὁ ναὸς τῆς σκηνῆς τοῦ μαρτυρίου ἐν τῷ οὐρανῷ, 6 καὶ ἐξῆλθον οἱ ἑπτὰ ἄγγελοι [οἱ] ἔχοντες τὰς ἑπτὰ πληγὰς ἐκ τοῦ ναοῦ ἐνδεδυμένοι λίνον καθαρὸν λαμπρὸν καὶ περιεζωσμένοι περὶ τὰ στήθη ζώνας χρυσᾶς). The transition into the third heavenly scene of the chapter (vv. 5–8) includes the temporal note, "after these things" as well as the third occurrence of "and . . . I saw" (καὶ . . . εἶδον). John previously highlighted the events of this section by using the historical present in v. 3a to introduce the song of vv. 3–4. The vision now records the equipping and heavenly authorization of the seven angels for the work of judgment that they will carry out in 16:1–21. These angels emerge from the presence of God in his heavenly temple, dressed impressively like emissaries of God (vv. 5–6). Earlier in the book, communication from the temple represented God's authorization to act (9:13–14; 14:17–18). This opening of the heavenly temple itself (v. 5) repeats an image from 11:19, and in both places it represents the ominous appearance of God himself, ready to exact his judgment on rebellious humanity (cf. 3 Macc 6:18–19). Because the heavenly temple is a prototype of the earthly tabernacle and its later counterpart in Jerusalem's temple (cf. Exod 25:9, 40; Heb 8:5), it can be described as "the tabernacle of testimony" (τῆς σκηνῆς τοῦ μαρτυρίου; cf. Exod 29:42; 40:34; Acts 7:44).[19] It bears witness to the Lord's presence in heaven, just as he was among his people Israel in the wilderness or in Jerusalem.

In a partial return to the summary image of v. 1, John describes the impressive emergence (v. 6) of "the seven angels who had the seven plagues"[20] from the now open temple. They are wearing garments of "pure bright linen," a reflection of their heavenly glory influenced by the Old Testament accounts of angelic appearances (e.g., Dan 10:5; 12:6–7; Ezek 9:3–4, 11; 10:2, 6–7). The word "bright" (λαμπρός) denotes a shining appearance (Acts 10:30; Rev 22:1, 16), but also suggests impressive, resplendent robes indicating high position (Luke 23:11; Jas 2:2–3; Rev 18:14; 19:8). Likewise, their "gold sashes" mark them out as important figures and emissaries of a powerful Lord (e.g., 1:13).

15:7–8 And one of the four living creatures gave the seven angels seven golden bowls filled with the anger of the God who lives forever and ever. 8 And the temple was filled with smoke from the glory of God and from his power, and no one could enter the temple until the seven plagues of the seven angels were completed (καὶ ἓν ἐκ τῶν τεσσάρων ζῴων ἔδωκεν τοῖς ἑπτὰ ἀγγέλοις ἑπτὰ φιάλας χρυσᾶς γεμούσας τοῦ θυμοῦ τοῦ θεοῦ τοῦ ζῶντος εἰς τοὺς αἰῶνας τῶν αἰώνων. 8 καὶ ἐγεμίσθη ὁ ναὸς καπνοῦ ἐκ τῆς δόξης τοῦ θεοῦ καὶ ἐκ τῆς δυνάμεως αὐτοῦ, καὶ οὐδεὶς ἐδύνατο εἰσελθεῖν εἰς τὸν ναὸν ἄχρι τελεσθῶσιν αἱ ἑπτὰ πληγαὶ τῶν ἑπτὰ ἀγγέλων). The specific act to commission these angels for their divinely ordained tasks is carried out by one of the beings closest to God's very presence in the heavenly temple. The "four living creatures" appeared prominently in the visions of God's throne room in chapters 4–5 and played a central role in the early seal judgments (6:1–8), but were seen only sporadically since then (7:11; 14:3). Now in v. 7a one of them hands over to the seven angels the "seven golden bowls" that symbolize the acts of judgment they will inflict on the earth in 16:1–21. These "bowls" (φιάλαι) are shallow dishes or basins used for sacred libations or to carry incense in the

---

19. BDAG 619. The phrase "of the tabernacle" is a genitive of apposition to "the temple" (i.e., "the temple which is the tabernacle").

20. Both "angels" and "plagues" have (anaphoric) articles in v. 6 to refer back to their initial mention in v. 1.

temple ritual (5:8; see Exod 27:3; 1 Kgs 7:50; 2 Kgs 25:15; Zech 14:20; cf. Josephus, *Ant.* 3.143).[21] At this point John changes his description of the seven angels: he previously said they "hold" or possess "the seven plagues" that represent the completion of God's anger (vv. 1, 6), but now they are entrusted with "seven bowls filled with God's anger" (v. 7). The two images represent the same actions of judgment to come (in 21:9 both descriptions occur together). Using the imagery of "bowls" of judgment, John notes that they are "filled with the anger of God" (γεμούσας τοῦ θυμοῦ τοῦ θεοῦ; see note on v. 1), implying that God has held back the full measure of his righteous indignation against human sin, but it is about to be poured out (as ch. 16 will portray). Describing God as "liv[ing] forever and ever" (v. 7c; see also 4:9–10; 10:6) is not perfunctory in this context. It identifies the Lord as the only true God in contrast to all the false gods that humans worship. As the living God, he is the sovereign over the whole world (cf. Dan 4:34–35; 6:26–27; 12:7) and can be expected one day to exact his judgment and justice against all rebels. Christians living amid Rome's claim to universal dominion and a world of many gods would benefit from reminders of the living God who surpasses all such supposed rivals.

God's awesome presence in this commissioning scene, especially his "glory" and "power," is symbolized by the "smoke" that filled the heavenly temple as the next event in John's vision (v. 8a). Smoke permeated the temple in Isaiah's vision of God in his heavenly sanctuary (Isa 6:4), and God's powerful presence was represented by fire and smoke on Mount Sinai (Exod 19:18; cf. Pss 18:7–9; 104:32). A cloud of smoke or incense symbolized God's glory as he dwelt among Israel in the tabernacle (Exod 40:34–35; Lev 16:2, 12–13) as well as in the temple (1 Kgs 8:10–11; 2 Chr 5:13–14; 7:1–2). In several of these accounts the smoke of God's glorious manifestation prevented Moses or the priests from entering the sanctuary for a time (e.g., Exod 40:35; 2 Chr 7:2). So also in John's vision, no one is permitted to intrude into God's presence during the time that his glory and power are displayed on earth in "the seven plagues of the seven angels" (v. 8b–c) that will be seen in the next chapter. The overpowering glory of God's presence and his display of wrath heighten the sense of his holy uniqueness from his creatures and call for this respite from contact.[22] But with this vision the stage is set for God's anger in judgment to be "completed" (vv. 1c, 8c; an *inclusio* emphasizing the climactic nature of the bowls that are introduced in this chapter).

Theology in Application

The Song of Those Set Free

Why is there jubilation in the theater when the evil villain gets his comeuppance? Why does the whole class go home encouraged when the bully finally gets sent to the principal's office? Why do we feel so satisfied at hearing the stories of Harriet Tubman's exploits along the Underground Railroad in the American South? It is

---

21. LSJ 1930; BDAG 1055. The KJV translation "vials" is misleading since that English word has changed in sense over the centuries.

22. Osborne, *Revelation*, 572.

because we have a built-in sense of justice that craves to see the right prevail and tyrants get their due. And the darker the injustice and the evil becomes, the stronger and deeper the rejoicing will be over its defeat. This passage reflects that same sober exultation over God's truth and justice winning out at last. The parallels with Israel at the exodus giving thanks for deliverance from Pharaoh help us to catch the nuances: the oppression of slavery to sin and evil broken by God's incomparable glory and power; the Lord Almighty, King of the nations, finally making things right for his people (vv. 2–4). Though we are sobered by the prospects of divine wrath being poured out on the world's evil (vv. 1, 7–8), it reminds us about who is truly in charge of this world in its present and in its future. We can find strength to fight injustice or tolerate oppression as necessary if we know that the Lord God exemplifies perfect justice and will do what is right in the end. Even if we know that our troubles are in many ways self-inflicted, we can glorify God for deliverance from the tyrannical powers that take advantage of our predicament. We worship and revere God not just because he is gentle and gives us warm feelings but because we long for his righteousness and truth to prevail in our world and set us free from its evil.

Revelation 16:1–21

Literary Context

After the heavenly introduction to the bowls given in chapter 15, this chapter now presents the seven bowls narrated in numbered sequence. These conclude the three series of God's judgments that began in chapter 6, and they continue the pattern of greater intensity seen in the movement through the three series. The bowl judgments represent the greatest outpouring of God's wrath that culminates his judgment against the sinful empires of the world led by the dragon, the beast, and the false prophet. The bowls prepare the way for the dominion of the Lord God and his Messiah. Their victory was announced in 11:15–19 and will be directly portrayed in 19:11–21. The section that intervenes (17:1–19:10) records the destruction of Babylon as the focus of those hostile world empires, a story that is previewed here in 16:19.

Main Idea

Seven angels pour out bowls of God's wrath on the earth and its inhabitants, reprising the plagues on Egypt and previewing the destruction of Babylon and the great eschatological battle.

Translation

Revelation 16:1–21

1a	Action/Preview	And **I heard a loud voice from the temple saying to the seven angels,**
b	Authorization	*"Go and pour out the seven bowls of God's anger on the earth."*
2a	Action/1st Bowl	And **the first went and poured out his bowl on the earth,**
b	Effect	and **evil and malignant sores appeared on the humans**
c	Specification	who **had the mark of the beast and worshiped his image.**
3a	Action/2nd Bowl	And **the second poured out his bowl on the sea,**
b	Effects	and **it became blood as from a dead person,**
c		and **every living creature of the things in the sea died.**
4a	Action/3rd Bowl	And **the third poured out his bowl on the rivers and springs of water,**
b	Effect	and **they became blood.**
5a	Action	And **I heard the angel of the waters saying,**
b	Praise	*"You are righteous—the one who is and who was, the holy one—*
c	Reason	*because you decreed these judgments.*
6a	Reason/ Premise	*For they poured out the blood of saints and prophets,*
b	Effect	*and you have given them blood to drink,*
c	Description	*which they deserve."*
7a	Action	And **I heard the altar saying,**
b	Affirmation	*"Yes, Lord God Almighty, your judgments are true and righteous."*
8a	Action/4th Bowl	And **the fourth poured out his bowl on the sun,**
b	Effects	and **it was allowed to burn people with fire.**
9a		And **people were burned severely,**
b	Effects of 8b–9a	and **they blasphemed the name of God**
c		who had authority over these plagues,
d		and **they did not repent**
e	Result	so as to give him glory.
10a	Action/5th Bowl	And **the fifth poured out his bowl on the throne of the beast,**
b	Effect of 10a	and **his kingdom became darkened,**
c	Effect of 2b, 8b	and **people gnawed their tongues because of pain,**
11a	Effects of 10b–c	and **they blasphemed the God of heaven because of their pains and their sores,**
b		and **they did not repent from their deeds.**

12a	Action/6th Bowl	**And the sixth poured out his bowl on the great river Euphrates,**
b	Effect	**and its water was dried up**
c	Purpose	to prepare the way for the kings from the east.

13a	Action/Preview	**And I saw three unclean spirits**
		like frogs
b	Description	coming out from the mouth of the dragon and
		from the mouth of the beast and
		from the mouth of the false prophet.

14a	Explanation	**For they are spirits, that is,**
		demons,
b	Descriptions	performing signs,
c		who go out to the kings of the whole inhabited world
d	Purpose	to gather them for the battle of the great day of God Almighty.

15a	Parenthetical	*"Indeed I am coming as a thief.*
	Declaration	
b	Beatitude	*Blessed is the one who is alert and*
		keeps his garments on
c	Purpose	*so that he may not walk around naked*
d		*and his shamefulness be exposed."*

16	Effect of 14c–d	**And they gathered them at the place called Armageddon in Hebrew.**
17a	Action/7th Bowl	**And the seventh poured out his bowl on the air,**
b	Effect	**and a loud voice came out of the temple from the throne, saying,**
c	Announcement	*"It has happened."*
18a	Effects	**And there came flashes of lightning and**
		rumblings and
		peals of thunder,
b		**and a great earthquake took place**
c	Description/	such as has not occurred from the time when humankind came to be on the earth,
	Comparison	so mighty an earthquake it was—so great!

19a	Effects	**And the great city split into three parts,**
b		**and the cities of the nations fell.**
c		**And Babylon the great was remembered before God**
d	Purpose	to give her the cup of the wine of the fury of God's wrath.
20a	Effects	**And every island fled,**
b		**and no mountains were to be found.**
21a		**And huge hail,…**
		each stone weighing about a hundred pounds,
		… came down from heaven on people,
b		**and people blasphemed God**
		because of the plague of hail,
c	Reason	because its plague was exceedingly severe.

Structure

After a very brief introduction (v. 1) the seven angels pour out their bowls in numbered sequence, steadily visiting God's wrath in the form of the most severe plagues seen yet: plagues on the beast's followers (v. 2), the natural world (vv. 3–9), and the beast's throne (vv. 10–11), preparing the way for the ultimate eschatological battle (vv. 12–16) and the destruction of Babylon itself (vv. 17–21).

Exegetical Outline

III. Second Vision: Heavenly Throne Room and Three Judgment Cycles (4:1–16:21)

    A. Vision of God in His Heavenly Throne Room (4:1–11)

    B. The Seven-Sealed Scroll and the Slain Lamb (5:1–14)

    C. The Seven Seals and the Interlude of the Two Multitudes (6:1–8:1)

    D. The Seven Trumpets and Further Interludes (8:2–14:20)

    E. The Seven Bowl Judgments (15:1–16:21)

        1. Heavenly Preparation for the Bowl Judgments (15:1–8)

➡   **2. The Seven Bowls of God's Wrath Poured Out (16:1–21)**

           a. Introduction: heavenly authorization for pouring out the seven bowls (16:1)

           b. The seven bowls of God's wrath and their effects (16:2–21)

               (1) The first bowl poured on the earth: sores on followers of the beast (16:2)

               (2) The second bowl poured on the sea: sea turned to blood (16:3)

               (3) The third bowl on rivers and springs: they turn to blood as recompense for the death of saints and prophets (16:4–7)

               (4) The fourth bowl poured on the sun: searing heat but no repentance (16:8–9)

               (5) The fifth bowl poured on the beast's throne: severe pain, no repentance (16:10–11)

               (6) The sixth bowl poured on the Euphrates: preparation for Armageddon (16:12–16)

               (7) The seventh bowl poured on the air: preview of Babylon's destruction (16:17–21)

Explanation of the Text

16:1 And I heard a loud voice from the temple saying to the seven angels, "Go and pour out the seven bowls of God's anger on the earth" (Καὶ ἤκουσα μεγάλης φωνῆς ἐκ τοῦ ναοῦ λεγούσης τοῖς ἑπτὰ ἀγγέλοις, Ὑπάγετε καὶ ἐκχέετε τὰς ἑπτὰ φιάλας τοῦ θυμοῦ τοῦ θεοῦ εἰς τὴν γῆν). After the previous chapter's three visions preparing the way for the seven bowl judgments, John now narrates those judgments in numbered sequence. They are briefly introduced in v. 1 by the divine instruction that John heard from the temple, authorizing the seven angels for their judicial task. The "loud voice" that he heard "from the temple" in heaven (v. 1a; cf. 7:15; 11:1–2, 19; 15:5, 8) is another in the series of commands given from God's throne room to commission acts of judgment that follow (cf. 9:13–14;

14:17–18). Some commentators understand this "voice" to belong to God himself,[1] but it belongs more likely to an overseeing angel expressing God's will (see note at 9:13 on such heavenly voices in Rev and see the reference here in v. 1b to "God's anger" not "my anger"). The seven angels had previously appeared as a portent "in heaven" (15:1), but now the heavenly voice tells them to "go and pour out"[2] their bowls "on the earth" (v. 1b), authorizing this series of judgments in summary.[3] The image of "pouring out" divine "anger" on rebellious humanity is drawn from a wide range of Old Testament prophetic texts that describe heaven's judgment on disobedient Israel as well as on the pagan empires of the world (e.g., Jer 10:25; 44:6; Lam 2:4; 4:11; Ezek 7:5; 9:8; 14:19; 36:18; Zeph 3:8). This combines easily with the figure of "bowls of God's anger" (v. 1b)[4] to be poured out from heaven (similar to 8:5 where a filled censer is used to "throw" fires of judgment onto the earth).[5]

16:2 And the first went and poured out his bowl on the earth, and evil and malignant sores appeared on the humans who had the mark of the beast and worshiped his image (Καὶ ἀπῆλθεν ὁ πρῶτος καὶ ἐξέχεεν τὴν φιάλην αὐτοῦ εἰς τὴν γῆν,

καὶ ἐγένετο ἕλκος κακὸν καὶ πονηρὸν ἐπὶ τοὺς ἀνθρώπους τοὺς ἔχοντας τὸ χάραγμα τοῦ θηρίου καὶ τοὺς προσκυνοῦντας τῇ εἰκόνι αὐτοῦ). The numbered sequence of seven angels pouring out bowls of judgment begins here in v. 2 and follows a consistent pattern of presentation until its conclusion with the seventh angel in vv. 17–21. The pattern is: "The [ordinal number referring to one of the seven angels][6] poured out his bowl [on a location] and [certain effects] came about or appeared [ἐγένετο] and [further effects resulted with various verbs used]." In a few cases some of these elements do not appear and other elements are added, but the broad pattern is clear.[7] Only in this verse do we find the initial verb "went" (ἀπῆλθεν; v. 2a) as a transition from the heavenly scene; for the remaining bowls the attention falls on the earthly effects of the judgments. The first angel emptied his bowl "on the earth" itself (v. 2a), in contrast to the sea or other water sources, the sun or the air, and so on as in subsequent verses. But the rest of the verse pays attention to its effect on the earth's human population spread out over the entire world (cf. 13:3; 14:3 for "earth" as referring to its inhabitants). Its effect is to inflict "evil and malignant sores" (v. 2b) on the humans who had accepted "the mark of the beast"

---

1. Aune, *Revelation 6–16*, 882; Beale, *Revelation*, 812; Smalley, *Revelation*, 400. A potential support for the idea that this is God's voice is the possibility that this is an allusion to Isa 66:6, "a sound/voice from the temple [φωνὴ ἐκ ναοῦ], the sound/voice of the Lord [φωνὴ κυρίου], giving recompense to his enemies." If it is not specifically the Lord's voice (see above), it reflects God's will in launching the culminating judgments of the seven bowls.

2. The imperative "pour out" (ἐκχέετε) is present (imperfective aspect) because it brings out the repeated acts of seven "pourings" that will follow (cf. Fanning, *Verbal Aspect*, 160–61; 364–65; contra Aune, *Revelation 6–16*, 855; Smalley, *Revelation*, 400, who say it is conative or inceptive).

3. "On the earth" in v. 1 has a broader reference than the more specific focus of "on the earth" in v. 2, "on the sea" in v. 3, and other locative phrases that follow in vv. 4, 8, 10, 12, 17.

4. See 16:19 for the lexical sense of "anger" (θυμός) here ver-

sus "wrath" (ὀργή) used also in Rev. Here "of anger" is a genitive of content to "bowls," and "God's" is a subjective genitive to "anger" (cf. Aune, *Revelation 6–16*, 855).

5. The suggestion (e.g., Aune, *Revelation 6–16*, 883; Beale, *Revelation*, 813) that "pouring out bowls" carries a symbolic reference to acts of sacrifice in the OT worship ritual (pouring out blood at the altar or drink offerings) is hard to fit into the context of dispensing judgment in full measure onto the earth. How is wrath like a sacrifice to be offered in worship? The imagery works better as a representation of the fullness of judgment that is dispensed (similar to the judgment "thrown" from a full censer to the earth in 8:5 and to the picture of the blood of the righteous "poured out" widely in 16:6).

6. Because "the seven angels" have been clearly in focus since 15:1, John can refer to them now with simply the ordinal numeral, "the first," "the second," and so on.

7. Aune, *Revelation 6–16*, 868–69, lays this out clearly.

(v. 2c; 13:16; 14:9) and "worshiped his image" (v. 2c; 13:14–15; 14:9; 15:2). These sores are a terrible kind of boil or skin ulcer (cf. Deut 28:27, 35; Job 2:7; Luke 16:20–21), mirroring the sixth plague against Egypt (Exod 9:9–11). They constitute another example of corresponding punishment or the penalty matching the crime (cf. v. 6; also 2:22): for receiving the beast's mark on their skin they now suffer grievous marks of judgment on their bodies.[8]

16:3–4 And the second poured out his bowl on the sea, and it became blood as from a dead person, and every living creature of the things in the sea died. 4 And the third poured out his bowl on the rivers and springs of water, and they became blood (Καὶ ὁ δεύτερος ἐξέχεεν τὴν φιάλην αὐτοῦ εἰς τὴν θάλασσαν, καὶ ἐγένετο αἷμα ὡς νεκροῦ, καὶ πᾶσα ψυχὴ ζωῆς ἀπέθανεν τὰ ἐν τῇ θαλάσσῃ. 4 Καὶ ὁ τρίτος ἐξέχεεν τὴν φιάλην αὐτοῦ εἰς τοὺς ποταμοὺς καὶ τὰς πηγὰς τῶν ὑδάτων, καὶ ἐγένετο αἷμα). The second and third bowls are closely related and are narrated quickly (vv. 3–4), followed by a doxological interlude that responds to both of them together (vv. 5–7). They also parallel and intensify the effects of the second and third trumpet judgments (8:8–11). These mirror the first plague on Egypt (Exod 7:17–21; Pss 78:44; 105:29) that turned all the water of Egypt into blood. Here likewise "the sea" is turned to blood, and all its creatures die (v. 3), and other water sources, "rivers and springs," are also turned to blood (v. 4). The two trumpet judgments in chapter 8 affected a third of the waters, but that is escalated here to include the sea, rivers, and springs without limitation, and "every creature" in the sea is killed. In the trumpet judgments, the effect on human life and commerce

was mentioned (8:9, 11), and such effects are likely here but are not made explicit.[9] The main point about these catastrophic effects on the sea (v. 3) in John's first-century context of writing is how disruptive this would be for food supplies and trade in general (cf. 18:17–19).[10] The same will be true in the end-times. It seems less likely that the sea as a source of all evil and of archetypal opposition to God (cf. 13:1; 21:1) is in view in this judgment.[11]

16:5–7 And I heard the angel of the waters saying, "You are righteous—the one who is and who was, the holy one—because you decreed these judgments. 6 For they poured out the blood of saints and prophets, and you have given them blood to drink, which they deserve." 7 And I heard the altar saying, "Yes, Lord God Almighty, your judgments are true and righteous" (καὶ ἤκουσα τοῦ ἀγγέλου τῶν ὑδάτων λέγοντος, Δίκαιος εἶ, ὁ ὢν καὶ ὁ ἦν, ὁ ὅσιος, ὅτι ταῦτα ἔκρινας, 6 ὅτι αἷμα ἁγίων καὶ προφητῶν ἐξέχεαν καὶ αἷμα αὐτοῖς [δ]έδωκας πιεῖν, ἄξιοί εἰσιν. 7 καὶ ἤκουσα τοῦ θυσιαστηρίου λέγοντος, Ναί κύριε ὁ θεὸς ὁ παντοκράτωρ, ἀληθιναὶ καὶ δίκαιαι αἱ κρίσεις σου). In response to these plagues inflicted on the waters of the earth, the angel charged with their oversight affirms the judicial aptness of such punishments (vv. 5–6), and a further heavenly voice adds its agreement (v. 7), both addressing God directly as the source of these judgments. John hears first "the angel of the waters" (v. 5a), a reference to God's heavenly servant charged with controlling and overseeing the earth's waters (see comments at 7:1; cf. 1 En. 60:11–22; 66:2; 69:22; Jub. 2:2). He testifies (v. 5b) to God's character as just and holy (δίκαιος and ὅσιος; see Rev 11:17; 15:4; also Deut 32:4; Pss

---

8. Beasley-Murray, *Revelation*, 240; Roloff, *Revelation*, 188–89.

9. This may be left unexpressed here because John will portray the wider effects of all these judgments in a different way in 18:3–8, 11, 17–19.

10. Osborne, *Revelation*, 580.

11. E.g., Boxall, *Revelation*, 226–27; Resseguie, *Narrative Commentary*, 210–11.

119:137; 145:17) as well as to his eternal existence ("the one who is and who was"; ὁ ὢν καὶ ὁ ἦν; see comments at 1:4; 11:17) that sets him off as utterly separate and unique from his creation. The angel ascribes righteousness and holiness to God because of his actions just witnessed: "Because you decreed these judgments" (ὅτι ταῦτα ἔκρινας; v. 5c).[12]

God's just actions are seen further in the principle of corresponding punishment (see 2:22; also v. 2 above) expressed in v. 6: they have shed righteous blood, and so they deserve blood to drink instead of water. The reference to "they" in the verb "they poured out" (ἐξέχεαν) does not have a specific antecedent in the preceding context, but it refers generally to those rebellious humans who suffered from the judgments on the waters (vv. 3–4; "these judgments" of v. 5c), like the followers of the beast punished in the first bowl judgment (v. 2). The idea of "blood for blood" will become a refrain in describing God's judgment of the harlot Babylon (17:6; 18:24; 19:2). This shared human guilt for shedding the blood "of saints and prophets" (16:6a) was demonstrated earlier in the earthly celebrations at the murder of the two witnesses (11:9–10; cf. 11:18) and is seen also in the Old Testament (e.g., 2 Chr 36:15–17; Neh 9:26; cf. Luke 11:49–51). The phrase translated "which they deserve" (v. 6c) is more literally "they are worthy" (ἄξιοί εἰσιν), but here the adjective "worthy" that usually carries a positive connotation ("deserving of good"; cf. 3:4) carries a negative sense instead

(e.g., Deut 25:2; Luke 12:48; Rom 1:32; cf. Herm. Sim. 6.3.3; 8.11.1).[13]

John hears another heavenly affirmation (v. 7), this one originating from "the altar" in the heavenly temple.[14] This is phrased cryptically as "I heard the altar saying" (καὶ ἤκουσα τοῦ θυσιαστηρίου λέγοντος), but this is likely to be an elliptical expression for what is phrased more fully in 9:13, "I heard a voice from . . . the altar . . . saying."[15] It is possible that this is the voice of the angel associated with the altar in 14:18, but John does not identify it further. As in vv. 1 and 5, this not the divine voice since it expresses its declaration to God with the vocative "Lord" and second-person pronoun "*your* judgments" (v. 7b). The address to "Lord God Almighty" continues from v. 5 the exalted view of God, here as the all-powerful sovereign who alone has the might and authority to effect justice on earth.[16] The declaration that his judgments are "true and righteous" (ἀληθιναὶ καὶ δίκαιαι) mirrors texts like Deuteronomy 32:4, Psalms 19:9 and 119:137, and Daniel 3:27 (LXX)[17] and is repeated almost verbatim in Revelation 19:2 in a similar heavenly doxology. His assessment always accords with what is actually the case and with what is fair and right.

16:8–9 And the fourth poured out his bowl on the sun, and it was allowed to burn people with fire. 9 And people were burned severely, and they blasphemed the name of God who had authority over these plagues, and they did not

---

12. Here the verb normally translated "judge" (κρίνω) refers to "mak[ing] a legal decision" (LN §56.20) or "impos[ing] . . . punishments" (BDAG 568–69). See CSB, NET.

13. BDAG 94.

14. This is the incense altar in the heavenly temple; see note on 6:9.

15. This is best taken as a genitive direct object with the verb "hear" (ἀκούω), a common enough usage in the NT and in Rev (cf. 16:1, 5; BDAG 38). This could be a partitive genitive, "[someone] from the altar" (see comment on 5:9; cf. Aune, *Revelation 6–16*, 888), but such partitive expressions elsewhere

in Rev use the preposition "from" (ἐκ), not the genitive case alone. A few manuscripts add ἐκ here (046, 2329), but the simple genitive is clearly the harder reading and is supported by superior manuscripts. The voice could also belong to the angel described in 14:18 who "came out from the altar . . . and cried with a loud voice."

16. See comments on the OT background of "Almighty" at 1:8.

17. See also Jewish texts like Tob 3:2; T. Job 43:13; Pss. Sol. 8:23–25; Apoc. Mos./LAE 27:5.

repent so as to give him glory (Καὶ ὁ τέταρτος ἐξέχεεν τὴν φιάλην αὐτοῦ ἐπὶ τὸν ἥλιον, καὶ ἐδόθη αὐτῷ καυματίσαι τοὺς ἀνθρώπους ἐν πυρί. 9 καὶ ἐκαυματίσθησαν οἱ ἄνθρωποι καῦμα μέγα καὶ ἐβλασφήμησαν τὸ ὄνομα τοῦ θεοῦ τοῦ ἔχοντος τὴν ἐξουσίαν ἐπὶ τὰς πληγὰς ταύτας καὶ οὐ μετενόησαν δοῦναι αὐτῷ δόξαν). The sequence of judgments resumes here with the pouring out of the fourth bowl, in this case on "the sun" (v. 8a).[18] The sun and other heavenly bodies were partially darkened in several earlier judgments (6:12; 8:12), but here the sun flares instead with intense heat and is permitted by God[19] to "burn" people with fire (v. 8b; καυματίσαι). John reinforces this in v. 9a by repeating the same verb in a passive form: people "were burned" (ἐκαυματίσθησαν),[20] adding the intensifier "severely."[21] This horrific judgment constitutes a direct contrast to the promise in 7:16 that God's people who had come from the final tribulation would be sheltered so that neither the sun nor any heat (καῦμα) would ever harm them.

The godless humans who suffer this punishment, however, respond with slanderous defiance (v. 9b–c). They "blasphemed the name of God"[22] instead of repenting of their rebellion against the great God they themselves know to have judged them in this way (this seems to be the point of John's description, "blasphemed . . . God who had authority over these plagues"; v. 9b–c).[23] Mention of "these plagues" alludes also to the judgments on Egypt and to Pharaoh's stubborn resistance

against the God of Israel despite the blows he and his nation were suffering (e.g., Exod 7:13, 22; 8:15, 19, 32; 9:7, 12, 34–35). Like Pharaoh, the humans in John's vision failed to repent before God and "give him glory" (δοῦναι αὐτῷ δόξαν; an infinitive of result). To give God glory (i.e., to acknowledge him as God; cf. Rom 1:21–23) is the appropriate response in such a situation (cf. Rev 11:13; 14:7; also T. Job 16:4), but as we have seen (e.g., Rev 9:20–21), this will be rare in those future days.

16:10–11 And the fifth poured out his bowl on the throne of the beast, and his kingdom became darkened, and people gnawed their tongues because of pain, 11 and they blasphemed the God of heaven because of their pains and their sores, and they did not repent from their deeds (Καὶ ὁ πέμπτος ἐξέχεεν τὴν φιάλην αὐτοῦ ἐπὶ τὸν θρόνον τοῦ θηρίου, καὶ ἐγένετο ἡ βασιλεία αὐτοῦ ἐσκοτωμένη, καὶ ἐμασῶντο τὰς γλώσσας αὐτῶν ἐκ τοῦ πόνου, 11 καὶ ἐβλασφήμησαν τὸν θεὸν τοῦ οὐρανοῦ ἐκ τῶν πόνων αὐτῶν καὶ ἐκ τῶν ἑλκῶν αὐτῶν καὶ οὐ μετενόησαν ἐκ τῶν ἔργων αὐτῶν). The fifth bowl produces similar defiant resistance but is focused more narrowly on the beast's locus of authority rather than the whole world, as the fourth bowl was. The beast's "throne" was mentioned in 13:2 along with his "power" and "great authority," all of which was given to him by the dragon, Satan. The immediate effect of the fifth angel's bowl was that "his kingdom became darkened" (v. 10b),[24]

---

18. The voice of v. 1 commanded the seven judgments to be poured out "on the earth," and "the sun" would normally be distinguished from the earth as a part of the lower heavens or sky (5:13; 10:6; 14:7). But the ultimate effects of this judgment are felt on the earth.

19. See the comments on the use of "it was allowed," "it was given" (ἐδόθη) in 6:4; 13:5.

20. "People" constitutes a generic use of the articular plural οἱ ἄνθρωποι (as in 8:11; 9:6, 10, 15, 18, 20; 13:13; 14:4; 21:3; cf. BDAG 81).

21. "Severely" is expressed in v. 9a by a cognate accusative

phrase (cf. BDF §153.1); lit., "they were burned a great burn" (ἐκαυματίσθησαν . . . καῦμα μέγα).

22. See comments on "blaspheme [God's] name" at 13:6; cf. also vv. 11, 21 below where the parallel expression is to "blaspheme God."

23. Cf. 6:15–17 where those who are judged are aware that God and the Lamb are behind their suffering, but choose to flee and hide in desperation rather than repent.

24. "Became darkened" is the translation of a Greek periphrastic verb phrase (ἐγένετο . . . ἐσκοτωμένη) that is unusual in using the verb "become" (γίνομαι) instead of the normal

reflective of the ninth plague of Egypt (Exod 10:21–23) as well as the fourth trumpet judgment (Rev 8:12). This darkness is not destruction itself but a frightening symbol of ongoing distress and impending cataclysmic judgment (cf. day-of-the-Lord texts like Joel 2:2; Amos 5:20; Zeph 1:15). In vv. 10c–11 John cites the ongoing severe distress that accompanies the darkness: their "pain" that causes them to "gnaw their tongues" is not due to the darkness per se but the physical afflictions that come from the previous bowls of judgment. One of them is mentioned specifically in v. 11a ("their sores") along with a repetition of "their pains."[25] Again the tragic further result is their continued blaspheming of "the God of heaven" and their refusal to "repent from their deeds" (v. 11b; cf. vv. 9, 21; also 9:20–21). Just as the beast himself is a notorious blasphemer (13:1, 5, 6), so his pitiable followers mimic his implacable rejection of God.

16:12–13 And the sixth poured out his bowl on the great river Euphrates, and its water was dried up to prepare the way for the kings from the east. 13 And I saw three unclean spirits like frogs coming out from the mouth of the dragon and from the mouth of the beast and from the mouth of the false prophet (Καὶ ὁ ἕκτος ἐξέχεεν τὴν φιάλην αὐτοῦ ἐπὶ τὸν ποταμὸν τὸν μέγαν τὸν Εὐφράτην, καὶ ἐξηράνθη τὸ ὕδωρ αὐτοῦ, ἵνα ἑτοιμασθῇ ἡ ὁδὸς τῶν βασιλέων τῶν ἀπὸ ἀνατολῆς ἡλίου. 13 Καὶ εἶδον ἐκ τοῦ στόματος τοῦ δράκοντος

καὶ ἐκ τοῦ στόματος τοῦ θηρίου καὶ ἐκ τοῦ στόματος τοῦ ψευδοπροφήτου πνεύματα τρία ἀκάθαρτα ὡς βάτραχοι). John allocates much longer descriptions to the final two bowls compared to the preceding five, and in both instances he introduces episodes of judgment that will be described in more detail in coming chapters. The sixth bowl occupies vv. 12–16 (with v. 15 as a parenthetical announcement of Christ's imminent arrival as conqueror; cf. 19:11–21). The events of the sixth bowl center on the final battle of the world's rulers against Christ when he comes to establish his universal rule from Jerusalem (cf. 13:4; 17:12–14; 19:19). The scene begins to unfold when the sixth angel targets "the great river Euphrates" and as a result its water is "dried up" (v. 12a–b). The Euphrates was a significant element in the account of the sixth trumpet (9:14), and here as well as there it is associated with attacks by vast forces from outside Israel. This association is due to historical patterns of warfare across the Euphrates, both actual invasions from Israel's past as well as fears of attack from the east in the first-century Roman world (see comments at 9:14, 16). The language of "drying up" the waters of the great river is drawn from accounts of Israel's miraculous passage through the Red Sea and also of God's ability either to bring his people back across from exile in Mesopotamia or to allow hostile armies to cross as instruments of his disciplinary judgment (Ps 106:9; Isa 11:15–16; 44:27; 51:10; Jer 50:38; 51:36; Zech 10:6–12; cf. 4 Ezra

---

"be" (εἰμί), so it means "became dark/darkened" rather than "was dark/darkened" (contra Mathewson, *Handbook*, 209, 215; Osborne, *Revelation*, 587). See Fanning, *Verbal Aspect*, 310; see also note on 3:2.

25. Beale's view (*Revelation*, 824; see also Smalley, *Revelation*, 406) is that the darkness is not literal but a symbol of separation from God that the ungodly become aware of at various times throughout their lives: "times of anguish and horror when they realize that they are in spiritual darkness, that they are separated from God and that eternal darkness awaits them." The pain John describes is "spiritual and psychological 'tor-

ment'" and is perhaps "linked with the removal of some forms of earthly security, which causes the wicked to focus on their lack of spiritual security" (p. 824). This articulation fits well into the therapeutic culture of the modern West, but it is doubtful that John or his readers would have caught this point from the imagery. Beale's appeal to Wis 17–18 (the spiritual agony that accompanied the plagues on Egypt) imposes an "either-or" dichotomy on such judgments that even Wisdom itself does not espouse. Yes, such physical judgment and pain will also cause spiritual and psychological distress, but eliminating the former in favor of the latter alone is not the best reading of the text.

13:39–50).[26] In this context what is in view is the threat of judgment using human forces of destruction. John fleshes out this connection by describing God's purpose in drying up the river: "To prepare the way for the kings from the east" (v. 12c).[27] In the first-century land of Israel as well as the wider Roman Empire, the "east" meant Mesopotamia and Persia or Parthia (e.g., Isa 41:2, 25; 46:11; cf. 1 En. 56:5–8; Sib. Or. 4:135–39; 8:145–55; T. Mos. 3:1, 13), often in connection with fears of invasion and conquest from empires to the east.[28] Verse 12 speaks only of preparing the way; it does not explicitly declare that these kings will cross the river to do battle against God and his messiah, but those details are added in vv. 14 and 16 below.

This typological connection of the Euphrates with the threat of an outside attack should affect our understanding of the reference to "the kings from the east" in v. 12c. The intensification of this pattern in its future fulfillment may involve armies from Mesopotamia or Parthia, but it is more likely that it represents forces invading Israel from "the

whole inhabited world" (v. 14; cf. 11:18; 19:19), not from the east alone.[29] It is unfortunate to read popular interpreters who look to the Far East and confidently speak of "Oriental rulers" and forces from countries such as "communist China" or Japan, the "Land of the Rising Sun."[30] In previous centuries interpreters confidently cited Ottoman Turks and other Muslims invading Eastern Europe as the eastern powers.[31] To declare that these specific modern nations are the "fulfillment" of what John speaks of has invariably been an embarrassment to prophetic interpretation in subsequent generations.

A further point of preparation is given in v. 13, the campaign of satanic deception that will lure the world's rulers to gather for battle against the Lord. John witnesses (v. 13a, "and I saw"; καὶ εἶδον) the emergence of "three unclean spirits" (whose deceiving work will be specified in v. 14). In a grotesque combination these are said to be "like frogs" coming "from the mouths" of the satanic trinity introduced earlier in the book.[32] The repulsive image of "frogs," seen then and now as slimy, unhealthful,

---

26. For this judgment also (see v. 11), Beale, *Revelation*, 828–29, and Smalley, *Revelation*, 408, understand the "drying up" of the river not literally but as a symbol for "disenchantment with Babylon" on the part of "multitudes of [its] religious adherents throughout the world" (Beale, *Revelation*, 828). While we may take this "drying up" as metaphorical for smoothing the way for an invasion from beyond Israel's borders, and marshaling this outside force is clearly done via spiritual deception (v. 14), the Euphrates as a metaphor for Babylon's spiritual influence seems quite foreign to the OT background of eschatological warfare and to this context.

27. The phrase "from the east" is a smoother translation of "from the rising of the sun" (ἀπὸ ἀνατολῆς ἡλίου), a standard way to refer to the "east" (BDAG 74; cf. 7:2; also 21:13 that says simply "from the rising"; often plural in LXX: "risings of the sun" [Deut 4:41; Judg 11:18]).

28. See comments at 9:14 about the typology of judgment related to the "Euphrates" and its influence on understanding the end-time events these verses predict.

29. The ten kings allied with the beast in 17:12–18 (who first attack Babylon itself) seem to be part of this contingent who will join the final battle against the Lamb (19:19) that 16:12–16 portrays.

30. Smith, *Revelation*, 233; Walvoord, Rawley, and Hitchcock, *Revelation*, 245–46.

31. Kovacs and Rowland, *Revelation*, 173–75. Albert Barnes, *Notes Explanatory and Practical on the Book of Revelation* (New York: Harper & Brothers, 1852), 408–9; and E. B. Elliott, *Horae Apocalypticae* (5th ed.; London: Seeley, Jackson, and Halliday, 1862), 3:455–60, both thought the "Euphrates" was a symbol for how the Ottoman Empire obstructed conversions from "eastern peoples" but when it weakened (i.e., "dried up"), then they would come and be "conquered" by the gospel, a spiritual reading of the war mentioned in v. 14. It is ironic that Scott, *Exposition*, 332, decries identifying the kings of the east with the "Turkish empire" since it was a fading power even in his day (1900), but he later mentions Russia as one of the leading nations that will invade Israel.

32. See mention of the dragon or Satan in 12:3–4, 8–9, 13, 17; 13:2; the beast in 11:7; 13:1, 6–7; and the beast from the land (13:11, 15–17), called here for the first time "the false prophet" (cf. 19:20; 20:10).

and ritually unclean (cf. Exod 8:2–6; Lev 11:10; Ps 78:45; 105:30),[33] communicates at a visceral level how evil these spirits (and the hosts who disgorged them) were. The trio of evil (dragon, beast, and false prophet) is relevant to this developing scene because, from their first mention in Revelation, they have been associated with "battle" (πόλεμος) or hostility against God, his witnesses, and his people (e.g., 11:7; 12:17; 13:7). The nature of this particular battle is shown in the next set of verses.

16:14–16 For they are spirits, that is, demons, performing signs, who go out to the kings of the whole inhabited world to gather them for the battle of the great day of God Almighty. 15 "Indeed I am coming as a thief. Blessed is the one who is alert and keeps his garments on so that he may not walk around naked and his shamefulness be exposed." 16 And they gathered them at the place called Armageddon in Hebrew (εἰσὶν γὰρ πνεύματα δαιμονίων ποιοῦντα σημεῖα, ἃ ἐκπορεύεται ἐπὶ τοὺς βασιλεῖς τῆς οἰκουμένης ὅλης συναγαγεῖν αὐτοὺς εἰς τὸν πόλεμον τῆς ἡμέρας τῆς μεγάλης τοῦ θεοῦ τοῦ παντοκράτορος. 15 Ἰδοὺ ἔρχομαι ὡς κλέπτης. μακάριος ὁ γρηγορῶν καὶ τηρῶν τὰ ἱμάτια αὐτοῦ, ἵνα μὴ γυμνὸς περιπατῇ καὶ βλέπωσιν τὴν ἀσχημοσύνην αὐτοῦ. 16 καὶ συνήγαγεν αὐτοὺς εἰς τὸν τόπον τὸν καλούμενον Ἑβραϊστὶ Ἁρμαγεδών). The foreboding effects of the sixth bowl are presented in clearest terms in vv. 14 and 16 with an important parenthetical exhortation in v. 15. Here John clarifies (explanatory "for," γάρ; v. 14a) both the evil character of the "unclean spirits" seen in v. 13 as well as their fateful role in gathering the nations for the coming eschatological battle. These "spirits" are "demons,"[34] evil supernatural beings that act in opposition to what is good (cf. 9:20).[35] Here, however, their evil deception serves God's larger purpose to exact divine judgment and justice on earth, just as he used a lying spirit to entice Ahab to his death in battle in 1 Kings 22:19–23. These evil spirits are allowed to work miraculous "signs" (σημεῖα), like the false prophet is said to perform in 13:13, as they go out to "the kings of the whole inhabited world" to entice them to battle (v. 14c–d). The broader scope of this phrase (cf. "the whole world" in 3:10; also Matt 24:14; Acts 11:28) as compared to "kings of the east" in v. 12 shows that the coming conflict will not be limited to traditional enemies from across the Euphrates. What is coming is a defiant but futile uprising of all the powers of the earth against the rule of Christ (Ps 2:2–3; Rev 11:15; 12:10) under the nefarious influence of Satan, the deceiver of "the whole world" (12:9).

As John explicitly notes (v. 14d), this battle is a feature of "the great day of God Almighty," a reference to "the day of the Lord" that the Old Testament prophets predicted (see also Rev 6:17, "the great day of their wrath"). Warfare by the nations against God and his people in Jerusalem is a common feature of such prophecies about that day, and they sometimes refer to attacks close at hand in the history of Israel or Judah and at other times to a distant fulfillment (Isa 2:10–21; 34:4; 63:1–3; Ezek 38–39; Joel 2–3; Zech 12:1–9; 14:1–11; cf. 4 Ezra 13:29–50). But either way they are part of a pattern of fulfillment that points to an ultimate earthly battle in the last

---

33. The frogs of the second plague on Egypt were offensive not because they existed in the Nile but because they swarmed into Egyptian palaces, bedrooms, beds, ovens, kneading troughs, and onto the people great and small (Exod 8:2–14; cf. Jos. *Ant.* 2.296–98).

34. The phrase, "spirits, that is, demons," is a Greek construction using a genitive of apposition or epexegetical geni-

tive ("spirits of demons"; πνεύματα δαιμονίων), in which the genitive clarifies or specifies the sense of the head term. See Wallace, *Grammar*, 95–100; Aune, *Revelation 6–16*, 895. The three words used in vv. 13b–14a (spirits, unclean, demons) are used in combination in several other NT texts (e.g., Luke 4:33; 9:42; Rev 18:2).

35. BDAG 210; LN §12.37.

days more intense and more decisive than any that has occurred before. At that time God will show himself truly "Almighty"[36] as he defeats all enemies and brings his heavenly rule to earth through his Messiah. Ironically the nations gather, intending to destroy God's people and God's work, but this will lead instead to their destruction.[37]

The fact that these events are associated with Christ's imminent return to earth[38] prompts a brief parenthesis (v. 15) in which Christ himself addresses the reader through John and pronounces a blessing on the person who will be ready for his return. The direct address is made more powerful by the lack of an introductory conjunction (see note on this at 9:11) and the word of affirmation or validation, "indeed" (ἰδού).[39] Christ affirms that he will come[40] to earth at a time no one can anticipate, that is, "as a thief" (v. 15a; see discussion at 3:3). The unpredictability of his coming demands moral alertness and attention, but the Lord phrases it not merely as a demand but as a blessing[41] that will come for the one who is prepared (v. 15b–d). The call for watchfulness (γρηγορέω) is a call for Christians to be morally alert and awake.[42] A parallel source of blessing is carefulness to maintain conduct that is upright. This is phrased with a clothing metaphor that John employed earlier with different particulars: Christ has provided them with pure

garments through his death on the cross for them (3:18; 7:13–14), and when they appear with him in heaven they will be robed in such (6:11; 7:9; 22:14). But between those two points, Christians are called on to maintain ("keep," τηρέω) firm faith and godly conduct that reflects this provision from Christ (3:4–5; cf. 2:26; 3:3, 8, 10; 12:17; 14:12). Otherwise their lack of such godliness will be obvious to their great shame and dismay (3:18; cf. 1 John 2:28). The clothing metaphor thus points to a righteousness that is given freely, not earned, but is then lived out in faithful and godly conduct.

After the parenthesis of v. 15, John resumes the main line of thought briefly in v. 16. He signals the thematic link with v. 14 by repeating the primary verb and its referents from v. 14d as the main thought here: "they gathered them" (συνήγαγεν αὐτούς),[43] that is, the spirits assembled the kings of the earth as v. 14 indicated. The rest of v. 14d (assembled "for the battle of the great day of God Almighty") is repeated in v. 16 too but in more enigmatic and ominous terms: "At the place called Armageddon in Hebrew." This foreboding reference is more powerful because John leaves it undeveloped at this point in the text. The entire scene of eschatological battle that he has set forth in vv. 12–16 simply sets the stage for its detailed narration that will come in 19:11–21.

---

36. In the later chapters of Rev, John uses the distinctive title "Almighty" for God in contexts that describe or celebrate the decisive establishment of God's rule on earth (11:17; 15:3; 19:6, 15).

37. Beasley-Murray, *Revelation*, 244–45; Smalley, *Revelation*, 408, 411.

38. See the parallels to v. 15a ("behold, I am coming as a thief") in 22:7, 12 ("behold, I am coming quickly"; cf. similar expressions in 3:11 and 22:20; see also the note on 2:5).

39. LN §91.10; cf. note at 1:7.

40. The verb "I am coming" (ἔρχομαι) is a futuristic present, a common idiom with this verb (e.g., 2:5, 16; cf. also 1:7; see too John 14:3, 18, 28; Fanning, *Verbal Aspect*, 223–24). This points to the events described in 19:11–21.

41. This is the third of seven beatitudes in Rev, most of which occur in the later chapters. See note on 1:3.

42. See note on 3:2.

43. The Greek verb translated "they gathered" (συνήγαγεν) is a third-person singular (one Greek manuscript, א, has the plural συνήγαγον, but this is almost certainly a scribal correction), so it could mean "he gathered" (KJV), referring to God from v. 14. But the implied subject of "gather" in v. 14 is "spirits," a neuter plural. In Greek the normal pattern is that neuter-plural subjects take singular verbs (e.g., ἐκπορεύεται in v. 14b; see Aune, *Revelation 6–16*, 858; Charles, *Revelation*, 1:cxli for details of usage in Rev). For English idiom "they gathered" (referring to the spirits) is the better sense (cf. ESV, NASB, NIV, NRSV, RSV).

IN DEPTH: The Significance of Armageddon

Even in today's world the mention of Armageddon evokes powerful images that are widely dispersed throughout popular culture. Sometimes they have almost no connection to the book of Revelation itself. But even if people know very little about Revelation, Armageddon looms large in their awareness of the book, all too often sensationalized by Christian writers. The name "Armageddon" itself in v. 16 is puzzling. What is explicit is that it is the name of a place and comes from Hebrew, but further details are debated. The two main views[44] of its basic meaning are that it refers to (1) the "Mount of Megiddo";[45] Megiddo is a well-known geographical location near Mount Carmel in northwest Israel and the site of many notable battles in biblical history (Judg 5:19–21; 2 Kgs 23:29–30; 2 Chr 35:22; also Judg 4 and 7; 1 Sam 31); or (2) the "mountain of assembly," understood as the place where Babylon's king desired to exalt himself even to divine status (Isa 14:13),[46] and so in Revelation 16:16 a place where the kings of the earth gather to do battle against God and his Messiah. Both views have unresolved questions.[47] Megiddo does not show up as a site of end-time conflict in apocalyptic literature prior to Revelation. Moreover, Megiddo is not itself a "mountain," but it is situated at the most strategic pass through the Mount Carmel ridge where a main road from Egypt to Damascus and Mesopotamia crossed and entered the Jezreel (or Esdraelon) Valley, so "mountain" may not be out of place in its name. On the other hand, it is hard to explain the Hebrew spelling changes from "mountain of assembly" to "mountain of Megiddo," and the context of Isaiah 14 does not easily support a reference to kings gathering for battle.[48]

All in all, the reference to Megiddo as the site of notable military engagements makes more sense in this context. It alludes to a place where, in past history, vast empires fought for strategic advantage, and victories or defeats had far-reaching consequences. Like John's references to Jezebel and Balaam (Rev 2:14, 20) or to Sodom and Egypt (11:8), Armageddon in 16:16 represents not the literal location of Megiddo[49] but an actual decisive battle in the future like those

44. See Aune, *Revelation 6–16*, 898–99; Beale, *Revelation*, 838–41 for further details.

45. The Greek word Ἁρμαγεδών (spelled "Harmagedon" in CEB, NRSV) is a transliteration of the Hebrew for "mountain of Magedon" (adding a consonant at the end as in LXX Judg 1:27; 2 Kgs 9:27; and MT Zech 12:11).

46. This assumes that "Harmagedon" is a corrupt spelling of *har-mo'ed*, the mountain of gathering or assembly in Isa 14:13.

47. J. Jeremias, "Ἀρ Μαγεδών," *TDNT* 1:468.

48. Fekkes, *Prophetic Traditions*, 202–4.

49. For Megiddo in northwest Israel as the literal site of this future battle, see Patterson, *Revelation*, 312–14; Smith, *Revelation*, 236; Thomas, *Revelation 8–22*, 270–71; Walvoord, Rawley, and Hitchcock, *Revelation*, 247–48 (all but Smith see this as one battlefield in a larger war).

that were fought there in the past.[50] This picture coheres with other references to a great eschatological battle in the end times in which nations gather for battle against God and his Messiah at Jerusalem and are summarily defeated by God, leading to peace for Israel (e.g., Ezek 38:14–23; Joel 3:1–17; Zeph 3:8; Zech 12:1–9; 14:2–3, 12–13; 4 Ezra 13:39–50; 1 En. 56:5–8; Sib. Or. 3:657–701). Armageddon as a typological symbol points to this greater fulfillment of the pattern of pivotal warfare and victory in the end times, that is, to Christ's decisive defeat of the nations gathered against him prior to his millennial reign as described in 19:19–21.[51]

What some interpreters say about Armageddon in v. 16 is representative of how they understand the imagery of the bowl judgments in general. Just as with the trumpet judgments (see comments at 9:9), we must ask what realities in the world of the final days (or of any time) do these portrayals represent? Are they symbols for spiritual or psychological pain and of God's final judgment that he will exact in spiritual terms only? This is the view of the bowls that Beale espouses (and Smalley in large measure follows).[52] What this approach gets right is that ultimately the bowls are poured out because of humanity's sinful rebellion against God, and these images are meant to urge John's Christian readers to remain loyal to God despite persecution from the satanically evil world around them. But those fundamental truths are not lost if we see the spiritual and religious issues bound up with physical and earthly judgments.

The fact that a typological pattern from the Old Testament is involved in these verses does not mean that the New Testament escalation must be exclusively spiritual, as Beale implies in a few places.[53] This is a common misunderstanding of typology (i.e., the OT antitype was earthly, physical, geographical, but the NT intensification leaves that behind and moves to the spiritual and heavenly). For example, the typology of sacrifice in Hebrews and elsewhere (e.g., 1 Cor 5:7) did not mean that Christ offered himself only spiritually or only in the heavenly realms to deal with sin. He experienced real physical suffering, death, and resurrection in time and space, and that suffering provided real spiritual, eternal

---

50. This is the difference between the typological view adopted here and the view of Beale, *Revelation*, 838–41; Michaels, *Revelation*, 188–89, who understand these images to represent spiritual judgments (or the final spiritual judgment) but not actual physical suffering or conflict. Boring, *Revelation*, 175–76, is similar. See also Smalley, *Revelation*, 412–13 (who takes Armageddon as "a symbolic figure for the whole world. . . . a mythical formulation which represents the apocalyptic and universal mountain" where God defeats evil in the end (413).

See the further discussion that follows in the comments above.

51. Hoskins, *Revelation*, 297–99; Osborne, *Revelation*, 594–96; Scott, *Exposition*, 334.

52. Beale articulates this view at the outset of his treatment of the bowls (*Revelation*, 812–13) and then repeats it as details of the judgments are presented in his subsequent pages; e.g., 824, 828, 838–41, 842. Some of these details were discussed above in comments on specific verses.

53. Cf. Beale, *Revelation*, 838, 842.

blessings for the redeemed. There is no theological dichotomy between the two, no either-or choice to make between them.

We have seen at various places that the eschatology of Revelation is in theological continuity with the Old Testament prophets and psalms (see comments at 10:6–7; 11:15–18; 12:5), and this is true of John's visions of the coming eschatological battle that centers on Jerusalem and will result in the Messiah's victory and the establishment of God's rule on earth centered in Jerusalem (Rev 19–21). The Christian theme that John brings to his essentially Old Testament prophetic picture of God's future triumph over the nations is the role of Jesus as Messiah, whose sacrificial death on earth has already gained the decisive victory. Moreover, Christ will return to establish his reign completely, not only in heaven but also on earth where evil nations under satanic influence now rule.[54] While images of spiritual judgment and eternal punishment against sin are mixed into this presentation, we are not forced to collapse one into the other. Such an approach does not do justice to the text of Revelation seen in its biblical as well as in its ancient religious and historical setting.

16:17–18 And the seventh poured out his bowl on the air, and a loud voice came out of the temple from the throne, saying, "It has happened." 18 And there came flashes of lightning and rumblings and peals of thunder, and a great earthquake took place such as has not occurred from the time when humankind came to be on the earth, so mighty an earthquake it was—so great! (Καὶ ὁ ἕβδομος ἐξέχεεν τὴν φιάλην αὐτοῦ ἐπὶ τὸν ἀέρα, καὶ ἐξῆλθεν φωνὴ μεγάλη ἐκ τοῦ ναοῦ ἀπὸ τοῦ θρόνου λέγουσα, Γέγονεν. 18 καὶ ἐγένοντο ἀστραπαὶ καὶ φωναὶ καὶ βρονταί καὶ σεισμὸς ἐγένετο μέγας, οἷος οὐκ ἐγένετο ἀφ᾽ οὗ ἄνθρωπος ἐγένετο ἐπὶ τῆς γῆς τηλικοῦτος σεισμὸς οὕτω μέγας). Remarkably (compared to the seals and the trumpets) John moves directly from the sixth bowl to the seventh without interlude or delay. The seventh angel pours out his judgment "on the air" (v. 17a), a part of the earth to be sure (cf. v. 1), but more pervasive since

it covers the earth (cf. 9:2; Acts 22:23)[55] and includes the atmospheric plague of a great hailstorm crashing down on humans (v. 21). The broader effects that are described likewise involve the whole world and its inhabitants (vv. 18–21). The immediate result is in fact a heavenly declaration that takes us back to the start of this series of divine judgments. As in v. 1, there comes "a loud voice . . . out of the temple," more specifically "from the throne" of God within the heavenly temple (v. 17b). This voice expresses God's testimony, whether it is spoken by him directly or by one of his angels (see v. 1 and note at 9:13). The declaration itself, "it has happened" (γέγονεν; v. 17c), should be understood in light of v. 1 and of other heavenly declarations recorded by John in recent chapters (10:6–7; 11:15; 12:10–12; 14:7–8; see also 15:1). The voice in v. 1 characterizes the seven bowl judgments as the pouring out of "God's anger" on the earth, which

---

54. McNicol, *Conversion*, 14–16, 56–61.

55. BDAG 23.

in turn points back to 15:1 where it is said that in them "God's anger will be completed." So what "has happened" or taken place (v. 17c) is the sevenfold outpouring of God's anger that has now reached its conclusion.[56] As in other heavenly announcements in these chapters (see 18:2 in addition to the verses cited above), this is recorded as already accomplished from heaven's point of view, even though it is yet to be fully portrayed in John's account of all that it entails. Moreover, it is of course still future in terms of actual events that will consummate God's coming judgment and redemption on earth.

Accompanying the announcement of v. 17 are the awesome phenomena of "flashes of lightning and rumblings and peals of thunder" as well as "a great earthquake" (v. 18a–b). These represent God's terrifying presence originally experienced at Sinai (Exod 19:16–19) and repeated often thereafter in the Old Testament as typological symbols of God's presence and as portents of coming judgment.[57] They have been features of John's visions of judgment at key places: as part of the grounding vision in 4:5, then at 8:5 (related to the seventh seal), and then at 11:19 (related to the seventh trumpet). Here they signal the conclusion of the bowl judgments and God's imminent appearance on earth through the return of his Messiah as king and judge (19:11–21).[58] This will constitute a greater intensification of the pattern of judgment than has ever been seen before, as John explicitly notes regarding the earthquake (v. 18c). The comparative phrasing ("such as . . .") and reference to a range of past occurrences that are now exceeded ("from the

time when humankind came to be on the earth") are characteristic features of this typology and its escalation (most notably in Dan 12:1; Matt 24:21; Mark 13:19; but see also Exod 9:18, 24; Jer 30:7; Joel 2:2; cf. T. Mos. 8:1; 1QM 1:12). The "great" or violent (NRSV, REB) earthquake is specifically noted as completely unprecedented, and John reinforces its severity by adding two phrases at the end to reinforce what was already said, "so mighty an earthquake it was—so great" (τηλικοῦτος σεισμὸς οὕτω μέγας).[59] The occurrence of a "great earthquake" is a notable parallel to Ezekiel 38:18–20 (e.g., 38:19 LXX: σεισμὸς μέγας) that describes an invasion of many nations against the land of Israel and the violent shaking of whole earth that is the Lord's response to their attack.

16:19–21 And the great city split into three parts, and the cities of the nations fell. And Babylon the great was remembered before God to give her the cup of the wine of the fury of God's wrath. 20 And every island fled, and no mountains were to be found. 21 And huge hail, each stone weighing about a hundred pounds, came down from heaven on people, and people blasphemed God because of the plague of hail, because its plague was exceedingly severe (καὶ ἐγένετο ἡ πόλις ἡ μεγάλη εἰς τρία μέρη καὶ αἱ πόλεις τῶν ἐθνῶν ἔπεσαν. καὶ Βαβυλὼν ἡ μεγάλη ἐμνήσθη ἐνώπιον τοῦ θεοῦ δοῦναι αὐτῇ τὸ ποτήριον τοῦ οἴνου τοῦ θυμοῦ τῆς ὀργῆς αὐτοῦ. 20 καὶ πᾶσα νῆσος ἔφυγεν καὶ ὄρη οὐχ εὑρέθησαν. 21 καὶ χάλαζα μεγάλη ὡς ταλαντιαία καταβαίνει ἐκ τοῦ οὐρανοῦ ἐπὶ τοὺς ἀνθρώπους, καὶ ἐβλασφήμησαν οἱ ἄνθρωποι τὸν θεὸν ἐκ τῆς

---

56. English translations almost universally render γέγονεν here as "it is done," and this has some claim to legitimacy (cf. BDAG 197 [2.a], "be performed . . . be done"). The sense "it has happened, taken place" is an attempt to retain a more commonly occurring sense for the verb γίνομαι and still contrast this perfect with the aorists of γίνομαι in 11:15; 12:10 as well as in 16:18 (4x).

57. See OT texts cited in comments on 4:5 and 6:12.

58. See Bauckham, *Climax*, 199–204, and comments on 4:5; 8:5; 11:19.

59. Zerwick and Grosvenor, *Grammatical Analysis*, 767, and BDAG 1001 call these phrases redundant or pleonastic, but they simply reinforce the point strongly.

πληγῆς τῆς χαλάζης, ὅτι μεγάλη ἐστὶν ἡ πληγὴ αὐτῆς σφόδρα). The next two verses (vv. 19–20) directly trace the results of the violent earthquake, while v. 21 describes the additional great portent that accompanies the list of theophanic phenomena in v. 18a–b (cf. 11:19 that also adds hail to the series of lightning, rumblings, thunder, and earthquake). As could be expected, the unprecedented force of the earthquake wreaks horrific damage (v. 19a–b) on both "the great city"—it is divided into three parts—and "the cities of the nations"—they crumble to the ground (see 11:13; cf. Matt 7:25, 27; Luke 13:4).[60] Records of quake damage throughout history, especially of the effects of severe earthquakes, show how terrible such damage can be in great population centers.

The identity of "the great city" mentioned here is disputed,[61] but given the earlier mention of "the great city" in 11:8 and its clear identification as Jerusalem in that context (see discussion there), it is evident that Jerusalem is in view in this verse as well.[62] The importance of Ezekiel as a background to this vision makes this the most natural reading: Ezekiel 5:1–13 (Jerusalem symbolically divided into threes to represent God's discipline for her sins) and Ezekiel 38:17–23 (great earthquake in response to invasion of Israel by pagan nations). The clear contrast in v. 19a–b (the great city vs. cities of the nations, i.e., the gentiles) supports this identification from the passage itself. The fact that "Babylon the great" is mentioned in v. 19c and is regularly described as "the great city" in the next two chapters (17:18; 18:10, 16, 18 [2x], 21) does not weaken this conclusion for 16:19a. Babylon is added in v. 19c as a specific (and greatest) example of "the cities of the nations" (v. 19b), and from here on in Revelation it represents a typological contrast to Jerusalem: the dragon's or the world's city as opposed to God's city (both viewed as women, either sinful or holy).[63] Here John notes that, among all the pagan world's cities, God has not overlooked Babylon's sins.[64]

Babylon is in fact "remembered"[65] in order to "give her" the judgment she deserves (v. 19c). This punishment is described in a metaphorical and fulsome way (v. 19d): she will be made to drink "the cup of the wine of the fury of his [God's] wrath" (τὸ ποτήριον τοῦ οἴνου τοῦ θυμοῦ τῆς ὀργῆς αὐτοῦ).

---

60. Cf. BDAG 815: "collapse."

61. Ford, *Revelation*, 264; Edmondo F. Lupieri, *A Commentary on the Apocalypse of John*, ITSORS (Grand Rapids: Eerdmans, 2006), 245–46; Thomas, *Revelation 8–22*, 275 (also Jauhiainen, *Zechariah*, 118–21) hold that "the great city" in v. 19a is Jerusalem, while Aune *Revelation 6–16*, 900–1; Charles, *Revelation*, 2:52; and Osborne, *Revelation*, 598–99, take it as Babylon. Several others argue that "the great city" is the whole world in opposition to God, including Jerusalem, Babylon/Rome, etc. (Beale, *Revelation*, 843–44; Koester, *Revelation*, 668–69; Smalley, *Revelation*, 414–15).

62. The larger context of the final two bowls (16:12–21; i.e., the nations' attack on Jerusalem in the final days), as well as previous interludes like 14:1–20 (the Lamb on Mount Zion and great judgment "outside the city"), also makes Jerusalem the most natural identification of "the great city" in 16:19. See too the expectation in Zech 14:4–5 that at the time of the eschatological battle centering on Jerusalem, a great earthquake will split the Mount of Olives east of Jerusalem. See Fekkes, *Prophetic Traditions*, 79, who argues that Rev 19:11–21 (the eschatological battle at Jerusalem) follows immediately on 16:21, with 17:1–19:10 (the fall of Babylon) as an interlude.

63. This verse (as well as 17:18; see comments there) makes it quite unlikely that for John the "great city" and "Babylon the great" here and in chs. 17–18 refer to the same place (Beagley, *Apocalypse*, 90–91; Chilton, *Days of Vengeance*, 414–16; Ford, *Revelation*, 264–65). The awkward redundancy of adding v. 19c to v. 19a is difficult for any position that sees the two clauses referring to the same city (whether Babylon/Rome or Jerusalem).

64. On Babylon as a type in Rev, see comment on 14:8 and discussion in the introduction under "Use of the Old Testament: Prophecy and Typology."

65. This is what Aune, *Revelation 6–16*, 901, has called God's "punitive remembrance," an OT theme about God's unfailing justice toward the good and the evil (cf. Neh 6:14; 13:29; Ps 137:7; Jer 14:10; Hos 7:2; 8:13; 9:9).

Drinking a "cup of wine" as a figure for judgment has appeared already in Revelation, and it will be repeated in the coming chapters (14:10; 18:6; 19:15; cf. 14:8; 17:2; 18:3).[66] Just as the sixth bowl (vv. 12–16) gave a preview of judgments to be described in more detail in 19:11–21, so this mention of wrath against Babylon introduces the content of chs. 17–18.

Two broader effects of the great earthquake of v. 18 are described briefly in v. 20. On the face of it, these are quite catastrophic results: "every island fled" (i.e., vanished, disappeared from sight; cf. 20:11)[67] and "no mountains were to be found" (i.e., they disappeared from view or from earthly existence; cf. 18:21; 20:11; Heb 11:5).[68] But these are likely to be hyperbolic descriptions of political and economic catastrophe for Babylon/Rome as a system, along with fearsome portents in the natural world of greater destruction to come. The use of "every, all" is often hyperbolic (cf. 1 Sam 25:1; Isa 40:4; Luke 5:17; 1 Cor 13:2), and the text itself indicates that the world did not immediately come to an end. People had time to respond with

blasphemy against God amid severe disruptions in nature (v. 21), and the armies who devastate Babylon (previewed here and recounted in 17:16) will go on from there to gather for battle against Christ and suffer catastrophic defeat (17:14; 19:19–21).[69]

As mentioned above (v. 18), the fearful portents that signal God's own presence (i.e., lightning, rumblings, thunder, and earthquake) can also include hailstones (v. 21a; cf. 11:19).[70] This is another feature that mirrors Ezekiel 38:17–23, where v. 22 describes "hailstones" (λίθοις χαλάζης) that God rains down on the armies of many nations invading Israel. In this case it is "huge hail," weighing nearly a hundred pounds apiece,[71] that crashes down on people from heaven in the ultimate intensification of the pattern of the seventh plague of Egypt (Exod 9:22–26; Ps 105:32–33; cf. also Josh 10:11).[72] The severity of such hail as a "plague" or blow from heaven (see note at 9:18) is reiterated in the final clause of the verse (v. 21c). Sadly, the response of people who suffer this intense judgment is defiance against God (v. 21b): they blaspheme (cf. vv. 9, 11) rather than repent of their godless ways.

---

66. The use of both words for "anger, wrath" (θυμός, ὀργή) in this phrase (cf. 19:15) serves primarily to intensify the reference to God's judicial displeasure against sin (perhaps alluding to Ezek 38:18–19 where the LXX text uses both words as well as "zeal," ζῆλος). But Rev can use θυμός to mean "fury, passion, intense desire" (cf. 14:8; 18:3; LN §25.19; BDAG 461), while ὀργή may denote God's more settled indignation against evil (LN §38.10; BDAG 721). In this string of genitives "of the wine" denotes the content of "cup"; "of the fury" is epexegetical (i.e., a genitive of apposition), filling in the more particular meaning of "the wine" (see Wallace, Grammar, 95–96; often the head noun is metaphorical, and the epexegetical genitive specifies the referent); "of the wrath" is a genitive of source; and "his" is subjective. See Aune, Revelation 6–16, 860; Mathewson, Handbook, 221, for a slightly different construal.

67. BDAG 1052.

68. BDAG 411.

69. Similar hyperbole regarding "mountains" is used in Ps 97:5; Isa 40:4; 42:15; 45:2; 54:10; Ezek 38:20. See also comments at Rev 6:14.

70. The verb "came down" (καταβαίνει) is a historical present verb amid the more normal narrative aorists that predominate in vv. 17–21. It serves to highlight the response that follows (see 5:5 on the historical present): blasphemy against God instead of repentance, even in the face of such calamities.

71. The phrase "about a [or one] hundred pounds" as found in most recent English versions translates the Greek ὡς ταλαντιαία ("about a talent"). A "talent" was a unit of measure that varied somewhat across the ancient world, but it weighed something like 65 to 90 pounds (30 to 40 kilograms).

72. Exod 9:24 is one of the verses (cited in comments on v. 18 above) that speaks of comparison in the pattern of woes: such heavy hail had never fallen in Egypt since it had become a nation.

Theology in Application

Blessed Are the Vigilant

Anyone who has lived in places plagued by tornados or hurricanes knows the drill. When storm season comes, you make it a habit to stay tuned to what the weather may hold in the days ahead. You look ahead and learn to expect the unexpected. Jesus issues a call to a similar kind of alertness in this chapter and promises that vigilance will bring blessing. Amid describing one catastrophe after another that will culminate God's outpouring of righteous anger on the sinful world, John pauses to record Jesus's pronouncement of blessing on the person who stays morally aware and "well-dressed" (v. 15). This is not a call to watch for visible "signs" of Christ's return but to maintain conduct that is godly and faithful, because God has promised that justice will prevail in the end. The imagery of clothing is used to refer to holiness given to us freely by the Lamb's sacrifice for us, a holiness that we live out in consistent faith and obedience toward God. We must not be overwhelmed or paralyzed by what the future holds, no matter how bleak it will be when the storms of judgment arrive. Nor can we be oblivious to what is coming or be distracted with things that take us away from commitment to Christ, but instead we must be aware and occupied with God's work in this world in the time that he gives us. Blessed are the vigilant.

The Strange Allure of Armageddon

Among the seven bowls of judgment described in this chapter, horrific as they are, the sixth one stands out from all the rest in popular imagination and attention. Somehow the specter of vast armies assembling from across the world "for the battle of the great day of God Almighty" at a place called "Armageddon" (vv. 12–16) has a perennial fascination. Many are drawn to ponder it, in part because the modern world already knows what warfare on that scale can mean for humanity, and in part because this battle seems to outstrip anything we have seen before. Unfortunately, such popular fascination all too often produces unsupportable speculation and outlandish claims about how recent events relate to these verses. Just as with guesses about the beast and his mark (ch. 13), conjectures about Armageddon and its relation to specific modern nations and locations that will be its "fulfillment" have invariably been an embarrassment to prophetic interpretation in subsequent generations (see comments on vv. 12–16).[73] It is true that we should expect Armageddon to proceed like an earthly military engagement (although it will not end like one; cf. 19:19–21), but we must resist the temptation to identify ahead of time the particular details of the campaign. Revelation simply does not give us such information. These will be

---

73. See also various chapters in Boyer, *When Time Shall Be No More*, for examples of how stale and false much of popular prophetic preaching can appear a couple of decades after it is delivered.

evident when the battle itself comes, but no ingenious decoding will fill us in before that time arrives.

It is tempting and somewhat understandable to read about fairly recent wars in the Middle East between the modern state of Israel and the countries that surround her (e.g., in the years of 1948, 1967, and 1973) or about the build up of arms by neighboring countries that seem to presage viable threats to her existence and assume that surely this is what Revelation 16:12–16 predicted. But such assumptions cannot be presented as valid expositions of Scripture. They are conjectures, not interpretations, and they should have no part in our preaching and teaching of Revelation. There is so much of value that we can communicate based on these texts. Why resort to speculative flash and splash when solid and life-changing biblical instruction is our calling?

Along this line, here is another all too common error to avoid in our thinking about the situation in the modern Middle East. Some popular preaching about the end-times—perhaps accompanied rightly by defending Israel against anti-Semitic bias—comes across, deservedly or not, as ethnically anti-Arab. We must be careful not to assume or seem to assume that all Arab nations currently opposed to the modern state of Israel are satanically inspired and deserve God's wrath. We must diligently avoid any semblance (perhaps unconscious) of relishing their destruction. The Arab peoples are among the nations of the world for whom Christ died and whom we want to reach with the gospel. Many Arabs are already faithful followers of Christ, sometimes in situations of great difficulty because of their Christian commitment. These points should be clear in all that we say about "Armageddon."[74]

What this calls for then is a healthy dose of discernment, for clear biblical teaching that informs people with the truth and guards against error or misunderstanding. Prophetic preaching or teaching should call for response to the gospel, for holiness and endurance, for making Christ the Lord of our lives even now, and for careful discernment not to be led away from the truth.[75]

---

74. See Tony Maalouf, *Arabs in the Shadow of Israel: The Unfolding of God's Prophetic Plan for Ishmael's Line* (Grand Rapids: Kregel, 2003), 31–37, 222–24.

75. See these five "practicalities of prophecy" discussed by C. Marvin Pate, *What Does the Future Hold: Exploring Various Views on the End Times* (Grand Rapids: Baker, 2010), 139–45.

Revelation 17:1–18

Literary Context

The phrase "he carried me away in the Spirit" in 17:3 (cf. 21:10) mirrors the expression "I came to be in the Spirit" (1:10; 4:2) in signaling the third of four high-level transitions between major units in the whole book of Revelation (see the introduction). The intervention of a heavenly mediator who carries John away "in the Spirit" reveals a new phase in the complex of visions that began in 1:9–10 and was extended in 4:1–2. Now in 17:1–3a the vision is extended again (although its content was previewed in 16:19: God's wrath on Babylon). This third phase of John's visions, focusing on Babylon's fall, runs from 17:1 to 19:10. In this section Babylon is portrayed as "a great prostitute" allied to the beast and leading the whole world astray, but devastated in the end by internal strife (17:1–18). Those who benefited from her rich luxuries and misdeeds bewail her devastation and its effects on the world (18:1–24), but in heaven there is rejoicing over God's just punishment on the prostitute and an introduction to the Lamb's pure bride who contrasts with her (19:1–10).

The fourth extension of the vision will come at 21:9–10, introduced likewise by "one of the seven angels who had the seven bowls," who also carries John away "in the Spirit" (a unit of text intervenes in 19:11–21:8 to transition between the two final sections). The third and fourth visionary complexes match each other in contrasting the great prostitute who represents the evil city of human civilization opposed to God (17:1, 18) with the bride of the Lamb who is also "the holy city Jerusalem that comes down from heaven from God" (21:10).[1]

---

1. Bauckham, *Climax*, 3–7. The parallels in how these two complexes open (the seven angels; John carried away in the Spirit) are matched by parallels in how they conclude in 19:9–10 and 22:6–9 (God's true words; worship God, not an angel).

I. Prologue (1:1–8)

II. First Vision: The Exalted Christ and His Messages to the Churches (1:9–3:22)

III. Second Vision: Heavenly Throne Room and Three Judgment Cycles (4:1–16:21)

➡ **IV. Third Vision: The Destruction of Babylon the Great (17:1–19:10)**

   A. Babylon, the Great Prostitute, and the Beast She Rides (17:1–18)

   B. The Effects of Babylon's Destruction (18:1–24)

   C. Celebration of Babylon's Judgment and Preparation of the Lamb's Bride (19:1–10)

Main Idea

Babylon the great city, for all its luxury and worldwide domination through alliance with Satan's henchman the beast, is depraved and idolatrous and will be devastated in the end by civil war.

Translation

Revelation 17:1–18

1a	Action/Vision Introduction	And **one of the seven angels ...** who had the seven bowls **... came and spoke with me saying,**
b	Invitation	*"Come, I will show you the judgment of the great prostitute*
c 2a	Descriptions	*who lives beside many waters, with whom the kings of the earth committed sexual immorality and*
b		*those who inhabit the earth became drunk with the wine of her sexual immorality."*
3a		And **he carried me away into a desert place in the Spirit.**
b	Action/Character Entrance	And **I saw a woman sitting on a scarlet beast**
c d	Descriptions	that was covered with blasphemous names and had seven heads and ten horns.

4a   Descriptions   **And the woman was clothed in purple and**
                                                     scarlet and

                               adorned with gold and
                                             precious stones and
                                             pearls,

 b   having a golden cup in her hand,
 c   filled with abominations and
                                               the impurities of her sexual immorality.

5a   Identification   **And a name was written on her forehead,**
                       a mystery,

 b   Apposition   *"Babylon the great,*
                              the mother of prostitutes and
                                   of the abominations of the earth."

6a   Action/Description   **And I saw the woman drunk with the blood of the saints and**
                                                    with the blood of Jesus's witnesses.

 b   Effect of 6a   **And I was greatly astonished when I saw her.**

7a   Response to 6b   **And the angel said to me,**

 b   Question   *"Why are you astonished?*
 c   Promise/Preview   *I will tell you the mystery concerning the woman and*
                                                        the beast that bears her,
 d   Description   *who has the seven heads and the ten horns.*
8a   Description   *The beast that you saw was and*
                                             is not and
                                             is about to come up out of the bottomless pit and
                                                        go to destruction.
 b   Effect of 8a   *And those*
                             who live on the earth,...
 c   *whose names are not written from the foundation of the earth in the book of life,*
 d   *... will marvel when they see the beast,*
 e   Basis of 8d   *that he was and*
                                       is not and
                                       will be present.

9a   Narrator's Aside   **(Here is the mind that has wisdom.)**
 b   Explanation of 7d   *The seven heads are seven mountains*
 c   *on which the woman sits,*
9d/10a Explanation of 7d   *and they are seven kings.*
10a/b   Explanation of 9d   *Five have fallen, one is, and the other has not yet come,*
 b/c   Time   *and when he comes*
 c/d   *he must remain for a little time.*

Continued on next page.

Continued from previous page.

11a   Explanation of 8a   *And the beast ...*
                                        who was and is not
                                            ... is also himself an eighth and
                                                is of the seven,

b   *and he goes to destruction.*
12a   Explanation of 3d   *And the ten horns that you saw are ten kings*
b   *who have not yet received ruling authority,*

c   *but   with the beast*
                           they receive authority
                                as kings
                                for one hour.

13a   Description of 12a   *These have a single purpose,*
b   Explanation of 13a   *and they give their power and authority to the beast.*
14a   Explanation of 12a   *These will make war against the Lamb,*
b   *and the Lamb will conquer them,*
c   Reason for 14b   *because   he is Lord of lords and*
                                              King of kings, and

d   *those with him are called and*
                                                         chosen and
                                                         faithful."

15a   Further Response   **And he said to me,**
       to 6b

b   Explanation of 1c   *"The waters that you saw, ...*
c   Place   *where the prostitute lives,*
d   *... are peoples and*
                                          multitudes and
                                          nations and
                                          languages.

16a   Explanation of 3d   *And the ten horns that you saw and*
                                the beast   *will hate the prostitute and*
b   *will make her desolate and naked and*
c   *will devour her flesh and*
d   *will burn her with fire.*
17a   Reason for 16   *For God put it in their hearts*
b   Purposes   *to accomplish his purpose and*
c   *to act with one purpose and*
d   *to yield their ruling authority to the beast*
e   Time   *until God's words are completed.*

18a   Concluding   *And the woman that you saw is the great city*
       Explanation

b   *that has ruling authority over the kings of the earth."*

Structure

This chapter falls naturally into three sections, beginning with a brief narration of John's angelic escort "carrying him away in the Spirit" to see the judgment of Babylon (vv. 1–6). This section includes the angel's summary assessment of "the great prostitute" as well as a brief record of what John saw of her in his vision. The rest of the chapter consists of two lengthy explanations given by the angelic guide, focusing first on the beast she rides (vv. 7–14) and then on the woman herself (vv. 15–18), with some mixture between the two in each section.

Exegetical Outline

IV. Third Vision: The Destruction of Babylon the Great (17:1–19:10)

→ **A. Babylon, the Great Prostitute, and the Beast She Rides (17:1–18)**

    1. A Vision of the Great Prostitute and the Beast She Rides (17:1–6)

        a. Journey in the Spirit to see the prostitute's judgment (17:1–3a)

        b. The abominable woman and her evil beast (17:3b–6)

    2. The Significance of the Beast (17:7–14)

        a. Introduction to the angel's interpretation (17:7)

        b. Origin and influence of the beast (17:8)

        c. The beast's seven heads: seven successive rulers plus an eighth (17:9–11)

        d. The beast's ten horns: ten client kings, his allies in war against the Lamb (17:12–14)

    3. The Significance of the Prostitute (17:15–18)

        a. The worldwide coalition that she dominates (17:15)

        b. Her devastation when God brings the beast and his allies against her (17:16–17)

        c. Summary explanation: she is the great city that rules the earth (17:18)

Explanation of the Text

17:1–3a And one of the seven angels who had the seven bowls came and spoke with me saying, "Come, I will show you the judgment of the great prostitute who lives beside many waters, 2 with whom the kings of the earth committed sexual immorality and those who inhabit the earth became drunk with the wine of her sexual immorality." 3 And he carried me away into a desert place in the Spirit (Καὶ ἦλθεν εἷς ἐκ τῶν ἑπτὰ ἀγγέλων τῶν ἐχόντων τὰς ἑπτὰ φιάλας καὶ ἐλάλησεν μετ' ἐμοῦ λέγων, Δεῦρο, δείξω σοι τὸ κρίμα τῆς πόρνης τῆς μεγάλης τῆς καθημένης ἐπὶ ὑδάτων πολλῶν, 2 μεθ' ἧς ἐπόρνευσαν οἱ βασιλεῖς τῆς γῆς καὶ ἐμεθύσθησαν οἱ κατοικοῦντες τὴν γῆν ἐκ τοῦ οἴνου τῆς πορνείας αὐτῆς. 3 καὶ ἀπήνεγκέν με εἰς ἔρημον ἐν πνεύματι). The beginning of chapter 17 signals a major thematic transition in Revelation (see "Literary Context" above). The revelation of the risen Christ that John presented beginning in 1:9–10 (encompassing 1:9–3:22) was expanded with a parallel beginning in 4:1–2 (4:1–16:21). Now, in developing the theme introduced at 16:19 (God's wrath on

Babylon), John records a new phase of the original vision (17:1–19:10) that will be complemented by a contrasting scene (21:9–22:9) introduced in very much the same way.[2] In both 17:1–3a and 21:9–10 we find one of the seven-bowl angels transporting John away "in the Spirit" to "show" him a notable woman who represents a city, either Babylon representing human society opposed to God, or the heavenly Jerusalem come to earth. Both sections conclude in remarkably parallel ways as well (see comments on 19:9b–10 and 22:6–9).[3]

It is appropriate that "one of the seven angels who had the seven bowls" (v. 1a) will be John's revelatory guide here (as well as in 21:9), since their bowls constitute the "seven last plagues" that will finish "God's anger" (15:1) and usher in his final renewal of all things. Evil must be dealt with before this restoration, and so the angel addresses John and invites him to view the decisive "judgment" (v. 1b) previewed already in 16:19, in which God pours out the cup of his furious wrath against Babylon the great. Here in v. 1, however, the angel does not name the object of judgment just yet (this comes out in v. 5). Instead he describes her as "the great prostitute who lives beside many waters,"[4] a richly connotative image that draws together several important themes from the Old Testament. Israel's prophets had used the figure of a "whore" (KJV, NRSV), "harlot" (NASB, RSV), or "prosti-

tute" (CSB, ESV, NET, NIV, NLT) to connote the unfaithful and outrageous conduct of various city-states or nations, from Jerusalem itself (Isa 1:21; Jer 3:3; Ezek 16:15–35; 23:1–21 [Samaria and Jerusalem])[5] to Tyre (Isa 23:15–17) and Nineveh (Nah 3:4–5).[6] More broadly, sexual infidelity appears in the Bible as a metaphor of turning away from the Lord to worship a false god (e.g., 2 Kgs 9:22; 1 Chr 5:25; Ps 73:27; Jer 3:6; Ezek 23:19, 29–30; cf. also Rev 2:14, 20). But the angel calls this one "the *great* prostitute" (τῆς πόρνης τῆς μεγάλης), the one who above all others is guilty of reprehensible conduct and of influencing others toward it,[7] and he adds the significant description, "who lives beside many waters"[8] (v. 1c). This reflects a conventional description of the city of Babylon, situated on the Euphrates with its tributaries and canals (Jer 51:13; Ps 137:1; see comments on Rev 17:15 for the interpretation of this detail). A reader with awareness of this background would assume that this prostitute represents Babylon even prior to v. 5, especially after the earlier association of "Babylon the great" in 14:8 with prostitution (πορνεία). For the referent or symbolic meaning of this "great prostitute [Babylon]," see comments on v. 5.

The prostitution theme continues in v. 2 with the added explanation of the significant influence she has across the whole world. The earth's kings "committed sexual immorality" (ἐπόρνευσαν) with

---

2. A set of transitional visions traces the significant events that intervene between the destruction of Babylon and the coming to earth of the new Jerusalem (19:11–21:8).

3. Bauckham, *Climax*, 3–7.

4. ESV, NIV have "the great prostitute"; CSB has "the notorious prostitute."

5. The fact that "harlot" imagery was used of various cities in the OT makes it doubtful that this element identifies Babylon "the great prostitute" in 17:1, 5 as Jerusalem. See 16:19 and 17:18 for further comment.

6. For a valuable summary of how John uses themes from the OT about ancient Babylon as well as Tyre, see Fekkes, *Prophetic Traditions*, 89–91.

7. Here the use of the positive adjective "great" (μέγας) stands for the superlative "greatest" in intensity or importance (the true superlative itself is almost never used in the NT; cf. BDAG 624; BDF §60). The English phrase with "great" carries a similar sense.

8. The phrase "lives beside" uses the verb "sit, be seated" (κάθημαι), but in the sense of "live, dwell" (BDAG 491; cf. 14:6). The preposition "beside" (ἐπί) can mean "on, upon" (with κάθημαι: 6:16; 9:17), but "near, beside" fits this context better (cf. Matt 21:19; John 21:1). For translations that read "sit" or "seated" with "on" or "upon," see CSB, ESV, KJV, NASB, NRSV, RSV.

her (v. 2a), a figure for drawing other nations into Babylon's profane behavior (repeated in 18:3, 9; interpreted as political and cultural domination in 17:18). The latter half of the verse rephrases this as drunkenness or moral incapacitation on the part of "those who inhabit the earth" (cf. 18:23, she misled all the nations). The world got drunk "with the wine of her sexual immorality" (v. 2b; ἐκ τοῦ οἴνου τῆς πορνείας αὐτῆς;[9] cf. 14:8; 18:3), and they with her will suffer punishment for it.[10] In light of the Old Testament background mentioned above, these references to "sexual immorality" promoted by a sensuous "prostitute" should be read as symbolic for spiritual and moral sins: she leads the nations away from the true God into idolatrous worship, and away from what is just and decent into moral failings of various kinds. In the world of John's readers, this "sexual immorality" took the form of temptations to engage in emperor worship and other idolatrous associations that enticed them on a daily basis in their lives in Roman Asia Minor.[11] This picture will be expanded to include greed and financial exploitation in chapter 18.

Verse 3a completes the thematic transition mentioned above. John's angelic guide bore him away "into a desert place in the Spirit" (cf. 1:9–10; 4:1–2; 21:9–10).[12] John was aware of being transported to a remote, wilderness place, but whether this happened bodily or in his vision only is hard to determine (cf. 2 Cor 12:1–5). The place is perhaps influenced by Isaiah 21:1–2 where the prophet received a "vision of the desert by the sea" (concerning southern Mesopotamia perhaps) in which he heard the message, "Fallen, fallen is Babylon" (Isa 21:9; cf. Rev 14:8; 18:2).[13]

17:3b–4 And I saw a woman sitting on a scarlet beast that was covered with blasphemous names and had seven heads and ten horns. 4 And the woman was clothed in purple and scarlet and adorned with gold and precious stones and pearls, having a golden cup in her hand, filled with abominations and the impurities of her sexual immorality (καὶ εἶδον γυναῖκα καθημένην ἐπὶ θηρίον κόκκινον, γέμον[τα] ὀνόματα βλασφημίας, ἔχων κεφαλὰς ἑπτὰ καὶ κέρατα δέκα. 4 καὶ ἡ γυνὴ ἦν περιβεβλημένη πορφυροῦν καὶ κόκκινον καὶ κεχρυσωμένη χρυσίῳ καὶ λίθῳ τιμίῳ καὶ μαργαρίταις, ἔχουσα ποτήριον χρυσοῦν ἐν τῇ χειρὶ αὐτῆς γέμον βδελυγμάτων καὶ τὰ ἀκάθαρτα τῆς πορνείας αὐτῆς). When "the great prostitute" (v. 1b) comes into John's view ("and I saw," καὶ εἶδον), she appears as "a woman sitting on a scarlet beast," and "woman" (γυνή) is the term used more frequently in the following verses (5x, all with an anaphoric article) instead of "prostitute" (πόρνη; twice in vv. 15–16 and once in 19:2). In v. 3b the woman is seen riding[14] on a "beast" (i.e., a wild animal; θηρίον) with bizarre features, including its color, "scarlet" (κόκκινος), an unusual hue for a natural animal but not for

---

9. "Of her immorality" is a genitive of apposition ("immorality" interprets the figure of "wine"); cf. Wallace, *Grammar*, 95–96; David E. Aune, *Revelation 17–22* (WBC 52c; Nashville: Thomas Nelson, 1998), 908.

10. Jer 51:7 uses this imagery to speak of Babylon as an instrument of God's judgment against the nations: she was his "golden cup" of wrath (cf. Rev 17:4) that they drank from—and then she in turn would be judged for her sins. Rev also intermingles these uses of the "cup" or "wine" that God will cause Babylon to drink after she forced it on others (14:8; 16:19; 18:3, 6; cf. 14:10).

11. As J. Nelson Kraybill, *Imperial Cult and Commerce in John's Apocalypse*, JSNTSup 132 (Sheffield: Sheffield Academic Press, 1996), 17, says, John "was concerned about the interplay of idolatry, military power and commerce." See comments on 2:14, 20–21.

12. See comments on "in the Spirit" at 1:10.

13. Seeing the prostitute after being taken away into a "desert place" (ἔρημος) perhaps sets up a wordplay, since the vision shows her "made desolate" (the related verb, ἐρημόω) in 17:16; 18:17, 19.

14. "Sitting" (καθημένην) here means "mounted, riding" on (cf. 6:2; 9:17; 19:11; phrased as being "carried," using βαστάζω, in v. 7).

an apocalyptic or symbolic one.[15] More bizarre—and patently symbolic—are the two additional descriptions (v. 3c–d): "covered with blasphemous names,"[16] representing its diabolical character, and "seven heads and ten horns,"[17] a reference to the animal's ruling power (see comments at 13:1 on the background of this in Dan 7 and also the interpretation given in comments at 17:7–13).[18] More significant is the immediate association of the woman with the first "beast" of 13:1 that these descriptions signal. "Blasphemous names," "seven heads," and "ten horns" are repeated verbatim from 13:1 except that the order of heads and names is reversed. Revelation 17:7–8 confirms this identification. What was initially described as "*a beast*" (no article; indefinite) is quickly seen even here in v. 3b to be *the* beast already known from 13:1

(and 11:7), presented as in some way allied to or in service of the woman Babylon.[19]

The woman for her part is described in powerful images of both royal beauty and revolting abomination (v. 4). She appears in regal robes of "purple and scarlet"[20] and jewelry of "gold, precious stones, and pearls," and she carries a fine "golden cup" in her hand.[21] But the cup is brimming over with "abominations and the impurities of her sexual immorality," a reference to the defilements and idolatries that she leads the nations into (vv. 2, 4; cf. Deut 12:31; 2 Chr 28:3; Isa 2:8; Jer 13:27; Matt 24:15; Mark 13:14).[22]

17:5–6 And a name was written on her forehead, a mystery, "Babylon the great, the mother of prostitutes and of the abominations of the earth."

---

15. The "red" or "fiery red" of the horse in 6:4 and the dragon in 12:3 is a different word in Greek (πυρρός), one that could be a natural color (see note on 6:4).

16. The verb in v. 3c translated "covered with" (γέμω) normally means "full of"; the meaning "covered with" occurs also in 4:6, 8. In v. 4c γέμω has its more normal sense.

17. The two participles in v. 3c–d describe "beast" (θηρίον, a neuter accusative noun) but exhibit irregular agreement in gender (they are masculine according to the most likely textual readings). This is due to agreement according to sense since "beast" symbolizes a person, not a thing. The participle translated "had" also fails to agree in case (it is nominative), but this seems to be part of John's idiolectic style. Such participles often should be nominative in agreement with nominative subjects, and he reverts to that here (e.g., 6:2, 5; 8:3; for similar agreement issues, see 1:16; 4:7; 5:6).

18. It is important to note that these symbolize two different kinds of ruling authority: the heads are seven kings preceding the beast in the line of rule that he represents, and the horns are ten kings allied to the beast (vv. 7–13). These two will diverge in civil war when the beast and his ten client kings attack the woman (i.e., Babylon/Rome), with whose power the seven kings (including the beast) were previously identified (vv. 16–18).

19. This association or alliance does not, however, equate the symbolic meaning of the woman (as referring, say, to Rome) with the referent of the beast (related to Rome but not identical with it). Verse 16 will show that a distinction must be maintained.

20. These colors usually indicated a person of wealth and high status (2 Sam 1:24; Dan 5:7; Mark 15:17–18; Luke 16:19; cf. 1 Esd 3:6; 1 Macc 10:20).

21. See Jer 51:7 for the association of such a "golden cup" (LXX 28:7: ποτήριον χρυσοῦν) with Babylon, but the imagery is used in a different way here.

22. The woman clearly exerts religious or spiritual influence over those she dominates politically and economically, as vv. 4c and 5b imply. But there is no convincing basis in the text of Rev 17–18 for seeing two different entities portrayed here: ecclesiastical Babylon in ch. 17 (i.e., an apostate church, whether papal Rome or ecumenical Protestantism) and political or commercial Babylon in ch. 18, as stated by Smith, *Revelation*, 241–43, 248, 251; Thomas, *Revelation 8–22*, 304–8; and Walvoord, Rawley, and Hitchcock, *Revelation*, 253, 256–59, 265–67. See Thomas R. Edgar, "Babylon: Ecclesiastical, Political, or What?," *JETS* 25 (1982): 333–41; and Charles H. Dyer, "The Identity of Babylon in Revelation 17–18, Part 1," *BSac* 144 (1987): 305–16, who persuasively argue against this approach. Such ideas seem to be rooted in the Reformers' view of the pope as the antichrist (cf. Kovacs and Rowland, *Revelation*, 153–59, 182–86), filtered through the antipathies of the fundamentalist-modernist controversies of a century ago. See Ian Boxall, "The Many Faces of Babylon the Great: *Wirkungsgeschichte* and the Interpretation of Revelation 17," in Moyise, *Studies in the Book of Revelation*, 51–52, 56–66, for hermeneutical reflections on various interpretations of the great prostitute over the centuries.

6 And I saw the woman drunk with the blood of the saints and with the blood of Jesus's witnesses. And I was greatly astonished when I saw her (καὶ ἐπὶ τὸ μέτωπον αὐτῆς ὄνομα γεγραμμένον, μυστήριον, Βαβυλὼν ἡ μεγάλη, ἡ μήτηρ τῶν πορνῶν καὶ τῶν βδελυγμάτων τῆς γῆς. 6 καὶ εἶδον τὴν γυναῖκα μεθύουσαν ἐκ τοῦ αἵματος τῶν ἁγίων καὶ ἐκ τοῦ αἵματος τῶν μαρτύρων Ἰησοῦ. Καὶ ἐθαύμασα ἰδὼν αὐτὴν θαῦμα μέγα). The transparent identity of the woman is made explicit in v. 5, but John indicates that the stated identification is an artifice giving insight into what she really represents. Frequently in Revelation a name or mark on the person or on the "forehead" identifies the owner or ruler of that person (3:12; 7:3; 9:4; 13:16–17; 14:1, 9; 20:4; 22:4), but only here and in 19:12, 16 does it identify the person himself or herself. The extent of the actual name is not entirely clear, but it is more likely that the word "mystery" is not part of the actual name (as ASV, KJV take it: "Mystery, Babylon the great . . .") but is an appositive to "name," explaining its character (CSB, NASB, NET, NIV, NRSV, REB; cf. ESV, RSV: "a name of mystery").[23] The standard sense of "mystery" in the New Testament is to denote a secret formerly hidden and unknowable but now revealed, especially God's plan for world redemption (cf. 10:7; Mark 4:11; Rom 16:25–26; Eph 3:3–6, 9; Col 1:26–27). But it can also mean something puzzling or enigmatic, a symbol that needs interpretation to be understood completely (Rev 1:20; cf. Dan 2:18–47; 2 Thess 2:7). That seems to be its sense here, but with the ad-

ditional nuance of a verbal ploy or artifice that enriches the plain meaning.[24]

Her primary name then is given as "Babylon the great" (v. 5b). Additional phrases describe her as "the mother of prostitutes and of the abominations of the earth," representing the widespread effect that her influence exerts. She is "the mother"[25] in the sense that she produces others who engage in "prostitution" (i.e., misusing valuable or sacred things for personal gain; violating what is right and good for evil or self-centered purposes) as she herself does.[26] So also she is the origin above all others of detestable, repulsive deeds—especially idolatrous acts (see comment on "abominations" in v. 4c above). None of these names are likely to be what she would call herself (much like Jezebel in 2:20), especially not the additional phrases. These constitute the Spirit's characterization of her as given in John's vision.

But the enigmatic name "Babylon the Great" still leaves room for debate regarding who or what John and his readers would understand this woman to be, and the further details given in chapters 17–18 provide more information to consider. The name "Babylon" has occurred without much description earlier in the book (14:8; 16:19). The preferred identification stated there was that this represents the Roman Empire in John's day as a pointer to a world power with similar but intensified evil characteristics in the end times. See the related section, "In Depth: The Identity of Babylon" for further discussion.

---

23. Almost all English translations take the phrases that follow "Babylon the great" as part of the name, and that seems likely, but it makes for a rather long name to be written on a woman's forehead, even in an apocalyptic vision. It is possible that "the mother of prostitutes and of the abominations of the earth" is an added description rather than part of the name itself.

24. John signals a similar ploy about the true referent of a name by using the phrase "in spiritual terms" (πνευματικῶς) in

11:8, "the great city, which in spiritual terms is called Sodom and Egypt, where their Lord also was crucified." It is clear in context that Jerusalem is intended, but "Sodom and Egypt" deepens the connotative sense.

25. The article in Greek carries its par excellence sense: she exemplifies this above all others (cf. Wallace, *Grammar*, 222–23).

26. BDAG 649; cf. Tob 4:13: "Idleness is the mother of starvation."

IN DEPTH: The Identity of Babylon

Three primary suggestions for identifying "Babylon the Great" are put forward by interpreters. One is that "Babylon" is the ancient city in Mesopotamia, restored in the end times to be a dominant power in world affairs and to oppose God again as it did in biblical days. Supporters of this view claim that it is the only one that "honors the literal method of interpretation."[27] The problem with this view is that it is both too literal and not literal enough. It is too literal (in the sense of woodenly following the "letter" of the text without noting that a figurative meaning is intended by the author) because it fails to account for hyperbolic language in the Old Testament texts about Babylon's destruction[28] as well as John's use of typological figures in Revelation (see comments at 2:14, 20; 11:8; 14:8; 16:8). And it is not literal enough in interpreting 17:9–11 (one "king" who presently exists [ἔστιν] at the time John writes; v. 11 shows that "kings" are personal throughout the unit)[29] and 18:17, 19 (verses lamenting Babylon's demise as a center of maritime trade). The Mesopotamian city does not fit either of these descriptions.

A second view is that "Babylon" symbolizes Jerusalem as the "great city" that persecuted the prophets (11:8), prostituted herself in her disloyalty to God and his covenant (e.g., Isa 1:21; Jer 3:3), rejected her Messiah (and adopted an anti-Christian, militaristic nationalism according to some).[30] Difficulties for this view show up most clearly in 16:19 and 17:18 (see comments) as well as at other points.[31]

The third and most common interpretation, and the one adopted here, is that "Babylon" refers to Rome and its empire in the first century as a pattern of godless rule exemplified in ancient Babylon in the Old Testament and in Rome in John's day and anticipates the extreme manifestation of the pattern in the end times (see comments on Babylon as a type in 14:8; 16:19 and in the section, "Use of the Old Testament: Prophecy and Typology" in the introduction). Many interpreters espouse this approach, some of them with differing emphases.[32]

27. Kenneth W. Allen, "The Rebuilding and Destruction of Babylon," *BSac* 133 (1976): 19–20; cf. Charles H. Dyer, "The Identity of Babylon in Revelation 17–18, Part 2," *BSac* 144 (1987): 443–49. Thomas, *Revelation 8–22*, 289–90, 307, also holds the view that Babylon is the ancient city restored.

28. Beale, *Revelation*, 829–30; Homer Heater, "Do the Prophets Teach That Babylonia Will Be Rebuilt in the *Eschaton*?," *JETS* 41 (1998): 23–43.

29. G. Biguzzi, "Is the Babylon of Revelation Rome or Jerusalem?," *Bib* 87 (2006): 372.

30. Beagley, *Apocalypse*, 92–100; Ford, *Revelation*, 283–86;

Lupieri, *Apocalypse*, 248–67; Rick van de Water, "Reconsidering the Beast from the Sea (Rev 13.1)," *NTS* 46 (2000): 245–61.

31. Also Biguzzi, "Babylon," 380–83.

32. Aune, *Revelation 17–22*, 959–61; Koester, *Revelation*, 675, 683–84; Osborne, *Revelation*, 608–9. Beale, *Revelation*, 888, says that Babylon is "the entire evil economic-religious system of the world throughout history" with influence also "over the political realm" until the rebellion "in the end time" seen in 17:15–17. He emphasizes the "transtemporal nature" of both the woman (858–59) and the beast (869–70) as facets of the evil or ungodly "world system" of all times (883–86),

This interpretation goes all the way back to Victorinus of Pettau (third century).[33] It fits more of the details of the text in more places than the other options. The typological pattern suggests, however, that the godless and oppressive influence over the world, not the geographical location, is what will be replicated in an extreme form in the end time. Its presence in Mesopotamia or Italy is not the focus of the pattern. Popular expectations of a "revived Roman empire" or a "ten-nation confederacy" centered in Europe should be adjusted accordingly.

As John peers at the woman further ("and I saw"; καὶ εἶδον, as in v. 3b), he discerns that she is "drunk with the blood" of God's people whom she has killed (v. 6a). The verb "be drunk" (μεθύω) in this context does not so much emphasize her intoxication in the sense that she is reeling crazily and has lost all judgment (although there might be some of that). Instead the point is that she has drunk "freely," drunk "a great deal" or is sated, gorged with murders (cf. Isa 58:11; 1 Cor 11:21).[34] She has shed the blood of "the saints" (i.e., God's people in general; cf. comment on 5:8) and more specifically the blood of "Jesus's witnesses" (τῶν μαρτύρων Ἰησοῦ), those who have loyally testified about him (objective genitive). The actual or threatened death of people because of their faithfulness to Christ is mentioned repeatedly in Revelation (2:13; 6:9; 11:7; 16:6; 20:4), and Babylon especially will be held accountable for her role in this persecution (18:20, 24).

The final part of v. 6 begins the transition from the vision of the woman that John has been shown (vv. 1–6; reinforced here by the phrase, "when I saw her"; ἰδὼν αὐτήν) to the angelic explanation of the vision (vv. 7–18). The verb "to be astonished" (θαυμάζω) occurs in v. 6b and v. 7b to signal the change. The sense of "astonished"[35] here is a mix of "appalled by fear and dismay" and "confused, perplexed."[36] This reaction is found frequently in apocalyptic texts at the literary seam where a symbolic visionary experience is followed by a heavenly interpretation. The response of "perplexed fear" (sometimes expressed by θαυμάζω or ἀποθαυμάζω, sometimes by their synonyms) is what typically characterizes the human recipient of the vision (e.g., Dan 4:19; 7:15; 8:27; cf. 4 Ezra 10:27–37; 12:4–9; 13:14–20).[37]

17:7–8 And the angel said to me, "Why are you astonished? I will tell you the mystery concerning the woman and the beast that bears her, who has the seven heads and the ten horns. 8 The beast that you saw was and is not and is about to come up out of the bottomless pit and go to destruction. And those who live on the earth, whose names are not written from the foundation of the earth in the book of life, will marvel when they see the

---

but he includes first-century Rome as "the contemporary embodiment of the beast" (869) or of Babylon (843, 885–86). He does not call this "typology" but an analogy applied "in an escalated manner" (830) or OT imagery "reapplied" (883) to the end times.

33. Biguzzi, "Babylon," 373–74. See also Weinrich, "Oecumenius," 72–76, who also identifies the woman as Rome.

34. BDAG 626; LN §23.37.

35. The phrase "I was greatly astonished" is more literally

"I was astonished with a great astonishment" (ἐθαύμασα ... θαῦμα μέγα), the use of a cognate accusative (a direct object noun from the same root as the verb itself; cf. 16:9 and BDF §153.1), with the adjective "great" modifying the accusative.

36. BDAG 444.

37. See also Lev 26:32; Job 17:8; 18:20 where the context is different, but the Greek words θαυμάζω or θαῦμα are used to translate the Hebrew/Aramaic verb שמם that appears in Dan 4:19 [4:16 MT]; 8:27.

beast, that he was and is not and will be present
(καὶ εἶπέν μοι ὁ ἄγγελος, Διὰ τί ἐθαύμασας; ἐγὼ ἐρῶ
σοι τὸ μυστήριον τῆς γυναικὸς καὶ τοῦ θηρίου τοῦ
βαστάζοντος αὐτήν τοῦ ἔχοντος τὰς ἑπτὰ κεφαλὰς
καὶ τὰ δέκα κέρατα. 8 τὸ θηρίον ὃ εἶδες ἦν καὶ
οὐκ ἔστιν καὶ μέλλει ἀναβαίνειν ἐκ τῆς ἀβύσσου
καὶ εἰς ἀπώλειαν ὑπάγει, καὶ θαυμασθήσονται οἱ
κατοικοῦντες ἐπὶ τῆς γῆς, ὧν οὐ γέγραπται τὸ ὄνομα
ἐπὶ τὸ βιβλίον τῆς ζωῆς ἀπὸ καταβολῆς κόσμου,
βλεπόντων τὸ θηρίον ὅτι ἦν καὶ οὐκ ἔστιν καὶ
παρέσται). John's angelic guide (cf. v. 1) challenges
his response to the vision but pledges to explain
what it means (v. 7) and begins right away to do
so (v. 8ff.). The angel's words are quoted directly
from here to the end of the chapter with only two
short insertions by John (vv. 9a, 15a). His explanation centers first on the significance of the beast
(vv. 8–14) and then on the woman (vv. 15–18) with
some intermixture in each section.[38]

The angel witnesses John's astonishment (v. 6b)
and apparently wonders whether it may have taken
a wrong turn toward worship. The question ("Why
are you astonished?" διὰ τί ἐθαύμασας;) and the
statement that follows in v. 8b–d (the worldlings
"will marvel"; θαυμασθήσονται) suggests a fear that
John may be drawn over from perplexed astonishment to worshipful admiration of the woman or
the beast (cf. 13:3–4).[39] The assumption, however,
is that a true understanding will squelch such a
response, so the angel promises to explain "the
mystery" (τὸ μυστήριον), the cryptic symbolism
(cf. v. 5), concerning both the woman and the

beast.[40] Verse 7c mentions the woman and the beast
in the order in which they appeared in v. 3b, but the
later explanation moves in reverse order: first the
beast (vv. 8–14) and then the woman (vv. 15–18).
The final part of v. 7 repeats from v. 3d several of the
most puzzling features of the beast ("seven heads
and ten horns") that will be explained in the verses
that follow (vv. 9–11 and vv. 12–14 respectively).
Explanatory help from an angelic interpreter is a
common feature of apocalyptic visions, since the
imagery is often puzzling.[41]

As John records the angel's interpretation, the
initial topic is put at the front of the clause, "the
beast that you saw," without an initial conjunction
(v. 8a).[42] The interpretation focuses first on the
beast itself (v. 8), then its heads (vv. 9–11), and
finally its horns (vv. 12–14). As often in apocalyptic literature (e.g., Dan 7:23–27; 9:25–27), the
"explanation" remains rather cryptic while giving
important clues to the identification or significance
of the visionary contents. This is especially true of
what is said about the beast itself in v. 8a. To say,
"the beast . . . was and is not and is about to come
up out of the bottomless pit and go to destruction"
does not seem to clarify very much, and it certainly
does not name a specific referent like Daniel 4:22
("the tree is you, O king") or 8:20–21 ("the kings
of Media and Persia . . . and the king of Greece").[43]
But some reflection on what had already been said
about the beast in 11:7 and 13:1–3 in light of their
current historical circumstances would give the
readers the insight they needed.

---

38. The angel's quoted explanation reflects a pattern of tense usage (i.e., mixture of presents, futures, imperfects, and aorists) characteristic of report or descriptive mode, not narrative (see note on 4:5).

39. BDAG 444–45; G. Bertram, "θαυμάζω," *TDNT* 3:41.

40. The phrase "concerning the woman and the beast" (τῆς γυναικὸς καὶ τοῦ θηρίου) reflects an objective-genitive sense with a word like "mystery" (i.e., about or concerning; cf. Wallace, *Grammar*, 116–19).

41. E.g., Dan 7:15–28; 8:15–25; Zech 1:7–11; 4:1–14; cf. 1 En. 52:2–9; 4 Ezra 12:1–39; 2 Bar. 55–56.

42. This word order signals "the beast" as the topic of what follows (cf. Runge, *Discourse Grammar*, 187–92).

43. See note at Rev 13:18 for discussion of why such a direct identification would be avoided.

The beast "was" (ἦν; i.e., "existed in the past") and "is not" (οὐκ ἔστιν; i.e., does not at the time John is writing exist in the world of the living) and "is about to come up out of the bottomless pit" (v. 8a; cf. 11:7, he will arise from the realm of the dead; see note on 9:1). All this is true because he had been put to death but was expected to return to life soon. He appears in 13:3 as one with a mortal wound ("as though slain unto death"), whose deathblow had been "healed" (13:3, 12), that is, he had "the wound of the sword but came to life" (13:14). The response of the non-Christian world (those not recorded in "the book of life," v. 8c; 13:8; cf. 3:5) to this remarkable recovery is worshipful amazement (they "will marvel," v. 8d; 13:3) at what appears to be a supernatural recovery. Verse 8d–e repeats 13:3, 12 in different words when it says they will worship "when they see"[44] that the beast "was and is not and will be present" (ἦν καὶ οὐκ ἔστιν καὶ πάρεσται; the first two verbs repeated from v. 8a). The only negative thing said about the beast here is the final clause in v. 8a, that he goes "to destruction" (repeated in v. 11b as an *inclusio* bracketing off vv. 8–11 as a unit). The career of the beast will seem wildly successful until he turns his satanic-inspired hostility against the returning Christ. His defeat at that point will be swift and overwhelming (19:19–21; cf. 2 Thess 2:8).

17:9–11 (Here is the mind that has wisdom.) The seven heads are seven mountains on which the woman sits, and they are seven kings. 10 Five have fallen, one is, and the other has not yet come, and when he comes he must remain for a little time. 11 And the beast who was and is not is also himself an eighth and is of the seven, and he goes to destruction

(ὧδε ὁ νοῦς ὁ ἔχων σοφίαν. αἱ ἑπτὰ κεφαλαὶ ἑπτὰ ὄρη εἰσίν, ὅπου ἡ γυνὴ κάθηται ἐπ᾽ αὐτῶν. καὶ βασιλεῖς ἑπτὰ εἰσιν· 10 οἱ πέντε ἔπεσαν, ὁ εἷς ἔστιν, ὁ ἄλλος οὔπω ἦλθεν, καὶ ὅταν ἔλθῃ ὀλίγον αὐτὸν δεῖ μεῖναι. 11 καὶ τὸ θηρίον ὃ ἦν καὶ οὐκ ἔστιν καὶ αὐτὸς ὄγδοός ἐστιν καὶ ἐκ τῶν ἑπτά ἐστιν, καὶ εἰς ἀπώλειαν ὑπάγει). The angel's interpretation of visionary details concerning the beast continues (focusing on the "heads" in vv. 9–11), interrupted by a parenthetical aside here in v. 9a. The parenthesis should be understood as John's editorial insertion amid the angel's explanation that starts in v. 7 and runs to v. 14. The parallel expressions in 13:10, 18 indicate that "here is . . ." could be paraphrased as "this requires . . . ," signaling that the beast's cryptic story (v. 8a, e, "he was and is not," etc.) needs careful reflection in order to unpack the intended sense.[45] Unfortunately, the explanation that follows is also puzzling. Part of the enigma is that the beast's "seven heads" are said to represent "seven mountains" (v. 9b) as well as "seven kings" (v. 9d/10a).[46] The details added with each phrase help to differentiate their meanings. The beast's heads are "mountains" in that they show the woman's location (v. 9b–c), but they are "kings" in that they characterize his role and that of others

---

44. The participle translated "when they see" (βλεπόντων) modifies the main verb "will marvel," so it is expected to be nominative agreeing with the subject, "those who live on the earth" (οἱ κατοικοῦντες ἐπὶ τῆς γῆς). But it has been attracted to the case of the genitive relative pronoun (ὧν) that intervened. See Mathewson, *Handbook*, 230. It is not a genitive absolute with the genitive pronoun omitted (cf. BDF §423.6) as Aune, *Revelation 17–22*, 910, and others suggest.

45. Aune, *Revelation 17–22*, 941, seems correct that the initial reference in v. 9a ("here" or "this requires . . .) is to what comes before (v. 8a, e).

46. Because of the individual treatment of the seven kings in vv. 10–11, it is highly unlikely that the number "seven" in this context is merely figurative for "completeness," as some commentators argue (Beale, *Revelation*, 869; Aune, *Revelation 17–22*, 948; Osborne, *Revelation*, 620; Resseguie, *Narrative Commentary*, 224). It also neglects the point that numbers like words may be both denotative (referring to specific items) as well as connotative (suggesting a larger sense or ethos). See comments about the seven churches of 1:4, 11 and the 144,000 of 7:3–8.

associated with him in that role (vv. 9d/10a–11). The woman was said to sit on the beast (v. 3) and be carried by the beast (v. 7), so any information about the location of the beast's heads perhaps identifies also the woman's location. What sitting on "seven mountains" indicates is that the woman is associated with Rome, widely known in the ancient world as "the city of seven hills."[47]

That the seven heads of the beast are also "seven kings" (v. 9d in Greek texts; v. 10a in many English versions) shifts away from a brief focus on the woman to an extended explanation of the beast's own ruling authority as well as the history of a line of rulers associated with him (vv. 10–11). In parallel with Daniel's vision of beasts with multiple heads and horns (Dan 7:17–27), these "kings" could represent either the *person* who exercises rule or the *kingdom* (or empire) over which he rules— and there could be an overlap of person and realm in the intended meaning. Both options have been suggested for these seven "kings." A complicating

factor for these verses is the specific set of details that are given ("five have fallen, one is," etc.), which make it harder to settle for a general metaphorical meaning. Which option best explains the specific details? Most interpreters see the need to correlate the specifics in some way with a line of rulers or empires that John and his readers could have had in mind in the first-century world.[48] But trying to correlate vv. 10–11 with a list of Roman *emperors* (i.e., "kings"; cf. 1 Tim 2:2; Pet 2:13, 17)[49] can be frustratingly confusing:[50] Which seven fit vv. 10–11 in a way that makes sense?[51] This has led many to argue instead that seven historic *empires* that have impacted Jewish-Christian affairs are in view: for example, Egypt, Assyria, Babylon, Medo-Persia, Greece, and Rome (with a future version of Babylon-Rome as the eighth).[52]

A plausible scheme in listing kings rather than kingdoms—more likely to be John's point but not without its own complications—begins with the understanding that what would be more mean-

---

47. See Cicero, *Att.* 6.5; Pliny, *Nat.* 3.66–67; Vergil, *Aen.* 6.781–84. Aune, *Revelation 17–22*, 944–45, lists seven other ancient texts that refer to Rome in this way. Citing these sources is not an argument that John's audience must have read these authors (as Andrew M. Woods, "Have the Prophecies in Revelation 17–18 about Babylon Been Fulfilled? Part 1," *BSac* 169 [2012]: 99–100 implies), but that Rome as "seven-hilled" would have been a part of general cultural knowledge even in Roman Asia Minor of the first century. The close connections between Asia Minor and Rome at that time (see Thompson, *Revelation*, 146–67) likewise mutes another objection Woods raises (citing others): that ancient authors who identify Rome as seven-hilled all come from the western Mediterranean, and we cannot be sure that people in Asia Minor would be familiar with the description.

48. A strictly futurist interpretation could try to sidestep this question about the ancient setting and explain the sense only in regard to rulers or empires that will arise in the end times, but Rev precludes that option here. The book seems to show throughout its chapters that we should not choose between a purely historical-critical (first-century) reading vs. a purely futurist (end-times) reading. The typology of Rev (and of the Bible in general) suggests that these "kings" would have significance both in John's time and in that ultimate future day.

49. BDAG 170.

50. See the range of possibilities in the chart on p. 445. For further discussion, see Aune, *Revelation 17–22*, 947–48; Beale, *Revelation*, 872–75; and Koester, *Revelation*, 72–73.

51. If we begin with Julius Caesar, the sixth emperor would be Nero, a possible solution to the puzzle (option "a" on the chart on p. 445). But the early emperors did not oppose Christ or resist Christianity, and there are other reasons for rejecting a date for the book during the reign of Nero (see introduction). Another option ("b") is to start with Augustus as the first one proclaimed as emperor, which makes Galba the sixth and allows for knowledge of Nero's death in the pattern that the beast reflects (revived after a fatal wound, 13:3; 17:8).

52. Ladd, *Revelation*, 227–31; Thomas, *Revelation 8–22*, 296–98; Walvoord, Rawley, and Hitchcock, *Revelation*, 262–63. This was suggested early on by Andrew of Caesarea (sixth century); see Weinrich, "Andrew of Caesarea," 178. A problem for this view is that "king" seems to refer to a personal ruler in v. 11a (the beast who appeared to have died and was revived), and he is cited as "of the seven." Ladd (p. 227) argues that mountains in v. 9b are symbols of ruling powers/kingdoms (e.g., Isa 2:2; Jer 51:25; Dan 2:35) rather than personal kings, but he then has no clear explanation of the seventh and "eighth" in the listing in vv. 10–11 (p. 231).

ingful for John and his first-century Christian readers would be the Roman emperors who had impacted the Christian movement in a negative way since its inception, those who distinctly fit the pattern that the antichrist to come would fulfill.[53] The list would start with Caligula, Claudius, and Nero, all of whom acted in self-exalting ways that threatened Christian security in Jerusalem as well as in Rome and the wider Mediterranean world.[54] The three generals who vied for Roman rule during the tumultuous single year after Nero's demise could plausibly be omitted since it is debated whether they actually "ruled,"[55] and their threat to Christians was negligible. Vespasian and Titus would certainly fit the list because of their destruction of Jerusalem and would complete the tally of five who "have fallen" (v. 10a/b). Domitian would then be the one who "is" (sixth in the list), as John writes toward the end of his reign in the mid-90s AD. The angel then anticipates a successor (the seventh), whose tenure is subject to God's timing,[56] who must rule for an unspecified "little" time (v. 10c/d). He means by this an extent of time that God controls and that cannot be reckoned specifically. While the seventh is not described further, he is presumably the ruler in control in the final days to come when the rebellion against the empire (i.e., the prostitute) occurs (vv. 16–17).

Returning to the beast himself in v. 11a, the angel repeats the cryptic description from v. 8a, c ("who was and is not") and then connects him to the series of seven kings, "he is also an eighth and is of the seven." This beast who had been killed but was expected to come back to life (cf. 13:3, 12, 14) would be the successor to the seventh emperor (the beast is "eighth"), a king in the same line ("of the seven"). As discussed at 13:18, this beast pictures Nero as a type of the future antichrist. Here his apparent revival to life is associated with a return to Rome/Babylon accompanied by allies who will help him briefly gain power again, but at the cost of devastating results for the empire itself (v. 16; 18:17, 19). To be clear, John's typology does not picture Nero himself returning but one in the end times

The Kings of Revelation 17:9–11			
Emperors (Dates)	**a**	**b**	**c**
Julius Caesar (49–44 BC)	1		
Augustus (31/27 BC–AD 14)	2	1	
Tiberius (AD 14–37)	3	2	
Gaius Caligula (AD 37–41)	4	3	1
Claudius (AD 41–54)	5	4	2
Nero (AD 54–68)	6	5	3
Galba (AD 68–69)		6	
Otho (AD 69)			
Vitellius (AD 69)			
Vespasian (AD 69–79)			4
Titus (AD 79–81)			5
Domitian (AD 81–96)			6
Nerva (AD 96–98)			
Trajan (AD 98–117)			
Hadrian (AD 117–138)			

---

53. This is the approach of Arie W. Zwiep, "Eight Kings on an Apocalyptic Animal Farm: Reflections on Revelation 17:9–11," in *Paul, John, and Apocalyptic Eschatology: Studies in Honour of Martinus C. Boer*, ed. Jan Krans et al. (Leiden: Brill, 2013), 225–37. Glasson, *Revelation*, 99–100, proposes the same list of emperors with largely the same rationale as Zwiep. This is option "c" on the chart above.

54. Not starting with Tiberius can be questioned since Jesus was crucified under his rule (a distinctly antichrist-like act), but the cross was not a self-exalting vendetta against Christ on his part. The personal tone of imperial claims to worship changed under Caligula.

55. Suetonius, *Vesp.* 1.1 and *Sib. Or.* 5:35 call them "three rebel princes."

56. For the use of "must" (δεῖ) in Rev to imply God's sovereign determination of times, see comment on 1:1.

who will be like Nero, characterized by even greater savagery and madness. But his terrible reign is destined not to last long. He "goes to destruction" (v. 11b), as v. 8a also declared, summarily defeated by the returning Christ (19:19–21). The victory that Christ will gain over the beast leads to the angel's explanation of the beast's ten horns that follows (vv. 12–14).

17:12–14 And the ten horns that you saw are ten kings who have not yet received ruling authority, but with the beast they receive authority as kings for one hour. 13 These have a single purpose, and they give their power and authority to the beast. 14 These will make war against the Lamb, and the Lamb will conquer them, because he is Lord of lords and King of kings, and those with him are called and chosen and faithful" (καὶ τὰ δέκα κέρατα ἃ εἶδες δέκα βασιλεῖς εἰσιν, οἵτινες βασιλείαν οὔπω ἔλαβον, ἀλλὰ ἐξουσίαν ὡς βασιλεῖς μίαν ὥραν λαμβάνουσιν μετὰ τοῦ θηρίου. 13 οὗτοι μίαν γνώμην ἔχουσιν καὶ τὴν δύναμιν καὶ ἐξουσίαν αὐτῶν τῷ θηρίῳ διδόασιν. 14 οὗτοι μετὰ τοῦ ἀρνίου πολεμήσουσιν καὶ τὸ ἀρνίον νικήσει αὐτούς, ὅτι κύριος κυρίων ἐστὶν καὶ βασιλεὺς βασιλέων καὶ οἱ μετ᾽ αὐτοῦ κλητοὶ καὶ ἐκλεκτοὶ καὶ πιστοί). After focusing on the beast's heads (vv. 9–11), the angel now explains the "ten horns" John saw (vv. 12–14). They symbolize "ten kings" (v. 12a), but not kings that rule one after another and stretch from the past into the future as represented by the heads (vv. 9–11). Instead, these ten exercise authority simultaneously "with the beast" for a short period of time, for "one hour," and their rule has not yet begun: they "have not yet received ruling authority" (v. 12b–c; cf. "ruling authority" or "kingdom rule,"

βασιλεία, in vv. 17, 18). They fit the pattern of the subordinate client kings that Rome found it convenient to use in governing their vast empire (like Herod the Great at an earlier period). When the beast arises from the bottomless pit and assumes overall sovereignty like that of the seven hostile emperors specified in vv. 10–11, these ten client kings will be his allies. The angel explains (v. 13) that as the beast's allies they will wholeheartedly[57] put their political and military strength at his disposal and serve his diabolical ambitions.

Verse 14 jumps ahead to the ultimate demise of this alliance when they turn their military efforts against Christ, as will be portrayed in 19:19. Their "war against the Lamb" (v. 14a) reflects the theme of eschatological warfare that comes up again and again in the final chapters of Revelation (e.g., 12:17; 13:7; 16:10, 12–16; 19:11–21; 20:7–10). The final campaign that the beast and his allies will undertake together will be a short and utterly futile battle against the returning Lord Jesus Christ: "They will make war against the Lamb, and the Lamb will conquer them" (v. 14a–b).[58] The beast's defeat and judgment at the hands of the Lamb was previewed already in vv. 8a, 11b ("he goes to destruction"). This battle is described later in 19:11–21, as v. 14b signals. In v. 14c the reason cited for the Lamb's complete victory is that "he is Lord of lords and King of kings," a distinctive combination that occurs in 19:16 in reverse order, "King of kings and Lord of lords."[59] Reference to the allies of the beast (the ten client kings) then calls forth a corresponding mention of those who will accompany the Lamb in his victory, that is, his people, those humans whom God has "called and chosen" (v. 14d), who show themselves "faithful" in their persevering loyalty to him.

---

57. They will "have a single purpose" (μίαν γνώμην ἔχουσιν); v. 17 uses the same word "purpose, intention" to assert that it is actually God's will that they will serve in these actions.

58. Their intermediate battle will be an attack against Babylon itself, as vv. 16–17; 18:8–10; 19:2 describe.

59. Phrases like these appear in Deut 10:17; Ps 136:3; Dan 2:47; cf. 2 Macc 13:4; 3 Macc 5:35; 1 En. 9:4; 63:4, 7; 84:2; 1QM 14:16.

These show up again (unspecified) in 19:14 as part of Christ's heavenly armies (see details there).

17:15–16 And he said to me, "The waters that you saw, where the prostitute lives, are peoples and multitudes and nations and languages. 16 And the ten horns that you saw and the beast will hate the prostitute and will make her desolate and naked and will devour her flesh and will burn her with fire (Καὶ λέγει μοι, Τὰ ὕδατα ἃ εἶδες οὗ ἡ πόρνη κάθηται, λαοὶ καὶ ὄχλοι εἰσὶν καὶ ἔθνη καὶ γλῶσσαι. 16 καὶ τὰ δέκα κέρατα ἃ εἶδες καὶ τὸ θηρίον οὗτοι μισήσουσιν τὴν πόρνην καὶ ἠρημωμένην ποιήσουσιν αὐτὴν καὶ γυμνὴν καὶ τὰς σάρκας αὐτῆς φάγονται καὶ αὐτὴν κατακαύσουσιν ἐν πυρί). John again cites the interpreting angel from v. 1 ("and he said to me," v. 15a),[60] whose explanation of the vision was previously quoted beginning in v. 7b (the quoted words extended through v. 14). His interpretation focused first on the beast and his heads and horns (vv. 8–14), but now shifts to the prostitute or woman of the vision, with occasional overlap of topic in each section (vv. 15–18; here the quoted words are vv. 15b–18). To grasp the prostitute's significance, one must understand "the waters" that identify her location as well as her influence (v. 15b–c).[61] The angel explains that they represent "peoples and multitudes and nations

and languages" (v. 15d). This is the last of seven occurrences of a set of remarkably similar terms that refer to the varied people groups of the whole world.[62] Citing this list as the interpretation of the "waters" indicates a broader sense than was alluded to by the phrase "beside many waters" in v. 1. There the reference identified "the great prostitute" as Babylon, the city-state located on the canals and tributaries of the southern Euphrates. But "waters" in the Old Testament are sometimes used with a wider reference, especially in a context of impending warfare. A range of Old Testament texts use "overflowing waters" to represent invading armies from Assyria, Egypt, Babylon, or many nations that are about to overwhelm Israel or Judah (e.g., Isa 8:7–8; 17:12–13; Jer 46:8; 47:2), and that is the point intended here. This multinational character for the prostitute is not at odds with her identification as Babylon the great, since Babylon is typological of future world powers allied against God, but it more clearly identifies her as the center of a worldwide coalition or empire that she dominates (cf. v. 18).

That coalition will experience the ravages of civil war, however, as v. 16 reveals. Returning to the alliance of ten client kings with the beast[63] who will wage war with the Lamb according to vv. 12–14 (his ten "horns" previously seen), the angel explains that

---

60. The verb "he said" (λέγει) in v. 15a could be a historical present "draw[ing] attention to the following speech [vv. 15–18]," as Mathewson, *Handbook*, 234, says. The verb that introduces speech in v. 7a is a narrative aorist, so the mode of this chapter seems to be narrative, not description or report (as, e.g., λέγει in 14:13; 18:7). The aorist variant reading (εἶπεν; A, vg) could be a solution to this issue, but it seems to be a scribal correction to match v. 7. A more consistent function for the historical present would be to highlight not the speech immediately following but the *next* event or speech (i.e., the vision of 18:1; see notes at 5:5; 10:9). Elsewhere in Rev when λέγει is used as a historical present, it introduces short dialogue (5:5; 10:9; 19:9; 21:5; 22:9, 10, 20), not a long speech as here. But an emphasis on 18:1ff. seems to be the best conclusion here. For other historical presents that anticipate the following chapter, see λέγουσιν in 6:16; 10:11.

61. Describing her again as "the prostitute" who "lives" beside "waters" is a clear return to the introduction given in v. 1 where these terms occurred together, and the sense of "lives" (κάθημαι) is the same as in v. 1 (see note there). Although "waters" were not mentioned explicitly as part of the description of the vision, they were part of what John witnessed, so the angel can cite them here as "the waters that you saw" (v. 15b).

62. See comments on 5:9 for a listing of occurrences in Rev and their roots in Daniel (cf. Bauckham, *Climax*, 326–37, for discussion).

63. Instead of "the ten horns . . . and the beast" (τὰ δέκα κέρατα . . . καὶ τὸ θηρίον) in v. 16a, the TR (cf. KJV, NKJV) reads "the ten horns on the beast" (τὰ δέκα κέρατα . . . ἐπὶ τὸ θηρίον), but this has no basis in Greek manuscripts (Thomas, *Revelation 8–22*, 309–10).

their hostile force will first be directed against the prostitute Babylon itself (v. 16a). Shifting to future tenses as in v. 14, he declares that their alliance "will hate" her and devastate her wealth and power. This devastation is pictured in three vivid images (v. 16b–d), also familiar from Old Testament pictures of national ruin: they "will make her desolate and naked" (Ezek 16:37–39; 23:29; 26:19; Hos 2:3; cf. Rev 18:17, 19), they "will devour her flesh" (Ps 27:2; Mic 3:3), and "will burn her with fire" (Lev 21:9; Jer 34:22; cf. Rev 18:8). Following the same pattern that Jeremiah 50:39–42 predicted for ancient Babylon (she would be ruined when attacked by many nations from the ends of the earth) as well as that of Ezekiel 38:21 (God will turn his enemies' swords against one another), this future Babylon will likewise be laid waste when she is attacked by those who were her former allies. Here again John utilizes fears in the Roman world that Nero would return from the east to attack Rome itself (see comments on vv. 9–13).[64]

17:17–18 For God put it in their hearts to accomplish his purpose and to act with one purpose and to yield their ruling authority to the beast until God's words are completed. 18 And the woman that you saw is the great city that has ruling authority over the kings of the earth" (ὁ γὰρ θεὸς ἔδωκεν εἰς τὰς καρδίας αὐτῶν ποιῆσαι τὴν γνώμην αὐτοῦ καὶ ποιῆσαι μίαν γνώμην καὶ δοῦναι τὴν βασιλείαν αὐτῶν τῷ θηρίῳ ἄχρι τελεσθήσονται οἱ λόγοι τοῦ θεοῦ. 18 καὶ ἡ γυνὴ ἣν εἶδες ἔστιν ἡ πόλις ἡ μεγάλη ἡ ἔχουσα βασιλείαν ἐπὶ τῶν βασιλέων τῆς γῆς). The ten kings' unity of purpose (mentioned already in v. 13) will not originate from solely human intent but is prompted by the sovereign God who controls the events of his world, even the

actions of evil, God-opposing powers (v. 17). The angel makes this clear by repeating the key word from v. 13 (intention, purpose; γνώμη) two times, showing that the unified purpose that the ten kings will execute will be God's intention that he places within them (v. 17b–c).[65] Part of their single intention, cited in v. 13 as well as v. 17, is to give their allegiance to the beast in this struggle against Babylon—expressed in v. 13 as giving him "their power and authority" (τὴν δύναμιν καὶ ἐξουσίαν αὐτῶν) and in v. 17d as giving him "their ruling authority" (τὴν βασιλείαν αὐτῶν, their kingship or royal power; cf. vv. 12, 18).[66] The fact that God is the one who prompts them to these actions leads to the ultimate accomplishment of his "purpose" that is described in a temporal clause in v. 17e, "until God's words are completed" (ἄχρι τελεσθήσονται οἱ λόγοι τοῦ θεοῦ). The parallel with 10:7c (ἐτελέσθη τὸ μυστήριον τοῦ θεοῦ) suggests that "God's words" are those communicated to his prophets (cf. 10:7d) as he declared his intention through them ahead of time.

The angel's interpretation of the prostitute or woman of John's vision that began in a focused way in v. 15 (and digressed a bit in v. 17) now comes to its most distinct form in v. 18. He identifies the woman that John saw as "the great city" (ἡ πόλις ἡ μεγάλη; v. 18a). The attribute "great" has already been used of the prostitute herself in the angel's introduction of her in v. 1 and of the city-state "Babylon the great" in v. 5 (the name written on the woman's forehead; cf. also 14:8; 16:19c). The epithet, "the great city," is used earlier in 16:19a and later in 18:10. But here the angel's identification does not stop with "the great city" alone; he adds the significant description, "that has ruling author-

---

64. Kraybill, *Imperial Cult*, 161–63; Bauckham, *Climax*, 407–23, 429–31; cf. *Sib. Or.* 4:115–24, 137–51; 5:137–60.

65. Three infinitives in v. 17b–d give the purpose of God's

action in v. 17a. For the idiom of "put in their hearts" (v. 17a), see Exod 7:3; Ezra 7:27.

66. BDAG 168.

ity over the kings of the earth."[67] In John's day the Old Testament typology of imperial Babylon ruling the nations from the shores of the Euphrates would transparently refer to a similar empire controlling the world of its day from the shores of the Tiber. Rome, the great city, clearly replicated the pattern of fallen human civilization opposed to God and his values.

Theology in Application

Following a Notorious Prostitute?

This passage may be awkward to preach to a typical Sunday congregation, but it is important not to be too quick to dispense with the powerful imagery in favor of the dry abstract principles that it represents. The symbolism gets our attention and shocks us into realizing what is really at stake in the verses. We'd rather not dwell on the repulsive image of prostitution, but no one can sugarcoat how wrong it is to trade on what is most personal and valuable in order to gain things that have little worth.[68] Yet because of how deceptive and dazzling sin can be, we are prone to sell out what should be most sacred and personal, to betray the loyalties that are most intimate and should be most important to us, for the sake of cheap substitutes. This "great prostitute" has that outward look of respectability: she is opulently dressed in fine garments and dazzling jewels. But a closer look reveals sordid abomination and gross uncleanness. She represents the reversal of true values that Christians should resist vehemently. It is the benefit of God's revelation that we can see through sin's enticements and deceptions and grasp what they really represent: values that are depraved and idolatrous.

Everybody's Doing It

Similar to the lessons of chapter 13 (all the world taken in by the beast's skillful deceptions), this chapter confronts us again with the prospect of delusion on a grand scale. Those who think that an individual or two can be misled but the majority is usually right should pay attention to the society-wide, systemic delusion portrayed here. What John sees in his vision is an interconnected network of godless values

---

67. This phrase in v. 18b renders very unlikely the identification of "the great city Babylon" with Jerusalem (e.g., Beagley, *Apocalypse*, 107–8; Ford, *Revelation*, 292–93; Lupieri, *Apocalypse*, 280–81; van de Water, "Reconsidering," 259–60). Several cite Ezek 16:12–14 (references to Jerusalem as a woman finely dressed, with a crown and royal status and fame among the nations) as a parallel, but that hardly pictures Jerusalem as possessing "ruling authority over the kings of the earth" (v. 18b). The detailed picture in ch. 18 of a city at the center of the world's commerce and (especially) maritime trade fails to

fit even the most hyperbolic view that first-century Jerusalem could have had of itself. See Biguzzi, "Babylon," 380–83, for an extended critique of this identification.

68. This image challenges the temptation to sordid disloyalties in us all (male and female) and should not be reduced to sermonizing against "wicked women." It is valuable to realize that women and girls are often swept into prostitution against their will, and "respectable" males play a major role in victimizing them by supporting the burgeoning business of internet pornography.

embraced by the world at large, a combination of religious, economic, and political ideologies affirmed seemingly by all. According to v. 2, "those who dwell on the earth" follow the prostitute gladly, although it is because they are "made drunk" by her enticements. They are drawn into her godless system unthinkingly, and the wider society is astonished that anyone would resist her ways. It is, however, a mixture of materialistic greed with certain "spiritual" sensitivities that are in reality utterly opposed to the true God. The world seems unaware that the prostitute "rides the beast," subject to powerful spiritual, cosmic forces at work beneath the surface. These are allowed to operate in God's sovereign plan, but actually represent avowed enemies of God and his people. And this system "reigns over the kings of the earth" (v. 18). Scripture presents this godless system that functions under Satan's control in other places (Eph 2:1–3; Jas 4:4; 1 John 2:15–16), but this passage shows us its ultimate intensification in the end times. Then as now it seems invincible and irresistible, but it is ultimately unstable and doomed. The seeds of its own destruction are already sown (Rev 17:16–17; cf. John 16:11). Christians are called and empowered to resist such enticements (Eph 6:10–17; 1 John 4:4) and to exemplify a different set of values, even if the whole world seems to be set against us.

Revelation 18:1–24

Literary Context

This chapter is the second part of the larger unit of 17:1–19:10 portraying God's judgment on Babylon. In chapter 17 John saw Babylon as "a great prostitute" riding the beast and together dominating the world, but then devastated in the end when God causes their alliance to fall apart (vv. 16–17). In chapter 18 the effects of that judgment are recorded. Her destruction that was previewed in 14:8 ("fallen, fallen is Babylon the great") is presented now in its full effects, not by viewing the act of devastation itself, but by hearing a series of dramatic lamentations uttered by those who previously benefitted from her evil ways. God's justice in judging Babylon will be celebrated in heaven in the final part of this unit (19:1–10).

> I. Prologue (1:1–8)
>
> II. First Vision: The Exalted Christ and His Messages to the Churches (1:9–3:22)
>
> III. Second Vision: Heavenly Throne Room and Three Judgment Cycles (4:1–16:21)
>
> **IV. Third Vision: The Destruction of Babylon the Great (17:1–19:10)**
>
>   A. Babylon, the Great Prostitute, and the Beast She Rides (17:1–18)
>
> ➡   **B. The Effects of Babylon's Destruction (18:1–24)**
>
>   C. Celebration of Babylon's Judgment and Preparation of the Lamb's Bride (19:1–10)

Main Idea

All who benefit from Babylon's rich luxuries and idolatry will in the end bewail her downfall when God judges her and vindicates those she has persecuted.

Translation

(See pages 452–55.)

Revelation 18:1–24

1a	Vision Intro/ Character Entrance 1	**After these things I saw another angel coming down from heaven,**
b	Description	**having great authority,**
c		**and the earth was illuminated by his glory.**
2a	Action	**And he cried out with a mighty voice saying,**

b	Announcement	*"Fallen, fallen is Babylon the great,*
c	Effect	*and she has become the dwelling place of demons and*
		the haven of every unclean spirit and
		the haven of every unclean bird and
		the haven of every unclean and detestable beast,

3a	Reasons for 2b	*because from the wine of her passionate immorality*
		all the nations have fallen and
b		*the kings of the earth committed sexual immorality with her and*
c		*the merchants of the earth got rich from her excessive luxury."*

| 4a | Action/Character Entrance 2 | **And I heard another voice from heaven saying,** |

b	Command	*"Come out from her, my people,*
c	Purpose	*so that you may not share in her sins and*
		may not receive any of her plagues,

5a	Reason	*because her sins have piled up to heaven and*
b		*God has remembered her crimes.*
6a	Command	*Render to her*
b	Comparison/ measure	*as she too has rendered*
c	Commands	*and pay her double*
		according to her works;

| d | | *in the cup that she mixed* |
| | | *mix her a double portion.* |

7a	Comparison/ measure	*Just as she glorified herself and lived in luxury,*
b	Command	*in the same measure*
		give her torment and grief,
c	Reason	*because in her heart she says,*
d	Assertions	*'I sit as a queen*
		and I am not a widow
		and I will never see grief.'

8a	Results of 7c–d	*For this reason in one day*
		her plagues will come,
		pestilence and
		grief and
		famine,
b		*and she will be burned with fire,*
c	Reason for 8a–b	*because the Lord God who judged her is mighty.*
9a	Action/Lament 1	*And the kings of the earth ...*
b	Description	*who committed sexual immorality and*
		lived in luxury with her
c		*... will weep and*
		mourn over her
d	Time	*while they watch the smoke of her burning,*
10a	Place	*standing far away in fear of her torment saying,*
b	Lament	*'Woe, woe, the great city, Babylon,*
		the mighty city,
c	Reason	*because in one hour your judgment has come.'*
11a	Action/Lament 2	*And the merchants of the earth weep and*
		grieve over her
b	Reason	*because no one buys their cargoes any longer,*
12a	Specification	*cargoes of gold and silver and*
		precious stones and pearls and
b		*linen and purple and*
		silk and scarlet and
c		*every kind of fragrant wood and*
		every article of ivory and
d		*every article of costly wood and*
		bronze and iron and marble, and
13a		*cinnamon and spice and*
		incense and perfumed ointment and frankincense and
b		*wine and oil and fine flour and grain and*
c		*cattle and sheep and horses and carriages and*
		bodies, that is, the souls of people.
14a	Declaration (by merchants of 11a)	*'And the fruit your soul desired has left you,*
b		*and all the luxurious and splendid things have been lost to you,*
c		*and they will never be found again.'*

Continued on next page.

Continued from previous page.

15a Resumption of   *The merchants of these things,...*
   Lament 2
  b   Description   *who got rich from her,*
  c   *... will stand*
                                                 far away
                                                 in fear of her torment,
                                                 weeping and
                                                 grieving,
16a   *saying,*

  b   Lament   *'Woe, woe, the great city,*
  c   Descriptions   *the one clothed in linen and purple and scarlet and*
  d   *adorned with gold and precious stones and pearls*

17a   Reason   *because in one hour such great riches were made desolate.'*
  b Action/Lament 3 *And every ship's captain and*
                          everyone who travels by boat and
                          sailors and
                          all who work on the sea ...

  c   Place   *... stood far away*
18a Action   *and*   *were crying out*
  b   Time   *as they watched the smoke of her burning saying,*

  c   Exclamation   *'Who was like the great city?'*
19a Response to 18b *And they threw dust on their heads and*
                            were crying out,

  b   Manner   *weeping and*
                             grieving,
                             saying,
  c   Lament   *'Woe, woe, the great city,*
  d   Description   *in which all those who had ships on the sea got rich*
                                                  from her prosperity,

  e   Reason   *because in one hour she was made desolate.'"*

20a Invitation   *"Rejoice over her, O heaven and*
   (by voice of 4a)   *saints and*
                                  apostles and
                                  prophets,

  b   Reason   *because God has exacted judgment for you against her."*

21a	Action/Character Entrance 3	**And a mighty angel took up a rock like a large millstone and threw it into the sea saying,**
b	Pronouncement	*"So will Babylon the great city be thrown down violently,*
c	General Effect	*and she will never be found again.*
22a	Specific Effects	*And the sound of kithara players and*
		musicians and
		flute players and
		trumpeters will never be heard in you again,
b		*and no craftsman of any craft will ever be found in you again,*
c		*and the sound of a mill will never be heard in you again.*
23a		*And the light of a lamp will never appear in you again,*
b		*and the sound of bridegroom and*
		bride will never be heard in you again.
c	Reasons for 21b–23b	*Because your merchants were the great ones of the earth,*
d		*because by your sorcery all the nations were led astray, and*
24		*in her the blood of prophets and*
		saints were found and
		of all those slain on the earth."

Structure

Different schemes have been suggested for structuring the content of chapter 18, partly because it is difficult to sort out the different speakers and actors that appear in this dramatic chapter. The most likely organization centers on the three explicit introductions of heavenly actors or speakers that John provides at vv. 1, 4, and 21. The first and last sections are relatively brief, giving a heavenly announcement of Babylon's fall (vv. 1–3) and a dramatic enactment of her judgment with accompanying pronouncements (vv. 21–24). The middle section is the longest and most diverse (vv. 4–20), but in summary it addresses God's people (vv. 4–8), records lamentation over Babylon's fall by three groups who benefitted from her rule over the earth (vv. 9–19), and issues a final call for heaven and earth to rejoice over her demise (v. 20).

Exegetical Outline

IV. Third Vision: The Destruction of Babylon the Great (17:1–19:10)

    A. Babylon, the Great Prostitute, and the Beast She Rides (17:1–18)

➡   **B. The Effects of Babylon's Destruction (18:1–24)**

        1. Announcement of Babylon's Fall (18:1–3)

        2. Warning to God's People and Laments from Babylon's Cronies (18:4–20)

           a. Commands to God's people about Babylon's fall (18:4–8)

           b. Laments over Babylon's fall (18:9–19)

               (1) Lament by kings (18:9–10)

               (2) Lament by merchants (18:11–17a)

               (3) Lament by seafarers (18:17b–19)

           c. Invitation to rejoice over Babylon's fall (18:20)

        3. Symbolic Enactment of Babylon's Fall (18:21–24)

           a. Her violent overthrow (18:21a–b)

           b. Effects of her overthrow (18:21c–23b)

           c. Reasons for her overthrow (18:23c–24)

Explanation of the Text

18:1 After these things I saw another angel coming down from heaven, having great authority, and the earth was illuminated by his glory (Μετὰ ταῦτα εἶδον ἄλλον ἄγγελον καταβαίνοντα ἐκ τοῦ οὐρανοῦ ἔχοντα ἐξουσίαν μεγάλην, καὶ ἡ γῆ ἐφωτίσθη ἐκ τῆς δόξης αὐτοῦ). Although chapters 17 and 18 are closely related under the theme previewed in 16:19 (God's judgment on Babylon the great), the phrase "after these things I saw" (μετὰ ταῦτα εἶδον) signals a transition to a new segment of that theme.[1] In this vision John sees a glorious and mighty angel, different from the interpreting angel (one of the seven bowl angels) who guided him in chapter 17 (e.g., 17:1, 7, 15). Here the angel descends from heaven (cf. 10:1; 20:1) to proclaim the effects of Babylon's judgment by God (vv. 2–3).

This impressive messenger possesses "great authority" and "glory" that lights up the earth, reinforcing the credibility of his proclamation.[2]

18:2–3 And he cried out with a mighty voice saying, "Fallen, fallen is Babylon the great, and she has become the dwelling place of demons and the haven of every unclean spirit and the haven of every unclean bird and the haven of every unclean and detestable beast, 3 because from the wine of her passionate immorality all the nations have fallen and the kings of the earth committed sexual immorality with her and the merchants of the earth got rich from her excessive luxury" (καὶ ἔκραξεν ἐν ἰσχυρᾷ φωνῇ λέγων, Ἔπεσεν ἔπεσεν Βαβυλὼν ἡ μεγάλη, καὶ ἐγένετο κατοικητήριον

---

1. This formula can indicate an entirely new section (e.g., 4:1) or a change within a larger section (7:9; 15:5).

2. The same verb "to illuminate" (φωτίζω) occurs in 21:23;

22:5 to refer to the glory of God and the Lamb that will light up the new Jerusalem (cf. Ezek 43:2; Luke 2:9, using forms of a different verb, λάμπω).

δαιμονίων καὶ φυλακὴ παντὸς πνεύματος ἀκαθάρτου καὶ φυλακὴ παντὸς ὀρνέου ἀκαθάρτου [καὶ φυλακὴ παντὸς θηρίου ἀκαθάρτου] καὶ μεμισημένου, 3 ὅτι ἐκ τοῦ οἴνου τοῦ θυμοῦ τῆς πορνείας αὐτῆς [πέπτωκαν] πάντα τὰ ἔθνη καὶ οἱ βασιλεῖς τῆς γῆς μετ᾽ αὐτῆς ἐπόρνευσαν καὶ οἱ ἔμποροι τῆς γῆς ἐκ τῆς δυνάμεως τοῦ στρήνους αὐτῆς ἐπλούτησαν). The glorious angel moves directly into the main point of the chapter by declaring the fall of Babylon for all to hear (cf. "cried out with a loud voice" in 7:2; 10:3; 19:17) with a focus on the *effects* of her collapse rather than the process or event itself (vv. 2–3). The chapter as a whole consists of a series of voices either rejoicing or lamenting over Babylon's resulting devastation and reflecting on why this came upon her. As in 14:8 the proclamation of her demise in v. 2b is drawn from Isaiah 21:9 (cf. also Amos 5:2): "Fallen, fallen is Babylon the great" (ἔπεσεν, ἔπεσεν Βαβυλὼν ἡ μεγάλη). These aorist verbs declare what has, from heaven's viewpoint, just occurred (English idiom uses a present perfect, "has/is fallen," for this sense).[3] In the literary sequence of John's visions this has been anticipated for several chapters but not until 19:11–21 is it portrayed as accomplished on earth itself. And the actual earthly fulfillment of what John portrays awaits the future return of Christ.[4]

A vivid symbolic description of Babylon's devastation (cf. 17:16) follows in v. 2c. According to Old Testament imagery, when a city is completely destroyed it is no longer suitable for human habitation but will become a haunt for savage creatures and possibly evil spirits (Isa 13:21–22; 34:11–15; Jer 50:39; 51:37; Zeph 2:14).[5] So Babylon is seen as "a dwelling place of demons" (cf. Jer 9:10; also Bar 4:35) and a "haven"[6] for every kind of[7] "unclean spirit" (i.e., demons; cf. Luke 4:33; 9:42; Rev 16:13), "unclean bird" (regarded as undesirable due to the strictures of Lev 11:13–19 or because they are symbolic of demonic beings that prey at night), and "unclean and detestable beast" (savage animals, hated because of the danger they pose; e.g., jackals, hyenas).[8] These creatures typify a great city laid waste.

In keeping with a structure repeated several times in this chapter (cf. vv. 7b–8, 23), the angel's observations about Babylon's desolate condition (v. 2b–c) are followed by a statement (v. 3) of why she deserved such a horrible judgment ("because," ὅτι; v. 3a). The first two clauses of the verse repeat and supplement the charges that were leveled against Babylon the great prostitute in 14:8 and 17:2. In those passages she is said to have enticed her victims by intoxicating them into sharing her immorality and thus misled "all the nations" and "the kings of the earth" into her profane and evil actions. But here the image from 14:8 and 17:2 of drinking "the wine of her passionate immorality"[9] (v. 3a) moves one step further. According to 14:8 she "caused them to drink" (πεπότικεν) and in 17:2b "they became drunk" (ἐμεθύσθησαν), but in the first clause of 18:3 they "have fallen" (πέπτωκαν)

---

3. See notes on 14:8; 15:4 for further discussion.

4. This mixture of temporal viewpoints explains why the tenses shift throughout this chapter, as Biguzzi, "Figurative and Narrative Grammar," 391–92, observes.

5. The contemporary genre of postapocalyptic books and films reflects this imagery as well.

6. The word translated "haven" (φυλακή) often means "prison" (BDAG 1067; cf. NASB), but a better sense here is "refuge, preserve" or "haunt" (most modern English translations).

7. In these examples the sense of "every" (πᾶς with singular, anarthrous nouns) is "every kind of, all sorts of" (BDAG 784).

8. The final phrase in v. 2c ("the haven of every unclean and detestable beast") is omitted in some manuscripts (ℵ, 2053, 2080, most Byzantine minuscules). The omission is reflected in KJV and NKJV, while most recent translations include the words. The parallels in this verse have caused different types of variation in the extant copies, but the reading with the final words included has superior external evidence, and they were probably left out accidentally.

9. See the note at 14:8 on how to construe the genitives of this phrase in Greek.

due to her "wine"[10] according to the best textual reading,[11] an image of stumbling into disaster due to intoxication ("have collapsed, gone to pieces").

The second clause (v. 3b) shifts purely to the image of prostitution as in 17:2a, the earth's kings "committed sexual immorality with her" (ἐπόρνευσαν). This recalls the same image used in 17:2 where sexual sin is a metaphor for spiritual and moral infidelity. In the context of chapter 18 this image is nuanced to add the sins of greed and materialism alongside idolatrous worship. These kings appear again in v. 9 to lament her catastrophic judgment, seemingly not from genuine contrition but in shock that material wealth could not insulate her from disaster. A different note is sounded in v. 3c where the earth's "merchants" (οἱ ἔμποροι τῆς γῆς; these appear again as mourners in vv. 11, 15) are described as getting wealthy[12] "from her excessive luxury" (cf. the related verb "live in luxury," στρηνιάω, in vv. 7, 9).[13] This phrase mirrors the portrait of Babylon's extravagance given in 17:4 and adds her baleful influence on the world's economic life to her list of sins. Reference to her "luxury" represents a materialistic focus on the part of the empire's elite and their conspicu-ous consumption of material goods leading to arrogant self-sufficiency and lack of concern for others.[14] But the larger picture of Babylon/Rome in v. 3 is its deadly mix of blasphemous idolatry wedded to greed and economic exploitation. To supply the luxurious goods they required, the elite were happy to countenance production and trade based on slave labor and ruthless mistreatment of its provincial partners across the empire, all held together by imperial power and worship offered to the emperor as the source of all prosperity.[15]

18:4–5 And I heard another voice from heaven saying, "Come out from her, my people, so that you may not share in her sins and may not receive any of her plagues, 5 because her sins have piled up to heaven and God has remembered her crimes (Καὶ ἤκουσα ἄλλην φωνὴν ἐκ τοῦ οὐρανοῦ λέγουσαν, Ἐξέλθατε ὁ λαός μου ἐξ αὐτῆς ἵνα μὴ συγκοινωνήσητε ταῖς ἁμαρτίαις αὐτῆς, καὶ ἐκ τῶν πληγῶν αὐτῆς ἵνα μὴ λάβητε, 5 ὅτι ἐκολλήθησαν αὐτῆς αἱ ἁμαρτίαι ἄχρι τοῦ οὐρανοῦ καὶ ἐμνημόνευσεν ὁ θεὸς τὰ ἀδικήματα αὐτῆς). A second communication from heaven rings out, spoken by someone different from the angel of

---

10. The phrase "from the wine" uses the preposition ἐκ in a causal sense (BDAG 297).

11. There is a difficult text-critical choice to be made in v. 3a between various spellings of the verb "drink" (πέπωκαν, πεπώκασιν, πέπωκεν; perfects of πίνω) as in most English translations (see NA[28]; UBS[5]; TCGNT2, 683; Beale, Revelation, 897; Smalley, Revelation, 422), or spellings of the verb "fall" (πέπτωκαν, πεπτώκασιν, πέπτωκεν; perfects of πίπτω) as in ASV, NET, NLT (see SBLGNT; Aune, Revelation 17–22, 965–66; Koester, Revelation, 698; Osborne, Revelation, 661). The external support strongly favors "fall" (only P, 051, 2053, 2329, and several ancient versions read "drink," while ℵ, A, C, 046, 1006, 1611, 1841, 1854, 2062, and most Byzantine minuscules read "fall"). Internal evidence is disputed, but "fall" seems more likely to be the harder reading that scribes would have corrected to "drink." It is narrowly preferred (the UBS[5] editors decided the other way with a "D" rating: "great difficulty in arriving at a decision"). Combining the nations' "fall" with "wine" in v. 3 is a wordplay that builds on Babylon's "fall" in v. 2.

12. "Got wealthy" (ἐπλούτησαν) reflects an ingressive use of the aorist of the verb "to be wealthy." Verbs denoting a state or condition are often ingressive in the aorist (Fanning, Verbal Aspect, 93–94, 137–38, 261–62).

13. "Her excessive luxury" (cf. BDAG 263, 949) is the likely sense of a Greek phrase that literally means "the power of her luxury" (τῆς δυνάμεως τοῦ στρήνους αὐτῆς). The genitive "of luxury" could be source or subjective (power coming from or effected by her luxury; cf. Mathewson, Handbook, 239), but in this verse "power" seems to be a trait attributed to "luxury" rather than coming from it (i.e., an attributed genitive; Wallace, Grammar, 89–91).

14. The noun "luxury" in v. 3c (στρῆνος) denotes an uncontrolled or outrageous extravagance or even sensuality (not so much sexual as simply self-absorbed). See BDAG 949; LN §88.254; LSJ 1654. The related verb (cf. 18:7, 9) is used of bulls "running wild" (P.Oxy. 36.2783, line 24).

15. Bauckham, Climax, 343–50; Kraybill, Imperial Cult, 15–17, 102–17.

vv. 1–3, and in this case John hears the voice, but the speaker is unseen (v. 4a).[16] The words from heaven are cited directly, the quotation probably running all the way through v. 20,[17] since it is only at v. 21 that we see a transition parallel to vv. 1 and 4 (an angel or voice from heaven) to signal a change. The voice from heaven initially addresses God's people (vv. 4b–5) and then certain agents of judgment who carry out God's will against Babylon (vv. 6–8), before describing others who will witness Babylon's future collapse (vv. 9–19) and then closing with an invitation for God's people to rejoice over these events (v. 20).

The command to God's people is, "come out from her" (ἐξέλθατε . . . ἐξ αὐτῆς; v. 4b), a pattern of instruction seen first in Genesis 19:12–22 (Lot commanded to escape Sodom before God's judgment falls) and repeated in Jeremiah 50:8–10; 51:6–10, 45–48 (Israel must flee Babylon before her fall at the hands of a devastating invasion by opposing nations). In both of those Old Testament books, the command to "come out" is quite literal, but similar texts in Isaiah 48:20–22 and 52:11–12 appear to be metaphorical (cf. 2 Cor 6:17), referring to rejection of the spiritual and moral values of the surrounding culture. This seems to be the point here as well, although the impending judgment (parallel to the setting in Jer 50–51) is quite literal in this context. The goal of this spiritual and moral exodus is similar to Jeremiah also: to escape complicity with Babylon's "sins" (cf. Eph 5:11; 2 John 11) and the "plagues" of judgment that such evil is about to bring upon her (v. 4c).[18] Finally, v. 5 cites the

reason they must "come out" (related to the reasons that she deserves judgment as in vv. 3, 7c–8, 23, but not quite the same). They must not conform to her values because her sins are immense in their extent and severity (they "have piled up to heaven," v. 5a), and God has not forgotten[19] or exempted her from punishment for her "crimes" (ἀδικήματα, v. 5b; cf. Acts 18:14; 24:30).[20]

In its first-century setting this command was a call to reject enticing associations with Rome's economic and political practices that inevitably led to religious compromises and idolatrous rituals tied to emperor worship.[21] While those Christians could not withdraw physically and geographically from life in first-century Asia Minor, they were called to follow different moral and religious convictions in their everyday social and economic conduct. In modern life there are similar challenges, if not as overt, that arise as Christians engage a world of commerce and finance whose values often sharply diverge from God's ways. See "Theology in Application" below.

18:6–8 Render to her as she too has rendered and pay her double according to her works; in the cup that she mixed mix her a double portion. 7 Just as she glorified herself and lived in luxury, in the same measure give her torment and grief, because in her heart she says, 'I sit as a queen and I am not a widow and I will never see grief.' 8 For this reason in one day her plagues will come, pestilence and grief and famine, and she will be burned with fire, because the Lord God who judged her is mighty (ἀπόδοτε αὐτῇ ὡς καὶ αὐτὴ

---

16. The speaker seems initially to be God, because he speaks of "my people" in v. 4. But v. 5b refers to God in the third person (also v. 8c, assuming it is part of the same quotation). It is more likely that an angel is speaking for God here, as with other heavenly voices in Rev (see note at 9:13).

17. Aune, *Revelation 17–22*, 975–76; Bauckham, *Climax*, 340–41.

18. The phrase "any of her plagues" in v. 4c reflects a Greek

partitive phrase with the preposition ἐκ (see note at 2:10). Occurrence of the word "plague" (πληγή) relates her judgment to the severe woes (like those against Egypt) described in 9:18, 20; 15:1; 16:21.

19. See the use of a related verb in 16:19 and the note at that verse about the OT background of this concept.

20. BDAG 20.

21. Kraybill, *Imperial Cult*, 16–17.

ἀπέδωκεν καὶ διπλώσατε [τὰ] διπλᾶ κατὰ τὰ ἔργα αὐτῆς, ἐν τῷ ποτηρίῳ ᾧ ἐκέρασεν κεράσατε αὐτῇ διπλοῦν, 7 ὅσα ἐδόξασεν αὐτὴν καὶ ἐστρηνίασεν, τοσοῦτον δότε αὐτῇ βασανισμὸν καὶ πένθος. ὅτι ἐν τῇ καρδίᾳ αὐτῆς λέγει ὅτι Κάθημαι βασίλισσα καὶ χήρα οὐκ εἰμὶ καὶ πένθος οὐ μὴ ἴδω· 8 διὰ τοῦτο ἐν μιᾷ ἡμέρᾳ ἥξουσιν αἱ πληγαὶ αὐτῆς, θάνατος καὶ πένθος καὶ λιμός, καὶ ἐν πυρὶ κατακαυθήσεται, ὅτι ἰσχυρὸς κύριος ὁ θεὸς ὁ κρίνας αὐτήν). Verse 6 raises a number of questions that require careful interpretation. The first is to decide the group to whom these commands are addressed. Based on what they are told to do we can label them generally as agents of God's judgment against Babylon, since the "her" and "she" of v. 6 is clearly the "her" of vv. 4b–5 (i.e., Babylon). The most likely understanding in the near context is that these agents of judgment (the "you" who receive the commands of v. 6) are likewise the "you" of v. 4b–c since no shift in addressee is signaled. So God's people are the ones who must pay Babylon back at this future time of reckoning with a double portion "according to her works."[22] Such a spectacle of God's people taking vengeance against their persecutors, however, seems a flagrant violation of biblical instructions to leave vengeance to the Lord and never to repay evil for evil to anyone (Rom 12:17; 1 Thess 5:15;

1 Pet 3:9). Some have therefore suggested that, broadening out the context a bit, it must be angels of judgment who are addressed here (Rev 14:15, 18; cf. Ezek 9:1–11)[23] or evil earthly agents such as the kings allied with the beast (cf. Rev 17:15–17), who are here urged to accomplish God's purpose in punishing Babylon for her sins.[24] Another suggestion is that specific addressees or agents of judgment are deliberately left out of view, but the rhetorical force of the commands emphasizes the certainty of Babylon's recompense.[25] These alternatives are more congenial to wider sensitivities about Christian morality, but they are hard to square with the wording of the text.[26]

It seems better to understand the imperatives of vv. 6–7 to describe actions that God's people in that period of ultimate conflict are told to share in when the world's armies gather under the beast's leadership to oppose God with all their might and Christ himself returns with a host of holy angels to conquer them.[27] At that time all those who are on God's side are called to join with Christ to bring God's swift vengeance against Babylon. This is not permission to exact personal revenge but participation in the vengeance that the Lord himself will ultimately carry out.[28]

What the Lord desires is judicial recompense

---

22. Several ancient Jewish texts picture Israel participating in God's judgment on evil nations, e.g., 1 En. 90:19; 91:12; 1QM 6:5–6; 11:13–14; Apoc. Ab. 29:14–21.

23. Boxall, *Revelation*, 257–58; Osborne, *Revelation*, 661; Smalley, *Revelation*, 448.

24. L. Goppelt, "ποτήριον," *TDNT* 6:151; Thomas, *Revelation 8–22*, 323; Robert W. Wall, *Revelation*, NIBC 18 (Peabody, MA: Hendrickson, 1991), 215.

25. Ruiz, *Ezekiel in the Apocalypse*, 402–3; Beckwith, *Apocalypse*, 711, 714 (speaks of unspecified "spirits of vengeance" but emphasizes that no addressees are given and says that "the passage is rhetorical in form, proclaiming the certainty of vengeance and its cause"); Koester, *Revelation*, 700, is hesitant about any specific addressees but allows that Christians, if they are addressed, are summoned to "pronounc[e] divine judgment," not inflict it themselves.

26. One could argue that John's visionary description is elliptical and subject to rapid shifts of viewpoint and addressees, and so the change of addressee here from vv. 4b–5 to vv. 6–7 is left for the reader/listener to discern based on the content. But John shows that he is capable of signaling such changes in other places (e.g., 9:14; 14:15, 18; 16:1).

27. See 17:14; 19:14–16, 19–20. In both passages the human (and angelic) role appears to be minimal or nonexistent, since Christ's power and authority is said to secure complete and immediate victory.

28. Aune, *Revelation 17–22*, 993–94; Susan M. Elliott, "Who Is Addressed in Revelation 18:6–7?," *Biblical Research* 40 (1995): 98–113.

against Babylon according to the measure—and above the measure—that she meted out to others in her oppression and sin. The command to "render to her as she too has rendered" (v. 6a–b)[29] calls for equivalent payback, but the next two clauses appear to exact an additional penalty: "Pay her double" and "mix her a double portion" (vv. 6c–d).[30] The language of "doubling" her recompense is also debated. Sometimes "double" in the Scripture means a matching or equivalent measure, something commensurate but not twice the extent or degree (perhaps Gen 43:15; Matt 23:15).[31] This certainly fits a strict reading of "according to her works" (v. 6c; cf. Jer 50:29) and "just as . . . in the same measure" (ὅσα . . . τοσοῦτον; v. 7a–b). In a few places "double" seems metaphorical or hyperbolic for "ample, full," but likewise not literally two times the amount (perhaps 2 Kgs 2:9; Isa 61:7; Zech 9:12; 1 Tim 5:17).[32] But "double" in texts that stipulate penalties for wrongdoing often appears to mean something more literal: an actual double assessment, a penalty beyond just an equivalent recompense (Exod 22:4, 7, 9; Jer 16:18; 17:18; cf. Exod 22:1; 2 Sam 12:6; Luke 19:8 where the penalty is four or five times the offence).[33] The purpose seems to be to display how serious the violation is and to deter future offences. In v. 6c–d the call for double the penalty is expressed using the image of

the cup of anger seen already in 14:10 and 16:19. For Babylon who intoxicated all the nations with her immorality (14:8; 17:2; 18:3; "the cup that she mixed," v. 6d), the heavenly command is to prepare "a double portion" for her.[34]

The comparative motif begun in v. 6b ("as she too has rendered") continues in v. 7 ("just as . . . in the same measure"), setting Babylon's grievous record of sins alongside the severe judgment that she is now to receive (v. 7a–b) and illustrating her arrogant self-sufficiency with her own words (v. 7c–d). Her sinful influence on the wider world included claiming an exalted status for herself, which inherently leads to denial of God's supreme glory (cf. 15:4; Rom 1:19–23) and requiring excessive material wealth for her own use (and those with her, v. 3c) to the detriment of others.[35] So it is only right for God to exact through his agents a commensurate penalty: instead of glory and comfortable luxury, she will receive "torment and grief" (cf. the similar reversal in Luke 6:24–26; Jas 4:9). As in v. 3 the basis for her judgment in this way is expressed through a causal clause (ὅτι, v. 7c) that reveals her inner sense (what she says "in her heart") of self-sufficiency and privilege over others. Her thoughts that are quoted in v. 7d are modeled closely on Isaiah 47:5–9, the claims of Babylon to be queen over the nations. There God declares

---

29. See this use of the verb "pay back" (ἀποδίδωμι) in 22:12; cf. Ps 137:8; Matt 16:27; 2 Tim 4:14.

30. The aorist imperatives of vv. 6–7 ("render," "pay," "mix," "give") illustrate its use to call for specific action on a given occasion, not repeated or customary acts of judgment (BDF §§335, 337; Fanning, *Verbal Aspect*, 327–29, 334–35).

31. Gerhard von Rad, "כִּפְלַיִם in Jes 40:2 = Äquivalent?," *ZAW* 79 (1967): 80–82, and Meredith G. Kline, "Double Trouble," *JETS* 32 (1989): 176–78, argue for this sense in several OT texts that speak of "double" punishment (e.g., Jer 16:18; 17:18). Kline argues for this sense in Rev 18 as well.

32. LN §60.75 suggests "much more" rather than strictly double.

33. See also Deut 21:17; Job 42:10 (cf. 1:3; 42:12); Jer 16:5 where "double" means twice as much.

34. "A double portion" (διπλοῦν) probably means a drink that is double strength. Wine in the ancient world was generally diluted with three to five parts of water before drinking. Here a stronger mixture is in view, representing harsher judgment.

35. The words of v. 7 provide a further reminder that Babylon's wealth is not objectionable in and of itself; rather, it is how it lured her into arrogant self-centeredness based on material riches. Self-glorification (seeing oneself or one's community as superior to others), self-sufficiency ("I am secure both now and for the future"), and self-absorption (lack of concern for the needs of others) based on material possessions are exactly the dangers of wealth that the Bible warns against (Luke 12:13–21; 1 Tim 6:6–10, 17–19; Jas 2:1–7, 14–16).

that his judgment will come to her in punishment for showing no mercy to Israel and for supposing that her rule supersedes even God's sovereignty. In this context, being "a widow" and suffering "grief" represents the loss of her client kingdoms, a stripping away of her ruling authority that she cannot conceive will ever occur.

However, such bereavement will come on her "in one day" (v. 8a) because of her arrogant godlessness.[36] The heavenly declaration shifts from imperatives (vv. 4b–7) to future indicative verbs in v. 8 to preview the "plagues" of judgment (cf. v. 4) that are soon to fall on Babylon. Several specific plagues or blows[37] are mentioned: "pestilence and grief and famine,"[38] as well as burning "with fire" (v. 8b; cf. 8:7; 16:8–9; 17:16). These show that the entire series of divine judgments associated with the seals, trumpets, and bowls are in view, but they will culminate in a cataclysm of woes in the final punishments within each series (cf. 9:18, 20; 15:1; 16:21). Her supposed invincibility is put in perspective by v. 8c that cites the surpassing might and power of the "Lord God" who is her judge.[39] This is the reason (ὅτι) that her desolation will come so swiftly and surely.

18:9–10 And the kings of the earth who committed sexual immorality and lived in luxury with her will weep and mourn over her while they watch the smoke of her burning, 10 standing far away in fear of her torment saying, 'Woe, woe, the great city, Babylon, the mighty city, because in one hour your judgment has come' (Καὶ

κλαύσουσιν καὶ κόψονται ἐπ' αὐτὴν οἱ βασιλεῖς τῆς γῆς οἱ μετ' αὐτῆς πορνεύσαντες καὶ στρηνιάσαντες, ὅταν βλέπωσιν τὸν καπνὸν τῆς πυρώσεως αὐτῆς, 10 ἀπὸ μακρόθεν ἑστηκότες διὰ τὸν φόβον τοῦ βασανισμοῦ αὐτῆς λέγοντες, Οὐαὶ οὐαί, ἡ πόλις ἡ μεγάλη, Βαβυλὼν ἡ πόλις ἡ ἰσχυρά, ὅτι μιᾷ ὥρᾳ ἦλθεν ἡ κρίσις σου). As the heavenly voice continues to describe future events related to Babylon's demise, it records the reaction of three closely related groups of observers: kings (vv. 9–10), merchants (vv. 11–17a), and seafarers (vv. 17b–19). Their lament over her desolation, taken in large part from Ezekiel's dirge songs about Tyre (Ezek 26:16–18; 27:30–32; also Isa 23:1–18), provides a vivid portrait as well as further insight into her evil ways.[40] The first group of mourners is the earth's kings or rulers (v. 9a), described here (also in 17:2; 18:3) as misled into evil and excess with her (they "committed sexual immorality" and "lived in luxury" under her political and cultural sway; cf. 17:18).[41] They will wail in shock and sadness (as if at a funeral wake; cf. Matt 2:18; Luke 8:52; 23:27) over her utter downfall, as they gaze at "the smoke of her burning" (v. 9d; cf. v. 8b). Their vantage point, however, is not close at hand as though hoping to help her in distress; they are "standing far away" (v. 10a; also vv. 15, 17b) due to their fear of what she is suffering (cf. "torment" in v. 7) and their awareness of their own complicity in her evils. Nevertheless, they cry out, addressing Babylon directly with their repeated laments over her condition[42] and their dismay that such a great power could suffer destruction so quickly

---

36. "For this reason" (διὰ τοῦτο) in v. 8a refers to the attitude expressed in v. 7d.

37. See the note on 9:18 on the sense of "plague" in Rev.

38. See note on 6:8 for "pestilence" as the sense for θάνατος in this context.

39. The aorist tense of the Greek participle translated "who judged" (κρίνας) focuses on God's act of future judgment against Babylon viewed as a single whole.

40. Kraybill, *Imperial Cult*, 153, observes, "Tyre's combi-

nation of economic prowess and idolatrous arrogance made it useful to John's purpose." Kraybill's larger treatment of this theme can be found on 152–61.

41. See the discussion of the sense of these two verbs at 17:2 and 18:3, 9.

42. See note on 8:13 about the meaning of "woe" (οὐαί) in such a context.

(v. 10b–c). They are dismayed that her judgment came "in one hour."[43]

18:11–13 And the merchants of the earth weep and grieve over her because no one buys their cargoes any longer, 12 cargoes of gold and silver and precious stones and pearls and linen and purple and silk and scarlet and every kind of fragrant wood and every article of ivory and every article of costly wood and bronze and iron and marble, 13 and cinnamon and spice and incense and perfumed ointment and frankincense and wine and oil and fine flour and grain and cattle and sheep and horses and carriages and bodies, that is, the souls of people (Καὶ οἱ ἔμποροι τῆς γῆς κλαίουσιν καὶ πενθοῦσιν ἐπ' αὐτήν, ὅτι τὸν γόμον αὐτῶν οὐδεὶς ἀγοράζει οὐκέτι 12 γόμον χρυσοῦ καὶ ἀργύρου καὶ λίθου τιμίου καὶ μαργαριτῶν καὶ βυσσίνου καὶ πορφύρας καὶ σιρικοῦ καὶ κοκκίνου, καὶ πᾶν ξύλον θύϊνον καὶ πᾶν σκεῦος ἐλεφάντινον καὶ πᾶν σκεῦος ἐκ ξύλου τιμιωτάτου καὶ χαλκοῦ καὶ σιδήρου καὶ μαρμάρου, 13 καὶ κιννάμωμον καὶ ἄμωμον καὶ θυμιάματα καὶ μύρον καὶ λίβανον καὶ οἶνον καὶ ἔλαιον καὶ σεμίδαλιν καὶ σῖτον καὶ κτήνη καὶ πρόβατα, καὶ ἵππων καὶ ῥεδῶν καὶ σωμάτων, καὶ ψυχὰς ἀνθρώπων). In a parallel but longer section (vv. 11–17a), the heavenly voice of v. 4 describes how the earth's "merchants" also lament Babylon's

fall, just as the kings did (vv. 9–10). Their tears and grief over her (v. 11a)[44] are initially quite self-interested: their sales prospects are completely wiped out. Because she was their primary customer and presumably their channel to wider commerce in her far-flung client states, their amazingly diverse stock of goods has no market any longer (v. 11b). The final part of v. 11 mentions the general term for this, "their cargoes" (τὸν γόμον αὐτῶν),[45] and vv. 12–13 fill this out with specific items, going into great detail. The portrayal that the heavenly voice provides thus shifts from the merchants' commercial setback to Babylon's wider wealth and extravagance (cf. also v. 16).

The list of specific cargoes, reflecting in many ways the recitation of Tyre's multifaceted commerce in Ezekiel 27:12–25, covers a remarkable array of fine goods as well as basic trade commodities. Beginning with precious metals and stones (gold, silver, gems, pearls; v. 12a), the list moves to luxury fabrics (linen, purple cloth, silk, scarlet; v. 12b)[46] and then to articles of various kinds[47] made of precious materials (fragrant wood, ivory, costly wood, bronze, iron, marble; v. 12c–d). Various expensive aromatic goods are included (cinnamon, spice, incense, perfumed ointment, frankincense; v. 13a) as well as a full array of basic commodities

---

43. The same phrase, "in one hour" (μιᾷ ὥρᾳ), occurs in similar statements in vv. 17, 19. The phrase "in one day" (ἐν μιᾷ ἡμέρᾳ, v. 8) allows for a slightly wider frame of events but carries essentially the same sense: "all too quickly," "suddenly," "unexpectedly." The aorist "has come" (ἦλθεν) expresses a recent past event (see note on 6:17, and Fanning, *Verbal Aspect*, 260–61).

44. Verse 11a has the same verb "weep," κλαίω, as in v. 9a, but a different verb of lament compared to v. 9a (here it is "grieve," πενθέω, as also in vv. 15, 19; see the related noun πένθος in vv. 7, 8). The passage is filled with mourning. The description in v. 11 shifts to present tenses from the futures of vv. 8–9 (but the future returns in v. 15).

45. The word "cargoes" (γόμος) is a collective singular in Greek, like our word "load, freight," describing various kinds of merchandise conveyed from one place to another (BDAG 205;

cf. Acts 21:3). The Greek collective singular is expressed as a plural to fit English idiom more naturally.

46. The first eight items in the list are expressed as genitives of content (BDAG 205) related to "cargoes" (γόμον) at the start of the verse, which is in apposition to the same word in v. 11b. The next three items are accusatives joined by "and" to "cargoes" in v. 12a. That third accusative is continued with a preposition "of" (ἐκ) that has four objects showing the material from which those items are made. In v. 13 the list continues with mainly accusatives, but three items toward the end shift to genitives (horses and carriages and bodies), probably implying an accusative like "cargoes" (γόμον) with eight genitives in v. 12a–b, as Swete, *Apocalypse*, 231, suggests. The final item awkwardly reverts to accusative (souls).

47. The word "article" (σκεῦος) in v. 12c–d denotes items like dishes or other vessels used for various purposes (BDAG 927).

and livestock (wine, oil, fine flour, grain, cattle, sheep, horses, and carriages [as closely related to horses]; v. 13b–c). Finally, at the end of this list of objects and animals, the term "bodies" (σωμάτων) appears, referring to slaves (v. 13c).[48] This word was common enough as a reference to enslaved people, but it is a dehumanizing term (the value of these humans was only as a physical instrument for labor or service on behalf of the owner). The added description, "that is, the souls of people" (καὶ ψυχὰς ἀνθρώπων),[49] is intended to set the record straight: such mere "bodies" are actually human beings created by God as living souls (Gen 1:26–27; cf. 2:7 ["man became a living soul"]; Ezek 27:13]).[50]

18:14 'And the fruit your soul desired has left you, and all the luxurious and splendid things have been lost to you, and they will never be found again' (καὶ ἡ ὀπώρα σου τῆς ἐπιθυμίας τῆς ψυχῆς ἀπῆλθεν ἀπὸ σοῦ, καὶ πάντα τὰ λιπαρὰ καὶ τὰ λαμπρὰ ἀπώλετο ἀπὸ σοῦ καὶ οὐκέτι οὐ μὴ αὐτὰ εὑρήσουσιν). Just as the kings of the earth addressed their lament directly to Babylon in v. 10, so here the earth's merchants speak to her in the second person as they mourn her losses (v. 14).[51] The wealth of goods just detailed (vv. 12–13) is in mind when they mourn that "the fruit your soul desired"[52] is now gone.[53] Likewise "all the luxurious and splendid things" refer to her extravagant, even flashy, material riches (REB renders this "all the glitter and glamour"). These are now "lost" or have perished (ἀπώλετο) as far as she is concerned.[54] And they will never be recovered as v. 14c says, shifting to a future of the verb "find" (εὑρήσουσιν),[55] anticipating the use of this verb later in vv. 21–22.

---

48. E.g., Gen 36:6; cf. Tob 10:10; 2 Macc 8:11; see BDAG 984.

49. "That is" in v. 13c translates an epexegetical use of the conjunction καί (usually "and").

50. There is disagreement about the larger significance of the list of cargoes in vv. 11–13. Bauckham, *Climax*, 350–71, takes them to represent the "conspicuous wealth and extravagance" (352) of first-century Rome, "derived from the conquest and plunder of the empire" and its "economic exploitation" of its subject peoples (368). Provan, "Foul Spirits," 85–89, counters that Rev 18 says nothing explicit about exploitation and warns against reading this into the text based on modern political and economic ideas. His view is that since the list of products is largely drawn from the critique of Tyre in Ezek 27, they represent the more typical OT emphasis on idolatrous nations: godless rulers swollen with arrogance because of their kingdoms' prosperity for which they themselves take credit. For Provan "economic sins are only ever a function of idolatry, so far as the Old Testament is concerned, and it is on the idolatry that the emphasis falls, rather than upon the economics" (88). He objects to such a focus on Rome also because, along with a few others, he understands "Babylon" in Rev to symbolize apostate Jerusalem rather than Rome (91–98; see comments against this view in the present commentary at 11:1–2 and 17:5) and because he takes John's portrayal of Babylon in Rev 17–18 to have greater typological significance than simply a historical-critical critique of first-century Rome's economy (98–100). On the narrower points (no reference to Roman economic exploitation; "Babylon" equals Jerusalem) I think Provan is wrong, but his larger point ("Babylon" is a type for godless human society across the ages and most pointedly in the final days) is certainly correct (see comments on 17:5 and discussion of typology in the introduction to this commentary).

51. The speaker(s) of the words of v. 14 are not stated explicitly, and no introductory participle (e.g., "saying") occurs here as in vv. 2, 4, 10, 16, 18, 19, 21. This could be the heavenly voice (v. 4) addressing Babylon directly, but references to the merchants before and after this (vv. 11, 15) make it more likely that they are the speakers.

52. The word "fruit" (ἡ ὀπώρα) is figurative of the harvest of riches she enjoyed (BDAG 718; e.g., Jer 40:10, 12; 48:32 [LXX 47:10, 12; 31:32]). In this string of genitives "your" (σου) is possessive to "fruit" in the Greek construction. The words translated "soul" and "desired" are also genitives in Greek (lit., "of the desire of the soul," τῆς ἐπιθυμίας τῆς ψυχῆς), and "soul" is a subjective genitive, while "desire" is a genitive of apposition explaining the figurative sense of "fruit" (cf. Wallace, *Grammar*, 95–96).

53. The aorists "have left" (ἀπῆλθεν) and "have been lost" (ἀπώλετο) refer to recent past events (see note on v. 10).

54. The Greek phrasing in v. 14a–b says these fine things have left or departed "from you" and perished "from you," emphasizing her loss.

55. The phrase in v. 14c, "they will never be found again," uses the Greek future indicative with οὐ μή to express emphatic negation (see note on 9:6), along with an impersonal "they" to express a passive sense (lit., "they will no longer find them [i.e., the things of v. 14b] at all"; see notes on this impersonal use at 10:11; 12:16).

This declaration, though it is ironic coming from the lips of her trading partners, helps to clarify that the list of "cargoes" just cited is not intended to condemn trade or commerce per se, nor are the luxury goods included in the list regarded as sinful in and of themselves.[56] Much of Rome's bustling commercial life provided prosperity and basic necessities for its far-flung provinces as well as for its urban poor. The problem specified in this verse is the tendency to regard material goods, especially luxury goods, as the goal and focus of life. Human existence does not consist of the material things people possess, even when they have the most or the best on offer (Luke 12:15–21). To make them the "soul's desire," as Babylon did, tragically misconceives what is most central in human identity and prosperity. It worships and draws meaning from a false god instead of the true One.

18:15–17a The merchants of these things, who got rich from her, will stand far away in fear of her torment, weeping and grieving, 16 saying, 'Woe, woe, the great city, the one clothed in linen and purple and scarlet and adorned with gold and precious stones and pearls 17 because in one hour such great riches were made desolate' (οἱ ἔμποροι τούτων οἱ πλουτήσαντες ἀπ᾿ αὐτῆς ἀπὸ μακρόθεν στήσονται διὰ τὸν φόβον τοῦ βασανισμοῦ αὐτῆς κλαίοντες καὶ πενθοῦντες 16 λέγοντες, Οὐαὶ οὐαί, ἡ πόλις ἡ μεγάλη, ἡ περιβεβλημένη βύσσινον καὶ πορφυροῦν καὶ κόκκινον καὶ κεχρυσωμένη [ἐν] χρυσίῳ καὶ λίθῳ τιμίῳ καὶ μαργαρίτῃ, 17 ὅτι μιᾷ ὥρᾳ ἠρημώθη ὁ τοσοῦτος πλοῦτος). After the merchants' brief address to Babylon in v. 14, the heavenly voice resumes a description of their reaction to her destruction (v. 15).[57] The merchants (v. 11), who deal in the varied wares just mentioned (i.e., "these things" of vv. 12–14), gained their wealth due to trade in and through Babylon (cf. v. 3c). Despite their direct involvement in her materialism and oppression—and their fear as they witness her suffering (same wording as in v. 10a)—they "will stand far away" (cf. vv. 10, 17a),[58] as though distant from her guilt, and they lament her fate with "weeping and grieving" (same verbs as in v. 11a).

Their expression of lament is quoted in vv. 16–17a in phrases quite close to v. 10 ("woe, woe, the great city" because of her destruction "in one hour") and even closer to the wording of 17:4. The extensive description of the city as "the one clothed in linen and purple and scarlet and adorned with gold and precious stones and pearls" is an almost exact duplicate of how the woman on the beast is described in 17:4. This ties chapters 17 and 18 together more closely, but of course their thematic links are already quite strong. Here the descriptions reinforce the focus on Babylon's great extravagance and ostentatious material wealth. As in vv. 10 and 19, the merchants' mourning is grounded in an expression of dismay over how quickly "such great riches" were wiped out (v. 17a). The verb "made desolate" (ἠρημώθη; also v. 19) provides another link to chapter 17 where in v. 16 it is said that the beast and his allies will make Babylon "desolate" (ἠρημωμένην; cf. the same language used of Tyre in Ezek 26:19).

18:17b–18 And every ship's captain and everyone who travels by boat and sailors and all who work on the sea stood far away 18 and were crying out as they watched the smoke of her burning saying, 'Who was like the great city?' (Καὶ πᾶς κυβερνήτης καὶ πᾶς ὁ ἐπὶ τόπον πλέων καὶ ναῦται καὶ ὅσοι τὴν θάλασσαν ἐργάζονται, ἀπὸ μακρόθεν ἔστησαν 18 καὶ

---

56. Wright, *Revelation for Everyone*, 163–64.

57. The focus on the merchants is resumed without an explicit conjunction (asyndeton) because the topic is still clear despite the parenthetical quotation of v. 14.

58. Here the description shifts back to the future, anticipating what will come soon (cf. vv. 8–9).

ἔκραζον βλέποντες τὸν καπνὸν τῆς πυρώσεως αὐτῆς λέγοντες, Τίς ὁμοία τῇ πόλει τῇ μεγάλῃ). The third group witnessing Babylon's demise and mourning over it (see overview at v. 9) is those who travel and work on the sea (vv. 17b–19). Like the earth's rulers and merchants, they have a vested interest in her prosperity because her political and economic power was expanded through extensive contact and travel connections carried on mainly by sea in the ancient Mediterranean world (cf. Ezek 27:3, 33). This pattern of empire was reflected in God's denunciation of Tyre's evil in Ezekiel 26–27, and it is replicated in John's day in the power of "Babylon" (Rome). The collapse of the central power would lead to worldwide disruption for seafaring interests, and here they lament her fall and their loss (e.g., v. 19). These seafaring interests are described in five overlapping phrases, and the first four are in v. 17b. "Every ship's captain" and "everyone who travels by boat" cover the full range of involvement from most central to most casual: the "ship's captain" (κυβερνήτης) would be the commander or pilot,[59] while the one "who travels by boat" (ὁ ἐπὶ τόπον πλέων)[60] would be an occasional traveler or even a tourist. The other two refer to seafaring occupations: "sailors" (a ship's crew) and "all who work on the sea" (perhaps fishermen).[61] All of these are portrayed as standing "far away" (v. 17c) in their mourning, like the rulers and merchants (see comments at vv. 10, 15). In the narration of this scene[62] their "crying out" is presented more vividly (imperfect verb here and in v. 19) to emphasize their dismay. As they witness the effects

of her destruction ("the smoke of her burning"; cf. vv. 8, 9; 17:16), they are struck by the incongruity of such a reversal: "Who was like the great city?" (v. 18c; cf. 13:4).[63] This exclamation is drawn from Ezekiel 27 (specifically v. 32), which influences several expressions in the next verse also.

18:19–20 And they threw dust on their heads and were crying out, weeping and grieving, saying, 'Woe, woe, the great city, in which all those who had ships on the sea got rich from her prosperity, because in one hour she was made desolate.'" 20 **"Rejoice over her, O heaven and saints and apostles and prophets, because God has exacted judgment for you against her"** (καὶ ἔβαλον χοῦν ἐπὶ τὰς κεφαλὰς αὐτῶν καὶ ἔκραζον κλαίοντες καὶ πενθοῦντες λέγοντες, Οὐαὶ οὐαί, ἡ πόλις ἡ μεγάλη, ἐν ᾗ ἐπλούτησαν πάντες οἱ ἔχοντες τὰ πλοῖα ἐν τῇ θαλάσσῃ ἐκ τῆς τιμιότητος αὐτῆς, ὅτι μιᾷ ὥρᾳ ἠρημώθη. 20 Εὐφραίνου ἐπ᾽ αὐτῇ, οὐρανέ καὶ οἱ ἅγιοι καὶ οἱ ἀπόστολοι καὶ οἱ προφῆται, ὅτι ἔκρινεν ὁ θεὸς τὸ κρίμα ὑμῶν ἐξ αὐτῆς). The seafarers continue to express their profound grief over Babylon in gesture and speech, accompanied by a generous mixture of self-pity as with the other two groups (v. 19). In a graphic display of mourning, they throw "dust on their heads" (cf. Josh 7:6; Job 2:12; Lam 2:10; Ezek 27:30), bewailing her fate with "weeping and grieving" (cf. vv. 11, 15). They cry out like the kings and merchants did, "Woe, woe, the great city" (cf. vv. 10, 16), but reflect on what this means for their own interests going forward (v. 19d). In v. 19d we find the fifth description of seafarers, "all those who had ships on the sea," who gained great

---

59. BDAG 573–74; cf. Ezek 27:8, 27–28.

60. The phrase is more literally "one who sails to a place" (BDAG 825).

61. To "work (on) the sea" (τὴν θάλασσαν ἐργάζονται) is comparable to "work (on) the land" as in Gen 2:5 LXX (BDAG 389).

62. Aorists and imperfects are used to trace the main line of the story in vv. 17b–19.

63. The Greek construction of v. 18c implies a linking verb, but does not express one explicitly. It could be taken as present, "is" (KJV, NASB, NET), or past, "was" (CSB, ESV, NIV, NRSV, REB, RSV), but the latter fits the context better. The point of their exclamation is her former incomparability in wealth and status, not her current incomparable destruction (although both are true).

wealth "from her prosperity," a prosperity amassed through conquest and greed (see vv. 3–5, 14–16). Again, their shock over her fate is greater in view of how quickly such a rich and powerful city had been "made desolate" (v. 19e; cf. vv. 10, 17a).

The identity of the speaker in v. 20 is unclear. It would be easy at first glance to take the verse as a continuation of the seafarers' lament from v. 19, since there is no reference to a separate speaker, and v. 20 is clearly a direct address (second-person singular verb and vocatives). But the addresses ("heaven and saints and apostles and prophets") and substance of what is said ("rejoice" because God's judgment on Babylon has come) are not likely to come from the lips of godless seamen shocked at Babylon's loss (and theirs).[64] A similar call for heaven to "rejoice" is found in 12:12, spoken by a "voice from heaven" as here (v. 4), so it is better to understand v. 20 as a final interjection by the heavenly voice that provided the account of Babylon's judgment from vv. 4–20.[65] Invoking joy in heaven (εὐφραίνω) is found in Old Testament contexts celebrating God's rule and redemption (Ps 96:10–11; Isa 44:23; 49:13), but here it is also an invitation to rejoice concerning his vindication against a persecutor (cf. Jer 51:48, rejoicing over Babylon's demise), and it addresses not heaven alone but God's servants who have suffered at her hand. The vocative in v. 20a, "heaven" (οὐρανέ), is followed by three nominatives used as vocatives: "the saints" (i.e., God's people, set apart for him; cf. 5:8), "the apostles" (meaning the Twelve; cf. 21:14),

and "the prophets" (including NT era prophets like the two in 11:10, but also probably OT prophets who in various ways foretold these days of fulfillment; cf. 10:7; 22:6, 9). In fact, in view of the reference in v. 24 to Babylon's killing of "saints and prophets" (also 16:6; cf. 11:18), it is likely that in typological terms both "saints and prophets" should be understood to include God's people and his spokespersons from all the ages of salvation history.

All these people are called to rejoice because God's vindication of their righteous suffering has come (v. 20b). Babylon, as the representation of the world's evil agents through the ages, has persecuted and martyred God's people and deserves his retribution for her hostile acts (cf. v. 6), and now God "has exacted judgment" against her. The wording of this in v. 20b is dense, and while the general sense is clear it can be nuanced in two different ways.[66] The literal phrasing is "God has judged your judgment from her" (ἔκρινεν ὁ θεὸς τὸ κρίμα ὑμῶν ἐξ αὐτῆς). This can mean that Babylon judged them, and now God has paid her back (taking "your" as objective genitive and "from her" as expressing agency), or God has assessed against her the judgment they deserve to have assessed ("your" as genitive of reference or purpose and "from her" as source).[67] The latter sense is preferred because "from" (ἐκ) carries this sense in other vindication texts in Revelation (6:10; 19:2). Another clarification is that "judge" in this verse does not mean "pronounce judgment" (NASB, NET) but "exact judgment or penalty." The sense of both the verb and the noun of judging used

---

64. One possible parallel where the godless acknowledge God's role in the judgment that has come is 6:16b–17, but the call to rejoice makes 18:20 different.

65. Aune, *Revelation 17–22*, 1006–7; Koester, *Revelation*, 708.

66. BDAG 567 helpfully summarizes the options as (1) "God has pronounced judgment for you against her," or (2) "God has pronounced on her the judgment she wished to impose on you."

67. In this context "from" (ἐκ) indicates source through a metaphor of assessing payment of a debt: judgment is exacted "from" (i.e., "against") her. The translation "against" is used because "from" fails to carry the appropriate sense in English. Cf. BDAG 298 and the use of the Hebrew preposition מִן "from" in 2 Kgs 9:7; Ps 119:84; Isa 1:24 (translated in LXX as some combination with ἐκ). See this sense for ἐκ also in Rev 6:10; 19:2.

here (κρίνω, κρίμα) often shades over into "punish" and "punishment,"[68] and that is what the scene in 18:9–20 portrays.

18:21–22 And a mighty angel took up a rock like a large millstone and threw it into the sea saying, "So will Babylon the great city be thrown down violently, and she will never be found again. 22 And the sound of kithara players and musicians and flute players and trumpeters will never be heard in you again, and no craftsman of any craft will ever be found in you again, and the sound of a mill will never be heard in you again (Καὶ ἦρεν εἷς ἄγγελος ἰσχυρὸς λίθον ὡς μύλινον μέγαν καὶ ἔβαλεν εἰς τὴν θάλασσαν λέγων, Οὕτως ὁρμήματι βληθήσεται Βαβυλὼν ἡ μεγάλη πόλις καὶ οὐ μὴ εὑρεθῇ ἔτι. 22 καὶ φωνὴ κιθαρῳδῶν καὶ μουσικῶν καὶ αὐλητῶν καὶ σαλπιστῶν οὐ μὴ ἀκουσθῇ ἐν σοὶ ἔτι, καὶ πᾶς τεχνίτης πάσης τέχνης οὐ μὴ εὑρεθῇ ἐν σοὶ ἔτι, καὶ φωνὴ μύλου οὐ μὴ ἀκουσθῇ ἐν σοὶ ἔτι). In a final climactic section "a mighty angel" (cf. 5:2; 10:1) symbolically enacts Babylon's fall and declares repeatedly her irreversible destruction and the reason for it (vv. 21–24). The angel adapts a script set forth in Jeremiah 51:63–64 for this dramatic representation (v. 21a).[69] The "rock" (λίθος), perhaps better a "boulder" because it is the size of a large millstone,[70] is thrown into the sea with the

declaration (v. 21b) that Babylon's future judgment will be like this: violent and forceful[71] as well as irrevocable and eternal. The strong denial (v. 21c), "she will never be found again,"[72] is reminiscent of Ezekiel 26:21 and launches a series of five additional statements like this in vv. 22–23b. The angel's pronouncement about Babylon's ruin is phrased in third person at the beginning and end ("she/her," vv. 21, 24) and second person in the middle ("you," 7x in vv. 22–23).

The shift to "you," declaring Babylon's fall to her directly, and the emphatic repetition of "will never . . . again" begins in v. 22. The first of these strong denials in v. 21c gives the summary statement (Babylon herself will disappear forever as a result of God's judgment). The remaining clauses in the series take up specific aspects of her everyday life— the beautiful and the mundane—that will be gone forever. First, pleasing music "will never be heard in you again," with mention in v. 22a of those who play the kithara (cf. 5:8; 14:2; 15:2), general music (cf. Ezek 26:13),[73] the flute (Matt 11:17; 1 Cor 14:7), and the trumpet (1 Cor 14:8; Rev 8:2, etc.). Also gone forever (v. 22b) will be artisans and their useful crafts or trades (cf. Acts 17:29; 18:3; 19:24–25) and one of the background sounds of basic life: "the sound of a mill" to grind grain for bread (v. 22c; this feature is clearly drawn from Jer 25:10).[74]

---

68. BDAG 567, 569.

69. Jer 51:63–64 describe Jeremiah's scroll that foretells disaster against Babylon, tied to a stone and thrown into the Euphrates, with the pronouncement, "so will Babylon sink never to rise again."

70. Not a stone from a small hand-mill but a stone large enough to require a donkey to turn it (BDAG 661; see related word in Mark 9:42).

71. The word translated "violently" (ὁρμήματι) is a dative of manner of a word that means a violent impulse or assault (BDAG 724). In the LXX it is used of an eagle's swooping attack (Deut 28:49) or of God's wrath and indignation (Hos 5:10; Amos 1:11; Hab 3:8).

72. This is the first of six occurrences of a subjunctive verb with "never . . . again" (οὐ μή . . . ἔτι) in vv. 21c–23b, an em-

phatic denial of these future possibilities (BDF §365; Wallace, *Grammar*, 468–69).

73. In addition to this connection to Ezek 26:21, the music cited in v. 22a is broadly dependent also on Jer 25:10 where the Lord's judgment on Jerusalem will be marked by the disappearance of "every sound of joy or gladness." Jer 25:10 adds that the sound of bridegroom and bride and of the grinding mill as well as the light from every lamp will disappear also (cf. v. 22c–23b here).

74. The fulfillment of this prophecy comes in a patterned way at the fall of ancient Rome, but comes in its fullest consummation at the defeat of the end-time empires opposed to God at the return of Christ (Rev 19:11–21). See further discussion in the introduction under "Use of the Old Testament: Prophecy and Typology."

18:23–24 And the light of a lamp will never appear in you again, and the sound of bridegroom and bride will never be heard in you again. Because your merchants were the great ones of the earth, because by your sorcery all the nations were led astray, 24 and in her the blood of prophets and saints were found and of all those slain on the earth" (καὶ φῶς λύχνου οὐ μὴ φάνῃ ἐν σοὶ ἔτι, καὶ φωνὴ νυμφίου καὶ νύμφης οὐ μὴ ἀκουσθῇ ἐν σοὶ ἔτι· ὅτι οἱ ἔμποροί σου ἦσαν οἱ μεγιστᾶνες τῆς γῆς, ὅτι ἐν τῇ φαρμακείᾳ σου ἐπλανήθησαν πάντα τὰ ἔθνη, 24 καὶ ἐν αὐτῇ αἷμα προφητῶν καὶ ἁγίων εὑρέθη καὶ πάντων τῶν ἐσφαγμένων ἐπὶ τῆς γῆς). Two other features of normal life that Babylon will never experience again are cited (v. 23a–b), followed by the reasons for her judgment (vv. 23c–24). The two remaining features, also under the direct influence of Jeremiah 25:10, are "the light of a lamp" and the sounds of joy from a "bridegroom and bride" at their wedding celebration. These poignant reminders of the everyday as well as the special days of life reinforce the tragic loss that stubborn resistance to God ultimately brings upon itself. The causal clauses that begin in v. 23c (cf. two uses of ὅτι) bring reminders of the worldwide impact of Babylon's evil hostility against God and his ways. They give the grounds for the destructive effects on Babylon described in vv. 21–23b. The reasons are set forth in two stages, with v. 23c beginning the thought and v. 23d adding to it. First, the point that Babylon's businessmen ("your merchants") carried great influence across the world: they were "the great ones of the earth" (οἱ μεγιστᾶνες τῆς γῆς).[75] In world trade they were the "magnates" (NRSV) or "tycoons" (NET), which in itself would not be objectionable. But v. 23d adds the evil influence that their elite stature produced: leading "all the nations" away from God and his ways. This evil deception (cf. 13:14) was accomplished through Babylon's "sorcery" (φαρμακεία), a word that with its cognates refers to the practice of magic, the use of potions, spells, or related rituals to gain power over spirits or humans.[76]

Verse 24 adds a further reason for Babylon's guilt: her role in violently opposing God's spokesmen and God's people as well as others all across the earth. This is ironically phrased as finding "the blood of prophets and saints" as well as all the earth's slain[77] "in her" (v. 24). Her guilt could not be hidden, but none of the activities of normal life would ever be found in her again (vv. 22–23b).

Theology in Application

Lessons from the Aftermath

There is something heartbreaking but reassuring about listening to people interviewed after a natural disaster has struck (e.g., flood, tornado, fire), even when it has wiped out everything they owned. After watching video footage of whole neighborhoods burned to the foundations or swept away by floodwaters, we look into the

---

75. The word translated "great ones" (μεγιστᾶνες) is derived from a superlative form of "great" (μέγας), denoting "a person of high rank . . . magnate" (BDAG 625; cf. Mark 6:21; Rev 6:15).

76. BDAG 1049–50. See Gal 5:20 and related words in Rev 9:21; 21:8; 22:15.

77. "All those slain on the earth" (v. 24) seems to be a hyperbolic reference to others across the world (non-Christians) whose lives the empire treated as worthless.

faces of those who have lost all the material trappings of life and hear them express relief and gratitude that what is really important has not been taken. Their family and friends and their own lives are okay. Often they reflect on God's protection and goodness to them even in great material loss. This is the opposite of the laments recorded in this chapter in the aftermath of the destruction of the great city Babylon. Her political allies and business partners are in similar shock over her sudden devastation, but they never appear to see the true lessons to be learned from their losses. This chapter forcefully reminds us not to build a life on "the finer things" that really mean nothing in the long run. Babylon's extravagant, flashy riches and the "excessive luxury" of her business partners (vv. 3, 14) were suddenly taken, and with them went all that they longed for in life. Sadly, this is a picture of many people caught up in the consumerism and materialism of the modern world: more and more expensive toys piled up in larger and larger homes and storage units do not lead to a richer life. Too frequently, however, they lead away from obedience and dependence on God and into proud self-sufficiency and indifference to the needs of people around them (v. 7). These dangers are just the things that Timothy was to warn "those who are rich in this world" against (1 Tim 6:17–19). What are we truly committed to above all else? What values and desires mark our lives and identity as humans in a world that seems intoxicated with superficial things? Do we have nice things or do nice things have us? These are lessons to sort out whether disaster or blessing lies in our path.

In the World but Not of It

The heavenly voice in Revelation 18:4 gives the command, "Come out from her, my people." This is a sobering word about divine judgment and the instability of all the things apart from God that humans depend on for their security. It also forms an essential part of a complementary theme that runs throughout Revelation, the theme of Christian witness. The theme of witness holds two important lessons for Christian living.[78] First is its call for us to reach out to an unwelcoming world with our witness about Jesus, conveyed by our conduct and verbal witness even when it may cause us great difficulty (1:9; 2:13; 6:9; 12:11, 17; 19:10; 20:4). We must testify to the truth about God's gracious salvation in Jesus Christ, offered even to those who are antagonistic to him. Instead of withdrawing from the hostile world and leaving it to its deserved judgment, we are called to bear winsome witness by our conduct and our verbal testimony to the Lamb who "redeemed for God with [his] blood people from every tribe and language and people and nation" (5:9). An active, witnessing presence of Christians truly *in* the world rather than separate from it (John 17:11–19)

---

78. On both points, see Bauckham, *Theology*, 159–64. The paragraphs that follow are adapted from Buist M. Fanning, "Discipleship in Revelation," in *Following Jesus Christ: The New Testament Message of Discipleship for Today*, ed. John K. Goodrich and Mark L. Strauss (Grand Rapids: Kregel, 2019).

mirrors the seeking, self-giving love of God (John 3:16) and of Christ (Mark 10:45; Luke 19:10).

The second lesson also reflects Jesus's rubric in John 17: though *in* the world, we cannot be *of* the world but must be set apart from it by God's truth (John 17:15–19). Revelation communicates this by its constant warnings against complacency and assimilation to the godless ideology and conduct of the surrounding culture (2:2, 20, 24; 3:17–19; 14:9–10). This is where the command to "come out from her" fits in. It means not physical isolation from "Babylon" but moral distinctiveness: not assimilating to the spiritual and moral values of the godless culture. We must exemplify Christ's values, in our personal and family lives as well as in our business, employment, and civic dealings. If we fail to love God and people or care little for holiness and faithfulness or adopt the "truth" that appeals most to the world around us, then we will have little to offer to our contemporaries and will not be witnesses for the Messiah whom we claim to follow.

Revelation 19:1–21

Literary Context

This chapter falls on the dividing line between two major divisions of Revelation. Its first part (19:1–10) completes the book's third vision, the account of Babylon's destruction (17:1–19:10). This passage ends with vv. 9–10 that display close parallelism with verses at the end of the fourth vision (22:6–9) to signal the literary structure (see comments on v. 9 and "Literary Context" for ch. 17). The second part of the chapter begins the section on events that intervene between Babylon's fall and the descent of the new Jerusalem (19:11–21:8). This larger section consists of a series of seven shorter visions that portray those intervening events. The first three of these visions come in 19:11–21.

Main Idea

All of heaven rejoices over Babylon's judgment and over the coming marriage supper of the Lamb (19:1–10); Christ comes to earth as King of kings and Lord of lords to achieve a decisive victory over Satan and the world's armies gathered in futile resistance (19:11–21).

Translation

Revelation 19:1–21

1a	Action/Vision Introduction	**After these things I heard something like the loud voice of a great multitude in heaven saying,**
b	Praise	*"Hallelujah, salvation and glory and power belong to our God,*
2a	Reasons	*because true and righteous are his judgments*
b		*because he has judged the great prostitute*
c	Description	*who corrupted the earth with her sexual immorality, and*
d		*he has avenged on her the blood of his servants."*
3a	Action	**And a second time they said,**
b	Praise	*"Hallelujah!*
c	Reason	*And the smoke goes up from her forever and ever."*
4a	Action/Character Entrance	**And the twenty-four elders and the four living creatures. fell down and worshiped God who sits on the throne saying,**
b		*"Amen. Hallelujah!"*
5a	Action	**And a voice came out from the throne saying,**
b	Praise	*"Praise our God, all you servants of his and those who fear him, the small and the great."*

Continued on next page.

Continued from previous page.

6a Action/Comparison   **And I heard something like the voice of a great multitude and**
     like the sound of many waters and
     like the sound of strong peals of thunder saying,

   b   Praise   *"Hallelujah,*
   c   Reason   *because the Lord our God*
         the Almighty   has begun to reign.

7a   Exhortation   *Let us rejoice and*
       be glad and
       give him glory,

   b   Reasons   *because the wedding of the Lamb has come and*
   c   *his bride has prepared herself.*
8a   *And it was granted to her to be clothed in pure, bright, fine linen.*
   b   Explanation of 8a   *For the fine linen is the righteous deeds of the saints."*

9a Action   **And he said to me,**
   b   Command/   *"Write: Blessed are those who are invited to the marriage banquet of the Lamb."*
       Beatitude
   c Action   **And he said to me,**
   d   Affirmation   *"These words of God are true."*
10a Response to 8–9   **And I fell at his feet to worship him.**
   b Response to 10a   **And he said to me,**
   c   Prohibition   *"Don't do that.*
   d   Reason   *I am a fellow servant of yours and*
         of your brothers and
         sisters
   e   Description   *who hold to the testimony of Jesus.*
   f   Command   *Worship God!*
   g   Reason   *For the testimony of Jesus is the Spirit of prophecy."*

11a Action/Vision   **And I saw heaven standing open,**
     Introduction
   b Character Entrance   **and behold, a white horse and**
       the one sitting on it,
   c   Identification   **called faithful and true,**

   d Descriptions   **and in righteousness he judges and**
       wages war.

12a   **Now his eyes are like a flame of fire,**
   b   **and on his head are many diadems;**
   c   **he has a name written**
   d   Description   **that no one knows except he himself,**

13a Descriptions   **and he is clothed in a robe dipped in blood,**
   b   **and his name is called the Word of God.**

14a	Action/Character Entrance	And **the armies in heaven,…**
b	Description	dressed in pure, white fine linen,
c		**… were following him on white horses.**

15a	Actions	And **from his mouth a sharp sword comes out**
b	Purpose	so that with it he might strike the nations,
c		and **he will shepherd them with a rod of iron** (Ps 2:9)
d		and **he treads the winepress of the wine of the fury of the wrath of God the Almighty,**
16a	Description	and **he has on his robe at the thigh a name written,**
b	Identification	*"King of kings and Lord of lords."*
17a	Vision Intro/ Character Entrance	And **I saw an angel standing on the sun,**
b	Action	and **he cried out with a loud voice,**
c	Address/ Recipients	saying to all the birds flying high in the sky,
d	Invitation	*"Come gather for the great supper of God*
18	Purpose	*that you may eat the* flesh of kings and
		flesh of commanders and
		flesh of mighty ones and
		flesh of horses and
		those who sat on them and
		flesh of all,
		both free and slaves and
		small and great."*

19a	Vision Intro/ Character Entrance	And **I saw the beast and**
		the kings of the earth and
		their armies
b	Description/Purpose	gathered to wage war against the one sitting on the horse and against his army.

20a	Action	And **the beast was captured and**
		with him
		the false prophet
b	Description	who performed before him the miracles
c	Description	by which he deceived those who had received the mark of the beast and those who worshiped his image.
d	Action	**The two were thrown alive into the lake of fire**
e	Description	that burns with sulfur.
21a	Action	And **the rest were killed by the sword**
b	Description	that comes out from the mouth of the one sitting on the ✍ horse,
c	Effect	and **all the birds were gorged with their flesh.**

Structure

This chapter is divided into two sections that bridge between major divisions of the book as described above in "Literary Context." The first section (19:1–10) consists of two units signaled by the words "I heard something like the voice of a great multitude" (vv. 1, 6). These contain praise to God centering on his judgment of Babylon the prostitute (vv. 1–5) and then praise to God centering on the preparation of the Lamb's bride and ending with a beatitude and John's interaction with the angel who revealed these things to him (vv. 6–10).

The second section consists of three units signaled by "and I saw" (vv. 11, 17, 19). John describes Christ as he comes in judgment (vv. 11–16), hears an invitation to feast on the evil armies (vv. 17–18), and records Christ's decisive victory over them (vv. 19–21).

Exegetical Outline

IV. Third Vision: The Destruction of Babylon the Great (17:1–19:10)

    A. Babylon, the Great Prostitute, and the Beast She Rides (17:1–18)

    B. The Effects of Babylon's Destruction (18:1–24)

➡   **C. Celebration of Babylon's Judgment and Preparation of the Lamb's Bride (19:1–10)**

       1. Praise for God's Judgment of Babylon the Prostitute (19:1–5)

       2. Praise for the Preparation of the Lamb's Bride (19:6–10)

V. Intervening Events: From Babylon to the New Jerusalem (19:11–21:8)

    A. The Heavenly Warrior's Overwhelming Victory (19:11–21)

       1. Appearance and Description of the Messianic Warrior and Judge (19:11–16)

       2. Angelic Summons to God's Victory Supper (19:17–18)

       3. Defeat of the Beast, the False Prophet, and their Allied Kings and Armies (19:19–21)

Explanation of the Text

19:1–2 After these things I heard something like the loud voice of a great multitude in heaven saying, "Hallelujah, salvation and glory and power belong to our God, 2 because true and righteous are his judgments because he has judged the great prostitute who corrupted the earth with her sexual immorality, and he has avenged on her the blood of his servants" (Μετὰ ταῦτα ἤκουσα ὡς φωνὴν μεγάλην ὄχλου πολλοῦ ἐν τῷ οὐρανῷ λεγόντων, Ἁλληλουϊά· ἡ σωτηρία καὶ ἡ δόξα καὶ ἡ δύναμις τοῦ θεοῦ ἡμῶν, 2 ὅτι ἀληθιναὶ καὶ δίκαιαι αἱ κρίσεις αὐτοῦ· ὅτι ἔκρινεν τὴν πόρνην τὴν μεγάλην ἥτις ἔφθειρεν τὴν γῆν ἐν τῇ πορνείᾳ αὐτῆς, καὶ ἐξεδίκησεν τὸ αἷμα τῶν δούλων αὐτοῦ ἐκ χειρὸς αὐτῆς). The first portion of this chapter constitutes the final phase (19:1–10) of John's visionary experiences portraying the judgment of Babylon (17:1–19:10).[1] This portion focuses on what John "heard" (ἤκουσα; vv. 1, 6) because here a crescendo of heavenly voices celebrates God's victory over Babylon (vv. 1–5) and anticipates the "marriage of the Lamb" (vv. 6–10; cf. 21:2, 9), a picture of God's communion with his people in the millennium and the New Jerusalem to come. These voices offer praise to God reminiscent of the extracts of heavenly worship John has heard in preceding chapters (e.g., 11:15–18; 12:10–12; 15:3–4; 16:5–7), but here they are also a response to the call in 18:20 to "rejoice ... O heaven." The despondent laments over Babylon's fall in chapter 18 are followed now by exuberant celebrations that God has finally judged her wickedness.

The two sections of praise that John hears are both said to come from "something like the voice of a great multitude" (vv. 1, 6), and here in v. 1a he adds "in heaven," without defining further who the speaker(s) might be.[2] What John hears is praise to God and the grounds for it (vv. 1b–2), beginning with the liturgical term "Hallelujah" (Ἀλληλουϊά), a transliteration of the Hebrew for "praise the LORD," drawn from the Old Testament book of Psalms.[3] These verses (vv. 1, 3, 4, 6) are the only New Testa-

ment uses of the transliteration, but it was becoming a common part of Jewish and Christian liturgy in the first century.[4] The declaration that "salvation and glory and power belong to God" (v. 1b) is a worshipful acknowledgment that these attributes are rightfully his ("belong to ... God" translates the possessive genitive τοῦ θεοῦ)[5] and that he deserves praise when he acts in his glorious power to bring deliverance and wholeness to his people (see discussion of these terms at 4:11; 7:10, 12; 12:10).[6]

The reason for this praise is God's righteous judgment of "the great prostitute" Babylon, whose punishment was portrayed so powerfully in chapter 18.[7] This central reason is expressed in two stages (two occurrences of "because," ὅτι, in v. 2a–b; similar to 18:23). First is the conviction that God's judgments in general are "true and righteous" (v. 2a), asserted earlier in 16:7 (see also 6:10; 15:3; 16:5).[8] The second causal clause clarifies how God's judgment of "the great prostitute" constituted a faithful and just act of judgment (v. 2b–d). Babylon's role in leading the people of the earth to moral ruin or "corruption" (φθείρω, cf. 11:18; Jer 51:25, διαφθείρω)[9] by her evil and profane deeds (her "sexual immorality"; cf. 14:8; 18:3, "all the nations") demonstrates God's righteousness

---

1. The transition is familiar: "After these things I heard" (v. 1a; cf. 4:1; 7:9; 15:5; 18:1). See "I saw" in 17:3b; 18:1; and "I heard" in 18:4 for other explicit transitions in this section of the book. "These things" in v. 1a refers to the multifaceted portrayal of Babylon's destruction in ch. 18.

2. It is clear that the speaker is not God, since "our God" is referred to in the third person in v. 1b. A similar phrase in Dan 10:6, "like the voice of a multitude," describes an angel's authoritative voice. The fact that the same phrase "a great multitude" (from every nation, etc.) is used in 7:9 (who also extol God for his "salvation," 7:10) is insufficient grounds to conclude that this is the same group as in 7:9.

3. The Hebrew phrase הַלְלוּ־יָהּ, "hallelujah" or "praise the LORD," occurs 24x in the Psalms, at the beginning or end of a psalm (e.g., 104:35; 106:1, 48; 111:1; 117:1–2; 135:1, 21; 146–50).

4. For example, Tob 13:17–18; 3 Macc 7:13; Apoc. Mos./ LAE 43:4; as the ending of almost all the Odes of Solomon; see

G. W. H. Lampe, *A Patristic Greek Lexicon* (Oxford: Clarendon, 1961), 75.

5. In Ps 3:8 [LXX 3:9] where the Hebrew has, lit., "salvation to the Lord" (לַיהוָה הַיְשׁוּעָה; cf. the dative used in Rev 7:10), the Greek uses a genitive (τοῦ κυρίου ἡ σωτηρία).

6. See note at 7:10 on the sense and OT background of this use of "salvation" (σωτηρία).

7. The two verbs in v. 2b, d, "has judged" and "has avenged" (ἔκρινεν, ἐξεδίκησεν) express the heavenly description of what was just witnessed in ch. 18. They are Greek aorists because they show what is already true in heaven, though yet to be accomplished on earth. See examples of this in 16:5; 18:20.

8. See note at 16:7 for the OT and wider Jewish background of this phrasing.

9. The verb translated "corrupted" (ἔφθειρεν) can be parsed as an imperfect (e.g., NASB) or aorist (ESV, NIV, NRSV), but this instance, surrounded by other aorists, is best understood as an aorist.

in judging her. The further grounding of his just judgment is that she had slaughtered God's people for their faithful service to him (symbolized in "the blood of his servants"; cf. 18:24) and thus rightly deserved God's vengeance (see same verb "avenge," ἐκδικέω, in 6:10) exacted "on her."[10]

19:3–4 And a second time they said, "Hallelujah! And the smoke goes up from her forever and ever." 4 And the twenty-four elders and the four living creatures fell down and worshiped God who sits on the throne saying, "Amen. Hallelujah!" (καὶ δεύτερον εἴρηκαν, Ἀλληλουϊά· καὶ ὁ καπνὸς αὐτῆς ἀναβαίνει εἰς τοὺς αἰῶνας τῶν αἰώνων. 4 καὶ ἔπεσαν οἱ πρεσβύτεροι οἱ εἴκοσι τέσσαρες καὶ τὰ τέσσαρα ζῷα καὶ προσεκύνησαν τῷ θεῷ τῷ καθημένῳ ἐπὶ τῷ θρόνῳ λέγοντες, Ἀμὴν Ἀλληλουϊά). Here the heavenly voice from v. 1 repeats its declaration of praise in much the same terms as in v. 2, followed by a gesture of divine worship and an antiphonal response offered by the two groups of heavenly beings seen in John's original throne room vision in chapters 4–5. The second occurrence of the voice is phrased as "they said" (εἴρηκαν; v. 3a)[11] since it sounded originally like a great "multitude" (v. 1; a collective singular that is plural in sense). Again their expression of praise begins with "hallelujah," but then cites not an instance of God's righteous action in redemption as in v. 1b (deliverance comes from him) but an indication of his punishment against

evil: "The smoke . . . from her" (i.e., from her burning)[12] "goes up forever and ever" (v. 3c), referring to the complete effectiveness of Babylon's destruction (18:9, 18; cf. 14:11; Isa 34:10).[13] Verse 4 records the reverential response of the heavenly elders and living creatures like those John saw around God's throne in 4:4 and 4:6. They have appeared in scenes of heavenly worship at several places in Revelation since that initial throne room vision (7:11; 11:16; 14:3), but this verse is their last mention in the book. Their appearance here is a reminder that all the judgments of chapters 6–18 have been directed from the heavenly throne room and watched with rapt attention from there. In their deep reverence they fall in worship again before God on his throne (just as the elders did in 4:11; 5:14; 11:16 and as both groups did in 7:11; see comments on this at 4:11). They also respond in their worship to what the heavenly voice had said in v. 3 by affirming it with an "amen"[14] and a concluding "hallelujah" (see both terms in Ps 106:48; similar ending in 1 Chr 16:36; Neh 5:13; many psalms end in "hallelujah"; e.g., 104:35; 106:48; 111:1; 135:21; 150:6).

19:5 And a voice came out from the throne saying, "Praise our God, all you servants of his and those who fear him, the small and the great" (Καὶ φωνὴ ἀπὸ τοῦ θρόνου ἐξῆλθεν λέγουσα, Αἰνεῖτε τῷ θεῷ ἡμῶν πάντες οἱ δοῦλοι αὐτοῦ [καὶ] οἱ φοβούμενοι αὐτόν, οἱ μικροὶ καὶ οἱ μεγάλοι).

---

10. There is debate over the sense of "on her" (lit., "from her hand," ἐκ χειρὸς αὐτῆς; cf. 2 Kgs 9:7) in v. 2d. It can signify agency (or means): she shed the blood (Aune, *Revelation 17–22*, 1026; Mathewson, *Handbook*, 257), but the better sense is source: vengeance is taken from or on her (BDAG 298). See 6:10 and note on 18:20.

11. Some manuscripts (046, 1854, 2344) read a singular "it/he said" (εἴρηκεν), but the plural has better support (א, A, 2329) and best explains the origin of the singular as a scribal correction to agree with the singular "voice." This verb is perfect tense, but it should be read as an aoristic perfect (see discussion at 5:7; 7:14).

12. The phrase "from her" is expressed in Greek as a gen-

itive of source attached to the noun "smoke" (καπνός), recast here to suit English idiom better (as in NRSV, NET).

13. The statement in v. 3c that follows "hallelujah" could be a parenthetical comment from John, but it is best to take it as part of the praise declaration like the last part of v. 1. Out of context it seems incongruous as a statement of praise, but here the praise centers on God's vindication of his people against Babylon.

14. "Amen" (Ἀμήν) is another transliteration of a Hebrew liturgical term (אָמֵן) expressing agreement with what has been said or prayed (BDAG 53). In the NT it often concludes prayers, doxologies, and other liturgical formulas (cf. 1:6, 7; 5:14; 7:12; 22:20).

An additional voice, this one "from the throne" itself (v. 5a), joins the chorus of worship from heaven. Like the voices in 9:13 (from the altar before God) and 16:17 (from the temple from the throne), this one speaks with heavenly authority, but it is unlikely to be God himself speaking since it refers to him as "our God" (v. 5b). The call that it adds is a command to "praise our God,"[15] which is a more explicit form of the transliterated Hebrew "hallelujah" ("praise the LORD"). This command is addressed to the wider circle of those who serve and honor God across all the strata of humanity, so that the worship of heaven (v. 4) will expand to the whole world as well (v. 5b). God's "servants" are his people, whose defining trait is that they belong to him and do his bidding (see comments on 1:1; also used in calls to worship in Pss 134:1; 135:1). Another way to describe them[16] is that they "fear him" or give honor and reverence to him (see comments on 11:18; cf. also in a call to worship in Ps 135:20). The final phrase, "the small and the great," extends the call across all groups of God's people regardless of their status (cf. 13:16; 19:18; 20:12). The combination of "those who fear him, the small and the great" is derived from Psalm 115:13 and appears also in Revelation 11:18.

19:6–8 And I heard something like the voice of a great multitude and like the sound of many waters and like the sound of strong peals of thunder saying, "Hallelujah, because the Lord our God the Almighty has begun to reign. 7 Let us rejoice and be glad and give him glory, be-cause the wedding of the Lamb has come and his bride has prepared herself. 8 And it was granted to her to be clothed in pure, bright, fine linen. For the fine linen is the righteous deeds of the saints" (καὶ ἤκουσα ὡς φωνὴν ὄχλου πολλοῦ καὶ ὡς φωνὴν ὑδάτων πολλῶν καὶ ὡς φωνὴν βροντῶν ἰσχυρῶν λεγόντων, Ἁλληλουϊά, ὅτι ἐβασίλευσεν κύριος ὁ θεὸς [ἡμῶν] ὁ παντοκράτωρ. 7 χαίρωμεν καὶ ἀγαλλιῶμεν καὶ δώσωμεν τὴν δόξαν αὐτῷ, ὅτι ἦλθεν ὁ γάμος τοῦ ἀρνίου καὶ ἡ γυνὴ αὐτοῦ ἡτοίμασεν ἑαυτὴν 8 καὶ ἐδόθη αὐτῇ ἵνα περιβάληται βύσσινον λαμπρὸν καθαρόν· τὸ γὰρ βύσσινον τὰ δικαιώματα τῶν ἁγίων ἐστίν). With the repetition of several key words from v. 1 ("I heard something like the . . . voice of a great multitude"), John moves to a second acclamation of heavenly joy at God's triumph for his people, in this case anticipating their intimate communion with him as "the bride" of the Lamb (vv. 6–10). It is truly an impressive voice that John hears since he tries to capture its power and intensity with three similes, comparing it to the sound of a "great multitude" (as in v. 1) as well as the sounds of "many waters" (cf. 1:15; 14:2) and of "strong peals of thunder" (14:2).[17] As in v. 1 the voice calls first for praise to be offered to the Lord, "hallelujah," grounded in God's supreme rule that is about to be established throughout the earth (cf. 11:15–17; 12:10). To say that God "has begun to reign" (ἐβασίλευσεν; v. 6c) carries an ingressive sense like the verb in 11:17 (ἐβασίλευσας). It refers to the inauguration of his rule through Christ (cf. 11:15) to be described in 20:4–6.[18] In such a setting,

---

15. The imperative "praise" (αἰνεῖτε) is a Greek present tense, used to express a general precept (i.e., a customary present calling for conduct that is characteristic of the lives of the listeners; cf. BDF §335; Fanning, *Verbal Aspect*, 327–40).

16. The "and" (καί) does not appear in some manuscripts (א, C, P), but it is probably original. In this context, however, it is explanatory ("that is") rather than adding a different group.

17. The same Greek word for "voice, sound" (φωνή) occurs three times in v. 6a, but it is translated differently to suit the English phrases better. See 1:15 for comments on the OT

background of these images. Despite the comparisons with things that are plural (a great crowd, waters, peals), this "voice" appears to come from a single heavenly being, the angel who interacts with John in vv. 9–10. See v. 9a for discussion. Here the words of the "voice" consist of the direct quotation of vv. 6b–8.

18. See Beale, *Revelation*, 932; Ladd, *Revelation*, 246, and comments on 11:15 earlier. Almost all English translations default to a present tense, "reigns," but see NABR, NJB, REB for the ingressive sense. Here it is translated as a recent past event like the aorists in 11:15–16.

looking back to his judgment of the seemingly invincible Babylon (18:10, 18) and forward to his reign over all the earth, it is evident that God is truly "the Almighty" (ὁ παντοκράτωρ),[19] to be praised for his sovereignty over all of history.

Such joyful praise and worship is what is urged in v. 7a with the exhortation for all who listen to join the heavenly company as they together "rejoice and [are] glad and give [God] glory."[20] The first two of these verbs, "rejoice and be glad" (χαίρωμεν καὶ ἀγαλλιῶμεν) are synonyms used together to reinforce the sense (as in Matt 5:12; also Ps 96:12; Hab 3:18; cf. Tob 13:15).[21] Glorifying or exalting God is the fitting accompaniment to such rejoicing since it acknowledges that he alone is the source of such blessedness (cf. 14:7; 15:4). Another influence toward the exhortation to double rejoicing in v. 7a is Isaiah 61:10 (see also 62:5) that speaks of celebrating and being glad (LXX verbs: εὐφραίνω, ἀγαλλιάω) when the Lord restores Israel and Jerusalem and robes his people with salvation, adorning them like a bridegroom or a bride. This conceptual influence is likely because the wedding imagery is invoked here in v. 7b as the reason for such joy.[22]

The "wedding of the Lamb" (v. 7b) has a broader resonance in biblical texts, since the Old Testament pictures the Lord as a husband to Israel, his beloved but often unfaithful wife (Isa 50:1; 54:4–8; Jer 3:20;

Hos 2:16–20). God's future restoration of Israel after exile is portrayed as a joyful reestablishment of the union after a period of estrangement (Isa 54:6–8; 61:10; 62:4–5), and such imagery is central to the meaning of Revelation 19:7–9 and 21:2, 9. In the New Testament Jesus is the bridegroom to the church (Mark 2:19–20; 2 Cor 11:2; Eph 5:25–32), and his presence in the world is a cause for rejoicing (Matt 9:15; John 3:29). The imagery is used here to represent not the ongoing *status* of a marital relationship (i.e., marriage) but a renewal or full *entrance* into the marriage (i.e., wedding ceremony; cf. "wedding banquet" in v. 9).[23] These verses alone (vv. 7–9) do not fill out the picture but anticipate John's return to the theme in 21:2, 9. There it becomes clearer that the marriage imagery represents the ultimate fulfillment of God's loving and personal communion with his people (cf. 21:3, 7).[24]

The first stage of that fulfillment is at hand as the verb "has come" (ἦλθεν) denotes,[25] and already the Lamb's "bride"[26] has been preparing for the ceremony (v. 7c). She "has prepared herself" (ἡτοίμασεν ἑαυτήν), on the one hand, by her own actions of keeping herself chaste and faithful to her bridegroom—this is not stated explicitly but is implied by the active verb and reflexive pronoun used here as well as the common biblical imagery

19. See comments at 1:18 and 11:17 for the significance of this title and its usage in Rev.

20. These hortatory subjunctives in the Greek of v. 7a express appeals for action that the speakers as well as the listeners will participate in.

21. The second verb "be glad" (ἀγαλλιάω) is very common in contexts of joyful worship (used frequently in LXX Psalms), while the first, "rejoice" (χαίρω), is relatively rare in the Psalms but is the more general word for human rejoicing in various settings (BDAG 1074–75). However, such rejoicing is often seen as the Christian's characteristic attitude in view of God's deliverance to come, even when suffering is their present experience.

22. Fekkes, *Prophetic Traditions*, 269–70.

23. BDAG 188. See J. Jeremias, "νύμφη," *TDNT* 4:1099–106;

and S. Safrai, "Home and Family," in *The Jewish People in the First Century* (Philadelphia: Fortress, 1976), 2:754–60, for Jewish wedding procedures and terminology. These are illustrated in part by Jesus's life (Matt 1:18–25; John 2:1–11) and parables (Matt 22:1–14; 25:1–13).

24. For the identity of those people (the bride of the Lamb), see discussion below.

25. See similar uses of "has come" (ἦλθεν) in 6:17; 14:7, 15; 18:10; and see 11:15; 12:10; 15:4; 19:6 for the aorists of other verbs denoting events seen as already done in heaven and about to be accomplished on earth.

26. The word translated "bride" in v. 7c is the Greek word that often means "wife" (γυνή). In Jewish wedding terminology, these two terms are interchangeable, as 21:9 shows. See also Gen 29:21; BDAG 209; Jeremias, "νύμφη," 1099.

of faithful versus unfaithful brides or wives (cf. the OT passages cited above; also 2 Cor 11:2 and Rev 21:2). She has also been prepared by God's gift (v. 8a, "it was granted to her," ἐδόθη αὐτῇ, implying God as the giver as in 6:4; 13:5) of wedding garments so that she is fully and beautifully dressed for her wedding day: "Clothed in pure, bright, fine linen."[27] An interpretation of this imagery is provided (as rarely in Rev; cf. 1:20; 4:5; 5:8; 17:9, 12, 15, 18) in the explanatory "for" (γάρ) clause of v. 8b (this is still probably the angel's words, not John's addition). These robes of "fine linen" (βύσσινον)[28] represent the "righteous deeds of the saints."[29]

The timing of this "wedding" (v. 7) or "marriage banquet" (v. 9) is not entirely clear from the context, and the articulation by different interpreters of when it will occur is bound up with their views of eschatological events in general. One possibility is that the wedding or marriage has already taken place in heaven prior to Jesus's coming to earth (19:11–21).[30] This is not likely to be correct, since it is based on a misunderstanding of the aorist verb "has come" in v. 7b (the tense does not demand that the wedding has already occurred at the time of Jesus's coming; see note at v. 7b). A better choice is that the wedding and its accompanying banquet of celebration (vv. 7, 9) represent God's loving intimacy and restoration of blessing for his people after Christ's second coming. This fits better with

the sense that "has come" in some way anticipates the results of Christ's victory in 19:11–21 (either a proleptic aorist or, as explained above, already true in heaven and about to be realized on earth). Differences among interpreters who take this broad understanding depend on their larger view of eschatological events after the second coming. Some speak of the wedding as a symbol for the New Jerusalem, which is identified with the bride in 21:2, 9–10. The personal presence of God and the Lamb with the saints in the renewal of all things correspond to the intimacy of a marriage entered into fully. Following this line of thinking, some identify the wedding with the blessedness pictured in chapters 21–22 whether they see that as in heaven or on a renewed earth.[31] Others understand the wedding and its banquet to refer to both the millennium (ch. 20) and the new heavens and new earth (chs. 21–22).[32] The intermediate reign of Christ launches the period of restoration for God's people, but the eternal state takes that renewal to its ultimate level of fullness and intimacy with God. This final option seems best for several reasons. The millennium is what the text portrays as immediately following Christ's victory in 19:11–21. In the Old Testament (e.g., Isa 54; 60–62) the restoration of the bride is linked to the return of Israel from exile and her rule from Jerusalem among the nations. In the New Testament God's rule on

---

27. See Acts 10:30; Jas 2:2–3; Rev 15:6; 19:14 for clothing described as "pure, clean" (καθαρόν) or "bright, resplendent" (λαμπρόν).

28. There is an intended contrast between v. 8 and 18:16, the clothing of the great prostitute also in "fine linen."

29. The same theological motif using this imagery appears elsewhere in Rev (3:4–5; 3:18; 7:14): the "clothing" of righteousness is on the one hand given by God based on the Lamb's act of sacrifice, and on the other hand lived out in actual conduct. The Christian's righteous deeds flow from God's gift of cleansing and forgiveness; they are not the means or cause of that forgiveness (Eph 2:8–10).

30. See Paul N. Benware, *Understanding End Times Prophecy: A Comprehensive Approach*, rev. ed. (Chicago: Moody, 2006), 232–33; J. Dwight Pentecost, *Things to Come: A Study in Biblical Eschatology* (Grand Rapids: Zondervan, 1964), 226–27; Scott, *Exposition*, 379.

31. Ladd, *Revelation*, 246–50; Mounce, *Revelation*, 347; Smalley, *Revelation*, 482.

32. Charles, *Revelation*, 2:126–29; Thomas, *Revelation 8–22*, 366. Two others who seem to hold this view are David J. MacLeod, *The Seven Last Things: An Exposition of Revelation 19–21* (Dubuque, IA: Emmaus College Press, 2003), 15–17, 27 (who speaks only of the millennium) and Willitts, "Bride of Messiah," 245–54 (who speaks only of the new Jerusalem).

earth is likened to a banquet similar to the wedding supper cited in v. 9 (Matt 8:11; Mark 14:25; Luke 13:28–29; 14:14–15; cf. Isa 25:6–9). And even here in 19:6–7 the beginning of God's rule on earth and the wedding of the Lamb are linked together as parallel reasons for heavenly celebration, so it is more likely that they occur together in time.

19:9–10 And he said to me, "Write: Blessed are those who are invited to the marriage banquet of the Lamb." And he said to me, "These words of God are true." 10 **And I fell at his feet to worship him. And he said to me, "Don't do that. I am a fellow servant of yours and of your brothers and sisters who hold to the testimony of Jesus. Worship God! For the testimony of Jesus is the Spirit of prophecy"** (Καὶ λέγει μοι, Γράψον· Μακάριοι οἱ εἰς τὸ δεῖπνον τοῦ γάμου τοῦ ἀρνίου κεκλημένοι. καὶ λέγει μοι, Οὗτοι οἱ λόγοι ἀληθινοὶ τοῦ θεοῦ εἰσιν. 10 καὶ ἔπεσα ἔμπροσθεν τῶν ποδῶν αὐτοῦ προσκυνῆσαι αὐτῷ. καὶ λέγει μοι, Ὅρα μή· σύνδουλός σού εἰμι καὶ τῶν ἀδελφῶν σου τῶν ἐχόντων τὴν μαρτυρίαν Ἰησοῦ· τῷ θεῷ προσκύνησον. ἡ γὰρ μαρτυρία Ἰησοῦ ἐστιν τὸ πνεῦμα τῆς προφητείας). The heavenly voice of v. 6 now addresses John directly with a message of encouragement for his readers (v. 9a–b).[33] In a reminder of John's role throughout the book as the vehicle of God's revelation (1:1–2, 11; 22:6–8), the angel instructs him to record for others to read ("write," γράψον; cf. 1:11, 19; 10:4; 14:13; 21:5) a pronouncement of blessing for all who will take part in the coming "marriage of the Lamb" (cf. vv. 7–8). This is the fourth of

seven beatitudes in Revelation (see 1:3 for a list of occurrences and their significance as a group). Here the "blessedness" comes from participation in the eschatological fulfillment of God's redemption. This fulfillment was pictured in v. 7 by the imagery of the "wedding" and "bride" and in v. 8 by the celebratory garments worn at such an occasion. Verse 9 adds the elements of a "banquet" or feast (δεῖπνον) and invited guests (οἱ . . . κεκλημένοι) who will share in the joy and table fellowship of the wedding. These features continue the biblical imagery of God's restoration of the full communion he desires to have with his people viewed as a marriage celebration. But it adds to it the portrayal of God's eschatological fulfillment as a messianic banquet (Matt 8:11; Mark 14:25; Luke 12:36–38; 13:28–29; 14:14–15).[34] Jesus also combines these elements, sometimes for different purposes, in his parables of the kingdom. In Luke 12:36–38 and 14:14–15 the banquet imagery carries with it the promise of blessing, as it does here. In Matthew 22:1–14 the kingdom is pictured as a wedding feast, and special attention is paid to those who are "invited" but refuse to attend (different from the sense of "invited" here) and also to the guests' clothing (not the bride's as here in v. 8).

Here "those invited" (v. 9b) denote the people chosen to participate in the celebratory table fellowship that is coming, a picture of intimate communion with Christ. The metaphor changes from vv. 7b–8 (the bride represents God's people) to v. 9 (the guests represent God's people).[35] The imagery of v. 9 is closer to how wedding banquets

---

33. Since no change in subject is indicated, the speaker in vv. 9–10a ("and he said to me," καὶ λέγει μοι, used three times) appears to be the same as the "voice" in vv. 6–8. As v. 10 will show, this speaker is an angel whose impressive voice and presence overawed John. The historical presents in v. 9 highlight the following interaction between John and the angel (v. 10; see note on historical present at 5:5).

34. See also 3 En. 48A:10; T. Isaac 6:22. For discussion of other ancient Jewish sources, see J. Priest, "A Note on the

Messianic Banquet," in *The Messiah: Developments in Earliest Judaism and Christianity*, ed. James H. Charlesworth (Minneapolis: Fortress, 1992), 222–38.

35. Beale, *Revelation*, 945, notes that vv. 7–8 use a corporate metaphor ("the corporate church . . . about to wed the Lamb"), but v. 9 shifts to an individual metaphor ("guests at the marriage banquet"). Both "portray the intimate communion of Christ with believers."

are portrayed in Jesus's parables as a representation of his relationship to his disciples. For example, note the guests' joy while the groom is with them (Mark 2:19) and prepared versus unprepared guests (Matt 22:1–14; 25:1–13). The bride is not even mentioned in these parables, just the groom and his guests.[36] This change in imagery within the span of three verses has led some to conclude that the bride (v. 7) and the guests (v. 9) represent different groups among the redeemed.[37] But for the reasons cited above, it makes more sense to see the images referring to the same group, the redeemed who are chosen in God's great love to be his people through the Lamb's redemptive sacrifice and who will be brought into fullness of intimate fellowship with God and the Lamb in the millennium and then beyond in the new Jerusalem. So based on the beginnings of the bridal imagery in the Old Testament and its continuation in the New, there is no rationale to see the church as distinct from Israel in this picture of redemption's consummation, even though other distinctions should be made. The church is not the new Israel, and Israel has not been rejected, but believing ethnic Israel along with believing gentiles will share together in that future day as the corporate bride of the Lamb and as individual guests at his wedding banquet.[38]

In addition to the command to write (v. 9b), the angel reassures John and his readers that the preceding content is a reliable revelation from God (v. 9c–d). The affirmation, "these words of God are true," is similar to that of 22:6. When coupled with beatitudes in both places (v. 9b and 22:7) and the dual accounts of John's attempted worship of an angel (v. 10 and 22:8–9), these textual features suggest a literary parallel to signal a transition from one major unit to another. In this case there is a transition from the section about Babylon (17:1–19:10) to a section about the all-important eschatological events (19:11–21:8) that lead to the New Jerusalem (21:9–22:5).[39] The parallels recur in 22:6–9 to signal the transition into the epilogue of the book (22:6–21).

So when the angel declares, "These words of God are true" (v. 9d), the referent of "these words" is most likely the entire preceding section about Babylon's judgment as a prelude to the fulfillment of God's redemption (17:1–19:9b), not just to v. 9b alone.[40] And the affirmation that they constitute "the true words of God" (οἱ λόγοι ἀληθινοὶ τοῦ θεοῦ)[41] should be understood in light of the prologue that describes the whole book as a revelation from God through John, a witness to "the word of God and the testimony of Jesus Christ" (τὸν λόγον

---

36. Jeremias, "νύμφη," 1104; Ladd, *Revelation*, 247, 250.

37. For example, Walvoord, Rawley, and Hitchcock, *Revelation*, 284–86 (the bride is the church, i.e., saints of the church age between Pentecost and the pretribulational rapture, and the guests are saints of the OT era and the tribulation period); Thomas, *Revelation 8–22*, 367–73 (similar to Walvoord, Rawley, and Hitchcock). But virtually the opposite is Willitts, "Bride of Messiah," 253 (the bride is "God's restored Israel," and the guests are "righteous gentiles," "the nations who will participate in the eschatological kingdom").

38. Saucy, *Case for Progressive Dispensationalism*, 183–86. On the "bride" in Rev 21–22, see Turner, "New Jerusalem," 288, who cites the twelve tribes and the twelve apostles represented in the new Jerusalem (21:12, 14) and speaks of "the transdispensational continuity of Israel and the church as the one people of God."

39. See "Literary Context" at 17:1 and the detailed discussion in Bauckham, *Climax*, 3–7.

40. "These words" in 22:6, however, since they introduce the epilogue, seem to refer to the entire book as it comes to a conclusion.

41. Most English translations take "true" (ἀληθινοί) as an attributive adjective and "these" (οὗτοι) as a subject pronoun: "These are (the) true words of God" (e.g., KJV, NIV, ESV, NASB). But the Greek adjective arrangement is best taken as predicate in sense (e.g., CSB, "these words of God are true"). One manuscript, A (quite a reliable one), has an article that clearly makes the adjective attributive, but this seems to be an attempt to correct an awkward phrasing (the predicate adjective comes between the noun "word" and the genitive "of God," but this is not unworkable).

τοῦ θεοῦ καὶ τὴν μαρτυρίαν Ἰησοῦ Χριστοῦ, 1:1–2). The readers can rely on these accounts as God's truth.

Something about the impressiveness of this angel and his authoritative words causes John to drop to the ground in worship (v. 10a). The angel immediately forbids this (v. 10b–c), with a deferential reminder that in all his heavenly magnificence he simply shares with John and other Christians in servitude to God (a "fellow servant," v. 10d),[42] who alone is worthy of worship ("worship God," v. 10f; cf. 22:8–9).[43]

The angel's description of Christians as those "who hold to the testimony of Jesus" (τὴν μαρτυρίαν Ἰησοῦ, v. 10e) denotes their loyalty to him in maintaining their commitment to Christian teaching about Christ (an objective genitive; i.e., testimony about Jesus, as in 12:17; 20:4; cf. 6:9; 12:11; 17:6).[44] A few interpreters take "testimony of Jesus" in both places here (v. 10e, g) as subjective genitives, meaning the faithful witness that Jesus gave,[45] and some argue for an ambiguity that includes both subjective and objective senses, a "witness by and to Jesus."[46] But the objective reading is more likely.

The statement in v. 10g ("for the testimony of Jesus is the Spirit of prophecy") can be taken as John's explanation of the angel's words in v. 10c–f,

but it is more likely the reason the angel himself gives for his commands, concluding the quoted material (the conjunction "for," γάρ, can accommodate either sense). With two ambiguous genitive expressions, a confusing use of "is" (ἐστιν), and a potentially ambiguous reference to "spirit" or "Spirit" (πνεῦμα), this clause seems to defy understanding. Most translations are content to pass on the ambiguities with a plain rendering that leaves all options open for the reader (even The Message plays this verse right down the middle: "The witness of Jesus is the spirit of prophecy"). As argued above, the first phrase seems to mean "testimony about Jesus" (objective sense). Reference to the "Spirit" or "spirit" is somewhat vexed by how to construe the connection that "is" seems to provide (more on that below), as well as by the sense of the genitive "of prophecy" (τῆς προφητείας). But some progress can be made by acknowledging that "spirit" (πνεῦμα, singular) in this book commonly refers to God's Spirit, the Holy Spirit (1:10; 2:7, 11, 17, 29; 3:6, 13, 22; 4:2; 14:13; 17:3; 21:10; 22:17) and that a common activity of the Holy Spirit in ancient Jewish or Christian literature is to inspire "prophecy."[47] It is highly unlikely that πνεῦμα in this text means "essence" or "heart" or "gist" (cf. NLT).[48] If "spirit" means "Spirit," then the genitive phrase "of

---

42. See similar human-angelic interchanges in Mart. Ascen. Isa. 7:21–22; 8:5; Tob 12:16–18; Apoc. Zeph. 6:11–15; Jos. Asen. 15:11–12. The significance of these and of Rev 19:10 and 22:8–9 for monotheistic worship ("worship God alone" rather than angels) in a book that celebrates the worship of Jesus alongside God himself (e.g., Rev 5:8–12) is discussed in Bauckham, *Climax*, 118–49, and Loren T. Stuckenbruck, *Angel Veneration and Christology: A Study in Early Judaism and in the Christology of the Apocalypse of John*, WUNT 77 (Tübingen: Mohr Siebeck, 1995), 245–65.

43. The command to "worship God" is expressed as an aorist imperative, which lends greater urgency and insistence than the present tense (Fanning, *Verbal Aspect*, 369–70, 380–82).

44. See Aune, *Revelation 17–22*, 1038–39; see also comments at 12:17.

45. Beckwith, *Apocalypse*, 729; Thomas, *Revelation 8–22*, 376; cf. Bauckham, *Climax*, 161; J. Beutler, "μαρτυρία," EDNT 2:392–93.

46. Beale, *Revelation*, 947; Koester, *Revelation*, 731–32; Smalley, *Revelation*, 487. Similar to the view of Koester is the idea that "the testimony of Jesus" refers to his witness in this book itself (cf. 1:2; 22:18, 20), and so to hold to his testimony means loyalty to what is written here. This is the argument of Sarah Underwood Dixon, *The Testimony of the Exalted Jesus: The "Testimony of Jesus" in the Book of Revelation* (London: Bloomsbury T&T Clark, 2017).

47. See references in BDAG 835–36 and the ancient texts cited by Koester, *Revelation*, 732.

48. Michaels, *Revelation*, 213–14; Witherington, *Revelation*, 234. As Beasley-Murray, *Revelation*, 276, notes this is "too impersonal" for an ancient Jewish-Christian reference to prophecy. It is easy in English to read "spirit" as "essence, heart," but it is doubtful whether πνεῦμα ever carried that sense in ancient Greek.

prophecy" carries the sense of product: the Spirit who produces or inspires prophecy.[49] A reference to God's Spirit in this verse fits better as a reason not to worship an angel but the God from whom these words of truth come (vv. 9c–10f).[50] With these other pieces in place, the sense of "is" cannot be a mere equation (e.g., A is B) but a statement of association or exemplification: testimony to Jesus reflects or represents the Spirit who reveals God's truth through his prophets because it also is God's message.[51] Those who maintain a faithful testimony to God's message about Jesus reveal the same Spirit who inspired the prophets to be powerfully at work in their own lives as well.

19:11–13 And I saw heaven standing open, and behold, a white horse and the one sitting on it, called faithful and true, and in righteousness he judges and wages war. 12 Now his eyes are like a flame of fire, and on his head are many diadems; he has a name written that no one knows except he himself, 13 and he is clothed in a robe dipped in blood, and his name is called the Word of God (Καὶ εἶδον τὸν οὐρανὸν ἠνεῳγμένον, καὶ ἰδοὺ ἵππος λευκός καὶ ὁ καθήμενος ἐπ᾽ αὐτὸν [καλούμενος] πιστὸς καὶ ἀληθινός, καὶ ἐν δικαιοσύνῃ κρίνει καὶ πολεμεῖ. 12 οἱ δὲ ὀφθαλμοὶ αὐτοῦ [ὡς] φλὸξ πυρός, καὶ ἐπὶ τὴν κεφαλὴν αὐτοῦ διαδήματα πολλά, ἔχων ὄνομα γεγραμμένον ὃ οὐδεὶς οἶδεν εἰ μὴ αὐτός, 13 καὶ περιβεβλημένος ἱμάτιον βεβαμμένον αἵματι, καὶ κέκληται τὸ ὄνομα αὐτοῦ ὁ λόγος τοῦ θεοῦ). Having completed his major section portraying the destruction of Babylon (17:1–19:10), John moves into the next, all-important portion of the book (19:11–21:8), covering significant eschatological events foreshadowed in the preceding chapters. These events are portrayed in a series of visions that John recounts, each introduced by "and I saw" (19:11, 17, 19; 20:1, 4, 11; 21:1).[52] The first vision (vv. 11–16) presents the return of Jesus Christ to earth as the messianic warrior and judge, but in language and imagery strangely unlike what we might expect in comparison with other New Testament passages about his second coming (e.g., Matt 24:27, 37; Acts 1:11; 1 Cor 1:7; 15:20–28; Phil 3:20–21; 1 Thess 4:13–18; 2 Thess 1:6–10; 2:3–12; 1 Tim 6:14; Titus 2:13; Heb 9:28; Jas 5:8; 1 Pet 4:7; 5:4; 1 John 2:28).[53] John's presentation of Christ's coming in vv. 11–16 is influenced more by Old Testament and Jewish imagery than by language found more commonly in the rest of the New Testament.[54]

This is a further confirmation of John's profound immersion in and dependence on the Old Testament prophets and Psalms for his understanding of the eschatological events to come (see comments

49. See Wallace, *Grammar*, 106–7, and his illustrations from Rom 15:5, 13, 33 (the God of endurance, encouragement, hope, peace). As he says, this is like an objective genitive, but the head noun does not carry an explicit verbal sense. Objective genitive is the label used by Osborne, *Revelation*, 698; Smalley, *Revelation*, 487.

50. Beasley-Murray, *Revelation*, 276; Mounce, *Revelation*, 349–50.

51. See Beasley-Murray, *Revelation*, 276, for related ideas; also Bruce, "Spirit in the Apocalypse," 337–38, for a similar treatment of 19:10 as a whole.

52. The words "and I saw" or "I saw" occur also in 20:12 and 21:2 in ways that continue a section rather than opening a new one.

53. Aune, *Revelation 17–22*, 1046, 1053; Boring, *Revelation*, 195–96. R. J. McKelvey, "The Millennium and the Second

Coming," in Moyise, *Studies in the Book of Revelation*, 85–100, observes these differences from other NT accounts, but decides that 19:11–21 does not describe Jesus's second coming at all. He follows Giblin in seeing recapitulation throughout the book (see introduction to this commentary for discussion) and especially in chs. 19–21 (see notes on 19:17–18 and 20:7–10). He fails to understand how John's previews of victory over the nations in earlier chapters point forward to the climactic battle and actual regime change portrayed in Rev 19–20.

54. For example, there are no terms in this passage like "come" (ἔρχομαι)—but Rev uses this word elsewhere (e.g., 16:15; 22:7, 12, 17, 20)—"appear" (φανερόω), "unveil" (ἀποκαλύπτω), "coming/presence" (παρουσία). This passage does, however, depict Christ "coming" with power and glory (Matt 24:30; Mark 13:26, a figure drawn from Dan 7). On the Jewish roots for the imagery John does use, see discussion in verses below.

at 10:7). While he knows the traditions about Jesus and the New Testament preaching of his saving work, the predominant themes of his visions are drawn from Old Testament portrayals of the divine warrior coming to defeat the nations and regather repentant Israel in a restored Jerusalem from which a Davidic king will rule both faithful Israel and believing gentiles. These are not scattered bits of obscure prophecy that fail to cohere or that have been reimagined in purely spiritual and heavenly terms but a consistent framework drawn from the Old Testament that John expects to come to pass in earthly and geographical terms.[55]

In his vision John witnesses "heaven standing open" (v. 11a; cf. 4:1; 11:19; 15:5), and what captures his attention immediately[56] is "a white horse and the one sitting on it" (v. 11b),[57] although he neither names the rider nor portrays any specific action on his part until later in the passage (see discussion below). The general descriptions, however, make clear that this is Jesus Christ returning in great power to conquer and judge all enemies and establish his righteous rule on earth. The names "faithful and true" ($\pi\iota\sigma\tau\grave{o}\varsigma \ldots \kappa\alpha\grave{\iota} \, \dot{\alpha}\lambda\eta\theta\iota\nu\acute{o}\varsigma$, v. 11c) are clearly descriptions of Christ (1:5; 3:7, 14), the one completely faithful to his promises and the genuine Messiah over against all false messiahs who may arise (cf. Matt 24:23–24; Mark 13:21–23). Verse 11d portrays his actions in general terms (customary presents): "In righteousness he judges and makes war" ($\dot{\epsilon}\nu \, \delta\iota\kappa\alpha\iota\sigma\sigma\acute{\nu}\eta \, \kappa\rho\acute{\iota}\nu\epsilon\iota \, \kappa\alpha\grave{\iota} \, \pi\omega\lambda\epsilon\mu\epsilon\hat{\iota}$). This reflects the Old Testament theme of God as the one who is the righteous Judge and who comes

to judge the world and its peoples with equity and justice (Pss 9:7–8; 72:2; 96:13; 98:9). This is done especially through the anointed one from the line of David (Isa 11:1, 4–5; cf. Rev 19:15) or the heavenly son of man (Dan 7:13–14, 22–27), both of whom accomplish righteous judgment against God's enemies and for God's faithful people (cf. Rev 6:9–11; 18:8, 20; 19:2).[58] In addition to judgment, the rider also "wages war," a theme anticipated in previous chapters (12:17; 13:4, 7; 16:14–16; 17:14)[59] and filled out in greater detail in verses that follow (vv. 13–21). The warrior Messiah comes to earth to establish in full the victory he has already accomplished at the cross (3:21; 5:5; 17:14).

As John describes further the appearance of this warrior Messiah (vv. 12–13), it becomes clear that this is Jesus Christ and that he has come to exact judgment against rebellious humanity. His eyes stand out "like a flame of fire" (v. 12a; cf. 1:14; 2:18; Dan 10:6), which here speaks of holy zeal against sin. On his head are "many diadems" (v. 12b), representing his royal authority that eclipses the ruling power of the dragon and his beast (cf. 12:3; 13:1). He has "a name written" (it is unclear where or how it is written), a name of which he alone understands the meaning (v. 12c–d). This has similarities to 2:17 and 3:12 (where the overcomer is promised a new private name or Christ's own new name respectively) and to Isaiah 62:2 (a new name for Jerusalem when the Lord restores her). These texts reflect the biblical idea that the name of a person is indicative of his or her true essence and role, and so a "new name" can symbolize a change of character

55. See McNicol, *Conversion*, 82–84.

56. For the use of "behold" ($\dot{\iota}\delta\omega\acute{\upsilon}$) in v. 11b, see notes on 4:1; 12:3.

57. Such a horseman is clearly a military image in the ancient world (cf. Jer 8:6; 12:5; Rev 9:7, 9; also 2 Macc 3:25). For contrasts with the rider on the white horse in 6:2, see discussion at that verse.

58. The messianic warrior from David's line appears also in

Pss. Sol. 17:21–32; Tg. Neof. Gen 49:11. In T. Mos. 10:3–7 the heavenly warrior who brings God's righteous judgment seems to be a mighty angel such as Michael.

59. This is also rooted in images of God as mighty warrior who will defeat Israel's enemies in battle (e.g., Deut 20:1–3; Isa 42:13; Zech 14:3).

or status.[60] Likewise a new circumstance can reveal that an existing name, one already known, has a depth of meaning and relevance not previously appreciated. That seems to be the point here, since Christ's private name (v. 12c–d) is likely to be either the name given in v. 13b ("the Word of God") or v. 16b ("King of kings and Lord of lords").[61] In both cases his authority and power now seen in judgment reveal him to be God's Word or ruler over all in a more profound sense than previously understood (the nearer one, v. 13b, is the more likely). See discussion of these titles below.

In a gruesome and sobering description he is said to be "clothed in a robe dipped in blood" (v. 13a). The image of a garment that has been "dipped" (βεβαμμένον)[62] or stained completely with "blood" is drawn from Isaiah 63:1–6, a picture of the Lord's wrath against the nations of the world, using the imagery of someone treading out grapes in a winepress (cf. Rev 14:19–20; 19:15). But his garment is stained not with dark grape juice but with the lifeblood of those he has judged.[63] The close dependence on Isaiah 63 shows that in this context "blood" refers not to Jesus's atoning sacrifice of himself (as in 1:5; 5:9; 7:14) but to the blood of his enemies that will be shed in his overwhelming victory against all resistance that hostile earthly

powers mount against him at his return (as in 14:17–20).[64]

The final description in this series is his name, "the Word of God" (v. 13b), which is likely to be the name in v. 12c–d that others previously failed to grasp (see discussion there). It is natural to connect this title to John 1:1, and that is certainly correct in part. But there the name is simply "the Word," and it carries a different sense (i.e., the one who shares the being of God and became incarnate is the ultimate revealer of God; cf. John 1:14, 18).[65] Here the more important influence seems to be Wisdom 18:15 where God's "all-powerful word" (ὁ παντοδύναμός σου λόγος) is said to come from heaven as a "stern warrior" (cf. Exod 15:3) with a "sharp sword" to bring death to the firstborn of Egypt. This best fits the related imagery of the divine warrior (Rev 19:11) and the bloody winepress of God's judgment against hostile nations (vv. 13a, 15). At his second coming Christ is revealed as God's word or message in a previously unfathomed sense in bringing divine judgment to bear on human evil.

19:14–16 And the armies in heaven, dressed in pure, white fine linen, were following him on white horses. 15 And from his mouth a sharp sword comes out so that with it he might strike

---

60. L. Hartman, "ὄνομα," *EDNT* 2:519–20.

61. Koester, *Revelation*, 754–55 (the name is "King of kings and Lord of lords") and Roloff, *Revelation*, 218–19 (the name is "the Word of God"). Either of the names from the context itself is better than the possibilities sometimes suggested by commentators: the tetragrammaton (Beale, *Revelation*, 953–56; Smalley, *Revelation*, 490–91) or an unknown name not revealed until the eschaton (Osborne, *Revelation*, 682; Thomas, *Revelation 8–22*, 385). Both Beale and Smalley echo the point made above about understanding the deeper significance of an existing name.

62. This is a perfect participle, denoting not the action of dipping or dyeing the robe but its resulting condition as he wears it (cf. BDAG 165–66).

63. Under the influence of Isa 63 this imagery of God's judgment appears also in Wis 18:15–16; Tg. Neof. Gen 49:11.

64. A few recent interpreters understand the blood on his garment to be Jesus's own blood, representing his atonement (e.g., Koester, *Revelation*, 755–56, 765) because in the sequence of events in vv. 13–15 his garments are red prior to the battle and because the savage imagery of Isa 63 has been Christianized. But as Fekkes, *Prophetic Traditions*, 196–98, argues, this is to "overliteralize" John's sequence (his visions often present things impressionistically rather than in their natural order). On the Christianizing of OT imagery, see vv. 17–18, 21 (birds gorged with flesh) and Iain Provan, "Foul Spirits, Fornication, and Finance: Revelation 17 from an Old Testament Perspective," *JSNT* 64 (1996): 83 ("the ghost of Marcion still haunts the Christian mansion").

65. The wording of 1 John 1:1 ("the Word of life") is clearly an allusion to John 1:1, but it continues the focus on Jesus's role in revealing God and the true life that comes from God.

the nations, and he will shepherd them with a rod of iron and he treads the winepress of the wine of the fury of the wrath of God the Almighty, 16 and he has on his robe at the thigh a name written, "King of kings and Lord of lords" (καὶ τὰ στρατεύματα [τὰ] ἐν τῷ οὐρανῷ ἠκολούθει αὐτῷ ἐφ᾽ ἵπποις λευκοῖς, ἐνδεδυμένοι βύσσινον λευκὸν καθαρόν. 15 καὶ ἐκ τοῦ στόματος αὐτοῦ ἐκπορεύεται ῥομφαία ὀξεῖα, ἵνα ἐν αὐτῇ πατάξῃ τὰ ἔθνη, καὶ αὐτὸς ποιμανεῖ αὐτοὺς ἐν ῥάβδῳ σιδηρᾷ, καὶ αὐτὸς πατεῖ τὴν ληνὸν τοῦ οἴνου τοῦ θυμοῦ τῆς ὀργῆς τοῦ θεοῦ τοῦ παντοκράτορος, 16 καὶ ἔχει ἐπὶ τὸ ἱμάτιον καὶ ἐπὶ τὸν μηρὸν αὐτοῦ ὄνομα γεγραμμένον· Βασιλεὺς βασιλέων καὶ κύριος κυρίων). The power and glory of Christ's return to earth is enhanced as John lifts his gaze for a moment from the warrior Messiah to take in the heavenly "armies" that accompanied him to earth (v. 14).[66] These are "the armies in heaven," also riding in military glory "on white horses" (cf. v. 11) and garbed in "pure, white fine linen" like the bride of the Lamb (v. 8) and like groups of earthly followers of Christ seen in heaven earlier in Revelation (6:11; 7:9, 13–14). Heavenly forces that come with God or his Messiah to bring judgment to earth are seen primarily in Zechariah 14:1–5 (the Lord attended by "his holy ones" when he comes to do battle against the nations who threaten Jerusalem), but the broader idea is influenced by texts that see the Lord served in heaven by myriads of angels or "holy ones" (Deut 33:2; Ps 68:17; Dan 7:10). These texts are picked up in New Testament verses about the coming of the Son of Man in judgment (Matt 16:27; 25:31; Mark 8:38; Luke 9:26; 1 Thess 3:13; 2 Thess 1:7; Jude 14, quoting 1 En. 1:9). Most of these verses take the "holy ones" who will come

from heaven explicitly as angels (1 Thess 3:13 and Jude 14 leave it as "holy ones").

There is debate over the composition of the heavenly armies here in v. 14, but it seems that John understands this group to include resurrected earthly followers of Christ already present in heaven as he writes (cf. Rev 6:11; 7:9, 13–14) as well as angelic warriors. The wording of 17:14 and 18:6–7 seems to imply this, and several noncanonical, early-Christian texts understand Zechariah 14:5 in this way as well (Did. 16:7; Mart. Ascen. Isa. 4:14–16).

The focus turns back to Christ himself again in v. 15 where Old Testament messianic warrior imagery occurs again. The metaphor (vv. 15a–b) of "a sharp sword" (ῥομφαία ὀξεῖα) coming "from his mouth" (cf. 1:16; 2:12, 16) as a weapon to "strike the nations" is drawn from Isaiah 11:4 and 49:2 (and to a lesser degree Ps 45:3). This refers to his power to effect judgment simply by declaring it done (see Job 4:9; 2 Thess 2:8; and comments at 1:16; cf. Gen 1:3; Ps 33:6). Also clearly messianic are the words from Psalm 2:9 (used earlier in Rev 2:27; 12:5) that "he will shepherd them with a rod of iron" (v. 15c), words that picture his irresistible control over all opposition to his rule (see comments at 2:27 on this use of "shepherd").[67] Verse 15d returns to the general picture given in v. 13a (drawn clearly from Isa 63:2–3; also Lam 1:15; Joel 3:13). This metaphor sees divine judgment as treading out grapes in a "winepress," graphically portraying the complete destruction or crushing under foot of all opposition to God's will. This picture of judgment was previewed in 14:19–20, and in a related verse (14:10) John uses the additional image of the "wine" that is

---

66. In changing his focus of attention, John shifts briefly from description using customary presents, participles, a stative perfect, and one future indicative (vv. 13–16, 14b–16) to an imperfect verb ("were following," ἠκολούθει) that also is descriptive of what he saw in his vision.

67. The verb "he will shepherd" shifts to a future (amid present tenses) under the influence of the future verb in LXX Ps 2:9 ("you will shepherd") and to anticipate when this will actually occur. See the note at 4:5 and Mussies, *Morphology*, 334–36, 340.

produced in this winepress as consisting in God's fury and his wrath or, as worded here, "the fury of the wrath of God."[68] The fearfulness of this wrath is heightened by the further title that is added, "the Almighty" (see v. 6).

As a complement to the description in v. 12c–d (a name that no one knows at that point except Christ himself), v. 16 unveils one of his names for all to see, a name that characterizes his essence (see comments at 2:3): he is "King of kings and Lord of lords" (v. 16b). This revelation of his complete sovereignty over all kings or lords was mentioned already in 17:14 (in reverse order) and in a more general form in 1:5 ("ruler of the kings of the earth"), but here it is seen in its full reality as it is about to be accomplished on earth.[69] This title was written "on his robe at the thigh,"[70] and the significance of this location is unclear (in 14:1 and 17:5 names are written on the forehead). But in the imagery of a mounted warrior, a name written there would perhaps be more prominent for all to see than anywhere else.

19:17–18 And I saw an angel standing on the sun, and he cried out with a loud voice, saying to all the birds flying high in the sky, "Come gather for the great supper of God 18 that you may eat the flesh of kings and flesh of commanders and flesh of mighty ones and flesh of horses and those who sat on them and flesh of all, both free and slaves and small and great" (Καὶ εἶδον ἕνα ἄγγελον ἑστῶτα ἐν τῷ ἡλίῳ καὶ ἔκραξεν [ἐν] φωνῇ μεγάλῃ λέγων πᾶσιν τοῖς ὀρνέοις τοῖς πετομένοις ἐν μεσουρανήματι, Δεῦτε συνάχθητε εἰς τὸ δεῖπνον τὸ μέγα τοῦ θεοῦ 18 ἵνα φάγητε σάρκας βασιλέων καὶ σάρκας χιλιάρχων καὶ σάρκας ἰσχυρῶν καὶ σάρκας ἵππων καὶ τῶν καθημένων ἐπ᾽ αὐτῶν καὶ σάρκας πάντων ἐλευθέρων τε καὶ δούλων καὶ μικρῶν καὶ μεγάλων). Here we have a brief recounting of John's second vision in this series (v. 17a, "and I saw"; cf. vv. 11, 19), adding to the picture of Christ's victorious return to earth as the messianic warrior and king. This vision anticipates the overwhelming defeat of all the forces that futilely resist his coming (cf. vv. 19–21), but it is a gruesome sight even when recounted indirectly, as done here. The imagery is drawn directly from Ezekiel 39 as a typology of judgment, where God predicted a rout of the forces of Gog that will invade Israel (Ezek 39:4, "You will fall on the mountains of Israel and I will give you as food for birds of prey and wild animals").[71] So many bodies will fall that it will take seven months to bury the dead from Gog's armies (39:11–16), but in the interim God invites the wild creatures to eat their fill of dead bodies (39:17–20). What John sees here is an angel "standing on the sun,"[72] summoning "all the birds flying high in the sky" to assemble for a great feast (v. 17). The command to "gather" (συνάχθητε) is taken from Ezekiel 39:17, but the phrase "the great supper of God" (τὸ δεῖπνον τὸ μέγα τοῦ θεοῦ) is likely to be a gruesome parody of

---

68. For the sense of the string of genitives in v. 15d ("of the wine of the fury of the wrath of God"), see the explanation of a similar phrase in a note on 16:19. The same note mentions the sense of these two words for "anger, fury" and "wrath."

69. See note at 17:14 for the OT background of the title "King of kings and Lord of lords."

70. This phrase is literally "on the robe and on his thigh" (ἐπὶ τὸ ἱμάτιον καὶ ἐπὶ τὸν μηρὸν αὐτοῦ), but the "and" is likely to be explanatory rather than additive. See Aune, *Revelation 17–22*, 1044.

71. This pattern of invasion and gruesome results as seen in Ezek 38–39 will be repeated in the events of Rev 20:7–10. This is not the same invasion recapitulated in two places, but different attacks that mirror the same pattern. See McNicol, *Conversion*, 67, and discussion of recapitulation at 20:7–10. The typological nature of this image is shown by its use also to describe the defeat of Egypt's Pharaoh (Ezek 29:2–5; 32:2–8).

72. The angel's location "on the sun" probably reflects not a mythical or religious significance but simply a prominent vantage point for an announcement to birds flying "high in the sky" (see note on this expression at 8:13).

the messianic banquet that the blessed will enjoy (cf. Rev 19:9).[73]

Instead of rich foods and wine at the messianic banquet, this feast for the carrion birds of the world will consist of the slain bodies of the vast armies mustered by the beast (19:19; cf. 13:4; 16:14; 17:14) to fight against the Lord and his Messiah, and none will be spared from the least to the greatest of them (v. 18). In solemn and gruesome repetition, the angel announces the purpose of their gathering ("that," ἵνα; v. 18a). It is for the birds to devour "the flesh"[74] of the corpses of them all, from their leaders (kings and commanders; cf. 6:15) to their seemingly invincible ones (the mighty, the war horses and their riders)—all of them, whatever their status (free and enslaved, small and great; cf. 6:15; 13:16). Such a grotesque "feast" represents the crushing defeat of all these enemies of God as well as the ignominy of dying in a dishonorable, profane cause. Leaving bodies unburied to be eaten as carrion constituted the worst dishonor (cf. 1 Sam 17:44; 2 Kgs 9:36; Ps 79:2; see comments at 11:9).

19:19–21 And I saw the beast and the kings of the earth and their armies gathered to wage war against the one sitting on the horse and against his army. 20 And the beast was captured and with him the false prophet who performed before him the miracles by which he deceived those who had received the mark of the beast and those who worshiped his image. The two were thrown alive into the lake of fire that burns with sulfur. 21 And the rest were killed by the sword that comes out from the mouth of the one sitting on

the horse, and all the birds were gorged with their flesh (Καὶ εἶδον τὸ θηρίον καὶ τοὺς βασιλεῖς τῆς γῆς καὶ τὰ στρατεύματα αὐτῶν συνηγμένα ποιῆσαι τὸν πόλεμον μετὰ τοῦ καθημένου ἐπὶ τοῦ ἵππου καὶ μετὰ τοῦ στρατεύματος αὐτοῦ. 20 καὶ ἐπιάσθη τὸ θηρίον καὶ μετ᾽ αὐτοῦ ὁ ψευδοπροφήτης ὁ ποιήσας τὰ σημεῖα ἐνώπιον αὐτοῦ, ἐν οἷς ἐπλάνησεν τοὺς λαβόντας τὸ χάραγμα τοῦ θηρίου καὶ τοὺς προσκυνοῦντας τῇ εἰκόνι αὐτοῦ· ζῶντες ἐβλήθησαν οἱ δύο εἰς τὴν λίμνην τοῦ πυρὸς τῆς καιομένης ἐν θείῳ. 21 καὶ οἱ λοιποὶ ἀπεκτάνθησαν ἐν τῇ ῥομφαίᾳ τοῦ καθημένου ἐπὶ τοῦ ἵππου τῇ ἐξελθούσῃ ἐκ τοῦ στόματος αὐτοῦ, καὶ πάντα τὰ ὄρνεα ἐχορτάσθησαν ἐκ τῶν σαρκῶν αὐτῶν). What was anticipated in John's second vision in this series (vv. 17–18) is now seen as accomplished[75] in the third vision beginning with "and I saw" (v. 19a). This time John witnesses directly the fate of the forces opposed to Christ, "the beast and the kings of the earth and their armies" (v. 19a). These have figured in several of John's preceding visions (13:1; 17:2; and verses cited below), but in ways that were mostly previews of this climactic scene. Here they are "gathered" for battle against Christ, the warrior Messiah of v. 11, and his heavenly army of v. 14. Such a mustering of the military forces of the earth's kings (under the deceptive influence of the dragon, the beast, and the false prophet) was foreseen already in 16:13–14, and their warfare against the Lamb (and their anticipated defeat at his hands) was described in 17:13–14.[76] This final battle by world forces "gathered" against Jerusalem and her Lord is anticipated also in Zechariah 12:2–10 and 14:2–5, and the re-

---

73. In Ezek 39:17, 19 the invitation is to a great "sacrifice" or sacrificial meal God has "sacrificed" (39:17, 20).

74. The words translated "flesh" are plurals in Greek (σάρκας; "fleshes" or "fleshly parts"; see 17:16; Jas 5:3; cf. Gen 40:19), referring to the material parts of the physical bodies of humans or animals (BDAG 914). Since flesh is a mass

noun (not a count noun) in English, it is more idiomatic to translate these plurals as collective singulars (as all the standard English translations do).

75. Note the shift to aorist narration in vv. 19–21 in comparison with the largely descriptive report given in vv. 11–18.

76. See also preliminary skirmishes in 11:7; 12:17; 13:7.

sult foreseen in Zechariah is what John witnesses in his vision: their swift and complete ruin.[77]

This ruin is narrated in rapid sequence by four aorist verbs in vv. 20–21 that carry the main story,[78] with a few modifying clauses to clarify background details. With no apparent struggle or resistance, the leader of this anti-God coalition, the beast, "was captured" (ἐπιάσθη) and his "false prophet" with him (v. 20a). Several parenthetical clauses then fill in the history of the false prophet's support for the beast: his miracles that deceived people into accepting the beast's "mark" and into worshiping the beast's image (v. 20b–c; see 13:13–17 for comments). What follows swiftly for both of them (the lack of an introductory conjunction in v. 20d reinforces this abrupt sequence) is to be "thrown alive" (ζῶντες ἐβλήθησαν) into the punishment of eternal fire.[79] The image of a "lake of fire" (here and in 20:10, 14–15; 21:8) is not a common one in the Old Testament or ancient Jewish texts, but some possible antecedents can be found (e.g., Isa 30:33; 66:24; cf. Dan 7:10, a river of fire coming out from God's presence; also Sib. Or. 2:286, a fiery river of judgment).[80] The description of the lake "burning with sulfur" (τῆς καιομένης ἐν θείῳ)[81] connects back to the pattern of judgment seen at Sodom

and Gomorrah (Gen 19:24; see note at 14:10). But here the pattern is intensified to denote eternal condemnation as in 20:10 and 21:8 (cf. 14:10–11). The savage beast's destruction, foreshadowed in 17:8 and 11, has now been accomplished.

With the two leaders of the world's rebellion having been judged, v. 21 completes the account with the summary defeat of "the rest" (i.e., the earth's kings and their armies, v. 19), recounted with the third aorist-passive verb in the sequence, "were killed" (ἀπεκτάνθησαν).[82] These succumb to the irresistible power of "the sword that comes out from the mouth" of Christ (v. 21a–b; cf. v. 15), the mounted warrior Messiah of v. 11 who rides out to establish his righteous rule (cf. Ps 45:3–7). Their corpses are then left to be consumed by "all the birds" summoned to the scene of this slaughter (vv. 17–18), who eat their fill (they "were gorged," ἐχορτάσθησαν) of the flesh of the fallen.

Three further interpretive points should be taken up regarding vv. 11–21. One is that the heavenly armies that accompany Christ (vv. 14, 19b), including both angels and resurrected humans who come from heaven with him, do not appear to play an active role in this great battle. The picture that emerges (vv. 15, 19–21) is that the all-powerful

---

77. The echoes of Ps 2 can be seen here as well: the resistance of "the kings of the earth" and their alliances "against the Lord and his Messiah" (vv. 1–3); the Messiah will "break them with a rod of iron" and inherit "the ends of the earth as his possession" (vv. 8–9; cf. Rev 19:15).

78. As in vv. 11–16, the victory is recounted rather indirectly since these four verbs are all passive voice, with Christ as the implied but not stated agent of the most important three ("was captured"; "were thrown"; "were killed"; vv. 20–21a).

79. This picture is possibly influenced by Num 16:30–35; Ps 55:15 (violators going down alive into Sheol; cf. also 1 En. 56:8).

80. A relatively close parallel is 1 En. 54:1–5 recounting the judgment of Satan's (Azazel's) armies, who are thrown into a deep valley of fire for leading earth-dwellers astray.

81. The phrase in v. 20d–e, "the lake of fire that burns with sulphur" (τὴν λίμνην τοῦ πυρὸς τῆς καιομένης ἐν θείῳ) exhibits irregular agreement of the Greek adjectival participle:

its gender agrees with "lake" (feminine), while its case agrees with "fire" (genitive). There is a certain logic to this since the participle could easily describe either noun. It is probably another example of the grammatical flexibility of John's idiolect. The suggestion of BDR §§249.2, 423.10 that the article reflects an archaic use as a demonstrative pronoun (τῆς for ταύτης) functioning in a genitive-absolute construction ("while it [the lake] was burning with sulfur") is highly unlikely.

82. Careful attention to the details of this passage shows that the "rest" who were killed after the beast and false prophet are dispatched are the kings and their armies (v. 19). This is not the obliteration of all unbelievers on the entire earth, as some interpreters understand it (e.g., J. Webb Mealy, *After the Thousand Years: Resurrection and Judgment in Revelation 20* [Sheffield: JSOT Press, 1992], 25, 89–92; Kim Riddlebarger, *A Case for Amillenniallism: Understanding the End Times* [Grand Rapids: Baker, 2003], 203–4). See McNicol, *Conversion*, 65–66.

divine warrior summarily defeats all the forces arrayed against them (cf. 2 Thess 2:8) without their joining the battle. There is no warrant here for literal armies of holy warriors mustering to fight the enemies of God.

The second is that this nevertheless appears to be a real battle in the earthly realm between actual military forces in the end times. Even though this portrayal is highly symbolic with metaphors that are clearly not to be read with wooden literalism (e.g., the sword coming from his mouth, forces mounted on horses), it is not a reference to a transcendent, spiritual battle only.[83] There is no convincing evidence that these Old Testament prophetic images have been reborn, reimagined, or "Christianized" by John into something purely spiritual. The symbols picture real earthly events in the political and geographical realms of this world as well as its transcendent, spiritual one (this is not an either/or choice in a universe infused with the God of the Bible). Just as the plagues secured Israel's release from Egypt, and the ancient empire of Babylon was eventually destroyed, and the Lamb was physically slain to provide redemption but

was then resurrected, so this eschatological battle will involve human armies who will be defeated by the return of this world's true "King of kings and Lord of lords."[84] This will ultimately lead to God's complete transformation of heaven and earth (chs. 20–22).

The third point follows on this last statement: as climactic as 19:11–21 seems in comparison to the preceding chapters (i.e., Christ as divine warrior finally comes to earth to defeat the enemies who have waged war against his people), it does not yet constitute the final consummation. It is the penultimate or perhaps antepenultimate stage of God's redemption. Two members of the infernal trinity of chapters 13–19 and their earthly allies have been decisively defeated, and those two have been consigned to judgment, but nothing is said here about the dragon, Satan, who empowered them. His fate is discussed right away in 20:1–3, but the story stretches out a thousand years from there (20:7–10). The King of kings will rule with his redeemed over this earth (20:4–6), but a new heaven and new earth are still to come (chs. 21–22). God's full restoration has not yet been accomplished.

Theology in Application

The Ways of Two Women

This passage comes at a major literary seam in the last part of the book, the dividing line between two sections that contrast two cities and two women, Babylon the great prostitute (17:1–19:10) and the new Jerusalem, the bride of the Lamb (19:11–21:8). The first part of the passage (19:1–10) exploits this connection to contrast the two female images in a kind of cosmic morality play. We see heaven rejoicing over both, but it is a solemn celebration of the downfall of the prostitute (vv. 1–6) followed by exultation over the anticipated marriage feast of the Lamb and his bride (vv. 7–10). To be sure, even the rejoicing over Babylon's fall soon turns away from her to focus

---

83. The spiritualized interpretation can be found in Boring, *Revelation*, 195–200; Hughes, *Revelation*, 203–8; Koester, *Revelation*, 764; Prigent, *Apocalypse*, 546–49.

84. Ladd, *Revelation*, 252–53; McNicol, *Conversion*, 59–61; Thomas, *Revelation 8–22*, 384. See comments at 9:7–9; 11:15; 16:14–16 for further defense of this view.

on the establishment of God's just rule over the earth (vv. 4–6). The crescendo of praise in v. 6 (along with 11:15–17) provides the inspiration for Handel's immortal "Hallelujah Chorus." Its lines reflect overflowing joy at God's coming victory: "For the Lord God Omnipotent reigneth" and "the kingdom of this world is become the kingdom of our Lord and of his Christ, and he shall reign forever and ever."

But the character contrasts between the evil prostitute and the pure bride provide instructive lessons as well. The prostitute, defiant against God and tainted by corruption that infects everything she touches, goes to her deserved judgment. The bride, devoted to her groom, is clothed with fine linen, bright and clean, that signifies her righteous deeds. The two women represent entire communities and characteristic life choices: the world deceived by Satan and opposed to God versus the community of God's people betrothed to Christ and anticipating personal intimacy with him in the new Jerusalem to come. They represent ultimate destinies as well: the smoke of judgment rising up forever (v. 3) versus a joyous marriage banquet of rich provision and communion forever (v. 9; 22:1–5). Morality plays are supposed to dispel our confusion and make ethical choices clear, and this one certainly does that.[85]

We Are on the Winning Side

Most of us have sports memories, both good and bad, that stick with us through life. My favorite recollections of competitive sports revolve around playing with my brothers in an almost grass-free backyard (we made it that way), where most of the neighborhood kids gathered to play whatever was in season. Or playing pickup basketball with friends and students at a nearby gym where you win or sit down and then negotiate "who's got next?" with the others who are waiting to play. In both cases it was strategic to arrange to have the right player or players on your team. If you could manage to get the right guy or gal on your side, you always knew who to get the ball to so that the game was bound to come out right.

In Revelation 19:11–21 we see the ultimate extension of that strategy. The entire experience of the church since Jesus's ascension to heaven has been an eager anticipation of his return to defeat evil in this world once and for all and to redeem his people completely. In Revelation everything since 1:7 ("indeed, he is coming with the clouds, and every eye will see him") has pointed forward to this culminating event. And when the time comes, our King and Lord does not disappoint. He comes trailing heavenly glory as the one who is "faithful and true" (v. 11), "the Word of God" (v. 13), "the King of kings and Lord of lords" (v. 16), and he proves himself worthy

---

85. It should go without saying that this passage is not the place to give heated denunciations of prostitutes or paeans of approval for virtuous brides. Those are important sermon or lesson topics, but other biblical texts will serve better for such messages. It is also important to remember that prostitutes are often the most victimized participants in their trade, and males as well as females have a major role to play in the sin or virtue of both marriage and prostitution. But this passage has a larger lesson in view.

beyond measure of each of those titles. "In righteousness he judges and wages war" (v. 11). He will assert complete sovereignty, ruling "with a rod of iron" and exacting "the fury of the wrath of God the Almighty" (v. 15). The "sharp sword" (v. 15) of his pronouncement of judgment and victory enables him to bring swift and complete ruin on the enemies assembled against him (vv. 19–21). With irresistible power he sets aside all resistance and establishes his righteous rule on earth (chs. 20–22).

This picture of what the end of the game will look like should be constantly on our minds when we are on the ropes or the odds seem hopelessly stacked against us in the contest set before us (1 Cor 9:24–27; Heb 12:1–3). We must exercise endurance and discipline, but the ultimate victory will come not by our skills or effort but by the One who heads our team.

Revelation 20:1–15

Literary Context

This chapter continues the major section of the book that began in chapter 19 (19:11–21:8). The section contains a series of seven visions introduced by "and I saw" (19:11, 17, 19; 20:1, 4, 11; 21:1), the first three of which came in chapter 19.[1] These events intervene between the third and fourth major visions of the book that focus on Babylon's fall (17:1–19:10) and the descent of the new Jerusalem (19:11–21:8), visions clearly set in contrast to each other (Babylon, the beast's great but evil city and great prostitute, versus the Lamb's bride, the holy city, the new Jerusalem). The intervening events tell the story of movement from negative to positive (God's judgment of the one to establish the other in its preliminary and then its final form), a movement that naturally suggests chronological succession of the events described in the visions (see discussion below). Chapter 20 presents three of these visions.

I. Prologue (1:1–8)

II. First Vision: The Exalted Christ and His Messages to the Churches (1:9–3:22)

III. Second Vision: Heavenly Throne Room and Three Judgment Cycles (4:1–16:21)

IV. Third Vision: The Destruction of Babylon the Great (17:1–19:10)

V. Intervening Events: From Babylon to the New Jerusalem (19:11–21:8)

    A. The Heavenly Warrior's Overwhelming Victory (19:11–21)

→   **B. The Millennial Reign and Judgment at the Great White Throne (20:1–15)**

    C. The New Heaven and the New Earth (21:1–8)

---

1. See note on 19:11.

Main Idea

The millennial reign of Christ and his resurrected saints will witness the binding of Satan for a thousand years and at its end his ultimate condemnation following a short-lived final rebellion against Christ's rule (20:1–10). In final preparation for the coming of God's renewed creation, the existing earth and heaven disappear while God judges all the unrighteous dead and condemns them to the lake of fire (20:11–15).

Translation

Revelation 20:1–15

1a	Vision Intro/ Character Entrance	**And I saw an angel coming down from heaven,**
b	Description	having the key to the bottomless pit and a great chain in his hand.
2a	Action/Character Entrance	**And he seized the dragon, the ancient serpent,**
b	Description	who is the devil and Satan,
c	Action	**and he bound him for a thousand years,**
3a	Action	**and he threw him into the bottomless pit and shut it and sealed it over him,**
b	Purpose	so that he might not deceive the nations any longer
c	Time Extent	until the thousand years were completed.
d	Preview of v. 7	**After these things he must be released for a little while.**
4a	Vision Intro	**And I saw thrones,**
b	Character Entrance	**and people sat on them,**
c	Action	**and they were granted authority to judge,**
d	Action	**and I saw the souls of those beheaded because of the testimony of Jesus and because of the word of God and**
e	Description	who did not worship the beast or his image and did not receive the mark on their forehead and on their hand.
f	Action	**And they came to life and reigned with Christ for a thousand years.**

5a	Action	**The rest of the dead did not come to life**
b	Time Extent	until the thousand years were completed.
c	Explanation	**This is the first resurrection.**
6a	Beatitude	**Blessed and holy is the one who has a part in the first resurrection.**
b	Explanation	**Over these the second death has no authority,**
c	Effects	**but they will be priests for God and Christ,**
d		**and they will reign with him for a thousand years.**

7a	Time	And when the thousand years are completed,
b	Actions	**Satan will be released from his imprisonment,**
8a		**and he will go out**
b	Purposes	to deceive the nations in the four corners of the earth,
		Gog and Magog,
c		to gather them for battle,
d	Description of 8b	whose number will be like the sand of the seashore.
9a	Action	And **they came up across the breadth of the earth,**
		and **they surrounded the camp of the saints and**
		the beloved city,
b	Response	and **fire came down from heaven and consumed them.** (2 Kgs 1:10, 12)
10a	Action/Description	And **the devil ...**
		who deceived them
		... was thrown into the lake of fire and sulfur
b	Place	where the beast and
		the false prophet were,
c	Result of 10a	and **they will be tormented**
		day and night
		forever and ever.

11a	Vision Intro/ Character Entrance	And **I saw a great white throne and**
		the one sitting on it,
b	Description	from whose face earth and heaven fled,
c	Result of 11b	and **no place was found for them.**
12a	Character Entrance	And **I saw the dead, great and small,**
b	Description/Place	standing before the throne.
c	Actions	And **books were opened,**
d		and **another book was opened,**
e	Identification	which is the book of life,
f	Actions	and **the dead were judged**
		from the things written in the books,
		according to their works.

Continued on next page.

Continued from previous page.

13a		And **the sea gave back the dead that were in it,**
b		and **Death and Hades gave back the dead that were in them,**
c		and **they were judged each one according to their works.**
14a		And **Death and Hades were thrown into the lake of fire.**
b	Explanation	This is **the second death,**
		the lake of fire.
15a	Premise	And if anyone was not found written in the book of life,
b	Consequence	**he was thrown into the lake of fire.**

Structure

The series of shorter visions that reveal various events leading from the destruction of the great prostitute Babylon (17:1–19:10) to the unveiling of the new Jerusalem, the bride of Christ (21:9–22:9) continue in this chapter. The passage covers three visions that John received, signaled by "and I saw" (20:1, 4, 11). These visions can be clustered into two larger sections regarding their content: the millennial reign of Christ and his followers (vv. 1–10, the first two visions tied together by the temporal motif, "a thousand years"), with thematic subsections as shown below, followed by the judgment at the great white throne (vv. 11–15).

Exegetical Outline

V. Intervening Events: From Babylon to the New Jerusalem (19:11–21:8)

    A. The Heavenly Warrior's Overwhelming Victory (19:11–21)

➡   **B. The Millennial Reign and Judgment at the Great White Throne (20:1–15)**

        1. The Millennial Reign of Christ and His Followers (20:1–10)

            a. The binding of Satan (20:1–3)

            b. The resurrection of Christ's followers and their co-rule with him (20:4–6)

            c. Satan's final rebellion and condemnation (20:7–10)

        2. The Judgment at the Great White Throne (20:11–15)

            a. God on his throne of judgment while the old heaven and earth disappear (20:11)

            b. The ungodly dead are resurrected to face God's condemnation (20:12–13)

            c. Death and Hades are consigned to the fiery lake of condemnation (20:14)

            d. Condemned humans are likewise consigned to the fiery lake (20:15)

Explanation of the Text

20:1–3 And I saw an angel coming down from heaven, having the key to the bottomless pit and a great chain in his hand. 2 And he seized the dragon, the ancient serpent, who is the devil and Satan, and he bound him for a thousand years, 3 and he threw him into the bottomless pit and shut it and sealed it over him, so that he might not deceive the nations any longer until the thousand years were completed. After these things he must be released for a little while (Καὶ εἶδον ἄγγελον καταβαίνοντα ἐκ τοῦ οὐρανοῦ ἔχοντα τὴν κλεῖν τῆς ἀβύσσου καὶ ἅλυσιν μεγάλην ἐπὶ τὴν χεῖρα αὐτοῦ. 2 καὶ ἐκράτησεν τὸν δράκοντα, ὁ ὄφις ὁ ἀρχαῖος, ὅς ἐστιν Διάβολος καὶ ὁ Σατανᾶς, καὶ ἔδησεν αὐτὸν χίλια ἔτη 3 καὶ ἔβαλεν αὐτὸν εἰς τὴν ἄβυσσον καὶ ἔκλεισεν καὶ ἐσφράγισεν ἐπάνω αὐτοῦ, ἵνα μὴ πλανήσῃ ἔτι τὰ ἔθνη ἄχρι τελεσθῇ τὰ χίλια ἔτη. μετὰ ταῦτα δεῖ λυθῆναι αὐτὸν μικρὸν χρόνον). John's next vision ("and I saw," v. 1a) immediately picks up the chronological storyline set out in the previous vision (the defeat of the beast and the false prophet together with their armies in 19:19–21) by recounting the capture of "the dragon" or Satan, the third and most powerful member of the evil triad. These three were closely associated in their deception of the world's inhabitants, especially in gathering them to the great battle just portrayed (13:2, 4, 12, 14; 16:13–14; see the link word "deceive" in 19:20; 20:3, 10). Now they are associated

in defeat and judgment, as Satan himself is dealt with by a single angel who comes "from heaven" to earth (where Satan's campaign has just been crushed) for this very purpose (v. 1a; cf. 10:1; 18:1). He brings with him both "the key to the bottomless pit" (a place of unfathomable depth thought of as below the earth; see comments at 9:1) and "a great chain" (v. 1b) to restrain Satan with absolute security. The angel's actions to secure the dragon (who is identified in v. 2a–b by three other titles used earlier in 12:9)[2] are narrated rapidly by five aorist verbs in vv. 2–3a. First he "seized" him and "bound him" (i.e., with the great chain he brought with him).[3] The intended duration of this restraint is said to be for a very long time (v. 2c), "for a thousand years" (χίλια ἔτη, an accusative of time; cf. vv. 3c, 4f, 5b, 6d, 7a).[4]

Three more actions add to this security: "He threw him into the bottomless pit and shut it and sealed it over him" (v. 3a). John's description is repetitive and somewhat redundant, since the first verb alone, or the first and second alone, would have made the point.[5] But he emphasizes that God's intent as executed by his angel was to seal Satan off completely for the time period specified, with absolutely no access to the earth and no chance of escape or release "until the thousand years were completed" (v. 3c).[6] This kind of captivity in an inaccessible, secure place to prevent escape

---

2. For the significance of these titles ("the ancient serpent, who is the devil and Satan"), see comments at 12:9.

3. The image of "binding" or "chaining" evil spirits to prevent or punish their opposition to God's people is a common one in ancient Jewish texts (e.g., 1 En. 10:4, 12; 54:3–4; 2 Bar. 56:13; Jub. 48:15, 18; Sib. Or. 2:289–90; T. Levi 18:12; see also 2 Pet 2:4; Jude 6).

4. For the significance of the thousand years, see comments at v. 3c and vv. 4–6.

5. Beasley-Murray, *Revelation*, 285.

6. This emphatic description makes the standard explanation of this "binding of Satan" by amillennialists quite implausible. Beale, for example, argues that it is "a curtailment of Satan's ability to deceive the nations and to annihilate the church," "a restraint on his deceiving abilities," and power to "mount hostile attack" during the church age but not an absolute restriction (Beale, *Revelation*, 984–88). See Matthew Waymeyer, "The Binding of Satan in Revelation 20," *MSJ* 26 (2015): 19–46; William J. Webb, "Revelation 20: Exegetical Considerations," *Baptist Review of Theology* 4 (1994): 7–39, for further arguments against such claims.

and to shut off even contact or influence on the outside world is also a common motif in ancient Jewish and Christian texts (e.g., Isa 24:21–23; Luke 8:30–33; Rev 9:1–6; cf. 1 En. 10:4–6, 11–13; 18:13–16; 21:1–10; 54:1–5; Jub. 10:5–6). References to binding a spiritual being with a chain and sealing him in a deep pit underground are symbolic rather than woodenly literal descriptions, but what they symbolize is absolute imprisonment and cessation of influence.[7] The specific purpose in this context for sealing Satan off in such a secure place is "so that he might not deceive the nations any longer" (v. 3b) as he had been doing prior to this capture (cf. 12:9; 16:13–14; 19:20).[8]

The binding of Satan in vv. 1–3 is one of the places where interpreters debate the chronological relationship between 19:11–21 and 20:1–10. If Satan's binding to prevent him from deceiving the nations "any longer" (20:1–3) *follows* Christ's second advent when he defeats the nations assembled by Satan to resist him (16:13–14; 19:11–21), then it cannot be a restraint that operated during the symbolic "thousand years" of the church from Christ's first coming (or his cross, resurrection, and exaltation) to his second coming as the amillennial view portrays it. The events of 20:1–10 must be a repetition or recapitulation of visions that occurred earlier to avoid this chronological problem. For the issue of binding Satan, the focus of this question is whether Revelation 20:1–6 is a repeat of the events

of Revelation 12:7–11 in a different symbolic form. This is in fact what some have argued.[9] Beale (followed by Riddlebarger) displays a chart showing seven parallels between the two passages that at first glance seem convincing.[10] But attention to the details shows that the chart "focuses on superficial points of similarity between Rev 12:7–11 and 20:1–6 while ignoring differences between the two passages which make it impossible for them to be describing the same events or time period."[11] For example, 12:9 gives Satan's titles, including "deceiver of the whole world," and 20:2–3 gives his titles and says he is restrained from "deceiving the nations until the thousand years are completed," but the chapters in between record how he deceives the nations and brings them under his authority (13:3–8, 14; 16:14)—difficult to do if the sealing of 20:3 is already in effect from 12:9 on. Also, in 12:9, 12 Satan is "cast down" from heaven to earth and because he has only "a little time" he brings great wrath to the earth, while in 20:2–3 he is "cast down" from earth to the abyss for a thousand years, after which he gains release for "a short time." The catchwords are the same, but their significance is quite different. These parallels do not portray the same events but the beginning of a narrative of conflict and deception in 12:7–10 that leads eventually to the conclusion of the story in 19:11–21 and 20:1–10. It reinforces the chronological sequence of the events symbolized in chapters 19–20.

---

7. It does not require an excessive literalism (as Beale, *Revelation*, 987–88, implies and Riddlebarger, *Case*, 199–200, asserts) to appreciate the absolute restriction on Satan's activities that is represented here. See Waymeyer, "Binding," 24–30.

8. It is a logical error to argue that v. 3b (not deceiving the nations or not leading them to assemble for battle against the Lord) is the only purpose for Satan's binding, enclosing, and sealing. In light of the other texts cited above it is better to see this as the most contextually relevant among various purposes for his imprisonment. The amillennial argument that except for this restriction Satan is free to exert his evil influence on the earth in multiple other ways throughout the "millennium"

(i.e., the church age) is unpersuasive. This certainly does not fit the case of Luke 8 or Rev 9 where being consigned to the bottomless pit entails no effect on humans or involvement in earthly life. See Waymeyer, "Binding," 30–35.

9. Hendriksen, *More Than Conquerors*, 184–96, pushes the parallels back into chs. 11–14, but ch. 12 is the key text.

10. Beale, *Revelation*, 991–95; Riddlebarger, *Case*, 200–202.

11. Waymeyer, "Binding," 43–45. James M. Hamilton, *Revelation: The Spirit Speaks to the Churches* (Wheaton, IL: Crossway, 2012), 251–52, has a convenient chart laying out the *differences* between the passages.

The final clause of v. 3 clarifies the relevance of the time period of the "thousand years" for Satan's imprisonment and previews where the story will go in vv. 7–10. "After these things" (v. 3d) means after the thousand-year period and its momentous events have taken place, as v. 7 indicates. At that point, in God's sovereign plan Satan "must be released" (δεῖ λυθῆναι; cf. "released" in v. 7),[12] but only for a short time, "a little while" (μικρὸν χρόνον). This temporal expression is almost identical to the phrase "a little while longer" (ἔτι χρόνον μικρόν) in 6:11, where the martyrs in heaven are assured that from the time of the fifth seal judgment God's vindication for them is not far away. This final temporal note in 20:3d (as well as v. 7) helps to clarify what the "thousand years" means in vv. 3–6. In the contextual contrast "a little while" is quite brief but not specifically defined, while the "thousand years" is quite long but does not continue forever—it has a limit; it is not symbolic for "eternity." See comments at the end of v. 6 for further discussion.

20:4 And I saw thrones, and people sat on them, and they were granted authority to judge, and I saw the souls of those beheaded because of the testimony of Jesus and because of the word of God and who did not worship the beast or his image and did not receive the mark on their forehead and on their hand. And they came to life and reigned with Christ for a thousand years (Καὶ

εἶδον θρόνους καὶ ἐκάθισαν ἐπ᾽ αὐτούς καὶ κρίμα ἐδόθη αὐτοῖς, καὶ τὰς ψυχὰς τῶν πεπελεκισμένων διὰ τὴν μαρτυρίαν Ἰησοῦ καὶ διὰ τὸν λόγον τοῦ θεοῦ καὶ οἵτινες οὐ προσεκύνησαν τὸ θηρίον οὐδὲ τὴν εἰκόνα αὐτοῦ καὶ οὐκ ἔλαβον τὸ χάραγμα ἐπὶ τὸ μέτωπον καὶ ἐπὶ τὴν χεῖρα αὐτῶν. καὶ ἔζησαν καὶ ἐβασίλευσαν μετὰ τοῦ Χριστοῦ χίλια ἔτη). In a new phase of the same vision about the thousand years during which Satan is imprisoned (vv. 1–3), John receives insight about what else occurs during those thousand years[13] (the resurrection and rule of the faithful in vv. 4–6 and then the rebellion and final judgment of Satan in vv. 7–10). The initial verb "and I saw" has a grammatical connection with two objects ("thrones" in v. 4a and "souls" in v. 4d), each of which is explained further by the clauses that follow them. As is sometimes true of his visionary accounts, John's narration here is impressionistic, not always in logical order, somewhat elliptical, and does not reveal the full picture until the end is reached. It is common for him to mention first thrones (4:2, 4; 20:11) or horses (6:2–8; 9:17; 19:11) or a cloud (14:14) by themselves before portraying those who sit on them, and this is what he does in v. 4a. His description of those seated on these thrones is at first minimal: "And people sat on them, and they were granted authority to judge" (v. 4b–c).[14] In subsequent clauses John comes around again to fill out both who these "people" are (v. 4d–e; Christian martyrs along with other faithful Christians) and

---

12. W. Popkes, "δεῖ," *EDNT* 1:280. See the use of "must" (δεῖ) with temporal expressions in 1:1; 4:1; 22:6; also Matt 24:6; Mark 13:7; Luke 21:9; cf. Dan 2:21. This divine necessity seems to stem from one of the purposes of the millennium (see "In Depth: The Nature and Purpose of the Millennium" located after the comments on 20:5–6): it demonstrates Satan's incorrigible evil and the susceptibility of fallen humanity to his deceptive influence.

13. Note the thematic linkage signaled by the phrase "thousand years" in vv. 2–3 (2x) and then in vv. 4–7 (4x). See comments at 19:11 about the seven important visions (of

which this is the fifth) that make up this larger unit of the book (19:11–21:8).

14. "People sat on them" is the translation of an impersonal plural in Greek (ἐκάθισαν ἐπ᾽ αὐτούς), lit., "they sat on them," where "they" has no definite referent but indicates "some (unidentified) individuals, people" (as in 16:15; 18:14; cf. Luke 16:4). It is highly unlikely that the referents of "they" in the verb ἐκάθισαν are the people included in 19:14 (the humans who were part of Christ's army from heaven) as suggested by Thomas, *Revelation 8–22*, 413–14; MacLeod, *Seven Last Things*, 141–42.

what this "authority to judge" looks like (v. 4f; it means "ruling").[15]

The second object of "I saw" is "the souls of those beheaded" (v. 4d), and the next series of clauses describe them further. The phrase follows an "and" (καί), but no main verb is stated in the Greek text of the new clause. Since "souls" is an accusative, it is natural to take it as a further object of "I saw" (see similar ellipses in 1:20; 4:4; 7:9; 14:14).[16] Here as in 6:9 "souls" (ψυχάς) means dead humans seen in regard to their immaterial, disembodied selves.[17] In this case it is those people who had been killed for their loyalty to Christ. John refers to a particular kind of execution common in the Roman world, decapitation with an axe (πελεκίζω), but this is certain to be simply a representative example of all the martyrdoms of faithful Christians, however they were killed.[18] In another close parallel to 6:9 the reasons for these beheadings are given as "the word of God" and "the testimony" they had, referring to their loyalty to God's message and their obedient witness to Jesus in the face of persecution.

A further description follows in v. 4e, echoing the specific challenges to Christian loyalty mentioned earlier in the book: "Who did not worship the beast or his image" (cf. 13:4, 8, 12–15; 14:9, 11; 16:2) and "did not receive the mark on their forehead and on their hand" (13:16; 14:11; 16:2). What is debated about these further clauses is whether they denote a second group of "souls" (cf. "and those who . . ."; ESV, NASB) or describe the same group in more detail (cf. varied phrasing to this effect in CSB, KJV, NIV, NRSV, REB). The latter is the more likely interpretation of the linking words "and who,"[19] thus characterizing these martyrs by both their allegiance to Jesus and their refusal to honor his adversary. The effect then is to focus on God's vindication of faithful martyrs: they will be resurrected and share in Christ's rule (vv. 4f and v. 6d). John does not comment here on faithful Christians who will not be martyred but survive the intense persecutions and judgments of those final days and join in Christ's reign also, but their share in Christ's rule is pledged in 2:26–28; 3:21; 5:10. Martyrdom is never said to be the universal fate of God's people in those days (cf. 7:3–8; 14:1–5 for one group of survivors) or cited as a condition for co-ruling with Christ (cf. 1 Cor 6:2–3; 2 Tim 2:12; Heb 2:5–9). The martyrs are cited explicitly, but they are representative of the larger group

---

15. Here the simple noun "judgment" (κρίμα) is used as a metonymy for the activity of judging or authority for judging, i.e., ruling (BDAG 567; LN §§37.49, 56.22; M. Rissi, "κρίμα," *EDNT* 2:318–19). The end of the verse shows that "judgment" here denotes "ruling, reigning," as in Matt 19:28; 1 Cor 6:2–3; cf. Wis 3:7–8. See comments at 2:26 on the background of this theme in LXX Dan 7:18, 22, where what the saints receive or are given is the "kingdom" and "dominion" (βασιλεία, βασίλειον). Given this background, it is unlikely that the clause (v. 4c) means "judgment was given in their favor" (i.e., "God has judged them favorably"; Koester, *Revelation*, 771). Koester (also Beale, *Revelation*, 997; Smalley, *Revelation*, 506) rejects the sense "authority to judge" was given "to them" because Rev does not picture saints "passing judgment" on anyone (*Revelation*, 771–72). Yet this ignores a perfectly good sense for "judge, judgment" (κρίνω, κρίμα), well attested elsewhere and perfectly appropriate here. In addition, a dative "to them" with the verb "give" in the NT is almost always a simple indirect object, not a dative of interest or advantage.

16. Aune, *Revelation 17–22*, 1073; Mussies, *Morphology*, 100. Virtually all translations supply the verb "I saw" to smooth out the English (e.g., CSB, ESV, KJV, NASB, NIV, NRSV).

17. See Matt 10:28; Acts 20:10; cf. BDAG 1098.

18. See Aune, *Revelation 17–22*, 1086–88 for various methods of Roman capital punishment. Rev mentions martyrdom as simply "killing" (2:13; 6:11; 11:7; 13:15) or "killing with a sword" (13:10) or "slaying" (6:9; 18:24).

19. The connecting words "and who" (καὶ οἵτινες) are used in 1:7 to describe the same group further ("every eye will see him, even those who pierced him"). The conjunction with the singular pronoun "and anyone who" (καὶ ὅστις) can denote a separate group by implying its own generic antecedent (e.g., Matt 5:41; 23:12), but the plural with or without the "and" seems always to have an antecedent that it describes further (e.g., Rom 11:4).

of faithful people who will reign with him. John focuses on the martyrs in this verse to emphasize that costly fidelity—even to the point of death if necessary—is the pathway to glory and exaltation, a pathway that Christ himself exemplified.

Having described these "souls" who were the second object that "he saw" earlier, John rounds out the verse by adding two further actions (v. 4f) that tie together in reverse order both objects that he saw (the thrones with people sitting on them and the souls of the martyrs). "They came to life" (ἔζησαν), referring to the bodily resurrection of these who for their faith had suffered loss of physical life, and they "reigned with Christ for a thousand years" (ἐβασίλευσαν μετὰ τοῦ Χριστοῦ χίλια ἔτη), defining the character of their thrones and the "judgment" he saw delegated to them earlier. The aorist form of the verb "to live" often carries an ingressive sense as here,[20] and in a context describing humans who have died it clearly denotes resuscitation to physical life (13:14; cf. 2 Kgs 13:21; Mark 5:23) or the restoration of the whole person in bodily resurrection (Rev 2:8; 20:5; see too Ezek 37:10; Rom 14:9; cf. the future of this verb with this sense in Matt 9:18; John 5:25; 11:25). The description of this in v. 5 as "resurrection" (ἀνάστασις) shows that bodily resurrection of those who have died physically is in view here (see further discussion at v. 5).[21] After their resurrection "they reigned with Christ," the future consummation of an expectation of earthly rule mentioned repeatedly in Revelation (1:6; 5:10; 11:15; 20:6; 22:5) and grounded in Daniel 7, the story that John began with in Revelation 1:7 and has alluded to again and again (1:13–14; 2:26; 3:21; 5:11; 11:3, 7, 15; 12:3, 14; 13:1–7; 14:14; 17:12; 19:20).

In one sense Christians already share Christ's rule in heaven, but the full exercise of his rule awaits its establishment also on earth in the final days when all things are subjected to him (1 Cor 15:20–28; Heb 2:5–9) and to his people with him as well (see the verses from Rev just cited).[22] This "already/not yet" motif about Christ's and the saints' rule means that Koester is off the mark when he argues that seeing this "millennial" reign as parallel to the intermediate messianic rule portrayed in Jewish apocalyptic literature (e.g., 4 Ezra 7:26–30) is somehow invalid because in Revelation "the Messiah reigns throughout the process, from his birth and exaltation to God's throne (12:5), to his return as King of kings (19:16), and to his sharing of God's throne in new Jerusalem (22:1, 3). Those redeemed by the Messiah already constitute 'a kingdom' (1:6; 5:9–10)."[23] Related to this is his argument that "many interpreters have assumed that the millennium will be the time when the prophetic texts will be fulfilled," but in his view, "Rev 20:1–6 makes almost no allusion to OT texts."[24] This estimate, while narrowly true, misrepresents the rich Old Testament background of the millennial reign referred to in Revelation 20 and implied by its establishment at this point in the book.[25] It leaves out the larger flow of the surrounding chapters from 10:6–7; 11:15–18; 15:3–4; 16:14–16; 19:6–7; to 19:11–21, in which what has been pictured is the coming "regime change" (not in heaven but on earth),[26] when the nations that rage against the Lord and his Messiah will gather under satanic influence to wage war against the Lord but be summarily defeated by the Messiah. Christ will then restore his people and reign from Jerusalem as the

---

20. Fanning, *Verbal Aspect*, 261–62.

21. See the note on v. 5c about the consistent use of the word "resurrection." Explaining this as spiritual revival or as dying and so achieving the intermediate state in heaven does not fit the context.

22. See comments at 5:10; 11:15.

23. Koester, *Revelation*, 749.

24. Koester, *Revelation*, 749.

25. See the treatment of this point in Helyer, *Witness of Jesus, Paul and John*, 361–64.

26. Koester, *Revelation*, adds these points himself on pp. 750–52, but fails to incorporate them in his statement on p. 749.

prophets and Psalms have predicted (most notably Pss 2, 45; Isa 11, 24, 60–63; Ezek 38–39; Dan 2, 7, 11–12; Zech 12, 14). What Revelation 20:1–10 portrays is the decisive fulfillment of that victory, and it is shortsighted to overlook this.

Part of Koester's point is that some of the theological debate over millennial views gives too large a place to Revelation 20 in the structure of the book itself and its place in the biblical canon, and he is correct to point that out. The millennium is, to be sure, the *penultimate* fulfillment of the biblical story, not the *ultimate* one—the ultimate will come as Koester indicates in Revelation 21–22.[27] But it is simply not true that Old Testament "messianic reign" texts do not fit Revelation 20 but fit Revelation 21–22 instead. They fit both in differing senses. Psalm 72 and Isaiah 11, among other examples, picture the kind of ideal rule from Jerusalem on this existing earth prior to its complete transformation (i.e., the Rev 20 scenario).[28] The appropriateness of God restoring such a rule on the present earth as a vindication of his work in the history and politics of earthly nations is an important motif in the biblical story.[29] The fact that this rule of God and his Messiah will continue in a new way in the new Jerusalem (21:5; 22:1, 3) does not mute this theme.

Similarly myopic and also reductionistic is Bauckham's contention that "the theological point of the millennium is solely to demonstrate the triumph of the martyrs." He adds further that John "has given the image of the millennium a very specific function [i.e., vindication of the martyrs]. But once we take the image literally—as predicting an actual period in the future history of the world—it is impossible to limit it to this function. . . . The millennium becomes incomprehensible once we take the image literally."[30] He advocates a minimalist, symbolic interpretation because John has not given clear answers to all the questions that we might ask about such a millennium. This is a strange approach to interpreting apocalyptic, especially if we resist the answers that the visions do seem to give.

Nevertheless, it is certainly appropriate to pay attention to John's emphasis here in vv. 4–6 on the exalted position given to the martyrs (and all faithful Christians; see comments above on v. 4e). Throughout his book John is at pains to encourage believers in their costly conflict with godless opponents (suffered either through persecutions or temptations to assimilate) that faithful endurance will be worth it in the end. Their present suffering will lead to matchless future blessings (see all the promises to the overcomer in chs. 2–3 among other reassurances in the book). Thus, to see persecuted believers now resurrected and reigning together with Christ reinforces the earlier exhortations. It also captures a creation-restoration theme that runs throughout the Bible and receives an appropriate place here in Revelation 19–22 as part of John's "climax" of prophecy, his pulling together of the entire storyline of the Bible.[31] Here the glory and honor God originally intended for humans to possess in reflecting his image and exercising his dominion over the creation (Gen 1:26–28; 2:15–17; Ps 8:3–8; Rom 8:18–25; Heb 2:5–9) is restored through Christ's redemption. With him they

27. Koester, *Revelation*, 748–50.

28. See Michael J. Vlach, "The Kingdom of God and the Millennium," *MSJ* 23 (2012): 227–40, for a more detailed survey of OT texts that find their fulfillment in a messianic reign like the one Rev 20 portrays, as distinct from what Rev 21–22 presents.

29. Caird, *Revelation*, 251–56; George Eldon Ladd, *A Theology of the New Testament*, rev. ed., ed. Donald A. Hagner (Grand Rapids: Eerdmans, 1993), 680–82.

30. Bauckham, *Theology*, 107–8.

31. J. Richard Middleton, *A New Heaven and a New Earth: Reclaiming Biblical Eschatology* (Grand Rapids: Baker Academic, 2014), 57–73.

rule once again over this earth, God's good creation (see Rev 22:1–5).

20:5–6 The rest of the dead did not come to life until the thousand years were completed. This is the first resurrection. 6 Blessed and holy is the one who has a part in the first resurrection. Over these the second death has no authority, but they will be priests for God and Christ, and they will reign with him for a thousand years (οἱ λοιποὶ τῶν νεκρῶν οὐκ ἔζησαν ἄχρι τελεσθῇ τὰ χίλια ἔτη. αὕτη ἡ ἀνάστασις ἡ πρώτη. 6 μακάριος καὶ ἅγιος ὁ ἔχων μέρος ἐν τῇ ἀναστάσει τῇ πρώτῃ· ἐπὶ τούτων ὁ δεύτερος θάνατος οὐκ ἔχει ἐξουσίαν, ἀλλ᾽ ἔσονται ἱερεῖς τοῦ θεοῦ καὶ τοῦ Χριστοῦ καὶ βασιλεύσουσιν μετ᾽ αὐτοῦ [τὰ] χίλια ἔτη). John's account of this vision-segment (vv. 4–6) continues to fill in the wider sense of what he has seen as he moves into vv. 5–6. The phrase "the rest of the dead" (v. 5a) reinforces the point that all the humans he saw in v. 4a–e (whether one group or two) were physically dead. He saw the souls of people who had died, and their resurrection and thousand-year reign with Christ (v. 4f) will now be contrasted with the remaining group of "dead" humans who were not mentioned in v. 4 and whose fate is different (they will be raised to experience condemnation; vv. 11–15). These will not "come to life" (ἔζησαν as in v. 4f) until the end of the thousand years (v. 5b).

The use of the same aorist verb (ἔζησαν) in vv. 4f and 5a (along with the references in vv. 5c and 6a to "the first resurrection"; ἡ ἀνάστασις ἡ πρώτη) brings us back to one of the interpretive cruxes of Revelation 20, one that has theological

ramifications for larger views of the Bible and its theology. The most natural reading of these references to "coming to life" and "the first resurrection" in a context that speaks of "the dead" and "those beheaded" is to understand them to refer primarily to physical or bodily resurrection of individual humans. Any other connotative meaning that comes along with that (e.g., signifying also vindication of the martyrs or national restoration or cosmic renewal) is secondary to this more basic and transparent sense.[32] Because this is such a crux of interpretation a complicated body of literature has grown up to justify various readings of "came to life" and "first resurrection" that cohere readily (or at least do not directly refute) one's preferred theological approach arrived at mostly by other means. The debates rage over whether "came to life" means the same thing in both places (vv. 4f, 5a): is it a coming to *spiritual* life in the first and a transformed *physical* or bodily life in the second? If it is a "spiritual resurrection" in v. 4f, does it refer to spiritual regeneration or to entrance into the intermediate state by dying and thus passing into the life of heaven? Likewise does "resurrection" in v. 5c and 6a mean a spiritual or physical rising? Does the adjective "first" denote primarily a *sequence* of "resurrections" or a *quality* of "resurrections"? These are complex questions and they are debated interminably with varying degrees of earnest conviction and sometimes vitriol. This commentary is not the place to resolve all these issues.[33] On the face of it, the wording of this passage in its context in the book seems more naturally to bring us to

---

32. See Andrew Chester, "Resurrection and Transformation," in *Auferstehung—Resurrection*, ed. Friedrich Avemarie and Hermann Lichtenberger, WUNT 135 (Tübingen: Mohr Siebeck, 2001), 73: "A literal, physical resurrection" but also "a powerful and evocative symbol for a metaphorical, communal and cosmic resurrection."

33. For the view preferred here, one of the best surveys and evaluation of the complicated literature on these issues is Matthew Waymeyer, "The First Resurrection in Revelation 20," *MSJ* 27 (2016): 3–32. For other views see Beale, *Revelation*, 1004–17; Riddlebarger, *Case*, 216–23; C. Samuel Storms, *Kingdom Come: The Amillennial Alternative* (Fearn, Scotland: Mentor, 2013), 462–66.

the view that physical, bodily resurrection of the dead is in view in both verses and that "first resurrection" refers to the same thing, the raising of God's faithful people from physical death to life in transformed bodies like the one Jesus possesses.[34] One of the problems for views that read these as primarily spiritual "resurrections" of one kind or another is that it requires amazingly complicated explanations of why the wording does not mean what a straightforward reading of it appears to yield.[35] It is true that sometimes a text does not mean what a superficial reading would indicate, but this seems to be an extreme example.

To move on in v. 5, a picture of who will constitute "the rest of the dead" does not come until John adds the further details of vv. 5c–6. The start of this clarification comes with the statement, "this is the first resurrection" (v. 5c).[36] On the face of it, the demonstrative "this" (αὕτη) could refer to both "revivals to life" mentioned in the preceding clauses, one at the start of the millennium (v. 4f) and one that will not occur until its end (v. 5a–b). But the strong contrast between the two groups suggests that "first resurrection" (v. 5c) refers to the one John saw as already accomplished (v. 4f) and not to the one in v. 5a–b. The raising of "the rest of the dead" constitutes a second or later resurrection,

not another phase of the first one. Verse 5, taken as a whole, seems to confirm this.

Exploration of backgrounds to the phrase "the first resurrection" (ἡ ἀνάστασις ἡ πρώτη) can help. While the exact phrase is not found elsewhere in ancient Jewish or Christian literature, some texts do speak of a broad division between a resurrection "of the just" and "of the unjust" (Acts 24:15; cf. Luke 14:14 "of the just" as a group) or a resurrection "to life" and "to judgment" (John 5:29). So here it seems likely that "the first resurrection" denotes the eventual raising of all the faithful (viewed as one group) along with Christ, whose resurrection guarantees theirs (cf. 1 Cor 15:20–22; Phil 3:20–21; 1 Thess 4:13–18; cf. Dan 12:2). In contrast, the raising of "the rest of the dead" at the end of the millennium (v. 5a–b) refers to a resurrection of the unjust for judgment, as vv. 11–15 seem to describe.[37] Seeing the continuation of the story (vv. 11–15) that v. 5a–b explicitly cites shows that "the rest of the dead" does not mean "the rest of the faithful dead," as some interpreters take it.[38]

This binary division of resurrection and judgment finds further support in the beatitude (v. 6) that John pronounces in response to his declaration about the first resurrection. Anyone "who has a part in the first resurrection" will truly be "blessed"

---

34. See Ladd, *Revelation*, 265–66. Regarding the view that the verses speak of dying and so passing into the intermediate state of the soul, N. T. Wright, *The Resurrection of the Son of God*, vol. 3 of *Christian Origins and the Question of God* (Minneapolis: Fortress, 2003), 474, says, "to use the word 'resurrection' to *refer to* death in an attempt to invest it with a new meaning seems to me to strain usage well beyond the breaking point."

35. About Kline's article on these questions (Meredith G. Kline, "The First Resurrection," *WTJ* 37 [1975]: 366–75), Harold W. Hoehner, "Evidence from Revelation 20," in *A Case for Premillennialism*, ed. Donald K. Campbell and Jeffrey L. Townsend (Chicago: Moody, 1992), 255, says, "The complexity of this view makes it suspect." Anyone who reads the treatment of the issues cited in an earlier note from Beale, *Revelation*, 1004–17; Riddlebarger, *Case*, 216–23; or Storms, *Kingdom*,

462–66, may certainly wonder why such convoluted explanations are needed.

36. John's word choice here provides further evidence that bodily resurrection is in view in these verses; the word ἀνάστασις is used in the NT of bodily resurrection 41x out of a total of 42 occurrences; only Luke 2:34 denotes another kind of "rising" (i.e., spiritual good fortune), and there it does not refer to a spiritual rebirth or renewal like some interpreters suggest for "came to life" in v. 4.

37. The label "second resurrection" is not used in vv. 11–15 or elsewhere, but the results of the judgment in that vision are uniformly negative (cf. vv. 14–15).

38. Wright, *Resurrection*, 473–74. Those who see "the rest of the dead" as the unrighteous dead (as preferred here) include Ladd, *Revelation*, 267–68, and Osborne, *Revelation*, 707–8.

by God (μακάριος; the fifth of seven beatitudes in Rev; see comments at 1:3) and will also be seen as "holy" (ἅγιος), set apart to God (v. 6a; see notes at 3:7 and 22:11). The grounds or explanation of this blessedness are expressed in the three clauses that follow (without an explicit conjunction to introduce them; see note at 9:11). The first of these clauses (v. 6b) reinforces the binary division by speaking of the negative counterpart: to share in the first resurrection means that "the second death" (ὁ δεύτερος θάνατος) has no claim over the person. This bifurcation seems to come from the contrast reflected in John 5:29 (resurrection to life vs. resurrection to judgment) and is reinforced in Revelation 20:14 and 21:8 (the unjust will experience the second death, i.e., punishment in the lake of fire).

The further explanation that v. 6b–d brings to what has come before, however, reaches back beyond the phrase "first resurrection" (v. 5c) to the group that is said to experience that resurrection: those who "came to life and reigned with Christ a thousand years" (v. 4f). If we just had v. 4 to go on, we would say that only Christian martyrs will be raised and reign in this way, since the earlier part of the verse mentions only them. But in light of how v. 6b–d rounds things out, we should understand that John focused on the martyrs for a particular purpose (see comments above), but they must be seen as representative of all Christians, not the martyrs only.[39] This comes out clearly because the blessings cited in v. 6b–d are promised earlier in Revelation not to martyrs only but to all Christians. This is true of the exemption from the second death just discussed, since 2:11 pledges this to the "one who overcomes," a victory that is available to all faithful

Christians, not just martyrs. The privilege of being "priests for God and Christ" (v. 6c) is attributed elsewhere to all Christians (1:6; 5:10), as also the destiny of "reigning" with Christ (v. 6d; cf. 5:10; 11:15; 22:5) for the thousand years.

One of the issues that attracts attention all along in vv. 1–7 is the interpretation of the time period, "a thousand years" (χίλια ἔτη), repeated six times in these verses (vv. 2c, 3c, 4f, 5b, 6d, 7a). This is, of course, bound up with the other questions of how this passage relates to the surrounding chapters of the book and to a scheme of God's salvation viewed more broadly. For some the meaning of the "thousand years" can be quickly settled with the declaration that, since it is surrounded on all sides by patently symbolic language (sword coming from the warrior's mouth, spiritual beings bound by a chain, etc.), this time period also must be symbolic rather than in any way literal.[40] Some then assert some version of the "all numbers in Revelation are symbolic" argument, and so this one must be also.[41] Smalley makes this observation too, but when he begins to cite examples of symbolic numbers, the first one mentioned demonstrates his point to be incorrect or at least misstated: the number seven in 1:4.[42] Actually John shows in 1:11 that the number seven has a literal sense (in its denotation), although it has also a connotative value marking completeness or totality (see comments on 1:4; 7:4). The same could be true of the number "thousand" here. Ladd also starts by citing "the obvious symbolic value of numbers" in the book, but when he ventures to give the figurative meaning ("A thousand equals the third power of ten—an

---

39. Just as "those beheaded" (v. 4d) represented all who were martyred by whatever means; cf. comments on v. 4. For the view that vv. 4, 6 imply that all the faithful, not just martyrs, "will reign with Christ" during the millennium, see Koester, *Revelation*, 771.

40. E.g., Smalley, *Revelation*, 502; Riddlebarger, *Case*, 210.
41. E.g., Hughes, *Revelation*, 209.
42. Smalley, *Revelation*, 502.

ideal time"), it is not so obvious that this makes sense in its first-century setting.[43]

When we look at the use of "thousand" in Revelation and in its Jewish background and reflect on the time periods cited for the intermediate messianic reign in early Jewish and Christian literature, the number "thousand" seems more likely to be essentially literal (a round number to be sure, not a precise count, and with connotative value as well as a literal sense). In Revelation we find a "thousand" used with obvious hyperbolic meaning (5:11; 14:20; probably 21:16), but there are other uses that in my judgment are "literal plus connotative" in sense (7:4–8; 11:13; 14:1, 3) and some that are plainly literal (11:3; 12:6). Ancient texts that refer to an intermediate messianic reign (1 En. 91:12–17; 2 Bar. 29:1–30:5; 40:1–4; 4 Ezra 7:26–44; Sib. Or. 3:703–31; 5:414–30; Ascen. Isa. 4:1–18; Barn. 15:1–9) do not usually specify its duration,[44] but the ones that do suggest that a more literal sense

rather than a purely symbolic one is intended. The time period in 4 Ezra 7:28–29 (four hundred years) is of course different than Revelation 20, but the rationale behind it shows the writer thought of the number as literal with connotative value. The four hundred years are God's recompense for the four hundred years spent in Egyptian bondage (Gen 15:13; Ps 90:15).[45] Likewise, the calculation in Barnabas 15 projects the course of world history based on God's seven days of creation, with Psalm 90:4 as the multiplier: "With the Lord a day is as a thousand years." The millennial reign of Christ is the seventh day, a day of rest, followed by an eighth, "the beginning of another world" (Barn. 15:5, 8).[46] Again the sense of "thousand" is essentially literal but with allusive or connotative value. It does not mean an indefinite but lengthy period or denote in itself a period that is ideal or perfect. With this background in view, "a thousand years" does not seem to be purely symbolic after all.

IN DEPTH: The Nature and Purpose of the Millennium

Discussions of "the millennium" in Christian theology and in Revelation 20 are often consumed primarily with competing evidence for the various views (pre-, post-, a-), surveys of support for these views through church history, and debates about how literal the number "one thousand" is in a book like Revelation. It is sometimes added that this is the only biblical text that teaches a "millennium" and that the verses themselves are rather vague in defining what this doctrine

43. Ladd, *Revelation*, 262. Osborne, *Revelation*, 701, opts for a symbolic rather than literal sense and says, "Multiples of ten were commonly used in Jewish writings symbolically, and it is likely that it refers to an indefinite but perfect period of time." But he does not cite examples of Jewish writings that illustrate this "common" usage.

44. See the surveys in Philip Alexander, "Towards a Taxonomy of Jewish Messianisms," in Ashton, *Studies in Apocalyptic*, 57–67; Margaret Barker, *The Revelation of Jesus Christ* (Edinburgh: T&T Clark, 2000), 347–54; Satake, *Offenbarung*, 389–92; Schürer, *History*, 2:529–38; Strecker, *Theology*, 542–43.

45. Schürer, *History*, 2:536–37; Michael E. Stone, *Fourth Ezra: A Commentary on the Book of Fourth Ezra* (Minneapolis: Fortress, 1990), 215.

46. Cf. E. Lohse, "χιλιάς, χίλιοι," *TDNT* 9:470–71. This "cosmic week" of seven or eight thousand years appears also in 2 En. 33:1; b. Sanh. 97a; Irenaeus, *Haer.* 5.28.3; cf. 5.30.4; 5.33.1. Other early patristic writers who held to a future, literal thousand-year reign of Christ were Papias (according to Eusebius, *Hist. eccl.* 3.39.11–12); Justin, *Dial.* 80.4; 81.3–4; and Tertullian, *Marc.* 3.24.3–6; *Res.* 19, 25. See discussion of these texts in Hoehner, "Evidence," 236–38.

entails. While the latter two points are true, some wider perspective is needed. So a few points about the larger significance of John's "millennium" are in order.

First, as in many doctrinal discussions, it is not the presence of a specific defining term that is central (e.g., "election," or "Trinity") but the engagement with a certain concept that makes a passage relevant to the topic. The stage of messianic rule (cf. 20:4, 6) that is presented in 20:1–6 (in the context of 19:11–21:8) has many biblical parallels, including other texts elsewhere in Revelation (e.g., 11:15–18; 15:3–4; 16:14–16; 19:6–7) that shed further light on the nature and purpose of this period without referring to "a thousand years."

Second, regarding the *nature* of the millennium, the evidence of Revelation 20:1–10 together with its biblical parallels shows that it consists of the initial phase of the future earthly reign of Jesus Christ that will be established by his bodily return to earth as "King of kings and Lord of lords" (19:11–21). Christ's return and reign will bring God's rule to earth, in keeping with the church's petition to the Father through the centuries: "May your kingdom come, may your will be done, on earth as it is in heaven" (Matt 6:10). This is a distinct period in the larger messianic kingdom revealed in Scripture from Genesis to Revelation and is fulfilled in stages stretching from Christ's first coming (the kingdom present in the Messiah's presence and activity on earth; Matt 12:28), to his exaltation at God's right hand (his invisible rule already established in heaven but not yet consummated on earth; Acts 2:26; Eph 1:20–23; Heb 2:8–9), to his glorious return from heaven to earth to bring "times of refreshing" and "the restoration of all things that God spoke about through his holy prophets long ago" (Acts 3:19–21).[47]

As Acts 3 suggests, Christ's future coming and earthly reign represent God's faithful fulfillment of Old Testament promises, patterns, and prophecies communicated to his people long ago. God's intent from the beginning was that humans, as the glory of his creation, would share his rule and express his dominion over the world he created (Gen 1:26–28; Ps 8:3–8). Sin and judgment did not derail this divine design that will ultimately be restored by Christ's earthly reign, which he will share with the saints (Dan 7:13–27; Matt 19:28; 1 Cor 6:2–3; Rev 2:26–27; 5:10; 20:4–6). God began this restoration by choosing Abraham as the channel of divine blessing for the wider world, promising him descendants and the land of Canaan as their possession (Gen 12:1–3; 15:18–21; 17:1–8). Later he brought to Israel the royal line of David, to whom he promised loving-kindness and lasting rule from Zion (2 Sam 7:8–29; Pss 72; 89; 132). These promises were

---

47. See Craig A. Blaising, "The Kingdom That Comes with Jesus," in *The Return of Christ: A Premillennial Perspective*, ed. David Lewis Allen and Steve Lemke (Nashville: B&H Academic, 2011), 141–46, on stages of Jesus's kingdom rule.

affirmed through the Old Testament prophets, who warned of God's judgment against Israel and Judah for their unfaithfulness but reassured them of the ultimate defeat of their enemies and their national restoration to peace and security in the land of Israel. The prophecies speak of this restoration against the backdrop of evil nations gathered against the Lord and his Messiah. This warrior Messiah will overwhelmingly defeat them and then reign over the peoples of the world from Jerusalem, as the prophets and Psalms predicted (most notably Pss 2, 45, 89; Isa 11, 24, 60–63; Jer 30–33; Ezek 38–39; Dan 2, 7, 11–12; Zech 12, 14). Revelation 19–20 portray the decisive earthly accomplishment of that victory.

God's kingdom in Jesus Christ brings to fallen humanity the spiritual as well as physical and earthly renewal that is desperately needed. This is why God promised "a new covenant with the house of Israel and the house of Judah" (Jer 31:31), namely, to provide eternal forgiveness of sin, for both the physical offspring of Abraham as well as all non-Israelites who share Abraham's faith in the true God (Rom 4:9–16; Gal 3:10–18). Christ's sacrifice on the cross provided this forgiveness and spiritual restoration (Mark 14:22–25; 1 Cor 11:23–26; Heb 10:11–18), a sacrifice remembered in the Lord's Supper that also anticipates the coming of his messianic kingdom at his return from heaven (Luke 22:18; 1 Cor 11:26). But the whole physical creation groans for deliverance from the corruption to which it was subjected due to human sin (Gen 3:17–19; Jer 12:4, 11; Rom 8:18–25), and the biblical hope is that all things, spiritual and physical, will be made new (Isa 65:17–19; 66:22; Rom 8:21; 2 Pet 3:13; Rev 20–22).[48]

In the course of predicting this glorious future for humanity and for God's creation, the prophets combine two scenarios that are difficult at first glance to hold together: (1) peace, justice, harmony, idyllic conditions, and great fruitfulness of the earth under the rule of the Messiah at Jerusalem, yet the continued presence of wickedness and rebellion that must be judged and of physical death that humans suffer even if they are blessed with greater longevity of life on earth (e.g., Isa 11:1–16; 65:17–25; Zech 14:9–21); and (2) peace and justice on earth with abundant provision for every need and great rejoicing in God's presence under the rule of the Messiah at Jerusalem that includes the end of all warfare, sorrow, and death (Isa 2:2–4; 9:1–7; 25:6–9; Micah 4:1–8). While these two are not clearly differentiated into two separate phases in the Old Testament prophets,[49]

---

48. Both spiritual and physical blessings of the millennium are surveyed by Alva J. McClain in a chapter ("The Blessings of the Prophetic Kingdom") in his classic book, *The Greatness of the Kingdom: An Inductive Study of the Kingdom of God* (Chicago: Moody, 1959), 217–54.

49. A common feature of prophetic perspective is to cluster certain events or features together that come to be understood later as clearly separated in time (e.g., Isa 61:1–2).

they naturally feed into the two stages of the future messianic kingdom on earth that was revealed to John, one prior to the final judgment of the wicked (Rev 20:11–15) and one subsequent to it.[50] The first of these, the millennium or intermediate messianic kingdom (20:1–10), includes a further rebellion of the nations led by Satan after his release (vv. 7–10) that is summarily crushed—all in keeping with the first prophetic scenario given above. The second of these, the eternal state or new heaven and new earth (21:1–22:5), escalates the idyllic conditions of messianic rule to include the complete renewal of creation and the end of all sin, sorrow, and death forever.[51]

This phasing of the earthly messianic kingdom into a preliminary stage (the millennium) and a culminating stage (eternity in the new creation) means that the two periods have some differences as well as some shared features. What will be markedly different is that in the millennial phase evil will still raise its ugly head, although Satan himself will be prevented from having any influence until the very end. The entrance of some redeemed humans into the millennial age who physically survive the horrors of the tribulation period (see comments on 20:4) means that the earth's inhabitants will be a mixture of resurrected martyrs as well as humans in their natural physical state (see Isa 65:20). Over time this will result in the propagation of a population of humans who are subject to messianic rule but perhaps not people of genuine faith and devotion to Christ. This explains—however perverse it will be, given their ideal conditions for life and their physical nearness to Christ—their deception by Satan when he is released and their abortive rebellion against divine rule at the end of the thousand years (20:7–10).

In both stages God and Christ will exert a beneficent, righteous reign over all the nations and regions of the earth, administered through faithful saints who rule with them. God's people will be active and engaged, tending and planting, designing and producing, learning and growing, using their gifts and creativity in the service of God and one another (see comments on 21:24–26). The world and its peoples will enjoy peace and harmony among each other, justice will prevail in human relations, abundant provision will be available for every need, and ideal conditions for life and human prospering will exist. Best

---

50. This sequence shows up also in Jewish apocalyptic literature from John's day (1 En. 91:12–17; 2 Bar. 29:1–30:5; 40:1–4; 4 Ezra 7:26–44; Sib. Or. 3:657–795).

51. See comments on 21:1–2 for discussion of the material character of the new heaven and new earth. Many recent interpreters are happy to argue for the physical, this-worldly character of the new creation and rely on OT passages that refer to Israel's restoration to its land and nations streaming to Jerusalem (e.g., Isa 2, 11, 60, 65) to support this view. But they reject a material, earthly millennium and universalize the land of Israel to denote the world in general rather than seeing the restored earthly Jerusalem as the center of God's new creation (see comments on 21:2). Steven L. James, *New Creation Eschatology and the Land: A Survey of Contemporary Perspectives* (Eugene, OR: Wipf & Stock, 2017), xv–xvi, 95–120, points out the hermeneutical inconsistency of such argumentation.

of all, people will experience the direct earthly presence of Christ and of God. All these benefits will be intensified in the new creation as compared with life in the millennium. God will live with his people, and they with him, in direct communion as a return to and even an advance on Edenic conditions in his restored creation, now cleansed of all evil and corruption. All mourning, sorrow, and death will be abolished forever. Jerusalem will continue to be the focal point of the new creation as the city of the true God (Ps 48:1–2; Ezek 5:5; 38:12; Matt 5:35; cf. 1 En. 26:1; Jub. 8:12), to which the world's nations will come in devoted worship of their great King and Creator.[52]

The *purpose* of the millennium, then, can be discerned from how it is presented in Revelation 20 as well as from these wider connections to the rest of Revelation and to the whole canon of Scripture. Six related points will help to unpack its purpose and theological significance.[53] First, it provides the proper context for God's vindication and reward of the martyrs and other faithful Christians who give unwavering allegiance to him through the dark days that immediately precede Christ's return as king. Other resurrected saints of all ages who accompany Christ from heaven will join in this reward as well (see comment on 19:14). As Irenaeus observes (*Haer.* 5.32.1), it is only right that they should receive their reward in the same creation where they labored and suffered faithfully and so be raised to life and reign with Christ in the same creation where they died in costly service for him. This is the fulfillment of Christ's promise to overcomers in Revelation 2:26–27 and 3:21 as well as the arrival of God's time to "reward [his] servants the prophets and the saints and those who fear [his] name, the small and the great" (11:18).

Second, the millennium confirms the "goodness of creation and of God as creator."[54] Establishing messianic rule over this world of woe even prior to its ultimate re-creation shows that God is unwilling to abandon the universe to the evil that has corrupted it. Instead he will judge those who have defiled it (11:18; 19:2) and restore righteousness and peace in the very real world of history, politics, and economics that was previously under a curse (Gen 3:17; 6:12; Rom 8:20–21).

Closely related is the third purpose for the millennium, to show the "importance of human history in God's salvific plan"[55] and of the divinely intended role

---

52. A helpful survey of life in Christ's future earthly rule (both phases treated together) is John W. Schmitt and J. Carl Laney, "Life in the Messianic Age," in *Messiah's Coming Temple: Ezekiel's Prophetic Vision of the Future Temple*, updated ed. (Grand Rapids: Kregel, 2014), 171–79.

53. Several of these are drawn from Judith L. Kovacs, "The Purpose of the Millennium: Perspectives Ancient and Modern on Revelation 20:1–6," in *New Perspectives on the Book of Revelation*, ed. Adela Yarbro Collins (Leuven: Peeters, 2017), 367–75.

54. Kovacs, "Purpose," 371.

55. Kovacs, "Purpose," 373.

for humans in the administration of his creation (Gen 1:26–28; Ps 8:3–8; Dan 7:22, 27; Heb 2:5–9). Revelation 20 demonstrates a belief "in the importance of the life men lead and the history nations fashion on this earthly scene. . . . [God's] purpose is worked out in history and must be vindicated in history. There must come a time on earth when it is true to say: 'the sovereignty of the world has passed to our God and to his Christ.'"[56] Human life in this world was important to the entire Old Testament from Genesis 1–2 on and formed a central part of the Old Testament prophets' vision of the future. In recording what he saw of the millennium in Revelation 20, John is continuing this expectation and moving it to its climax.

Fourthly, the millennium demonstrates the sovereignty of God and his fidelity to the promises he made to Abraham and David and through them to Israel and the world (Gen 12:1–3; 2 Sam 7:12–16).[57] The Lord's word through Jeremiah (Jer 32:19–26) declares the ironclad certainty of the divine promise to restore Israel to her land of blessing. All the spiritual and earthly forces of evil cannot stand against God's power to defeat them (Rev 19:20–20:3; 20:9–10) and to accomplish his purpose in this world. Israel by God's election is "beloved because of the patriarchs, for the gifts and calling of God are irrevocable" (Rom 11:28–29), and through her the nations will also experience the Messiah's just and prosperous rule on earth.

Fifthly, the perverse and paradoxical rebellion at the end of the thousand years against Christ's idyllic reign (Rev 20:7–10) demonstrates God's righteousness in judging human sin and ultimately removing evil completely from his creation.[58] Such susceptibility by humans to satanic influence under even the best of conditions shows the necessity of the devil's final consignment to judgment (20:10) as well as the exclusion from the new creation of all that is receptive to evil and deception (21:8, 27; 22:15).

Sixthly, the millennium "serves to motivate and direct human action in the present."[59] Both future phases of Christ's earthly rule (millennium and new creation) give disciples hope that human life on this earth in all of its diversity of "tribe and language and people and nation" (Rev 5:9; 7:9; 10:11; 11:9; 13:7; 14:6; 17:15) can be lived in harmony and mutual respect and in care of God's good creation. This requires the saving and restoring grace of God in Christ to deal with human brokenness and then mutual submission on the part of his people under the rule of Christ to align their lives not for self but for God and for

---

56. Caird, *Revelation*, 254.
57. Cf. Irenaeus, *Haer.* 5.34–35.

58. Osborne, *Revelation*, 717.
59. Kovacs, "Purpose," 373.

others.[60] Their future destiny as God's people should embolden disciples to live differently in the present and establish microcosms of God's coming kingdom on earth even now.

20:7–9 And when the thousand years are completed, Satan will be released from his imprisonment, 8 and he will go out to deceive the nations in the four corners of the earth, Gog and Magog, to gather them for battle, whose number will be like the sand of the seashore. 9 And they came up across the breadth of the earth, and they surrounded the camp of the saints and the beloved city, and fire came down from heaven and consumed them (Καὶ ὅταν τελεσθῇ τὰ χίλια ἔτη, λυθήσεται ὁ Σατανᾶς ἐκ τῆς φυλακῆς αὐτοῦ 8 καὶ ἐξελεύσεται πλανῆσαι τὰ ἔθνη τὰ ἐν ταῖς τέσσαρσιν γωνίαις τῆς γῆς, τὸν Γὼγ καὶ Μαγώγ, συναγαγεῖν αὐτοὺς εἰς τὸν πόλεμον, ὧν ὁ ἀριθμὸς αὐτῶν ὡς ἡ ἄμμος τῆς θαλάσσης. 9 καὶ ἀνέβησαν ἐπὶ τὸ πλάτος τῆς γῆς καὶ ἐκύκλευσαν τὴν παρεμβολὴν τῶν ἁγίων καὶ τὴν πόλιν τὴν ἠγαπημένην, καὶ κατέβη πῦρ ἐκ τοῦ οὐρανοῦ καὶ κατέφαγεν αὐτούς). As the irrefutable demonstration of satanic evil and human depravity, the devil's earlier attempt to defeat God's purpose by assembling a vast army to resist Christ's coming (19:19–21) is repeated as John describes in vv. 7–10. Not having reformed in the least as a result of his long captivity in the bottomless pit, Satan mounts another rebellion at the end of the thousand years, and a large number of humans for their part are prepared to enlist in his cause even after experiencing the ideal conditions of rule by Christ on the earth. The thematic and narrative link of this section to the preceding is signaled by (1) the temporal clause, "when the thousand years

are completed" (v. 7a); (2) the repetition of the verb "released" from v. 3, a preview of this event; and (3) the reference to Satan's "imprisonment" (v. 7b) summarizing the story of his capture, binding, and enclosure in the bottomless pit at the start of the thousand years (vv. 2–3). These narrative links to what was just described show that the events of vv. 7–10 are subsequent to those of vv. 4–6 (within the second vision), lending support to the idea that the events of all seven visions from 19:11–21:8 are chronologically sequenced across the visions.

Continuing his evil habits from the earlier episode, Satan will "deceive the nations" (v. 8b) into assembling for battle again (16:13–16; 17:13–14; 19:19; 20:3) to attack God's people centered in Jerusalem. He "will go out" to the nations to gather them from far-flung places, "the four corners of the earth" (v. 8a–b; cf. 7:1; Ezek 7:2; also T. Ash. 7:2), and he will muster an innumerable military force "like the sand of the seashore" (v. 8c–d; a common idiom, used of fearfully large armies in Josh 11:4; Judg 7:12; 1 Sam 13:5). John calls these nations of the earth that will threaten Jerusalem "Gog and Magog" (v. 8b; cf. Ezek 38:2–3), not to identify them as specific kingdoms or peoples but as a reminder of the pattern of attack and deliverance that Israel has seen throughout her history.[61] Just as he cited Balaam (Rev 2:14), Jezebel (2:20), and Sodom and Egypt (11:8) earlier as types of evil that recur over and over, so here "Gog and Magog" are reminders of the prophecy of Ezekiel 38–39. Those chapters

---

60. See the "Theology in Application" section at the end of ch. 21: "What's Wrong with This Picture?"

61. E.g., the pattern of Satan being released after a period of

imprisonment to trouble God's people further is cited in Jub. 48:15–19, an account of "Prince Mastema" and his allies being set free to oppose Israel again at the time of the exodus.

tell the story of an international coalition attacking a nation restored from ruin and brought back from exile across the world and how God will show himself great by defeating their invasion. The events of vv. 7–10 are the ultimate replication of such a pattern.[62]

The description that John gave using future verbs in vv. 7–8 now switches to aorist verbs narrating the invasion and defeat of Satan's rebellion as John witnessed it in his vision (vv. 9–10b).[63] Verse 9a is an indication of the distance Satan's forces had to travel and the goal of their attack: "They came up across the breadth of the earth."[64] In biblical usage one always "goes up" (ἀναβαίνω) to Jerusalem, partly because it was a city set in the hills along the central mountain range of Israel, but mainly because of its status.[65] So their strategic target is clear, "the camp of the saints and the beloved city," a paradoxical reference to Jerusalem as both an armed garrison to be attacked (a barracks or military camp; cf. Acts 21:34; 23:10) and a city of people loved by God (cf. Pss 78:68; 87:2; Jer 11:15; 12:7; also Sir 24:11).[66] This place "they encircled" in preparation for a military attack (cf. 2 Kgs 6:14–15). But as in 19:19–21, this attacking force is dealt a crushing blow directly from God when "fire came down from heaven and consumed them" (v. 9b). This description is taken almost verbatim from the story of Elijah's escape from arrest in 2 Kings 1:10, 12 (cf. Rev 11:5), but it is similar also to Ezekiel 38:22 and 39:6 and more broadly of the stories of God's miraculous defeat of invading

forces in 2 Kings 7:5–15 and Isaiah 37:33–38 (cf. Pss 46:4–7; 48:1–8; 1 En. 56:5–8; 4 Ezra 13:5–15).

20:10 And the devil who deceived them was thrown into the lake of fire and sulfur where the beast and the false prophet were, and they will be tormented day and night forever and ever (καὶ ὁ διάβολος ὁ πλανῶν αὐτοὺς ἐβλήθη εἰς τὴν λίμνην τοῦ πυρὸς καὶ θείου ὅπου καὶ τὸ θηρίον καὶ ὁ ψευδοπροφήτης, καὶ βασανισθήσονται ἡμέρας καὶ νυκτὸς εἰς τοὺς αἰῶνας τῶν αἰώνων). The final verse of this unit (v. 10) caps off the plotlines of John's previous two visions together. The vision of vv. 1–3 told the story of the binding of Satan as the complement to the judgment of his two evil companions in 19:19–21, but that binding was just the prelude to his full judgment recorded here. The vision of vv. 4–10 traces especially the vindication of the saints who were martyred in the onslaught instigated by Satan and his companions. Those martyrs suffered for a brief period but were resurrected to rule with Christ for a thousand years and into eternity, and the torments of their murderers will continue forever also, as recorded here. The devil's armies from the nations of the world are destroyed by fire from heaven (v. 9), so it is only right that he "who deceived them" (v. 10a) will suffer fiery judgment of a more horrible kind. Like his evil comrades, the beast and the false prophet, the devil also is now "thrown into the lake of fire and sulfur" (v. 10a–b; cf. 19:20; 21:8), and his opposition to God's ways will finally be over (cf. T. Mos. 10:1, "then the devil will have an end"). The final part of the verse

---

62. Thomas, *Revelation 8–22*, 423–24; see also note at 19:17 on Gog and Magog as a type.

63. See note on 4:5 for discussion of John's modes of presentation.

64. The reference of "the breadth of the earth" (τὸ πλάτος τῆς γῆς) is not to a specific geographical area or type of terrain ("broad plain") but to the dimension or distance of their journey (BDAG 364, 823; cf. Hab 1:6; LXX Dan 12:2; also Sir 1:3).

65. BDAG 58; Aune, *Revelation 17–22*, 1096; Barker, *Revelation*, 359, notes that this is the verb used of Gog's invasion of Israel in Ezek 38:9, 11, 16 (cf. 1 En. 56:6–7, nations going up to attack Jerusalem).

66. The "camp of the saints" and the "beloved city" both refer to the same entity, the latter picturing God's beloved people as a community centered in a place God chose for them and radiating out from there into the whole world. See comments on 21:2.

solemnly projects into the future to describe their horrible fate, "and they will be tormented" (βασανισθήσονται; cf. 14:10–11; Matt 8:29) and not just occasionally or temporarily (Rev 9:5) but "day and night forever and ever" (v. 10c).[67]

The important conclusion to be drawn from the account of vv. 7–10 is that God's rule on earth established by the victory of his Messiah in 19:11–21 cannot be overturned. Satan's brief and final uprising only proves again his own incorrigible character and the gullibility of humans[68] who fall for his deception while living in a world ruled by Christ himself. But this time he is finished forever and will never again be a threat to the rule of God and his Messiah.[69]

The similarities in the battle accounts in 19:17–21 and 20:7–10 have led some to insist that they depict the same conflict seen from different points of view.[70] It is true that both draw from the imagery of Ezekiel 38–39 and picture the summary defeat of a satanic-led coalition of nations opposed to God. But the differences are just as great as the similarities.[71] There is no mention of "Gog and Magog" in 19:17–21, although 19:17–18 utilize the macabre "supper of God" imagery from Ezekiel 39:4, 17–20. The birds feast on the bodies of military forces killed by the sword of the divine warrior (19:21), and the beast and false prophet are thrown alive into the lake of fire (19:20). Nothing is said of Satan's fate in 19:17–21, but that is the storyline picked up immediately in 20:1–3 as though it were the missing piece. On the other hand, in 20:7–10 "Gog and Magog" are named as the leaders or nations whom Satan assembles, and they move to attack

Jerusalem. The attack is, as in 19:20–21, summarily defeated, but in 20:9 fire from heaven "devours" the armies (no slain carcasses for the "supper of God"). Satan is then thrown into the lake of fire "where the beast and the false prophet were" (20:10). Why not say he was thrown in "with" them if it is the same battle with the same result? All in all, the two accounts are much more likely to be different replications of the Gog and Magog typology at different times, and they reflect a chronological sequence of events (not just of John's reception or recounting of his visions) across the sections of 19:11–21:8.

20:11 And I saw a great white throne and the one sitting on it, from whose face earth and heaven fled, and no place was found for them (Καὶ εἶδον θρόνον μέγαν λευκὸν καὶ τὸν καθήμενον ἐπ᾽ αὐτόν, οὗ ἀπὸ τοῦ προσώπου ἔφυγεν ἡ γῆ καὶ ὁ οὐρανὸς καὶ τόπος οὐχ εὑρέθη αὐτοῖς). With the transition "and I saw" John moves into the next-to-last visionary experience of this larger unit (19:11–21:8). This paragraph gives the all-important transition between Satan's final judgment at the end of the millennium (vv. 7–10) and God's full blessing of his people in renewing all of creation (21:1–8). Before the ultimate renewal occurs, the fate of the ungodly dead who followed Satan's way during their lifetime must be settled, and John records their destiny here in vv. 11–15. Yet equally important is his mention of an all-important detail for the history of the world, the disappearance of the earth as we have known it (v. 11b–c) in preparation for its complete renewal (21:1–8).[72] As in v. 4 (see comments there), John mentions a "throne" first and then describes the person sitting on it (v. 11a). But here it is a ma-

---

67. See comments at 14:10–11 defending the theology of eternal punishment.

68. Osborne, *Revelation*, 717.

69. McNicol, *Conversion*, 67–68.

70. Riddlebarger, *Case*, 204–6.

71. Webb, "Revelation 20," 10–19.

72. This is similar to 4 Ezra 7:113–14, which locates the day of judgment at "the end of this age and the beginning of the immortal age to come, in which corruption has passed away, sinful indulgence has come to an end, unbelief has been cut off, and righteousness has increased and truth has appeared."

jestic and holy throne, "a great white throne."[73] The adjectives "great" and "white" represent the throne's unrivaled authority (cf. Solomon's "great throne," 1 Kgs 10:18) and sterling righteousness (see note on "white" as a symbol of holiness at 7:14). John mentions and describes the throne's occupant but does not identify him explicitly. It is clear that the Lord God is "the one sitting on it," as frequently in Revelation (e.g., 4:2–3; 5:7, 13; 6:16; 7:10),[74] because his awesome presence is such that no created thing can stand before him unchanged (v. 11b).

The statements of v. 11b–c raise interpretive questions that we have faced before (cf. 6:12–14; 16:20). Should we take "earth and heaven fled, and no place was found for them" to be hyperbolic? (As similar phrasing in 6:12–14 and 16:20 seems to be; see comments there.) Or do these words describe in brief and cryptic fashion the cosmic change that John seems to presuppose just a few verses later? (See 21:1b–c: "The first heaven and the first earth passed away and the sea exists no longer.") Because of its placement in the book and its close relation to 21:1, it makes more sense to understand 20:11 to refer to the dissolution and disappearance of all creation in preparation for its renewal. See 21:1–5 for the cosmological and theological significance of this interpretation.

The picture of judgment that this vision presents as it moves on in vv. 12–15 is, like many of John's vision accounts (cf. 20:4–6), somewhat elliptical and not always in logical order, but the pieces fit together once the end is reached. The imagery here is strongly influenced by Daniel 7:9–10 where Daniel beholds "thrones set in place" and the eternal God sitting on "his fiery throne," attended by myriads of angels in his heavenly court with "books" of

judgment opened. In its immediate sense Daniel 7 speaks of God's decree to bring about the earthly defeat and judgment of the "little horn," who represents ultimately the "beast" of Revelation, the human leader of the world's hostility to God in the final days (Rev 13:1–8; 19:19–21).[75] But John adapts this further as a pattern for God's terrifying judgment against all evil, including the dragon or Satan (20:10) as well as those humans who resisted God's will throughout humanity's history.[76] It is important not to read this unthinkingly against the conceptual background of universal judgment drawn from later Christian theology (as pictured, for example, in Michelangelo's "Last Judgment" in the Sistine Chapel or John Wesley's "Great Assize" sermon in March 1758), that is, the dead and living, godly and ungodly of all ages standing to give an account before God. See discussion below.

20:12–13 And I saw the dead, great and small, standing before the throne. And books were opened, and another book was opened, which is the book of life, and the dead were judged from the things written in the books, according to their works. 13 And the sea gave back the dead that were in it, and Death and Hades gave back the dead that were in them, and they were judged each one according to their works (καὶ εἶδον τοὺς νεκρούς, τοὺς μεγάλους καὶ τοὺς μικρούς, ἑστῶτας ἐνώπιον τοῦ θρόνου. καὶ βιβλία ἠνοίχθησαν, καὶ ἄλλο βιβλίον ἠνοίχθη, ὅ ἐστιν τῆς ζωῆς, καὶ ἐκρίθησαν οἱ νεκροὶ ἐκ τῶν γεγραμμένων ἐν τοῖς βιβλίοις κατὰ τὰ ἔργα αὐτῶν. 13 καὶ ἔδωκεν ἡ θάλασσα τοὺς νεκροὺς τοὺς ἐν αὐτῇ καὶ ὁ θάνατος καὶ ὁ ᾅδης ἔδωκαν τοὺς νεκροὺς τοὺς ἐν αὐτοῖς, καὶ ἐκρίθησαν ἕκαστος κατὰ τὰ ἔργα αὐτῶν). When we

---

73. This is the only place in Rev where a throne is described with additional modifiers (besides possessive genitives like "his," "God's," etc.).

74. Some NT texts refer to Christ's role in judgment (e.g.,

22:12; cf. Matt 25:31; John 5:26–27), but this should be seen as a complement to God's role, not a replacement of it.

75. Collins, *Daniel*, 299–304.

76. Bauckham, *Theology*, 106–7; Woods, *Daniel*, 187–92.

read in v. 12 that "the dead, great and small [were] standing before the throne" (v. 12a–b) and there to be "judged" (vv. 12f, 13c), it is evident that this is a scene of God's judgment, not of God's rule alone or of heavenly worship and adoration as in chapters 4–5.[77] And this judgment will be not a matter of earthly punishment and defeat (as in, e.g., Dan 7:9–10; Joel 3:1–3, 9–12),[78] since it concerns the dead (vv. 12a, 12f, 13a–b), not the living, and it is the dead from all strata of humanity ("great and small," v. 12a; cf. 11:18). The presence of these dead humans before God raises several important questions that are not answered explicitly but can be resolved satisfactorily when the whole picture comes into view.

First, the fact that these are "standing before the throne" (v. 12b) by itself could imply existence in a disembodied form (pre-resurrection; like the "souls" of 6:9) or a resurrected form. But the picture of "giving back" the dead (v. 13) tips the scale in favor of resurrected dead. In ancient Jewish thought, handing back the dead from whatever their previous location was (sea, Death, Hades) implies resurrection (see further at v. 13).[79] Second, if these are resurrected dead, do they include the godly and the ungodly (e.g., as in Dan 12:1–2; Matt 25:31–46)? What is the relationship of these dead to the resurrected martyrs (and probably others) in 20:4 and "the rest of the dead" in 20:5? A few of the visions of final judgment that appear in ancient Jewish texts outside the Bible portray an assessment of righteous and unrighteous together with resulting blessing or condemnation to follow (e.g., 2 Bar. 50:1–51:3; T. Benj. 10:6–9; 4 Ezra 7:31–44; Sib. Or. 4:40–49, 179–93).[80] But this scene in Revelation pictures only negative results (the "lake of fire") in vv. 14–15,[81] and the reference to "the second death" in v. 14b forms a likely contrast to "the first resurrection," that is, those whom the second death cannot touch (vv. 5–6). It makes more sense to understand these dead (vv. 12–13) as the unrighteous now raised to face God's evaluation.[82]

The judgment scene in Daniel 7:10 (also Dan 12:1) includes the opening of "books" or scrolls (v. 12c–f) in connection with God's judgment of those standing before him (a common element in ancient Jewish and Christian texts).[83] Here John mentions that "books were opened" and then specifies that "another book was opened" that he identifies as "the book of life" (v. 12d–e). This is one of his distinctive Christian additions to the tradition about records of human life and destiny:

---

77. John uses the phrase "and I saw" to begin v. 12, but it is clear that vv. 12–15 continue the same theme as in v. 11 (note the link word "throne" in both verses); this is a subsection of the same vision.

78. T. Francis Glasson, "The Last Judgment in Rev. 20 and Related Writings," *NTS* (1982): 528–29.

79. Bauckham, *Climax*, 56–70.

80. An older view in Jewish sources is that judgment comes immediately at death and only at a later time will the righteous be resurrected (1 En. 22:13; Pss. Sol. 2:31; 3:11–12; 9:4–5; Josephus, *Ant.* 18.1.3; *J.W.* 2.8.14). For a valuable survey of changing views of judgment in ancient Jewish sources, see Glasson, "Last Judgment," 530–36.

81. There is a place for the "book of life" in this judgment (vv. 12e, 15a) but its role is negative (the absence of one's name leads to second death, v. 15a). See further discussion of v. 12c–f above.

82. For this view, see Jan Lambrecht, "Final Judgments and Ultimate Blessings: The Climactic Visions of Revelation 20,11–21,8," *Bib* 81 (2000): 368–70. The view of Beale, *Revelation*, 1032, and Osborne, *Revelation*, 721–24, that this is the general judgment of righteous and unrighteous depends too much on traditional views of the great assize (see comments on v. 11) and does not give enough weight to the continuity of this scene with v. 10 (assignment of the devil to the lake of fire) and its contrast with vv. 4–6 (resurrection of righteous martyrs at the start of the millennium and implicitly other righteous as part of the first resurrection who escape the second death).

83. E.g., Exod 32:32–33; Ps 69:28; Ezek 13:9; Dan 7:10; 12:1–2; Mal 3:16; 1 En. 47:3; 90:20; 108:3; Jub. 30:19–23; 36:10; *Jos. Asen.* 15:3–4; 1QM 12:2; Luke 10:20; Phil 4:3 contain references to heavenly "books" or records of deeds.

the distinction between "books" (of works) and a "book" (of life). For John the presence of a person's name in "the book of life" (vv. 12e, 15a) represents the Lamb's atoning death for that person (13:8; 21:27) as well as the divine initiative to mark that person out as God's own from before time began (17:8).[84] It functions like "a citizenship list of the righteous in the heavenly Jerusalem,"[85] here functioning negatively in anticipation of the next vision (21:1–8), but viewed positively in 21:27.

The role of the opened "books" (plural; v. 12c) is specified in vv. 12f and 13c. These dead "were judged from the things written in the books," which is clarified further as "according to works" (v. 12f; also v. 13c), that is, according to what a person "had done" (ESV, NIV). These books are records of human deeds, a symbol of God's complete and lasting knowledge of human actions, which ensures that his judgment will be informed and just. The theological point of this (in light of the absence of these dead in "the book of life"; vv. 12d–e, 15) is that apart from God's electing and redeeming love in the Lamb all humans will fall short when God's righteous judgment comes (Acts 17:31; Rom 2:16). The statements in vv. 12f and 13c indicate God's negative verdict pronounced on these dead: they "were judged" or condemned (ἐκρίθησαν in both verses).[86] The description of what their punishment will be as a result of that legal decision will come in v. 15.

In between these decisive statements about the judgment of these dead, John describes their "resurrection to judgment" (John 5:29) as a "giving back" of the dead, referencing both some from "the sea" and some from "Death and Hades" (v. 13a–b).

The concept of "giving back" the dead derives from the idea that God hands deceased humans over in custody to a certain location "for safekeeping," and that place, as Bauckham says, "does not therefore own them, but owes them to God and must return them when he reclaims them at the time of the resurrection. . . . The dead actually belong to God; he entrusts them to Sheol for safekeeping, but retains the right to reclaim them."[87] This can be seen in texts like 1 Enoch 51:1; 4 Ezra 7:32; and 2 Baruch 42:8; 50:2. But why is "the sea" set in distinction from "Death and Hades" as locations for the dead? It seems that "the sea" represents the dead who did not receive a normal burial: those who were lost at sea or in the desert or were eaten by animals or perished in fires. Dead like these were a special concern because they were thought to be out of reach of either blessing or judgment (cf. 1 En. 61:5; Sib. Or. 2:234–38). In contrast, Death and Hades are the standard terms for the realm of the dead, representing those who died in more "normal" ways (see comments on 1:18; 6:8). The distinction does not seem to depend on regarding the sea as a symbol of primordial evil (as perhaps implied by 21:1).[88]

20:14–15 And Death and Hades were thrown into the lake of fire. This is the second death, the lake of fire. 15 And if anyone was not found written in the book of life, he was thrown into the lake of fire (καὶ ὁ θάνατος καὶ ὁ ᾅδης ἐβλήθησαν εἰς τὴν λίμνην τοῦ πυρός. οὗτος ὁ θάνατος ὁ δεύτερός ἐστιν, ἡ λίμνη τοῦ πυρός. 15 καὶ εἴ τις οὐχ εὑρέθη ἐν τῇ βίβλῳ τῆς ζωῆς γεγραμμένος, ἐβλήθη εἰς τὴν λίμνην τοῦ πυρός). Verse 14 represents the final step in God's judgment of the evil forces that have

---

84. See extended comments at 3:5.

85. Baynes, *Heavenly Book Motif*, 164–67, 197 (quotation from p. 167).

86. BDAG 568; LN §56.30.

87. Bauckham, *Climax*, 62. See his full treatment and other supporting ancient texts on pp. 56–70.

88. See Koester, *Revelation*, 780 (who suggests the view taken above); Osborne, *Revelation*, 722 (sea personifies evil); Bauckham, *Climax*, 68 (sea is just a synonym for death or Hades as a realm of the dead).

oppressed humanity over the centuries. At the time of Christ's second coming two members of the infernal trinity, the beast and the false prophet, were consigned to the fiery lake that represents God's condemnation (19:20). Then the third, the devil himself, met that fate at the conclusion of the millennium (20:10). Now, closely following him at the consummation of the old order, Death and Hades (as personifications of humanity's last enemy; cf. 1 Cor 15:26, 54–55; Heb 2:14–15) are consigned to that fate as well (v. 14a). This is a dramatic way of communicating the truth of Isaiah 25:8 (death swallowed up) that will be evoked in Revelation 21:4 (no more death). Life for God's people in the new Jerusalem will face this threat no longer. To reinforce both the glory of its absence for the redeemed and the horror of its reality for the condemned, John concludes the chapter with two more uses of the phrase "the lake of fire." The first of these is in v. 14b, as he explains[89] the sig-

nificance of that fiery lake in contrast to the "first resurrection" (the gift of lasting and blessed life for the redeemed) mentioned back in v. 6. The words of v. 14b, "this is the second death," capture the finality of spiritual death that follows on physical death for those who are condemned.

The final use of "the lake of fire" comes in John's summary in v. 15 of this vision segment (vv. 11–15). It is his reminder, again in a negative way, of the significance of enrollment in the "book of life" mentioned in v. 12e for each individual person. He had spoken in the previous verses primarily of groups of people ("the dead" in vv. 12a, 12f, 13a, 13b), but here (as in v. 13c "each one") he speaks of "anyone [τις] . . . not found written in the book of life" (v. 15a). The fate of such an individual is to be "thrown" (ἐβλήθη) into the fiery lake of condemnation just as the infernal trinity along with Death and Hades were "thrown" into it previously (19:20; 20:10, 14).

Theology in Application

Suffering, Then Glory

Revelation 20:4–6 (along with Rev 21–22 to follow) provides the important positive conclusion to John's repeated encouragement to Christians that the faithful endurance of suffering will be worth it in the end. This is part of a consistent biblical paradigm that human glory does not come from self-exaltation but from submission to God as supreme and from obedience to him despite harsh opposition (1 Sam 2:30; Isa 57:15; Matt 23:12). This is, of course, the pathway that Jesus walked, and he calls his people to follow it as well (Mark 8:34–38; 10:42–45; Phil 2:1–11; Heb 2:9–10). Such followers are the ones who will someday share his rule in the future kingdom: "If we endure, we will also reign with him" (2 Tim 2:12). "They reigned with Christ" (v. 4) is the fulfillment of the earthly rule of God's people mentioned repeatedly in Revelation (1:6; 5:10; 11:15; 20:6; 22:5) and grounded in Daniel 7. It also begins the

---

89. Verse 14b is John's explanatory aside (using present tense) amid the narration of his vision (using aorists). See Mussies, *Morphology*, 333; see too the comments on modes of presentation at 4:5. No conjunction is used (asyndeton) because it is closely related to the surrounding material (Levinsohn, *Discourse Features*, 118).

fulfillment of the glory and honor God originally intended for humans to possess as his image-bearers and dominion-keepers over his good creation (Gen 1:26–28; 2:15–17; Ps 8:3–8; Rom 8:18–25; Heb 2:5–9). It begins here and finds its ultimate consummation in the new heaven and new earth of Revelation 21–22. Paul's opinion is profoundly true, that "our present sufferings are not worthy to be compared with the glory that will be revealed to us" (Rom 8:18). In our present "groaning" and longing for complete redemption for ourselves and for the whole creation, we must live in hope, that eager expectation of what we do not yet possess but can be confident of in Christ. God is refining our character even now through our faithful endurance of suffering (Rom 5:3–5; Jas 1:2–4; 1 Pet 1:3–9), but the best is yet to be.

The Sting of Death

Revelation 20 brings both good news and bad news about "the last enemy, death" (1 Cor 15:26) and the eternal future of every human who has ever lived. On the one hand, we see people who died gruesome physical deaths (e.g., beheadings with an axe), not because of any criminal deeds on their part but because of their witness for Christ and their faithfulness to the true God (v. 4). But this was not their "end," as final and tragic as their killing may have seemed. The enemy death had been defanged for them. The "sting of death" had been removed because of Christ's victory over death, namely, his resurrection, which guarantees the same for all his followers (1 Cor 15:55–57). They appear in v. 4 as resurrected like Christ was, and "they came to life" to join him in his reign over the earth. The second of the seven beatitudes of Revelation speaks directly to this transformation of death (14:13): "Blessed are the dead who die in the Lord." Likewise, the fifth beatitude, occurring right here in 20:6, elucidates this change further: "Blessed and holy is the one who has a part in the first resurrection. Over these the second death has no authority." As explained above, the "first resurrection" includes all those who will share with Christ in a "resurrection to life" (John 5:29), a resurrected, unending life of communion with God and the Lamb (Rev 21–22). While they died physically, they are not subject to the "second death" (v. 6; cf. 2:11; 20:14) that leads to eternal judgment. For Christ's followers, the sting of death is gone, and its enslaving power has been broken forever (Heb 2:14–15).

But vv. 11–14 present the opposite destiny for the multiplied billions of non-Christian dead who will experience the "resurrection of judgment" (John 5:29) to stand before God's great white throne and be "judged" (vv. 12, 13). They will not escape the second death, which is consignment to the "lake of fire" (v. 14). This fate will subject them to eternal punishment and separation from the life of God forever (20:10; cf. 14:9–11; 19:20), the "sting" and power of death that will never be overcome. How can we fathom the depths of this vast human tragedy! As Christians we are usually numbed by it. As Francis Chan has written, it is easy for us to react with theological or defensive musings and "miss the main point. This is real. We're talking about the fate of actual people." He adds:

> Every time my thoughts wander to the future of unbelievers, I quickly brush them aside so they don't ruin my day. But there is a reality here that I can't ignore. Even as the conversations of people around me fill my ears, the truth of Scripture penetrates my heart with sobering statements about their destinies. We can talk about the fate of some hypothetical person, but as I look up and see their smiles, I have to ask myself if I really believe what I have written in this book. Hell is for real. *Am I?*[90]

The Christian response cannot be numbness or, worse, smug relief that we won't face this sting. It must be dedication to God's business instead of our comfort and safety and to sacrificial and humble outreach toward those who need to hear the good news of God's gracious salvation in Christ.

---

90. Francis Chan and Preston Sprinkle, *Erasing Hell: What God Said about Eternity and the Things We've Made Up* (Colorado Springs: David C. Cook, 2011), 104, 107–8. Their book presents a solid biblical and theological defense against recent evangelical trends that dispense with hell. It gives an urgent call to Christian holiness and gospel outreach.

CHAPTER 27

Revelation 21:1–27

Literary Context

This chapter (like chs. 19 and 20) is divided between two closely related major sections of the book. It adds the final segment to the section covering significant eschatological events that intervene between Babylon and the new Jerusalem (19:11–21:8). This section consists of a series of visions introduced by "and I saw" (19:11, 17, 19; 20:1, 4, 11; 21:1), and 21:1–8 is the last vision in that series. The second part of the chapter is the longer passage describing the glorious details of the new Jerusalem (21:9–22:9). These verses open with the features that have signaled the start of each of the four overarching visions of the book (John "carried away in the Spirit" by an angelic agent of revelation; see "Literary Context" in ch. 17 for details). The first part of the chapter (vv. 1–8) is one of the most quoted, most comforting and beloved passages in the entire book. This larger set of passages (21:1–22:9) prior to the epilogue can easily be seen as the climax of the entire book and a summary of the message of Revelation.

Main Idea

God makes all things new in the coming of the new heaven and earth and the new Jerusalem, in which God dwells with his redeemed peoples personally and abolishes all death, grief, weeping, and pain (21:1–8). The Lamb's bride, the glorious new Jerusalem, appears as a city lavishly supplied with abundant provision and security for the vibrant life of God's people in communion with God and with one another (21:9–27).

Translation

Revelation 21:1–27

1a	Action/Vision Introduction	**And I saw a new heaven and a new earth.**
b	Explanation	**For the first heaven and the first earth passed away,**
c		**and the sea exists no longer.**
2a	Action	**And the holy city,**
		the new Jerusalem, I saw
b	Descriptions	**coming down out of heaven from God,**
c		**prepared like a bride adorned for her husband.**
3a	Action	**And** **I heard a loud voice from the throne saying,**
b	Announcement	*"Look, the dwelling of God is with humans*
c		*and he will dwell with them,*
d		*and they will be his peoples*
e		*and God himself will be with them as their God.*
4a		*And he will wipe away every tear from their eyes* (Isa 25:8)
b		*and there will be no more death or*
		mourning or
		crying or
		pain
		any more,
c	Reason	*because the first things passed away."*
5a	Action/Character Entrance	**And the one sitting on the throne said,**
b	Assertion	*"Indeed I am making all things new,"*
c	Action	**and he said,**
d	Command	*"Write this down*
e	Reason	*because these words are faithful and true."*

6a	Action	**And he said to me,**
b	Announcement	*"They have happened!*
c	Basis of 6b	*I am the Alpha and the Omega,*
		the beginning and the end.
d	Promises	*To the one who thirsts I will give*
		freely
		from the spring of the water of life.
7a		*The one who overcomes will inherit these things*
b		*and I will be his God*
c		*and he will be my son.* (2 Sam 7:14)
8a	Warning	*But* *for the* *cowardly and*
		unfaithful and
		vile and
		murderers and
		fornicators and
		sorcerers and
		idolaters and
		all liars,...
		... their part will be
		in the lake
		that burns with *fire and*
		sulfur,
b	Identification	*which is the second death."*
9a	Action/Character Entrance	**And one of the seven angels ...**
b	Description	who had the seven bowls filled with the seven last plagues
c		**... came and spoke with me saying,**
d	Invitation/Preview	*"Come, I will show you the bride,*
		the wife of the Lamb."

Continued on next page.

Continued from previous page.

10a Actions　　　　**And he carried me away**
　　　　　　　　　　　in the Spirit
　　　　　　　　　　　onto a great and high mountain,

　b　　　　　　　**and he showed me the holy city Jerusalem**

　c　Descriptions　　coming down out of heaven from God,
11a　　　　　　　　having the glory of God.
　b　Description/　　Its radiance was　like a most precious gem,
　　　Comparison　　　　　　　　　　　like a transparent jasper stone,

12a　Descriptions　　having a　great and
　　　　　　　　　　　　　　high wall,
　b　　　　　　　　having　　　　　twelve　gates and
　　　　　　　　　　at the gates
　　　　　　　　　　　　　　　　twelve　angels and
　　　　　　　　　　　　　　　　　　names written
　　　　　　　　　　　　　　　　　　　　on the gates,

　c　　Identification　　　　　　　　　　which are the names of the twelve tribes of the sons of Israel,

13　　　　　　　　　on the east　　three gates and
　　　　　　　　　　on the north　　three gates and
　　　　　　　　　　on the south　　three gates and
　　　　　　　　　　on the west　　three gates.

14a　Descriptions　　And the wall of the city had　　　　　twelve foundation stones and
　b　　　　　　　　　　　　on them were the　twelve names
　　　　　　　　　　　　　　　　　　　　of the twelve apostles of
　　　　　　　　　　　　　　　　　　　　　the Lamb.

15a　Action　　**And the one who was speaking with me had a gold measuring rod**
　b　　Purpose　　　　　　　　　to measure　the city and
　　　　　　　　　　　　　　　　　its gates and
　　　　　　　　　　　　　　　　　its wall.

16a　Descriptions　**And the city is laid out in a quadrilateral plan,**
　b　　　　　**and its length is the same as its width.**
　c　Action　　**And he measured the city with the rod at twelve thousand stadia;**
　d　Result　　**its length and width and height are equal.**
17a　Action　　**And he measured its wall at**　　**one hundred and forty-four cubits,**
　　　　　　　　　　　　　　　a human measurement,
　b　　Description　　　　　　which is an angel's.

18a	Descriptions	And the building material of its wall is	jasper,
b		and the city is	pure gold like clear glass.
19a	Description: General	The foundation stones	
		of the city's wall	
		are adorned with	every kind of precious stone.

b	Description:	The first foundation stone is	jasper,
	Specifics	the second	sapphire,
		the third	chalcedony,
		the fourth	emerald,
20		the fifth	sardonyx,
		the sixth	carnelian,
		the seventh	chrysolite,
		the eighth	beryl,
		the ninth	topaz,
		the tenth	chrysoprase,
		the eleventh	hyacinth,
		the twelfth	amethyst.

21a	Descriptions	And the twelve gates are	twelve pearls—
b		each one of the gates was from	a single pearl—
c		and the square of the city was	pure gold like transparent glass.

22a	Action	And I did not see a temple in it,	
b	Explanation	for the Lord God Almighty and	
		the Lamb	are its temple.

23a	Description	And the city has no need for the sun or	
			for the moon to shine in it,
b	Explanations	for the glory of God gave it light,	
c		and its lamp was the Lamb.	
24a	Actions	And the nations will walk in its light,	
b		and the kings of the earth will bring their glory into it,	
25a	Action	and its gates will never close by day,	
b	Explanations	for there will be no night there,	
26		and the glory and honor of the nations will be brought into it.	
27a	Action	And nothing unclean	will ever come into it nor
		anyone who commits what is abominable and false, but	
b	Contrast	only those who are recorded in the Lamb's book of life.	

Structure

As noted above, 21:1–8 provides the final of seven vision accounts (introduced by "and I saw") in a series that bridges between the prostitute Babylon's destruction (17:1–19:10) and the unveiling of the new Jerusalem, the bride of the Lamb (21:9–22:9). Then with clear literary parallels to 1:9–10; 4:1–2; and 17:1–3 John signals the opening of the fourth major vision of the book, the description of the bride of the Lamb, the new Jerusalem (21:9–22:9). After the verses that mark this transition (vv. 9–10), John describes the city's general impressiveness (v. 11), its walls and gates (vv. 12–14), its dimensions (vv. 15–17), its building materials (vv. 18–21), and features of life in the city (vv. 22–27).

Exegetical Outline

V. Intervening Events: From Babylon to the New Jerusalem (19:11–21:8)

    A. The Heavenly Warrior's Overwhelming Victory (19:11–21)

    B. The Millennial Reign and Judgment at the Great White Throne (20:1–15)

➡   **C. The New Heaven and the New Earth (21:1–8)**

        1. The Vision of the New Heaven and Earth and the New Jerusalem (21:1–2)

        2. Heavenly Announcement of God's Presence with His People (21:3–4)

        3. God's Declaration of All Things Made New (21:5–8)

VI. Fourth Vision: The Coming of the New Jerusalem (21:9–22:9)

    A. God's Glorious City, the Lamb's Bride (21:9–27)

        1. John Carried Away in the Spirit to See the Lamb's Bride, the New Jerusalem (21:9–10)

        2. General Impression of the City: Brilliant Glory (21:11)

        3. Its Walls and Gates (21:12–14)

        4. Its Astounding Dimensions (21:15–17)

        5. Its Costly Building Materials (21:18–21)

        6. Its Vibrant Life of Communion with God and between Humans (21:22–27)

Explanation of the Text

21:1–2 And I saw a new heaven and a new earth. For the first heaven and the first earth passed away, and the sea exists no longer. 2 And the holy city, the new Jerusalem, I saw coming down out of heaven from God, prepared like a bride adorned for her husband (Καὶ εἶδον οὐρανὸν καινὸν καὶ γῆν καινήν. ὁ γὰρ πρῶτος οὐρανὸς καὶ ἡ πρώτη γῆ ἀπῆλθαν καὶ ἡ θάλασσα οὐκ ἔστιν ἔτι. 2 καὶ τὴν πόλιν τὴν ἁγίαν Ἰερουσαλὴμ καινὴν εἶδον καταβαίνουσαν ἐκ τοῦ οὐρανοῦ ἀπὸ τοῦ θεοῦ ἡτοιμασμένην ὡς νύμφην κεκοσμημένην τῷ ἀνδρὶ αὐτῆς). John's repeated phrase, "and I saw" (καὶ εἶδον; v. 1a), launches this final vision in the series of climactic scenes that take the world and its peoples from Babylon to the new Jerusalem (19:11–21:8). The vision (vv. 1–8) encompasses two complementary prospects that John sees (vv. 1–2) and then two speakers that he hears (vv. 3–4, 5–8). What John sees in v. 1a is "a new heaven and a new earth," a panorama of God's glorious future for his creation taken from the prophecy of Isaiah (Isa 65:17; 66:22). This is followed immediately by an explanatory clause (v. 1b; introduced by "for," γάρ) showing the contrast with the former creation, "the first heaven and the first earth," as well as its complete replacement by the "new" that has come: they "have passed away" (ἀπῆλθαν). To say that the former heaven and earth "passed away" is a reference to 20:11 where heaven and earth were said to have "fled, and no place was found for them." Wording such as this is a bit ambiguous, but it means at least that their previous condition or mode of existence came to an end in favor of the new.[1] It does not explicitly denote destruction or obliteration, but "passing away" (i.e., going out of existence) may imply that.

A parallel passage, 2 Peter 3:10–13 (that also follows Isa 65–66 closely), does seem to speak of the fiery destruction or dissolution (λύω) of the present heavens and earth (vv. 10–12) prior to the appearance of "new heavens and new earth" (v. 13).[2] But 2 Peter 3 also uses strong language about the world of Noah's day "perishing" or "being destroyed" (ἀπόλλυμι) in the flood, so this could refer to some radical renewal or reforming of the present creation instead of obliteration and starting over afresh. The statement in v. 5b, "I am making all things new," is likewise ambiguous but seems to imply radical renewal instead of destruction and then creation again. Ancient Jewish texts can be cited in support for both sides of this question, and many of them are equally ambiguous (e.g., 1 En. 91:16 and Rev 21:1 have very similar wording).[3] The word "new" (vv. 1a, 2a, 5b; καινός)[4] is sometimes thought to provide the key to whether this will be a "brand new" or "renewed" creation, but individual words normally cannot be expected to carry such a point by themselves—explicit statements or combinations of words are required, and John has simply not given us such explicitness. He does not pay attention to the process by which this "newness" comes but focuses instead on the result: a new, transformed world instead of the old disordered one.[5]

By focusing on the result that John does portray here and how the rest of the book has prepared the way for this change from old to new, we can come to some further understanding of the significance of this new creation. Several points are clear. First, a radical change has come, and the old evil world seen at its worst in the preceding chapters has come to an end. Death, darkness, deprivation, threat, conflict, and rebellion against God are replaced by life, light, provision, security, community, and intimacy with God. There is clear discontinuity between the two creations. Second, at no place is this

---

1. The verb, "pass away" (ἀπέρχομαι), often means simply to go away, leave, or depart to a different location (e.g., Mark 5:20; John 4:8). But it can also refer to a state or condition coming to an end or discontinuing (e.g., leprosy, Luke 5:13; luxurious living, Rev 18:14; distress or judgments, Rev 9:12; 11:14; cf. BDAG 102). The related verb (παρέρχομαι) is used in Matt 5:18; Mark 13:31; Luke 16:17 to assert the lasting validity of divine revelation in comparison to heaven and earth that will "pass away."

2. Gale Z. Heide, "What Is New about the New Heaven and the New Earth? A Theology of Creation from Revelation 21 and 2 Peter 3," *JETS* 40 (1997): 46–55.

3. David Mathewson, *A New Heaven and a New Earth*, JSNTSup 238 (Sheffield: Sheffield Academic Press, 2003), 36, provides a brief list of ancient texts on both sides. Also Adams, *Stars Will Fall*, 96–100; Harry Alan Hahne, *The Corruption and Redemption of Creation: Nature in Romans 8:19–22 and Jewish Apocalyptic Literature*, LNTS 336 (London: T&T Clark, 2006), 153–68.

4. On the meaning and use of the word "new" (καινός), see BDAG 496–97, 669; LN §§58.71; 67.115 (who note that the two Greek words for "new," καινός and νέος, can overlap in sense).

5. Beckwith, *Apocalypse*, 750; Mathewson, *New Heaven*, 38–39.

change grounded in a cosmological dualism that regards physical existence and the material world as evil as opposed to the spiritual or heavenly realm as good. The existing material world is God's good creation despite the ravages caused by the sin of his creatures. This passage shows heaven and earth brought together as the dwelling place of God and his people. And heaven is brought to earth instead of earth being eclipsed and left behind for heaven. Third, signs of continuity with the old as created by God appear in the new creation, however radically it has been reformed. The new Jerusalem bears the same name as the old, and its layout and daily life are pictured in terms similar to the better features of the old. The paradise of Revelation 22:1–3 mirrors the garden where God placed his creatures originally (Gen 1–2). And fourth, however much the new mirrors the old and is continuous with it, it clearly transcends and supersedes the old. It is far better and far more like what the Creator intended for the original creation. In this way it is analogous to the relationship between the mortal body and the resurrected body of Christ and of all who are his. There is unmistakable continuity with the old, but the new is better by far.[6]

In addition to the passing of the former heaven and earth, John specifically declares the fate of the "sea" as well, that "the sea exists no longer" (v. 1c).[7] This certainly signals the end of the sea as a source of evil in the world (cf. 13:1; Dan 7:4–6) and possibly alludes to the absence of any threat of destruction by water as at Noah's time.[8] The potential of the new creation reverting to evil and incurring judgment as the old once did is now completely removed.[9] John's later description pictures other bodies of water in the new creation (springs, rivers), but there is no mention of seas or oceans (cf. 21:6; 22:1).

John reports an additional object that he witnessed in his vision, "the holy city, new Jerusalem" (v. 2a), in this case repeating the verb "I saw" (εἶδον) in the middle of its clause.[10] The repetition of "new" in this verse connects it thematically to the "new heaven and new earth" of v. 1 (also v. 5). In addition, the title "the holy city" shows a clear continuity with the earthly Jerusalem of Israel's past since this was a common way to refer to the place that was the center of the nation's life, political as well as religious.[11] But it is also set off from that earthly city by the attribute "new" as well as by

---

6. Many interpreters articulate themes of continuity as well as discontinuity like these in dealing with the issues of how the new creation relates to the old in Rev 21–22. Some (Adams, *Stars Will Fall*, 237–39, 251, 254–56; Aune, *Revelation 17–22*, 1117; Osborne, *Revelation*, 720–21, 730, 742–43; Thomas, *Revelation 8–22*, 439–40) do this while emphasizing discontinuity (the old is destroyed to give way to a brand-new creation). Others (Bauckham, *Theology*, 47–51; Chester, "Chaos and New Creation," 344–47; Ladd, *Revelation*, 275–77; McNicol, *Conversion*, 71–72; Christopher Rowland, *Christian Origins: An Account of the Setting and Character of the Most Important Messianic Sect of Judaism*, 2nd ed. (London: SPCK, 2002], 296) emphasize continuity (this is a renewal, not a replacement, of God's creation). The latter approach seems more likely in Rev 21 (see also parallels in Rom 8:18–22; Heb 12:22–29). Mathewson, *New Heaven*, 35–39, has a nice balance between the two. See Weinrich, "Oecumenius," 95, and Weinrich, "Andrew of Caesarea," 195, for two of the earliest interpreters, both of whom emphasize continuity between the old and new creation

along the lines of Rom 8 (they cite Rom 8:21).

7. The sea is the third part of creation that John includes elsewhere alongside of heaven and earth (e.g., 5:13; 10:6; cf. 14:7; Exod 20:11; Ps 146:6).

8. Bauckham, *Theology*, 52–53, suggests the latter point.

9. This is the conclusion of Jonathan Moo, "The Sea That Is No More: Rev 21:1 and the Function of Sea Imagery in the Apocalypse of John," *NovT* 51 (2009): 148–67.

10. Since the verb "I saw" is separated from the sentence-opening conjunction "and" (καί) by the object phrase ("the holy city," etc.), this is not quite like John's standard transition "and I saw." However, in context it seems similar to 20:11–12 where "and I saw" appears in two consecutive verses as complementary parts of the same vision.

11. See "holy city," sometimes with "Jerusalem" added and sometimes not, in texts such as Neh 11:1, 18; Isa 48:2; 52:1; also the LXX of Isa 64:9; 66:20; Dan 3:28; Joel 4:17 [ET 3:17]; Tob 13:10.

the description "coming down out of heaven from God" (v. 2b). Both qualifiers were used already in 3:12 where Christ's promise to the overcomer anticipates this blessing to come.

For some interpreters a new Jerusalem coming from heaven (or the "Jerusalem above," Gal 4:26; the "heavenly Jerusalem," Heb 12:22) denotes a spiritual city, a nonmaterial place of eternal, heavenly existence in which the physical, material world is left behind.[12] But for the Jewish-Christian reader of the first century there is ample evidence pointing to a different sense. Ancient Jewish texts speak frequently of a preexistent heavenly counterpart to the earthly Jerusalem, a city that God has founded and built already in heaven.[13] When the time is right, God will reveal that city by bringing it to earth and establishing it here as the center of his restored people Israel, and all the nations of the world will come to it to worship the true God (1 En. 53:6; 90:29; 4 Ezra 7:26; 8:52; 10:27, 39–59; 13:36; 2 Bar. 4:2–7; 59:4). The description "comes down out of heaven" means its establishment on earth, not earth's eclipse in favor of a heavenly, ethereal city.[14]

So the connection of the "new Jerusalem" (v. 2) to the "new heaven and new earth" (v. 1) seems to be a part-to-whole relationship—it will be the center or focal point of the new creation[15] in the same way that the old Jerusalem became the center of the original creation since it was the city of the true God, the Creator (Ps 48:1–2; Ezek 5:5; 38:12; Matt 5:35; cf. 1 En. 26:1; Jub. 8:12).[16] There is no indication that the new Jerusalem is identical to or coextensive with the new heaven and new earth. The fact that it is presented in a separate but related vision indicates that it is associated but distinct (in a part-to-whole relationship). Thus vv. 1–2 provide a summary vision of God's new world to come, which the speeches of vv. 3–8 and the descriptions of vv. 9–27 will expand further.

The final description of the new Jerusalem in v. 2c, "prepared as a bride adorned for her husband," also gives a preview of the glories of that city (21:9–22:5). John introduced this bridal theme previously in 19:7, and he saw its initial fulfillment in the culminating events of Christ's return and intermediate reign on earth (19:11–20:10). He repeats the imagery here because the intimate relationship of Christ (and God) to his people (see comments on 19:7) will continue and be heightened throughout eternity in the new creation centered on the new Jerusalem. The connection of the city and the bride comes up again in vv. 9–10.

21:3–4 And I heard a loud voice from the throne saying, "Look, the dwelling of God is with humans and he will dwell with them, and they will be his peoples and God himself will be with them as their God. 4 And he will wipe away every tear from their eyes and there will be no more death or mourning or crying or pain any more, because the first things passed away" (καὶ ἤκουσα φωνῆς μεγάλης ἐκ τοῦ θρόνου λεγούσης, Ἰδοὺ ἡ σκηνὴ τοῦ

---

12. E.g., Michael Wilcock, *The Message of Revelation* (Downers Grove, IL: InterVarsity Press, 1975), 203, 207.

13. E.g., 4 Ezra 7:26; 10:54; 13:36; 2 Bar. 4:2–7. See Aune, *Revelation 17–22*, 1052–53; William Horbury, "Land, Sanctuary and Worship," in *Early Christian Thought in Its Jewish Context*, ed. John Barclay and John Sweet (Cambridge: Cambridge University Press, 1996), 208–11; Stone, *4 Ezra*, 213–14, 403.

14. Sean M. McDonough, "Revelation: The Climax of Cosmology," in *Cosmology and the New Testament*, ed. Jonathan T. Pennington and Sean M. McDonough (London: T&T Clark, 2008), 179–83, 188; McNicol, *Conversion*, 72; Elke Toenges,

"'See, I Am Making All Things New': New Creation in the Book of Revelation," in *Creation in Jewish and Christian Tradition*, ed. Henning Graf Reventlow and Yair Hoffman (Sheffield: Sheffield Academic Press, 2002), 139–41.

15. Ladd, *Theology of the New Testament*, 682; Toenges, "New Creation," 146–49.

16. This comes out again later in the vision when "the kings of the earth will bring their glory into it . . . and the glory and honor of the nations will be brought into it" (vv. 24, 26). The city itself is not the entirety of the new creation, but it is likely to be the center of it.

θεοῦ μετὰ τῶν ἀνθρώπων, καὶ σκηνώσει μετ᾽ αὐτῶν, καὶ αὐτοὶ λαοὶ αὐτοῦ ἔσονται, καὶ αὐτὸς ὁ θεὸς μετ᾽ αὐτῶν ἔσται [αὐτῶν θεός] 4 καὶ ἐξαλείψει πᾶν δάκρυον ἐκ τῶν ὀφθαλμῶν αὐτῶν, καὶ ὁ θάνατος οὐκ ἔσται ἔτι οὔτε πένθος οὔτε κραυγὴ οὔτε πόνος οὐκ ἔσται ἔτι, [ὅτι] τὰ πρῶτα ἀπῆλθαν). As on many occasions what John sees is accompanied by what he hears in his visionary experience (vv. 3–4, 5–8). The first audition is "a loud voice from the throne" in heaven[17] (v. 3a; cf. 9:13; 16:1, 17; 19:5), which is most likely an angel speaking with God's authority rather than the voice of God himself (see notes at 9:13; 16:1) since God is spoken of in third person ("God's dwelling"). This "loud voice" also calls for careful attention ("look"; see note on 4:1) to what is now presented, that is, the remarkable blessing of God's own presence among his redeemed hu-

manity. For God's "dwelling"[18] to be "with humans" (μετὰ τῶν ἀνθρώπων; v. 3b)[19] is a return to and an advance on the Edenic condition of direct communion with God (Gen 1–2) prior to their hiding from God and expulsion from the garden in Genesis 3. This is reinforced in v. 3c, "and he will dwell with them" (σκηνώσει μετ᾽ αὐτῶν), using a verb form of the same root as in v. 3b (see also 7:15; cf. Zech 2:10–13). The blessing of direct communion with God is shown to have an even more intimate character and basis by the final two declarations of the verse: "They will be his peoples"[20] and "God himself will be with them as their God"[21] (v. 3d–e).

The plural "peoples" (v. 3d) contrasts with Old Testament texts that speak in similar terms but refer to God's *people* (i.e., Israel): Leviticus 26:11–12; Ezekiel 11:20; 37:27; Jeremiah 31:1, 33; Zechariah

---

17. Instead of "from the throne" (ἐκ τοῦ θρόνου) some manuscripts read "from (the) heaven" (ἐκ τοῦ οὐρανοῦ; cf. KJV, NKJV). The reading "throne" has stronger external support (ℵ, A, 94 versus P, 046, and a number of Byzantine and non-Byzantine minuscules) and was likely changed due to the familiar "I heard a voice from heaven" in related verses (e.g., 10:4, 8; 14:2, 13; 18:4).

18. The word "dwelling" (σκηνή) resonates with biblical allusions to God's residence among his people in the wilderness tabernacle or the temple of the OT (Exod 40:34; Lev 26:11–12; 2 Sam 7:2; 1 Chr 6:32; 2 Chr 1:3) despite the paradox of the majestic God living on earth (1 Kgs 8:27). This is projected into the future in some ancient noncanonical texts (e.g., T. Dan 5:12–13; Sib. Or. 3:785–87). The same root "dwell" is used to describe Jesus becoming incarnate as the Word who was God coming to dwell among humans (John 1:1, 14).

19. The phrase "with humans" is the Greek μετὰ τῶν ἀνθρώπων, using a generic article to refer to the class of persons, "with humankind, with people" (BDAG 81). This alludes perhaps to Ps 78:60 that speaks of the opposite situation: God abandoning "the tent he had pitched among humans" at Shiloh due to Israel's sin. Such a generic sense can be expressed by the plural either with or without the article (LXX Ps 77:60 lacks the article), but John's idiomatic way to refer to humankind is the plural articular phrase (cf. 8:11; 14:4). However, a plural generic may or may not refer to "every member in the class"; that depends on the context. See the nonuniversalistic uses in 9:4, 6, 10 (not harming grass or trees but humans who do not have God's seal). This phrase in and of itself cannot be a support for universal salvation as Bauckham, *Climax*, 310–11,

seems to say: "We should take τῶν ἀνθρώπων to mean, not just (some) human beings as opposed to angels or animals, but the human race. It has the universalistic sense which it commonly has in Revelation's usage" (310). Koester, *Revelation*, 805–6, understands him to argue for universal salvation here. But Bauckham's words in *Climax*, 310, probably are intemperate; in his *Theology*, 139–40, he still uses the term "universalism" but adds, "it should not be taken to mean that Revelation predicts the salvation of each and every human being" (139). He cites verses that refer to the unrepentant being excluded from the new Jerusalem (21:8, 27; 22:15).

20. Modern printed Greek texts (NA[28]; UBS[5]; SBLGNT) as well as most recent commentaries prefer the variant "peoples" (λαοί) over the singular "people" (λαός) in 21:3d, although many recent translations still give the rendering "people" (e.g., ESV, KJV, NABR, NASB, NET, NIV, NJB) instead of "peoples" as in CSB, NRSV. The plural has better external support (pl.: ℵ, A, 046, 2050, 2053, 2329; sg.: P, 1006, 1611, 1841, 1854), and echoes of the OT phrase "people of God" in contexts like this make the plural a harder reading, likely to have been corrected by a scribe either consciously or unconsciously.

21. In v. 3e the phrase "as their God" (αὐτῶν θεός) is textually uncertain, but it is the preferred reading. Some form of it is included in many manuscripts (the ones that omit it are: ℵ, 046, and some of the Byzantine minuscules). When it is included, it appears in several different forms, but the reading as printed above shows up in A, 2030, 2050, and 2329. The omission or alteration seems to come from attempts to deal with an awkward existing text rather than additions to a shorter one.

8:8.[22] It is significant that the humans (Rev 21:3b) who make up the new Jerusalem, the bride of the Lamb (vv. 2, 9–10), are viewed not as a "people" but as "peoples," a multiethnic community whose unity and intimate communion with the one true God does not efface their differing national backgrounds even into eternity.[23] In particular this verse does not indicate that gentiles will be incorporated into the one *people* of God, "the true Israel,"[24] nor that the ethnic heritage of Jewish followers of Jesus will become irrelevant to God. Instead, believing Israel will continue to be God's channel of blessing to all the nations of the world as always intended (Gen 12:1–3; Rev 5:9; 7:9). Through Christ the new-covenant community of those who know the true God is expanded to include other nations in addition to Israel (Jer 31:33; Ezek 37:27) without effacing their ethnic diversity. This is symbolized later in the passage by memorials in the new Jerusalem to both the twelve tribes of Israel and the twelve apostles of the Lamb (21:12, 14), as well as the geographical arrangement with Jerusalem as the focal point of a new earth whose redeemed nations stream into the city to honor God and the Lamb (21:22–22:5).

The renewal of intimate relationship with God and the restoration of human life as God always intended it to be lived is brought home to the reader by John's further description of what this renewal will mean in specific terms (v. 4). In some of the best loved, most quoted, most uplifting words in the entire book John declares the significant

changes that will come then compared to humanity's condition through the ages. This starts with the most intimate and tender of his descriptions, "he will wipe away every tear from their eyes" (v. 4a). This note of God's compassionate care for humans in their sorrows is drawn directly from Isaiah 25:8 (a passage about God's rule from Zion over all the nations), a verse John has already cited as a promise to Christian martyrs in Revelation 7:17. Everything that people weep over, whether publicly or alone, will be taken away[25] when God's new creation arrives. Also influenced by Isaiah 25 (vv. 7–8) is the prospect of death's complete destruction, "there will be no more death" (θάνατος; v. 4b). Because sin has been dealt with completely in Christ's death and resurrection, and his own victory over death was the firstfruits of the resurrection of his people (1 Cor 15:20–22), the victory over death as the last enemy will be accomplished forever when God's fulfillment comes (1 Cor 15:24–28; Heb 2:8–9, 14–15). A wider catalog of related woes that plague humans is added to death with a repetition of the "any more" (ἔτι) at the end: "There will be no ... mourning or crying or pain any more" (οὔτε πένθος οὔτε κραυγὴ οὔτε πόνος οὐκ ἔσται ἔτι).[26] This listing of human troubles that are gone forever also mirrors Old Testament prophetic passages about God's coming victory over evil (e.g., Isa 35:10; 51:11; 65:14, 19; Jer 31:16; cf. 4 Ezra 8:52–54; 2 Bar. 73:1–7). The final declaration from the heavenly voice (v. 4c) grounds these glorious changes in the truth that John saw at the start of

---

22. However, even in the OT the term "people" could be used for gentiles who turn to the true God (e.g., 1 Kgs 8:43; Isa 19:24–25; 25:6–7; 55:3–5; Zech 2:11).

23. Saucy, *Case for Progressive Dispensationalism*, 188–90; Smith, *Revelation*, 282, 289; Thomas, *Revelation 8–22*, 444; Willitts, "Bride of Messiah," 247–53.

24. Contra Beale, *Revelation*, 1047; 1070; Smalley, *Revelation*, 538; Ladd, *Presence of the Future*, 246–61.

25. Removal of "tears" is a metonymy of effect for cause: not

just the sadness or the outward sign of sadness but the reasons for it will be taken away.

26. "Mourning" (πένθος) refers to deep grief over death or other serious loss (cf. 18:11, 15, 19; also Gen 50:10; Deut 34:8; 2 Sam 13:37). "Crying" (κραυγή) is loud shouting or wailing, as here, in despair or sadness (cf. Exod 3:7; 2 Sam 22:7; Heb 5:7). "Pain" (πόνος) is hard labor or, as here, severe anguish or physical torment (cf. 16:10–11; see too Exod 2:11; 1 Kg 15:23; Ps 90:10).

this vision: "Because the first things passed away" and are gone forever in favor of God's new heaven and new earth (v. 1).

21:5–6 And the one sitting on the throne said, "Indeed I am making all things new," and he said, "Write this down, because these words are faithful and true." 6 And he said to me, "They have happened! I am the Alpha and the Omega, the beginning and the end. To the one who thirsts I will give freely from the spring of the water of life" (Καὶ εἶπεν ὁ καθήμενος ἐπὶ τῷ θρόνῳ, Ἰδοὺ καινὰ ποιῶ πάντα, καὶ λέγει, Γράψον, ὅτι οὗτοι οἱ λόγοι πιστοὶ καὶ ἀληθινοί εἰσιν. 6 καὶ εἶπέν μοι, Γέγοναν. ἐγώ [εἰμι] τὸ Ἄλφα καὶ τὸ Ὦ, ἡ ἀρχὴ καὶ τὸ τέλος. ἐγὼ τῷ διψῶντι δώσω ἐκ τῆς πηγῆς τοῦ ὕδατος τῆς ζωῆς δωρεάν). After the voice of an angel speaking authoritatively from the heavenly throne room (vv. 3–4), John now records the voice of God himself, "the one sitting on the throne" in heaven, who speaks in two short utterances (v. 5) followed by a longer one (vv. 6–8) that, taken together, bring the whole book to a climax and summarize the message of Revelation. In this long book God in fact speaks directly only here and in 1:8 (and possibly in 16:17, though this is unclear). Here the reference of "the one sitting on the throne" is certainly God himself (cf. 4:2–3; 5:7, 13; 6:16; 7:10; 20:11), and the repeated first-person references show that he is the speaker in vv. 5–7 (and v. 8 should be included since it contrasts with v. 7). God's first declaration is emphatic,[27] "Indeed, I am making all things new" (v. 5b), referring to the renewal of creation that John saw in v. 1. This statement mirrors the Lord's words

in Isaiah 43:19 (also 42:9; 48:6), but "all things" is added here to suit the expansion to "a new heavens and a new earth" (Isa 65:17; 66:22). That God will renew all things is a central part of John's message in Revelation, one that his readers must grasp fully and live out in faithful obedience. This is why God's next statement[28] to John is a command, "Write this down" (γράψον; v. 5d),[29] referring to what has just been said. A further reason for writing is given: "Because these words are faithful and true" (v. 5e). Here the reference of "these words" is likely to be the statement just made ("I am making all things new"), but see 22:6 where the scope includes the whole book, and that is possible here as well.

For a third time in these two verses John records that God spoke to him ("and he said to me," v. 6a), but this time the quoted content is longer, running through to the end of v. 8. In these verses God pronounces his decree about the coming renewal of all things, declares his own character that guarantees its fulfillment, and makes several promises about how the readers should respond to them. When God says, "They have happened" (γέγοναν), he is declaring the reality of the new creation that John has just seen and heard about (vv. 1–4), which God's words in v. 5 described. This is parallel to the anticipatory pronouncement of 16:17 (that God's judgment had come to a conclusion, γέγονεν). From heaven's point of view these things are already accomplished (cf. the perfect tense of γίνομαι, to take place, come to pass), while their actual fulfillment in the earthly sphere is yet to come (note how the future dimension comes to the

---

27. The word "indeed" translates the Greek ἰδού, sometimes rendered "look" or "behold" (CSB, ESV, NASB, NRSV, RSV). For the meaning "indeed" or "I tell you," see note at 2:10.

28. The verb "he said" in v. 5c is a historical present in Greek (λέγει). Its force is to anticipate and highlight the statement that follows the one it introduces (and its reason; v. 5d–e): the declaration "they have happened!" (v. 6a–b). See note on 5:5.

29. The Greek has no object stated with the command, "write" (γράψον). The other occurrences of "write" in Rev include an explicit object clause to be recorded (e.g., 1:11, 19; 14:13; 19:9; also seven occurrences in chs. 2–3). The command by itself is awkward in English, so the words "this down" are added to smooth out the idiom (as in ESV, NIV).

fore in the future verbs of vv. 6d–7). What guarantees the fulfillment in the interim is God's eternal character and sovereign control over the events of earthly time and space: "I am the Alpha and the Omega, the beginning and the end" (v. 6c). These two phrases are complementary since alpha, as the first letter of the Greek alphabet, could also be used as a cardinal or ordinal numeral (i.e., one or first), and so the mention here of alpha and omega could represent the first and last members of a sequence (see discussion at 1:8). This is then quite similar to "the beginning and the end" (here and in 22:13) as well as to "the first and the last" in 1:17 and 22:13 (used of the Lord's control of all things in Isa 44:6; 48:12). God is asserting here that he is the origin and goal of everything, especially regarding the beginning and end of history. He has formed all things, and he moves his creation along toward its divinely intended purpose, as this chapter shows.

Based on his sovereign character, God issues two promises to encourage anyone who reads what John will write (cf. v. 5) to respond to the glorious prospect of the new creation that he will bring about in the future (vv. 6d–7). These are reminiscent of the promises made in the messages to the churches in chapters 2–3.[30] First, for anyone who is spiritually thirsty (v. 6d),[31] God will provide abundant, life-giving refreshment, "the spring of the water of life" (see 7:17; 22:1, 17; cf. Isa 55:1; Jer 2:13; Zech 14:8; John 7:37–38), and it will be given "freely" (without charge, as a gift, δωρεάν; also 22:17; cf. Rom 3:24). The second promise follows in v. 7.

21:7–8 The one who overcomes will inherit these things and I will be his God and he will be my son. 8 But for the cowardly and unfaithful and vile and murderers and fornicators and sorcerers and idolaters and all liars, their part will be in the lake that burns with fire and sulfur, which is the second death" (ὁ νικῶν κληρονομήσει ταῦτα καὶ ἔσομαι αὐτῷ θεὸς καὶ αὐτὸς ἔσται μοι υἱός. 8 τοῖς δὲ δειλοῖς καὶ ἀπίστοις καὶ ἐβδελυγμένοις καὶ φονεῦσιν καὶ πόρνοις καὶ φαρμάκοις καὶ εἰδωλολάτραις καὶ πᾶσιν τοῖς ψευδέσιν τὸ μέρος αὐτῶν ἐν τῇ λίμνῃ τῇ καιομένῃ πυρὶ καὶ θείῳ, ὅ ἐστιν ὁ θάνατος ὁ δεύτερος). Adding another promise based on his ability to accomplish the renewal of all things that John has seen, God speaks about "the one who overcomes" (ὁ νικῶν), the Christian referred to seven times in the messages to the churches (chs. 2–3), who through faith in Christ and obedience to him gains victory in the age-long struggle against all that is opposed to God (see discussion at 2:7). God pledges that this one "will inherit these things" (v. 7a), referring to his future share in the cosmic renewal and victory over death and sorrow described in vv. 1–6. In most of the New Testament what the Christian receives as a son or daughter of God is often described as an "inheritance" freely given, either already or in the future.[32] But this specific theme (using κληρονομέω and related words) does not appear at all in John's Gospel and Epistles, and only here in Revelation. Nevertheless, the wider concept of adoption or becoming members of God's family or people is one shared widely in early Christian teaching and is grounded also in the Old Testament (e.g., the covenant language of Gen 17:7; 2 Sam 7:14; Jer 31:33; Ezek 34:24). Here the promise of inheritance is supported and supplemented by the pledge that follows in v. 7b–c: "I will be his God and he will be my son," taken quite closely

---

30. See "I will give" in 2:7, 17, 26, 28; 3:21; "the one who overcomes" in 2:7, 11, 17, 26; 3:5, 12, 21.

31. "The one who thirsts" (τῷ διψῶντι) is a figure drawn from Isa 49:10 picturing God as a careful shepherd who feeds his needy sheep and leads them by "springs of water" to ensure they have all that is necessary; cf. Rev 7:16; 22:17; see also John 4:14; 7:37–38.

32. J. H. Friedrich, "κληρονομέω," *EDNT* 2:298–99.

from 2 Samuel 7:14.[33] What is promised to the king in David's line is generalized to apply also to those who identify with him in faith and obedience (see the same broader application in Rev 2:26–27; 3:21). In this broader sense the intimate reciprocal relation of God to his "son" or child who is the heir (v. 7)[34] repeats the essence of v. 3: God will dwell with them, and they will be his people, and he will be their God.

After such pledges to the readers to encourage them toward costly perseverance, it would not be right to mention only the positive side (vv. 6d–7) without the negative counterpart (v. 8). In difficult struggles against evil all around, it always seems easier to yield and escape persecution than to live in faith and obedience. But a major focus of the "unveiling" that John has received is to see fully the larger reality of the universe, both now and in the future. The perspective of the present earthly scene is insufficient. So here as elsewhere (v. 27; also 9:20–21; 22:15) God reveals through John the radical division that divine judgment and redemption will finally bring to all humans. Over against God's redeemed who experience his renewal of all creation will be those who resisted him and chose evil instead.[35] These people and their horrifying

eternal fate are described in v. 8, beginning with eight descriptions of characteristic patterns of evil conduct.[36] For such people, their "part"[37] will be "the lake burning with fire and sulfur" (v. 8), the fate of Satan, the beast, and the false prophet (19:20; 20:14–15). The further identification of this as "the second death" (cf. 2:11; 20:6, 14) adds to the finality and tragedy of such a fate. It is to be avoided no matter what suffering or persecution it may cost.

The images used in 21:1–8 as well as in 21:9–22:9 that continue the same themes are replete with allusions to the Old Testament. Turner has a convenient listing of over fifty Old Testament allusions in these verses,[38] and a good general impression of this can be gained by simply scanning the marginal cross references for this passage in the NA[28] Greek text or a good study Bible. This is a good indication of how Revelation as a whole (see comments on the "climax of prophecy" at 10:6–7) and these verses in particular express "the full flowering of the Old Testament eschatological hope."[39] In fact, they represent a rich collection of themes to provide a fitting conclusion to the whole story of the Bible. See further the "Theology in Application" section for chapter 22.

---

33. The pronouns "his" and "my" in v. 7b–c are datives of possession in Greek (αὐτῷ, μοι). They duplicate the form of the Hebrew expression in 2 Sam 7:14 (the preposition -לְ with the verb "to be," showing possession), but this is an accepted idiom in Greek as well (without, however, the classical distinctions from the genitive of possession; see BDF §189).

34. The connection of inheriting (v. 7a) to sonship (v. 7c) is exploited also in Rom 8:17; Gal 4:7.

35. One Greek article is used to unify in some sense the first seven descriptions (three adjectives and four nouns), but this is not a case of the so-called "Granville Sharp rule" or construction. Because these are plurals and because they mix adjectives and nouns together, the rule that Granville Sharp formulated to define when such strings of words attribute all the descriptions to the same person or persons does not apply. See Wallace, *Grammar*, 278–86. The eighth ("all liars") is set off with its own article.

36. Most of these are self-evident sins that are cited elsewhere in Rev. "Cowardly" (δειλός) is related closely to "unfaithful" (ἄπιστος) or unbelieving regarding God's promises when faced with opposition or threat (e.g., Josh 1:9; Deut 1:21; Isa 13:7; Mark 4:40). "Vile" (from βδελύσσομαι) or "detestable" is the trait that results from idolatry (cf. Rev 21:27; a related word occurs in 17:4–5; see BDAG 172). On "sorcerers" (φάρμακος) and "liars" (ψευδής), see comments on 9:21; 14:5; 21:27; and 22:15.

37. The word "part" in v. 8a (μέρος) means a share, what is apportioned out to someone (BDAG 634). In the nearby verses their "part" contrasts with what the overcomer inherits (v. 7a), and in the wider context the word is used of sharing in the first resurrection (20:6) or losing a share in the tree of life and the holy city (22:19). It is used of one's eternal destiny also in Matt 24:51 and Luke 12:46.

38. Turner, "New Jerusalem," 278–80.

39. Turner, "New Jerusalem," 280.

21:9-11 And one of the seven angels who had the seven bowls filled with the seven last plagues came and spoke with me saying, "Come, I will show you the bride, the wife of the Lamb." 10 And he carried me away in the Spirit onto a great and high mountain, and he showed me the holy city Jerusalem coming down out of heaven from God, 11 having the glory of God. Its radiance was like a most precious gem, like a transparent jasper stone (Καὶ ἦλθεν εἷς ἐκ τῶν ἑπτὰ ἀγγέλων τῶν ἐχόντων τὰς ἑπτὰ φιάλας τῶν γεμόντων τῶν ἑπτὰ πληγῶν τῶν ἐσχάτων καὶ ἐλάλησεν μετ' ἐμοῦ λέγων, Δεῦρο, δείξω σοι τὴν νύμφην τὴν γυναῖκα τοῦ ἀρνίου. 10 καὶ ἀπήνεγκέν με ἐν πνεύματι ἐπὶ ὄρος μέγα καὶ ὑψηλόν, καὶ ἔδειξέν μοι τὴν πόλιν τὴν ἁγίαν Ἰερουσαλὴμ καταβαίνουσαν ἐκ τοῦ οὐρανοῦ ἀπὸ τοῦ θεοῦ 11 ἔχουσαν τὴν δόξαν τοῦ θεοῦ, ὁ φωστὴρ αὐτῆς ὅμοιος λίθῳ τιμιωτάτῳ ὡς λίθῳ ἰάσπιδι κρυσταλλίζοντι). This verse signals a major transition in these final chapters of the book. Having briefly mentioned the Lamb's "bride" in 19:7 (and more vaguely in 21:2), John now returns to that topic as he surveys in detail her glorious appearance, although in this section she is viewed through the related figure of "the holy city Jerusalem" (v. 10). As he resumes this theme, John launches the final major section of Revelation, parallel to 17:1–19:10, in which he completes the contrast between the great prostitute representing Babylon, Satan's evil city, and the Lamb's bride rep-

resenting Jerusalem, God's holy city. These sections begin and end in corresponding ways to reinforce the contrast. Here in v. 9a, as in 17:1, the vision is initiated when "one of the seven angels who had the seven bowls . . . came" (exactly the wording from 17:1; cf. 15:1; 16:1).[40] Here John adds that the bowls were "filled with the seven last plagues" (cf. 15:1, 7).[41] Verse 9c continues, "and spoke with me saying, 'Come, I will show you . . .'" (the same wording as in 17:1).[42] After such strong parallels, the contrast that follows is even stronger: instead of showing John the great prostitute's judgment (17:1), here the object is "the bride, the wife of the Lamb" (τὴν νύμφην τὴν γυναῖκα τοῦ ἀρνίου, v. 9d).[43] She was already said to have "prepared herself" for her wedding (19:7), and the new Jerusalem was portrayed as "prepared like a bride adorned for her husband" (21:2). This adornment will be set forth in detail beginning in v. 11.

Just prior to those details, however, John completes the literary parallelism that reinforces the start of this new major section (v. 10a) and reestablishes the alternate image (as in 21:2), the bride as a glorious city prepared by God (v. 10b). "And he carried me away in the Spirit"[44] is again a close parallel to 17:3, with only the destination being different. Instead of "into a desert place" (17:3), here John is taken "onto a great and high mountain" (v. 10a), a phrase reflecting Ezekiel 40:2.[45] From that vantage point the angel was able to reveal to John "the holy

---

40. It is appropriate, though paradoxical, that these angels who poured out God's wrath have a role in the vision of Babylon's judgment as well as in the revelation of the glories of the new Jerusalem, the climax of God's redemption. The full renewal of God's creation and restoration of his intimate fellowship with human beings required the final judgment of the evil that originally ruptured that communion and corrupted that creation.

41. The participle "filled" (γεμόντων) in v. 9b clearly modifies "bowls" (accusative; φιάλας) as in 5:8; 15:7, but here it has been drawn over to agree with the previous noun "angels" (genitive; ἀγγέλων) instead. This is another example of John's

idiolect (greater tolerance for lax agreement when the sense is clear).

42. In Rev the verb "show" (δείκνυμι/δεικνύω) used in vv. 9d, 10b denotes revelation from God (here through his angel). See 1:1; 4:1; 17:1.

43. See comments on 19:7 for the significance of Jesus Christ, the Lamb, having a "bride."

44. See the parallel phrase, "in the Spirit," i.e., a state receptive to revelatory experience, also in 1:10; 4:2.

45. God took Ezekiel to "a very high mountain," from which he glimpsed a glorious restored Jerusalem (Ezek 40–48).

city Jerusalem" (cf. Rev 21:2 that adds "new"; in 11:2 the earthly Jerusalem is called "the holy city," but without the explicit name "Jerusalem"; see note on 21:2). As in 3:12 and 21:2, the city is described as "coming down out of heaven from God," a holy place already existing in heaven that God will in the future establish on earth in his new creation. It will be the vibrant center of a redeemed humanity enjoying eternal communion with God.[46]

The surprising correlation that the angel makes in vv. 9–10 ("the bride, the wife of the Lamb" is "the holy city Jerusalem") shows that what these symbols represent is both a people and a place. Despite the figurative language used in both phrases and throughout the following description, we are not forced to choose between these two symbols. The two ideas of people living in intimacy with the God who loved them and chose them to be his forever (the bride) and living in vibrant community with one another, enjoying God's abundant provision and security (the city, a place), easily cohere. Both figures bring something important to our understanding of the future reality they point to. This does not require an either-or choice.[47]

The mention of the Jerusalem from heaven (v. 10) leads into John's detailed portrayal of various features of the city (21:11–22:5), recounted in generally descriptive mode (see note on 4:5). Verse 11 begins this by presenting the general appearance of the city as something glorious and splendid to behold. Most importantly, it shines with God's glory, an evidence of God's presence among his people

(cf. Isa 58:8; 60:1–3; Ezek 43:2–5). Its "radiance" (φωστήρ) or splendor[48] could be compared with "a most precious gem" or, to cite one such example, "like a transparent jasper stone" (cf. 4:3 where "jasper" is used in attempting to portray God's splendor). The city, with God present within it, is so dazzling that John struggles to describe it.

Before we tackle the details of walls and gates and measurements and priceless building materials that follow (vv. 12–23), this is an opportune place to comment on how to handle the astonishing images that John uses in the coming verses. The brief survey of "hermeneutics of the new Jerusalem" that Turner gives in his essay on this passage has much to offer on this topic.[49] He tries to steer a middle course between what he calls "excessive literalism" on the one hand and "the opposite error of spiritualizing the imagery in a Platonic dualism between matter and spirit" on the other.[50] As Turner points out, the mistake made by "excessive literalism" is to suppose that allowing any symbolic meaning is to deny the realities to which they point (i.e., "literal" equals "real, actual," while figurative equals "only imaginary, nonexistent").[51] But to understand the image of the "Lamb" in 5:6 as symbolic of Christ is not to deny the reality of Jesus or his sacrifice; it actually enhances it. Related to this is that John's vivid pictures are usually "descriptions of the symbols, not of the reality conveyed by the symbols."[52] John gives detailed pictures of what he has seen not because they correspond in a point-by-point way to the reality they represent but because they

---

46. See comments at 21:2 and the picture of a bustling, vibrant urban center for all the nations in vv. 24–27.

47. Robert H. Gundry, "The New Jerusalem: People as Place, Not Place for People," *NovT* 29 (1987): 254–64, argues that the passage symbolizes people only. This is the view of Beale, *Revelation*, 1062–65, also. But see Aune, *Revelation 17–22*, 1122 (implies that it is both); McNicol, *Conversion*, 72 ("not . . . an either/or proposition"; "The new Jerusalem is a revived Jerusalem as a place populated by faithful, renewed people"); and Osborne, *Revelation*, 733.

48. The word "radiance" can be used of a star, a heavenly luminary (cf. Gen 1:14, 16; Dan 12:3; Phil 2:15) or of the brilliant quality of such a heavenly body, its brightness or brilliance (BDAG 1073).

49. Turner, "New Jerusalem," 275–78.

50. Turner, "New Jerusalem," 278.

51. This is the kind of mistake made by people who say, "He literally threw me under the bus," meaning "he really did betray me."

52. Metzger, *Breaking the Code*, 14.

communicate facets of that real entity in powerful and vivid ways.[53]

The opposite extreme is to spiritualize all the symbols into general references to the glories of heaven in the future or of the Christian's personal religious blessings in the present.[54] This misses John's consistent portrayal of God's future intervention in this world's history and politics in order to establish his kingdom on earth in space and time (Rev 20) and then in his new creation (Rev 21–22). Spiritualizing it loses "the earthiness of biblical eschatology."[55] So while much of the picture of the new Jerusalem does not correspond literally to that future reality, it does represent it as life in a city[56] of redeemed and resurrected people, living in direct worshipful communion with God and Christ and engaging in vibrant contact with a wider renewed world while enjoying his good creation. Working out what the specific symbols mean and how much they mirror that future reality will still demand good judgment, but this is the broad approach taken in the present commentary.

21:12–14 having a great and high wall, having twelve gates and at the gates twelve angels and

names written on the gates, which are the names of the twelve tribes of the sons of Israel, 13 on the east three gates and on the north three gates and on the south three gates and on the west three gates. 14 And the wall of the city had twelve foundation stones and on them were the twelve names of the twelve apostles of the Lamb (ἔχουσα τεῖχος μέγα καὶ ὑψηλόν, ἔχουσα πυλῶνας δώδεκα καὶ ἐπὶ τοῖς πυλῶσιν ἀγγέλους δώδεκα καὶ ὀνόματα ἐπιγεγραμμένα, ἅ ἐστιν τῶν δώδεκα φυλῶν υἱῶν Ἰσραήλ· 13 ἀπὸ ἀνατολῆς πυλῶνες τρεῖς καὶ ἀπὸ βορρᾶ πυλῶνες τρεῖς καὶ ἀπὸ νότου πυλῶνες τρεῖς καὶ ἀπὸ δυσμῶν πυλῶνες τρεῖς. 14 καὶ τὸ τεῖχος τῆς πόλεως ἔχων θεμελίους δώδεκα καὶ ἐπ' αὐτῶν δώδεκα ὀνόματα τῶν δώδεκα ἀποστόλων τοῦ ἀρνίου). John's description of the new Jerusalem moves from his general impression of its glory in v. 11 to a more detailed account of its features, size, and precious materials (vv. 12–21). First, he describes the city wall with its gates and its foundations (vv. 12–14). It has[57] "a great and high wall" (v. 12a), signifying to an ancient reader its security and prosperity as a well-designed, well-maintained city.[58] The impressive wall possesses additional features that represent both its security against any

---

53. As Wright (*Resurrection*, xix) points out, "literal" is concerned with "*the way words refer to things*, not to the things to which the words refer." To take the illustration he uses a different direction than he takes it, to say "that greasy spoon at the corner" is not to describe an actual spoon (although it may be greasy). It is not "a literal spoon." The fact that "greasy spoon" is a metaphor does not make its referent imaginary or unreal. But the metaphor communicates something about the real restaurant that is harder to say in a literal description.

54. E.g., Hendriksen, *More Than Conquerors*, 196–202; Milligan, *Revelation*, 367–71; Smalley, *Revelation*, 578–80; Swete, *Apocalypse*, 298. See Jerome's comment about this passage in his "Letters": "Evidently this description cannot be taken literally (in fact, it is absurd to suppose a city the length, breadth and height of which are all twelve thousand furlongs), and therefore the details of it must be mystically understood" (Philip Schaff and Henry Wace, eds., *A Select Library of the Nicene and Post-Nicene Fathers of the Christian Church, Second Series* [New York: Christian Literature Company, 1893], 6:63).

55. Turner, "New Jerusalem," 278.

56. The parallels with Babylon/Rome of chs. 17–18 (as set out in Boxall, *Revelation*, 297–99) show that behind the symbolism John envisions a real, if transformed, city that forms the center of a world it influences.

57. The participles "having" (ἔχουσα) in vv. 12a and 12b continue to describe "the city" (τὴν πόλιν; accusative) of v. 10, but the case reverts to the more typical nominatives used in descriptive clauses throughout the book. See the clauses that follow in vv. 12–14 that contain mostly present participles and verbless (nominal) clauses (and the nominative participle, ἔχων, in v. 14a).

58. In the modern world a walled city seems unwelcoming and fearful, but this would not be the case in ancient times. See Nehemiah's concern to rebuild Jerusalem's wall first in his return to Judah in the fifth century BC. The fact that all enemies have been vanquished when the new Jerusalem appears does not diminish the figurative significance of its walls.

threat to its inhabitants and its role as a vibrant center of human interaction. It has "twelve gates"[59] (v. 12b) that provide ready access in and out of the city—see the indication in vv. 24–26 that these gates never close and that people come in and out from all parts of the renewed earth. It also has "twelve angels" posted "at the gates," reinforcing the imagery of supernatural protection from any hostile force. A further feature of the gates, closely following Ezekiel 48:30–31, is a set of names placarded on them: there are "names written on the gates" (v. 12b), and these are "the names of the twelve tribes of the sons of Israel" (v. 12c). These names remind all who come and go within the city about God's promises to Abraham, Isaac, Jacob or "Israel," and their descendants. The city itself represents the ultimate fulfillment of those promises made by God to the people of Israel as a nation. While others from other ethnic groups will have entered into those blessings over the centuries (cf. the names on the foundations, v. 14), the faithful descendants of Israel will have a prominent place among God's people throughout eternity. God's redemption started with them and expanded to include others without revoking or canceling God's promises to Israel.[60] So this detail about the gates signifies (as in 7:4–8; see discussion there) the fulfillment of the widespread ancient Jewish expectation that all the tribes of Israel will be regathered in the end-times from their exile among the nations.

As a further development of the idea of ready access to the city and under the influence of Ezekiel 48:31–34, John specifies that the twelve gates are arranged symmetrically around the city (v. 13). There are three gates on each of its four sides: on the east, north, south, and west sides.[61] John does not list the tribal names for each side as Ezekiel does, and his order is slightly different (Ezekiel has north, east, south, west), but the accounts are clearly similar.

The foundations of the city's walls are described briefly in v. 14 with a focus, as with the gates, on what they represent theologically. John says that the "wall of the city" has (literally) "twelve foundations," meaning that the wall rests on massive foundation stones (i.e., it is a permanent, lasting city; cf. Heb 11:10),[62] whose precious materials are specified in vv. 19–20. But the point here is that there are twelve of them, signifying completeness. They are also inscribed with twelve significant names, like the gates in v. 12. Here the names are those of "the twelve apostles of the Lamb" (v. 14b). This represents the fullness of the New Testament church, a "building" of God founded on the apostles and prophets with Christ himself as the cornerstone (Eph 2:20; cf. 1 Cor 3:11), encompassing believers in Christ from both Jewish and gentile backgrounds. The names of the twelve apostles in the new Jerusalem will forever represent God's expansion of the promises of redemption to include others besides his people Israel.[63] Citation of "the Lamb" here, instead of saying "Christ" or "the Lord," recalls his self-sacrifice to redeem all the citizens of this city and perhaps connects to the starting point of this section in v. 9, "the bride, the wife of the Lamb."

21:15–17 And the one who was speaking with me had a gold measuring rod to measure the city and its gates and its wall. 16 And the city is laid

---

59. This number has a literal sense but is not merely or only literal; "twelve tribes" connotes the idea of the fullness or completeness of God's restoration of Israel as a nation (see the discussion of numbers in Rev at 1:4; 7:4; 20:2–3).

60. See the similar recognition of two groups within God's redeemed people earlier in Rev in 7:4–8 and 7:9–17.

61. See also Luke 13:29 (people coming from east, west, north, and south to the messianic banquet).

62. BDAG 448.

63. The two sets of twelve names in vv. 12 and 14 are complementary but not identical, just as the two groups in 7:4–8 and 7:9–17 are complementary but not identical.

out in a quadrilateral plan, and its length is the same as its width. And he measured the city with the rod at twelve thousand stadia; its length and width and height are equal. 17 And he measured its wall at one hundred and forty-four cubits, a human measurement, which is an angel's (Καὶ ὁ λαλῶν μετ' ἐμοῦ εἶχεν μέτρον κάλαμον χρυσοῦν, ἵνα μετρήσῃ τὴν πόλιν καὶ τοὺς πυλῶνας αὐτῆς καὶ τὸ τεῖχος αὐτῆς. 16 καὶ ἡ πόλις τετράγωνος κεῖται καὶ τὸ μῆκος αὐτῆς ὅσον τὸ πλάτος. καὶ ἐμέτρησεν τὴν πόλιν τῷ καλάμῳ ἐπὶ σταδίων δώδεκα χιλιάδων, τὸ μῆκος καὶ τὸ πλάτος καὶ τὸ ὕψος αὐτῆς ἴσα ἐστίν. 17 καὶ ἐμέτρησεν τὸ τεῖχος αὐτῆς ἑκατὸν τεσσεράκοντα τεσσάρων πηχῶν μέτρον ἀνθρώπου, ὅ ἐστιν ἀγγέλου). Another significant way to portray the new Jerusalem is to focus on its measurements, both its size and its symmetry, as John's vision proceeds to do in vv. 15–17. The change to a new segment is signaled by a reference again to the angel who appeared in v. 9 to show John the city. Now the angel is seen with "a gold measuring rod" with which he could measure "the city and its gates and its wall" (v. 15). This angel is similar to the figure in Ezekiel's vision who appeared with a "measuring rod" to show the size of the temple Ezekiel saw (Ezek 40:3, 5; 42:16; cf. Zech 2:2, an angel measuring Jerusalem). In Revelation 11:1–2, a measuring rod and temple measurements represent God's promise to restore and rebuild after destruction (see discussion there), but here as in Ezekiel the angel's measurements are a vehicle to represent important characteristics of the new city.

The action of measuring the city is not recorded, but v. 16 gives its results.

First, the measurements reveal that the city is "laid out in a quadrilateral plan,"[64] and more specifically as a square ("its length is the same as its width"; v. 16a–b). This was a common scheme for a city in the ancient world where it was geographically possible,[65] and it perhaps represents a well-designed, proper functioning community. More important seems to be the proportionality communicated in the final clause (v. 16d, skipping over v. 16c for the moment): the measurements reveal that the city is not only a square but is in fact a cube, "its length and width and height are equal." This would make it a replication on a vast scale of the most holy chamber in the temple in Jerusalem (1 Kgs 6:20; cf. Jub. 8:19, Eden as the holy of holies, God's dwelling place). The symmetrical proportions of the new Jerusalem replicate the place where God's presence was localized among his people, where his glory was to be found on earth, a typological pattern here fulfilled on a grand scale in God's presence with his people in the renewed creation.

The equal measurements that were cited in the preceding clause show the enormous size of the city: it was "twelve thousand stadia" on each side (v. 16c). As the capital city and center of the new creation, this city will have no equal in power or grandeur.[66] The impressive scale of the city and its structures appears again in v. 17 with the measuring of its "wall" (cf. v. 15). Its dimension comes in at "one hundred and forty-four cubits," or about

---

64. The phrase "in a quadrilateral plan" translates the word τετράγωνος that means simply "four-cornered" or "having four sides," but it commonly refers to objects with four equal sides, as here (cf. BDAG 1000; LSJ 1780).

65. Aune, *Revelation 17–22*, 1160–61, cites cities that ancient writers described as laid out in a square (e.g., Nineveh, Babylon, Nicaea, Rome).

66. BDAG 940, calculates one stadion at one-eighth of a mile (192 meters), so 12,000 stadia would be 1400 to 1500 miles (2300 to 2400 kilometers), a huge size for a literal city. The Talmud tractate b. Meg. 6b cites the size of Rome at 9,000 stadia (1100 mi/1700 km). Sib. Or. 5:249–54 pictures Jews in "the city of God" in the eschaton, whose "great wall" stretches to Joppa (about 40 mi/65 km). Security against invading nations is the sense given to this in the context.

seventy-two yards (sixty-six meters).[67] This dimension is probably to be understood as its width rather than its height, but either way it is massive. John adds an explanation of the scale being used: "A human measurement, which is an angel's." He means by this that the reader should not think that this large dimension (or the measurement of v. 16) is somehow not analogous to the normal human scale of things. The units of measure used by the angel in his vision are the normal earthly ones (see Deut 3:11 for the same idiom, "of a man"). However, these measurements should not be taken as purely literal despite the assurance that a human scale is being used. It is true that the width and length of the new Jerusalem may not be staggering if we consider all the people of God of all ages who should be pictured as dwelling in it. It is true also that God could construct something in any mode and size he desires in a renewed creation.[68] But a city described as a cube structure is likely to be a figurative rather than literal depiction, especially with a height of approximately 1500 miles.[69] See further comments at v. 26 on how to interpret the descriptions used in this passage.

21:18–21 And the building material of its wall is jasper, and the city is pure gold like clear glass. 19 The foundation stones of the city's wall are adorned with every kind of precious stone. The first foundation stone is jasper, the second sapphire, the third chalcedony, the fourth emerald, 20 the fifth sardonyx, the sixth carnelian, the seventh chrysolite, the eighth beryl, the ninth topaz, the tenth chrysoprase, the eleventh hyacinth, the twelfth amethyst. 21 And the twelve gates are twelve pearls—each one of the gates was from a single pearl—and the square of the city was pure

gold like transparent glass (καὶ ἡ ἐνδώμησις τοῦ τείχους αὐτῆς ἴασπις καὶ ἡ πόλις χρυσίον καθαρὸν ὅμοιον ὑάλῳ καθαρῷ. 19 οἱ θεμέλιοι τοῦ τείχους τῆς πόλεως παντὶ λίθῳ τιμίῳ κεκοσμημένοι· ὁ θεμέλιος ὁ πρῶτος ἴασπις, ὁ δεύτερος σάπφιρος, ὁ τρίτος χαλκηδών, ὁ τέταρτος σμάραγδος, 20 ὁ πέμπτος σαρδόνυξ, ὁ ἕκτος σάρδιον, ὁ ἕβδομος χρυσόλιθος, ὁ ὄγδοος βήρυλλος, ὁ ἔνατος τοπάζιον, ὁ δέκατος χρυσόπρασος, ὁ ἑνδέκατος ὑάκινθος, ὁ δωδέκατος ἀμέθυστος, 21 καὶ οἱ δώδεκα πυλῶνες δώδεκα μαργαρῖται, ἀνὰ εἷς ἕκαστος τῶν πυλώνων ἦν ἐξ ἑνὸς μαργαρίτου. καὶ ἡ πλατεῖα τῆς πόλεως χρυσίον καθαρὸν ὡς ὕαλος διαυγής). In addition to its measurements another insight into the significance of the new Jerusalem is gained by a focus on the materials from which it is made (vv. 18–21). Here John returns to the principle of v. 11 that a city in which God is present must be filled through and through with dazzling splendor. Again, we encounter brilliant extravagance and opulent treasures at every turn, an overwhelming display that John can hardly put into words. First, he gives a general statement of the substances used to build the features of the city already seen. The word translated "building materials" (ἐνδώμησις; v. 18a) can mean the action of building, but by metonymy it denotes the materials used in the construction.[70] The city's walls are made of "jasper," a return to the gem used in 4:3 to portray God's glorious appearance and in 21:11 of the city as possessing God's glory (see also v. 19). The city itself is made of "pure gold" (v. 18b; cf. v. 21), a gold beyond the splendor of earthly gold because it was so pure as to be translucent, glowing "like clear glass" (similar words in v. 21).

The city wall's twelve massive foundation stones were described in v. 14, and their materials are now specified in great detail (vv. 19–20). They are

---

67. A cubit was about 18 inches (45 centimeters) according to BDAG 812.

68. Thomas, *Revelation 8–22*, 466–68.

69. Turner, "New Jerusalem," 277.

70. BDAG 334.

"adorned with every kind of precious stone," but the sense of "adorn" in this context may be more than just "decorated outwardly," as though gems are embedded in them here and there. At times the word "adorn" (κοσμέω) means to "make something beautiful" or "build a thing of beauty,"[71] and the context suggests that sense here. As vv. 19b–20 show, the "precious stones" are not merely outward decorations but the very substance of the foundation stones. These verses list in detail the twelve costly and beautiful jewels of which the foundations are made (see translation above). Many of these appear in Old Testament lists of gems; for example, they appear in the twelve on Aaron's breastplate representing Israel's tribes in the Lord's presence (Exod 28:17–20), the stones that adorn the king of Tyre in his claims to be like God (Ezek 28:12–13), and the precious materials used to build the restored Jerusalem (Isa 54:11–12; cf. Tob 13:15–18). Three of them appear in Revelation 4:3 as a representation of God's splendor and glory (jasper, emerald, carnelian), and that is the best guide to their symbolic significance here. The foundation stones of the walls are described as dazzling and costly gems to represent God's glorious presence with his people in this city.

The "twelve gates" likewise are huge specimens of another sort of costly and beautiful material: they are "twelve pearls" (v. 21a).[72] John clarifies that each of the massive gates is formed or carved from "a single pearl" (v. 21b), something almost beyond imagination but intended to portray the impressiveness and magnificence of God's new Jerusalem. The material substance of one final

feature of the city is mentioned, its main "square" (v. 21c). The word translated "square" (πλατεῖα) means "wide space," and it is often used of "streets" in the Gospels and Acts (e.g., Matt 6:5; Luke 10:10; 14:21; Acts 5:15), but these are always in the plural. The word appears in the singular in the New Testament only in Revelation (11:8; 21:21; 22:2), and in these places the sense "main plaza" or "public square" is more fitting (cf. Gen 19:2; Judg 19:15–20; Ezra 10:9), notwithstanding the popular conception of heaven's "streets" paved with gold. The material of this main square is similar to how the city itself is described in v. 18: it is made of "pure gold like transparent glass" (v. 21c; see comments at v. 18).

21:22–23 And I did not see a temple in it, for the Lord God Almighty and the Lamb are its temple. 23 And the city has no need for the sun or for the moon to shine in it, for the glory of God gave it light, and its lamp was the Lamb (Καὶ ναὸν οὐκ εἶδον ἐν αὐτῇ, ὁ γὰρ κύριος ὁ θεὸς ὁ παντοκράτωρ ναός αὐτῆς ἐστιν καὶ τὸ ἀρνίον. 23 καὶ ἡ πόλις οὐ χρείαν ἔχει τοῦ ἡλίου οὐδὲ τῆς σελήνης ἵνα φαίνωσιν αὐτῇ, ἡ γὰρ δόξα τοῦ θεοῦ ἐφώτισεν αὐτήν, καὶ ὁ λύχνος αὐτῆς τὸ ἀρνίον). Beyond the city's measurements and materials John notes two features that are *not* present in the new Jerusalem and explains how these absences indicate God's direct presence in the city. Using a familiar verb "I saw" (εἶδον, v. 22a), but here with a negative, John refers in summary to the lack of a sanctuary or "temple" of worship in this community of God's people.[73] Scholars puzzle over this lack of a temple in the new Jerusalem that descended to earth "out of heaven from God" (vv. 2, 10; cf. 3:12), since heaven's throne

---

71. E.g., κοσμέω is used in Luke 21:5 (the temple was "adorned with beautiful stones and offerings," perhaps carved decorations on the walls); also Matt 23:29, where κοσμέω is parallel to οἰκοδομέω (to build, construct) in describing decorated tombs.

72. Pearls are mentioned earlier as costly adornments or commodities associated with Babylon, the great prostitute (17:4; 18:12, 16).

73. This word occurs frequently in earlier parts of Rev, either of a temple in the earthly Jerusalem (11:1–2) or of the heavenly temple (e.g., 11:19; 14:17; 15:5; 16:1, 17).

room itself was understood to serve as a temple (see discussion at 4:5–6). But the preexistence of this city in heaven does not mean that it is coextensive with God's throne-room/temple.[74]

Another puzzle is why John departs from the common Jewish expectation of a rebuilt temple in the restored Jerusalem of the last days (e.g., Isa 60:13; 63:18; Ezek 37:26–27; Zech 6:12–15; cf. Tob 13:10; Jub. 1:15–18; 5Q15 1:3). Many take Ezekiel's detailed temple vision (Ezek 40–48) to be a symbol for what John sees here in Revelation 21–22 (the new Jerusalem with its walls and gates).[75] More consistent with the broader context of Ezekiel 33–48 is the view that Ezekiel describes primarily the millennial temple to be restored when God regathers Israel in its land at the time of Christ's second coming and his reign from the earthly Jerusalem for a thousand years (19:11–20:10).[76] That restored temple representing God's presence among his people in the interim messianic kingdom will be typologically related to, but finally eclipsed by, God's presence among his people in the ultimate way in the new creation.[77] There are a few Jewish parallels to this conception of a coming Jerusalem without a temple. Jeremiah 3:14–18 is a possible parallel,[78] but a more likely conceptual background

can be seen in a midrash on Exodus 27:20 (the lamp in the sanctuary) that pulls in Psalm 132:17 and Isaiah 60:19 (the Messiah and the Lord will be Israel's light).[79] In any case in v. 22b John provides a plausible explanation ("for," γάρ) for his vision of a new Jerusalem without a temple: the majestic God himself[80] and the Lamb are personally present in the city, and they "are its temple." The need for a physical building to serve as the locus of worship is eclipsed when God himself is present with them, as v. 3 says, "the dwelling of God is with humans and he will dwell with them, and they will be his peoples and God himself will be with them as their God."

The other feature no longer needed in the new Jerusalem is an external source of light such as the sun or moon "to shine in it" (v. 23a). This reality, which is repeated in many of the same terms in 22:5 (cf. also v. 25b), is based on Old Testament texts such as Isaiah 24:23 and 60:2, 19–20 that speak of a future for Jerusalem when the sun and moon are eclipsed because the Lord's "glory" will be its light (cf. Sib. Or. 3:785–88). John has introduced this idea already in v. 11, and it comes out more clearly in the explanatory clause of v. 23b: "For the glory of God gave it light." The dual role of God and the Lamb among God's people in the new creation is

---

74. While the heavenly sanctuary is not replicated in the new Jerusalem that comes down from heaven, the throne of God and of the Lamb does appear as the locus of his eternal rule over the new creation (22:1, 3).

75. E.g., Beale, *Revelation*, 1068–70, 1090–91; Osborne, *Revelation*, 759–60; Smalley, *Revelation*, 556–57.

76. Ralph H. Alexander, "Ezekiel," in *Zondervan NIV Bible Commentary, Volume 1: Old Testament*, ed. Kenneth L. Barker and John R. Kohlenberger III (Grand Rapids: Zondervan, 1994), 1326–47; Cooper, *Ezekiel*, 351–53; and Richard S. Hess, "The Future Written in the Past: The Old Testament and the Millennium," in *A Case for Historic Premillennialism: An Alternative to "Left Behind" Eschatology*, ed. Craig L. Blomberg and Sung Wook Chung (Grand Rapids: Baker Academic, 2009), 27–35. For discussion of issues related to the restoration of the sacrificial ritual in this millennial temple, see Alexander, "Ezekiel," 1340–47.

77. In the "Apocalypse of Weeks" the eighth week (1 En. 91:12–13) represents an interim messianic age with a rebuilt temple. The tenth week includes final judgment followed by departure of the first heaven and the appearance of a new heaven (91:15–16).

78. Jer 3:15–18 speaks in ways very similar to Rev 21:22–26 about a future time when Israel is regathered to Zion and the nations assemble likewise to worship God in Jerusalem. At that time no one will remember the ark of the covenant in the wilderness because Jerusalem itself will be God's throne.

79. David Flusser, "No Temple in the City," in *Judaism and the Origins of Christianity* (Jerusalem: Magnes, 1988), 454–65; Aune, *Revelation 17–22*, 1167. See also 1QS 8:1–9 where the community itself is the sanctuary.

80. The name "Lord God Almighty" in v. 22b is the final of nine occurrences of this title in Rev (mostly in chs. 11–21; see the discussion of its significance at 1:8 and 11:17).

reinforced by v. 23c, "and its lamp was the Lamb" (cf. v. 22b; 22:1, 3).

21:24–26 And the nations will walk in its light, and the kings of the earth will bring their glory into it, 25 and its gates will never close by day, for there will be no night there, 26 and the glory and honor of the nations will be brought into it (καὶ περιπατήσουσιν τὰ ἔθνη διὰ τοῦ φωτὸς αὐτῆς, καὶ οἱ βασιλεῖς τῆς γῆς φέρουσιν τὴν δόξαν αὐτῶν εἰς αὐτήν, 25 καὶ οἱ πυλῶνες αὐτῆς οὐ μὴ κλεισθῶσιν ἡμέρας, νὺξ γὰρ οὐκ ἔσται ἐκεῖ, 26 καὶ οἴσουσιν τὴν δόξαν καὶ τὴν τιμὴν τῶν ἐθνῶν εἰς αὐτήν). The influence of Isaiah 60 on v. 23 carries over to these verses, because Isaiah speaks of the nations and kings of the earth coming in and out of Jerusalem with rich products for trade as well as to offer worship to the true God (Isa 60:3, 5–7, 11, 14). This is a common theme in the Old Testament, beginning with the promise in Genesis 12:1–3 that through Abraham all the nations would be blessed, and it is repeated with further details subsequently (e.g., Pss 68:29, 31; 72:10–11; Isa 2:2–3; Mic 4:1–2; Zech 8:20–23; cf. Tob 13:11). The consummation of this theme will come partly in the millennial kingdom, but will come in a greater way in the new creation that follows. As he moves into vv. 24–27, John switches to future verbs (and a futuristic present, v. 24b) to anticipate the scenes of his vision becoming a reality in the end times. It yields a picture of vibrant human commerce and interaction across the renewed earth with Jerusalem as its center.

People from "the nations" will commingle freely "in its light" (v. 24a; cf. vv. 11, 23),[81] and their leaders ("the kings of the earth," here no longer hostile to God as in 6:15; 19:19; cf. Ps 2:2) come to enter into the life of the city as well as to honor the Lord God and the Lamb whose glory is its light (v. 24b).[82]

John adds that the impressive gates described earlier are not obstacles to these lively connections since they "will never close by day" (v. 25a).[83] This appears to be specifically designed to build on the pattern of Isaiah 60:11 (Jerusalem's gates will "never be shut by day or night"), but to show its intensification in the new Jerusalem. There is no need to speak of "by day or night," since "there will be no night there" (v. 25b; cf. vv. 11, 23; 22:5). Thus "the glory and honor of the nations" will freely and continually be "brought into it" (οἴσουσιν . . . εἰς αὐτήν).[84] As in v. 24 the nations' "glory" (δόξα), this time with "honor" (τιμή) added, constitutes a metonymy where abstract qualities are used to refer to concrete things that are associated with them. They do not bring their abstract status or even their impressive apparel that could reflect that status. Instead, they bring various useful products and necessary commodities that enhance their nations' reputations (and bring honor to their God; see earlier note).

Verses 24–26 (as well as 22:1–5) reflect lively, productive human life and commerce on a renewed earth. Its redeemed people move in and out of the city that forms the center of God's new creation. They use their creative skills and crafts (21:24,

---

81. See BDAG 223–24 for this sense of the preposition "in" (διά). The expression "walk in its light" (v. 24a) seems to be a combination of Isa 60:3 (nations coming "to" God's light) with the sentiment of Isa 2:3, 5: God's redeemed from the nations as well as from Israel "walking in his paths, in his light." See Bauckham, *Climax*, 314–15; McNicol, *Conversion*, 77.

82. For the kings of the earth to "bring their glory into" the new Jerusalem indicates in part their transformation from self-glory to divine worship. Their "glory" in abstract refers to their honored position or status, but in this case not flaunted to

enhance their own reputation but to add to the praise and glory of the God they come to worship (cf. BDAG 257; Matt 4:8; 6:29; Luke 4:6; 12:27). See Bauckham, *Climax*, 315–16.

83. The phrase "will never close" illustrates the Greek emphatic negative construction with οὐ μή and the subjunctive (see note on 18:21; this occurs again in 21:27).

84. The Greek phrase uses an impersonal "they" (third-person plural) form of the active verb ("they will bring . . . into it") to express a passive meaning. See 10:11; 12:6; 13:16.

26), till and tend the fruitful earth (22:2–3a), learn and grow (22:2e), and worship God with direct intimacy and commitment (21:3, 22; 22:3–4). This is not a "heaven" spent floating in the clouds and strumming harps or eternally contemplating the face of God with an inward but not physical vision. Many longstanding (and somewhat off-putting) impressions of what "heaven" and eternal life will be like are not informed sufficiently by the picture John has given here.[85] See comments at 22:2 and 22:5 for further reflections on this point.

21:27 And nothing unclean will ever come into it nor anyone who commits what is abominable and false, but only those who are recorded in the Lamb's book of life (καὶ οὐ μὴ εἰσέλθῃ εἰς αὐτὴν πᾶν κοινὸν καὶ [ὁ] ποιῶν βδέλυγμα καὶ ψεῦδος εἰ μὴ οἱ γεγραμμένοι ἐν τῷ βιβλίῳ τῆς ζωῆς τοῦ ἀρνίου). In keeping with the city's holy status (v. 2, "the holy city") as the dwelling of God among his people (vv. 3, 7), those who will participate in the vibrant life of the new Jerusalem will all have come to share in the holiness of God and the Lamb. The contrast between these holy people and those who lack such holiness was already set forth in v. 8 (cf. also 22:14–15). The theological point of v. 8 is a valid one here in v. 27 as well: the wicked will have already been consigned to their judgment in the lake of fire at the time when the new Jerusalem appears and so are eternally excluded from the blessings of life with God there. The terms used in v. 27 to describe the wicked are influenced by Old Testament verses that speak of restrictions on those who enter holy Jerusalem (Isa 35:8; 52:1)[86] but also by descriptions of Babylon in Revelation (17:4–5; see comments there). These will never "come into it" (cf. 22:14), nor those who deal in falsehood and dishonesty (cf. 14:5; 22:15). In contrast, the ones who participate in the life of the holy city will be those "who are recorded in the Lamb's book of life" (cf. Isa 4:3; see comments at Rev 3:5; 20:12).

Theology in Application

In the Sweet By-and-By

Christian hymns and worship songs—and even popular music—often focus on heaven as our destiny when our days on earth are past. Songs like "The Sweet By-and-By," "When the Roll is Called Up Yonder," "I'll Fly Away," and "This World Is Not My Home" are only a few that could be cited. There is much that is good and comforting about these songs, so it seems picky to find fault with them, but this chapter in Revelation shows that they can promote an incomplete picture of our future life with God in eternity. Yes, it is true—as many of these songs celebrate— that the Christian will enjoy direct communion with our God and with Christ our Savior (vv. 2–3). It will mean complete deliverance from death, grief, weeping, and pain: our God "will wipe away every tear" (v. 4). We will come to enjoy life with God not merely as individuals face-to-face with him, wonderful as that will be, but also as a community of God's people in "the holy city, the new Jerusalem" (v. 10).

---

85. Blaising, "Premillennialism," 160–81; Middleton, *New Heaven and a New Earth*, 21–34; Sauer, *Triumph*, 181–82; Turner, "New Jerusalem," 289–92; Wright, *Surprised by Hope*, 17–20, 93–108.

86. The LXX of Isa 35:8; 52:1 uses ἀκάθαρτος ("unclean, impure"), but the sense is the same as κοινός, "unclean" or "common, ritually impure," used here (cf. BDAG 552; see Acts 10:14, 28; 11:8 where the two terms are synonymous).

There we will be active in using and developing our gifts to serve God and others and in worshiping God together with the people of God of all ages and nations (and yes, in reunion with loved ones who have gone before us into God's presence). But one problem with many of these songs is a tendency to reinforce the dualistic conception in popular Christian culture that at death we leave this evil, physical life behind and go to be with God in heaven forever in a kind of nonbodily, spiritual existence in the clouds. Revelation itself gives glimpses of God's people in God's heavenly presence after earthly life is over (6:9–11; 7:9–17), but in both cases the verses indicate that it's not their final destination. They enjoy God's presence, to be sure, but they await the day when heaven comes down to earth in the form seen here in 21:1–8 and later in 22:1–5. The earth itself will be restored and joined to heaven as God's eternal dwelling place with his redeemed peoples. The idea that anything material is evil and temporary while only what is spiritual is good and lasting cannot be supported from the Bible. This "picky" point is important because of what it means for the value of our physical bodies and the work we do with them as well as for the natural world that God created (Gen 1:1, 31; Ps 19:1–6). They will not be discarded as worthless or temporary but resurrected and renewed (respectively) to fit them for a useful and creative eternity. Therefore, it matters even now how we use our bodies (not for immorality but to glorify God according to 1 Cor 6) and how we steward and protect God's creation as his good gift (the creation mandate of Gen 1:26–31). Conservation and environmental concerns cannot be left for secularists to dominate, with their tendency to elevate nature as a new deity and demote humans to the level of snail darters. It should be the concern of Christians as well, who can bring biblical values to the task.[87]

What's Wrong with This Picture?

The mess we have grown accustomed to seems just fine until we catch sight of something far better. My fellow manager's productive, happy department wakes me up to my own sloppy, inattentive leadership. My neighbor's organized garage shames me into clearing out the piles of stuff that keep me from ever parking a car in mine. Similarly, a glimpse of the rule of God and Christ over this world in the millennium and in the new creation (especially 21:1–8; 22:1–5) shows us how far short all human society comes in this sinful age that is passing away. Political and business leaders that serve their own interests instead of the people's, disease and starvation in a world of medical miracles and agricultural abundance, racism and isolation among humans who share God's image and have infinite value to him, unimaginable violence and

---

87. See Jonathan Moo, "Continuity, Discontinuity, and Hope: The Contribution of New Testament Eschatology to a Distinctively Christian Environmental Ethos," *TynBul* 61 (2010): 21–44; and idem, *Let Creation Rejoice: Biblical Hope and the Ecological Crisis* (Downers Grove, IL: InterVarsity Press, 2014), 80–96, 146–61.

warfare—all of this is so common to our experience in this fallen world that we too easily accept it as unchangeable.

One of the most important values of eschatology—that takes us beyond the individualistic focus that we often see (e.g., my reward in heaven, my encouragement to endure hardship in this life)—is the corporate and civic vision that it provides. These chapters give us a glimpse of human life as it can be, of the justice and community and human flourishing that can exist in this world that God has made. It is true that this will never be reached until God deals ultimately with the sin problem that caused everything to spin out of control in the first place. But the church corporately is "an inaugurated form of the future kingdom of God"[88] on earth. It should display ahead of time what God's redeemed and reconciled human society can look like in pursuing righteousness, justice, joy, and peace among people of diverse backgrounds. Its members should truly care not just for their own needs but for one another and for the wider world, especially those who are weak, disadvantaged, or suffering.[89] Our anticipated future has a strong influence on our present identity and conduct, and if we live in light of that future now, we will bear living witness to the world around us that human life can be different from what we all have come to accept as the status quo.

88. Blaising and Bock, *Progressive Dispensationalism*, 286; cf. 285–91.

89. Marva J. Dawn, *Joy in Our Weakness: A Gift of Hope from the Book of Revelation*, rev. ed. (Grand Rapids: Eerdmans, 2002), 203–6.

Revelation 22:1–21

Literary Context

The initial portion of the chapter (vv. 1–9) is the final segment of the book's fourth major vision describing the bride of the Lamb, the New Jerusalem, including a hinge paragraph (vv. 6–9) that contributes both to what comes before and to what follows. The latter portion is the epilogue to the whole book (vv. 10–21) that looks back to the themes of the introduction (1:1–8) and looks forward to the imminent coming of Jesus to consummate all that the book has revealed.

I. Prologue (1:1–8)

II. First Vision: The Exalted Christ and His Messages to the Churches (1:9–3:22)

III. Second Vision: Heavenly Throne Room and Three Judgment Cycles (4:1–16:21)

IV. Third Vision: The Destruction of Babylon the Great (17:1–19:10)

V. Intervening Events: From Babylon to the New Jerusalem (19:11–21:8)

VI. Fourth Vision: The Coming of the New Jerusalem (21:9–22:9)

    A. God's Glorious City, the Lamb's Bride (21:9–27)

→   **B. God's Eden Restored and the Angel's Instructions (22:1–9)**

VII. Epilogue (22:10–21)

Main Idea

The new Jerusalem will be like an enhanced Eden where God's people will forever experience his full provision, enjoy his presence in face-to-face fellowship, and reign with him over a renewed creation as he intended for them from the beginning (vv. 1–9). This book's authoritative revelation from God about the imminent return of Jesus as King and Judge should cause all people to seek his free gift of life forever in his eternal city (vv. 10–21).

Translation

Revelation 22:1–21

1a	Action (angel of 21:9)	And **he showed me a river**
		of the water of life,
		clear as crystal,
b	Descriptions	flowing
		from the throne of God and
		of the Lamb
2a		through the middle of the city square.
b	Description/Place	And **on either side of the river was the tree of life**
c	Descriptions	producing twelve kinds of fruit,
d		yielding its fruit every month,
e	Purpose	and **the leaves of the tree were for the health of the nations.**
3a	Descriptions	And **there will no longer be any curse.**
b		And **the throne of God and**
		of the Lamb will be in the city,
c	Actions	and **his servants will worship him,**
4a		and **they will see his face,**
b		and **his name will be on their foreheads.**
5a	Descriptions	And **there will be no more night,**
b		and **they will have no need for the light of a lamp or**
		the light of the sun,
c	Reason	because the Lord God will shine over them,
d	Action	and **they will reign forever and ever.**
6a	Action (angel of 21:9; 22:1)	And **he said to me,**
b	Affirmations	*"These words are faithful and true,*
c		*and the Lord,*
		the God of the spirits of the prophets,
		… sent his angel
d	Purpose	*to show his servants what must happen soon."*
7a	Parenthetical Words of Jesus	*("And indeed, I am coming soon.*
b	Beatitude	*Blessed is the one who obeys the words of the prophecy of this book.")*
8a	Identification	And **I, John, am the hearer and**
		eyewitness
		of these things.
b	Time	And when I heard and saw them,

c	Response to 6	**I fell to worship at the feet of the angel**
d	Description	who showed them to me.
9a	Response to 8c	And **he said to me,**
b	Prohibition	*"Don't do that.*
c	Reason	*I am a fellow servant of yours and*
		of your brothers the prophets and
		of those who obey the words of this book.
d	Command	*Worship God!"*
10a	Action	And **he said to me,**
b	Prohibition	*"Do not seal up the words of the prophecy of this book,*
c	Reason	*for the time is near.*
11a	Commands	*Let the one who does wrong still do wrong,*
b		*and let the one who is defiled still stay defiled,*
c		*and let the righteous one still do what is righteous,*
d		*and let the holy one still stay holy."*
12a	Affirmation of	*"Indeed, I am coming soon,*
	10–11 by Jesus	
b		*and my reward is with me*
c	Purpose	*to render to each one*
d	Measure	*as his work deserves.*
13	Basis of 12	*I am the Alpha and the Omega,*
		the first and the last,
		the beginning and the end.
14a	Beatitude	*Blessed are those who wash their robes*
b	Purposes	*so that they may have the right to the tree of life and*
c		*they may enter by the gates into the city.*
15	Contrast to 14c	*Outside are the dogs and*
		the sorcerers and
		the sexually immoral and
		the murderers and
		the idolaters and
		everyone who loves and practices falsehood.
16a	Action	*I, Jesus, sent my angel*
b	Purpose	*to testify to you about these things for the churches.*
c	Identification	*I am the shoot and*
		the descendant of David,
		the bright morning star."
17a	Action	And **the Spirit and the bride say,**
b	Invitation	*"Come."*
c	Invitation	And **let the one who hears say,**
d	Invitation	*"Come."*

Continued on next page.

Continued from previous page.

e	Invitation	And **let the one who thirsts come;**
f	Invitation	**let the one who desires it take the water of life freely.**
18a	Warning	**I testify to everyone who hears the words of the prophecy of this book:**
b	Condition	*"If anyone adds to them,*
c	Consequence	*God will inflict on him the plagues*
d	Description	*that are written about in this book,*
19a	Condition	*and*
		if anyone takes away from the words of the book of this prophecy,
b	Consequence	*God will take away his portion from the tree of life and the holy city*
c	Description	*that are written about in this book."*
20a	Action	**The one who testifies about these things says,**
b	Affirmation	*"Surely I am coming soon."*
c	Response	**Amen. Come, Lord Jesus!**
21	Benediction	**The grace of the Lord Jesus be with all.**

Structure

In the early verses of the chapter John continues to describe what the revealing angel has shown him about the new Jerusalem, particularly its character as a garden city, the enhanced Eden (vv. 1–5). Verses 6–9 present John's interaction with that angel (parallel to 19:9–10), which concludes the vision of the new Jerusalem (see "Literary Context" for chs. 17 and 19), and anticipates the themes of the epilogue (vv. 10–21). The epilogue echoes many of the points of the prologue (1:1–8) about the source and themes of the entire book, including its focus on Jesus's return to earth to consummate "what must happen soon" (1:1). Its subsections are hard to delineate because it takes the form of a lively dialogue between various speakers (the angel, John, Jesus, the Spirit, the bride, and even the readers or hearers of the book). Their conversation moves broadly through two larger subsections (vv. 10–15 and vv. 16–20 as shown below), followed by a benediction that concludes the book. These subsections have some thematic coherence, and similar topics appear in both of them.

Exegetical Outline

VI. Fourth Vision: The Coming of the New Jerusalem (21:9–22:9)

A. God's Glorious City, the Lamb's Bride (21:9–27)

➡ **B. God's Eden Restored and the Angel's Instructions (22:1–9)**

    1. God's Eden Restored (22:1–5)

    2. John and the Revealing Angel (22:6–9)

VII. Epilogue (22:10–21)

A. The Righteous and the Unrighteous Face Jesus's Imminent Return (22:10–15)

B. Jesus Affirms the Authority of This Book (22:16–20)

C. Epistolary Benediction (22:21)

Explanation of the Text

22:1–2 And he showed me a river of the water of life, clear as crystal, flowing from the throne of God and of the Lamb 2 through the middle of the city square. And on either side of the river was the tree of life producing twelve kinds of fruit, yielding its fruit every month, and the leaves of the tree were for the health of the nations (Καὶ ἔδειξέν μοι ποταμὸν ὕδατος ζωῆς λαμπρὸν ὡς κρύσταλλον, ἐκπορευόμενον ἐκ τοῦ θρόνου τοῦ θεοῦ καὶ τοῦ ἀρνίου. 2 ἐν μέσῳ τῆς πλατείας αὐτῆς καὶ τοῦ ποταμοῦ ἐντεῦθεν καὶ ἐκεῖθεν ξύλον ζωῆς ποιοῦν καρποὺς δώδεκα, κατὰ μῆνα ἕκαστον ἀποδιδοῦν τὸν καρπὸν αὐτοῦ, καὶ τὰ φύλλα τοῦ ξύλου εἰς θεραπείαν τῶν ἐθνῶν). John's final vision of the book that started in 21:9–10 concludes here in vv. 1–5, followed by a hinge section (vv. 6–9) that connects this vision to the epilogue of the book (vv. 10–21). The verb "he showed me" (v. 1a) that starts the final part of this vision refers to the

action by the angel who began in 21:9–10 to show John the bride of the Lamb, the new Jerusalem (his actions are cited also in 21:15, 17). Now in these verses John is shown features of the city that are significant for its relationship to the storyline of the Bible as a whole. He sees that the new Jerusalem is the expanded counterpart to Eden, God's paradise for humans in his original creation (Gen 2–3).[1] In the end time God will replicate in escalated fashion what his design for humans was at the creation. The first feature that shows this connection is the "river of the water of life" (v. 1a) that parallels the "river watering the garden that flowed out of Eden" in Genesis 2:10 (Eden was a place of abundant waters, Gen 13:10). In this case the water gives "life,"[2] both physically and spiritually (cf. Rev 7:17; 21:6; 22:17; cf. John 4:14; 7:38). This water is pure and inviting for all to partake of: it is "clear as crystal" (v. 1a)[3] as it flows through the "city square" (v. 2a).[4]

---

1. For several clear ancient Jewish texts that also connect the new Jerusalem to Eden, see T. Dan 5:12–13; 4 Ezra 8:52; 2 Bar. 4:2–7.

2. The phrase "water of life" reflects a Greek genitive of product (Wallace, *Grammar*, 106–7).

3. The adjective translated "clear" (λαμπρός) can mean "bright, shining" (cf. 18:14; 19:8), but in this context it denotes "clear, transparent" (cf. LSJ 1028; BDAG 585). This implies

purity, and some manuscripts actually add the word "pure" (καθαρός) to the text (051 supplement, 2030, 2377, part of the Byzantine minuscules; KJV and NKJV translate this inclusion), but it is an inferior reading both externally and internally.

4. See 21:21 for discussion of the word translated "square" (πλατεία). Here the phrase is actually "its square," with "its" referring to the city in 21:23. The antecedent has been made explicit to clarify the reference.

The source of this water is the very focal point of the entire vast city (cf. 21:16) as well as its surrounding renewed earth, that is, "the throne" on which both God and the Lamb were seated among their redeemed people (v. 1b).[5] John has already specified that no temple like the former earthly or heavenly one was found in the city because God himself and the Lamb are its temple (21:22), but here (and in v. 3) he makes clear that the new Jerusalem has a divine throne presumably in its center (as in the heavenly temple), where God's servants can see him and worship him freely (vv. 3b–4a). The phenomenon of living water flowing from the divine presence has its Old Testament parallels, most notably Ezekiel 47:1–12,[6] but the clear symbolism here is that God and the Lamb are the ever-abundant source of life and health for their people.

As reflected in the translation above, the phrase in v. 2a ("through the middle of the city square") goes better with the verb in v. 1b, and a new construction begins with the "and" of v. 2b.[7] Here we find a second feature that parallels Genesis 2–3 (specifically 2:9), the "tree of life" (ξύλον ζωῆς).[8] Here the "tree" is found on either side of the river that flows from the throne (v. 2b). It seems odd to have a tree planted on both sides of a river, but this is a play on words. It alludes to the singular "tree" in Genesis 2, but with a collective singular sense here ("wood, trees") as an escalation of Genesis 2:9.[9] This happens perhaps under the influence of Ezekiel 47:12 where first a singular is used with a wider sense, "every tree for eating" (v. 12a), and later it

is referred to with a plural, "their leaves" (v. 12b). Again, the larger point is that God provides abundantly for his people by means of the tree: it bears "twelve kinds of fruit" and yields "its fruit every month" (v. 2c–d). This also has a clear parallel in Ezekiel 47:12 that speaks of various fruit trees on both sides of the stream that comes from the sanctuary. They constantly produce fruit because of their abundant water supply. Ezekiel also adds that "their fruit will be for food and their leaves for healing" (47:12; cf. Gen 3:6; also 4 Ezra 7:123), and John reflects that here as well: its leaves were "for the health of the nations" (Rev 22:2e). John expands on Ezekiel's wording to include the redeemed non-Israelite peoples that will stream to Jerusalem also (cf. 21:24–27; see OT background discussed there).

It is impossible to resolve all the interesting questions that could arise from the descriptions in vv. 1–2. What will be the character of human life in the new heaven and new earth? Clear water flowing from the throne and the "tree of life" yielding abundant fruit can certainly be figurative representations of God's abundant provision for his people there. They will have all that they need for life, and with the curse removed, harsh toil to scratch out daily sustenance will not be required. But will resurrected bodies eat and drink? Will the nations still need "healing" in the renewed Eden of eternity? The text does not give explicit answers to such questions. But a few suggestions can be made here (and later in comments on v. 5). One important point is that even in resurrected, glorified bod-

---

5. The singular word "throne" in v. 1b (also in v. 3b) indicates the shared rule of God and the Lamb (cf. 3:21).

6. John draws repeatedly from the imagery of Ezek 47:1–12 (abundant water "flowing," ἐκπορευόμενον, from inside the temple and giving life to the whole land; perhaps also itself an allusion to Gen 2:10); see also Joel 3:18 (a fountain from the Lord's house); Zech 14:8 (living water from Jerusalem).

7. This differs from the punctuation in the NA[28] and UBS[5] Greek texts, but is followed by SBLGNT and Aune, *Revelation 17–22*, 1139. See BDAG 635 on the translation "through" in v. 2a.

8. The word "tree" (ξύλον) can be a Greek accusative as a second object of "he showed" or a nominative as the subject of a nominal sentence. The latter seems better and is followed in the translation above.

9. The word "tree" is articular in Gen 2:9 (also in Rev 2:7; 22:19). The translation "tree of life" (singular) in this verse more clearly preserves the allusion to Gen 2:9 (singular also in T. Levi 18:11).

ies and a renewed world, humans will not become gods. Their dependence on God will still be total and will never come to an end. They will continue to be creatures rather than the Creator, although they will be delivered from sin's corrupting effects on their creaturely existence. Likewise, God's good creation, even renewed, will continue to display his glory in its operation, apparently with plants that grow and yield useful fruits to meet human needs, and perhaps they will require tending or at least harvesting. Humans for their part will not become omniscient, but it seems likely that human potential for growth in knowledge and skills, for creativity and satisfying labor, for management of God's good creation to his glory—that is, for greater and greater expression of the divine image—will continue eternally.[10] See comments on v. 5 for further development of these ideas.

22:3–5 And there will no longer be any curse. And the throne of God and of the Lamb will be in the city, and his servants will worship him, 4 and they will see his face, and his name will be on their foreheads. 5 And there will be no more night, and they will have no need for the light of a lamp or the light of the sun, because the Lord God will shine over them, and they will reign forever and ever (καὶ πᾶν κατάθεμα οὐκ ἔσται ἔτι. καὶ ὁ θρόνος τοῦ θεοῦ καὶ τοῦ ἀρνίου ἐν αὐτῇ ἔσται, καὶ οἱ δοῦλοι αὐτοῦ λατρεύσουσιν αὐτῷ 4 καὶ ὄψονται τὸ πρόσωπον αὐτοῦ, καὶ τὸ ὄνομα αὐτοῦ

ἐπὶ τῶν μετώπων αὐτῶν. 5 καὶ νὺξ οὐκ ἔσται ἔτι καὶ οὐκ ἔχουσιν χρείαν φωτὸς λύχνου καὶ φῶς ἡλίου, ὅτι κύριος ὁ θεὸς φωτίσει ἐπ᾽ αὐτούς, καὶ βασιλεύσουσιν εἰς τοὺς αἰῶνας τῶν αἰώνων). John adds a third parallel with the story of Eden in Genesis 2–3 (v. 3a) before returning to some of the traits of the new Jerusalem that were mentioned in earlier lines. The complete absence of "any curse" (v. 3a)[11] is cited under the influence of Zechariah 14:11, but with an escalation and broadening compared to the sense in Zechariah. Zechariah 14 describes no more ban or oath of destruction against an invading army, but the reference here is to the end of God's universal curse on human beings and on the earth's fecundity as a consequence of sin (cf. Gen 3:17 and the contrast with Rev 22:2 above).[12] Continuing with mostly future-tense verbs (vv. 3–5), John projects what he has seen into the time of its future fulfillment. Again he mentions God and the Lamb ruling together "in the city"[13] (v. 3b; cf. v. 1) and available to receive their people's worship (v. 3c). The singular pronouns ("his servants will worship him") refer here to God as supreme (as in 7:15), but Revelation elsewhere views Christ (the Lamb) as fully worthy of worship alongside God (e.g., 5:9–14). The personal engagement of God's people rejoicing and worshiping in his immediate presence (as in 21:3, 7) is portrayed further in v. 4: "They will see his face" (v. 4a).

The ability to "see" God was previously only partial and available to a choice few (Exod 33:18–23;

---

10. Ladd, *Presence of the Future*, 62–64; Turner, "New Jerusalem," 289–90. Daniel K. K. Wong, "The Tree of Life in Revelation 2:7," *BSac* 155 (1998): 220–21, suggests that "health of the nations" (v. 2e) denotes not recovery from disease but God's spiritual care of his redeemed. Turner suggests that it concerns "developing physical, social, and spiritual capacities to serve God, neighbor, and nature more lovingly and faithfully" (290).

11. The sense "any curse" arises from the combination of "every" (πᾶν) with the negative (cf. 7:1; 9:4; BDAG 782; BDF §302.1). The word for "curse" (κατάθεμα) is used only here in the NT, but it is a synonym for ἀνάθεμα (cf. Rom 9:3; 1 Cor

12:3; Gal 1:8–9) and their related verbs (καταθεματίζω and ἀναθεματίζω) are used interchangeably in Matt 26:74; Mark 14:71. Some understand "curse" (κατάθεμα) here in a concrete sense (something or someone accursed or devoted to destruction; cf. BDAG 517; ESV; NLT is similar), but the abstract sense is better (the condition of being under a curse).

12. Jauhiainen, *Zechariah*, 125–26.

13. The words "in the city" in v. 3b have been used (as in CSB, NIV) to translate ἐν αὐτῇ ("in it/her") and clarify the reference of "it/her" to the city, last cited in 21:23.

Isa 6:1; John 1:18), but this ability will be open to all his redeemed people at that time when they come to share his holiness (cf. Ps 17:15; Matt 5:8; 1 Cor 13:12; Heb 12:14; 1 John 3:2). These verses, including v. 4a, incorporate the attractive parts of the view of heaven as an eternal "beatific vision" of God but without its unbiblical features of ethereal, nonmaterial existence.[14] The restored and enhanced Eden represents an earthly, material existence of some transformed kind. It is life on God's good earth, but in a "regenerated" form (Matt 19:28).[15]

Also as in 21:3 and 21:7 they will be clearly identified as his people and he as their God, which is expressed symbolically here as bearing "his name . . . on their foreheads" (v. 4b) to mark them as his (cf. 3:5, 12; 7:3; 14:1). Finally, John repeats the future blessing that God's people will no longer experience the darkness of night (representing ignorance and evil) but will live in the light of God's glory in the new Jerusalem. In God's presence "there will be no more night" (v. 5a; cf. 21:25), and this is not due to lamplight or sunlight but because "God will shine on them" (v. 5b–c; cf. 21:11, 23; Isa 60:19–20), a symbol of his personal communion with them and his blessing on them forever (cf. Num 6:24–27). And there in communion with him before his throne in the new Jerusalem, God's servants will share his rule over the new creation: "They will reign forever and ever" (v. 5d), in fulfillment of Daniel 7:18, 27 and as an intensification of their millennial rule with Christ and God (Rev 20:6; cf. 1:6; 5:10; 11:15; see also Matt 19:28; 1 Cor 6:2; 15:24–28; cf. 1 En. 92:4).

Another dimension of the "reign" of the saints that is suggested by the surrounding imagery of the new earth as a restored (and improved) Eden is the installation of humankind once again as image-bearers and dominion-keepers, ruling over and tending God's good creation as vice-regents for God and the Lamb (Gen 1:26–28; 2:15–17; Ps 8:3–8; cf. 1 Cor 15:20–28; Eph 1:20–23; Heb 2:5–10). This is central to the "already/not yet" eschatology of Hebrews 2 (humans restored to the exalted position God intended them to have in his original creation; already seen in Christ's exaltation, but not yet established on earth). Middleton argues correctly that it is central to the plotline of the whole Bible.[16] It is likely that this is part of the concept of the saints ruling in God's enhanced Eden, but John has not developed it in detail (no clear allusions to Gen 1:26–28 or Ps 8:3–9 in the book).

22:6–7 And he said to me, "These words are faithful and true, and the Lord, the God of the spirits of the prophets, sent his angel to show his servants what must happen soon." 7 ("And indeed, I am coming soon. Blessed is the one who obeys the words of the prophecy of this book.") (Καὶ εἶπέν μοι, Οὗτοι οἱ λόγοι πιστοὶ καὶ ἀληθινοί, καὶ ὁ κύριος ὁ θεὸς τῶν πνευμάτων τῶν προφητῶν ἀπέστειλεν τὸν ἄγγελον αὐτοῦ δεῖξαι τοῖς δούλοις αὐτοῦ ἃ δεῖ γενέσθαι ἐν τάχει. 7 καὶ ἰδοὺ ἔρχομαι ταχύ. μακάριος ὁ τηρῶν τοὺς λόγους τῆς προφητείας τοῦ βιβλίου τούτου). The vision of the new Jerusalem that started in 21:9–10 is brought to its conclusion here in 22:6–9.[17] At the same time vv. 6–9

---

14. See comments on 21:26; see also Blaising, "Premillennialism," 160–70; Middleton, *New Heaven and a New Earth*, 21–34; Wright, *Surprised by Hope*, 17–20.

15. Smalley, *Revelation*, 563, 579–80, speaks about these things as symbols of "the covenant relationship between God and his servants" and "the perfected indwelling of God with his people" in "the spiritual dimension of eternity," but he seems to have lost the conclusion to the biblical story in leaving it as something purely spiritual.

16. Middleton, *New Heaven and a New Earth*, 57–73.

17. See the structural parallels described at 1:9–10; 4:1–2; 17:1–3; and 21:9–10. Bruce W. Longenecker, "'Linked Like a Chain': Rev 22.6–9 in Light of an Ancient Transition Technique," *NTS* 47 (2001): 105–17, discusses the verbal links that mark vv. 6–9 as the conclusion of the preceding unit (21:9–22:9) as well as "springboard" into the new one (22:10–21).

also begin the transition into the epilogue of the book (vv. 10–21) by establishing clear thematic links back to John's prologue in 1:1–8. So even as the climactic vision of the new creation is winding down, John repeats the larger themes of the whole book as a "revelation of Jesus Christ" concerning "what must happen soon" (1:1–3). The angel who had shown John the new Jerusalem (21:9, 15; 22:1) now addresses John again ("and he said to me," v. 6a; also v. 9), but what he says has a broader import than the content of the previous vision. So "these words are faithful and true" (v. 6b; cf. 19:9; 21:5) may refer only to the preceding descriptions of the new Jerusalem as reliable, but the following verses suggest that the whole book is in view. The next clause (v. 6c–d) begins with "and" (καί), but it provides the basis for the reliability asserted in v. 6b: these words can be trusted because God who inspires his prophets has revealed them. The description of the Lord as "the God of the spirits of the prophets" anchors this revelation in the inspiration of the prophets by God's Spirit across the generations (see 10:6–7).[18] The words that follow in v. 6c–d provide explicit verbal links back to the opening verses of the book (1:1–3).

This Lord, according to John's angelic guide, "sent his angel to show his servants what must happen soon" (v. 6c–d). Every one of these key words occurs in 1:1 (in virtually the same form), and every one of the key agents in the prologue appears in these verses as well (beginning with "God," 21:6; cf. 1:1). The angel speaking in v. 6 (one of the seven bowl angels, cf. 21:9, 15; 22:1) is not referring to himself when he cites God's "angel" in v. 6c but to a different revealing angel singled out back in 1:1, who was God's agent for revealing the larger portion of the book. That angel was "sent" (v. 6c; see 1:1) in order to "show" (v. 6d; see 1:1) to God's "servants" (v. 6d; see 1:1) all the coming events that would culminate God's work of judgment and redemption: "What must happen soon" (v. 6d; see 1:1; cf. 1:19; 4:1; Dan 2:28–29, 45).[19] Two other key players from 1:1–3 will show up here in v. 7 (Jesus Christ) and v. 8 (John).

The mention of "what must happen soon" (v. 6d) triggers John's insertion of a parenthetical declaration in v. 7, using the same key word "soon": "And indeed, I am coming soon."[20] The speaker is not identified explicitly, but in Revelation as a whole (especially 2:16; 3:11; 22:20) it is clear that Jesus is the one who declares his imminent coming.[21] Identifying the speaker in v. 7 as Jesus adds another key player from 1:1–3 to the cast here. In vv. 7, 12, and 20 the statement "I am coming soon" is reinforced by confirmatory words to strengthen the assertion.[22] The fact that Jesus could appear without delay turns the beatitude that follows in v. 7b into a more urgent appeal. His soon return

---

18. As often true in biblical usage, reference to the human "spirit" or "spirits" reflects the work of God's "Spirit" in the background (BDAG 833; e.g., Mark 8:12; John 4:23; Acts 17:16; 1 Cor 4:21; Gal 6:1). The phrase "God of the spirits" is a genitive of subordination (Wallace, *Grammar*, 103–4): God who influences the prophets' spirits by means of his own Spirit at work in them; this wording is close to Num 27:16, but the wider concept is seen in Neh 9:30; Zech 7:12; Mark 12:36; Acts 1:16; 2:30–31; 1 Cor 14:32; 1 Pet 1:10–11. See Bruce, "Spirit in the Apocalypse," 339.

19. See 1:1 for discussion of the temporal sense of "soon" (ταχύ).

20. In addition to cementing the connection with God's words through the prophets (v. 6, "soon"), v. 7a ties vv. 6–9 to the epilogue by beginning a sevenfold repetition of the verb "come" that runs to v. 20 (Resseguie, *Narrative Commentary*, 259–60). No more appropriate conclusion could be found for the whole book than to anticipate again and again the imminent return of Christ.

21. Isa 40:10; 62:11 show the Lord God "coming" to rule and judge, and that image is invoked in Rev 22:12, but in v. 7 and v. 12 the more likely sense is that Jesus is coming to carry out God's purpose on earth.

22. The words are "indeed" or "behold" (ἰδού) in v. 7a, 12a; see notes on this use at 2:10 and 21:5; and "yes" or "surely" (ναί) in v. 20b.

makes it more important to obey "the words of the prophecy of this book" (v. 7b; cf. vv. 9, 18), a clear parallel to the beatitude of 1:3. The use of "obey" (or "keep," as τηρέω is often rendered; cf. CSB, ESV, NIV)[23] is a reminder of the hortatory content of this entire book. Its intent is not simply to convey information about the future but to communicate moral demands to be obeyed in the present. But the one who lives out what the book calls for will enjoy the transcendent happiness that God's favor brings.[24]

22:8–9 And I, John, am the hearer and eyewitness of these things. And when I heard and saw them, I fell to worship at the feet of the angel who showed them to me. 9 And he said to me, "Don't do that. I am a fellow servant of yours and of your brothers the prophets and of those who obey the words of this book. Worship God!" (Κἀγὼ Ἰωάννης ὁ ἀκούων καὶ βλέπων ταῦτα. καὶ ὅτε ἤκουσα καὶ ἔβλεψα, ἔπεσα προσκυνῆσαι ἔμπροσθεν τῶν ποδῶν τοῦ ἀγγέλου τοῦ δεικνύοντός μοι ταῦτα. 9 καὶ λέγει μοι, Ὅρα μή· σύνδουλός σού εἰμι καὶ τῶν ἀδελφῶν σου τῶν προφητῶν καὶ τῶν τηρούντων τοὺς λόγους τοῦ βιβλίου τούτου· τῷ θεῷ προσκύνησον). An additional parallel in vv. 6–9 to the themes and actors of 1:1–3 is this acknowledgment (22:8a) of John's role as the recipient of God's revelation of what must happen soon (cf. 1:1, 4, 9). John speaks directly about that role in v. 8a and then confesses

once again (vv. 8b–9) to succumbing to the temptation to offer worship to the glorious angel (as he had done at the end of his vision of Babylon; cf. 19:10). He describes his role using present participles in a nominal clause,[25] with "the hearer and eyewitness" (ὁ ἀκούων καὶ βλέπων)[26] as the predicates (v. 8a). These present participles focus on the action of hearing and seeing as repeated or characteristic events, but the present time sense of the normal translation ("the one who hears and sees") does not fit the context very well since he is not currently experiencing "these things." Because of John's allusions back to 1:1–3 and his explicit reference to the entire book in v. 7, the scope of "these things" in v. 8a must be the whole book as well.

Repeating the same two verbs (this time as aorists summarizing his visionary experiences up to this point), John acknowledges that when "he heard and saw,"[27] he prostrated himself in worship before the angel (v. 8b–d).[28] In this clause John seems to return to his more immediate visionary experience, since "the angel who showed them to me" seems more likely to describe the bowl angel who had guided John through the new Jerusalem vision (cf. 21:9, 15; 22:1, 6). This also better preserves the structural parallels with 19:9–10. The reply of the angel to John's worship[29] is very close to the wording of 19:10 (see comments there). However, instead of citing "of your brothers and sisters

---

23. BDAG 1002.

24. BDAG 610. This is the sixth of seven beatitudes in Rev (see 1:3 for listing; the final one is in 22:14). This beatitude (v. 7b) could be taken as John's words, parallel to the first beatitude in 1:3 about heeding this prophecy, and thus the parenthetical words of Jesus would consist of v. 7a only. But John explicitly shifts to himself in v. 8, so it seems more likely that both parts of v. 7 are the words of Jesus.

25. Here the verb "am" is implied; the clause structure implicitly links the subject "I, John" with the participles as predicate nominatives.

26. Zerwick and Grosvenor, *Grammatical Analysis*, 77, suggest this rendering for the participles.

27. These aorists could be put into English as past perfects to show the sequence of tenses, "when I had heard and seen, I fell . . ." (NIV, NJB, REB), an issue more important to English idiom than to Greek. See Burton, *Moods and Tenses*, 22–23.

28. See the combination of "fell and worshiped" also in 4:10, a physical expression of devotion and obeisance.

29. There is a historical present in v. 9a, translated "he said" (λέγει). While introducing the words about proper worship in vv. 9b–d, it also points forward to the angel's words in vv. 10–11. See note on the historical present at 5:5 and the significance of historical presents occurring one after another in Runge, *Discourse Grammar*, 139–41.

who hold to the testimony of Jesus" (19:10), the additional description reflects what has just been said in vv. 6–7: "Of your brothers the prophets and of those who obey the words of this book" (v. 9c). John is rightly grouped with "the prophets" since this book is a "prophecy" (vv. 7, 18; see 1:3), and reinforcing the noble calling of living out what this book calls for (v. 7b) is a relevant addition in this context. The angel's final command in v. 9d, "worship God!" has significance at all times for John and for the readers, but especially here as the book's conclusion draws near.

22:10–11 And he said to me, "Do not seal up the words of the prophecy of this book, for the time is near. 11 Let the one who does wrong still do wrong, and let the one who is defiled still stay defiled, and let the righteous one still do what is righteous, and let the holy one still stay holy" (καὶ λέγει μοι, Μὴ σφραγίσῃς τοὺς λόγους τῆς προφητείας τοῦ βιβλίου τούτου, ὁ καιρὸς γὰρ ἐγγύς ἐστιν. 11 ὁ ἀδικῶν ἀδικησάτω ἔτι καὶ ὁ ῥυπαρὸς ῥυπανθήτω ἔτι, καὶ ὁ δίκαιος δικαιοσύνην ποιησάτω ἔτι καὶ ὁ ἅγιος ἁγιασθήτω ἔτι). Verses 6–9 already set out various thematic links with the opening passage (1:1–3), and now vv. 10–21 continue that linkage as they conclude the whole composition. In addition to repeating the source and reliability of the book from 1:1–3, this epilogue drives home to the readers their urgent need to respond in obedience to what the book records. Such urgency appears in the final words of the revealing angel (i.e., the one in vv. 1, 6, 9; the angel of 21:9), addressed to John and to his readers (vv. 10b–11).[30] First he instructs John not to "seal up" (μὴ σφραγίσῃς) the book's prophetic words (v. 10b). To "seal up" here

denotes keeping something secure so that it is secret or inaccessible.[31] In some contexts the purpose has a temporal component: to keep something safe for a long period of time so that it will be available at a much later date (e.g., the visions in Dan 8:26; 12:4, 9; words kept safe until the time of the end; cf. T. Mos. 1:16–18). In Revelation 10:4 John was told not to write what he had heard but to seal it up in the sense of "keeping secret, not disclosing" the mysteries of God that humans can never know (see comments there). This prohibition is the opposite of both: God desires what John has written to be widely known in his own day and in subsequent generations up to the actual fulfillment of the prophecies it contains. The supportive clause ("for," γάρ) in v. 10c shows that preservation for a far distant generation is not the point of this sealing. The well-known season or occasion ("the time," ὁ καιρός) "is near" when the things John writes about will take place (cf. 1:3; also see John's use of "soon" in 1:1; 2:16; 3:11; 22:6, 7, 12, 20).

Following his prohibition to John in v. 10, the angel addresses four imperatives to the readers more broadly (v. 11), commands that seem rather fatalistic (similar to 13:10).[32] The four imperatives are arranged in two pairs, the first pair expressing an ungodly or resistant response to what Revelation says (v. 11a–b) and the second pair embodying a godly response (v. 11c–d). All four contain the adverb "still, yet, more" (ἔτι), implying simply the continuation of a person's existing moral or religious course with no possibility of change even in the pressing present and future crises that John has recorded. This is in part an acknowledgement of the biblical theme that human stubbornness and

---

30. The use of the historical present in v. 10a (λέγει, translated as "said") is to emphasize not the angel's utterance in vv. 10–11 but the words of Jesus about his coming and his character in vv. 12–13. So again features of vv. 6–9 lead us forward into the central points of vv. 10–21. See previous note on v. 9a.

31. BDAG 980.

32. This sequence of thought perhaps mirrors the ideas of Dan 12:9–10. See also Ezek 3:26–27.

evil are so ingrained that even the worst distresses or warnings cannot dislodge them, as Pharaoh demonstrated at the exodus (Exod 7–12), as Isaiah was told about his audience (Isa 6:8–10), and as Jesus understood when he spoke in parables (Matt 13:10–15). Revelation shows that this will be true when God's future judgments fall (e.g., 6:15–17; 9:20–21; 16:9–11, 21). But the two outward allowances to normal human evil[33] in v. 11a–b ("go ahead and do wrong still; go ahead and stay defiled") confront a reader with the question, "Is this your true condition or will you turn away from it?" They provide an ironic challenge to clarify what is at stake: "Go ahead and be stubborn—there is an eternal price to pay for such resistance." The two positive commands in v. 11c–d ("do what is righteous; stay holy") present the alternative pathway.[34] They call John's faithful readers to perseverance until the end despite severe opposition (and deliverance is near; cf. Isa 56:1), but they also appeal to the ungodly to turn toward God in view of the future reckoning John describes in his book. Either way these commands warn that one's response to the appeals presented in this book will settle that person's destiny forever.

22:12–13 "Indeed, I am coming soon, and my reward is with me to render to each one as his work deserves. 13 I am the Alpha and the Omega, the first and the last, the beginning and the end (Ἰδοὺ ἔρχομαι ταχύ, καὶ ὁ μισθός μου μετ᾽ ἐμοῦ ἀποδοῦναι ἑκάστῳ ὡς τὸ ἔργον ἐστὶν αὐτοῦ. 13 ἐγὼ τὸ Ἄλφα καὶ τὸ Ὦ, ὁ πρῶτος καὶ ὁ ἔσχατος, ἡ ἀρχὴ

καὶ τὸ τέλος). The epilogue incorporates a variety of voices to reinforce the themes of the book, and John switches now to the words of Jesus directly (probably including vv. 12–16), but in vv. 12–13 they develop the points just communicated by the angel in vv. 10–11. The time for all the things John has described is truly near (v. 10c), because Jesus himself is "coming soon" to consummate those events (v. 12a; cf. vv. 7, 20; the latter verse explicitly identifies the one coming as the Lord Jesus).[35] And those who hear must give heed to the angel's commands (v. 11) because Jesus himself will recompense "each one as his work deserves" (v. 12b–d; cf. 2:23; 11:18).[36]

In his "coming" to earth to bring his "reward," Jesus is assuming the role that Yahweh takes in Isaiah 40:10 (the same key terms occur here as in the LXX translation; see also Isa 62:11) especially in blessing his faithful people. The close identification of Jesus, the Lamb, with Yahweh, the Lord God, throughout Revelation (e.g., Rev 1:4–5; 5:13; 6:16–17) makes it appropriate for Jesus to confirm his faithfulness to his people by taking on his lips a series of titles that could also be used (and are used) of Yahweh (22:13; cf. Isa 41:4; 44:6; 48:12).[37] Jesus is "the Alpha and the Omega," just as God is (see discussion at Rev 1:8; 21:6), he is "the first and the last" (see discussion at 1:17), and he is "the beginning and the end," just as God is (see 21:6).[38] These titles all represent his eternal being and his sovereign direction of history toward the fulfillment of his purposes.

---

33. These are permissive imperatives with an ironic sense (Wallace, *Grammar*, 488–89).

34. See Koester, *Revelation*, 840–41, for understanding these imperatives as an appeal to the readers.

35. See comments at v. 7 for arguments showing that Jesus is the speaker in vv. 7, 12.

36. The phrase "as his work deserves" (v. 12d) is a smoother English rendering of "as his work is" (ὡς τὸ ἔργον ἐστὶν αὐτοῦ). This is similar to "according to [one's] works" (κατὰ τὰ ἔργα;

cf. 2:23; 20:12; see too Prov 24:12; Rom 2:6) whether positive or negative. See theological discussion of this at 19:8.

37. Verse 13 begins with no explicit conjunction (asyndeton), but it is closely connected to v. 12, and the implied connection is that it shows his timeless sovereignty that will enable him to accomplish what v. 12 says he will do in the near future (the basis of the actions of v. 12).

38. Cf. Bauckham, *Theology*, 23–28, 54–58.

22:14–15 "Blessed are those who wash their robes so that they may have the right to the tree of life and they may enter by the gates into the city. 15 Outside are the dogs and the sorcerers and the sexually immoral and the murderers and the idolators and everyone who loves and practices falsehood (Μακάριοι οἱ πλύνοντες τὰς στολὰς αὐτῶν, ἵνα ἔσται ἡ ἐξουσία αὐτῶν ἐπὶ τὸ ξύλον τῆς ζωῆς καὶ τοῖς πυλῶσιν εἰσέλθωσιν εἰς τὴν πόλιν. 15 ἔξω οἱ κύνες καὶ οἱ φάρμακοι καὶ οἱ πόρνοι καὶ οἱ φονεῖς καὶ οἱ εἰδωλολάτραι καὶ πᾶς φιλῶν καὶ ποιῶν ψεῦδος). The final of the seven beatitudes in Revelation appears here (see 1:3 for discussion and listing). Its parallel with the sixth one in 22:7 (closely associated with Christ's "I am coming soon"; cf. v. 12 above) gives support for taking this as a further statement by Jesus. He pronounces blessing on those who "wash their robes" and so are able to participate in the blessings of God's favor in the new Jerusalem (v. 14).[39] The expression "who wash their robes" (οἱ πλύνοντες τὰς στολὰς αὐτῶν)[40] appears in a similar form in 7:14 (cf. also 3:4) and represents the human response of turning to Christ for cleansing from sin (see 7:14, "washed their robes and made them white in the blood of the Lamb"). Christ himself has provided the spiritual cleansing needed to enter God's presence (cf. OT parallels in Exod 19:10, 14; Num 8:7, 21). The goal of this washing ("so that," ἵνα; v. 14b) is to give Christians the privilege to partake from

the abundant sustenance of the "tree of life" in the center of the new Jerusalem (v. 14b; cf. 2:7; 22:2) as well as ready access "by the gates into the city" (v. 14c; see 21:12, 21, 25; cf. Ps 118:19–20). The strictly logical sequence of these actions would be "entering the city and then partaking of the tree at its center," but the order of occurrence is not important here (as often in Rev). The point is that spiritual washing leads to both blessings. The references in v. 14b–c to features of the new Jerusalem as just cited are examples of significant promises made also to "the overcomer" in several messages to the churches in chapters 2–3 that find their fulfillment in chapters 20–22 of the book (cf. 2:7, 11, 26–28; 3:5, 12, 21).[41]

As a reinforcement of the privilege of cleansing from sin and entrance into the city (v. 14), Christ portrays in v. 15 those who continued in their sin and were thus judged and cast into the lake of fire prior to the arrival of the new Jerusalem on earth (described in 20:11–15). He cites in contrast a listing of people who practice various sins and are consequently excluded from the city (they are "outside," ἔξω; cf. the lists in 21:8, 27).[42] The first group on the list, "dogs" (κύνες), is a somewhat common biblical metaphor for people who engage in disgusting practices of various kinds. In much of the ancient world, canines were regarded not as lovable pets but despicable scavengers (e.g., Prov 26:11; Luke 16:21; 2 Pet 2:22). To use "dogs" as a metaphor for people was a vivid way to characterize

---

39. A textual variation that makes a significant difference in the translation and sense of the verse occurs here. Most of the Byzantine manuscripts (and a few others: 046, etc.) read "who do his commands" (οἱ ποιοῦντες τὰς ἐντολὰς αὐτοῦ; cf. KJV, NKJV). But the reading given above has stronger and earlier manuscript support (א, A, 1006, etc.) and fits the idiom of Rev better. See Metzger, *TCGNT*2, 690; contra Stephen Goranson, "The Text of Revelation 22.14," *NTS* 43 (1997): 154–57; J. M. Ross, "Further Unnoticed Points in the Text of the New Testament," *NovT* 45 (2003): 220–21.

40. All but one of the seven beatitudes of Rev are expressed using Greek present-tense participles to give a generic sense:

"anyone or all who" act in a certain way. They are not progressive or iterative in a narrow way ("are washing, repeatedly wash"). See Fanning, *Verbal Aspect*, 209–11, 411–12. The exception is 19:9 (a perfect participle referring to those "invited" to the wedding banquet and thus authorized to attend).

41. Boxall, *Revelation*, 312, has a valuable chart displaying these parallels.

42. See 1 Cor 6:9–10; Gal 5:19–21; Eph 5:5 for a similar "will not enter" motif; cf. also Rom 1:29–32.

depraved human behavior (e.g., Isa 56:10–11; Matt 7:6; Phil 3:2).[43] The second group is "sorcerers" or those who practice magic arts (φάρμακοι; Gal 5:20; Rev 9:21; 18:23; 21:8; see note at 9:21). The remaining ones named in v. 15 are all proscribed in the Decalogue (Exod 20:13–15) and are cited elsewhere in Revelation or in the New Testament in lists of sinful people or conduct (e.g., Rev 9:20–21; 21:8, 27). The final group (shifting to generic singular) is "everyone who loves and practices falsehood." In a list citing other violations of the Decalogue, this also refers most likely to people who lack general integrity or honesty (contra the ones in 14:5). But it is possible that a more specific sense is in view and that it refers to anyone who follows the false prophet's "lie" (ψεῦδος) or deception about the beast (13:11–17; 16:13). The effect of v. 15 overall is to give another implicit appeal, like v. 11, to turn away from such practices and accept the water of life from Jesus free of charge (v. 17).

22:16–17 "I, Jesus, sent my angel to testify to you about these things for the churches. I am the shoot and the descendant of David, the bright morning star." 17 And the Spirit and the bride say, "Come." And let the one who hears say, "Come." And let the one who thirsts come; let the one who desires it take the water of life freely (Ἐγὼ Ἰησοῦς ἔπεμψα τὸν ἄγγελόν μου μαρτυρῆσαι ὑμῖν ταῦτα ἐπὶ ταῖς ἐκκλησίαις. ἐγώ εἰμι ἡ ῥίζα καὶ τὸ γένος Δαυίδ, ὁ ἀστὴρ ὁ λαμπρὸς ὁ πρωϊνός. 17 Καὶ τὸ πνεῦμα καὶ ἡ νύμφη λέγουσιν, Ἔρχου. καὶ ὁ ἀκούων εἰπάτω, Ἔρχου. καὶ ὁ διψῶν ἐρχέσθω, ὁ θέλων λαβέτω ὕδωρ ζωῆς δωρεάν). The words spoken directly by Jesus (vv. 12–16) come to an end here at v. 16, but only for a brief interlude before

he speaks again in vv. 18–20. Here again we find reflections back to the opening of the book that identified it as a "revelation" from Jesus Christ (1:1) that God gave to him so that it could be communicated to John and to God's people through "his angel" (1:1) as a "testimony" to them (1:2). A bit later in the opening, the book is addressed to seven specific churches in the province of Asia (1:4, 11), and then later Jesus speaks by the Spirit directly to those churches (and through them to other churches both then and now; see 2:7, etc. at the end of each of the messages of chs. 2–3: "What the Spirit says to the churches"). This chain of revelation and witness helps to explain the puzzling combination of a plural pronoun, "to you" (ὑμῖν) plus a reference to "the churches" in 22:16b. The "you" seems to refer to the seven specific churches originally addressed, while "the churches" is the larger group of Christians to whom the Spirit also speaks through this book. So, in v. 16a–b Jesus attests again to the reliability of the book's contents as a testimony that he revealed through his messengers (cf. this point also in vv. 18–20a).

The book's reliability is enhanced by his "I am" declaration in v. 16c, where Jesus reveals himself again as the one who fulfills God's long-expected deliverance for Israel and all the earth's peoples through his Messiah. As "the shoot and the descendant of David" (ἡ ῥίζα καὶ τὸ γένος Δαυίδ),[44] Jesus is the personal focus of God's redemptive plan spoken of in Isaiah 11:10 ("shoot of Jesse"; also Rom 15:12) and revealed more broadly in 2 Samuel 7; Psalms 2; 89; 110; 132; Isaiah 9; Jeremiah 23; 33; Ezekiel 34; Amos 9; Zechariah 12 (cf. Luke 1:31–33, 69; Rom 1:3). A different image that speaks of this

---

43. In one OT passage, Deut 23:19 in Hebrew (v. 18 in English), "dog" is figurative for a male cult prostitute, but that specific practice is not in view here.

44. For the rendering "shoot" instead of "root" for ῥίζα, see note at 5:5. Here the word means "shoot, scion" ("that which grows from a root," BDAG 903–4; cf. C. Maurer, "ῥίζα," *TDNT* 6:989).

same saving purpose of God is his identification as "the bright morning star," a messianic title drawn from Numbers 24:17 that refers to the one who brings God's light to shine on the world as the dawn of his age of salvation (cf. Isa 60:1–3; Luke 1:78–79; 2 Pet 1:19; Rev 2:28).[45] References such as 2:27; 3:7; 5:5; 11:15; 12:5; 19:15 show the importance of the Davidic (and thus Israelite) connection of Jesus for the theology of Revelation. This is a feature of John's focus on what the Old Testament prophets and psalms have said regarding the events "that must happen soon" to consummate the history of this world.

Jesus's speech that began in v. 12 with "indeed, I am coming soon" (and a previous "I am" declaration) comes to a temporary end with v. 16. It is interrupted by a brief response and three related exhortations (v. 17). This verse is best taken as John's report of what he perceives to be the heavenly and earthly response to Jesus's promise of his imminent coming to earth. Both "the Spirit and the bride" urge him on with their appeal, "Come" (v. 17a–b). The "Spirit" is the divine Spirit through whom Jesus spoke to the churches (chs. 2–3; see note on 2:7), but here he speaks through John as a Christian prophet to urge Christ's return. Likewise, John discerns the voice of the corporate, spiritual entity of God's redeemed people of all ages, pictured through the imagery of the "bride" he has chosen, who longs for her groom's coming to take her as his own (cf. 19:7; 21:2, 9).[46]

Their appeal to Jesus to come and fulfill God's saving purpose on earth leads John to add three related instructions of his own, addressed to all who hear this appeal (v. 17c–f). First, he urges anyone hearing this passage as it is read in the churches

(cf. 1:3) to join in with the Spirit and the bride to invite Jesus to come soon (John models this himself in v. 20c): that person should say "come" in response to what was just heard (v. 17c–d).[47] Next he adds two more commands to anyone whose longing for true spiritual life has been stirred by Jesus's words: "Let the one who thirsts come" (v. 17e). Here in a wordplay, the term "come" (ἔρχομαι) changes from an invitation for Jesus to return to earth (v. 17b) into an invitation for the spiritually needy to turn to God for true satisfaction. The final command reinforces this image: anyone who wants to slake his or her spiritual thirst may "take the water of life freely" (v. 17f; see 21:6 for parallels and OT background). Here the earlier implicit appeals to the reader or hearer of the book (vv. 11, 15) become explicit and cogent.

22:18–19 I testify to everyone who hears the words of the prophecy of this book: "If anyone adds to them, God will inflict on him the plagues that are written about in this book, 19 and if anyone takes away from the words of the book of this prophecy, God will take away his portion from the tree of life and the holy city that are written about in this book" (Μαρτυρῶ ἐγὼ παντὶ τῷ ἀκούοντι τοὺς λόγους τῆς προφητείας τοῦ βιβλίου τούτου· ἐάν τις ἐπιθῇ ἐπ᾽ αὐτά, ἐπιθήσει ὁ θεὸς ἐπ᾽ αὐτὸν τὰς πληγὰς τὰς γεγραμμένας ἐν τῷ βιβλίῳ τούτῳ, 19 καὶ ἐάν τις ἀφέλῃ ἀπὸ τῶν λόγων τοῦ βιβλίου τῆς προφητείας ταύτης, ἀφελεῖ ὁ θεὸς τὸ μέρος αὐτοῦ ἀπὸ τοῦ ξύλου τῆς ζωῆς καὶ ἐκ τῆς πόλεως τῆς ἁγίας τῶν γεγραμμένων ἐν τῷ βιβλίῳ τούτῳ). The speaker in vv. 18–19 ("I testify," v. 18a) could be John, continuing the comments begun in v. 17. But it is much more likely that Jesus steps back in after the brief interlude of v. 17 as the one

---

45. See discussion of this image at 2:28.

46. This seems to be the spirit of 2 Tim 4:8 about "those who love [Christ's] appearing." They do so because they love him

and eagerly wait to be in his presence (cf. Phil 1:23).

47. Bruce, "Spirit in the Apocalypse," 343.

who testifies to the contents of vv. 18–19.[48] Jesus is identified as the speaker in v. 20 where "testifies to these things" looks back to these verses, and then Jesus states, "I am coming soon" (v. 20b). "Testify" in this context means "confirms the truth of, supports the validity of"[49] in a way similar to an oath formula, solemnly declaring what follows to be reliable. The confirmation is directed to anyone who listens to what John's book says (described formally in v. 18a in words similar to 1:3; cf. 22:7, 10; 19a). The repeated description of the book is significant because of what it says about the divine origin of Revelation itself. Because it contains "words of . . . prophecy" that come from God (as 1:1–3; 22:6–7, 10, 16 assert), it has a privileged authority beyond merely human words.

The substance of what Jesus affirms is a set of severe punishments pledged against anyone who violates the integrity of what God has revealed in this book (vv. 18b–19). The strict integrity of its contents is described in words that reflect Moses's warnings in Deuteronomy 4:2 (cf. Deut 12:32; Prov 30:5–6) that there must be no additions or deletions from the things he is teaching Israel because they constitute "commandments from the LORD your God."[50] No alterations to make them purely human words or teachings can be allowed. In these LXX passages (Deut 4:2; 12:32 [31:1 LXX]; Prov 30:6) the verb that is translated "add to" is προστίθημι, while in Revelation 22:18 it is a near synonym, ἐπιτίθημι.[51] The same word for "take away" (ἀφαιρέω) occurs in Deuteronomy 4:2, 12:32

[13:1 LXX], and Revelation 22:19. This leads to the balanced conditional statements, first in v. 18b–d: if someone "adds to" the words of Revelation, God will "inflict on him" the very woes against the wicked that the book describes (the word for "plagues, afflictions," πληγαί, is used often, e.g., in 9:18, 20; 15:1; 16:9). Likewise (v. 19) if anyone "takes away" anything from its wording or teaching, God will "take away" that person's share in the eschatological blessings described in the book (cf. Gal 1:6–7; Jas 3:1). The blessings are central to the life of the godly in the new creation: "the tree of life" and "the holy city."

22:20–21 The one who testifies about these things says, "Surely I am coming soon." Amen. Come, Lord Jesus! 21 The grace of the Lord Jesus be with all (Λέγει ὁ μαρτυρῶν ταῦτα, Ναί, ἔρχομαι ταχύ. Ἀμήν, ἔρχου κύριε Ἰησοῦ. 21 Ἡ χάρις τοῦ κυρίου Ἰησοῦ μετὰ πάντων [τῶν ἁγίων. ἀμήν][52]). After Jesus's solemn confirmation or testimony (v. 18a) to the preceding words, John adds a brief but significant concluding coda and benediction. Jesus as "the one who testifies" to what was just said now affirms again his sure and imminent return (as in vv. 7, 12; cf. 2:16; 3:11). The confirmatory particle "surely" (ναί; "in solemn assurance")[53] is new to the expression (but see John's use of it in response to the OT prophecies about Jesus's coming in 1:7). This is exactly the word from the Lord—both assuring and challenging—that any reader can welcome at the end of such a book so filled with fearful, momentous

48. Osborne, *Revelation*, 778–79, includes all of vv. 12–19 as the words of Jesus (cf. also p. 794). Koester, *Revelation*, 844; Michaels, *Revelation*, 257–58; Mounce, *Revelation*, 409–10, agree that vv. 18–19 are Jesus's words. Seeing John as the speaker in vv. 18–19 are Beale, *Revelation*, 1154; Boxall, *Revelation*, 319; Smalley, *Revelation*, 582–83.

49. BDAG 618.

50. Very similar wording appears in later texts about divinely revealed teaching (1 En. 104:10–11; Josephus, *Ag. Ap.* 1.8; Did. 4:13).

51. The word used for "add to" in v. 18b and v. 18c (ἐπιτίθημι) is possibly a shift to allow for a wordplay across both clauses, since it can mean "inflict, lay on" punishment (e.g., Acts 16:23) as well as "put on, add to" (BDAG 384; Aune, *Revelation 17–22*, 1230–31).

52. See comments on this textual uncertainty in what follows.

53. BDAG 665.

events of cosmic and lasting import. John for his part follows the counsel offered in v. 17c–d and welcomes the Lord's coming with a hearty affirmation: "Amen. Come, Lord Jesus!"[54] Such an appeal and heartfelt longing should be the disciple's spoken and unspoken request to Christ at all times.

The benediction that formally closes the composition follows a standard epistolary form (cf. notes about epistolary genre at 1:4–5), but it focuses appropriately on "grace" from the Lord Jesus, who has just been the focus and is the center of God's redeeming work throughout the book. The phrase "with all" at the end is subject to a wide variety of textual variations (e.g., μετὰ τῶν ἁγίων. ἀμήν, "with the saints. Amen"), but "with all" is the shortest reading and thus best explains how the others arose, although its external evidence is thin (A, vg).[55] In any case "with all" in this context implies "with all the Christian readers in the churches addressed by this composition" (cf. 1:4, 11; 2:7).

Theology in Application

How Did We Get Here, and Where Are We Going?

Revelation 22:1–5 cries out to be preached or taught as the conclusion to the grand story of the Bible: Eden renewed and human life as it is meant to be lived. No preacher should leave this theme unmentioned in giving an exposition of any part of 21:1–22:9. Too often our preaching or teaching of Scripture is piecemeal and atomistic, focused on a single text without giving the larger picture. But in a world where even churchgoers are often biblically illiterate, we should constantly try to show the important connections across the themes of the Bible. This is not just an academic concern. People facing the ups and downs of life need to see God's grand scheme of things. Why is life on this earth so hard at times and yet so glorious at others? How can people be capable of such good and noble things and, on the other hand, such horror and cruelty? Romans 8 is an example of Paul setting out the full story in brief (sin, the law, the incarnation, present groaning and future glory, God's goal to conform all believers to Christ, his unconquerable love) so that his readers can see what the problem is and what God's solution will be, that they might live in hope and obedience. This passage can serve in a similar way to instruct and encourage God's people.

"The End Is Not an Event but a Person"

The line in the title above, taken from Caird's commentary on Revelation 21:6,[56] can be understood in the wrong way (i.e., Rev provides no idea of what will actually happen in the future, it just shows us more about Jesus). But the sense of 21:6 (God is "the Alpha and the Omega, the beginning and the end") and of Revelation 21–22 as

---

54. The combined title "Lord Jesus" in vv. 20–21 (used together only here in Rev) reflects the traditional Aramaic phrase that appears in 1 Cor 16:22 (cf. Did. 10:6), "Maranatha ["our Lord, come"; μαράνα θά]."

55. *TCGNT2*, 690–93. English versions vary a great deal in including one or another of these additional words.

56. Caird, *Revelation*, 266.

a whole is that the central focus of eternal life will be God and the Lamb in the midst of their peoples. God is the one who planned our redemption and accomplished it through Jesus, and the chief blessedness of the new Jerusalem will be to enjoy face-to-face communion with God: "The dwelling of God is with humans, and he will dwell with them, and they will be his peoples, and God himself will be with them as their God" (21:3). Note also 22:3–4: "The throne of God and of the Lamb will be in the city, and his servants will worship him, and they will see his face." More blessed than the lavish surroundings or abundant provision in the new Jerusalem will be the presence of the Lord God among his people.

But the focus on the person of God or of God and the Lamb in the earlier passages changes in 22:6–21 to a yearning for Jesus our Savior to return. He is the groom for whom the bride longs and prepares herself (19:7; 21:2; 22:17). The anticipation of the bridegroom's appearance builds, as three times John records Jesus's affirmation that he will come soon (22:7, 12, 20). This eager expectation is how the book began (cf. 1:1–3, 7). After Jesus's second declaration of his coming in 22:12, John reports the ardent response of the Spirit (who revealed the book), of the bride corporately, and of the individual Christian reading the book, all of whom invite him to "come" (v. 17). After the third affirmation, "Surely I am coming soon" (v. 20), John's plaintive appeal, "Amen. Come, Lord Jesus!" is the book's fitting conclusion along with the benediction, "The grace of the Lord Jesus be with all" (v. 21). The Lord Jesus is the person whose coming every Christian should love, long for, and pray for. His grace and his presence should be the center of our lives from beginning to end and in all our moments in between.

Free Water for Those Who Thirst

The same word "come," used repeatedly to invite Jesus to return, appears in a wordplay in v. 17 to appeal to the unconverted to respond also, in this case to accept the gift of salvation provided freely by Christ. At the end of a book detailing God's sober judgment against sin and his rich blessings for the redeemed, it is only right for the conclusion to focus on the urgency for the spiritually needy to turn to God for true satisfaction ("let the one who thirsts come") and for its wide-open availability to be advertised ("let the one who desires it take the water of life freely"). In reading about the blessings of the new Jerusalem and the celebration of the bride and groom in the marriage feast of the Lamb (19:7–9; 21:2, 9; 22:17), no one who sees his or her spiritual lack and desires to slake that thirst should feel excluded. The invitation to step into real life with God is extended without cost to anyone who desires it (21:6; 22:17). This is the most appropriate beginning point for someone who is not a Christian to "obey the words of the prophecy of this book" and find the blessedness about which it speaks (v. 7). To change the imagery, Christ's sacrifice is the only way to have our "robes washed clean and have access to the tree of life and enter into the city" (v. 12, the book's final beatitude). And all are welcome!

Theology of Revelation

Introductory Summary

Revelation is above all else a book centered on the true and living God engaged with his good creation.[1] It confronts us with who God is and what he is doing in this world, with a special focus on what is to come and how we should live now in anticipation of that future. It is filled with powerful images of God's glory, power, holiness, and sovereignty. But in his majesty and dominion, God is not distant but remains present and engaged with his world across all the ages. We see him as the eternal God (1:8; 4:8; 21:6), the Almighty (9x), on his heavenly throne (e.g., 1:4; 4:2; 5:13; 19:4; 20:11; 22:1–3), extolled as creator (3:14; 4:11; 10:6; 14:7; 21:5) and redeemer (5:9; 7:10; 12:10; 19:1), and feared as the judge to whom all will give an account (6:16–17; 11:18; 14:10, 19; 19:15; 20:11). These titles portray God as the all-powerful ruler and sovereign over all things, who created and now sustains his universe while bringing all things to their divinely intended fulfillment. The worship that John shows being offered to God in heaven serves as a model of the fitting and proper worship to be offered to him on earth by all its inhabitants. It shows us that devotion to and communion with such a God are the most important things—the central things—to which we could give ourselves.

More particularly, Revelation is a book about God's work of judgment and redemption through Christ, leading to the renewal of all things. From beginning to end John's topic is "things that must soon take place" (1:1; 22:6; cf. 1:19; 4:1), for "the time is near" (1:3; 22:10) and Christ is "coming quickly" (3:11; 22:7, 12, 20). As in the rest of the New Testament, Jesus Christ is seen as the focal point of history, for God's people Israel and the diverse nations of the world as well as for all creation. His incarnation, death, resurrection, and exaltation as the slain but glorified Lamb ensure God's victory over evil for all time (1:5–6, 17–18; 3:7; 5:6, 9–10; 11:15). But we await his return as the Lion of Judah, the King of kings and Lord of lords,

---

1. This summary is adapted from Fanning, "Discipleship in Revelation."

to bring this victory to earth in its fullness (1:6; 5:5; 10:6–7; 11:15–18; 14:1; 19:11–21; 21:1–5; 22:16).

In many ways then Revelation recaps the entire story of the Bible from creation to new creation. It is firmly anchored in the Old Testament story of Israel's kings and prophets and in the gospel of God's saving grace in Christ. To these it adds the glorious climax of biblical revelation, visions of deliverance and renewal that will bring humans into direct worship of and communion with God and the Lamb forever in a restored creation (21:1–22:5). In the process, it shows the privileged status and responsibility that Christians possess now while the ongoing story of God's redemption works its way out in the real world in which we live.[2]

God and His World

Revelation is a God-saturated book.[3] Only when we see God in the ways that John saw him in this book's visions can we grasp the significance of all the other things he records. Among the most distinctive descriptions of God in Revelation are the divine titles "Almighty" (9x in Rev; only once elsewhere in the NT), "Alpha and Omega" (used of God the Father in 1:8 and 21:6), "the beginning and the end" (21:6), and "who was and is and is to come" (1:4, 8; 4:8; cf. 11:17; 16:5).[4] These are rooted in the Old Testament picture of the eternal, incomparable God (especially Exod 3:14; Isa 44:6; Amos 4:13; Hag 2:6–9). The final part of the latter title ("who . . . is to come") refers not only to God's existence in the future but his actual "coming" now and in the future into the affairs of this world, his intervention in judgment and redemption that will constitute the culminating earthly events that Revelation describes. He is not distant or absent but is engaged with his creation, accomplishing his purposes.

There are also descriptions of God and his ways that Revelation shares with other New Testament books, which also carry important weight in its own portrayal of him. These include the descriptors "holy" (4:8; 6:10; 16:5), "just" (15:3; 16:5–7; 19:2), and "true" (16:7; 19:2). He is also called "Father [of Jesus]" (1:6; 3:5; 14:1), "Creator" (4:11; 10:6; 14:7; 21:5), and "King" (15:3). Acknowledging God as the Creator is to recognize his right to control the course of this world and its creatures according to

---

2. The theological points included in what follows attempt to gather up the distinctive features of the theology of Rev as discussed in the commentary itself. For details, see the commentary on the verses that are cited. The question of whether there is a shared theology across all the NT books traditionally attributed to John the Apostle (Gospel, Epistles, Revelation) is vitally connected, of course, to decisions about their authorship (see the introduction for discussion). Even if they are all understood to come from the same author, one could argue that the theology of Rev is distinctive enough so that treatment of Rev apart from the theology of the Gospel and Epistles is the

best option. Marshall, *New Testament Theology*, 574, follows this approach. It is followed here as well.

3. See Bauckham, *Theology*, 23–53, and G. K. Beale, "Revelation (Book)," in *New Dictionary of Biblical Theology* (Downers Grove, IL: InterVarsity Press, 2000), 356–57.

4. Bauckham, *Theology*, 27, says about the title "Alpha and Omega" that "God precedes all things, as their Creator, and he will bring all things to eschatological fulfillment. He is the origin and goal of all history. He has the first word, in creation, and the last word, in new creation."

his own intent and timing. This coheres with images of God's supreme authority and his sovereign control over all things (similar to the title "Almighty"). The overwhelming sense of God's sovereignty is reflected also in the pervasive picture of God on his heavenly throne (in 14 of 22 chs. in Rev) and in the repeated divine passive "was given" (ἐδόθη) used to denote actions that occur only because he allows them to (e.g., 6:8; 9:3; 13:7; even evil agents serve his larger purposes). He is clearly in control and will act according to his wise, just, and good plans for his creatures and for his own glory (4:11; 7:12; 14:7; 15:4; 19:7).[5]

According to Revelation, divine glory also belongs to Jesus Christ (5:12–13; 21:23). He bears the titles "the Alpha and the Omega, the first and the last, the beginning and the end" (22:13; cf. 1:17; 2:8; the first and third of these phrases are used of God in 1:8; 21:6). These names signify Christ's eternal being and his sovereign direction of the universe according to the divine purpose. He is the one through whom God's dominion will be exerted on this earth: Christ is "the ruler of the kings of the earth" (1:5) and "the King of kings and Lord of lords" (19:16; cf. 17:14).[6] He is the fulfillment of God's Old Testament promises to rule through his Messiah in the line of David (3:7; 5:5; 12:5; 19:15; 22:16; cf. Gen 49:9; 2 Sam 7:12–16; Ps 2:1–12; Isa 11:1, 10)[7] and to exert everlasting dominion, along with his people, over the nations of the world as the "Son of Man" (1:13; 14:14; cf. Dan 7:13–14, 27). He shares with God the worship of the whole heavenly company and all creation (5:13–14).[8] But most pointedly his sacrificial death became the focal point of God's redemption, the turning point of human history and salvation (1:5–6; 5:9–12; 12:5, 11).[9] Rev emphasizes this by its most distinctive and most frequently used title for Jesus, "the Lamb" (ἀρνίον; 29x), an image that combines both self-sacrificing weakness and conquering power.[10] This image, once introduced in the throne-room vision of 5:6, is carried on throughout the rest of the book. The picture of the "Lamb standing as though slain" who has "gained the victory" (5:5) signifies his worthiness to open the scroll (i.e., to set in motion God's plan for judgment and redemption), including his role in divine wrath (6:16–17; 14:10), in defeating the powers of evil (12:11; 17:14), in restoring and preserving faithful Israel (14:1, 4), in sharing with God the position of greatest authority (5:13; 21:22–23; 22:1, 3), and in providing resurrected life and

5. Osborne, *Revelation*, 31–33.

6. The other title used of Jesus Christ in 1:5, "the firstborn of the dead," is significant for both roles mentioned above: it refers to his ascension to kingly rule (Ps 89:27) as well as his victory over death that guarantees resurrection for all the faithful.

7. The title "Christ" (Χριστός) appears seven times in Rev, three times as "Jesus Christ" where it is more of a combined proper name (1:1–2, 5) and four times with the article in the sense of "the Messiah, the Anointed One" (11:15; 12:10; 20: 4, 6). See Strecker, *Theology*, 523–24.

8. Hurtado, *Lord Jesus Christ*, 592–93, regards the visions of chs. 4–5 in which the Lamb "receives heavenly worship along with God" as the most "direct and forceful way to express Jesus's divine status."

9. Jan A. du Rand, "Soteriology in the Apocalypse of John," in *Salvation in the New Testament: Perspectives on Soteriology*, ed. Jan G. van der Watt (Leiden: Brill, 2005), 492–95.

10. W. Hall Harris, "A Theology of John's Writings," in *A Biblical Theology of the New Testament*, ed. Roy B. Zuck and Darrell L. Bock (Chicago: Moody, 1994), 193–94; Strecker, *Theology*, 528–30.

communion with God for all the redeemed throughout all eternity (5:9–10; 7:9–10, 14; 13:8; 19:9; 21:9, 27).[11]

Satan's defeat in his opposition to God was decisively secured at the cross (5:5), and the full extension of that victory will be accomplished when Jesus returns to earth in power and great glory (19:11–21). There he will be seen in full measure as "the ruler of the kings of the earth" (1:5), "the Word of God" (19:13),[12] and as "King of kings and Lord of lords" (19:16). Remarkably, in tracing this glorious and powerful work that Jesus accomplished for our redemption, Revelation does not lose sight of the characteristic theme from John's Gospel and Epistles that this work of God and Christ is grounded in divine, self-sacrificing love. One of the first descriptions of Jesus in the book is "the one who loves us and freed us from our sins by his blood" (1:5; cf. 3:9), and one of the last is the image of the bridegroom waiting for intimate life together with his bride for whom he gave himself (19:7–9; 21:2, 9).

Less is said about the Spirit in Revelation, but he appears in important places in his role of revealing the Father and the Son to the world. The epistolary opening in 1:4–5 has a striking Trinitarian motif in referring to God and to Jesus Christ and, in between, to "the seven spirits before [God's] throne" (1:4; cf. 4:5), an image of the full-orbed Holy Spirit drawn from Isaiah 11:2 and Zechariah 4:1–6. He is closely associated with Jesus (cf. 3:1; 5:6), and the messages to the churches in chapters 2–3 are spoken directly by Christ (see the start of each message), but they are also said to be "what the Spirit says to the churches" (see the ending of each). Beyond that we see the Spirit active in revealing John's visions to him (1:10; 4:2; 17:3; 21:10) and interjecting his oracles at other places (14:13; 22:17). In another important text he is said to be the one who inspires all the prophets in their testimony about Jesus (19:10).[13]

Humanity and Creation

The picture of the majestic, sovereign God who effects his salvation on the earth is counterbalanced in Revelation by the reality of evil that has corrupted both humankind and the wider creation. God's good creation itself is not evil, but it has been co-opted for evil purposes in resistance to its Creator. An important dimension of this aggressive, satanic evil directed against God, his Messiah, and his people is its cosmic and age-long character. It will intensify in the days immediately preceding

---

11. As Strecker, *Theology*, 526–28, observes, the central christological titles in Rev are dependent on OT terms and categories in a way that is unique in the NT, while incorporating also NT traditions about Jesus's person and work. This is perfectly in keeping with his pervasive use of the OT throughout the book (see the introduction).

12. This title is similar to John 1:1, 14 ("the Word") in revealing to the world what God is like (cf. John 1:18). But

"the Word of God" in Rev 19:13 draws from the background of God's "all-powerful word" (ὁ παντοδύναμός σου λόγος) in Wis 18:15. There the "Word" is said to come from the heavenly throne as a "stern warrior" (cf. Exod 15:3) with a "sharp sword" to bring death to Egypt at the exodus. At his second coming Christ is revealed as God's "Word" in the sense of bringing God's sovereign judgment to bear on human evil.

13. Osborne, *Revelation*, 36–37.

Christ's return (12:10–13, 17; 13:7), but Satan's implacable struggle against God began long ago and continues through the present age despite the decisive defeat he suffered in Christ's death and resurrection (Rev 2:10–13; 12:3–9).[14] Satan in his opposition to God has subverted God's original intent for humanity and for the creation itself. Humans were intended to be the glory of God's creation and to embody his dominion over the earth by ruling and tending his creation and expressing his likeness in all that they do (Gen 1:26–28; 2:15–17; Ps 8:3–8).[15] Instead they turned away from God in distrust and disobedience to serve their own ends. The natural world itself became corrupted and cursed (Gen 3:17–19; Rom 8:20–22). Both are forms of enslavement to evil from which neither humans nor the wider creation could free themselves, and so the need for God's redemption (i.e., release, ransom; cf. 1:5; 5:9; 14:3–4) through the death of Christ is made clear.

Revelation portrays this ongoing enslavement to deception and corruption by Satan and his minions (2:20; 12:9; 13:14; 19:2) as warfare against God and his saving work (11:7; 12:17; 13:7). His rule over the present age and his relentless attacks on God's people and their witness in the world will not be stymied until Christ's victory is brought to its fulfillment on the earth. Such attacks come at times in the form of overt persecution, including social ostracism, personal slander, economic discrimination, physical assault or imprisonment, and even death (1:9; 2:9–10, 13; 11:7; 13:15–17). But Satan's opposition can also manifest itself in times of peace and prosperity in the form of false teachings (2:2, 20, 24) or temptations that lull Christians into complacency (3:17–19) and easy conformity to the sinful practices of the world (2:20; 18:3–4).

This ongoing history of evil and enslavement is why salvation in Revelation is presented in "two-tone colors":[16] it requires judgment of evil as well as renewal for both humanity and the creation in order to bring God's saving work to its completion. Satan and those who persist in following his evil ways must be defeated and condemned if restoration is to be accomplished. So the story of Revelation is a story of an imminent "regime change" on earth,[17] God's victory over its current rulers (Satan and the rebellious "nations" or "kings of the earth") so that "the kingdom of the world" can "become the kingdom of our Lord and of his Messiah" (11:15–18; 12:10; 19:6). The invisible rule of God and the Lamb is already firmly in place in heaven (2:27; 3:21; chs. 4–5; 12:5), but it remains to be established visibly and fully on earth (19:11–21; 20:1–6; 22:1–5). This reign will come in two stages: first the intermediate rule of the Messiah for a thousand years (20:1–10) and then the eternal

---

14. Helyer, *Witness of Jesus, Paul and John*, 357–59; Ladd, *Theology of the New Testament*, 675–76.

15. Sauer, *King of the Earth*, 72–100.

16. Ladd, *Theology of the New Testament*, 678. See also du Rand, "Soteriology in the Apocalypse of John," 472.

17. Guttesen, *Leaning into the Future*, 123–41; and McNicol, *Conversion*, 56–57.

rule of God and the Lamb over the new heaven and new earth (chs. 21–22).[18] Both of these are works of both spiritual and physical or material renewal, not spiritual only.

When God establishes his reign again over the fallen and defiant earth, his work of creation and salvation will have come full circle, to a restored and enhanced Eden (22:1–5) in which humans are likewise restored to the original divine intent for them.[19] They will rule with God and the Lamb over his good creation in its renewed form (1:6; 2:26–27; 3:21; 5:10; 22:5) as saints of the Most High, governing the formerly rebellious empires of the world under the authority of the Ancient of Days and the glorious Son of Man (Dan 7:13–14, 27). Thus, while the book includes past and present dimensions of God's saving work, its orientation is toward salvation's final fulfillment, "not merely a terminus but a goal, an end that is purposed and fulfilled."[20]

The New Community for a New World

The community of God's redeemed humanity is presented in different facets in Revelation. John begins by addressing the book to particular churches (ἐκκλησίαι) in his sphere of ministry, the seven churches of first-century Asia Minor (1:4, 11; also 22:16). As the specific messages to these churches unfold, we discover that they are representative of all the congregations like them addressed by the exalted Jesus ("hear what the Spirit says to the churches," 2:7, etc.). These are the individual local congregations in various cities made up of God's "servants" (δοῦλοι; 1:1; 2:20; 22:6) who need exhortation to remain faithful in the struggle against Satan's deceptions. By showing them "what must happen soon," God intends to bolster their fidelity and perseverance in displaying the characteristic traits of Christ's followers despite opposition (e.g., love, faith, endurance, obedience, discernment, holiness, and zeal in serving God). While God promises to deliver them from the time of severe suffering immediately preceding Christ's return (3:10), they must remain steadfast in light of the hope and assurance of future victory and renewal that Revelation communicates to them.

The term "church" does not appear after chapters 1–3 in Revelation (until the epilogue, 22:16), but John continues to portray the character and history of God's re-

---

18. Seyoon Kim, "Kingdom of God," in *DLNT* 634–37. He suggests that "kingdom of God" is the central theme of the book. Jan A. du Rand, "'Your Kingdom Come 'on Earth as It Is in Heaven': The Theological Motif of the Apocalypse of John," *Neotestamentica* 31 (1997): 69–72, discusses the themes of God's sovereignty and his kingdom's establishment on earth and prioritizes the latter as the overarching theme. While this is certainly important in Rev, I prefer to nuance "God's kingdom" as secondary to "God's salvation completed on earth," that is, the sovereign God completing his work of salvation on this earth through Christ (both judgment and restoration).

More recently du Rand himself seems to shift to the theme of God's salvation as the integrative core of Rev's theology. See du Rand, "Soteriology in the Apocalypse of John," 468–72, 490–92.

19. Middleton, *New Heaven and a New Earth*, 57–73.

20. Eugene H. Peterson, *Reversed Thunder: The Revelation of John and the Praying Imagination* (San Francisco: Harper & Row, 1988), 9. See also Strecker, *Theology*, 530, who says about Rev that "the real goal of the work is the future end of history, to which all visions and events in the world are directed. Here they find their final fulfillment in chaps. 21–22."

deemed humanity through other images and descriptions. Those who follow Christ during the severe period of final tribulation to come will face unique and greatly intensified suffering (e.g., warfare waged by Satan and his minions in a paroxysm of wrath at his impending doom, 12:12; 13:7), including martyrdom for many of them (7:14; 16:6; 17:6; 19:2). They, like John's churches, are called to endure in faith and obedience when these intense trials come (13:10; 14:12). One group of them will be set apart for absolute divine protection during the tribulation period (a remnant of believing Jews taken from all the tribes constituting the full regathering and survival of Israel as a nation through its time of restorative discipline; see 7:3–8; 14:1–5). But many other Christians, Jewish and gentile, will not survive the terrible judgments of those days (6:9–11; 7:9–17; 16:6; 20:4).

When the visions of Revelation give us glimpses of the consummation of God's salvation, however, these different groups are united in a single redeemed community drawing near to God in worship, devotion, and fellowship with him and with one another, first in heaven (5:9–10; 7:9–17) and then on the earth (19:7–9; 20:4–6; 21:1–14; 22:1–5). Revelation enters into the larger story of the Bible in reflecting how God's saving purpose for fallen humanity started with one person, Abraham, through whose descendants he promised to bring blessing to "all the families of the earth" (Gen 12:1–3). From him God formed "a holy nation," Israel, his "kingdom of priests," to be his channel of salvation for humanity at large (Exod 19:5–6). Through Israel he brought forth an anointed deliverer, one who would be exalted as ruler over all the nations (Ps 2:2, 9; Rev 12:1–5). His deliverance and victory over rebellious nations would be accomplished by his sacrificial death as the Lamb, who is also the Lion of the tribe of Judah, the promised deliverer and king from Zion (Rev 5:5–6; 12:10–11). He also fulfills the role of the glorious Son of Man whose everlasting dominion over "the peoples, nations, and languages . . . under the whole heaven" will be shared with "the saints of the Most High" (Dan 7:13–14, 27; Rev 1:13).

Others who are not from Israel will enter into the blessings of this redemption, being set free from sin and appointed also as a royal priesthood, just as Israel was (1:5–6; 5:10). Believers in Christ from among ethnic Israel are not rejected or excluded from this new community but constitute the "firstfruits" of the redeemed (14:4), the initial ingathering that anticipates God's full harvest of those set aside as his own. Thus the "saints" who collectively form "the bride of the Lamb" (19:7–9) are viewed not as a people but as *peoples* (21:2–3, 9–10), a multiethnic community whose unity and intimate communion with the one true God does not efface their differing national backgrounds even into eternity. Thus, it is not that gentiles will be incorporated into the one *people* of God, "the true Israel," nor that the ethnic heritage of Jewish followers of Jesus will become irrelevant to God. Through Christ the new-covenant community of those who know the true God is expanded to include other nations in addition to Israel (Jer 31:33; Ezek 37:27), while valuing their ethnic diversity within the larger unity they share in Christ.[21] The new Jerusalem itself incorporates memorials to the twelve tribes of Israel as well as to the twelve apostles of the Lamb (21:12, 14). Likewise, the geographical arrangement of the new earth with Jerusalem as the focal point, to which the redeemed nations constantly come to honor God and the Lamb (21:22–22:5), reflects this unity and diversity in the lineage of their salvation.

These visions of final salvation depicting a vibrant, diverse corporate entity rejoicing together in God and in the renewal provided for them are significant. Eternal life will not be a privatized, individual enjoyment of God in isolation from others, a personal renewal experienced all alone. It will be the restoration of human society, people living in mutual and supportive relationships with one another.[22] To be sure, entrance into this community is individualized (21:6; 22:17), and each one on this side of that renewal must take exhortations to be faithful as a personal call to fidelity regardless of what others may do (2:7; 13:9; 22:7, 11). The Lamb's book of life contains individual names (3:5; 20:15; 21:27), and each person will find in that future life with Christ his or her unique identity, the full flowering of individual character that God has in mind for each of his children (2:17). Moreover, that future life will have its tender personal moments (e.g., "he will wipe away every tear from their eyes," 21:4; "if anyone hears my voice and opens the door, I will come in to him and share a meal with him and he with me," 3:20). But the new heaven and new earth will constitute a rich and varied community, redeemed from "every tribe and language and people and nation" (5:9) across the ages and cultures and unified under the covenant-keeping God.[23] Life in the new Jerusalem will be carried out in vital corporate union and communion with one another and with God. The individual and the corporate will be complementary, not opposed to each other.[24]

On this side of heaven, the role of this unified community of God's "servants" and "saints," regardless of their ethnic background, gender, or age, is to bear faithful testimony to God and to Christ by verbal witness and by godly character in all their dealings with the wider world. The fact that they are devoted to his service does not mean isolation or withdrawal from a hostile world. It means truly living in the fallen

21. Saucy, *Case for Progressive Dispensationalism*, 188–90.

22. See William J. Dumbrell, *The End of the Beginning: Revelation 21–22 and the Old Testament* (Homebush West, NSW: Lancer, 1985), 194–96, and Wright, *Surprised by Hope*, 80 (who both emphasize *cosmic* renewal, not just individual), and Hays, *Moral Vision*, 176–81, 193–200 (who sees "the corporate participatory character of the people of God" [196] as one of the focal points of the Bible's story that should guide us in moral living today in anticipation of God's coming renewal of all things).

23. Middleton, *New Heaven and a New Earth*, 173–74.

24. This corporate picture of the future of God's redeemed peoples should have an effect on how Christians relate to one another even now in witness to the wider world. As Blaising and Bock, *Progressive Dispensationalism*, 285–91, point out, the church corporately is "an inaugurated form of the future kingdom of God on earth" (286). It displays ahead of time what God's redeemed and reconciled human society can look like in pursuing righteousness, joy, and peace among peoples of diverse backgrounds. This provides a vision for the church to stand for human freedom and justice today without denying traditional Christian doctrines (e.g., judgment for sin) or collapsing eschatology into a completely realized mode as found in Pablo Richard, *Apocalypse: A People's Commentary on the Book of Revelation*, BLS (Maryknoll, NY: Orbis, 1995), 170–73.

world and with its inhabitants, while maintaining their distinctiveness as those who belong not to this age and its values but to the true and living God (cf. John 17:13–19). In this, Christians are called to follow Christ himself ("the faithful witness," 1:5) who did not remain distant and did not prove unfaithful in testifying about God and accomplishing his saving purpose, despite great cost. Thus Revelation constantly warns Christians against complacency and assimilation to the godless ideology and conduct of the surrounding culture (2:2, 20, 24; 3:17–19; 14:9–10; 18:3–4), while urging vital engagement and devoted testimony (2:13; 6:9; 12:11, 17; 19:10) about the one whose sacrificial love provides free and full salvation (1:5; 22:17).[25]

The devoted service of God's community of saints does not end when the ultimate renewal of all things arrives (21:1–2). The continuity and change that comes in cosmology (i.e., God's fallen creation not obliterated but radically reformed and renewed)[26] is mirrored in the transformation that comes in their eternal worship, communion, and service with and for God and the Lamb (21:1–7, 22–27; 22:1–5). It is not that the sinful material earth is left behind for the purely spiritual realm of heaven but that the fallen world's rebellion, corruption, and subjection to Satan are left behind (along with their consequences; 21:4; 22:3). Redeemed humanity is likewise set free from sinful self-sufficiency and self-centeredness to enjoy face-to-face communion with God and the Lamb while supplied with abundant provision of all that is needed for their well-being (21:3; 22:1–2).[27] It is true that "life in the New Jerusalem is one long experience of worship" since God is present with his people there.[28] But all of life in that future existence will redound to God's glory and constitute worship. Humans will be restored to the image-bearing, dominion-keeping, and God-exalting role he originally intended for them (Gen 1:26–28). In resuming their role as the glory of God's creation (Ps 8:3–8; Heb 2:8–10), humans will remain creatures in need of God and in subjection to him; they do not become gods. But their creaturely human life with God will be lively and productive, and their work will not be burdensome but fulfilling (22:3). They will use their creative skills and crafts and conduct commerce with one another and from place to place (21:24, 26). They will till and tend the fruitful earth (22:2–3), learn and grow (22:2), and worship God and the Lamb with direct intimacy and joyful devotion, offering it to the God to whom all glory belongs (4:11; 5:13; 21:3, 22; 22:3–4).[29]

---

25. Bauckham, *Theology*, 161–63; Hays, *Moral Vision*, 176–81.

26. Bauckham, *Theology*, 48–51; Ladd, *Revelation*, 275–77; Middleton, *New Heaven and a New Earth*, 21–34.

27. Bauckham, *Theology*, 132–35.

28. Osborne, *Revelation*, 49.

29. J. Scott Duvall, *The Heart of Revelation: Understanding the 10 Essential Themes of the Bible's Final Book* (Grand Rapids: Baker, 2016), 157–75; Middleton, *New Heaven and a New Earth*, 172–75; Turner, "New Jerusalem," 289–90; Michael E. Wittmer, *Heaven Is a Place on Earth: Why Everything You Do Matters to God* (Grand Rapids: Zondervan, 2004), 197–21.

Scripture Index

Leviticus

Numbers

Jeremiah

Mark

Luke

Other Ancient Literature Index

3 Baruch

1 Enoch

2 Enoch

3 Enoch

Patristic Writings

Subject Index

Author Index